THE GOOD NEWS ABOUT CAREERS

THE GOOD NEWS ABOUT CAREERS

HOW YOU'LL BE WORKING IN THE NEXT DECADE

BARBARA MOSES, Ph.D.

FOREWORD BY JANE HUTCHESON

Stoddart

Copyright © 1999 by Barbara Moses

All rights reserved. No part of this publication may be reproduced
or transmitted in any form or by any means, electronic or mechanical,
including photocopying, recording, or any information storage and
retrieval system, without permission in writing from the publisher.

Published in 1999 by Stoddart Publishing Co. Limited
34 Lesmill Road, Toronto, Canada M3B 2T6

Distributed by General Distribution Services Limited
325 Humber College Blvd., Toronto, Canada M9W 7C3
Tel. (416) 213-1919 Fax (416) 213-1917
Email customer.service@ccmailgw.genpub.com

03 02 01 00 99   2 3 4 5

Stoddart Books are available for bulk purchase for sales promotions, premiums, fundraising, and
seminars. For details, contact the **Special Sales Department** at the above address.

Canadian Cataloguing in Publication Data
Moses, Barbara

The good news about careers:
how you'll be working in the next decade

ISBN 0-7737-3181-4

1. Career development. I. Title.

HF5549.5.C35M68 1999   650.14   C99-930090-3

Portions of this book first appeared, in different form, in columns published by
the *Globe and Mail*. The piece entitled "TempWorld Manifesto" first appeared in
the author's *Career Intelligence* (Stoddart Publishing, 1997). "Recession-Proofing Your
Career" first appeared, in different form, in *Report on Business Magazine*, December 1998.

Cover Design: Bill Douglas @ The Bang
Text Design: Tannice Goddard

Printed and bound in Canada

*We acknowledge for their financial support of our publishing program the Canada Council,
the Ontario Arts Council, and the Government of Canada through the
Book Publishing Industry Development Program (BPIDP).*

To my son Nathaniel
and to the next generation:
may you live and work well.

Contents

Foreword

*T*his is a book about the world of work. We complain about work, often experience stress as a result of it, but it is a critical part of our lives. Work is, of course, about economic survival, but more importantly it is at the heart of our humanity. It helps define our identity and sense of self, our ability to contribute to an organization, community, society, and our families, and to grow and develop as individuals.

This is the world that Barbara Moses knows and writes about so well. I met Barbara in the early 1980s. We have had countless conversations about work and careers over the years, some funny, some serious, some absurd, some creative and thought-provoking. In my view, Barbara is at her best as an observer and commentator on the world of work.

This book provides practical strategies and techniques that can be used by everyone to increase their marketability and personal satisfaction in the workplace of today. Barbara gets behind the buzzwords and describes how you can be more effective in communicating in a frenetic world, how to make the most of your opportunities to network, how to prepare yourself for an increasingly uncertain future, how to career-proof your children, how to be a better coach to others – as well as how to be more "coachable" – and how to choose work that you will enjoy and at which you are most likely to be successful.

All of these tactics and techniques make for extremely insightful and useful reading, but I believe the real value of this book is even deeper. I read the manuscript in two long sessions while I was on holidays. As I finished it, I was struck by the unique perspective that characterized the writing throughout. What came across was enlightening, compassionate, and humorous at times, but more than that it actually caused me to *think*. The areas being discussed are an everyday part of my life as a human-resources consultant working with large corporations. Many concepts have become the equivalent of unassailable truths – networking is always good, busy is better, you need to be an extrovert to be successful, and everyone who is highly evolved as a person loves getting feedback.

As I read a different and original point of view on each of these topics, I was forced to question some long-held ideas. Then I thought about how seldom I do *that* anymore. I realized that one of the true losses in our frantic and time-impoverished lives is an understanding of the value of reflection. We are so obsessed with doing, with being productive all the time, that we no longer see the benefits of taking time to think differently about ourselves, our situations, and the way things are. And isn't that ability what separates us from the animals? As Socrates said, the unexamined life is not worth living.

Finally, despite painting a realistic and accurate picture of the challenges facing us in today's world of work, Barbara ultimately presents us with hope. The good news is that there really is greater flexibility and room for variety in how we work. There are people loving the new world of work and thriving in a host of different circumstances. If you believe there is room for greater meaning in what *you* do for a living, then I recommend that you read on. Take the opportunity to reflect, make some choices for *you*, and reposition your own views on work and its importance in the total fabric of your life.

JANE HUTCHESON

Senior Consultant

Hay Management Consultants

Acknowledgments

I'm privileged to count as my clients, colleagues, and friends some very insightful and committed people. This book is full of their stories. I have worked with many people in many organizations and have learned from all. Unfortunately, space does not permit me to thank each one.

I would like to thank the following friends, clients, and colleagues for their anecdotes and wry insights: Helen Bozinovski at Heart and Stroke Foundation; John Bryan of Core International; Heather Campbell at Nesbitt Burns; Carolyn Clark at CP Hotels and Resorts; Sue Cunningham and Debbie Glover at Lattice Learning; Heather Faire at PPG Industries; Michelle Gerber at PricewaterhouseCoopers; Margo Gordon at Warner Lambert; Keith Hollihan at Linkage Incorporated; Susannah Kelly at Herman Smith Executive Initiatives; Pam MacIntyre at Crown Life; Margot McKinnon at Body Harmonics; Jeff Novak; Anne Peel at Voices for Children; Lauri Reed at CTG; Harvey Schachter; Connie Simington at Enbridge Consumers Gas; Keith Southey at CIBC; Barbara Steinberg at the United Nations; Irene Taylor; Nadia Valerio at Bank of Montreal; Judy Westover; Leslee Wilson; John Young at Four Seasons Hotels and Resorts.

Acknowledgments

I have been fortunate to gain insight into young professionals as a result of the leading-edge work of the public-accounting firms. I thank in particular the partners and education leaders I have worked with, including Wayne McFarlane, Chris Gillespie, and Judy Elliott at PricewaterhouseCoopers; Lori Pearson and Halia Bonner at Ernst & Young; Michelle Johnston at Deloitte & Touche.

My many clients should be congratulated on the outstanding work they have done in helping people respond to new work realities, in particular: George Sallay and Darlene Brushett at the Bank of Montreal; Sharon Wingfelder and other leaders in the Royal Bank Learning Network; and Sharon Rose at the Nortel/CAW Return to Learning Program.

I owe a special debt of gratitude to my long-time colleagues and friends Tamara Weir-Bryan and Joan Hill, whose insightful observations, generosity, and outstanding work have nourished me, and to my other committed associates: Laurie Hillis and Ann Toombs in Calgary, JoAnne Maurer in Vancouver, Frank Rambeau in Ottawa, Denise Lapointe in Montreal, my American associates Joan Caruso and B.J. Chakiris, Elaine Christie in New Zealand, and Howard Elias in Hong Kong.

Thank you Bill Pallett at Delta Hotels and Resorts for your outstanding generosity and friendship; Garth Toombs of Garth Toombs & Associates in Alberta, and Dick Knowdell of Career Research and Testing in California, for your consistent and long-time support. Also, my fine speaker's agents including Speakers' Spotlight, CanSpeak, and National Speakers' Bureau, and the associations and organizations they represent, for linking me up with audiences who are a constant source of inspiration and real experiences.

Thank you also to my friend and literary agent Bruce Westwood and Gordon Pitts, my wonderful editor at the *Globe and Mail*, who has given me free rein in my column writing. I remain grateful to the team at Stoddart and in particular thank Don Bastian, my fine editor; wry marketing whiz Stephen Quick; and Mary Giuliano, my savvy publicist.

Thank you Jane Hutcheson and Jeff Davidson for your thought-provoking, sometimes irritating, and always stimulating conversations.

This book could not have been written without the extraordinary support of my husband, Andrew Weiner, the toughest and most insightful editor, and the best partner, anyone could ask for.

Introduction

When my book *Career Intelligence* first came out, two years ago, people recognized it as an accurate description of the new workplace. But many found the description – of a world without any certainty or job security, where every individual must take responsibility for managing their own career, and where one must constantly reprove one's competence – scary and depressing.

Since then, however, I've noticed a shift in how people feel about the changing landscape of work. While they recognize there are tough realities associated with the new employment contract and the new work order – including the constant uncertainty and the sheer volume and pace of work – many have also found in it significant reasons for celebration.

Rather than simply saying, "Well, this is the way it is, there is nothing I can do about it," people are starting to take what I've called an activist stance in relation to their careers. They are engaged in active thinking and dialogue about how they work, why they work, and what they need to do to earn a living.

As I show in this book, individuals are finding creative and fresh ways to manage some of the complexities of a life on fast forward. They are more open, not only to change and to experiencing the exciting aspects of a new career but also to sharing their feelings and experiences. They are looking for work that reflects who they are, for work in which they are free to bring their entire personality and spirit.

If there is any phrase that captures the new thinking about work, it's *take it personally*. Work is no longer experienced as an impersonal force of nature over which one has no control. Instead people are asking, indeed demanding, that work meet their personal needs. Everywhere, people are questioning what I call in this book the "cult of busyness" – the preoccupation with doing, acting, and achieving for its own sake, rather than being mindful of what we care about and what we are trying to accomplish.

At the same time, organizations are also beginning to recognize the new personal realities of their employees' over-committed, hyper-metabolic lives and to make some accommodations. In this book, besides helping individuals create a better work future, I will examine ways of shaping more *life-friendly organizations* that are in tune with individual rhythms and the human need for challenge and emotional security.

It's not all good news out there, of course. A friend of mine, a vice-president of a large financial institution, was asked whether she wanted to see a scary movie. She said, "I have a policy against seeing scary movies these days. If I want to be frightened, I just go into work in the morning."

Organizations continue to slash overhead costs and associated payroll and to obsessively monitor the bottom line; parents continue to be spooked about the prospect of their kids not making it in the new workplace; organizations continue to be puzzled about how best to manage under the new deal at work; boomer bosses are perplexed by their 20-something staff (not to mention children), who seem to have a very different attitude towards work; and everyone is grappling with the competing demands of managing very complicated work and personal lives.

In this book, I don't pull any punches. I describe some of the more hard-hitting truths, the scary stuff, if you will, about work and how we'll be working over the next 10 years. But at the same time, I see much to be optimistic about.

Over the course of the past two years I have been encouraged by the number of people who have found interesting and inventive ways to craft a future that allows them to withstand whatever curves the economy might throw at them. Many people have also told me that as little as three years ago they couldn't have possibly imagined themselves having made such a successful adaptation to an uncertain work world — much less finding real joy and liberation in new ways of working.

Freedom, flexibility, opportunities to test yourself in new roles . . . these will be the cornerstones of life and work in the next decade. As traditional authoritarian workplace structures crumble under the onslaught of the new economy, people are gaining a new sense of *control* and *autonomy* in their lives and careers. A new style of worker is emerging, based on a new, unique psychology.

What are the new workers like? What motivates them, and how does that differ from what motivated their predecessors? What will they need to do to be successful? How will organizations need to rethink how they reward, motivate, and retain people? These are some of the questions I address in this book. I also look at:

- where careers are going, and how we, as individuals, managers, and parents, can profit from future work trends;
- how to operate as a self-managing career activist;
- how to achieve a creative balance between the new work and personal realities;
- the search for authenticity in a shifting career landscape; and
- how managers and organizations can lead today's and tomorrow's workers.

Introduction

There are numerous myths about the new workplace, such as: in the future you will constantly need to reinvent yourself; in order to market yourself successfully you will have to become a walking billboard of your accomplishments, endlessly networking and parading your skills; in order for your children to be successful they should be crammed with as much extracurricular skill-building activity as possible, while being encouraged to make early career choices.

In this book I challenge conventional wisdom and show you how elastic the new workplace really is. There are many ways to design work that plays to your own strengths, preferences, and values. I show how to use this elasticity to your benefit – and that of your children.

One of the questions I ask early career professionals in my workshops is: "Do you feel that your parents and managers understand the impact of the new work order on your future career?" Sadly, only a handful of people indicate that their parents or managers do understand.

In this book, I present and answer the questions I am most asked by 20-somethings about how to kick start their careers. I also share what boomer bosses think of their young workers – and vice versa – and how managers can engage their young staffs.

How can parents career-proof their children for this new work world? This continues to one of the most pressing challenges facing us as parents and as a society. Indeed, of all the issues I write and speak on, this is one of the ones that elicits the most intense response. As you will see throughout this book, I believe that we can create a work world that we would be proud to pass on to our children.

And that will be the best news of all.

part one

The New Workplace

The Cult
of Busyness

*L*inda, a senior vice-president in the financial-services industry, just got back to the office from a vacation at the cottage – a week early. "I was calling in every day on my cellphone, checking e-mail on my laptop, faxing memos back and forth . . . and still I had to be there. My kids are mad at me, my husband is mad at me, but what can you do? The work has to be done."

Jim, a former geologist, has been semi-retired for years, although hardly anyone knows it. Jim has deeply internalized society's belief that visible work equals visible worth. He takes frequent vacations, but tells his friends and neighbors that he is going away to look after overseas business interests.

Both Linda and Jim are, each in their own way, victims of what I call the cult of busyness. Today, one's busyness is worn like a badge of honor, a measure of one's status in the modern workplace. Ask someone how they are, and almost invariably they'll say something like, "I'm so busy" or "Things are crazy around here."

It's become almost banal to comment on how busy and overworked people are today. While the unemployed and underemployed complain about not having enough meaningful or challenging work, people with full-time jobs have too much. Statisticians document it, journalists report on it, almost everyone complains about it.

"I Work, Therefore I Am"

To some degree, of course, this frantic pace of work is driven by economic realities. Organizations demand improved productivity and competitiveness to please demanding shareholders and other stakeholders. Employees, uncertain about their job security, scramble to comply.

But there are other factors at work here. Somewhere along the way, many people have become addicted to this relentless, hyper-metabolic pace of work. It's almost as if they need to be continually *doing, acting,* and *achieving* to feel fully alive: "I work, therefore I am." Even when they seem to be complaining about the pressure they are under, they are actually making a kind of *boast*: "I'm so busy, therefore I must be important." It's as if you need to be demonstrably over-committed and exhausted to be a fully functioning contributor to your organization and paid-up member of the global economy.

Indeed, it's interesting to see what happens to these people when, for whatever reason, they are forced to stop in their tracks. One comment you often hear from people who are between jobs or work assignments is the feeling that their life is empty. As one person put it, "I'm starting to feel like I'm a phantom, that I'm not real. There's nothing that gives my life shape or meaning."

Other people are profoundly ambivalent about the new work realities. If you ask them in workshops how they are feeling, they will tell you that their most significant relationships are suffering. When asked how they would like to spend their time outside work, they say, "Forget spending time with friends, just spending time with my children is a luxury." They are tired, distracted, grumpy. But they don't see any way out. "I have no choice," they say. Typically, in fact, it is those who complain the least about their busyness, the quietly desperate ones, who are suffering the most.

Consider Carol, a 45-year-old single mother with two teenage children who works as a human resources consultant. "Lately, every time I schedule a family event or outing such as a birthday dinner, I have to cancel at the last minute because of a so-called important meeting," she says. "At this point, my children don't believe me when I make a commitment to them to do something with them. It's just the way it is." Despite the fact that her children are experiencing difficulties at school, she couldn't make the last parent-teachers night. She used to work out, but she hasn't done anything for the past year. Every time she thinks about her life she gets more depressed, but feels that she's caught between meeting her financial commitments and her children's needs.

But whether people embrace busyness or resent it, they rarely stop to question it. If you ask people *why* they are working so hard, you find that most people haven't given any thought to it: It's simply the way things are. Busyness has become a fact of nature, like the weather, or gravity.

The Price We Pay

Ultimately, though, we may pay a heavy price for our unthinking acceptance of this ever-escalating cyclone of busyness. You have to wonder: What will be the long-term impact on people's physical and mental health and on their personal relationships? And what, exactly, are we teaching our children about work?

A few years ago, when I gave a talk about careers to my son's Grade 6 class, I asked the students what they thought their parents felt about their work. The children started to compete about whose parents were more miserable: "My mother hates her job." "Oh yeah? Well both my mother and father hate their jobs." "At least your parents have a job to hate." And so on.

Children develop many of their initial ideas about work from what their parents say and from what they observe for themselves. Is it any wonder that they develop the belief that work is unpleasant? This impression is exacerbated by their resentment for the tremendous number of hours their parents work, and the intrusion of work into their family's time together. Many feel abandoned by their parents, who seem to prefer to meet their never-ending work commitments. An educational psychologist colleague tells me that a significant number of the children she sees suffering from behavioral and cognitive difficulties say, "I'm so lonely."

Similarly, I often hear the 20-something children of workaholic baby boomer parents express resentment about their abandonment in favor of work, along with cynicism about the ultimate payoff of those sacrifices. "My father worked for the same company for 25 years," one young accountant told me. "He worked nights, weekends, vacation days. We never got to spend any time with him. He worked his heart out for them. And when he was 50 they tossed him out like a piece of garbage. I'm never going to make the mistake of believing that my work is more important than my personal life."

Boomer managers sometimes complain about the attitudes of their 20-something staff, their reluctance to put in long hours, and their emphasis on balancing work and personal life. I find it a healthy development, and one that may well be a more adaptive response to the future of work.

Work in the future will almost certainly be of a more *intermittent* nature than it is today. Rather than working continuously for the same employer for a long period of time, more and more of us will move between assignments or contracts of varying lengths with different employers or clients, punctuated by varying periods of so-called downtime. During these periods we may be looking for work, or upgrading our skills, or simply re-energizing ourselves through personal pursuits.

We will need to be able to manage these periods of downtime not only financially but *psychologically*. We will need to know not only how to be busy but how to *stop* our busyness, how to use these breaks as times to nourish ourselves, reconnect with people, explore new avenues of work and play. We will need to find something other than our own busyness to validate our self-worth.

What Organizations Can Do

Although we may not have the power to change the way that people's sense of self-esteem has become attached to being productive, we can lobby inside our organizations. What behaviors are valued?

For example, are meetings routinely called at 7:00 in the morning or at 6:00 at night or on weekends? Are vacations interrupted at the behest of anxious customers? Is it okay to take off in the middle of the day to help out at your kid's school? Do you have to cancel training events at the last minute because managers say they're too busy?

One of the key steps in creating what I call "life-friendly organizations" is to provide people with the opportunity to reflect on how they are living their lives and spending their time through career planning or self-assessment. Here people have the opportunity to reflect on such questions as:

- Is your work really meeting your most important needs?
- Are you defining yourself purely in terms of your accomplishments?
- Why are you working so hard? To what personal ends?
- Are you making significant sacrifices in favor of your work? What is the impact of your work on other people important in your life?

One executive vice-president in the financial-services industry invited his department to a career-management experience with the following words:

"You've given us a significant investment of your time. Now it's time to invest in yourself. Take this day to think about your work and your life and how you can be as satisfied and meaningfully engaged as possible."

The New
Obsession with Work

*R*ecently, at the hairdresser, I overheard a 20-something reception-ist telling a teenage assistant: "Don't quit school. Did you know that a university education today is worth what a high-school education was worth 10 years ago?"

Everywhere, people today are talking about work: How to find it, how to keep it, how to get greater satisfaction from it, how to control it so that you still have a life. This new obsession with work, and the sophistication with which people are talking about work, is symptomatic of a profound sea change in our society.

When I went to university in the late 1960s, like so many of my generation I didn't particularly consider whether my education would be instrumental in finding work. To the extent we thought about work at all, we assumed opportunities would be available. Indeed, there was a definite snob-bery among liberal-arts students about our more "careerist" contemporaries who were pursuing professional degrees with clear-cut job prospects, whether engineering or accounting or physiotherapy.

Of course, people *have* to be highly career conscious today, with the stakes being so much higher than they used to be. Work, particularly "good" work – challenging and with decent pay and professional content – has become a highly valued commodity. And the specter of ending up as one of the have-nots instead of the haves creates ever-intensifying anxiety in a society that is increasingly divided.

What are the consequences of this new work obsession? On the one hand, people who don't have work – from newly graduated 20-somethings to so-called early retirees – are desperate to find it. But among people who do have work, there is a growing tendency to reevaluate how they are spending their lives. They are asking: "Why am I working so hard for so little – financially, emotionally, and personally? What is the cost of this work to my family, to my relationships, to things that are important to me?"

This is not the same thing as a mid-life crisis. It stems from a realistic reappraisal of the relationship between effort at work and traditional rewards such as advancement, salary, status, and protection against the vagaries of the marketplace. As these extrinsic rewards diminish, people pay more attention to the *intrinsic* qualities of their work, asking: Is it skill-building? Fun? Challenging? Does it provide opportunities to balance work and personal life? While these qualities were always important, they have become much more salient today as work is stripped of its traditional rewards.

Essentially people are saying, "I may no longer be able to aspire to the traditional trappings of success. But that gives me the freedom to make life choices that reflect my needs and values." Obviously these choices will be moderated by economic realities. But increasingly, people seem more willing to make tradeoffs, giving up more work and income for more time for family and personal interests.

Ultimately, this reevaluation of work and its rewards may prove liberating for individuals, freeing people to make decisions independent of traditional pressures and to pursue personal passions rather than the brass ring.

At the same time, this new hyperconsciousness about work may be a healthy trend for society. As more people actively *think* about how and why they are working, it is to be hoped that this will lead to a dialogue about the nature of the contemporary workplace, the distribution of work, and the new employment contract between individuals and organizations.

Living and
Working in TempWorld

Ken and Doug, camera operators with a network news organization, worked side-by-side for more than 10 years on similar assignments. They now find themselves victims of downsizing. The two men are equally employable in terms of their portfolio of skills and experiences. But where Ken has lined up various freelance assignments, Doug sits at home, depressed and immobilized by his unemployment.

The major difference between them is that Ken, who had been working on a renewable temporary contract, has always seen himself as a freelancer, even though he was with the same employer so long. All along, he has maintained an active network and sought out information about the assignments of his counterparts working for other employers. Doug, in contrast, was a permanent, full-time employee and continues to see himself as someone who needs a conventional job.

In many ways, being a temporary worker is more a state of mind rather than a hard-and-fast employment status. And in this sense, it often seems to me that the world is divided into two types of people.

Some people like to think of themselves as living in a world that is unpredictable and ever-changing. If they have a job, they view it as one step in a series of short-term commitments to a job or organization. That commitment may stretch out several years, but they still have the mindset of temporary workers. For them, too much predictability is boring and stifling.

But there are others who, no matter how much turbulence they may have experienced in the employment market, still believe in the fundamental rightness and goodness of the traditional employment contract. Often, they have been the victim of downsizing or reengineering in a number of job settings. And yet they still crave the "security" of a conventional full-time job and react with anxiety to a lack of predictable employment.

This latter group is still very much in the majority. A recent poll, conducted for Shell by Peter D. Hart Research Associates and reported in the *Globe and Mail*, found that 72% of the 1,123 randomly selected adults who participated in the survey said they preferred "the security of staying with one employer for a long time and moving up the ladder."

Unfortunately for this latter group, the conventional, full-time, "permanent" job is a rapidly vanishing commodity. Today, like it or not, we all have to see ourselves as temporary workers, no matter what our official employment status is. We may have something that *appears* to be a conventional full-time job, governed by a so-called traditional employment contract. Or we may, like a steadily growing proportion of the workforce, be contingent, contract, or freelance workers. But either way, we are living and working in what I call "TempWorld."

Everything Is Temporary

In TempWorld everything shifts rapidly. Nothing is forever, everything is temporary: where you work, what you do there, the skills you use, the people you work with. Or, as the late Andy Warhol might have put it, in the future, everyone will have a good job — for fifteen minutes.

In TempWorld, as in Hollywood, the past counts for little or nothing. You are only as good as your last hit – or presentation, or quarterly results, or sales figures. Whatever your experience or accomplishments, you have to constantly re-earn your right to employment. Under such circumstances, work becomes an endless audition as you constantly re-prove that you have the savvy, skills, and know-how to be the "best person for the job."

As one person put it, "Just when you think you can relax for a minute, despite the fact you've been killing yourself and achieved outstanding results, there's another reorganization and there you are, résumé in hand, reciting your list of accomplishments over the past six months."

I like to compare the new career pattern to a date, the old one to marriage. Many of us crave the relative security, comfort, commitment, and intimacy provided by marriage. But marriage can also be, well, predictable. A date, on the other hand, can be exciting. You don't know how it will end until you get there. But you always have to hold your stomach in.

Young Workers Show the Way

For many people, the new work realities demand a very difficult adjustment. Organizations used to offer more than just job security. They also offered people a sense of *psychological* security as well – a feeling of belonging to and contributing to something bigger than themselves. Now, in most organizations, that sense of psychological security is gone, leaving people feeling unprotected and without moorings.

There are considerable generational differences in how people respond to this uncertain new work world. Many pre-boomers and baby boomers mourn the loss of stable and predictable employment. Under the old psychological contract between the individuals and the organization they had felt protected, experiencing both financial and career benefits from that protection.

In contrast, their 20-something and early 30-something counterparts never learned to expect a secure and stable work environment, and so have a completely different set of beliefs about work life. Unlike their pre-boomer and boomer predecessors, they often welcome the challenges of this new and unpredictable work world.

For the past seven years, I have been working with early career professionals in public accounting firms. A few years ago, when asked about their future aspirations, a significant percentage saw partnership as a viable and desirable career goal. Although some see partnership as a possible career goal, they can also think of any number of other options: moving into industry, owning their own business, working for themselves, perhaps even running a café.

Of course, even within the pre-boomer and baby boomer contingents, there have long been those who, whether by accident or design, have embraced temporariness: freelancers, consultants, contract workers, and the like. And when we compare these people with those who have pursued the security of full-time employment, we see that in most respects – in education, experiences, skills – they are similar if not identical. The primary difference is *attitudinal*.

As one 40-something woman, a highly successful contract worker, put it, "I love going from contract to contract, even if at times it's a bit scary. Each assignment is different, so it's an opportunity to learn something new. And then, I get bored after a while, so I like knowing there is a discrete end and I can move on to something else."

Her words reflect a key underlying psychological dimension. For some people the very idea of a predictable work relationship is stultifying. They thrive on change, on testing themselves in new situations where the outcome is uncertain. Indeed, when provided with too much security they become depressed and look for ways to undermine their security by making career-endangering moves. When they find themselves in relatively secure environments they say things like, "I feel like I'm being choked."

Where some people embrace temporariness, others have it forced on them. Can these reluctant temporary workers, with no previous predilection for risk and change, make the necessary attitudinal shift when they find themselves thrust into an insecure work world? In many cases they can.

Jack, a longtime editor, was forced into freelancing by the closing of his magazine. Initially, he saw this as a way of "keeping his show on the road" while he looked for another "real" job. But real jobs proved elusive — while freelancing proved to be highly rewarding, both financially and personally. "The more feedback I got on what I was doing, the more confident I was in my ability to do it well," Jack says. "I realized that I could make it on my own, and I found that very liberating. All those years, I wanted to belong to something. Now I belong to myself." Two years later, when he was offered a plum full-time editing job, Jack turned it down flat.

Ultimately, there is little difference between freelancing and a supposed full-time job. Today, we are all free agents. Like multimillionaire sports stars, we go wherever the work takes us, changing jobs or assignments with the ebb and flow of the economy, seeking to better ourselves in terms of challenge and rewards. And like sports stars, too, if our services are no longer necessary, or considered too expensive, we will be cast aside. The key difference is that the freelancer — the psychological free agent — already has the mind-set to move on quickly to the next challenge.

Tips for Living and Thriving in TempWorld

Think like a temporary worker: Even if you have a so-called "permanent" job, start to think of yourself as a temporary worker. Temps know they can make no assumptions about any kind of predictability in their work.

Temporary workers know that it is up to them to demonstrate that they have the skills for the job — now. They will not receive any kind of training to bring them up to speed, so it is up to them to get whatever training they need.

In TempWorld there is no tolerance for error, no protection for a job less well done. Social Darwinism is at work, and competition for resources is fierce.

Earlier, I compared the old career pattern to a marriage, the new one to a date. Let's extend that comparison to temporary work. In a marriage, both sides will often be prepared to slog it out when things are not moving along in the happiest manner. But in a date, there is no serious commitment on either side, and when the going gets tough there are no serious consequences – emotionally or financially – to ending the relationship.

Under these circumstances, all relationships need to be redefined. For example, workers should look on their bosses as their clients. What are their critical business priorities? How is your work contributing to their goals and adding value to the enterprise? Are you managing your relationship with your boss with the same care and vigilance that you manage your relationship with clients and customers?

Try to define yourself in terms that are independent of your job title. For example, would you describe yourself as a comptroller for ABC Trust Company, or do you consider yourself as a financial professional, with business-planning and problem-solving skills, adept at working with diverse teams, currently applying your knowledge in the financial-services industry? Think of yourself as having a portfolio of skills that you could potentially apply in a variety of work settings.

Build financial independence: Temps know they cannot afford to make any assumptions about economic continuity. If you lost your income tomorrow, do you have sufficient savings to tide you over until you find a replacement source of income? Financial planners typically recommend that you keep six months' salary in the bank to provide you with the barest level of protection.

Ensure your marketability: Although you can't have job security, you can have security in the *marketability* of your skills. If you had to find new work tomorrow, do you know what skills you could sell? Do you know who to contact as potential buyers of those skills? Are your skills sufficiently broad that they have a number of possible business applications? Or are your skills tied to only one industry or one narrow business challenge?

Going through a process of self-assessment will help you know your product: the skills you have to offer, the kinds of environments in which you are most effective, and the ways in which you can add value to an employer or client. At the same time, you can enhance your self-confidence by evaluating your past accomplishments, in both your work and personal life, and the skills you used to achieve them.

Keep your portfolio up to date: With constantly changing work and shifting skill requirements, "lifelong learning" has become a necessity. Moreover, in our hit-the-ground-running business culture, it's up to you to do what is necessary to ensure the currency of your skills portfolio. Stay current in your field and continue to develop skills and knowledge outside it.

TempWorld offers many challenges to how we think about working life, as well as opportunities. Or as Frank Sinatra sang in "That's Life," you may be shot down in May, but you're "back on top in June."

Life in TempWorld

1. You will always have to re-prove yourself.
2. Success is conditional on your last hit.
3. You are affected by external factors and may move up and down economically, subject to these factors.

4. Your skills portfolio, interpersonal skills, and resilience will help safeguard you against external factors.
5. Relationships will be fluid, and you will have changing alliances as you move in and out of different projects, assignments, work situations.
6. There will be more commuter families as individuals go "where the work is," leaving others behind.
7. Communities will weaken as people leave family and friends to chase work opportunities globally.

If you want to thrive in TempWorld you will need to take personal responsibility for your career and your life. Understand future work trends so that you can be best positioned to seek out and make the most of every opportunity.

On Being
a Player

*D*ave, 50 years old, recently "early retired" from a large accounting firm. After spending close to a year on a job search, he came up with two offers: one, a well-paying position with a company in a suburb, the other part-time, and for less money, but in the financial district of a big city. He took the big-city offer. "Getting up in the morning, putting on a suit, and walking around all those tall buildings makes me feel like I'm still part of the action," he said.

Thirty-three-year-old Carol is torn. She wants to take 10 months off to "paint, think about things, test myself in new ways, feel what it's like to not be working." She can afford to do this, but feels held back by one concern. "What am I going to tell people if I bump into them on the street? It's not like I can say I'm taking time off to spend time with my children, or to go back to school. People will think I don't count anymore, that I've lost my edge."

Fifty-five-year-old Peter has just sold his very successful business in a deal that leaves him free of any financial concern for the future. And yet he is desperately pursuing new business ideas, however unsuitable. By Peter's own admission, these ventures are more appropriate to someone half his age. Nor do they make good use of his skills as a highly accomplished professional who still has something to contribute.

What do these three people have in common? They all want to be players, they all want to be "in the game." Our society uses work as its currency to determine an individual's worth. So much of our sense of self is tied up with working, doing, achieving, and, most importantly, being *seen* to be achieving. And for some people, being a player is so crucial a part of their self-image that they make unusual or even misguided career choices to keep that status.

Being seen to be a player means you are important, an opinion-maker, a mover and shaker, someone who is going somewhere. Players are engaged and connected. Other people seek out their friendship and support. To not be a player is to be unimportant, almost irrelevant, inconsequential.

Sarah, newly downsized and disengaged from the workforce, tells a story of bumping into a former supplier at a party who used to actively cultivate a relationship with her. "When I told him I was no longer working, I saw a flicker of what looked like pity in his eyes. Then he just got up and walked away, as if I had ceased to exist."

This is truly a tragic reflection on what we value today. Most of us complain about the demands of our work, yet it does provide us with a vital source of identity and self-esteem. Many people say that if they could, they would stop working. But most of them, if actually confronted with that as an option, would likely continue working anyway. And successful small-business owners often refuse to let go long after they should, because their whole sense of identity is tied up with their business.

By the same token, we feel uncomfortable around people who aren't working. We have trouble finding a point to connect with, and we even feel sorry for them, as if they are no longer valuable contributors to society.

Players and Non-Players

Who wants to be a player? Obviously, everyone wants to feel important, to feel they are doing work that makes a difference. If the opposite of being a player is being a schlep, no one would tell you that they want to be a schlep. But certainly, some people are more driven to be players than others.

Everyone has different views on what it means to be a player. For some it means being in the know, having your hand on the pulse, being connected. For others, it means being a leader in your field, or being an innovator. And for yet others it means being the best. Many talented professionals and accomplished artists have left their field once they learned that they would fall short of greatness: being "really good" was just not good enough.

For some people, *where* they are a player is as important as what work they are doing. Linda, for example, a human-resources consultant in a large financial-services company, was offered the opportunity to be the vice-president of a high profile organization in the public sector. But she worried that being in the public sector wasn't as sexy or high profile as being in financial services. I've come across this quandary many times: people are attracted to working in the public sector but worried they will no longer be seen as a player because the work is not as closely related to the bottom line.

People are motivated to become players for different, although sometimes overlapping, reasons. One common element is the search for some kind of *recognition* or acclaim – being seen as making the best deals, getting the biggest advances, or having the largest consulting firm. But people differ in the *kind* of recognition they seek.

For some, the only acclaim that counts is the *public* variety, as measured in newspaper inches and TV appearances. But for others the playing field may not be so public. Some "players" turn to a relatively small community for their acclaim. For example, the back-room boys quietly wielding power behind the scenes, or the key adviser to the CEO. They are in the thick of things, with the people and in the places where big decisions are made. It doesn't matter to them whether the public knows about their contribution, as long as they are recognized as players by their peers.

This hunger for recognition, whether public or private, may or may not be tied to a drive to achieve. Some people are happy just to be *seen* as players: to have the title, the corner office, the high profile. But for others the title is not enough. You actually have to *own* the achievement, to have done something only *you* could have done. Typically, for this group, the achievement must be *quantifiable* – whether it's the size of the deal, the return to shareholders, or the number of employees working for you.

Some people cannot bear to be "one of" – that is, one of 20 computer programmers or one of 10 human-resource consultants. Jenny, for instance, took a cut in pay to be *the* director of marketing for a small organization, rather than one of any army of analysts working for a large organization.

There are also people who have been thrown into the game reluctantly. Because they have to work, they feel *forced* to become a player, and at this point their competitiveness kicks in and they find themselves playing hard. But at best they are ambivalent and uneasy. All things being equal, they would rather not be in the game.

For many, the desire to be a player likely can be traced back to childhood, as reflected in some children's excessive achievement strivings to be the best at whatever they do, or in children who constantly put themselves forward to be in the limelight whether to star in the school play or play the class clown.

Witness Pulitzer-prize-winning columnist and best-selling novelist Anna Quindlen. She told Jan Wong in a *Globe and Mail* column of how her "perfection complex" at age 16 drove her to "get all A's, be editor of the school paper, be a cheerleader. I wanted to be a star."

High expectations, though, are not always met. When we are young, we are seen as having all kinds of potential. But by the time we are in our 40s, we have largely played out that potential. By then it's apparent whether we are players or not. Many people in their 40s are grappling with the recognition that they will never be the players they thought they would be. Facing up to that reality can be a very painful adjustment, indeed.

The Dark Side of Being (or Not Being) a Player

Unfortunately, there is almost always a point when you "lose it" and fall out of the game. Perhaps the market takes a dive, business has turned sour, or someone younger and more capable has arrived on the scene. For those so heavily invested psychologically in being players, the price is huge, as their very sense of self is challenged. As television personality Ralph Benmergui told the *Toronto Star* of his own highly checkered career, "I think there's a certain lack of puffiness in what I do because I had to deflate myself and no longer be a major motion picture inside my own head." Players unable to adjust to life in the minor leagues may retreat and fall into depression.

Typically, players are never satisfied. They become addicted to the adrenaline rush of being "Mr. or Ms. *It*." Witness, for example, the number of highly paid CEOs who complain that they must retire at the age of 67. They are driven by a hunger that can never be filled. Instead of taking joy in achievements and tasks, they look for the next set of challenges to be overcome, the next mountain to be scaled.

Others seem unencumbered by the need to be a player. They can make life and career choices free of the burden of image. Being in the limelight, being seen to be doing work of visible prestige and status, simply are not important sources of their self-esteem. They are not motivated by external validation, or by the need to wield power and influence. Unfortunately, there is a downside here as well. Because they care little for prestige or status, they fail to seek out high-profile assignments perceived to have importance to management. As a result, they may be regarded by managers and colleagues as apathetic or uncommitted to their work. And yet they will often complain about being passed over for work that they would enjoy doing.

We are all motivated by different things. The key to going after what you want and making effective career decisions is being aware of what makes you feel important. Know yourself. If you want to be a player, don't be embarrassed about it. Some people, especially women, feel it's somehow unseemly to want to be a player, or to demonstrate the necessary competitiveness to become one.

Try to identify what it means to you to be a player, and identify the stage on which you wish to play. Instead of simply driving to become a player in your professional life, look for ways to be a player in your whole life.

What We
Didn't Do on Vacation

*T*here is a new epidemic in today's workplace . . . weariness. Recently, I put a question to a workshop for some 200 middle managers and first-line supervisors in customer-service work. I asked the attendees to identify their personal goals. What came through was a palpable feeling of being depleted, of having nothing more left to give. Almost to a person, they said their goals were to be reinvigorated, re-energized, renewed.

Most of these people, I thought, could benefit from a good long vacation. But I knew that they were unlikely to get one.

Taking a vacation used to be a simple matter. You booked your time off, and away you went. But in today's time-urgent, compressed workplace, what was once a simple decision has become fraught with complexities.

Harry, a sales manager, was finally able to get away with his family for a one-week vacation. But he was called back after five days to soothe an important customer.

Linda, a communications specialist, studied her vacation options for months, finally settling on a kayaking vacation in the Yukon. "I work so hard, and my free time is so precious, that when I do get away, I want to make sure it's a really meaningful experience."

Mel, a senior manager, recently returned from two weeks at the family cottage. "It was great to be reading and canoeing and fishing," he says. "But coming back to work was a nightmare. There were the usual thousands of faxes, e-mails, and voice messages, but I just couldn't motivate myself to process it. Re-entry was a real problem."

Laptops at the Beach

How do you stack up? Do you take your full allotment of vacation days? Do you completely de-wire while on vacation, or do you routinely check on e-mail and voice-mail? Are you able to mentally disengage yourself from work or is your mind back at the office? Do you return from vacation refreshed and reinvigorated? Do you come back feeling you have had a great time but looking forward to getting back to work?

Leisure experts suggest that most people need two consecutive weeks to really benefit from a vacation. But for many people today, that is no longer a viable option. The pressure of work demands and deadlines is such that they are able to get away for a few days or at most a week at a time. Even then, like Harry, they may be called back early to deal with some real or imagined crisis.

How often, these days, do you get someone's voice-mail only to hear, "I'm away on vacation this week but I will be calling in to check my messages." How often do you see travelers toting their laptops along with their golf bags, so that they can continue to work on that proposal or gather up their e-mail, or carrying their beepers and cell phones to the beach? Under pressure from both employers and customers, people feel unable to make a clean break – and technology makes it that much harder to do so. The result: vacations don't accomplish what they should.

Organizational expectations can weigh heavy. As one professional reports, "In my organization, long days are demanded, vacation weeks are often postponed, and all-nighters are all too common. These expectations are underscored by a second in command who works late – sometimes until midnight – most nights, works almost every weekend, and whose one-week vacation turns into three days off because she finds it necessary to be in the office. The company has a policy of allowing all employees to take four Fridays off in July and August. In reality, many of these are not taken, either because workload won't permit it or because senior management schedules important meetings with you and clients on the very days you have booked off."

Those who do swim against the current and take exceptionally long vacations often create consternation among their colleagues. "I wish I could afford to get away for so long," they say, meaning, "*My* work is far too important to let me get away for so long."

Then, too, many people seem afraid to take a longer vacation for fear of what will happen on their return. They know that, like Mel, they will face a mountain of work that has accumulated in their absence, but with a diminished will to get through it. "Every time I start to really relax, I pay the price," Mel says. "I start to question why I'm working so hard all the time. I lose my edge. Eventually I get back up to speed. But it's always a struggle."

Indeed, some people worry about whether they'll be able to rev themselves up sufficiently after vacation to go back to what they've been doing. It's almost as if they feel their commitment to work is so fragile and tenuous that once out of the work environment they will lose it completely.

The decision of how much vacation time to take becomes a kind of cost-benefit analysis: "How relaxed can I afford to get? Do I take the kind of vacation I need and suffer the consequences later, or do I take a shorter vacation and minimize the downside when I get back to work?"

And then there are those who fear that if they go away for an extended period of time, their employers will discover that they can manage well enough without them. We might call this the Ted Baxter syndrome, after the classic episode of the old *Mary Tyler Moore Show* in which newscaster Ted is forced to take a vacation, and discovers that he is all too replaceable. After a decade of downsizing, this may appear a perfectly reasonable fear.

The self-employed may find it even more of a challenge to take a vacation. They worry about losing customers, missing potential sales – the out-of-sight, out-of-mind anxiety. Then there is the question of whether there is anyone they can trust to cover for them while they are away. Along with these complexities, they may also have difficulty in disengaging, because so much of themselves is tied up with what they do. Many small-business owners are so overly identified psychologically with their business that when they are away from it for any length of time they lose their sense of meaning and direction.

The self-employed can also be victims of their own empowerment. Because they are in charge of what they do and when they do it, they can in theory take a vacation any time they choose. On the other hand, there is no compelling reason to take a vacation at any given time, or indeed to take one at all. There is no one telling them when to take off, and they are not going to lose any paid vacation days.

Productivity Suffers

In the short term, organizations may appear to benefit from having employees so willing to cut back on their vacation time. But there is a longer-term cost. Ultimately, exhausted and depleted staff are not high-performing staff. Indeed, intelligent organizations might well wonder about the *emotional wellness* of individuals who do not insist on taking the time they are entitled to in order to refresh themselves.

To their credit, at least some organizations have become concerned about people who never take a long enough break to be properly refreshed and rejuvenated and have taken steps to discourage such compulsive "presenteeism." They have tried to communicate to their staff the importance of taking a vacation by limiting the number of vacation days staff can carry over from one year to the next. Some innovative organizations have gone even further, treating additional vacation days as a negotiable benefit staff can "buy" – reinforcing the value of vacation time in people's minds. Similarly, some organizations encourage staff to take sabbaticals of up to six months to engage themselves in new pursuits, whether it be trekking in the Himalayas, landscape gardening, or volunteer work. Organizations who have adopted these strategies report that they are reaping gains in creativity and productivity.

Such enlightened attitudes, however, remain the exception rather than the rule. Most organizations continue to tolerate, even encourage, their people's avoidance of longer breaks, while many managers think nothing of interfering with their workers' vacation plans.

Consuming Leisure

As average vacation times shrink, many people are gripped by much the same imperative that drives their work: to do more with less. It's no longer enough just to have a pleasant break. Instead, people feel driven to cram a month's worth of experience into a few days. Whether it's helicopter skiing or white-water rafting or climbing Mount Everest, it's almost as if we've become so tired and jaded that an ordinary vacation doesn't do it for us anymore – we need a Technicolor experience to experience it at all.

Then, too, we have become so accustomed to acting, doing, and achieving that we become uncomfortable when confronted with the blank canvas of leisure time. So we buy an experience to fill it.

There's an element of conspicuous consumption here as well. That African safari may be enjoyable in itself (or it may be dull and grueling), but the experience of it is immeasurably enhanced by being able to brag about it when you get back to the office.

Even when people go away to a retreat, there is often the same tendency to reduce experience to a consumable commodity. Indeed, when presented with a menu of stress reducers, people may get even more stressed out deciding what to do. "Should I go for homeopathic medicine at 10:00 or aromatherapy? Should I do Pilates or go for a 10-mile hike?"

For the most part, then, what we *don't* do on vacation is what we could benefit from most: relax and recuperate from the strains of work, and renew ourselves through personally meaningful pursuits.

Why the Grass
Isn't Always Greener . . .

When I was young, I would look into the homes of my Christian friends and neighbors and wonder at the delights and treats and family bonhomie that lay beneath the twinkling lights. It was only when I was an adult that I realized how romanticized my beliefs were. Christmas, although joyous for many, can also be fraught with disappointments, repressed tensions, and bubbling resentments.

There are certain times of the year, such as post-vacation September and just after New Year's, when people return to work with feelings of disappointment, looking at their day-to-day lives with a jaundiced eye. They believe secretly – or not so secretly – that other people have better jobs, make more money for less work, get better bonuses, are more appreciated by bosses and colleagues, have work that better meets their personal needs, and just generally have more fun. They believe, in other words, that the grass is greener elsewhere.

This myth of the better job – or life – next door, or perhaps across the street, is widely held. Partly it stems from the tremendous pressures that people are under today. People everywhere feel overworked and under-rewarded. It's not surprising that they tend to overestimate how much fun other people are having at work, while underestimating their own career and life satisfaction.

This belief is also formed, in part, by a lack of understanding of workplace realities. I do a lot of work with early career individuals in professional-service environments. Their picture of the working world is largely excerpted from stories told by their friends. So, for example, they will insist that professionals in private sector companies make more money than they do and are paid double time for any hours over 35 in a week. When challenged about the origin of their beliefs, they almost always mention the proverbial friend's friend.

For many people, the notion that the grass is greener elsewhere is exacerbated by the notion that it was somehow an accident that they have ended up in a particular professional course – that they never really *chose* to become what they've become. Looking back, it all seems arbitrary, somehow: If a particular company had not been aggressively recruiting on campus, or if a friend had not referred them to their employer, or if they had not made a spur-of-the-moment reply to a recruitment ad, they would not have embarked on the series of events that culminated in their doing the work they are doing now.

If your career choice was an accident rather than a matter of choice, if it seems to you that you merely "fell into" what you are doing, you might well ask, "How do I know I wouldn't be happier doing something else?" This is, in fact, the most common type of career angst one sees among educated managers and professionals in First World countries.

When people believe that the grass is greener elsewhere, the danger is that they will jump jobs or careers prematurely. Instead of doing a thorough assessment of both their short-term interests and long-term needs, they move on at the first opportunity, in the belief that all kinds of things will work out in their new job. Unfortunately, in many cases, they discover that their new job is not a panacea — that in many ways they were actually happier before. Moving on may solve one problem (for example, getting a higher salary) while creating new ones (bad management, tighter resources, etc.).

Rather than jumping from an imagined frying pan into a real fire, you should first take stock of your current situation, and ask: In what way is it meeting my needs, both in the short- and long-term? What am I giving up by staying where I am? What is disturbing me? How will moving on lead to my achieving greater fulfillment?

Interestingly, when people go through a meaningful and rigorous self-assessment, they typically discover a number of things. First, they learn that they have indeed made career choices. Rather than being the servant of a series of accidents and arbitrary career events, they have gravitated into certain areas because they were good at them and because doing that type of work was satisfying. By the same token, they have moved away from work situations and environments that did not play to their personal preferences and aptitudes.

They also often discover that they are enjoying their work much more than they realized. It's just that one or two things have taken on disproportionate significance in coloring how they feel about their work. For example, 33-year-old Jane, after a self-assessment of what she really cared about and what she was good at, observed, "Hey, I really like doing what I'm doing. The only thing that's really bugging me is that I'm not getting enough recognition and I guess now that I've identified that I can do something about it."

Similarly, people often will say, "Although there are one or two things that are disturbing me — and I'm going to look for ways to minimize them — on balance, when I look at all the things that are positive, these things seem to pale in importance."

Living in Real Time

Effective career management means making informed choices. You may not be able to get everything you want right now, but you may be able to get much of it. For example, in the short-term you may choose to put up with a boss you don't particularly care for because you are being exposed to a new technology and are getting great experience.

As a general rule, however, the older you are, the less flexible you should be about making tradeoffs. I thought it odd when a highly accomplished 45-year-old engineer was going to move into what he described as a "killer environment" where he would be working 80 hours a week because the experience would look good on his résumé. At what point, I wondered, would he see himself as living in real time, as opposed to continuously upgrading his credentials in preparation for some imagined future where he would at last be rewarded for his sacrifices.

Sometimes, of course, it is time to move on — not necessarily because your job is horrible, or because the grass is greener elsewhere, but because it is too easy to be lulled by the daily predictable comforts of a well-worn routine. Perhaps it's time to test yourself, to go out on the edge, put yourself on the line.

The path to renewal may be across the street, or it may be in your own backyard.

part two

The New Worker

The Search
for Authenticity

*I*n my 20s, while completing my Ph.D., I worked under contract for a large petrochemical organization. Coming from a family of small-business owners, I thought corporate life the absolute height of glamour.

Desperately hoping this contract position would lead to full-time employment, I studied the behaviors, dress, and deportment of the successful women in that organization and tried to emulate them. But despite my best efforts to "act corporate," I did not receive a job offer. I was torn between extreme disappointment and relief. In retrospect I realize that the awkwardness of my impersonation, and the ambivalence behind it, must have come through.

Sacrificing the Self

Traditionally, much as in the book *The Man in the Gray Flannel Suit*, "acting corporate" has meant being "in role," wearing a mask, donning a false persona, numbing yourself: never letting people know what you're really thinking, never displaying too much enthusiasm (you might say "that's quite good" but not "that's wonderful!"), never being emotional or self-expressive or spontaneous.

But where once people accepted the need to conform to corporate norms as a fact of life, today there is a widespread perception of organizations as demanding the sacrifice of individual selfhood.

Across the board, from senior managers to the most junior employees, people are no longer so willing to act different from "who they really are," repressing important aspects of their personality, in exchange for employment. More and more, people list the need for personal authenticity among their key criteria for satisfying work. It's not only "I want challenge" or "I want a good salary" but also "I want to be myself at work . . . I don't want to have to hang up my values and personal style at the door."

Women, of course, have always struggled with the demand to check their emotions and expressiveness. For example, Sandra P., a senior manager in the communications industry who has an amazingly loyal and committed staff, has often been criticized by her executives for being "too complimentary" to her staff. They say she is too effusive, too open. Basically she is too Technicolor for them, too willing to show her hand. "What kind of world are we living in, when you're criticized for being enthusiastic?" she asks.

Similarly, it was no accident in the 1970s and 1980s that many women railed against a "dress for success" dress code based on the thoughtless and silly feminization of the male suit, designed to make them look as sexless as possible.

Although women may have borne more of the brunt of having to fit into what many of them experienced as a hostile culture based on traditional male values of toughness and competition, this is certainly not an exclusively female issue. When David P. was fired from his senior-management job in manufacturing, his life went into a tailspin. As he went through a rigorous self-assessment as part of his outplacement, he realized that he had spent the last 15 years "first play-acting, and then *becoming* that role. I had become someone I didn't like – cold, impersonal, obsessed with the bottom line – and in the process had sacrificed some of my most fundamental values. And I had bought into a lifestyle to support my role as a senior executive that had nothing to do with what I cared about as a person. I lived where I was supposed to live, sent my kids to the right private schools, played golf even though I found it pointless and boring."

Generational Pressures

When I asked a group of 20-something engineers working for a civil engineering consulting firm what was most important to them in a job, one man said, "Being able to be my authentic self at work." His comment was met with widespread agreement.

The search for authenticity has become a major issue for 20-somethings, who ask questions like:

– "What's the big deal about a second hole in my ear as long as I'm well-groomed?"
– "Why can't I wear jeans to work if I'm not meeting with a client?"
– "Why can't I work closely with important customers without being micromanaged?"
– "Why can't I take time off to run in a marathon if I'm putting in the hours to make up for it?"
– "Why do I have to give up my personal life to get ahead?"

This is a generation that grew up in a period of social, economic, and environmental upheaval, when all traditional North American values were being questioned and all our institutions were under fire. It is not surprising that they are so irreverent and detached, so lacking in respect for traditional organizational norms. It's not like the "suits" have done such a great job, they say.

Indeed, if the organizational climate is now shifting to allow people greater freedom of dress and expression, it is at least partly in response to pressure from these authenticity-seeking 20-somethings. Organizations are increasingly aware that if they want to attract, hire, and retain the best of this generation, they need to accommodate their demands for a freer environment.

Of course, the nature of the people who run organizations has changed, too. The pre-baby boomer generation who once dominated organizational life are heading into retirement, taking with them a set of values shaped by Depression and war that stressed the need for hard work, sacrifice, and toughness.

Taking their place in the upper reaches of the corporate hierarchy are front-end baby boomers, born in the late 1940s and 1950s. These boomer bosses are more sceptical about the value of corporate conformity, and more tolerant of diversity. They are also, in many cases, themselves working much too hard in their downsized organizations to sweat, in the way their predecessors might have done, the small details of what's acceptable versus unacceptable behavior.

When Work and Personal Boundaries Blur

Alongside this demographic changing of the guard, the structure of organizations has been changing, too. The old hierarchies are breaking down under the pressure of new technology, a newly diverse workforce, and new ways of working such as project work and, in particular, telecommuting.

It's not surprising that research shows that telecommuters are happier than other employees. For one thing, telecommuting provides enhanced flexibility in the use of time — allowing individuals to better balance work and personal life. But perhaps just as important, it permits something closer to a seamless connection between work domains and personal domains. For example, if you want to work in your pajamas while listening to Bach, or have your lunch at 3:00 in the afternoon, you can. The more time people spend outside traditional work settings, the freer they feel to be who they are – and the greater the "slippage" from organizational norms. One of the more common comments I hear from telecommuters is that when they do have to go to the office, they forget what is considered acceptable dress.

Marsha G., a long-term bank employee who now telecommutes, describes the blurring of boundaries this way: "When you do come into work, you bring more of your personality with you. Every time I come in, people say, 'You look so happy. You can't be working hard enough – you don't look very stressed.'"

The example set by these telecommuters helps to subvert the norms even for those who remain in the office as they gradually start to set new standards for such things as dress, office hours, and behavior.

The sheer pace and pressure of contemporary work life is also helping to raise consciousness of the cost of inauthenticity. It's one thing to have to conform a little when you're working in a job you enjoy in a relatively convivial environment with time to reflect and prospects for promotion. But when you're working 80 hours a week under intense pressure to produce in exchange for what you see as insufficient rewards, that's a long time to spend being something other than yourself. People start to ask themselves: *Why* am I doing this? Is my work really meeting my needs? What am I giving up?

The recent upsurges of interest in spirituality in the workplace, as demonstrated by the number of conferences devoted to this topic across North America, is testimony in part to this hunger for authenticity at work. So is the increasingly influential movement towards "voluntary simplicity," in which people give up their high-paying jobs and luxurious lifestyles in favor of doing work that reflects their real needs and values.

It could be argued that this new hunger for authenticity is fundamentally a First World luxury, a privilege of highly educated people who have a range of choices. And indeed, when your primary concern is simply to put food on the table, you can't afford to spend much time worrying about whether you are acting in tune with your authentic self.

But when you do have choices, you should exercise them. Ask yourself, "What is the cost to me over time of working in a job that's not a good match for me?" For short periods, we may indeed be capable of making tradeoffs, doing work that represents less than a good fit with our interests and values in favor of pursuing other goals. But in the long term, we pay a heavy price when we deny our need to live an authentic life.

What Kind of
New Worker Are You?

*T*he project team had gone the limit, putting in several all-nighters and weekends to meet a demanding deadline. Management, in turn, put a lot of thought into choosing their way of expressing appreciation: an alarm clock with a big gold company logo, and a hundred-dollar-a-plate dinner at one of the city's fanciest hotels. They were therefore puzzled by the response of team members. Instead of responding with gratitude, most of the people looked, well, disappointed. "It's enough that I gave them my soul for the past four weeks, I don't want to have to go to bed and wake up with them," commented one of the team members, 27 years old. Another person enjoyed the dinner and the company of his co-workers, but said, "My idea of fun is not putting on a suit and eating in the kind of restaurants my parents go to."

Across the street, a similar organization called together their staff to celebrate the outstanding quarterly results they had just posted. The CEO said, "I wanted to thank you for your superhuman efforts. I'm not going to take up much of your time. I just wanted you to know that you are each going to get a cheque equal to five per cent of your salary. And you can choose an additional reward from a menu that includes extra vacation time, club memberships, or course or conference tuition." People walked out with huge smiles on their faces.

These examples illustrate some of the ways in which rewards can go awry from intention to reception – and some of the ways in which rewards can delight individuals when they are customized to individual needs and preferences.

I am often asked, "How do you motivate the new worker?" But there is really no such thing as a single type of clearly definable new worker. Today's workers do have certain shared experiences, attitudes, and beliefs, including an awareness that in an uncertain work world it is up to them to plan and manage their careers and keep their skills portfolio updated. But they also bring to the table a complex constellation of psychological motivators.

People are different, in other words – and this is hardly news. Still, the range of motivators driving today's new workers is broader than ever. And people have become much more assertive in expressing their individual preferences.

Understanding your own motivational profile can help you identify what is most important to you in a work setting. For managers and organizations, understanding the profile of staff members can help in designing effective rewards and systems to attract and retain the best talent.

I have grouped what motivates the new worker into six idealized profiles. While each profile has its own defining characteristics, individuals may share characteristics from more than one:

Independent thinkers or entrepreneurs: "I need to be free to choose and be in charge of what I do, for whom, and when." These independent problem-solvers want to own or build their own work, whether working inside an organization on a project or in their own independent business. They are impatient with corporate norms and procedures and have little allegiance to the corporation. Hanging around the office too long or being forced to go to an endless round of meetings makes them antsy. They are motivated by autonomy, and need to feel they are living in a free-form world that they can shape.

Almost by definition, independent thinkers are uncomfortable with "received wisdom," preferring to create or invent their own way. They are prepared to take full responsibility for their successes and failures. But in order to do so, they have to be in charge. They also need to be doing work that in their own terms is meaningful and has impact – whether it is a project important to management, the development of a new customer-retention strategy, or the creation of their own business.

As employees, independent thinkers are responsive to having money at risk – whether a bonus, commission, or other type of pay for performance. Hell for them is the off-site "team-building event" complete with highly pro-grammed activities for golf, tennis, and the scavenger hunt that allow them no freedom of choice.

Lifestylers: "I work to live, not live to work. I want to enjoy my work, but it's also a means to an end. I want the flexibility to pursue my own personal passions." A range of people fall into this category: young resort workers who want the opportunity to pursue their love of outdoor activities; 30-something parents determined to balance their work and family life; mid-career individuals saddled with eldercare responsibilities along with commitments to children; young professionals who value the freedom to pursue personal priorities.

As one example, many young professionals I work with in Vancouver say they would be loath to take a transfer to a bigger job in Toronto, because it would take them away from the mountains and into harsh winters. They are typically prepared to work hard to do whatever is necessary to get the job done. But they expect their hard work to pay off, by buying them free time they can enjoy in the way they prefer.

Personal developers: "As long as I'm learning, I'm happy." This category includes many 20-something contract workers, frequent job changers, as well as independent consultants. Most Information Technology professionals fall into this group.

Personal developers evaluate their work in terms of whether they're being stretched, or whether they are acquiring a new skill. They are very quick to become bored, particularly if they are in what they see as a dead-end job. Although not risk-takers by nature, they are prepared to take career risks if it will stretch them or expose them to a new arena in which they can acquire new skills.

Personal developers are not without ambition. For many of them, it's important to advance in their careers and become players in their profession. But their identification is very much to their profession and their work, and not to any particular employer.

Interestingly enough, despite most people's beliefs about young MBAs being motivated primarily by money, nearly half of 1998's crop of U.S. business-school grads turned down their highest-paying job offer, opting instead for ones that offered more room for personal growth (*Business Week*, May 22, 1998).

Careerists: "I want to get ahead, and I am willing to make the necessary sacrifices." Obviously, this category is not new. In fact, most careerists resemble the profile of traditional baby boomers who evaluated their success in terms of opportunities for advancement and increasing work responsibility.

Although some careerists want to be players in their profession, they are more likely to want to move into general management. They tend to take a longer-term view of their career, but differ from the old-style careerist who saw a predictable future within a given organization. Although they are prepared to entertain the possibility of having a long career with their present employer, they also recognize it could just as likely take place elsewhere, and their horizons are more likely to stretch across an entire industry, several industries, or types of work settings.

Careerists are ambitious, motivated by prestige and status. They recognize that as they move up the ladder, they may be moving into other areas that reflect increasing responsibilities. A young lawyer looking down the road, for example, may equally see himself as partner in a large firm, a chief corporate secretary, or head of his own firm.

Authenticity-seekers: "I gotta be me." Individuals motivated by authenticity refuse to "hang up their personality" at the door. They won't sacrifice their own personal expressiveness in order to play a corporate role. Don't ask them to put on a uniform, or to repress their personal values in favor of "what's good for the company."

In some ways, this group shares characteristics with the independent thinkers, because of their demands to be self-expressive. If they run their own business, they will typically infuse it with a strong personality that reflects their own style.

Authenticity-seekers can be quite creative, but difficult to manage if their employer demands conformity to corporate norms. This does not mean they cannot be happy working for an organization under any circumstances. Indeed, many disaffected mid-career changers complaining about the soullessness of the corporate sector's pursuit of the bottom line have moved into the not-for-profit sector to do work more in line with their personal values.

Self-expressive 20-somethings choosing to work for a small, hip software developer ("I can wear jeans to work, have a lip ring, shoot hoops at night") or starting a webzine because it is more in sync with their personal style, are also often authenticity-seekers.

Collegiality-seekers: "I need to work with people. I'm a people person." Collegiality-seekers associate strongly with their team or work group and derive much of their identity from belonging to it. They are extremely loyal to whatever group they belong to. Fun for them is going out for a drink after work with other members of the group. They welcome signifiers of their group membership, whether a photo of the team or a plaque commemorating a particular project.

Members of this group regard careers as important, but when asked what is most important they usually say it is working with people they enjoy. As one woman manager who had just recently moved into a new job from a role as an independent consultant put it, "I need to have a tribe."

Although collegiality-seekers are often attracted to working for large organizations, they may also choose to work in smaller firms, so long as their needs for affiliation are met. Unlike their independent-thinking or entrepreneurial counterparts, this group loves the team-building events that take place at off-site meetings. They are not happy working by themselves. As a general rule they are not drawn to telecommuting.

Many contract workers who are collegiality-seekers complain about the lack of belonging they experience going from contract to contract. Unfortunately, as independent work becomes the norm for them – whether as project workers, contractors, or independent consultants – these "people-persons" may be disadvantaged.

Tailoring Rewards

Savvy employers can take advantage of understanding the different types of new worker by tailoring rewards and systems to reflect different motivations. They need to offer a variety of options, such as additional vacation time, flexible time to accommodate caring for elderly parents, money to attend a conference, or the opportunity to own a high-profile project. In this way, employers will be able to individualize rewards and meet the broad range of preferences that characterize the new worker.

The New Worker

Type	Motivation
Independent Thinkers/Entrepreneurs	Autonomy
Lifestylers	Flexibility
Personal Developers	Learning/Growth
Careerists	Advancement
Authenticity-Seekers	Self-Expression
Collegiality-Seekers	Belonging/Loyalty to Team

Career-Defining
Moments

When Carol received her performance appraisal, her boss told her, "You're doing outstanding work — with a little more seasoning, you'll be an excellent candidate for my job."

Carol was surprised at her own response. "I knew I should feel flattered and excited. But I just felt flat. I had always *assumed* that this was what I wanted, but once it became a reality, I realized that it wasn't what I wanted at all. It would be more of the same, only with more headaches."

Ted, a 50-something professional with his own practice, got a letter from his building's management company offering him a 10-year lease renewal on his office suite. "Suddenly I found myself asking, am I really going to be doing this for another 10 years?"

Most of us don't spend a lot of time thinking about our future lives and careers. We are busy enough just keeping our show on the road, doing, working. And there may also be the nagging, largely unacknowledged fear that if we looked too hard at what we are doing now, we might not like what we saw. Most of us just keep on keeping on. Until, like Carol or Ted, we hit one of life's *career-defining moments*.

A career-defining moment is one that forces us to take stock of where we are right now, and where we want to go in the future. It's a sense of having reached a kind of crossroads – a moment of decision as to our future paths.

Sometimes a career-defining moment is a dramatic incident that jars us out of our well-worn ruts: we lose a job, a close friend battles a life-threatening illness, we win the lottery. But just as often, it emerges from a relatively ordinary life situation, like Carol's performance review.

A career-defining moment is, typically, a signal that you need to change your course – or at the very least, sit down and think very carefully about your future.

At different times in our lives, most of us find ourselves doing work that is in some way wrong for us, from taking a job we really don't want, because it will "round out our résumé," to doing work that is mind-numbingly dull because we can't galvanize ourselves to seek out something better. For whatever reason, we lose the plot. Our work is out of line with our values and priorities, or else it lacks meaning and purpose for us. It is then that we are ripe for a career-defining moment.

Of course, such a moment need not lead us to change our lives. We can always ignore it, and hope it goes away. Ralph, a commercial lawyer, had a career-defining epiphany early in his career. "I saw that the only difference between what I was doing now and what I would be doing in 20 years was that the deals would be bigger and the consequences of error would be more severe. But otherwise I would be doing exactly the same thing."

Ralph, however, chose to ignore that insight. He has continued to practice the same kind of law, consciously trading-off the tedium of repetition against the status and monetary rewards his work offers him. In this he is no different from many other professionals who are similarly bored with the repetitiveness of their work, from CAs to management consultants to doctors. "Whoever said work was *supposed* to be fun?" Ralph asks.

Often, as in Ralph's case, failure to embrace a career-defining moment stems from a streak of Puritanism. So what if we're unhappy and dissatisfied with our work? Life is tough, we tell ourselves. Get over it. Don't be so indulgent. Stop taking your emotional temperature.

We may be sceptical, too, about our ability to reinvent our lives, asking, "What if I try to do something different, and I fail? I don't want to look like a pathetic wannabe." Feeling unequal to the challenge, we retreat instead into what we know, to the secure and predictable.

Often, we exaggerate the consequences of trying and failing. Old scripts, particularly ideas about our financial needs, may hold us back.

Sally, for example, was part of the management team of a company that was taken over. She received a large lump sum on being let go. At first, she felt a great sense of release. She had been bored with her work for some years, and this was a perfect opportunity to get into a business she had long dreamed of, designing and leading eco-tours. It was a venture that would bring together her love and knowledge of travel and fitness. But on second thought, she was afraid this was too risky. Perhaps she should simply look for another job.

After sitting down with her financial planner, Sally realized that she was being overcautious. Her house was paid for, her children had finished university, she had considerable savings. Even if her business venture failed, she would still have food on her table and a roof over her head. She could afford to take a chance.

Change is always scary. Reinventing yourself and your life always involves some risks. It's important to carefully examine the possible tradeoffs involved. But you shouldn't underestimate your own capacity to rise to the occasion, or to find the internal resources that will allow you to withstand setbacks and overcome obstacles.

So when you feel a career-defining moment, don't try to shrug it off. Instead, embrace it, and let it show you where you want to go.

Who Will Win?
Introverts vs. Extroverts

Carolyn L. is an independent management consultant who makes her living giving speeches and delivering workshops and seminars. Many people who know her think of her as being sociable and outgoing. They also consider her the consummate networker, with her Filofax full of business contacts and professional associates. And in fact if you knew her only through her work, you would probably describe her as socially highly skilled. Despite such appearances, Carolyn insists that she is actually an extreme introvert.

"When I'm giving a workshop," she says, "I always arrive just before it starts, so I don't have to stand around making small talk. And when I'm finished I don't linger to mingle, but get away as soon as possible. I rarely attend professional network events, and when I go to parties I never stay long. And perhaps most telling of all, I never have business lunches and I don't carry business cards."

The concepts of introversion and extroversion have become part of our everyday vocabulary. Parents, in describing the personality characteristics of their children, will label them as "shy" or "outgoing." In fact, one of the first distinguishing characteristics we invoke in describing what "someone is like" is their sociability: the extent to which they are friendly and outgoing.

Who Is More Successful?

There is still a lot of misunderstanding about the personality characteristics of introversion and extroversion, despite the efforts of psychologists like Carl Jung and H. J. Eysenck to explain the concept, and despite the remarkable popularity of the Myers-Briggs Type Indicator, which assesses these attributes, among others (and which has become as much a cornerstone of corporate life as the personal computer).

Typically, we equate social skill with extroversion so that we tend to think of people as being either social skilled extroverts or emotionally klutzy introverts. And because of the apparent connection to social skills, we attribute all kinds of other positive characteristics to extroverts, such as warmth, friendliness, authoritativeness . . . in essence, success. By the same token, we ascribe negative characteristics to introverts: they are withdrawn, quiet, passive, "won't set the world on fire."

And historically, at least, it has been the *apparent* extroverts who have been most valued in business circles for their ability to mix easily, establish relationships, put people at their ease, and facilitate team-building, all key attributes for success in managers. Indeed, when I ask people in workshops whether they believe there is a connection between leadership and sociability, they typically describe their senior managers as being extroverted. After all, being a leader means that you have to be "good with people" – the implication being that introverts are *not* good with people. This attitude is reflected in executive searches where the word "outgoing" is commonly used as an adjective for "leader."

Actually, this is a rather simplistic set of assumptions. The fact is that both introverts and extroverts can be "good with people," depending on the circumstances. Many introverts like Carolyn are extremely effective and successful in business. Their interpersonal success, however, is a function of *situational* characteristics, that is, the degree to which the situation is structured and task-focused or unstructured and open-ended.

For example, if you bumped into Carolyn on the street, you might think that she was awkward, standoffish, even arrogant, though in fact she is simply shy. (Nine times out of ten, when I hear people described as "arrogant," I know that they are probably shy or uncomfortable in social situations.) But in a more structured situation such as a workshop, with a clear purpose and set of objectives to be accomplished, Carolyn shines.

Indeed, when we look at senior managers, we see that very few of them are in fact extroverted. Most are in the middle of the scale (so-called "ambiverts") or on the introverted side. Being friendly and outgoing can only carry you so far. Typically, in order to achieve a senior-management position, you not only need to be able to establish relationships quickly and relate to diverse kinds of people, you also have to spend considerable time by yourself behind closed doors, thinking and planning. (Notable exceptions to this are senior managers in customer-service environments such as hotels, stores, and retail banks, where a significant aspect of management is accomplished by "walking around.")

Are you more extroverted or introverted? Do you get your energy from being around other people? Or do you prefer to spend time working by yourself? How comfortable are you in teamwork environments? Does an open-office concept energize you – there is always someone you can relate to. Or does it depress you – no privacy, you can't hear yourself think, there is always someone bothering you.

The answer to these questions could have significant implications for everything from your choice of work setting to your preferred style of learning (extroverts thrive in a classroom setting with lots of opportunity for discussion, while introverts are comfortable spending time by themselves quietly hitting the books).

Indeed, I am often surprised at how little thought people give to understanding their own sociability, how defensive they become when it is suggested they are more introverted than extroverted, and how little attention they pay to their own sociability in making important career choices.

John P., for example, was happy as a marketing manager in a field office, heading up a successful sales team. It was a noisy environment with a lot of social interaction and spontaneous meetings. The team was close-knit and often would end the day going to a bar together or to someone's house for an impromptu barbecue.

John was then moved to head office to examine the feasibility of introducing a new product. Now he spends most of his time doing research on the Internet, reading reports, and crunching numbers on a computer terminal, and he is miserable. Although he has all the technical skills to handle his new assignment, he is unable to function effectively in a work environment that provides so little interaction with people. John is now thinking about making a career move. With a little more insight into his own personality, he could have avoided this situation in the first place.

Understanding your own preference can also help you in your relations with colleagues and others you work with. For example, Bill, an extremely gregarious vice-president of human resources, liked to drop by the office of Susan, his training director, whenever he was working on a report – to "talk it out." Susan, an introvert, found these unplanned meetings extremely irritating. "Can't he do anything himself? Do we have to live out of each others' pockets?" she complained. Bill's reaction? That Susan was rigid, abrupt, and "uptight." Developing an appreciation for each other's preferred way of working led to a significant improvement in their relationship.

Leveraging Your Own Style

A little self-knowledge can also help you successfully navigate in today's emerging new workplace. That workplace is characterized by *temporariness*. Work is increasingly organized around teams that coalesce around a particular project and then dissolve once its objectives have been achieved. Some people work on these projects as full-time employees, some as part-time or contract staff, some as independent contractors, but all share the same need to market themselves for new assignments once the current project is over.

So who will be more successful? At first glance, extroverts might appear to be at an advantage in this freewheeling economy. Whether as employees or independent contractors, they would seem better able to network their way into the best projects, to work effectively in teams, to establish relationships with a broad range of people, and to market themselves effectively for new positions or contracts.

And yet, on closer examination, the picture may not be quite so one-sided. One of the paradoxes of the new workplace is that while you need the ability to work in groups, you also need the discipline to work by yourself, whether at home, in the office or on an airplane. Indeed, with the pressure to reduce office overhead and to meet people's needs for more flexible hours, many people find themselves spending more time working from home or on the road. Moreover, many types of work are increasingly being outsourced to independent consultants who work alone much of the time, often from their homes. For extroverts, who get their energy from others, working this way can be uncomfortable and dispiriting. One frequently hears about people who left corporate life to set up their businesses only to discover that they are extremely lonely and miss the collegiality of the office.

Introverts, on the other hand, may actually prefer the more temporary and superficial working relationships that characterize today's projects. They don't need to *bond* with anyone to get the work done. And in today's task-focused, get-to-the-point-quickly business culture this can be an asset.

And while they may be at an initial disadvantage when it comes to networking and selling themselves in the more traditional manner, introverts can still be successful if they can develop marketing strategies that suit their personalities.

I know a number of highly successful consultants who have established their professional credentials by making presentations at conferences, writing articles for professional journals, becoming media commentators. In other words, they have established themselves as experts in their field, so although they may be seen as short on "schmooze," they are high on knowledge and credibility.

Indeed, with sufficient effort, introverts can become more effective marketers than many extroverts – particularly the ones who confuse having lunch with people and collecting business cards with the meaningful exchange of information that will establish your credentials or help sell business. (One of the most common mistakes independently employed extroverts make is to confuse the number of social interactions they have with live business potential.)

By the same token, extroverts can develop strategies to compensate for their own difficulties in the new workplace. For example, some chatty extroverts say that they had to learn how to repress their natural desire to establish *personal* relationships with people with small talk before a meeting begins, or to go off on interesting tangents in the meeting itself.

Extroverts can also work happily and successfully as independent contractors, so long as they build regular social contact with clients, associates, and professional colleagues into their daily schedules. Other common strategies include joining professional associations, establishing weekly lunches or workouts at the gym with a friend, setting up brainstorming sessions with colleagues and customers.

Some will achieve this by finding a business partner – a good idea so long as it doesn't result in *two* unemployed consultants sitting around schmoozing rather than seeking contracts. (Unfortunately, there is a tendency for extroverts to be attracted to extroverts and introverts to be attracted to introverts instead of seeking out a partner who will offset weaknesses.)

Both introverts and extroverts, then, can thrive in the new workplace. The key to doing so will be *self-knowledge* — understanding the environments in which you will excel. Work is elastic: it can take many shapes and forms. The trick will be not just finding but also *shaping* work to play to your own strengths and preferences. That will mean looking beyond the received wisdom — that says, for example, that the only way to market yourself and your services is to attend every possible network event and to "schmooze" with everyone and anyone you can. The challenge then is to find new ways to reach the same objectives. If you understand yourself, you will be able to achieve them your way.

20-Something
Career Angst

"I look at bios of successful people and they've done far more than me by this stage of their lives. These past few years are the time people really get the kind of credentials and experiences that look great on their résumé and last them a lifetime. And what have I accomplished? Basically I've blown it . . ."
– DANNY J., 26-YEAR-OLD STUDENT

*D*anny was everyone's golden boy – high-school valedictorian, winner of scholarships to top universities, college football star, straight-A student. But after completing a master's degree in economics, Danny's effortless progress began to falter. He enrolled in a doctoral program in political science, but dropped out after six months: it just didn't seem to be what he wanted to do. He enrolled in law school, but that didn't feel right, either. Now he's contemplating an MBA. He's interested in business, and he has the analytical skills employers are looking for. But he's really not sure.

"What if I'm wrong again?" Danny asks. "If I make another mistake, I'll just fall that much further behind the eight-ball. I look at my friends who went straight into professional schools such as law or computer science or whatever, and they're doing great. But I still don't know what I want to do. I really should *know* by now."

Moreover, like many perpetual students, Danny is guilt-ridden about accepting any further financial help from his parents. Worse, he's worried about disappointing them yet again. He feels under pressure – whether real or imagined – from them and from others to grow up, get a career, and get it *right* this time. Terrified of making any commitment, Danny marks time as an office temp, profoundly confused and depressed.

Danny is suffering from 20-something career angst – something I see a lot of these days:

> *"Should I go for my doctorate, or start earning big money right now?"*
> *"Should I stay with a big public accounting firm or get a job in industry?"*
> *"What kind of work would really suit me?"*
> *"What should I be when I grow up?"*

Twenty-somethings, of course, are not the only demographic group prone to such angst. But they are particularly vulnerable to it. And it must be admitted that people in their 20s have *always* been prone to career confusion and indecision. If you had asked me when I was that age what I wanted to do I would have said, "I don't have a clue." Like Danny I was troubled that I did not have a clear sense of direction. I was also convinced that that meant there was something wrong with me, and that everyone else had it more "together" than I did. I was envious of friends who seemed more certain about their own eventual place in the world. It was only later that I came to realize that few people are as certain as they appear, and in fact, most of my friends were just as confused as I was: they just didn't talk about it.

But if 20-something career angst is not new, it is certainly more pronounced, and more intense, than ever. In today's fast-shifting economy, the stakes are much higher for early career individuals, the margin for error much slimmer. The cost of a university education has spiraled at a time when many parents are cash-strapped. The pressure is on early to make the "right" decision. Kids feel that ambling along, making it up as you go, is not an option.

Career Pressures

This anxiety is exacerbated by a heightened consciousness about careers. These days, college and university students are bombarded with career advice. Career centers are located right on the campus. Career planning is part of the core curriculum. Among the bestselling issues of newsstand magazines are the ones that feature cover stories on "where the hot jobs are." The clear implication is that you *should* know what you want to do when you grow up.

Moreover, with the exception of an elite group with in-demand skills, such as engineering and computer technology, 20-somethings face an extremely challenging job market. Whereas in the past organizations hired for potential, today they are more likely to seek new hires who can "hit the ground running" and deliver value *now*, rather than taking their time to learn the ropes.

The traditional effort-reward equation has changed, so that 20-somethings don't believe that the rewards − that is, challenging, well-paying work − will be there relative to their efforts. And they may be right. A recent report shows the earnings of men and women 18 to 24 have declined about 20% over the past 20 years, even among those who are university educated (*Globe and Mail*, July 29, 1998).

Moreover, the work landscape is shifting fast with new specialties appearing while old ones disappear. Managing your career in this new workplace requires both assessing your own skills and interests and evaluating a multiplicity of options to see where you might best fit in. Of course, for young people with limited or no work experience, making career decisions can present a real conundrum. And so many ask, "How do I know I'll like it if I haven't done it?"

Adding to this anxiety and confusion is the ambivalence that many 20-somethings feel about working for an organization. Having seen their parents make significant sacrifices in terms of their personal lives, working long hours and giving unswerving loyalty to their corporations only to be cast aside in the great downsizing purges of the past decade, they are hesitant to commit to follow in their footsteps.

It's not surprising, then, that so many 20-somethings are so frightened of making a bad career choice, and so anxious to make the "right" decision.

Fear of Career Commitment

There are a number of strategies that 20-somethings can use to manage their career anxiety. But first, I'd like to offer a word of advice to the *parents* of these Hamlets for hire: *Chill out.* Don't put so much pressure – or even the appearance of pressure – on your kids.

We live in a society where everything – and not the least, education – is assumed to have an end-product. As early as grade school we ask children, "What do you want to be when you grow up?" – as though they should already know and should be preparing themselves for a particular job right now. We shouldn't be surprised that children internalize these societal pressures to decide what they want to be. Or that, as young adults, unable to live up to those perceived pressures, they may become completely paralyzed, unable to decide anything.

For the 20-something individual wrestling with career angst, the starting point is to recognize that there's nothing wrong with not knowing what you want to do. *Don't overestimate the consequences of making a "mistake."*

Instead of chasing after that elusive "right" decision, recognize that there are many possible career paths. When you are 45 years old, you are not going to look back and say, "If only when I was 25 years old I had done A, B, and C." That decision may appear momentous in the present – all the more so if there are debts from student loans or parental pressures to contend with. But, in the long term, the decision will have little or no impact on prospects for successful participation in the work force.

The long term usually takes care of itself. Indeed, given the fast-changing nature of work and the accelerating shift towards an economy based on temporary employment, it makes little sense to try to plan out an entire career. Entering a workplace where even a "full-time" job may last only a few years, and work is increasingly done by contract workers and self-employed external suppliers, you should focus on building a portfolio of skills and experiences that will ensure longer-term employability. *There is no beginning line and no finish line* in careers – and no right or wrong time to pursue a particular career option.

In this context, every experience counts. Even bad work experiences, painful though they may be at the time, can be valuable and important. I know of few successful people who have not at one time or another had some really hideous work experience. It's simply part of growing up. And it's part of how we learn what we like and don't like.

Career angst is itself a painful kind of experience, full of indecision and soul-searching. Some people try to avoid this process by closing down their options. Rather than seeking work that will best match their interests and skills, they surrender to the marketplace and pursue some "hot" career path or other whether or not they are suited to it.

But if instead you engage with your career angst, and struggle with it, you will come out on the other side with a much clearer sense of your values and priorities, and a renewed commitment to career success.

"Hey 40-Something,
I'm Talking to You!"

*H*ey 40-something, get a life! You're obsessed with work, you measure yourself by short-term, narrow-minded, quarterly results, you think exercise and work-life balance comes from hopping on a treadmill, you don't know your kids.

You talk about values, but you don't have the balls to actually live them. So don't bore me by trying to sell me on your value statements.

You hired me because you said you wanted outside-the-box thinking, but every time I make a suggestion, you look at me like I'm crazy. You don't really want outside-the-box thinking. You do the same things you've always done, or you change the color of the box and tell us all about it in a company-wide e-mail.

We sit around in endless meetings and talk about what's wrong and what needs to be done. You tell us you understand, yet after the meeting things stay the same. If you spent a little bit more time actually *doing* something – being bold, shaking things up – and worried less about office politics and the way things have always been, you might actually get somewhere.

You say that this workplace cares about young people, but if I want to live, dress, talk, or act like a young person, you can't handle it.

You hold yourself up as a model and call yourself my mentor. You tell me that when you were my age, you were prepared to put in your time and earn your own way. Think about this for a second: I'm way overqualified for this job. And the truth of the matter is that you wouldn't even have gotten this job with your skills and qualifications today. You think I'm impatient and not willing to wait my turn just because I want to do something meaningful with my time.

You say all we're interested in is money. That's a conceit. You guys jump for money, too – it's just that you end up getting it.

We live in different worlds. You complain about how big your mortgage is and how expensive private schools are. But it was you who got us into this spot – bidding up the price of housing, overburdening the social system – and yet you still ended up with the great career and the two cars. Now we have to have roommates to get by and spend all of our time marketing ourselves for the next contract.

You stuck me in this cubicle and gave me e-mail. I spend half my life sending messages to the friends I never see, and listening to the calls going on around me, trying not to tune in on the ones where my cube-mates are working out their relationships, whispering, "I can't talk now," and quietly hanging up the phone.

I know I've got a lot to offer – I'm creative, independent, technically savvy, and prepared to take risks. Unfortunately, you don't seem to know how to take advantage of those skills and you never take my new ideas seriously.

I'm prepared to kill myself for my projects, even if it means working my butt off for a month around the clock, but I expect something back.

Don't tell me I'm your most important resource, because if you really cared about me and my career, you would treat me like I'm more than just a unit of productivity and not just a leverage for your career.

P.S. Just because you ordered Starbucks roast for the coffee maker and put in recycling bins doesn't mean you understand.

"Hey 20-Something, I'm Talking to You!"

*H*ey, 20-something, get real! You talk about how you are ideally suited to this new workplace because you grew up with a life on fast-forward – what do you think, I can't breathe and talk at the same time?

You think you've discovered independence and learning, like you're the first generation who was ever concerned about being challenged at work. You think you're so precious and unique, with your lattes (you didn't discover cafés), and your cute little shirts. But you're arrogant and you overestimate your qualifications. You may have knowledge in your head, but you have no experience.

You talk about office politics as if it's a contagious disease. Actually, it's how a lot of important information is exchanged and you can learn an awful lot about what's really going on.

You want everything to come easily to you and you want it now – high-profile projects, interesting work, contact with senior management. But you're never going to get ahead if you're not prepared to make some sacrifices, if you don't learn to play the game and what it takes to make a success of yourself in this organization.

You're not entitled to any damn thing except what you earn. The world is not going to offer you anything on a platter. You have a lot of potential, but you won't be able to realize it with this attitude. You need to learn to take a long-term view. You need to learn how to delay gratification, to pay your dues. You're not a kid anymore.

Your generation prides itself on its ability to take risks and deal with uncertainty. But ironically, you're always looking for guarantees that whatever you do is going to give you an immediate payoff, that it's going to lead to the right job or the right project or the right career path. Guess what — there are no guarantees. Getting ahead is not simply a question of following a formula and checking off the ingredients. You're never going to get the clarity or reassurance you're looking for.

And stop asking me for constant feedback. Sometimes I feel that you're always saying, "Feed me, stroke my ego." Of course you want to know how well you are doing. But you're not my only priority. And although I respect your need for feedback, sometimes you're going to have to live with either getting no feedback or waiting your turn.

You have no sense of the commitment I've made, or respect for anything that went on before you were here. You think everything was invented yesterday. You have no appreciation for the knowledge, wisdom, and know-how we have accumulated over the years, and trust me, being able to deal with people and touchy issues is no different today than it ever was.

You talk about this workplace not being sympathetic to your style and values. Why should I design a special workplace just for you?

Do you have to be so cocky? I know you want to make a meaningful contribution, and I know your opinions are important, but there are some skills you need to develop before you will be seen as a serious player here.

Yes, we want to hire you, but don't hold me to ransom with your signing bonuses like we are so desperately in search of talent that we will do anything to court you.

You have no sense of loyalty. All you care about is money. You would jump ship for an extra few dollars. You don't understand how to weigh up money relative to the kind of skills and opportunities you can get here. Balancing your work and personal life is all you ever talk about – your marathons, your time with friends. What, you don't think I care about my family, that I don't have a life?

P.S. I'm really sick of hearing how your generation is so much better adapted to the workplace because of your use of technology. Yes, I know how to work with new technology, I can use a computer, can multitask, and can take risks. But there is nothing wrong with being a team-player or being able to spell.

"Hey 20-Something/
40-Something, Shut Up Already!"

I'm tired of you boomers thinking you define the world, and I'm sick of hearing how hip and happening you 20-somethings are. I'm 35 and I can't wait around forever. When does my big career start? Why can't we have our shot at the brass ring, too?

Our problem? We grew up with all the big expectations for the big jobs, the big careers. But we just got there a little bit too late. You boomers got the great careers and the great houses. All we got were two huge recessions and your dregs. Instead of the big houses, the housettes; instead of the big jobs, the jobettes; instead of the luxury sports utilities, the minivans. I'm sick of my two-hour commute to a sterile subdivision in the middle of nowhere, being forced to live in the middle of beyond just to make ends meet. But you're not about to retire tomorrow, so please don't tell me to wait my turn.

Every time I pick up the newspaper I read about some hip young entrepreneur making millions on the net, doing something "cool" with a hot new webzine, or developing a line of street clothing, because "it came out of my culture." And now organizations want to hire young talent because of their voice. Don't you think I have a voice, too?

We're the ones paying the price for boomer excesses. When we arrived in the job market in the late '80s and early '90s there were no jobs. Everyone was downsizing. We couldn't even get unpaid internships. We missed out on all the opportunities to get ahead. So we traveled, or went back to school, just to do something.

Now I'm doing the same job that people who are younger and much less experienced are doing. And everyone wants to hire 20-somethings, because they're cheaper and organizations think they're more current and more flexible — more easily molded into the company's image. So they have them leapfrogging ahead of me even though I've got way more experience.

Stuck in the middle with you — that's how I always feel. I look above me and see a big pampered mass of boomers complaining about their investments and I look behind me and I see a whole bunch of self-consciously precious 20-somethings nibbling at my backside, who don't think I'm prepared to take risks. I *am* prepared to take risks, but I also want security. Wait till you have kids. Security will be important to you, too.

And both you guys, you 20-somethings with no kids and you 40-somethings with teenagers, can't you figure out a way to schedule important meetings that takes into account that I've got a young family and baby-sitting responsibilities? No, I'm not prepared to pull a whole bunch of all-nighters — are you going to look after my kids?

Sure I want the big jobs, the promotions, this is what I was brought up to expect. But I also want challenge and learning. When I look at a job, my first question is, how will this add to my résumé or my portfolio of skills? Not, "Will it lead to a promotion?" Unlike my boomer bosses I don't see my job as a lifetime commitment but as a short-term engagement. Work to me is a means to an end, not an end in itself. But I'm also capable of lots of loyalty.

I feel squeezed on all fronts, like the proverbial middle kid. Our generation wasn't sexy enough to be endlessly profiled or hip enough to be courted for its style and pluckiness.

So here I am, expected to be a good parent, spend time with my kids, go to the school and run interference with the teachers. And at the same time, I have 5,000 competing priorities at work. So the work isn't getting done the way I want it, and by the time I get home I'm so wiped I have nothing left for my kids, much less my partner. A personal life? I barely get through the day. Excuse me if sometimes I seem a little bit tired or sour.

So 20-somethings, could you please shut up about how our workplace isn't cool enough, and how sick you are of going from contract to contract? At least you *have* work, and the opportunity to get some great experience. And 40-somethings, stop whining about how you'll never have enough money to retire. No one told you to spend so much money and get so much in debt.

P.S. We're the real Generation X — the anonymous generation nobody notices or cares about, with no identity of our own. You can look it up if you like (in Douglas Coupland's *Generation X: Tales for an Accelerated Culture*).

What 20-Somethings
Ask About Work and Careers

I started my organizational career doing career counseling for young professionals at a large petrochemical company in the late 1970s. The most common questions I was asked was: "What do I have to do to become vice-president in the next five years?" and "I've been offered a promotion which involves a transfer to Pipsypoo – will my career be dead-ended if I refuse?"

These days, I deliver many career-planning workshops to young professionals. Their questions are for the most part very different. They ask fewer questions about advancement and career-limiting moves. Here are the questions I am asked most frequently.

If you're a 40-something, understand what is on the hearts and minds of your young staff. You may discover that many of these concerns are not that different from those you once grappled with. And if you're in your 20s, or even your 30s, look at these questions relative to your own questions about your career and your life.

1. I have devoted all this time and money to pursuing a particular professional course. What if I've made a mistake? With so many career possibilities, how do I know if this is really right for me?

This is an existential question – and one of the questions I'm most frequently asked. With career choices, much as in the choice of a house or partner, you can never be absolutely certain that there isn't something better out there.

This kind of doubt and second-guessing is hardly unique to 20-somethings. Still, with the stakes so high, this generation has a greater fear of making a "career mistake" than their predecessors. When boomers entered the workforce it seemed that there was an endless amount of opportunity. If things didn't work out, you could always "go across the street" and get another job. Today, people don't feel they have that luxury – the bar for participation in the good life has moved into the stratosphere. And so they worry that if they take the wrong job they will be left even further behind the eight-ball.

Often, people seem to believe that there is one *perfect job* out there for them. In fact, there is no magic bullet, no one perfect job. Some matches are simply better than others. Very few people know what kind of work will represent a good fit for them until they actually *do* it, so there is often a period of trial and error. If you do end up in a job that is a bad match, that's not such a tragedy. The worst thing that can happen is that you will learn more about what is important to you in your working environment, and will be able to use that knowledge to make future career decisions.

In the meantime, you can significantly increase the likelihood of finding work that is a good match for you by gaining a clear sense of your own skills and interests and using this information to evaluate opportunities presented to you. For example, if you know you need a lot of autonomy, and get impatient with office politics, then in your job interviews ask targeted questions relating to those subjects. Discover how decisions get made (will you be endlessly second-guessed?) and how much freedom you will have on the job (will you be endlessly micromanaged?). Is this the type of environment where everything is done in teams and by consensus, or is there latitude for individual decision-making?

The good news is that most people do end up making decisions that put them on the right professional course. Trust yourself.

2. I left my previous job because my boss was a jerk. How do I explain this in job interviews?

Without savaging your former boss, talk about how you had fundamental differences in the way you viewed the work. Most employers are sensitive today about person-job match issues. They understand that in one environment you may experience difficulties because of what is often referred to as "personal chemistry," but in another you may thrive.

You would be surprised at how many people leave jobs because of a serious conflict with the boss. They may love the work content, and the organization, but over time a boss who is a jerk will take a significant toll on self-esteem and attitudes towards work — especially when it occurs early in your career.

An interviewer may grill you about the circumstances of your parting. Show how you tried to solve the problems when they occurred. Personally, I think people who leave an unhappy work situation are demonstrating emotional maturity and a strong belief in their own marketability.

3. Should I take a job I don't want just to make some money?

There's no problem with this, particularly if you have serious financial obligations to meet. While the work may not, at first blush, rate highly in terms of being challenging or personally meaningful for you, all experience counts.

At the same time, consider the opportunity costs. Taking a job that does not relate to your personal interests, or the skills you want to acquire at this stage of your career, may lead to your missing out on better opportunities that you could have found by devoting yourself to a more rigorous job search.

4. When they hired me they said they were looking for outside-the-box thinking. But every time I express an opinion, they basically tell me to shut up. Are there any organizations out there which really mean what they say and will treat me like I've got something to contribute?

At a recent meeting of senior human-resource professionals, a 28-year-old with multiple degrees complained that although she had been hired because of her educational credentials, she was basically doing clerical work. There was widespread agreement in the meeting that many of the larger and more traditional organizations in this country talk a good line but have failed miserably to actually follow through in using the extraordinary talents of the 20-somethings.

As a general rule you will have greater opportunities to have a direct impact on the business in smaller, more flexible organizations, younger industries such as high-tech and entertainment, and startup environments. Larger organizations can provide meaningful opportunities for contribution when each division is organized as if it is an independent company or autonomous work unit.

5. Where can I find a 35-hour-a-week job with good benefits and security?

Nowhere. The reality is that no job today is completely secure. Even so-called traditionally secure environments like government and health care have been rocked by productivity pressures, downsizing, and restructuring.

In fact, as mentioned above, today we all have to think of ourselves as temp workers, whether we have a so-called traditional job governed by the traditional employment contract or whether we are temporary, contingent, or contract workers.

A full-time position may not be any more secure than temporary work, but it does typically offer some kind of benefits package. Many companies now provide a menu of benefits that allows employees to tailor their own package based on their personal circumstances. Single people, for example, can drop family dental care coverage or life insurance in favor of vision care benefits or access to Employee Assistance Programs.

As for a 35-hour work week – dream on! Few salaried jobs involve less than 40 hours per week, with most people routinely putting in 50 hours and some up to 60 or 70.

6. My boss doesn't have a life. Does that mean I can't have one either?

Being able to balance work and personal life has become a critical workplace issue. Increasingly, in evaluating work opportunities people are putting personal time and having a life on the table as a key ingredient in negotiations.

There is, however, a significant generational difference in expectations of just exactly what an appropriate work week is and the importance of balancing work and personal life.

Forty-something bosses say: "Get real. All my 20-something staff care about is whether they'll be able to run in a marathon or leave work at six to meet their friends. When I was their age, if the boss asked me to work late, I did. After all, that was what was expected of me."

Twenty-something staff say: "Don't hold yourself up as a model. You're out of shape, you never see your family, and your boss still doesn't appreciate you."

Your boss came from a generation which believed there was a strong link between hard work and fast promotion up the corporate ladder. Today, the effort-reward equation has changed, but the boomers have not changed their expectations, of themselves and others around them.

Within this context, it's your responsibility to manage your boss. Without being unrealistic, make it clear what you are prepared to give up in personal time, and what you will not bend on. For example, you may need to pull a few all-nighters to get a project in on deadline, but it is reasonable to expect some personal time in return. If your boss still doesn't "get it" and you don't feel that the effort-reward equation justifies the excessive demands, then start looking for other work. You can't enjoy your job or be an effective contributor if you resent being there.

7. I've been offered a promotion to a managerial role at my company, but I'm not convinced that it's right for me. After hearing what the job involves, I'm worried that it's going to take me away from doing the type of projects I really love to do.

Your concern is that if you turn down this promotion, you will not be seen as being ambitious. Not too long ago, people would have thought you were crazy to turn down more responsibility, the money that goes with it, and the opportunity to advance your career. Today there is more appreciation of people who are thoughtful in choosing to do the kind of work that suits them and plays to their strengths. In other words, there's no longer the knee-jerk reaction that a promotion is good and you should automatically take it.

You may also prefer to play more of a specialist role than a role in management. Unfortunately, higher-level positions typically do involve managerial responsibilities. Be frank with your boss about your concerns. They may be able to modify the position to give you a better blend of professional and leadership responsibilities.

8. Why should I kill myself in this job? There's no place to go in this organization, and even if I do make a superhuman effort, no one seems to notice.

Actually, you'd be surprised at how much people do notice. The problem is, most people are too busy, pressured, and self-absorbed themselves to acknowledge the extra efforts of others. Also, consider the consequences of doing poor work. Today the expectation is that everyone will be working at 100%. You can be sure if you're not pulling your weight you will be noticed.

While we all want external confirmation − being noticed and thanked for a job well done − defining your value in those terms ultimately is very limiting. You need to be able to reward yourself by monitoring your accomplishments and taking credit where it's due, rather than relying on others for feedback. Don't be shy about tooting your own horn. Keep people you work with informed of your achievements and how you have added value to the work. Ensure you are producing the kind of work you can be proud of − that's what usually gets people noticed − work that, perhaps more importantly, gives you a sense that what you are doing is significant and worthy of celebration.

9. I've been offered a job in an organization I'm really interested in working for in the long term but I know my circumstances will change in the short term (I'm planning to go to Europe to study Italian/to start a family/to take time off to finish my Ph.D. thesis). Should I take the job here knowing that I'm not going to stay and risk pissing them off?

As John Lennon observed, life is what happens when you're making other plans. The world rarely unfolds the way we expect it to. You may have plans to get pregnant, or take a trip, but obviously things beyond our control are also at work. Rather than worrying about what would happen if you left in the near future, think about the learning experiences you would be losing by not working for this organization and the missed opportunity to demonstrate your value.

Organizations are made up of human beings who understand that life is unpredictable. If you decide to leave for a personal reason, they probably will not hold your job until you return. But if you are doing an outstanding job, you are definitely in a privileged position among job seekers when you get back into the workforce. If nothing else, you have developed marketable skills and have established good contacts for the future.

Women in this situation who are planning to have children often worry that people will assume they have only taken the job to collect maternity benefits. Bear in mind that it may take years to get pregnant, you will likely be able to work throughout your pregnancy, and you can't possibly know now whether you will want to return to work after the baby is born anyway. So take the opportunity to get some experience and demonstrate your value when you have it.

10. In the future, who will be more in demand, specialists or generalists?

This is no longer a black-and-white dichotomy. The question today is really: Should I be *more* of a specialist or *more* of a generalist? So-called specialist work is usually tied to a particular professional area, for example environmental law, forensic accounting, or computer-based animation. Generalist work typically requires the use of a broader range of skills such as managing projects, coordinating resources, and implementing programs.

Today, of course, everyone needs such general skills as being a good team member, giving effective presentations, being able to establish credibility, working under pressure, and so on.

If you choose the specialist route, you will need both depth and breadth of knowledge at a very elite level. If you cannot say, "I am among the best people in my field in this city/country," this is not the route for you.

Remember also that the demand for specialists changes with technology, world events, environmental regulations, and so on, so *don't give up on your generalist skills*. Be sure to have a fall-back position.

On the other hand, the demand for generalists – people who can work with others from a broad range of disciplines – will increase as the world becomes increasingly complex. That said, you still need something to give you a competitive edge, professional expertise to "hang your hat on" – be it a good understanding of biomechanics, marketing, agribusiness, or something else.

11. I've been trained as an engineer/accountant/lawyer. I don't want to be limited to that role. How can I branch out into other areas?

This is one of the most common concerns I hear from young professionals who worry about being stereotyped. No sooner do they receive their professional designation, be it in law, engineering, or accounting, than they decide they really want to do something else.

In today's highly competitive job market, there is an easy way to change disciplines when you are starting out. Establish your skills and demonstrate your value to the enterprise in the area in which it is easiest to secure employment by virtue of your professional credentials. This is good advice whether you are an accountant who wants to move out of finance into marketing, or a lawyer who wants to move into communications. In other words, demonstrate your generalist skills to your employer before trying to compete with marketing professionals who hold specialized degrees in that area. You can then leverage the skills and experiences you have acquired to move into other areas.

One woman, after a short stint as a lawyer, parlayed her background in law into a career in journalism specializing in legal issues. Another lawyer used problem-solving and analytical skills to become a systems consultant.

A third combined her curiosity about people, her appreciation of individual differences, and her broad professional network to move into executive recruitment.

12. Do I need to do a lot of research on the job market? Can't I just go to a headhunter?

A headhunter is hired and paid for by companies looking for job candidates. You may want to approach a search firm that specializes in your field to increase your odds of getting interviewed by organizations you'd like to work for. But remember, recruiters do not necessarily have your interests at heart. They are not career counselors. They don't work for you, and it's not their job to find the best match for you. And they can only interview you for spots they have been hired to fill if your qualifications fit.

By all means talk to headhunters – but only as part of a careful and thorough job search of your own. Be aware also that, as a general rule, headhunters work at more senior levels, focusing on seasoned workers, or in high-end specialties such as information technology.

13. Do I have to work on my birthday?

Regrettably, your birthday is not a public holiday. Unless you choose to take it as a vacation day or a personal day, you will almost certainly have to work. Very few organizations have a policy of allowing their employees to take their birthdays off (although it's a nice idea).

14. If I'm called for an interview for something I'm really not interested in, should I go?

Yes. It's an opportunity to hone your interviewing skills, as well as to learn about another industry or type of work. Even if the job doesn't appear to interest you, you may be surprised and find that the job is a better match than you thought. You also don't know where the interview may lead, as the interviewer may well identify other opportunities that could prove more suitable.

15. I really want to travel for a while. Will a year off look bad on my résumé?

There used to be much more rigid ideas about what looked good or bad on a résumé – and periods of non-gainful employment were definitely considered bad. In the new work environment, however, we have very different concepts about what employment continuity means. It used to be that people would go to school, then maybe "take a year off" and go travel in Europe, and then get down to the serious business of earning a living – all in a more or less linear fashion, with an expected and predictable linear professional progression. The path today is far less straightforward.

Essentially, we are all working in what I have called TempWorld. Work life will consist of a series of short-term assignments and we will be constantly moving back and forth between different life domains, whether it be travel, work, family, recreation, and education, without any rigid boundaries between them. As such it no longer makes sense to talk about the idea of taking a year off as if that year has no value.

In a fast-changing global economy, independence, the capacity to take risks, self-management skills, and experience and knowledge of other cultures will be highly valued – precisely the behaviors and skills you will acquire in your adventure.

16. Should I do an MBA?

Pursue a higher-level business degree – for that matter any degree – only if it will help you achieve your *personal* goals. Don't undertake any kind of education simply because it's a "hot" professional qualification, or will give you entry to an area where you think the jobs will be in the future. In the long run, your time would have been better invested in upgrading your education in an area of personal interest.

The perceived value and demand for MBAs is extremely cyclical. Some years they are all the rage, while a few years later, employers are saying that people with the degrees are great with the spreadsheets but lack the creativity and depth of thought we need. You shouldn't pursue something just because you think that's what the market wants you to do.

17. What are the "hot" skills or occupations?

I'm not a great fan of preparing for the future by trying to second-guess where the hot occupations will be. I call it the "top 10" or "what's hot/what's not" approach to career planning. What's hot today can well be rendered meaningless tomorrow by any number of factors such as global events, the Asian flu, changes in government policy, and new technology. In fact, if you were to look at a list of what are currently considered hot jobs, you probably couldn't pronounce half of them, much less know what they are. Hot jobs change almost as fast as the weather.

Still, you can take advantage of business trends. For example, looking into the future we know that environment issues will continue to grow in importance. Similarly, as society continues to cut back on spending in the public health sector, anything that keeps people healthier longer will be a winner, as will anything that combines technology with biology. In an age of continuous learning combined with a generation weaned on media, being able to use the media to promote life-long learning in the field known as edutainment will be a hot area. Finally, keep in mind that aging boomers are tired and jaded, and have a growing interest in the environment: anything that packages recreation and physical fitness with environmental awareness – be it hiking in the rainforest or birdwatching – will continue to grow in popularity.

When making career choices, know what you care about. Don't try to second-guess the marketplace. Identify your own personal passions and pursue them.

18. What are the hot or best companies to work for?

To some extent this is a matter of individual preference. To one person, "hot" may mean a company that's growing, doing a lot of R&D, and has lots of young people to shoot hoops with in the office. For another, it may mean great international opportunities and working with leading-edge technology. As a general rule, many young people today prefer smaller, more entrepreneurial organizations that are growing in so-called hot areas such as edutainment, biotechnology, and other high-tech industries.

But you can't really stereotype by size. For example, I do a lot of work with the large accounting firms, where there is tremendous opportunity – if, that is, you are interested in the areas where they are growing.

For many people, the best companies are the ones that offer more autonomy and the opportunity to really make a difference.

19. I love my work but have been offered more money elsewhere. Should I tell my boss or will she think I'm blackmailing her?

Talent is scarce and very expensive to replace. If the issue is really one of money and that is all it will take to keep you, then you should tell your boss, and make it very clear that you are not blackmailing her. Given the cost of hiring and training a replacement, she probably has a real interest in ensuring you stay put.

On the other hand, if you are jumping ship for just a few extra dollars, it may prove short-sighted in the long run. Ask yourself, is everything equal in both positions in terms of training and development opportunities, in terms of people you can really learn from? If the answer is no, you may be much better off where you are.

20. If I'm well-groomed, why can't I wear a lip ring?

Good question. Much of this is determined by organizational climate. Are you working in a more conservative environment, like financial services, or a creative one, like advertising? If your boss is saying you can't wear a lip ring because clients will react negatively, check out how realistic this perception is. Many baby boomer bosses are projecting onto younger generations their own beliefs about what's acceptable.

As one young person in advertising put it, "We went to make the call, and the client had a nose ring, a lip ring, and was dressed more like I wanted to look than the way my boss was dressed."

What it comes down to is, how much does this mean to you? How much will you have to sacrifice personally? Is this worth a confrontation?

21. I'm in a dead-end job. Should I quit? How can I make the most of my time here?

You may have to rethink what you mean by a "dead-end" job. Even so-called McJobs can provide opportunities for making significant accomplishments over and above the day-to-day work. It's up to you to be vigilant in identifying potential opportunities. Make the most of your time in your current position by thinking strategically about how you can use your skills at a higher level. Look for opportunities to add value – for example by finding a problem and solving it – and take advantage of every potential learning experience.

Another strategy you can use is "shadowing." Are there people in your work environment from whom you can learn? Ask your boss or other people whose work interests you if you can follow them around for the day or accompany them on an important assignment.

At this stage in your career, you should not be thinking of the prestige associated with your job title, but what experience you can get from the job. Think in terms of accomplishments that you can add to your résumé: for example, taking over a project from your supervisor, winning the employee-of-the-month award, or making an innovative suggestion for service delivery.

Finally, remember that you're not in prison. If your job isn't meeting your needs, look for better work.

22. How do I move up in this organization? No one seems to notice the work I'm doing, and I don't want to be at this level forever.

Today's organizations are flat, making the competition for higher level work much more intense. There are more people chasing fewer opportunities. Rather than getting caught up in the prestige associated with your title or the number of salary increases you have received, ask yourself a few questions. Are you learning on the job? Are you gaining skills? Are you improving your own employability? Those are the real measures of success. Measure your progress not by your promotions but by the content of your work. Is it increasing in complexity? Does it have more of an impact on the success of the enterprise?

23. Some people seem so comfortable passing out their business cards, calling up acquaintances, meeting people for lunch. But to me all this networking seems a little forced. I know I'm supposed to be constantly marketing my skills, but at what point is enough enough?

People vary in their attitudes towards networking and the degree to which they are comfortable networking. One reason some avoid it is that they worry that they will be seen as using people, or else think it means acting phony.

However, studies show that successful people actively cultivate and maintain broad networks. Rather than looking at networking as using people to "get them to do something for you," they think of it as being one of the many resources they use in managing their career and work — as, in this instance, a knowledge resource. Other people are vital stores of information and knowledge about how things get done, new ways of thinking about a problem, potential new clients, new ideas, new opportunities. Don't think purely in instrumental terms, evaluating the usefulness of a network member in terms of their ability to "pay off" by delivering a job lead or client contact. Think of yourself as developing mutually supportive relationships in which you may be helping someone who helps someone else, and eventually the favor returns to you.

Keep your network as broad as possible. Stay in touch with people you went to university with and former managers who can be an important source for references and work leads. (See Part IV for more on networking.)

24. I really hate office politics. Is there any workplace out there where being political isn't part of the package?

A lot of people say they don't like office politics, but as often as not the politics turns out simply to be different groups of people expressing different points of view and trying to influence each other or make them understand their opinions. In fact, this can be an extremely healthy and creative way to communicate. If, however, you are referring to a level of politics that is simply petty whining about personalities, you have control over your entry into the fray.

What is often thought to be negative about office politics is people venting and expressing their feelings. But in fact, we all need that kind of exchange where we are testing out our own feelings. For example, in an office where politics did not exist, you might find a whole group of people who feel that "there is something wrong with them" because they can't get along with their boss. Given the chance to compare notes with co-workers, they would realize the boss is actually insensitive and abusive.

Remember, office politics is often an important source of information about what is actually going on and can help keep you "tied in" to the decisions being made. Information picked up at meetings does not always tell the complete story. The nuances of people's motivations, feelings about what has been proposed – all this adds the real meat to information and helps you to know what is important and what isn't.

25. I'm sick of going from contract to contract and always having to sell myself, not having any money, and not being able to make any plans. Is there such a thing as a real job out there?
Sorry, Virginia, you will be hard pressed to find a "job" in the traditional sense of the word – something with security and a predictable pension. But that doesn't mean there isn't a lot of interesting and challenging work out there. Make sure your skills are up to date, that you have a skills portfolio that you could sell to other potential employers, and that you have money in the bank for any downtime.

If it's security that you crave, knowing that you are capable of managing your own career and selling your services to others will be your security.

26. Some of my friends have been offered signing bonuses. How do I get one?
You have to have a special set of skills in a profession where there is intense competition for talent. Signing bonuses were once offered only to senior executives to lure them away from one lucrative position to another. More recently they have been used to attract professionals in high-demand areas, such as information technology and edutainment, software development, and to reel in much-sought-after seasoned project managers.

If you are offered a signing bonus, be aware that it will probably come with strings attached. Your new employer will probably want you to stay with their company for two to three years to get their money's worth, and may prorate it over that period to ensure you do stick around.

Career-Development Tips for 20-Somethings

To summarize . . .

- Find a mentor – someone you can learn from.
- Look to increase your experience: "eavesdrop" in important meetings, leverage your skills, volunteer.
- Expand your skills portfolio.
- Shadow someone who is doing work that interests you.
- Pursue education at the highest broadest level.
- Increase your personal profile/network.
- Look at opportunities in terms of learning, not the effort-reward equation.
- Understand the mind-set of 40-something bosses.
- Recognize that there are no "right" career choices.

How to Career-Proof
Your Children

*E*lizabeth's 11-year-old son just returned home from summer camp, proudly proferring a gift: a hand-carved wooden duck. Elizabeth is concerned about this new and unexpected talent. "He used to say he was going to be a doctor," she says. "What if he wants to be a woodworker now?"

Doug arranged a summer job volunteering at a senior citizens home for his 14-year-old daughter – not because it was a good thing for her to do, but because "it will look good on her résumé."

Bob is sending his seven-year-old son to a summer camp that he really can't afford: "It's never too early to start making the right kind of contacts," he says.

"My kid didn't do anything this summer," complains Linda. "Next year it'll be time for him to get down to business and use his time more productively." Linda's son is 13.

Career Hypersensitivity

When parents start to apply the same productivity obsession to their children's summer activities as they do to their own work, you know that the world has changed. People have become so anxious and hyper-vigilant about the future that they take everything their children do and filter it through the template of future careers.

For example, a comment on a project that little Dougie is sometimes intolerant of his fellow team members is heard as "little Dougie is not a good team player and will never make it in a team-oriented work environment." Similarly, a report that Sally failed to take initiative in French class is interpreted as "Sally lacks leadership skills."

We have become obsessed with the new marketplace. It is telling, in this context, to see to whom parents and the media turn for career advice: senior industrial managers and leaders. We seek their advice about the future of work in this country, and how the educational system can better meet the needs of industry. Certainly, they have a handle on some of the challenges facing us. But just because someone understands a business plan doesn't mean she has an understanding of child and adolescent development, or the psychological process that underlies how people make career choices, or individual differences in temperament. Nor does she necessarily have any special insight into the future of work.

One of the most common questions I hear from senior managers is not about their staff's career concerns, or even their own, but about their children. They ask, "What should I tell my kids about careers? What advice and support should I give them?"

Parents have always been concerned about their children's future, and they have usually expressed some sort of expectations for what their children might accomplish. But never before have so many tried to micromanage every detail of their children's educational curriculum and career choices. There are good reasons, of course, for this level of concern. The stakes are so much higher. The world of work continues to change drastically. Many people have a hard time seeing where *they* will fit into the job picture a few years from now, let alone what will become of their children.

At the same time, the cost of post-secondary education has soared. It's not surprising that cash-strapped parents want to ensure that they are investing their dollars on the right program of study. They must also wrestle with a plethora of choices, between schools that specialize in science and technology and those that emphasize languages and arts; mainstream and alternative schools; public and private schools; community colleges and universities.

What About the Kids?

The result of this no-time-to-waste mentality is anxious, stressed-out kids overloaded with never-ending round of extracurricular activities (builds leadership and team-skills; broadens their skills base), jobs (résumé-building), and enrichment classes, to ensure they will make it among the "haves" in the future. Children are expected to decide early on their future careers, and then stick to that decision.

Indeed, in one much-lauded school board in California, high-school guidance counselors have an extremely sophisticated curriculum to help children make career choices as early as Grade 8 — and if they haven't decided by Grade 10, they get assistance from peer counselors.

One of the most common complaints I hear from parents about their teenage and post-teenage children is, "My kid isn't focused." These parents say their children can't make up their minds what programs they want to study or to what end, or keep changing university majors and are not using their time seriously.

I believe that it's a mistake to force children into premature career choices. Grade 9 or 10 is still too young to make decisions about the rest of your life. At this age, children are still too young to vote, they're supposed to call home if they're coming back late, and they haven't had sex yet (we hope) — so why should we expect them to know what they want to be doing at work when they're 40?

Children at this age will indeed often have ideas about what kind of work they might want to do. But they need some experience of the world of work before they can be clear about their skills, interests, and values, and where they will best fit in.

And after all, is the main challenge of childhood and adolescence to make our children future workers, ready to engage in the marketplace? I don't believe so. The main challenge should be to develop an interest in and curiosity about the world around us. Forcing kids to make premature career decisions only sets up a paradigm that the world is full of right or wrong answers – A or B, black or white, yes or no – denying them the more nuanced view that the world is ambiguous and free form and contains many possibilities.

Obviously, as parents we all want to make sure that our children end up equipped to look after themselves, to be able to participate economically in our society, and to have meaningful and challenging work. The question is, what is the best way of doing that?

Some Tips for Career-Proofing Your Children

Promote self-knowledge: Instead of encouraging your children to prepare themselves for jobs, encourage them to know themselves and discover what they do well.

In what areas does your child excel? Do you give her feedback on those skills and abilities? Do you help her reflect on her experiences so that she can start the process of self-discovery? For example, does she prefer to study alone or in groups? Does she take feedback well? Does she have difficulty disciplining herself to do private work as opposed to projects with classmates? What has she learned about herself from the feedback of other people when working in groups?

Avoid the top-10 syndrome: As we've seen, it's all too easy to become seduced by the yearly predictions of soothsayers of what is going to be "hot" or "not" in the next decade. But too many factors, whether the Asian flu, new technology, changes in legislation, or new inventions around the globe, can render today's hot career choice quickly obsolete. Instead, you and your child should think about roles and areas of competence, rather than preparation for specific occupations. For example, is your child a social organizer at school, a natural leader, theatrical, a great presenter, critic, or devil's advocate?

Even if you could second-guess the market, it's unwise to encourage children to mold themselves to fit market needs or trends. Their skills, talents, and preferences – not just the marketplace – should drive their career choices.

This doesn't mean kids can't begin exploring their options and considering different occupations – this process can be an exercise for them in self-discovery. For example, a teenager drawn to filmmaking can begin by asking himself what he finds interesting about it as a career, and what kind of working environment he imagines it will be. Or consider Sam L. He writes extremely well and has a wonderful command of language. He also has strong graphic and design skills and a good sense of storylines. Instead of having him focus on a particular occupation, he should be encouraged to think about a number of different possibilities, including photojournalism, video-game design, film direction, and advertising.

Above all, encourage your children to *pursue their personal passions.* Although this may sound blissfully naive, it in fact makes good career-planning sense, for the most effective choices are based on strengths and interests. And in the future, finding work that meets and reflects personal values as well as economic needs will increasingly become a prime determinant of career choices.

Lighten up: Don't try to force your children into premature career choices. Doing so may close down options which they don't have enough information to understand when they are 14 or 17. As a career counselor, I have met a lot of people who thought they had it right early in life, who have only now discovered the negative consequences of those decisions.

But really there is no such thing as getting it right. It's simply a question of better or worse choices. In the final analysis, whether our children are happily on their way in the workplace at the age of 24 or whether it takes another five years for them to find work they like will not really make any difference, except in the cost of additional education. Although it may be unnerving when kids start out in psychology, then move to engineering, then decide that's not right either, you have to understand that it is very difficult for your child to know what it is like to work as a psychologist or an engineer. Even if children have received career counseling, they still haven't had any hands-on experience to reflect and react to.

Putting undue pressure on your kids makes them anxious and resentful. It doesn't get them there any faster.

Don't impose your boomer values and world view on your kids: Parents, in talking about their kids who have not been able to focus or commit to a particular field of study, will often say, "When I was their age I knew exactly what I wanted to do." But what was true then is not true now, and saying this does nothing but irritate. We have entered a free-form career world where young people face intense competition for work, often with a sense that the chances for finding well-paid, challenging, and meaningful work are slim. In other words, consider the possibility that your experience may no longer be relevant.

Be careful, the kids are listening: When returning your e-mails from home are you muttering under your breath, "My boss the jerk . . ."? Or at the end of the day, do you complain about the "idiots" you work with? Well, guess what, congratulations, for once your child is listening.

Many young people are ambivalent about work because of what their parents have said over the years. Parents who are frustrated, who feel they have been passed over for promotions, who never share their joys or satisfactions but only their day-to-day irritations, have a profound impact on their children's long-term beliefs and feelings about work.

Share the positives as well as the negatives. Discuss real issues: budgets, plans that have gone awry, projects that were changed midstream, or the interpersonal skills you employed to turn around a difficult situation.

Pursue education at the highest and broadest level: A recent poll found that Ontario residents believe the skills acquired through a college or apprenticeship program provide better future jobs preparation than a university degree. This takes a very limited view of the future, ignoring the incredible global, technical, demographic, and environmental complexities with which workers will be grappling. Children should strive for the best education that is financially feasible, to the highest possible level. An understanding and appreciation of history, literature, and all the traditional humanities prepares people for dealing with a complex world. Learning how to learn and learning how to think are going to be critical imperatives for the future.

Promote self-esteem and emotional resilience: Make sure your children have the emotional wherewithal to deal with the failures as well as the successes associated with work, and the emotional breadth to relate maturely to people of diverse backgrounds and positions. Model for your children the skills they will need to withstand the emotional disappointments, stresses, and pressures that go hand in hand with work.

Foster trade and service skills: When I was a teenager, I used to help my father in his business on Saturdays, selling bridal veils. I wasn't that interested in bridal veils, but I gained a lot from the experience. In the first place, I learned something about myself: that I liked to sell, and that I was good at it. I also picked up some valuable business skills that have served me well throughout my career. I learned how to establish contact with customers, how to negotiate and close a sale, how to deal with a lot of people at the same time, and how to understand people's needs and respond to them.

Early opportunity to gain such skills will serve your children well, whether they ultimately go into business for themselves, go to work for an organization, or – as will most likely be the case – move in and out of different types of employment relationships. In a "Me, Inc." future, we will be managing our own careers much like a business – and that means knowing your own worth, being able to sell yourself, being able to negotiate contracts, and managing customer, client, and employer relationships well.

There are many ways trade skills can be acquired, from the traditional staples like lemonade stands, newspaper routes, lawn mowing, and baby-sitting, to running garage sales, buying, selling, and trading baseball cards or comic books, to starting an actual business. One 15 year old, for example, turned his passion for model cars into a highly profitable business trading them on the Internet.

You can use your children's business experiences to promote the development of trade skills by sharing your own business expertise and encouraging them to be reflective about what they have been doing, what they have learned, and how they can do things differently and better in the future.

Prepare your children to be good citizens: Your children will not only be units of economic productivity, but also global citizens. Think of the kind of roles you would like your children to play in society and the skills they will need to be effective contributors — and not just as workers but as leaders, volunteers, and members of the community. Help them embrace the values they will be expressing in those roles.

part three

The New Manager

The New Employment
Contract Comes Home to Roost

*P*icture this scene. It is an all-staff meeting. Management has just unveiled its business plan for the next 24 months. Significant change has been promised. But instead of getting the excited response from their staff they had anticipated, this is what they hear.

"You've told us this is going to unleash our creativity and enable us to stay closer to the customer and provide more value to them," one employee says. "But all I'm hearing is that I'll have even less resources for my job, and will have to work even longer and harder in this new super-lean organization. So, if I'm going to be giving you all this effort, and at the same time take responsibility for continuing learning, what I don't understand is what are you going to give me back? I can see what is in it for *you*. But what's in it for *me*?"

This question pinpoints some of the underlying tensions and difficulties with the new employment contract, a point I usually illustrate in my speeches with a pair of overhead slides.

The first slide shows how the organization defines the new contract: *"You are responsible for your own employability. We will provide you with meaningful, challenging, and skill-building work that will be good for your résumé, so long as you continue to add value."*

People nod. They have all heard the litany, ad nauseam. It has, after all, become the new corporate mantra.

The other slide shows what people really hear when organizations recite their mantras: *"We offer no job security. We will fire you when we have no more need for you. We will work you to the bone. We don't pay particularly well. And we will tell you that you are our most important resource."*

This second slide is greeted by the rueful laughter of recognition by everyone, including senior managers – in particular, senior managers.

Under the new employment contract, there is no loyalty between individual and organization; no commitment beyond the short term; no history beyond yesterday's results. Considered as a contract, it is extraordinarily one-sided. The organization gets the flexibility to hire and fire at will, without obligation and without guilt. Individuals get only vague promises of continuing growth and development, so long as they demonstrate their continuing usefulness. As one friend put it, "They call that a contract? I mean, would you sign it?"

In the days of the buyers' employment market, organizations didn't need to worry what their people thought. They could rely on economic insecurity and fears about job loss to keep people in line. Turnover was not a concern. Indeed, retention of staff was more often seen as a problem rather than a goal.

Talent Wars

There are signs, however, that the pendulum is beginning to swing back. Organizations describe talent wars as they compete for staff. The job market for managers and professionals has improved, particularly for in-demand knowledge workers in the systems area and in professional-service firms such as accounting, advertising, and consulting. Emboldened by growing demand for their skills, the very people whom organizations "empowered" to manage their own careers have become cocky enough to do exactly that. After all, being empowered means always being on the lookout to ensure that you are doing work that meets your needs, contributes to your employability, and adds to your résumé. So suddenly, for the first time in years, organizations are worrying about turnover and retention.

Turnover always increases in an improving job market. What is apparent today, though, is the apparent absence of any trace of loyalty on the part of staff to their current organizations. The chickens, as they say, are coming home to roost. Or as one job-hopper put it, "How can organizations expect us to remain loyal, given the shabby treatment we've received over the past few years?" Paradoxically, despite managers' lament of the loss of loyalty, that quality may still exist more strongly than they believe. For example, in a survey of 2,020 American employees, the Loyalty Institute found that approximately 66% intend to stay with their current company for the next several years and 50% would stay, even if they were offered a similar job with slightly higher pay elsewhere (*Canadian HR Reporter*, April 20, 1998).

There's no doubt that some organizations have handled their restructurings and downsizings of recent years clumsily, even downright callously. But even in the most humane and well-managed organizations, turnover is on the increase. And that's only to be expected: it's the flipside of the new employment contract.

Like it or not, we are all free agents now. Whether we work as freelancers, on contract, or as "permanent" staff, we are ultimately disposable when our services are no longer required. But by the same token, we can – and will – choose to move on to work that looks more rewarding or challenging. That is now the way of the world. And no matter how much individuals or organizations may want to turn the clock back to the old way of doing things, that simply isn't going to happen.

Rethinking Turnover

In this new atmosphere, organizations need to think what turnover means and whether it really is a problem. People move on for a variety of reasons. Some are reacting to a bad situation, such as a poor match with their skills, lack of future career prospects, or lack of opportunities for personal growth. Others are moving because they think – often unrealistically – that the grass is greener elsewhere. They believe that other people in other organizations are working fewer hours, have more resources, get more recognition, and are better rewarded. By providing staff with career-planning assistance, organizations can help people understand their own work situation better and realistically appraise their opportunities elsewhere.

But there will always be some people who, no matter how much they may like their current work, still want to go elsewhere to acquire new skills or be stretched in new ways. There is very little that organizations can do about this. Nor is it necessarily a bad thing.

I like to compare this to moving house. Sometimes you move because the house is falling apart or the neighborhood is going downhill – in other words, unpleasant things have happened since you've moved in. But sometimes you move because your needs have changed. It doesn't mean that there is anything wrong with the house or community. Rather, there is something out there that better meets your changing needs.

Organizations should certainly monitor the reasons for turnover to make sure that it doesn't reflect any internal problems. But insofar as there is no identifiable indication that such problems exist, then there's no reason to panic about people exiting the organization. Indeed, it could be argued that an organization that sees turnover as a *healthy byproduct* of empowerment has been effective in implementing the new employment contract.

Organizations may well bemoan investing time and resources to train and develop people who then move to another organization. But what goes around comes around. Often these organizations will themselves benefit from hiring people who have been developed elsewhere — who may represent a better match than the people they lose to turnover. In the long run, the result is greater flexibility for individuals and organizations.

A more mobile society, by extension, means more rapid and more frequent movement between jobs. Higher turnover was always a predictable outcome under the new employment contract. It's just that organizations are only now beginning to read the fine print.

Ten Strategies for
Managing the New Worker

I asked the senior-management team, "What do you want first, the good news or the bad news?"

Some years ago this organization had recognized that the nature of work performed by their front-line, mostly 20-something staff had changed significantly. Before, they were essentially expected to follow procedures and clearly defined policies. Now they were expected to be independent problem-solvers, capable of responding to a wide range of scenarios, acting as if they owned the business. The organization had gone out to hire individuals who filled this bill. Now they were struggling with the consequences.

"The good news," I told the senior managers, "is that you have risen effectively to the challenge of hiring the kind of front-line staff you want: people who are autonomous, who can take initiative, and who are independent problem-solvers. The bad news is that you have hired people who are autonomous, who can take initiative, and who are independent problem-solvers!"

The problem was that although they were hiring the right people, they couldn't seem to keep them. Morale and motivation were poor, turnover undesirably high. Management blamed this on a lack of loyalty.

Organizations often complain about the end of loyalty. But "loyalty" is a catchall word for describing a broad range of behaviors. It's true that in recent years we've seen the death of the unswerving identification of the individual to that abstract entity, the organization, that characterized old-style corporatism. But there still exists strong commitment on the part of individuals to their work. And after all, when managers say they want loyalty, what they really mean is they want people who display a high level of task dedication. The underlying motivation of such employees for this intense work commitment – whether to meet their own personal growth needs, advance their careers, or show commitment to the team – doesn't really matter.

"I was told that I was being hired to think outside the box. But every time I express an opinion, they look at me like I have some kind of contagious disease." This highlights some of the underlying tensions of the new work-place.

New workers, regardless of their individual psychological profiles, share a number of common characteristics:

- Concerns about employability. Workers today need to ensure that they have the skills to be capable of earning a living.
- A commitment to their work, team members, or profession over blind loyalty to their employing organization.
- A need to manage their complicated and harried lives.

Given the death of corporatism, forget the expensive company-logoed gift, unless it is a small token. There are several more successful ways to attract and retain good people, some of which have broad appeal and some which are more tailored to the individual.

I have already mentioned some of the different psychological profiles that dictate how individuals approach their work and careers. Some are independent thinkers or entrepreneurs, some are mainly motivated by lifestyle or personal growth, and some are careerists, authenticity seekers, or collegiality seekers.

Here are 10 general motivational and reward strategies that organizations can use to address some of the common concerns of the new worker, along with some specific strategies in response to the differing profiles of individual staff members.

1. Provide skill-building opportunities: Everyone can take a lesson from the 35-year-old manager who pitched a job applicant by writing down the three new skills she would be able to put on her résumé after she had completed her first project. All work can be potentially skill building, but it is up to the employer to articulate what the learning will be and how it can be useful to the individual. It's also important to remember that a skill-building opportunity is valuable to the extent that individuals perceive the skills to be meaningful to them in terms of their own career interests.

Skills can be acquired in a number of different ways, even in apparently dead-end jobs. Managers can encourage the process by matching workers with people they can learn from, giving workers opportunities to participate in cross-departmental task forces, setting up opportunities for them to shadow other workers in other jobs, and promoting cross-functional training. Some managers believe that their people can best acquire new skills by being thrust into situations that stretch them beyond their comfort level. Such managers are to be commended, so long as they provide a safety net.

2. Offer a personal pot of money: One life-insurance company, which takes its learning organization credo seriously, gives all staff a percentage of their salary to use for developmental purposes, whether for courses, travel to conferences, or books. Staff do not have to justify or explain their expenditures. Moreover, there are no expectations that the investment will pay off immediately on the job. Long-term career interests and ensuring one's ongoing employability are equally valid.

The sum of money does not need to be large, and managers don't need to prescribe how it is spent. One hotel chain with resorts staffed by many 20-somethings recognized the different needs of its staff by providing a small sum of money as a reward. The money could be applied to course tuition, spa services in their hotel, or ski lessons – you name it.

3. Use sabbaticals: With so many people today working to the point of exhaustion, smart organizations will encourage staff to take sabbaticals whether to recharge themselves, reflect on their next steps if they have come to a career crossroads, pursue a personal passion such as hiking in the Himalayas, or to finish a university program. A sabbatical as short as two months can be beneficial, though some people may need up to a year to truly recharge.

Sabbaticals shouldn't be tied to levels of hierarchy in an organization or length of service. Rather, they should be used to recognize that in the new work landscape people will have an ongoing need to retool. This means that weary baby boomers grappling with mid-life crises and 20- and 30-somethings seeking time off to travel or to test themselves in new ways are equally likely to welcome this sojourn from their everyday lives. Given the cost of replacing talent, this is a highly effective strategy for keeping people who may otherwise have jumped ship.

Interestingly enough, many people who take sabbaticals don't want to protect their jobs after their sabbaticals out of insecurity over their income. Rather, they really like their organization and want to ensure they can come back later. However, if they had not been given the sabbatical they would have quit.

4. *Provide career planning:* This is one of the interventions most frequently requested by staff and one that has a significant benefit both to the individual and the organization. The organization concretely demonstrates its commitment to individuals' employability. Individuals, meanwhile, typically discover that they like their work more than they thought and their company is not so bad after all. People establish goals based on their own interests, values, and strengths so that learning and developmental planning are tied to their personal needs.

In simple terms, career planning allows organizations to honor their side of the new employment contract, ensuring that staff have the skills to manage their careers.

5. *Establish company alumni clubs:* Savvy organizations will want to maintain contact with their talent, even after it has walked out of the door. Instead of seeing it as a rejection of the corporate culture, they will treat former staff members as ombudsmen who can refer new talent or clients and, more importantly, as valuable members of a potential talent pool who already understand the culture and may return to the organization with new skills in hand. One client organization, for example, routinely sends out a newsletter to its alumni. Organizations can also set up Internet chat rooms open to current staff as well as alumni. Instead of treating the exit interview as the final goodbye, managers can use it to communicate, where appropriate, an attitude of "good luck and we hope to see you again."

6. *Build on personal relationships:* Rather than assuming people have strong emotions about year-end results, build on the rapport that people naturally develop with team members and managers. People are committed to people and tasks, not to profit-and-loss statements. It is extraordinary how often it is the small and often banal gestures that are the most meaningful. People will often say things like, "I'm not really happy but I'm not yet prepared to jump ship because my boss was really good to me when my mother was sick." Or, "This project really needs me and we're a really tight team."

7. Provide flexible benefits: The Toronto Stock Exchange recently sent each staff member a toy dinosaur to underscore the extinction of their old benefits package. The old packages were being replaced by tailored packages to appeal to the diverse needs of different employee groups. Today's complicated personal and family configurations mean that people differ in the kinds of benefits they need and want. Increasingly, organizations are providing employees with a menu of benefits they can choose from, no longer assuming that everyone has the same tolerance of risk and need for long-term protection. While a young family, for example, may want orthodontic coverage, older workers may prefer higher drug benefits.

Nor is everyone a member of a nuclear family. Almost a quarter of urban, educated women born between 1946 and 1964, for example, are childless. Today, the U.S. Bureau of Labor Statistics calculates that the single and the childless are the fastest-growing segment of the workforce, a trend that demographers predict will continue.

Many large U.S. corporations now give everyone "benefit accounts" from which one can pay for health insurance for children, college tuition, child care, even legal insurance. In a similar vein, Kodak has changed its postpartum leave to a personal leave that provides employees with extended unpaid time to use as they wish, whether it be to prepare for a marathon, take a spiritual trek, or spend time with an infant.

Given the highly mobile nature of today's workforce, long-term pension plans may not be as attractive as self-managed portable investment portfolios. Young workers, for instance, know they have to take responsibility for their finances both in the short term and for retirement. They do not believe that government pension programs will be around for them when they retire.

8. *Provide opportunities for eavesdropping:* In my first job my boss, a therapist, invited me to hang out in her office when she was on the phone. I listened in on her returned calls to patients and learned a lot about how to handle many of the more difficult situations that arise in a clinical practitioner's profession. Eavesdropping is one of the simplest and most powerful ways to help someone pick up new skills. It can be accomplished in a number of ways. You could invite a sales associate to accompany you on a client call to an important customer, or to sit in on important meetings with management or clients.

9. *Promote mentoring:* Careerists and skill builders particularly benefit from being provided the opportunity to be counseled in everything from their career development to how to solve tricky political problems. Organizations can establish formal programs where they match employees with mentors from within the company, or they can let people select mentors from a pool. Ideally, individuals should partner with one or more persons who can teach them the basics or act as sounding boards.

10. *Allow for project ownership:* Many employees, particularly those who are more entrepreneurial, want to have the same kind of experiences they might have if they were running their own businesses. They need to feel that they own their own work, with both the upsides and downsides. They are prepared to take risks, including putting some of their own income at risk in return for a greater stake in the profits. If you allow staff to own a project, you must trust in their capacity and avoid micromanagement. Be there to provide support when needed, but don't force yourself into the picture.

Twenty-somethings, disdainful of large hierarchically organized companies, will be particularly responsive to management with this philosophy: "We trust you, we will support you in your risk-taking even if you make a mistake, we will fast-forward you to the highest level of responsibility where you can have a direct impact on the business, and if you're not having fun then there is something wrong."

Recognizing Personal Needs

One way or another, the 10 strategies above boil down to *recognizing personal needs*. One would be hard-pressed today to find an organization that doesn't pay at least lip service to the importance of work-family balance. Unfortunately, lip service doesn't take you to your kid's mid-afternoon soccer game, get you to the dentist, let you take unexpected time off to attend an out-of-town friend's wedding, or let you check out retirement homes for your aging parents. To the extent that organizations do have work-life programs in place – and it often seems to me that the more they talk about their policies, the less they are actually used – they are largely built around responding to emergencies such as child or elder care issues. In fact, all of today's workers are saying that opportunities for work-life balance are critical factors in determining job satisfaction.

Responsive employers will create what I call life-friendly organizations – cultures that support all individuals in their needs for personal time, whether for nourishing themselves and recovering from deadline-driven lives or in order to attend to family matters. This means more than flexible work arrangements or on-site daycare. It means ensuring that people can complete their work to their level of satisfaction while not making significant sacrifices in their personal relationships or other things they care about. It also means avoiding the "politics of overwork." One 33-year-old accountant who left an employer that did have a much-touted work-life policy put it succinctly: "I was prepared to give this job 100% in a 40-hour work week that would leave me 100% for the rest of my life, but 40 hours was never enough. Why should this company get the best of me, and my family only the dregs?"

Tired, Tired, Tired

Organizations that continue to reward staff with "command performance" off-site golf games and evenings at the racetrack may well be accused of suffering from a serious lack of creativity, not to mention insensitivity to the very demanding lives of their employees. As one 40-year-old director of marketing said about a day of corporate golf, "I hate golf. I resent spending money on clothes I'll never wear. I really like the people I work with but that doesn't mean I want to hang out with them, nor do I think we will be a more effective team because we shared some intimate expletives around a ball."

Organizations need to redesign their reward strategies to recognize the diverse needs of the new worker as well as each individual's unique values and interests so that the rewards are meaningful gifts.

Old Worker
vs. New Worker

Then	*Now*
Commitment is to company	Commitment is to self or work
Loyalty is to company	Loyalty is to team or manager
Other-directed	Self-directed
Seeks direction	Solves problems independently
Takes direction	Self-managed
Pursues career	Pursues challenge
Seeks promotion	Seeks self-fulfillment
Takes continuous career path	Follows zigzag career path
Long-term focus	Short-term focus
Values job satisfaction	Values work-life balance

The Coaching
Boom

At a recent meeting of industry executives, I was struck by the presence of a new group of people. In addition to the usual assortment of employed and unemployed managers and professionals, about 25% of the participants introduced themselves as "personal coaches."

Suddenly, personal coaching has become the hottest management trend since reengineering. From coaches helping small-business owners become more effective, to organizations hiring coach-consultants to work with their executives, to motivational guru Tony Robbins coaching President Clinton, it seems that everyone is getting in on the act.

Of course, the need to receive advice and counsel is not new. People have always sought informal advice and counsel, whether from a manager, friend, mentor, parent, or priest or rabbi. What is new is the *professionalization* of personal coaching. (Witness the number of courses, schools, and professional designations devoted to coaching now sprouting up across North America.)

In part, these new professional coaches are simply filling a vacuum. Previously, people could routinely seek advice from their managers. Today that's not always possible. Many managers are simply too beleaguered themselves to spend much time coaching their staff. And where in less harried times one might have sought out a friend to use as a sounding board, today one worries about taking up that friend's precious time – assuming, that is, that you can coordinate your busy schedules to even sit down together once. Enter, therefore, the personal coach to pick up the slack.

In addition, the growing fragmentation of society means that traditional social networks – whether based in community, religion, or family – have broken down. Many people are feeling lost and unprotected. These feelings are exacerbated by the complexity of the times we live in. As people struggle with a free-form world in which all the old rules about life and work and how to get ahead are no longer true, the promise of professional coaching becomes more enticing. In a world where we feel increasingly anonymous, a coach is someone on *our* side, someone who takes our interests seriously, who will help us to be the best we can be.

In sports, coaching is what happens when things get *serious*. You don't see coaches in the school playground, where children play informal pickup games. You see them when play becomes competitive, from t-ball leagues and up. Similarly, the new popularity of coaching in business circles is a direct reflection of the toughness of the contemporary workplace. The bar is set so high these days, and the competition is so fierce, that people feel the need for a coach to pump them up to a higher level of performance.

Coaching vs. Counseling

In a recent meeting a manager went through verbal contortions to avoid using the word "counseling," saying that she had gone to see someone for "counseling . . . I mean, um, advice . . . I mean, coaching."

The fact is that coaching is a much easier sell in the business world than counseling. Seeing a counselor has significant clinical overtones, and may be viewed as a sign of weakness or neediness. (There is no room for wimps in this tough new work world.) But going for coaching with its connotation of hard-edged, skill-based improvement is much more socially acceptable.

Indeed, given the glamour of big-time professional sports these days, going for personal coaching is more than just acceptable. It's seen as admirable, even sexy. It shows you are taking your work seriously indeed and making yourself as effective as possible as part of your ongoing improvement plan.

Organizations, therefore, will often willingly pay for something labeled as coaching while hesitating to contribute to counseling, which is seen as "touchy-feely," "mucking about in people's heads," not oriented to the bottom line, and so on. Male managers, in particular, are more comfortable with the sports-based language of coaching, with its promise of measurable improvements in performance and productivity, kind of like a *personal trainer* for the boardroom.

I find this distinction between coaching and counseling somewhat disturbing in that it can lead to an extremely narrow way of thinking about coaching. People go to coaches for a variety of reasons. In some cases, they are simply looking for some tips they can apply right away to improve their presentation skills, their dress and deportment, or their boardroom polish. The support they want is tactical and after one to three short sessions, they feel their needs have been met.

But there are also those who seek coaching for deeper life and career issues. They are working so hard, they feel that they have somehow lost sight of what's really important in their lives. They are asking whether their work is really meeting their needs. Or they may be feeling that something is missing in their lives. Sometimes they are experiencing a profound sense of emptiness: they have achieved everything they set out to achieve . . . and now what?

Then again, perhaps they have experienced a personal crisis, such as the death of a parent, the end of a relationship, sending children off to university.

In other words, there are many situations in which people are seeking much more than instrumental advice on how to improve their performance, catch the eye of the boss, or get that promotion.

Characteristics of a Good Coach

John D. is very proud of his coaching skills. He boasts about his success rate in turning around two troubled companies and his understanding of the new market forces. He feels particularly qualified to coach CEOs and senior vice-presidents because he's "been there."

I watched John try to sell himself as a coach to a senior manager wrestling with the fallout of a merger – significant layoffs. What John failed to understand was that the manager wasn't asking for help with a business decision – that part he had taken care of – but for help with dealing with his emotions about having to let so many people go.

In addition to understanding the business environment, good coaches will also be *capable counselors*. They will show many, or all, of the following characteristics:

- A holistic approach to the individual.
- An ability to tailor the intervention to the needs of the client.
- Knowledge of when to back off and when to push.
- Sensitivity to individual differences.
- An understanding of the new work landscape.
- A genuine desire to help.

Let's look at each in turn.

A holistic approach to the individual: A good coach works with individuals to increase their effectiveness in *all* areas of their life, both personal and professional. That involves helping them identify how they want to live, how they can achieve what they want from life, and what might be getting in the way of their being who they want to be.

By this definition, many of today's self-styled personal coaches like John D. fall short. Indeed, many have no real qualifications to fill the role. Often they are former managers with impressive management and leadership experience and a solid understanding of business issues. This may equip them to coach on pragmatic issues, such as working with people on their leadership styles or thinking through long-term business strategies. But these presenting issues often mask deeper underlying conflicts interfering with people's effectiveness, such as questions of personal fulfillment, authenticity, and fit.

David P., a 45-year-old executive, was having problems as a team leader, and the morale of his staff was suffering. He was sent for coaching. But what was supposed to be a relatively straightforward intervention to improve his leadership skills turned into something more complicated. The coach found that David was suffering from a profound career malaise, which was spilling into his work environment. Basically, David was having a values crisis and was unsure that he wanted to spend the next chapter of his life "producing more widgets." It was this *values crisis*, rather than weaknesses in his leadership style, that needed addressing.

An ability to tailor the intervention to the needs of the client: A good coach recognizes and appreciates the unique strengths and goals of the persons they are counseling. Rather than using a "one-size-fits-all" approach, they tailor their intervention to reflect what would best meet the needs of their clients. At their best, they see hidden strengths and can recognize, describe, and articulate those strengths.

For one woman, this was almost an epiphany. "I always thought I wasn't good at presenting in groups because I would get so nervous," she said. "But my coach saw my nervous energy in a different way. He said it was like a magnet in drawing and holding an audience's attention. So now, rather than avoiding giving presentations and trying to repress my nervousness, I've learned to cultivate it and use it as an asset."

Knowledge of when to back off and when to push: A good coach knows when to withdraw: they recognize that they have no more to offer their clients, or they realize that their own vision of what the clients can be does not match the clients' own goals. In some cases, they may recommend someone else who they feel will do a better job. Clearly this is a very difficult and challenging call, requiring a *sensitivity to individual differences*. Unfortunately, it is one that many self-styled coaches are quite unable to make.

Sensitivity to individual differences: A good coach will often want to stretch you beyond your comfort level. Sometimes, though, a coach will be so convinced about what her client is capable of achieving, that she may not be able to hear what her client actually *wants* to achieve. Either the coaches don't see the same barriers and obstacles that the client sees, or else they discount them.

For example, Carol C., a marketing manager, had always flirted with the idea of self-employment and was increasingly feeling that she did not fit corporate life. On the other hand, as a single parent, she had genuine needs for some kind of financial stability and income predictability. Carol's coach was so convinced of her ability to make it on her own that she dismissed her financial concerns. This was in part because the coach had never valued financial security herself.

A coach is sensitive to these underlying issues and understands concepts of individual differences, adult development, and career and life stages, as well as the complex interpersonal dynamics of business relationships. (Many have a background in psychology or other behavioral sciences and therefore have a good grounding in personality theory.) This sensitivity should be accompanied by the cognitive capabilities and business skills to see and understand the big picture.

An understanding of the new work landscape: A good coach understands the new work landscape, whether it be the frenzied schedules of workers, their struggle to balance work and personal life, or the new complexities of how work gets done. If coaches are from a different generation than their clients, they should be sensitive to realities of that generation, rather than imposing ideas and concepts based on old expectations or what used to be true.

A genuine desire to help: When you ask coaches why they like coaching, they often mention having the opportunity to "make a difference in someone else's life," "contribute to someone's development," or "give something back to the people."

Perhaps most important of all, then, a good coach is also someone who has a *genuine* desire to play a role in supporting and facilitating the development of other human beings. Unfortunately, many of the coaches I've met define their own success in terms of the status of their clients.

One woman in describing her coaching business talked at length about the CEOs she has coached, and then indicated at the end of her presentation that she could occasionally fit people with less lofty positions into her consulting practice. The subtext, essentially, was "I must be an important person, because I work with CEOs." For such people, the motivation to coach is tied up with a need to confirm their own self-worth, along with a desire to be close to senior management and feel themselves to be on the inside, and "in the know."

How a Coach Can Help

How can a coach help you? Often, people think they need to be coached in identified areas of weakness. For example, a small-business owner with no aptitude for marketing wants to learn how to market, or a middle manager wants to develop skills in networking. With concerted effort, it is possible to develop skills in areas where you have difficulty.

However, unless improvement in specified areas of weakness is *critical* to your work, you are usually better advised to focus on what you already do well. Spend your time developing further skills in those areas, rather than focusing on areas where you have no underlying aptitude. Typically, you will get more return for your investment of time and effort. Ask yourself what the cost would be of *not* improving yourself in those areas. How likely are you to be successful in your efforts? What will the cost of those efforts be in terms of time and money? Are there other areas you could be focusing on that will give you a greater return on your development investment?

At the same time, if you are entering a coaching relationship consider this an opportunity to examine your life, both professional and personal, at the broadest level. Instead of limiting yourself to enhancing one skill so that you will be more effective in your work, be prepared to take a journey to unexpected places. The results may be both surprising and rewarding.

The Manager
as Career Coach

*D*ave L., a 40-something administrator, has always been a good performer. But lately his work has deteriorated and he often seems cranky and irritable, sometimes getting into conflict with other team members. The reason: David is exhausted due to a combination of work and family pressures. Following reengineering, he is working much longer hours while also grappling with the problem of organizing living arrangements for an aging parent in another city. Dave has asked his manager for a meeting to discuss modifying his workload.

Sharon C., a high-performing sales representative, is unhappy due to a restructuring of her work. Where she was once relatively autonomous and able to act on her own initiative, Sharon's job now involves much more teamwork and consensus decision-making, a process she finds tedious and irritating. She is planning to ask her manager for a move.

Who Are You Going to Call?

Where do people who work for organizations turn first for career advice?

Usually to their managers. Like it or not – and many managers clearly don't like it – it has become part of the manager's role to act as a kind of career counselor. And this is particularly true in today's fast-shifting economy.

These are challenging times for managers, who have to maintain the morale and productivity of the people reporting to them even though insecurity about the future is rampant; traditional rewards for performance, such as promotion or salary increases, may be limited or unavailable; and individuals are facing extreme pressures both at work and in their personal lives.

To support the people reporting to them, managers must become involved in a broad range of work and career issues, in some cases going well beyond the traditional management role. They need to be attuned to the complexities of people's lives – to their anxieties about financial pressures, concerns about balancing work and personal life, and worries about future job security.

Making this situation all the more challenging is the fact that the manager may be grappling with some of these same issues themselves. They, too, may be feeling over-stretched and underappreciated. They can understand what members of their staff are going through, but may feel overwhelmed by the demand for personal attention just when they themselves are feeling overwhelmed by their work.

From the individual's point of view, seeking career advice from their managers makes good sense. The manager, after all, is in the best position to observe their work at first hand, offer feedback on their skills and potential, and help match up their aspirations with current and future organizational requirements. Moreover, where appropriate, the manager can refer individuals to other sources of information and can advance their plans at higher levels in the organization.

When managers hold regular career discussions with staff there are significant benefits for the individual, the manager, and the organization as a whole.

The individual gains better understanding of the links between performance, organizational expectations, and career opportunities. The manager opens up new channels of communication with staff, has the opportunity to renew enthusiasm and motivation, and is given the opportunity to provide practical career support. The organization benefits, too, gaining new and better information on the individual's skills, interests, and aspirations — information that can be put to good use in assessing training and development requirements, and in succession planning.

And yet despite these potential benefits, managers are often ill-prepared to take on a career-counseling role. Many are extremely uncomfortable with the whole idea.

Why Managers Can't Coach

Why do so many managers dislike acting as a career counselor to staff? Usually because they see this role as onerous. They see it, in fact, as much more burdensome than it really is — or at least, much more burdensome than it ought to be.

Counseling staff on career issues can be a relatively straightforward, even enjoyable, process — if organizations provide managers with appropriate support for their efforts.

Let's examine some of the most common objections raised by managers to counseling staff:

"I'm not a therapist." Many managers have found career counseling to be a painfully one-sided process. Typically, as they describe it, the individual presents a problem or concern ("I'm bored," "Where should I go next?", "What should I be good at?"). The individual then sits back, expecting the manager to do all the hard work of drawing out their ideas, extracting and interpreting information about their skills and abilities, and matching all

this up with career opportunities and work assignments.

A thankless task indeed. Small wonder that so many managers complain about having to "play therapist" and "mess about in people's heads." Such a one-sided exchange makes heavy demands on people who are not trained in this area. Indeed, it would be difficult enough even for people who are. Professional counselors, after all, don't usually *tell* their clients what to do. Instead, they provide structured frameworks to enable individuals to discover that for themselves.

Structure is precisely what is missing in the typical manager-employee career discussion. And usually it is the organization that has failed both parties – by failing to provide individuals with the necessary tools to hold up their end of the discussion.

Giving staff the tools to plan their careers – whether through workshops or self-study career-planning materials – makes them articulate about their career interests. Instead of offering empty platitudes ("I enjoy working with people"), they can spell out precisely what they are looking for to build their portfolios, and what they see as their key strengths and developmental needs.

What ensues is a dialogue based on mutual respect between two human beings rather than the more authoritarian doctor-patient model, where the patient describes the symptoms to an all-knowing professional who diagnoses the problem and prescribes the remedies.

Managers no longer have to perform a marathon to draw out individuals but can instead simply respond to their well-framed questions and concerns and offer realistic feedback on their strengths, weaknesses, and goals. (As one manager, whose organization recently provided staff with career-planning tools, commented: "It was great. I could just sit back and listen. It was the best career discussion I'd ever had, resulting in some very concrete developmental decisions.")

This doesn't mean that you abdicate all responsibility to provide support. In fact, your role is more pivotal than ever. The difference is that, working within a well-structured context, you are much better able to provide useful help.

"We don't have clear career paths." In the days when organizations could confidently construct elaborate career paths, career development was a matter of showing staff how to get from job A to job B to job C. Today, no organization can provide such precise career-pathing information. The world is changing too fast. It's hard enough to keep abreast of current changes in jobs and staffing requirements, let alone to make meaningful predictions about future needs.

That's why, increasingly, organizations are placing responsibility for career planning on the individual. Individuals, after all, are in the best position to assess their own skills and interests, and decide on future work and life options that are satisfying and personally meaningful.

Rather than showing people how to get from job A to job B, career planning should *educate* them as to who they really are and what they really do at work. Instead of narrowly focusing on their job titles, and preparing themselves for jobs that may not even exist, people should look at *what they do* at work. They should examine not only their current position and specific technical skills, but also the *broader context* of their work to understand how to achieve greater satisfaction. They should be looking at the "Five Ws" of career planning (these are covered in more detail in the Conclusion to this book):

- *Who* do I want to work with? And how much interaction do I require with my co-workers?
- *Why* do I work? What is the purpose of my job, and how does it fit into the bigger organizational picture? And how well does it mesh with my own values?
- *Where* should I work? What kind of work setting suits my own work style and allows me to perform most effectively?

- *What* skills do I want to use? Technical skills, such as computer programming, marketing, accounting – skills acquired through special training? Or more general skills – leadership, writing, oral presentations, team-building – that are readily transferable from environment to environment?
- *When*? Do I prefer a fast-paced work environment, where I handle many tasks simultaneously, or a slower, more deliberate pace?

When people say they are unhappy with a job, for example, they may be *confusing the technical aspects* of the job as representing all the elements of the job. Typically, it's not the technical aspects (the *what* of the job) that are bothering them, but one or more other aspects (the *who*, *why*, etc., of the job).

By examining all these elements, people can look beyond their current job titles to discover their real skills, values, and preferences. They can then identify the areas in which they are most likely to be able to contribute, so that they can make informed decisions and set realistic career and life goals.

"With so much change, how can we talk about career planning?"
Actually, the rapid pace of change makes career planning *more crucial than ever*. Unless we develop and pursue a vision, we will simply drift, buffeted by successive waves of change, never sure exactly where we're heading. By setting goals, we take control over the future.

Career planning today means thinking about the landscape of work and opportunities in a radically different way. It means keeping your skills portfolio updated so that you can make the most of opportunities for satisfying and meaningful work.

"We'll be asked questions about future jobs we don't know."
The further we look into the future, the more difficult it is to say what opportunities will exist, or what skills and experience will be required to take advantage of them. But we can still have a good sense of the general skills and competencies people will need.

Given the rapid pace of change, it no longer makes sense to prepare for jobs. We need to prepare for areas of competence, types of work, and roles. Encourage your staff to look at their competencies in the light of probable organizational needs, and to develop learning goals that support their future employability – inside and outside the organization.

"Won't career planning raise expectations?" Sometimes managers express concern that talking about career development will spark unrealistic expectations of opportunities for advancement.

Most people *already* have expectations, realistic or not, about their careers. Far from raising expectations, career planning helps people develop a much better understanding of the realities of organizational life. It asks them to match up their skills, interests, and goals with the opportunities that are realistically available to them, taking into account both their own skills and potential and the requirements of the organization. And where their current goals prove to be unrealistic, it assists in identifying alternate routes to career satisfaction.

"Everyone will want a career change." Occasionally, some managers are reluctant to encourage staff to explore other functional areas, fearing that they will be deluged with requests for transfers to other areas of the organization, or worse, staff will want to leave. Engineers will want to move into marketing, marketing analysts will yearn to manage, and so on.

Of course, many people like to muse about the idea of career change. They *think* they're unhappy in their current job, and they wonder if the grass might not be greener elsewhere. But most people, once they go through the career-planning process, conclude that their current work, with perhaps some minor adjustments, is fundamentally a good match for them.

Sometimes people will want to make more use of certain strengths, or to develop skills required to attain future career goals. But these requirements can often be satisfied by enriching current work. Requests for dramatic changes, as opposed to shifts in emphasis, are the exception rather than the rule.

In any case, when an organization supports individual career self-management, it does not assume a responsibility to meet everyone's expressed desires. Its only responsibility is to provide the tools and mechanisms that will enable people to plan and manage their careers effectively.

"I'm over-stretched already." In today's leaner organizations, many managers are already feeling beleaguered. Whole layers have been cut out, both above and below them. Administrative support has been reduced. Prospects for their own advancement appear more limited than before. These managers, as a result, see themselves as working harder than ever for less rewards. And they feel doubly beleaguered when staff clamor for help with their careers.

This is, in fact, a very strong argument in favor of providing career-planning assistance to managers as well as to their staff. Once managers go through a career-planning process themselves, they feel more positive about their own careers and more enthusiastic about helping staff members.

At the same time, assuming that staff are provided with effective career-planning tools, the pressure on the manager is actually reduced. In my experience, most managers *are* genuinely concerned about their staff and would like to help them with their careers – if they only had the time and the skills. Giving individuals appropriate tools reduces the demands on the manager on both fronts.

Common Career Concerns

People come to their managers with a variety of questions and problems. In some cases, these concerns will be specific to the organization: apprehension about the future, for example, in the light of a merger or acquisition. Other questions will be more general. Managers need to understand the roots of these concerns in order to provide effective coaching assistance.

Let's examine some of the common career issues on which individuals consult their managers:

"I'm bored/dissatisfied." Gary W. is an excellent technical trainer. But lately he has become increasingly bored with his work. "I teach the same courses over and over again," he tells his boss. "I'd really like the chance to try some internal consulting." Because Gary is such a good trainer, his boss is reluctant to have the courses taught by someone else. But she knows that if she doesn't give Gary some new challenges, his performance may suffer, or he may start to look for work elsewhere.

Boredom and dissatisfaction are always warning signals. When they are ignored, performance will typically decline, or else the individual may quit and move elsewhere in search of new challenges. In some cases, the individual may be heading for a full-fledged burn-out, as discussed below.

Some staff members, like Gary W., have no difficulty articulating their feelings of boredom and dissatisfaction. Others need some help defining exactly what is bothering them.

As a career coach, you can point to some of the possibilities. For example, has the person's job changed to become a poor match with his personal work style and preferences? Has the job become less challenging, or has it perhaps become *too* challenging because of increasing volume of work? Does the person get enough opportunity for visibility to senior management – or would he or she actually prefer less exposure? Or is the problem just a nagging feeling that other people in other jobs seem to be having more fun?

You can suggest areas to look at. But the individual contributor is the person who can best define the problem. If he is unable to pinpoint the causes of his distress, discussion should be postponed until he has gone through a careful process of self-assessment.

Once contributors define the problem, you will have to consider what you can do to meet their needs. It is not your responsibility as a manager to provide work that is constantly exciting and stimulating. Certainly, you should be as responsive as possible to the individual's requirements. But it is up to the individual to frame those requirements, and to ensure that they are realistic within the context set by your business objectives and available resources.

Sometimes you will be unable to meet their needs. Perhaps you don't have the flexibility or the resources, or the request is simply unreasonable. But often you will be able to arrive at a compromise that gives more of what they want. Gary W.'s boss, for example arranged for him to spend one day a week working as an organizational consultant. The company retained his excellent training skills the rest of the time.

You should also be careful not to impose your own values on the individual. You may think, for example, that a person is bored or dissatisfied because you know that you would be if you were in the same position. But actually that person may still be perfectly happy.

"What should I be when I grow up?" Peter K. thinks he might want to specialize in his field. But then again, perhaps he would be happier and more successful as a manager. "I don't know," he tells his manager. "I just don't know. What do you think I should do?"

No matter how strongly an organization communicates the message that individuals are responsible for planning their own careers, there will always be some holdouts – people who expect their managers to decide for them. They will ask, in effect, "What should I be when I grow up?"

Don't get drawn in. Send them back to do their homework.

"I'm burnt-out." Sandra G. used to be a high performer. But these days she seems listless and depressed. "I used to look forward to coming to work. But lately I don't feel like I'm accomplishing anything to my own satisfaction. There's always some new project demanding my attention. I try to keep up with everything, but it's hopeless."

At one time or another, most of us will experience feelings of being burnt-out and devitalized. This is a particularly common form of distress today, given the pressures that people are dealing with on so many fronts. People like Sandra G. feel involved in a never-ending routine of too much work and not enough recognition. Over-stretched, but under-stimulated, they feel that they are not learning anything new and have nothing to look forward to.

The burnt-out individual often appears over-stressed and emotionally fatigued – "flaring up" at the smallest cue, or appearing withdrawn and apathetic. Often they will complain of "losing their edge." Performance typically will decline.

Burn-out can have a variety of causes. Sometimes, the cause of the stress may be partly or wholly personal (financial or marital difficulties, for example). But it may also be strongly work-related. The person may be overstretched by current workloads.

Encourage the individual to undertake a thorough self-assessment, paying particularly close attention to:

1. Pacing and volume of work.
2. Nature and amount of stress on the job. Can it be reduced, or is it a function of role ambiguities or conflicts?

In some cases, the solution will be to restructure staff members' current jobs. In others, it may be necessary to reassign them to a position that provides a better match with their work style and preferences. Those who are clearly in psychological difficulty might best be referred for professional counseling.

"How did I get from there to here?" Ed H. is manager for an airline company. He is rated as a good performer and seems happy in his job. But lately he often finds himself lying awake, wondering, "I'm from a family of lawyers. How did I end up working in the airline industry?" Looking back on his career, it all seems arbitrary, somehow. Did he make the right choices? Did he make any choices at all?

One very common form of distress today among managers and professionals is the sense that their career is somehow accidental, arbitrary. They feel that they just "fell into" their line of work, that they never chose to become what they have become.

However, as we've already seen, our career choices are rarely arbitrary or accidental. Most of us are doing work to which we are well matched. But when we're under pressure, it may not seem that way. As mentioned above, most people who go through the self-assessment process conclude that their work — with perhaps some adjustments — is fundamentally a good match.

"I'm stuck." When Douglas C. joined his firm as a purchasing manager five years ago, he looked above him and saw four management levels between him and the president. He saw plenty of room to grow and develop and advance in his career. Douglas is still in the same job. But as a result of reengineering and de-layering, there are now only two management levels between Douglas and the president, and, he says, "A lot of people with better qualifications than me are quadruple-parked on the few spots likely to open up." Douglas is tired of being stuck in the same job, and depressed at

the thought that he has nowhere else to go.

Everyone's career ultimately reaches a plateau: a point from which further advancement in an organization becomes unlikely. Today, due to both widespread restructuring and demographic realities – too many people chasing too few opportunities to advance – people like Douglas C. are often hitting a plateau at a relatively early stage in their careers. A career plateau may be either:

- *situational:* the individual still has potential to move up, but the organization has no place for them to go, or
- *personal:* the individual has achieved his or her full potential.

When individuals hit a plateau, there is always the danger that they will become demotivated and apathetic. As a result, they may well perform below their previous level. In some cases, too, they may become embittered, blaming the organization for their situation. Worse, they may "export" their bitterness to colleagues and subordinates, by bad-mouthing the organization to anyone who will listen. As a result, the morale and performance of their co-workers may suffer, too.

The starting point in managing plateaued individuals is the recognition that they can still make a contribution to the organization. Research shows that most people can adjust to the loss of upward career mobility. As a manager, it's your responsibility to ensure that they do. What they deeply resent is being treated as second-class citizens, unable to contribute in any significant way.

Work with plateaued individuals to find ways of keeping their jobs interesting and challenging. For example, you can provide them with:

- Job enrichment.
- Lateral moves.

- Opportunities to mentor younger staff members.
- The chance to work in cross-departmental task forces.
- Enrollment in meaningful and prestigious training programs.

These are all ways of saying that "we care about you, and we still value your skills."

At the same time, encourage the individual to develop new interests outside work to meet needs that cannot be met inside the organization, such as leadership in a charity or volunteer group.

"I'm worried I won't be able to cut it." Marjorie P., a bank teller, adapted successfully to the introduction of new technology. But she is having difficulty adjusting to the new emphasis on selling. Marjorie is a quiet, shy person who balks at the very idea. "Once it was enough just to process transactions efficiently," she said. "Now I'm expected to do that, and sell customers on new services. If I was any good at selling, I would have got a job in retail." Marjorie is making no effort to sell anyone anything.

Skills obsolescence happens when an individual's job has been changed dramatically, or made redundant, by new technology or market change. What can be done to salvage the situation?

Most people use a mixture of specialist and generalist skills in their work. When specialist skills become outdated, they may still have other, more generalized strengths to build on for the future. By going through a process of self-assessment, they can identify these strengths and investigate other work in which they can apply them. With the rapid pace of change, the threat of skills obsolescence is present in almost every industry. Encourage your people to:

- Anticipate and make plans for change; be flexible and adaptive in their thinking.

- Be aware of the downside of overspecialization.
- Build on transferable skills.
- Continue to update skills.

Marjorie's manager initially thought about sending her on a course in sales skills. But after Marjorie went through a searching self-assessment, it became clear that she would never be very happy or effective in a sales role. But she had some considerable strengths in other areas, including problem-solving and analyzing information. She opted to move into the Information Systems area, where she is both happy and productive.

"I've been in this job a year. When is my next move?" Some people, although they have not yet hit a plateau, are moving up much less rapidly than they would like. They are rated as having high potential. They have been told that the organization sees them as tomorrow's leaders – but for now, there is no room to promote them.

The risk is that these high achievers will jump to another organization in search of speedier advancement. Faced with that risk, managers may try to hold on to them with promises of advancement they cannot keep.

By making such promises, managers only undermine their credibility and store up trouble for the future. It's much better to confront the situation now. Managers should be honest and realistic with these impatient high achievers, encouraging them to develop a better understanding of their situation through career planning.

In some cases, as a result of such planning, the high achiever will decide to look for opportunities outside the organization. But almost certainly they would have done so anyway, sooner or later. And typically they will discover that most organizations are operating under the same constraints.

In the meantime, you should work with your high achievers to make their current positions as stimulating and challenging as possible. They will appreciate the opportunity to learn new skills that will be instrumental to their long-term career success. They are also extremely responsive to psychological rewards, such as status and prestige, or being given responsibility for a high-profile project with major visibility to senior management.

"I'm ready for promotion — don't you agree?" It's a common aggravation. A staff member believes it is time for an upward move, but as her manager you don't share that assessment. And no matter how bluntly you explain this, the individual continues to overrate her abilities and potential.

Almost immune to criticism, unable to distinguish between politeness and fulsome praise, such individuals might be thought of as "pronoids" (a term first coined by Queens College sociologist Fred H. Goldner). Where paranoids suffer from delusions of persecution, pronoids have delusions of admiration. They can be extremely exasperating people to have around.

Faced with a pronoid individual, some managers become quite infuriated ("How can I make him understand that he just isn't ready?"). But your responsibility here is only to give clear and honest feedback, not to persuade the individual of its accuracy. Some people will indeed choose not to hear what you are saying. But so long as the individual is doing his or her job well, it's really not worth getting upset about.

A Coach — Not a Fortuneteller

People look to their managers for assistance on a whole range of career-related issues. And managers can indeed provide valuable help – so long as the ground rules are clearly defined, and individuals are empowered to acquire the information they need to make informed and realistic career choices.

Managers are not psychiatrists or fortunetellers. But in a well-structured counseling situation, they can be highly effective coaches.

Mentors
Show the Way

Fred and Ken W. graduated from the same MBA program in the same year and started their careers in similar jobs with similar companies. Five years later, Fred has done quite well and is a director of marketing. But Ken has done even better: he was recently appointed assistant vice-president.

When Fred and Ken compare notes, one key difference emerges. Ken has always had a mentor – someone who has taken an interest in his development, and has been a source of advice, guidance, and support in his career.

A mentor is someone who typically acts as a sounding board, coaching you in effective behaviors and providing insight into everything from how to handle a tricky situation, to how to pitch a client or get a bank loan, to how to deal with corporate politics. Sometimes he or she may also open doors for you and act as an advocate on your behalf.

Research shows that successful people almost always have had one or more mentors. The classic mentor-mentoree bond in these studies was an informal one. But by the late 1970s, with growing recognition of the importance of mentors in career development, organizations had begun to experiment with more formal mentoring programs. Today, interest in mentoring, whether formal or informal, is exploding. At the same time, the mentoring relationship itself is changing to reflect new pressures and new work realities.

There are a number of reasons why mentoring has become such a hot topic. In a quicksand economy where the old rules of career success no longer apply and productivity pressures demand that you get it right the first time, many people are looking for direction. And typically, their own managers, overwhelmed by their own productivity pressures and besieged with other demands, are unable to offer that support. Instead people look to a mentor for advice.

Organizations, too, have begun to take an interest in mentoring, in some cases sponsoring formal programs. This renewed interest goes well beyond a recognition of the positive impact that mentors can play in people's long-term career development. Organizations understand that their managers don't have the time to provide traditional career support for staff, and that mentors can help pick up some of the slack. Moreover, in organizations that have been largely denuded of wisdom by massive restructuring and downsizing, mentoring offers a mechanism for capturing and transmitting the embedded wisdom of the older staff who remain.

Mentoring programs have also been introduced in recognition of the fact that many people need "a leg up" and don't have access to informal mentoring assistance. In organizations, for example, informal mentoring relationships have always existed between male senior managers and high-potential young men – while women have had few such sources of informal support available to them. Providing women with formal mentors helps level the playing field.

Similarly, there are many groups – whether people starting their own businesses, young people entering the workforce, immigrants upgrading their skills – who are starting to benefit from mentoring initiatives.

The first step in a formal mentoring program is to identify potential mentors. Not everyone has the right psychological makeup. There are no hard and fast rules, but here are some key attributes:

- Ideal mentors derive a genuine pleasure from promoting others' interests.
- They are proud of the accomplishments of their protégés rather than threatened by them — even where the protégés go on to surpass them.
- They are adept at reading people and situations.
- They have an intuitive sense of what different types of work require in terms of personal characteristics, and where different work experiences can lead.
- They understand the business and can balance its needs against the needs of their protégés.
- They are sensitive to individual differences in personality and values.
- They welcome the opportunity to give something back, and to make a difference.
- Perhaps most important of all, they have a generosity of spirit.

Once potential mentors have been identified, some programs, almost like a dating service, match them up with mentorees. A potential difficulty with this approach is that if the match proves a poor one, the mentoree may be too embarrassed to change it.

It's important to recognize that mentoring is a *human* relationship with a strong emotional component. The mutual respect between mentor and mentoree can be facilitated, but it cannot be legislated. One approach that works well is to let mentorees pick from a pool of potential designated mentors (indicating their second and third choices as well, to help the organization ensure a balanced workload).

More Than Practical Guidance

Some programs legislate how often mentor and mentoree should meet, for how long, and what they should discuss. But while a framework can be helpful, don't look at the relationship mechanistically, or you risk stripping it of its vibrancy. Different people have different needs to talk to a mentor at different points in time. What they want to talk about will vary, too, depending on their age, personality, and their life and work situation. Carol, for example, may be looking at a career move into a high-profile project and seeks advice, while Peter is concerned about the balance between his work and personal life.

But while people differ in what they look for in a mentor, in general it seems clear that today they are looking for more than just practical guidance. Increasingly, they are looking for *broader emotional and psychological support* from someone who genuinely cares about them as human beings.

With the breaking of the traditional ties of loyalty between the individual and the organization, and the growing depersonalization of contemporary society, people are looking to mentors to act as their defenders and provide feelings of being nurtured. And in some cases – depending on the personality of the mentor – they may be expecting too much.

Jane C., for example, was deeply disturbed by an unpleasant work incident. She ran into her mentor's office and blurted out the problem, expecting her mentor to reassure her and intervene on her behalf, the way her mother might have done. But her mentor was preoccupied with something else and reacted coolly to the interruption, saying, "This is not the right time or place."

Other people expect a mentor to act as a kind of personal agent for them – not just guiding them but also promoting their interests and marketing them into new projects or positions within the organization. In fact, mentors do not necessarily do those things. Typically it would be rare to have a single mentor who would both offer career guidance *and* act as a marketing agent – although some people are fortunate enough to have multiple mentors who share these roles.

Finding a Mentor

If you don't have a mentor, you can find one. Look for someone either inside or outside your organization with a more developed career intelligence – someone from whom you can learn and who meets the criteria discussed above.

Your ideal mentor may be a previous manager; a manager in another area of the organization (giving you access to other areas); a client; an external consultant; a family friend; or someone you worked with on a project team.

In the past, a mentor typically was *older* than his or her protégé. In the classic mentoring relationship, a senior manager would take a younger high-potential version of himself under his wing and steer him into plum assignments. Today, though, this model is increasingly being turned on its head, with the changing composition of the workforce and the flattening of hierarchy. Today, an older worker may be able to benefit as much from mentoring by a young employee as vice versa. Where a younger worker may learn about "how things often get done around here," and who the key players are, from an older mentor, the older worker may benefit from having their traditional beliefs about work challenged by younger, more irreverent colleagues.

You may have more than one mentor. After all, given the multiple roles we play, many people are potential sources of support.

Traditionally, in finding a mentor, people thought about "chemistry." In fact, you may be better off with someone whose approach, style, and world view is dramatically different from yours. You can then take advantage of new ways of thinking about things.

The most important step in finding a mentor is determining how you can benefit from someone else's know-how and expertise. Start with a self-assessment. What are your relative areas of weakness given your longer-term interests? Who can help you develop in these areas?

One question people ask is, "How do I approach someone? For example, do I call them up and say, I'd like you to be my mentor?" The mentoring relationship need not be that formal. It can in fact be very fluid. For example, there are a number of younger women who call me for advice every now and then when they are wrestling with a problem. Consider approaching people whose opinions you value to ask them out for coffee. Tell them you'd like to pick their brain or use them as a sounding board.

Many people don't avail themselves of the help of a potential mentor because they worry that it's an imposition. Actually, having their opinions sought can be deeply satisfying to mentors. Far from feeling imposed on, they appreciate the recognition that they have some knowledge and wisdom to share.

How to Give
People a Belief in the Future

Ann Sanders, a vice-president with a large financial-services company, is a success by most people's standards. She has moved ahead rapidly in her career, while managing to maintain a strong family life. But lately, she feels close to the breaking point. "Most days I go into work early and stay late, but somehow I never catch up with the work. There's always some new priority, some new fire to fight. And every time I have to travel, the work piles up even higher. My boss is mad at me because I'm not delivering; my husband is mad because I'm always home late; and my kids are upset because they hardly see me. More and more I find myself thinking: Is it really worth it? If not for the money, I would quit tomorrow."

Mark Miller, a manager for a high technology company, is coping with the aftermath of a major downsizing. Forced to produce more work with fewer resources, he feels under siege. "Before I finish one project to my own satisfaction, I have to start on another," he says. "I'm not managing anymore, I'm just reacting to events. I really feel as if I'm losing my edge."

Linda Graves, a compensation specialist in an HR department that has shrunk from 12 people to 5, is being called upon to function in a generalist's role, juggling a broad range of issues. "I'm not happy in this new work, nor do I feel like I'm doing a good job," she says.

Jack Thompson was once a highly effective sales manager in a midsize manufacturing company, reporting to the vice-president of marketing. Following a corporate restructuring, Jack reports directly to the CEO and is being asked to play a more strategic marketing role. "I'm great at selling, but handling these more strategic issues just isn't my strength," Jack says. "More and more, I feel that I just can't do what they're asking me to do. It makes me start to question myself: Am I stupid? Incompetent? I never used to feel that way."

Fewer Rungs Left to Climb

Restructuring. Downsizing. Organizational change. As we have seen, these have become fixtures in the new landscape of work as companies scramble to meet the challenges of an increasingly competitive marketplace. Widespread elimination of jobs and reporting levels has created increased workloads for managers and professionals, while other jobs have changed to the point where they demand different competencies. And, always, there is the relentless pressure to produce.

Many people caught up in these sweeping changes are feeling beleaguered by the demands placed upon them now, and chronically anxious about the future. Often, they

- are working at such a frantic pace they are losing any sense of satisfaction or accomplishment in their work;
- are worried about the security of their income;
- no longer feel that they are making a meaningful contribution;
- have begun to doubt their own competence;

- are having increasing difficulty balancing work demands with their personal and family life.

At the same time, many people feel that the whole effort-reward equation has become unbalanced. Not only are they working harder than ever, they are often doing so for what they perceive as fewer rewards. Their career progress has slowed to a crawl. And when they look ahead they find it difficult to see where they can go. As reporting levels have been eliminated, there are fewer rungs left to climb on the traditional career ladder. And they know that jobs that exist now may not do so five years from now.

This sense of malaise is compounded when people are in the wrong job or work environment – something that happens all too often in the wake of restructuring and downsizing. Highly competent specialists like Linda Graves, in the example above, are turned into barely competent generalists. People with real strengths, like Jack Thompson, are shuffled into positions where their weaknesses come to the fore.

Perhaps the most pervasive stressor of all, however, is coping on a daily basis with the all-encompassing state of *ambiguity* that characterizes contemporary organizational life. People are plagued with such questions as:

- Will my organization restructure/downsize (again)?
- How will I be affected? Will I still have a job? What will it be?
- Who will I be reporting to?
- What will happen to the people reporting to me?
- Will this company/unit/division still exist a year from now?

Most people who work for organizations have been socialized to expect a much more orderly world – one in which the future is relatively predictable, and in which it is possible to engage in particular tasks to achieve particular outcomes. What we are seeing today is a pervasive anxiety, as people try to come to grips with a world in which the present is uncertain and the future almost completely unpredictable and uncontrollable. Faced with this chronic ambiguity, their whole sense of personal efficacy is being eroded.

Helping People Cope

People work to derive a variety of rewards: not only salary and the prospect of advancement, but also a sense of collegiality with co-workers; a feeling of purpose in their work; opportunities for development; identification with the goals of the organization; a sense that their activities are instrumental in contributing to producing desirable outcomes in the future. When these rewards are progressively stripped away, morale and performance will inevitably suffer.

The pressures on people in organizations are unlikely to abate for the foreseeable future. Instead we will likely see much more of the same. Jobs will continue to change or disappear entirely; companies will continue to sell off, or shut down, whole business areas; new technology will continue to transform how people do their work; market changes will require an ever-shifting mix of skills. There will be more restructuring, more downsizing – and even more pressure on the individuals caught up in these changes.

The challenge facing organizations is to help their people cope with these pressures by providing them with a *renewed sense of purpose*. People need to feel that they are making a real contribution in their jobs and that they are valuable both to themselves and to the organization.

What can organizations do to help their people cope, and restore their sense of the future? Here are five strategies:

1. Recognize that people are a nonrenewable resource. People today are juggling demands on many fronts: work, family, finances. They don't have endless resources for coping with the pressures placed upon them. Eventually they will be worn down, and their performance and productivity will decline. There is only so much you can ask of them.

2. *Communicate clearly and honestly.* Whether the issue is a downsizing, a potential merger or sell-off of assets, or simply the need to cut costs and improve productivity, organizations need to let their people know what is going on. When organizations keep their people in the dark, gossip and rumor will flourish – usually with a much more devastating impact on morale and productivity than the plain truth would have had.

The organization must paint a *compelling picture of the future* so that the staff will have a sense of how they can benefit from the coming changes. All too often, senior managers hide behind closed doors during a significant organizational change. When they come out, they walk about mournfully, looking like they just lost their best friend. They should recognize what they are actually communicating through such behavior, and fulfill their responsibility to deal openly and positively with staff.

3. *Demonstrate an appreciation for individuals.* Organizations can show that they care about their people in a variety of ways, ranging from simple gestures (like taking the trouble to say thank you for a job well done) to more complex interventions, such as the provision of opportunities for self-assessment and self-determination (see below).

4. *Live up to the new employment contract.* By now everyone knows that no organization can guarantee its people lifelong job security. But what organizations can and should do is ensure that their staff remain marketable, whether inside or outside the organization. And what that requires is supporting individuals in taking responsibility for managing their own careers. Loyalty can no longer be bought with promises of security – but it can be earned, by treating people with dignity and respect.

5. Provide opportunities for self-assessment and self-determination. As well as encouraging people to take responsibility for managing their careers, organizations should provide them with the proper tools to do the job. People should have the opportunity to go through a meaningful process of self-assessment that enables them to plan out their goals. This can be provided in a number of ways, from the "Cadillac option" of executive coaching to career-planning workshops and one-on-one counseling.

How Effective Career-Management Programs Can Help

At first glance, this may seem to be a paradoxical suggestion. Why undertake a career-management program when, for most organizations and industries, so many question marks abound about future jobs or careers?

But it is precisely the uncertainty that makes career planning so vital. Career planning promotes morale and employability by:

- Fostering self-knowledge.
- Restoring a sense of self-efficacy.
- Communicating "we care."
- Preparing people for the future.
- Improving job fit.

Let's look at these benefits in detail:

Fostering self-knowledge: Career management helps staff move beyond identification with their existing jobs and job titles. Individuals no longer see themselves as filling a specific job (e.g., "I'm a marketing manager for ABC Company"). Instead, they recognize themselves as the *owner of a portfolio of skills and experiences* (e.g., "competencies and knowledge in marketing and sales; knowledge of financial products aimed at baby boomers;

team-building abilities"). They can then *reconfigure these skills* and experiences in new ways, either in the organization or outside it.

Restoring a sense of self-efficacy: Providing people buffeted by change with the opportunity for self-assessment can be extremely valuable in promoting individual and organizational renewal. The career-planning experience builds confidence and boosts self-esteem by reminding individuals of their accomplishments. It promotes an understanding of their marketability, both within and outside the organization.

Through self-assessment, people have the opportunity to sit back and reflect on how much they really *are* contributing now, if they only had the time to realize it. Reviewing their accomplishments gives people a renewed sense of self-efficacy in their work. As a result, their morale and commitment are renewed, too.

Communicating "we care": Supporting individuals in their career management shows them that management cares and is living up to its side of the new employment contract. The message is that people do have a future, whether it's inside the organization or outside.

Some senior managers might fear that introducing career planning in a period of uncertainty will only create panic by leading staff to believe they are about to lose their jobs. That's an old-fashioned concern, however. Today's workers aren't fools. They understand the challenges of the new employment contract and all but a few realize, at least intellectually, that they are responsible for managing their own careers. Implementing a career-planning initiative doesn't communicate they are about to lose their jobs. It communicates that the company wants them to be the strongest and most capable individuals they can be, and is willing to invest in them.

Some executives, of course, might harbor an opposite fear: that the initiative will only encourage their best staff to leave. In my experience, that fear is unfounded. If the organization is properly communicating with its staff, career planning won't encourage people to jump ship.

Indeed, the opposite has been the case. People come to career-planning workshops excited and appreciative that the company is finally doing something to support them in ensuring their employability, rather than simply paying lip service to the new employment contract. And even if at times they are nervous because their jobs are vulnerable, they come out feeling significantly more competent. Participants realize that they are much more employable than they thought, whether inside or outside the organization. People say, "I recognize that I'm marketable, and I'm comfortable waiting out this change, because this could represent an exciting opportunity."

Consider, also, whether you want individuals working for your organization who aren't highly employable elsewhere – and are clueless about their appeal?

Preparing people for the future: Self-assessment also assists people in preparing themselves to adapt to change in the future. It shows them how to look beyond their job titles to identify key underlying skills that can be transferred to other work settings. Once people gain a sense of their own "marketability," whether inside or outside the organization, they will be more confident in themselves and less anxious about the future.

Going through a career-planning experience typically assures staff that they have the strength to thrive in the future organization, whatever its shape – or that if they do lose their jobs, they have skills that can be used in other work. That makes them less defensive, more willing to accept change.

Improving "fit": It's crucial that organizations, as they change and evolve, ensure that people don't wind up in the wrong slots. By helping people understand their abilities and by boosting their confidence, career planning reduces the chance that individuals will grab at any opening just for the sake of continuing to hold a job with the company. Instead, they will understand what roles they are best geared to fit and which ones will further growth and advancement.

Take George, for example. A policy analyst at a large firm, he saw himself only as capable of continuing in that role after a merger. But through career planning, he realized that what had made his unit so successful was not its analytical research skills but the ability of people within it to build team relationships. When an opportunity presented itself that put a premium on team-building skills, he was comfortable in making the switch, thanks to his heightened self-awareness.

Self-assessment gives people who are currently in a job or work environment that represents a mismatch with their interests and skills the opportunity to identify the causes of their stress and do something about it. In some cases the solution will be some modification to their current work, to give them more of what suits them best. In other cases, a move – whether inside or outside the company – will be necessary to achieve a more satisfactory match.

Delivering Support

There are a number of vehicles for delivering career-management support for staff during periods of apprehension and change. The one I prefer is that which an organization would normally use for support in career self-management, whether it be a corporate university, leadership institute, management development program, or learning center.

I am less enthusiastic about some of the other vehicles. Making an Employee Assistance Program the sole mechanism to respond to staff apprehensions, for example, can send an implicit message that anyone having problems is not as emotionally strong as his or her colleagues. After all, an EAP is where you go when you are suffering from a personal problem. Obviously the EAP must continue to be promoted during this period. But HR should also be stressing more positive and less clinical approaches.

Career centers have also been used with varied success to help smooth transitions. When the career center is viewed as a vehicle for promoting employability and change, it has been successful. But when it is confined to delivering one-on-one counseling support, it can become like an EAP program, preoccupied with people who are *hurting*. That can become expensive and also result in the career center eventually losing touch with the many individuals it should be helping.

In other words, career planning should be positioned to help people:

- get started on the process of framing meaningful and realistic career and life goals;
- identify their unique work style and preferences profile;
- learn how to look beyond their job titles and identify key underlying skills and competencies that can be applied in future work assignments;
- identify the new skills they may need to develop to adapt to new corporate directions;
- make informed decisions about future job assignments;
- develop and implement personal career and life plans.

Making the Right Move

To see the potential impact of an effective career-management program, let's look briefly at the experience of a financial-services company. This company had already gone through a downsizing and was about to place one of its divisions up for sale. A company-wide meeting was called to brief people on the situation. Although no promises could be made about job security, management wanted people to understand that they recognized their apprehension and demoralization.

Subsequently, the company offered a series of career self-management workshops. The workshops were open to everyone, and over 80% of the employees opted to participate. Through these workshops, people were able to regain a sense of their own marketability. As a result, they were able to face an uncertain future with much greater confidence. The program had an obvious and direct impact on morale – including the receipt by senior management of dozens of unsolicited thank-you letters.

Giving Something Back

Obviously, organizations stand to gain some significant benefits from providing self-assessment and career-planning assistance to their people. Individuals become more flexible and adaptive. Morale and commitment are renewed.

Perhaps even more important, however, is the opportunity for organizations to show that they really do care about what their people are going through in these difficult times, and to demonstrate their concern by *giving something back*. And what they are giving back is nothing less than the individual's sense of well-being and personal efficacy.

part four

A New Set of Skills

Become a
Career Activist

Lately, I've been struck by the number of people who are unhappy in their work but unwilling, or unable, to do anything about it. They recite the usual millennial litany of being overworked and underappreciated, of managing their families at long distance, of "not having a life anymore." But for all their complaints that they aren't going anywhere, they also make statements like: "I'm just waiting for the package." Or, "Better the devil you know than the one you don't know." Or, "Maybe when X retires next year things will change."

The very language is revealing: fatalistic, unquestioning, resigned. At its extremes it reflects the helplessness associated with depression: "There's no point in trying to make a move. It's the same everywhere . . ." (Do you recognize yourself in this language?)

And then there are people who, poised to take advantage of a hot job market, *are* looking to move – with the number-one criteria being money, rather than what kind of life they want to lead or whether their work meets their underlying values. They say, in effect, "If I'm going to have to go to the wall for my work, I might as well get a whack of money for it."

Career Passivity

These are, in fact, two sides of the same coin. Both groups, in their own ways, are demonstrating career *passivity*. It's a paradox that in these days of empowerment and self-management many people who otherwise see themselves as independent, take-charge types demonstrate a kind of helplessness when it comes to how they spend their working lives. They act as if their work is an implacable force of nature, something they are powerless to change, and can only accept with resignation. Where once people complained angrily about their excessive workloads, now they seem only resigned to putting up with a kind of ongoing, low-level malaise.

Most of us understand that today we have to take an activist stance in relation to our health, our personal finances, or our children's education. We no longer trust in the goodness of others, or of institutions, to look after our interests. We act at the first sign of a problem in these other domains to protect our rights and try to control our own destiny.

And yet work — which plays such a critical role in determining how we feel about ourselves, how effective we are as parents, family members, and members of society — has become the last area for such personal activism. It's as if *we don't see ourselves as being worthy of protection.*

Ask people *why* they are working so hard and they typically don't have an answer. Routinely working 12 hours a day plus a day on the weekend has become their reality, and they no longer think about things being different. Probe further and you'll get passive responses like "you just get sucked in," "you know how it is," or "that's just the way things are these days."

This career passivity is not limited to overworked middle managers. Indeed, senior managers who see themselves as self-determining at work — making choices and redesigning their organizations at will — are just as likely to describe their work as though it were an immutable truth, saying matter-of-factly, "I can't go on vacation (or go to parent-teachers night or visit with friends) because I have work to do." Asked what the consequences of *not* working might be, they can't even entertain the thought.

In part, perhaps, we are just too tired, busy, and distracted to look after ourselves. But we are also, typically, ill-prepared to think like career activists and recognize that we *do* have control over many aspects of our careers, if only we choose to exercise it.

In contrast to people waiting for the package or moving jobs purely for money are those who are introspective, thoughtful, and activist in their attitudes to their work. As one woman observed, "I wouldn't allow myself to be abused in a relationship, so why would I put up with being abused in a job? When you're doing work for which you're not well-suited, or which doesn't make you feel good about yourself, over time it feels like abuse."

Career activism means *becoming an intelligent actor in your own life*: developing a thorough understanding of your current situation, and then taking steps to change it for the better. And that means first of all having a vision of oneself as *worthy* of meaningful work and a fulfilling personal life. You need to become vigilant on your own behalf in routinely scanning your environment to ensure that your work continues to meet your needs. Ask yourself:

- Am I engaged? Am I feeling stretched in a positive way?
- Am I learning, am I contributing to my employability?
- Do I feel I'm doing work that's important?
- Are my personal needs outside of work being met?

To be a successful career activist, you need to understand the external economic and social landscape, educating yourself about the new work and career realities and knowing what you need to do to ensure your continued marketability. But you also need to be attuned to your own internal, personal world: what engages you, what you care about, what gives your life meaning. Only by knowing yourself will you be able to make the right decisions about your career – decisions that reflect your most important personal values and concerns rather than the external measures of success such as salary.

You will then be able to think about yourself and your career differently, to rise above the frenetic busyness of everyday working life, to make choices in terms of your own agenda, to pursue your own goals. And you will learn to trust yourself – your own ideas, instincts, and perceptions.

People need to think about the long-term cost to themselves, not to mention their families, their workplace, and their society, of sacrificing that which gives their life meaning. Becoming a career activist is not a luxury. It's the key to a successful and rewarding career and life.

On Selling
Yourself

"*I*f I'm good, my work should speak for itself. I shouldn't have to continually trumpet my accomplishments."

If you ask people, as I do frequently in speeches and workshops, to what extent they agree with this statement, the response is typically one of profound ambivalence.

Intellectually, at least, most people understand that one of the central themes of the new economy is the need to always look after one's own employability – which means, among other things, continually having to sell oneself. And yet many people, particularly managers and professionals of a certain age, feel that this sort of self-promotion is somehow unseemly and unprofessional, and that they really *shouldn't* need to do it.

We have all had to sell ourselves at one time or another, whether in interviewing for a job or selling the services of our business to a client. But in today's tenuous, shape-shifting workplace, we need to sell ourselves *hard* all the time. People who work for large organizations now find themselves in the same position as consultants and other freelancers, constantly having to gather testimonials, document their achievements, and pitch new work.

It is no longer enough just to perform well. You must also manage other people's impressions of how well you are performing. Like it or not, the only way to secure your employability is to turn yourself into a valued commodity, constantly selling yourself so that others will buy your services.

Many people *don't* like it. Reducing themselves to a package of assets and selling features ("I'm a customer-responsive, client-centered, profit-driven, value-adding, flexible, results-oriented team player . . .") leaves them feeling somehow less human.

There is also an interesting paradox at work here. In today's teamwork-sensitive environment, where the emphasis is very much on *we* rather than *I*, some people are extremely uneasy about drawing the line between what *I* did and what *we* did in order to claim credit for their individual contributions.

Often, too, people are at a loss as to *how* to go about selling themselves. They are unsure where to draw the line between simply drawing attention to their attributes and accomplishments and being obnoxiously self-promoting. And they wonder what the proper mechanics are for doing so: should they waylay people in the hall, take them out for lunch, or what?

I should note that there is a strong *generational difference* in attitudes to self-promotion. At a recent workshop at a bank I probed those feelings by asking participants to choose which of two statements more accurately described them:

- "I understand why I have to keep people informed of my accomplishments, but, to be perfectly honest, I feel very uncomfortable constantly promoting myself. After all, if I'm really good other people should know."
- "I feel comfortable letting people know about my accomplishments. After all, if I don't, how are they going to know?"

There was almost a perfect generational divide between these alternatives. Participants who were in their 20s and early 30s found the second statement reflected them perfectly. They were comfortable marketing themselves. They had entered the workplace at a time when opportunities were scarce and when the old employment contract was under siege. They understood, or at least learned very quickly, that the only way they could secure work was by aggressively selling themselves. They had no expectation that some benevolent employer would look after them and their career.

But almost to a person, those in their late 30s and 40s picked the first option – they simply weren't at ease in the self-marketing role, even though intellectually they understand the need for self-promotion.

A typical comment from that older group is, "I'm 45 years old – I shouldn't still be *proving* my competence."

Still, as one 20-something observed, while the 40-somethings may have difficulty in selling themselves, they, at least for the most part, have some place in which to do so. She and her friends, she said, had absolutely no problem marketing themselves – if only they could find a potential purchaser.

Suggestions for Reluctant Self-Marketers

Reappraise what it means to talk about your skills and accomplishments: Many people are self-conscious about talking about themselves, fearing that they will be seen as shamelessly self-promoting. Get over this self-consciousness – think of yourself as communicating useful information about how you can contribute to people who might be interested to hear about it. If you don't tell them what you are capable of, they may never find out.

Recognize that what is obvious to you may not be obvious to others: Don't assume that because you have told people something once, they will necessarily remember it. A friend was upset because she was passed over for a role on a high-profile project. "They knew I was the best person for the assignment," she complained. Six months before, when the project was first discussed, she had made a strong pitch for her inclusion, based on her skills and experience. I often hear stories like this one, and usually the problem is that "they" *don't* know or don't remember. People are so busy these days, and so buried in information, that they won't necessarily remember something you told them months ago. It's incumbent on you to remind them at appropriate intervals.

Avoid the "ego-dump": There's nothing I find more suffocating and off-putting than having to listen to someone recite a self-congratulatory litany of commendations, client bookings, sales results, or whatever else. Marketing yourself is no different from marketing any other product. *Edit your information* for your market. Focus on what they want and need to know about you. Make sure what you say interests *them* — not just *you*.

Remember the other person's ego: If you go too far in touting your own accomplishments, you run the risk of making the other person feel insignificant. He may feel his only value to you is as a repository for your achievements, or may compare himself with you and feel inadequate. You are providing potential purchasers of your skills information about what you can do. You should not be seeking affirmation or validation from them about your value as a human being.

Track your strengths and accomplishments: To do an effective job of marketing yourself, you need to identify your key strengths and accomplishments. Don't expect your boss or your client to do it for you. In today's often-thankless work world, they may well be too busy to notice what you're doing, much less give you meaningful feedback. Going through a careful self-assessment will help you determine what you have to sell, as well as giving you the confidence to point out your strengths to others.

Properly done, self-marketing can be an enormous boost to your career. It also can become, in time, second nature. The key is to be yourself. Avoid being overbearing, obnoxious, or mindlessly repetitive. But at the same time, don't fall into the trap of being so complacent that your golden deeds remain buried treasures.

The Right and
Wrong Ways to Network

*T*he fall seems to be a time of year when many people approach their careers with renewed seriousness. Perhaps they've done some stock-taking at the cottage and have returned to work determined to get back into high gear. Or perhaps they've come back to find the same problems they placed on hold for the summer: the job is still a poor match with their skills, the boss is still a jerk, another reorganization is coming down the pike.

Whatever the reason, every fall I get a flurry of "networking" calls from people looking for advice, information, and contacts. Typically they are thinking seriously about changing jobs, or going out on their own as a consultant, or changing their business strategy.

Networking is an increasingly important career skill. We all need to be plugged into a variety of networks to keep up with developments in our field and position ourselves to take advantage of new opportunities – particularly in today's fluid workplace, with its growing emphasis on short-term assignments and multidisciplinary project teams. And yet many people are very clumsy, if not misguided, in their networking efforts.

We all know people who are so highly *instrumental* in their networking that they completely turn us off. When Gary T. calls me, as he does every year or so, I know he's either lost his job, or is looking for some other type of help. In between these calls, I may as well not exist – and Gary's hearty congeniality when he does call does not conceal the fact that this is clearly a fair-weather friendship.

Other people, however, are so uncomfortable about the whole idea of networking that they do it as little as possible. They think of it as being manipulative and exploitative – *using* other people to help them get ahead. Or they feel it is somehow *unseemly* for them to have to schmooze or glad-hand. They see networking as fundamentally insincere – feigning interest in people when all you really want is to use them for your own ends.

Rather than being about using people, networking is really about expanding your relationships and developing *mutually supportive relationships*. It is as much about being there for someone else as about using someone else to get ahead. When you network properly, the other person is as likely to be the beneficiary as you are. You might learn about a possible merger at a customer's company, for example, while she gets the name of a great contact for raising money for a community association she belongs to.

Indeed, a general goal you should set for yourself in every networking contact is to find something out about the other person. You should leave networking conversations knowing something new about them, either about their additional business lines, trends affecting their business, or some of the challenges they are facing. The exchange of information may or may not lead to an immediate payoff. Relationships take time to nurture, and one doesn't enter every relationship looking for something of immediate economic value. *Don't measure your networking by its economic utility or the immediacy of the payback.*

How Not to Measure Networking

Networking should not be based on pure exchange. I routinely receive phone calls from people who want to meet to discuss a potentially "mutually rewarding relationship." This often leaves me feeling queasy. Perhaps I would have been quite happy to meet with this person – not to satisfy some need of my own, but simply to help him. The promise of a mutually rewarding relationship completely undermines this desire to be helpful and removes any motivation to make further contact. I also find it extremely presumptuous for someone I don't know to "know" what would be good for me.

If you are looking for help, don't sugarcoat it by implying you are doing the other person as much of a favor as they are doing for you.

Types of Networkers

The robotic networker: Erica C. was invited to a get-together with a group of talented and accomplished women from a broad range of professional fields. While the other women were having animated discussions, punctuated by gales of laughter, about everything under the sun, from work and careers to relationships and children to pure gossip, Erica was going around collecting business cards. "That was great," she told her hostess at the end of the evening. "I've got 15 business cards!" Erica was concerned only to identify potential resources to assist her with work-related problems. If she had allowed herself to participate in the spirit of the evening, she could have learned much that could enrich her *life* as well as her career.

The information interviewer: "I'm currently exploring my career options. I'd like to meet with you and learn about what you do." Everyone gets these calls. We've been getting them ever since the job-search gurus began to advocate "information interviewing" as a strategy for making contacts and positioning oneself for opportunities ("I'd really appreciate if you could critique my résumé . . ."). This was once an ingenious notion: most people like to be helpful, after all, and are usually flattered to be asked for advice. But it's a strategy that's getting tired. People have heard it too often.

Most people today don't have the luxury of time to meet face to face with each caller. At best, they may be able to spend some time on the phone. Information-seekers who insist on a face-to-face meeting will usually be disappointed. And trust me, the promise of a free lunch is not going to make a meeting more likely.

If you are seeking information, be mindful of the other person's time. One strategy is to make contact by e-mail. This grants the recipient more control over when, if ever, to deal with your request. But don't let the ease of transmitting e-mail lead you into besieging your contacts with a lot of information, or requiring them to take an inordinate amount of time responding. If you hope to get a useful response, be targeted. (And if you get a response, make sure you thank the person afterward!)

The incessant networker: Recently I was telling a client how I avoid talking to fellow passengers on airplanes. He was horrified, asking, "But what if the person sitting next to you was a potential client?" I admire entrepreneurial zeal as much as the next person. But you don't have to approach every interaction as a potential business lead.

The out-of-left-field networker: The caller says, "Hello, this is Jill. I'm in the process of changing my career direction, and I'd like your opinion. You were so helpful before . . ." And you wonder: "Who the hell is Jill?"

When you're calling someone you haven't seen or spoken to in years, don't assume the person will instantly remember you – particularly if the previous encounter was fleeting. If in doubt, provide some clues as you initiate the conversation so the other person can recall you ("Hello, this is Jill Smith. You may not remember me, but I'm a friend of Fred Jones and we met . . ."). Don't overestimate your own importance in your contacts' lives.

The narrow networker: It's amazing how parochial some people are in their networking. Bankers hang out with bankers, accountants with accountants, programmers with programmers. As a result, they develop a very narrow view of the world. In today's work world, where *breadth* is an increasingly key requirement for career success, expanding your network horizons will increase your understanding of critical business and social trends. Developing a broad network of contacts both inside your workplace and outside it – for example by participating in professional associations, social-interest groups, and community organizations – gives you a broader perspective on your work, as well as enriching your life.

Moreover, even from a purely practical point of view, it makes little sense to network only with people in your profession or industry. If there is a downturn in your area, you could find yourself in a network of people all looking for the same kind of work. Getting involved in multiple networks will increase your exposure to potential opportunities if you need to make a career transition.

Networking as Good Social Relations

The best networkers I know are conscious of the other person in the equation. They know what that person needs or values. They take genuine pleasure in doing something that makes a small difference in the other person's life. They are willing to spend a little extra effort helping out, and they don't begrudge the time they spend helping. Neither do they view it as a *quid pro quo*.

Communicating
on Fast Forward

A group of senior managers met for hours, developing a series of recommendations. The next day, when a copy of the recommendations was circulated among the members of the group, there was widespread consternation. "I don't remember agreeing to *that*," said one manager. Another asked, "Are you sure we were at the same meeting?"

Communication breakdown. It's become something of an epidemic these days. Lately it seems that we're all too busy and preoccupied to communicate clearly, or to listen to what other people are trying to tell us.

How often these days do you make a phone call, only to hear the other person tapping away on a keyboard or clicking a mouse — or even *eating* — as they talk? When attention is diluted like this, both the task at hand *and* the quality of the communication suffer.

Even when people appear to be taking part in a dialogue, their minds are often elsewhere. You are just one of five thousand things competing for their attention. They're thinking, "I'm exhausted, my boss is breathing down my neck, my partner is pissed off because she hasn't seen me in two weeks, my kid has three studs in his nose. I really don't have time to pay attention to you."

When I'm talking to people I often have the feeling that they really don't want to listen because in their minds the inevitable result will simply be more things to do — more to e-mail, fax, delegate, or report on — as if they don't have enough to do already.

An Escalation in Hyperbole

Given how difficult it has become to capture anyone's attention for more than a nanosecond, it's not surprising that there has been a steady escalation in hyperbole. It's no longer enough to say that something is "interesting" or "quite good" or "notable." Instead we have to throw around adjectives like the titles of old science-fiction magazines. Either something is the most extraordinary, amazing, astounding, and fantastic idea, book, theory, or event since the dawn of civilization, or it's hardly worth considering.

And then there are the miscommunications that occur when people working in overdrive leap to conclusions. Too impatient to process an entire communication, they fixate on key words or phrases, trying to speed-read the meaning. Metaphorically, they become like teenagers rolling their eyes at nagging parents, insisting that they *get the point* when they don't really get it at all.

This rush to get to the point — even the *wrong* point — is certainly understandable. But you wouldn't want your surgeon to skim over the results of your x-rays, or your lawyer to surf through the fine print. The consequences of not listening carefully — whether to a friend, a colleague, a boss, or a family member — can be equally disastrous.

Then again, even when you listen carefully, the other person may not really be saying anything. How often these days do you hear someone lapsing into "yadda, yadda, yadda"? It's as if we can't be bothered, or are too tired, to take the time to actually *think* about the content of the information — or else afraid that our listeners are too restless and bored and impatient to listen to any details. Instead we go through the *motions* of having communicated, skimming the surface rather than immersing ourselves in the content of the information.

And even when we *do* appear to be providing information, we are often only exchanging what are really meaningless abstractions: "globalization," "impact of technology," "profound cultural change," and so on. These are merely headings for whole pages of hypertext yet to be properly discussed, or even thought about. For all the meaning this impatient shorthand conveys, we might just as well be saying, "yadda, yadda, yadda."

The irony, of course, is that communication skills have never been at a greater premium. Given the pace of work and the tremendous amount of information to be exchanged and processed, it's crucial to be able to communicate effectively. Moreover, the new configuration of the workplace, and in particular the growing emphasis on project work, compels us to communicate in new ways. Members of a project team, for example, must be able to establish rapport quickly and build relationships with people they may never have met before – and in some cases may never meet face to face. And they must communicate clearly with people from different disciplines across borders and time zones.

Improving Communication

Traditional management-development courses in communication, with their focus on skills such as good listening, clarification, feedback, and being nonjudgmental, remain valuable and worthwhile. But at the same time they largely miss the most fundamental point: How do you connect with someone when you are just one of a multitude of things competing for their attention?

There are no easy answers to this question. But there are, at least, some strategies that improve your chances of being not only heard but understood. You need to be able to communicate in a way that is both *graphic* and *to the point*. Ask yourself:

- Can I quickly capture my listener's attention and get my message across?
- Can I use words to paint a picture, tell a story, make information vivid? Can I talk in headlines?
- Can I write clearly, persuasively, and with impact?
- Can I zero in on key concepts and translate them appropriately for my listener's requirements? Or do I embellish needlessly and bury vital points in useless information?
- Am I aware of what my listener is interested in – as opposed to what I feel a need to say?
- Can I quickly establish relationships and credibility with people I've never met?

At the same time, think about the kind of behaviors you are demonstrating both as a communicator and as a listener. Are you contributing to the hysterical din of miscommunication, or are you taking the time both to understand and to make yourself understood?

It's very easy to fall into the trap of thinking you have heard something before, when this time it has a different twist. Pay attention carefully to what you are hearing and make sure you can summarize the essence of what you have just heard.

If you're not really hearing something that somebody else is saying, be honest. Tell the person that you're overloaded and you'd prefer to deal with it at some other point. It's better to admit you haven't fully processed something than to do the other person the disservice of pretending to listen. You may have missed something important that they really needed you to hear.

In a faster-paced world, we will increasingly be working with people we've never met, or who come from different disciplines. Given the shape of work to come, and the growing complexity of communications, the ability to communicate powerfully and persuasively, and to decode what others are trying to tell you, will be critical to career success.

"Don't Take
This Personally, But . . ."

"*D*o you mind if I give you some feedback?" How often, when asked this question, do you really want to say, "Well actually, I do." But in an era when we are all supposed to be continuously learning, we worry that this would reflect an underlying defensiveness.

Well, the reasons one might be less than enamored of receiving such *unsolicited* feedback are simple enough. (Note that we are not talking about a formal coaching situation where there is a meaningful expectation that your behavior will be helpfully assessed by someone else.)

Unsolicited Feedback

To begin with, when people ask, "Do you want feedback?", almost invariably what they really mean is, "I'd like to criticize you." After all, if they were going to praise you, would they ask for permission? And in that statement, "I'd like to criticize you," they are making two major assumptions.

First, they are assuming that they know something that you don't already know – that they can tell you something significant about your behavior that you were not aware of, and that their opinion counts for something. In fact, by the time most people are in their 30s, they have fairly accurate insight into their own behavior. It is unusual that someone can make an off-the-cuff observation about a problem behavior that you are completely unaware of. So if you have just made a complete idiot of yourself, you probably already know that, and don't necessarily need the point to be driven home any further. As one person commented, "I'm 40 years old and I've been doing presentations for 15 years now. When I've completely missed it, I usually already know."

Another assumption is that you will benefit from the feedback – that the behavior being commented on is *something you can change*. Some behaviors are changeable. But given the relative consistency of personality characteristics, the chances are that if you continue to exhibit this area of so-called weakness for a long time, you are probably aware of the difficulty. You have either tried to change it without success, or else focused on improving in other areas.

Unsolicited feedback is also often essentially trivial in nature. It's as if people feel an expectation they *should* give you feedback, so they make a comment on the smallest detail in order to say anything at all.

One woman, for example, had just delivered a successful sales presentation on which she had worked long and hard. Her efforts paid off and her company stole the account from a competitor. Her boss's comment was, "On the fifth slide, you misspelled the word 'people.'" True enough, she thought, but in the bigger scheme of things, would it not have made more sense to have said, "Congratulations, great presentation, and by the way, on a very minor note for your future reference, you had a typo . . ."?

Often this focus on tiny details says more about their own need to puff up their self-importance than it does about you. What is particularly galling is that such comments are typically purely *descriptive* ("You look really tired") rather than *prescriptive*, making suggestions as to what you could do differently.

"Don't Take It Personally"

And then there's that old chestnut, "Don't take it personally." Janice, for example, as part of what she described as a "group dump masquerading as team-building," was told that she was "rude, arrogant, and condescending." She asked the group, in a somewhat sarcastic manner, "Is there anything else you would like to share with me?", only to be told, "Don't be defensive, you're not supposed to take it personally . . ."

You have to wonder, if someone is being criticized, who owns that behavior, the world or that person? Experts on communication will insist that it is your behavior that is being criticized, not you as a person. Indeed, this is one of the fundamental precepts of performance appraisals. But the behavior is grounded in the individual. How else should Janice take it if not personally?

One especially nasty variation of feedback is what an organizational consultant colleague of mine calls "the s___-filled Twinkie . . . ," in which criticism comes with a perfunctory sugarcoating. For example, "I really liked the way you answered questions in that presentation. Unfortunately, I don't think your content showed the level of preparation I expect of you. But good job on the Q&A."

All this said, it's true that people will often *say* they want feedback, when in fact they don't like it at all. As part of my Ph.D. thesis I did research on how people respond to praise and criticism from their bosses. The situations described real-life events such as writing a report or giving a presentation with the boss providing behavioral feedback. For example, "You captured the key concepts in a vivid and compelling manner," versus "I think you could have got to the key points faster."

My research showed when people were praised, their moods or emotions were significantly altered in a positive manner. When given negative feedback, even so-called helpful and constructive feedback, they reacted with anger, disappointment, and confusion.

So when people say they want feedback, what they often really want is unqualified admiration and affirmation.

Individual Differences

There are significant differences in how people respond to feedback. Some people are more sensitive to criticism, while others are more dispassionate and capable of shrugging it off. For example, some people, when told that their report is "quite good," hear "your report was a disaster." Or, after having given a presentation that 90% of participants described as "excellent" and 10% said "needs improvement," some will focus obsessively on the minority opinion. On the other hand, there are those who fail to recognize even the most damning criticism.

Some people are simply more sensitive to, and more strongly affected by, the way others see them. They feel better about themselves to the extent that they've been praised. They are quicker to pick up subtle interpersonal cues related to others' reactions to them – for example, that their listeners look bored, or that their joke died.

Other people are less sensitive, even impervious, to how the world sees them. They are less likely to pick up cues and are also less affected by negative feedback.

Some think that people whose feelings about themselves are more easily affected by how others see them must have low self-esteem. But in my experience, people who are more sensitive are just as likely as their less-sensitive counterparts to see themselves as being capable and effective, and are not particularly more prone to depression – in fact, they are equally optimistic in their expectations of the world.

Giving Feedback

What is true of unsolicited feedback is just as true of the feedback you may get through such official mechanisms as performance appraisal or coaching and counseling situations. Most people resent getting negative feedback from their boss or team leader — all the more so if their compensation or prospects for advancement are at stake.

Organizations continue to spend millions of dollars constantly revising their performance appraisal systems. But the sad fact remains that, no matter how couched the comments may be, most people don't like negative feedback. Although in the long term people may actually benefit from it, don't be surprised that they are less than enthusiastic to hear it right now.

The following principles will increase the probability that the person getting the feedback will actually benefit from it:

- Remember to describe the positive. People are usually more aware of their faults than strengths, so don't emphasize the negative at the expense of the positive.
- Show how something could have been done differently. Focus on behaviors that can be changed.
- Consider extenuating circumstances. For example, "I know you've been under a lot of pressure lately, so your recent performance may reflect the fact that you are really tired. However, in the future . . ."
- Don't insist that the other person share your views of their relative inadequacies. You are entitled to an opinion on their behavior, but you don't have the right to demand that they agree with your assessment.
- People are often aware of faults. Articulating them can motivate them to change, as long as it isn't soul destroying.
- Tailor your feedback in relation to the person's personality, remembering that some people are more sensitive to criticism than others.
- Check out whether your feedback is truly wanted.

The Politics
of Bad Fit

*R*ebecca, a three-year employee of an advertising agency, had been put on probation as a result of a number of performance problems: she did not follow through on commitments, failed to deliver projects on time, and was ill-prepared for important meetings. Weekly conscientious coaching sessions with her manager improved her performance significantly.

Still, her boss, Eric, remained unhappy. He acknowledged that the performance issues had been addressed, and that Rebecca was now following through on her assignments and performing well.

"The real problem is I just don't like her," he said. "I find her silly, I can't stand her fake laugh, she's always dropping by my office, and it's driving me crazy. And yet I realize that many people find her very charming, so this may be as much of a statement about myself and what I like in people as it is about her. So I don't know where to go from here. Where do you draw the line between where it is acceptable for management to intervene and asking someone to change their basic personality?"

Authentically Obnoxious

This is indeed a thorny problem. Organizations like to flatter themselves in believing that almost everything an individual does in the workplace can be described and commented on in behavioral terms — and that individuals with problems can be coached for performance improvement. But the reality is that when people come to work, they bring their whole personalities with them. And that whole personality, in some cases, will cause some people to cringe. They are too loud, pushy, manipulative, political, dense, and so on.

We like to believe that today's organizations celebrate diversity and individual differences. People are supposed to be freer to bring their authentic selves to work. But what if that authentic self is objectionable?

Of course, annoying habits or distasteful characteristics are essentially a *subjective* question rather than something that can be *objectively* described and corrected. What one person finds unattractive, another might actually like. Organizational culture also plays a part in determining what is acceptable. A brash, aggressive person might flourish in sales but get on people's nerves in a research department.

Organizations cannot legislate desirable personality characteristics, nor do they have the right to change them. And yet problems of clashing personalities are ubiquitous and can often lead to dysfunctional or toxic work environments.

Managers like Eric wonder: How do you comment on such behaviors? Do you even have the right to comment on them? They often feel embarrassed having to "muck about" in such potentially emotive areas. Traditionally, these matters are seen as lying outside the realms of acceptable feedback. On the other hand, these behaviors not only may be irritating to co-workers, they may also significantly interfere with the person's effectiveness and advancement.

Michael, for example, had to deal with a subordinate who wanted to move into management, but whose abrasive manner made the move impossible. Without a change of style, the individual was told, he would not achieve his goals. No one likes to hear this kind of information, but it was useful feedback all the same.

Saving Face

One way that organizations can manage these situations is by referring people to coaches. Coaches have the interpersonal sensitivity and the psychological skills to describe the questionable behavior and its impact on others in a way that allows the individual to save face. And the coach can provide clear descriptions of alternative behaviors.

Coaching can be particularly helpful when the behavior is experienced by others in a way that is not intended by the individual. Very shy people, for example, may come across as arrogant and contemptuous of their team members when in fact they are simply socially uncomfortable.

It should be recognized, though, that coaching is far from a panacea. Some people simply lack any insight into their behavior, or its impact on others, and not even the most skillful coach can bring them to recognize the source of their problems. Other people don't *want* to change: they like themselves just the way they are and think it's the people around them who have the problem, not they. And in at least some cases, they are right.

Where an individual is unwilling or unable to change, there are really only a few options. You can learn to live with what you experience as obnoxious behavior. You can move away from the problem person – requesting a transfer, or finding another job. Or, if you are in a position to do so, you can fire the person.

However, one would be hard-pressed to make a legal case for firing someone for talking too loudly, having an irritating laugh, or being too political. That's why irreconcilable personality conflicts are usually dealt with quietly:

the individual is shown the door as part of a "restructuring" or because – using that favorite managerial chestnut – they are a "bad fit."

Indeed, we often use such euphemisms as "style," "culture," "chemistry," or "fit" to describe these situations. But the reality is that when we say someone had a problem fitting into the culture, it's usually just a polite way of saying that we don't like them.

A Matter of Style?

A whole other category of conflicts surrounds the question of personal taste and style. Is it all right to come to work wearing nose rings? Eyebrow rings? Visible tattoos? This is becoming a major source of intergenerational conflict in the workplace.

Styles and tastes change over time: just a decade ago, the idea that men in business suits would wear earrings would have seemed utterly fantastic to most people. But there are still boundaries set by prevailing cultural norms. You can push the edges of the envelope, but you still have to be able to get *into* the envelope.

How free we really are to be ourselves is a complex issue today, when many think of their life as a work of art that they are creating. Looking down the road, the impact of personal style issues on the workplace is likely to be magnified.

Teenagers have always celebrated personal style in their identification with a particular subculture, be it hippie, street, or preppie. But today we are witnessing an unprecedented number of subcultures or "tribes" among teenagers, who are adopting the dress, mannerisms, music, and style of their preferred subculture at an increasingly early age – and defending their memberships aggressively as anti-corporate punk-rockers, party-loving ravers, materialistic preppies, or whatever else.

These kids are growing up with a belief that expressing their personal style is their right, their entitlement. When they enter the workplace, will they make the kind of transitions that their boomer parents did and be prepared to grow up, build a career, and conform?

Or will they simply become the obnoxious person in the next cubicle?

Recession-Proofing
Your Career

*T*here's a recession coming. There's *always* a recession coming, sooner or later. Is your career recession-proof?

Let's be clear. We are *not* talking here about the security of your current job, because these days no job is secure. Even through the boom years, organizations continued to restructure and downsize to become ever-more effective and competitive. Another downturn in the business cycle will only accelerate the pace of change – and make careful career management even more crucial.

These days, as discussed throughout this book, no matter what our official employment status, we are all temporary workers. Whether we have a conventional full-time job, or are contingent, contract, or freelance workers, we are all living and working in TempWorld. In TempWorld everything shifts rapidly. Nothing is forever, everything is temporary: where you work, what you do there, the skills you use, the people you work with.

In this fast-shifting world, there can be no guarantees attached to any particular job. But there is much that you can do to insulate yourself from change and economic upheaval, by equipping yourself with the skills to manage your career more effectively. And what that involves is becoming a *career activist*.

Hillary, a 27-year-old systems analyst, quit her job to study French for six months. Longer term, she wants to be able to parlay her information technology skills into work with an international organization.

Zack, 30, a conference producer, is devoting all of his free time away from work to networking with consultants as well as furiously saving his money. Next year, he hopes to become a ghost writer for management consultants.

Forty-year-old Jane has just sold her home in downtown Toronto and moved to a small town. She is using the proceeds from her house to subsidize her pursuit of a law degree.

Twenty-five-year-old Peter does not have a business card. He chose to work for an international petrochemical company as a contractor because of its reputation for attracting top talent and doing leading-edge work. He's managed to stretch out a six-month contract into two years, acquiring important business skills, by understudying pregnant women and then taking over from them when they go on maternity leave.

Taking Charge of Careers

Each of these people, in their different ways, has become a career activist. Instead of taking a passive approach to their work they have *taken charge* of their careers, organizing their lives to ensure their long-term career and personal interests are met.

Being a career activist means stepping back from the frenzy of daily business to reflect on what you are doing, why you are doing it, and whether it meets your short- and long-term needs. It means taking the long view of your career, rather than only taking your "career temperature" when you feel a chill.

Let's look at some of the rules for this new world of work:

Ensure your employability: If you lost your main source of income tomorrow, could you find an alternate source to replace it? How do you evaluate the currency of your skills? By the standards set by your current employer? Or by wider industry and professional standards?

Do you actively pursue learning and development opportunities, including ones that will stretch you? Can you describe one important thing you have learned over the past six months and one that you will be acquiring in the next? The more you learn, the more options you have.

The most important imperative in protecting yourself now and in the future is ensuring that you have *choices*. Don't let yourself be held back by a lack of skill portability ("I've been working for this company so long, I'll never be able to get another job"), or fear of change.

All too often I meet people who have been good performers in their own organization who have discovered that they are in effect stuck. Because they have become so closely identified with a particular company or industry, their skills are not perceived as being readily transferable to other settings. Measure yourself against community as well as internal standards. Your professional association and network can assist you.

Have a fallback position — develop a new mind-set: Human resource manager Carol K. works for a large public utility. Anticipating the impact of regulatory changes in her industry, she is pursing a diploma in alternative dispute resolution. "I know my job may be vulnerable," she said. "This way, if the worst happens, I can always hang out a shingle as a conflict mediator."

Don't put all your eggs in one basket. If you limit yourself to one particular area or sector, you limit your opportunities, too. Today it is critical to have multiple options, multiple avenues, and multiple roles. If you only see yourself, for example, in the role of an employee, your work options are significantly more limited than if you understand how your skills can be applied in different types of employment relationships in different sectors and industries. Having a fallback position means that you can equally see yourself selling your skills as a contract worker, as a freelance consultant, or as a small-business owner, even if these other roles are less desirable to you than that of full-time employee. In other words, redefine the way in which you work, and your relationship to potential purchasers of your skills and knowledge, to ensure your future employability. This means developing a new mind-set.

Know your key skills — think Lego: We've all heard the statement that in the future we will hold five to seven careers. When I discuss this in workshops, many people find it alarming. They think it means they are without substance, with no enduring value, programmed to self-destruct every few years. They fear they will be required to constantly reinvent themselves.

Actually, most people will not be embarking on entirely new careers (architect becomes farmer) so much as *reconfiguring* existing skills and experience in new ways (architect hobby farmer starts business designing and building greenhouses).

The first step in career management is to know your underlying or core skills. Like a child's Lego pieces, these are the building blocks that you can continually reassemble, though in slightly new configurations, as you move through your career. Identifying your key strengths and skills requires going through a rigorous self-assessment. Ask yourself, what are your unique talents, what are the special skills you bring to the table?

Develop a work identity independent of your job, defining yourself by what you do rather than simply by your job title. Look at yourself as the owner of a self-managed group of skills and abilities that you can apply in a wide range of jobs and projects. For example, 29-year-old chartered accountant John D. put it this way, "If I see myself as a financial professional with strong technical experience in telecommunications and effective team-building and leadership skills, currently leasing my knowledge to ABC Company, I have significantly more mobility than if my whole work identity is tied to my professional designation."

Prepare for areas of competence, not jobs: A global marketplace means jobs come and go as quickly as changes in the stock market. Today's hottest jobs may not exist tomorrow. Some people, worried about their employability, are responding to current, much-trumpeted predictions of a severe shortage of information technology workers by enrolling in Information Technology courses. If you love computers, then this work represents a great choice. But don't enter a field just because you think that's where the hot jobs are. To begin with that work may not exist. But even if it does, it may not represent a good match with your own skills and abilities. Start with an assessment of your own strengths and interests, then look to see where you may match up best in the job market.

Instead of preparing yourself for specific jobs, think in terms of the areas in which you want to contribute, whether it be technical areas such as software design or market analysis, or non-technical areas such as team-building, leadership of knowledge workers, or relationship-building.

Market! Market! Market! In the new workplace, people must perform at an exceedingly high level *now*, while at the same time always marketing for the *future* – keeping one eye on the next work assignment and positioning themselves for it.

This leads some people to wonder, "If I'm spending all my time marketing, how can I be producing at the same time?" But marketing yourself doesn't mean endlessly parading your list of credentials and accomplishments to the world at large. It does mean letting other key people know about your skills and how they can add value. Do you keep potential clients informed of significant accomplishments and how they can be applied to meeting their needs? Do you cultivate and maintain an active network both inside your profession and outside it?

You need to be continuously networking, but in a *thoughtful* way. That means building *knowledge networks*, not simply handing out business cards or e-mail addresses at business or association meetings. Good networkers are "wired." Their networks are broad, ranging well beyond their own professional boundaries. They cultivate relationships with people who know how to get things done. They know who to go to for information or referrals or plum work assignments.

Good networkers above all leave an impression on you because they have engaged your attention and listened to you as if what you had to say was interesting and important.

If you are uncomfortable in face-to-face networking, develop alternative strategies. For example, if you have something to say, you can become known as an expert in a particular field by writing articles for trade magazines, speaking at professional events, setting up your own web page, or chairing a professional conference.

It can be argued, in fact, that in today's hyperkinetic business environment, in which potential clients are too busy just to be schmoozed, being able to give people hard information that they can use will be much more desirable.

Develop *long-term relationships* with people. In the future, increasingly, we will be moving back and forth between different employers, and you may well find yourself five years down the road working for a previous employer. Treat everyone with whom you work – whether a boss, co-worker, customer, or client – as a potential client.

Learn to walk a delicate line between bugging people and being responsive to their information-overloaded minds.

Act Type A, but Be Type B: The Type A, hard-driving, achievement-oriented, coronary-prone behavior style used to be *the* model for success in our society. And in the current economic environment, the Type-A individual's focus, commitment, stamina, and excessive achievement-orientation may continue to be highly desired assets.

As executive recruiter Susannah Kelly of Herman Smith International observes, "Today, you must perform in a way that exceeds expectations, not just meets them. In these volatile times, to just meet expectations means you are in maintenance mode, not in change or leadership mode."

Work-intoxicated Type A's may well be better able to sustain these intense productivity pressures than their more relaxed Type B counterparts. So we need to *Act Type A*.

But at the same time, the work world we are living is far more thankless than it used to be. We don't get the kind of rewards, compliments, and positive feedback we used to because everyone's too busy. Moreover, there will typically be periods where employment is interrupted, and we have no work in which to play out our achievement-strivings. This is bad news for Type A's, whose whole sense of self is tied to doing, performing, achieving, and acting. So we also have to *Think Type B* – able to feel good about ourselves both when we are producing and when we are not, both when it is recognized and when it is not. That means cultivating a sense of self that is not completely tied to our achievements and accomplishments.

Cultivate emotional resilience: Can you withstand disappointment, juggle stressful situations, and handle pressure with aplomb? In today's workplace, do you have the resilience to deal with failures as well as successes? Can you learn from those failures so that you are not immobilized by them but can use them to your advantage in the future? Successful people reflect on things that didn't go well in an honest way, but they don't beat themselves up for it, endlessly revisiting the event.

Stay culturally current: I'm frequently amazed at how culturally parochial so many senior business and professional people are. Given the complex economic, cultural, and demographic global environment in which we operate, it is critical to stay tuned to larger cultural trends that affect the landscape and context of work.

Do you read outside your professional milieu? This means reading broadly, whether it be book reviews, international business magazines, non-fiction in areas related to general social trends, magazines such as *Fast Company* and *Rolling Stone*, alternative press digests such as *Utne Reader*, or going on-line to participate in discussion groups. Stay in tune with pop culture and be engaged by viewpoints from different sectors of the economy and demographic groups. World and cultural events have a direct impact on your work.

Try to glean from these sources important trends that will affect how your work is carried out, new potential applications, sources of competition, and customs. Never before has public opinion played such an important role in day-to-day political and business decision-making.

Sometimes, older people tell me they feel discriminated against because of their age. While that certainly happens, I find that often these individuals are somewhat disconnected from the world around them. Being in the know – in tune with the *Zeitgeist* – is important for being able to establish personal relationships with others, as well as for managing your career effectively.

Be a compelling communicator: Every time you talk to someone today you are competing with five thousand other priorities against a background of almost chronic sleep deprivation.

Our hit-the-ground-running culture means that today we must immediately establish credibility with co-workers, clients, and project members without benefit of what was once the "getting to know someone and exchanging pleasantries" stage. The person you are communicating or working with today may also be halfway around the world and/or from a different discipline. Can you translate what you do in a way that someone who doesn't share your professional expertise will readily understand?

Manage your finances: The most important source of protection we can have is knowing that we are not "owned" by debt. Given the temporary nature of the future of work, we cannot make any assumptions about employment continuity, nor can we make any assumptions about income continuity. Ensure that your finances are in order so that you're not gripped by fear of a downturn in the economy.

If you lost your job or a major client tomorrow, do you have enough money in the bank to tide you over until you replace them? Are you doing the work you choose to do, or is your work governed by fear of economic instability? Are you making significant personal sacrifices to maintain a standard of living?

Perhaps we can take a lesson here from many of the post-boomers. Having grown up in a period of economic instability, and with no illusions of any corporate or government pension plan being available to provide for them adequately in their senior years, many of them are already aggressive savers.

We can take a lesson, too, from the generations of immigrants who came to North America with little more than the clothes on their back. *Thinking like an immigrant* means understanding the importance of having *multiple income streams* whether from a business, renting out a basement apartment, owning vending machines, or giving violin lessons. We can no longer afford to rely on all of our income coming from one source. Whether you are a full-time employee or an independent contractor, cultivate other sources of income as an invaluable fallback in difficult times.

Act like an insider, think like an outsider: There is a paradox in contemporary business. Management gurus wax lyrical about thinking independently, being inventive, "thinking out of the box." But most large organizations place a heavy and in many cases contradictory emphasis on teamwork and group solidarity.

I have met people who have spent so much time in an organization that they have lost the "I." Ask them a question about how they think or feel about something and they immediately respond, "Well, at the ACME Company, *we* do *x* . . . ," as if the way their company does it is justification of the value of that activity and behavior.

Managing your career effectively requires balancing these apparently mutually competitive imperatives. In a teamwork environment, you need to be able to work effectively in groups. But at the same time you need to be able to work independently and to evaluate the team's work from an external perspective, rising above the "group think" in which it is so easy to become mired.

Some organizations mouth the rhetoric of "thinking independently" but actually want to customize everything to reflect their own internal corporate values and culture. If you find yourself routinely using jargon that only someone who works in your company or work team understands, you may be losing your capacity to think independently.

As a general rule, successful people get involved in teamwork very judiciously. They recognize that teamwork can be extremely valuable where the combined talents of a group can deliver a better product than an individual working alone. But they don't regard this way of working as good for its own sake, nor do they value consensus achieved at any cost.

Being able to think independently will become even more important as people are increasingly forced to make quick decisions without benefit of group input. People often become successful, in fact, because they didn't know how things "should" be done. Without the benefit of building on accumulated wisdom, they have invented their own solutions.

Be capable of rewarding yourself: You need to be able to give yourself the pat on the back for a job well done – the chances are good that no one else will take the time to notice. Be realistic in your expectations, celebrate your successes, and learn how to nourish yourself. Don't define your worth only in terms of your measurable accomplishments. Do you punish yourself for things that don't work out? Can you live with less than perfect? Do you celebrate your own success?

The ability to celebrate your successes, and *know* you *deserve* to celebrate them, may well be the most important skill of all.

Conclusion:
The Good News About Careers

*D*oug has just taken a job with a company he describes as having a reputation for being a career killer, "chewing people up and spitting them out." When asked why he would possibly commit career hara-kiri by joining such an organization, he says, "I'll be getting much more out of this than they will – moving to another city, being exposed to a new industry, and learning a very hot new technology. And if it doesn't work out, we'll just rent a U-Haul, load it up, and try something else."

Sheila and Joe are a husband-and-wife team who started a very successful advertising agency. They have just entered into a strategic partnership with another agency, which gives that agency the option to buy them out. When asked what they would do if presented with an offer, Sheila says, "We'd travel in Asia for a year, and while we are traveling decide on a new business. I have no idea what that business might be, but I know we'll be successful at whatever we do."

Louise, a marketing manager, has just been downsized out of a job for the third time. "The first time it happened, I was shocked and scared," she says. "I thought I had done something wrong. I thought I would never find work again. Now I know the drill. In fact, this time I saw it coming and I welcomed it, because the settlement will buy me time to finish my MBA and move on to a new chapter in my life."

We have seen some sweeping changes in the world of work over the past decade. In my previous book, *Career Intelligence*, I looked at the impact of these changes on people's lives. Many people have suffered profoundly the end of job security; the loss of identification with a supposedly benevolent and all-protective organization; and the tremendous increase in both the pace and volume of work. Some people are still reeling from these changes. But for many others, time has been a healer. These people have come to recognize that many of the new work realities actually provide tremendous opportunities. There are in fact at least as many positives as negatives about the shape of the new career – *if* you are able to respond to the new work realities in a creative way, taking responsibility for managing your own career.

The Armies of the Day

When I started my career working at a large petrochemical company, I watched armies of brown- and black-suited women and men pouring in through the giant portals each morning. In my mind's eye, I always imagined row upon row of employee lockers lining the grand lobby, each identified by an employee number. The workers would go to their lockers to hang up their personality, sexuality, and anything else that made them real as human beings. They would emerge in full corporate mask, ready to meet the day head on.

We have lived through the breakdown of these old-style corporate monoliths with their rigid bureaucracy, ossified roles and policies, and clearly defined expectations of "how things are done around here." Marxists once insisted that the state would wither away after a communist revolution. That didn't happen. But there *has* been a revolution in the world of work.

Traditional organizations, if not quite withering away, have been profoundly transformed. At the same time, new organizations have emerged with very different corporate cultures. The result? The creation of a much more diverse world of work. This new world is potentially liberating for the individual, offering much greater opportunities for empowerment and self-expression. It is much more in tune with individual needs and personal characteristics.

So let's look at some of the *good* news about careers.

The End of Paternalism

In the old world of work, the relationship between the individual and the organization was characterized by fear and insecurity. The company was all-knowing and all-powerful. If you did what was required of you, the organization would reward you with advancement and salary increases, guiding you along a clearly marked career path towards your ultimate destiny.

Old-style organizations were benevolent in their own way, providing job security, benefits, and developmental experiences. But the relationship was one-sided. The price of corporate success was conformity and a permanent state of dependence.

Today there is a new relationship between the individual and his or her employer – a "new employment contract." Under this new deal, neither side is beholden to the other, and both sides understand that the relationship is based on *mutual exchange*. As a result, individuals are on a more equal footing with the organization. People no longer feel "owned" or enchained. They work because they *want* to contribute to the achievement of mutual goals.

This sort of relationship, of course, has to be earned and cultivated on both sides. As we have seen, for their part, organizations need to provide individuals with the tools to manage their own careers in the light of the new work realities. Only when people are empowered by a belief in their own employability can they develop a more equal, rather than fear-driven, relationship to their organization.

Individuals, meanwhile, increasingly recognize their responsibility in managing their own careers. They understand that they no longer can rely on a benevolent organization to do it for them. And we see this happening. People are taking a stand on what they want from their work. At the extremes, the formerly beholden individual may even be seen as cocky. When they are not saying, "Show me the money," they are saying, "Show me the learning, show me the opportunity."

In the new world of work, you have the freedom to choose your work, your colleagues, your clients, your workspace. Employers used to be the buyers. Now they have to do a selling job. Individuals ask, "Why should I work here, what will I learn, what will I walk out with at the end of the day that I didn't have before?" If the organization tries to sell them a bill of goods, they are quite willing to walk away.

Forty-one-year-old Glenna, an accomplished independent consultant, was hired to facilitate a company's two-day off-site team-building event. After the fifth meeting with her clients reviewing her design for the event line by line, she said, "You hired me because I am a professional, and presumably you thought I could do the work. But I'm too old for this. If you can't trust me to work at the level I've been contracted to, then find yourself another consultant."

If one word can be used to characterize the new career, it is *self-reliance*. That means you believe in your own competence and can deal with all the uncertainties associated with the new work world, because you know you have the skills to sell and you know your own value. And you are ready and able to move on when necessary.

A recently survey by Royal Bank shows that about half of Canadians have an up-to-date résumé. Perhaps more than anything else, this shows that people truly understand the importance of being ready to move on, that they no longer hold a simple belief in secure employment.

When my son was born, I said to a friend, half jokingly, "I guess the choice is independence, or dependence. If I promote his independence, I have to fully expect him to be calling me from a different time zone when he is an adult." In the future, we will all be free agents, moving from work assignment to work assignment, city to city, country to country in pursuit of challenging and lucrative work. Greater mobility means greater opportunity. At the same time, we will need creativity to ensure that friendship, family, and a sense of community survive, and that our relationships are not virtual and digitally expressed, but are living, dynamic, and rooted.

The New Security

In the new workplace, contract workers and independent consultants work alongside people who still have traditional full-time jobs. But no matter what your official work status, there is no security other than that you create for yourself: the security of knowing you are employable in other work settings.

Indeed, many people who have made the transition from traditional employment to contract work or consulting report that they feel *more* security now than when they worked for an organization. Rather than waiting around passively for the axe to fall – to be fired, downsized, or restructured – they have become active players in managing their own lives.

As a marketing consultant puts it, "My life used to depend on the whims of my boss or the attitudes of consultants hired to reinvent the corporation. I was in a permanent state of anxiety. Now that I work for myself, I'm much less anxious, even though I frequently face times when I have no work."

Security today comes in a completely different package: no one can find complete protection from the vagaries of the marketplace, or the whims of employers. But what you can do is develop a mind-set that security lies in your own personal competence and effectiveness, and keep your repertoire of skills in line with market needs. You will then have the ultimate security: knowing that you are the principal player in what happens in your career and your life.

Freedom to Design Your Own Work

As the old monolithic corporate culture has fragmented, a new diversity in ways of working has emerged. When I was starting out my career, organizations typically made great protestations about their unique corporate culture, but there was in fact very little to distinguish between company A and company B. Today there is a much broader range of options in terms of work environments, and you can choose the one that best meets your needs.

If you want hip, find a small software developer where you can shoot pool on your break – and where *you* decide when you need or want a break. If you want collegiality, look for a team-focused environment. If you want freedom, work for yourself, telecommute, or find an employer who promotes individual autonomy. With a little research, you can *design your own work situation* to fit your own needs.

Before you can do this, though, you must first of all *know yourself.* Greater self-awareness means you can craft a work environment tailored to the "Five Ws," the critical determinants of what you are looking for in a work environment:

Who? What kinds of people do you want to work with and for? And what kinds of people interactions do you want to have? If, for example, you are more introverted, you may shy away from team-focused environments, preferring work that provides you with more time for one-on-one interactions and "back-room" work.

Why? Why do you work? What do you care about at this stage of your career? What are the core values you need to honor to feel good about yourself? If you have a young family, for example, you may decide to trade off a more challenging job that requires a lot of out-of-town travel for work that allows you to spend more time with your family. Of course, your values will change over time. In your 20s, for example, skill-building opportunities may be most important to you; in your 40s, you may be looking for work that enables you to give something back to the community.

What? What skills do you want to use and develop? That includes both *technical* skills — for example, software development, tax expertise, or designing training curriculum materials — and *general* skills, such as team-building, leading a group, and written communication. Some people who have very strong general skills may get more pleasure out of using these skills. For others, thinking about problems associated with their technical specialty is a key motivator in crafting a work environment.

Where? Increasingly, people are thinking about where they want to work, whether it be in a large metropolis or a small rural community, or even from home, via telecommuting. In some cases, in fact, people are telecommuting from a city across the country, with face-to-face contact kept to just two or three meetings a year.

As one human-resources professional recently e-mailed me, "For the first time in my professional life, I am telecommuting. I am thoroughly enjoying working from my ranch in Texas. Yesterday I was working at my dining-room table that sits in front of a huge picture window, when I discovered my two billy goats having quite an argument. I was just thinking how nice it is to be able to get my clothes out of the dryer while downloading my mail." This trend reaches right to the top. A recent newspaper article profiled a number of CEOs who were leading companies in countries other than where they lived.

When? We all vary in how many balls we want to juggle at any given time. If you get your energy from juggling several competing priorities, never quite having enough time to attend to everything, you will want to seek out a more fast-paced environment. If you are someone who prefers to work on a few things and put them to bed before going on to the next, you will want to look for a work environment and a way of working that will give you more control over your work.

Granted, it is nearly impossible today to find a *slow*-paced work environment, but with a little creativity you should be able to modify your work so that it better fits your needs. For example, you may choose telecommuting a couple of days a week to avoid the spontaneous distractions that occur as a result of ongoing office life. Or you might enjoy running a business where you're only working with a few clients at a time.

The good news is that the new business environment will increasingly be able to accommodate individual differences as people craft their work and work environment to play to their strengths and preferences. Instead of adapting yourself to fit an existing work environment, you can seek out a niche that fits you.

Competence Counts

As little as five years ago, one person in three would tell you a story about incompetent bosses with bloated egos enjoying long alcohol-fuelled lunches or networking on the golf course. You don't hear these stories nearly as often today. With the bar so high in business, and with organizations so flat, only the competent survive, and only the extremely competent thrive. The ability to *do* the work, add value, and be seen as adding value – not only by the people above you but also the people below you – is the most important determinant of success.

Competence counts, not titles: Merit, rather than who you know or how much experience you have, drives careers. Although some say that experience is the great teacher, it does not carry as much weight today. If someone says to you they have 20 years of experience, the question will be what *kind* of experience was it, good experience, bad experience, indifferent experience? What's important is what you have learned from that experience, and how you will express that learning in achieving results today.

Work is Fun: Business and Life Intermingle

Twenty-seven-year-old Tom K. borrowed $500 from his father and with two friends, a marketer and a recent design graduate from Ryerson Polytechnic University, developed a line of "streetwear" clothing, now being sold in the U.S. He did this without benefit of a marketing plan, an MBA, or a bank loan. "I'm part of this culture, I watch what my friends are wearing and listening to. I see what the Club Kids are doing. My inspiration comes from my life."

With the erosion of traditional boundaries that defined personal life and work life, people are enjoying their work more. They see work, like play, as an arena in which to express who they are. Indeed, as the boundaries between work and play break down, people increasingly describe their work as play. Work environments, too, have become more playful, especially in the newer high-tech startup organizations, where you can bring your dog to work, have a latte or a beer at 7 p.m., or go home and talk to a client while weeding your garden.

Life-Friendly Organizations

I talked on the telephone recently to four people in rapid succession. I was puzzled after I got off the phone with the fourth caller: there was something different about our conversation that I couldn't quite put my finger on. Then I realized what it was. In the background of the first three conversations was the sound of children. It was this "white noise" that I had missed when talking to the fourth caller. Increasingly, the sounds of life, whether it be dishes clinking or children playing, will not seem foreign in professional conversations.

People have a wide range of work options today, whether it be flextime, telecommuting, or various configurations of part-time, contingent, and contract work. This provides greater flexibility in shaping a work schedule in sync with our personal values and familial responsibilities.

Today we are seeing the beginnings of what I like to call *life-friendly* organizations. These organizations provide people with greater flexibility in balancing their work and personal lives. Daycare, whether on-site or subsidized by the employer off-site, and eldercare programs are increasingly common. They may soon become fixtures of the new work landscape.

Life-friendly organizations will value all contributors, whether they be full-time, contingent, or part-time 20-somethings or 50-somethings. They will be sensitive to the *entire* human life-cycle, reflecting the fact that people at different ages and career stages have varying needs, interests, commitments, and responsibilities. They will also recognize that people who *don't* have child care or eldercare responsibilities may still have personal needs and passions and commitments that need to be addressed.

At work, physical space will be organized to accommodate people working late at night, with TVs and couches for people who want to lie down and take a quick break. And instead of the traditional authoritarian structures of fixed spaces, spaces will become more fluid and flexible, with tactile, soft furniture. Traditional office chairs will be replaced with moveable futons. Recognizing the turbo-charged, over-committed lives of their employees, organizations will provide concierge-type services to help them, whether it be to pick up dry-cleaning, go to the shoemaker, or make special provisions for elderly parents.

You also have more flexibility in terms of how long you may choose to stay in a particular organization. In the days of fixed-benefit pension plans, people often felt compelled to continue in jobs they had come to detest. It was too expensive for them to move elsewhere and give up their accumulated future benefits (or "golden handcuffs"). Now, with portable pensions designed to reflect a more mobile and fluid economy, people are freer to move on without as much concern about the long-term financial consequences.

Freedom to Change: Role Fluidity

Elsewhere I have described the new workplace as "TempWorld," an arena where nothing is fixed or certain. In TempWorld, what we do to earn a living will constantly shift, from the content of our work to where we work and how we work. The result is more uncertainty – but also more *freedom* to take on new roles. Instead of being tied to fulfilling a particular role, or being stereotyped in that role throughout an entire career, we are now freer to sample different kinds of work and experience ourselves in different roles, whether as full-time employees, independent contractors, small-business owners, or professional temps.

This new fluidity of roles offers the prospect of tremendous liberation for those who dread being trapped in a particular role and who can't bear the thought that "I'm going to be doing the same thing for the rest of my life." Playing out different roles means we can develop a different understanding of ourselves in relation to our work environment and become freer to test out different aspects of our personality.

New career patterns reflect this shift from the old straight-line career. Instead of a predictable stride up a linear ladder, people will zigzag between different kinds of work situations, continually redeploying themselves in new ways as their work changes. Instead of, for example, being a corporate lawyer working your way up to partnership in the firm, you may be a recruiter specializing in hiring legal professionals, a legal textbook writer, or a corporate treasurer.

In fact, people today are increasingly playing multiple work roles. For example, combining teaching an evening course at university with consulting to startup companies and a regular two-day-a-week gig as a marketing manager. In this way, we can do a variety of stimulating work that reflects and plays to different aspects of our diverse interests and strengths.

Redefining Failure

In a work world of greater fluidity and mobility, the ability to take risks – to try on new roles, new challenges, and new ways of working – is a key determining factor in career success. But if risk-taking is celebrated, then we also need to adjust our reactions to the potential flipside of risk.

When people take risks, they sometimes fail. Indeed, when we look at the track record of successful entrepreneurs in starting new businesses, we see that many failed repeatedly before they finally got it right. Career activists, like entrepreneurs, must accept the potential to fail, and must learn to see failure in a different light.

In today's highly mobile economy, people lose jobs for a variety of reasons, most of them due to *change*. Personnel changes, for example, may lead to personality clashes; changing job requirements, to a bad person-job fit. Moreover, the more often we move around, the greater the probability of running into an untenable work situation. We need to learn to think of job loss in a new light, as simply being part of a new work landscape, something that happens as we move in and out of different income producing domains.

Indeed, people's attitudes to failure are already shifting. We are so information-overloaded and time-committed these days, and so prone to move around from one work situation to another, that our memories of our own and other people's failures has grown much shorter. Losing a job used to be an anguishing experience filled with a sense of failure. A friend's father-in-law, for example, still remembers being fired from his first job more than 40 years ago, and still wonders why. These days, few people who lose a job pause to look back. They simply get on with their lives.

Indeed, the time may come when we take a dim view of those who have never experienced any kind of failure. We may suspect them of not being sufficiently engaged by their world to take a calculated risk. People who have never failed may appear to us as overly rigid and programmed, unwilling to take an activist stance towards their career, always making "safe" choices.

Opportunity to Test Yourself

Increasingly, individuals who work for organizations are being empowered to make many more decisions regarding how they do their work and how they please customers. Organizations have become much flatter, with bureaucratic top-down decision-making being replaced by decision-making much closer to the front lines. At the same time, the sheer *speed* with which decisions must be made in today's volatile marketplace means there is no time for endless group decision-making, review, and discussion until consensus is achieved.

As decision-making gets pushed further and further down the line, people have more of an opportunity to test their individual effectiveness and judgment. One 40-year-old marketing professional, part of the senior-management group that had bought out his previous employer, told me, "It's the same products, and the same kind of decisions have to be made. But whereas before I would come to my team with pages of figures and pros and cons associated with making investments, I now have to make that decision myself without the benefit of group input or even the luxury of time. What's exciting is knowing you were the key person instrumental in the decision, and you're responsible for what happens."

Think of some of the words I have used to define some of the character-istics of the new workplace: zigzag between jobs and work domains, testing yourself, uncertainty. These words all suggest movement and change.

In the old-style career, you typically knew exactly where you were head-ing, whether you wanted to get there or not. The new career is much less predictable, and much more exciting. You can take steps to design your future, but you can never quite know where things will go. To use that trite expression, it's a journey of discovery, and in the true sense. If you have the fortitude, confidence in your skills, and emotional resilience to embrace it, it can be an exhilarating trip.

Redefining Time

When I was 22, having just graduated from McGill University, I went to Europe to travel. My parents told all their friends that I was "taking a year off." I was puzzled by their description of my behavior, as it seemed to imply that I had somehow ceased to exist in a meaningful way – as if the only way of being engaged in the world was either as a student or a worker.

In the new career, increasingly, we won't talk about time "on" and "off." All time will count, whether or not the way it was spent was instrumental in producing an income. This will be liberating in terms of the choices that people can make about how they spend their time after their earlier formal education.

Forty-nine-year-old Jocelyn B., for example, is at a crossroads in her career, finding herself doing work that is increasingly unsatisfying and unchallenging. She has decided to take a sabbatical to backpack in Asia. "Look at me," she says. "Isn't this extraordinary? Who would have thought a 49-year-old conservative executive would have aggressively lobbied to take a sabbatical with no particular plans as to whether I will return to my job?"

It used to be that the starting line was the first job, post-college or university. One then moved in a relatively predictable way through a series of linearly-structured career opportunities. Today, movement is much more fluid as we shuttle between different life spheres, be it work, education, leisure, or family commitments. And if there is no starting line or finishing line, then one is free to try out various kinds of career and life challenges.

In this scenario, all activity is legitimate. A career becomes a rich pattern of work and life experiences orchestrated by the individual spanning a broad range of potential experiences. That pattern will include work, study, travel, family, and time spent pursuing personal passions.

When you have belief in your own competence, you don't need to worry about taking time "off" or about an uncertain future. Instead, you can allow your career and your life to unfold through different spheres of experience, whether traveling the world, enhancing your education, or raising a family.

We will also see much greater acceptance of the possibility of successful *mid-career change* – something that in the past was often seen as misguided and bound to fail. For example, the legendary French writer Colette, approaching 60, decided to open a beauty salon in 1932. It was a bad time for the arts, and the effects of the Depression were beginning to be felt in France, so she needed a practical way to earn a living. Unfortunately, Parisians reacted negatively and scornfully. "My crime is serious," she wrote in French *Vogue*. "Starting a whole new career at an age when women are supposed to be over the hill."

In the past, when someone made a change in mid-career it was considered a huge deviation from the norm. Today, there is widespread recognition that we can and will reconfigure ourselves in different ways throughout our careers.

There is also no finishing line. Retirement is no longer the end of working life. The erosion of social programs, and doubts about the viability of government pension plans, mean that many people will need to continue to earn a living past 65. At the same time, we are living longer and healthier lives and need to remain intellectually and emotionally engaged, so that continuing to work meets our psychological needs as well.

So if you don't like what you are doing now, it's never too late to change things. You might find something else that is more to your liking – or someone might invent a job tomorrow that will fit you better.

Redefining Success

Darryl K., 48, was formerly the vice-president of marketing for a large petrochemical organization. When he was fired, he pounded the street. But like so many of his cohorts, he was not successful. But as a child, Darryl had always had a passion to act. "All of a sudden," he says, "I had an idea, which 10 years ago would have been unthinkable. I wanted to act. I told my wife, and thought she would think I was crazy. But instead, she said, 'Go for it.'" Darryl has taken a huge decrease in income, but for the first six months has managed to earn about $20,000 as a film extra and doing the occasional commercial.

Increasingly, the way in which we evaluate work is being liberated from pure considerations of money to a focus on the actual content of our work: what we like doing, what we do best, what is personally meaningful.

It's true, of course, that people always cared about the nature of their work and whether it was challenging. But they were also motivated by such external considerations as prestige, financial security, and status. Today the importance of these external considerations has been reduced, at least in relative terms, and internal rewards, such as personal fulfillment, have come to the forefront.

In part this is because for many people these external rewards are no longer so readily available: their prospects for further advancement are slim, or like Darryl they are having difficulty finding any kind of work. This forces them to look inward for their sense of career satisfaction. At the same time, the search for greater personal authenticity leads people to place greater value on the intrinsic qualities of work – in some cases rejecting prestige and money in favor of personal satisfaction and growth.

In the new career, rather than viewing career success purely in terms of status and monetary considerations, we will use other measures. When we look at our work, we will ask: Will I be free to pursue a passion? Will I learn? Will I be engaged? When redefined in this way, career success is within everyone's reach.

Opportunities for Authenticity

Laura F. was a 30-something successful lawyer with rosy prospects for becoming a partner in her high-profile firm. As a result of a messy divorce, she became increasingly worried about the effects of her 60-hour work week on her children. This in turn made her concerned about the psychological well-being of children in general. After doing some serious soul-searching, she took a significant decrease in income to start up a nonprofit agency devoted to promoting the wellness of children.

Today, people are demanding that their work reflect what they care about emotionally and intellectually. There has always been a tendency for people in mid-career to reevaluate whether they are doing work that is personally meaningful. Now, this is becoming a critical issue for everyone, including job entrants just out of school.

Being authentic means no longer pretending you are somebody else when you come to work. It means bringing your whole personality to work and doing work that is expressive of who you are in all aspects. Witness the many startups in high tech that have taken this to heart: the design of their offices, style of clothing, visual representation of the physical space reflect who the staff are and the nature of the work they are doing.

People in business are now much more open and self-expressive rather than impression-managing. They will tell people more personal things – that they don't like their job, for example, or that they are feeling stuck – where in the past they would have worried about saying something that might reflect badly on them. I've noticed, too, that people are more open in their business dealings. They used to be cagey when it came to talking about things like their budget for a particular project. Today, people are much more honest in expressing where they stand and what they are thinking and feeling. After all, who has time to play games?

Opportunity to Make Big Money

One can barely pick up a newspaper or magazine these days without reading about 20- or 30-somethings who parlayed their understanding of technology or popular culture, or their skills in some high-level scientific endeavor, into a fortune.

In an era where what you know, your ability to read the environment, extreme focus, and capacity to take risks count more than experience, anyone can potentially become the next Bill Gates at any age. And if you can't become the next Bill Gates, perhaps you can work for him or her – and get rich with them. Startup companies in high-growth areas such as high technology often offer stock options instead of a higher salary. In this way they can attract talented people with the promise of future wealth when the stock is publicly traded or the company is acquired. Sometimes these stock options prove to be very valuable – as witness the number of millionaires who work for Microsoft.

Even in more conventional organizations, an increasingly common feature of today's compensation schemes is having money at risk. Betting on the quality of your work can lead to significant rewards, whether it be in bonus, commission, or stock options.

Talent Pushes Back

As hyper-frenetic work schedules become the norm, people will increasingly demand of their employer that their hard work be recognized and rewarded with time off. People will refuse to be the servant of productivity-obsessed organizations. They will look at work and free time as coins to be bartered. They will say in essence, "I rose to the challenge of doing the work that needed to be done, but in exchange for these past eight days of round-the-clock work, I expect you to honor my time by giving me time off." In other words, hard work buys time for play.

Being an activist means that individuals will be prepared to *protest* about work expectations they perceive to be unreasonable. Freed up from a psychological mind-set that enforces dependence, they will see themselves as worthy of having all their work sacrifice honored. They will expect time in exchange for time, not a modest token such as "you can leave work early today."

Start Spreading the News

Heather was offered what she thought was the job of her dreams: she was going to be given complete autonomy to create and manage a new function that would develop a new marketing strategy. Unfortunately, the billing of the job far exceeded the reality. She had numerous conversations with her boss, but when he said, "There's going to be some changes around here, just hold on a bit longer and I promise you it will be worth your while," she quit.

"Life is too short," she said, "and work is too important to be living with this frustration. I deserve better than this. I'm out of here."

When you believe in your personal competence, are aware of your skill portfolio, and understand the new work landscape, you will have the confidence not only to expect but also to *demand* that your work meets your personal needs.

Conclusion

Work plays a crucial role in determining how we feel about ourselves: our self-esteem, our mental well-being, our ability to experience the world with joy and optimism, how we parent our children, and how we contribute to our individual workplaces, our communities, and our society. Given such significance, having work that engages us, makes us feel good about ourselves and allows us to play all the critical roles in our lives – partner, parent, friend, child, individual contributor, as well as citizen – is not a luxury, but a necessity.

It would be Pollyanna-ish of me not to acknowledge that there is a dark side to the new work landscape. But if we cultivate resilience, pluckiness, and a belief in the future, we can shape a work world that we will be proud to leave for the next generation.

Bon voyage!

About

Barbara Moses

"Canadian career guru" (Fast Company, October 1998)

Dr. Barbara Moses, North America's leading expert in career self-management, is the best-selling author of *Career Intelligence* and is the work issues columnist for Canada's national newspaper, the *Globe and Mail*.

Dr. Moses is also the author of the acclaimed *Career Planning Workbook* and *Manager's Career Coaching Guide*. Since its first publication in 1982, the *Career Planning Workbook* has become a "corporate bestseller," completed by over a million people in more than 2,000 organizations worldwide.

A sought-after presenter and keynote speaker for senior business and professional audiences, Dr. Moses is consistently praised for her practical insights into new work and personal realities, her stimulating and compelling delivery, and her tell-it-like-it-is style.

Dr. Moses' innovative approach to career self-management has been reported on extensively in numerous publications across North America. She has appeared frequently on network and local TV and radio and has been quoted and profiled in major North American publications, including *Fast Company* magazine, the *New York Times*, *Los Angeles Times*, *EnRoute*, *Parenting*, *Toronto Star*, the *Globe and Mail*, and *Report on Business Magazine*.

Dr. Moses holds degrees in psychology from McGill University, the London School of Economics, and the University of Toronto.

Clients

More than 2,000 organizations worldwide in every sector of the economy, including education, financial services, government, health care, high technology, mass media, oil and petrochemical, public accounting, telecommunications, and travel and hospitality.

Career Management Programs from
BBM Human Resource Consultants

The most pressing issues facing individuals and organizations today are self-management, managing change, employability, and learning for the future. Dr. Moses' firm, BBM Human Resource Consultants, provides proven interventions to prepare staff at all levels to meet these challenges and thrive in the new knowledge economy.

BBM shows organizations and individuals buffeted by change how to respond to the new career and work realities – promoting self-reliance and adaptation to change, managing work and personal life, motivating different demographic groups, advancing continuous learning, mentoring, and fostering renewal and revitalization. Over the past decade, BBM has helped thousands of organizations deliver career development and career self-management programs. A full-service firm, BBM provides career planning materials, workshops, and consulting support.

With its head office in Toronto, BBM has representative offices in Montreal; Calgary; Ottawa; Vancouver; New York; Chicago; Auckland, New Zealand; and London, UK.

Career Planning Workbook

A corporate best-seller, the *Career Planning Workbook* has helped over a million people worldwide manage their careers in the light of the new work and personal realities. It is a highly user-friendly, innovative, and cost-effective approach to providing comprehensive and practical career planning guidance.

Completing the *Career Planning Workbook* is like having your own personal career coach and counselor. Through a series of easy-to-complete self-assessment instruments, people identify core strengths and competencies; their unique profile of personal work style and preferences; and how to better balance competing demands of work and personal life, among other issues.

A highly flexible tool, the *Workbook* can be used on a self-study basis or in workshops, and is available in two editions – managerial/professional and clerical/technical – to provide professional quality career planning support to all staff.

Manager's Career Coaching Guide

This companion piece to the *Career Planning Workbook* prepares managers for their crucial role in developing and counseling staff; providing information and how-to advice on the new employment contract at work; dealing with coaching concerns; supporting career self-management; helping people cope with new work realities; and handling common career issues including burnout, plateauing, and Managing Generation X.

Workshops

A range of workshops are offered for different employee groups, including:
- Executive Overview
- Personal Career Self-Management Workshops
- Manager's Career Planning and Coaching Workshop
- Train-the-Trainer to Implement Career Self-Management

Keynote Speeches / Events by Dr. Barbara Moses

Extraordinary changes in the workplace have transformed the fundamental relationship between the individual and the organization. How do we have a sense of career, when everything we have been socialized to believe to be true is no longer true? In her lucid, compelling speeches, Dr. Moses provides insight into the new work and personal realities, along with practical strategies for dealing with them, and shows you how to profit from the good news about careers. Speeches are tailored to meet the needs and interests of different audiences, including women, managers, individual contributors, early-career professionals, and so on.

For more information on services from BBM Human Resource Consultants visit our web site at: http://www.BBMcareerdev.com

FREQUENTLY USED SYMBOLS

α alpha coefficient, a measure of a portfolio's "value added" return

APT   arbitrage pricing theory

AUM   assets under management

β beta coefficient, a measure of an asset's systematic riskiness

C   call option value

CAPM   capital asset pricing model

CF   cash flow; CF_t is cash flow in period t

CML   capital market line

COV_{ij} covariance of the returns between assets i and j

D   dividend per share of stock; D_t is dividend per share during period t

D_p Macaulay duration measure of portfolio p

DDM   dividend discount model

€   euro currency

EBIT   earnings before interest and taxes

EBITDA   earning before interest, taxes, depreciation, and amortization

EMH   efficient market hypothesis

EPS   earnings per share

E(R)   expected return; $E(R_t)$ is the expected return during period t

F   futures or forward contract delivery price

FV   future value

FVIF   future value interest factor for a lump sum

FVIFA   future value interest factor for an annuity

FX   foreign exchange

G   geometric mean

g growth rate in earnings, dividends, or stock prices

h hedge ratio

HML   value-growth ("high minus low") risk factor

HPR   holding period return

HPY   holding period yield

I rate of inflation; $E(I)$ is the expected rate of inflation

IR_p information ratio portfolio performance measure

k required rate of return

£   pound currency

NAV   net asset value

OAS   option-adjusted spread

P   price of a share of stock or put option; P_O is the current price

P/BV   price/book value ratio

P/CF   price/cash flow ratio

P/E   price/earnings ratio

PPP   purchasing power parity

P/S   price/sales ratio

PV   present value

PVIF   present value interest factor for a lump sum

PVIFA   present value interest factor for an annuity

r_{ij} correlation coefficient between assets i and j

RFR   rate of return on a risk-free asset

ROA   return on assets

ROE   return on equity

RR   fraction of a firm's earnings retained rather than paid out. It is equal to $(1 - D/E)$, where D/E is the ratio of dividends (D) to earnings (E)

S_p Sharpe ratio portfolio performance measure

SMB   size ("small minus big") risk factor

SML   security market line

Σ summation sign (capital sigma)

σ standard deviation (lowercase sigma)

σ_{ij} covariance between returns for security i and j

t tax rate or time when used as a subscript (e.g., D_t-the dividend in year t)

T   time to expiration

TE   tracking error

V   value of an asset; V_j is the value of asset j

w_i proportion of portfolio invested in asset i

WACC   weighted average cost of capital

X   option exercise price

¥   yen currency

YTC   yield to call

YTM   yield to maturity

Investment Analysis and Portfolio Management

FIRST CANADIAN EDITION

FRANK K. REILLY
University of Notre Dame

KEITH C. BROWN
University of Texas at Austin

PEGGY L. HEDGES
Haskayne School of Business, University of Calgary

PHILIP C. CHANG
Haskayne School of Business, University of Calgary

NELSON / EDUCATION

Investment Analysis and Portfolio Management, First Canadian Edition

by Frank K. Reilly, Keith C. Brown, Peggy L. Hedges, and Philip C. Chang

Vice President and Editorial Director:
Evelyn Veitch

Editor-in-Chief, Higher Education:
Anne Williams

Senior Acquisitions Editor:
Craig Dyer

Executive Marketing Manager:
Dave Ward

Senior Developmental Editor:
Elke Price

Photo Researcher:
Kristiina Paul

Permissions Coordinator:
Kristiina Paul

Senior Content Production Manager:
Anne Nellis

Production Service:
Integra

Copy Editor:
Mike Kelly

Proofreader:
Integra

Indexer:
Integra

Production Coordinator:
Ferial Suleman

Design Director:
Ken Phipps

Managing Designer:
Franca Amore

Interior Design:
Katherine Strain

Cover Design:
Peter Papayanakis

Cover Image:
Courtesy of DeGroote School of Business at McMaster University

Compositor:
Integra

Printer:
Edwards Brothers

COPYRIGHT © 2010 by Nelson Education Ltd.

Adapted from *Investment Analysis and Portfolio Management,* Ninth Edition, by Frank K. Reilly and Keith C. Brown. Copyright © 2009 South-Western, a part of Cengage Learning.

Printed and bound in the United States
1 2 3 4 12 11 10 09

For more information contact Nelson Education Ltd., 1120 Birchmount Road, Toronto, Ontario, M1K 5G4. Or you can visit our Internet site at http://www.nelson.com

Statistics Canada information is used with the permission of Statistics Canada. Users are forbidden to copy this material and/or redisseminate the data, in an original or modified form, for commercial purposes, without the expressed permissions of Statistics Canada. Information on the availability of the wide range of data from Statistics Canada can be obtained from Statistics Canada's Regional Offices, its World Wide Web site at <http://www.statcan.ca>, and its toll-free access number 1-800-263-1136.

ALL RIGHTS RESERVED. No part of this work covered by the copyright herein may be reproduced, transcribed, or used in any form or by any means—graphic, electronic, or mechanical, including photocopying, recording, taping, Web distribution, or information storage and retrieval systems—without the written permission of the publisher.

For permission to use material from this text or product, submit all requests online at www.cengage.com/permissions. Further questions about permissions can be emailed to permissionrequest@cengage.com

Every effort has been made to trace ownership of all copyrighted material and to secure permission from copyright holders. In the event of any question arising as to the use of any material, we will be pleased to make the necessary corrections in future printings.

Library and Archives Canada Cataloguing in Publication

Investment analysis and portfolio management / Frank K. Reilly. . . [et al.]. – 1st Canadian ed.

Previous eds. by F. Reilly and K. Brown.

Includes bibliographical references and index.
ISBN 978-0-17-650069-6

1. Investments—Textbooks.
2. Investment analysis—Textbooks.
3. Portfolio management—Textbooks. I. Reilly, Frank K.

HG4521.I495 2010
332.6 C2009-906082-5

ISBN-13: 978-0-17-650069-6
ISBN-10: 0-17-650069-3

Cover Image: Undergraduate commerce students experience the real-world relationships and interactions of the financial markets in the state-of-the-art Allen H. Gould Trading Floor at the DeGroote School of Business at McMaster University.

To my best friend & wife,
Therese,
and the greatest gifts and
sources of our happiness,
Frank K. III, Charlotte, and Lauren
Clarence R., II, Michelle, Sophie, and Cara
Therese B., and Denise
Edgar B., Lisa, Kayleigh, Madison J. T., and Francesca
—F.K.R.

To Sheryl, Alexander, and Andrew who make it all worthwhile
—K.C.B.

For the two who give me so much, Wayne and Jonathan.
—P.L.H.

To my wife Joanna,
who loves teaching,
learning, and the classroom
as much as I do.
—P.C.C.

CONTENTS

The pleasure of authoring a textbook comes from writing about a subject that you enjoy and find exciting. As an author, you hope that you can pass on to the reader not only knowledge but also the excitement that you feel for the subject. In addition, writing about investments brings an added stimulant because the subject can affect the reader during his or her entire business career and beyond. We hope what readers derive from this book will help them enjoy better lives through managing their financial resources properly.

To accomplish this, you need to learn about the investment alternatives that are available today and, what is more important, to develop a way of analyzing and thinking about investments that will remain with you in the years ahead when new and different investment opportunities become available.

Because of its dual purpose, the book mixes description and theory. The descriptive material discusses available investment instruments and considers the purpose and operation of capital markets in Canada and around the world. The theoretical portion details how you should evaluate current investments and future opportunities to develop a portfolio of investments that will satisfy your risk-return objectives.

Preparing this first Canadian edition has been challenging for two reasons. First, many changes have occurred in the securities markets during the last few years in terms of theory, new financial instruments, trading practices, and a significant credit/liquidity disruption. Second, capital markets continue to become very global in nature. Consequently, early in the book we present the compelling case for global investing. Subsequently, to ensure that you are prepared to function in a global environment, almost every chapter discusses how investment practice or theory is influenced by the globalization of investments and capital markets. This completely integrated treatment is to ensure that you develop a broad mindset on investments that will serve you well in the 21st century.

Intended Market

This text is addressed to both graduate and advanced undergraduate students who are looking for an in-depth discussion of investments and portfolio management. The presentation of the material is intended to be rigorous and empirical, without being overly quantitative. A proper discussion of the modern developments in investments and portfolio theory must be rigorous. The discussion of numerous empirical studies reflects the belief that it is essential for alternative investment theories to be exposed to the real world and be judged on the basis of how well they help us understand and explain reality.

Key Features of the First Canadian Edition

When planning the Canadian edition of *Investment Analysis and Portfolio Management,* we wanted to retain the original text's traditional strengths and capitalize on new developments in the investments area to make it the most comprehensive investments textbook available.

First is the unparalleled international coverage. Investing knows no borders, and although the total integration of domestic and global investment opportunities may seem to contradict the need for separate discussions of international issues, it in fact makes the need for specific information on foreign markets, instruments, conventions, and techniques even more compelling.

Second, today's investing environment includes derivative securities not as exotic anomalies but as standard investment instruments. We felt that *Investment Analysis and Portfolio Management* must reflect that reality. Consequently, our two chapters on derivatives are written to provide the reader with an intuitive, clear discussion of the different instruments, their markets, valuation, trading strategies, and general use as risk-management and return-enhancement tools.

Third, Chapter 17, "Professional Money Management, Alternative Assets, and Industry Ethics," includes an extensive discussion of the hedge fund and private equity industries. In a very short period of time, these forms of "alternative" assets have emerged as some of the most important vehicles for attracting investment capital throughout the world. We provide a discussion of how these industries are structured and how they have evolved over the past decade, as well as a breakdown of the myriad portfolio strategies that hedge fund and private equity managers employ. We also contrast the salient characteristics of these funds with more traditional professional money management products, such as mutual funds.

Fourth, as well as many questions and problems in the end-of-chapter material, we have included an appendix containing a significant number of CFA exercises, to provide more student practice on executing computations concerned with more sophisticated investment problems.

Fifth, throughout the book, we have included an analysis of Shoppers Drug Mart. Web Chapters 19, "Analysis of Financial Statements," and 20, "An Introduction to Security Valuation," provide a review of accounting and fundamental analysis along with an extensive analysis of Shoppers. A review of these two Web chapters before studying Chapter 9 will be beneficial for those students who have not had extensive exposure to financial statement analysis.

Major Content Highlights

While retaining many of the key features of the U.S. text, the Canadian edition has thoroughly updated, reorganized, and streamlined the materials.

Chapter 2 In this asset allocation chapter, there is an extended discussion of the importance of the policy statement and its components. We discuss several tax considerations and how they impact the asset allocation decision, and provide an example of a risk tolerance questionnaire and examples of asset allocations across risk tolerances. We also demonstrate the importance of investing early and regularly. We emphasize not only what should be done but also some common mistakes by investors. Finally, we consider in detail how the asset allocation decision affects long-run risk-return results, and how asset allocation differs among foreign countries and is changing.

Chapter 3 The review of current and historical returns supports the notion of global diversification, and a new study of global assets supports the use of a global measure of systematic risk to explain asset returns. We consider new investment instruments available for global investors, including global index funds and, notably, exchange-traded funds (ETFs) for numerous countries that trade continuously.

Chapter 4 Because of the significant growth in trading volume experienced by the electronic communication networks (ECNs), this chapter reflects the new and rapidly evolving secondary market for stocks. We also consider the rationale for the continuing consolidation of global exchanges across asset classes of stocks, bonds, and derivatives. In addition, we note that the corporate bond market also experienced major changes in how and when trades are reported and the number of bond issues involved. We discuss growth and value style stock indices and analyze the relationship among indices.

Chapter 5 This chapter considers various studies that both support the efficient market hypothesis and provide new evidence of anomalies. We describe behavioural finance and discuss how it explains many of the anomalies. There is a discussion of the practical implications of the recent findings and how they relate to the efficient market hypothesis for analysts, portfolio managers, and individual investors.

Chapter 6 This chapter builds the foundation for the theory of portfolio management. We develop the Markowitz portfolio theory from mean and variance of a two-security portfolio all the way to efficient frontier and optimal portfolio.

Chapter 7 This chapter presents the important transition between modern portfolio theory and the capital asset pricing model (CAPM) in an intuitive way. The discussion also contains several examples of how the CAPM and beta are measured and used in practice. We include a discussion of the theory and practice using multifactor models of risk and expected return. We stress the connection between the arbitrage pricing theory (APT) and empirical implementations of the APT, both conceptually and with several examples.

Chapter 8 This chapter presents economic and industry analysis for investments. We consider both the macroeconomic variables that affect capital markets and the industry factors that impact on stock performance. We also discuss how to conduct an industry analysis.

Chapter 9 Following a unique discussion of a growth company and a growth stock, we provide a valuation of Shoppers Drug Mart stock using the alternative techniques. We consistently emphasize a key point that an outstanding company like Shoppers can have a fully valued or overvalued stock. There is also a discussion dealing with the importance of quarterly earnings estimates. We conclude the chapter with a consideration of several models that can be used to value true growth companies.

Chapter 10 With the mixed views on the role of technical analysis in investment and portfolio management, we introduce a number of measures and provide a discussion of the studies that have tested the successes of the various rules. Some technical analysis rules are applied to Shoppers Drug Mart to demonstrate how these rules may be interpreted.

Chapter 11 Because of the credit-liquidity problems encountered in the U.S. bond market during 2007 and 2008 that impacted security markets around the world, we have included several discussions about the various bond types and their role in the credit-liquidity crisis.

Chapter 12 This chapter contains discussions on the various ways to calculate bond yields and their respective meaning. Macaulay duration, modified duration, and bond price volatility are examined. We also consider the concept of convexity, its calculation, and its determinants.

Chapter 13 We begin this chapter with traditional discussions of the "fundamentals" associated with using derivative securities (e.g., interpreting price quotations, basic payoff diagrams, basic strategies) and provide examples of both basic and intermediate risk management applications using derivative positions. This includes the role that forward and futures contracts play in managing exposures to equity, fixed-income, and foreign exchange risk.

Chapter 14 We present a discussion linking valuation and applications of futures and options in the context of investment management and offer examples designed to illustrate how investors use futures and options in practice. We have also included a discussion of credit default swaps (CDSs) and collateralized debt obligation (CDO); both received much attention during the recent global financial crisis.

Chapter 15 This chapter contains a discussion of the relative merits of passive versus active management techniques for equity portfolio focusing on the important role of tracking error. We discuss equity investment style analysis in detail and explore asset allocation strategies.

Chapter 16 This chapter on bond portfolio management strategies includes an extended discussion comparing active and passive fixed-income strategies, as well as examples of how the bond immunization process functions. We have included material on how the investment style of a fixed-income portfolio is defined and measured in practice.

Chapter 17 This chapter contains a discussion of the organization and participants in the professional asset management industry. Of particular note is an extensive update of the structure and strategies employed by hedge funds as well as new analysis of how private equity funds function. The chapter concludes with a discussion of ethics and regulation in the asset management industry.

Chapter 18 In this chapter, we provide an application of the performance measurement techniques that are introduced throughout the chapter. The discussion includes a section on how the concept of risk can be incorporated into the performance measurement process. We also cover evaluation techniques beyond risk-adjusted measures, the challenges of benchmarking, bond portfolio evaluation, and how to report investment performance.

Web Chapter 19 Alongside the more traditional ratio analysis, this chapter also contains a detailed comparison of alternative cash flow specifications and how they are used in valuation models and credit analysis. We include a discussion of how to analyze operating leases and demonstrate how the capitalization of these leases and the implied interest impacts the financial risk ratios for retail firms like Shoppers Drug Mart. We also demonstrate how to measure operating leverage related to business risk.

Web Chapter 20 We emphasize the two alternative approaches to valuation (present value of cash flows and relative valuation). We discuss how and when they should be implemented and consider the estimation of the variables that are relevant for all valuation models.

Supplement Package

The preparation of the first Canadian edition gave us the opportunity to create a supplement product that provides more than just basic answers and solutions. We are indebted to the supplement writers who devoted their time, energy, and creativity to making this the best supplement package.

Instructor's Resource CD-ROM (0-17-647836-1)   Instructors can get quick access to all of these ancillaries from the easy-to-use Instructor's Resource CD-ROM (IRCD), which lets the user electronically review, edit, and copy what's needed. The CD contains an *Instructor's Manual,* a *Solutions Manual,* a *Test Bank* in Microsoft® Word and in ExamView®, and PowerPoint® slides.

- **Instructor's Manual.** The *Instructor's Manual,* written by the text authors, contains a brief outline of each chapter's key concepts and equations that can be easily copied and distributed to students as a reference tool.

- **Solutions Manual.** This contains all the answers to the end-of-chapter questions and solutions to end-of-chapter problems. It also includes all of the solutions for the CFA questions and problems found in Appendix A. The text authors and technical checker, Ann Miciak, were ever diligent in the preparation of these materials, ensuring the most error-free solutions possible.
- **Test Bank.** The *Test Bank* includes an extensive set of questions and problems and complete solutions to the testing material.
- **Computerized Test Bank.** The ExamView® computerized testing program contains all of the questions in the *Test Bank.* ExamView® is an easy-to-use test-creation software compatible with Microsoft® Windows® operating systems or Macintosh® computers. Instructors can add or edit questions, instructions, and answers, and select questions by previewing them on the screen, selecting them randomly, or selecting them by number. Instructors can also create and administer quizzes online, whether over the Internet, a local-area network (LAN), or a wide-area network (WAN).
- **PowerPoint® Slides.** A comprehensive set of PowerPoint® slides is available on the IRCD. Each chapter has a self-contained presentation that covers all the key concepts, equations, and examples within the chapter. The files can be used as is for an innovative, interactive class presentation. Instructors who have access to Microsoft® PowerPoint® can modify the slides in any way they wish, adding or deleting materials to match their needs.

Rotman Portfolio Manager (RPM) is one of the most robust Portfolio Simulations available. The software has been designed to simulate the look, feel, and functionality of proprietary applications that are used in leading financial institutions. The application allows students to manage a fantasy portfolio of stocks, bonds, futures, and options using real market data. RPM offers students advanced trading and portfolio management features that give them the ability to focus their time on the portfolio design and management process, rather than tedious trade execution and portfolio trading. Professors can register and have their students trading within minutes! Nelson Education can provide access to Rotman Portfolio Manager at substantial savings to students.

Product Support Web Site *Investment Analysis and Portfolio Management*'s web site at www.reilly.nelson.com includes a variety of up-to-date teaching and learning aids for both instructors and students. Students can also go directly to the text web site to link to the Internet addresses in the text margins.

So many people have helped us in so many ways that we hesitate to list them, fearing that we may miss someone. Accepting this risk, we will begin with the University of Calgary because of their direct support. We are also grateful to the following who participated in the reviewing of the first Canadian edition and its original proposal:

Ata Assaf, *University of Windsor*
David Grusko, *Red River College*
Larbi Hammami, *McGill University*
Sergey Isaenko, *Concordia University*
W. M. Lawson, *Carleton University*
Mary M. Oxner, *St. Francis Xavier University*
Wulin Suo, *Queen's University*
Francis Tapon, *University of Guelph*
Jun Yang, *Acadia University*

We truly appreciate the dedication of the many people responsible for the development and production of *Investment Analysis and Portfolio Management*. Special thanks to the always supportive and professional staff at Nelson Education Ltd.: Elke Price, Senior Developmental Editor; Craig Dyer, Senior Acquisitions Editor; Anne Nellis, Senior Content Production Manager; Dave Ward, Executive Marketing Manager; Ferial Suleman, Production Coordinator; and Valarmathy Munuswamy, Project Manager; and thanks also to our Copy Editor, Michael Kelly; our proofreader, Integra; and our Technical Checker, Ann Miciak. And finally, special thanks to Francis Tapon at the University of Guelph for providing the *Alternative Viewpoint* features.

We are convinced that professors who want to write a book that is academically respectable and relevant, as well as realistic, require help from the "real world." We have been fortunate to develop relationships with a number of individuals (including a growing number of former students) whom we consider our contacts with reality.

Peggy Hedges would like to thank her colleagues, former clients, and former students. I appreciate their desire to have information presented in a meaningful and straightforward fashion. In particular, thank you to Larry A. Wood, who continues to be an inspiration, mentor, and business partner. As well, I would have been lost in data without the skilled assistance of Katrina Montgomery, resource librarian at the Haskayne School of Business.

Philip Chang would like to thank his colleagues at Haskayne School of Business for supporting his development of the investments and portfolio management courses over the years. The tradition of teaching excellence at Haskayne continues to challenge us to be better teachers.

We would like to thank all of our former students, too; their curious eyes and critical minds are always an inspiration. Special thanks go to the following individuals for their assistance with analysis of data and creation of graphics: Dan Zuniga, Karen Chang, Sarah Mody, Dawei Zhang, and Tony Zaremba, CFA.

Peggy L. Hedges
Philip C. Chang
Calgary, AB

Frank K. Reilly is the Bernard J. Hank Professor of Finance and former dean of the Mendoza College of Business at the University of Notre Dame. Holding degrees from the University of Notre Dame (B.B.A.), Northwestern University (M.B.A.), and the University of Chicago (Ph.D.), Professor Reilly has taught at the University of Illinois, the University of Kansas, and the University of Wyoming in addition to the University of Notre Dame. He has several years of experience as a senior securities analyst, as well as experience in stock and bond trading. A Chartered Financial Analyst (CFA), he has been a member of the Council of Examiners, the Council on Education and Research, the grading committee, and was Chairman of the Board of Trustees of the Institute of Charted Financial Analysts and Chairman of the Board of the Association of Investment Management and Research (AIMR) (now the CFA Institute).

Professor Reilly was named on the list of *Outstanding Educators in America* and has received the University of Illinois Alumni Association Graduate Teaching Award, the Outstanding Educator Award from the M.B.A. class at the University of Illinois, and the Outstanding Teacher Award from the M.B.A. class and the Senior Class at Notre Dame. He also received from the CFA Institute both the C. Stewart Sheppard Award for his contribution to the educational mission of the Association and the Daniel J. Forrestal III Leadership Award for Professional Ethics and Standards of Investment Practice.

Keith C. Brown holds the position of University Distinguished Teaching Professor of Finance and Fayez Sarofim Fellow at the McCombs School of Business, University of Texas. He received his B.A. in Economics from San Diego State University. He received his M.S. and Ph.D. in Financial Economics from the Krannert Graduate School of Management at Purdue University. He has specialized in teaching Investment Management, Portfolio Management and Security Analysis, Capital Markets, and Derivatives courses at the undergraduate, M.B.A., and Ph.D. levels and has received numerous awards for teaching innovation and excellence, including election to the University's prestigious Academy of Distinguished Teachers. In addition to his academic responsibilities, he has also served as President and Chief Executive Officer of The MBA Investment Fund, L.L.C., a privately funded investment company managed by graduate students at the University of Texas.

Professor Brown has published more than 40 articles, monographs, chapters, and papers on topics ranging from asset pricing and investment strategy to financial risk management.

In August 1988, Professor Brown received his charter from the Institute of Chartered Financial Analysts (ICFA). He has served as a member of AIMR's CFA Candidate Curriculum Committee and Education Committee, and on the CFA Examination Grading staff.

Professor Brown is the co-founder and senior partner of Fulcrum Financial Group, a portfolio management and investment advisory firm located in Austin, Texas, and Las Vegas, Nevada, that currently oversees portfolios holding a total of $60 million in fixed-income securities. He is an Advisor to the Boards of the Texas Teachers Retirement System and the University of Texas Investment Management Company and serves on the Investment Committee of LBJ Asset Management Partners.

He has lectured extensively throughout the world on investment and risk management topics in the executive development programs for such companies as Fidelity Investments, JP Morgan Chase, BMO Nesbitt Burns, Merrill Lynch, Chase Manhattan Bank, Chemical Bank, Lehman Brothers, Union Bank of Switzerland, Shearson, Chase Bank of Texas, The Beacon Group, Motorola, and Halliburton.

Peggy L. Hedges is a Senior Instructor at the Haskayne School of Business at the University of Calgary. Her background includes education and experience in financial services. Before joining the Haskayne School of Business in 1990, Peggy worked for the Canadian Imperial Bank of Commerce (CIBC) as both an administration and commercial lending manager.

Peggy received a B.Sc. and M.B.A. from the University of Calgary. She has a Ph.D. in Environmental Planning from the University of Strathclyde and is a Fellow of the Institute of Canadian Bankers (FICB) and a Fellow of the Canadian Securities Institute (FCSI).

Peggy has published articles on topics ranging from small business financing, alternative funding for defined-benefit pension plans, and risk analysis of catastrophic bonds. She has co-authored another textbook with William Lasher and Terry Fegarty entitled *Practical Financial Management;* this textbook is in its second Canadian edition.

Peggy has developed and taught undergraduate and graduate courses in corporate, personal, investment, institutional, and public finance for the University of Calgary, University of Northern British Columbia, Athabasca University, and Mount Royal College. She has received the Dean's Award for Teaching Excellence and has been nominated several times for teaching awards. As well, she is a co-owner of a company that specializes in financial education to executives.

Philip C. Chang is an Associate Professor of Finance at the Haskayne School of Business at the University of Calgary. He has formerly served as Chair of Finance and Operations Management and Associate Dean (International) at Haskayne.

Philip received his Ph.D. in Economics from University of Illinois at Urbana-Champaign and his M.A. and B.A. in Economics from National Taiwan University. He has taught in the fields of economics, statistics, investments, and corporate finance at the business schools of University of Illinois, University of Calgary, National Chengchi University in Taipei, and Peking University in Beijing. He has received many teaching excellence awards over the years. Philip's publications range from mergers, risk management, cost of capital, and bank fund reallocation, to the linkage between finance and corporate social responsibility.

We are responsible for the complete revision and Canadianization of this text, so we invite you to send your comments, suggestions, or questions about the book directly to us.

Peggy L. Hedges
University of Calgary
hedges@haskayne.ucalgary.ca

Philip C. Chang
University of Calgary
philip.chang@haskayne.ucalgary.ca

The Investment Background

The chapters in this section will provide a background for your study of investments by answering the following questions:

- Why do people invest?
- How do you measure the returns and risks for various investments?
- What factors should you consider when you make asset allocation decisions?
- What investments are available?
- How do securities markets function?
- How and why are securities markets in the world changing?
- What are the major uses of security-market indices?
- How can you evaluate the market behaviour of common stocks and bonds?
- What factors cause differences among stock- and bond-market indices?

We begin by considering why an individual would invest, how to calculate an investment's return, and what factors determine an investor's required return on a particular investment. The latter point will be important in subsequent analyses when we work to understand investor behaviour, the securities marketplace, and the valuation of various investments.

Because the ultimate decision facing an investor is the makeup of his or her portfolio, Chapter 2 deals with the all-important asset allocation decision. This includes specific steps in the portfolio management process and factors that influence the makeup of an investor's portfolio over his or her life cycle.

To minimize risk, investment theory asserts the need to diversify. Chapter 3 begins our exploration of investments available to investors by making an overpowering case for investing globally rather than limiting choices to only Canadian securities. Building on this premise, we discuss several investment instruments found in global markets. We conclude the chapter with a review of the historical rates of return and measures of risk for a number of different asset groups.

In Chapter 4, we examine how markets work in general, and then specifically focus on the purpose and function of primary and secondary bond and stock markets. Significant changes have occurred in the operation of the securities markets, and after discussing these changes and the rapid development of new capital markets around the world, we speculate about how global markets will continue to consolidate and increase available investment alternatives. We finish the chapter by examining and comparing a number of stock-market and bond-market indices available for the domestic and global markets.

1

The Investment Setting

This initial chapter discusses several topics basic to the subsequent chapters, beginning with the definition of the term investment and discussing the returns and risks related to investments. This leads to a presentation of how to measure the expected and historical returns for an individual asset or a portfolio of assets. In addition, we consider how to measure risk for an individual investment and for an investment that is part of a portfolio.

Next we discuss the factors that contribute to an asset's total risk and that impact the return demanded. Because most investors hold portfolios, it is necessary to consider an asset's risk when it is a part of a large portfolio.

The final section provides an overview of how macroeconomic and microeconomic events can affect an asset's required rate of return over time.

1.1 May You Live in Interesting Times

Whether a curse or a blessing, we certainly are now living in interesting times. At the time of writing this text, the news of the day talked about the new global financial crisis, there were bailouts offered to some industries and asked for by others. We knew the markets were in a downturn—was this downturn to be a recession or would it free-fall into a depression? There was speculation by analysts and commentators daily on whether we had hit bottom, were we to expect further declines, or were we on a recovery. Many questioned why governments and analysts didn't see this coming, or if they did why they didn't do anything sooner. Surely we have learned from the downturns in the markets before. By the time this text is in print, you hopefully will be in a position to answer some of these questions.

Over time, there have certainly been a number of interesting examples of incredibly high prices and speculative booms that have, in some cases, been fuelled by easy credit terms. For example, there was the tulip-bulb craze of the mid-1600s, the South Sea bubble in the early 1700s, the market crash of 1929, Black Monday in 1987, and even the Internet bubble of 2000.[1] Even though we have seen

---

1 See Burton Malkiel's *A Random Walk Down Wall Street* (2007, W.W. Norton & Company Inc., New York) for a very detailed and interesting discussion of historical bubbles and busts.

numerous examples, no one has a good method for predicting whether we are in a speculative boom or when and if the bubble will collapse. Haven't we learned from our mistakes? That leaves us to agree with Mark Twain when he noted that investing is fraught with uncertainty: "October. This is one of the peculiarly dangerous months to speculate in stocks in. The others are July, January, September, April, November, May, March, June, December, August and February."

There are numerous reasons and explanations for what has happened and how even when a number of investors are losing money, many other investors continue to invest and make money. So this leaves us to question whether, in these interesting times, there are still good opportunities to invest? If so, where and how can we identify such investments? That is the purpose of this textbook: to learn about what makes a good investment, how to construct a portfolio, and how to evaluate the results.

1.2   What Is an Investment?

For most of your life, you will be earning and spending money. Rarely, though, will your current income exactly balance with your consumption desires. When current income exceeds current consumption desires, people tend to save the excess. They can do any of several things, including giving up the immediate possession of these savings for a future larger amount of money that will be available for future consumption. This trade-off of present consumption for a higher level of future consumption is the reason for saving. What you do with the savings to make them increase over time is investment.[2] Conversely, those who consume more than their current income (i.e., borrow) must be willing to repay more than they borrowed.

The rate of exchange between *future consumption* (future dollars) and *current consumption* (current dollars) is the *pure rate of interest*. People's willingness to pay this difference for borrowed funds as well as their desire to receive a surplus on their savings give rise to an interest rate referred to as the *pure time value of money*. This interest rate is established in the capital market by a comparison of the supply of excess income available (savings) to be invested and the demand for excess consumption (borrowing) at a given time. An exchange of $100 of certain income today for $104 of certain income one year from today means that the pure rate of return on a risk-free investment (i.e., the time value of money) is 4% (104/100 − 1).

The investor who gives up $100 today in order to consume $104 of goods and services in the future assumes that the general price level in the economy stays the same. Such price stability is rare as we have seen inflation rates vary from almost 0% in 1994 to over 12% in 1981, with an average of about 4.7% per year between 1970 and 2008. If investors expect a change in prices, they will require higher returns to compensate for it. For example, if our investor expects 2% inflation over the investment period, he or she will require $106 in the future to defer the $100 of consumption during an inflationary period (a 6% nominal, risk-free rate will be required instead of 4%).

Further, if the future payment from the investment is not certain, the investor will demand a rate higher than the nominal risk-free rate. The uncertainty of the payments from an investment is the investment risk. The additional return added to the nominal, risk-free rate is called a risk premium. Thus, in our example, the investor demanded $110 one year from now to compensate for the uncertainty; the extra $4 (4%) would be considered a risk premium.

There are a number of interesting websites that discuss investing manias. Check out one recent article at http://www.forbes.com/2008/10/21/bubble-tulipmania-crash-pf-ym-in_avb_1020youngmoney_inl.html.

---

2 In contrast, when current income is less than current consumption desires, people borrow to make up the difference. Although we will discuss borrowing on several occasions, the major emphasis of this text is how to invest savings.

1.2.1 INVESTMENT DEFINED

Investment is the current commitment of dollars for a period of time in order to derive future payments that compensate the investor for (1) the time the funds are committed, (2) the expected rate of inflation, and (3) the uncertainty of the future payments. Similarly, this definition includes all types of investments, including investments by corporations in plant and equipment and investments by individuals in stocks or shares,[3] bonds, commodities, or real estate. In all cases, the investor is trading a *known* dollar amount today for some *expected* future stream of payments that will be greater than the current outlay.

At this point, we have answered the questions about why people invest and what they want from their investments. How investors select investments that will give them their **required rates of return** is a central question of this book.

1.3 Measures of Risk and Return

In order to choose among various investments, you need to estimate and evaluate the expected risk-return trade-offs. Therefore, you must understand how to properly measure the investment's return and the risk. To meet this need, we examine how to measure both *historical* and *expected* rates of return and risk. Given the historical returns, we will then review the traditional measures of risk for a historical time series of returns (i.e., variance and standard deviation).

Lastly, we must estimate an investment's *expected* rate of return. Obviously, such an estimate contains a great deal of uncertainty, and we present measures of this uncertainty or risk.

1.3.1 MEASURES OF HISTORICAL RATES OF RETURN

Often you need to compare alternative investments with widely different prices or lives. For example, you might want to compare a stock currently selling for $10 that pays no dividends with a stock selling for $150 that pays an annual dividend of $5. To properly evaluate these two, their historical returns must be compared.

When we talk about an investment's return we are concerned with the *change in wealth* resulting from this investment. This change can either be due to cash inflows, such as interest or dividends, or be caused by a change in the price of the asset (positive or negative).

Suppose a $200 investment at the beginning of the year is worth $220 at the end of the year: What is your return for the period? The period over which you own the investment is called its *holding period*, and the return over that period is the **holding period return (HPR)**. In this example, the HPR is 1.10, calculated as follows:

1.1

$$\text{HPR} = \frac{\text{Ending Value of Investment}}{\text{Beginning Value of Investment}}$$

$$= \frac{\$220}{\$200} = 1.10$$

This value will be greater than one (1.0) if you received a positive return during the period. A value less than one means that wealth declined or you experienced a negative return. A zero HPR indicates that you lost all your money.

---

3 We will use the term stock and shares interchangeably.

Although HPR helps express the change in an investment's value, investors generally evaluate returns in *percentage terms on an annual basis* so that it is easier to directly compare investments with markedly different characteristics. To convert an HPR to an annual percentage rate or the **holding period yield (HPY)**, simply subtract 1 from the HPR.

1.2
$$\text{HPY} = \text{HPR} - 1$$

In our example:

$$\text{HPY} = 1.10 - 1 = 0.10, \text{ or } 10\%$$

Our simple equation can be adjusted to derive an annual HPY when the investment horizon is not annual. First compute an *annual* HPR as follows, and then subtract 1. Annual HPR is found by:

1.3
$$\text{Annual HPR} = \text{HPR}^{1/n}$$

where:
n = number of years the investment is held

Consider an investment that cost $250 and is worth $350 after two years:

$$\text{HPR} = \frac{\text{Ending Value of Investment}}{\text{Beginning Value of Investment}} = \frac{\$350}{\$250}$$
$$= 1.40$$
$$\text{Annual HPR} = 1.40^{1/n}$$
$$= 1.40^{1/2}$$
$$= 1.1832$$
$$\text{Annual HPY} = 1.1832 - 1 = 0.1832, \text{ or } 18.32\%$$

For a decline in wealth, the computation becomes:

$$\text{HPR} = \frac{\text{Ending Value}}{\text{Beginning Value}} = \frac{\$400}{\$500} = 0.80$$
$$\text{HPY} = 0.80 - 1.00 = -0.20, \text{ or } -20\%$$

A multiple-year loss over two years would be computed as follows:

$$\text{HPR} = \frac{\text{Ending Value}}{\text{Beginning Value}} = \frac{\$750}{\$1,000} = 0.75$$
$$\text{Annual HPR} = (0.75)^{1/n} = (0.75)^{1/2}$$
$$= 0.866$$
$$\text{Annual HPY} = 0.866 - 1.00 = -0.134, \text{ or } -13.4\%$$

In contrast, the annual HPY for a $100 investment that earned $12 over a six-month period would be:

$$\text{HPR} = \frac{\$112}{\$100} = 1.12 \, (n = 0.5)$$
$$\text{Annual HPR} = 1.12^{1/5}$$
$$= 1.12^2$$
$$= 1.2544$$
$$\text{Annual HPY} = 1.2544 - 1.00 = 0.2544, \text{ or } 25.44\%$$

Note that when converting the HPY to an annual basis we implicitly assume a constant annual yield for each year. In the two-year investment, we assumed an 18.32% return each year, compounded. In the partial-year HPR that was annualized, we assumed that the return earned during the first half of the year is likewise earned on the second half of the year. The 12% six-month return compounds to 25.44% for the full year.[4] Given the uncertainty of being able to earn the same return in the future six months, institutions typically do not compound partial-year results.

1.3.2 COMPUTING MEAN HISTORICAL RETURNS

Now that we have calculated the HPY for a single investment for a single year, we want to consider **mean rates of return** for a single investment and for a portfolio of investments. Because a single investment will likely have high returns some years and low, or possibly negative, returns during others, your analysis should consider each of these returns individually as well as the return you should expect to receive if you held this investment over a long period of time.

Alternatively, you might want to evaluate a portfolio of investments. In this instance, you would calculate the portfolio's mean rate of return.

Single Investment Given an individual investment's set of annual returns (HPYs), there are two summary measures of return performance. The first is the arithmetic mean return; the

---

4 To check that you understand the calculations, determine the annual HPY for a three-year HPR of 1.50 (answer: 14.47%). Compute the annual HPY for a three-month HPR of 1.06 (answer: 26.25%).

second is the geometric mean return. To find the **arithmetic mean (AM)**, the sum (Σ) of annual HPYs is divided by the number of years (n) as follows:

1.4	$$AM = \Sigma HPY/n$$

where:

$$\Sigma HPY = \text{the sum of annual holding period yields}$$

An alternative computation, the **geometric mean (GM)**, is the nth root of the product of the HPRs for n years.

1.5	$$GM = [\pi HPR]^{1/n} - 1$$

where:
$\pi =$ the product of the annual holding period returns as follows:

$$(HPR_1) \times (HPR_2) \times \ldots \times (HPR_n)$$

To illustrate, consider an investment with the following values:

Year	Beginning Value	Ending Value	HPR	HPY
1	100.0	115.0	1.15	0.15
2	115.0	138.0	1.20	0.20
3	138.0	110.4	0.80	-0.20

$$
\begin{aligned}
AM &= [(0.15) + (0.20) + (-0.20)]/3 \\
&= 0.15/3 \\
&= 0.05, \text{ or } 5\% \\
GM &= [(1.15) \times (1.20) \times (0.80)]^{1/3} - 1 \\
&= (1.104)^{1/3} - 1 \\
&= 1.03353 - 1 \\
&= 0.03353, \text{ or } 3.353\%
\end{aligned}
$$

As investors are typically concerned with long-term performance when comparing various investments, GM is considered a superior measure of the long-term mean return because it indicates the compound annual return based on the ending value of the investment versus its beginning value.[5] So, using the prior example, if we compound 3.353% for three years, $(1.03353)^3$, we would get an ending wealth value of 1.104, or 11.04%.

---

5 Note that the GM is the same whether you compute the geometric mean of the individual annual holding period yields or the annual HPY for a three-year period.

Although AM return provides a good indication of the investment's expected return during any one year, it is biased upward when measuring an asset's long-term performance. Consider, for example, a security that increases in price from \$50 to \$100 during year one and falls to \$50 during year two would show the following HPYs:

Year	Beginning Value	Ending Value	HPR	HPY
1	50	100	2.00	1.00
2	100	50	0.50	−0.50

The GM return would be:

$$(2.00 \times 0.50)^{1/2} - 1 = (1.00)^{1/2} - 1$$
$$= 1.00 - 1 = 0\%$$

The AM return would be:

$$[(1.00) + (-0.50)]/2 = 0.50/2$$
$$= 0.25, \text{ or } 25\%$$

So which return is correct? This investment brought no change in wealth and therefore no return, yet the AM return is 25%. The GM return of 0% accurately measures the fact that there was no change in wealth from this investment over the two-year period.

When returns are the same for all years, the GM equals the AM. However, if the returns vary over time, the GM will always be lower than the AM. The difference between the two mean values will depend on the year-to-year changes in the returns. Larger annual changes in the returns—that is, more volatility—will result in a greater difference between the mean values.

Understanding the two methods of computing mean returns is important because most published accounts of long-run investment performance or descriptions of financial research use both.

A Portfolio of Investments The mean historical return (HPY) for a portfolio can be measured as the weighted average of the HPYs for the individual investments in the portfolio, or simply the overall change in value of the original portfolio. The weights used to calculate the averages are the relative *beginning* market values for each investment; this is referred to as *dollar-weighted* or *value-weighted* mean rate of return. This is shown in Exhibit 1.1. Notice that the HPY is the same (9.5%) whether computing the weighted average return using the beginning market-value weights or computing the overall change in the total value of the portfolio.

Although historical performance is useful, selecting investments for your portfolio requires you to predict the returns you *expect* to prevail.

1.3.3 CALCULATING EXPECTED RATES OF RETURN

Risk is the uncertainty that an investment will not earn its expected return. In the earlier examples, we examined *realized* or historical rates of return. In contrast, an investor evaluating an investment alternative expects or anticipates a certain return. The investor might say that he or she *expects* that they will get a 10% return, but this is a *point estimate*. Pressed further, the investor might admit that, under certain conditions, the investment's annual return might be as low as −10% or as high as 25%.

To determine how certain the investment's returns are, the investor might begin by analyzing expected return estimates. To do this, the investor assigns probability values to all *possible* returns.

	Number of Shares	**Beginning Price**	**Beginning Market Value**	**Ending Price**	**Ending Market Value**	**HPR**	**HPY**	**Market Weight[a]**	**Weighted HPY**
Investment									
A	100,000	$10	$1,000,000	$12	$1,200,000	1.20	20%	0.05	0.01
B	200,000	20	4,000,000	21	4,200,000	1.05	5	0.20	0.01
C	500,000	30	15,000,000	33	16,500,000	1.10	10	0.75	0.075
Total			$20,000,000		$21,900,000				0.095

EXHIBIT 1.1   Determining Holding Period Yield for a Portfolio

$$HPR = \frac{21{,}900{,}000}{20{,}000{,}000} = 1.095$$

$$HPY = 1.095 - 1 = 0.095, \text{ or } 9.5\%$$

[a]**Weights** are based on beginning values.

These probability values range from zero (no chance of return) to one (complete certainty that the investment will yield the specified return). Typically, these probabilities are subjective estimates based on the historical performance of the investment or similar investments that are modified by the investor's expectations for the future.

To calculate an investment's expected return, we weight the possible returns and then sum the results where:

1.6 $$\text{Expected Return} = \sum_{i=1}^{n} (\text{Probability of Return}) \times (\text{Possible Return})$$

$$E(R_i) = \left[(P_1)(R_1) + (P_2)(R_2) + (P_3)(R_3) + \dots + (P_n)(R_n) \right]$$

$$E(R_i) = \sum_{i=1}^{n} (P_i)(R_i)$$

Let us begin our risk analysis with an example of perfect certainty. The investor is absolutely certain of a 5% return. Perfect certainty allows only one possible return, so the probability of receiving that return is 1.0 and there is only one value for $P_i R_i$:

$$E(R_i) = (1.0)(0.05) = 0.05$$

What would happen if the investor believes an investment could provide several different returns depending on various economic conditions? The investor believes that with a strong economic environment with high corporate profits and little or no inflation, the expected return on common stocks could go as high as 20% in the upcoming year. In contrast, if there is an economic decline with a higher-than-average rate of inflation, the investor might expect the common stock returns to be −20%. Finally, with no major change in the economic environment, the return during the next year would probably approach the long-run average of 10%.

The investor might estimate probabilities for each of these economic scenarios based on past experience and the current outlook as follows:

Economic Conditions	Probability	Rate of Return
Strong economy, no inflation	0.15	0.20
Weak economy, above-average inflation	0.15	−0.20
No major change in economy	0.70	0.10

The expected return $[E(R_i)]$ is calculated as follows:

$$E(R_i) = [(0.15)(0.20)] + [(0.15)(-0.20)] + [(0.70)(0.10)]$$
$$= 0.07, \text{ or } 7\%$$

Obviously, the investor is less certain about the expected return from this investment than the prior investment with its single possible return.

Lastly, what happens with an investment with 10 possible outcomes ranging from −40% to 50%, each with the same probability? In this case, there are numerous outcomes from a wide range of possibilities. The expected return $[E(R_i)]$ for this investment would be:

$$E(R_i) = (0.10)(-0.40) + (0.10)(-0.30) + (0.10)(-0.20) + (0.10)(-0.10)$$
$$+ (0.10)(0.0) + (0.10)(0.10) + (0.10)(0.20) + (0.10)(0.30)$$
$$+ (0.10)(0.40) + (0.10)(0.50)$$
$$= (-0.04) + (-0.03) + (-0.02) + (-0.01) + (0.00) + (0.01) + (0.02)$$
$$+ (0.03) + (0.04) + (0.05)$$
$$= 0.05, \text{ or } 5\%$$

The *expected* return for this investment is the same as the certain return for the first example; but, in this case, the investor is highly uncertain about the *actual* return. This would be considered a risky investment because of that uncertainty. An investor faced with the choice between this risky investment and the certain (risk-free) case would most certainly select the certain alternative. This expectation is based on the belief that most investors are **risk averse**, which means that if everything else is the same, they will select the investment that offers greater certainty (i.e., less risk).

1.3.4 MEASURING THE RISK OF EXPECTED RETURNS

We can calculate an investment's expected return and evaluate the uncertainty, or risk, by identifying the range of possible returns and assigning each possible return a weight based on the probability that it will occur. Most investors want to quantify this dispersion using statistical techniques that allow you to compare the return and risk measures for alternative investments directly. Two possible measures of risk (uncertainty) have received support in theoretical work on portfolio theory: the *variance* and the *standard deviation* of the estimated distribution of expected returns.

We will work with the examples discussed earlier.

Variance The larger the **variance** for an expected return, the greater the dispersion of expected returns and the greater the uncertainty, or risk, of the investment. The formula for variance is as follows:

$$
\begin{aligned}
\textbf{1.7} \quad \textbf{Variance}\,(\sigma^2) &= \sum_{i=1}^{n} (\textbf{Probability}) \times \begin{pmatrix} \textbf{Possible} & - & \textbf{Expected} \\ \textbf{Return} & & \textbf{Return} \end{pmatrix}^2 \\
&= \sum_{i=1}^{n} (P_i)\,[R_i - E(R_i)]^2
\end{aligned}
$$

The variance for the perfect-certainty (risk-free) example would be:

$$
\begin{aligned}
(\sigma^2) &= \sum_{i=1}^{n} P_i\,[R_i - E(R_i)]^2 \\
&= 1.0\,(0.05 - 0.05)^2 = 1.0\,(0.0) = 0
\end{aligned}
$$

With perfect certainty, there is no deviation from expectations and, hence, *no risk*. The variance for the second example would be:

$$
\begin{aligned}
(\sigma^2) &= \sum_{i=1}^{n} P_i\,[R_i - E(R_i)]^2 \\
&= [(0.15)(0.20 - 0.07)^2 + (0.15)(-0.20 - 0.07)^2 \\
&\quad + (0.70)(0.10 - 0.07)^2] \\
&= [0.002535 + 0.010935 + 0.00063] \\
&= 0.0141
\end{aligned}
$$

Standard Deviation The **standard deviation** is the square root of the variance:

$$
\textbf{1.8} \quad \textbf{Standard Deviation} = \sqrt{\sum_{i=1}^{n} P_i\,[R_i - E(R_i)]^2}
$$

For the second example, the standard deviation would be:

$$
\begin{aligned}
\textbf{HPR} = \sigma &= \sqrt{0.0141} \\
&= 0.11874, \text{ or } 11.874\%
\end{aligned}
$$

Therefore, you would say that you expect a 7% return from this investment, but the standard deviation of your expectations is 11.87%.

A Relative Measure of Risk In some cases, an unadjusted variance or standard deviation can be misleading. For example, if there are major differences in the expected returns for two or more investment alternatives, it is necessary to use a measure of *relative variability* to indicate risk per unit of expected return. The **coefficient of variation (CV)** controls for the size of the mean and is calculated as follows:

$$1.9 \quad \text{Coefficient of Variation (CV)} = \frac{\textbf{Standard Deviation of Returns}}{\textbf{Expected Rate of Return}}$$

$$= \frac{\sigma_i}{E(R)}$$

The *CV* for the preceding example would be:

$$CV = \frac{0.11874}{0.07000}$$

$$= 1.696$$

As an illustration, consider the following:

	Investment A	Investment B
Expected return	0.07	0.12
Standard deviation	0.05	0.07

Comparing absolute measures of risk, investment B appears to be riskier because it has a higher standard deviation than investment A. However, the *CV* figures show that investment B has less *relative* variability or lower risk per unit of expected return because it has a substantially higher expected return:

$$CV_A = \frac{0.05}{0.07} = 0.714$$

$$CV_B = \frac{0.07}{0.12} = 0.583$$

1.3.5 RISK MEASURES FOR HISTORICAL RETURNS

To measure the risk for a series of historical returns, we use the same measures as for expected returns (variance and standard deviation) except that we consider the historical holding period yields (HPYs) as follows:

$$1.10 \quad \sigma^2 = \left[\sum_{i=1}^{n} [\text{HPY}_i - E(\text{HPY})]^2 \right] \Big/ n$$

where:

$$\sigma^2 = \text{the variance of the series}$$
$$\text{HPY}_i = \text{the holding period yield during period } i$$
$$E(\text{HPY}) = \text{the expected value of the holding period yield that is equal to the arithmetic}$$
$$\text{mean (AM) of the series}$$
$$n = \text{the number of observations}$$

Web Appendix 1A, "A Review of Statistics and the Security Market Line," available at www.reilly.nelson.com, provides a numeric example.

1.4 Determinants of Required Rates of Return

In this section, we continue to examine factors that must be considered when selecting securities for an investment portfolio. Recall that the selection process involves finding securities that provide a return that compensates the investor for the time value of money, the expected rate of inflation, and the risk involved.

Summing these three components gives the *required rate of return* or the minimum return that an investment should provide to compensate you for deferring consumption.

The analysis and estimation of the required return are complicated by the behaviour of market rates over time. First, a wide range of rates are available for various investments at any time. Second, returns on specific assets change dramatically over time. Third, the difference between the returns available (the spread) on different assets changes over time.

The yield data in Exhibit 1.2 for various debt instruments demonstrate these three characteristics. First, even though all these securities have promised returns based upon bond contracts, the annual yields during any year differ substantially. For example, during 2001 the average yields ranged from 3.74% on T-bills to 7.64% for BBB corporate bonds. Second, the changes in yields for a specific asset are shown by the three-month Treasury bill rate that went from 2.22% in 2004 to 4.12% in 2007. Third, an example of a change in the difference between yields over time (referred to as a spread) is shown by the BBB–AA spread.[6] The yield spread in 2001 was 106 basis points (7.64–6.58), but the spread in 2004 was only 50 basis points. A basis point is 0.01%.

EXHIBIT 1.2	**Promised Yields on Various Debt Instruments**						
Type of Bond	**2001**	**2002**	**2003**	**2004**	**2005**	**2006**	**2007**
Government of Canada 3-month Treasury bills	3.74%	2.55%	2.85%	2.22%	2.73%	4.04%	4.12%
Government of Canada 10-year bonds	5.78	5.66	5.28	5.08	4.39	4.30	4.34
AA long-term corporate bonds	6.58	6.10	5.77	5.74	4.70	4.69	4.94
BBB long-term corporate bonds	7.64	7.07	6.42	6.24	5.66	5.79	7.10

Source: Calculations by authors using Bloomberg data.

---

6 Bonds are rated by rating agencies based upon the credit risk of the securities, that is, the probability of default. AAA is the top rating DBRS and S&P gives to bonds with almost no probability of default. BBB is a lower rating given to bonds of generally high quality that have some possibility of default under adverse economic conditions.

Because differences in yields result from the riskiness of each investment, you must understand the risk factors affecting required returns and include these in your assessment of investment opportunities.

1.4.1 THE REAL RISK-FREE RATE (RRFR)

We begin our review with a discussion of the **real risk-free rate (RRFR)**. This is the basic interest rate, assuming no inflation and no uncertainty about future flows. An investor in an inflation-free economy who knew with certainty what cash flows he or she would receive at what time would demand the RRFR on an investment. Earlier, we called this the *pure time value of money* because the only sacrifice the investor made was deferring the use of the money for a period of time.

Two factors, one subjective and one objective, influence this rate. The subjective factor is the time preference of individuals for the consumption of income. If there is a greater desire to spend now, the RRFR will increase to attract savings. By the same token, the desire to spend less means that it is easier to attract savings, thus the RRFR will decrease. Time preferences vary among individuals, and the market creates a composite rate that includes the preferences of all investors. This composite rate changes gradually over time because it is influenced by all the investors in the economy, whose changes in preferences may offset one another.

The objective factor that influences the RRFR is the set of investment opportunities available. The investment opportunities are determined in turn by the *long-run real growth rate of the economy*. A rapidly growing economy produces more and better opportunities to invest funds and experience positive rates of return. A change in the economy's long-run real growth rate causes a change in investment opportunities and a change in the required returns. Just as investors supplying capital demand higher returns when growth is higher, those seeking funds should be willing and able to pay higher returns to use the funds for investment because of the higher growth rate. Thus, a *positive* relationship exists between the real growth rate in the economy and the RRFR.

1.4.2 FACTORS INFLUENCING THE NOMINAL RISK-FREE RATE (NRFR)

When we discuss interest rates, we need to differentiate between *real* interest rates, which adjust for changes in the general price level, and *nominal* interest rates, which are stated in money terms. That is, nominal rates that prevail in the market are determined by real rates of interest, plus factors that will affect the nominal rate, such as the expected rate of inflation and the monetary environment.

As noted earlier, variables that determine the RRFR change gradually, therefore you might expect the return on a risk-free investment to be quite stable over time. Recall from your earlier corporate finance course that investors view T-bills as a prime example of a default-free investment because the government has the ability to increase taxes or to create money in order to pay interest. Therefore, one could expect that T-bill returns should change only gradually. However, referring back to Exhibit 1.2, we can see that rates on three-month T-bills were *not* stable over the period from 2001 to 2007. In fact, looking back even further we see a highly erratic pattern: In 1981, T-bill yields were close to 18%, dropping to just under 10% by 1984 and back up to almost 13% by 1990. Clearly, the nominal interest rate on a default-free investment is *not* stable in the long run or the short run, even though the underlying determinants of the RRFR are quite stable. The point is that two other factors influence the *nominal risk-free rate (NRFR)*: (1) the relative ease or tightness in the capital markets, and (2) the expected inflation rate.

Conditions in the Capital Market The purpose of capital markets is to bring together those with surplus cash with those who need capital to expand or to finance deficits. The cost of funds at any time (the interest rate) is the price that equates the current supply and demand for capital. A change in the relative ease or tightness in the capital market is a short-run phenomenon caused by a temporary disequilibrium in the supply and demand of capital.

An unexpected change in monetary policy or fiscal policy will produce a change in the NRFR of interest, but the change should be short-lived because, in the longer run, the higher or lower interest rates will affect capital supply and demand. For example, an increase in the federal deficit due to increased government spending (easy fiscal policy) will increase the demand for capital and increase interest rates. In turn, this increase in interest rates will cause an increase in savings and a decrease in the demand for capital by corporations and individuals. These changes in market conditions will bring rates back to the long-run equilibrium, which is based on the long-run growth rate of the economy.

Expected Rate of Inflation As discussed earlier, if investors expected the price level to increase over their investment horizon, they would require a return to compensate them for the expected rate of inflation. Assume that you require a 4% real return on a $100 risk-free investment but you expect prices to increase by 3% during the investment period. In this case, you should increase your required return to about 7% [(1.04 × 1.03) − 1]. If you do not, the $104 you receive at year-end will represent a real return of about 1%, not 4%. Because prices have increased by 3% during the year, what previously cost $100 now costs $103, so you can consume only about 1% more at the end of the year [($104/$103) − 1]. Had you demanded a 7.12% nominal return, your real consumption could have increased by 4% [($107.12/$103) − 1]. Therefore, an investor's nominal required return on a risk-free investment should be:

1.11

$$\text{NRFR} = (1 + \text{RRFR}) \times (1 + \text{Expected Rate of Inflation}) - 1$$

Rearranging the formula, the RRFR on an investment is calculated as follows:

1.12

$$\text{RRFR} = \left[\frac{(1 + \text{NRFR})}{(1 + \text{Rate of Inflation})} - 1 \right]$$

For example, assume that the nominal return on T-bills was 9% during a given year, when the inflation rate was 5%. In this instance, the RRFR on these T-bills was 3.8%, as follows:

$$\text{RRFR} = \left[\frac{(1 + 0.09)}{(1 + 0.05)} \right] - 1$$
$$= 1.038 - 1$$
$$= 0.038, \text{ or } 3.8\%$$

This discussion makes it clear that the nominal rate on a risk-free investment is not a good estimate of the RRFR because, in the short run, the nominal rate can change dramatically in reaction to temporary ease or tightness in the capital market, or because of changes in the expected rate of inflation.

The Common Effect All the factors discussed thus far affect the required return on any investment. If the inflation rate increases from 2% to 6%, the investor's required return should increase by 4%. Similarly, if a decline in the economy causes a decline in the RRFR of 1%, the required return on all investments should decrease by 1%.

1.4.3 RISK PREMIUM

Recall from our earlier discussion that most investors demand higher returns if they perceive that there is any uncertainty about the returns they can expect. This increase in return over the NRFR is the **risk premium (RP)**. Although the RP represents a composite of all uncertainty, it is possible to consider several fundamental sources of uncertainty, including: (1) business, (2) financial (leverage), (3) liquidity, (4) exchange rate, and (5) country (political) risk.

Business risk is the uncertainty of income flows caused by the nature of a firm's business. The less certain the income flows of the firm, the less certain the income flows to the investor. Therefore, the investor will demand a RP that is based on the uncertainty caused by the basic business of the firm. For example, over time a grocery retailer would typically have stable sales and earnings growth. Its business risk would be low when compared to a firm in the automotive industry, where sales and earnings fluctuate substantially over the business cycle, implying high business risk.

Financial risk is the uncertainty resulting from a firm's choice of financing. If a firm uses only common stock to finance investments, it incurs only business risk. However, if a firm borrows money to finance itself, it must pay fixed financing charges (interest to creditors) prior to providing income to the common shareholders, so the uncertainty of returns to the equity investor increases. This increase in uncertainty as a result of fixed-cost financing is called *financial risk* or *financial leverage* and causes an increase in the stock's RP. For an extended discussion on this, see Brigham (2007).

Liquidity risk is the uncertainty introduced by the secondary market for an investment. An investor expects that the investment they have made will mature (as with a bond) or that it will be easily saleable; that is, the investor expects to be able to convert the security into cash. The more difficult it is to convert to cash, the greater the liquidity risk. An investor must consider two questions when assessing the liquidity risk of an investment: (1) How long will it take to convert the investment into cash? (2) How certain is the price to be received? Similar uncertainty faces an investor who wants to acquire an asset: How long will it take to acquire the asset? How uncertain is the price to be paid?[7] Uncertainty regarding how fast an investment can be bought or sold, or the existence of uncertainty about its price, increases liquidity risk.

Exchange rate risk is the uncertainty of returns to an investor who purchases securities denominated in a currency different from his or her own. The likelihood of incurring this risk is becoming greater as investors buy and sell assets around the world, as opposed to only assets within their own countries. A Canadian investor who buys Japanese stock denominated in yen must consider the foreign firm's business and financial risk, the security's liquidity risk, and the additional uncertainty of the return when it is converted from yen to Canadian dollars.

---

7 You may recall from prior courses that the capital market is composed of the primary and secondary market. Securities are initially sold in the primary market, and all subsequent transactions take place in the secondary market. These concepts are discussed in Chapter 4.

The more volatile the exchange rate between two countries, the greater the exchange rate risk, and the larger the exchange rate RP you would require. For an analysis of pricing this risk, see Jorion (1991).

However, there can also be exchange rate risk for a Canadian firm that is extensively multinational in terms of sales and components (costs). In such a case, the firm's foreign earnings can be affected by changes in the exchange rate. As will be discussed later, this risk can generally be hedged, albeit, at a cost.

Country risk, or *political risk*, is the uncertainty of returns caused by the possibility of a major change in the political or economic environment of a country. When investing globally (which is emphasized throughout the book), investors must consider these additional uncertainties. How liquid are the secondary markets for stocks and bonds in the country? Are any of the country's securities traded on major stock exchanges? What will happen to exchange rates during the investment period? What is the probability of a political or economic change that will adversely affect your return? Exchange rate risk and country risk differ among countries.

This discussion of risk components can be considered a security's *fundamental risk* because it deals with the intrinsic factors that should affect a security's volatility of returns over time. In subsequent discussion, the standard deviation of returns is referred to as a measure of the security's *total risk*, which considers the individual stock by itself—that is, the stock is not considered as part of a portfolio.

Risk Premium = f (Business Risk, Financial Risk, Liquidity Risk, Exchange Rate Risk, Country Risk)

1.4.4 Risk Premium and Portfolio Theory

Extensive work in portfolio and capital market theory by Markowitz (1952, 1959) and Sharpe (1964) have resulted in an alternative view of risk. Although these theories are dealt with in greater detail in Chapters 6 and 7, their impact on a stock's RP should be mentioned briefly at this point. These prior works indicated that investors should use an *external market* measure of risk. Under a specified set of assumptions, all rational, profit-maximizing investors want to hold a completely diversified market portfolio of risky assets, and they borrow or lend to arrive at a risk level that is consistent with their risk preferences. Under these conditions, they showed that the relevant risk measure for an individual asset is its *comovement with the market portfolio*. This comovement, measured by an asset's covariance with the market portfolio, is referred to as an asset's **systematic risk**, the portion of an individual asset's total variance that is attributable to the variability of the total market portfolio. In addition, because of an individual asset's unique features, there exists variance that is unrelated to the market portfolio (the asset's non-market variance). This non-market variance, or *unsystematic risk*, is generally considered unimportant because its effects are mostly eliminated in a large, diversified portfolio. Therefore, under these assumptions, *the risk premium for an individual asset is a function of the asset's systematic risk with the aggregate market portfolio of risky assets*. The measure of an asset's systematic risk is referred to as its *beta*:

Risk Premium = f (Systematic Market Risk)

1.4.5   **FUNDAMENTAL RISK VERSUS SYSTEMATIC RISK**

Some might expect a conflict between the market measure of risk (systematic risk) and the fundamental determinants of risk (business risk, and so on). A number of studies have examined the various relationships and have generally concluded that *a significant relationship exists between the market measure of risk and the fundamental measures of risk.* This consistency seems reasonable because, in a properly functioning capital market, the market measure of risk should reflect the fundamental risk characteristics of the asset. However, as we discuss in Chapter 7, a firm that has a high level of fundamental risk and a large standard deviation of return on stock can have a lower level of systematic risk simply because its earnings and stock price variability are not related to the aggregate economy or the aggregate market. Therefore, one can specify the RP for an asset as either:

Risk Premium = *f* (Business Risk, Financial Risk, Liquidity Risk, Exchange Rate Risk, Country Risk)

or

Risk Premium = *f* (Systematic Market Risk)

1.5   Relationship between Risk and Return

Exhibit 1.3 graphs the expected relationship between risk and return. It shows that investors increase their required rates of return as perceived risk (uncertainty) increases. The line that reflects this combination is referred to as the **security market line (SML)**. Investors would select investments that are consistent with their risk preferences; some would consider only low-risk investments, whereas others welcome high-risk investments.

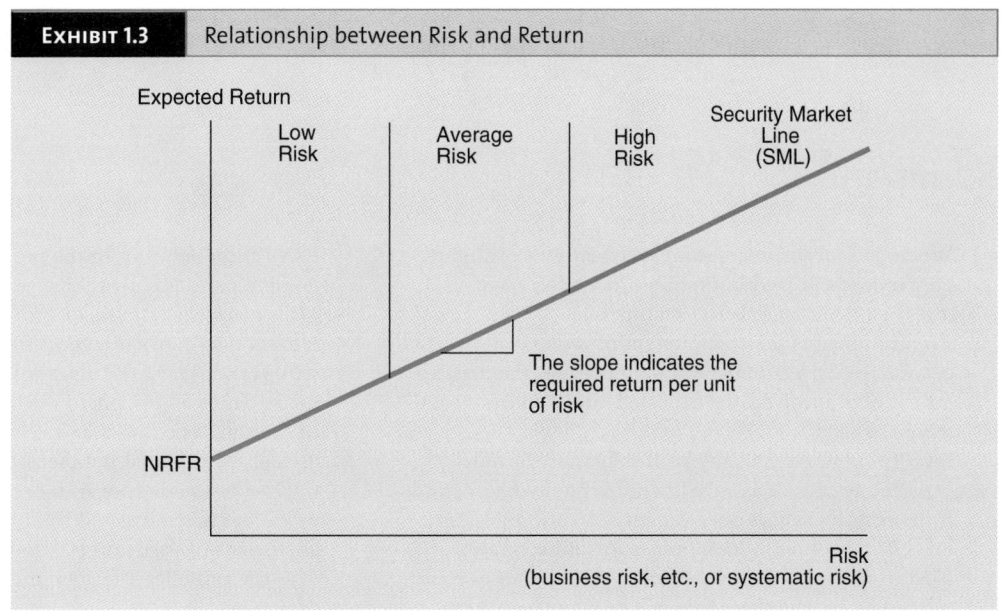

EXHIBIT 1.3   Relationship between Risk and Return

Starting with an initial SML, three changes can occur. First, individual investments can change positions on the SML because of changes in the perceived risk of the investments. Second, the slope of the SML can change because of a shift in investor attitudes toward risk; that is, investors can change the returns they require per unit of risk. Third, the SML can experience a parallel shift due to a change in the RRFR or the expected rate of inflation—that is, a change in the NRFR. These three possibilities are discussed in more detail in Web Appendix 1A (www.reilly.nelson.com) to this chapter.

1.6   Road Map for the Rest of the Book

Now that we've had a chance to review some of the basics from our economics, corporate finance, and statistics classes, we need to put the rest of the book in perspective. The remainder of Part 1 delves into the asset allocation decisions that need to be made, whether for an individual or for an institutional investor. Any investor needs to understand what investments are available and what impacts that various economic factors may have on those investments.

In Part 2, we examine the capital markets—how information is embedded in prices, how we know whether we are being adequately compensated, and why we should use portfolios. We review concepts already introduced and explore further the evidence for and against various theories.

Parts 3 and 4 examine the specific tools that we can use to value financial instruments and how analysts examine value: Is value readily identifiable from analysis of the company, price and volume characteristics, or some combination? We have included two Web chapters, Chapter 19, "Analysis of Financial Statements," and Chapter 20, "An Introduction to Security Valuation," for those needing a quick refresher on financial statement analysis and valuation basics (www.reilly.nelson.com).

We next scrutinize derivative instruments: What are they, how are they used, and can they be used to protect a portfolio? Do they create value and how exactly do they have value? Part 5 attempts to address these questions.

Lastly, for those interested in portfolio management, Part 6 deals with specific issues faced by professional portfolio managers. Certainly they need to understand the basics of investing, but what other issues must they consider? From an investor's perspective, how do we evaluate the performance of these managers?

Summary

1. When current income needs exceed current consumption, individuals (and institutions) invest the excess so that they can have future consumption.
2. An investment is the commitment of savings for a period of time to derive a return that compensates the investor for the time involved, the expected rate of inflation, and the uncertainty.
3. Investors typically measure both the historical and expected return on an investment over a holding period. If the period exceeds one year, investors use an arithmetic and geometric mean return. Arithmetic mean (AM) is the sum of annual holding period rates of return divided by the number of years. The geometric mean (GM) is the nth root of the product of the annual holding period returns for n years minus 1.

4. Most investors want to quantify the uncertainty in the returns that they can expect from an investment. A first step in measuring distributions of expected returns is to use variance and standard deviation. Variance is the sum of the squares of a return's deviation from the mean, divided by the total number of returns. Standard deviation is the square root of the variance. If the standard deviations are calculated using different means, then a coefficient of variation (CV) needs to be calculated. The CV provides a relative measure of risk per unit of return.

5. A number of factors contribute to the return that investors require on various investments, but estimating the required return is complicated. Rates on individual investments change over time, there is a wide range of returns available on various investments, and the differences between required returns on various investments (e.g., the yield spreads) likewise change over time.

6. Some of the macroeconomic and microeconomic factors that contribute to changes in the required rate of return for investments include: (1) the real risk-free rate (RRFR), which is based on the real rate of growth in the economy; (2) the nominal risk-free rate (NRFR), which is influenced by capital market conditions and the expected rate of inflation; and (3) a risk premium (RP), which is a function of fundamental factors, such as business risk, or the systematic risk of the asset relative to the market portfolio.

Key Terms

arithmetic mean (AM), p. 8
business risk, p. 17
coefficient of variation (CV), p. 13
country risk, p. 18
exchange rate risk, p. 17
financial risk, p. 17
geometric mean (GM), p. 8

holding period return (HPR), p. 5
holding period yield (HPY), p. 6
investment, p. 5
liquidity risk, p. 17
mean rates of return, p. 7
real risk-free rate (RRFR), p. 15
required rates of return, p. 5

risk, p. 9
risk averse, p. 11
risk premium (RP), p. 17
security market line (SML), p. 19
standard deviation, p. 12
systematic risk, p. 18
variance, p. 12

Suggested Readings

Fama, Eugene F., and Merton H. Miller. *The Theory of Finance.* New York: Holt, Rinehart and Winston, 1972.

Fisher, Irving. *The Theory of Interest.* New York: Macmillan, 1930, reprinted by Augustus M. Kelley, 1961.

 For Chapter CFA Questions and Problems, please see Appendix A at the end of this text.

Questions

1. Discuss the overall purpose that people have for investing. Define investment.

2. As a student, are you saving or borrowing? Why?

3. Divide a person's life from ages 20 to 70 into 10-year segments and discuss the likely saving or borrowing patterns during each period.

4. Discuss why you would expect the saving–borrowing pattern to differ by occupation (e.g., for a doctor versus a plumber).

5. *The Globe and Mail* reports that the yield on common stocks is about 2%, whereas a study at the University of Chicago contends that the annual returns on common stocks since 1926 has averaged about 12%. Reconcile these statements.

6. Some financial theorists consider the variance of the distribution of expected returns to be a good measure of uncertainty. Discuss the reasoning behind this measure of risk and its purpose.

7. Discuss the three components of an investor's required return on an investment.

8. Discuss the two major factors that determine the market nominal risk-free rate (NRFR). Explain which of these factors would be more volatile over the business cycle.

9. Briefly discuss the five fundamental factors that influence the risk premium of an investment.

10. You own stock in the Gentry Company, and you read in the financial press that a recent bond offering has raised the firm's debt/equity ratio from 35% to 55%. Discuss the effect of this change on the variability of the firm's net income stream, other factors being constant. Discuss how this change would affect your required return on the common stock of this firm.

11. Draw a properly labelled graph of the security market line (SML) and indicate where you would expect the

following investments to fall along that line. Discuss your reasoning.
a. Common stock of large firms
b. Government of Canada bonds
c. U.K. government bonds
d. Low-grade corporate bonds
e. Common stock of a Japanese firm

12. Explain why you would change your nominal required return if you expected the rate of inflation to go from 0 (no inflation) to 4%. Give an example of what would happen if you did not change your required return under these conditions.

13. Assume the long-run growth rate of the economy increased by 1% and the expected rate of inflation increased by 4%. What would happen to the required returns on government bonds and common stocks? Show graphically how the effects of these changes would differ between these investments.

14. You see in *The Globe and Mail* that the yield spread between BBB corporate bonds and AAA corporate bonds has gone from 350 basis points (3.5%) to 200 basis points (2%). Show graphically the effect of this change in yield spread on the SML and discuss its effect on the required returns for common stocks.

15. Give an example of a liquid investment and an illiquid investment. Discuss why you consider each of them to be liquid or illiquid.

Problems

1. On February 1, you bought a stock for $34 and sold it one year later for $39. During the year, you received a cash dividend of $1.50 per share. Compute your HPR and HPY on this investment.

2. On August 15, you purchased shares of stock in the Cara Cotton Company at $65 a share, and a year later you sold it for $61 a share. During the year, you received dividends of $3 per share. Compute your HPR and HPY on your investment in Cara Cotton.

3. At the beginning of last year, you invested $4,000 in 80 shares of the Chang Corporation. During the year, Chang paid dividends of $5 per share. At the end of the year, you sold the 80 shares for $59 a share. Compute your total HPY on these shares and indicate how much was due to the price change and how much was due to the dividend income.

4. The returns computed in Problems 1, 2, and 3 are nominal returns. Assuming that the rate of inflation during the year was 4%, compute the real returns on these investments. Compute the real returns if the rate of inflation was 8%.

5. During the past five years, you owned two stocks that had the following annual rates of return:

Year	Stock T	Stock B
1	0.19	0.08
2	0.08	0.03
3	−0.12	−0.09
4	−0.03	0.02
5	0.15	0.04

a. Compute the arithmetic mean annual return for each stock. Which stock is most desirable by this measure?

b. Compute the standard deviation of the annual return for each stock. (Use the Chapter 1 Web Appendix if necessary.) By this measure, which is the preferable stock?

c. Compute the coefficient of variation for each stock. (Use the Chapter 1 Web Appendix if necessary.) By this relative measure of risk, which stock is preferable?

d. Compute the geometric mean return for each stock. Discuss the difference between the arithmetic and the geometric mean return for each stock. Discuss the differences in the mean returns relative to the standard deviation of the return for each stock.

6. You are considering acquiring shares of common stock in the Hudson Bay Beer Corporation. Your return expectations are as follows:

HUDSON BAY BEER CORP.

Possible Rate of Return	Probability
−0.10	0.30
0.00	0.10
0.10	0.30
0.25	0.30

Compute the expected return $[E(R_i)]$ on your investment in Hudson Bay Beer.

7. A stockbroker calls you and suggests that you invest in the Light Computer Company. After analyzing

the firm's annual report and other material, you believe that the distribution of expected returns is as follows:

LIGHT COMPUTER CO.

Possible Rate of Return	Probability
−0.60	0.05
−0.30	0.20
−0.10	0.10
0.20	0.30
0.40	0.20
0.80	0.15

Compute the expected return $[E(R_i)]$ on Light Computer stock.

8. Without any formal computations, do you consider Hudson Bay Beer in Problem 6 or Light Computer in Problem 7 to present greater risk? Discuss your reasoning.

9. During the past year, you had a portfolio that contained T-bills, long-term government bonds, and common stocks. The returns on each of them were as follows:

T-bills	5.50%
Government of Canada long-term bonds	7.50
Canadian common stocks	11.60

During the year, the consumer price index, which measures the rate of inflation, went from 160 to 172

(1982–1984 = 100). Compute the rate of inflation during this year. Compute the real returns on each of the investments in your portfolio based on the inflation rate.

10. You read in *The Globe and Mail* that a panel of economists has estimated that the long-run real growth rate of the Canadian economy over the next 5-year period will average 3%. In addition, a bank newsletter estimates that the average annual rate of inflation during this five-year period will be about 4%. What nominal return would you expect on T-bills during this period?

11. What would your required return be on common stocks if you wanted a 5% risk premium to own common stocks given what you know from Problem 10? If common stock investors became more risk averse, what would happen to the required return on common stocks? What would be the impact on stock prices?

12. Assume that the consensus required return on common stocks is 14%. In addition, you read in the *Bank of Canada Review* that the expected rate of inflation is 5% and the estimated long-term real growth rate of the economy is 3%. What interest rate would you expect on T-bills? What is the approximate risk premium for common stocks implied by these data?

2

The Asset Allocation Decision*

After you read this chapter, you should be able to answer the following questions:

1. Why is a policy statement important to the planning process?

2. What objectives and constraints should be detailed in a policy statement?

3. How and why do investment goals change over a person's lifetime?

4. What are the four steps in the portfolio management process?

5. What is involved in the asset allocation process?

6. What is the role of asset allocation in investment planning?

7. Why do asset allocation strategies differ across national boundaries?

8. What are some issues that institutional investors must deal with?

The last chapter reminded us that risk drives return. Therefore, the practice of investing funds and managing portfolios should focus primarily on managing risk rather than on managing returns.

This chapter examines some of the practical implications of risk management in the context of asset allocation. **Asset allocation** is the process of deciding how to distribute an investor's wealth among different countries and asset classes for investment purposes. An **asset class** is comprised of securities with similar characteristics, attributes, and risk/return relationships. A broad asset class, such as *bonds*, can be divided into smaller asset classes, such as government, corporate, and high-yield bonds. We will see that, in the long run, the highest compounded returns will most likely accrue to those investors with larger exposures to risky assets. We will also see that there are no shortcuts or guarantees to investment success, but maintaining a reasonable and disciplined approach to investing will increase the likelihood of investment success over time.

The asset allocation decision is not an isolated choice; rather, it is a component of a structured four-step portfolio management process. The first step in the process is to develop an investment policy statement, or plan, that will guide all future decisions. Much of an asset allocation strategy depends on the investor's policy statement, which includes the investor's goals or objectives, constraints, and investment guidelines.

Regardless of who the investor is or how simple or complex the investment needs, he or she should develop a policy statement before making long-term investment decisions. Although most of our examples will be in the context of an individual investor (institutional investors will be dealt with in much more detail in Chapters 15 through 18), the concepts we introduce here—investment objectives, constraints, benchmarks, and so on—apply to any investor, individual or institution. We'll review historical data to show the importance of the asset allocation decision and discuss the need for investor education, an important issue for companies that offer retirement or savings plans to their employees. The chapter concludes by examining asset

* The authors acknowledge the collaboration of Professor Edgar Norton of Illinois State University on this chapter.

allocation strategies across national borders to show the effect of regulations, market environment, and culture on investing patterns; what is appropriate for a Canadian-based investor is not necessarily appropriate for a foreign-based investor.

2.1 Individual Investor Life Cycle

Financial plans and investment needs are as different as each individual. Investment needs change over a person's life cycle. How individuals structure their financial plans should be related to their age, financial status, future plans, risk aversion characteristics, and needs.

2.1.1 THE PRELIMINARIES

Before embarking on an investment program, we need to make sure other needs are satisfied. No serious investment plan should be started until the investor has adequate income to cover living expenses and has a safety net should the unexpected occur.

Insurance One of the first steps in developing a financial plan is to purchase adequate life insurance. Life insurance protects loved ones against financial hardship should death occur before our financial goals are met. The death benefit paid by the insurance company can help pay medical bills and funeral expenses and provide cash that family members can use to maintain their lifestyle, retire debt, or invest for future needs (e.g., children's education, spouse retirement). Therefore, one of the first steps in developing a financial plan is to purchase adequate life insurance.

Insurance can also serve more immediate purposes, including being a means to meet long-term goals, such as retirement planning. On reaching retirement age, the cash surrender value of the life insurance policy can be used for retirement or estate-planning purposes.

Insurance coverage also provides protection against other uncertainties. *Health* insurance helps to pay additional medical bills. *Disability* insurance provides continuing income should you become unable to work. *Automobile and home* (or rental) insurances provide protection against accidents and damage to cars or residences.

Although nobody ever expects to use his or her insurance coverage, the lack of insurance can ruin the best-planned investment program.

There are a number of insurance companies that provide free life insurance calculators; for example, check out http://www.insurecan.com/lifeinsurance/life-insurance-calculator-canada.

Cash Reserve Emergencies, job layoffs, and unforeseen expenses happen, and good investment opportunities emerge. It is important to have a cash reserve to help meet these occasions. In addition to providing a safety cushion, a cash reserve reduces the likelihood of being forced to sell investments at inopportune times to cover unexpected expenses. Most experts recommend a cash reserve equal to about six months' living expenses. Calling it a "cash" reserve does not mean the funds should be in cash; rather, the funds should be in investments you can easily convert to cash with little chance of a loss in value. Money market mutual funds, Canada Savings Bonds, and bank accounts are appropriate vehicles for the cash reserve.

Similar to the financial plan, an investor's insurance and cash reserve needs will change over his or her life. The need for disability insurance declines in retirement but other insurance, such as supplemental medical coverage or long-term-care insurance, may become more important.

2.1.2 LIFE-CYCLE NEW WORTH AND INVESTMENT STRATEGIES

Assuming the basic insurance and cash reserve needs are met, individuals can start a serious investment program with their savings. Because of changes in their net worth and risk tolerance, individuals' investment strategies will change over their lifetime. In the following sections, we review various phases in the investment life cycle. Although each individual's needs and preferences are different, some general traits affect most investors over the life cycle.

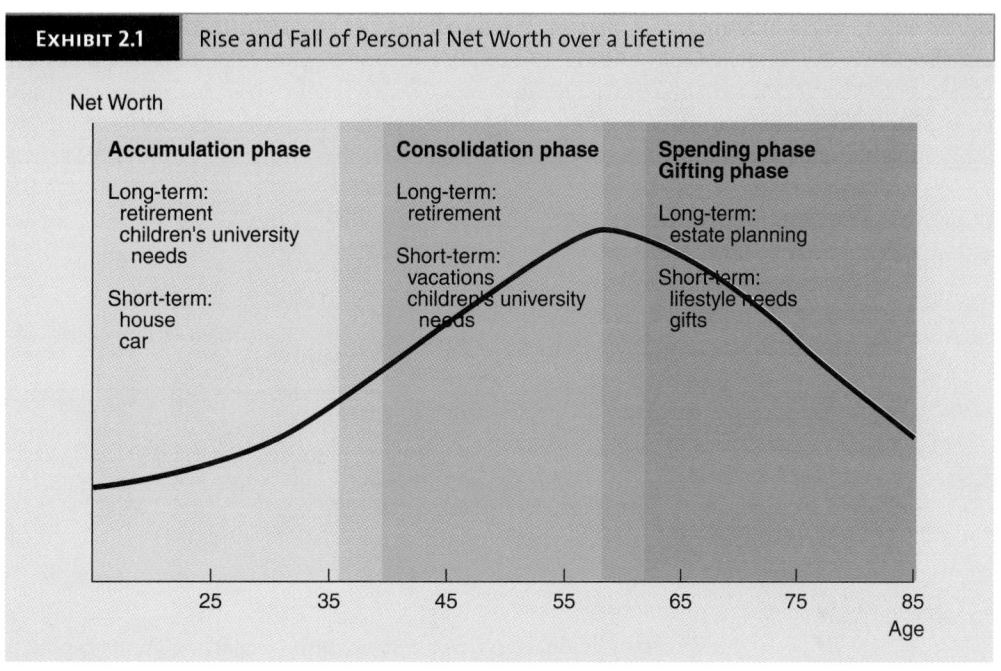

EXHIBIT 2.1   Rise and Fall of Personal Net Worth over a Lifetime

The life-cycle phases are shown in Exhibit 2.1 (the spending and gifting phases are shown as concurrent) and described below.

Accumulation Phase Individuals in the early-to-middle years of their working careers are in the **accumulation phase**. These individuals are attempting to accumulate assets to satisfy fairly immediate needs (e.g., a down payment for a house) or longer term goals (children's higher education, retirement). Typically, their net worth is small, and debt from car loans or their own past student loans may be heavy. As a result of their typically long investment time horizon and their future earning ability, individuals in this phase are willing to make relatively high-risk investments in the hopes of making above-average nominal returns over time.

Here we must emphasize the wisdom of investing early and regularly. Funds invested in early life-cycle phases, with returns compounding over time, reap significant financial benefits during later phases. Exhibit 2.2 shows growth from an initial $10,000 investment over 20, 30, and 40 years at annual returns of 4% and 6%. The middle-aged person who invests $10,000 "when he or she can afford it" will reap the benefits of compounding for 20 years or so before retirement. The person who begins saving at a younger age will enjoy the much higher benefit of having the funds invested for 30 or 40 years. Regularly investing $2,000 a year results in large benefits over time, as well. As shown in Exhibit 2.2, an initial $10,000 investment followed by $2,000 annual investments over 40 years (total $90,000) at 4% annually will result in nearly $250,000 being accumulated. If the funds are invested more aggressively and earn the 6% return, the accumulation will be over $400,000.

Consolidation Phase Individuals in the **consolidation phase** are typically past the midpoint of their careers, have little or no debt, and perhaps have paid, or have the assets to pay, their children's university expenses. Earnings exceed expenses, so the excess can be invested to provide for future retirement or estate-planning needs. The typical investment horizon for this phase is still long (20 to 30 years), so moderately high-risk investments are attractive.

EXHIBIT 2.2	Benefits of Investing Early			
		The Future Value of an Initial $10,000 Investment	The Future Value of Investing $2,000 Annually	The Future Value of the Initial Investment Plus the Annual Investment
Interest rate	4.0%			
20 years		$21,911.23	$59,556.16	$81,647.39
30 years		$32,433.98	$112,169.88	$144,603.86
40 years		$48,010.21	$190,051.03	$238,061.24
Interest rate	6.0%			
20 years		$32,071.35	$73,571.18	$105,642.53
30 years		$57,434.91	$158,116.37	$215,551.28
40 years		$102,857.18	$309,523.93	$412,381.11

Source: Calculations by authors.

However, individuals in this phase are also concerned about capital preservation; they do not want to take very large risks that may put their current nest egg in jeopardy.

Spending Phase The **spending phase** typically begins when individuals retire. Living expenses are covered by CPP and income from prior investments, including employer pension plans. Because their earning years have ended for the most part, they seek greater protection of their capital. At the same time, they must balance their desire to preserve the nominal value of their savings with the need to protect themselves against a decline in the *real* value of their savings due to inflation. The average 65-year-old in Canada has a life expectancy of about 20 years, which means they still need some risky growth investments, such as common stocks, for inflation (purchasing power) protection.

The transition into the spending phase requires sometimes a difficult change in mindset: Throughout our working life we are trying to save; suddenly we can spend. We tend to think that if we spend less, say 4% of our accumulated funds annually instead of 5%, 6%, or 7%, our wealth will last far longer. Although this is correct, a bear market early in our retirement can greatly reduce our accumulated funds. Fortunately, there are planning tools that can give a realistic view of what can happen to our retirement funds should markets fall early in our retirement years; this insight can assist in budgeting and planning to minimize the chance of spending (or losing) all the saved retirement funds. Annuities, which transfer risk from the individual to the annuity firm (most likely an insurance company), are another possibility. With an annuity, the recipient receives a guaranteed, lifelong stream of income. Options can allow for the annuity to continue until both spouses die.

Gifting Phase The **gifting phase** is similar to, and may be concurrent with, the spending phase. In this stage, individuals may believe they have sufficient income and assets to cover their current and future expenses while maintaining a reserve for uncertainties. Excess assets can be used to provide financial assistance to relatives or friends, to establish charitable trusts, or to fund trusts as an estate-planning tool to minimize estate taxes.

2.1.3   LIFE-CYCLE INVESTMENT GOALS

During an individual's investment life cycle, he or she will have a variety of financial goals. **Near-term, high-priority goals** are shorter term financial objectives that individuals set to fund purchases that are personally important to them, such as accumulating funds to make a house down payment, buy a new car, or take a trip. Parents with teenage children may have a near-term, high-priority goal to accumulate funds to help pay for university. Because of the emotional importance of these goals and their short time horizon, high-risk investments are not usually considered suitable for achieving them.

Long-term, high-priority goals typically include some form of financial independence, such as the ability to retire at a certain age. Because of their long-term nature, higher risk investments can be used to help meet these objectives.

Lower priority goals are just that—it might be nice to meet these objectives, but it is not critical. Examples include the ability to purchase a new car every few years, redecorate the home with expensive furnishings, or take a long, luxurious vacation. A well-developed policy statement considers these diverse goals over an investor's lifetime.

2.2 The Portfolio Management Process

The process of managing an investment portfolio never stops. Once the funds are invested according to the plan, the real work begins in evaluating the portfolio's performance and updating the portfolio based on changes in the environment and the investor's needs.

The first step in the portfolio management process, as seen in Exhibit 2.3, is for the investor, either alone or with an investment advisor, to construct a **policy statement**. The policy statement is a road map; in it, investors specify the types of risks they are willing to take and their investment goals and constraints. All investment decisions are based on the policy statement to ensure they are appropriate for the investor. Because investor needs change over time, the policy statement must be periodically reviewed and updated.

The second step is to develop an investment strategy, based on current financial and economic conditions and forecast future trends, alongside the investor's policy statement. Economies are dynamic; they are affected by numerous industry struggles, politics, and changing demographics and social attitudes. Thus, the portfolio will require constant monitoring and

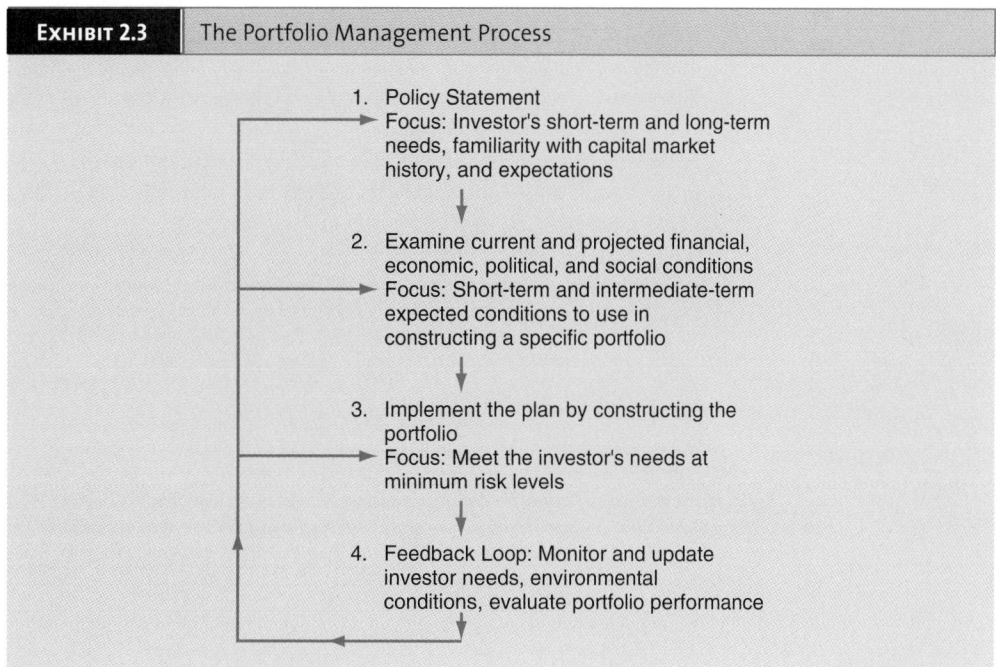

EXHIBIT 2.3 | The Portfolio Management Process

1. Policy Statement
    Focus: Investor's short-term and long-term needs, familiarity with capital market history, and expectations

2. Examine current and projected financial, economic, political, and social conditions
    Focus: Short-term and intermediate-term expected conditions to use in constructing a specific portfolio

3. Implement the plan by constructing the portfolio
    Focus: Meet the investor's needs at minimum risk levels

4. Feedback Loop: Monitor and update investor needs, environmental conditions, evaluate portfolio performance

updating to reflect changes in financial market expectations. We examine the process of evaluating and forecasting economic trends in Chapter 8.

The third step is to **construct the portfolio**. With the investor's policy statement and financial market forecasts as input, the advisor implements the investment strategy and determines how to allocate available funds across different countries, asset classes, and securities. This involves constructing a portfolio that will minimize the investor's risks while meeting the needs specified in the policy statement. Financial theory frequently assists portfolio construction; this will be discussed in Part 2.

Continual monitoring of the investor's needs and capital market conditions, and when necessary, updating the policy statement and modifying the investment strategy, is the last step in the process. An important component of the monitoring process is the evaluation of a portfolio's performance and comparison of the relative results to the expectations and the requirements listed in the policy statement.

2.3 The Need for a Policy Statement

When asked about their investment goals, people often say, "to make a lot of money," or some similar response. There are two important reasons for constructing a policy statement: First, it helps the investor decide on realistic investment goals, and second, it creates a standard by which to judge the portfolio manager's performance.

In terms of helping investors understand their own needs, objectives, and investment constraints, the policy statement encourages investors to learn about financial markets and the risks of investing. This background will help them specify realistic goals and become more informed about the risks and costs of investing.[1]

One expert in the field recommends that investors should think about the following set of questions and explain their answers as part of the process of constructing a policy statement:

1. What are the real risks of an adverse financial outcome, especially in the short run?
2. What probable emotional reactions will I have to an adverse financial outcome?
3. How knowledgeable am I about investments and financial markets?
4. What other capital or income sources do I have? How important is this particular portfolio to my overall financial position?
5. What, if any, legal restrictions may affect my investment needs?
6. How would any unanticipated consequences of fluctuations in portfolio value affect my investment policy?

Source: Adapted from Charles D. Ellis, *Investment Policy: How to Win the Loser's Game* (Homewood, IL: Dow Jones-Irwin, 1985), 25–26. Reproduced with permission of the McGraw-Hill Companies.

---

1 Market values of assets, whether they be stocks, bonds, or real estate, can fluctuate dramatically. For example, during the October 1987 crash, the Dow Jones Industrial Average (DJIA) fell more than 20% in one day; in October 1997, the Dow fell "only" 7%. A review of market history shows that it is not unusual for asset prices to decline from 10% to 20% over several months. Investors typically focus on a single statistic, such as an 11% average annual rate of return on stocks, and expect the market to rise 11% every year. Such thinking ignores the risk of stock investing. Part of the process of developing a policy statement is for the investor to become familiar with the risks of investing, because we know that a strong positive relationship exists between risk and return.

Constructing a policy statement is mainly the investor's responsibility and is necessary in order for the investor to adequately communicate his or her needs to the portfolio manager. Without this input from investors, the portfolio manager cannot construct a portfolio that will satisfy clients' needs. Bypassing this step will most likely result in future aggravation, dissatisfaction, and disappointment.

The policy statement also assists in judging the performance of the portfolio manager. Performance cannot be judged without an objective standard; the policy statement provides that objective standard. The portfolio's performance should be compared to guidelines specified in the policy statement, not on the portfolio's overall return. For example, a low-risk investor might find their portfolio does not perform as well as the risky S&P/TSX Composite index. Because risk drives returns, the investor's lower risk investments, as specified in the investor's policy statement, will likely earn lower returns than if all the investor's funds were placed in the stock market.

The policy statement will typically include a **benchmark portfolio**, or comparison standard. The risk of the benchmark, and the assets included in the benchmark, should agree with the client's risk preferences and investment needs. Notably, both the client and the portfolio manager must agree that the benchmark portfolio reflects the client's risk preferences and appropriate return requirements. In turn, the investment performance of the portfolio manager should be compared to this benchmark. For example, an investor specifying a low-risk investment policy statement should compare the portfolio manager's performance against a low-risk benchmark portfolio. Likewise, an investor seeking high-risk, high-return investments should compare the portfolio's performance against a high-risk benchmark portfolio, such as 30% S&P/TSX Composite index, 30% S&P 500 (Canadian dollars), and 40% MSCI EAFE (Canadian dollars)

Because it sets an objective performance standard, the policy statement acts as a starting point for periodic portfolio review and client communication with managers. Questions concerning portfolio performance or the manager's faithfulness to the policy can be addressed in the context of the written policy guidelines. Managers should mainly be judged by whether they consistently followed the client's policy guidelines. A manager who makes unilateral deviations from policy is not working in the best interests of the client, even if those deviations result in higher portfolio returns.

Thus, we see the importance of the client constructing the policy statement: The client must first understand his or her own needs before communicating them to the portfolio manager. In turn, the portfolio manager must implement the client's desires by following the investment guidelines. As long as policy is followed, performance shortfalls should not be a major concern. Remember that the policy statement is designed to impose an investment discipline on the client and on the portfolio manager. The less knowledgeable they are, the more likely clients are to inappropriately judge the performance of the portfolio manager.

2.3.1 OTHER BENEFITS

Few things in our lives remain constant, and your portfolio manager could be promoted, be dismissed, or take a better job, leaving your portfolio under the management of someone you do not know and who does not know you. To prevent costly delays during this transition, a clearly written policy statement can ensure that the new manager "hits the ground running." It should prevent delays in monitoring and rebalancing your portfolio and help create a seamless transition from one portfolio manager to another.

An appropriate policy statement should satisfactorily answer the following questions:

1. Is the policy carefully designed to meet the specific needs and objectives of this particular investor? (Cookie-cutter or one-size-fits-all policy statements are generally inappropriate.)
2. Is the policy written so clearly and explicitly that a competent stranger could use it to manage the portfolio in conformance with the client's needs? In case of a manager transition, could the new manager use this policy statement to handle your portfolio in accordance with your needs?
3. Would the client have been able to remain committed to the policies during the capital market experiences of the past 60 to 70 years? That is, does the client fully understand investment risks and the need for a disciplined approach to the investment process?
4. Would the portfolio manager have been able to maintain the policies specified over the same period? (Discipline is a two-way street; we do not want the portfolio manager to change strategies because of a disappointing market.)
5. Would the policy, if implemented, have achieved the client's objectives? (Bottom line: Would the policy have worked to meet the client's needs?)

Source: Adapted from Charles D. Ellis, *Investment Policy: How to Win the Loser's Game* (Homewood, IL: Dow Jones-Irwin, 1985), 62. Reproduced with permission of the McGraw-Hill Companies.

2.4 Input to the Policy Statement

Before an investor and advisor can construct a policy statement, they need to have an open and frank exchange of information, ideas, fears, and goals. To build a framework for this information-gathering process, the client and advisor need to discuss the client's investment objectives and constraints. To illustrate this framework, we discuss the investment objectives and constraints that may confront "typical" 25-year-old and 65-year-old investors.

2.4.1 INVESTMENT OBJECTIVES

The investor's **objectives** are his or her investment goals expressed in terms of both risk and returns. Expressing goals only in terms of returns can lead to inappropriate investment practices, such as the use of high-risk investment strategies or account *churning,* which involves moving quickly in and out of investments in an attempt to buy low and sell high.

For example, a person may have a stated return goal such as "double my investment in five years." Before such a statement becomes part of the policy statement, the client must become fully informed of investment risks associated with such a goal, including the possibility of loss. *A careful analysis of the client's risk tolerance should precede any discussion of return objectives.* It makes little sense for a person who is risk averse to have his or her funds invested in high-risk assets. Investment firms survey clients to gauge their risk tolerance and many self-help tests are available (see Exhibit 2.4). From that, an initial asset allocation can be constructed such as those contained in Exhibit 2.5.

Risk tolerance is more than a function of an individual's psychological makeup; it is affected by other factors, including a person's current insurance coverage, cash reserves, family situation (e.g., marital status and the number and ages of children), and his or her age. We know that older individuals generally have shorter investment time frames within which to make up any losses; they also have years of experience, including living through various market gyrations and

A number of financial institutions provide risk assessment tools and surveys to help you determine the kind of investor you are. Go to http://www.rbcam.com/ and click the "What are my investment options?" link.

EXHIBIT 2.4	How Much Risk Is Right for You?

You've heard the expression "no pain, no gain"? In the investment world, the comparable phrase would be "no risk, no reward."

How you feel about risking your money will drive many of your investment decisions. The risk-comfort scale extends from very conservative (you don't want to risk losing a penny regardless of how little your money earns) to very aggressive (you're willing to risk much of your money for the possibility that it will grow tremendously). As you might guess, most investors' tolerance for risk falls somewhere in between.

If you're unsure of what your level of risk tolerance is, this quiz should help.

1. You win $300 in an office football pool. You: (a) spend it on groceries, (b) purchase lottery tickets, (c) put it in a money market account, (d) buy some stock.

2. Two weeks after buying 100 shares of a $20 stock, the price jumps to over $30. You decide to: (a) buy more stock—it's obviously a winner, (b) sell it and take your profits, (c) sell half to recoup some costs and hold the rest, (d) sit tight and wait for it to advance even more.

3. On days when the stock market jumps way up, you: (a) wish you had invested more, (b) call your financial advisor and ask for recommendations, (c) feel glad you're not in the market because it fluctuates too much, (d) pay little attention.

4. You're planning a vacation trip and can either lock in a fixed room-and-meals rate of $150 per day or book standby and pay anywhere from $100 to $300 per day. You: (a) take the fixed-rate deal, (b) talk to people who have been there about the availability of last-minute accommodations, (c) book standby and also arrange vacation insurance because you're leery of the tour operator, (d) take your chances with standby.

5. The owner of your apartment building is converting the units to condominiums. You can buy your unit for $75,000 or an option on a unit for $15,000. (Units have recently sold for close to $100,000, and

prices seem to be going up.) For financing, you'll have to borrow the down payment and pay mortgage and condo fees higher than your present rent. You: (a) buy your unit, (b) buy your unit and look for another to buy, (c) sell the option and arrange to rent the unit yourself, (d) sell the option and move out because you think the conversion will attract couples with small children.

6. You have been working three years for a rapidly growing company. As an executive, you are offered the option of buying up to 2% of company stock: 2,000 shares at $10 a share. Although the company is privately owned (its stock does not trade on the open market), its majority owner has made handsome profits selling three other businesses and intends to sell this one eventually. You: (a) purchase all the shares you can and tell the owner you would invest more if allowed, (b) purchase all the shares, (c) purchase half the shares, (d) purchase a small amount of shares.

7. You go to a casino for the first time. You choose to play: (a) quarter slot machines, (b) $5 minimum-bet roulette, (c) dollar slot machines, (d) $25 minimum-bet blackjack.

8. You want to take someone out for a special dinner in a city that's new to you. You pick a place by: (a) reading restaurant reviews in the local newspaper, (b) asking co-workers if they know of a suitable place, (c) calling the only other person you know in this city who eats out a lot but only recently moved there, (d) visiting the city sometime before your dinner to check out the restaurants yourself.

9. The expression that best describes your lifestyle is: (a) no guts, no glory, (b) just do it! (c) look before you leap, (d) all good things come to those who wait.

10. Your attitude toward money is best described as: (a) a dollar saved is a dollar earned, (b) you've got to spend money to make money, (c) cash and carry only, (d) whenever possible, use other people's money.

SCORING SYSTEM: Score your answers this way: (1) a-1, b-4, c-2, d-3 (2) a-4, b-1, c-3, d-2 (3) a-3, b-4, c-2, d-1 (4) a-2, b-3, c-1, d-4 (5) a-3, b-4, c-2, d-1 (6) a-4, b-3, c-2, d-1 (7) a-1, b-3, c-2, d-4 (8) a-2, b-3, c-4, d-1 (9) a-4, b-3, c-2, d-1 (10) a-2, b-3, c-1, d-4.

What your total score indicates:

- 10–17: You're not willing to take chances with your money, even though it means you can't make big gains.

- 18–25: You're semi-conservative, willing to take a small chance with enough information.

- 26–32: You're semi-aggressive, willing to take chances if you think the odds of earning more are in your favour.

- 33–40: You're aggressive, looking for every opportunity to make your money grow, even though in some cases the odds may be quite long. You view money as a tool to make more money.

Source: Adapted from *Feathering Your Nest: The Retirement Planner.* Copyright © 1993 by Lisa Berger. Used by permission of Workman Publishing Company, Inc., New York. All Rights Reserved.

Money Central has an interesting asset allocation tool at
http://moneycentral.msn.com/investor/calcs/assetall/main.asp.

EXHIBIT 2.5	Initial Risk and Investment Goal Categories and Asset Allocations Suggested by Investment Firms

FIDELITY INVESTMENTS SUGGESTED ASSET ALLOCATIONS

	Cash/Short-Term	Bonds	Domestic Equities	Foreign Equities
Conservative	30%	50%	20%	0%
Balanced	10%	40%	45%	5%
Growth	5%	25%	60%	10%
Aggressive growth	0%	15%	70%	15%

VANGUARD INVESTMENTS SUGGESTED ASSET ALLOCATIONS

Overall Objective	Risk Level	Cash/Short-Term	Bonds	Stocks
Income-oriented	Conservative	0%	100%	0%
	Moderate	0%	80%	20%
	Aggressive	0%	70%	30%
Balanced	Conservative	0%	60%	40%
	Moderate	0%	50%	50%
	Aggressive	0%	40%	60%
Growth	Conservative	0%	30%	70%
	Moderate	0%	20%	80%
	Aggressive	0%	0%	100%

Source: Based on data sampled from Personal Fidelity.com and Vanguard.com.

Canada Life has a good questionnaire at
http://www.canadalife.com/web5?groups/common/@public/documents/we_content.s%_009444.pdf.

"corrections" (a euphemism for downtrends or crashes) that younger people have not experienced or the effect of which they do not fully appreciate. Risk tolerance is also influenced by one's current net worth and income expectations. All else being equal, individuals with higher incomes have a greater propensity to undertake risk because their incomes can help cover any shortfall. Likewise, individuals with larger net worths can afford to place some assets in risky investments while the remaining assets provide a cushion against losses.

A person's return objective may be stated in terms of an absolute or a relative percentage return, but it may also be stated in terms of a general goal, such as capital preservation, current income, capital appreciation, or total return.

Capital preservation means that investors want to minimize their risk of loss, usually in real terms: The return needs to be no less than the inflation rate. Generally, this is a strategy for strongly risk-averse investors or for funds needed in the short run, such as for next year's tuition or a down payment on a house.

Capital appreciation is an appropriate objective when the investors want the portfolio to grow in real terms over time to meet some future need. Under this strategy, growth mainly occurs through capital gains. This is an aggressive strategy for investors willing to take on risk to meet their objective. Generally, longer term investors seeking to build a retirement or university education fund may have this goal.

When **current income** is the return objective, the investors want the portfolio to concentrate on generating income rather than capital gains. This strategy sometimes suits investors who want to supplement their earnings with income generated by their portfolio to meet their living expenses. Retirees may favour this objective for part of their portfolio to help generate spendable funds.

The objective for the **total return** strategy is similar to that of capital appreciation; namely, the investors want the portfolio to grow over time to meet a future need. Whereas the capital appreciation strategy seeks to do this primarily through capital gains, the total return strategy seeks to increase portfolio value by both capital gains and reinvesting current income. Because the total return strategy has both income and capital gains components, its risk exposure lies between that of the current income and capital appreciation strategies.

Investment Objective: 25-Year-Old What is an appropriate investment objective for our typical 25-year-old investor? Assume he holds a steady job, is a valued employee, has adequate insurance coverage, and has enough money in the bank to provide a cash reserve. Let's also assume that his current long-term, high-priority investment goal is to build a retirement fund. Depending on his risk preferences, he can select a strategy carrying moderate to high amounts of risk because the income stream from his job will probably grow over time. Further, given his young age and income growth potential, a low-risk strategy, such as capital preservation or current income, is inappropriate for his retirement fund goal; a total return or capital appreciation objective would be most appropriate. Here's a possible objective statement:

> Invest funds in a variety of moderate- to higher-risk investments. The average risk of the equity portfolio should exceed that of a broad stock-market index, such as the S&P/TSX composite index. Foreign and domestic equity exposure should range from 80% to 95% of the total portfolio. Remaining funds should be invested in short- and intermediate-term notes and bonds.

Investment Objective: 65-Year-Old Assume our typical 65-year-old investor likewise has adequate insurance coverage and a cash reserve. Let's also assume she is retiring this year. She will want less risk exposure than the 25-year-old investor, because her employment income will soon be ending; she will not be able to recover any investment losses by saving more out of her paycheque. Depending on her CPP and employer pension plan income, she may need additional income from her retirement portfolio to meet living expenses. She expects to live another 20 years, so she will need protection against inflation. A risk-averse investor will choose a combination of current income and capital preservation strategy; a more risk-tolerant investor will choose a combination of current income and total return in an attempt to have principal growth outpace inflation. Here's an example of such an objective statement:

> Invest in stock and bond investments to meet income needs (from bond income and stock dividends) and to provide for real growth (from equities). Fixed-income securities should comprise 55% to 65% of the total portfolio; of this, 5% to 15% should be invested in short-term securities for extra liquidity and safety. The remaining 35% to 45% of the portfolio should be invested in high-quality stocks with risk that is similar to the S&P/TSX composite index.

More detailed analyses for our 25-year-old and our 65-year-old would make more specific assumptions about the risk tolerance of each, as well as clearly enumerate their investment goals, return objectives, the funds they have to invest now, the funds they expect to invest over time, and the benchmark portfolio that will be used to evaluate performance.

2.4.2 INVESTMENT CONSTRAINTS

In addition to the investment objective that sets limits on risk and return, certain other constraints also affect the investment plan. Investment constraints include liquidity needs, an investment time horizon, tax factors, legal and regulatory constraints, and unique needs and preferences.

Liquidity Needs An asset is **liquid** if it can be quickly converted to cash at a price close to fair market value. Generally, assets are more liquid if many traders are interested in a fairly standardized product. Treasury bills are a highly liquid security; real estate and venture capital are not.

Investors may have liquidity needs that the investment plan must consider. For example, although an investor may have a primary long-term goal, several near-term goals may require available funds. Wealthy individuals with sizable tax obligations need adequate liquidity to pay their taxes without upsetting their investment plan. Some retirement plans may need funds for shorter term purposes, such as buying a car or a house.

Our typical 25-year-old investor probably has little need for liquidity as he focuses on his long-term retirement fund goal. This may change, however, should he face a period of unemployment or should near-term goals, such as honeymoon expenses or a house down payment, enter the picture. Should any changes occur, the investor needs to revise his policy statement and financial plans accordingly.

Our soon-to-be-retired 65-year-old investor has a greater need for liquidity. Although she may receive regular cheques from her pension plan and CPP, it is not likely that they will equal her working paycheque. She will want some of her portfolio in liquid securities to meet unexpected expenses, bills, or special needs such as trips or cruises.

Time Horizon Time horizon as an investment constraint briefly entered our earlier discussion of near-term and long-term high-priority goals. A close (but not perfect) relationship exists between an investor's time horizon, liquidity needs, and ability to handle risk. Investors with long investment horizons generally require less liquidity and can tolerate greater portfolio risk: less liquidity because the funds are not usually needed for many years; greater risk tolerance because any shortfalls or losses can be overcome by earnings and returns in subsequent years.

Investors with shorter time horizons generally favour more liquid and less risky investments because losses are harder to overcome during a short time frame.

Because of life expectancies, our 25-year-old investor has a longer investment time horizon than our 65-year-old investor. However, this does not mean the 65-year-old should place all her money in short-term investments; she needs the inflation protection that long-term investments such as common stock can provide. Still, because of the time horizon constraint, the 25-year-old can have a greater proportion of his portfolio in equities—including stocks in small firms, as well as international and emerging market firms—than the 65-year-old.

Tax Concerns Investment planning is complicated by taxes, and the situation is even more complicated if international investments are part of the portfolio. Taxable income from interest, dividends, or rents is taxable at the investor's marginal tax rate. Exhibit 2.6 shows the federal, Ontario, and Alberta tax rates for different levels of taxable income 2009.

Capital gains or losses arise from changes in an asset's price and are taxed only when an asset is sold and the gain or loss, relative to its initial cost or adjusted cost base, is realized. **Unrealized capital gains** (or *losses*) reflect the price change in currently held assets that have *not* been sold; the tax liability on unrealized capital gains can be deferred indefinitely. **Realized capital gains** occur when an appreciated asset has been sold; taxes are due on the realized capital gains. **Dividends** are subject to a lower tax rate through the use of a dividend-tax credit system.

Some find the difference between average and marginal income tax rates confusing. The **marginal tax rate** is the tax paid on the next dollar in income. Thus, in 2009 an Ontario

Exhibit 2.6	Tax Rates for Individuals, 2009

Federal	
Taxable Income	**Tax Rate**
$0–$40,726	15%
$40,727–$81,452	22%
$81,453–$126,264	26%
$126,265–Unlimited	29%

Ontario	
Taxable Income	**Tax Rate**
$0–$36,848	6.05%
$36,849–$73,698	9.15%
$73,699–Unlimited	11.16%

Alberta	
Taxable Income	**Tax Rate**
$0–Unlimited	10.0%

Source: http://www.cra-arc.gc.ca/tx/ndvdls/fq/txrts-eng.html.

resident with income of $81,452 had a marginal tax rate of 37.16% (= 26 + 11.16). The 37.16% marginal tax rate would be used to determine after-tax returns on investments.

The **average tax rate** is simply a person's total tax payment divided by their total income. It represents the average tax paid on each dollar the person earned. From Exhibit 2.6, in 2009 an Albertan would have paid $13,149.18 in tax on $50,000 total income [$6,108.90 + 0.22($50,000 − $40,726) + 0.1($50,000)]. This average tax rate is $13,149.18/$50,000 or 26.30%. Note that the average tax rate is a weighted average of the marginal tax rates paid on each dollar of income.

The after-tax return on taxable investment income is:

After-Tax Income Return = Pre-Tax Income Return × (1 − Marginal Tax Rate)

Tax liabilities from investments can be reduced through the use of a *registered retirement savings plan (RRSP or RSP)*. Contributions can often be deducted in order to reduce current taxes, and taxes on any investment returns of an RSP, including any income, are deferred until the funds are withdrawn from the account. Any funds withdrawn from an RSP are taxable as current income, regardless of whether growth in the RSP occurs as a result of capital gains, income, or both. For this reason, to minimize taxes advisors recommend investing in stocks in taxable accounts and bonds in tax-deferred accounts such as RSPs. When funds are withdrawn from a tax-deferred account such as a regular RSP, assets are taxed at the investor's highest marginal rate, even if the source of the stock return is primarily capital gains. In a taxable account, only half the capital gain is taxed.

The benefits of deferring taxes can dramatically compound over time, as we saw in Chapter 1. For example, $1,000 invested in an RSP at a rate of 8% grows to $10,062.66 over

30 years; in a taxable account (for simplicity, assuming a 28% marginal provincial and federal tax rate), the funds would grow to only $5,365.91. After 30 years, the value of the tax-deferred investment has grown to be nearly twice as large as the taxable investment. With various stipulations, as of 2009, tax-deductible contributions of up to $21,000 (to be raised to $22,000 in 2010) can be made to a traditional RSP.

Another tax-deferred investment is the cash value of life insurance contracts; these accumulate tax-free until the funds are withdrawn. Also, employers may offer plans that allow the employee to reduce taxable income by making tax-deferred investments. Often, employee contributions are matched by employer donations (up to a specified limit), thus allowing the employees to double their investment with little risk.

At times, investors face a trade-off between taxes and diversification needs. If entrepreneurs concentrate much of their wealth in equity holdings of their firm, or if employees purchase substantial amounts of their employer's stock through payroll deduction plans during their working life, their portfolios may contain a large amount of unrealized capital gains. In addition, the risk position of such a portfolio may be quite high because it is concentrated in a single company. The decision to sell some of the company stock in order to diversify the portfolio's risk by reinvesting the proceeds in other assets must be balanced against the resulting tax liability.

Our typical 25-year-old investor probably is in a fairly low tax bracket, so detailed tax planning will not be a major concern. Nonetheless, he should still invest as much as possible into such tax-deferred plans as RSPs for the retirement portion of his portfolio. If other funds are available for investment, they should be allocated based on his shorter and longer term investment goals.

Our 65-year-old investor may face a different situation. If she had been in a high tax bracket prior to retiring—and therefore has sought tax-deferred investments—her situation may change shortly after retirement. After her retirement, without large regular paycheques, the need for tax-deferred investments becomes less important. If her employer's stock is a large component of her retirement account, she must make careful decisions regarding the need to diversify versus the cost of realizing large capital gains (in her lower tax bracket).

Legal and Regulatory Factors Both the investment process and the financial markets are highly regulated and subject to numerous laws. At times, these legal and regulatory factors constrain the investment strategies of individuals and institutions.

For example, funds removed from a registered retirement savings plan are taxable. You may also be familiar with the tag line, "interest penalty upon early withdrawal." Regulations and rules such as these may make such investments unattractive for investors with substantial liquidity needs in their portfolios.

Regulations can also constrain the investment choices available to someone in a fiduciary role. A *fiduciary,* or trustee, supervises an investment portfolio of a third party, such as a trust account or discretionary account.[2] The fiduciary must make investment decisions in accordance with the owner's wishes; a properly written policy statement assists this process. In addition, trustees of a trust account must meet the prudent investor standard, which means that they must invest and manage the funds as a prudent person would manage his or her own affairs. Notably, the prudent investor is based on the composition of the entire portfolio, not each individual asset.[3]

All investors must respect certain laws, such as insider-trading prohibitions against the purchase and sale of securities on the basis of important information that is not publicly known.

---

2 A discretionary account is one in which the fiduciary, many times a financial planner or stockbroker, has the authority to purchase and sell assets in the owner's portfolio without first receiving the owner's approval.

3 As we discuss in Chapter 6, it is sometimes wise to hold assets that are individually risky in the context of a well-diversified portfolio, even if the investor is strongly risk averse.

Security transactions based on access to insider information violates the fiduciary trust the shareholders have placed with management because the managers seek personal financial gain from their privileged position as agents for the shareholders.

For both our investors, legal and regulatory matters will be of little concern, with the possible exception of insider-trading laws. Our 25-year-old should find a financial advisor to assist him in constructing a financial plan; that advisor would have to follow the regulations pertinent to a client-advisor relationship. Our advice to the 65-year-old investor is similar; if she wants to do estate planning and set up trust accounts, she should seek legal and tax advice to ensure her plans are properly implemented.

Unique Needs and Preferences This category covers the individual, and sometimes idiosyncratic, concerns of each investor. Some investors may want to exclude certain investments from their portfolio solely on the basis of personal preference or for social consciousness reasons. For example, firms that manufacture or sell tobacco, alcohol, pornography, or environmentally harmful products may be excluded from their portfolio. Some mutual funds screen according to this type of social responsibility criterion.

Another example of a personal constraint is the time and expertise a person has for managing his or her portfolio. Some people may prefer to relax during non-working hours while others may have the time but believe they lack the expertise to choose and monitor investments, so both may have a trusted advisor manage their investments.

In addition, a business owner with a large portion of her wealth—and emotion—tied up in her firm's stock may be reluctant to sell even when it may be financially prudent to do so and then reinvest the proceeds for diversification purposes. Further, if the stock holdings are in a private company, it may be difficult to find a buyer unless shares are sold at a discount from their fair market value. Because each investor is unique, the implications of this final constraint differ for each person; there is no "typical" 25-year-old or 65-year-old investor. Each individual will have to decide on—and then communicate—specific goals in a well-constructed policy statement.

2.4.3 Some Common Mistakes

When constructing their policy statements, participants in employer-sponsored retirement plans need to realize that these plans may invest in their employer's stock. Having so much money invested in one asset violates diversification principles and could be costly. To put this in context, most mutual funds are limited to having no more than 10% of their assets in any one company's stock; a firm's pension plan can invest no more than 10% of their funds in its own stock. As noted by Schulz (1996), individuals are unfortunately doing what government regulations prevent many institutional investors from doing. In addition, some studies point out that the average stock allocation in retirement plans is lower than it should be to allow for growth of principal over time—i.e., investors tend to be too conservative.

Another consideration is the issue of stock trading. A number of studies[4] have shown that individual investors typically trade stocks too often (driving up commissions), sell stocks with gains too early (prior to further price increases), and hold onto losers too long (as the price continues to fall). These costly mistakes are especially true for males and online traders.

Lastly, it seems that many investors seem to neglect that important first step to achieve financial success: They do not plan for the future. Studies of retirement plans show that Canadians are not saving enough to finance their retirement years and they are not planning sufficiently for what will happen to their savings after they retire.

---

4 Barber and Odean (1999, 2000, 2001) and Odean (1998, 1999).

2.5 The Importance of Asset Allocation

Guided by the policy statement, the investor must allocate funds into different asset classes. This process, *asset allocation,* is usually expressed in ranges. This allows the investment manager some freedom, based on his or her reading of capital market trends, to invest toward the upper or lower end of the ranges. For example, suppose a policy statement requires that common stocks be 60% to 80% of the value of the portfolio and that bonds should be 20% to 40% of the portfolio's value. If a manager is particularly bullish about stocks, she will increase the allocation of stocks toward the 80% upper end of the equity range with bonds making up the remaining 20%. Should she be optimistic about bonds or bearish on stocks, that manager may shift the allocation closer to 40% invested in bonds with the remainder in equities.

A review of historical data and empirical studies provides strong support for the contention that a critical component of the portfolio management process is the asset allocation decision. In general, there are four decisions involved in constructing an investment strategy:

- What asset classes should be considered for investment?
- What policy weights should be assigned to each eligible asset class?
- What are the allowable allocation ranges based on policy weights?
- What specific securities or funds should be purchased for the portfolio?

The asset allocation decision involves the first three points. How important is the asset allocation decision to an investor? In a word, *very.* Several studies[5] have examined the effect of the normal policy weights on investment performance, using data from both pension funds and mutual funds, during time periods extending from the early 1970s to the late 1990s. The studies all found similar results: About 90% of a fund's returns over time can be explained by its target asset allocation policy. Exhibit 2.8 shows the relationship between returns on the target or policy portfolio allocation and actual returns on a sample mutual fund.

Rather than looking at just one fund and how the target asset allocation determines its returns, some studies have looked at how much the asset allocation policy affects returns on a variety of funds with different target weights. For example, Ibbotson and Kaplan (2000) found that, across a sample of funds, about 40% of the difference in fund returns is explained by differences in asset allocation policy. And what does asset allocation tell us about the *level* of a particular fund's returns? The studies by Brinson and colleagues (1986, 1991) and Ibbotson and Kaplan (2000) answered that question as well. They divided the policy return (what the fund return would have been had it invested in indices at the policy weights) by the actual fund return (which includes the effects of varying from the policy weights and security selection). Thus, a fund that was passively invested at the target weights would have a ratio value of 1.0, or 100%. A fund managed by someone with skill in market timing (for moving in and out of asset classes) and security selection would have a ratio less than 1.0 (or less than 100%); the manager's skill would result in a policy return less than the actual fund return. The studies showed the opposite: The policy-return/actual-return ratio averaged over 1.0, showing that asset allocation explains slightly more than 100% of the level of a fund's returns. Because of market efficiency, fund managers practising market timing and security selection, on average, have difficulty surpassing passively invested index returns, after taking into account the expenses and fees of investing.

Thus, asset allocation is a very important decision. Across all funds, the asset allocation decision explains an average of 40% of the variation in fund returns. For a single fund, asset

---

5 Ibbotson and Kaplan (2000); Brinson, Hood, and Beebower (1986); and Brinson, Singer, and Beebower (1991).

allocation explains 90% of the fund's variation in returns over time and slightly more than 100% of the average fund's level of return.

Good investment managers may add some value to portfolio performance, but the major source of investment return—and risk—over time is the asset allocation decision (Brown, 2000).

2.5.1   Real Investment Returns after Taxes and Costs

Exhibit 2.7 provides additional historical perspectives on returns. It indicates how an investment of $1 would have grown over the 1988–2008 period and, using fairly conservative assumptions, examines how investment returns are affected by taxes and inflation.

Focusing first on stocks, funds invested in 1988 in the S&P/TSX composite index would have averaged a 10.0% annual return by mid-2008. Unfortunately, this return is unrealistic because if the funds were invested over time, taxes would have to be paid and inflation would erode the real purchasing power of the invested funds.

But the major reduction in the value of our investment is caused by inflation. The real after-tax average annual return on a stock over this time frame was only 7.6%, which is quite a bit less than our initial unadjusted 10.0% return!

Exhibit 2.7	The Effect of Taxes and Inflation on Investment Returns: 1988–2008			
	Before Taxes and Inflation	After Taxes	After Taxes and Inflation	After Inflation Only
Common Stocks	10.00%	8.00%	5.60%	7.60%
Long-Term Bond	8.70%	6.26%	3.86%	6.30%
T-Bill	5.75%	4.14%	1.74%	3.35%

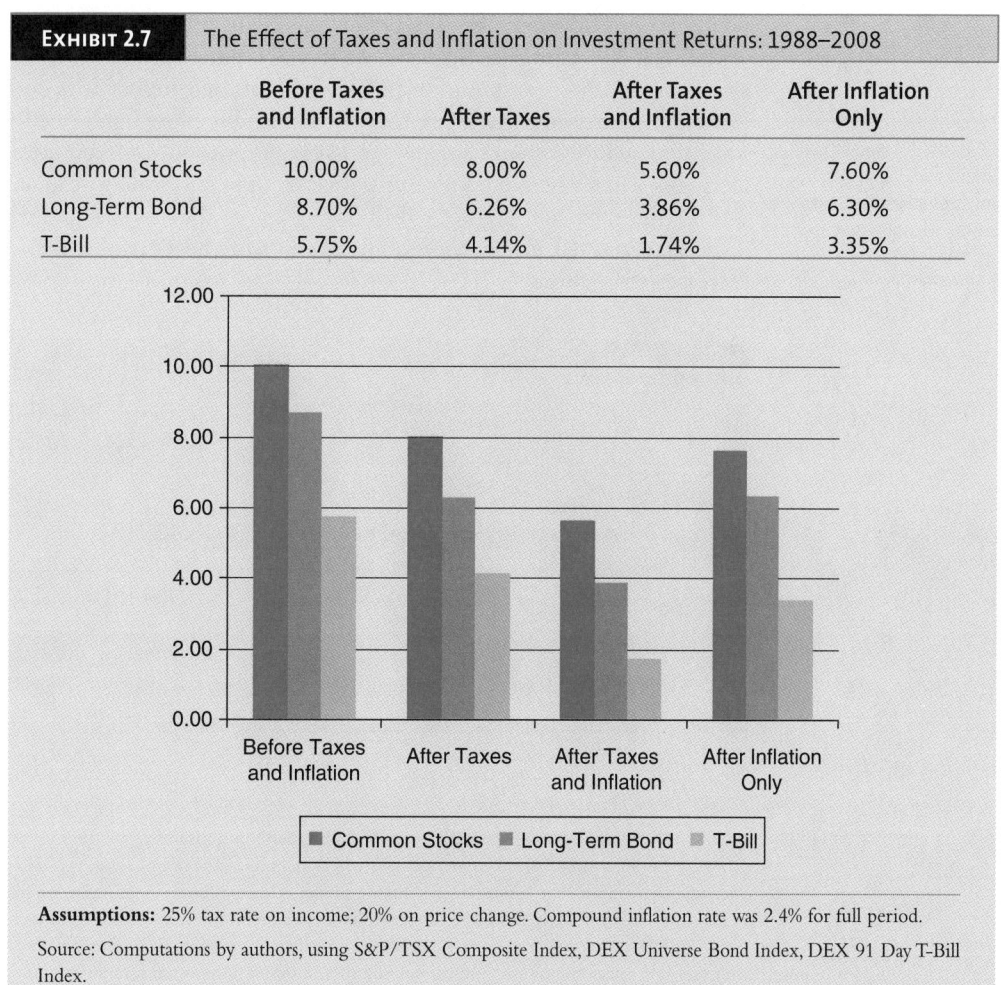

Assumptions: 25% tax rate on income; 20% on price change. Compound inflation rate was 2.4% for full period.

Source: Computations by authors, using S&P/TSX Composite Index, DEX Universe Bond Index, DEX 91 Day T-Bill Index.

The example in Exhibit 2.7 shows the long-run impact of taxes and inflation on the real value of a stock portfolio. For bonds and T-bills, however, the results in Exhibit 2.7 show something even more surprising. After adjusting for taxes, bonds[6] maintained their purchasing power; T-bills barely provided value in real terms. One dollar invested in bonds in 1988 gave the investor an annual average after-tax real return of 3.86%. An investment in T-bills earned an average rate of only 1.74% after taxes and inflation.

This historical analysis demonstrates that for a taxable portfolio that does not include a substantial commitment to common stocks makes it difficult for the portfolio to maintain real value over time.[7]

Notably, the fourth column, labelled "After Inflation Only," is more encouraging because it refers to results for a tax-free retirement account that is only impacted by inflation. These results should encourage investors to take advantage of tax-free opportunities.

2.5.2 Returns and Risks of Different Asset Classes

By focusing on returns, we have ignored its partner—risk. Assets with higher long-term returns have these returns to compensate for their risk. Exhibit 2.8 illustrates returns (unadjusted for costs and taxes) for several asset classes over time. As expected, the higher returns available from equities (both large cap and small cap) come at the cost of higher risk. This is precisely why investors need a policy statement and why the investor and manager must understand the capital markets and have a disciplined approach to investing. Safe T-bills will sometimes outperform equities, and, because of their higher risk, common stocks sometimes lose significant value. These are times when undisciplined and uneducated investors become frustrated, sell their stocks at a loss, and vow never to invest in equities again. In contrast, these are times when disciplined investors stick to their investment plan and position their portfolios for the next bull market.[8] By holding on to their stocks and continuing to purchasing more at depressed prices, the equity portion of the portfolio will experience a substantial increase in the future.

Ibbotson is a wealth of information helpful to the investor education and asset allocation process; go to http://www.ibbotson.com.

Exhibit 2.8	Summary Statistics of Annual Returns, 1981–2007, Canadian Securities		
	Geometric Mean (%)	Arithmetic Mean (%)	Standard Deviation (%)
Large company stocks (S&P/TSX Composite)	9.86%	10.80%	14.28%
Small company stocks (S&P/TSX Small Cap)	12.25%	12.79%	11.42%
Government of Canada (CANSIM)	7.97%	8.00%	2.88%
Corporate bonds (CANSIM)	8.93%	8.97%	2.88%
30-day Treasury bill	7.17%	7.25%	4.11%
Consumer Price Index (CANSIM)	3.14%	3.16%	2.08%

Source: Calculations by authors, using data noted. Small Cap from 2003–2006.

---

6 The DEX Universe Bond Index tracks the broad Canadian Bond Market.

7 Of course, other equity-oriented investments, such as venture capital or real estate, may also provide inflation protection after adjusting for portfolio costs and taxes. Future studies of the performance of inflation-protected securities (real return bonds, or RRBs) will likely show their usefulness in protecting investors from inflation as well.

8 Newton's law of gravity seems to work two ways in financial markets. What goes up must come down; it also appears over time that what goes down may come back up. Contrarian investors and some "value" investors use this concept of reversion to the mean to try to outperform the indexes over time.

The asset allocation decision determines to a great extent both the returns and the volatility of the portfolio. Looking at Exhibit 2.8 we can quickly conclude that stocks are riskier than bonds or T-bills. If we were to investigate the annual returns of these various investments we would find that stocks have sometimes experienced returns lower than those of T-bills, in some cases for extended periods of time (see Exhibit 2.9). Thus, having the discipline to stick with an investment policy through difficult times is necessary to provide attractive long-term rates of return.[9]

EXHIBIT 2.9	Holding Period Returns between Equities and T-Bills: 1981–2007
Length of Holding Period (calendar years)	Percentage of Periods that Stock Returns Trailed T-Bill Returns[*]
1	40.7%
5	34.8%
10	27.8%

[*] Price change plus reinvested income

Source: Authors' calculations.

Although we often measure risk by examining the variability of returns over time (standard deviation), this measure alone does not give the whole story. Another intriguing measure of risk is the probability of *not* meeting your investment return objective. From this perspective, the results in Exhibit 2.9 show that if the investor has a long time horizon, the risk of equities is small and that of T-bills is large because of their differences in long-term expected returns.[10] That is, investing in T-bills may actually be a riskier strategy than investing in common stocks because of the risk of not meeting long-term investment return goals after considering the impact of inflation and taxes.

Cultural Differences Thus far, our analysis has focused on Canadian investors. Foreign investors make their asset allocation decisions in much the same manner; but because they face different social, economic, political, and tax environments, their allocation decisions differ from those of Canadian investors. Exhibit 2.10 shows the equity allocations of pension funds in several countries. As shown, the equity allocations vary dramatically from 64% in Hong Kong to 46% in Japan and only 28% in Germany.

National demographic and economic differences can explain much of the divergent portfolio strategies. Of these nations, Germany and Japan have the greatest population over age 60, and the lowest is in the United States and the United Kingdom, which helps explain the greater use of equities in the U.S., as well as the government privatization programs during the 1980s in the U.K. that encouraged equity ownership among individual and institutional investors. Further, since 1980, the cost of living in the U.K. has increased at nearly double that of Germany, and this inflationary bias favours higher equity allocations. Further, many Germans are more risk averse and consider stock investing a form of gambling. Although this attitude is changing, the

---

9 The added benefits of diversification—combining different asset classes in the portfolio—may reduce overall portfolio risk without harming potential return. The topic of diversification is discussed in Chapter 6.

10 The percentage of periods that stock returns trailed T-bills is somewhat higher than one might expect. This is owed in part to the short time period used (27 years) and the high-interest-rate environment of the early 1980s.

EXHIBIT 2.10	Equity Allocations in Pension Fund Portfolios, 2007

Country	Percentage in Equities
Hong Kong	64%
United Kingdom	64%
Ireland	62%
United States	59%
Canada	52%
Japan	46%
Germany	28%

Source: 2008 Global Pension Assets Study, Watson Wyatt Worldwide, January 2008

German stock market remains relatively illiquid. Exhibit 2.11 shows a positive relationship between the level of inflation in a country and its pension fund allocation to equity. These results indicate that the general economic environment and its demographics have an effect on the asset allocation in a country.

EXHIBIT 2.11	Asset Allocation and Inflation for Different Countries' Equity Allocation as of December 2007; Average Inflation Measured over the 2003–2007 Period

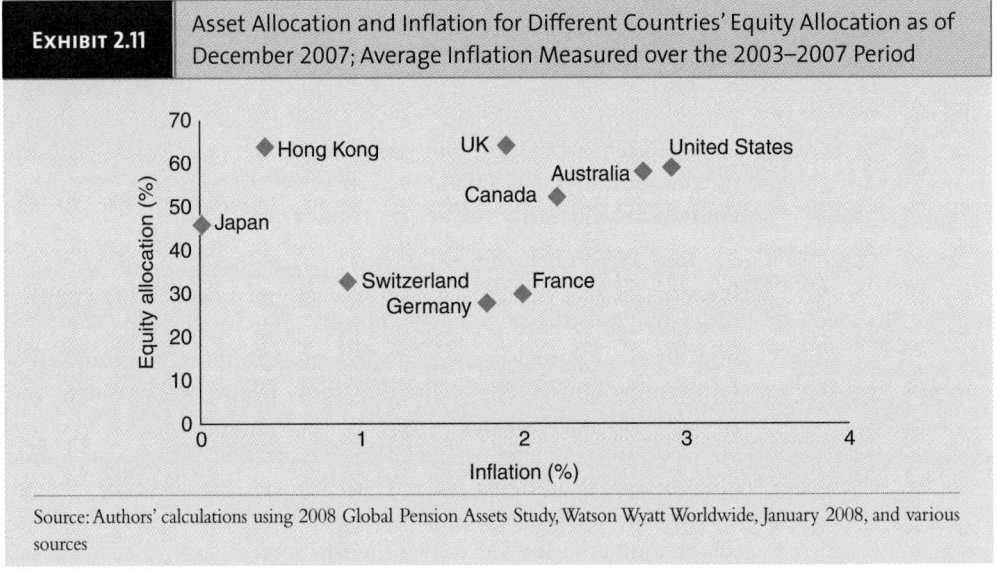

Source: Authors' calculations using 2008 Global Pension Assets Study, Watson Wyatt Worldwide, January 2008, and various sources

Other Organisation for Economic Co-operation and Development (OECD) countries place regulatory restrictions on institutional investors. For example, in Germany, institutional investors must have more than 35% of their assets in listed equities. Finland places a 10% limit on investments outside its borders by pension funds while French pension funds must invest a minimum of 50% in EU government bonds.

Thus, while asset allocation policy and strategy are determined in the context of an investor's objectives and constraints, there are many factors that explain differences in investor behaviour across countries, including their demographics, as well as the political and economic environments.

Summary

1. Investors need to prudently manage risk within the context of their investment goals and preferences.
2. An investment policy statement must be prepared before implementing an investment plan. By forcing investors to examine their needs, risk tolerance, and familiarity with the capital markets, policy statements help investors correctly identify appropriate objectives and constraints. In addition, the policy statement provides a standard by which to evaluate the performance of the portfolio manager.
3. Income, spending, and investing behaviour will change over a person's lifetime. How individuals structure their financial plans should be related to their age, financial status, future plans, risk-aversion characteristics, and needs.
4. The portfolio management process begins with establishing a policy statement; from there an investor can develop an investment strategy to address his or her needs. Once that has been done, the investor then implements the strategy by purchasing the various investments. Finally, the investor must monitor and update both the portfolio and policy in light of changes in the marketplace and the investor's situation.

5. The asset allocation decision, not the selection of specific stocks or investments, determines most of the portfolio's returns over time. Although seemingly risky, investors seeking capital appreciation, income, or even capital preservation over the long term should allocate a sizable proportion of their portfolio to equities.
6. Asset allocation decisions impact on a portfolio's returns. An investor must carefully examine which asset classes are suitable to invest in, what weights should be allocated and what ranges are acceptable, and whether various securities or funds are the better investment.
7. Asset allocation strategies differ across national boundaries for cultural, political, tax, and economic reasons.
8. Institutional investors must deal with many issues similar to individual investors; however, they also find there are a number of additional regulations and tax issues that must be addressed. Each type of institution has a set of investment objectives and constraints that are similar; however, given the wide variety of needs that these institutions have, each need a specific set of objectives and investment strategies.

Key Terms

accumulation phase, p. 27
asset allocation, p. 25
asset class, p. 25
average tax rate, p. 37
benchmark portfolio, p. 31
capital appreciation, p. 34
capital preservation, p. 34
consolidation phase, p. 27

construct the portfolio, p. 30
continual monitoring, p. 30
current income, p. 35
dividend, p. 36
gifting phase, p. 28
liquid, p. 36
long-term, high-priority goal, p. 29
lower priority goal, p. 29

marginal tax rate, p. 36
near-term, high-priority goal, p. 28
objectives, p. 32
policy statement, p. 29
realized capital gains, p. 36
spending phase, p. 28
total return, p. 35
unrealized capital gains, p. 36

Suggested Readings

Miller, Janet T., ed. *Investment Counseling for Private Clients, III.* Charlottesville, VA: AIMR, 2001.

Mitchell, Roger S., ed. *Investment Counseling for Private Clients, II.* Charlottesville, VA: AIMR, 2000.

Pompian, Michael M., *Behaviorial Finance and Wealth Management: How to Build Optimal Portfolios that Account for Investor Biases,* John Wiley & Sons, 2006.

Solin, Daniel, *Smartest Investment Book You'll Ever Read,* Canadian Edition, Viking Canada, 2007.

For Chapter CFA Questions and Problems, please see Appendix A at the end of this text.

Questions

1. "Young people with little wealth should not invest money in risky assets such as the stock market, because they can't afford to lose what little money they have." Do you agree or disagree with this statement? Why?

2. Your healthy 63-year-old neighbour is about to retire and comes to you for advice. From talking with her, you find out she was planning on taking all the money out of her company's retirement plan and investing it in bond mutual funds and money market funds. What advice should you give her?

3. Discuss how an individual's investment strategy may change as he or she goes through the accumulation, consolidation, spending, and gifting phases of life.

4. Why is a policy statement important?

5. Use the questionnaire "How much risk is right for you?" (Exhibit 2.4, p. 33) to determine your risk tolerance.

Use this information to help write a policy statement for yourself.

6. Your 45-year-old uncle is 20 years away from retirement; your 35-year-old older sister is about 30 years away from retirement. How might their investment policy statements differ?

7. What information is necessary before a financial planner can assist a person in constructing an investment policy statement?

8. Use the Internet to find the websites for some financial-planning firms. What strategies do they emphasize? What do they say about their asset allocation strategy? What are their firms' emphases—for example, value investing, international diversification, principal preservation, retirement and estate planning?

Problems

1. Suppose your first job pays you $45,000 annually. What percentage should your cash reserve contain? How much life insurance should you carry if you are unmarried? How much if you are married with two young children?

2. What is the marginal tax rate for an Ontario resident if her taxable income is $20,000? $40,000? $80,000? What is her tax bill for each of these income levels? What is her average tax rate for each of these income levels? Use the 2009 rates on page 37.

3. a. Someone in the 29% tax bracket can earn 9% annually on her investments in a tax-exempt RSP account. What will be the value of a one-time $10,000 investment in 5 years? 10 years? 20 years?

   b. Suppose the preceding 9% return is taxable rather than tax-deferred and the taxes are paid annually. What will be the after-tax value of her $10,000 investment after 5, 10, and 20 years?

4. a. An Ontario resident in the lowest tax bracket (21.05% combined in 2009) can earn 10% on his investments in a tax-exempt RSP account. What will be the value of a $10,000 investment in 5 years? 10 years? 20 years?

   b. Suppose the preceding 10% return is taxable rather than tax-deferred. What will be the after-tax value of his $10,000 investment after 5, 10, and 20 years?

5. An investor is deliberating between a term deposit at a bank with a guaranteed return of 4% per annum and a credit union's inflation protection fixed date deposit that pays 2% per annum plus annual inflation rate. Both investments are for two years.

   a. If the investor anticipates inflation in the first year will be 1.5%, what is the maximum inflation rate that can occur in the second year in order to make the investor indifferent to either deposit?

   b. Which investment is likely safer, at least from a potential return standpoint?

OBJECTIVES AND CONSTRAINTS OF INSTITUTIONAL INVESTORS

Institutional investors manage large sums of money in the course of their business. They include mutual funds, pension funds, insurance firms, endowments, and banks. In this appendix, we review the characteristics of various institutional investors and discuss their typical investment objectives and constraints.

Mutual Funds

A number of mutual funds publish their investment objectives and strategies. An example can be found at Ethical Global Equity Fund's website at https://www.ethicalfunds. com/en/Investor/ Investments/ FundsAndSolutions/ EthicalFunds/Pages/ EthicalGlobalEquity FundClassA.aspx.

A mutual fund pools sums of money from investors, which are then invested in financial assets. Each mutual fund has its own investment objective, such as capital appreciation, high current income, or money market income. A mutual fund will state its investment objective, and investors choose the funds in which to invest. Two basic constraints face mutual funds: those created by law to protect mutual fund investors and those that represent choices made by the mutual fund's managers. Some of these constraints will be discussed in the mutual fund's prospectus, which must be given to all prospective investors before they purchase shares in a mutual fund. Mutual funds are discussed in more detail in Chapter 17.

Pension Funds

Pension funds are a major component of retirement planning for individuals. As of 2007, pension assets were nearly $25 trillion in the 11 largest pension markets. Basically, a firm's pension fund receives contributions from the firm, its employees, or both. The funds are invested with the purpose of giving workers either a lump-sum payment or the promise of an income stream after their retirement. **Defined benefit pension plans** promise to pay retirees a specific income stream after retirement. The size of the benefit is usually based on factors that include the worker's salary, or time of service, or both. The company contributes a certain amount each year to the pension plan; the size of the contribution depends on assumptions concerning future salary increases and the rate of return to be earned on the plan's assets. Under a defined benefit plan, the company carries the risk of paying the future pension benefit to retirees; should investment performance be poor, or should the company be unable to make adequate contributions to the plan, the shortfall must be made up in future years. "Poor" investment performance means the actual return on the plan's assets fell below the assumed **actuarial rate of return**. The actuarial rate is the discount rate used to find the present value of the plan's future obligations and thus this rate determines the size of the firm's annual contribution to the pension plan.

Defined contribution pension plans do not promise set benefits but only specified contributions to the plan. As a result, employees' benefits depend on the size of the contributions made to the pension fund and the returns earned on the fund's investments. Thus, the plan's risk related to the rates of return on investments is borne by the employee. Unlike a defined benefit plan, employees' retirement income is not an obligation of the firm.

A pension plan's objectives and constraints depend on whether the plan is a *defined benefit plan* or a *defined contribution plan*. We review each separately below.

Defined Benefit

The plan's risk tolerance depends on the plan's funding status and its actuarial rate. For **underfunded plans** (where the present value of the fund's liabilities to employees exceeds the value of the fund's assets), a more conservative approach toward risk is taken to ensure that the funding gap is closed over time. This may entail a strategy whereby the firm makes larger plan contributions and assumes a lower actuarial rate. **Overfunded plans** (where the present value of the pension liabilities is less than the plan's assets) allow a more aggressive investment strategy, which implies a higher actuarial rate. This allows the firm to reduce its contributions and increases the risk exposure of the plan. The return objective is to meet the plan's actuarial rate of return, which is set by actuaries who estimate future pension obligations based on assumptions about future salary increases, current salaries, retirement patterns, worker life expectancies, and the firm's benefit formula. Obviously, the actuarial rate helps determine the size of the firm's plan contributions over time.

The liquidity constraint on defined benefit funds is mainly a function of the average age of employees. A younger employee base means less liquidity is needed; an older employee base generally means more liquidity is needed to pay current pension obligations to retirees. The time-horizon constraint is also affected by the average age of employees, although some experts recommend using a 5- to 10-year horizon for planning purposes. Taxes are not a major concern to the plan, because pension plans are generally exempt from paying tax on investment returns. The major legal constraint is that the plan must be run in accordance with the pension standards legislation that is governed provincially, and investments must satisfy the "prudent-person" standard when evaluated in the context of the overall pension plan's portfolio.

Defined Contribution

Notably, the individual employee decides how his or her contributions to the plan are to be invested. As a result, the objectives and constraints for defined contribution plans depend on the individual. Because the employee, rather than the firm, carries the risk of inadequate retirement funding, defined contribution plans are generally more conservatively invested (the majority of research indicates that employees tend to be too conservative). If, however, the plan is considered part of an estate-planning tool for a wealthy founder or officer of the firm, a higher risk tolerance and return objective are appropriate because most of the plan's assets will ultimately be owned by the individual's heirs.

The liquidity and time horizon needs for the plan differ depending on the average age of the individual employees and the degree of employee turnover within the firm. Similar to defined benefit plans, defined contribution plans are generally tax-exempt and are governed by the provisions of various provincial legislation.

Endowment Funds

Endowment funds arise from contributions made to charitable or educational institutions. Rather than immediately spending the funds, the organization invests the money for the purpose of providing a future stream of income to the organization. The investment policy of an endowment fund is the result of a "tension" between the organization's need for current income and the desire for a growing future stream of income to protect against inflation.

To meet the institution's operating budget needs, the fund's return objective is often set by adding the spending rate (the amount taken out of the funds each year) and the expected inflation rate. Funds that have more risk-tolerant trustees may have a higher spending rate than those overseen by more risk-averse trustees. Because a total return approach usually serves to meet the return objective over time, the organization is generally withdrawing both income and capital gain returns to meet budgeted needs. The risk tolerance of an endowment fund is largely affected by the collective risk tolerance of the organization's trustees.

Due to the fund's long-term time horizon, liquidity requirements are minor except for the need to spend part of the endowment each year and maintain a cash reserve for emergencies. Many endowments are tax-exempt, although income from some can be taxed. Regulatory and legal constraints arise on the state level, where most endowments are regulated. Unique needs and preferences may affect investment strategies, especially among university or religious endowments, which may have strong preferences about social investing issues.

Insurance Companies

The investment objectives and constraints for an insurance company depend on whether it is a life insurance company or a non-life (such as a property and casualty) insurance firm.

Life Insurance Companies

Except for firms dealing only in term life insurance, life insurance firms collect premiums during a person's lifetime that must be invested until a death benefit is paid to the insurance contract's beneficiaries. At any time, the insured can turn in her policy and receive its cash surrender value. Discussing investment policy for an insurance firm is also complicated by the insurance industry's proliferation of insurance and quasi-investment products.

Basically, an insurance company wants to earn a positive "spread," which is the difference between the return on investment minus the return it credits its various policyholders. This concept is similar to a defined benefit pension fund that tries to earn a return in excess of its actuarial rate. If the spread is positive, the insurance firm's surplus reserve account rises; if not, the surplus account declines by an amount reflecting the negative spread. A growing surplus is an important competitive tool for life insurance companies. Attractive investment returns allow the company to advertise better policy returns than those of its competitors. A growing surplus also allows the firm to offer new products and expand insurance volume.

Because life insurance companies are quasi-trust funds for savings, fiduciary principles limit the risk tolerance of the invested funds. The Office of the Superintendent of Financial Institutions (OSFI) establishes risk categories for bonds and stocks. Regulation of these companies is the shared responsibility of the federal and provincial governments.

Insurance companies' liquidity needs have increased over the years due to increases in policy surrenders and product-mix changes. A company's time horizon depends upon its specific product mix. Life insurance policies require longer term investments, whereas guaranteed insurance contracts (GICs) and shorter term annuities require shorter investment time horizons.

Non-life Insurance Companies

Cash outflows are somewhat predictable for life insurance firms, based on their mortality tables. In contrast, the cash flows required by major accidents, disasters, and lawsuit settlements are not as predictable for non-life insurance firms.

Due to their fiduciary responsibility to claimants, risk exposures are low to moderate. Depending on the specific company and competitive pressures, premiums may be affected by both the probability of a claim and the investment returns earned by the firm. Typically, casualty insurance firms invest their insurance reserves in relatively safe bonds to provide needed income to pay claims; capital and surplus funds are invested in equities for their growth potential. As with life insurers, property and casualty firms have a stronger competitive position when their surplus accounts are larger than those of their competitors. Many insurers now focus on a total return objective as a means to increase their surplus accounts over time.

Because of uncertain claim patterns, liquidity is a concern for property and casualty insurers who also want liquidity so that they can switch between taxable and tax-exempt investments as their underwriting activities generate losses and profits. The time horizon for investments is typically shorter than that of life insurers, although many invest in long-term bonds to earn the higher yields available on these instruments. Investing strategy for the firm's surplus account focuses on long-term growth.

Regulation of property and casualty firms is more permissive than for life insurers. Similar to life companies, federal or provincial regulations specify classes and quality of investments for a certain percentage of the firm's assets. Beyond this restriction, insurers can invest in many different types and qualities of instruments, although some provinces limit the proportion that can be invested in real estate assets.

Banks

Pension funds, endowments, and insurance firms obtain virtually free funds for investment purposes. Not so with banks. To have funds to lend, they must attract investors in a competitive interest rate environment. They compete against other banks and also against companies that offer other investment vehicles, from bonds to common stocks. A bank's success relies primarily on its ability to generate returns in excess of its funding costs.

A bank tries to maintain a positive difference between its cost of funds and its returns on assets. If banks anticipate falling interest rates, they will try to invest in longer term assets to lock in the returns while seeking short-term deposits, whose interest cost is expected to fall over time. When banks expect rising rates, they will try to lock in longer term deposits with fixed-interest costs, while investing funds short term to capture rising interest rates. The risk of such strategies is that losses may occur should a bank incorrectly forecast the direction of interest rates. The aggressiveness of a bank's strategy will be related to the size of its capital ratio and the oversight of regulators.

Banks need substantial liquidity to meet withdrawals and loan demand. A bank has two forms of liquidity. *Internal liquidity* is provided by a bank's investment portfolio that includes highly liquid assets. A bank has *external liquidity* if it can borrow funds in the interbank markets (where banks lend reserves to other banks), from the Bank of Canada, or if it can sell certificates of deposit at attractive rates.

Banks have a short time horizon for several reasons. First, they have a strong need for liquidity. Second, because they want to maintain an adequate interest revenue–interest expense spread, they generally focus on shorter term investments to avoid interest rate risk and to avoid getting "locked in" to a long-term revenue source. Third, because banks typically offer short-term deposit accounts (demand deposits, chequing accounts, and such) they need to match the maturity of their assets and liabilities to avoid taking undue risks.[11] This desire to match the maturity of assets and liabilities is shared by virtually all financial institutions.

Banks are heavily regulated, with the OSFI, Bank of Canada, and the Canada Deposit Insurance Corporation overseeing various components of bank operations. Unique situations that affect each bank's investment policy depend on their size, market, and management skills in matching asset and liability sensitivity to interest rates.

Institutional Investment Summary

Among the great variety of institutions, each institution has its "typical" investment objectives and constraints. This discussion has indicated the differences that exist among types of institutions and some of the major issues confronting them. Notably, just as with individual investors, "cookie-cutter" policy statements are inappropriate for institutional investors. The specific objectives, constraints, and investment strategies must be determined on a case-by-case basis.

Key Terms

actuarial rate of return, p. 47
defined benefit pension plan, p. 47
defined contribution pension plan, p. 47

overfunded plan, p. 48
underfunded plan, p. 47

---

11 An asset/liability mismatch caused the ultimate downfall of savings and loan (S&Ls) associations in the U.S. They attracted short-term liabilities (deposit accounts) and invested in long-term assets (mortgages). When interest rates became more volatile in the early 1980s and short-term rates increased dramatically, S&Ls experienced negative spreads and suffered significant losses.

Selecting Investments in a Global Market*

After you read this chapter, you should be able to answer the following questions:

1. Why should investors have a global perspective regarding their investments?

2. What has happened to the relative size of Canadian and foreign stock and bond markets?

3. What are the differences in the rates of return on Canadian and foreign securities markets?

4. Is there additional advantage to diversifying in international markets beyond the benefits of domestic diversification?

5. What alternative securities are available? What are their cash flow and risk properties?

Individuals are willing to defer current consumption for many reasons. Thus far, we have said little about the investment opportunities available in financial markets. In this chapter, we address this issue by surveying investment alternatives. This is an essential background for making the asset allocation decision discussed in Chapter 2, as well as for later chapters where we analyze investments, such as bonds, common stock, and other securities. It is also important when we consider how to construct and evaluate portfolios of investments.

As an investor in the 21st century, you have an array of investment choices unavailable a few decades ago. A combination of dynamic financial markets, technological advances, and new regulations have resulted in many new investment instruments and expanded trading opportunities in both domestic and global markets. Telecommunications networks enable brokers to reach security exchanges in London, Tokyo, and other European, Asian, and American cities as easily as those in Toronto. The competitive environment in the brokerage industry and the deregulation of the banking sector have made it possible for more financial institutions to compete for investor dollars. This has spawned investment vehicles with a variety of maturities, risk-return characteristics, and cash flow patterns. In this chapter, we examine some of these choices.

As an investor, you need to understand the differences among investments so that you can build a properly diversified **portfolio** that conforms to your objectives. If chosen carefully, such portfolios minimize risk for a given level of return because low or negative returns on some investments over time are offset by above-average returns on others. Your goal should be to build a balanced portfolio of investments with a relatively stable return. An appreciation of alternative security types is the starting point for this analysis.

This chapter is divided into three main sections. Because investors can choose securities from around the world, we initially look at a combination of reasons why investors *should* include both foreign and domestic securities in their portfolios. Secondly, we

---

* The authors acknowledge data collection help on this chapter from Edgar Norton of Illinois State University, David J. Wright from the University of Wisconsin—Parkside, and Katrina Montgomery and Tony Zaremba from the University of Calgary.

describe the main features and cash flow patterns of securities in domestic and global markets. You will see that the varying risk-return characteristics of alternative investments suit the preferences of different investors. Lastly, we examine the historical risk and return performance of several investments from around the world and the relationship among the returns for many of these securities. These results provide strong empirical support for global investing.

3.1 The Case for Global Investments

Twenty years ago, the bulk of investments available to individual investors consisted of stocks and bonds. Now, however, the click of a button or a call to your broker gives you access to a wide range of securities sold throughout the world.

Several changes have caused this explosion of investment opportunities. For one, the growth and development of numerous foreign financial markets, such as those in Japan, the United Kingdom, and Germany, as well as emerging markets, such as China and India, have made these markets accessible and viable for investors around the world. Investment firms have recognized this opportunity and established facilities in these countries aided by advances in technology that allow constant contact with offices and financial markets around the world. In addition, foreign firms and investors undertook counterbalancing initiatives, including significant mergers of firms and security exchanges. As a result, investors and investment firms can easily trade securities in markets around the world.

Three interrelated reasons investors should think of constructing global investment portfolios can be summarized as follows:

1. When investors compare the absolute and relative sizes of foreign markets for stocks and bonds, they see that ignoring foreign markets reduces their choices of available investment opportunities. Because more opportunities broaden the range of risk-return choices, it makes sense to evaluate foreign securities when selecting investments and building a portfolio.
2. The returns available on foreign securities often have substantially exceeded those for Canadian-only securities. The higher returns on these foreign *equities* can be justified by the higher growth rates for the countries where they are issued.
3. A major tenet of investment theory is that investors should diversify their portfolios. Because the relevant factor when diversifying a portfolio is low correlation between asset returns over time, diversification with foreign securities that have very low correlation with Canadian securities can substantially reduce portfolio risk.

In this section, we analyze these reasons to demonstrate the advantages to a growing role of foreign financial markets for investors and to assess the benefits and risks of trading in these markets.

3.1.1 RELATIVE SIZE OF FINANCIAL MARKETS

Prior to 1970, 65% of the securities traded in world capital markets were U.S. stocks and bonds. Therefore, an investor selecting securities strictly from U.S. markets had a fairly complete set of investments available. However, that situation has changed dramatically over the past four decades whereby almost 66% of the securities traded in world capital markets are outside the U.S. markets. Currently, investors who ignore stock and bond markets outside their borders limit their investment choices substantially.

This is confirmed with a quick glance at Exhibit 3.1. We can see that not only has the overall value of all securities increased dramatically (to $103 trillion), but the composition has also changed.

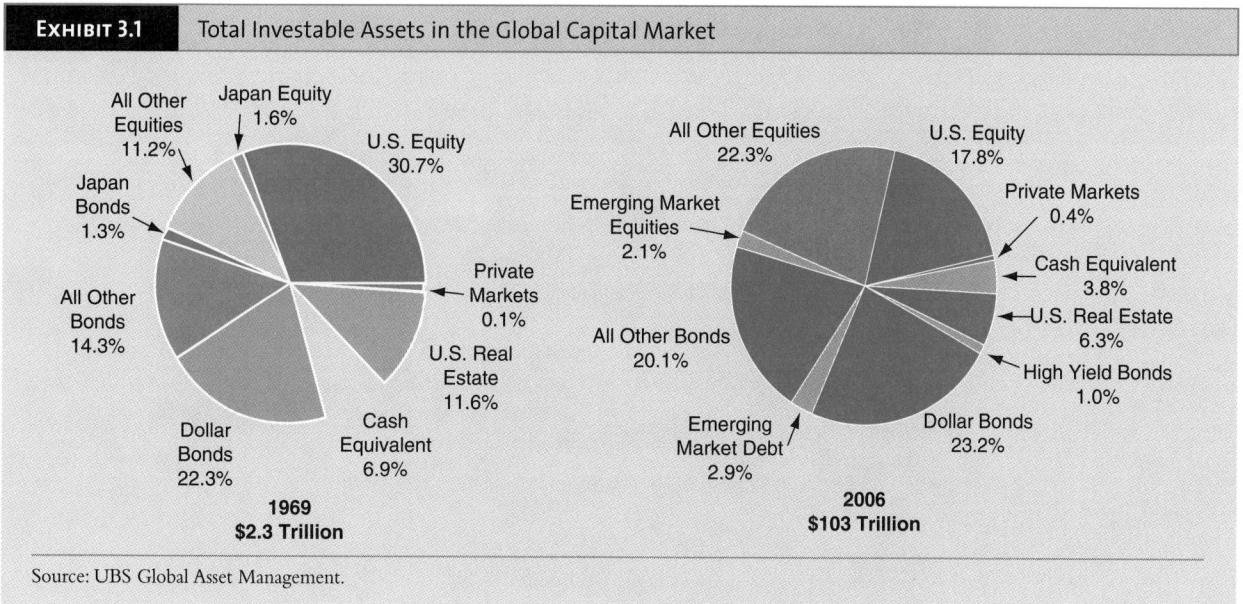

EXHIBIT 3.1   Total Investable Assets in the Global Capital Market

1969
$2.3 Trillion

2006
$103 Trillion

Source: UBS Global Asset Management.

3.1.2   RETURN ON DOMESTIC AND FOREIGN SECURITIES

An examination of the returns on Canadian and foreign securities not only demonstrates that many foreign securities provide superior return but also shows the impact of the exchange rate risk discussed in Chapter 1.

Global Bond-Market Returns   Exhibit 3.2 reports annual compound returns (in Canadian dollars) for several major international bond markets between 1999 and 2008. Exhibit 3.3 shows much the same, but in local currency terms. An analysis of the returns in Exhibit 3.2 indicates that the performance of the Canadian bond market ranked higher than the United States Part of the reason for the better performance had to do with the weaker Canadian dollar during this time frame (although it performed reasonably well against other currencies). Looking at Exhibit 3.3, we can see that, in local currency terms, the Canadian five-year average annual returns were higher than the other seven countries listed. The result was that foreign investors investing in Canadian bond markets enjoyed a boost to their returns.

EXHIBIT 3.2   Government Bond Annual Rates of Return in Canadian Dollars: 1999–2008

	Geometric Mean (%)
Canada	6.38
France	6.80
Germany	6.81
Japan	2.01
United Kingdom	1.72
United States	3.92

Source: Bloomberg.

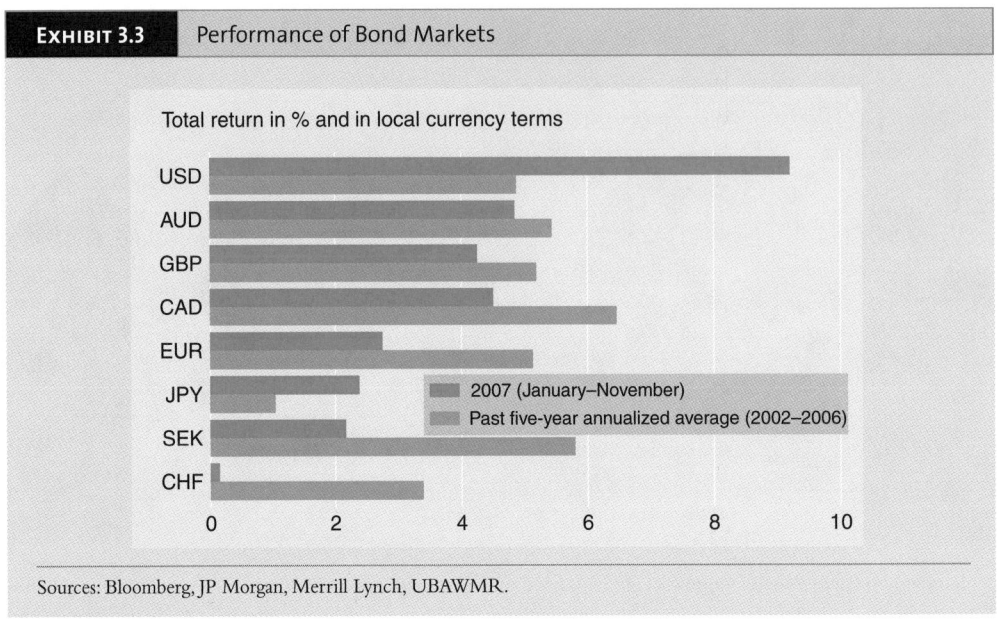

| Exhibit 3.3 | Performance of Bond Markets |

Sources: Bloomberg, JP Morgan, Merrill Lynch, UBAWMR.

Global Equity-Market Returns Exhibit 3.4 shows the annual returns in Canadian dollars for six major equity markets from 2002 through 2008. Note that the Canadian and Mexican markets had stellar results from 2003 through 2006.

These results for equity and bond markets around the world indicate that investors who limit themselves to their own domestic market may well experience returns below those in many other countries.

| Exhibit 3.4 | Annual Returns, in Canadian Dollars |

Performance of Various Indices

	Year 2008 Returns	Year 2007 Returns	Year 2006 Returns	Year 2005 Returns	Year 2004 Returns	Year 2003 Returns	Year 2002 Returns
Canada—S&P/TSX composite	−33.38	9.83%	17.26%	24.13%	14.48%	26.72%	−12.44%
United Kingdom— FTSE 100	−34.41	−7.27%	30.77%	4.81%	10.80%	7.25%	−14.02%
Japan—Nikkei 225	−8.05	−20.16%	7.12%	19.14%	4.76%	14.06%	−9.94%
Mexico—Bolsa	−25.02	−3.82%	47.82%	42.52%	39.14%	9.80%	−15.31%
Swiss	−10.69	−10.12%	27.27%	12.68%	7.56%	10.17%	−11.65%
United States—DJIA	−15.82	−7.44%	19.08%	−1.66%	−2.50%	5.16%	−15.75%
United States— S&P 500	−22.07	−10.28%	15.90%	1.41%	2.64%	5.59%	−22.78%

Source: Bloomberg.

3.1.3   RISK OF COMBINED COUNTRY INVESTMENTS

In Chapter 1, we considered the idea of combining a number of assets into a portfolio and noted that investors should create diversified portfolios to reduce the variability of the returns over time. To measure whether two investments will contribute to diversifying a portfolio we compute the correlation coefficient between their return over time. Correlation coefficients can range from +1.00 to −1.00. Combining investments that are perfectly positively correlated would not help diversify the portfolio because they have identical rate-of-return patterns over time. In contrast, combining two investments with large negative correlation in a portfolio would be ideal for diversification because it would stabilize the return over time, reducing the standard deviation of the portfolio returns and hence the risk of the portfolio. Therefore, if you want to diversify your portfolio and reduce your risk, you want an investment that has either *low positive correlation, zero correlation,* or, ideally, *negative correlation* with the other investments in your portfolio. With this in mind, the following discussion considers the correlations of returns among various investments globally.

Global Bond Portfolio Risk Exhibit 3.5 lists the correlation coefficients between Canadian bonds and bond returns for other countries in Canadian dollar terms from 1993 to April 2009. These low positive correlations among returns indicate that investors have substantial opportunities for risk reduction through global diversification of bond portfolios.

  Why do these correlation coefficients for returns between Canadian bonds and those of the other countries differ? That is, why is the Canada–U.S. correlation is 0.37 whereas the Canada–Japan correlation is only 0.093? The answer is because the international trade patterns, economic growth, fiscal policies, and monetary policies of the countries differ. We do not have an integrated world economy but, rather, a collection of economies that are related to one another in different ways. For example, the Canadian and U.S. economies are closely related due to geographic proximity, similar domestic economic policies, and the fact that each is the other's largest trading partner. In contrast, Canada has less trade with Japan and the fiscal and monetary policies of the two countries differ dramatically. For example, the Canadian economy was growing during much of the 1990s while the Japanese economy was in a recession.

Exhibit 3.5	Correlation Coefficients between Rates of Return on Government Bonds in Canada and Selected Foreign Markets: 1993–April 2009 (monthly data, in Canadian dollars)	
		Correlation Coefficient
	United States	0.370
	United Kingdom	0.282
	Germany	0.590
	Japan	0.093
	Switzerland	0.216

Source: Bloomberg.

  Therefore, macroeconomic differences cause the correlation of bond returns between the various countries to differ and these differing correlations make it worthwhile to diversify with foreign bonds. Keep in mind though that *the correlation of returns between a single pair of countries changes over time* because the factors influencing the correlations, such as international trade, economic growth, fiscal policy, and monetary policy, change over time. A change in any of these variables will produce a change in how the economies are related and in the relationship between returns on bonds.

  Exhibit 3.6 shows what happens to the risk-return trade-off when we combine Canadian and foreign bonds in a portfolio. Combining the two portfolios in different proportions provides

| **EXHIBIT 3.6** | Risk-Return Trade-Off for International Bond Portfolios |

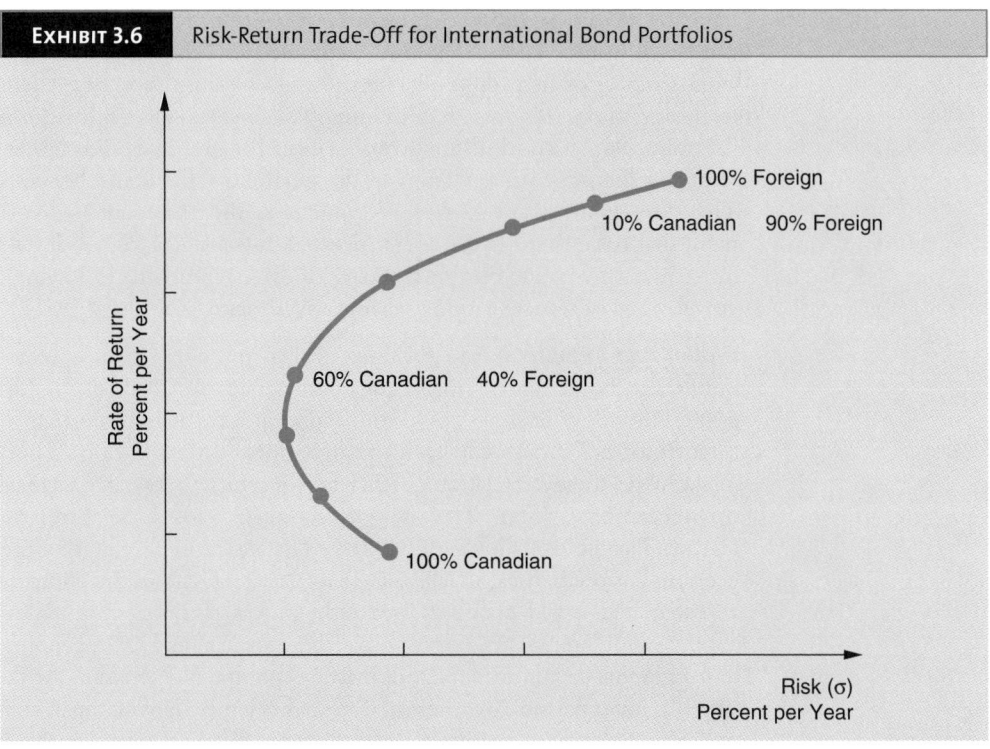

an interesting set of points. Because the correlations are less than one, the risk levels of the combined portfolios decline below those of the individual portfolios. Therefore, by adding foreign bonds that have low correlation with a portfolio of Canadian bonds, a Canadian investor is able to not only increase the bond portfolio's expected return but also reduce its risk as compared to a total Canadian bond portfolio.

Global Equity Portfolio Risk The correlation of world equity markets resembles that for bonds. Exhibit 3.7 lists the correlation coefficients in Canadian dollars between monthly equity returns of each country and the Canadian market between 1993 to March 2009.

These relatively small positive correlations between Canadian stocks and foreign stocks have similar implications to those derived for bonds. Investors can reduce the overall risk of their stock portfolios by including foreign stocks.

| **EXHIBIT 3.7** | Correlation Coefficients between Rates of Return on Common Stocks in Canada and Other Foreign Stock Markets: 1993–March 2009, in Canadian Dollars |

	Correlation Coefficient
United States—S&P 500	0.635
United States—DJIA	0.537
United States—Russell 3000[a]	0.692
Japan—Nikkei 225	0.389
United Kingdom—FTSE 100	0.538

[a] Russell 3000 data from 1996

Source: Correlation table computed by the authors using monthly data from Bloomberg.

Exhibit 3.8 demonstrates the impact of international equity diversification. These curves demonstrate that as you increase the number of randomly selected securities in a portfolio, the standard deviation will decline due to the benefits of diversification *within your own country.* This is referred to as *domestic diversification.* After a certain number of securities (30 to 40), the curve will flatten out at a risk level that reflects the basic market risk for the domestic economy. The lower curve illustrates the benefits of international diversification. This curve demonstrates that adding foreign securities to a Canadian portfolio to create a global portfolio enables an investor to experience lower overall risk because the foreign securities are not correlated with our economy or our stock market, allowing the investor to eliminate some of the basic market risks of the Canadian economy.

To see how this works, consider, for example, the effect of inflation and interest rates on all Canadian securities. As discussed in Chapter 1, all Canadian securities will be affected by

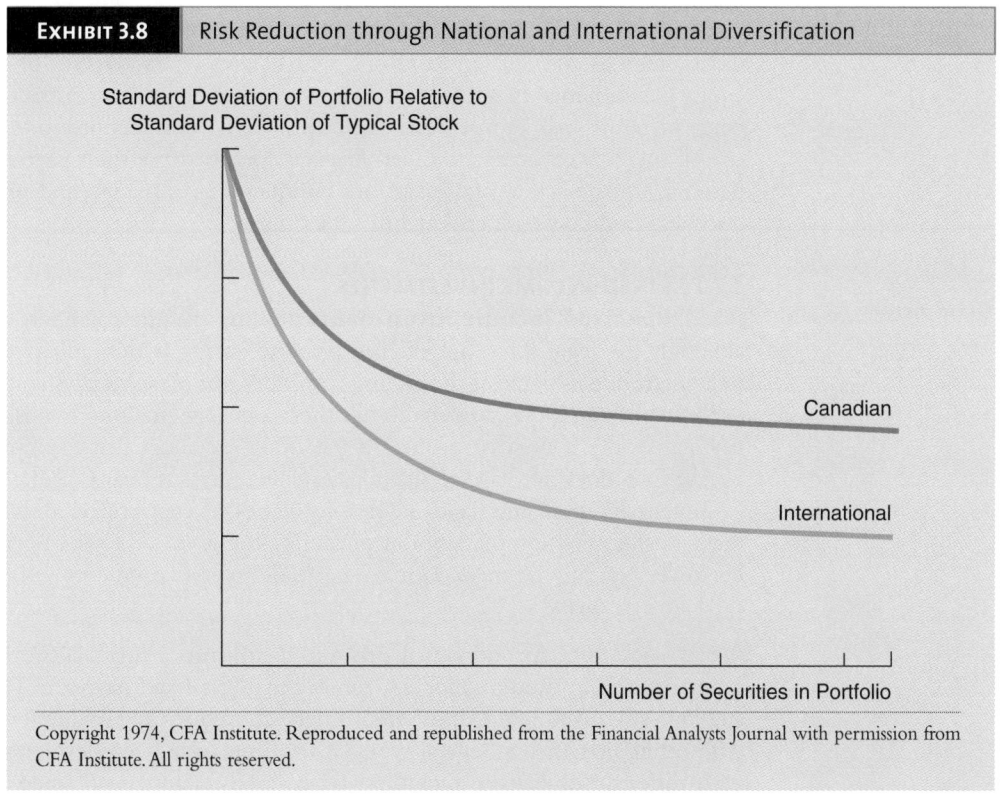

| **EXHIBIT 3.8** | Risk Reduction through National and International Diversification |

Copyright 1974, CFA Institute. Reproduced and republished from the Financial Analysts Journal with permission from CFA Institute. All rights reserved.

these variables. In contrast, a Japanese stock is mainly affected by what happens in the Japanese economy and will typically not be affected by changes in Canadian variables. Thus, adding Japanese, German, and Italian stocks to a Canadian stock portfolio reduces the portfolio risk of the global portfolio to a level that reflects only worldwide systematic factors.

Summary on Global Investing As promised, several rather compelling reasons exist for adding foreign securities to a Canadian portfolio. Therefore, developing a global investment perspective is important because such an approach has been shown to be justified, and this current trend in the investment world is expected to continue. Implementing this new global investment perspective will not be easy because it requires an understanding of new terms, instruments (such as Eurobonds), and institutions (such as foreign stock and bond markets). Still, the effort is justified because you are developing a set of skills and a way of thinking that will enhance your investing results.

The next section presents an overview of investment alternatives from around the world, beginning with fixed-income investments and progressing through numerous alternatives.

3.2 Global Investment Choices

This section provides an important foundation for subsequent chapters in which we describe techniques to value individual investments and combine alternative investments into properly diversified portfolios that conform to your risk-return objectives. In this section, we briefly describe the numerous investment alternatives available. Most of these assets will be described in greater detail in subsequent chapters.

The investments are divided by asset classes. First, we briefly describe fixed-income investments, including bonds and preferred stocks. In the second subsection, we discuss equity investments, and the third and fourth subsections contain a discussion of special equity instruments, such as warrants and options, which have characteristics of both fixed-income and equity instruments. In subsection five, we consider futures contracts that allow for a wide range of return-risk profiles. The sixth subsection considers investment companies.

All these investments are called *financial assets* because their payoffs are in money. In contrast, *real assets,* such as real estate, art, antiques, coins, stamps, and precious gems are briefly discussed in the seventh and eighth subsections.

3.2.1 FIXED-INCOME INVESTMENTS

Recall that **fixed-income investments** promise specific payments at predetermined times, although the legal force behind the promise varies, which affects their risks and required returns. At one extreme, if the issuing firm does not make its payment as agreed, creditors can declare the issuing firm in default. In other cases (e.g., income bonds), the issuing firm makes payments only if it earns profits. In yet other instances (for example, preferred stock), the issuing firm does not have to make payments unless its board of directors votes to do so.

Investors purchasing fixed-income securities (except preferred stock) are really lenders to the issuers. You lend some amount of money, the *principal,* to the borrower and in return, the borrower typically promises to make periodic interest payments and to repay the principal at the loan's maturity.

Savings Accounts An individual depositing funds in a financial institution is really lending money to the institution and, as a result, earning a fixed payment. These convenient, liquid, and low-risk investments (most are insured) consequently provide lower returns as compared with other alternatives. Several types of accounts have been developed to appeal to investors with differing objectives, including term deposits and guaranteed investment certificates, which require minimum deposits and have fixed durations (usually in months).

Investors with larger sums of money ($10,000 or more) can choose to invest in Treasury bills (T-bills) of the Canadian (and sometimes provincial) government. To compete against T-bills, banks issue money market certificates, which require minimum investments and maturities.

Capital Market Instruments These are fixed-income obligations that trade in the secondary market and there are two general categories: (1) government and (2) corporate.

Government Securities All government securities, whether issued by the federal government, the various provincial and territorial governments, by municipalities and the various agencies of the governments, are fixed-income instruments. They may be bills, notes, or bonds depending on their times to maturity. Specifically, bills mature in one year or less, notes in over one to 10 years, and bonds in more than 10 years from time of issue. Although default in the government (and their agencies) bonds is rare, the federal government obligations are considered to have the least credit risk in terms of both default and liquidity.

It should be noted that in the United States, the interest earned on municipal bonds is tax-exempt. The interest earned from them is exempt from taxation by the federal government and by the state that issued the bond, provided the investor is a resident of that state. For this reason, municipal bonds are popular with investors. For example, an investor with a marginal tax rate of 35% would net only 5.2% after taxes on an 8% coupon bond whereas a tax-free bond of equal risk may yield 6%. The tax-exempt status allows these municipal bonds to offer yields that are generally 20% to 30% lower than yields on comparable taxable bonds.

Agency Securities Agency securities are sold by various agencies or Crown corporations of the various governments to support specific programs, but they are not direct obligations of the issuing government. An example of an agency is the Canada Mortgage and Housing Corporation, which sells bonds and uses the proceeds to purchase mortgages from Canadian financial institutions.

Although these securities are not direct obligations of the government, they are virtually default-free because it is almost inconceivable that the government would allow them to default. Also, they are fairly liquid. As a result of the potential for default and the lower liquidity, they typically have slightly higher returns than comparable government issues.

Corporate Bonds These fixed-income securities issued by corporations can be broken down by issuer (industrial or utility), in terms of credit quality (measured by the ratings assigned by an agency on the basis of probability of default), in terms of maturity (short, intermediate, or long term), or based on some component of the indenture (sinking fund or call feature).

All bonds include an **indenture**, which is the legal agreement listing the obligations of the issuer to the bondholder, including the payment schedule and features such as call provisions and sinking funds. **Call provisions** specify when a firm can issue a call for the bonds prior to their maturity, at which time current bondholders must submit the bonds to the issuing firm, which redeems them (i.e., pays back the principal and a small premium). A **sinking fund** provision specifies payments the issuer must make to redeem a given percentage of the outstanding issue prior to maturity.

Corporate bonds fall into various categories based on their contractual promises to investors. Brief descriptions of many of these features are located in the Web Appendix 3A, "A Review of Bond Categories and Terminology," as many of these terms are likely familiar to you from earlier introductory finance classes. The Web appendix is available at www.reilly.nelson.com.

Preferred Stock **Preferred stock** is classified as a fixed-income security because its yearly payment is stipulated as either a coupon (e.g., 5% of the face value) or a stated dollar amount (e.g., $5 preferred). Preferred stock differs from bonds because its payment is a dividend and therefore not legally binding. For each period, the firm's board of directors must vote to pay it, similar to a common stock dividend. Even if the firm earned enough money to pay the preferred stock dividend, the board of directors could theoretically vote to withhold it. Because most preferred stock is cumulative, the unpaid dividends would accumulate to be paid in full at a later time.

Although preferred dividends are not legally binding, as are the interest payments on a bond, they are considered *practically* binding because of the credit implications of a missed dividend. For many Canadian corporations, the dividends received from other taxable Canadian corporations are tax exempt; preferred stocks have therefore become attractive investments. For example, a corporation that owns preferred stock of another firm and receives $100 in dividends can exclude 100% of this amount. Due to this tax benefit (recall that individuals also pay a lower effective tax rate on dividends), the yield on high-grade preferred stock is typically lower than that on high-grade bonds.

3.2.2 INTERNATIONAL BOND INVESTING

As noted earlier, more than half of all fixed-income securities available to Canadian investors are issued by firms in countries outside Canada. Investors identify these securities in different ways: by the country or city of the issuer (e.g., United States, United Kingdom, Japan); by the location of the primary trading market (e.g., Tokyo, London); by the home country of the major buyers; and by the currency in which the securities are denominated (e.g., dollars, yen, euros). We identify foreign bonds by their country of origin and include these other differences in each description.

A **Eurobond** is an international bond denominated in a currency not native to the country where it is issued. Specific kinds of Eurobonds include Eurodollar bonds, Euroyen bonds, and Eurosterling bonds. A Eurodollar bond is denominated in U.S. dollars and sold outside the United States to non-U.S. investors. For example, General Electric could issue a U.S. dollar bond and Nippon Steel could issue a Euroyen bond, both for sale in London. Eurobonds are typically issued in Europe, with the major concentration in London. Further, if it appears that investors are looking for foreign currency bonds, a Canadian corporation could issue a Euroyen bond in London.

Maple bonds are Canadian dollar–denominated bonds sold in Canada by foreign corporation or governments. This allows a Canadian to buy the bond of a foreign firm or government but receive all payments in Canadian dollars, eliminating exchange risk.

An example would be a Canadian dollar–denominated bond issued by British Airways. Similar bonds are issued in other countries, including the Bulldog Market, which involves British sterling–denominated bonds issued in the United Kingdom by non-British firms; the Samurai Market, which involves yen-denominated bonds issued in Japan by non-Japanese firms; and, of course, Yankee bonds, or U.S. dollar–denominated bonds issued in the United States by foreign issuers.

International domestic bonds are sold by an issuer within its own country in that country's currency. An example would be a bond sold by Nippon Steel in Japan denominated in yen. A Canadian investor purchasing such a bond would receive maximum diversification but would incur exchange rate risk.

3.2.3 EQUITY INSTRUMENTS

Recall that the returns from equity investments are not contractual; as a result, you can receive returns that are much better or much worse than what you would receive on a bond. We begin this section with common stock, the most popular equity instrument and probably the most popular investment instrument.

Common stock represents *ownership* of a firm. Owners of the common stock share in the company's successes and problems. If the company prospers, the investor receives high returns and can become wealthy. In contrast, the investor can lose money if the firm does not do well or even goes bankrupt, as did the once formidable Nortel and Enron. In these instances, the firm may be forced to liquidate its assets and pay off its creditors. The firm's preferred stockholders and common stock owners receive what is left, which is usually little or nothing. Investing in common stock entails all the advantages and disadvantages of ownership and is a relatively risky investment when compared with fixed-income securities.

Common Stock Classifications When considering an investment in common stock, people tend to divide the vast universe of stocks into categories based on general business lines and by industry within these business lines. The division includes broad classifications for industrial firms, utilities, transportation firms, and financial institutions. Within each of these broad classes are industries. The industrial group, which is very diverse, includes such industries as automobiles, industrial machinery, chemicals, and beverages. Utilities include electrical power companies, gas suppliers, and the water industry. Transportation includes airlines, trucking firms, and railroads. Financial institutions include commercial banks, insurance companies, and investment firms.

An alternative classification scheme might separate domestic (Canadian) and foreign common stocks. We avoid this division because the business line–industry breakdown is more appropriate and useful when constructing a diversified portfolio of global common stock investments. With a global capital market, the focus of analysis should include all the companies in an industry viewed in a global setting. It isn't relevant whether a large chemical firm is located in Canada or Germany, just as it doesn't matter whether a computer firm is located in Montreal or Calgary. Therefore, when considering, say, the automobile industry, it is necessary to consider auto firms from throughout the world, such as Honda Motors, Porsche, Daimler, Nissan, Toyota, and Fiat.

Buying Foreign Equities Many investors may recognize the benefits of investing in foreign common stocks, but they may be intimidated by the transaction logistics. Currently, there are a couple of different ways to buy foreign common stock:

1. Direct purchase or sale of foreign shares listed on a foreign stock exchange
2. Purchase or sale of international or global mutual funds or exchange-traded funds (ETFs)

Direct Purchase or Sale of Foreign Shares The most difficult, complicated, and cumbersome foreign-equity transaction takes place in the country where the firm is located because it must be carried out in the foreign currency and the shares must then be transferred to Canada. A second alternative is buying or selling shares of a multinational firm such as Sun Life Financial, Bombardier, and Alcan. A third alternative is to purchase the stock at a stock exchange where the securities originated. For example, if you purchased shares of a French company listed on the London Stock Exchange (LSE), the shares would be denominated in pounds and the transfer would be swift, assuming your broker is able to trade on the LSE.

Purchase or Sale of American Depository Receipts Another way to buy foreign shares directly is through **American Depository Receipts (ADRs)**. These are certificates of ownership issued by a U.S. bank or the firms themselves that represent indirect ownership of a certain number of shares of a specific foreign firm on deposit in a bank in the firm's home country. The U.S. bank purchases the foreign shares and then issues claims (the ADR) to those shares in the United States. The investor buys and sells ADRs in U.S. dollars and receives all dividends in U.S. dollars. An ADR price can reflect the fact that it represents multiple shares—for example, an ADR can be for 5 or 10 shares of the foreign stock. ADRs can be issued at the discretion of a bank based on the demand for the stock. The shareholder absorbs the additional handling costs of an ADR through higher transfer expenses, which are deducted from dividend payments.

ADRs are quite popular because of their diversification benefits. By the end of 2006, 462 foreign companies had stocks listed on the New York Stock Exchange, and 356 of these were available through ADRs, including all the stock listed from Japan, the United Kingdom, Australia, Mexico, and the Netherlands. A Canadian buying ADRs could purchase stocks from many countries but deal only with a U.S. exchange.

Purchase or Sale of Global Mutual Funds or ETFs Numerous mutual funds and exchange-traded funds (ETFs) make it possible for investors to indirectly acquire the stocks of firms from outside Canada. The alternatives range from *global funds,* which invest in both Canadian and foreign stocks, to *international funds,* which invest almost wholly outside Canada. In turn, international funds can (1) diversify across many countries, (2) concentrate in a segment of the world (for example, Europe, South America, the Pacific basin), (3) concentrate in a specific country (for example, the Japan Fund, the Germany Fund, the Italy Fund, or the Korea Fund), or (4) concentrate in types of markets (for example, emerging markets, which would include stocks from countries such as Thailand, Indonesia, India, and China). A mutual fund is a convenient path to global investing, particularly for a small investor, because the purchase or sale of one of these funds is similar to a transaction for a comparable Canadian mutual fund.

A recent innovation in the world of index products are ETFs, which are depository receipts for a portfolio of securities deposited at a financial institution in a unit trust that issues a certificate of ownership for the portfolio of stocks (similar to ADRs discussed earlier). The stocks in a portfolio are those in an index like the S&P/TSX Composite, and dozens of country or industry indices. A significant advantage is that ETFs can be bought and sold (including short sales) continuously on an exchange like common stock. Another advantage is that they do not have management fees, but there is the typical transaction cost for the purchase or sale of ETF shares.[1]

3.2.4 SPECIAL EQUITY INSTRUMENTS: OPTIONS

In addition to common stock investments, it is also possible to invest in equity-derivative securities, which are securities that have a claim on the common stock of a firm. This would include **options**—rights to buy or sell common stock at a specified price for a stated period of time. The two kinds of option instruments are (1) warrants and (2) puts and calls.

Warrants Recall that warrants are options issued by a corporation that gives the holder the right to purchase a firm's common stock from the company at a specified price within a designated time period. The warrant does not constitute stock ownership, only the option to buy the stock.

Puts and Calls A **call option** is similar to a warrant because it allows the holder to buy the common stock of a company within a certain period at a specified price called the *striking price.* A call option differs from a warrant because it is not issued by the company but by another investor who is willing to assume the other side of the transaction. Options also are typically valid for a shorter time period than warrants; call options are generally valid for less than one year, whereas a warrant's life often exceeds five years. The owner of a **put option** has the right to sell a given stock at a specified price during a designated time period. Puts are useful to investors who expect a stock price to decline during the specified period or to investors who own the stock and want hedge protection from a price decline.

---

1 Mutual funds and ETFs are discussed further in the next section and in Chapters 15 and 18.

3.2.5 FUTURES CONTRACTS

Another instrument providing an alternative to an investment purchase is a **futures contract**. This agreement provides for the future exchange of a particular asset at a specified delivery date (usually within nine months) in exchange for a specified payment at the time of delivery. Although the full payment is not made until the delivery date, a good-faith deposit, the **margin**, is made to protect the seller. This is typically about 10% of the value of the contract.

The bulk of trading on the commodity exchanges is in futures contracts. The current price of the futures contract is determined by the participants' beliefs about the future for the commodity. For example, in June of a given year, a trader could speculate on the ICE Futures Canada exchange for canola in July and November of that year, and January, March, and May of the next year. If the investor expected the commodity price to rise, he or she could buy a futures contract on one of the commodity exchanges for later sale. If the investor expected the price to fall, he or she could sell a futures contract on an exchange with the expectation of buying similar contracts later when the price had (hopefully) declined to cover the sale.

Several differences exist between investing in an asset through a futures contract and investing in the asset itself. One is the use of a small good-faith deposit, which increases the volatility of returns. Because an investor puts up only a small portion of the total value of the futures contract (10% to 15%), the change in the total value of the contract (up or down) is large compared to the amount invested when the price of the commodity changes. Another unique aspect is the term of the investment: Although stocks can have infinite maturities, futures contracts typically expire in less than a year.

Financial Futures In addition to futures contracts on commodities, there also has been the development of futures contracts on financial instruments, such as T-bills, Treasury bonds, and Eurobonds. For example, it is possible to buy or sell a futures contract that promises future delivery of $100,000 of T-bills at a set price and yield. The major exchange for financial futures is the CME Group.[2] These futures contracts allow individual investors, bond portfolio managers, and corporate financial managers to protect themselves against volatile interest rates. Certain currency futures allow individual investors or portfolio managers to speculate on or to protect against changes in currency exchange rates. Finally, there are futures contracts on various stock market series, such as the S&P 500, the *Value Line* Index, and the Nikkei 225.

3.2.6 INVESTMENT COMPANIES

Rather than a direct investment in an individual stock or bond, you may choose to buy these investments indirectly by purchasing shares or units in an **investment company** or **mutual fund** that owns a portfolio of individual stocks, bonds, or a combination of the two. Specifically, an investment company sells shares or units in itself and uses these proceeds to purchase bonds, stocks, or other investments. As a result, an investment company investor is a partial owner of the investment company's portfolio of stocks or bonds. We will distinguish between investment companies by the types of investment instruments they acquire.

Money Market Funds These are investment companies that purchase high-quality, short-term investments (*money market* instruments), such as T-bills and high-grade commercial paper (public short-term loans) from various corporations. Money market portfolio yields surpass those on typical bank deposits because the investment by the money market fund is larger and the fund can commit to longer maturities than the typical individual. Typically the

---

2 The CME Group is a result of the merger of the Chicago Mercantile Exchange (CME) and the Chicago Board of Trade (CBOT) in July 2007.

minimum initial investment in a money market fund is $1,000, there are no sales commissions, and minimum additions are allowed. Usually you can easily withdraw funds from your money market fund without penalty by writing a cheque on the account, and you receive interest up to the day of withdrawal.

Individuals tend to use money market funds as alternatives to savings accounts because they are generally quite safe (although not insured, they typically limit their investments to high-quality, short-term investments), they provide yields above what are available on most savings accounts, and the funds are readily available. Because of relatively high yields and extreme flexibility and liquidity, the total value of these funds reached more than $2.5 trillion in 2007.

Bond Funds Bond funds generally invest in various long-term government or corporate bonds. They differ by the type and quality of the bonds included in the portfolio as assessed by various rating services. Some bond funds invest only in risk-free government bonds and high-grade corporate bonds while others concentrate in lower rated corporate bonds, called **high-yield bonds** or *junk bonds.* The expected returns from various bond funds will differ, with the low-risk government bond funds paying the lowest returns and the high-yield bond funds expected to provide the highest returns.

Common Stock Funds Numerous common stock funds invest to achieve stated investment objectives, which can include aggressive growth, income, precious metal investments, and international stocks. Such funds offer smaller investors the benefits of diversification and professional management. They include different investment styles, such as growth or value, and concentrate in alternative-sized firms, including small-cap, mid-cap, and large-capitalization stocks. To meet the diverse needs of investors, numerous funds have been created that concentrate in one industry or sector of the economy, such as chemicals, electric utilities, health, housing, and technology. These funds are diversified within a sector or an industry, but are not diversified across the total market. Investors who participate in a sector or an industry fund bear more risk than investors in a total market fund because the sector funds will tend to fluctuate more than an aggregate market fund that is diversified across all sectors. Also, international funds that invest outside Canada and global funds that invest in Canada and in other countries offer opportunities for global diversification by individual investors.

Balanced Funds **Balanced funds** invest in a combination of bonds and stocks of various sorts depending on their stated objectives.

Index Funds Index funds are mutual funds created to equal (track) the performance of a market index like the S&P/TSX Composite. Such funds appeal to *passive* investors who want to simply experience returns equal to some market index either because they do not want to try to "beat the market" or they believe in efficient markets and do not think it is possible to do better than the market in the long run. Given the popularity of these funds, they have been created to emulate numerous stock indices including very broad indexes like the Dow Jones Wilshire 5000 and broad foreign indexes like the EAFE index. In addition, numerous bond indices have been created for those who want passive bond investing.[3]

Exchange-Traded Funds (ETFs) A problem with mutual funds in general and index funds in particular is that they are only priced daily at the close of the market and all transactions take place at that price. As a result, if you are aware of changes taking place for the aggregate market due to some economic event during the day and want to buy or sell to take advantage of this, you can put in an order for a mutual fund, but it will not be executed until the end of the day

---

3 Stock and bond indices are discussed in Chapter 4.

at closing prices. In response to this problem, the Toronto Stock Exchange in 1987 introduced the world's first exchange traded fund. The Toronto Index Participation Units or TIPS value was tied to the Toronto 35 (TSE35) index. This exchange-traded fund or ETF could be traded continuously like a share because the prices for the underlying 35 stocks were updated continuously. Since then, a number of exchanges have occurred and now a number of EFTs are available. This concept of an ETF has been applied to numerous foreign and domestic indices including the Morgan Stanley Capital International (MSCI) indexes. Barclay's Global Investors (BGI) have created "i shares," using the MSCI indexes for numerous individual countries.

For a list of Exchange Traded Funds available, go to http://www.tmxmoney.com/en/sector_profiles/exchange_traded_funds/funds/by_type.html.

3.2.7 REAL ESTATE

Like commodities, most investors view real estate as an interesting and profitable investment alternative but believe that it is only available to a small group of experts with a lot of capital to invest. In reality, some feasible real estate investments require no detailed expertise or large capital commitments. We will begin by considering low-capital alternatives.

Real Estate Investment Trusts (REITs) A **real estate investment trust** is an investment fund designed to invest in various real estate properties. There are several types of REITs.

Construction and development trusts lend the money required by builders during the initial construction of a building. *Mortgage trusts* provide long-term mortgages on properties once construction is completed. *Equity trusts* own various income-producing properties, such as office buildings, shopping centres, or apartment houses. Therefore, an investor who buys shares in an equity real estate investment trust is buying part of a portfolio of income-producing properties.

REITs have experienced periods of great popularity and significant depression in line with changes in the aggregate economy and the money market. Although subject to cyclical risks depending on the economic environment, they offer small investors a way to participate in real estate investments.

Direct Real Estate Investment The most common type of direct real estate investment is the purchase of a home, which is the largest investment most people ever make. A home purchase is considered an investment because the buyer pays a sum of money either all at once or over a number of years through a mortgage. Subsequently, a homeowner hopes to sell the house for its cost plus a gain. Aside from home ownership, an investor can purchase raw land with the intention of selling at a profit or developing it in the future. Over the time you own that property, you have negative cash flows from mortgage payments, property maintenance, and taxes, so an obvious risk is the uncertainty of the future real estate market.

Lastly, an investor may purchase property for rental purposes with the intention of deriving enough rental income from the rents to pay the expenses of the structure, including the mortgage payments. For the first few years following the purchase, the investor generally has no reported income from the building because of tax-deductible expenses, including the interest component of the mortgage payment and amortization on the structure. Subsequently, rental property provides a cash flow and an opportunity to profit from the sale of the property.

3.2.8 LOW-LIQUIDITY INVESTMENTS

Most of the investment alternatives we have described thus far are traded on securities markets and, except for real estate, have good liquidity. In contrast, the investments discussed in this section have very poor liquidity and high transaction costs. Many of these assets are sold at auctions, where prices can vary substantially. Because there is generally no national market for these investments, local dealers must be compensated for the added carrying costs and the cost of searching for buyers or sellers. Therefore, many financial theorists view these low-liquidity investments more as hobbies than investments, even though studies have indicated that some of these assets have experienced substantial rates of return.

Antiques If we gauge an antique's value based on prices established at large public auctions, it appears that many serious collectors enjoy substantial returns. In contrast, the average investor who owns a few pieces to decorate his or her home finds such returns elusive. The high transaction costs and illiquidity of antiques may erode any profit that the individual may expect to earn when selling these pieces.

Art We often see stories reporting the results of major art auctions, such as when Van Gogh's *Irises* and *Sunflowers* sold for $59 million and $36 million, respectively. Obviously, these examples and others indicate that the value of some art has increased significantly and thereby generated large returns for their owners. However, such investments typically require an in-depth knowledge of art and the art world, along with substantial capital, patience, and an ability to absorb high transaction costs. For investors who enjoy fine art and have the resources, these can be satisfying investments; for most small investors, it is difficult to get sufficient returns that compensate for the uncertainty, illiquidity, and high transaction costs.

Coins and Stamps The market for coins and stamps is fragmented compared to the stock market, but it is more liquid than the art and antiques market as indicated by the weekly and monthly price list publications. An investor can get a widely recognized grading specification on a coin or stamp, and once graded, a coin or stamp can usually be sold quickly through a dealer. It is important to recognize that the percentage difference between the bid price the dealer will pay to buy the stamp or coin and the asking or selling price the investor must pay the dealer is going to be substantially larger than the bid-ask spread on stocks and bonds.

eBay and other sites have improved liquidity of some of these items. Check out http://www.sothebys.com for information on collectibles.

Diamonds Diamonds can be and have been good investments during many periods. Still, investors who purchase diamonds should realize that (1) diamonds can be highly illiquid, (2) the quality grading process is quite subjective, (3) most investment-grade gems require substantial capital, and (4) they generate no positive cash flow during the holding period until the stone is sold. In fact, during the holding period, the investor must cover costs of insurance and storage, and there are appraisal costs before selling.

3.3 Historical Risk-Returns on Alternative Investments

How do investors weigh the costs and benefits of owning investments and make decisions to build portfolios that will provide the best risk-return combinations? To help investors answer this question, financial theorists have examined extensive data to provide information on the return and risk characteristics of various investments.

There have been numerous studies of the historical returns on common stocks (both large-capitalization stocks in terms of aggregate market value and small-capitalization stocks)[4] and bonds. Because inflation has been so pervasive, many studies examine both nominal and real investment returns. Still other investigators have examined the performance of such assets as real estate, foreign stocks, art, antiques, and commodities to help you to make decisions on building your investment portfolio and on the allocation to the various asset classes. We'll focus our review on stocks and bonds.

---

4 Small-capitalization stocks were broken out as a separate class of asset because several studies have shown that firms with relatively small capitalization (stocks with low-market value) have experienced returns and risk significantly different from those of stocks in general. Therefore, they were considered a unique asset class. We will discuss these studies in Chapter 5, which deals with the efficient markets hypothesis. The large-company stock returns are based upon the S&P/TSX Composite Index (described in Chapter 4).

3.3.1   WORLD PORTFOLIO PERFORMANCE

A brief review of the performance of a number of assets for the period from 1993 to March 2009 is shown in Exhibit 3.9. Generally, the results confirm the expected relationship between annual rates of return and the total risk (standard deviation) of these securities. The riskier assets—those that had higher standard deviations—experienced higher returns. For example, the S&P/TSX composite index had a relatively high return (8.47%) and large standard deviation (17.68%) whereas the risk-free 90-day T-bill had low returns (4.02%) and the smallest standard deviation (1.28%).

Return and Systematic Risk Also shown in Exhibit 3.9 is the systematic risk, which is the volatility of an asset relative to a market portfolio of risky assets (or beta, discussed briefly in Chapter 1). These results are graphed in Exhibit 3.10 and show that the systematic risk measure (beta) does a better job of explaining the returns during the period than the total risk measure.[5]

EXHIBIT 3.9	Summary Risk-Return Results for various Capital Market Assets (Canadian dollars): 1993–March 2009			
Index	Arithmetic Mean Return	Geometric Mean Return	Standard Deviation Annual Return	Beta with S&P/TSX Composite Index
S&P/TSX Composite Index	10.08%	8.47%	17.68%	1.00
Russell 3000 Index[a]	5.46%	3.87%	18.24%	0.71
S&P 500 Index	8.05%	6.39%	18.77%	0.67
Dow Jones Industrial Average	9.58%	8.37%	16.09%	0.49
FTSE 100 Index	7.83%	5.98%	19.07%	0.58
Nikkei 225 Index	0.90%	−1.47%	21.90%	0.48
MSCI EAFE Index[b]	1.92%	0.13%	18.35%	0.72
MSCI World Index[b]	−1.16%	−2.27%	15.78%	0.60
91 Day Cdn T-bill Rate	4.03%	4.02%	1.28%	0.00
Inflation (CPI Index)	1.93%	1.93%	0.64%	0.00

[a] Statistics for Russell 3000 index are based on 1996–March 2009 data.
[b] Statistics for MSCI EAFE and MSCI World Index are based on 2002–March 2009 data.

Note: MSCI EAFE is monthly from 2002–2008
Note: MSCI World Index is monthly from Feb. 2002–2008
Note: Russell 3000 Index is monthly from 1996–2009

Source: Bloomberg and author calculations.

Correlations between Asset Returns Exhibit 3.11 is a correlation matrix of Canadian versus world assets. The first column shows that Canadian equities have a reasonably high correlation with U.S. and U.K. stocks but low correlation with Japanese stocks. Also, Canadian equities show almost zero correlation with T-bills (as do all of the indices shown). Recall from our earlier discussion that you can use this information to build a diversified portfolio by combining those assets with low positive or negative correlations.

---

5 For those interested in a more comprehensive review of risk-return profiles, including real assets, see Frank K. Reilly and David J. Wright, "An Analysis of Risk-Adjusted Performance for Global Market Assets," *Journal of Portfolio Management* 30, no. 3 (Spring 2004): 63–77.

EXHIBIT 3.10	Geometric Mean Return versus S&P/TSX Composite Beta for Various Capital Market Assets, 1993–March 2009

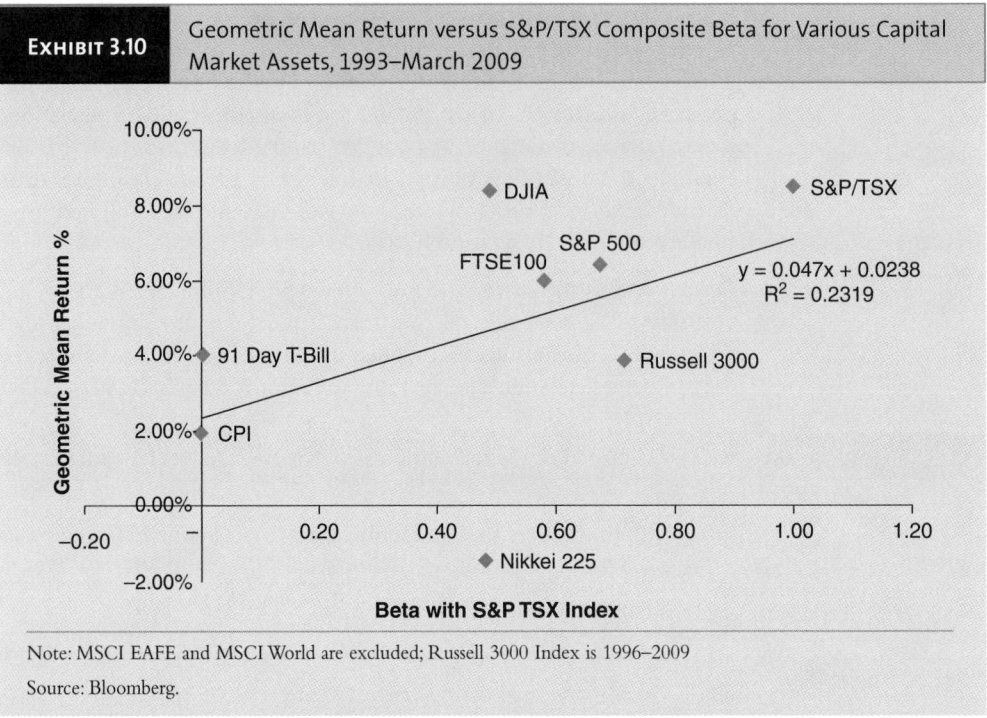

Note: MSCI EAFE and MSCI World are excluded; Russell 3000 Index is 1996–2009

Source: Bloomberg.

The correlation of returns with inflation has implications regarding the ability of an asset class to be an inflation hedge—a good hedge should have a strong positive correlation with inflation. All assets shown have negative correlations, which implies that they are poor inflation hedges.

EXHIBIT 3.11	Correlations among Various Capital Market Assets Annual Returns (Canadian dollars): 1993–March 2009

Index	S&P/TSX Composite	DJIA	MSCI EAFE	MSCI World
S&P/TSX Composite	1.000	0.537	0.696	0.676
S&P 500	0.635	0.918	0.821	0.955
DJIA	0.537	1.000	0.737	0.878
Russell 3000[a]	0.692	0.892	0.835	0.961
FTSE 225	0.538	0.672	0.909	0.892
Nikkei 100	0.389	0.373	0.645	0.533
MSCI EAFE[b]	0.696	0.737	1.000	0.953
MSCI World[b]	0.676	0.878	0.953	1.000
T-bill-90 day	0.410	0.138	0.098	0.102
Inflation (CPI Canada)	−0.220	−0.156	−0.291	−0.238

[a] Statistics for Russell 3000 index are based on 1996–March 2009 data.
[b] Statistics for MSCI EAFE and MSCI World Index are based on 2002–March 2009 data.

Source: Bloomberg and author calculations.

Summary

1. Many foreign securities offer investors higher risk-adjusted returns than do domestic securities. In addition, the low positive or negative correlations between foreign and Canadian securities make them ideal for building a diversified portfolio.
2. Continued economic growth worldwide has resulted in a need for capital. At the same time, some economies have become world powerhouses, shifting the flow of cash from the more established markets to those with growth opportunities.
3. Various exhibits summarized the risk and return characteristics of the investment alternatives described in this chapter. Some of the differences are due to unique factors specific to those investments, and we noted that foreign investments can be riskier than domestic ones because of the unavoidable uncertainty due to exchange rate risk and country risk.
4. There is an additional advantage to diversifying in international markets beyond the benefits of domestic diversification. Increasing the number of randomly selected securities in a portfolio will reduce the portfolio's standard deviation. Adding foreign securities to a Canadian portfolio to create a global portfolio enables an investor to further lower overall portfolio risk because the foreign securities are not correlated with the Canadian economy or stock market.
5. In addition to describing many direct investments in stocks and bonds in domestic and foreign markets, we also discussed investment companies that allow investors to buy investments indirectly. For investors who want to take advantage of professional management and instant diversification with a limited amount of funds this can be an attractive option, whether investing in a mutual fund or an ETF.

Now that we know the range of domestic and foreign investment alternatives, our next task is to learn about the markets in which they are bought and sold. That is the objective of the next chapter.

Key Terms

American Depository Receipts (ADRs), p. 61
balanced fund, p. 64
call option, p. 62
call provisions, p. 59
capital market instruments, p. 58
common stock, p. 60
Eurobonds, p. 60

fixed-income investments, p. 58
futures contract, p. 63
high-yield bond, p. 64
indenture, p. 59
international domestic bonds, p. 60
investment company, p. 63
maple bonds, p. 60
margin, p. 63

mutual fund, p. 63
options, p. 62
portfolio, p. 51
preferred stock, p. 59
put option, p. 62
real estate investment trusts (REITs), p. 65
sinking fund, p. 59

Suggested Readings

Grabbe, J. Orlin. *International Financial Markets.* New York: Elsevier Science Publishing, 1986.

Hamao, Yasushi. "Japanese Stocks, Bonds, Inflation, 1973–1987." *Journal of Portfolio Management* 16, no. 2 (Winter 1989).

Lessard, Donald R. "International Diversification." In *The Financial Analyst's Handbook*, 2nd ed., ed. Sumner N. Levine. Homewood, IL: Dow Jones-Irwin, 1988.

Malvey, Jack. "Global Corporate Bond Portfolio Management." In *The Handbook of Fixed-Income Securities*, 7th ed., ed. Frank J. Fabozzi. New York: McGraw-Hill, 2005.

Rosenberg, Michael R. "International Fixed-Income Investing: Theory and Practice." In *The Handbook of Fixed-Income Securities*, 7th ed., ed. Frank J. Fabozzi. New York: McGraw-Hill, 2005.

Siegel, Laurence B., and Paul D. Kaplan. "Stocks, Bonds, Bills, and Inflation around the World." In *Managing Institutional Assets*, ed. Frank J. Fabozzi. New York: Harper & Row, 1990.

Solnik, Bruno, and Dennis McLeavey. *International Investments*, 5th ed. Reading, MA: Addison-Wesley, 2004.

Steward, Christopher. "International Bond Markets and Instruments." In *The Handbook of Fixed-Income Securities*, 7th ed., ed. Frank J. Fabozzi. New York: McGraw-Hill, 2005.

CFA **For Chapter CFA Questions and Problems, please see Appendix A at the end of this text.**

Questions

1. What are the advantages of investing in the common stock rather than the corporate bonds of a company? Compare the certainty of returns for a bond with those for a common stock. Draw a line graph to demonstrate the pattern of returns you would envision for each of these assets over time.

2. Discuss three factors that cause investors to consider including various global securities in their portfolios.

3. Discuss why international diversification reduces portfolio risk. Specifically, why would you expect low correlation in the rates of return for domestic and foreign securities?

4. Discuss why you would expect a difference in the correlation of returns between securities from the Canada and from alternative countries (for example, Japan, the United States, South Africa).

5. Discuss whether you would expect any change in the correlations between Canadian stocks and the stocks for different countries. For example, discuss whether you would expect the correlation between United States and Japanese stock returns to change over time. If so, why?

6. When you invest in Japanese or German bonds, what major additional risks must you consider besides yield changes within the country?

7. Some investors believe that international investing introduces additional risks. Discuss these risks and how they can affect your return. Give an example.

8. What alternatives to direct investment in foreign stocks are available to investors?

9. You can purchase convertible bonds from a rapidly growing company or from a utility. Speculate on which convertible bond would have the lower yield and discuss the reason for this difference.

10. Compare the liquidity of an investment in raw land with that of an investment in common stock. Be specific as to why and how the liquidity differs. (Hint: Begin by defining *liquidity*.)

11. What are warrants and call options? How do they differ?

12. Discuss why financial analysts consider antiques and art to be illiquid investments. Why do they consider coins and stamps to be more liquid than antiques and art? What must an investor typically do to sell a collection of art and antiques? Briefly contrast this procedure to the sale of a portfolio of stocks listed on the TSX.

13. You have a fairly large portfolio of Canadian stocks and bonds. You meet a financial planner at a social gathering who suggests that you diversify your portfolio by investing in emerging market stocks. Discuss whether the correlation results in Exhibit 3.11 support this suggestion.

Problems

1. Using a source of international statistics, compare the percentage change in the following economic data for Japan, Germany, the United States, and Canada for a recent year. What were the differences, and which country or countries differed most from Canada?
   a. Aggregate output (GDP)
   b. Inflation
   c. Money supply growth

2. Using a recent edition of Barron's, examine the weekly percentage change in the stock price indices for Japan, Germany, United Kingdom, the United States, and Canada. For each of three weeks, which foreign series moved most closely with the Canadian series? Which series diverged most from the Canadian series? Discuss these results as they relate to international diversification.

3. Using published sources (for example, the FP Infomart, Barron's, Bank of Canada), look up the exchange rate for Canadian dollars with Japanese yen for each of the past

10 years (you can use an average for the year or a specific time period each year). Based on these exchange rates, compute and discuss the yearly exchange rate effect on an investment in Japanese stocks by a Canadian investor. Discuss the impact of this exchange rate effect on the risk of Japanese stocks for a Canadian investor.

4. You are given the following long-run annual returns for alternative investments:

Government of Canada T-bills	3.50%
Large-cap common stock	11.75%
Long-term corporate bonds	5.50%
Long-term government bonds	4.90%
Small-capitalization common stock	13.10%

The annual inflation rate during this period was 3%. Compute the real return on these investment alternatives.

CHAPTER 4

Securities Markets and the Economy*

After you read this chapter, you should be able to answer the following questions:

1. What characteristics determine the quality of a market?

2. What is the difference between a primary and secondary capital market, and how do these two markets support each other?

3. For secondary equity markets, what are the two basic trading systems?

4. What are call markets and how are they typically used?

5. What is meant by "passing the book"?

6. What are the third market and Electronic Communication Networks (ECNs)?

7. What are the major types of orders available to investors and market makers?

8. What are some uses of security-market indices, and what are the main computational differences in various indices?

9. Why are bond-market indices more difficult to create and maintain than stock indices?

The stock market and the bond market are part of our everyday experience. Each evening on television we find out how stocks and bonds fared; each morning we read in the newspapers about expectations for a market rally or decline. Yet most people have an imperfect understanding of how domestic and world capital markets actually function. To be a successful investor in a global environment, you must know what financial markets are available around the world and how they operate.

In this chapter we take a broad view of securities markets and provide a detailed discussion of how major stock markets function. We also consider how global securities markets have changed during recent years and conclude with a discussion of how they will change in the future.

We begin with a discussion of securities markets and the characteristics of a good market. We describe two components of the capital markets: primary and secondary. Our main emphasis is on the secondary stock market, including the national stock exchanges around the world and how these markets, separated by geography and by time zones, are becoming linked into a 24-hour market. We also consider how alternative exchange markets operate, including the Electronic Communication Networks (ECNs). We then reflect on the numerous changes that have occurred and consider the significant mergers, as well as future changes expected. These changes will have a profound effect on what investments are available from around the world and how we buy and sell them.

Next we consider the various stock-market indices. A fair statement regarding **security-market indices** is that everybody talks about them but few people understand them. Even those investors familiar with widely publicized stock-market series, such as the Dow Jones Industrial Average (DJIA), usually know little about indices for the bond market or for foreign stock markets such as Tokyo or London.

Although portfolios are obviously composed of many different individual stocks, investors typically ask, "What happened to the

---

* The authors acknowledge helpful comments on this chapter from Robert Battalio and Paul Schultz of the University of Notre Dame.

market today?" The reason for this question is that if an investor owns more than a few stocks or bonds, it is cumbersome to follow each stock or bond individually to determine the composite performance of the portfolio. Also, there is an intuitive notion that most individual stocks or bonds move with the aggregate market. Therefore, if the overall market rose, an individual's portfolio probably also increased in value. To supply investors with a composite report on market performance, some financial publications or investment firms have created and maintain stock-market and bond-market indices.

4.1   What Is a Market?

A **market** is the means through which buyers and sellers are brought together to aid in the transfer of goods and/or services. Several aspects of this general definition seem worthy of emphasis. First, a market need not have a physical location. It is only necessary that the buyers and sellers can communicate regarding the relevant aspects of the transaction.

Second, the market does not necessarily own the goods or services involved. For a good market, ownership is not involved; the important criterion is the smooth, cheap transfer of goods and services. In most financial markets, those who establish and administer the market do not own the assets but simply provide a physical location or an electronic system that allows potential buyers and sellers to interact. They help the market function by providing information and facilities to aid in the transfer of ownership.

Finally, a market can deal in any variety of goods and services. For any commodity or service with a diverse clientele, a market should evolve to aid in the transfer of that commodity or service. Both buyers and sellers benefit from the existence of a market.

4.1.1   Characteristics of a Good Market

Throughout this book, we will discuss markets for stocks, bonds, options, and futures in Canada and throughout the world. We will refer to these markets using various terms of quality such as *strong, active, liquid,* or *illiquid*. There are many financial markets, but they are not all equal—some are active and liquid, others are relatively illiquid and inefficient in their operations. To appreciate these discussions, you should be aware of the characteristics investors look for when evaluating the quality of a market.

One enters a market to buy or sell a good or service quickly at a price justified by the prevailing supply and demand. To determine the appropriate price, participants must have timely and accurate information on the volume and prices of past transactions and all currently outstanding bids and offers. Therefore, one attribute of a good market is **timely and accurate information**.

Another requirement is **liquidity**, or the ability to quickly buy or sell an asset and at a price not substantially different from the prices for prior transactions, assuming no new information is available. The likelihood of an asset being sold quickly, sometimes referred to as its *marketability*, is a necessary, but not a sufficient, condition for liquidity. The expected price should also be fairly certain, based on the recent history of transaction prices and current bid-ask quotes.[1]

A component of liquidity is **price continuity**, which means that prices do not change much from one transaction to the next unless substantial new information becomes available. Suppose no new information is forthcoming, and the last transaction was at a price of $20; if

---

1 For a formal discussion of liquidity, see Handa and Schwartz (1996) and AIMR's articles on *Best Execution and Portfolio Performance* (Jost, 2001).

the next trade were at $20.10, the market would be considered reasonably continuous.[2] A continuous market without large price changes between trades is a characteristic of a liquid market.

To have price continuity there must also be *depth*, meaning that there are numerous potential buyers and sellers willing to trade at prices above and below the current market price. These investors enter the market in response to changes in supply, demand, or both, and thereby prevent drastic price changes. In summary, liquidity requires marketability and price continuity, which, in turn, requires depth.

Another factor contributing to a good market is the **transaction cost**. Lower costs (as a percent of the value of the trade) make for a more efficient market. An individual comparing transaction costs between markets would choose the one that charges 2% of the value of the trade compared with one that charges 5%. This attribute is referred to as *internal efficiency*.

Finally, an investor wants the prevailing price to adequately reflect all the information available regarding supply and demand factors in the market. If such conditions change as a result of new information, the price should change quickly and accordingly. This attribute is referred to as **external (or informational) efficiency**. We discuss this attribute extensively in Chapter 5.

In summary, a good market for goods and services has the following characteristics:

1. Timely and accurate information on the price and volume of past transactions.
2. Liquidity, meaning an asset can be bought or sold quickly at a price close to the prices for previous transactions (has price continuity), assuming no new information has been received. In turn, price continuity requires depth.
3. Low transaction costs, including the cost of reaching the market, the actual brokerage costs, and the cost of transferring the asset.
4. Prices that rapidly adjust to new information, so the prevailing price is fair because it reflects all available information regarding the asset.

4.1.2 ORGANIZATION OF THE SECURITIES MARKET

Before we discuss the specific operation of the securities market, we need to understand its overall organization. The principal distinction is between **primary markets**, where new securities are sold, and **secondary markets**, where outstanding securities are bought and sold. Each of these markets is further divided based on the economic unit that issued the security. We will consider each of these major segments of the securities market, with an emphasis on the individuals involved and the functions they perform.

4.2 Primary Capital Markets

The primary market is where new issues of bonds, preferred stock, or common stock are sold by government units, municipalities, or companies to acquire new capital.[3]

4.2.1 GOVERNMENT OF CANADA BOND ISSUES

Canadian government issues are subdivided into three segments based on their original maturities. **Treasury bills** are negotiable, non-interest-bearing securities with original maturities of one year or less; medium-term bonds have 3- to 10-year maturities; and long-term bonds are typically issued with initial maturities over 10 years.

---

2 You should be aware that common stocks are sold in decimals (dollars and cents), which is a significant change from a time when they were priced in eighths and sixteenths.

3 For a review of studies on the primary market, see Jensen and Smith (1986).

4.2.2 PROVINCIAL AND MUNICIPAL BOND ISSUES

Nearly all of the provinces, territories, and municipalities borrow money to finance public works and other such investments. Bonds issued by provinces and territories (including bonds issued by provincial authorities that are guaranteed by the province) are typically called provincial bonds, while those issued by municipalities are called municipals.

4.2.3 CORPORATE BOND ISSUES

Corporate bond issues are almost always sold through a negotiated arrangement with an investment banking firm that maintains a relationship with the issuing firm. In a global capital market that involves an explosion of new instruments, the design of the security in terms of characteristics and currency is becoming more important. As a result, the expertise of the investment banker can help reduce the issuer's cost of new capital.

Once a stock or bond issue is specified, the underwriter will put together an underwriting syndicate of other major underwriters and a selling group of smaller firms for its distribution, as shown in Exhibit 4.1.

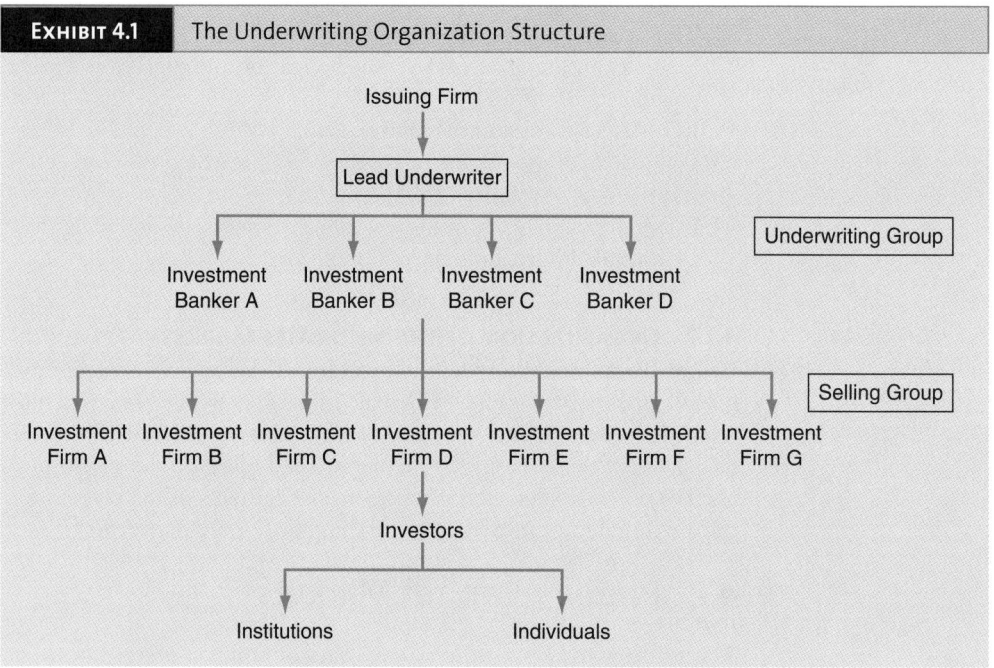

EXHIBIT 4.1 The Underwriting Organization Structure

4.2.4 CORPORATE STOCK ISSUES

In addition to the ability to issue fixed-income securities to get new capital, corporations can also issue equity securities—generally, common stock. For corporations, new stock issues are typically divided into two groups: (1) seasoned equity issues and (2) initial public offerings (IPOs).

Seasoned equity issues are new shares offered by firms that already have stock outstanding. An example would be George Weston Limited, a large, well-regarded firm that has been listed on the TSX for a number of years. If George Weston Limited needed additional capital, it could sell additional common stock to the public at a price very close to the stock's current market price.

Initial public offerings (IPOs) involve a firm selling its common stock to the public for the first time. At the time of an IPO, there is no existing public market for the stock; that is, the company has been closely held. An example was an IPO by Tim Hortons at $23.16 US per share. At the time, the company was being sold off by Wendy's International Inc. the purpose of the offering was twofold: to establish a trading volume and to provide funds to repay debt owed to Wendy's.

New issues (seasoned or IPOs) are typically underwritten by investment bankers, who acquire the total issue from the company and sell the securities to interested investors. The underwriter gives advice to the corporation on the general characteristics of the issue, its pricing, and the timing of the offering. The underwriter also accepts the risk of selling the new issue after acquiring it from the corporation.[4]

You can view a copy of the preliminary and final form prospectus for Tim Hortons at http://www.sedar.com/DisplayCompanyDocuments.do?lang=EN&issuerNo=00023027. Scroll down to the bottom of the page.

Relationships with Investment Bankers The underwriting of corporate issues typically takes one of three forms: negotiated, competitive bids, or best-efforts arrangements. As noted, negotiated underwritings are the most common.

With a competitive bid, the corporation typically specifies the type of securities to be offered (common stock, preferred stock, or bonds) and then solicits competitive bids from investment banking firms. Although this process typically reduces the cost of an issue, it also means that the investment banker gives less advice but still accepts the risk-bearing function, by underwriting the issue, and fulfills the distribution function.

Alternatively, an investment banker can agree to sell an issue on a *best-efforts basis.* This is usually done with speculative new issues. In this case, the investment banker does not underwrite the issue, the stock is owned by the company and the investment banker acts as a *broker* to sell whatever it can at a stipulated price. Because it bears no risk, the investment banker earns a lower commission on such an issue than on an underwritten issue.

Short Form Prospectus Distribution To reduce the repetitive filing requirements for large firms, the Ontario Securities Commission (OSC) Short Form Prospectus Distribution (SPDF) system allows issuers to file their annual and interim financial statements on a continuous basis, whether or not they intend on issuing securities. If the issuer needs to issue new securities, they need only provide supplementary material and the approval process then drops to a matter of days. Such a system appeals to underwriters as it reduces their pricing risk.[5]

4.2.5 PRIVATE PLACEMENTS

Rather than a public sale using one of these arrangements, primary offerings can be sold privately. In such an arrangement, referred to as a *private placement,* the firm designs an issue with the assistance of an investment banker and sells it to a small group of institutions. The firm enjoys lower issuing costs because it does not need to prepare the extensive registration statement required for a public offering. The institution buying the issue typically benefits because the issuing firm passes some of these cost savings on to the investor as a higher return. In fact, the institution should require a higher return because of the absence of any secondary market for these securities, which implies higher liquidity risk.[6] Depending upon the issuer, the type of security, and the type of purchases, these securities may or may not be subsequently resold.

---

4 For further discussion, see Brealey and Myers (2004, Chapter 15).

5 In the United States, the short form prospectus is called a shelf registration, governed by Rule 415. See Rogowski and Sorensen (1985) for further discussion.

6 The private placement market changed dramatically when Rule 144A was introduced by the U.S. Securities and Exchange Commission (SEC). This rule allows corporations—including non-U.S. firms—to place securities privately with large, sophisticated institutional investors without extensive registration documents. These securities may be subsequently traded among these large sophisticated investors (those with assets in excess of $100 million). See Milligan (1990) and Hanks (1990). Presently, more than 85% of high-yield bonds are issued as 144A issues.

4.3 Secondary Financial Markets

Secondary markets permit trading in stocks or bonds that have already been sold to the public. The proceeds from a sale in the secondary market do not go to the issuer (the government or company), but rather to the current owner of the security.

4.3.1 WHY SECONDARY MARKETS ARE IMPORTANT

Because the secondary market involves the trading of securities initially sold in the primary market, *it provides liquidity to the individuals who bought these securities.* After purchasing securities in the primary market, investors may want to sell them. The primary market benefits greatly from the liquidity provided by the secondary market because investors would hesitate to purchase securities if they thought they could not subsequently sell them in the secondary market. That is, without an active secondary market, potential issuers of stocks or bonds in the primary market would have to provide much higher returns to compensate investors for the substantial liquidity risk.

Secondary markets are also important to those selling seasoned securities because the prevailing market price of the securities (*price discovery*) is determined by transactions in the secondary market. New issues of outstanding stocks or bonds to be sold in the primary market are based on prices and yields in the secondary market.[7]

4.3.2 SECONDARY BOND MARKETS

The secondary market for bonds distinguishes among those issued by the federal government, provinces and municipalities, or corporations.

In Canada, most trading in bonds occurs **over-the-counter (OTC)**, that is, there is no formal market—just a network of dealers standing ready to buy and sell. For the government issues, many of the bonds are held as investments by the dealers as well as by large institutional investors. Many investors, individual and institutional, are also active in the corporate bond market; however, corporate bond trading is somewhat limited when compared to the fairly active trading in government bonds. As a result, corporate bond dealers do not carry extensive inventories of specific issues. Rather, they hold a limited number of bonds desired by their clients, and when someone wants to do a trade, they work more like brokers than dealers.

Transparency of the bond market remains an issue. Although on a daily basis there are fewer trades in the fixed-income markets than on the stock market, the dollar volume per trade far exceeds the stock market. The progress toward increased transparency is slow.[8]

4.3.3 FINANCIAL FUTURES

In addition to the market for the bonds, a market has developed for futures contracts related to these bonds. These contracts allow the holder to buy or sell a specified amount of a given bond issue at a stipulated price. The two major futures exchanges, the Chicago Board of Trade (CBOT) and the Chicago Mercantile Exchange (CME), merged during 2007 to become the CME Group. We discuss these futures contracts and the futures market in Chapter 14. The Montreal Stock Exchange offers a limited range of products.

The Investment Industry Regulatory Organization of Canada (IIROC) has proposed new rules to address fair pricing OTC traded securities including fixed income securities. You can find them at http://docs.iiroc.ca/DisplayDocument.aspx?DocumentID=18FBA2EF91264AA39A9179A97A465D5D&Language=en. Check the IIROC website periodically to see how the new rules are progressing.

---

7   Notably, the secondary market also has an effect on market efficiency and price volatility, as discussed by Foster and Viswanathan (1993) and Jones, Kaul, and Lipson (1994). Even forthcoming IPOs are priced based on the prices and values of comparable stocks or bonds in the public secondary market.

8   See Blythe, Scott, "Can Bonds Go Electric?" *Canadian Investment Review,* Summer 2003.

4.3.4 SECONDARY EQUITY MARKETS

Before 2000, the secondary equity markets in Canada and elsewhere were divided into three segments: national stock exchanges, regional stock exchanges, and OTC markets for stocks listed on an exchange. Following our background discussions on alternative trading systems and call versus continuous markets, we will describe the market types listed in Exhibit 4.2[9] and discuss how they complement and compete against each other to provide price discovery and liquidity to individual and institutional investors.

Basic Trading Systems Although stock exchanges are similar in that only qualified stocks can be traded by individuals who are members of or participating organizations in the exchange, they can differ in their *trading systems.* There are two main trading systems, and an exchange can use one or a combination of them. One is a *pure auction market* (also referred to as an *order-driven market*), in which interested buyers and sellers submit bid-and-ask prices (buy and sell orders) for a given stock to a central location where the orders are matched. Participants also refer to this system as *price-driven* because shares are sold to the investor with the highest bid price and bought from the seller with the lowest offering price. Advocates of an auction market argue for a very centralized market that ideally will include all the buyers and sellers of the stock.

The other major trading system is a *dealer market* (also referred to as a *quote-driven* market) where individual dealers provide liquidity for investors by buying and selling the shares of stock for themselves. Ideally, with this system there will be numerous dealers who will compete against each other to provide the highest bid prices when you are selling and the lowest asking price when you are buying stock. Clearly, this is a very decentralized system that derives its benefit from the competition among the dealers to provide the best price for the buyer and seller. When we discuss the various equity markets, we will indicate the trading system used.

EXHIBIT 4.2	Secondary Equity Markets: Classification and Examples
Market Type	**Examples**
Primary listing markets	New York Stock Exchange
	London Stock Exchange
	Toronto Stock Exchange
	NASDAQ National Market System (NMS)
Regional markets	Boston Stock Exchange
	Chicago Stock Exchange
	Cincinnati Stock Exchange
Third-market dealers/brokers	Madoff Investment Securities
	Knight Trading Group
Alternative Trading Systems (ATSs)	
Electronic Communications Networks (ECNs)	Alpha Trading Systems Instinet
Electronic Crossing Systems (ECSs)	Instinet Canada Crossing

Source: Adapted from Larry Harris, *Trading and Exchanges* (Oxford University Press, 2003), p. 49.

---

9 This classification has been suggested by Harris (2003) in response to the numerous changes that have occurred.

Call versus Continuous Markets Beyond the different trading systems for equities, the operation of exchanges can differ in terms of when and how the stocks are traded.

In a **call market**, the intent is to gather all the bids and asks for the stock at a point in time and attempt to arrive at a single price where the quantity demanded is as close as possible to the quantity supplied. Call markets are generally used during the early stages of development of an exchange when there are few stocks listed or a small number of active investors-traders. For an exchange that is strictly a call market with a few listed stocks and traders, a designated market maker would call the roll of stocks and ask for interest in one stock at a time. After determining the available buy and sell orders, exchange officials specify a single price that will satisfy *most* of the orders, and all orders are transacted at this price.

A number of interesting statistics on stock exchanges worldwide can be found at the World Federation of Exchanges website at
http://www.
world-exchanges.org/.

Notably, call markets are also used at the opening for stocks on a large exchange if there is an overnight buildup of buy and/or sell orders, in which case the opening price can differ from the prior day's closing price, or if trading is suspended during the day because of some significant new information. In either case, the specialist or market maker would attempt to derive a new equilibrium price using a call-market approach that would reflect the imbalance and take care of most of the orders. For example, assume a stock has been trading at $42 and some significant, new, positive information was released overnight or during the day. If it happened overnight, it would affect the opening price; if it happened during the day, trading would be temporarily suspended and a call-market process would be used to determine a new equilibrium price that reflects the supply and demand due to the new information. If the buy orders were three or four times as numerous as the sell orders, the new price based on the call market might be $44.[10] Several studies have shown that using the call-market mechanism contributes to a more orderly market and less volatility in such instances.

In a **continuous market**, trades occur at any time the market is open wherein stocks are priced either by auction or by dealers. In a dealer market, dealers make a market in the stock, which means that they are willing to buy or sell for their own account at a specified bid-and-ask price. In an auction market, enough buyers and sellers are trading to allow the market to be continuous; that is, when one investor comes to buy stock, there is another investor available and willing to sell stock. A compromise between a pure dealer market and a pure auction market is a combination structure wherein the market trading system is basically an auction market, but there exists an intermediary (specialist) who is willing to act as a dealer if the pure auction market does not have enough activity. These intermediaries who act as both brokers and dealers provide temporary liquidity to ensure the market will be liquid and continuous.

Many continuous auction market exchanges employ a call-market mechanism in specific occasions at the open and during trading suspensions.

4.4   Classification of Secondary Equity Markets

In this section we consider the different secondary equity markets as listed in Exhibit 4.2.

4.4.1   PRIMARY LISTING MARKETS

Primary listing markets are formal exchanges or markets where a corporate stock is primarily or formally listed.

Toronto Stock Exchange (TSX) At one time, Canada had five stock exchanges; in 2000, a major realignment of the Canadian stock markets resulted in all equity trading to be handled by the TSX with the Montreal Exchange (ME) taking responsibility for the derivatives market. At

---

10 For an analysis of price movements surrounding trading halts, see Hopewell and Schwartz (1978) and Fabozzi and Ma (1988).

the time of writing, the TSX and ME were continuing to consider merging to form TMX Group. Our description below is current to time of writing.

The TSX has two tiers: Tier 1 (the TSX) is for companies having a certain level of earnings and net tangible assets, while tier 2 (the TSX Venture) is for more junior companies. Once a company trading on the TSX Venture Exchange meets the TSX listing requirements, it may apply to graduate to the TSX. A company failing to maintain the ongoing listing requirements of the TSX Venture Exchange move to the NEX platform, which is a trading forum that also allows opportunities for these companies to reinvest and reinvent themselves. At the end of 2008, the TSX had 1,570 listed companies while the TSX Venture Exchange (including NEX) had 2,076 listed companies. Combined, the two exchanges had a combined total listed-company market capitalization of $1.3 trillion.

In 2002, the TSX became a public company known as the TSX Group Inc. (ticker X). The result of this change meant that the TSX was no longer owned by member brokers but by the public at large. The idea behind this move was that separating exchange ownership from its members would result in more accountability and better responsiveness to the rapidly changing capital markets. In order to trade through the facilities of the TSX, a firm must be approved as a Participating Organization. Participating Organizations of the TSX and Members of TSX Venture Exchange may act as sponsors for listed issuers or issuers wanting to be listed on TSX Venture Exchange.

> The TSX Learning Academy provides a good overview of the market-maker role at http://www.tsx.com/en/pdf/MarketMakerPresentation.pdf.

Unlike the New York Stock Exchange, all trades on the Toronto Stock Exchange are conducted electronically; the buy and sell orders are matched electronically by the exchange's computerized system. The TSX still assigns a specialist role (market maker) to exchange participants to ensure that there is an orderly market for listed securities. The market maker will trade in the shares if there are unusual circumstances, such as a temporary disparity between demand and supply.

New York Stock Exchange (NYSE) The New York Stock Exchange (NYSE), the largest organized securities market in the United States, was established in 1817 as the New York Stock and Exchange Board. The name was changed to the New York Stock Exchange in 1863. In 2006, the NYSE went public, and in 2007 the NYSE Group Inc. merged with Euronext M.V. Although still referred to as the NYSE, the role of the NYSE Euronext (NYX) is to bring together major European and U.S. marketplaces. Because the renaming is still new, we will refer to the NYSE Euronext as the NYSE. At the end of 2007, approximately 2,850 companies had their stock listed on the NYSE with a total market value of more than $14 trillion.

The NYSE has dominated the other exchanges in the United States in trading volume. The average number of shares traded daily on the NYSE has increased steadily and substantially. Prior to the 1960s, the daily share-trading volume averaged less than 3 million shares, compared with the 2007 average daily volume of about 2.55 billion shares.

Given its stringent listing requirements and its prestige, most of the largest and best-known U.S. and Canadian companies are listed on the NYSE.

An Aside on Global Stock Exchanges The equity-market environment outside Canada is similar in that each country typically will have one relatively large exchange that dominates the market. Examples include the Tokyo Stock Exchange, the London Stock Exchange, the Frankfurt Stock Exchange, and the Paris Bourse.

Three points about these international exchanges: First, there has been a trend toward consolidations or affiliations that will provide more liquidity and greater economies of scale to support the technology required by investors. Second, many of the larger companies in these countries that can qualify for listing on another exchange become dual-listed. As a result, about 20% of the stocks listed on the NYSE are foreign firms (2% of firms listed on the TSX are foreign). Third, the existence of these strong international exchanges has made possible a global equity market wherein stocks that have a global constituency can be traded around the world continuously, as discussed in the following section. There is intense competition between the various exchanges.

The Global 24-Hour Market Our discussion of the global securities market will emphasize the markets in New York, London, and Tokyo because of their relative size and importance, and because they represent the major segments of a worldwide 24-hour stock market. You will often hear about a continuous market where investment firms "pass the book" around the world. This means the major active market in securities moves around the globe as trading hours for these three markets begin and end.

Consider the individual trading hours for each of the three exchanges, using a 24-hour eastern standard time (EST) clock:

	Local Time (24-hr. notations)	24-Hour EST
New York Stock Exchange (NYSE)	0930–1600	0930–1600
Tokyo Stock Exchange (TSE)	0900–1100	2300–0100
	1300–1500	0300–0500
London Stock Exchange (LSE)	0815–1615	0215–1015

Imagine trading starting in New York at 0930 and going until 1600 in the afternoon, being picked up by Tokyo late in the evening and going until 0500 in the morning, and continuing in London (with some overlap) until it begins in New York again (with some overlap) at 0930. Alternatively, it is possible to envision trading as beginning in Tokyo at 2300 hours and continuing until 0500, when it moves to London, then ends the day in New York. This latter model seems the most relevant, because the first question a London trader asks in the morning is, "What happened in Tokyo?" The U.S. trader asks, "What happened in Tokyo and what *is* happening in London?" The point is, the markets operate almost continuously and are related in their response to economic events. Therefore, investors are not dealing with three separate and distinct exchanges, but with one interrelated world market. Clearly, this interrelationship is growing daily because of numerous multiple listings where stocks are listed on several exchanges around the world (such as the NYSE and TSE) and the availability of sophisticated telecommunications. Examples of stocks that are part of this global market are General Electric, Johnson and Johnson, and McDonald's.

The NASDAQ Market[11] Historically this system was known as the OTC market, which included stocks not formally listed on the two major U.S. exchanges (NYSE and AMEX [the American Stock Exchange]). This description has changed since it was recognized that this is an equity market similar to the major exchanges with several minor differences. First, NASDAQ is a *dealer market,* in contrast to a broker/dealer (specialists) market as is the NYSE. Second, trading on NASDAQ takes place electronically rather than on a trading floor. What the NASDAQ has in common with the other exchanges is a set of requirements for a stock to be traded on the NASDAQ National Market System (NMS). Also, while NASDAQ

---

11 NASDAQ is an acronym for National Association of Securities Dealers Automated Quotations. The system is discussed in detail in a later section. To be traded on the NMS, a firm must have a certain size and trading activity and at least four market makers.

dealers do not have to pay for a seat (membership) on the exchange, they are required to be members of the National Association of Security Dealers (NASD) and abide by its rules.

The NASDAQ market is the second-largest U.S. secondary market in terms of the number of issues traded. More than 2,800 issues are actively traded on the NASDAQ NMS and almost 700 on the NASDAQ Small-Cap Market (SCM). The NASDAQ market is also the most diverse secondary market component in terms of quality because it has multiple minimum requirements. Stocks that trade on the NASDAQ market (NMS and SCM) range from those of small, unprofitable companies to large, extremely profitable firms such as Microsoft and Intel.

At the end of 2007 an estimated 650 issues of NASDAQ were either foreign stocks or American Depository Receipts (ADRs), representing over 8% of total NASDAQ share volume. About 300 of these issues trade on both NASDAQ and a foreign exchange such as the TSX. NASDAQ has developed a link with the Singapore Stock Exchange that allows 24-hour trading from NASDAQ in New York to Singapore to a NASDAQ/London link and back to New York.

Although the NASDAQ market has the greatest number of issues, the NYSE has a larger total value of trading. In 2007 the approximate value of average daily equity trading on the NYSE was about $52 billion and on NASDAQ was about $31 billion.

Operation of the NASDAQ Market As noted, stocks can be traded on the NASDAQ market as long as there are dealers willing to make a market by buying or selling for their own account.[12]

The NASDAQ Quotation System The *National Association of Securities Dealers Automated Quotation (NASDAQ) system* is an automated, electronic quotation system. Any number of dealers can elect to make markets in a NASDAQ stock. The actual number depends on the activity in the stock. In 2007, the average number of market makers for all stocks on the NASDAQ NMS was about eight.

NASDAQ makes all dealer quotes available immediately. The broker can check the quotation machine and call the dealer with the best market, verify that the quote has not changed, and make the sale or purchase. The NASDAQ quotation system has three levels to serve firms with different needs and interests.

Level 1 provides a single median representative quote for the stocks on NASDAQ. This quotation system is for firms that want current quotes on NASDAQ stocks but do not consistently buy or sell these stocks for their customers and are not market makers. This representative quote changes constantly to adjust for any changes by individual market makers.

Level 2 provides instantaneous current quotations on NASDAQ stocks by all market makers in a stock. This quotation system is for firms that consistently trade NASDAQ stocks. Given an order to buy or sell, brokers check the quotation machine, call the market maker with the best market for their purposes (highest bid if they are selling, lowest offer if buying), and consummate the deal.

Level 3 is for NASDAQ market makers. Such firms want Level 2, but they also need the capability to change their own quotations, which Level 3 provides.

Listing Requirements for NASDAQ Quotes and trading volume for the NASDAQ market are reported in two lists: a National Market System (NMS) list and a regular NASDAQ list. A company must meet all of the requirements under at least one of the three listing standards for initial listing and then meet at least one continued listing standard to maintain its listing

For the latest NASDAQ listing requirements go to http://www.nasdaq.com/about/listing_information.stm#fees. Under "Listing Guides and Resources" there are Listing Guides.

---

12 *Dealer* and *market maker* are synonymous.

on the NMS. For stocks on this system, reports include up-to-the-minute volume and last-sale information for the competing market makers as well as end-of-the-day information on total volume and high, low, and closing prices.

A Sample Trade Assume you are considering the purchase of 100 shares of Intel. Although Intel is large enough and profitable enough to be listed on the NYSE, the company has never applied for listing because it enjoys an active market on NASDAQ (ticker INTC). (It is one of the volume leaders, with daily volume typically above 25 million shares and often in excess of 50 million shares.) When you contact your broker, she will consult the NASDAQ quotation machine to determine the current dealer quotations for INTC.[13] The quote machine might show that over 30 dealers are making a market in INTC. An example of differing quotations might be as follows:

Dealer	Bid	Ask
1	30.60	30.75
2	30.55	30.65
3	30.50	30.65
4	30.55	30.70

Assuming these are the best markets available from the total group, your broker would call either dealer 2 or dealer 3 because they have the lowest offering prices. After verifying the quote, your broker would give one of these dealers an order to buy 100 shares of INTC at $30.65 per share. Because your firm was not a market maker in the stock, the firm would act as a broker and charge you $3,065 plus a commission for the trade. If your firm had been a market maker in INTC, with an asking price of $30.65 the firm would have sold the stock to you at $30.65 net (without commission). If you had been interested in selling 100 shares of Intel instead of buying, the broker would have contacted dealer 1, who made the highest bid ($30.60).

Changing Dealer Inventory Let's consider the price quotations by a NASDAQ dealer who wants to change his inventory on a given stock. For example, assume dealer 4, with a current quote of 30.55 bid–30.70 ask, decides to increase his holdings of INTC. The NASDAQ quotes indicate that the highest bid is currently 30.60. Increasing the bid to 30.60 would bring some of the business currently going to dealer 1. Taking a more aggressive action, dealer 4 might raise the bid to 30.63 and buy all the stock offered, because he has the highest bid. In this example, the dealer raises the bid price but does not change the ask price, which was above those of dealers 2 and 3. This dealer will buy stock but probably will not sell any. A dealer who had excess stock would keep the bid below the market (lower than 30.60) and reduce the ask price to 30.65 or less. Dealers constantly change their bid-and-ask prices, depending on their current inventories or changes in the outlook based on new information for the stock.

Other NASDAQ Market Segments Now that we are familiar with the NASDAQ system and its operation, we can easily describe the other segments of this market because the major differences relate to the size and liquidity of the stocks involved.

- **The NASDAQ Small-Cap Market (SCM)** initial listing requirements consider the same factors as the NMS but are generally about one-half to one-third of the values required for the NMS. As of late 2007, there were about 700 stocks listed in the NASDAQ small-cap segment. This compares to about 600 stocks listed in the section entitled "NASDAQ NM

---

13 Trading symbols are one- to four-letter codes used to designate stocks. Whenever a trade is reported on a stock ticker, the trading symbol appears with the figures.

Issues Under $100 Million Market Cap" and about 2,200 in the section entitled "NASDAQ National Market Issues."

- **The NASDAQ** *OTC Electronic Bulletin Board (OTCBB)* reports indications for smaller stocks sponsored by NASD dealers. As of late 2007, there were about 3,400 stocks included on the OTCBB.
- **The National Quotation Bureau (NQB) Pink Sheets** report order indications for the smallest publicly traded stocks in the United States. Pre-1970, these pink sheets (actually printed on pink sheets of paper) were the primary daily source of OTC stock quotes. With the creation of the NASDAQ electronic quotation system, the sheets were superseded. Currently, the NQB publishes a weekly edition on paper and distributes a daily edition electronically with these small-stock quotes.

4.4.2 REGIONAL STOCK EXCHANGES

The second category in Harris's classification of secondary markets (Exhibit 4.2) is the regional market. Regional exchanges typically have the same operating procedures as national exchanges in the same countries, but they differ in their listing requirements.

As discussed earlier, Canada no longer has regional stock exchanges; however, their presence in other countries warrants a review. Regional stock exchanges exist for two main reasons: First, they provide trading facilities for local companies not large enough to qualify for listing on a national exchange. Their listing requirements are typically less stringent than for national exchanges. Second, regional exchanges in some countries list firms that also list on one of the national exchanges to give local brokers access to these securities. For example, Wal-Mart and General Motors are listed on both the NYSE and several regional exchanges. This dual listing allows a local brokerage firm that is not a member of the NYSE to buy and sell shares of the dual-listed stock without going through the NYSE. In addition, regional exchanges can trade some stocks on the NASDAQ market under *unlisted trading privileges (UTP)* granted by the SEC. The majority of trading on regional exchanges is due to dual-listed and UTP stocks.

4.4.3 THE THIRD MARKET

The **third market** involves dealers and brokers who trade exchange-listed shares away from the exchange. Typically these investment firms are not a member of an exchange but make a market in a listed stock away from the exchange. Most third-market trading is in well-known stocks such as Coca-Cola, IBM, and Ford. The success or failure of the third market depends on whether the non-exchange market in these stocks is as good as the exchange market and whether the relative cost of the transaction compares favourably with the cost on the exchange. This market is critical during the relatively few periods when trading is not available on the larger exchanges (NYSE, TSX) either because trading is suspended or the exchange is closed. This market has also grown because of the quality and cost factors mentioned. Third-market dealers typically display their quotes on the *NASDAQ InterMarket* system. For articles that discuss the impact of third-market trading and the practice of purchasing order flow, see Battalio (1997); Battalio, Greene, and Jennings (1997); and Easley, Kiefer, and O'Hara (1996).

4.4.4 ALTERNATIVE TRADING SYSTEMS (ATSs)

The final category in Exhibit 4.2 is alternative trading systems, where the biggest changes have occurred during the last decade. *Alternative trading systems (ATSs)* are non-traditional, computerized trading systems that compete with or supplement dealer markets and traditional exchanges. These trading systems facilitate the exchange of millions of shares every day through electronic means. Notably, they do not provide listing services. The most well-known ATSs are the Electronic Communication Networks (ECNs) and the Electronic Crossing Systems (ECSs).

- *Electronic Communication Networks (ECNs)* are electronic facilities that match buy and sell orders directly via computer, mainly for retail and small institutional trading. ECNs do *not* buy or sell from their own account but act as very cheap, efficient electronic brokers.
- *Electronic Crossing Systems (ECSs)* are electronic facilities that act as brokers to match *large* buy and sell orders.

The trading of exchange-listed stocks using one of these ATSs has become the *fourth market*.

4.5 Detailed Analysis of Exchange Markets

IIROC has a listing of the current Canadian equity marketplaces at http://www.iiroc.ca/English/Documents/SumCompEquityMarkets_en.pdf.

The importance of listed exchange markets requires that we discuss them at some length. In this section, we discuss the major types of orders, as well as exchange market makers—a critical component of a good exchange market.

4.5.1 TYPES OF ORDERS

It is important to understand the different types of orders available to investors and the specialist as a dealer.

Market Orders The most frequent type of order is a **market order**, an order to buy or sell a stock at the best current price. An investor who enters a market sell order indicates a willingness to sell immediately at the highest bid available at the time the order reaches the trading floor; a market buy order indicates the investor is willing to pay the lowest offering price available. Market orders provide immediate liquidity for an investor willing to accept the prevailing market price.

Assume you are interested in Shoppers Drug Mart (ticker SC) and you look at your online trading account and see the current "market" on the stock. The site indicates that the prevailing market is 44.65 bid–44.68 ask. This means that the highest current bid on the books is 44.65 and the lowest offer is 44.68, that is, the lowest price anyone is willing to accept to sell the stock. If you placed a market buy order for 100 shares, you would buy 100 shares at $44.68 a share (the lowest ask price) for a total cost of $4,468 plus commission. If you submitted a market sell order for 100 shares, you would sell the shares at $44.65 each and receive $4,465 less commission.

Limit Orders The individual placing a **limit order** specifies the buy or sell price. You might submit a limit-order bid to purchase 100 shares of Shoppers Drug Mart stock at $44.50 a share when the current market is 44.65 bid–44.68 ask, with the expectation that the stock will decline to $44.50 in the near future.

You must also indicate how long the limit order will be outstanding. Alternative time specifications are basically boundless. A limit order can be instantaneous ("fill or kill," meaning fill the order instantly or cancel it). It can also be good for part of a day, a full day, several days, a week, or a month (good-till-date, or GTD). It can also be open-ended, or good-till-cancelled (GTC).

Rather than wait for a given price on a stock, because SC is listed on the TSX your broker will give the limit order to the specialist, who will put it in a limit-order book and act as the broker's representative. When and if the market price for SC reaches the limit-order price, the specialist will execute the order and inform your broker. The specialist receives a small part of the commission for rendering this service.

Short Sales Most investors purchase stock ("go long") expecting to derive their return from an increase in value. If you believe that a stock is overpriced, however, and want to take advantage of an expected decline in the price, you can sell the stock short. A **short sale** is the sale of stock that you do not own with the intent of purchasing it back later at a lower price. Specifically, through your broker you borrow the stock from another investor and sell it in the market. Subsequently you replace it at (you hope) a price lower than the price at which you had sold it (referred to as *covering your short position*). Although a short sale has no time limit, the lender of the shares can decide to sell the shares, in which case your broker must find another investor willing to lend the shares.[14]

Three technical points affect short sales. First, a short sale can be made only on an uptick or flat-tick (meaning the price of the short sale must be higher than or equal to the last trade price). This is because the exchanges do not want traders to force a profit on a short sale by pushing the price down through continually selling short. For an example of a flat-tick, consider the following set of transaction prices: 42, 42.25, 42.25. You could sell short at 42.25 even though it is no change from the previous trade at 42.25.[15]

The second technical point concerns dividends. The short seller must pay any dividends due to the investor who lent the stock. The purchaser of the short sale receives the dividend from the corporation, so the short seller must pay a similar dividend to the lender.

Finally, short sellers must post the same margin as an investor who had purchased stock. This margin can be in any unrestricted securities owned by the short seller.

Special Orders In addition to these general orders, there are several special types of orders. A *stop loss order* is a conditional market order whereby the investor directs the sale of a stock if it drops to a given price. Assume you buy a stock at 50 and expect it to go up. If you are wrong, you want to limit your losses. To protect yourself, you could put in a stop loss order at 45. In this case, if the stock dropped to 45, your stop loss order would become a market sell order, and the stock would be sold at the prevailing market price. The stop loss order does not guarantee that you will get the $45; you can get a little bit more or a little bit less. Because of the possibility of market disruption caused by a large number of stop loss orders, exchanges have, on occasion, cancelled all such orders on certain stocks and not allowed brokers to accept further stop loss orders on those issues.

A related stop loss tactic for an investor who has entered into a short sale is a *stop buy order.* Such an investor who wants to minimize loss if the stock begins to increase in value would enter this conditional buy order at a price above the short-sale price. Assume you sold a stock short at 50, expecting it to decline to 40. To protect yourself from an increase, you could put in a stop buy order to purchase the stock using a market buy order if it reached a price of 55. This conditional buy order would hopefully limit any loss on the short sale to approximately $5 a share.

Margin Transactions When investors buy stock, they can pay for the stock with cash or borrow part of the cost, leveraging the transaction. Leverage is accomplished by buying on margin, which means the investor pays for the stock with some cash and borrows the rest through the broker, putting up the stock for collateral.

After the initial purchase, changes in the market price of the stock will cause changes in the *investor's equity*, which is equal to the market value of the collateral stock minus the amount borrowed. Obviously, if the stock price increases, the investor's equity as a proportion

14 For discussions of both good and bad experiences with short-selling, see Power (1993), Loomis (1996), Weiss (1996), and Beard (2001).

15 Current rules on short selling in Canadian markets can be found at http://www.iiroc.ca/English/ComplianceSurveillance/RuleBook/Pages/UMIR.aspx.

The World Federation of Exchanges has an interesting commentary on short selling and bubble pessimism at http://www.world-exchanges.org/files/file/WFE%20Finadium%20Short%20Selling%20Jan%2009.pdf.

IIROC has an interesting study on short trades at http://docs.iiroc.ca/DisplayDocument.aspx?DocumentID=DE2E6F9F4AE442F5BC0AE75A9E812FE5&Language=en.

A listing of client debt margin accounts can be found at the IIROC web site at www.iiroc.ca. Under "Compliance/Surveillance," click on "Financial and Operational Compliance" and then "Resource Information."

of the total market value of the stock increases, that is, the investor's margin will exceed the initial margin requirement.

Assume you purchased 200 shares at $50 each for a total cost of $10,000. A 50% initial margin requirement allowed you to borrow $5,000, making your initial equity $5,000. If the stock price increases by 20% to $60 per share, the total market value of your position is $12,000, and your equity is now $7,000 ($12,000–$5,000), or 58% ($7,000/$12,000). In contrast, if the stock price declines by 20% to $40 per share, the total market value would be $8,000, and your investor's equity would be $3,000 ($8,000–$5,000), or 37.5% ($3,000/$8,000).

This example demonstrates that buying on margin provides all the advantages and the disadvantages of leverage. Lower margin requirements allow you to borrow more, increasing the percentage of gain or loss on your investment when the stock price increases or decreases. The leverage factor equals 1/percent margin. Thus, as in the example, if the margin is 50%, the leverage factor is 2, that is, 1/0.50. Therefore, when the return on the stock is plus or minus 10%, the return on your equity is plus or minus 20%. If the margin requirement declines to 33%, you can borrow more (67%), and the leverage factor is 3 (1/0.33). When you buy investments on margin, you are increasing the financial risk of the investment beyond the risk inherent in the security itself and hence you should increase your required return accordingly.

The following example shows how borrowing by using margin affects the distribution of your returns *before commissions and interest* on the loan. If the stock increased by 20, your return on the investment would be as follows:

1. The market value of the stock is $12,000, which leaves you with $7,000 after you pay off the loan.
2. The return on your $5,000 investment is

$$\frac{7{,}000}{5{,}000} - 1 = 0.40, \text{ or } 40\%$$

In contrast, if the stock declined by 20% to $40 a share, your return would be as follows:

1. The market value of the stock is $8,000, which leaves you with $3,000 after you pay off the loan.
2. The negative return on your $5,000 investment is

$$\frac{3{,}000}{5{,}000} - 1 = -0.40, \text{ or } -40\%$$

Notably, this symmetrical increase in gains and losses is only true ignoring commissions and interest. Assuming a 7% cost of borrowing (interest cost would be $5,000 \times 0.07 = $350) and a $100 commission on the transaction, the results would be as follows:

TD Waterhouse has a fairly complete list of margin requirements at http://www.tdcanadatrust.com/planning/investing/margin.jsp.

$$20\% \text{ increase: } \frac{\$12{,}000 - \$5{,}000 - \$350 - \$100}{5{,}000} - 1 = 0.31, \text{ or } 31\%$$

$$20\% \text{ decline: } \frac{\$8{,}000 - \$5{,}000 - \$350 - \$100}{5{,}000} - 1 = -0.49, \text{ or } -49\%$$

Margin requirements range from 30% to 100%, depending upon the price at which the stock is selling. The **maintenance margin**, which is the required proportion of your equity to the total value of the stock, protects the broker if the stock price declines. For example, if the stock price declines to the point where your investor's equity drops below 30% of the total value of the position, the account is considered undermargined, and you will receive a **margin call** to provide more equity. If you do not respond with the required funds in time, the stock will be sold to pay off the loan. The time allowed to meet a margin call varies between investment firms and is affected by market conditions. Under volatile conditions, the time allowed to respond to a margin call can be shortened drastically.

For example, say on our previous purchase of 200 shares there is a 30% margin requirement, how far can the stock price fall before you receive a margin call? If the price of the stock is P and you own 200 shares, the value of the position is 200P and the equity in the account is 200P − $5,000. The percentage margin is (200P − 5,000)/200P. To determine the price, P, that is equal to 30% (0.30), we use the following equation:

$$\frac{200P - \$5{,}000}{200P} = 0.30$$

$$200P - \$5000 = 60P$$

$$140P = \$5{,}000$$

$$P = \$35.71$$

Therefore, when the stock is at $35.71, the equity value is exactly 30%; so if the stock declines from $50 to below $35.71, you will receive a margin call.

To continue the previous example, if the stock declines to $30 a share, its total market value would be $6,000 and your equity would be $1,000, which is only about 17% of the total value ($1,000/$6,000). You would receive a margin call for approximately $1,143, which would give you equity of $2,143, or 30% of the total value of the account ($2,143/$7,143). If the stock declined further, you would receive additional margin calls.

4.5.2 EXCHANGE MARKET MAKERS

Earlier we briefly introduced the role of the market maker. Although the various markets may have a different structure (floor trading versus continuous electronic auction markets), the market maker has a role.

The specialist (or designated market maker, DMM) is an exchange member who applies to the exchange to be assigned stocks to handle. The typical specialist will handle 10 to 15 stocks.

Functions of the Specialist (DMM) Specialists (DMMs) have two major functions. First, they serve as *brokers* to match buy and sell orders and to handle special limit orders. As noted earlier, an individual broker who receives a limit order (or stop loss or stop buy order) leaves it with the specialist (DMM) who executes it when the specified price occurs.

The second major function of a specialist is to act as a *dealer* to maintain a fair and orderly market by providing liquidity when the normal flow of orders is not adequate. As a dealer, the specialist must buy and sell for his or her own account (like a NASDAQ dealer) when public supply or demand is insufficient to provide a continuous, liquid market.

Consider the following example: A stock is currently selling for $40 and the current bid and ask in an auction market (without the intervention of the specialist) is 40 bid–41 ask.

Under such conditions, random market buy and sell orders might cause the stock price to fluctuate between 40 and 41 constantly—a movement of 2.5% between trades. Most investors would probably consider such a price pattern too volatile; the market would not be considered liquid. Under such conditions, the specialist is expected to provide "bridge liquidity" by entering alternative bids and asks or both to narrow the spread and improve the stock's price continuity. In this example, the specialist could enter a bid of 40.25 or 40.50 or an ask of 40.50 or 40.75 to narrow the spread to one-half or one-quarter point.

Specialists can enter either side of the market, depending on several factors, including the trend of the market. Notably, they are expected to buy or sell against the market when prices are clearly moving in one direction. Specifically, they are required to buy stock for their own inventories when there is a clear excess of sell orders and the market is definitely declining. Alternatively, they must sell stock from their inventories or sell it short (i.e., borrow shares) to accommodate an excess of buy orders when the market is rising. Specialists are not expected to prevent prices from rising or declining, but only to ensure that *prices change in an orderly fashion* (i.e., to maintain price continuity).

Assuming that there is not a clear trend in the market, several factors will affect how specialists close the bid-ask spread. One factor is their current inventory position in the stock. For example, if they have large inventories of a given stock, all other factors being equal, they would probably enter on the ask (sell) side to reduce these heavy inventories. In contrast, specialists who have little or no inventory of shares because they had been selling from their inventories, or selling short, would tend toward the bid (buy) side of the market to rebuild their inventories or close out their short positions.

Second, the position of the limit-order book will influence how they narrow the spread. Numerous limit buy orders (bids) close to the current market and few limit sell orders (asks) might indicate a tendency toward higher prices because demand is apparently heavy and supply is limited. Under such conditions, a specialist who is not bound by one of the other factors would probably opt to accumulate stock in anticipation of a price increase.

Specialist Income The specialist derives income from the broker and dealer functions. The actual breakdown between the two sources depends on the specific stock. In an actively traded stock, a specialist has little need to act as a dealer because the substantial public interest in the stock creates a tight market (i.e., a narrow bid-ask spread). In such a case, the main source of income would come from maintaining the limit orders for the stock.

In contrast, a stock with low trading volume and substantial price volatility would probably have a fairly wide bid-ask spread, and the specialist would have to be an active dealer. The specialist's income from such a stock would depend on his or her ability to trade it profitably. Specialists should have a major advantage when trading because of their limit-order books. Officially, only specialists are supposed to see the limit-order book, which would contain important information regarding the current supply and demand for a stock. The fact is, most specialists routinely share the limit-order book with other brokers, so it is not a competitive advantage.

Most specialists attempt to balance their portfolios between strong broker stocks that provide steady, riskless income and stocks that require active dealer roles. It has been noted that an increase in dealer activity has been matched with an increase in return on capital for specialists. For further analysis of specialists, see Madhaven and Sofianos (1998) and Benveniste, Marcus, and Wilhelm (1992).

4.5.3 WHERE DO WE GO FROM HERE?

One cannot help but be struck by the significant changes that have taken place in global equity marketing during the new millennium. The technological advances have contributed to significant reductions in trading costs for institutional and retail investors. The rapid globalization of the markets wherein investors and investment firms are interested in trading continuously around the clock anywhere in the world in virtually any asset class and communication technology makes this possible.

4.6 Uses of Security-Market Indices

Security-market indices have at least five specific uses. A primary application is to use the index values to compute total returns and risk measures for an aggregate market or some component of a market over a specified time period and use the return–risk results as a *benchmark* to judge the performance of individual portfolios and professional money managers. A basic assumption when evaluating portfolio performance is that any investor should be able to experience a risk-adjusted return comparable to the market by randomly selecting a large number of stocks or bonds from the total market; hence, a superior portfolio manager should consistently do better than the market.

An obvious use of indices is to develop an index portfolio. If it is truly difficult for most money managers to consistently outperform specified market indices on a risk-adjusted basis over time,[16] an obvious alternative is to invest in a portfolio that will emulate this market portfolio. This notion led to the creation of **index funds** and **exchange-traded funds (ETFs)**, whose purpose is to track the performance of the specified market series (index) over time.[17] The development of comprehensive, well-specified bond-market indices and the inability of most bond-portfolio managers to outperform these indices have led to a similar phenomenon in the fixed-income area (bond-index funds).[18]

Securities analysts, portfolio managers, and academics doing research use security-market indices to examine the factors that influence aggregate security price movements and to compare the risk-adjusted performance of alternative asset classes (for example, stocks versus bonds versus real estate).

4.7 Differentiating Factors in Constructing Market Indices

Because an index is intended to reflect the overall movements of a group of securities, we need to consider three factors that are important when constructing an index designed to represent a total population.

4.7.1 THE SAMPLE

The first factor is the sample used to construct an index. The size, the breadth, and the source of the sample are all important.

A small percentage of the total population will provide valid indications of the behaviour of the total population *if* the sample is properly selected. In some cases, because of the economics of computers, virtually all the stocks on an exchange or market are included, with a few deletions of unusual securities. The sample should be *representative* of the total population; otherwise, its size will be meaningless. A large biased sample is no better than a small biased sample. The sample can be generated by completely random selection or by a non-random

---

16 Throughout this chapter and the book, we will use *indicator series* and *indices* interchangeably, although *indicator series* is the more correct specification because it refers to a broad class of series; one popular type of series is an index, but there can be other types and many different indices.

17 The original index funds were common-stock funds as discussed in Malkiel (2007), chapter 14; and Mossavar-Rahmani (2005).

18 See Hawthorne (1986) and Dialynas (2001).

selection technique designed to incorporate the important characteristics of the desired population. Finally, the *source* of the sample is important if there are any differences between segments of the population, in which case samples from each segment are required.

4.7.2 WEIGHTING SAMPLE MEMBERS

The second factor is the weight given to each member in the sample. Three principal weighting schemes are used for security-market indices: (1) a price-weighted index, (2) a market-value-weighted index, and (3) an unweighted index, or what would be described as an equal-weighted index. We will discuss each of these in detail.

4.7.3 COMPUTATIONAL PROCEDURE

The final consideration is the computational procedure used. One alternative is to take a simple arithmetic mean of the various members in the index. Another is to compute an index and have all changes, whether in price or value, reported in terms of the basic index. Finally, some prefer using a geometric mean of the components rather than an arithmetic mean.

4.8 Stock-Market Indices

As mentioned previously, we hear a lot about what happens to the Dow Jones Industrial Average (DJIA) each day. You might also hear about other stock indices, such as the S&P/TSX composite index, the NASDAQ composite, or even the Nikkei Average. If you listen carefully, you will realize that these indices experience different percentage changes (which is the way that the changes should be reported). Reasons for some differences are obvious, but others are not.

We have organized the discussion of the indices by the weighting of the sample of stocks. We begin with the price-weighted index because some of the most popular indices are in this category. The next group is the value-weighted index, which is the technique currently used for most indices. Finally, we will examine the unweighted indices.

4.8.1 PRICE-WEIGHTED INDEX

A **price-weighted index** is an arithmetic mean of current stock prices; this means that index movements are influenced by the differential prices of the components.

Dow Jones Industrial Average The best-known and oldest price-weighted index is the Dow Jones Industrial Average (DJIA). The DJIA is a price-weighted average of 30 large, well-known industrial stocks that are generally the leaders in their industry (blue chips). It is computed by totalling the current prices of the 30 stocks and dividing the sum by a divisor that has been adjusted to take account of stock splits and changes in the sample over time.[19] Exhibit 4.3 shows how a divisor is adjusted. The equation for the index is

$$DJIA_t = \sum_{i=1}^{30} \frac{P_{it}}{D_{adj}}$$

where:

$DJIA_t$ = the value of the DJIA on day t

P_{it} = the closing price of stock i on day t

D_{adj} = the adjusted divisor on day t

---

[19] A complete list of all events that have caused a change in the divisor since the DJIA went to 30 stocks on October 1, 1928, is contained in Phyllis S. Pierce, ed., *The Business One Irwin Investor's Handbook* (Burr Ridge, IL: Dow Jones Books, annual).

EXHIBIT 4.3	Example of Change in DJIA Divisor when a Sample Stock Splits	
Stock	Before Split	After Three-for-One Split by Stock A
	PRICES	PRICES
A	30	10
B	20	20
C	<u>10</u>	<u>10</u>
	60 ÷ 3 = 20	40 ÷ X = 20	X = 2
			(NEW DIVISOR)

When stocks split, the divisor becomes smaller (see Exhibit 4.3). The adjusted divisor ensures that the new value for the index is the same as it would have been without the split. In this case, the presplit index value was 20. Therefore, after the split, given the new sum of prices, the divisor is adjusted downward to maintain this value of 20. The divisor is also changed when there is a change in the sample makeup of the index. The DJIA divisor as of June 2009 was 0.132319135.

Because the index is price weighted, a high-priced stock carries more weight than a low-priced stock. As shown in Exhibit 4.4, a 10% change in a $100 stock ($10) will cause a larger change in the index than a 10% change in a $30 stock ($3). For Case A, when the $100 stock increases by 10%, the average rises by 5.5%; for Case B, when the $30 stock increases by 10%, the average rises by only 1.7%.

The DJIA has been criticized on several counts. First, the index sample used is limited to 30 non-randomly selected blue-chip stocks that cannot be representative of the thousands of U.S. stocks. Several studies have shown that the DJIA has not been as volatile as other market indices, and its long-run returns are not comparable to other NYSE stock indices.

EXHIBIT 4.4	The Impact of Differently Priced Shares on a Price-Weighted Index		
		Period T + 1	
Stock	Period T	Case A	Case B
A	100	110	100
B	50	50	50
C	<u>30</u>	<u>30</u>	<u>33</u>
Sum	180	190	183
Divisor	3	3	3
Average	60	63.3	61
Percentage change		5.5	1.7

---

20 For a discussion of specific differences between indices, see Ip (1998).

In addition, because the DJIA is price weighted, when companies have a stock split, their prices decline and therefore their weight in the DJIA is reduced—even though they may be large and important. Therefore, the weighting scheme causes a downward bias in the DJIA because high-growth stocks will have higher prices, and because such stocks tend to split, they will consistently lose weight within the index.[20]

Nikkei-Dow 225 Stock Average Also referred to as the Nikkei-Dow Jones Average, this index is an arithmetic mean of prices for 225 stocks on the First Section of the Tokyo Stock Exchange (TSE). This best-known series in Japan shows stock-price trends since the reopening of the TSE. Notably, it was formulated by Dow Jones and Company, and, similar to the DJIA, it is a price-weighted index. It is also criticized because the 225 stocks only comprise about 15% of all stocks on the First Section.

4.8.2 VALUE-WEIGHTED INDEX

A **value-weighted index** such as the S&P/TSX composite is generated by deriving the initial total market value of all stocks used in the index (Market Value = Number of Shares Outstanding [or freely floating shares] × Current Market Price). "Freely floating shares" exclude shares held by insiders. This initial figure is typically established as the base and assigned an index value (the most popular beginning index value is 100, but it can vary—for example, 10, 50). Subsequently, a new market value is computed for all securities in the index, and the current market value is compared to the initial "base" market value to determine the percentage of change, which in turn is applied to the beginning index value.

$$\text{Index}_t = \frac{\sum P_t Q_t}{\sum P_b Q_b} \times \textbf{Beginning Index Value}$$

where:

Index_t = index value on day t

P_t = ending prices for stocks on day t

Q_t = number of outstanding or freely floating shares on day t

P_b = ending price for stocks on base day

Q_b = number of outstanding or freely floating shares on base day

A simple example for a three-stock index in Exhibit 4.5 shows that there is an *automatic adjustment* for stock splits and other capital changes with a value-weighted index because the stock price decrease is offset by the increase in the number of shares outstanding. In a value-weighted index, the importance of individual stocks in the sample depends on the market value of the stocks. Therefore, a specified percentage change in the value of a large company has a greater impact than a comparable percentage change for a small company. As shown in Exhibit 4.6, if we assume that the only change is a 20% increase in the value of stock A, which has a beginning value of $10 million, the ending index value would be $202 million, or an index of 101. In contrast, if only stock C increases by 20% from $100 million, the ending value will be $220 million or an index value of 110. Because price changes for the large market value stocks in a value-weighted index will dominate changes in the index value over time, it is important to be aware of the large-value stocks in the index.

EXHIBIT 4.5	Example of a Value-Weighted Index Calculation

Stock	Share Price	Number of Shares	Market Value
December 31, 2008			
A	$10.00	1,000,000	$10,000,000
B	15.00	6,000,000	90,000,000
C	20.00	5,000,000	100,000,000
Total			$200,000,000
		Base Value Equal to an Index of 100	
December 31, 2009			
A	$12.00	1,000,000	$ 12,000,000
B	10.00	12,000,000[a]	120,000,000
C	20.00	5,500,000[b]	110,000,000
Total			$242,000,000

$$\text{New Index Value} = \frac{\text{Current Market Value}}{\text{Base Value}} \times \text{Beginning Index Value}$$

$$= \frac{\$242,000,000}{\$200,000,000} \times 100$$

$$= 1.21 \times 100$$

$$= 121$$

[a]Stock split two-for-one during the year.
[b]Company paid a 10% stock dividend during the year.

EXHIBIT 4.6	Demonstration of the Impact of Different Values on a Market-Value-Weighted Stock Index

	December 31, 2008			December 31, 2009			
				Case A		Case B	
Stock	Number of Shares	Price	Value	Price	Value	Price	Value
A	1,000,000	$10.00	$10,000,000	$12.00	$12,000,000	$10.00	$10,000,000
B	6,000,000	15.00	90,000,000	15.00	90,000,000	15.00	90,000,000
C	5,000,000	20.00	100,000,000	20.00	100,000,000	24.00	120,000,000
Index Value			$200,000,000		$202,000,000		$220,000,000
			100.00		101.00		110.00

4.8.3 UNWEIGHTED INDEX

In an **unweighted index**, all stocks carry equal weight regardless of their price or market value. A $20 stock is as important as a $40 stock, and the total market value of the company is unimportant. Such an index can be used by individuals who randomly select stock for their portfolio and invest the same dollar amount in each stock. One way to visualize an

EXHIBIT 4.7	Example of an Arithmetic and Geometric Mean of Percentage Changes

Share Price

Stock	T	T + 1	HPR	HPY
X	10	12	1.20	0.20
Y	22	20	0.91	−0.09
Z	44	47	1.07	0.07

$$\Pi = 1.20 \times 0.91 \times 1.07 \qquad \Sigma = 0.18$$
$$= 1.168 \qquad 0.18/3 = 0.06$$
$$1.168^{1/3} = 1.0531 \qquad = 6\%$$
$$\text{Index Value (T)} \times 1.0531 = \text{Index Value (T + 1)}$$
$$\text{Index Value (T)} \times 1.06 = \text{Index Value (T + 1)}$$

unweighted index is to assume that equal dollar amounts are invested in each stock in the portfolio (e.g., an equal $1,000 investment in each stock would work out to 50 shares of a $20 stock, 100 shares of a $10 stock, and 10 shares of a $100 stock). In fact, the actual movements in the index are typically based on *the arithmetic mean of the percent changes in price or value for the stocks in the index*. The use of percentage price changes means that the price level or the market value of the stock does not make a difference—each percentage change has equal weight. This arithmetic mean of percent changes procedure is being used in academic studies when the authors specify equal weighting.

In contrast to computing an arithmetic mean of percentage changes, both *Value Line* and the *Financial Times* Ordinary Share Index compute a geometric mean of the holding period returns and derive the holding period yield from this calculation. Exhibit 4.7, which contains an example of an arithmetic and a geometric mean, demonstrates the downward bias of the geometric calculation. Specifically, the geometric mean of holding period yields (HPY) shows an average change of only 5.3% versus the actual change in wealth of 6%.

4.8.4 STYLE INDICES

Financial service firms such as Dow Jones, Moody's, Standard & Poor's, Russell, and Wilshire Associates are generally very fast in responding to changes in investment practices. For example, in response to the growth in popularity of small-cap stocks following academic research in the 1980s suggesting small-cap stocks outperformed large-cap stocks on a risk-adjusted basis spurred the creation of a number of small-cap stock indices.[21] This led to sets of size indices, including large-cap, mid-cap, small-cap, and microcap, which were used to evaluate the performance of money managers who concentrated in those size sectors.

The next innovation was for money managers to concentrate in *types* of stocks—that is, *growth stocks* or *value stocks*. Again, financial services firms responded by creating indices of growth stocks and value stocks based on relative P/E, price-book value, price-cash flow ratios,

---

21 For a comparative analysis of these indices, see Reilly and Wright (2002).

and other metrics such as return on equity (ROE) and revenue growth rates. Eventually, these two factors (size and type) were combined into six major style categories:

Small-cap growth	Small-cap value
Mid-cap growth	Mid-cap value
Large-cap growth	Large-cap value

The most recent additions to style indices are those created to track ethical funds or socially responsible investment (SRI) funds. These SRI indices are further broken down by country and include a global ethical stock index.

The best source for style stock indices (both size and type of stock) is *Barron's*.

4.8.5 GLOBAL EQUITY INDICES

There are stock-market indices available for most individual foreign markets. While these local indices are closely followed within each country, a problem arises in comparing the results implied by these indices to one another because of a lack of consistency among them in sample selection, weighting, or computational procedure. To solve these comparability problems, several investment data firms have computed a set of consistent country stock indices. As a result, these indices can be directly compared and combined to create various regional indices (for example, Pacific Basin). We will describe the three major sets of global equity indices.

The indices are market value weighted and have a base date of December 31, 2002 = 200. The index results are typically reported in local currency although there are options to convert the index results to other currencies such as U.S. dollar, yen, and euros. In addition to the individual countries and the world index, there are several geographic subgroups.

In addition, the following relative valuation information is available: (1) price-to-book value (P/BV) ratio, (2) price-to-cash earnings (P/CE) ratio, (3) price-to-earnings (P/E) ratio, and (4) dividend yield (YLD). These ratios help in analyzing different valuation levels among countries and over time for specific countries.

Notably, the Morgan Stanley group index for Europe, Australasia, and the Far East (EAFE) is the basis for futures and options contracts on the international monetary section of the CME Group Exchange.

4.9 Bond-Market Indices[22]

Investors know little about the growing number of bond-market indices currently available because these are relatively new and not widely published. Knowledge regarding these is important because of the growth of fixed-income money managers and mutual funds and the consequent need to have a reliable set of benchmarks to use in evaluating their performance. Also, because the performance of many fixed-income money managers has been unable to match that of the aggregate bond market, interest has been growing in bond-index funds.

For a variety of reasons, it is more difficult to create and compute a bond-market index than a stock-market index. Ranging from T-bills to bonds in default, the universe of bonds is broader and changing constantly because of new issues, bond maturities, calls, and bond sinking funds. As well, the volatility of prices for individual bonds and bond portfolios changes because bond price volatility is affected by duration, which is likewise changing constantly

Many websites provide stock market indices for many foreign markets. Check out the market summary at http://ca.finance.yahoo.com.

Explore the FTSE Group indices at http://www.ftse.com, including the FTSE Global Equity Index Series. The FTSE Group creates a number of equity, bond, and alternative asset class indices. The FTSE Global Equity Index Series (GEIS) covers approximately 7,000 equity securities in 48 countries representing at least 98% of the world's investable market capitalization.

The indices available from Morgan Stanley Capital International (MSCI) can be reviewed at http://www.mscibarra.com/products/indices/equity/index.jsp, including the Morgan Stanley Capital International (MSCI) Indices. Among other activities, MSCI Barra provides a number of indices covering international, national, industry groups, and the like.

---

22 The discussion in this section draws heavily from Reilly and Wright (2005).

because of changes in maturity, coupon, and market yield (see Chapter 11). Finally, significant problems can arise in correctly pricing the individual bond issues in an index (especially corporate and mortgage bonds) compared to the current and continuous transactions prices available for most stocks used in stock indices.

4.9.1 INVESTMENT-GRADE BOND INDICES

Various firms have created and maintain indices for government bonds and other bonds considered investment grade, that is, the bonds are rated BBB or higher. As demonstrated in a subsequent section, the relationship among the returns for these investment-grade bonds is strong (that is, correlations average about 0.95), regardless of the segment of the market.

4.9.2 HIGH-YIELD BOND INDICES

One of the fastest growing segments of the bond market during the past 25 years has been the high-yield bond market, which includes bonds that are not investment grade (rated below BBB). Because of this growth, a few investment firms including Merrill Lynch created indices related to this market. For an analysis of the alternative high-yield bond benchmarks, see Reilly and Wright (1994); for an overall analysis of this market, see Reilly and Wright (2001).

4.9.3 GLOBAL GOVERNMENT BOND INDICES

The global bond market has experienced significant growth in size and importance during the past 15 years. Notably, this global bond segment is completely dominated by government bonds because few foreign countries have a viable corporate bond market. Once again, several major investment firms have created indices that reflect the performance for the global bond market.

4.10 Composite Stock-Bond Indices

Beyond separate stock and bond indices for individual countries, a natural step is the development of a composite index that measures the performance of all securities in a given country. With a composite index, investors can examine the benefits of diversifying with a combination of asset classes such as stocks and bonds in addition to diversifying within the asset classes of stocks or bonds. We'll examine two such indices.

First, a market-value-weighted index called the MCSI Global Capital Markets Index measures the total return performance of the combined MCSI All Country World Index (equity) and the MSCI Global Total Bond Index. As such, it tracks more than 11,500 stocks and bonds and, as of March 2006, the relative weights are about 42.5% bonds and 57.5% stocks.

A second composite index is the UBS Global Security Market Index (GSMI), which contains U.S. stocks and bonds as well as international and emerging markets equities and bonds along with an allocation to cash. The specific breakdown as of August 2007 was 65% equities and 35% bonds.

Because the GSMI contains U.S., international, and emerging-market stocks and bonds, it is clearly the most diversified benchmark available with a weighting scheme that approaches market values. As such, it is closest to the theoretically specified "market portfolio of risky assets" referred to in the capital asset pricing model (CAPM) literature.

4.11 Comparison of Indices Over Time

In Chapter 3, we discussed the correlation coefficients between various asset classes. A quick search of equity-market indices shows that most of the correlation differences that exist between global markets are attributable to the different sample of firms listed on the different stock exchanges. Not surprisingly, there is a high positive correlation between the S&P 500 and the several comprehensive U.S. equity indices, while the correlations with indices from Canada, the United Kingdom, Germany, and Japan support the case for global investing.

Various studies have shown the correlations between the S&P 500 and investment-grade bonds and high-yield bonds indicate significantly lower correlations (about 0.49) caused by definite equity characteristics of high-yield bonds; see Reilly and Wright (2001). The correlation of world government bonds (without the United States) is even lower (about 0.35), reflecting the different interest rate movements and exchange rate effects, further supporting global diversification of bond portfolios.

Summary

1. A good market has timely and accurate information on the price and volume of past transactions, liquidity, price continuity, low transaction costs, and prices that rapidly adjust to new information.

2. Primary markets are important sources of new capital for security issuers; the secondary markets provide the liquidity that is critical to the primary markets.

3. An exchange can use one or a combination of the two basic trading systems. A pure auction market has interested buyers and sellers submit bid-and-ask prices (buy and sell orders) for a given stock to a central location where the orders are matched. Shares are sold to the highest bidder and bought from the seller with the lowest offering price. In a dealer market, individual dealers provide liquidity for investors by buying and selling the shares of stock for themselves.

4. Call markets are generally used during the early stages of an exchange's development, when a stock is suspended from trading during the day due to new information or when there is an overnight buildup of buy or sell orders. All the bids and asks for a stock at a point in time are compiled and market administrators attempt to arrive at a single price where the quantity demanded is as close as possible to the quantity supplied.

5. Consolidations and affiliations between exchanges has made possible a global equity market where stocks that have a global constituency can be traded around the world continuously. This means the active market moves around the globe as trading hours for New York, London, and Tokyo begin and end. This provides a continuous market where investment firms "pass the book" around the world.

6. The third market involves dealers and brokers who trade exchange-listed shares away from the exchange. This market is critical when trading is not available on the larger exchanges (NYSE, TSX) either because trading is suspended or the exchange is closed. Electronic Communication Networks (ECNs) are electronic facilities that match buy and sell orders directly via computer, mainly for retail and small institutional trading. ECNs do not buy or sell from their own account but act as very cheap, efficient electronic brokers. Electronic Crossing Systems (ECSs) are electronic facilities that act as brokers to match large buy and sell orders. Neither ECNs nor ECSs have listing facilities. Trading of exchange-listed stocks using one ECNs or ESCs has become the fourth market.

7. To buy or sell a stock at the best current price, a market order is used. If the buy or sell price is specified, the investor has used a limit order. Limit orders must specify a time period they are outstanding, including instantaneous (fill or kill); good for part of a day, a full day, several days, a week, or a month (good-till-date or GTD); or open-ended, or good-till-cancelled (GTC). A short sale is the sale of borrowed stock with the intent of purchasing it back later at a lower price.

    A few of the more common specialty orders include a stop loss order, which is a conditional market order whereby the investor directs the sale of a stock if it drops to a given price; and similarly, a stop buy order, whereby an investor who has entered into a short sale may limit possible losses.

8. Indices maybe used as benchmarks to evaluate portfolio performance.[23] In this case, you must be sure the index (benchmark) is consistent with your investing universe. Investors need to examine numerous market indices to evaluate the performance of their investments.

    Three factors are important when constructing an index intended to represent a total population. Firstly, the sample should be representative of the total population. Secondly, there needs to be consideration of the weight given to each member in the sample. Three principal weighting schemes are used for security-market indices:

---

23 Chapter 18 includes an extensive discussion of the purpose and construction of benchmarks and considers the use of benchmarks in the evaluation of portfolio performance.

(1) a price-weighted index, (2) a market-value-weighted index, and (3) an unweighted or equal-weighted index. Lastly, is the computational procedure to be used. This may be (1) a simple arithmetic mean of the various members in the index; (2) reporting of all changes, whether in price or value, in terms of the basic index; or (3) using a geometric rather than an arithmetic mean of the components.

9. The creation and calculation of a bond-market index is more complicated than a stock-market index. This is because of the broad range of bonds, their numerous features and maturities, and that the volatility of prices for individual bonds and bond portfolios changes because bond price volatility is affected by duration, which is likewise changing constantly because of changes in maturity, coupon, and market yield. There are further complications in correctly pricing the individual bond issues in an index compared to the current and continuous transactions prices available for most stocks used in stock indices.

Key Terms

call market, p. 78
continuous market, p. 78
exchange-traded fund (ETF), p. 89
external, or informational, efficiency, p. 73
index fund, p. 89
initial public offering (IPO), p. 75
limit order, p. 84
liquidity, p. 72
maintenance margin, p. 87

margin call, p. 87
market, p. 72
market order, p. 84
new issue, p. 75
over-the-counter (OTC), p. 76
price continuity, p. 72
price-weighted index, p. 90
primary market, p. 73
seasoned equity issues, p. 74

secondary market, p. 73
security-market index, p. 71
short sale, p. 85
third market, p. 83
timely and accurate information, p. 72
transaction cost, p. 73
Treasury bill, p. 73
unweighted index, p. 93
value-weighted index, p. 91

Suggested Readings

Barclay, Michael, Terrence Hendershott, and D. Timothy McCormick. "Competition among Trading Venues: Information and Trading on Electronic Communications Networks." *Journal of Finance* 58, no. 6 (December 2003).

Fisher, Lawrence, and James H. Lorie. *A Half Century of Returns on Stocks and Bonds.* Chicago: University of Chicago Graduate School of Business, 1977.

Huang, Roger. "The Quality of ECN and Nasdaq Market-Maker Quotes." *Journal of Finance* 57, no. 3 (June 2002).

Hughes, Pamela S., and Ehsan Zargar. "Exchange Demutualization." Blake, Cassels and Graydon LLP (May 2006) retrievable at http://www.blakes.ca/english/publications/bsra/v143/Paper-Exchange_Demutualization-May2006.pdf.

Ibbotson Associates. *Stocks, Bonds, Bills, and Inflation.* Chicago: Ibbotson Associates, annual.

 For Chapter CFA Questions and Problems, please see Appendix A at the end of this text.

Questions

1. Define *market* and briefly discuss the characteristics of a good market.
2. You own 100 shares of TELUS stock and you want to sell it because you need the money to make a down payment on a car. Assume there is absolutely no secondary market system in common stocks. How would you go about selling the stock? Discuss what you would have to do to find a buyer, how long it might take, and the price you might receive.
3. Define *liquidity* and discuss the factors that contribute to it. Give examples of a liquid asset and an illiquid asset, and discuss why they are considered liquid and illiquid.

4. Define a primary and secondary market for securities and discuss how they differ. Discuss how the primary market is dependent on the secondary market.

5. Give an example of an initial public offering (IPO) in the primary market. Give an example of a seasoned equity issue in the primary market. Discuss which would involve greater risk to the buyer.

6. Find an advertisement for a recent primary offering in *The Globe and Mail*. Based on the information in the ad, indicate the characteristics of the security sold and the major underwriters. How much new capital did the firm derive from the offering before paying commissions?

7. Briefly explain the difference between a competitive-bid underwriting and a negotiated underwriting.

8. Which segment of the secondary stock market (listed exchanges or NASDAQ) is larger in terms of the number of issues? Which is larger in terms of the value of the issues traded?

9. Discuss the three levels of NASDAQ in terms of what each provides and who would subscribe to each.

10. a. Define the third market. Give an example of a third-market stock.
    b. Define the fourth market. Discuss why a financial institution would use the fourth market.

11. Briefly define each of the following terms and give an example.
    a. Market order
    b. Limit order
    c. Short sale
    d. Stop loss order

12. Briefly discuss the two major functions and sources of income for the NYSE specialist.

13. Discuss briefly several uses of security-market indices.

14. What major factors must be considered when constructing a market index?

15. Explain how a market index is price weighted. In such a case, would you expect a $100 stock to be more important than a $25 stock? Give an example.

16. Explain how to compute a value-weighted index.

17. Explain how a price-weighted index and a value-weighted index adjust for stock splits.

18. Describe an unweighted index and describe how you would construct such an index. Assume a 20% price

change in Research in Motion ($80/share and 565 million shares outstanding) and Tim Hortons Inc. ($30/share and 185 million shares outstanding). Explain which stock's change will have the greater impact on this index.

19. If you correlated percentage changes in the Wilshire 5000 equity index with percentage changes in the NYSE composite and the NASDAQ composite index, would you expect a difference in the correlations? Why or why not?

20. There are high correlations between the monthly percentage price changes for the alternative NYSE indices. Discuss the reason for this similarity: Is it size of sample, source of sample, or method of computation?

21. The Nikkei and the Tokyo (TSE) Composite Index have a correlation of 0.82 while the TSE and the S&P 500 index have a correlation of 0.33. Explain why these relationships differ.

22. You learn that the Wilshire 5000 market-value-weighted index increased by 16% during a specified period, whereas a Wilshire 5000 equal-weighted index increased by 23% during the same period. Discuss what this difference in results implies.

23. Why is it contended that bond-market indices are more difficult to construct and maintain than stock-market indices?

24. Suppose the Wilshire 5000 market-value-weighted index increased by 5%, whereas the Merrill Lynch–Wilshire Capital Markets Index increased by 15% during the same period. What does this difference in results imply?

25. Based on what you know about the *Financial Times* (FT) World Index, the Morgan Stanley Capital International World Index, and the Dow Jones World Stock Index, what level of correlation would you expect between monthly rates of return? Discuss the reasons for your answer based on the factors that affect indices.

26. How would you explain that the ML High-Yield Bond Index was more highly correlated with the NYSE composite stock index than the ML Aggregate Bond Index?

27. Assuming that the mandate to a portfolio manager was to invest in a broadly diversified portfolio of U.S. stocks, which two or three indices should be considered as an appropriate benchmark? Why?

Problems

1. You have $40,000 to invest in Sloppy Shoes, a stock selling for $80. The initial margin requirement is 60%. Ignoring taxes and commissions, show in detail the impact on your return if the stock rises to $100 per share and if it declines to $40 a share, assuming that (a) you

pay cash for the stock, and (b) you buy it using maximum leverage.

2. Shali has a margin account and deposits $50,000. Assume the initial margin requirement is 40%, commissions are ignored, and the Gentry Corporation is selling at $35 per share.

a. How many shares can Shali purchase using the maximum allowable margin?

b. What is Shali's profit (loss) if the price of Gentry's stock
   i. rises to $45?
   ii. falls to $25?

c. If the minimum margin is 30%, to what price can Gentry fall before Shali will receive a margin call?

3. Suppose you buy a round lot of Elmo Industries stock on 55% margin when the stock is selling at $20. The broker charges a 10% annual interest rate, and commissions are 3% of the stock value on the purchase and sale. A year later you receive a $0.50 per share dividend and sell the stock for $27. What is your return on Elmo Industries?

4. You decide to sell short 100 shares of Skippy Farms when it is selling at its yearly high of $56. Your broker tells you that your margin requirement is 45% and that the commission on the purchase is $155. While you are short the stock, Skippy pays a $2.50 per share dividend. At the end of one year, you buy 100 shares of Skippy at $45 to close out your position and are charged a commission of $145 and 8% interest on the money borrowed. What is your return on the investment?

5. You own 200 shares of Shamrock Enterprises that you bought at $25 a share. The stock is now selling for $45 a share.

   a. You put in a stop loss order at $40. Discuss your reasoning for this action.

   b. If the stock eventually declines in price to $30 a share, what would be your return with and without the stop loss order?

6. Two years ago, you bought 300 shares of Brown Cow Milk Co. for $30 a share with a margin of 60%. Currently, the Brown Cow Stock is selling for $45 a share. Assuming no dividends and ignoring commissions, compute (a) the annualized return on this investment if you had paid cash, and (b) your return with the margin purchase.

7. The stock of the Bay Street Travel Co. is selling for $28 a share. You put in a limit buy order at $24 for one month. During the month, the stock price declines to $20, then jumps to $36. Ignoring commissions, what would have been your return on this investment? What would be your return if you had put in a market order? What if your limit order was at $18?

8. You are given the following information regarding prices for a sample of stocks.

Stock	Number of Shares	Price T	Price T + 1
A	1,000,000	60	80
B	10,000,000	20	35
C	30,000,000	18	25

a. Construct a price-weighted index for these three stocks, and compute the percentage change in the index for the period from T to T + 1.

b. Construct a value-weighted index for these three stocks, and compute the percentage change in the index for the period from T to T + 1.

c. Briefly discuss the difference in the results for the two indices.

9. a. Given the data in Problem 8, construct an equal-weighted index by assuming $1,000 is invested in each stock. What is the percentage change in wealth for this portfolio?

   b. Compute the percentage of price change for each of the stocks in Problem 8. Compute the arithmetic mean of these percentage changes. Discuss how this answer compares to the answer in Part a.

   c. Compute the geometric mean of the percentage changes in Part b. Discuss how this result compares to the answer in Part b.

10. For the past five trading days, compute the daily percentage price changes for the following stock indices.
    a. DJIA
    b. S&P 500
    c. S&P/TSX Composite Index
    d. FT-100 Share Index
    e. Nikkei 225 Stock Price Average
    f. Discuss the difference in results for Parts a and b, a and c, a and d, a and e, and d and e. What do these differences imply regarding diversifying?

11.

Company	Price A	B	C	Shares A	B	C
Day 1	12	23	52	500	350	250
Day 2	10	22	55	500	350	250
Day 3	14	46	52	500	175[a]	250
Day 4	13	47	25	500	175	500[b]
Day 5	12	45	26	500	175	500

[a] Split at close of Day 2.
[b] Split at close of Day 3.

a. Calculate a Dow Jones Industrial Average for days 1 through 5.

b. What effects have the splits had in determining the next day's index? (Hint: Think of the relative weighting of each stock.)

12. Utilizing the price and volume data in Problem 11,

   a. Calculate a Standard & Poor's Index for days 1 through 5 using a beginning index value of 10.

   b. Identify what effects the splits had in determining the next day's index. (Hint: Think of the relative weighting of each stock.)

13. Based on the following stock price and shares out-standing information, compute the beginning and ending values for a price-weighted index and a market-value-weighted index.

	December 31, 2008		December 31, 2009	
	Price	Shares Outstanding	Price	Shares Outstanding
Stock K	20	100,000,000	32	100,000,000
Stock M	80	2,000,000	45	4,000,000[a]
Stock R	40	25,000,000	42	25,000,000

[a] Stock split two-for-one during the year.

a. Compute the percentage change in the value of each index during the year.
b. Explain the difference in results between the two indices.
c. Compute the percentage change for an unweighted index and discuss why these results differ from those of the other indices.

Developments in Investment Theory

Part 1 provided background on why individuals invest their funds and what they expect to derive. We also argued very strongly for a global investment program and showed the relationship among these instruments and markets.

In Part 2, we are now ready to discuss how to analyze and value various investment instruments available. In turn, valuation requires the estimating of expected returns (cash flows) and a determination of the risk involved in the securities. Before we can begin the analysis, we need to understand several major developments in investment theory that have influenced how we specify and measure risk in the valuation process.

We begin with the concept of efficient capital markets, which hypothesizes that security prices reflect the effect of all information.

We consider why markets should be efficient, discuss how one goes about testing this hypothesis, and review the results of numerous tests that both support the hypotheses and indicate the existence of anomalies that are inconsistent with the hypotheses. We also look at how behavioural finance provides a rationale for some of the results. We conclude the chapters with an extensive discussion of the implications of the results for those engaged in technical and fundamental analysis as well as portfolio management.

Chapter 6 provides an introduction to portfolio theory, which was developed by Harry Markowitz. This theory provided the first rigorous measure of risk for investors and showed how one selects alternative assets to diversify and reduce the risk of a portfolio. Following the development of the

Markowitz portfolio model, we examine the extensions into a general equilibrium asset pricing model that included an alternative risk measure for all risky assets. Chapter 7 contains a detailed description of these developments and an explanation of the relevant risk measure implied by this valuation model, referred to as the *capital asset pricing model (CAPM)*. Although the CAPM has long been the pre-eminent theoretical explanation in finance for the connection between risk and expected return, the past several decades have seen the rise of several competing models. The latter half of the chapter is devoted to exploring several of these alternative asset pricing models, which differ from the CAPM primarily by specifying multiple risk factors in lieu of a single-market portfolio-based variable.

5

Efficient Capital Markets

An **efficient capital market** is one in which security prices adjust rapidly to the arrival of new information and, therefore, the current prices of securities reflect all information about the security. Some of the most interesting and important academic research during the past 30 years has analyzed whether our capital markets are efficient. The results of this research has significant real-world implications for investors and portfolio managers. In addition, the question of whether capital markets are efficient is one of the most controversial areas in investment research. A new dimension has been added to the controversy because of the rapidly expanding research in behavioural finance that has implications regarding the concept of efficient capital markets and has been providing some intriguing insights on reasons for many of the anomalies identified.

We are considering the topic of efficient capital markets at this point for two reasons. First, it seems natural to consider the efficiency of these markets in terms of how security prices react to new information now that we have discussed how capital markets function. Second, the overall evidence on capital market efficiency is best described as mixed: Some studies support the hypothesis, and others do not. The implications of these diverse results are important to anyone involved in analyzing securities and building a portfolio.

5.1 Why Should Capital Markets Be Efficient?

Although the idea of an efficient capital market is relatively straightforward, we often fail to consider *why* capital markets *should* be efficient. What set of assumptions imply an efficient capital market? Before we continue, though, we need to be a bit more precise in our definition. If security prices adjust rapidly to new information, and, therefore, current security prices fully reflect all available information we have an **informationally efficient market**.

An initial and important premise of an efficient market requires that *a large number of profit-maximizing participants analyze and value securities,* each independently of the others.

A second assumption is that *new information regarding securities comes to the market in a random fashion*, and the timing of one announcement is generally independent of others.[1]

The third assumption is especially crucial: *the buy and sell decisions of all those profit-maximizing investors who adjust security prices rapidly to reflect the effect of new information.* Although the price adjustment may be imperfect, it is unbiased. This means that sometimes the market will over-adjust and other times it will underadjust, but you cannot predict which will occur at any given time. Security prices adjust rapidly because of the many profit-maximizing investors competing against one another.

The combined effect of (1) information coming in a random, independent, unpredictable fashion and (2) numerous competing investors adjusting stock prices rapidly to reflect this new information means that one would expect price changes to be independent and random. You can see that the adjustment process requires a large number of investors following the security, analyzing the impact of new information on its value, and buying or selling the security until its price adjusts to reflect the new information. This implies that informationally efficient markets require some minimum amount of trading and that more trading by numerous competing investors should cause a faster price adjustment, making the market more efficient. We will return to this need for trading and investor attention when we discuss some anomalies of the EMH.

Finally, because security prices adjust to all new information, these security prices should reflect all information that is publicly available at any point in time. Therefore, the security prices that prevail at any time should be an unbiased reflection of all currently available information, including the risk involved in owning the security. Therefore, in an efficient market, *the expected returns implicit in the current price of the security should reflect its risk,* which means that investors who buy at these informationally efficient prices should receive a return that is consistent with the perceived risk of the stock.

5.2 Alternative Efficient Market Hypotheses

Most of the early work related to efficient capital markets was based on the *random walk hypothesis*, which asserted that changes in stock prices occurred randomly. This early academic work contained extensive empirical analysis without much theory behind it. An article by Fama (1970) attempted to formalize the theory and organize the growing empirical evidence. Fama presented the efficient market theory in terms of a *fair game model*, contending that investors can be confident that a current market price fully reflects all available information about a security and, therefore, the expected return based upon this price is consistent with its risk.

In his original article, Fama divided the overall efficient market hypothesis (EMH) and the empirical tests of the hypothesis into three subhypotheses depending on the information set involved: (1) weak-form EMH, (2) semistrong-form EMH, and (3) strong-form EMH.

In a subsequent review article, Fama (1991) again divided the empirical results into three groups but shifted empirical results between the prior categories. Therefore, the following discussion uses the original categories, noted above, but organizes the presentation of results using the new categories.

5.2.1 WEAK-FORM EFFICIENT MARKET HYPOTHESIS

The **weak-form EMH** assumes that current stock prices fully reflect *all security market information*, including the historical sequence of prices, returns, trading-volume data, and other market-generated information, such as odd-lot transactions, block trades, and transactions by exchange specialists. Because it assumes that current market prices already reflect all past

---

1 New information, by definition, must be information that was not known before, and is not predictable. If it were predictable, it would have been impounded in the security price.

returns and any other security market information, this hypothesis implies that past returns and other historical market data should have no relationship with future returns (that is, returns should be independent). Therefore, this hypothesis implies that you should gain little from using any trading rule that decides whether to buy or sell a security based on past returns or any other past security market data.

5.2.2 SEMISTRONG-FORM EFFICIENT MARKET HYPOTHESIS

The **semistrong-form EMH** asserts that security prices adjust rapidly to the release of *all public information*, thus current security prices fully reflect all public information. The semistrong hypothesis encompasses the weak-form hypothesis, because all the market information considered by the weak-form hypothesis is public. Public information also includes all non-market information, such as earnings and dividend announcements, price-to-earnings (P/E) ratios, dividend-yield (D/P) ratios, price-book value (P/BV) ratios, stock splits, and political news. This hypothesis implies that investors basing their decisions on any important new information *after it is public* should not receive above-average risk-adjusted profits from their transactions because the security price already reflects all such information.

5.2.3 STRONG-FORM EFFICIENT MARKET HYPOTHESIS

The **strong-form EMH** contends that stock prices fully reflect *all information from public and private sources*. This means that no group of investors has monopolistic access to information relevant to the formation of prices and therefore, no group of investors should be able to consistently derive above-average risk-adjusted returns. The strong-form EMH encompasses both the weak-form and the semistrong-form EMH. Further, the strong-form EMH extends the assumption of efficient markets, in which prices adjust rapidly to the release of new public information, to assume perfect markets, in which all information is cost-free and available to everyone at the same time.

5.3 Tests and Results of Efficient Market Hypotheses

Like most hypotheses in finance and economics, the evidence on the EMH is mixed. Some studies have supported the hypotheses and indicate that capital markets are efficient. Results of other studies have revealed some **anomalies** related to these hypotheses, indicating results that do not support the hypotheses.

5.3.1 WEAK-FORM HYPOTHESIS: TESTS AND RESULTS

Researchers have formulated two groups of tests for the weak-form EMH. The first involves statistical tests of independence between rates of return. The second set of tests compares risk-return results for trading rules that make investment decisions based on past market information relative to the results from a simple buy-and-hold policy.[2]

Statistical Tests of Independence Two major statistical tests have been used to verify the EMH contention that security returns over time should be independent of one another because new information comes to the market in a random, independent fashion and security prices adjust rapidly to this new information.

First, **autocorrelation tests** of independence measure the significance of positive or negative correlation in returns over time. Does the return on day t correlate with the return on day $t - 1$, $t - 2$, or $t - 3$?[3] Those who believe that capital markets are efficient would expect insignificant correlations for all such combinations.

---

2 Buy-and-hold policy assumes that you buy stock at the beginning of a test period and hold it to the end.

3 For a discussion of tests of time-series independence, see DeFusco, McLeavey, Pinto, and Runkle (2004), Chapter 10.

Several researchers have examined the serial correlations among stock returns for several relatively short time horizons including 1 day, 4 days, 9 days, and 16 days. The results typically indicated insignificant correlation in stock returns over time. Some recent studies that considered portfolios of stocks of different market size have indicated that the autocorrelation is stronger for portfolios of small-market-size stocks. Therefore, although the older results tend to support the hypothesis, the more recent studies cast doubt on it for portfolios of small firms, although these results could be offset by the higher transaction costs of small-cap stocks and non-synchronous trading for small-cap stocks.

The second statistical test of independence, as discussed by DeFusco et al. (2004), is the **runs test**. Given a series of price changes, each price change is either designated a plus (+) if it is an increase in price or a minus (−) if it is a decrease in price. The result is a set of pluses and minuses as follows: + + + − + − − + + − − + +. A run occurs when two consecutive changes are the same; two or more consecutive positive or negative price changes constitute one run. When the price changes in a different direction, such as when a negative price change is followed by a positive price change, the run ends and a new run may begin. To test for independence, you would compare the number of runs for a given series to the number in a table of expected values for the number of runs that should occur in a random series.

Stock price run studies have confirmed the independence of stock price changes over time. The actual number of runs for stock price series consistently fell into the range expected for a random series.

Although short-horizon stock returns have generally supported the weak-form EMH, several studies that examined price changes for individual *transactions* on the NYSE found significant serial correlations. Notably, none of these studies attempted to show that the dependence of transaction price movements could be used to earn above-average risk-adjusted returns after considering the trading rule's substantial transaction costs.

Tests of Trading Rules A second group of tests of the weak-form EMH were developed in response to criticism that statistical tests of independence were too rigid to identify the intricate price patterns examined by technical analysts. As we will discuss in Chapter 10, technical analysts typically look for a general consistency in price trends over time, which might include both positive and negative changes. For this reason, technical analysts believed that their trading rules were too sophisticated and complicated to be properly tested by rigid statistical tests.

As a result, investigators attempted to test various technical trading rules through simulation. Efficient market advocates hypothesized that investors would be unable to derive abnormal profits above a buy-and-hold policy using any trading rule that depended solely on past market information.

The trading rule studies compared the risk-return results derived from trading-rule simulations, including transaction costs, to the results from a simple buy-and-hold policy. Three major pitfalls can negate the results of a trading-rule study:

1. The investigator should *use only publicly available data* when implementing the trading rule. For example, the trading activities of specialists as of December 31 may not be publicly available until February 1, so you should not factor in information about specialist trading activity until the information is public.
2. *All transaction costs* involved in implementing the trading strategy from a particular trading rule should be included when computing returns because most trading rules involve far more transactions than a simple buy-and-hold policy.
3. You must *adjust the results for risk* because a trading rule might simply select a portfolio of high-risk securities that should experience higher returns.

Researchers have encountered two operational problems in testing specific trading rules. First, some trading rules require too much subjective interpretation of data to simulate mechanically. Second, the almost infinite number of potential trading rules makes it impossible to test all of them. As a result, only the better-known technical trading rules have been examined.

Restricting the studies to relatively simple trading rules, which many technicians consider rather naïve, and using readily available data from the NYSE, which is biased toward well-known, heavily traded stocks, makes these studies open to further criticism. However, for securities with relatively few stockholders and little trading activity, the market could be inefficient simply due to fewer investors analyzing the effect of new information, and this limited interest would result in insufficient trading activity to move the price of the security quickly to a new equilibrium value that reflects the new information. Therefore, using only active, heavily traded stocks when testing a trading rule could bias the results toward finding efficiency.

Results of Simulations of Specific Trading Rules   In the most popular trading technique, filter rule, an investor trades a stock when the price change exceeds a filter value set for it. For example, an investor using a 5% filter would consider a positive breakout to have occurred if the stock were to rise 5% from some base, suggesting that the stock price would continue to rise. They would buy the stock to take advantage of the expected continued rise. Conversely, a 5% decline from some peak price would be considered a breakout on the downside, the investor would expect a further price decline and would sell any stock holdings and possibly even sell the stock short.

Studies of this trading rule have used a range of filters from 0.5% to 50%, and the results have indicated that small filters would yield above-average profits *before* taking account of trading commissions. However, small filters generate numerous trades and, therefore, substantial trading costs. When these trading costs were considered, all the trading profits turned to losses. Alternatively, trading using larger filters did not yield returns above those of a simple buy-and-hold policy.

Researchers have simulated other trading rules that used past market data other than stock prices. Trading rules have been devised that consider advanced-decline ratios, short sales, short positions, and specialist activities.[4] These simulation tests have generated mixed results. Most of the early studies suggested that these trading rules generally would not outperform a buy-and-hold policy on a risk-adjusted basis after commissions, although several recent studies have indicated support for specific trading rules. Therefore, most evidence from simulations of specific trading rules indicates that most trading rules tested have not been able to beat a buy-and-hold policy. Therefore, these test results generally support the weak-form EMH, but the results are far from unanimous.

5.3.2   SEMISTRONG-FORM HYPOTHESIS: TESTS AND RESULTS

Recall that the semistrong-form EMH asserts that security prices adjust rapidly to the release of all public information and security prices fully reflect all public information. Studies testing the semistrong-form EMH can be divided into the following:

1. *Studies to predict future returns using available public information beyond pure market information such as prices and trading volume considered in the weak-form tests.* These studies can involve either *time-series analysis* of returns or the *cross-section distribution* of returns for individual stocks. EMH advocates assert that it would not be possible to predict *future* returns using past returns or to predict the distribution of future returns (e.g., the top quartile or decile of returns) using public information.

---

4   Many of these trading rules are discussed in Chapter 10.

2. *Event studies that examine how fast stock prices adjust to specific significant economic events.* A corollary approach would be to test whether it is possible to invest in a security after the public announcement of a significant event (e.g., earnings, stock splits, major economic data) and experience significant abnormal returns. Again, EMH advocates would expect security prices to adjust rapidly, such that it would not be possible for investors to experience superior risk-adjusted returns by investing after the public announcement and paying normal transaction costs.

Before we examine these studies in further detail, we need to review adjustments for market effects.

Adjustment for Market Effects For any of these tests, the security's returns must be adjusted for the returns of the overall market during the period. A stock's 5% return during a period surrounding an announcement is meaningless until you know what the aggregate stock market did during the same period and how this stock normally acts under such conditions. If the market had experienced a 10% return during this period, the 5% return for the stock may be lower than expected.

Authors of pre-1970 studies generally recognized the need to make such adjustments for market movements. They typically assumed that the individual stocks should experience returns equal to the aggregate stock market. Thus, the market-adjustment process simply entailed subtracting the market return from the individual security's return to derive its **abnormal rate of return**:

5.1	$$AR_{it} = R_{it} - R_{mt}$$

where:
AR_{it} = abnormal rate of return on security i during period t
R_{it} = rate of return on security i during period t
R_{mt} = rate of return on a market index during period t

In the example where the stock experienced a 5% increase while the market increased 10%, the stock's abnormal return would be minus 5%.

Since the 1970s, many authors have adjusted the rates of return for securities by an amount different from the market return because they recognize that, based on work with the capital asset pricing model, all stocks do not change by the same amount as the market. Some stocks are more volatile than the market, while some are less volatile. Therefore you must determine an **expected return** for the stock based on the market return *and* the stock's relationship with the market (its beta). For example, suppose a stock is generally 20% more volatile than the market (so a beta of 1.20). Should the market experience a 10% return, you would expect this stock to deliver a 12% return. Therefore, you would determine the abnormal rate of return as the difference between the stock's actual return and its *expected return* as follows:

5.2	$$AR_{it} = R_{it} - E(R_{it})$$

where:
$E(R_{it})$ = the expected rate of return for stock i during period t based on the market rate of return and the stock's normal relationship with the market (its beta)

Thus the abnormal return for our stock that was expected to have a 12% return but only had a 5% return would be −7%. Over the long run, the abnormal returns for a stock would be expected to sum to zero. Specifically, during one period the returns may exceed expectations and the next period they may fall short.

In both sets of tests, the emphasis is on the analysis of abnormal returns that deviate from long-term expectations or returns that are adjusted for a stock's specific risk characteristics and overall market returns during the period.

Return Prediction Studies The first set of studies is referred to as **return prediction studies**. The investigators in these studies attempt to predict the time series of future returns for individual stocks or the aggregate market using public information. For example, is it possible to predict abnormal returns over time for the market based on public information such as specified values or changes in the aggregate dividend yield or the risk premium spread for bonds? Another example would be **event studies** that examine abnormal returns for a period immediately after an announcement of a significant event, such as a stock split, a proposed merger, or a stock or bond issue, to determine whether an investor can derive above-average risk-adjusted returns by investing after the release of public information. The **time-series analysis** assumes that in an efficient market the best estimate of *future* returns will be the long-run *historical* returns. The test's main objective is to determine whether any public information will provide superior estimates of returns for a short-run (one to six months) or a long-run period (one to five years).

Risk Premium Proxies These studies have shown limited success in predicting short-horizon returns, but the analysis of long-horizon returns has been quite successful. A prime example is dividend yield studies. After postulating that the aggregate dividend yield (D/P) was a proxy for the risk premium on stocks, they found a positive relationship between the D/P and future long-run stock market returns.

In addition, several studies have considered two variables related to the term structure of interest rates: (1) a *default spread*, which is the difference between the yields on lower and investment-grade long-term corporate bonds, and (2) the *term structure spread*, which is the difference between the long-term government bond yield and the yield on one-month Treasury bills. These variables have been used to predict stock and bond returns. Similar variables in foreign countries have also been useful for predicting returns for foreign common stocks.

The reasoning for these empirical results is as follows: When the two most significant variables—the dividend yield (D/P) and the bond default spread—are high, it implies that investors are demanding a high return on stocks and bonds. Notably, this occurs during poor economic environments. A poor economic environment also implies a low-wealth environment wherein investors perceive higher risk for investments. As a result, for investors to invest and shift consumption from the present to the future they require a high rate of return to entice them. In contrast, when these values are small, it implies that investors have reduced their risk premium and required returns and, therefore, future returns will be below normal.

Quarterly Earnings Reports These studies question whether it is possible to predict future returns for a stock based on publicly available quarterly earnings reports. The typical test examined firms that experienced changes in quarterly earnings that differed from expectations. The results generally indicated abnormal returns during the 13 or 26 weeks *following* the announcement of a large *unanticipated* earnings change—referred to as an **earnings surprise**. These results suggest that an earnings surprise is *not* instantaneously reflected in security prices.

An extensive analysis by Rendleman, Jones, and Latané (1982) and a follow-up by Jones, Rendleman, and Latané (1985) using a large sample and daily data from 20 days before a quarterly earnings announcement to 90 days after the announcement indicated that 31% of the total response in stock returns came before the earnings announcement, 18% on the day of the announcement, and 51% *afterward*.

Check out current earnings surprises at http://investdb. theglobeandmail.com/ invest/investSQL/gx.show_ surprise.

Several studies examined reasons for the earnings drift following earnings announcements and found that unexpected earnings explained more than 80% of the subsequent stock-price drift for the total time period. According to authors such as Benesh and Peterson (1986), Bernard and Thomas (1989), and Baruch (1989), who reviewed the prior studies, stock-price drift resulted from the *earnings revisions* that followed the earnings surprises and contributed to the positive correlations of prices.

Such results indicate that the market has not adjusted stock prices to reflect the release of quarterly earnings surprises as quickly as expected by the semistrong-form EMH. This implies that earnings surprises and earnings revisions can be used to predict returns for individual stocks. These results are evidence against the EMH.

The final set of calendar studies questioned whether some regularities in the returns during the calendar year would allow investors to predict returns on stocks. These studies include numerous studies on "the January anomaly" and studies that consider a variety of other daily and weekly regularities.

The January Anomaly Several years ago, Branch (1977) and Branch and Chang (1985) proposed a unique trading rule for those interested in taking advantage of tax selling. Investors (including institutions) tend to engage in tax selling toward the end of the year to establish losses on stocks that have declined. After the new year, the tendency is to repurchase these stocks or to buy similar stocks that look attractive. This scenario would produce downward pressure on stock prices in late November and December and positive pressure in early January. Such a seasonal pattern is inconsistent with the EMH because it should be eliminated by arbitrageurs who would buy in December and sell in early January.

A supporter of the hypothesis found that December trading volume was abnormally high for stocks that had declined during the previous year and that significant abnormal returns occurred during January for stocks that had experienced losses during the prior year. It was concluded that, because of transaction costs, arbitrageurs must not be eliminating the January tax-selling anomaly. Subsequent analysis showed that most of the January effect was concentrated in the first week of trading, particularly on the first day of the year.

Several studies provided support for a January effect inconsistent with the tax-selling hypothesis by examining what happened in countries that did not have similar tax laws or a December year-end. They found abnormal returns in January, but the results could not be explained by tax laws. It has also been shown that the classic relationship between risk and return is strongest during January, and there is a year-end trading volume bulge in late December–early January.

Despite numerous studies, the January anomaly poses as many questions as it answers.

Other Calendar Effects Several other "calendar" effects have been examined, including a monthly effect, a weekend/day-of-the-week effect, and an intraday effect. One study found a significant monthly effect wherein all the market's cumulative advance occurred during the first half of trading months.

An analysis of the weekend effect found that the mean return for Monday was significantly negative during five-year subperiods and a total period. In contrast, the average return for the other four days was positive.

A study decomposed the Monday effect that is typically measured from Friday close to Monday close into a *weekend effect* (from Friday close to Monday open), and a pure *Monday trading effect* (from Monday open to the Monday close). It was shown that the negative

Monday effect found in prior studies actually occurs from the Friday close to the Monday open (it is really a weekend effect). After adjusting for the weekend effect, the pure Monday trading effect was positive. Subsequently, it was shown that the Monday effect was on average positive in January and negative for all other months.

Finally, for *large firms* the negative Monday effect occurred before the market opened (it was a weekend effect), whereas for *smaller firms* most of the negative Monday effect occurred during the day on Monday (it was a Monday trading effect).

Predicting Cross-Sectional Returns The second set of studies are those that predict cross-sectional returns. In these studies, investigators look for public information regarding individual stocks that will allow them to predict the cross-sectional distribution of future risk-adjusted returns. For example, they test whether it is possible to use variables such as the price-earnings ratio, market value size, the price/book-value ratio, the P/E/growth rate (PEG) ratio, or the dividend yield to predict which stocks will experience above-average (e.g., top quartile) or below-average risk-adjusted returns in the future. Assuming an efficient market, *all securities should have equal risk-adjusted returns* because security prices should reflect all public information that would influence the security's risk. Therefore, studies in this category examine whether public information can be used to predict what stocks will enjoy above- or below-average risk-adjusted returns.

These studies typically examine the usefulness of alternative measures of size or quality to rank stocks in terms of risk-adjusted returns. Keep in mind that all of these tests involve a *joint hypothesis* because they consider the efficiency of the market and are dependent on the asset pricing model that provides the measure of risk used in the test. Specifically, if a test determines that it is possible to predict risk-adjusted returns, these results could occur because the market is not efficient, or they could be because the measure of risk is faulty and, therefore, the measures of risk-adjusted returns are wrong.

Price-Earnings Ratios Several studies, beginning with Basu (1977), have examined the relationship between the historical **price-earnings (P/E) ratios** and the returns on the stocks. Some have suggested that low P/E stocks will outperform high P/E stocks because growth companies enjoy high P/E ratios, but the market tends to overestimate the growth potential and thus overvalues these growth companies, while undervaluing low-growth firms with low P/E ratios. A relationship between the historical P/E ratios and subsequent risk-adjusted market performance would constitute evidence against the semistrong-form EMH, because it would imply that investors could use publicly available information regarding P/E ratios to predict future abnormal returns.

Performance measures indicated that low P/E ratio stocks experienced superior risk-adjusted results relative to the market, whereas high P/E ratio stocks had significantly inferior risk-adjusted results.[5] Subsequent analysis concluded that publicly available P/E ratios possess valuable information regarding future returns, which is inconsistent with semistrong efficiency.

Peavy and Goodman (1983) examined P/E ratios with adjustments for firm size, industry effects, and infrequent trading and likewise found that the risk-adjusted returns for stocks in the lowest P/E ratio quintile were superior to those in the highest P/E ratio quintile.

Price-Earnings/Growth Rate (PEG) Ratios During the past decade, there has been a significant increase in the use of the ratio of a stock's price-earnings ratio divided by the firm's expected earnings growth rate (referred to as the PEG ratio) as a relative valuation tool, especially for

---

5 Composite performance measures are discussed in Chapter 18.

stocks of growth companies that have P/E ratios substantially above average. Advocates of PEG ratio hypothesize that stocks with relatively low PEG ratios (i.e., less than one) will experience above-average returns while stocks with relatively high PEG ratios (i.e., in excess of three or four) will have below-average returns. A study by Peters (1991) using quarterly rebalancing supported the hypothesis of this inverse relationship. These results would constitute an anomaly and would not support the EMH. A subsequent study by Reilly and Marshall (1999) assumed annual rebalancing and divided the sample on the basis of a risk measure (beta), market value size, and expected growth rate. Except for stocks with low betas and very low expected growth rates, the results were not consistent with the hypothesis of an inverse relationship between the PEG ratio and subsequent returns.

In summary, the results for using the PEG ratio to select stocks are mixed.

The Size Effect Banz (1981) examined the impact of size (measured by total market value) on the risk-adjusted returns. The risk-adjusted returns for extended periods (20 to 35 years) indicated that the small firms consistently experienced significantly larger risk-adjusted returns than the larger firms. Reinganum (1981) contended that it was the size, not the P/E ratio, that caused the results discussed in the prior subsection, but this contention was disputed by Basu (1977).

Recall that abnormal returns may occur because the markets are inefficient or because the market model provides incorrect estimates of risk and expected returns.

It was suggested that the riskiness of the small firms was improperly measured because small firms are traded less frequently. An alternative risk-measure technique confirmed that the small firms had much higher risk, but the consideration of the higher betas did not account for the large difference in returns.

A study by Stoll and Whaley (1983) that examined the impact of transaction costs confirmed the size effect but also found that firms with small market value generally have low stock prices. Because transaction costs vary inversely with price per share, these costs must be considered when examining the small-firm effect. It was shown that there was a significant difference in the percentage total transaction cost for large firms (2.71%) versus small firms (6.77%). This differential in transaction costs, assuming frequent trading, can have a significant impact on the results. Assuming daily transactions, the original small-firm effects are reversed. Thus, size-effect studies must consider realistic transaction costs and specify holding period assumptions. Reinganum (1983) considered both factors over long periods and demonstrated that infrequent rebalancing (about once a year) is almost ideal—the results beat long-run buy-and-hold and avoid frequent rebalancing that generates excess costs. In summary, small firms outperformed large firms after considering higher risk and realistic transaction costs, assuming annual rebalancing.

Most studies on the size effect employed large databases and long time periods (over 50 years) to show that this phenomenon has existed for many years. In contrast, a study that examined the performance over various intervals of time concluded that *the small-firm effect is not stable*. During most periods investigators found the negative relationship between size and return, but during selected periods (such as 1967–1975), they found that large firms outperformed the small firms. Notably, this positive relationship held during the following recent periods: 1984–1987; 1989–1990; and 1995–1998. Reinganum (1992) acknowledges this instability but contends that the small-firm effect is still a long-run phenomenon.

In summary, firm size is a major efficient-market anomaly. The two strongest explanations are higher risk measurements due to infrequent trading and higher transaction costs. Depending on the frequency of trading, these two factors may account for much of the differential. These results indicate that the size effect must be considered in any event study that considers long time periods and contains a sample of firms with significantly different market values.

Neglected Firms and Trading Activity Arbel and Strebel (1983) considered an additional influence beyond size—attention or neglect. They measured attention in terms of the number of analysts who regularly follow a stock and divided the stocks into three groups: (1) highly followed, (2) moderately followed, and (3) neglected. They confirmed the small-firm effect but also found a neglected-firm effect caused by the lack of information and limited institutional interest. The neglected-firm concept applied across size classes. Contrary results are reported by Beard and Sias (1997) who found no evidence of a neglected-firm premium after controlling for capitalization.

James and Edmister (1983) examined the impact of trading volume by considering the relationship between returns, market value, and trading activity. The results confirmed the relationship between size and returns, but the results indicated no significant difference between the mean returns of the highest and lowest trading activity portfolios. A subsequent study hypothesized that firms with less information require higher returns. Using the period of listing as a proxy for information, they found a negative relationship between returns and the period of listing after adjusting for firm size and the January effect.

Book Value–Market Value Ratio This ratio relates the book value (BV) of a firm's equity to the market value (MV) of its equity. Rosenberg, Reid, and Lanstein (1985) found a significant positive relationship between current values for this ratio and future stock returns and contended that such a relationship between available public information on the BV/MV ratio and future returns was evidence against the EMH.[6]

Strong support for this ratio was provided by Fama and French (1992) who evaluated the joint effects of market beta, size, P/E ratio, leverage, and the BV/MV ratio (referred to as BE/ME) on a cross-section of average returns. They analyzed the hypothesized positive relationship between beta and expected returns and found that this positive relationship held pre-1969 but disappeared during the period 1963 to 1990. In contrast, the negative relationship between size and average return was significant by itself and significant after inclusion of other variables.

In addition, they found a significant positive relationship between the BV/MV ratio and average return that persisted even when other variables were included. Most importantly, *both* size and the BV/MV ratio are significant when included together and they dominate other ratios. Specifically, although leverage and the E/P ratio were significant by themselves or with size, they become insignificant when both size and the BV/MV ratio are considered.

In summary, studies that have used publicly available ratios to predict the cross-section of expected returns for stocks have provided substantial evidence in conflict with the semistrong-form EMH. Significant results were found for P/E ratios, market value size, and BV/MV ratios. Although the research by Fama and French indicated that the optimal combination appears to be size and the BV/MV ratio, a study by Jensen, Johnson, and Mercer (1997) indicates that this combination works only during periods of expansive monetary policy.

Results of Event Studies Recall that the intent of event studies is to examine abnormal returns surrounding significant economic information. Those advocating the EMH would expect returns to adjust quickly to announcements of new information such that investors should not experience positive abnormal returns by acting after the announcement. Because of space constraints, we can only summarize the results for some of the more popular events: stock splits, the sale of initial public offerings, exchange listings, unexpected world or economic events, and the announcements of significant accounting changes. Notably, the results for most of these studies have supported the semistrong-form EMH.

---

6 Many studies define this ratio as "book-to-market value" (BV/MV) because it implies a positive relationship, but most practitioners refer to it as the "price-to-book value" (P/B) ratio. Obviously the concept is the same, but the sign changes.

Stock Split Studies Many investors believe that the prices of stocks that split will increase in value because of increased demand for the now lower priced shares. In contrast, efficient-market advocates would not expect a change in value because the firm simply issued additional stock and nothing fundamentally affecting the value of the firm has occurred.

The classic study by Fama, Fisher, Jensen, and Roll (1969), referred to hereafter as FFJR, hypothesized no significant price change following a stock split, because any relevant information (such as earnings growth) that caused the split would have already been discounted. The FFJR study analyzed abnormal price movements surrounding the time of the split and divided the stock split sample into those stocks that did or did not raise their dividends. Both groups experienced positive abnormal price changes prior to the split. Stocks that split but did *not* increase their dividend experienced abnormal price *declines* following the split and within 12 months lost all their accumulated abnormal gains. In contrast, stocks that split and increased their dividend experienced no abnormal returns after the split.

These results support the semistrong-form EMH because they indicate that investors cannot gain from the information on a stock split after the public announcement. These results were confirmed by most (but not all) subsequent studies.

Initial Public Offerings (IPOs) During the past 20 years, a number of companies have gone public by selling some of their common stock (Exhibit 5.1). Because of uncertainty about the appropriate offering price and the risk involved in underwriting such issues, it has been hypothesized that the underwriters would tend to underprice these new issues.

Given this general expectation of underpricing, the studies in this area have generally considered three sets of questions: (1) What is the magnitude of the underpricing on average? Does the underpricing vary over time? If so, why? (2) What factors cause different amounts of underpricing for various issues? (3) How fast does the market adjust the price for the underpricing?

The answer to the first question is that an average underpricing does exist and varies over time. The main variables causing differential underpricing seem to be: various risk measures,

IPO Facts: A wealth of information on IPOs can be found at http://bear.cba.ufl.edu/ritter/ipodata.htm.
For specific information on IPOs and average underpricing in the U.S. markets, click on the link, "Some Factoids About the 2007 IPO Market."

EXHIBIT 5.1	Number of Offerings and Total Proceeds of Initial Public Offerings in 2000–2008	
Year	Number of Offerings[1]	Total Proceeds, $ Millions[2]
2000	87	6,260
2001	33	849
2002	32	853
2003	36	620
2004	60	3,116
2005	79	2,203
2006	94	3,134
2007	102	3,791
2008	59	705

[1]The number of offerings excludes capital pool IPOs. Common equity including units, flow-through, and convertible debt.
[2]Total proceeds data are including the proceeds from any overallotment options.
Source: fpinfomart.ca, "New Issues-IPOs by Industry."

firm size, underwriter prestige, and the status of the firm's accounting firms. On the question of direct interest to the EMH, results in Miller and Reilly (1987) and Ibbotson, Sindelar, and Ritter (1994) indicate that the price adjustment to the underpricing takes place within one day after the offering. Therefore, it appears that some underpricing occurs based on the original offering price, but the only ones who benefit from this underpricing are investors who receive allocations of the original issue. More specifically, institutional investors captured most (70%) of the short-term profits. This rapid adjustment of the initial underpricing would support the semistrong-form EMH. Studies by Loughran, Ritter, and Rydqvist (1994, updated March 2008) and Kooli and Suret (2004) have shown that the initial returns on first-day trading averaged 7.1% between 1971 and 2007 and 20.57% between 1991 and 1998. Further, these studies among others have examined the long-run returns on IPOs and found that investors acquiring the stock after the initial adjustment do *not* experience positive long-run abnormal returns.

New listings in the TSX and TSX Venture exchange can be found at

http://www.tmxmoney.com /en/market_activity/new_ listings_tsx_current.html.

Exchange Listing A significant economic event for a firm is listing its stock on a national exchange. Such a listing is expected to increase the market liquidity of the stock and add to its prestige. An important question is, can an investor derive abnormal returns from investing in the stock when a new listing is announced or around the time of the actual listing? The results are mixed. All the studies agreed that (1) the stocks' prices increased before any listing announcements, and (2) stock prices consistently declined after the actual listing. The crucial question is: What happens between the announcement of the application for listing and the actual listing (a period of four to six weeks)? A study by McConnell and Sanger (1989) points toward profit opportunities immediately after the announcement that a firm is applying for listing and there is the possibility of excess returns from price declines after the actual listing. However, other studies examining the impact of listing on the risk of the securities found no significant change in systematic risk or the firm's cost of equity.

Such evidence of short-run profit opportunities for investors using public information would not support the semistrong-form EMH.

Unexpected World Events and Economic News The results of several studies that examined the response of security prices to world or economic news have supported the semistrong-form EMH. An analysis of the stock-price reactions to unexpected world events found that prices adjusted to the news before the market opened or before it reopened after the announcement (generally, as with the World Trade Center attack, the exchanges are closed immediately for various time periods—e.g., one to four days). A study by Pierce and Roley (1985) that examined the response to announcements about money supply, inflation, real economic activity, and the discount rate found an impact that did not persist beyond the announcement day. Finally, Jain (1988) did an analysis of hourly stock returns and trading-volume response to surprise announcements and found that unexpected information about money supply impacted stock prices within one hour. For a review of studies that considered the impact of news on individual stocks, see Chan (2003).

Announcements of Accounting Changes Numerous studies have analyzed the impact of announcements of accounting changes on stock prices. In efficient markets, security prices should react quickly and predictably to such announcements. If, for example, an accounting change affects reported earnings but has no economic significance, it should not affect stock prices (i.e. a firm changing its amortization method for reporting purposes from accelerated to straight line will likely experience an increase in reported earnings but there is no economic consequence). An analysis of stock-price movements surrounding this accounting change indicates that the securities markets react quite quickly and adjust security prices as expected on the basis of changes in true value (that is, analysts pierce the accounting veil and value securities on the basis of economic events).

Corporate Events Events such as mergers and acquisitions, spin-offs, reorganization, and various security offerings (common stock, straight bonds, convertible bonds) have been examined, relative to two general questions: (1) What is the market impact of these various events? (2) How fast does the market adjust the security prices?

Regarding the reaction to corporate events, the answer is very consistent—stock prices react as one would expect based on the underlying economic impact of the action. For example, the reaction to mergers is that the stock of the firm being acquired increases in line with the premium offered, whereas the stock of the acquiring firm typically declines because of the concern that they overpaid for the acquisition. On the question of how quickly, the evidence indicates that the price adjustment is quite rapid (completed in about three days). Studies related to financing decisions are reviewed by Smith (1986), corporate control in mergers and reorganizations are reviewed by Jensen and Warner (1988), while interesting stock performance has resulted from corporate spin-offs as shown by Desai and Jain (1999) and Chemmanur and Yan (2004).

Summary on the Semistrong-Form EMH Clearly, the evidence from tests of the semistrong-form EMH is mixed. The hypothesis receives almost unanimous support from the numerous event studies on a range of events while mixed results come from exchange listing studies.

In sharp contrast, the numerous studies on predicting returns over time or for a cross-section of stocks present evidence counter to semistrong efficiency. This includes time-series studies on risk premiums, calendar patterns, and quarterly earnings surprises. Similarly, the results for cross-sectional predictors such as size, the BV/MV ratio (when there is expansive monetary policy), and P/E ratios indicate non-efficiencies.

5.3.3 STRONG-FORM HYPOTHESIS: TESTS AND RESULTS

The strong-form EMH contends that stock prices fully reflect *all information,* implying that no group of investors has access to *private information* that will allow them to consistently experience above-average profits.

Tests of the strong-form EMH have analyzed returns over time for different identifiable investment groups to determine whether any group consistently received above-average risk-adjusted returns. Such a group must have access to and act upon important private information or an ability to act on public information before other investors, which would indicate that security prices were not adjusting rapidly to *all* new information.

Investigators have tested this form of the EMH by analyzing the performance of four different investor types: (1) *corporate insiders,* (2) *stock exchange specialists,* (3) *security analysts* at *Value Line* and elsewhere, and (4) *professional money managers.*

Corporate Insiders Corporate insiders are required to report to the System for Electronic Disclosure by Insiders (SEDI) on their transactions (purchases or sales) in the stock of the firm for which they are insiders within 10 days of the trade date. Insiders include senior corporate officers, members of the board of directors, and owners of 10% or more of any equity class of securities. About one week after the reporting period, this information is made public. The insider-trading data has been used to determine whether the corporate insiders have bought or sold, on balance, before abnormally good or bad price movements for their stock. The results of studies, including Chowdhury, Howe, and Lin (1993) and Pettit and Venkatesh (1995), have generally indicated that corporate insiders consistently enjoyed above-average profits, heavily dependent on selling prior to low returns and not selling before strong returns. This implies that many insiders had private information from which they derived above-average returns on their company stock.

In addition, an earlier study found that *public* investors who consistently traded with the insiders based on announced insider transactions would have enjoyed excess risk-adjusted returns (after commissions), although a subsequent study concluded that the market had eliminated this inefficiency after considering total transaction costs.

Overall, these results provide mixed support for the EMH because several studies indicate that insiders experience abnormal profits, while subsequent studies indicate it is no longer possible for non-insiders to use this information to generate excess returns. Notably, because of investor interest in these data as a result of academic research, the *Wall Street Journal* currently publishes a monthly column entitled "Inside Track" that discusses the largest insider transactions.

The TSX publishes insider trades at

http://cxa.marketwatch. com/TSX/en/Market/ marketactivitycan.aspx

Stock Exchange Specialists Several studies have determined that specialists have monopolistic access to certain important information about unfilled limit orders, and they should be able to derive above-average returns from this information. This expectation is generally supported by the data. First, specialists generally make money because they typically sell shares at higher prices than their purchased price. Also, they apparently make money when they buy or sell after unexpected announcements and when they trade in large blocks of stock; see Ip (2001).

Security Analysts Several tests have considered whether it is possible to identify a set of analysts who have the ability to select undervalued stocks. The analysis involves determining whether, after a stock selection by an analyst is made known, a significant abnormal return is available to those who follow these recommendations. These studies and those that discuss performance by money managers are more realistic and relevant than those that considered corporate insiders and stock exchange specialists because these analysts and money managers are full-time investment professionals with no obvious advantage except emphasis and training. If anyone should be able to select undervalued stocks, it should be these "pros." We initially examine *Value Line* rankings and then analyze the usefulness of recommendations by individual analysts.

Check out the *Value Line* website at

http://www.valueline.com.

The Value Line Enigma *Value Line* (VL) is a large well-known advisory service that publishes financial information on approximately 1,700 stocks. Included in its report is a timing rank, which indicates *Value Line*'s expectation regarding a firm's common-stock performance over the coming 12 months. A rank of 1 is the most favourable performance and 5 is the worst. This ranking system, initiated in April 1965, assigns numbers based on four factors:

1. An earnings and price rank of each security relative to all others
2. A price momentum factor
3. Year-to-year relative changes in quarterly earnings
4. A quarterly earnings "surprise" factor (actual quarterly earnings compared with VL estimated earnings)

The firms are ranked based on a composite score for each firm. The top and bottom 100 are ranked 1 and 5, respectively; the next 300 from the top and bottom are ranked 2 and 4; and the rest (approximately 900) are ranked 3. Rankings are assigned every week based on the latest data. All the data used to derive the four factors are public information.

Several years after the ranking was started, *Value Line* contended that the stocks rated 1 substantially outperformed the market and the stocks rated 5 seriously underperformed the market (the performance figures did not include dividend income but also did not account for commissions).

Early studies on the *Value Line* enigma indicated that there was information in the VL rankings (especially either rank 1 or 5) and in changes in the rankings (especially going from 2 to 1). Recent evidence indicates that the market is fairly efficient, because the abnormal adjustments appear to be complete by Day + 2. An analysis of study results over time indicates a faster adjustment to the rankings during recent years. Also, despite statistically significant price changes, mounting evidence indicates that it is not possible to derive abnormal returns from these announcements after considering realistic transaction costs. The strongest evidence regarding not being able to use this information is that *Value Line*'s Centurion Fund, which concentrates on investing in rank-1 stocks, has consistently underperformed the market over the past decade.

Analysts' Recommendations There is evidence in favour of the existence of superior analysts who apparently possess private information. A study by Womack (1996) found that analysts appear to have both market timing and stock-picking ability, especially in connection with relatively rare sell recommendations. Jegadeesh et al. (2004) found that consensus recommendations do not contain incremental information for most stocks beyond other available signals (momentum and volume), but changes in consensus recommendations are useful. Alternatively, research by Ivkovic and Jegadeesh (2004) indicated that the most useful information consisted of upward earning revisions in the week prior to earnings announcements. A recent study by Goff, Hulbart, Keasler, and Walsh (2008) examined the information content of analyst recommendations after the passage of Regulation Fair Disclosure (REGFD—a U.S. regulation; Canada already had strong disclosure requirements) and concluded that recommendation changes continue to be informative.

Performance of Professional Money Managers Money managers typically do not have monopolistic access to important new information but are highly trained professionals who work full-time at investment management. Therefore, if any "normal" set of investors should be able to derive above-average profits, it should be this group. Also, if any outsider should be able to derive inside information, professional money managers should because they conduct extensive management interviews.

Most studies on money-manager performance have examined mutual funds because data are readily available for them (whether managed by a bank, a trust, an insurance company, or investment dealers). The original mutual fund studies indicated that most funds did not match the performance of a buy-and-hold policy.[7] When risk-adjusted returns were examined *without* considering commission costs, slightly more than half of the money managers did better than the overall market. When commission costs, load fees, and management costs were considered, approximately two-thirds of the mutual funds did *not* match aggregate market performance. It was also found that successful funds during individual years were inconsistent in their performance.

Now that it is possible to get performance data for pension plans and endowment funds, several studies have documented that the performances of pension plans did not match that of the aggregate market. Similarly, the results for a large sample of endowments confirm the inability to outperform the market.

Conclusions Regarding the Strong-Form EMH The strong-form EMH tests have also generated mixed results. The results for corporate insiders and stock exchange specialists did not support the hypothesis because both groups apparently have monopolistic access to important information and use it to derive above-average returns.

Tests to determine whether there are any analysts with private information concentrated on the *Value Line* rankings and publications of analysts' recommendations. The results for *Value Line* rankings have changed over time and currently tend toward support for the EMH.

---

7 These studies and others on this topic are reviewed in Chapter 17.

Specifically, the adjustment to rankings and ranking changes is fairly rapid, and it appears that trading is not profitable after transaction costs. However, individual analysts' recommendations and overall consensus changes seem to contain significant information.

Finally, recent performance by professional money managers provided mixed support for the strong-form EMH.

5.4 Behavioural Finance[8]

A number of papers related to behavioural finance can be found on Richard Thaler's website at http://faculty.chicagogsb.edu/richard.thaler/research.

Our discussion up to this point has dealt with standard finance theory and how to test within this theoretical context whether capital markets are informationally efficient. However, in the 1990s, a new branch of financial economics was added to the mix. **Behavioural finance** considers how various psychological traits affect how individuals or groups act as investors, analysts, and portfolio managers. Behavioural finance advocates recognize that the standard finance model of rational behaviour and profit maximization can be true within specific boundaries' but they assert that it is *incomplete* because it does not consider individual behaviour.

Specifically, according to Olsen (1998), behavioural finance

seeks to understand and predict systematic financial market implications of psychological decisions processes . . . behavioural finance is focused on the implication of psychological and economic principles for the improvement of financial decision-making. (p. 11)

While it is currently acknowledged that there is no unified theory of behavioural finance, the emphasis has been on identifying portfolio anomalies that can be explained by various psychological traits in individuals or groups, or pinpointing instances when it is possible to experience above-normal returns by exploiting the biases of investors, analysts, or portfolio managers.

Alternative Viewpoint: Behavioural Finance

Investors' emotions are now studied to explain investment performance. Conventional finance theory argues that in order to earn higher returns, one has to accept more risk irrespective of one's psychological make-up. Failure to measure up stems from a lack of intellect.

Ever the contrarian, Warren Buffett has repeatedly claimed that "success in investing doesn't correlate with I.Q." He uses the Mr. Market metaphor, taught to him by Ben Graham, to explain that the market is like a person suffering from manic depression. Every day Mr. Market offers to buy stocks from investors or offers them his holdings at prices he sets depending on his mood. Sometimes Mr. Market is depressed and his prices are ridiculously low; other times he is ebullient and his prices are unrealistically high. Mr. Market does not mind being ignored and will always reappear the next day with another set of prices. In order to be successful, it is up to investors to recognize these moods, to remain rational, and to take advantage of them. But our psychological make-up gets in the way.

Behavioural finance starts from the observation that people are remarkably irrational when it comes to money and this irrationality leads investors to disastrous results. One evolutionary explanation for this irrationality of *Homo sapiens* is that those of us who have survived carry a survival

(Continued)

---

8 The discussion in this section was enhanced by two outstanding survey articles by Barberis and Thaler (2003) and by Hirschleifer (2001), as well as presentations at the CFA Research Foundation Workshop in Vancouver (May 2008).

gene that tells us that there is safety in the herd and, failing that, in fleeing at the first sign of danger. These qualities are often disastrous for investors and lead to the following mistakes:

- We follow the herd because we assume that it "knows" and we don't want to stick it out (if we stick it out we may get eaten by the predator, or more appropriately for investors, we do not want to look ridiculous in being different).
- We are more upset by losses than we are happy about gains.
- We use a kind of mental accounting where we are ready to lose money we won unexpectedly at the casino but would be terribly upset if the same amount came from our paycheque.
- We are very reluctant to change away from the status quo.
- We are paralyzed and procrastinate when we face many different options.
- We like keeping things simple when we are gathering information for a new decision. Thus, we tend to focus on data points that we have recently run across or are stuck in our memories even if they are irrelevant.
- We like to draw conclusions from data that are at hand even if drawn from a limited sample.
- We confuse familiarity with knowledge and we fail to recognize our lack of understanding of complex situations.
- We suffer from overconfidence even after many instances when we have been proven to be wrong.
- We ascribe our successes to our cleverness and our failures to bad luck.

These psychological traits lower our results by leading us to:

- Trade excessively.
- Be unprepared for the future (money for retirement, for children's education, for a rainy day).
- Believe that we are skilled stock pickers.
- Believe that we can recognize which money managers' performance is due to luck and which ones to skill. This leads us to run after performance rather than to recognize it ahead of the crowd.
- Keep our money in one basket and to believe that we do not need to diversify.

Prepared by Francis Tapon, University of Guelph

5.4.1 EXPLAINING BIASES

Over time it has been noted that investors have a number of biases that negatively affect their investment performance. Behavioural finance advocates have been able to explain a number of these biases based on psychological characteristics such as the propensity of investors to hold on to "losers" too long and sell "winners" too soon. This is explained by *prospect theory*, which contends that utility depends on deviations from moving reference points rather than absolute wealth. That is, investors fear losses more than they value gains.

There are two related biases that seriously impact analysis and investment decisions. The first is *belief perseverance*, which means that once people have formed an opinion (on a company or stock) they cling to it too tightly and for too long. As a result, they are reluctant to search for contradictory beliefs, and even when they find such evidence, they are very skeptical about it or even misinterpret such information. A related bias is *anchoring*, wherein individuals who are asked to estimate something, start with an initial arbitrary (casual) value, and then adjust away from it. The problem is that the adjustment is often insufficient. Therefore, if your initial estimate is low, you may raise it with information, but it is likely you will not raise it enough and thus will end up below the "best estimates."

Another bias is *overconfidence* in forecasts, which causes analysts to overestimate growth rates for growth companies and overemphasize good news and ignore negative news for these firms. Analysts and many investors also believe that the stocks of growth companies will be "good" stocks. In some instances, investors look for information that supports prior opinions and decisions, a confirmation bias. As a result, they will misvalue the stocks of these generally popular companies. Overconfidence is also related to *self-attribution bias*; success is based on our talents while failure is a result of bad luck or bad timing. This, along with *hindsight bias* (the individual believes that he or she predicted the event), causes people to overestimate their talent.

Various researchers have examined *noise traders* (non-professionals with no special information) and found that when there is a shift in sentiment, these traders move together, which increases the prices and the volatility of these securities during trading hours. Noise traders tend to follow newsletter writers, who in turn tend to "follow the herd." These writers and "the herd" are almost always wrong, which contributes to excess volatility.

Shefrin (2001) describes *escalation bias*, which causes investors to put more money into a failure that they feel responsible for rather than into a success. This leads to the relatively popular investor practice of "averaging down" on an investment that has declined in value since the initial purchase rather than consider selling the stock if it was a mistake. The thinking is that if it was a buy at $40, it is a bargain at $30. Obviously, an alternative solution is to reevaluate the stock to see if some important bad news was missed in the initial valuation (therefore, sell it and accept the loss), or to confirm the initial valuation and acquire more of the "bargain." The difficulty for most investors though is to seriously look for the bad news and consider the negative effects of this news on the valuation.

5.4.2 FUSION INVESTING

According to Charles M. C. Lee (2003), *fusion investing* is the integration of two elements of investment valuation—fundamental value and investor sentiment. In Robert Shiller's (1984) formal model, the market price of securities is the expected dividends discounted to infinity (its fundamental value) plus a term that indicates the demand from noise traders who reflect investor sentiment. It is contended that when noise traders are bullish, stock prices will be higher than normal or higher than what is justified by fundamentals. Under this combination pricing model of fusion investing, investors will engage in fundamental analysis but also should consider investor sentiment in terms of fads and fashions. During some periods, investor sentiment is rather muted and noise traders are inactive, so fundamental valuation dominates market returns. In other periods, when investor sentiment is strong, noise traders are very active and market returns are more heavily impacted by investor sentiments. Both investors and analysts should be cognizant of these dual effects on the aggregate market, various economic sectors, and individual stocks.

Beyond advocating awareness of the dual components of fusion investing, results from other studies have documented that fundamental valuation may be the dominant factor but it takes much longer to assert itself—about three years. To derive some estimate of changing investor sentiment, Lee proposes several measures of investor sentiment, most notably analysts' recommendations, price momentum, and high trading turnover. Significant changes in these variables for a stock will indicate a movement from a glamour stock to a neglected stock or vice versa.

5.5 Implications of Efficient Capital Markets

Having reviewed the mixed results of numerous studies related to different facets of the EMH, it is important to consider the implications of this contrasting evidence so that we can ask, "What does this mean to individual investors, financial analysts, portfolio managers, and institutions?"

The Economist has an interesting article on market efficiency, bubbles, and behaviour at
http://www.economist.com/finance/displaystory.cfm?story_id=13240822.

The following discussion considers the implications of both sets of evidence. Specifically given results that support the EMH, we consider what techniques will not work and what you should do if you cannot beat the market. In contrast, because of the evidence that fails to support the EMH, we discuss what information and psychological biases should be considered when attempting to derive superior investment results through active security valuation and portfolio management.

5.5.1 EFFICIENT MARKETS AND TECHNICAL ANALYSIS

Technical analysis assumptions oppose the notion of efficient markets.[9] Technicians believe that when new information comes to the market, it is not immediately available to everyone but is typically disseminated from the informed professional to the aggressive investing public and then to the great bulk of investors. Also, technicians contend that investors do not analyze information and act immediately. Therefore, they hypothesize that stock prices move in a gradual manner to a new equilibrium after the release of new information, which causes trends in stock price movements that persist.

Technical analysts believe that nimble traders can develop systems to detect the beginning of a movement to a new equilibrium (called a "breakout"). Hence, they hope to buy or sell the stock immediately after its breakout to take advantage of the subsequent, gradual price adjustment.

The belief in this pattern of price adjustment directly contradicts EMH advocates' conviction that security prices adjust to new information rapidly. These practitioners realize that prices do not adjust perfectly, which implies a chance of an over- or under-adjustment. Still, because it is uncertain whether the market will over- or under-adjust at any time, you cannot derive abnormal profits from adjustment errors.

If the capital market is weak-form efficient as indicated by most of the results, then prices fully reflect all relevant market information, so technical trading systems that depend only on past trading data *cannot* have any value. By the time the information is public, the price adjustment has taken place. Therefore, a purchase or sale using a technical trading rule should not generate abnormal returns after taking into account risk and transaction costs.

5.5.2 EFFICIENT MARKETS AND FUNDAMENTAL ANALYSIS

As you know from our prior discussion, fundamental analysts believe that, at any time, there is a basic intrinsic value for the aggregate stock market, various industries, or individual securities and that these values depend on underlying economic factors. Therefore, investors should determine the intrinsic value of an investment at a point in time by examining the variables that determine value such as future earnings or cash flows, interest rates, and risk characteristics. If the prevailing market price differs from the estimated intrinsic value by enough to cover transaction costs, you should take appropriate action: buy if the market price is substantially below intrinsic value, or sell if the market price is above the intrinsic value. Investors engaged in fundamental analysis believe that occasionally market price and intrinsic value differ but eventually investors recognize the discrepancy and correct it.

An investor who can do a superior job of *estimating* intrinsic value can consistently make superior market timing (asset allocation) decisions or acquire undervalued securities and generate above-average returns. The divergent results from the EMH research have important implications for all of these components.

---

9 Chapter 10 contains an extensive discussion of technical analysis.

Aggregate Market Analysis with Efficient Capital Markets Chapter 8 makes a strong case that intrinsic value analysis should begin with aggregate market analysis. Still, the EMH implies that if you examine only *past* economic events, it is unlikely that you will outperform a buy-and-hold policy because the market rapidly adjusts to known economic events. Evidence suggests that the market experiences long-run price movements, but to take advantage of these movements in an efficient market, you must do a superior job of *estimating* the relevant variables that cause these long-run movements. If you only use *historical* data to estimate future values and invest on the basis of these "old news" estimates, you will *not* experience superior, risk-adjusted returns.

Industry and Company Analysis with Efficient Capital Markets As we discuss in Chapter 9, the wide distribution of returns from different industries and companies clearly justifies industry and company analysis. The EMH does not contradict the potential value of such analysis but implies that you need to (1) understand the relevant variables affecting returns and (2) do a superior job of *estimating future* values for these relevant variables. To demonstrate, Malkiel and Cragg (1970) developed a model that did an excellent job of explaining past stock price movements using historical data. When this model was used to project *future* stock price changes using *past* company data, however, the results were consistently inferior to a buy-and-hold policy. This implies that, even with a good valuation model, you *cannot* select stocks that will provide superior future returns using only past data as inputs.

A study by Benesh and Peterson (1986) showed that the crucial difference between the stocks that enjoyed the best and worst price performance during a given year was the relationship between professional analysts' earnings forecasts and actual earnings (that is, it was *earnings surprises*). Specifically, stock prices increased if actual earnings substantially exceeded expected earnings and stock prices fell if actual earnings were below expected levels. As suggested by Fogler (1993), if you can do a superior job of projecting earnings and your expectations *differ from the consensus* (i.e., you project earnings surprises), you will have a superior stock-selection record. Remember, if you are correct in your estimates but not different from the consensus, and the consensus was correct, this implies no surprise and no abnormal price movement.

The quest to be a superior analyst holds some good news and some suggestions. The good news is related to the strong-form tests that indicated the likely existence of superior analysts. It was shown that the rankings by *Value Line* contained information value, even though it might not be possible to profit from the work of these analysts after transaction costs. Also, the price adjustments to the publication of analyst recommendations also point to the existence of superior analysts. The point is, there are some superior analysts, but only a limited number, and it is *not* an easy task to be among this select group.

The suggestions for those involved in fundamental analysis are based on the studies that considered the cross-section of future returns. As noted, these studies indicated that P/E ratios, size, and the BV/MV ratios were able to differentiate future return patterns, with size and the BV/MV ratio appearing to be the optimal combination. Therefore, these factors should be considered when selecting a universe or analyzing firms. In addition, the evidence suggests that neglected firms should be given extra consideration. Although these ratios and characteristics have been shown to be useful in isolating superior stocks from a large sample, it is our suggestion that they are best used to derive a viable sample to analyze from the total universe (e.g., select 200 stocks to analyze from a universe of 3,000). Then the 200 stocks should be rigorously valued using the techniques discussed in subsequent chapters.

How to Evaluate Analysts or Investors To determine if an individual is a superior analyst or investor, you should examine the performance of numerous securities that the analyst or investor recommends over time in relation to the performance of a set of randomly selected stocks of the same risk class. The stock selections of a superior analyst or investor should *consistently* outperform the randomly selected stocks. The consistency requirement is crucial because you would expect a portfolio developed by random selection to outperform the market about half the time.

Conclusions about Fundamental Analysis An investment text can detail the relevant variables to be analyzed and describe the important analysis techniques, but the actual estimation of the relevant variables is as much an art and a product of hard work as it is a science. If the estimates could be done on the basis of some mechanical formula, a computer could be programmed to do it, and there would be no need for analysts. Therefore, the superior analyst or successful investor must understand what variables are relevant and have the ability and work ethic to do a superior job of *estimating* values for these variables. Alternatively, one can be superior if he or she has the ability to interpret the impact or estimate the effect of some public information better than others.

5.5.3 Efficient Markets and Portfolio Management

As discussed, studies have shown that the majority of professional money managers cannot beat a buy-and-hold policy on a risk-adjusted basis. One explanation is that there are no superior analysts and the cost of research and trading forces the results of adequate analysis into the inferior category. Another explanation, which is favoured by the authors and has some empirical support from the *Value Line* and analyst recommendation results, is that money management firms employ both superior and inferior analysts, and the gains from the recommendations by the few superior analysts are offset by the costs and the poor results derived from the inferior analysts' recommendations.

This raises the question: Should a portfolio be managed actively or passively? A portfolio manager with superior analysts or an investor who believes that he or she has the time and expertise to be a superior investor can manage a portfolio actively by looking for undervalued or overvalued securities and trading accordingly. In contrast, without access to superior analysts or the time and ability to be a superior investor, you should manage passively and assume that all securities are properly priced based on their levels of risk.

A portfolio manager (or investor) who does not have access to superior analysts should build a portfolio to match the risk preferences of his or her clients by investing a certain proportion of the portfolio in risky assets and the rest in a risk-free asset (see Chapter 7).

The manager then needs to *minimize transaction costs* because excessive transaction costs detract from your expected return. Three factors are involved in minimizing total transaction costs:

1. *Minimize taxes.* Methods of accomplishing this objective vary, but it should receive prime consideration.
2. *Reduce trading turnover.* Trade only to liquidate part of the portfolio or to maintain a given risk level.
3. *When you trade, minimize liquidity costs by trading relatively liquid stocks.* To accomplish this, submit limit orders to buy or sell several stocks at prices that approximate the specialist's quote. That is, you would put in limit orders to buy stock at the bid price or sell at the ask price. The stock bought or sold first is the most liquid one; all other orders should be withdrawn.

The Rationale and Use of Index Funds and Exchange-Traded Funds As discussed, efficient capital markets and a lack of superior analysts imply that many portfolios should be managed *passively* to match the performance of the aggregate market, minimizing the research and trading costs. In response to this demand, several institutions have introduced *index funds*, which are security portfolios designed to duplicate the composition, and performance, of a selected market index series.

Notably, this concept of stock-market index funds has been extended to other areas of investments and, as discussed by Gastineau (2001) and Kostovetsky (2003), has been enhanced by the introduction of exchange-traded funds (ETFs). Index bond funds attempt to emulate the bond-market indices discussed in Chapter 4. Also in Chapter 4 we discussed various index funds that focus on specific segments of the market such as international bond or stock-index funds, or stock-index funds that target specific countries, company size, or industry. When financial planners want a given asset class in their portfolios, they often use index funds or ETFs to fulfill this need. Index funds or ETFs are less costly in terms of research and commissions, and during almost all time periods they can provide the same or better performance than the majority of active portfolio managers.

Summary

1. Capital markets should be efficient because numerous rational, profit-maximizing investors react quickly to the release of new information. Assuming prices reflect new information, they are unbiased estimates of the securities' true, intrinsic value, and there should be a consistent relationship between the return on an investment and its risk.

2. In our previous discussions, we determined that timely and accurate information, liquidity, price continuity, and low transaction costs are important factors contributing to an informationally efficient markets.

3. Given the overall efficient market hypothesis (EMH), what are the three subhypotheses and what are the implications of each of them? The weak-form EMH states that stock prices fully reflect all market information, so any trading rule that uses past market data to predict future returns should have no value. The semistrong-form EMH asserts that security prices adjust rapidly to the release of all public information and this hypothesis test results are mixed. Several studies consistently support the semistrong hypothesis while others do not. The strong-form EMH states that security prices reflect all information, including insider information. Evidence on this is split as well. Some studies indicate certain investor groups may benefit from insider information while others, who may have significant information, are unable to profit from it.

4. There is voluminous research on the EMH. The weak-form tests include statistical tests of independence and tests of trading rules. Semistrong-form tests of this hypothesis either examine the opportunities to predict future returns (either a time series or a cross-section) or they involve event studies in which investigators analyze whether investors could derive above-average returns from trading on the basis of public information. Tests for the strong-form EMH analyze returns over time for different identifiable investment groups to determine which, if any, consistently achieve higher than average risk-adjusted returns.

5. During the past decade, there has been significant research in behavioural finance by those contending that some of the anomalies can be explained by recognizing some of the implications of psychological decisions made by individuals. Recognition of these behaviours can also help explain the existence of several biases and provide opportunities for excess returns. It is important to be aware of a number of biases because they can lead to inferior performance as an analyst and portfolio manager but they may also be exploited for excess returns.

6. Given the mixed results, it is important to consider the implications of all of this for technical or fundamental analysts and for portfolio managers. The EMH indicates that technical analysis should be of no value. All forms of fundamental analysis are useful, but they are difficult to implement because they require the ability *to estimate future values* for relevant economic variables. Superior analysis is possible but difficult because it requires superior projections. Without access to superior analytical advice, you should run your portfolio like an index fund or an ETF. In contrast, those with superior analytical ability should be allowed to make decisions, but they should concentrate their efforts on mid-cap firms and neglected firms where there is a higher probability of discovering misvalued stocks.

This chapter contains some good news and some bad news. The good news is that the practice of investment analysis and portfolio management is not an art that has been lost to the advances in computers and modelling. Viable professions still await those willing to extend the effort and able to accept the pressures. The bad news is that many bright, hard-working people with extensive resources make the game tough. In fact, those competitors have created a fairly efficient capital market in which it is extremely difficult for most analysts and portfolio managers to achieve superior results.

Key Terms

abnormal rate of return, p. 110
anomalies, p. 107
autocorrelation test, p. 107
behavioural finance, p. 121
earnings surprise, p. 111
efficient capital market, p. 105
event study, p. 111

expected return, p. 110
informationally efficient market, p. 105
price-earnings (P/E) ratio, p. 113
return prediction studies, p. 111
runs test, p. 108
semistrong-form efficient market hypothesis, p. 107

strong-form efficient market hypothesis, p. 107
time-series analysis, p. 111
weak-form efficient market hypothesis, p. 106

Suggested Readings

Ariely, Dan. *Predictably Irrational: The Hidden Forces that Shape Our Decisions,* New York: Harper Collins, 2008.

Arnott, Robert D., Jason C. Hsu, and John M. West. *The Fundamental Index.* New York: Wiley, 2008.

Ball, Ray. "The Theory of Stock Market Efficiency: Accomplishments and Limitations." *Journal of Applied Corporate Finance* 8, no. 1 (Spring 1995).

Barberis, Nicholas, and Richard Thalen. "A Survey of Behavioral Finance." *Handbook of the Economics of Finance,* ed. G.M. Constantianides, M. Harris, and Rene Stulz. New York: Elsevier Science, 2003.

Berkowitz, Stephen A., Louis D. Finney, and Dennis Logue. *The Investment Performance of Corporate Pension Plans.* New York: Quorum Books, 1988.

Fama, Eugene. "Market Efficiency, Long-Term Returns, and Behavioral Finance." *Journal of Financial Economics* 49, no. 3 (September 1998): 283–306.

Hartford, Tim. *The Logic of Life.* New York: Random House, 2008.

King, M., and M. Padalko. "Outing Insiders: A Look at Price and Volume Dynamics Ahead of Canadian Merger Announcements." *Canadian Investment Review,* Spring 2007.

Kryzanowski, L., S. Lasrak, and I. Rakita. "The Behaviour of Prices, Trades, and Spreads for Canadian IPOs." *Multinational Finance Journal* 9, no. 3/4, 2005.

Marin, Jose M., and Jacques P. Oliver. "The Dog That Did Not Bark: Insider Trading and Crashes." *The Journal of Finance* 63, no. 5, (October 2008).

Sadka, Ronnie E., and Anna Scherbina. "Analysts Disagreement Mispricing, and Liquidity." *The Journal of Finance* 62, no. 5, (October 2007).

Shefrin, Hersh. *A Behavioral Approach to Asset Pricing Theory.* Amsterdam: Elsevier-North Holland, 2005.

Shefrin, Hersh, and Meir Statman. "Behavioral Capital Asset Pricing Theory." *Journal of Financial and Quantitative Analysis* 30, no. 3 (September 1995a).

Shermer, Michael. *The Mind of the Market.* New York: Times Books, 2008.

Wood, Arnold S., ed. *Behavioral Finance and Decision Theory in Investment Management.* Charlottesville, VA: AIMR, 1995.

CFA **For Chapter CFA Questions and Problems, please see Appendix A at the end of this text.**

Questions

1. Discuss the rationale for expecting an efficient capital market. What factor would you look for to differentiate the market efficiency for two alternative stocks?

2. Define and discuss the weak-form EMH. Describe the two sets of tests used to examine the weak-form EMH.

3. Define and discuss the semistrong-form EMH. Describe the two sets of tests used to examine the semistrong-form EMH.
4. What is meant by the term *abnormal rate of return*?
5. Describe how you would compute the abnormal rate of return for a stock for a period surrounding an economic event. Give a brief example for a stock with a beta of 1.40.
6. Assume you want to test the EMH by comparing alternative trading rules to a buy-and-hold policy. Discuss the three common mistakes that can bias the results against the EMH.
7. Describe the results of a study that supported the semistrong-form EMH. Discuss the nature of the test and specifically why the results support the hypothesis.
8. Describe the results of a study that did *not* support the semistrong-form EMH. Discuss the nature of the test and specifically why the results did not support the hypothesis.
9. For many of the EMH tests, it is really a test of a "joint hypothesis." Discuss what is meant by this concept. What are the joint hypotheses being tested?
10. Define and discuss the strong-form EMH. Why do some observers contend that the strong-form hypothesis really requires a perfect market in addition to an efficient market? Be specific.
11. Discuss how you would test the strong-form EMH. Why are these tests relevant? Give a brief example.
12. Describe the results of a study that did *not* support the strong-form EMH. Discuss the test involved and specifically why the results reported did not support the hypothesis.

13. Describe the results of a study that *did* support the strong-form EMH. Discuss the test involved and specifically why these results support the hypothesis.
14. Describe the general goal of behavioural finance.
15. Why do the advocates of behavioural finance contend that the standard finance theory is incomplete?
16. What does the EMH imply for the use of technical analysis?
17. What does the EMH imply for fundamental analysis? Discuss specifically what it does not imply.
18. In a world of efficient capital markets, what do you have to do to be a superior analyst? How would you test whether an analyst was superior?
19. What advice would you give to your superior analysts in terms of the set of firms to analyze and variables that should be considered in the analysis? Discuss your reasoning for this advice.
20. How should a portfolio manager without any superior analysts run his or her portfolio?
21. Describe the goals of an index fund. Discuss the contention that index funds are the ultimate answer in a world with efficient capital markets.
22. At a social gathering, you meet a portfolio manager for a mutual fund company. He confides to you that he has been following the recommendations of six analysts for an extended period and has found that two are superior, two are average, and two are clearly inferior. What would you recommend that he do to run his portfolio?

Problems

1. Compute the abnormal returns for the following stocks during period t (ignore differential systematic risk):

Stock	R_{it}	R_{mt}
B	11.5%	4.0%
F	10.0	8.5
T	14.0	9.6
C	12.0	15.3
E	15.9	12.4

R_{it} = return for stock i during period t

R_{mt} = return for the aggregate market during period t

2. Compute the abnormal returns for the five stocks in Problem 1 assuming the following systematic risk measures (betas):

Stock	β_i
B	0.95
F	1.25
T	1.45
C	0.70
E	−0.30

3. Compare the abnormal returns in Problems 1 and 2 and discuss the reason for the difference in each case.

4. Look up the daily trading volume for the following stocks during a recent five-day period:
   - Bombardier Inc.
   - Yamana Gold Inc.
   - Royal Bank of Canada
   - Talisman Energy Inc.
   - BCE Inc.

Randomly select five stocks from the TSX and examine their daily trading volume for the same five days.

a. What are the average volumes for the two samples?

b. Would you expect this difference to have an impact on the efficiency of the markets for the two samples? Why or why not?

An Introduction to Portfolio Management

One of the major advances in the investment field during the past few decades has been the recognition that you cannot create an optimum investment portfolio by simply combining numerous individual securities that have desirable risk/return characteristics. Specifically, it has been shown that an investor must consider the relationship *among* the investments to build an optimum portfolio that will meet investment objectives. The recognition of how to create an optimum portfolio was demonstrated in the derivation of portfolio theory.

In this chapter we explain portfolio theory step by step. We introduce the basic portfolio risk formula for combining different assets. Once you understand this formula and its implications, you will understand why you should diversify your portfolio and also *how* you should diversify.

6.1   Some Background Assumptions

Before presenting portfolio theory, we need to clarify some general assumptions of the theory.

This includes not only what we mean by an optimum portfolio but also what we mean by the terms *risk aversion* and *risk*.

One basic assumption of portfolio theory is that investors want to maximize the returns from your total set of investments for a given level of risk. To adequately deal with such an assumption requires certain ground rules. First, your portfolio should include all of your assets and liabilities, not only your marketable securities but also your car, house, and less marketable investments such as coins, stamps, art, antiques, and furniture. The full spectrum of investments must be considered because the returns from all these investments interact, and this relationship among the returns for assets in the portfolio is important. Hence, a good portfolio is not simply a collection of individually good investments.

6.1.1   Risk Aversion

Portfolio theory also assumes that investors are basically risk averse, meaning that given a choice between two assets with equal returns, investors will select the asset with the least risk. Evidence that most investors are risk averse is that they purchase various types of insurance, including life insurance, car insurance, and health insurance. Buying insurance basically involves an outlay of a given known

Pensions & Investments: News for Money Managers (http://www.pionline.com).

amount to guard against an uncertain, possibly larger, outlay in the future. Further evidence of risk aversion is the difference in promised yield (the required return) for different grades of bonds with different degrees of credit risk. Specifically, the promised yield on corporate bonds increases from AAA (the lowest risk class) to AA to A, and so on, indicating that investors require a higher return to accept higher risk.

This does not imply that everybody is risk averse, or that investors are completely risk averse regarding all financial commitments. The fact is, not everybody buys insurance for everything. Some people have no insurance against anything, either by choice or because they cannot afford it. In addition, some individuals buy insurance related to some risks such as auto accidents or illness, but they also buy lottery tickets and gamble at race tracks or in casinos, where it is known that the expected returns are negative (which means that participants are willing to pay for the excitement of the risk involved). This combination of risk preference and risk aversion can be explained by an attitude toward risk that depends on the amount of money involved. Researchers such as Friedman and Savage (1948) speculate that this is the case for people who like to gamble for small amounts (in lotteries or slot machines) but buy insurance to protect themselves against large losses such as fire or accidents.

While recognizing such attitudes, we assume that most investors with a large investment portfolio are risk averse. Therefore, we expect a positive relationship between expected return and expected risk, which is consistent with historical results as shown in Chapter 3.

6.1.2 DEFINITION OF RISK

Although there is a difference in the specific definitions of *risk* and *uncertainty*, for our purposes and in most financial literature the two terms are used interchangeably. For most investors, *risk* means the *uncertainty of future outcomes*. An alternative definition might be the *probability of an adverse outcome*. In our subsequent discussion of portfolio theory, we consider several measures of risk that are used when developing and applying the theory.

6.2 Markowitz Portfolio Theory

Nobel Prize Laureate Harry M. Markowitz and his contributions are available at http://search.nobelprize.org/search/nobel/?q=markowitz&i=en.

In the early 1960s, the investment community talked about risk, but there was no specific measure for the term. To build a portfolio model, however, investors had to quantify their risk variable. The basic portfolio model was developed by Nobel Prize Laureate Harry Markowitz (1952, 1959), who derived the expected return for a portfolio of assets and an expected risk measure. Markowitz showed that the variance of the rate of return was a meaningful measure of portfolio risk under a reasonable set of assumptions. More important, he derived the formula for computing the variance of a portfolio. This portfolio variance formula not only indicated the importance of diversifying investments to reduce the total risk of a portfolio but also showed *how* to effectively diversify. The Markowitz model is based on several assumptions regarding investor behaviour:

1. Investors consider each investment alternative as being represented by a probability distribution of expected returns over some holding period.
2. Investors maximize one-period expected utility, and their utility curves demonstrate diminishing marginal utility of wealth.
3. Investors estimate the risk of the portfolio on the basis of the variability of expected returns.
4. Investors base decisions solely on expected return and risk, so their utility curves are a function of expected return and the expected variance (or standard deviation) of returns only.
5. For a given risk level, investors prefer higher returns to lower returns. Similarly, for a given level of expected return, investors prefer less risk to more risk.

Under these assumptions, *a single asset or portfolio of assets is considered to be efficient if no other asset or portfolio of assets offers higher expected return with the same (or lower) risk or lower risk with the same (or higher) expected return.*

6.2.1 ALTERNATIVE MEASURES OF RISK

One of the best-known measures of risk is the variance or standard deviation of *expected returns.*[1] It is a statistical measure of the dispersion of returns around the expected value whereby a larger variance or standard deviation indicates greater dispersion. The idea is that the more disperse the expected returns, the greater the uncertainty of future returns.

Another measure of risk is the *range of returns.* It is assumed that a larger range of expected returns, from the lowest to the highest, means greater uncertainty regarding future expected returns.

Instead of using measures that analyze all deviations from expectations, some observers believe that investors should be concerned only with returns below expectations, which means only deviations below the mean value. A measure that only considers deviations below the mean is the *semivariance.* An extension of the semivariance measure only computes expected returns *below zero* (that is, negative returns), or returns below the returns of some specific asset such as T-bills, the inflation rate, or a benchmark. These measures of risk implicitly assume that investors want to *minimize the damage* (regret) from returns less than some target rate. Assuming that investors would welcome returns above some target rate, the returns above such a target rate are not considered when measuring risk.

Although there are numerous potential measures of risk, we will use the variance or standard deviation of returns because (1) this measure is somewhat intuitive, (2) it is a correct and widely recognized risk measure, and (3) it has been used in most of the theoretical asset pricing models. The following sections are also a demonstration of applying the expected return, variance, and covariance concepts discussed in Chapter 1.

6.2.2 EXPECTED RETURN

We compute the expected return for an individual investment as shown in Exhibit 6.1. The expected return for an individual risky asset with the set of potential returns and an assumption of the different probabilities used in the example would be 10.3%.

The expected return for a *portfolio* of investments is simply the weighted average of the expected rates of return for the individual investments in the portfolio. The weights are the proportion of total value for the individual investment.

EXHIBIT 6.1	Computing the Expected Return for an Individual Asset	
Probability	Possible Rate of Return (%)	Expected Security Return (%)
0.35	0.08	0.0280
0.30	0.10	0.0300
0.20	0.12	0.0240
0.15	0.14	0.0210
		$E(R_i) = 0.1030$

---

1 We consider the variance and standard deviation as one measure of risk because the standard deviation is the square root of the variance.

EXHIBIT 6.2	Computing the Expected Return for a Portfolio of Risky Assets	
Weight (w_i) (percent of portfolio)	Expected Security Return (R_i)	Expected Portfolio Return ($w_i \times R_i$)
0.20	0.10	0.0200
0.30	0.11	0.0330
0.30	0.12	0.0360
0.20	0.13	0.0260
		$E(R_{port}) = 0.1150$

The expected return for a hypothetical portfolio with four risky assets is shown in Exhibit 6.2. The expected return for this portfolio of investments would be 11.5%. The effect of adding or dropping any investment from the portfolio would be easy to determine; we would use the new weights based on value and the expected returns for each of the investments. We can generalize computing of a portfolio's expected return $E(R_{port})$ as follows:

6.1

$$E(R_{port}) = \sum_{i=1}^{n} w_i R_i$$

where:

w_i = the weight of an individual asset in the portfolio, or the percent of the portfolio in Asset i

R_i = the expected rate of return for Asset i

6.2.3 STANDARD DEVIATION OF RETURNS FOR AN INDIVIDUAL INVESTMENT

As noted, we will be using the variance or the standard deviation of returns as the measure of risk. Therefore, at this point we review how to calculate the standard deviation of returns for an individual investment. Subsequently, after discussing some other statistical concepts, we will consider how to determine the standard deviation for a *portfolio* of investments.

Recall that variance, or standard deviation, is a measure of the variation of possible rates of return R_i from the expected return $E(R_i)$ as follows:

6.2

$$\text{Variance} = \sigma^2 = \sum_{i=1}^{n} [R_i - E(R_i)]^2 P_i$$

where:

P_i = probability of the possible rate of return R_i

6.3

$$\text{Standard Deviation} = \sigma = \sqrt{\sum_{i=1}^{n} [R_i - E(R_i)]^2 P_i}$$

EXHIBIT 6.3	Calculation of the Variance for an Individual Risky Asset				
Possible Rate of Return (R_j)	Expected Security Return $E(R_j)$	$R_j - E(R_j)$	$[R_j - E(R_j)]^2$	P_j	$[R_j - E(R_j)]^2 P_j$
0.08	0.103	−0.023	0.0005	0.35	0.000185
0.10	0.103	−0.003	0.0000	0.30	0.000003
0.12	0.103	0.017	0.0003	0.20	0.000058
0.14	0.103	0.037	0.0014	0.15	0.000205
					0.000451

Variance = σ^2 = 0.000451
Standard Deviation = σ = 0.021237

We show in Exhibit 6.3 the variance and standard deviation of return calculations for the individual risky asset in Exhibit 6.1.

6.2.4 STANDARD DEVIATION OF RETURNS FOR A PORTFOLIO

Two basic concepts in statistics, covariance and correlation, must be understood before we discuss the formula for the variance of the return for a portfolio.

Covariance of Returns In this subsection we discuss what the covariance of returns is intended to measure, give the formula, and show how it is used. **Covariance** is a measure of the degree to which two variables move together relative to their individual mean values over time. In portfolio analysis, we usually are concerned with the covariance of *rates of return* rather than prices or some other variable.[2]

A positive covariance means that the rates of return for two investments tend to move in the same direction relative to their individual means during the same time period. In contrast, a negative covariance indicates that the returns for two investments tend to move in different directions relative to their means during specified time intervals. The *magnitude* of the covariance depends on the variances of the individual return series, as well as on the relationship between the series.

Toronto Stock Exchange: http://www.tsx.com.

Exhibit 6.4 contains the monthly rates of return values for Canadian stocks (measured using the S&P/TSX Composite Index) and bonds (measured by the DEX Universe Overall Bond Index, formerly known as the Scotia Capital Universe Bond Index). Using end-of-month values for each index, we compute the percentage change in the index each month, which equals its monthly rates of return during the period July 2007 to June 2008. Exhibits 6.5 and 6.6 contain a time-series plot of these monthly returns. Although the returns for the two assets moved in opposite direction during some months, in other months they moved together. The covariance statistic provides an absolute measure of how they moved together over time.

---

2 Returns, of course, can be measured in a variety of ways, depending on the type of asset. We define returns (R_j) as:

$$R_i = \frac{EV - BV + CF}{BV}$$

where EV is ending value, BV is beginning value, and CF is the cash flow during the period.

Exhibit 6.4	Monthly Rates of Return for Canadian Stocks and Bonds, 2007–2008	
	S&P/TSX Composite Index Monthly Rate of Return (%)	**DEX Universe Overall Bond Index Monthly Rate of Return (%)**
Jul-07	−0.27	0.12
Aug-07	−1.50	0.85
Sep-07	3.21	0.72
Oct-07	3.73	0.63
Nov-07	−6.40	1.47
Dec-07	1.05	0.62
Jan-08	−4.90	0.62
Feb-08	3.25	1.34
Mar-08	−1.71	0.96
Apr-08	4.40	−0.52
May-08	5.58	−0.15
Jun-08	−1.68	−0.05
Mean	0.40	0.55

Source: Based on the S&P/TSX Composite Index and the DEX Universe Overall Bond Index.

For two assets, i and j, we define the covariance of rates of return as

6.4	$$\text{Cov}_{ij} = E\{[R_i - E(R_i)][R_j - E(R_j)]\}$$

When we apply this formula to the monthly rates of return for the S&P/TSX Composite Index and the DEX Universe Overall bond indices during 2007 and 2008, it becomes

$$\frac{1}{12} \sum_{i=1}^{12} [R_i - \bar{R}_i][R_j - \bar{R}_j]$$

Canadian bond indices can be found at PC-Bond Analytics at http://www.canadian-bondindices.com.

As can be seen, if the rates of return for one asset are above (below) its mean return $\overline{R}$ during a given period and the returns for the other asset are likewise above (below) its mean return during this same period, then the product of these deviations from the mean is positive. If this happens consistently, the covariance of returns between these two assets will be some large positive value. If, however, the return for one of the securities is above its mean return, while the return on the other security is below its mean return, the product will be

| **Exhibit 6.5** | Time-Series Plot of the Monthly Returns for S&P/TSX, 2007–2008 |

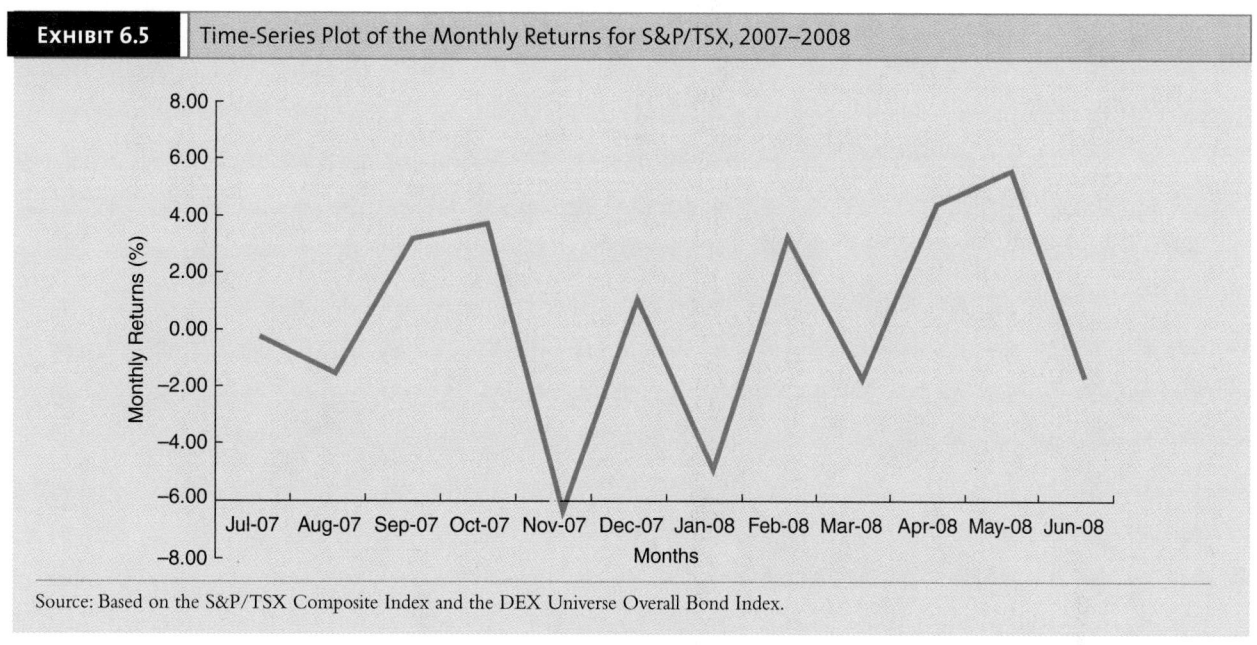

Source: Based on the S&P/TSX Composite Index and the DEX Universe Overall Bond Index.

| **Exhibit 6.6** | Time-Series Plot of the Monthly Returns for DEX Bond Index, 2007–2008 |

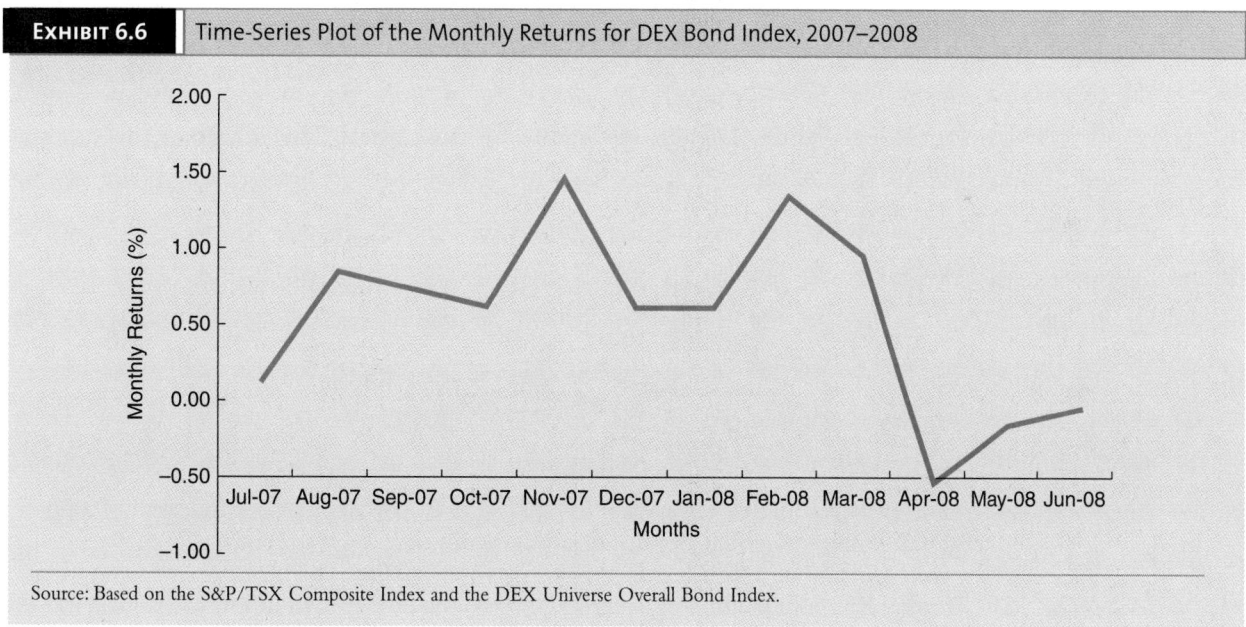

Source: Based on the S&P/TSX Composite Index and the DEX Universe Overall Bond Index.

Bond index and ratings can be found at the Standard & Poor's (S&P) website at http://www.standardandpoors.com.

negative. If this contrary movement occurs consistently, the covariance between the returns for the two assets will be a large negative value.

Exhibit 6.7 includes the monthly returns during 2007 and 2008 shown in Exhibit 6.4. One might expect returns for the two asset indices to have reasonably low covariance

EXHIBIT 6.7	Computation of Covariance of Returns for S&P/TSX Composite and DEX Bond Indices, 2007–2008				
	Monthly Return				
Date	**S&P/TSX Index (R_1)**	**DEX Universe Overall Bond Index (R_2)**	**S&P/TSX Index ($R_1 - \bar{R}_1$)**	**DEX Universe Overall Bond Index ($R_2 - \bar{R}_2$)**	**$(R_1 - \bar{R}_1) \times (R_2 - \bar{R}_2)$**
Jul-07	−0.27	0.12	−0.67	−0.43	0.29
Aug-07	−1.50	0.85	−1.90	0.30	−0.57
Sep-07	3.21	0.72	2.81	0.17	0.48
Oct-07	3.73	0.63	3.34	0.08	0.27
Nov-07	−6.40	1.47	−6.79	0.92	−6.24
Dec-07	1.05	0.62	0.66	0.07	0.04
Jan-08	−4.90	0.62	−5.30	0.07	−0.37
Feb-08	3.25	1.34	2.85	0.79	2.26
Mar-08	−1.71	0.96	−2.11	0.41	−0.87
Apr-08	4.40	−0.52	4.00	−1.07	−4.29
May-08	5.58	−0.15	5.18	−0.70	−3.65
Jun-08	−1.68	−0.05	−2.08	−0.60	1.25
Mean	**0.40**	**0.55**			**Covariance = −0.95**

Source: Based on the S&P/TSX Composite Index and the DEX Universe Overall Bond Index.

because of the differences in the nature of these assets. The means of the monthly returns were

$$(\bar{R}_i) = \frac{1}{12} \sum_{i=1}^{12} R_{it} = 0.40 \,(\text{stocks})$$

$$(\bar{R}_j) = \frac{1}{12} \sum_{j=1}^{12} R_{jt} = 0.55 \,(\text{bonds})$$

The average monthly return was 0.40% for S&P/TSX Composite Index and 0.55% for the DEX Universe Overall Bond Index. The results in Exhibit 6.7 show that the covariance between the rates of return for these two assets was −0.95.

Interpretation of a number such as −0.95 is difficult; is it high or low for covariance? We know the relationship between the two assets is generally negative, but it is not possible to be more specific. Exhibit 6.8 contains a scatterplot with paired values of R_{it} and R_{jt} plotted against each other. This plot demonstrates the linear nature and strength of the relationship. During 2007 and 2008, it appears there indeed is a negative linear relationship between Canadian stocks and bonds.

Covariance and Correlation Covariance is affected by the variability of the two individual return indices. Therefore, a number such as the −0.95 in our example might indicate a weak

| **Exhibit 6.8** | Scatterplot of Monthly Returns for the S&P/TSX Composite and DEX Bond Indices, 2007–2008 |

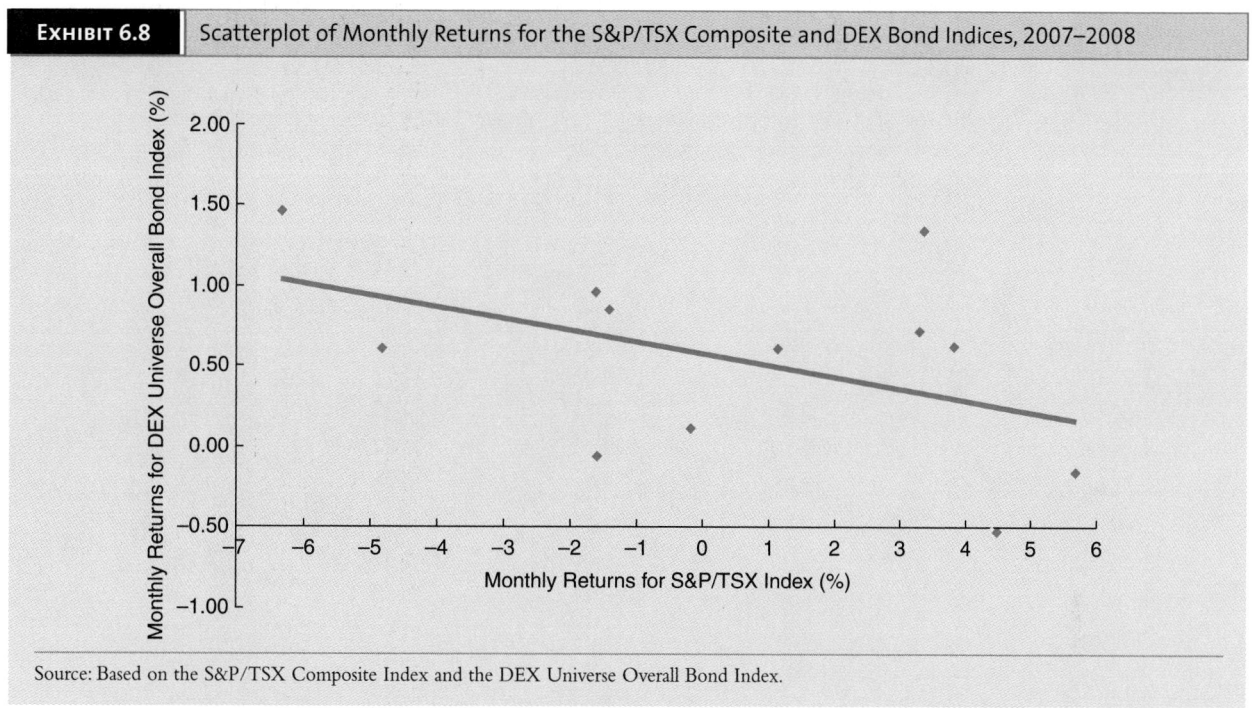

Source: Based on the S&P/TSX Composite Index and the DEX Universe Overall Bond Index.

negative relationship if the two individual indices were volatile, but would reflect a strong negative relationship if the two indices were stable. Obviously, we want to standardize this covariance measure. We do so by taking into consideration the variability of the two individual return indices, as follows:

6.5
$$r_{ij} = \frac{Cov_{ij}}{\sigma_i \sigma_j}$$

where:

r_{ij} = the correlation coefficient of returns
σ_i = the standard deviation of R_{it}
σ_j = the standard deviation of R_{jt}

Standardizing the covariance by the product of the individual standard deviations yields the **correlation coefficient** r_{ij}, which can vary only in the range −1 to +1. A value of +1 indicates a perfect positive linear relationship between R_i and R_j, meaning the returns for the two assets move together in a completely linear manner. A value of −1 indicates a perfect negative relationship between the two return indices so that when one asset's return is above its mean, the other asset's return will be below its mean by a comparable amount.

To calculate this standardized measure of the relationship, we need to compute the standard deviation for the two individual return indices. We already have the values for $(R_{it} - R_i)$ and $(R_{it} - \overline{R}_i)$ and $(R_{jt} - \overline{R}_j)$ in Exhibit 6.7. We can square each of these

EXHIBIT 6.9	Computation of Standard Deviation of Monthly Returns for the S&P/TSX Composite and the DEX Bond Indices

	S&P/TSX Composite Index		DEX Universe Overall Bond Index	
Date	$(R_1 - \bar{R}_1)$	$(R_1 - \bar{R}_1)^2$	$(R_2 - \bar{R}_2)$	$(R_2 - \bar{R}_2)^2$
Jul-07	−0.67	0.45	−0.43	0.19
Aug-07	−1.90	3.60	0.30	0.09
Sep-07	2.81	7.92	0.17	0.03
Oct-07	3.34	11.13	0.08	0.01
Nov-07	−6.79	46.17	0.92	0.84
Dec-07	0.66	0.43	0.07	0.00
Jan-08	−5.30	28.06	0.07	0.00
Feb-08	2.85	8.15	0.79	0.63
Mar-08	−2.11	4.44	0.41	0.17
Apr-08	4.00	16.00	−1.07	1.15
May-08	5.18	26.88	−0.70	0.49
Jun-08	−2.08	4.32	−0.60	0.36
Sum		157.54		3.97
Variance		13.13		0.33
Standard Deviation		3.62		0.57

Source: Based on the S&P/TSX Composite Index and the DEX Universe Overall Bond Index.

values, sum them, and divide by 12 as shown in Exhibit 6.9 to calculate the variance of each return series.

$$\sigma_i^2 = \frac{1}{12}\ 157.54 = 13.13$$

$$\sigma_i^2 = \frac{1}{12}\ 3.97 = 0.33$$

The standard deviation for each index is the square root of the variance for each, as follows:

$$\sigma_i = \sqrt{13.13} = 3.62$$
$$\sigma_i = \sqrt{0.33} = 0.57$$

In the above calculation of variance, we simply want to know the variance of the 12 observations. If we were to view the 12 months as a sample taken from a population, then following basic statistics, we would divide the sum by 11 or $(n - 1)$ to adjust for statistical bias. In practice, when the sample size is large—most financial time series are—there is no significant difference using n or $(n - 1)$ as the divider.

Thus, based on the covariance between the two indices and the individual standard deviations, we can calculate the correlation coefficient between returns for Canadian stocks and bonds during 2007 and 2008: -0.46. This means the two have a modest negative relationship; they fit a negatively sloped line "better" than a pair of variables with a correlation coefficient of -0.2 but "worse" than a pair of variables with a correlation of -0.8.

$$r_{ij} = \frac{\text{Cov}_{ij}}{\sigma_i \sigma_j} = \frac{-0.95}{(3.62)(0.57)} = \frac{-0.95}{2.06} = -0.46$$

6.2.5 Standard Deviation of a Portfolio

As noted, a correlation of $+1.0$ indicates perfect positive correlation, and a value of -1.0 means that the returns moved in completely opposite directions. A value of zero means that the returns had no linear relationship, that is, they were uncorrelated statistically. That does not mean that they are independent; they may have a non-linear relationship. The value of $r_{ij} = -0.454$ means there is a significant negative linear relationship between Canadian stocks and bonds during this period of time. If in another 12-month period, the correlation coefficient is -0.20 we can state that during 2007 and 2008, Canadian stocks and bonds have a stronger negative relationship than the comparison period.

Portfolio Standard Deviation Formula Now that we have discussed the concepts of covariance and correlation, we can consider the formula for computing the standard deviation of returns for a *portfolio* of assets, our measure of risk for a portfolio. In Exhibit 6.2, we showed that the expected return of the portfolio was the weighted average of the expected returns for the individual assets in the portfolio; the weights were the percentage of value of the portfolio. One might assume it is possible to derive the standard deviation of the portfolio in the same manner, that is, by computing the weighted average of the standard deviations for the individual assets. This would be a mistake. Markowitz (1959) derived the general formula for the standard deviation of a portfolio as follows:

6.6

$$\sigma_{\text{port}} = \sqrt{\sum_{i=1}^{n} w_i^2 \sigma_i^2 + \sum_{i=1}^{n} \sum_{\substack{j=1 \\ i \neq j}}^{n} w_i w_j \text{Cov}_{ij}}$$

where:

σ_{port} = the standard deviation of the portfolio

w_i = the weights of an individual asset in the portfolio, where weights are determined by the proportion of value in the portfolio

σ_i^2 = the variance of rates of return for asset i

Cov_{ij} = the covariance between the rates of return for assets i and j, where $\text{Cov}_{ij} = r_{ij}\sigma_i\sigma_j$

This formula indicates that the standard deviation for a portfolio of assets is a function of the weighted average of the individual variances (where the weights are squared), *plus* the weighted covariances between all the assets in the portfolio. The very important point is that the standard deviation for a portfolio of assets encompasses not only the variances of the individual assets but *also* includes the covariances between all the pairs of individual assets in the portfolio. Further, it can be shown that in a portfolio with a large number of securities, this formula reduces to the sum of the weighted covariances.

Impact of a New Security in a Portfolio Although in most of the following discussion we will consider a two-asset portfolio (because it is possible to show the effect in two dimensions), we will also demonstrate the computations for a three-asset portfolio. Still, it is important at this point to consider what happens to a large portfolio's standard deviation when we add a new security. As shown by the formula, we see two effects. The first is the asset's own variance of returns, and the second is the covariance between the returns of this new asset and the returns of *every other asset that is already in the portfolio.* The relative weight of these numerous covariances is substantially greater than the asset's unique variance; the more assets in the portfolio, the more this is true. This means that the important factor to consider when adding an investment to a portfolio containing a number of other investments is the average covariance of this new asset with all other investments in the portfolio; not the new security's own variance.

Portfolio Standard Deviation Calculation Because of the assumptions used in developing the Markowitz portfolio model, any asset or portfolio of assets can be described by two characteristics: the expected return and the expected standard deviation of returns. Therefore, the following demonstrations can be applied to two *individual* assets, two *portfolios* of assets, or two *asset classes* with the indicated return-standard deviation characteristics and correlation coefficients.

Equal Risk and Return—Changing Correlations Consider first the case in which both assets have the same expected return and expected standard deviation of return. As an example, let's assume

$$E(R_1) = 0.20, E(\sigma_1) = 0.10$$
$$E(R_2) = 0.20, E(\sigma_2) = 0.10$$

To show the effect of different covariances, we assume different levels of correlation between the two assets. We also assume that the two assets have equal weights in the portfolio ($w_1 = 0.50$; $w_2 = 0.50$). Therefore, the only value that changes in each example is the correlation between the returns for the two assets.

Now consider the following five correlation coefficients and the covariances they yield. Because $Cov_{ij} = r_{ij}\sigma_i\sigma_j$, the covariance will be equal to $r_{1,2}$ (0.10)(0.10) because the standard deviation of both assets is 0.10.

a. For $r_{1,2} = 1.00$, $Cov_{1,2} = (1.00)(0.10)(0.10) = 0.01$
b. For $r_{1,2} = 0.50$, $Cov_{1,2} = (0.50)(0.10)(0.10) = 0.005$
c. For $r_{1,2} = 0.00$, $Cov_{1,2} = (0.00)(0.10)(0.10) = 0.000$
d. For $r_{1,2} = -0.50$, $Cov_{1,2} = (-0.50)(0.10)(0.10) = -0.005$
e. For $r_{1,2} = -1.00$, $Cov_{1,2} = (-1.00)(0.10)(0.10) = -0.01$

Now let's see what happens to the standard deviation of the portfolio under these five conditions.

When we apply the general portfolio formula from Equation 6.6 to a two-asset portfolio, it is

6.7 $$\sigma_{port} = \sqrt{w_1^2\sigma_1^2 + w_2^2\sigma_2^2 + 2w_1w_2r_{1,2}\sigma_1\sigma_2}$$

or

$$\sigma_{\text{port}} = \sqrt{w_1^2 \sigma_1^2 + w_2^2 \sigma_2^2 + 2w_1 w_2 \text{Cov}_{1,2}}$$

Thus, in Case a:

$$\begin{aligned}
\sigma_{\text{port (a)}} &= \sqrt{(0.5)^2(0.10)^2 + (0.5)^2(0.10)^2 + 2(0.5)(0.5)(0.01)} \\
&= \sqrt{(0.25)(0.01) + (0.25)(0.01) + 2(0.25)(0.01)} \\
&= \sqrt{0.01} \\
&= 0.10
\end{aligned}$$

In this case, where the returns for the two assets are perfectly positively correlated, the portfolio standard deviation is, in fact, the weighted average of the individual standard deviations. Thus we get no real benefit from combining two assets that are perfectly correlated; they are like one asset already because their returns move together.

Now consider Case b, where $r_{1,2}$ equals 0.50.

$$\begin{aligned}
\sigma_{\text{port(b)}} &= \sqrt{(0.5)^2(0.10)^2 + (0.5)^2(0.10)^2 + 2(0.5)(0.5)(0.005)} \\
&= \sqrt{(0.0025) + (0.0025) + 2(0.25)(0.005)} \\
&= \sqrt{0.0075} \\
&= 0.0866
\end{aligned}$$

The only term that changed from Case a is the last term, $\text{Cov}_{1,2}$, which changed from 0.01 to 0.005. As a result, the standard deviation of the portfolio declined by about 13 %, from 0.10 to 0.0866. Note that *the expected return of the portfolio did not change* because it is simply the weighted average of the individual expected returns; it is equal to 0.20 in both cases.

You should be able to confirm through your own calculations that the standard deviations for Portfolios c and d are as follows:

c. 0.0707
d. 0.05

The final case, where the correlation between the two assets is -1.00, indicates the ultimate benefits of diversification.

$$\sigma_{\text{port(e)}} = \sqrt{(0.5)^2(0.10)^2 + (0.5)^2(0.10)^2 + 2(0.5)(0.5)(-0.01)}$$
$$= \sqrt{(0.0050) + (-0.0050)}$$
$$= \sqrt{0}$$
$$= 0$$

Here, the negative covariance term exactly offsets the individual variance terms, leaving an overall standard deviation of the portfolio of zero. *This would be a risk-free portfolio.*

Exhibit 6.10 illustrates a graph of such a pattern. Perfect negative correlation gives a mean combined return for the two securities over time equal to the mean for each of them, so the returns for the portfolio show no variability. Any returns above and below the mean for each of the assets are *completely offset* by the return for the other asset. No variability in total returns means no risk for the portfolio. Thus, a pair of completely negatively correlated assets provides the maximum benefits of diversification by completely eliminating risk.

The graph in Exhibit 6.11 shows the difference in the risk–return posture for our five cases. As noted, the only effect of the change in correlation is the change in the standard deviation of this two-asset portfolio. Combining assets that are not perfectly correlated does not affect the expected return of the portfolio, but it *does* reduce the risk of the portfolio (as measured by its standard deviation). When we eventually reach the ultimate combination of perfect negative correlation, risk is eliminated.

Combining Stocks with Different Returns and Risk We have seen what happens when only the correlation coefficient (covariance) differs between the assets. We now consider two assets

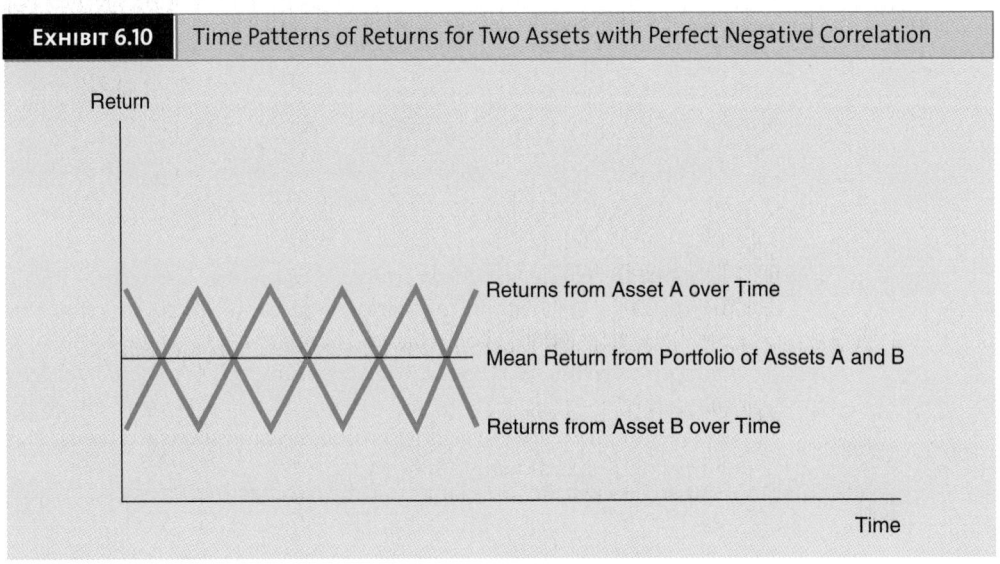

EXHIBIT 6.10	Time Patterns of Returns for Two Assets with Perfect Negative Correlation

Return

Returns from Asset A over Time

Mean Return from Portfolio of Assets A and B

Returns from Asset B over Time

Time

EXHIBIT 6.11	Risk–Return Plot for Portfolios with Equal Returns and Standard Deviations but Different Correlations

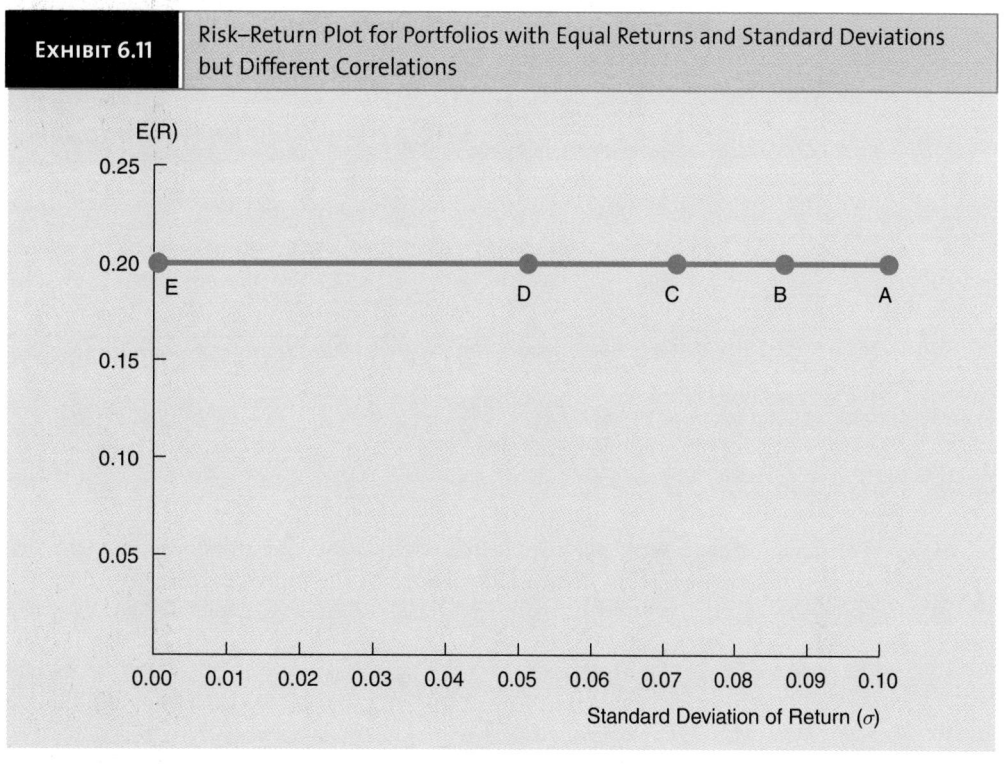

(or portfolios) with different expected returns and individual standard deviations.[3] We will show what happens when we vary the correlations between them. We will assume two assets with the following characteristics.

Asset	$E(R_i)$	w_i	σ_i^2	σ_i
1	0.10	0.50	0.0049	0.07
2	0.20	0.50	0.0100	0.10

We will use the previous set of correlation coefficients, but we must recalculate the covariances because this time the standard deviations of the assets are different. The results are shown in this table.

Case	Correlation Coefficient ($r_{1,2}$)	Covariance ($r_{1,2}\sigma_1\sigma_2$)
a	+1.00	0.0070
b	+0.50	0.0035
c	0.00	0.0000
d	−0.50	−0.0035
e	−1.00	−0.0070

---

3 As noted, these could be two asset classes. For example, Asset 1 could be low risk–low return bonds, and Asset 2 could be higher return–higher risk stocks.

Because we are assuming the same weights in all cases $(0.50 - 0.50)$, the expected return in every instance will be

$$E(R_{port}) = 0.50\,(0.10) + 0.50\,(0.20)$$
$$= 0.15$$

The portfolio standard deviation for Case a will be

$$\sigma_{port(a)} = \sqrt{(0.5)^2(0.07)^2 + (0.5)^2(0.10)^2 + 2(0.5)(0.5)(0.0070)}$$
$$= \sqrt{0.007225}$$
$$= 0.085$$

Again, with perfect positive correlation, the portfolio standard deviation is the weighted average of the standard deviations of the individual assets:

$$(0.5)(0.07) + (0.5)(0.10) = 0.085$$

As you might envision, changing the weights with perfect positive correlation causes the portfolio standard deviation to change in a linear fashion. This will be an important point to remember when we discuss the capital asset pricing model (CAPM) in the next chapter. For Cases b, c, d, and e, the portfolio standard deviations are as follows:[4]

$$\sigma_{port(b)} = \sqrt{(0.001225) + (0.0025) + (0.5)(0.0035)}$$
$$= \sqrt{(0.005475)}$$
$$= 0.07399$$
$$\sigma_{port(c)} = \sqrt{(0.001225) + (0.0025) + (0.5)(0.00)}$$
$$= 0.0610$$
$$\sigma_{port(d)} = \sqrt{(0.001225) + (0.0025) + (0.5)(-0.0035)}$$
$$= 0.0444$$
$$\sigma_{port(e)} = \sqrt{(0.003725) + (0.5)(-0.0070)}$$
$$= 0.015$$

---

4 In all the following examples, we will skip some steps because you are now aware that only the last term changes. You are encouraged to work out the individual steps to ensure that you understand the computational procedure.

EXHIBIT 6.12	Risk–Return Plot for Portfolios with Different Returns, Standard Deviations, and Correlations

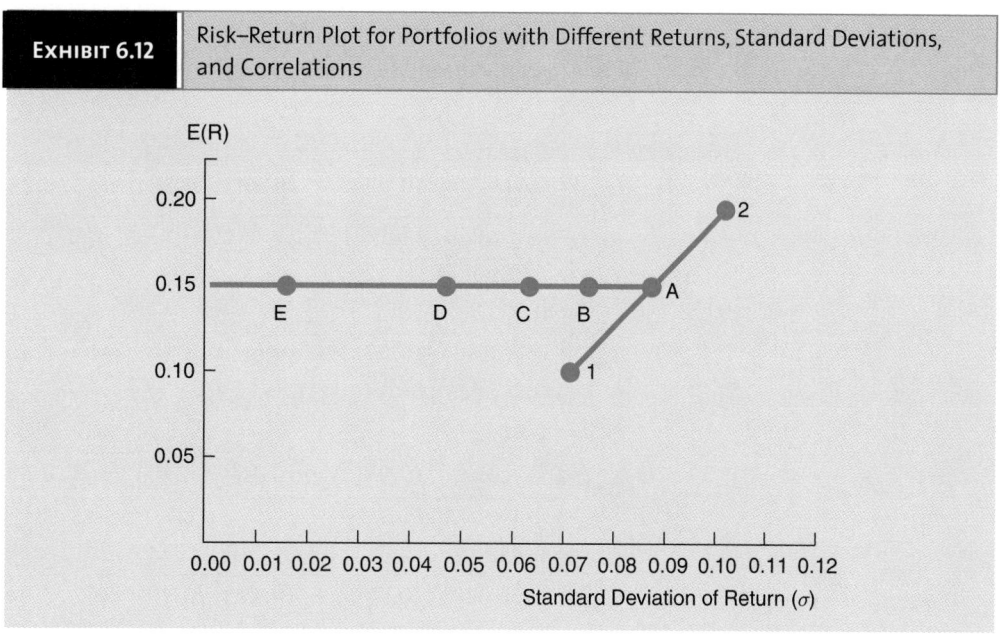

Note that, in this example, with perfect negative correlation the portfolio standard deviation is not zero. This is because the different examples have equal weights, but the asset standard deviations are not equal.[5]

Exhibit 6.12 shows the results for the two individual assets and the portfolio of the two assets assuming the correlation coefficients vary as set forth in Cases a through e. As before, the expected return does not change because the proportions are always set at 0.50–0.50, so all the portfolios lie along the horizontal line at the return, $R = 0.15$.

Constant Correlation with Changing Weights If we changed the weights of the two assets while holding the correlation coefficient constant, we would derive a set of combinations that trace an ellipse starting at Asset 2, going through the 0.50–0.50 point, and ending at Asset 1. We can demonstrate this with Case c, in which the correlation coefficient of zero eases the computations. We begin with 100% in Asset 2 (Case f) and change the weights as follows, ending with 100% in Asset 1 (Case l):

Case	w_1	w_2	$E(R_i)$
f	0.00	1.00	0.20
g	0.20	0.80	0.18
h	0.40	0.60	0.16
i	0.50	0.50	0.15
j	0.60	0.40	0.14
k	0.80	0.20	0.12
l	1.00	0.00	0.10

---

5 The two appendixes to this chapter show proofs for equal weights with equal variances and solve for the appropriate weights to get zero standard deviation when standard deviations are not equal.

We already know the standard deviations (σ) for portfolios f and l (only one asset) and portfolio (i). In Cases g, h, j, and k, the standard deviations are[6]

$$\sigma_{port(g)} = \sqrt{(0.20)^2(0.07)^2 + (0.80)^2(0.10)^2 + 2(0.20)(0.80)(0.00)}$$
$$= \sqrt{(0.04)(0.0049) + (0.64)(0.01) + (0)}$$
$$= \sqrt{0.006596}$$
$$= 0.0812$$

$$\sigma_{port(h)} = \sqrt{(0.40)^2(0.07)^2 + (0.60)^2(0.10)^2 + 2(0.40)(0.60)(0.00)}$$
$$= \sqrt{0.004384}$$
$$= 0.0662$$

$$\sigma_{port(j)} = \sqrt{(0.60)^2(0.07)^2 + (0.40)^2(0.10)^2 + 2(0.60)(0.40)(0.00)}$$
$$= \sqrt{0.003364}$$
$$= 0.0580$$

$$\sigma_{port(k)} = \sqrt{(0.80)^2(0.07)^2 + (0.20)^2(0.10)^2 + 2(0.80)(0.20)(0.00)}$$
$$= \sqrt{0.003536}$$
$$= 0.0595$$

The various weights with a constant correlation yield the following risk–return combinations.

Case	w_1	w_2	$E(R_i)$	$E(\sigma_{port})$
f	0.00	1.00	0.20	0.1000
g	0.20	0.80	0.18	0.0812
h	0.40	0.60	0.16	0.0662
i	0.50	0.50	0.15	0.0610
j	0.60	0.40	0.14	0.0580
k	0.80	0.20	0.12	0.0595
l	1.00	0.00	0.10	0.0700

A graph of these combinations appears in Exhibit 6.13. We could derive a complete curve by simply varying the weighting by smaller increments.

A notable result is that with low, zero, or negative correlations, it is possible to derive portfolios that have *lower risk than either single asset*. In our set of examples where $r_{ij} = 0.00$, this occurs in Cases h, i, j, and k. This ability to reduce risk is the essence of diversification.

As shown in Exhibit 6.13, assuming the normal risk–return relationship where assets with higher risk (larger standard deviation) provide high rates of return, it is possible for a conservative investor to experience both lower risk and higher return by diversifying into a higher risk–higher return asset, assuming that the correlation between the two assets is fairly low. Exhibit 6.13 shows that in the case where we used the correlation of zero (0.00), the low-risk investor at Point 1—who would receive a return of 10% and risk of 7%—could, by investing

---

6 Again, you are encouraged to fill in the steps we skipped in the computations.

Exhibit 6.13	Portfolio Risk–Return Plots for Different Weights when $r_{i,j} = +1.00; +0.50;$ 0.00; $-0.50; -1.00$

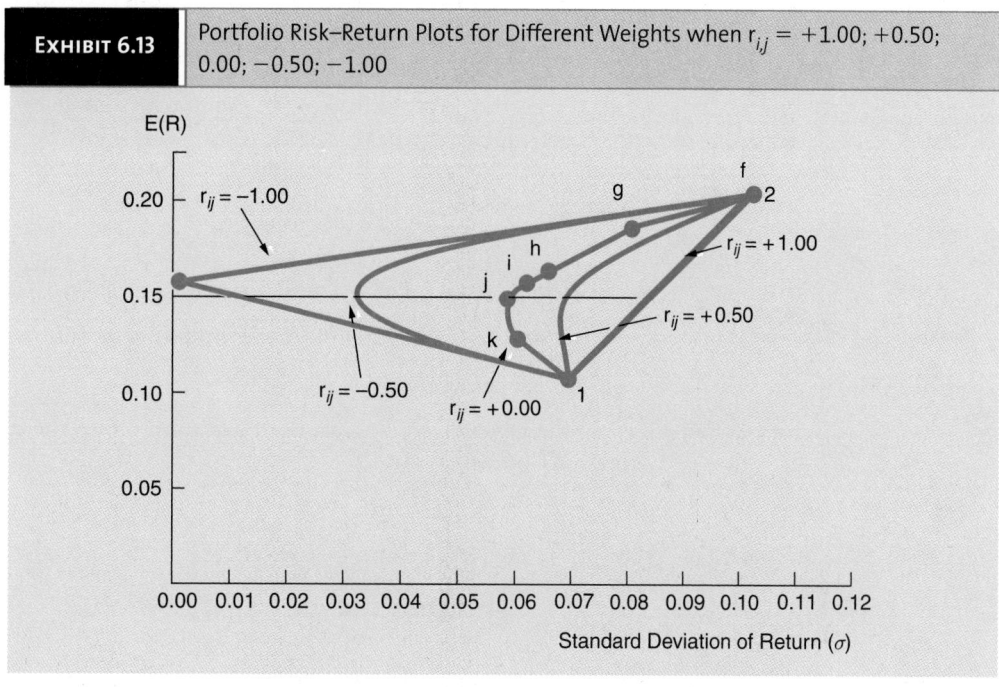

in portfolio j, *increase* the return to 14% and experience a *decline* in risk to 5.8% by investing (diversifying) 40% of the portfolio in riskier Asset 2. It is worth repeating that the benefits of diversification are critically dependent on the correlation between assets. The exhibit shows that there is even some benefit when the correlation is 0.50 rather than zero. Exhibit 6.13 also shows that the curvature in the graph depends on the correlation between the two assets or portfolios. With $r_{ij} = +1.00$, the combinations lie along a straight line between the two assets. When $r_{ij} = 0.50$, the curve is to the right of the $r_{ij} = 0.00$ curve; when $r_{ij} = -0.50$, it is to the left. Finally, when $r_{ij} = -1.00$, the graph would be two straight lines that would touch at the vertical line (zero risk) with some combination. As shown in Appendix 6B, it is possible to solve for the specified set of weights that would give a portfolio with zero risk. In this case, it is $w_1 = 0.412$ and $w_2 = 0.588$, which implies an E(R) of 0.1588.

6.2.6 A THREE-ASSET PORTFOLIO

A demonstration of what occurs with a three-asset portfolio is useful because it shows the dynamics of the portfolio process when assets are added. It also shows the rapid growth in the calculations required, which is why we will stop at three!

In this example, we will combine three asset classes we have been discussing: stocks, bonds, and cash equivalents.[7] We will assume the following characteristics:

Asset Classes	$E(R_i)$	$E(\sigma_i)$	w_i
Stocks (S)	0.12	0.20	0.60
Bonds (B)	0.08	0.10	0.30
Cash equivalent (C)	0.04	0.03	0.10

7 The asset allocation articles regularly contained in the *Wall Street Journal* generally refer to these three asset classes.

The correlations are

$$r_{S,B} = 0.25; \quad r_{S,C} = -0.08; \quad r_{B,C} = 0.15$$

Given the weights specified, the $E(R_{port})$ is

$$E(R_{port}) = (0.60)(0.12) + (0.30)(0.08) + (0.10)(0.04)$$
$$= (0.072 + 0.024 + 0.004) = 0.100 = 10.00\%$$

When we apply the generalized formula from Equation 6.6 to the expected standard deviation of a three-asset portfolio, it is

6.8
$$\sigma^2_{port} = (w^2_S \sigma^2_S + w^2_B \sigma^2_B + w^2_C \sigma^2_C)$$
$$+ (2w_S w_B \sigma_S \sigma_B r_{S,B} + 2w_S w_C \sigma_S \sigma_C r_{S,C} + 2w_B w_C \sigma_B \sigma_C r_{B,C})$$

From the characteristics specified, the standard deviation of this three-asset-class portfolio (σ_{port}) would be

$$\sigma^2_{port} = [(0.6)^2(0.20)^2 + (0.3)^2(0.10)^2 + (0.1)^2(0.03)^2]$$
$$+ \{[2(0.6)(0.3)(0.20)(0.10)(0.25)] + [2(0.6)(0.1)(0.20)(0.03)(-0.08)]$$
$$+ [2(0.3)(0.1)(0.10)(0.03)(0.15)]\}$$
$$= [(0.015309) + (0.0018) + (-0.0000576) + (0.000027)]$$
$$= 0.0170784$$
$$\sigma_{port} = (0.0170784)^{1/2} = 0.1306 = 13.06\%$$

6.2.7 ESTIMATION ISSUES

It is important to keep in mind that the results of this portfolio asset allocation depend on the accuracy of the statistical inputs. In the current instance, this means that for every asset (or asset class) being considered for inclusion in the portfolio, we must estimate its expected returns and standard deviation. We must also estimate the correlation coefficient among the entire set of assets. The number of correlation estimates can be significant—for example, for a portfolio of 100 securities, the number is 4,950 (that is, 99 + 98 + 97 + . . .). The potential source of error that arises from these approximations is referred to as *estimation risk*.

We can reduce the number of correlation coefficients that must be estimated by assuming that stock returns can be described by the relationship of each stock to a market index—that is, a single index market model, as follows:

6.9
$$R_i = a_i + b_i R_m + \varepsilon_i$$

where:
$\quad$ b_i = the slope coefficient that relates the returns for Security i to the returns for the
$\quad\quad$ aggregate stock market
$\quad$ R_m = the returns for the aggregate stock market

If all the securities are similarly related to the market and a slope coefficient b_i is derived for each one, it can be shown that the correlation coefficient between two securities i and j is

6.10

$$r_{ij} = b_i b_j \frac{\sigma_m^2}{\sigma_i \sigma_j}$$

where:
$\quad$ σ_m^2 = the variance of returns for the aggregate stock market

This reduces the number of estimates from 4,950 to 100—that is, once we have derived a slope estimate b_i for each security, we can compute the correlation estimates. Notably, this assumes that the single-index market model provides a good estimate of security returns.

6.3   The Efficient Frontier and Investor Utility

The Efficient Frontier:
http://www.efficient
frontier.com.

If we examined different two-asset combinations and derived the curves assuming all the possible weights, we would have a graph like that in Exhibit 6.14. The envelope curve that contains the best of all these possible combinations is referred to as the **efficient frontier**. Specifically, the efficient frontier represents that set of portfolios that has the maximum return for every given level of risk or the minimum risk for every level of return. An example of such a frontier is shown in Exhibit 6.15. Every portfolio that lies on the efficient frontier has either a higher return for equal risk or lower risk for an equal return than some portfolio beneath the frontier. Thus, we would say that Portfolio A in Exhibit 6.15 *dominates* Portfolio C because

EXHIBIT 6.14	Numerous Portfolio Combinations of Available Assets

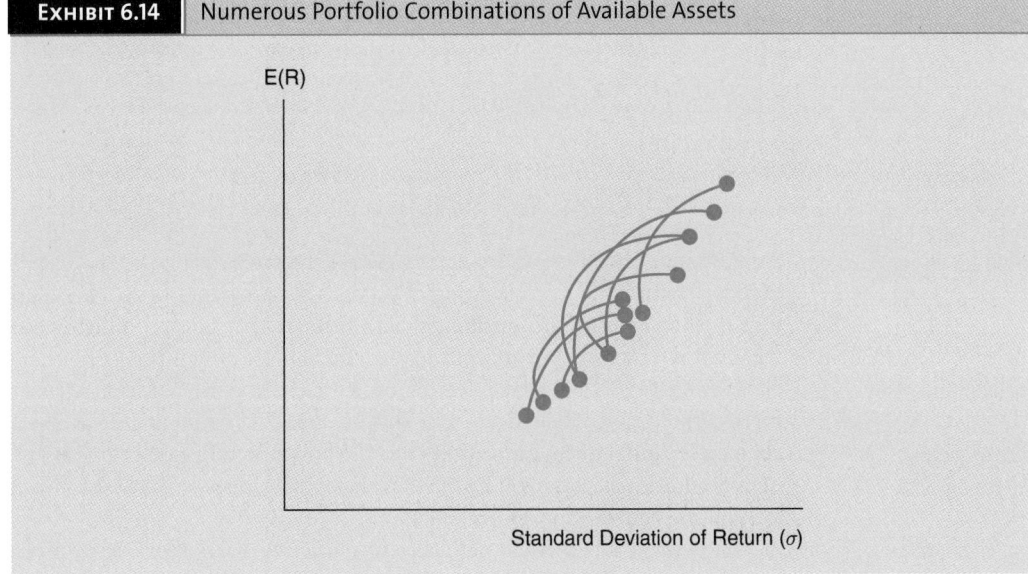

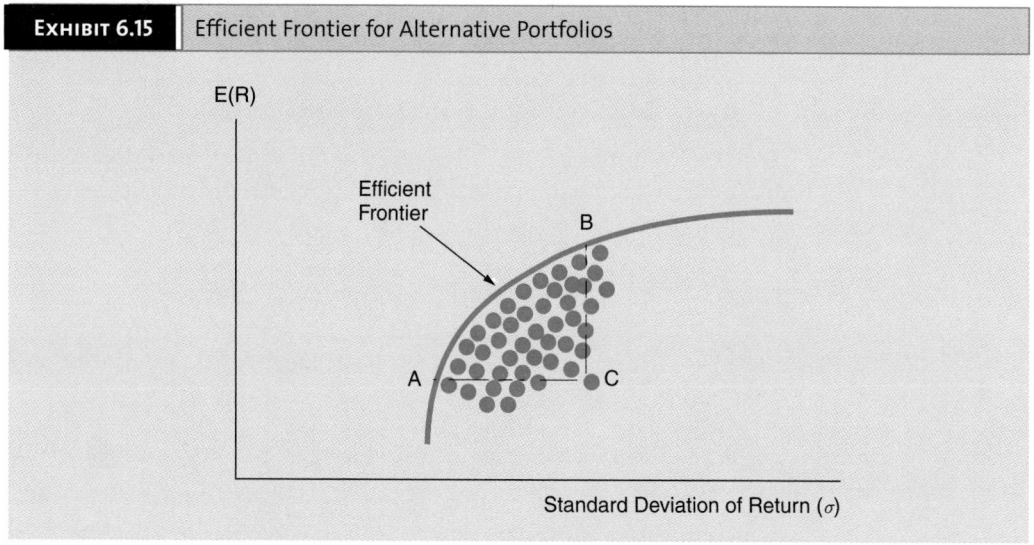

| **EXHIBIT 6.15** | Efficient Frontier for Alternative Portfolios |

it has an equal return but substantially less risk. Similarly, Portfolio B dominates Portfolio C because it has equal risk but a higher expected return. Because of the benefits of diversification among imperfectly correlated assets, we would expect the efficient frontier to be made up of *portfolios* of investments rather than individual securities. Two possible exceptions arise at the end points, which represent the asset with the highest return and the asset with the lowest risk.

As an investor, you will target a point along the efficient frontier based on your *utility function*, which reflects your attitude toward risk. No portfolio on the efficient frontier can dominate any other portfolio on the efficient frontier. All of these portfolios have different return and risk measures, with expected rates of return that increase with higher risk.

6.3.1   THE EFFICIENT FRONTIER

The curve in Exhibit 6.15 shows that the slope of the efficient frontier curve decreases steadily as we move upward. This implies that adding equal increments of risk as we move up the efficient frontier gives diminishing increments of expected return. To evaluate this situation, we calculate the slope of the efficient frontier as follows:

6.11
$$\frac{\Delta E\,(R_{port})}{\Delta E\,(\sigma_{port})}$$

An individual investor's utility curves specify the trade-offs he or she is willing to make between expected return and risk. In conjunction with the efficient frontier, these utility curves determine which *particular* portfolio on the efficient frontier best suits an individual investor. Two investors will choose the same portfolio from the efficient set only if their utility curves are identical.

Exhibit 6.16 shows two sets of utility curves along with an efficient frontier of investments. The curves labelled U_1, U_2, and U_3 are for a strongly risk-averse investor. These utility curves are quite steep, indicating that the investor will not tolerate much additional risk to obtain additional returns. The investor is equally disposed toward any E(R), E(σ) combinations along the specific utility curve U_1.

The curves labelled $U_{3'}$, $U_{2'}$, $U_{1'}$ characterize a less risk-averse investor. Such an investor is willing to tolerate a bit more risk to get a higher expected return.

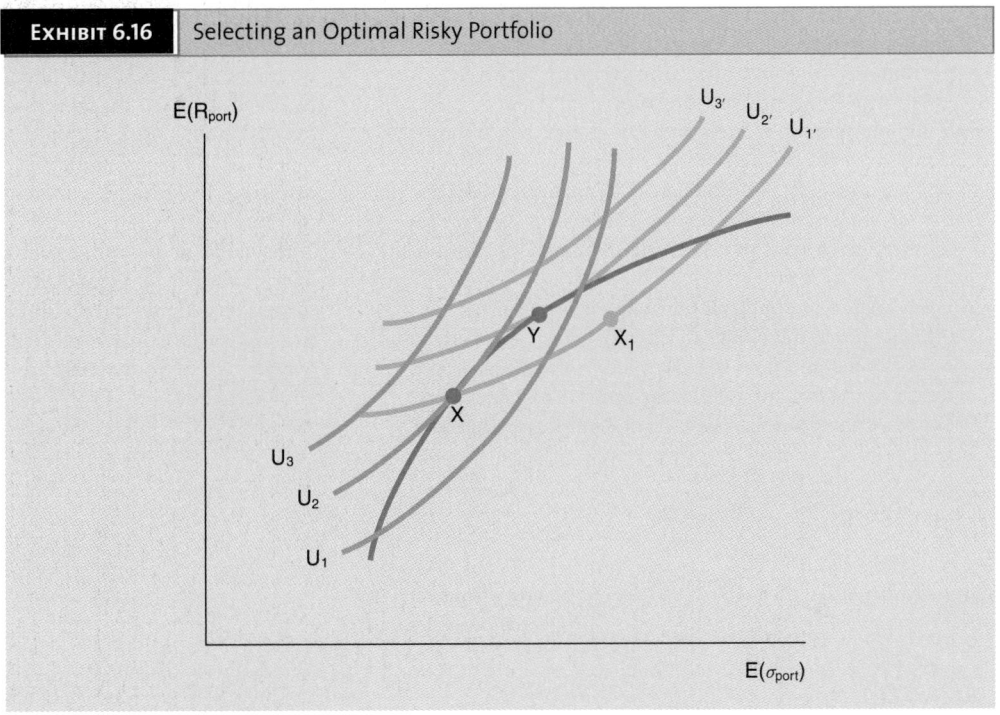

EXHIBIT 6.16 | Selecting an Optimal Risky Portfolio

The **optimal portfolio** is the efficient portfolio that has the highest utility for a given investor. It lies at the point of tangency between the efficient frontier and the U_1 curve with the highest possible utility. A conservative investor's highest utility is at Point X in Exhibit 6.16, where the U_2 curve just touches the efficient frontier. A less risk-averse investor's highest utility occurs at Point Y, which represents a portfolio on the efficient frontier with higher expected returns and higher risk than the portfolio at X.[8]

Summary

1. The Markowitz portfolio theory assumes that there is a probability distribution of expected returns. Investors maximize utility and estimate the risk of the portfolio on the basis of the variability of expected returns. Investors base decisions solely on expected return and risk as their utility curves are a function of expected return and the expected variance of returns only. For a given risk level, investors prefer higher returns to lower returns. Similarly, for a given level of expected return, investors prefer less risk to more risk.

2. The basic Markowitz portfolio model derives the expected return for a portfolio of assets and a measure of expected risk, which is the standard deviation of expected rates of return. Markowitz showed that the expected return of a portfolio is the weighted average of the expected return for the individual investments in the portfolio.

3. The standard deviation of a portfolio is a function not only of the standard deviations for the individual investments but also of the covariance between the rates of return for all the pairs of assets in the portfolio. In a large portfolio, these covariances are the important factors.

4. Different weights or amounts of a portfolio held in various assets yield a curve of potential combinations. Correlation coefficients among assets are the critical factor to

---

8 For a discussion on indifference curves in the context of investments, please see Appendix 6C, "Indifference Curves and Investor Utility." Readers who are not familiar with indifference curves in economics are referred to textbooks such as *Microeconomics,* 4th Canadian Edition, by N.G. Mankiw, R.D. Kneebone, K.J. McKenzie, and N. Rowe, Thomson Nelson, 2008.

consider when selecting investments. Investors can maintain their return while reducing the risk level of their portfolio by combining assets or portfolios that have low-positive or negative correlation.

5. Assuming numerous assets and a multitude of combination curves, the efficient frontier is the envelope curve that encompasses all of the best combinations. It defines the set of portfolios that has the highest expected return for each given level of risk or the minimum risk for each given level of return.

6. From this set of dominant portfolios, investors select the one that lies at the point of tangency between the efficient frontier and their highest utility curve. Because risk-return utility functions differ, the point of tangency and, therefore, the portfolio choice will differ among investors.

At this point, you understand that an optimum portfolio is a combination of investments, each having desirable individual risk–return characteristics that also fit together based on their correlations. This deeper understanding of portfolio theory should lead you to reflect back on our earlier discussion of global investing. Because many foreign stock and bond investments provide superior rates of return compared with Canadian securities and have low correlations with portfolios of Canadian stocks and bonds (as shown in Chapter 3), including these foreign securities in your portfolio will help you to reduce the overall risk of your portfolio while possibly increasing your return.

Key Terms

correlation coefficient, p. 139
covariance, p. 135

efficient frontier, p. 151
optimal portfolio, p. 153

Suggested Readings

Auger, Robert, and Denis Parisien. "Understanding Asset Allocation," *Canadian Investment Review* 4, no. 1 (Spring 1991).

Elton, Edwin J., Martin J. Gruber, Stephen J. Brown, and William N. Goetzmann. *Modern Portfolio Theory and Investment Analysis*, 6th ed. New York: Wiley, 2003.

Farrell, James L., Jr. *Portfolio Management: Theory and Application*, 2nd ed. New York: McGraw-Hill, 1997.

Kaplan, Paul D. "Asset Allocation Models Using the Markowitz Approach." January 1998. http://corporate.morningstar.com/ib/documents/MethodologyDocuments/IBBAssociates/MarkowitzApproach.pdf.

Korkie, B., and H. Turtle. "The Canadian Investment Opportunity Set. 1967–1993." *Canadian Journal of Administrative Sciences* 15, no. 3 (September 1998), 213–229.

Masinn, John L., Donald L. Tuttle, Jerold E. Pinto, and Dennis W. Mcleavy. *Managing Investment Portfolios: A Dynamic Process*, 3rd ed. Hoboken, NJ: John Wiley & Sons, 2007.

Potvin, Paul. "Passive Management, the TSE 300, and the Toronto 35 Stock Indexes." *Canadian Investment Review* 5, no. 1 (Spring 1992).

Strong, Robert. *Portfolio Construction, Management, and Protection*. Cincinnati: Thomson South-Western, 5th edition, 2008.

 For Chapter CFA Questions and Problems, please see Appendix A at the end of this text.

Questions

1. Why do most investors hold diversified portfolios?
2. What is covariance, and why is it important in portfolio theory?
3. Why do most assets of the same type show positive covariances of returns with each other? Would you expect positive covariances of returns between *different* types of assets such as returns on Treasury bills, General

Electric common stock, and commercial real estate? Why or why not?
4. What is the relationship between covariance and the correlation coefficient?
5. Explain the shape of the efficient frontier.
6. Draw a properly labeled graph of the Markowitz efficient frontier. Describe the efficient frontier in exact

terms. Discuss the concept of dominant portfolios, and show an example of one on your graph.

7. Assume you want to run a computer program to derive the efficient frontier for your feasible set of stocks. What information must you input to the program?

8. Why are investors' utility curves important in portfolio theory?

9. Explain how a given investor chooses an optimal portfolio. Will this choice always be a diversified portfolio, or could it be a single asset? Explain your answer.

10. Assume that you and a business associate develop an efficient frontier for a set of investments. Why might the two of you select different portfolios on the frontier?

11. Draw a hypothetical graph of an efficient frontier of Canadian common stocks. On the same graph, draw an efficient frontier assuming the inclusion of Canadian bonds as well. Finally, on the same graph, draw an efficient frontier that includes Canadian common stocks, Canadian bonds, and stocks and bonds from around the world. Discuss the differences in these frontiers.

12. Stocks K, L, and M each have the same expected return and standard deviation. The correlation coefficients between each pair of these stocks are:

K and L correlation coefficient = +0.8
K and M correlation coefficient = +0.2
L and M correlation coefficient = −0.4

Given these correlations, a portfolio constructed of which pair of stocks will have the lowest standard deviation? Explain.

Problems

1. Considering the world economic outlook for the coming year and estimates of sales and earning for the pharmaceutical industry, you expect the rate of return for Lauren Labs common stock to range between −20 % and +40 % with the following probabilities.

Probability	Possible Returns
0.10	−0.20
0.15	−0.05
0.20	0.10
0.25	0.15
0.20	0.20
0.10	0.40

Compute the expected rate of return $E(R_i)$ for Lauren Labs.

2. Given the following market values of stocks in your portfolio and their expected rates of return, what is the expected rate of return for your common stock portfolio?

Stock	Market Value ($Mil.)	$E(R_i)$
Disney	$15,000	0.14
Starbucks	$17,000	−0.04
Harley-Davidson	$32,000	0.18
Intel	$23,000	0.16
Walgreens	$7,000	0.12

3. The following are the monthly rates of return for Madison Cookies and for Sophie Electric during a six-month period.

Month	Madison Cookies	Sophie Electric
1	−0.04	0.07
2	0.06	−0.02
3	−0.07	−0.10
4	0.12	0.15
5	−0.02	−0.06
6	0.05	0.02

Compute the following.

a. Average monthly rate of return $\bar{R}_i$ for each stock
b. Standard deviation of returns for each stock
c. Covariance between the rates of return
d. The correlation coefficient between the rates of return

What level of correlation did you expect? How did your expectations compare with the computed correlation? Would these two stocks offer a good chance for diversification? Why or why not?

4. You are considering two assets with the following characteristics.

$E(R_1) = 0.15 \quad E(\sigma_1) = 0.10 \quad w_1 = 0.5$
$E(R_2) = 0.20 \quad E(\sigma_2) = 0.20 \quad w_2 = 0.5$

Compute the mean and standard deviation of two portfolios if $r_{1,2} = 0.40$ and −0.60, respectively. Plot the two portfolios on a risk–return graph and briefly explain the results.

5. Given: $E(R_1) = 0.10$
$E(R_2) = 0.15$
$E(\sigma_1) = 0.03$
$E(\sigma_2) = 0.05$

Calculate the expected returns and expected standard deviations of a two-stock portfolio in which Stock 1 has a weight of 60% under the following conditions.

a. $Cov_{1,2} = 1.00$
b. $Cov_{1,2} = 0.75$
c. $Cov_{1,2} = 0.25$
d. $Cov_{1,2} = 0.00$
e. $Cov_{1,2} = -0.25$
f. $Cov_{1,2} = -0.75$
g. $Cov_{1,2} = -1.00$

6. Given: $E(R_1) = 0.12$
$E(R_2) = 0.16$
$E(\sigma_1) = 0.04$
$E(\sigma_2) = 0.06$

Calculate the expected returns and expected standard deviations of a two-stock portfolio having a covariance of 0.70 under the following conditions.

a. $w_1 = 1.00$
b. $w_1 = 0.75$
c. $w_1 = 0.50$
d. $w_1 = 0.25$
e. $w_1 = 0.05$

Plot the results on a return-risk graph. Without calculations, draw in what the curve would look like first if the correlation coefficient had been 0.00 and then if it had been -0.70.

7. The following are monthly percentage price changes for four market indices.

Month	DJIA	S&P 500	Russell 2000	Nikkei
1	0.03	0.02	0.04	0.04
2	0.07	0.06	0.10	−0.02
3	−0.02	−0.01	−0.04	0.07
4	0.01	0.03	0.03	0.02
5	0.05	0.04	0.11	0.02
6	−0.06	−0.04	−0.08	0.06

Compute the following.

a. Average monthly rate of return for each index
b. Standard deviation for each index
c. Covariance between the rates of return for the following indices:
   DJIA–S&P 500
   S&P 500–Russell 2000
   S&P 500–Nikkei
   Russell 2000–Nikkei
d. The correlation coefficients for the same four combinations.
e. Using the answers from parts (a), (b), and (d), calculate the expected return and standard deviation of a portfolio consisting of equal parts of (1) the S&P and the Russell 2000 and (2) the S&P and the Nikkei. Discuss the two portfolios.

8. The standard deviation of Shamrock Corp. stock is 19%. The standard deviation of Sophie Co. stock is 14%. The covariance between these two stocks is 100. What is the correlation between Shamrock and Sophie stock?

A. PROOF THAT MINIMUM PORTFOLIO VARIANCE OCCURS WITH EQUAL WEIGHTS WHEN SECURITIES HAVE EQUAL VARIANCE

When $\sigma_1 = \sigma_2$, we have:

$$
\begin{aligned}
\sigma^2_{\text{port}} &= w_1^2(\sigma_1)^2 + (1 - w_1)^2(\sigma_1)^2 - 2w_1(1 - w_1)r_{1,2}(\sigma_1)^2 \\
&= (\sigma_1)^2[w_1^2 + 1 - 2w_1 + w_1^2 + 2w_1r_{1,2} - 2w_1^2r_{1,2}] \\
&= (\sigma_1)^2[2w_1^2 + 1 - 2w_1 + 2w_1r_{1,2} - 2w_1^2r_{1,2}]
\end{aligned}
$$

For this to be a minimum,

$$
\frac{\partial(\sigma^2_{\text{port}})}{\partial w_1} = 0 = (\sigma_1)^2[4w_1 \times 2 + 2r_{1,2} \times 4w_1r_{1,2}]
$$

Assuming $(\sigma_1)^2 > 0$,

$$
\begin{aligned}
4w_1 - 2 + 2r_{1,2} - 4w_1r_{1,2} &= 0 \\
4w_1(1 - r_{1,2}) - 2(1 - r_{1,2}) &= 0
\end{aligned}
$$

from which

$$
w_1 = \frac{2(1 - r_{1,2})}{4(1 - r_{1,2})} = \frac{1}{2}
$$

regardless of $r_{1,2}$. Thus, if $\sigma_1 = \sigma_2$, σ^2_{port} will *always* be minimized by choosing $w_1 = w_2 = 1/2$, regardless of the value of $r_{1,2}$, except when $r_{1,2} = +1$ (in which case $\sigma_{\text{port}} = \sigma_1 = \sigma_2$). This can be verified by checking the second-order condition

$$
\frac{\partial(\sigma^2_{\text{port}})}{\partial w_1^2} > 0
$$

Problem

1. The following information applies to Questions 1a and 1b. The general equation for the weight of the first security to achieve minimum variance (in a two-stock portfolio) is given by

$$w_1 = \frac{(\sigma_2)^2 - r_{1,2}(\sigma_1)(\sigma_2)}{(\sigma_1)^2 + (\sigma_2)^2 - 2r_{1,2}(\sigma_1)(\sigma_2)}$$

  a. Show that $w_1 = 0.5$ when $\sigma_1 = \sigma_2$.
  b. What is the weight of Security 1 that gives minimum portfolio variance when $r_{1,2} = 0.5$, $\sigma_1 = 0.04$, and $\sigma_2 = 0.06$?

B. DERIVATION OF WEIGHTS THAT WILL GIVE ZERO VARIANCE WHEN CORRELATION EQUALS −1.00

$$\begin{aligned}
\sigma_{port}^2 &= w_1^2(\sigma_1)^2 + (1 - w_1)^2(\sigma_2)^2 + 2w_1(1 - w_1)r_{1,2}(\sigma_1)(\sigma_2) \\
&= w_1^2(\sigma_1)^2 + (\sigma_2)^2 - 2w_1(\sigma_2)^2 + w_1^2(\sigma_2)^2 + 2w_1 r_{1,2}(\sigma_1)(\sigma_2) - 2w_1^2 r_{1,2}(\sigma_1)(\sigma_2)
\end{aligned}$$

If $r_{1,2} = -1$, this can be rearranged and expressed as

$$\begin{aligned}
\sigma_{port}^2 &= w_1^2[(\sigma_1)^2 + 2(\sigma_1)(\sigma_2) + (\sigma_2)^2] - 2w_1[(\sigma_2)^2 + (\sigma_1)(\sigma_2)] + (\sigma_2)^2 \\
&= w_1^2[(\sigma_1) + (\sigma_2)]^2 - 2w_1(\sigma_2)[(\sigma_1) + (\sigma_2)] + (\sigma_2)^2 \\
&= \{w_1[(\sigma_1) + (\sigma_2)] - (\sigma_2)\}^2
\end{aligned}$$

We want to find the weight, w_1, which will reduce (σ_{port}^2) to *zero*; therefore,

$$w_1[(\sigma_1) + (\sigma_2)] - (\sigma_2) = 0$$

which yields

$$w_1 \frac{(\sigma_2)}{(\sigma_1) + (\sigma_2)}, \text{ and } w_2 = 1 - w_1 = \frac{(\sigma_1)}{(\sigma_1) + (\sigma_2)}$$

Problem

1. Given two assets with the following characteristics:

$E(R_1) = 0.12$ $\sigma_1 = 0.04$
$E(R_2) = 0.16$ $\sigma_2 = 0.06$

Assume that $r_{1,2} = -1.00$. What is the weight that would yield a zero variance for the portfolio?

C. INDIFFERENCE CURVES AND INVESTOR UTILITY

Let us further examine the indifference curves in Exhibit 6.16 on page 153. Each point on a particular curve gives the investor equal satisfaction, that is same level of utility. Take point X on indifferent curve U1 for example. When moving from point X to point X_1, the risk and return combination has changed. The investor moves in the northeast direction, meaning she is taking on more risk on the horizontal but she is also compensated with higher return on the vertical. Because points X and X_1 are on the same utility curve, this means that the higher return she received at X_1 exactly what she needs to compensate for the higher risk, no more and no less; thus she feels indifferent between points X and X_1. This is a typical investor who, as discussed at the beginning of this chapter, strives to maximize investment returns but at the same time, dislikes risk. The only way to keep her as happy as at point X, after taking on more risk, is providing her with higher return.

The reason why indifference curves for investors are oriented in the northeastern and southwestern position can be explained through Exhibit 6C.1. Take point A on the map to begin with and the investor knows the risk and return of investment A. We can imagine that there are numerous other investment opportunities all over the map. We can tell what the preference of the investor is, that is, can we rank which investment opportunities are better than A and which are worse. Because we don't know this investor personally, we won't have all the answers until we ask her to rank each and every alternative for us. But if we accept the assumptions in Section 6.1 that this investor wishes to maximize return but avoid risk, then we can determine her preferences for her for a lot of the investment opportunities, if not all of them.

Consider investment B, which provides higher return but lower risk than A. If the investor is indeed a typical risk averse individual, she would prefer B to A. In fact, all points on the northwestern quadrant are better than A. Similarly, it is not difficult to see that all investments in the southeastern quadrant like point C, are worse than A as they are more risky than A and offer a lower return. So even without asking the investor about her preferences, we know she would favour alternatives northwest to A and shy away from investments southeastern to A. This is a universal principle an investment advisor should know.

The above intuitively appealing ranking principle for risk-averse investors is the mean-variance criterion, which states that investment i dominates investment j if

6C.1		$E(R_i) \geq E(R_j)$
	and	$\sigma_i \geq \sigma_j$

and at least one inequality is strict.

Now how about investments in the other two quadrants such as D and E? D provides more return but one has to put up with more risk as well. Would the extra return be sufficient to induce the investor to accept more risk? We really don't know the subjective trade-offs of the investor until we actually talk to her. By the same token, E is also in an unknown state because we don't know if the lower risk is low enough to make up for the lower return. In fact, all points in the northeastern and southwestern quadrants are in a "we don't know" kind of state. Then if northwest is better than A and southeast worse than A, where would we find investments viewed by the investor as same as A? They must be northeast and southwest to investment A. Therefore, investments viewed by the investor as "indifferent" from A must go southwest-northeast, and thus the orientation of the indifferent curves on Exhibit 6.16. The actual slope of the curve depends on how risk averse the investor is. Two possible sets are illustrated in that chart.

The return-loving and risk-hating "complex" of a typical investor can be captured by a utility function that reflects such characteristics:

6C.2

$$\text{Utility} = E(R) - \left(\frac{\sigma^2}{RT}\right)$$

$$= E(R) - \text{Risk Penalty}$$

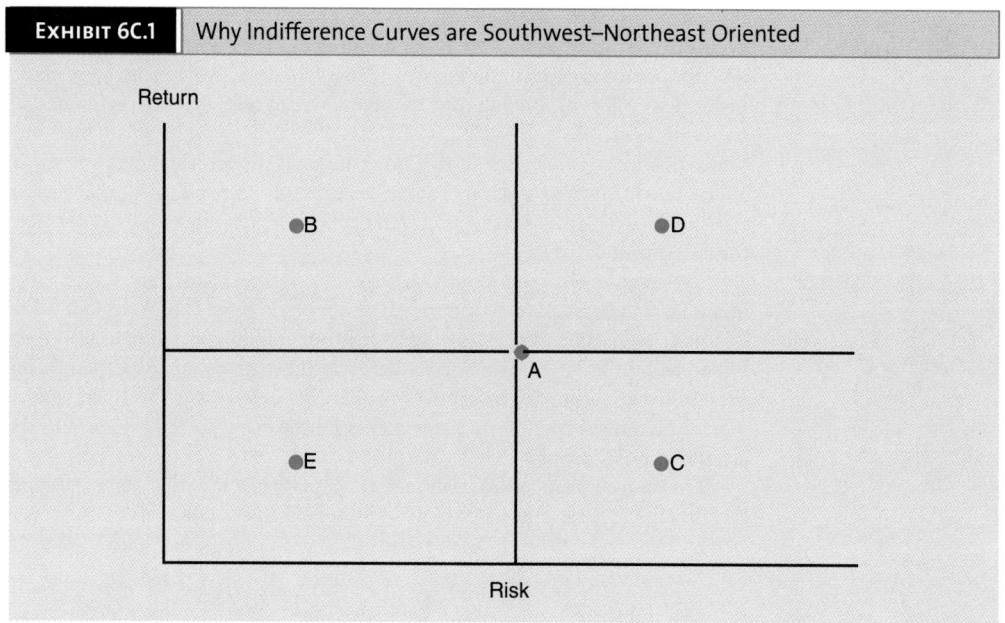

EXHIBIT 6C.1 | Why Indifference Curves are Southwest–Northeast Oriented

where R is the rate of return, σ^2 is the variance, and RT is the risk-tolerance factor for the investor. The risk-tolerance factor is an estimate intended to capture the essence of an investor's attitude toward risk bearing. In the equation, the signs tell us that expected return makes a positive impact on utility while variance a negative impact. Notice that the higher the risk-tolerance factor, the more risk tolerant the investor is and, hence, the less the investor's expected return "penalized" by its risk level. We will apply this formula again in section 15.5.1 in the context of asset allocation.

The Markowitz portfolio theory and risk-averse investors with mean-variance-based utility function are important building blocks of the capital asset pricing model (CAPM), which we will discuss in the next chapter. We will see that we start the development of CAPM with the assumption that all investors are Markowitz efficient investors who want to choose an investment from points on the efficient frontier. The exact choice on the efficient frontier will depend on each investor's risk–return utility function.

Asset Pricing Models: CAPM and APT

After you read this chapter, you should be able to answer the following questions:

1. How does capital market theory extend Markowitz portfolio theory to the capital market line (CML)? How does it enhance our understanding of the relationship between risk and expected return?

2. What is the market portfolio, and what role does it play in the investment process implied by the CML?

3. How does the capital asset pricing model (CAPM) extend the results of capital market theory? What special role does beta play in the CAPM?

4. What is the security market line (SML), and what are the similarities and differences between the SML and CML?

5. What are the challenges to the CAPM, and how was the APT developed as an alternative asset pricing model?

6. What is the main difficulty in implementing the APT?

7. What are macroeconomic and microeconomic approaches to overcome the difficulty?

Following the development of portfolio theory by Markowitz, two major theories have been derived for the valuation of risky assets. In this chapter, we first introduce the capital asset pricing model (CAPM). The background on the CAPM is important at this point in the book because the risk measure it implies is a necessary input for much of our subsequent discussion. The presentation concerns capital market theory and the capital asset pricing model that was developed almost concurrently by three individuals. An alternative asset valuation model—the arbitrage pricing theory (APT)—has led to the development of numerous other multifactor models and is the subject of Sections 7.5 and 7.6 of this chapter.

7.1 Capital Market Theory: An Overview

Because capital market theory builds directly on the portfolio theory we developed in Chapter 6, this chapter begins where our discussion of the Markowitz efficient frontier ended. In particular, capital market theory extends portfolio theory by developing a model for pricing all risky assets. The final product, the capital asset pricing model (CAPM), will allow you to determine the required return for any risky asset. As we will see, this development depends critically on the existence of a risk-free asset, which in turn will lead to the designation of the market portfolio, a collection of all of the risky assets in the marketplace that assumes a special role in asset pricing theory.

7.1.1 BACKGROUND FOR CAPITAL MARKET THEORY

With any theory, it is necessary to articulate a set of assumptions that specify how the world is expected to act. This allows one to concentrate on developing an explanation for how market participants will respond to changes in the environment. In this section, we consider the main assumptions that underlie the development of capital market theory.

Assumptions of Capital Market Theory Because capital market theory builds on the Markowitz portfolio model, it requires the same assumptions, along with some additional ones:

1. All investors are Markowitz-efficient in that they seek to invest in tangent points on the efficient frontier. The exact location of this tangent point and, therefore, the specific portfolio selected will depend on the individual investor's risk-return utility function.
2. Investors can borrow or lend any amount of money at the risk-free return (RFR). (Clearly, it is always possible to lend money at the nominal risk-free rate by buying risk-free securities such as government T-bills. It is not always possible to borrow at this risk-free rate, but we will see that assuming a higher borrowing rate does not change the general results.)
3. All investors have homogeneous expectations; that is, they estimate identical probability distributions for future rates of return. Again, this assumption can be relaxed with minimal effect.
4. All investors have the same one-period time horizon, such as one month or one year. The model will be developed for a single hypothetical period, and its results could be affected by a different assumption, as it requires investors to derive risk measures and risk-free assets consistent with their investment horizons.
5. All investments are infinitely divisible, which means that it is possible to buy or sell fractional shares of any asset or portfolio. This assumption allows us to discuss investment alternatives as continuous curves. Changing it would have little impact on the theory.
6. There are no taxes or transaction costs involved in buying or selling assets. This is a reasonable assumption in many instances. Neither pension funds nor charitable organizations pay taxes, and the transaction costs for most financial institutions are less than 1% on most financial instruments. Again, relaxing this assumption does not change the basic result.
7. There is no inflation or any change in interest rates, or inflation is fully anticipated. This is a reasonable initial assumption, and it can be modified.
8. Capital markets are in equilibrium. This means that we begin with all investments properly priced in line with their risk levels.

Some of these assumptions may seem unrealistic, but keep in mind two things. First, relaxing them would have only a minor effect on the model and would not change its main implications or conclusions. Second, a theory should never be judged on the basis of its assumptions but rather on how well it explains and helps us predict behaviour in the real world. If this theory and the model it implies help explain the rates of return on a wide variety of risky assets, it is useful, even if some assumptions are unrealistic.

More about Nobel Laureate William Sharpe and his contributions can be found at http://nobelprize.org.

Development of Capital Market Theory The major factor that allowed portfolio theory to develop into capital market theory is the concept of a risk-free asset. Following the development of the Markowitz portfolio model, several authors considered the implications of assuming the existence of a **risk-free asset**, that is, an asset with zero variance. As we will show, such an asset would have zero correlation with all other risky assets and would provide *the risk-free return (RFR)*.

This assumption of a risk-free asset allows us to derive a generalized theory of capital asset pricing under conditions of uncertainty from the Markowitz portfolio theory. This achievement is generally attributed to William Sharpe (1964), who received a Nobel Prize for it, but Lintner (1965) and Mossin (1966) derived similar theories independently. Consequently, you may see references to the Sharpe-Lintner-Mossin capital asset pricing model.

7.1.2 DEVELOPING THE CAPITAL MARKET LINE

We have defined a **risky asset** as one from which future returns are uncertain, and we have measured this uncertainty by the variance, or standard deviation, of expected returns. Because the expected return on a risk-free asset is entirely certain, the standard deviation of its expected return is zero ($\sigma_{RF} = 0$). The return earned on such an asset should be the risk-free return (RFR), which, as we discussed in Chapter 1, should equal the expected long-run growth rate of the economy with an adjustment for short-run liquidity. We now show what happens when we introduce this risk-free asset into the risky world of the Markowitz portfolio model.

Covariance with a Risk-Free Asset Recall that the covariance between two sets of returns is

$$\text{Cov}_{ij} = \sum_{i=1}^{n} [R_i - E(R_i)][R_j - E(R_j)]/n$$

Assume for the moment that Asset i in this formula is the risk-free asset. Because the returns for the risk-free asset are certain ($\sigma_{RF} = 0$), $R_i = E(R_i)$ during all periods. Thus, $R_i - E(R_i)$ will equal zero, and the product of this expression with any other expression will equal zero. Consequently, the covariance of the risk-free asset with any risky asset or portfolio of assets will always equal zero. Similarly, the correlation between any risky asset i, and the risk-free asset, RF, would be zero because it is equal to

$$r_{RF,i} = \text{Cov}_{RF,i}/\sigma_{RF}\sigma_j$$

Combining a Risk-Free Asset with a Risky Portfolio What happens to the expected return and the standard deviation of returns when you combine a risk-free asset with a portfolio of risky assets such as those that exist on the Markowitz efficient frontier?

Expected Return Like the expected return for a portfolio of two risky assets, the expected rate of return for a portfolio that includes a risk-free asset with a collection of risky assets (call it Portfolio M) is the weighted average of the two returns:

$$E(R_{port}) = W_{RF}(RFR) + (1 - w_{RF})E(R_M)$$

where:
w_{RF} = the proportion of the portfolio invested in the risk-free asset
$E(R_M)$ = the expected rate of return on risky Portfolio M

Standard Deviation Recall from Chapter 6 that the expected variance for a two-asset portfolio is

$$\sigma_{port}^2 = w_1^2\sigma_1^2 + w_2^2\sigma_2^2 + 2w_1w_2r_{1,2}\sigma_1\sigma_2$$

Substituting the risk-free asset for Security 1, and the risky asset portfolio for Security 2, this formula would become

$$\sigma_{port}^2 = w_{RF}^2 \sigma_{RF}^2 + (1 - w_{RF})^2 \sigma_M^2 + 2w_{RF}(1 - w_{RF})r_{RF,M}\sigma_{RF}\sigma_M$$

We know that the variance of the risk-free asset is zero, that is, $\sigma_{RF}^2 = 0$. Because the correlation between the risk-free asset and any risky asset, M, is also zero, the factor in the preceding equation also equals zero. Therefore, any component of the variance formula that has either of these terms will equal zero. When you make these adjustments, the formula becomes

$$\sigma_{port}^2 = (1 - w_{RF})^2 \sigma_M^2$$

The standard deviation is

$$\sigma_{port} = \sqrt{(1 - w_{RF})^2 \sigma_M^2}$$
$$= (1 - w_{RF})\sigma_M$$

Therefore, the standard deviation of a portfolio that combines the risk-free asset with risky assets is *the linear proportion of the standard deviation of the risky asset portfolio.*

The Risk-Return Combination With these results, we can develop the risk-return relationship between $E(R_{port})$ and σ_{port} by using a few algebraic manipulations

$$E(R_{port}) = (w_{RF})(RFR) + (1 - w_{RF})E(R_M) + \{RFR - RFR\}$$
$$= RFR - (1 - w_{RF})RFR + (1 - w_{RF})E(R_M)$$
$$= RFR + (1 - w_{RF})[E(R_M) - RFR]$$
$$= RFR + (1 - w_{RF})\{\sigma_M/\sigma_M\}[E(R_M) - RFR]$$

so that

7.1	$$E(R_{port}) = RFR + \sigma_{port}\left[\dfrac{E(R_M) - RFR}{\sigma_M}\right]$$

Equation 7.1 is the primary result of capital market theory. It can be interpreted as follows: Investors who allocate their money between a riskless security and the risky Portfolio M can expect a return equal to the risk-free rate plus compensation for the number of risk units (σ_{port}) they accept.

This outcome is consistent with the concept underlying all of investment theory that investors perform two functions in the capital markets for which they can expect to be rewarded. First, they allow someone else to use their money, for which they receive the risk-free return. Second, they bear the risk that the returns they have been promised in exchange for their invested capital will not be paid. The term $[E(R_M) - RFR]/\sigma_M$, is the expected compensation per unit of risk taken, which is more commonly referred to as the investor's expected *risk premium* per unit of risk.

The Capital Market Line The risk–return relationship shown in Equation 7.1 holds for every combination of the risk-free asset with *any* collection of risky assets. However, investors would obviously like to maximize their expected compensation for bearing risk (i.e., they would like to maximize the risk premium they receive). Let us now assume that Portfolio M is the single collection of risky assets that happens to maximize this risk premium. With this assumption, Portfolio M is called the *market portfolio* and, by definition, it contains all risky assets held anywhere in the marketplace. It has the property of receiving the highest level of expected return (in excess of the risk-free rate) per unit of risk for any available portfolio of risky assets. Under these conditions, Equation 7.1 is called the **capital market line (CML)**.

Exhibit 7.1 shows the various possibilities when a risk-free asset is combined with alternative risky combinations of assets along the Markowitz efficient frontier. Each of the straight lines depicted represents mixtures of a risky portfolio with the riskless asset. For instance, the risk-free asset could be combined in various weights with Portfolio A, as shown by the straight line *RFR*–A. Any combination on this line would dominate portfolio possibilities that fall below it because it would have a higher expected return for the same level of risk. Similarly, any combination of the risk-free asset and Portfolio A is dominated by some mixture of the risk-free asset and Portfolio B.

EXHIBIT 7.1	Portfolio Possibilities Combining the Risk-Free Asset and Risky Portfolios on the Efficient Frontier

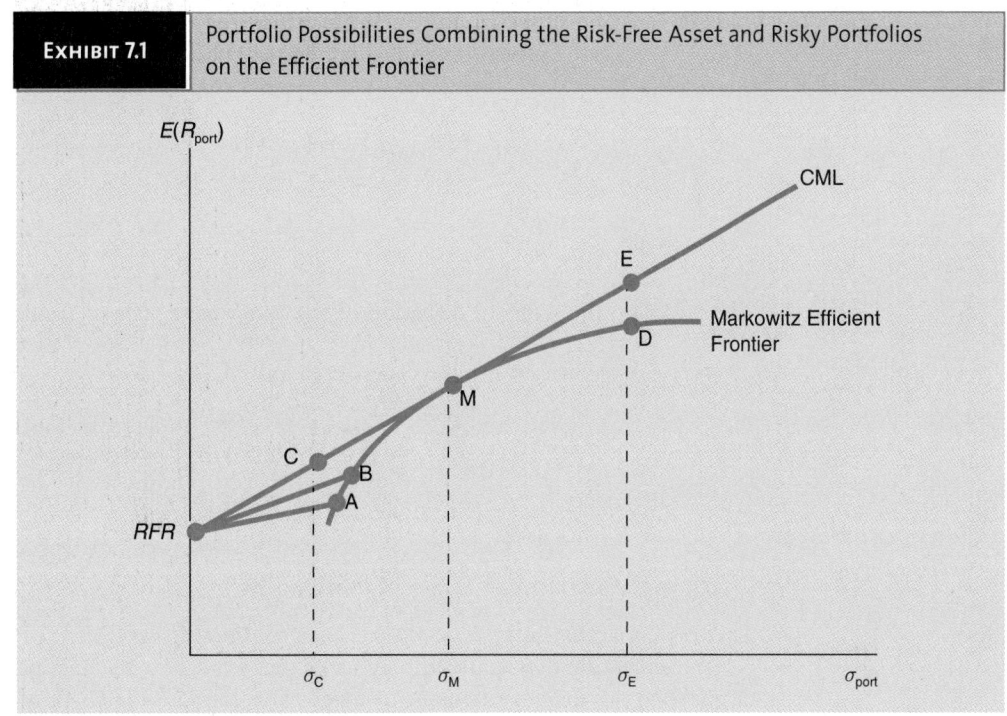

You can continue to draw lines from RFR to the efficient frontier with increasingly higher slopes until you reach the point of tangency at Portfolio M. The set of portfolio possibilities along the line *RFR–M*—which is the CML—dominates *all* other feasible combinations that investors could form. For example, Point C could be established by investing half of your assets in the riskless security (i.e., lending at *RFR*) and the other half in Portfolio M. Notice in Exhibit 7.1 that there is no way to invest your money and achieve a higher expected return for the same level of risk (σ_c). In this sense, *the CML represents a new efficient frontier* that results from combining the Markowitz efficient frontier of risky assets with the ability to invest in the risk-free security. Finally, the slope of the CML is $[E(R_M) - RFR]/\sigma_M$, which is the maximum risk-premium compensation that investors can expect for each unit of risk they bear.

Risk-Return Possibilities with Leverage An investor may want a higher expected return than is available at Point M in exchange for accepting higher risk. One alternative would be to invest in one of the risky asset portfolios on the efficient frontier beyond Point M such as the portfolio at Point D. A second alternative is to add *leverage* to the portfolio by *borrowing* money at the risk-free rate and investing the proceeds in the risky asset portfolio at Point M; this is shown as Point E. What effect would this have on the return and risk for your portfolio?

If you borrow an amount equal to 50% of your original wealth at the risk-free rate, w_{RF} will not be a positive fraction but, rather, a negative 50% $(w_{RF} = -0.50)$. The effect on the expected return for your portfolio is:

$$
\begin{aligned}
E(R_{port}) &= w_{RF}(RFR) + (1 - w_{RF})E(R_M) \\
&= -0.50(RFR) + [1 - (-0.50)]E(R_M) \\
&= -0.50(RFR) + 1.50E(R_M)
\end{aligned}
$$

The return will increase in a *linear* fashion along the CML because the gross return increases by 50%, but you must pay interest at the *RFR* on the money borrowed. If $RFR = 0.06$ and $E(R_M) = 0.12$, the return on your leveraged portfolio would be:

$$
\begin{aligned}
E(R_{port}) &= -0.50(0.06) + 1.5(0.12) \\
&= -0.03 + 0.18 \\
&= 0.15
\end{aligned}
$$

The effect on the standard deviation of the leveraged portfolio is similar.

$$
\begin{aligned}
\sigma_{port} &= (1 - w_{RF})\sigma_M \\
&= [1 - (-0.50)]\sigma_M = 1.50\sigma_M
\end{aligned}
$$

where:

σ_M = the standard deviation of Portfolio M

Therefore, *both return and risk increase in a linear fashion along the CML.* This is shown in Exhibit 7.2.

Our discussion of portfolio theory stated that when two assets are perfectly correlated, the set of portfolio possibilities falls along a straight line. Because the CML is a straight line, it implies that all the portfolios on the CML are perfectly positively correlated. This positive correlation

Exhibit 7.2	Derivation of Capital Market Line Assuming Lending or Borrowing at the Risk-Free Rate

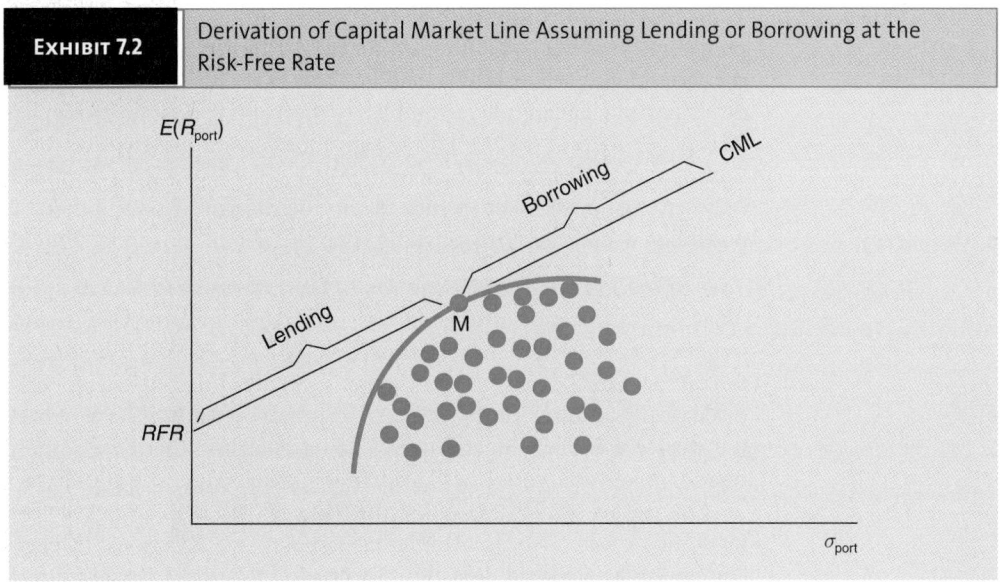

occurs because all portfolios on the CML combine the risky asset Portfolio M and the risk-free asset. You either invest part of your money in the risk-free asset (i.e., you *lend* at the RFR) and the rest in the risky asset Portfolio M, or you *borrow* at the risk-free rate and invest these funds in the risky asset portfolio. In either case, all the variability comes from the risky asset M portfolio. The only difference between the alternative portfolios on the CML is the magnitude of that variability, which is caused by the proportion of the risky asset portfolio held in the total portfolio.

7.1.3 Risk, Diversification, and the Market Portfolio

The investment prescription emerging from capital market theory is clear-cut: Investors should only invest in two types of assets—the risk-free security and risky asset Portfolio M— with the weights of these two holdings determined by the investors' tolerance for risk. Because of the special place that the market Portfolio M holds to all investors, it must contain *all risky assets* for which there is any value in the marketplace. This includes not just Canadian common stocks, but also foreign stocks, foreign bonds, real estate, private equity, options and futures contracts, art, antiques, and so on. Further, these assets should be represented in Portfolio M in proportion to their relative market values.

Because the market portfolio contains all risky assets, it is a **completely diversified portfolio**, which means that all risk unique to individual assets in the portfolio is diversified away. Specifically, the unique risk, or **unsystematic risk**, of any single asset is offset by the unique variability of all of the other holdings in the portfolio. This implies that only **systematic risk**, defined as the variability in all risky assets caused by macroeconomic variables, remains in Portfolio M. Systematic risk can be measured by the standard deviation of returns to the market portfolio and it changes over time whenever there are changes in the underlying economic forces that affect the valuation of all risky assets.[1] Such economic forces would be variability of money supply growth, interest rate volatility, and variability in industrial production or corporate earnings.

---

1 For analyses of changes in the standard deviation (volatility) of returns for stocks and bonds in the United States, see Schwert (1989); Ineichen (2000); Reilly, Wright, and Chan (2000); and Ang, Hodrick, Xing, and Zhang (2006).

How to Measure Diversification As noted earlier, all portfolios on the CML are perfectly positively correlated, which means that all portfolios on the CML are perfectly correlated with the completely diversified market Portfolio M. Lorie (1975) suggests a measure of diversification. Specifically, a completely diversified portfolio would have a correlation with the market portfolio of +1.00. This is logical because complete diversification means the elimination of all the unsystematic or unique risk. Once you have eliminated all unsystematic risk, only systematic risk is left, which cannot be diversified away. Therefore, completely diversified portfolios would correlate perfectly with the market portfolio, which has only systematic risk.

Diversification and the Elimination of Unsystematic Risk As discussed in Chapter 6, the purpose of diversification is to reduce the standard deviation of the total portfolio. This assumes imperfect correlations among securities. Ideally, as you add securities, the average covariance for the portfolio declines. How many securities must be included to arrive at a completely diversified portfolio? To discover the answer, you must observe what happens as you increase the sample size of the portfolio by adding securities that have some positive correlation. The typical correlation between Canadian securities ranges from 0.20 to 0.60.

One set of studies examined the average standard deviation for numerous portfolios of randomly selected stocks of different sample sizes. Evans and Archer (1968) and Tole (1982) computed the standard deviation for portfolios of increasing size up to 20 stocks. The results indicated that the major benefits of diversification were achieved rather quickly, with about 90% of the maximum benefit of diversification derived from portfolios of 12 to 18 stocks. Exhibit 7.3 shows a stylized depiction of this effect.

Two subsequent studies have modified this finding. Statman (1987) considered the trade-off between the diversification benefits and additional transaction costs involved with increasing the size of a portfolio. He concluded that a well-diversified portfolio must contain at least 30 to 40 stocks. Campbell, Lettau, Malkiel, and Xu (2001) demonstrated that because the idiosyncratic portion of an individual stock's total risk has been increasing in recent years, it now takes more stocks in a portfolio to achieve the same level of diversification. For instance, they showed that the level of diversification that was possible with only 20 stocks in the 1960s would require about 50 stocks by the late 1990s.

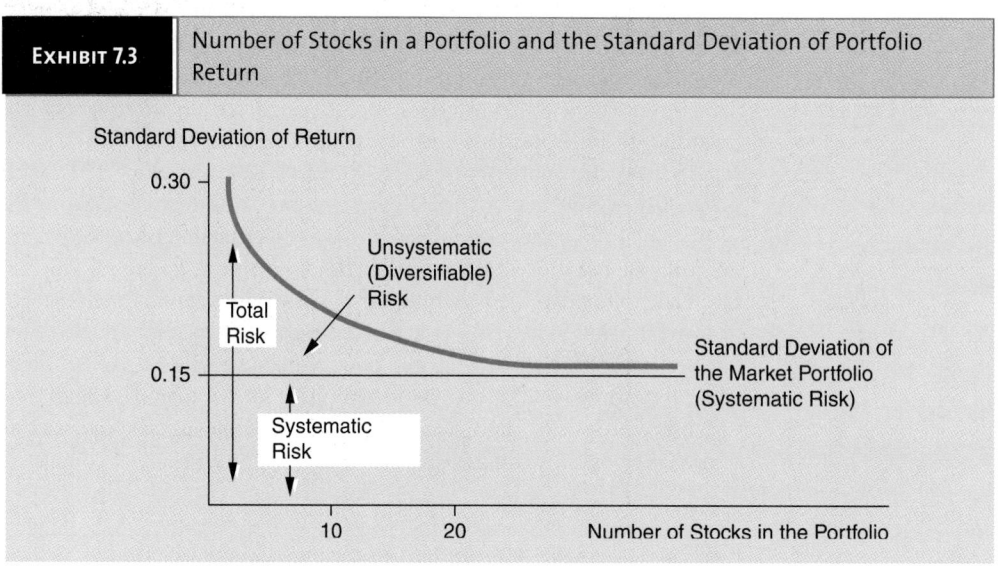

| **EXHIBIT 7.3** | Number of Stocks in a Portfolio and the Standard Deviation of Portfolio Return |

The important point to remember is that you can reduce the overall standard deviation of the portfolio, which will eventually reach the level of the market portfolio, by adding stocks that are not perfectly correlated with the other stocks in the portfolio. At that point, you will have diversified away all unsystematic risk, but you still have market or systematic risk. You cannot eliminate the variability and uncertainty of macroeconomic factors that affect all risky assets. Further, you can attain a lower level of systematic risk by diversifying globally versus only diversifying within Canada because some of the systematic risk factors in the Canadian market (such as Canadian monetary policy) are not perfectly correlated with systematic risk variables in other countries such as Germany and Japan. As a result, if you diversify globally, you eventually get down to a world systematic risk level.

The CML and the Separation Theorem As we have seen, the CML leads all investors to invest in the same risky asset Portfolio M. Individual investors should only differ regarding their position on the CML, which depends on their risk preferences. In turn, how they get to a point on the CML is based on their *financing decisions.* If you are relatively risk averse, you will lend some part of your portfolio at the *RFR* by buying some risk-free securities and investing the remainder in the market portfolio of risky assets (for example, Point C in Exhibit 7.1). In contrast, if you prefer more risk, you might borrow funds at the *RFR* and invest everything (all of your capital plus what you borrowed) in the market portfolio (Point E in Exhibit 7.1). This financing decision provides more risk but greater expected returns than the market portfolio. Because portfolios on the CML dominate other portfolio possibilities, the CML becomes the efficient frontier of portfolios, and investors decide where they want to be along this efficient frontier. Tobin (1958) called this division of the investment decision from the financing decision the **separation theorem**. Specifically, to be somewhere on the CML efficient frontier, you initially decide to invest in the market Portfolio M, which means that you will be on the CML. This is your *investment* decision. Subsequently, based on your risk preferences, you make a separate *financing* decision either to borrow or to lend to attain your preferred risk position on the CML.

A Risk Measure for the CML In discussing the Markowitz portfolio model, we noted that the relevant risk to consider when adding a security to a portfolio is *its average covariance with all other assets in the portfolio.* In this chapter, we have shown that *the only relevant portfolio is the market Portfolio M.* Together, this means that the only important consideration for any individual risky asset is its average covariance with all the risky assets in Portfolio M or *the asset's covariance with the market portfolio.* This covariance, then, is the relevant risk measure for an individual risky asset.

Because all individual risky assets are a part of the market portfolio, one can describe their rates of return in relation to the returns to Portfolio M using the following linear model:

7.2

$$R_{it} = a_i + b_i R_{Mt} + \varepsilon$$

where:

R_{it} = return for asset i during period t
a_i = constant term for asset i
b_i = slope coefficient for asset i
R_{Mt} = return for Portfolio M during period t
ε = random error term

The variance of returns for a risky asset can similarly be described as

7.3	

$$\begin{aligned} \text{Var}(R_{it}) &= \text{Var}(a_i + b_i R_{Mt} + \varepsilon) \\ &= \text{Var}(a_i) + \text{Var}(b_i R_{Mt}) + \text{Var}(\varepsilon) \\ &= 0 + \text{Var}(b_i R_{Mt}) + \text{Var}(\varepsilon) \end{aligned}$$

Note that $\text{Var}(b_i RM_t)$ is the variance of return for an asset related to the variance of the market return, or the asset's *systematic variance or risk*. Also, $\text{Var}(\varepsilon)$ is the residual variance of return for the individual asset that is not related to the market portfolio. This residual variance is the variability that we have referred to as the unsystematic or *unique risk* because it arises from the unique features of the asset. Therefore:

$$\text{Var}(R_{it}) = \textbf{Systematic Variance} + \textbf{Unsystematic Variance}$$

We know that a completely diversified portfolio has had all of its unsystematic variance eliminated. Therefore, the unsystematic variance of an asset is not relevant to investors, because they can eliminate it when holding an asset as part of a broad-based portfolio. As a consequence, investors should not expect to receive compensation for bearing this unsystematic risk. Only the systematic variance is relevant because it cannot be diversified away, because it is caused by economic forces that affect all risky assets.

7.1.4 INVESTING WITH THE CML: AN EXAMPLE

After doing considerable research on current capital market conditions, you have estimated the investment characteristics for six different combinations of risky assets. Exhibit 7.4 lists your expected return and standard deviation forecasts for these portfolios. You have also established that each of these portfolios is completely diversified so that its volatility estimate represents systematic risk only. The risk-free rate at the time of your analysis is 4%.

EXHIBIT 7.4	Investment Characteristics for Portfolios of Risky Assets (*RFR* = 4%)		
Portfolio	**Expected Return**	**Standard Deviation**	**$[E(R) - RFR]/\sigma$**
1	5%	5%	0.200
2	7	7	0.429
3	9	10	0.500
4	11	15	0.467
5	13	21	0.429
6	15	28	0.393

Based on your forecasts for $E(R)$ and σ alone, none of these portfolios clearly dominates the others as higher levels of expected return always come at the cost of higher levels of risk. Which portfolio offers the best trade-off between risk and return? The last column in Exhibit 7.4 calculates the ratio of the expected risk premium ($E(R) - RFR$) to volatility (σ) for each portfolio. As explained earlier, this ratio can be interpreted as the *amount of compensation that investors can expect for each unit of risk* they assume in a particular portfolio. For example, Portfolio 2 offers investors 0.429 ($= [7 - 4]/7$) units of compensation per unit of risk while the comparable ratio for Portfolio 6 is lower at 0.393 ($= [15 - 4]/28$) despite promising a much higher overall return. By this measure, it is clear that Portfolio 3 offers investors the best combination of risk and return. No other feasible collection of risky assets in this comparison can match the 0.500 units of expected risk premium per unit of risk promised by Portfolio 3. Consequently, Portfolio 3 should be considered as the market portfolio. Capital market theory would recommend that you only consider two alternatives when investing your funds: (i) lending or borrowing in the riskless security at 4% and (ii) buying Portfolio 3.

Suppose now that given your risk tolerance you are willing to assume a standard deviation of 8.5%. How should you go about investing your money, according to the CML? First, using Equation 7.1, the return you can expect is:

$$4\% + (8.5\%)(0.500) = 8.25\%$$

As we have seen, there is no way for you to obtain a higher expected return under the current conditions without assuming more risk. Second, the investment strategy necessary to achieve this return can be found by solving:

$$8.25\% = w_{RF}(4\%) + (1 - w_{RF})(9\%)$$

or $w_{RF} = (9 - 8.25)/(9 - 4) = 0.15$. This means that you would need to invest 15% of your funds in the riskless asset and the remaining 85% in Portfolio 3. Finally, notice that the expected risk premium per unit of risk for this position is 0.500 ($=[8.25 - 4]/8.5$), the same as Portfolio 3. In fact, all points along the CML will have the same risk–return trade-off as the market portfolio as this ratio is the slope of the CML.

As a last extension, consider what would happen if you were willing to take on a risk level of $\sigma = 15\%$. From Exhibit 7.4, you could realize an expected return of 11% if you placed 100% of funds in Portfolio 4. However, you can do better than this by following the investment prescription of the CML. Specifically, for a risk level of 15%, you can obtain an expected return of:

$$4\% + (15\%)(0.500) = 11.5\%$$

This goal is greater than the expected return offered by a 100% investment in the market portfolio (i.e., 9%), so you will have to use leverage to achieve it. Specifically, solving for the investment weights along the CML leaves $w_{RF} = (9 - 11.5)/(9 - 4) = -0.50$ and $(1 - w_{RF}) = 1.50$. Thus, for each dollar you currently have to invest, you will need to borrow an additional 50 cents and place all of these funds in Portfolio 3.

7.2   The Capital Asset Pricing Model

Capital market theory represented a major step forward in how investors should think about the investment process. The formula for the CML (Equation 7.1) offers a precise way of calculating the return that investors can expect for (1) providing their financial capital (*RFR*), and (2) bearing σ_{port} units of risk ($[E(R_M) - RFR]/\sigma_M$). This last expression is especially significant because it offers a tangible measurement for the expected risk premium prevailing in the marketplace.

Unfortunately, capital market theory is an incomplete explanation for the relationship that exists between risk and return. To understand why, recall that the CML defined the risk an investor bears by the total volatility (σ) of the investment. However, since we have seen that investors cannot expect to be compensated for any portion of risk that they could have diversified away (i.e., unsystematic risk), the CML must be based on the assumption that investors only hold *fully diversified portfolios,* for which total risk and systematic risk are the same thing. The limitation is that the CML cannot provide an explanation for the risk-return trade-off for *individual* risky assets because the standard deviation measures for these securities will contain a substantial amount of unique risk.

The **capital asset pricing model (CAPM)** extends capital market theory in a way that allows investors to evaluate the risk-return trade-off for both diversified portfolios *and* individual securities. To do this, the CAPM redefines the relevant measure of risk from total volatility to just the non-diversifiable portion of that total volatility (i.e., systematic risk). This new risk measure is called the **beta** coefficient and it calculates the level of a security's systematic risk compared to that of the market portfolio. Using beta as the relevant measure of risk, the CAPM then redefines the expected risk premium per unit of risk in a commensurate fashion. This in turn leads once again to an expression of the expected return that can be decomposed into (1) the risk-free rate and (2) the expected risk premium.

7.2.1   A CONCEPTUAL DEVELOPMENT OF THE CAPM

As noted earlier, Sharpe (1964), along with Lintner (1965) and Mossin (1966), developed the CAPM in a formal way. In addition to the assumptions listed before, the CAPM requires others, such as that asset returns come from a Normal probability distribution. Rather than repeat the mathematical derivation of the CAPM, we will present a conceptual development of the model that emphasizes its role in the natural progression that began with the Markowitz portfolio theory.

Recall that the CML expressed the risk-return trade-off for fully diversified portfolios as follows:

$$E(R_{port}) = RFR + \sigma_{port}\left[\frac{E(R_M) - RFR}{\sigma_M}\right]$$

When trying to extend this expression to allow for the evaluation of any individual risky asset *i*, the logical temptation is to simply replace the standard deviation of the portfolio (σ_{port}) with that of the single security (σ_i). However, as explained above, this would overstate the relevant level of risk in the *i*-th security because it does not take into account how much of that volatility the investor could diversify away by combining that asset with other holdings. One way to address this concern is to "shrink" the level of σ_i to include only the portion of risk in Security *i* that is systematically related to the risk in the market portfolio. This can be done by multiplying σ_i by the correlation coefficient between the returns to Security i and the market portfolio ($(r_{jM}$). Inserting this product into the CML and adapting the notation for the i-th individual asset leaves:

$$E(R_i) = RFR + (\sigma_i r_{iM}) \left[\frac{E(R_M) - RFR}{\sigma_M} \right]$$

This expression can be rearranged as:

$$E(R_i) = RFR + \left(\frac{\sigma_i r_{iM}}{\sigma_M} \right) [E(R_M) - RFR]$$

or:

7.4 $\qquad E(R_i) = RFR + \beta_i [E(R_M) - RFR].$

Equation 7.4 is the CAPM. Notice in particular that the CAPM redefines risk in terms of a security's beta (β_i), which captures the non-diversifiable portion of that stock's risk *relative to the market as a whole*. Because of this, beta can be thought of as *indexing* the asset's systematic risk to that of the market portfolio. This leads to a very convenient interpretation: A stock with a beta of 1.20 has a level of systematic risk that is 20% greater than the average for the entire market, while a stock with a beta of 0.70 is 30% less risky than the market. By definition, the market portfolio itself will always have a beta of 1.00.

Indexing the systematic risk of an individual security to the market has another nice feature as well. From Equation 7.4, it is clear that the CAPM once again expresses the expected return for an investment as the sum of the risk-free rate and the expected risk premium. However, rather than calculate a different risk premium for every separate security that exists, the CAPM states that only the overall **market risk premium** $(E(R_m) - RFR)$ matters and that this quantity can then be adapted to any risky asset by scaling it up or down according to that asset's riskiness relative to the market (β_i). As we will see, this substantially reduces the number of calculations that investors must make when evaluating potential investments for their portfolios.

7.2.2 THE SECURITY MARKET LINE

The CAPM can also be illustrated graphically as the **security market line (SML)** as shown in Exhibit 7.5. Like the CML, the SML expresses the trade-off between risk and expected return as a straight line intersecting the vertical axis (i.e., zero-risk point) at the risk-free rate. However, there are two important differences between the CML and the SML. First, the CML measures risk by the standard deviation (i.e., total risk) of the investment while the SML explicitly considers only the systematic component of an investment's volatility. Second, as a consequence of the first point, the CML can only be applied to portfolio holdings that are already fully diversified, whereas the SML can be applied to any individual asset or collection of assets.

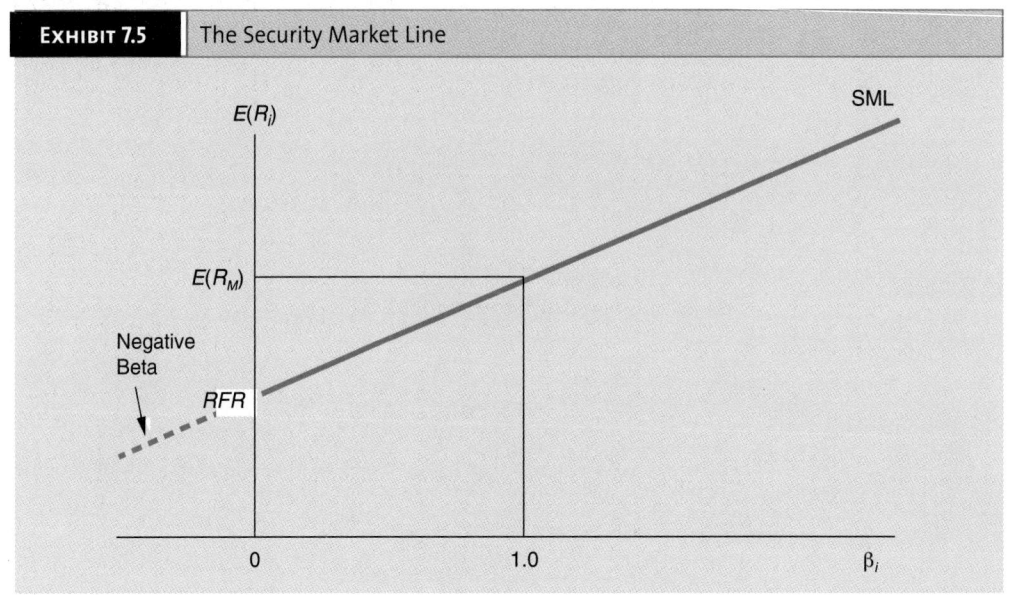

EXHIBIT 7.5 | The Security Market Line

Determining the Expected Return for a Risky Asset To demonstrate how you would compute expected or required rates of return, consider the following example stocks assuming you have already computed betas:

Stock	Beta
A	0.70
B	1.00
C	1.15
D	1.40
E	−0.30

Assume that we expect the economy's *RFR* to be 5% (0.05) and the expected return on the market portfolio ($E(R_M)$) to be 9% (0.09). This implies a market risk premium of 4% (0.04). With these inputs, the SML would yield the following required rates of return for these five stocks:

$$E(R_i) = RFR + \beta_i(E(R_M) - RFR)$$
$$E(R_A) = 0.05 + 0.7(0.09 - 0.05)$$
$$= 0.078 = 7.80\%$$
$$E(R_B) = 0.05 + 1.00(0.09 - 0.05)$$
$$= 0.09 = 9.00\%$$
$$E(R_C) = 0.05 + 1.15(0.09 - 0.05)$$
$$= 0.096 = 9.60\%$$
$$E(R_D) = 0.05 + 1.40(0.09 - 0.05)$$
$$= 0.106 = 10.60\%$$

$$E(R_E) = 0.05 + (-0.30)(0.09 - 0.05)$$
$$= 0.05 - 0.012$$
$$= 0.038 = 3.8\%$$

Stock A has lower risk than the aggregate market, so you should not expect its return to be as high as the return on the market portfolio of risky assets. You should expect Stock A to return 7.80%. Stock B has systematic risk equal to the market's (beta = 1.00), so its required return should likewise be equal to the expected market return (9%). Stocks C and D have systematic risk greater than the market's, so they should provide returns consistent with their risk. Finally, Stock E has a *negative* beta (which is quite rare in practice), so its required return, if such a stock could be found, would be below the *RFR* of 5%.

In equilibrium, *all* assets and *all* portfolios of assets should plot on the SML. That is, all assets should be priced so that their **estimated rates of return**, which are the actual holding period rates of return that you anticipate, are consistent with their levels of systematic risk. Any security with an *estimated* return that plots above the SML would be considered under-valued because it implies that you would receive a higher return on the security than its *required* return based on its systematic risk. In contrast, assets with estimated returns that plot below the SML would be considered overvalued (estimated return is below what should be required based on the asset's systematic risk).

In a completely efficient market, you would expect all assets to plot on the SML because, in equilibrium, all stocks should provide holding period returns equal to their required rates of return. Alternatively, a market that is fairly efficient but not completely efficient may misprice certain assets because not everyone will be aware of all the relevant information for an asset. As discussed in Chapter 5, a superior investor has the ability to derive value estimates for assets that consistently outperform the consensus market evaluation. As a result, such an investor will earn better returns than the average investor on a risk-adjusted basis.

Identifying Undervalued and Overvalued Assets Now that we understand how to compute the return one should expect or require for a specific risky asset using the SML, we can compare this *required* return to the asset's *estimated* return over a specific investment horizon to determine whether it is an appropriate investment. To make this comparison, you need an independent estimate of the return outlook for the security based on either fundamental or technical analysis techniques, which will be discussed in subsequent chapters.

Assume that analysts at a major brokerage firm have been following the five stocks in the preceding example. Based on extensive fundamental analysis, they provide you with expected price and dividend information for the next year, as shown in Exhibit 7.6. Given these projections, you can compute an estimated return for each stock by summing the expected capital gain ($[P_{t+1} - P_t]/P_t$) and the expected dividend yield (D_{t+1}/P_t). For example, the analysts' estimated future return for Stock A is 8.00% (= $[26 - 25]/25 + 1/25$). Exhibit 7.7 summarizes the relationship between the required return for each stock based on its systematic risk as computed earlier, and its estimated return. This difference between estimated return and expected return is sometimes referred to as a stock's expected alpha or its excess return. This alpha can be positive (the stock is undervalued) or negative (the stock is overvalued). If the alpha is zero, the stock is on the SML and is properly valued in line with its systematic risk.

EXHIBIT 7.6	Price, Dividend, and Return Estimates			
Stock	Current Price (P_t)	Expected Price (P_{t+1})	Expected Dividend (D_{t+1})	Estimated Future Rate of Return (Percent)
A	25	26	1.00	8.00%
B	40	42	0.50	6.25
C	33	37	1.00	15.15
D	64	66	1.10	4.84
E	50	53	—	6.00

EXHIBIT 7.7		Comparison of Required Return to Estimated Return (RFR 5%)			
Stock	Beta	Required Return $E(R_i)$	Estimated Return	Estimated Return Minus $E(R_i)$	Evaluation
A	0.70	7.80	8.00	0.20	Properly valued
B	1.00	9.00	6.25	−2.75	Overvalued
C	1.15	9.60	15.15	5.55	Undervalued
D	1.40	10.60	4.84	−5.76	Overvalued
E	−0.30	3.80	6.00	2.20	Undervalued

Plotting these estimated returns and stock betas on the SML gives Exhibit 7.8. Stock A is almost exactly on the line, so it is considered properly valued because its estimated return is almost equal to its required return. Stocks B and D are considered overvalued because their estimated returns during the coming period are substantially less than what an investor should expect for the risk involved. As a result, they plot below the SML. In contrast, Stocks C and E are expected to provide returns greater than we would require based on their systematic risk. Therefore, both stocks plot above the SML, indicating that they are undervalued.

If you trusted these analysts' forecasts, you would take no action regarding Stock A, but you would buy Stocks C and E and sell Stocks B and D. You might even sell Stocks B and D short, if you favoured such aggressive tactics.

Calculating Systematic Risk There are two ways that a stock's beta can be calculated in practice. First, given our conceptual discussion of the CAPM, a beta coefficient for Security i can be calculated directly from the following formula:

$$\text{7.5} \qquad \beta_i = \left(\frac{\sigma_i}{\sigma_M}\right)(r_{iM}) = \frac{Cov\,(R_i, R_M)}{\sigma_M^2}$$

where, in addition to the terms defined earlier, σ_M^2 is the return variance for the market portfolio and $Cov(R_i'\ R_M)$ is the covariance between returns to the Security i and the market.

Exhibit 7.8	Plot of Estimated Returns on SML Graph

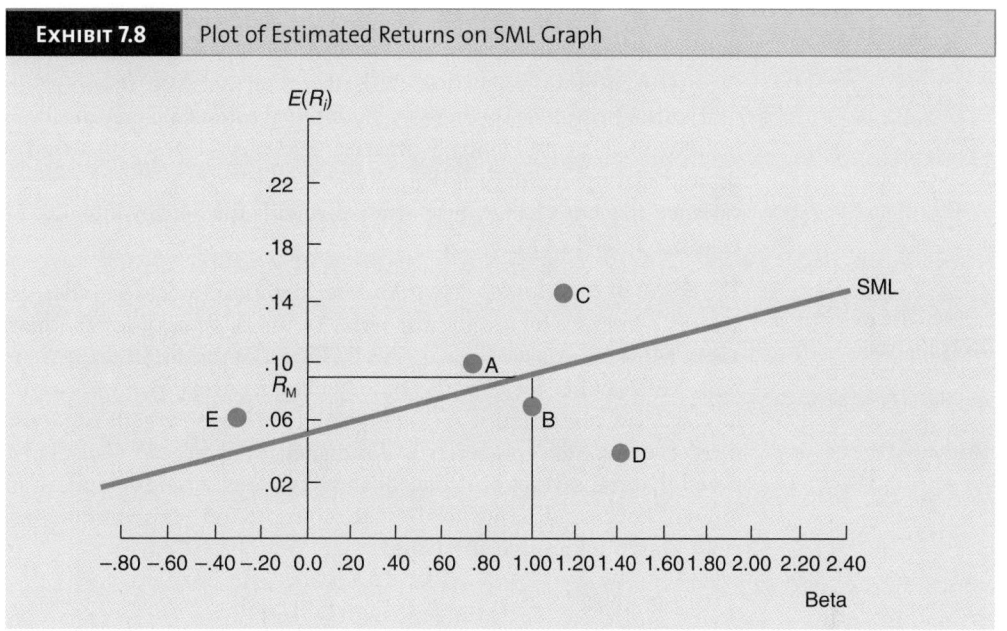

Alternatively, security betas can also be estimated as the slope coefficient in a regression equation between the returns to the security (R_{it}) over time and the returns (R_{Mt}) to the market portfolio:

<table>
<tr><td>7.6</td><td>$$R_{it} = a_i + \beta_i(R_{Mt}) + e_{it}$$</td></tr>
</table>

where a_i is the intercept of the regression and e_{it} is the random error term that accounts for the fact that not all of Security i's risk is systematically related to the market. Equation 7.6 is known as the security's **characteristic line** with the market portfolio.

Equations 7.5 and 7.6 will produce the same estimate of β_i for any given sample of security and market portfolio returns. However, the regression-based method in Equation 7.6 is often preferred because it is a formal estimation process, meaning that the statistical reliability of the estimate can be assessed (i.e., a t-statistic on the β_i estimate can be evaluated).

The Impact of the Time Interval In practice, the number of observations and the time interval used in the regression vary widely. For example, Morningstar derives characteristic lines for common stocks using monthly returns for the most recent five-year period (60 observations). Reuters Analytics calculates stock betas using daily returns over the prior two years (504 observations). Bloomberg uses two years of weekly returns (104 observations) in its basic calculations, although its system allows the user to select daily, weekly, monthly, quarterly, or annual returns over other time horizons. Because there is no theoretically correct time interval for this estimation, we must make a trade-off between enough observations to eliminate the impact of random rates of return and an excessive length of time, such as 15 or 20 years, over which the subject company may have changed dramatically. Remember that what you really want is the *expected* systematic risk for the potential investment. In this process, you are analyzing historical data to help you derive a reasonable estimate of the asset's future level of systematic risk.

Reilly and Wright (1988) analyzed the differential effects of return computation, market index, and the time interval and showed that the major cause of the differences in beta was the use of monthly versus weekly return intervals. Also, the interval effect depended on the sizes of the firms. The shorter weekly interval caused a larger beta for large firms and a smaller beta for small firms. Handa, Kothari, and Wasley (1989) concurred with this conclusion and showed that the reason was that an asset's covariance with the market and the market's return variance did not change proportionally with the return interval. They also confirmed that firm size influenced the effect.

Canadian company's beta and financials can be found at FPinfomart at http://www.fpinfomart.ca, and also at the *Financial Times* at http://www.FT.Com.

The Effect of the Market Proxy Another significant decision when computing an asset's characteristic line is which indicator series to use as a proxy for the market portfolio of all risky assets. Most investigators use the S&P/TSX Composite Index as a proxy for the market portfolio, because the stocks in this index encompass a large proportion of the total market value of Canadian stocks and it is a value-weighted series, which is consistent with the theoretical market series. Still, this series is dominated by large-cap Canadian stocks. Previously, it was noted that the market portfolio of all risky assets should include Canadian stocks and bonds, foreign stocks and bonds, real estate, coins, stamps, art, antiques, and any other marketable risky asset from around the world.

7.3   Relaxing the Assumptions

Earlier in the chapter, several assumptions were set forth related to the CAPM. In this section, we discuss the impact on the capital market line (CML) and the security market line (SML) when we relax several of these assumptions.

7.3.1   DIFFERENTIAL BORROWING AND LENDING RATES

One of the first assumptions of the CAPM was that investors could borrow and lend any amount of money at the risk-free rate. It is reasonable to assume that investors can *lend* unlimited amounts at the risk-free rate by buying government securities (e.g., T-bills). In contrast, it is quite unlikely that investors can *borrow* unlimited amounts at the T-bill rate. For example, when T-bills are yielding 4%, most individuals would have to pay about 6% or 7% to borrow at a bank.

Because of this differential, there will be two different lines going to the Markowitz efficient frontier, as shown in Exhibit 7.9. The segment *RFR-F* indicates the investment opportunities available when an investor combines risk-free assets (i.e., lending at the *RFR*) and Portfolio F on the Markowitz efficient frontier. It is not possible to extend this line any further if you are unable to borrow at this risk-free rate to purchase more units of Portfolio F. If you can borrow at R_b, the point of tangency from this rate would be on the curve at Portfolio K. This indicates that you could borrow at R_b and use the proceeds to invest in Portfolio K to extend the CML along the line segment K-G. Therefore, the CML is made up of *RFR-F-K-G*; that is, a line segment (*RFR-F*), a curve segment (F-K), and another line segment (K-G). As noted by Brennan (1969), this implies that you can either lend or borrow, but the borrowing portfolios are not as profitable as when it was assumed that you could borrow at the *RFR*. In this instance, because your cost to borrow is higher than the *RFR*, your net return is less. That is, the slope of the borrowing line (K-G) is below that for *RFR-F*.

7.3.2   ZERO-BETA MODEL

If the market portfolio (M) is mean-variance efficient (i.e., it has the lowest risk for a given level of return among the attainable set of portfolios), an alternative model, derived by

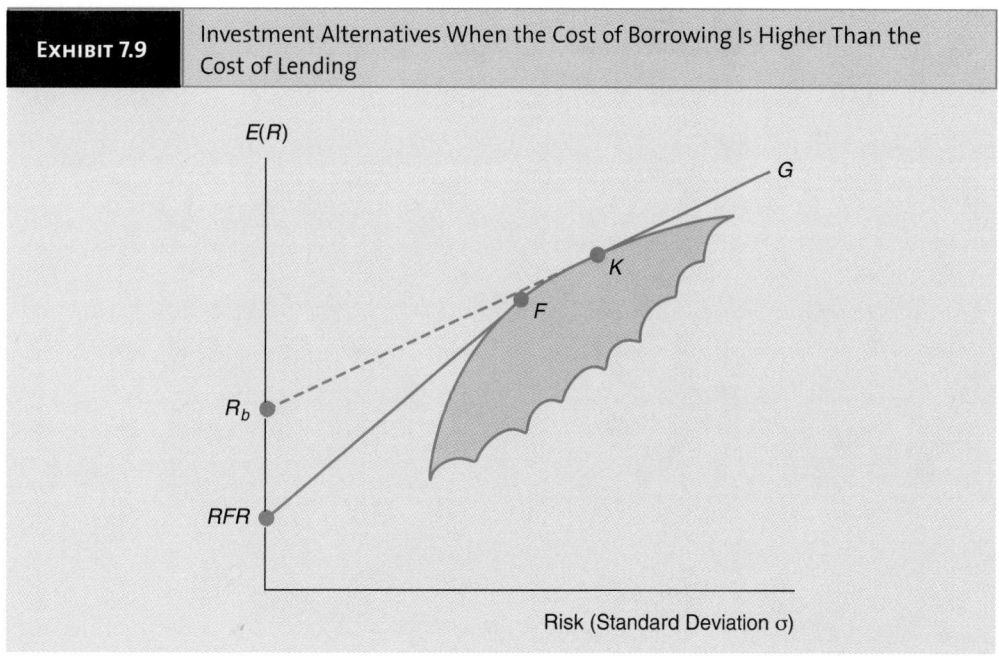

EXHIBIT 7.9 Investment Alternatives When the Cost of Borrowing Is Higher Than the Cost of Lending

Black (1972), does not require a risk-free asset. Within the set of feasible alternative portfolios, several exist where the returns are completely uncorrelated with the market portfolio; the beta of these portfolios with the market portfolio is zero. Among the several zero-beta portfolios, you would select the one with minimum variance. Although this portfolio does not have any systematic risk, it does have some unsystematic risk. The availability of this zero-beta portfolio will not affect the CML, but it will allow construction of a linear SML, as shown in Exhibit 7.10. The combinations of this zero-beta portfolio and the market portfolio will be a linear relationship in return and risk because the covariance between the zero-beta portfolio (R_z) and the market portfolio is similar to what it was with the risk-free asset. Assuming the return for the zero-beta portfolio is greater than that for a risk-free asset, the slope of the line through the market portfolio would not be as steep; that is, the market risk premium would be smaller. The equation for this zero-beta CAPM line would be:

7.7
$$E(R_i) = E(R_z) + b_i[E(R_M) - E(R_z)]$$

Obviously, the risk premiums for individual assets would be a function of the beta for the individual security and the market risk premium:

$$[E(R_m) - E(R_z)]$$

Several studies have specifically tested this model with its higher intercept and flatter slope and had conflicting results. Specifically, studies by Gibbons (1982) and Shanken (1985b) rejected the model, while a study by Stambaugh (1982) supported the zero-beta CAPM.

EXHIBIT 7.10	Security Market Line with a Zero-Beta Portfolio

7.3.3 TRANSACTION COSTS

The CAPM assumes there are no transaction costs, so investors will buy or sell mispriced securities until they plot on the SML. If there are transaction costs, investors will not correct all mispricing because in some instances the cost of buying or selling will be greater than any potential excess return. Therefore, securities will plot very close to the SML, but not exactly on it. Thus, the SML will be a band of securities, as shown in Exhibit 7.11, rather than a single line. Obviously, the width of the band is a function of the amount of the transaction costs. In a world with a large proportion of trading by institutions at pennies per share and with discount brokers available for individual investors, the band should be quite narrow.

Dimson (1979) considered how transaction costs affect the extent of diversification by investors. Recall earlier, we discussed the relationship between the number of stocks in a portfolio and the portfolio variance. Initially, the variance declined rapidly, approaching about 90% of complete diversification with around 20 securities. Thus an important question is, "How many securities must be added to derive the last 10%?" Because of transaction costs, Brennan and Subramanyam (1996) show that at some point the additional cost of diversification would exceed its benefit, especially when considering the costs of monitoring and analyzing the added securities. Degennaro and Robotti (2007) demonstrate that transaction costs can reduce the slope of the CML.

7.3.4 HETEROGENEOUS EXPECTATIONS AND PLANNING PERIODS

If all investors had different expectations about risk and return, each would have a unique CML or SML, and the composite graph would be a set (band) of lines with a breadth determined by the divergence of expectations. If all investors had similar information and background, the band would be reasonably narrow.

The impact of *planning periods* is similar. Recall that the CAPM is a one-period model, corresponding to the planning period for the individual investor. Thus, if you are using a

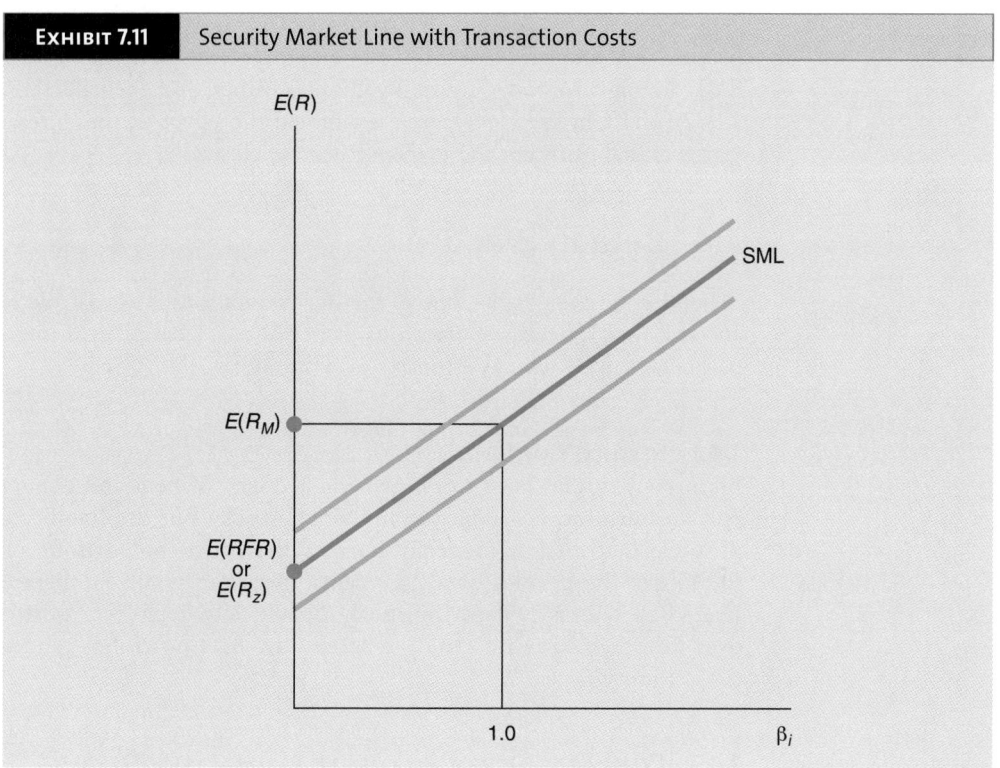

EXHIBIT 7.11 Security Market Line with Transaction Costs

one-year planning period, your CML and SML could differ from someone with a one-month planning period.

7.3.5 TAXES

The expected returns in the CAPM are pretax returns. In fact, the actual returns for most investors are affected as follows:

$$
7.8 \qquad E(Ri(AT)) = \frac{(P_e - P_b) \times (1 - T_{cg}) + (Div) \times (1 - T_i)}{P_b}
$$

where:

$R_i(AT)$ = after-tax rate of return
P_e = ending price
P_b = beginning price
T_{cg} = tax on capital gain or loss
Div = dividend paid during period
T_i = tax on ordinary income

Clearly, tax rates differ between individuals and institutions. For institutions that do not pay taxes, the original pretax model is correctly specified—that is, T_{cg} and T_i take on values of zero. As noted by Black and Scholes (1979) and Litzenberger and Ramaswamy (1979), because investors have heavy tax burdens, this could cause major differences in the CML and SML among investors. Studies by Elton, Gruber, and Rentzler (1983); Miller and Scholes (1982); and Christie (1990) have examined the effect of the differential taxes on dividends versus capital gains but the evidence is inconclusive.

7.4 Beta in Practice

When testing the CAPM, one of the major questions is how stable is the measure of systematic risk (beta). Because beta is our principal risk measure, it is important to know whether past betas can be used as estimates of future betas.

7.4.1 STABILITY OF BETA

Numerous studies have examined the stability of beta and generally concluded that the risk measure was *not* stable for individual stocks, but the stability of the beta for *portfolios* of stocks increased dramatically. Further, the larger the portfolio (e.g., over 50 stocks) and the longer the period (over 26 weeks), the more stable the beta estimate. Also, the betas tended to regress toward the mean. Specifically, high-beta portfolios tended to decline over time toward unity (1.00), whereas low-beta portfolios tended to increase over time toward unity.

Estimate of U.S. company betas may be found at Google Finance by entering the ticker symbol at http://www.google.com/finance, or at Yahoo Finance by entering ticker symbol at http://finance.yahoo.com/ and link to Key Statistics.

7.4.2 COMPARABILITY OF PUBLISHED ESTIMATES OF BETA

In contrast to deriving your own estimate of beta for a stock, you may want to use a published source for speed or convenience, such as Merrill Lynch's *Security Risk Evaluation Report* (published monthly) and the weekly *Value Line Investment Survey*. Both services use the following market model equation:

$$(R_{i,t}) = RFR + \beta_i R_{m,t} + E_t$$

Notably, they differ in the data used. Specifically, Merrill Lynch uses *60 monthly observations* and the S&P 500 as the market proxy, whereas the *Value Line* estimates beta using *260 weekly observations* and the NYSE composite series as the market proxy. They both use an adjustment process because of the regression tendencies.

As noted earlier, Statman (1987) documented a difference between the betas for the two services. Subsequently, Reilly and Wright (1988) showed that the reason for the difference was due to the return interval used (weekly vs. monthly) by the two services and demonstrated that market value also made a difference. Handa, Kothari, and Wasley (1989) concurred with the differences in betas and showed that the specific reason the return interval was the cause was that an asset's covariance with the market and the market's variance did not change proportionally with the return's interval. They also confirmed that size impacted the effect. Exhibit 7.12 is a sample of the betas of selected Canadian companies.

EXHIBIT 7.12	Beta of Canadian Companies		
Company	**Ticker**	**60-Month Beta**	**Industry**
Royal Bank	RY	0.53	Financial
Bank of Montreal	BMO	0.26	Financial
Canadian Natural Resources	CNQ	2.35	Energy
Husky Energy	HSE	1.54	Energy
Encana	ECA	1.63	Energy
TransCanada	TRP	0.35	Pipeline
TransAlta	TA	0.52	Power
Barrick Gold	ABX	0.71	Gold
Fording Canadian Coal Trust	FDG	1.22	Coal
Bombardier	BBD	1.41	Aerospace
Nortel Networks	NT	1.07	Communications
Research In Motion	RIM	1.51	Communications
Potash Corp. of Sask.	POT	0.99	Fertilizer
West Fraser Timber	WFT	0.49	Forest Products
Shoppers Drug Mart	SC	0.55	Drug Retail

Source: FPinformart (http://www.fpinfomart.ca) based on financials as of August 22, 2008.

7.5 Arbitrage Pricing Theory (APT)

7.5.1 FROM CAPM TO APT

So far we have highlighted many of the ways in which the CAPM has contributed to the investment management field. In many respects, the CAPM has been one of the most useful—and frequently used—financial economic theories ever developed. However, many of the empirical studies cited point out some of the deficiencies in the model as an explanation of the link between risk and return. For example, tests of the CAPM indicated that the beta coefficients for individual securities were not stable but that portfolio betas generally were. There was mixed support for a positive linear relationship between rates of return and systematic risk for portfolios, with some recent evidence indicating the need to consider additional risk variables or a need for different risk proxies. In addition, several papers criticized the tests of the model and its usefulness in portfolio evaluation because of its dependence on a market portfolio of risky assets that is not currently available.

One major challenge to the CAPM was the set of results suggesting that it is possible to use knowledge of certain firm or security characteristics to develop profitable trading strategies, even after adjusting for investment risk as measured by beta. Banz (1981) showed that portfolios of stocks with low market capitalizations (i.e., "small" stocks) outperformed "large" stock portfolios on a risk-adjusted basis, and Basu (1977) documented that stocks with low price-earnings (P/E) ratios similarly outperformed high P/E stocks. More recent work by Fama and French (1992) also demonstrates that "value" stocks (i.e., those with high book-to-market value ratios) tend to produce larger risk-adjusted returns than "growth" stocks (i.e., those with low book-to-market ratios). In an efficient market, these return differentials should not occur, meaning that either: (1) markets are not particularly efficient for extended periods of time (i.e., investors have been ignoring profitable investment opportunities for decades), or (2) market prices are efficient but there is something wrong with the way the single-factor models such as the CAPM measure risk.

Given the implausibility of the first possibility, financial economists began to consider the implications of the second. In the early 1970s the academic community searched for an alternative asset pricing theory to the CAPM that was reasonably intuitive, required only limited assumptions, and allowed for multiple dimensions of investment risk. The result was the **arbitrage pricing theory (APT)**, which was developed by Ross (1976, 1977) in the mid-1970s and has three major assumptions:

1. Capital markets are perfectly competitive.
2. Investors always prefer more wealth to less wealth with certainty.
3. The stochastic process generating asset returns can be expressed as a linear function of a set of K risk factors (or indexes), and all unsystematic risk is diversified away.

Equally important, some major assumptions used in the development of the CAPM are *not* required: (1) Investors possess quadratic utility functions, (2) normally distributed security returns, and (3) a market portfolio that contains all risky assets and is mean-variance efficient. Obviously, if such a model is simpler and can also explain differential security prices, it will be considered a superior theory to the CAPM.

Prior to discussing the empirical tests of the APT, we provide a brief review of the model basics. The theory assumes that the stochastic process generating asset returns can be represented as a K factor model of the form:

| 7.9 | $$R_i = E(R_i) + b_{i1}\delta_1 + b_{i2}\delta_2 + \ldots + b_{ik}\delta_k + \varepsilon_i \text{ for } i = 1 \text{ to } n$$ |

where:

$\quad R_i$ = the actual return on asset i during a specified time period, $i = 1, 2, 3, \ldots n$
$E(R_i)$ = the expected return for asset i if all the risk factors have zero changes
$\quad b_{ij}$ = the reaction in asset i's returns to movements in a common risk factor j
$\quad \delta_K$ = a set of common factors or indexes with a zero mean that influences the returns on all assets
$\quad \varepsilon_i$ = a unique effect on asset i's return (i.e., a random error term that, by assumption, is completely diversifiable in large portfolios and has a mean of zero)
$\quad n$ = number of assets

Two terms require elaboration: δ_k and b_{ij}. As indicated, δ terms are the multiple risk factors expected to impact on *all* assets returns. Examples of these factors might include inflation, growth in gross domestic product (GDP), major political upheavals, or changes in interest rates. The APT contends that there are many such factors that affect returns, in contrast to the CAPM, where the only relevant risk to measure is the covariance of the asset with the market portfolio (i.e., the asset's beta).

Given these common factors, the b_{ij} terms determine how each asset reacts to the jth particular common factor. Although all assets may be affected by growth in GDP, the impact or reaction to a factor will differ. For example, cyclical firms stock will have larger b_{ij} terms for the "growth in GDP" factor than will non-cyclical firms, such as grocery store chains. Likewise, all stocks are affected by changes in interest rates; however, some experience larger impacts. An interest-sensitive stock might have a b_j interest of 2.0 or more, whereas a stock that is relatively insensitive to interest rates have a b_j of 0.5. Other examples of common factors include changes in unemployment rates, exchange rates, and yield curve shifts. Note, however, *the factors are not identified* when we apply the theory. You will see this, when we discuss the empirical studies of the APT; the investigators will claim that they found three, four, or five factors that affect security returns, but *they will give no indication of what these factors represent.*

Similar to the CAPM model, the APT assumes that the unique effects (ε_i) are independent and will be diversified away in a large portfolio. The APT requires that in equilibrium the return on a zero-investment, zero-systematic-risk portfolio is zero when the unique effects are fully diversified. This assumption (and some theoretical manipulation using linear algebra) implies that the expected return on any asset i (i.e., $E(R_i)$), can be expressed as:

$$E(R_i) = \lambda_0 + \lambda_1 b_{i1} + \lambda_2 b_{i2} + \ldots + \lambda_k b_{ik} \text{ (APT)}$$

where:
λ_0 = the expected return on an asset with zero systematic risk
λ_j = the risk premium related to the jth common risk factor
b_{ij} = the pricing relationship between the risk premium and the asset; that is, how responsive asset i is to the jth common factor. (These are called factor betas or factor loadings.)

This equation represents the fundamental result of the APT. It is useful to compare the form of the APT's specification of the expected return-risk relationship with that of the CAPM from Chapter 6.

$$E(R_i) = RFR + \beta_i[E(R_M) - RFR] \text{ (CAPM)}$$

Exhibit 7.13 contrasts the relevant features of the two models. It should be clear that the ultimate difference between these two lies in the way systematic investment risk is defined: a single, market-wide risk factor for the CAPM versus a few (or several) factors in the APT that capture the salient nuances of that market-wide risk. However, both specify linear models based on the common belief that investors are compensated for performing two functions: committing capital and bearing risk. Finally, notice that the APT equation suggests a relationship that is analogous to the security market line associated with the CAPM. However, instead of a line connecting risk and expected return, the APT implies a *security market plane* with $(K + 1)$ dimensions—K risk factors and one additional dimension for the security's expected return. Exhibit 7.14 illustrates this relationship for two risk factors (i.e., $K = 2$).

7.5.2 Using the APT

As noted earlier, the primary challenge with using the APT in security valuation is identifying the risk factors. We will address the complexities of this issue later, and begin by illustrating how the model works by assuming that there are only two common factors: one related to unexpected changes in the level of inflation and another related to unanticipated changes in the real level of GDP. If the risk premium related to GDP sensitivity is 0.03 and

EXHIBIT 7.13	Comparing the Capital Asset Pricing Model (CAPM) and the Arbitrage Pricing Theory (APT)	
	CAPM	**APT**
Form of Equation	Linear	Linear
Number of Risk Factors	1	$K\,(\geq 1)$
Factor Risk Premium	$[E(R_M) - RFR]$	$\{\lambda_j\}$
Factor Risk Sensitivity	β_i	$\{b_{ij}\}$
"Zero-Beta" Return	RFR	λ_0

EXHIBIT 7.14	The Relationship between Expected Return and Two Common Risk Factors ($\lambda_0 = 4\%$, $\lambda_1 = 2\%$, $\lambda_2 = 3\%$)

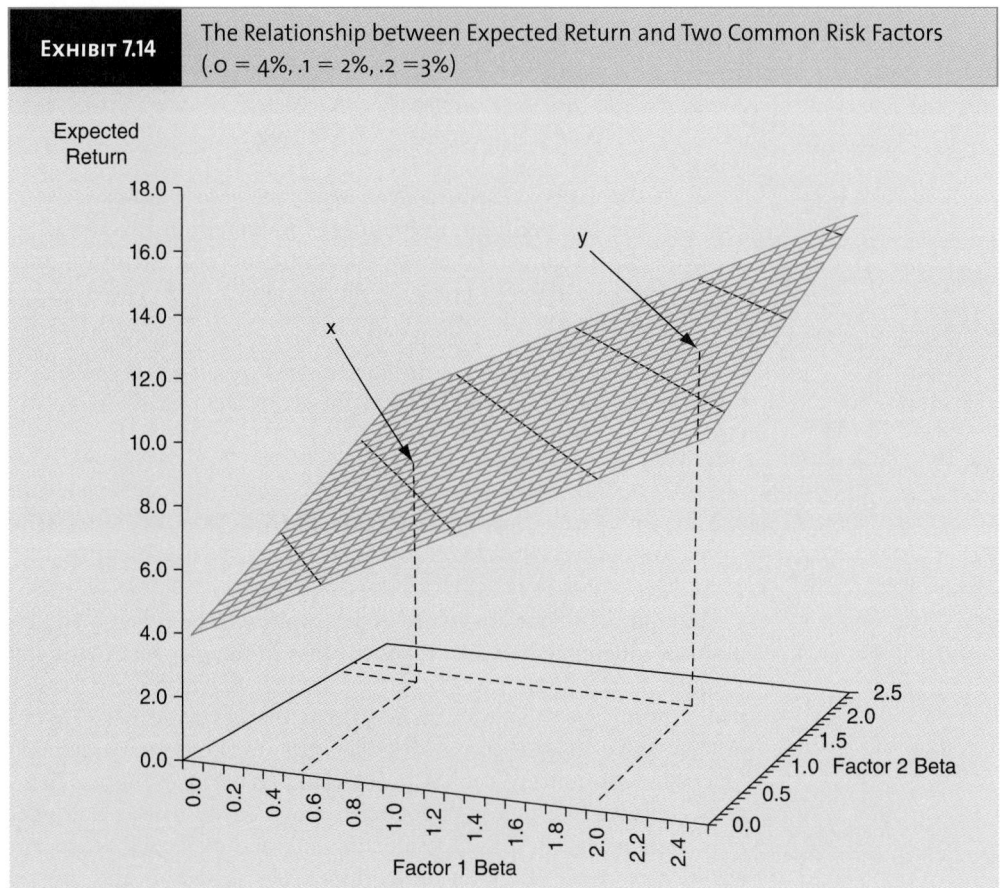

a stock that is sensitive to GDP has a b_j (where j represents the GDP factor) of 1.5, this means that this factor would cause the stock's expected return to increase by 4.5% (= 1.5 × 0.03).

To develop this notion further, consider the following example of two stocks and a two-factor model. First, consider these risk factor definitions and sensitivities:

δ_1 = unanticipated changes in the rate of inflation. The risk premium related to this factor is 2% for every 1% change in the rate ($\lambda_1 = 0.02$)

δ_2 = unexpected changes in the growth rate of real GDP. The average risk premium related to this factor is 3% for every 1% change in the rate of growth (λ_2 = 0.03)

λ_0 = the rate of return on a zero-systematic risk asset (i.e., zero beta) is 4% (λ_0 = 0.04)

Assume also that there are two assets (x and y) that have the following sensitivities to these common risk factors:

b_{x1} = the response of asset x to changes in the inflation factor is 0.50 (b_{x1} = 0.50)
b_{x2} = the response of asset x to changes in the GDP factor is 1.50 (b_{x2} = 1.50)
b_{y1} = the response of asset y to changes in the inflation factor is 2.00 (b_{y1} = 2.00)
b_{y2} = the response of asset y to changes in the GDP factor is 1.75 (b_{y2} = 1.75)

These factor sensitivities can be interpreted in much the same way as beta in the CAPM; that is, the higher the level of b_{ij}, the greater the sensitivity of asset i to changes in the jth risk factor. Thus, the response coefficients listed indicate that asset y is higher risk than asset x, and, therefore, its expected return should be greater. The overall expected return equation will be:

$$E(R_i) = \lambda_0 + \lambda_1 b_{i1} + \lambda_2 b_{i2}$$
$$= 0.04 + (0.02)b_{i1} + (0.03)b_{i2}$$

Therefore, for assets x and y:

$$E(R_x) = 0.04 + (0.02)(0.50) + (0.03)(1.50)$$
$$= 0.0950, \text{ or } 9.50\%$$

and

$$E(R_y) = 0.04 + (0.02)(2.00) + (0.03)(1.75)$$
$$= 0.1325, \text{ or } 13.25\%$$

The positions of the factor loadings and expected returns for these two assets are shown in Exhibit 7.14. If the prices of the two assets do not reflect these expected returns, we would expect investors to arbitrage whereby they would sell overpriced assets short and use the proceeds to purchase the underpriced assets until the relevant prices were corrected. Given these linear relationships, it should be possible to find an asset or a combination of assets with equal risk to the mispriced asset, yet providing a higher expected return.

7.6 Multifactor Models in Practice

When it comes to putting theory into practice, one advantage of the CAPM framework is that the identity of the single risk factor (i.e., the excess return to the market portfolio) is well specified. The empirical challenge in implementing the CAPM is to accurately estimate the market portfolio, a process that first requires identifying the relevant investment universe.

As we saw in previous sections, this is not a trivial problem as an improperly chosen proxy for the market portfolio (e.g., using the S&P 500 index to represent the market when evaluating a fixed-income portfolio) can lead to erroneous judgments. However, we also saw that once the returns to an acceptable surrogate for the market portfolio are identified (i.e., R_m), the process for estimating the parameters of the CAPM is straightforward and can be accomplished by either of the following regression equations:

1. A security or portfolio's *characteristic line* can be estimated via regression techniques using the *single-index market model:*

$$R_{it} = a_i + b_i R_{mt} + e_t$$

2. Alternatively, this equation can also be estimated in *excess return form* by netting the risk-free rate from the period t returns to security i and the market portfolio:

$$(R_{it} - RFR_t) = \alpha_i + b_i(R_{mt} - RFR_t) + e_{it}$$

In contrast to the CAPM, the primary practical problem associated with implementing the APT is that neither the identity nor the exact number of the underlying risk factors are developed by theory and therefore must be specified in an ad hoc manner. That is, before the APT can be used to value securities or measure performance, the investor must fill in a considerable amount of missing information about the fundamental relationship between risk and expected return.

As discussed earlier, the first attempts to implement a usable form of the APT relied on multivariate statistical techniques, such as principal components analysis and factor analysis, wherein many periods of realized returns for large number of securities are analyzed simultaneously in order to detect recognizable patterns of behaviour. A consistent finding of these studies is that there appear to be as many as three or four "priced" (i.e., statistically significant) factors, although researchers were not able to establish that the same set of factors was generated by different subsets of their sample. Indeed, we also saw that the inability to identify the risk factors is a major limitation to the usefulness of the APT. Jones (2001) and Ludvigson and Ng (2007) provide some recent extensions along these lines.

A different approach to developing an empirical model that captures the essence of the APT relies on the direct specification of the form of the relationship to be estimated. That is, in a multifactor model, the investor chooses the exact number and identity of risk factors in the following equation:

7.10

$$R_{it} = a_i + [b_{i1}F_{1t} + b_{i2}F_{2t} + \ldots + b_{iK}F_{Kt}] + e_{it}$$

where F_{jt} is the period t return to the jth designated risk factor and R_i can be measured as either a nominal or excess return to security i. The advantage of this approach is that the investor knows precisely how many and what things need to be estimated to fit the regression equation. The major disadvantage of a multifactor model is that it is developed with little theoretical guidance as to the true nature of the risk-return relationship. In this sense, developing a useful factor model is as much an art form as it is a theoretical exercise.

A wide variety of empirical factor specifications have been employed in practice. A hallmark of each alternative model developed is that it attempts to identify a set of economic influences that is simultaneously broad enough to capture the major nuances of investment risk but small enough to provide a workable solution to the analyst or investor. Two general approaches have been employed in this factor-identification process. First, risk factors can be viewed as *macroeconomic* in nature; they attempt to capture variations in the underlying reasons an asset's cash flows and investment returns might change over time (e.g., changes in inflation or real GDP growth). On the other hand, risk factors can also be viewed at a R_I level by focusing on relevant characteristics of the securities themselves, such as the size of the firm in question or some of its financial ratios. A few examples representative of each of these approaches are discussed next.

7.6.1 MACROECONOMIC-BASED RISK FACTOR MODELS

One particularly influential model was developed by Chen, Roll, and Ross (1986), who hypothesized that security returns are governed by a set of broad economic influences in the following fashion:

$$\boxed{7.11} \quad R_{it} = a_i + [b_{i1}R_{mt} + b_{i2} + MP_t + b_{i3}DEI_t + b_{i4}UI_t + b_{i5}UPR_t + b_{i6}UTS_t] + e_{it}$$

where:

R_m = the return on a value-weighted index of NYSE-listed stocks
MP = the monthly growth rate in U.S. industrial production
DEI = the change in inflation, measured by the U.S. consumer price index
UI = the difference between actual and expected levels of inflation
UPR = the unanticipated change in the bond credit spread (Baa yield − RFR)
UTS = the unanticipated term structure shift (long-term less short-term RFR)

In estimating this model, the authors used a series of monthly returns for a large collection of securities from the Center for Research in Security Prices (CRSP) database from 1958 to 1984. Exhibit 7.15 shows the factor sensitivities (associated *t*-statistics in parentheses) that they established. Notice two things about these findings. First, the economic significance of the designated risk factors changed dramatically over time. For instance, the inflation factors (DEI and UI) appear to only be relevant during the period 1968 to 1977. Second, the parameter on the stock market proxy is never significant, suggesting that it contributes little to the explanation beyond the information contained in the other macroeconomic risk factors.

EXHIBIT 7.15	Estimating a Multifactor Model with Macroeconomic Risk Factors						
Period	Constant	R_M	MP	DEI	UI	UPR	UTS
1958-1984	10.71	−2.40	11.76	−0.12	−0.80	8.27	−5.91
	(2.76)	(−0.63)	(3.05)	(−1.60)	(−2.38)	(2.97)	(−1.88)
1958-1967	9.53	1.36	12.39	0.01	−0.21	5.20	−0.09
	(1.98)	(0.28)	(1.79)	(0.06)	(−0.42)	(1.82)	(−0.04)
1968-1977	8.58	−5.27	13.47	−0.26	−1.42	12.90	−11.71
	(1.17)	(−0.72)	(2.04)	(−3.24)	(−3.11)	(2.96)	(−2.30)
1978-1984	15.45	−3.68	8.40	−0.12	−0.74	6.06	−5.93
	(1.87)	(−0.49)	(1.43)	(−0.46)	(−0.87)	(0.78)	(−0.64)

Source: Nai-fu Chen, Richard Roll, and Stephen A. Ross, "Economic Forces and the Stock Market," *Journal of Business* 59, no. 3 (April 1986).

Burmeister, Roll, and Ross (1994) analyzed the predictive ability of a model based on a different set of macroeconomic factors. Specifically, they define the following five risk exposures: (1) *confidence risk,* based on unanticipated changes in the willingness of investors to take on investment risk; (2) *time horizon risk,* which is the unanticipated changes in investors' desired time to receive payouts; (3) *inflation risk,* based on a combination of the unexpected components of short-term and long-term inflation rates; (4) *business cycle risk*, which represents unanticipated changes in the level of overall business activity; and (5) *market-timing risk*, defined as the part of the S&P 500 total return that is not explained by the other four macroeconomic factors. Using monthly data through the first quarter of 1992, the authors estimated risk premia (i.e., the market "price" of risk) for these factors:

Risk Factor	Risk Premium
Confidence	2.59%
Time horizon	−0.66
Inflation	−4.32
Business cycle	1.49
Market timing	3.61

They also compared the factor sensitivities for several different individual stocks and stock portfolios. Panel A and Panel B of Exhibit 7.16 show these factor beta estimates for Reebok International Ltd. versus the S&P 500 index and for a portfolio of small-cap firms versus a portfolio of large-cap firms. Also included in these graphs is the security's or portfolio's exposure to the BIRR composite risk index, which is designed to indicate which position has the most overall systematic risk. These comparisons highlight how a multifactor model can help investors distinguish the nature of the risk they are assuming when they hold with a particular position. For instance, notice that Reebok has greater exposures to all sources of risk than the S&P 500, with the incremental difference in the business–cycle exposure being particularly dramatic. Additionally, smaller firms are more exposed to business cycle and confidence risk than larger firms but less exposed to horizon risk.

7.6.2 Microeconomic-Based Risk Factor Models

In contrast to macroeconomic-based explanations of the risk and expected return relationship, it is also possible to specify risk in microeconomic terms using proxy variables that concentrate on certain characteristics of the underlying sample of securities. Typical of this characteristic-based approach to forming a multifactor model is the work of Fama and French (1993), who use the following functional form:

$$7.12 \qquad (R_{it} - RFR_t) = \alpha_i + b_{i1} (R_{mt} - RFR_t) + b_{i2} SMB_t + b_{i3} HML_t + e_{it}$$

where, in addition to the excess return on a stock market portfolio, two other risk factor proxies are defined:

SMB (i.e., small minus big) is the return to a portfolio of small capitalization stocks less the return to a portfolio of large capitalization stocks

HML (i.e., high minus low) is the return to a portfolio of stocks with high ratios of book-to-market values less the return to a portfolio of low book-to-market value stocks

In this specification, *SMB* is designed to capture risk elements associated with firm size while *HML* is intended to distinguish risk differentials associated with "growth" (i.e., low

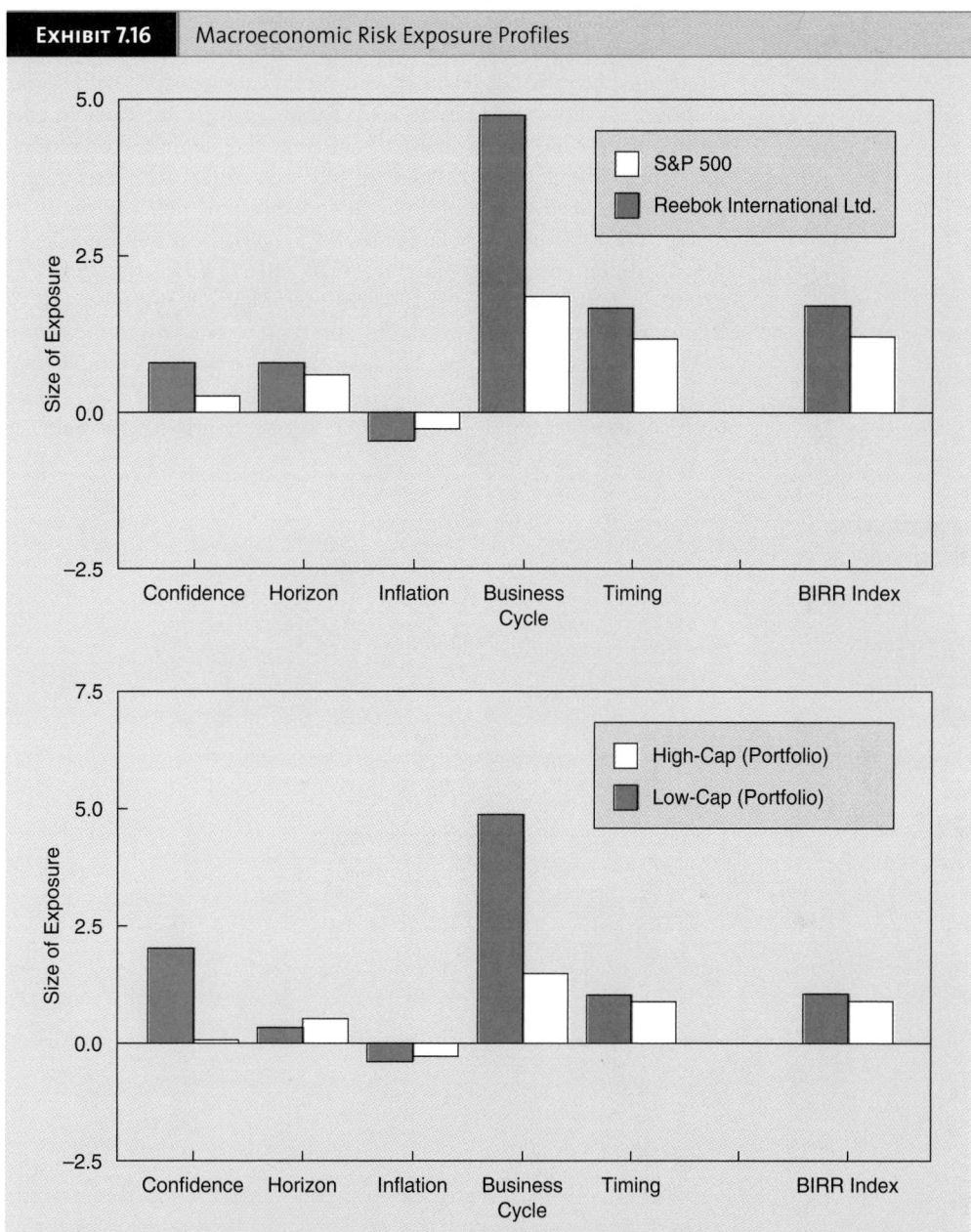

EXHIBIT 7.16 Macroeconomic Risk Exposure Profiles

Source: Copyright 1994, The Research Foundation of the Institute of Chartered Financial Analysts. Reproduced and republished from *A Practitioner's Guide to Arbitrage Pricing Theory* with permission from The Research Foundation of the Association for Investment Management and Research. All Rights Reserved.

Copyright 1994, CFA Institute. Reproduced and republished from A Practitioner's Guide to Factor Models with permission from CFA Institute. All rights reserved.

book-to-market ratio) and "value" (i.e., high book-to-market) firms. Recall, these two dimensions of a security or portfolio have consistently been shown to matter when evaluating investment performance. Also, notice that without *SMB* and *HML,* this model reduces to the excess returns form of the single-index market model.

Fama and French examined the behaviour of a broad sample of stocks grouped into quintile portfolios by their P/E ratios on a yearly basis from July 1963 to December 1991. The results for both the single-index and multifactor versions of the model for the two extreme quintiles are shown in Exhibit 7.17 (*t*-statistics for the estimated coefficients in parentheses). Notice that while the estimated beta from the single-factor model indicates that there are substantial differences between low and high P/E stocks (i.e., 0.94 vs. 1.10), this gap is dramatically reduced in the multifactor specification (i.e., 1.03 vs. 0.99). This suggests that the market portfolio in a one-factor model serves as a proxy for some, but not all, of the additional risk dimensions provided by *SMB* and *HML*. Further, low P/E stocks tend to be positively correlated with the small-firm premium, but the reverse is not reliably true for high P/E stocks. Finally, low P/E stocks also tend to have high book-to-market ratios while high P/E stocks tend to have low book-to-market ratios (i.e., estimated *HML* parameters of 0.67 and 0.50, respectively). Not surprisingly, relative levels of P/E and book-to-market ratios are both commonly employed in practice to classify growth and value stocks.

EXHIBIT 7.17 Estimating a Multifactor Model with Characteristic-Based Risk Factors

Portfolio	Constant	Market (1) Single-Index Model	SMB	HML	R²
Lowest P/E	0.46 (3.69)	0.94 (34.73)	—	—	0.78
Highest P/E	−0.20 (−2.35)	1.10 (57.42)	—	—	0.91
		(2) Multifactor Model			
Lowest P/E	0.08 (1.01)	1.03 (51.56)	0.24 (8.34)	0.67 (19.62)	0.91
Highest P/E	0.04 (0.70)	0.99 (66.78)	−0.01 (−0.55)	−0.50 (−19.73)	0.96

Source: Reprinted from Eugene F. Fama and Kenneth R. French, "Common Risk Factors in the Returns on Stocks and Bonds," *Journal of Financial Economics* 33, no. 1 (January 1993), with permission from Elsevier Science.

Carhart (1997) directly extends the Fama-French three-factor model by including a fourth common risk factor that accounts for the tendency for firms with positive (negative) past returns to produce positive (negative) future returns. He calls this additional risk dimension a *price momentum factor* and estimates it by taking the average return to a set of stocks with the best performance over the prior year minus the average return to stocks with the worst returns.

In this fashion, Carhart defines the momentum factor—labelled here as *MOM*—in a fashion similar to *SMB* and *HML*. Formally, the model he proposes is:

$$7.13 \quad (R_{it} - RFR_t) = \alpha_i + b_{i1}(R_{mt} - RFR_t) + b_{i2}SMB_t + b_{i3}HML_t + b_{i4}MOM_t + e_{it}$$

He demonstrates that the typical factor sensitivity (i.e., factor beta) for the momentum variable is positive and its inclusion into the Fama-French model increases explanatory power by as much as 15%. Equation 7.13 is often referred to as the four-factor Fama-French model.

7.6.3 EXTENSIONS OF CHARACTERISTIC-BASED RISK FACTOR MODELS

Another type of security characteristic-based method for defining systematic risk exposures involves the use of index portfolios (e.g., S&P 500, Wilshire 5000) as common factors. Intuitively, if the indexes themselves are designed to emphasize certain investment characteristics, they can act as proxies for the underlying exposure that determines returns to that characteristic. Examples of this include the Russell 1000 Growth index, which emphasizes large-cap stocks with low book-to-market ratios, or the EAFE (Europe, Australia, and the Far East) index that selects a variety of companies domiciled outside the United States. Typical of these index-based factor models is the work of Elton, Gruber, and Blake (1996), who rely on four indexes: the S&P 500, the Lehman Brothers aggregate bond index, the Prudential Bache index of the difference between large- and small-cap stocks, and the Prudential Bache index of the difference between value and growth stocks. Ferson and Schadt (1996) have developed an interesting variation on this approach, which, in addition to using stock and bond indexes as risk factors, also includes other "public information" variables, such as the shape of the yield curve and dividend payouts.

Summary

1. Capital market theory expanded the concepts introduced by Markowitz portfolio theory by introducing the notion that investors could borrow or lend at the risk-free rate in addition to forming efficient portfolios of risky assets. This insight led to the development of the *capital market line (CML)*, which can be viewed as a new efficient frontier that emanates from the risk-free rate and is tangent to the old Markowitz efficient frontier. The point of tangency is called the market portfolio.

2. The CML's main contribution is the relationship it specifies between the risk and expected return of a well-diversified portfolio. The CML makes it clear that the market portfolio is the single collection of risky assets that maximizes the ratio of expected risk premium to portfolio volatility. The investment prescription of the CML is that investors cannot do better, on average, than when they divide their investment funds between (1) the riskless asset and (2) the market portfolio.

3. The CML is a model of the risk-return trade-off that only applies to portfolios that have diversified away all unsystematic risk. The *capital asset pricing model (CAPM)* generalizes this relationship to individual securities as well as entire portfolios. To make this extension, the CAPM redefines the relevant measure of risk as beta, which is the systematic component of a security's volatility relative to that of the market portfolio.

4. Like the CML, the *security market line (SML)* shows that the relationship between risk and expected return is a straight line with a positive slope. The SML provides investors with a tool for judging whether securities are undervalued or overvalued given their level of systematic (beta) risk.

5. Although the CAPM is an elegant and appealing explanation of the risk and expected return relationship, a number of empirical anomalies—such as the small-firm effect—have caused researchers to seek other answers. Ross subsequently devised an alternative asset pricing model—the APT—that makes fewer assumptions than the CAPM and does not specifically require the designation of a market portfolio. Instead, the APT posits that expected security returns are related in a linear fashion to multiple common risk factors. Unfortunately, the theory does not offer guidance as to how many factors exist or what their identities might be. The results from the empirical tests of the APT have thus far been mixed.

6. Given that the common risk factors are not identified, the APT is difficult to put into practice in a theoretically rigorous fashion. Multifactor models of risk and return attempt to bridge this gap by specifying a set of variables thought to capture the essence of the systematic risk exposures that exist in the capital market. There have been a number of alternative risk factors suggested and tested by researchers.

7. One general approach has been to use macroeconomic variables—such as unexpected inflation, changes in consumer confidence, unanticipated shifts in the yield curve, or unexpected changes in real GDP—as surrogates for the types of exposures that will have an impact on all securities. Once selected, historical data are often employed to determine the risk premium (i.e., market "price") for each common factor. A second approach to proxying for the risk exposures in a multifactor model has focused on the characteristics of the securities themselves. Typical of this sort of microeconomic approach is the work of Fama and French, who posit that three risk factors should be employed: the excess returns to a broad market index, the return difference between portfolios of small- and large-cap stocks, and the return difference between portfolios of value- and growth-oriented stocks.

Key Terms

arbitrage pricing theory (APT), p. 184
beta, p. 172
capital asset pricing model (CAPM), p. 172
capital market line (CML), p. 165
characteristic line, p. 177

completely diversified portfolio, p. 167
estimated rate of return, p. 175
market risk premium, p. 173
risk-free asset, p. 162
risky asset, p. 163

security market line (SML), p. 173
separation theorem, p. 169
systematic risk, p. 167
unsystematic risk, p. 167

Suggested Readings

Black, Fischer. "Capital Market Equilibrium with Restricted Borrowing." *Journal of Business* 45, no. 3 (July 1972): 444–455.

Campbell, John Y., and John Ammer. "What Moves the Stock and Bond Markets? A Variance Decomposition for Long-Term Asset Returns." *Journal of Finance* 48, no. 1, 1993.

Elton, Edwin J., Martin J. Gruber, Stephen J. Brown, and William N. Goetzmann. *Modern Portfolio Theory and Investment Analysis,* 8th ed. New York: Wiley, 2010.

Grinold, Richard C., and Ronald N. Kahn. *Active Portfolio Management,* 2nd ed. New York: McGraw-Hill, 2008.

Kryzanowski, Lawrence, Simon Lalancette, and Minh Chau To. "Performance Attribution Using an APT with Prespecified Macrofactors and TIME-VARYING RISK PREMIA and betas," *Journal of Financial and Quantitative Analysis* 32, no. 2 (June 1997): 205–224.

Lehmann, B. N., and D. M. Modest. "The Empirical Foundations of the Arbitrage Pricing Theory." *Journal of Financial Economics* 21, no. 3 (September 1988).

Otuteye, Eben. "How Economic Forces Explain Canadian Stock Returns." *Canadian Investment Review* 4 (Spring 1991).

Peavy, John, ed. *A Practitioner's Guide to Factor Models.* Charlottesville, VA: Research Foundation of the CFA Institute, 1994.

Sharpe, William F. "Factor Models, CAPMs, and the APT." *Journal of Portfolio Management* 11, no. 1 (Fall 1984).

Sharpe, William F. *Investors and Markets: Portfolio Choices, Asset Prices, and Investment Advice.* Princeton, NJ: Princeton University Press, 2007.

CFA **For Chapter CFA Questions and Problems, please see Appendix A at the end of this text.**

Questions

1. Draw a graph that shows what happens to the Markowitz efficient frontier when you combine a risk-free asset with alternative risky asset portfolios on the Markowitz efficient frontier. Explain why the line from the *RFR* that is tangent to the efficient frontier defines the dominant set of portfolio possibilities.

2. What changes would you expect in the standard deviation for a portfolio of between 4 and 10 stocks, between 10 and 20 stocks, and between 50 and 100 stocks?

3. The capital asset pricing model (CAPM) contends that there is systematic and unsystematic risk for an individual security. Which is the relevant risk variable and why is it relevant? Why is the other risk variable not relevant?

4. What are the similarities and differences between the CML and SML as models of the risk-return trade-off?
5. Draw an ideal SML. Based on the early empirical results, what did the actual risk-return relationship look like relative to the ideal relationship implied by the CAPM?
6. According to the CAPM, what assets are included in the market portfolio, and what are the relative weightings? In empirical studies of the CAPM, what are the typical proxies used for the market portfolio? Assuming that the empirical proxy for the market portfolio is not a good proxy, what factors related to the CAPM will be affected?

7. Some studies related to the efficient market hypothesis generated results that implied additional factors beyond beta should be considered to estimate expected returns. What are these other variables and why should they be considered?
8. Suppose you are considering the purchase of shares in the XYZ mutual fund. As part of your investment analysis, you regress XYZ's monthly returns for the past five years against the three factors specified in the Fama and French models. This procedure generates the following coefficient estimates: market factor = 1.2, **SMB** factor = −0.3, **HML** factor = 1.4. Explain what each of these coefficient values means. What types of stocks is XYZ likely to be holding?

Problems

1. Assume that you expect the economy's rate of inflation to be 3%, giving an *RFR* of 6% and a market return (R_M) of 12%.
   a. Draw the SML under these assumptions.
   b. Subsequently, you expect the rate of inflation to increase from 3% to 6%. What effect would this have on the *RFR* and the R_M? Draw another SML on the graph from Part a.
   c. Draw an SML on the same graph to reflect an *RFR* of 9% and an R_M of 17%. How does this SML differ from that derived in Part b? Explain what has transpired.
2. a. You expect an *RFR* of 10% and the market return (R_M) of 14%. Compute the expected return for the following stocks, and plot them on an SML graph.

Stock	Beta	$E(R_i)$
U	0.85	
N	1.25	
D	−0.20	

   b. You ask a stockbroker what the firm's research department expects for these three stocks. The broker responds with the following information:

Stock	Current Price	Expected Price	Expected Dividend
U	22	24	0.75
N	48	51	2.00
D	37	40	1.25

   Plot your estimated returns on the graph from Part a and indicate what actions you would take with regard to these stocks. Explain your decisions.

3. You are evaluating various investment opportunities currently available and you have calculated expected returns and standard deviations for five different well-diversified portfolios of risky assets:

Portfolio	Expected Return	Standard Deviation
Q	7.8%	10.5%
R	10.0	14.0
S	4.6	5.0
T	11.7	18.5
U	6.2	7.5

   a. For each portfolio, calculate the risk premium per unit of risk that you expect to receive $([E(R) - RFR]/a)$. Assume that the risk-free rate is 3.0%.
   b. Using your computations in Part a, explain which of these five portfolios is most likely to be the market portfolio. Use your calculations to draw the capital market line (CML).
   c. If you are only willing to make an investment with $\sigma = 7.0\%$, is it possible for you to earn a return of 7.0%?
   d. What is the minimum level of risk that would be necessary for an investment to earn 7.0%? What is the composition of the portfolio along the CML that will generate that expected return?
   e. Suppose you are now willing to make an investment with $\sigma = 18.2\%$. What would be the investment proportions in the riskless asset and the market portfolio for this portfolio? What is the expected return for this portfolio?
4. You are an analyst for a large public pension fund and you have been assigned the task of evaluating two different

external portfolio managers (Y and Z). You consider the following historical average return, standard deviation, and CAPM beta estimates for these two managers over the past five years:

Portfolio	Actual Ave. Return	Standard Deviation	Beta
Manager Y	10.20%	12.00%	1.20
Manager Z	8.80	9.90%	0.80

Additionally, your estimate for the risk premium for the market portfolio is 5.00% and the risk-free rate is currently 4.50%.

a. For both Manager Y and Manager Z, calculate the expected return using the CAPM. Express your answers to the nearest basis point (i.e., xx.xx%).
b. Calculate each fund manager's average "alpha" (i.e., actual return minus expected return) over the five-year holding period. Show graphically where these alpha statistics would plot on the security market line (SML).
c. Explain whether you can conclude from the information in Part b if: (i) either manager outperformed the other on a risk-adjusted basis, and (ii) either manager outperformed market expectations in general.

5. Draw the security market line for each of the following conditions:
a. (1) $RFR = 0.08$; $R_M(\text{proxy}) = 0.12$
(2) $R_z = 0.06$; $R_M (\text{true}) = 0.15$
b. Rader Tire has the following results for the last six periods. Calculate and compare the betas using each index.

RATES OF RETURN

Period	Rader Tire (%)	Proxy Specific Index (%)	True General Index (%)
1	29	12	15
2	12	10	13
3	−12	−9	−8
4	17	14	18
5	20	25	28
6	−5	−10	0

c. If the current period return for the market is 12% and for Rader Tire it is 11%, are superior results being obtained for either index beta?

6. Consider the following data for two risk factors (1 and 2) and two securities (J and L):
$\lambda_0 = 0.05$ $b_{J1} = 0.80$
$\lambda_1 = 0.02$ $b_{J2} = 1.40$
$\lambda_2 = 0.04$ $b_{L1} = 1.60$
                $b_{L2} = 2.25$

a. Compute the expected returns for both securities.
b. Suppose that Security J is currently priced at $22.50 while the price of Security L is $15.00. Further, it is expected that both securities will pay a dividend of $0.75 during the coming year. What is the expected price of each security one year from now?

7. You have been assigned the task of estimating the expected returns for three different stocks: QRS, TUV, and WXY. Your preliminary analysis has established the historical risk premiums associated with three risk factors that could potentially be included in your calculations: the excess return on a proxy for the market portfolio (MKT), and two variables capturing general macroeconomic exposures (MACRO1 and MACRO2). These values are: $\lambda_{MKT} = 7.5\%$, $\lambda_{MACRO1} = -0.3\%$, and $\lambda_{MACRO2} = 0.6\%$. You have also estimated the following factor betas (i.e., loadings) for all three stocks with respect to each of these potential risk factors:

FACTOR LOADING

Stock	MKT	MACRO1	MACRO2
QRS	1.24	−0.42	0.00
TUV	0.91	0.54	0.23
WXY	1.03	−0.09	0.00

a. Calculate expected returns for the three stocks using just the MKT risk factor. Assume a risk-free rate of 4.5%.
b. Calculate the expected returns for the three stocks using all three risk factors and the same 4.5% risk-free rate.
c. Discuss the differences between the expected return estimates from the single-factor model and those from the multifactor model. Which estimates are most likely to be more useful in practice?
d. What sort of exposure might MACRO2 represent? Given the estimated factor betas, is it really reasonable to consider it a common (i.e., systematic) risk factor?

8. Consider the following information about two stocks (D and E) and two common risk factors (1 and 2):

Stock	B_{i1}	B_{i2}	$E(R_i)$
D	1.2	3.4	13.1%
E	2.6	2.6	15.4%

a. Assuming that the risk-free rate is 5.0%, calculate the levels of the factor risk premia that are consistent with the reported values for the factor betas and the expected returns for the two stocks.

b. You expect that in one year the prices for Stocks D and E will be $55 and $36, respectively. Also, neither stock is expected to pay a dividend over the next year. What should the price of each stock be today to be consistent with the expected return levels listed at the beginning of the problem?

c. Suppose now that the risk premium for Factor 1 that you calculated in Part a suddenly increases by 0.25% (i.e., from x% to $(x + 0.25)$%, where x is the value established in Part a). What are the new expected returns for Stocks D and E?

d. If the increase in the Factor 1 risk premium in Part c does not cause you to change your opinion about what the stock prices will be in one year, what adjustment will be necessary in the current (i.e., today's) prices?

Analysis and Management of Common Shares

In Parts 1 and 2 we learned about the purpose of investing and the importance of an appropriate asset allocation decision. We also studied the numerous investment instruments available on a global basis and the background regarding the institutional characteristics of the capital markets. In addition, we are now aware of the major developments in investment theory as they relate to efficient capital markets, portfolio theory, capital asset pricing, and multi-factor valuation models. Therefore, at this point we are in a position to consider the theory and practice of estimating the value of various securities, which is the heart of investing and leads to the construction of a portfolio that is consistent with our risk-return objectives. In Part 3, we focus on common stocks, and in Part 4, we deal with bonds.

The analysis and management of common stocks are presented through Chapters 8, 9, and 10. We first present a three-step economy-industry-company approach to stock valuation. This approach begins with a valuation of the aggregate economy and market and the examination of various industries and concludes with the analysis of individual companies and their securities. In Chapter 8, we develop the first two steps, economic and industry analysis, and in Chapter 9, we move on to the third step, company analysis.

The above approach is based on fundamentals of the business and the economic and industry forces that influence the business. Thus, this approach is known as fundamental analysis. Chapter 10 deals with technical analysis, an alternative or supplement to the fundamental approach. Rather than estimating value based on fundamental variables, the technical analyst believes that it is possible to project future stock price movements based on past stock price changes or other stock market data. Various techniques are discussed and demonstrated.

8

Economic and Industry Analysis

After you read this chapter, you should be able to answer the following questions:

1. What are the two major approaches to the investment process?

2. What are the specifics and logic of the top-down (three-step) approach?

3. What are the main variables an investor should look at in conducting economic analysis?

4. What are some of the key aspects that should be covered in a typical industry study?

5. What are the techniques available for conducting industry analysis?

This **investment decision process** is similar to the process we follow when deciding on a corporate investment or when shopping for clothes, a stereo, or a car. In each case, we examine the item and decide how much it is worth to us (its value). If the price equals its estimated value or is less, we would buy it. The same technique applies to securities except that the determination of a security's value is more formal.

We begin our discussion of security valuation by reviewing the **valuation process**. There are two general approaches: (1) the top-down, three-step approach; or (2) the bottom-up, stock valuation, stock-picking approach. Both of these can be implemented by either fundamentalists or technicians. The difference between the two approaches is the perceived importance of the economy and a firm's industry on the valuation of a firm and its stock.

Advocates of the top-down, three-step approach believe that both the economy/market and the industry effect have a significant impact on the total returns for individual stocks. In contrast, those using the bottom-up, stock-picking approach contend that it is possible to find stocks that are undervalued relative to their market price, and these stocks will provide superior returns *regardless* of the market and industry outlook.

Both of these approaches have numerous supporters, and advocates of both approaches have been quite successful.[1] In this book, we advocate and present the top-down, three-step approach because of its logic and empirical support. Although we believe that a portfolio manager or an investor can be successful using the bottom-up approach, we believe that it is more difficult to be successful because these stock pickers are ignoring substantial information from the market and the firm's industry.

Although we know that the value of a security is determined by its quality and profit potential, we also believe that the economic environment and the performance of a firm's industry influence the value of a security and its return. Because of the importance of these economic and industry factors, we present an overview of the valuation process that describes these influences and explains how they can be incorporated into the analysis of security value. Subsequently, we describe the theory of value and emphasize the factors that affect the value of individual securities.

---

1 For the history and selection process of a legendary stock picker, see Hagstrom (2001) or Lowenstein (1995).

At the start of this book, we defined an investment as a commitment of funds for a period of time to derive a return that would compensate the investor for time, inflation, and for the uncertainty involved. From this definition, we know that the first step in making an investment is determining our required return.

Once we have determined this rate, we must estimate the investment's value to determine if its current market price is consistent with our estimated intrinsic value. The intrinsic value estimate is based on the security's expected cash flows and our required return. After we have finished estimating a security's intrinsic value, we compare this estimated intrinsic value to the prevailing market price to decide whether we want to buy the security.

8.1   An Overview of the Valuation Process

Psychologists suggest that the success or failure of an individual can be caused as much by his or her social, economic, and family environment as by genetic gifts. Extending this idea to the valuation of securities means we should consider a firm's economic and industry environment during the valuation process. Regardless of the qualities or capabilities of a firm and its management, the economic and industry environment will have a major influence on the success of a firm and the realized return on its stock.

For example, assume we own shares of the strongest and most successful firm producing home furnishings. If we own the shares during a strong economic expansion, the sales and earnings of the firm will increase and our return on the stock should be quite high. In contrast, if we own the same stock during a major economic recession, the sales, earnings, and cash flows of this firm (and probably most or all of the firms in the industry) would likely experience a decline and the price of its stock would be stable or decline. Therefore, when assessing the future value of a security, it is necessary to analyze the outlook for the aggregate economy and the firm's specific industry.

The valuation process is like the chicken-and-egg dilemma. Do we start by analyzing the macroeconomy and various industries before individual stocks, or do we begin with individual securities and gradually combine these firms into industries and the industries into the entire economy? For reasons discussed in the next section, we contend that the discussion should begin with an analysis of aggregate economies and overall securities markets and progress to different industries with a global perspective. Only after a thorough analysis of a global industry are we in a position to properly evaluate the securities issued by individual firms within the better industries. Thus, we recommend a three-step, top-down valuation process as shown in Exhibit 8.1.

8.2   Why a Three-Step Valuation Process?

8.2.1   General Economic Influences

Monetary and fiscal policy measures enacted by various agencies of national governments influence the aggregate economies of those countries. The resulting economic conditions influence all industries and companies within the economies.

Fiscal policy initiatives, such as tax credits or tax cuts, can encourage spending, whereas additional taxes on income, gasoline, cigarettes, and liquor can discourage spending. Increases or decreases in government spending on defense, on employment insurance, on retraining programs, or on highways also influence the general economy. These fiscal policies influence the business environment for firms that rely directly on such government expenditures. In addition, we know that government spending has a strong multiplier effect. For example, increases in road building increase the demand for earthmoving equipment and concrete materials.

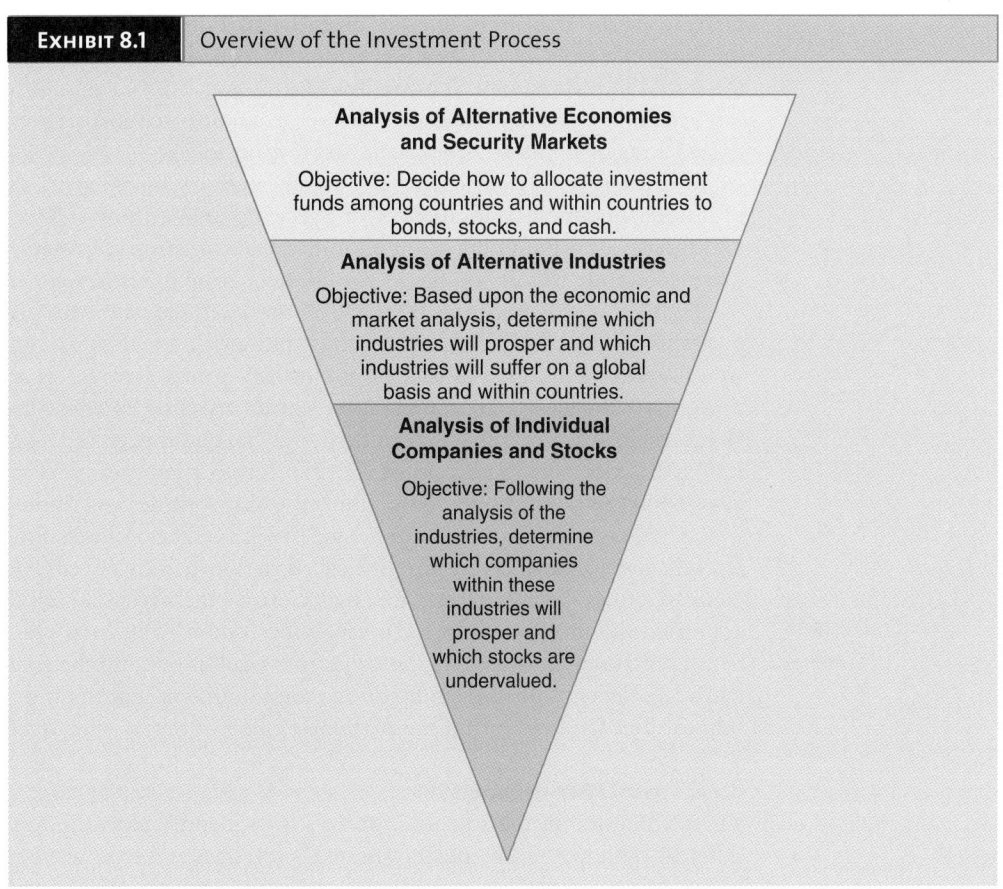

EXHIBIT 8.1 Overview of the Investment Process

Analysis of Alternative Economies and Security Markets

Objective: Decide how to allocate investment funds among countries and within countries to bonds, stocks, and cash.

Analysis of Alternative Industries

Objective: Based upon the economic and market analysis, determine which industries will prosper and which industries will suffer on a global basis and within countries.

Analysis of Individual Companies and Stocks

Objective: Following the analysis of the industries, determine which companies within these industries will prosper and which stocks are undervalued.

As a result, in addition to construction workers, the employees of industries that supply the equipment and materials have more to spend on consumer goods, which raises the demand for consumer goods, which, in turn, affects another set of suppliers.

Monetary policy produces similar economic changes. A restrictive monetary policy that reduces the growth rate of the money supply reduces the supply of funds for working capital and expansion for all businesses. Alternatively, a restrictive monetary policy that targets interest rates would raise market interest rates and therefore firms' costs and make it more expensive for individuals to finance home mortgages and to purchase other durable goods, such as cars and appliances. Monetary policy therefore affects all segments of an economy and that economy's relationship with other economies.

Any economic analysis must consider inflation. As discussed, inflation causes differences between real and nominal interest rates and changes the spending and savings behaviour of consumers and corporations. In addition, unexpected changes in the inflation rate make it difficult for firms to plan, which inhibits growth and innovation. Beyond the impact on the domestic economy, differential inflation and interest rates also influence the trade balance between countries and the currency exchange rates.

In addition to monetary and fiscal policy actions, such events as war, political upheavals, or global financial crisis produce changes in the business environment that add to the uncertainty of sales and earnings expectations and therefore the risk premium required by investors. For example, the political uncertainty in Russia during the late 1990s caused a significant increase in the risk premium for investors in Russia and a reduction in investment and spending in Russia. In contrast, the end of apartheid in South Africa and its open election in the mid-1990s were viewed as positive events and led to a significant increase in economic activity in the country. Similarly, the peace accord in Northern Ireland in the late 1990s caused a major influx of investment and tourist dollars.

In short, it is difficult to conceive of any industry or company that can avoid the impact of macroeconomic developments that affect the total economy. Because aggregate economic events have a profound effect on all industries and companies within these industries, these macroeconomic factors should be considered before industries are analyzed.

Taking a global portfolio perspective, the asset allocation for a country within a global portfolio will be affected by its economic outlook. If a recession is imminent in a country, we would expect a negative impact on its security prices. Because of these economic expectations, investors would be apprehensive about investing in most industries in the country. Given these expectations, the country will be underweighted in portfolios relative to its weight based on its market value. Further, given these pessimistic expectations, any funds invested in the country would be directed to low-risk sectors (industries) of the economy.

In contrast, optimistic economic and stock market outlooks for a given country should lead an investor to increase the overall allocation to this country (overweight the country compared to its weights determined by its relative market value). After allocating funds among countries, the investor looks for outstanding industries in each country. This search for the best industries is enhanced by the economic analysis because the future performance of most industries depends on the country's economic outlook and the industry's expected relationship to the economy during the particular phase of the business cycle.

8.2.2 INDUSTRY INFLUENCES

The second step in the valuation process is to identify global industries that will prosper or suffer in the long run or during the expected near-term economic environment. Examples of conditions that affect specific industries are strikes within a major producing country, import or export quotas or taxes, a worldwide shortage or an excess supply of a resource or product, or government-imposed regulations on an industry.

We should remember that alternative industries react to economic changes at different points in the business cycle. For example, firms typically increase capital expenditures when they are operating at full capacity at the peak of the economic cycle. Therefore, industries that provide plant and equipment will typically be affected toward the end of a cycle. In addition, alternative industries have different responses to the business cycle. As an example, cyclical industries, such as steel or autos, typically do much better than the aggregate economy during expansions, but they suffer more during contractions. In contrast, non-cyclical industries, such as retail food and household products, would not experience a significant decline during a recession but also would not experience a strong increase during an economic expansion.

Another factor that will have a differential effect on industries is demographics. For example, it is widely recognized that the U.S. and Canadian population is weighted toward baby boomers in their late 50s and that there has been a large surge in the number of citizens over age 65. These two groups have heavy demand for second homes and medical care and the industries related to these segments (for example, home furnishings and pharmaceuticals).

Firms that sell in international markets can benefit or suffer as foreign economies shift. An industry with a substantial worldwide market might experience low demand in its domestic market but benefit from growing demand in its international market. As an example, much of the growth for Coca-Cola and Pepsi and the fast-food chains, such as McDonald's and Burger King, has come from international expansion in Europe and the Far East.

In general, an industry's prospects within the global business environment will determine how well or poorly an individual firm will fare, so industry analysis should precede company analysis. Few companies perform well in a poor industry, so even the best company in an industry with a negative outlook is a bad prospect for investment. For example, a poor sales and earnings outlook in the farm equipment industry would have a negative impact on Deere and Co., a well-managed firm and probably the best firm in its industry. Though Deere would likely perform better than other firms in the industry (some might go bankrupt), its earnings and stock performance would still fall far short of its past performance, and the company would probably do poorly compared to firms in most other industries.

Notably, even money managers who are essentially "stock pickers" consider industry analysis important because it determines a firm's business risk due to sales volatility and operating leverage, and its profitability is impacted by the competitive environment in the industry.

8.2.3 COMPANY ANALYSIS

After determining an industry's outlook, an investor can analyze and compare an individual firms' performance relative to the entire industry using financial ratios and cash flow values. As we reviewed in Web Chapter 19, many financial ratios for firms are valid only when they are compared to the performance of their industries.

We undertake company analysis to identify the best company in a promising industry. This involves examining a firm's past performance, but more important, its future prospects. After we understand the firm and its outlook, we can estimate its value using one of several valuation models. An important point that will be emphasized is that it is our estimated inputs to the valuation models that are critical, and the quality of these inputs depends on our prior market-industry-company analysis. In the final step, we compare our estimated intrinsic value to the prevailing market price of the firm's stock and decide whether its stock is a good investment.

Our final goal is to select the best stock within a desirable industry and include it in our portfolio based on its relationship (correlation) with all other assets in our portfolio. As we discuss in more detail in Chapter 9, the best stock for investment purposes may not necessarily be issued by the best company because the stock of the finest company in an industry may be overpriced, which would cause it to be a poor investment. We cannot know whether a security is undervalued or overvalued until we have thoroughly analyzed the company, estimated its intrinsic value, and compared our estimated intrinsic value to the market price of the firm's stock.

8.2.4 DOES THE THREE-STEP PROCESS WORK?

Although we might agree with the logic of the three-step investment process, we might wonder how well this process works in selecting investments. The results of several academic studies have supported this technique. First, studies indicated that most changes in an individual firm's *earnings* could be attributed to changes in aggregate corporate earnings and changes in the firm's industry, with the aggregate earnings changes being more important. Although the relative influence of the general economy and the industry on a firm's earnings varied among individual firms, the results consistently demonstrated that the economic environment had a significant effect on firm earnings.

Second, studies by Moore and Cullity (1988) and Siegel (1991) found a relationship between aggregate stock prices and various economic series, such as employment, income, or production. These results supported the view that a relationship exists between stock prices and economic expansions and contractions. Third, an analysis showed that most of the changes in rates of return for individual stocks could be explained by changes in the rates of return for the aggregate stock market and the stock's industry.

These results from academic studies support the use of the three-step investment process. This investment decision approach is consistent with the discussion in Chapter 2, which contended that the most important decision is the asset allocation decision.[2] Recall that the asset allocation specifies: (1) what proportion of our portfolio will be invested in various nations' economies; (2) within each country, how we will divide our assets among stocks, bonds, or other assets; and (3) our industry selections, based on which industries are expected to prosper in the projected economic environment.

Now that we understand the rationale of a three-step, top-down approach, in the balance of this chapter, we discuss how to conduct step one, economic analysis, and step two, industry analysis. Chapter 9 deals with step three, company analysis. In the following discussions, we assume readers are familiar with basic approaches to equity valuation, including discounted cash flow and relative valuation techniques. A review of these concepts, however, is available in Web Chapter 20.

8.3 Economic Analysis

Canadian Economy Online: A one-stop guide to the Canadian economy at http://www.canadi-aneconomy.gc.ca.

This section is concerned with step one, economic analysis, which is an application of macroeconomics, as we believe that *security markets reflect what is expected to go on in the economy*. Because the value of an investment is determined by its expected cash flows and its expected required return (that is, its discount rate), both of these valuation factors are influenced by the aggregate economic environment. The objective is to consider what specific variables and economic series should be considered when attempting to project future market movements.

Fluctuations in security markets are related to changes in expectations for the aggregate economy. The prices of government bonds and investment-grade corporate bonds are determined by the level of interest rates, which is influenced by overall economic activity and the Bank of Canada's monetary policy. Aggregate stock prices reflect investor expectations about corporate performance in terms of earnings, cash flows, and the required return by investors. All of these expectations are heavily impacted by the economic outlook.

In the following, we organize our discussion on economic analysis into five components: understanding business cycles, knowing monetary variables, inflation and interest rates, forecasting performance of the stock market, and analysis of world security markets. The first three components are mainly applications of macroeconomics and readers are encouraged to consult textbooks in macroeconomics such as Mankiw, Kneebone, McKenzie, and Rowe's *Principles of Macroeconomics*.

8.3.1 Understanding Business Cycles

Economists examine the relationship of various economic series to the behaviour of the entire economy and have classified numerous economic series into three groups: leading, coincident, and lagging indicators. Further, extensive analysis of the relationship between the economy and the stock market has shown that stock prices are one of the better leading indicator series.

---

2 The classic studies that established the importance of asset allocation are Brinson, Hood, and Beebower (1986), followed by Brinson, Singer, and Beebower (1991). A subsequent well-regarded application of these concepts is contained in Cohen (1996).

There are two possible reasons why stock prices lead the economy. One is that stock prices reflect *expectations* of earnings, dividends, and interest rates. As investors attempt to estimate these future variables, their stock price decisions reflect expectations for *future* economic activity, not past or current activity. A second possible reason is that the stock market reacts to various leading indicator series, the most important being corporate earnings, corporate profit margins, interest rates, and changes in the growth rate of the money supply. Because these series tend to lead the economy, when investors adjust stock prices to reflect expectations for these leading economic series, it makes stock prices a leading series as well.

As noted, because research has documented that peaks and troughs in stock prices tend to occur prior to peaks and troughs in the economy, our consideration of relevant economic series concentrates on two broad categories of economic series that likewise lead the economy and should provide some insights regarding the future trend of stocks. The first is a set of economic series related to business cycles, and the second are monetary variables influenced by the monetary authority: in Canada, the Bank of Canada, and in United States, the Federal Reserve.

The Cyclical Indicator Approach The cyclical indicator approach to monitoring and forecasting the economy is built on the belief that the aggregate economy experiences periods of expansion and contraction that can be identified by the movements in economic activity reflected in specific economic series. In addition to the individual economic series, a composite time series combines these economic series—for example, the *composite leading indicator index*.

This composite leading indicator series is widely reported in the press each month as an indicator of the current and future state of the economy. There are also composite coincident and lagging indicator series. Some analysts have used a ratio of these composite series, contending that the ratio of the composite coincident series divided by the composite lagging series acts like a leading series, in some instances even leading the composite leading series. The rationale for expecting this leading relationship for the ratio is that the coincident series should turn before the lagging series, and the ratio of the two series will be quite sensitive to such changes. As a result, this ratio series is expected to lead both of the individual composite series, especially at turning points. Statistics Canada uses a set of 10 economic series as leading indicators, as listed in Exhibit 8.2, covering the financial and real sectors for the purpose of economic forecast.

Bank of Canada: http://www.bankofcanada.ca
Federal Reserve System of the United States: http://www.federalreserve.gov

Exhibit 8.2	Leading Indicators for Canada

1. Average work week, manufacturing
2. Housing index
3. United States composite leading index
4. Money supply
5. New orders, durable goods
6. Retail trade, furniture and appliances
7. Durable goods sales excluding furniture and appliances
8. Shipment to inventory ratio, finished products
9. Stock price index, S&P/TSX
10. Business and personal services employment

Source: Statistics Canada CANSIM Table 377-0003, *Business Leading Indicators for Canada*.

Based on the 10 leading indicators, Statistics Canada has developed a composite leading index as an overall gauge of the future direction of the Canadian economy. Exhibit 8.3 shows the association between percentage change of Canadian GDP and the composite leading index during the period 1971 to 2006. While the composite leading index seems to be linked to economic growth, we should take note that the S&P/TSX Composite Index itself is a component of the leading index and makes it less than perfect to use the composite index to predict the direction of the Canadian stock market. Nevertheless, there are still nine other series in the composite leading index, and it still gives us an overall sense of the direction of the economy and consequently the direction of the industry. It is through such a connection that forecasting of business cycles can help with the analysis of the valuation of common stocks.

EXHIBIT 8.3	Percentage Change of Composite Leading Index and GDP of Canada

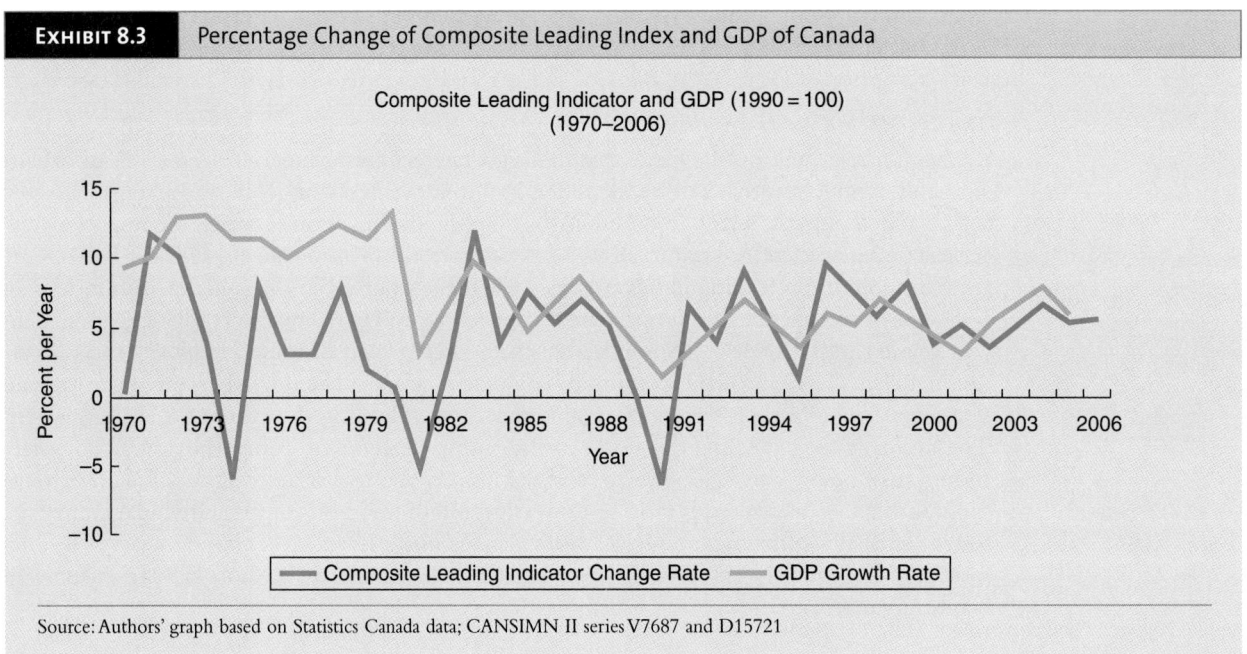

Source: Authors' graph based on Statistics Canada data; CANSIMN II series V7687 and D15721

8.3.2 KNOWING MONETARY VARIABLES

Many academic and professional observers hypothesize a close relationship between stock prices and various monetary variables that are influenced by monetary policy. The best-known monetary variable is the *money supply*. We will recall from our economics course that the money supply can be measured in several ways as described by Walter (1989). The government publishes numerous measures of the money supply, but M1 and M2 are the best known. The Bank of Canada and the U.S. Federal Reserve (the Fed) control the money supply of the respective countries through various tools, the most useful of which is open market operations.

Money Supply and the Economy In their classic work on the monetary history of the United States, Friedman and Schwartz (1963) thoroughly documented the relationship between changes in the growth rate of the money supply and subsequent changes in the economy. Specifically, they demonstrated that declines in the rate of growth of the money supply have preceded business contractions, while increases in the growth rate of the money supply have consistently preceded economic expansions.

Friedman (1969) suggests a transmission mechanism through which changes in the growth rate of the money supply affect the aggregate economy. He hypothesizes that to implement planned changes in monetary policy, the Fed engages in open market operations, buying or selling government bonds to adjust bank reserves and, eventually, the money supply. Because the Fed deals in government bonds, the initial liquidity impact when the Fed buys bonds affects the government bond market, creating excess liquidity for those who sold bonds to the Fed. The result is an increase in bond prices and lower interest rates. Rising government bond prices subsequently filter down to corporate bonds, and this change in liquidity eventually affects common stocks and then the real goods market. There is the opposite effect if the Fed sells bonds to reduce bank reserves and the money supply. The impact of money supply growth on stock prices is really part of the transmission process whereby money supply affects the aggregate economy. This liquidity transmission scenario implies that the effect of a change in monetary policy initially appears in financial markets (bonds and stocks) and only later in the aggregate economy.

In Canada, history shows that since 1915, each documented recession is always preceded by a decline in the growth of money supply.[3] Exhibit 8.4 shows money growth and business cycles in Canada from 1968 to 2007. During this period, the contraction of money supply indeed goes before each slowdown. However, this does not mean that contraction of money supply is a perfect predictor of recession. The chart shows that slowing down of monetary growth is not always followed by a recession.

EXHIBIT 8.4	Money Growth and Business Cycles in Canada (1968–2007)

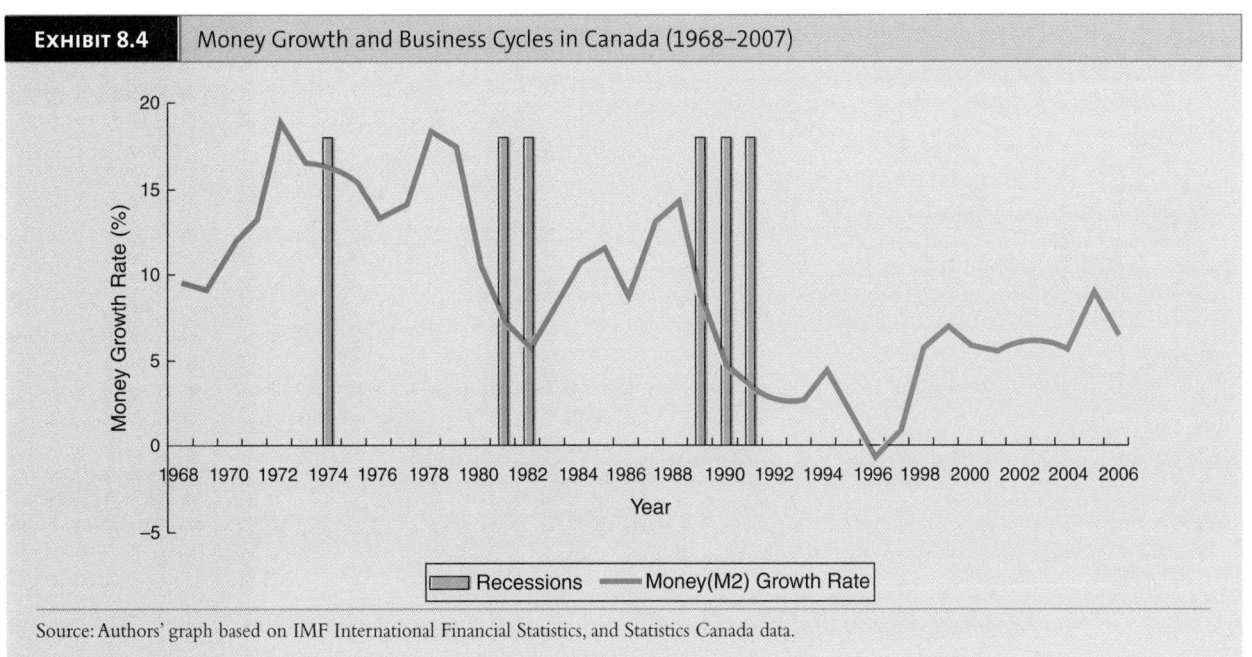

Source: Authors' graph based on IMF International Financial Statistics, and Statistics Canada data.

---

3 See Frederic S. Mishkin and Apostolos Serletis, *The Economics of Money, Banking, and Financial Markets*, Third Canadian Edition, Addison Wesley (2008), and also Cherie Metcalf, Angela Redish, and Ronald Shearer, "New Estimates of the Canadian Money Stock, 1871-1967," *The Canadian Journal of Economics* 31, no. 1 (Feb. 1998): 104-124.

8.3.3 INFLATION AND INTEREST RATES

We have noted throughout the book the critical role of expected inflation and nominal interest rates in determining the required return used to derive the value of all investments. We would expect these variables that are very important in microeconomic valuation to also affect changes in the aggregate markets.

Exhibit 8.5 shows the nominal interest rate and the inflation rate in Canada during the period 1956 to 2006. This graph demonstrates the strong relationship between inflation and interest rates. We contended in our earlier discussion that when investors anticipated an increase in the inflation rate, they would increase their required returns by a similar amount to derive constant real returns. The chart confirms the expected relationship overall. If the relationship was perfect and investors were accurate in their *predictions* of future inflation, the difference between the interest rate and the inflation rate (the spread between them) would be fairly constant, reflecting the real return on corporate bonds. As shown, the spread between these two curves changes over time.

| **EXHIBIT 8.5** | Nominal Interest Rate and Inflation in Canada |

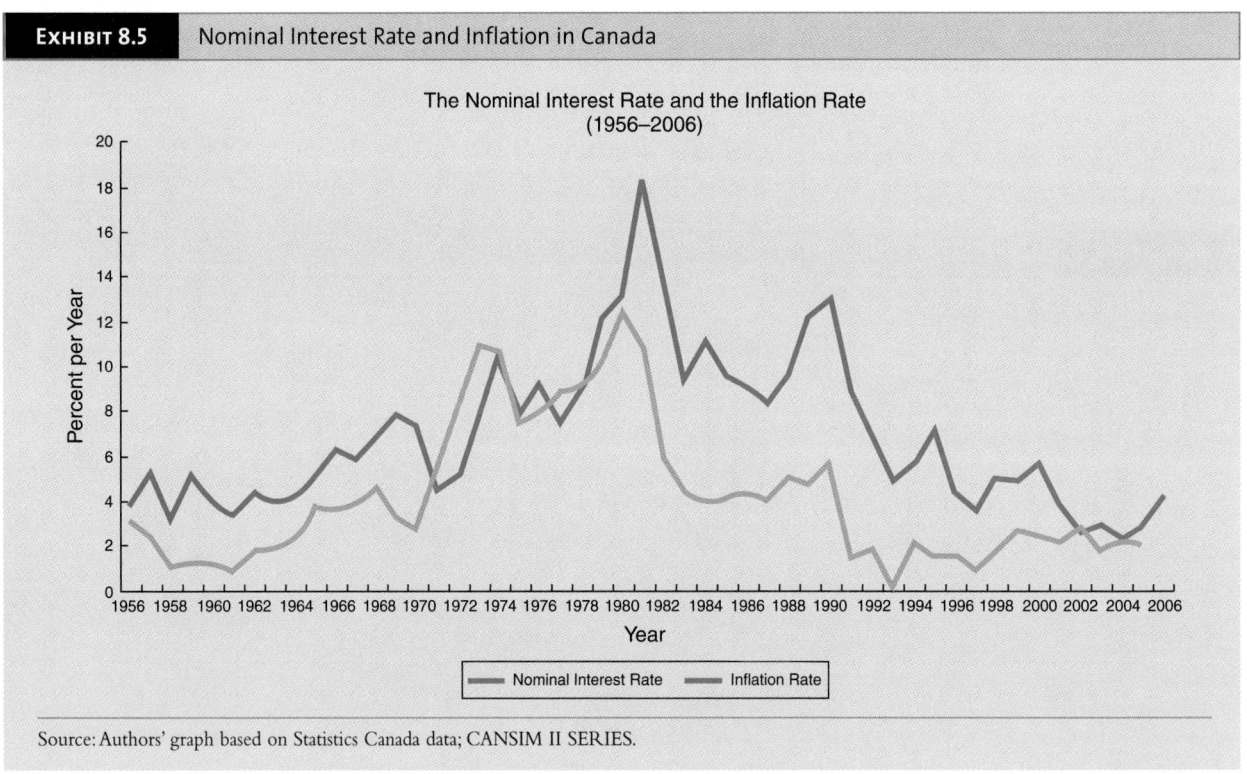

Source: Authors' graph based on Statistics Canada data; CANSIM II SERIES.

Interest Rates and Bond Prices There are many interest rates, but they usually move up and down together and thus when addressing the direction of interest rate changes, people usually simply use the term, interest rates, without being specific as to which interest rate it is. Exhibit 8.6 shows three Canadian interest rates based on three-month Treasury bills, long-term government bonds, and long-term corporate bonds, and how they generally move up and down in the same direction.

The relationship between interest rates and bond prices is clearly negative because the only variable that changes in the valuation model is the discount factor. Specifically, the

EXHIBIT 8.6	Interest Rates in Canada

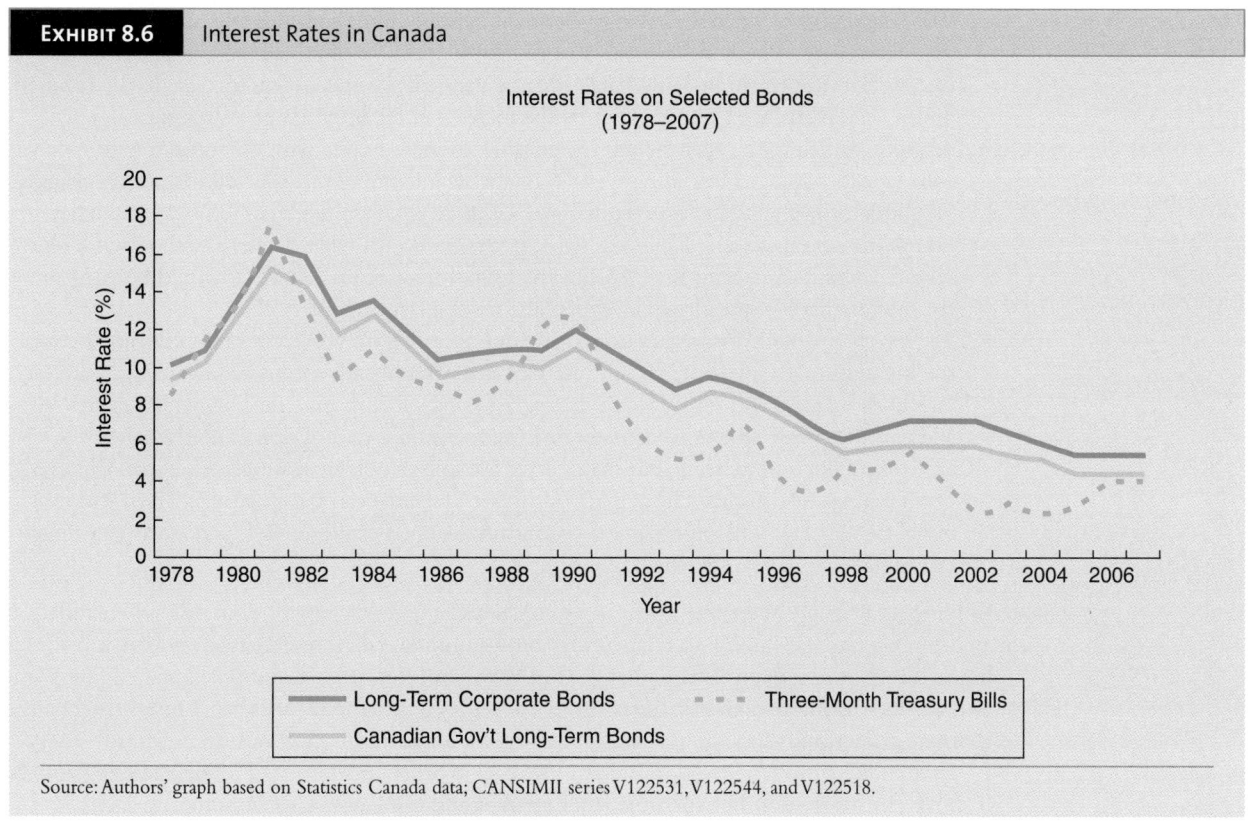

Interest Rates on Selected Bonds
(1978–2007)

Legend:
— Long-Term Corporate Bonds   - - - Three-Month Treasury Bills
— Canadian Gov't Long-Term Bonds

Source: Authors' graph based on Statistics Canada data; CANSIMII series V122531, V122544, and V122518.

expected cash flows from a straight non-callable bond would not change, so an increase in interest rates will cause a decline in bond prices and a decline in interest rates will boost bond prices. For example, if we own a 10-year bond with a coupon of 10%, when interest rates increase from 10% to 12%, the price of this bond will decline from $1,000 (par) to $885. In contrast, if rates decline from 10% to 8%, the price of the bond will increase from $1,000 to $1,136.

The size of the price change will depend on the characteristics of the bond. As will be discussed in Chapter 16, a longer term bond will experience a larger price change for a change in interest rates. Therefore, we can anticipate a negative relationship between inflation and the rates of return on bonds because inflation generally has a direct effect on interest rates; and, in turn, interest rates have an inverse effect on bond prices and rates of return. One example of empirical verification for this negative relationship is provided in Exhibit 3.11, which shows a correlation of −0.065 between inflation and returns on long-term investment-grade bonds.

Inflation, Interest Rates, and Stock Prices The relationship between inflation, interest rates, and stock prices is not direct and consistent. The reason is that the cash flows from stocks can change along with inflation and interest rates, and we cannot be certain whether this change in cash flows will augment or offset the change in interest rates. To demonstrate, consider the following potential scenarios following an increase in the rate of inflation and the effect on stock prices based on the dividend discount model (DDM).

1. *The positive scenario.* Interest rates rise due to an increase in the inflation rate, and corporate earnings likewise grow because firms are able to increase prices in line with cost increases. In this case, stock prices might be fairly stable because the negative effect of an increase in the required return (*k*) is partially or wholly offset by the increase in the growth rate of earnings and dividends (*g*), which means that the returns on stock increase in line with the inflation rate.

2. *Mild negative scenario.* Interest rates increase due to inflation, but expected cash flows change very little or not at all because firms are not able to increase prices in response to higher costs. This would cause a decline in stock prices similar to what happens with a bond. The required return (*k*) would increase, but the growth rate of dividends (*g*) would be constant. As a result, the *k–g* spread would widen and stock prices would decline.

3. *Very negative scenario.* Interest rates increase due to inflation, while cash flows decline because the inflation that caused the rise in interest rates has a negative impact on earnings. Interest rates may increase and remain high during a period of economic decline, which causes sales and earnings to decline. Alternatively, one can envision a period of inflation wherein the costs of production increase, but many firms are not able to increase prices, which causes a decline in profit margins. The impact of this set of events can be disastrous. Given this scenario, stock prices will experience a significant decline because *k* will increase as *g* declines, causing a large increase in the *k–g* spread.

In contrast to these scenarios, we can envision a comparable set of scenarios when inflation and interest rates decline. The relationship between inflation, interest rates, and stock prices is not as direct or consistent as the relationship between interest rates and bond prices. The point is, the effect of interest rate changes on stock prices will depend on what caused the change in interest rates and the effect of this event on the expected cash flows on common stock.

Exhibit 8.7 shows the relationship among stock market, inflation, and interest rate in Canada. It shows the association between the stock market and the key macroeconomic variables.

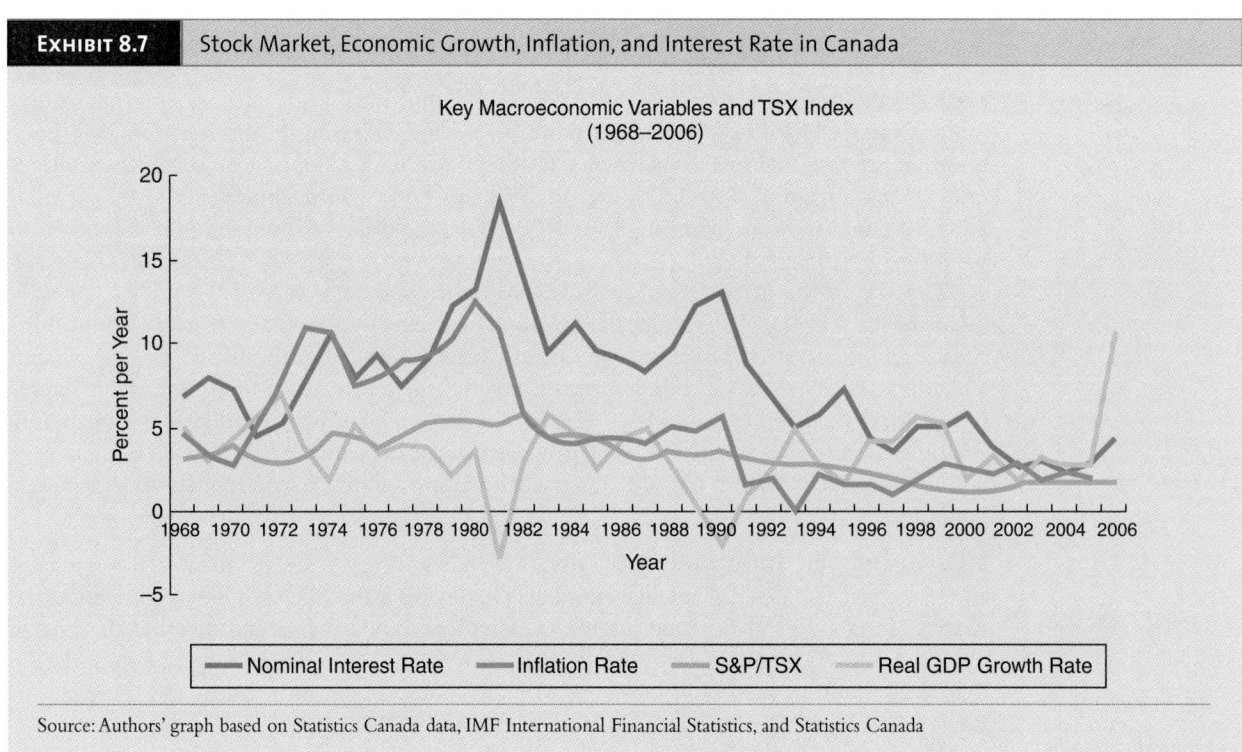

EXHIBIT 8.7   Stock Market, Economic Growth, Inflation, and Interest Rate in Canada

Source: Authors' graph based on Statistics Canada data, IMF International Financial Statistics, and Statistics Canada

8.3.4 FORECASTING PERFORMANCE OF THE STOCK MARKET

The Earnings Multiplier Approach From the capital asset pricing model (CAPM), we know there is a correlation between a stock and the overall market. Thus analysts would be very interested in knowing the overall direction of the stock market. We introduce the earnings multiplier version of the dividend discount model to value the stock market because it is a theoretically correct model of value assuming a constant growth rate of dividends for an infinite time period. The point is, these are reasonable assumptions for the aggregate stock market.[4] Also, this valuation technique is consistently used in practice.

The ultimate objective of forecasting stock market performance is to estimate the intrinsic market value for a major stock market series, such as the S&P/TSX Index. This estimation process has two equally important steps. One is to estimate the future earnings per share for the stock market series, and two is to estimate the appropriate earnings multiplier for the stock market series. If an analyst estimates that in the coming year, the aggregate earnings multiplier for the S&P/TSX would be 24 and the earnings per share of the companies that constitute the index would be $550, then the product of the above (= 13,200), would be her estimate for the overall performance for the Toronto Stock Exchange.

The challenge, of course, is how one would go about estimating those two aggregate parameters. We can assume that the aggregate earnings per share in the coming year is a function of overall economic condition and thus we can integrate this year's earning per share with a predicted economic growth rate of the coming year and come up with an estimate of next year's earnings. As to the earnings multiple (that is, P/E ratio), if there is a relatively stable relationship between aggregate P/E ratio and a certain financial variable, that variable can serve as a basis for the forecast. For instance, if we believe that the 1% average spread between long-term T-bill yield and S&P/TSX earnings yield (the inverse of P/E) in the past provides a reliable linkage, then if the current T-bill yield is 5%, our estimate for next year's earnings yield would be 5% − 1% = 4%. The inverse, 1/0.04 = 25, would be our estimate for the earnings multiplier for next year.

The advantage of the earnings multiplier approach is that it is easy to operate and understand, but the shortcoming is that it is difficult to tell if the inputs are reliable. Similar to other types of business forecasts, it would be prudent to construct different scenarios of the future and come up with a different estimate for each scenario.

The earnings multiplier is a relative valuation technique as it is based on a ratio or multiplier. Other relative valuation techniques include the price-to-book-value ratio (P/BV), the price-to-cash-flow ratio (P/CF), and the price-to-sales ratio (P/S). An alternative set of tools employs the discounted cash flow approach, also known as the absolute valuation techniques. These techniques include the dividend discount model (DDM), the operating free cash flow model, and the free cash flow to equity model. They provide an estimate of the stock market based on present value of cash flow. All of the above are consistent with the discounted cash flow and the relative valuation techniques discussed in Web Chapter 20, "An Introduction to Security Valuation." Due to space limitation, the details are not discussed here.[5]

Bank for International Settlements' link to Central Banks all over the world: http://www.bis.org/cbanks.htm

---

4 Recall that these assumptions may be unrealistic for many stocks, especially for stocks of growth companies. We consider these problems for growth companies and discuss alternative-growth company-valuation models that consider such conditions in Chapter 9.

5 For a detailed discussion on factors influencing the earnings multiplier approach, and an overview of all other relative and absolute valuation techniques, please see chapter 12, "Macroanalysis and Microvaluation of the Stock Markets," in *Investment Analysis and Portfolio Management,* 9th Edition, by F. K. Reilly and K. C. Brown, South-Western Cengage Learning, 2009.

On the Three-Step Approach

In this box, we are going to explain why Warren Buffett and Charlie Munger, two of the world's most successful investors, emphasize a deep understanding of companies before they spend a penny of Berkshire Hathaway's shareholders' money (it also helps that they are by far two of the largest owners of the company).

They stress that while businesses operate within specific economies and industries, the crucial fact to remember is that when investing, *one buys a partnership in a business that, if well-run, will produce cash flows that may be reinvested elsewhere or paid out to shareholders.* Ben Graham (Buffett's finance professor at Columbia) makes this case in *The Intelligent Investor* (1973: 286):

Investment is most intelligent when it is most *businesslike.*

While they do not spend time worrying about the state of the economy (Buffett has repeatedly stressed that he does not attempt to "time the market," although he has also said "be greedy when others are fearful and fearful when others are greedy"), they also point out that *industry factors* are important to their evaluations. One oft-repeated quote from Buffett illustrates their thinking: "I've said many times that when a management with a reputation for brilliance tackles a business with a reputation for bad economics, it is the reputation of the business that remains intact." In other words, it is a losing game to invest in industries with bad economics as Buffet learned when he took control of Berkshire Hathaway, a New England firm struggling in the textile industry.

The third step in security analysis, *company analysis,* tries to determine whether the company's performance will be sustained if it is already successful or will recover if it has fallen on hard times. In many speeches and letters to shareholders, Buffett has argued that the four questions Charlie Munger and he always try to answer are the following:

- Do we understand the business?
- Is it protected by deep moats that widen over time?
- Do we like the people running the business?
- Does the business sell for an attractive price?

Buffett and Munger consider only firms that have understandable businesses (within their "circle of competence"), and have bought many firms in seemingly unattractive industries (e.g., confectionery, shoes, uniforms, vacuum cleaners, books, bricks, manufactured homes, custom frame suppliers, fast food, cutlery, paints, underwear, furniture, carpets) but with wide and deepening moats.

The term "economic moat" is one that Buffett coined. It refers to the height of entry barriers protecting the company's business that give it a competitive advantage. The depth of economic moats refers to the durability of these entry barriers. Finding companies with a significant and *sustainable* competitive advantage has been the key to Buffett and Munger's outstanding performance. Entry barriers are most easily evaluated for simple businesses (e.g., Gillette, See's Candies, Coca Cola), although they are not simple to create, protect, and widen. Without these barriers, the profit-generating capability of the business would eventually crumble and vanish under the attacks of competitors.

As we have noted, quality of management is one of the prime determinants of Buffett and Munger's decision to invest because economic moats are created and deepened by the effort of managers. They evaluate the quality of management by studying the following variables:

1. Do the managers have "skin in the game"?
2. Do managers act with integrity and intelligence?
3. Is management candid with its shareholders?
4. Does management allocate capital rationally?

Source: Prepared by Francis Tapon, University of Guelph.

Country economic data are available at the World Bank site.

http://www.worldbank.org/

8.3.5 ANALYSIS OF WORLD SECURITY MARKETS

Although we have focused on Canada to demonstrate economic analysis, we must also consider a similar approach to numerous foreign markets to complete step one in the investment process, that is, the analysis of alternative economies and security markets. The analysis may include key industrialized countries such as the United States, Germany, the United Kingdom, and emerging economic powers such as the BRIC countries (Brazil, Russia, India, and China). While it is not feasible to consider a complete analysis of the global economy, the following discussion considers some of the variables and economic series.

Leading economic series are available for virtually all the developed countries, and the empirical relationships to the economy are similar to what we discussed in the last section.

Real GDP growth is typically consistent with what is implied by the leading series. Notably, the growth rate outlook may vary insubstantially between an industrialized country such as the United States and that of an emerging economy such as China. Recall that these estimates of real GDP growth will impact both the country's real rate of interest and the growth of its sales and earning cash flows.

The *monetary environment* of a country will clearly differ across the countries because the monetary authority in each country will be responsive to the economic outlook for *its* country.

The *inflation outlook* will depend on the monetary environment—that is, the ease or tightness of monetary policy. It also will be impacted by the economic environment and the point on the business cycle (recession or expansion). Again, there will be a wide range for the expected rate of inflation among countries, and the impact of these different inflation rates on security values will be as described earlier.

8.4 Industry Analysis[6]

Industry analysis is a crucial link between step one, macroeconomic analysis, and step three, company analysis. While the performance of individual companies within a particular industry may differ significantly, they are all being impacted in similar ways by a number of factors at the industry level. In the following, we discuss four important industry analysis tools, namely, business cycle, structural changes in the economy, the life cycle of the industry, and the competitive environment of the industry.

Industry Canada:

http://www.ic.gc.ca

8.4.1 WHAT IS AN INDUSTRY?[7]

Identifying a company's industry can be difficult in today's business world. Although airlines, railroads, and utilities may be easy to categorize, what about manufacturing companies with three different divisions, none of which is dominant? Perhaps the best way to test whether a company fits into an industry grouping is to compare the operating results for the company and an industry. For our purposes, an industry is a group of companies with similar demand, supply, and operating characteristics.

The following is a set of guidelines for preparing an industry appraisal, including the topics to consider and some specific items to include.

---

6 The authors acknowledge input to the discussions on "The Business Cycle and Industry Sectors" and "Structural Economic Changes and Alternative Industries" provided by Professor Edgar Norton of Illinois State University.

7 Reprinted and adapted with permission of Stanley D. Ryals, CFA; Investment Council, Inc: La Crescenta, CA 91214.

Characteristics to Study

1. **Price history reveals valuable long-term relationships.**
   a. Price/earnings ratios
   b. Common stock yields
   c. Price/book value ratios
   d. Price/cash flow ratios
   e. Price/sales ratios
2. **Operating data show comparisons of**
   a. Return on total investment (ROI)
   b. Return on equity (ROE)
   c. Sales growth
   d. Trends in operating profit margin
   e. Evaluation of stage in industrial life cycle
   f. Book-value-per-share growth
   g. Earnings-per-share growth
   h. Profit margin trends (gross, operating, and net)
   i. Evaluation of exchange rate risk from foreign sales
3. **Comparative results of alternative industries show**
   a. Effects of business cycles on each industry group
   b. Secular trends affecting results
   c. Industry growth compared to other industries
   d. Regulatory changes
   e. Importance of overseas operations

Factors in Industry Analysis

Markets for Products

1. Trends in the markets for the industry's major products, historical and projected
2. Industry growth relative to GDP or other relevant economic series; possible changes from past trends
3. Shares of market for major products among domestic and global producers; changes in market shares in recent years; outlook for market share
4. Effect of imports on industry markets; share of market taken by imports; price and margin changes caused by imports; outlook for imports
5. Effect of exports on their markets; trends in export prices and units exported; outlook for exports
6. Expectations for the exchange rates in major foreign countries; historical volatility of exchange rates; outlook for the level and volatility of exchange rates

Financial Performance

1. Capitalization ratios; ability to raise new capital; earnings retention rate; financial leverage
2. Ratio of capital assets to capital invested; amortization policies; capital turnover
3. Return on total capital; return on equity capital; components of ROE
4. Return on foreign investments; need for foreign capital

Operations

1. Degrees of integration; cost advantages of integration; major supply contracts
2. Operating rates as a percentage of capacity; backlogs; new-order trends
3. Trends of industry consolidation
4. Trends in industry competition

5. New-product development; research and development expenditures in dollars and as a percentage of sales
6. Diversification; comparability of product lines

Management

1. Management depth and ability to develop from within; organizational structure
2. Board of directors: internal versus external members; compensation package
3. Flexibility to deal with product demand changes; ability to identify and eliminate losing operations
4. Record and outlook regarding labour relations
5. Dividend policy and historical progression

Sources of Industry Information

1. Independent industry journals
2. Industry and trade associations
3. Government reports and statistics
4. Independent research organizations
5. Brokerage house research
6. Financial publishers (*S&P; Moody's; Value Line*)

FPinformart.Ca: Canadian industry and company information:
https://www.fpinfomart.ca

Canadian Cross-Sectional Industry Performance It is important to note that there are very substantial cross-sectional differences in the performance of the industry, and thus, when we attempt to conduct a three-step economy-industry-company analysis, we need to recognize that the impact of the economy and overall market on one industry can be very different from another sector. Based on stock indexes of industrial sectors, Exhibit 8.8 shows the cross-sectional risk and return of the stocks of Canadian industries during 1989 to 2006. The Canadian information technology sector is the most risky and profitable, with a standard deviation of 55% and an average annual return of 19%, while the consumer discretionary sector is the least risky (standard deviation = 7%) and the least profitable (average return = 12%). In between are important Canadian industries such as energy, financial, and telecommunications.

Exhibit 8.9 explicitly shows how the returns of the sectors fared over time. We can see that while the performance of the industries moved together in a general way, there is wide variation in any given year. For instance, in 1999, the Canadian information technology sector enjoyed an exceptional return of 186% but the financials suffered a loss of 13%. Similarly, for any given industry, the annual return also fluctuates over time. This illustrates the importance of industry analysis when we make asset allocation decisions across the industries.

8.4.2 THE BUSINESS CYCLE AND INDUSTRY SECTORS

Economic trends can and do affect industry performance. Our objective is to monitor the economy and gauge the implications of new information on our economic outlook and industry analysis. Recall that in order to beat the market on a risk-adjusted basis, our forecasts must differ from the market consensus *and* we must be correct more often than not. Economic trends can take two basic forms: **cyclical changes** that arise from the ups and downs of the business cycle, and **structural changes** when the economy is undergoing a major change in how it functions. For example, excess labour or capital may exist in some sectors whereas shortages of labour and capital exist elsewhere. The "downsizing" of corporate America during the 1990s, transitions from socialist to market economies in Eastern Europe,

Exhibit 8.8	Cross-Sectional Performance of Canadian Industries

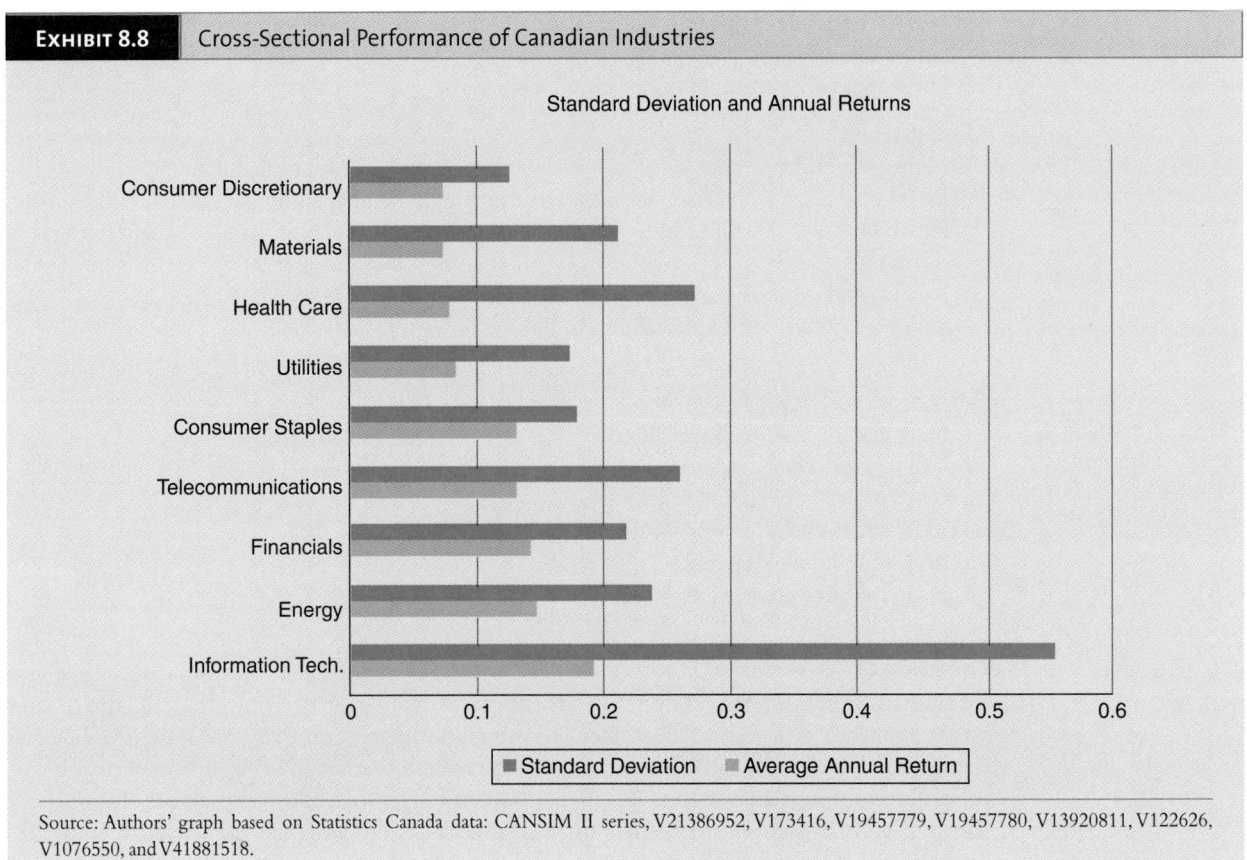

Source: Authors' graph based on Statistics Canada data: CANSIM II series, V21386952, V173416, V19457779, V19457780, V13920811, V122626, V1076550, and V41881518.

and the transition in the United States from a manufacturing to a service economy are all examples of structural change.[8] Industry analysts must examine structural economic changes for the implications they have for an industry under review.

While industry performance is related to the stage of the business cycle, the real challenge is that every business cycle is different, and those who look only at history miss the evolving trends that will determine future market and industry performance. Switching industry groups over the course of a business cycle is known as a *rotation strategy*. When trying to determine which industry groups will benefit from the next stage of the business cycle, investors need to monitor economic trends and changes in industry characteristics. Exhibit 8.10 presents a stylized graphic of which industry groups typically perform well in the different stages of the business cycle. For example, toward the end of a recession, financial stocks rise in value because investors anticipate that banks' earnings will rise as both the economy and loan demand recover. Brokerage houses become attractive investments because their sales and earnings are expected to rise as investors trade securities, businesses sell debt and equity, and there are more mergers during the economic recovery. These industry expectations assume that when the recession ends there will be an increase in loan demand, housing construction, and security offerings. Once the economy begins its recovery, consumer durable firms that produce items such as cars, personal

---

8 An excellent discussion of structural changes in the U.S. economy and the implications of these changes for the business cycle, the stock market, and some specific industries is contained in Dudley and McKelvey (1997).

EXHIBIT 8.9	Canadian Industry Returns

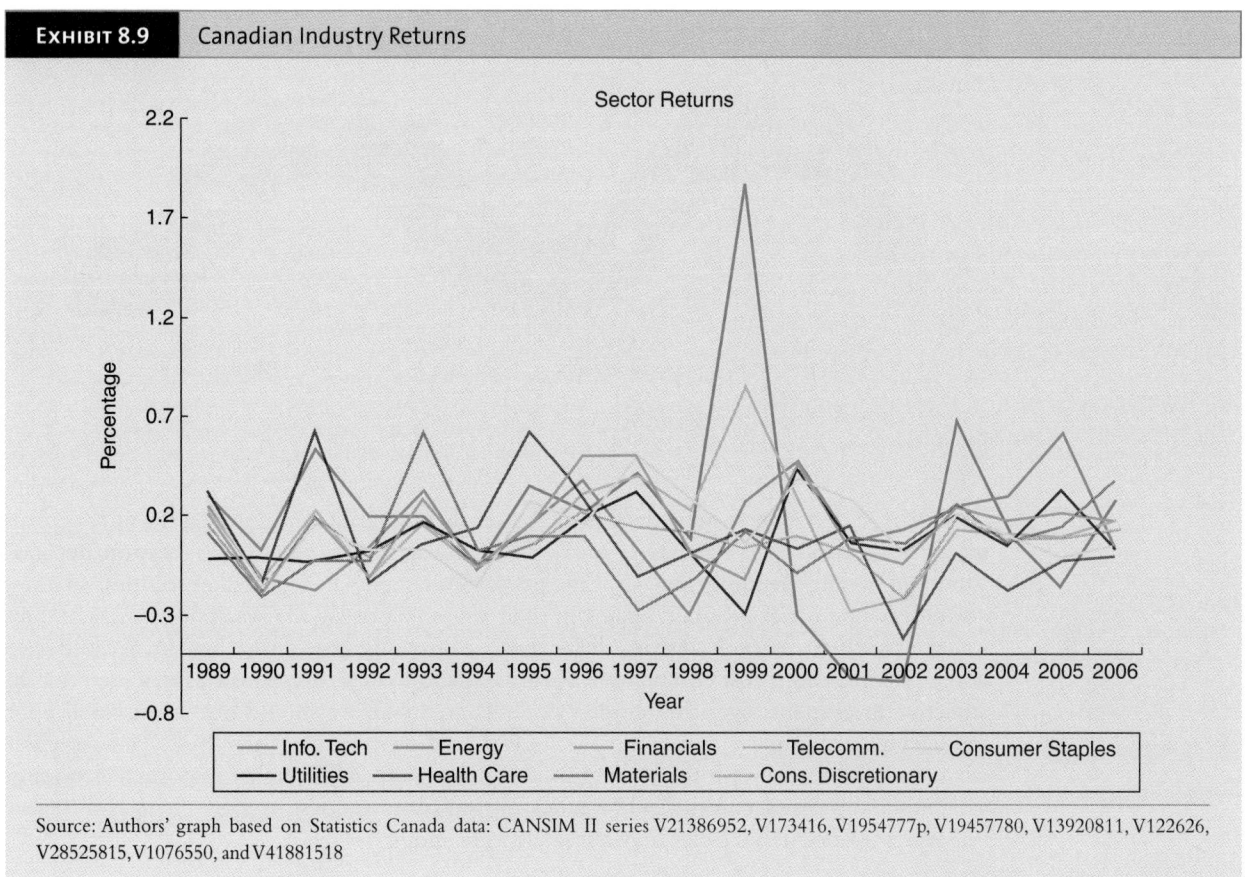

Source: Authors' graph based on Statistics Canada data: CANSIM II series V21386952, V173416, V1954777p, V19457780, V13920811, V122626, V28525815, V1076550, and V41881518

computers, refrigerators, lawn tractors, and snow blowers become attractive investments because a reviving economy will increase consumer confidence and disposable income. Once businesses recognize the economic recovery, they think about modernizing, renovating, or purchasing new equipment to satisfy rising demand and reduce costs. Thus, capital goods industries such as heavy equipment manufacturers, machine tool makers, and airplane manufacturers become attractive.

Cyclical industries whose sales rise and fall along with general economic activity are attractive investments during the early stages of an economic recovery. Because of their high degree of operating leverage, they benefit greatly from the sales increases during an economic expansion.[9] Industries with high financial leverage likewise benefit from rising sales volume.[10] Traditionally, toward the business cycle peak, inflation increases as demand starts to outstrip supply. Basic materials industries such as oil, metals, and timber, which transform raw materials into finished products, become investor favourites. Because inflation has less influence on the cost of extracting these products and companies can increase prices, these industries experience higher profit margins.

---

9 As discussed in Web Chapter 19, operating leverage arises from the existence of fixed costs in a firm's operating structure. Industries with large fixed expenses will have high degrees of operating leverage. This means a small percentage change in sales can result in a large percentage change in operating income.

10 As noted in Web Chapter 19, financial leverage arises from fixed financial costs (that is, interest expense) in a firm's capital structure. Industries that have extensive debt financing (such as banks or utilities) will have net income that is sensitive to small changes in operating income.

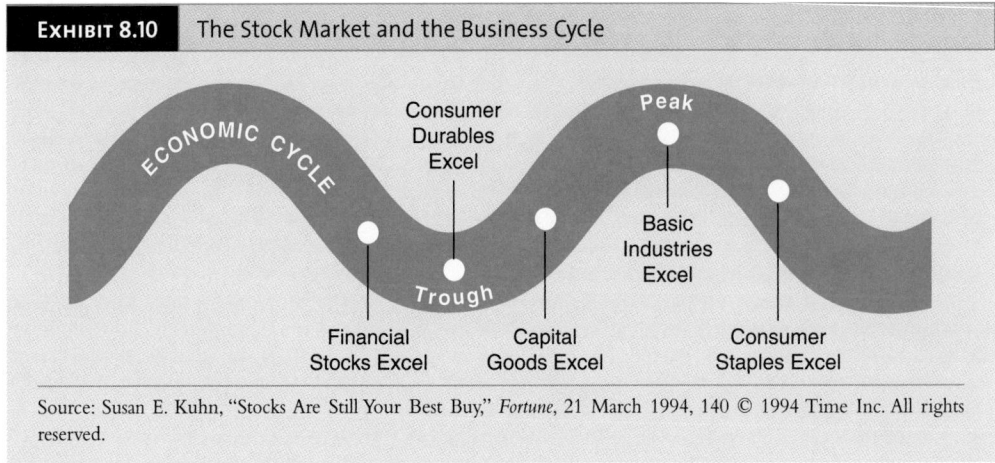

EXHIBIT 8.10 The Stock Market and the Business Cycle

ECONOMIC CYCLE

Peak

Consumer Durables Excel

Trough

Basic Industries Excel

Financial Stocks Excel

Capital Goods Excel

Consumer Staples Excel

Source: Susan E. Kuhn, "Stocks Are Still Your Best Buy," *Fortune*, 21 March 1994, 140 © 1994 Time Inc. All rights reserved.

During a recession, some industries do better than others. Consumer staples, such as pharmaceuticals, food, and beverages, outperform other sectors during a recession because, although overall spending may decline, people still spend money on necessities, so these "defensive" industries generally maintain their values. Similarly, if a weak domestic economy causes a weak currency, industries that export to growing economies benefit because their goods become more cost competitive. We have identified certain industries that are typically attractive investments over the business cycle. Remember, we should not invest based upon the current economic environment because the efficient market has already incorporated current economic news into security prices. Rather, we must *forecast* important economic variables and invest accordingly. The following subsections consider how changes in several important economic variables may affect different industries.

Inflation As noted in several chapters, higher inflation is generally negative for stocks, because it causes higher market interest rates, creates more uncertainty about future prices and costs, and harms firms that cannot pass through cost increases. Although these adverse effects are true for most industries, there are some industries that benefit from inflation. Natural resource industries benefit *if* their production costs do not rise with inflation, because their output will likely sell at higher prices. Industries with high operating leverage benefit because many of their costs are fixed in nominal (current dollar) terms whereas revenues increase with inflation. Industries with high financial leverage may also gain, because their debts are repaid in cheaper dollars.

Interest Rates Financial institutions, including banks, are typically adversely impacted by higher rates because they find it difficult to pass on these higher rates to customers (that is, lagged adjustment). High interest rates clearly harm the housing and the construction industry, but they might benefit industries that supply the do-it-yourselfer. High interest rates also benefit retirees whose income is dependent on interest income. A study by Reilly, Wright, and Johnson (2007) examines the interest rate sensitivity of a large cross-section of industries and types of stocks.

International Economics Both domestic and international events affect the value of the Canadian dollar. A weaker Canadian dollar helps Canadian industries because their exports become comparatively cheaper in overseas markets while the goods of foreign competitors become more expensive in Canada. A stronger Canadian dollar has an opposite effect. Economic growth in world regions or specific countries benefits industries that have a large presence in those areas. The creation of free trade zones, such as the European Community and the North American Free Trade Zone, assists industries that produce goods and services that previously faced quotas or tariffs in partner countries.

Consumer Sentiment Because it comprises about two-thirds of GDP, consumption spending has a large impact on the economy. Optimistic consumers are more willing to spend and borrow money for expensive goods, such as houses, cars, new clothes, and furniture. Therefore, the performance of consumer cyclical industries will be affected by changes in consumer sentiment and by consumers' willingness and ability to borrow and spend money.

8.4.3 STRUCTURAL ECONOMIC CHANGES AND ALTERNATIVE INDUSTRIES

Influences other than the economy are part of the business environment. Climate change, demographics, changes in technology, and political and regulatory environments also can have a significant effect on the cash flow and risk prospects of different industries.

GS Sustain: Goldman Sachs's study of climate change and equity valuation is available through its web site at http://www2. goldmansachs.com/

Climate Change Climate change has become an increasing significant factor influencing government regulations and industry behavior. Study of the impact of climate change on stock value has entered the main stream of the financial industry. In a 2009 study (see the link on the left margin), Goldman Sachs finds that in carbon-intensive industries such as utilities, energy, basic materials, and industrials, the association between carbon emission management and equity market valuations is already obvious. Understanding climate change, societal awareness, and regulatory and industry responses, would be increasingly important to financial analysts.

Demographics In the past 50 years, the United States and Canada have had a baby boom and a baby bust and are now enjoying a baby boomlet as members of the baby-boom generation (those born between the end of World War II and the early 1960s) have children or grandchildren. The influx of the baby boom and the "greying of the baby boom" have had a large impact on consumption, from advertising strategies to house construction to concerns over social security and health care. The study of demographics includes much more than population growth and age distributions. Demographics also includes the geographical distribution of people, the changing ethnic mix in a society, and changes in income distribution. Wall Street industry analysts carefully study demographic trends and attempt to project their effect on different industries and firms.

During the period from 1990 to 2005, the fastest growing age groups in North America were those in their 40s and 50s, teens, and those over 70; among the declining groups were those between ages 18 and 24. As of the early 2000s, more than one in eight North Americans were 65 years of age or older. The changing age profile has implications for resource availability, namely a possible shortage of entry-level workers leading to an increase in labour costs and difficulty in finding qualified persons to replace the retiring baby boomers. The aging North American population also affects savings patterns, as people in the 40-to-60 age bracket usually save more than younger people. This is good for the financial services industry, which offers assistance to those who want to invest their savings. Alternatively, fewer younger workers and more "saving seniors" may have a negative impact on some industries, such as the retailing industry.

Lifestyles Lifestyles deal with how people live, work, form households, consume, enjoy leisure, and educate themselves. Consumer behaviour is affected by trends and fads. The rise and fall of designer jeans, chinos, and other styles in clothes illustrate the sensitivity of some markets to changes in consumer tastes. The increase in divorce rates, dual-career families, population shifts away from cities, and computer-based education and entertainment have influenced numerous industries, including housing, restaurants, automobiles, catalogue shopping, services, and home entertainment. From an international perspective, some U.S.-brand goods—from blue jeans to movies—have a high demand overseas. They are perceived to be more in style and perhaps higher quality than items produced domestically. Several industries have benefited from this positive brand reputation.

Technology Technology can affect numerous industry factors, including the product or service and how it is produced and delivered. There are numerous examples of changes due to technological innovations. For example, demand has fallen for carburetors on cars because of electronic fuel injection technology. The engineering process has changed because of the advent of computer-aided design and manufacturing. Perpetual improvement of designs in the semiconductor and microprocessor industry has made that industry a difficult one to evaluate. Innovations in process technology allowed steel minimills to grow at the expense of large steel producers.

Advances in technology allow some plant sites and buildings to generate their own electricity, bypassing their need for power from the local electric utility. Trucks have reduced railroads' market share in the long-distance carrier industry. The information superhighway is becoming a reality and encouraging linkages between telecommunications and cable television systems. Changes in technology have spurred capital spending in technological equipment as a way for firms to gain competitive advantages. The future effect of the Internet is astronomical.

The retailing industry is a wonderful example of how an industry can use new technology. Some forecasters envision relationship merchandising, in which customer databases will allow closer links between retail stores and customer needs. Rather than market research on aggregate consumer trends, specialized retailers offer products that consumers desire in preferred locations. Technology allows retailers to become more organizationally decentralized and geographically diversified. Major retailers use barcode scanning, which speeds the checkout process and allows the firm to track inventory and customer preferences. Credit cards allow firms to track customer purchases and send customized sales announcements. Electronic data interchange (EDI) allows the retailer to electronically communicate with suppliers to order new inventory and pay accounts payable. Electronic funds transfer allows retailers to move funds quickly and easily between local banks and headquarters.

It is essential for an analyst to become aware of how technology can be a benefit or threat to an industry.

Politics and Regulations Because political change reflects social values, today's social trend may be tomorrow's law, regulation, or tax. The industry analyst needs to project and assess political changes relevant to the industry under study.

Some regulations and laws are based on economic reasoning. Due to utilities' positions as natural monopolies, their rates must be reviewed and approved by a regulatory body. Some regulation involves social ends. For example, Health Canada regulates food safety to protect the public; the federal government's Canadian Centre for Occupational Health and Safety (CCOHS) monitors occupational health and safety; and Environment Canada regulates the protection of environment. Notably, heavy regulation of an industry can increase a firm's costs but also can restrict entry into the industry. Regulatory changes have affected numerous industries. An example is the numerous regulations and inspections following the terrorist attacks of September 11, 2001. Changing regulations and technology are bringing participants in the financial services industry—banking, insurance, investment banking, and investment services—together. Regulations and laws affect international commerce. International tax laws, tariffs, quotas, embargoes, and other trade barriers have a significant effect on some industries and global commerce.

Again, an interesting example is how the retail industry is affected by numerous regulatory factors. First, the minimum-wage law impacts many retail employees. A second factor is employer-paid health insurance, which dramatically impacts the labour costs of service industries, such as retailing. Third, because goods must first be delivered to the stores, regulations that affect the cost of shipping by airplane, ship, or truck will affect retailers' costs. Finally, lower tariffs and quotas will allow retailers to offer imported goods at lower prices (e.g., Wal-Mart), which will expand their international production (outsourcing).

8.4.4 EVALUATING THE INDUSTRY LIFE CYCLE

An insightful analysis when predicting industry sales and trends in profitability is to view the industry over time and divide its development into stages similar to those that humans progress through: birth, adolescence, adulthood, middle age, old age. The number of stages in this **industry life cycle analysis** can vary based on how much detail we want. A five-stage model would include

1. Pioneering development
2. Rapid accelerating growth
3. Mature growth
4. Stabilization and market maturity
5. Deceleration of growth and decline

Exhibit 8.11 shows the growth path of sales during each stage. The vertical scale in logs reflects *rates* of growth, whereas the arithmetic horizontal scale has different widths representing different, unequal time periods. To estimate industry sales, we must predict the length of time for each stage. This requires answers to such questions as: How long will an industry grow at an accelerating rate (Stage 2)? How long will it be in a mature growth phase (Stage 3) before its sales growth stabilizes (Stage 4) and then declines (Stage 5)?

Besides being useful when estimating sales, this analysis of an industry's life cycle also can provide some insights into profit margins and earnings growth, although these profit measures do not necessarily parallel the sales growth. The profit margin series typically peaks very early in the total cycle and then levels off and declines as competition is attracted by the early success of the industry.

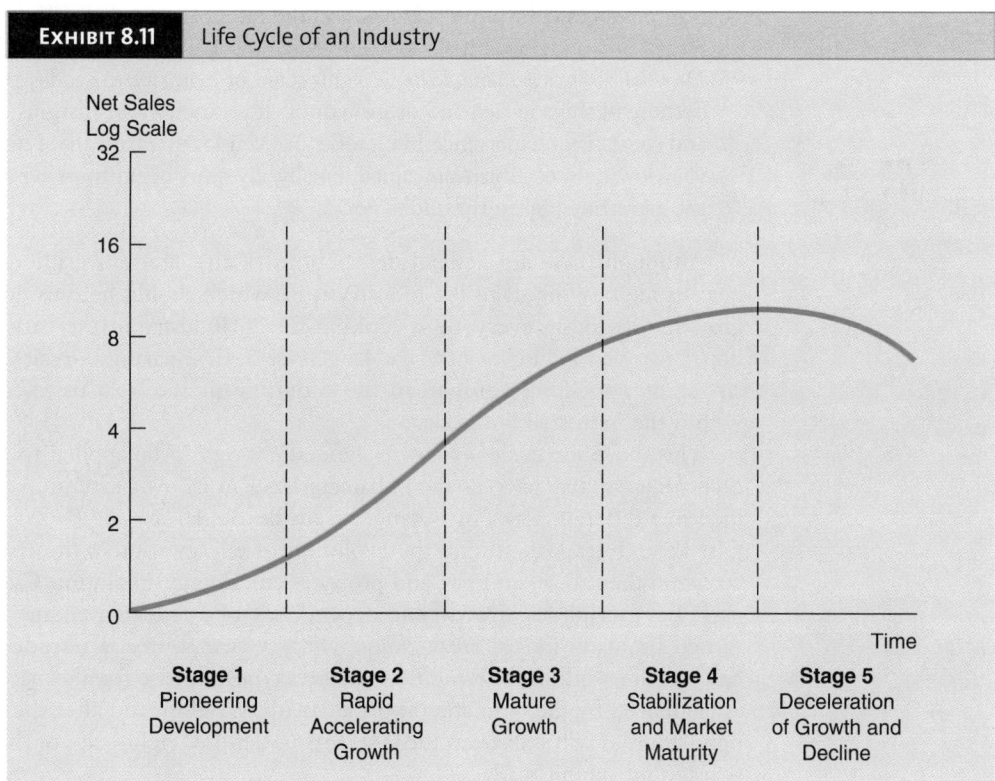

EXHIBIT 8.11   Life Cycle of an Industry

The following is a brief description of how these stages affect sales growth and profits:

1. *Pioneering development.* During this start-up stage, the industry experiences modest sales growth and very small or negative profit margins and profits. The market for the industry's product or service during this time period is small, and the firms involved incur major development costs.

2. *Rapid accelerating growth.* During this rapid growth stage, a market develops for the product or service and demand becomes substantial. The limited number of firms in the industry faces little competition, and individual firms can experience substantial backlogs. The profit margins are very high. The industry builds its productive capacity as sales grow at an increasing rate as the industry attempts to meet excess demand. High sales growth and high profit margins that increase as firms become more efficient cause industry and firm profits to explode. During this phase, profits can grow at over 100% a year as a result of the low earnings base and the rapid growth of sales and net profit margins.

3. *Mature growth.* The success in Stage 2 has satisfied most of the demand for the industry goods or service. Thus, future sales growth may be above normal but it no longer accelerates. Also, the rapid growth of sales and the high profit margins attract competitors to the industry, which causes an increase in supply and lower prices, which means that the profit margins begin to decline to normal levels.

4. *Stabilization and market maturity.* During this stage, which is probably the longest phase, the industry growth rate declines to the growth rate of the aggregate economy or its industry segment. During this stage, investors can estimate growth easily because sales correlate highly with an economic series. Although sales grow in line with the economy, profit growth varies by industry because the competitive structure varies by industry, and by individual firms within the industry because the ability to control costs differs among companies. Competition produces tight profit margins, and the rates of return on capital (e.g., return on assets, return on equity) eventually become equal to or slightly below the competitive level.

5. *Deceleration of growth and decline.* At this stage of maturity, the industry's sales growth declines because of shifts in demand or growth of substitutes. Profit margins continue to be squeezed, and some firms experience low profits or even losses. Firms that remain profitable may show very low rates of return on capital. Finally, investors begin thinking about alternative uses for the capital tied up in this industry.

Although these are general descriptions of the alternative life cycle stages, they should help us identify the stage the industry is in, which should help us estimate its potential sales growth. Obviously, everyone is looking for an industry in the early phases of Stage 2 and hopes to avoid industries in Stage 4 or Stage 5. Comparing the sales and earnings growth of an industry to similar growth in the economy should help us identify the industry's stage within the industrial life cycle.

The above life cycle analysis is general enough to be applied to almost any industry but each industry may have its own characteristics in its own evolution and each may be examined in a different way. For instance, in his book, *A Thousand Barrels a Second*, energy economist Peter Tertzakian studies the evolution of energy sources from whale oil to kerosene to coal, and then to oil and gas, and proposes an "Energy Evolution Cycle" (Exhibit 8.12). The cycle has four phases: growth and dependency of an existing energy source, pressure buildup caused by many forces, break point where a new source is introduced, and rebalances. He believes the world is entering into the break-point phase for alternative energy to replace oil as evidenced by the dramatic oil price volatility. Before and after the break point, investment opportunities will shift from those sectors under the "right half" of the cycle to the "left half" as listed in Exhibit 8.12.

EXHIBIT 8.12   Energy Evolution Cycle

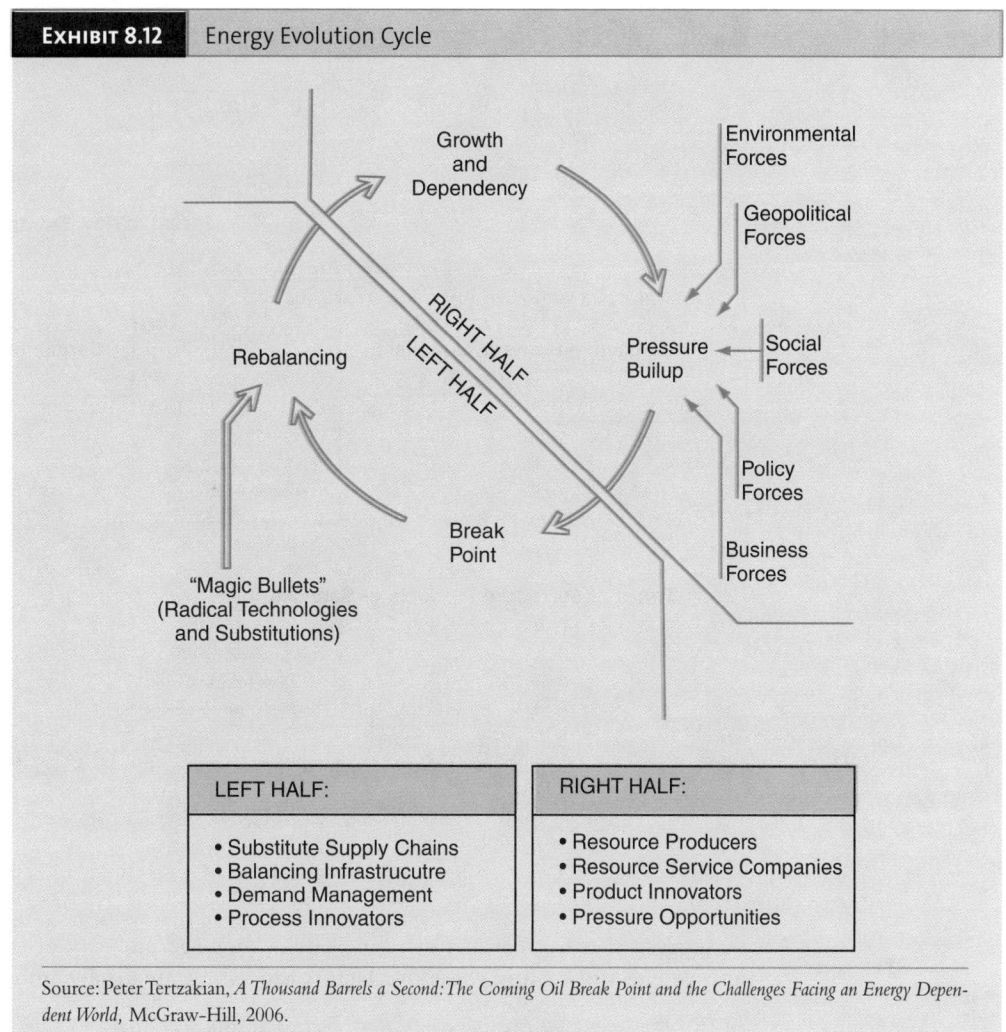

LEFT HALF:	RIGHT HALF:
• Substitute Supply Chains • Balancing Infrastrucutre • Demand Management • Process Innovators	• Resource Producers • Resource Service Companies • Product Innovators • Pressure Opportunities

Source: Peter Tertzakian, *A Thousand Barrels a Second: The Coming Oil Break Point and the Challenges Facing an Energy Dependent World,* McGraw-Hill, 2006.

8.4.5 ANALYSIS OF INDUSTRY COMPETITION

Similar to the sales forecast that can be enhanced by the analysis of the industrial life cycle, an industry earnings forecast should be preceded by the analysis of the competitive structure for the industry. Specifically, a critical factor affecting the profit potential of an industry is the intensity of competition in the industry, as Porter (1980a, b, 1985) has discussed.

Competition and Expected Industry Returns Porter's concept of **competitive strategy** is described as the search by a firm for a favourable competitive position in an industry. To create a profitable competitive strategy, a firm must first examine the basic competitive structure of its industry because the potential profitability of a firm is heavily influenced by the profitability of its industry. Analysts need to examine the factors that determine the relative competitive position of a firm within its industry.

Basic Competitive Forces Porter believes that the **competitive environment** of an industry (the intensity of competition among the firms in that industry) determines the ability of the firms to sustain above-average rates of return on invested capital. As shown in Exhibit 8.13,

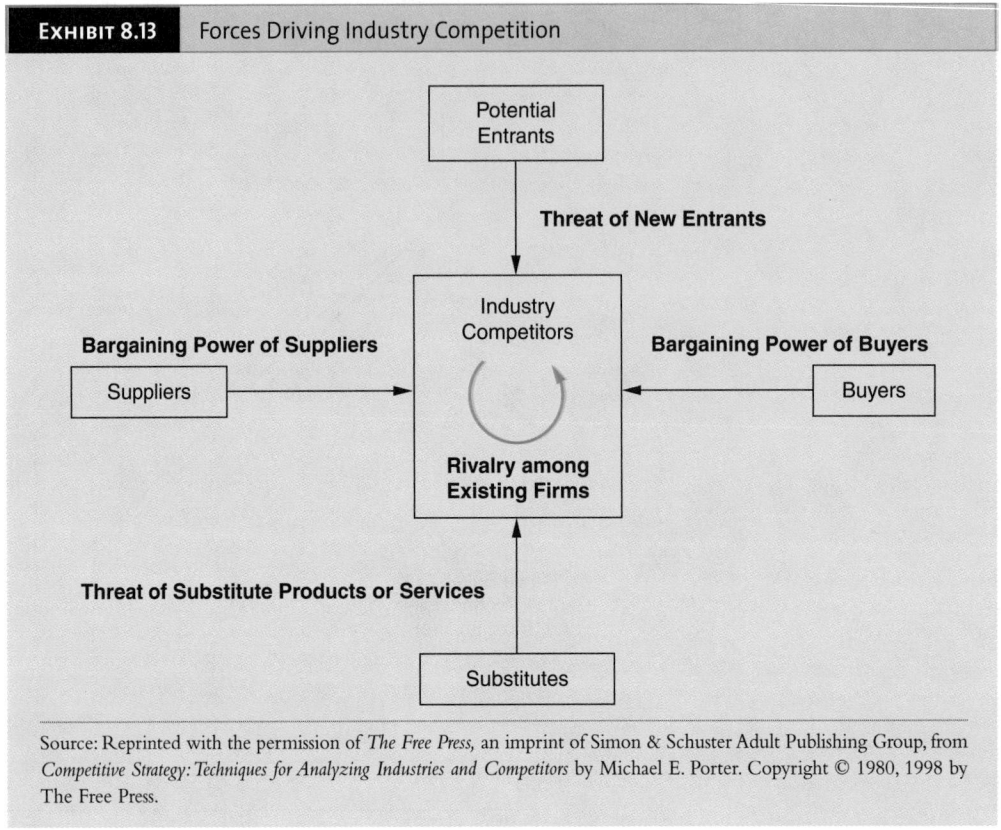

EXHIBIT 8.13 Forces Driving Industry Competition

Source: Reprinted with the permission of *The Free Press,* an imprint of Simon & Schuster Adult Publishing Group, from *Competitive Strategy: Techniques for Analyzing Industries and Competitors* by Michael E. Porter. Copyright © 1980, 1998 by The Free Press.

he suggests that five competitive forces determine the intensity of competition and that the relative effect of each of these five factors can vary dramatically among industries.

1. *Rivalry among the existing competitors.* For each industry analyzed, we must judge if the rivalry among firms is currently intense and growing, or if it is polite and stable. Rivalry increases when many firms of relatively equal size compete in an industry. When estimating the number and size of firms, be sure to include foreign competitors. Further, *slow growth* causes competitors to fight for market share and increases competition. *High fixed costs* stimulate the desire to sell at the full capacity, which can lead to price cutting and greater competition. Finally, look for *exit barriers,* such as specialized facilities or labour agreements. These can keep firms in the industry despite *below-average* or negative rates of return.
2. *Threat of new entrants.* Although an industry may have few competitors, we must determine the likelihood of firms entering the industry and increasing competition. *High barriers to entry,* such as low current prices relative to costs, keep the threat of new entrants low. Other barriers to entry include the need to invest large financial resources to compete and the availability of capital. Also, substantial economies of scale give a current industry member an advantage over a new firm. Further, entrants might be discouraged if success in the industry requires extensive distribution channels that are hard to build because of exclusive distribution contracts. Similarly, high costs of switching products or brands, such as those required to change a computer or telephone system, keep competition low. Finally, government policy can restrict entry by imposing licensing requirements or limiting access to materials (lumber, coal). Without

some of these barriers, it might be very easy for competitors to enter an industry, increasing the competition and driving down potential rates of return.

3. *Threat of substitute products.* Substitute products limit the profit potential of an industry because they limit the prices firms in an industry can charge. Although almost everything has a substitute, we must determine how close the substitute is in price and function to the product in the industry. For example, new energy such as solar is a rising threat to oil and gas, especially when the oil prices keep rising.

4. *Bargaining power of buyers.* Buyers can influence the profitability of an industry because they can bid down prices or demand higher quality or more services by bargaining among competitors. Buyers become powerful when they purchase a large volume relative to the sales of a supplier (e.g., Wal-Mart, Home Depot). The most vulnerable firm is a one-customer firm that supplies a single large manufacturer, as is common for auto parts manufacturers or software developers. Buyers will be more conscious of the costs of items that represent a significant percentage of the firm's total costs. This consciousness increases if the buying firm is feeling cost pressure from its customers. Also, buyers who know a lot about the costs of supplying an industry will bargain more intensely—for example, when the buying firm supplies some of its own needs and buys from the outside.

5. *Bargaining power of suppliers.* Suppliers can alter future industry returns if they increase prices or reduce the quality of the product or the services they provide. The suppliers are more powerful if they are few and if they are more concentrated than the industry to which they sell and if they supply critical inputs to several industries for which few, if any, substitutes exist. In this instance, the suppliers are free to change prices and services they supply to the firms in an industry. Ultimately, both the supplier and the buyer can undertake vertical integration and have their own division providing the same product or services. Finally, when analyzing supplier bargaining power, be sure to consider labour union's power and the supply and demand of labour and special talents that an industry needs.

An investor needs to analyze these competitive forces to determine the intensity of the competition in an industry and assess the effect of this competition on the industry's long-run profit potential. We should examine each of these factors and develop a relative competitive profile for each industry. We need to update this analysis of an industry's competitive environment over time, because an industry's competitive structure can and will change over time.

Summary

1. As investors, we want to select investments that will provide a return that compensates us for our time, the expected rate of inflation, and the risk involved. We consider the two investment decision processes, which are the top-down, three-step approach and the bottom-up, stock-picking approach.

2. Although it is recognized that either process can provide abnormal positive returns if the analyst is superior, we feel that a preferable approach is the top-down approach in which we initially consider the aggregate economy and market, then examine alternative global industries, and finally analyze individual firms and their stocks.

3. Economic analysis covers macroeconomic variables that would be related to stock market performance. These include business cycles, economic growth rate, monetary variables, inflation, and interest rates. The earnings multiplier approach can be used to forecast the performance of the aggregate stock market. It is also important to analyze the world security markets.

4. Industry analysis for investment purposes would cover price history, operating data, and alternative industries. Key factors in industry analysis include markets for products, financial performance, operations, and management.

5. Industry analysis is a crucial link between economic analysis and company analysis. We discussed four important industry analysis tools: business cycle, structural changes in the economy, the life cycle of the industry, and the competitive environment of the industry.

Key Terms

competitive environment, p. 225
competitive strategy, p. 225
cyclical change, p. 217

industry life cycle analysis, p. 223
investment decision process, p. 201

structural change, p. 217
valuation process, p. 201

Suggested Readings

Valuation

Brockman, Paul, Charles Mossman, and Dennis Olson. "What's the Value of Fundamental Analysis?" *Canadian Investment Review* 10, no. 3 (Fall 1997): 10.

Damodaran, Aswath. *Damodaran on Valuation*, 2nd ed. New York: Wiley, 2006.

Helfert, Erich A. *Techniques of Financial Analysis*, 11th ed. New York: McGraw-Hill Irwin, 2002.

Higgins, Robert C. *Analysis for Financial Management*, 8th ed. New York: McGraw-Hill Irwin, 2005.

Koller, Tim, Marc Goedhart, and David Wessels. *Valuation, Measuring and Managing the Value of Companies*, 4th ed. New York: Wiley, 2005.

Palepu, Krishna, and Paul Healy. *Business Analysis and Valuation*, 4th ed. Cincinnati, OH: South-Western, 2007.

Economic Analysis

Cherie Metcalf, Angela Redish and Ronald Shearer, "New Estimates of the Canadian Money Stock, 1871–1967," The *Canadian Journal of Economics* 31, no. 1 (Feb. 1998): 104-124.

Diermeier, Jeffrey J. "Capital Market Expectations: The Macro Factors." In *Managing Investment Portfolios: A Dynamic Process*, 2nd ed., eds. John L. Maginn and Donald L. Tuttle. Boston: Warren Gorham and Lamont, 1990.

Fama, Eugene F., and Kenneth French. "Business Conditions and Expected Returns on Stocks and Bonds." *Journal of Financial Economics* 25, no. 1 (November 1989).

Finnerty, John D., and Dean Leistikow. "The Behavior of Equity and Debt Risk Premiums." *Journal of Portfolio Management* 19, no. 4 (Summer 1993).

Mankiw, N. G., Kneebone, R. D., McKenzie, K. J., and N. Rowe. *Principles of Macroeconomics*, 4th Canadian Edition, Nelson, 2008.

Mishkin, Frederic S. and Serletis, Apostolos. *The Economics of Money, Banking, and Financial Markets*, 3rd Canadian Edition, Addison Wesley, 2008.

Shackalford, Aaron L., ed. *Economic Analysis for Investment Professionals.* Charlottesville, VA: AIMR, 1997.

Solnik, Bruno. Predictable Time-Varying Components of International Asset Returns. Charlottesville, VA: AIMR, 1993.

Industry Analysis

Goldman Sachs. *Introducing the GS SUSTAIN*, 2007. http://www.unglobalcompact.org/docs/summit2007/gs_esg_embargoed_until030707pdf.pdf

Goodman, D. A., and John W. Peavy, III. "Industry Relative Price-Earnings Ratios as Indicators of Investment Returns," *Financial Analysts Journal* 39, no. 2 (March–April 1983): 60–66.

Kan, J. *Handbook of Canadian Security Analysis*, Wiley, Volume One, 1997; Volume Two, 2000.

Porter, Michael E. "How to Conduct an Industry Analysis." In *The Financial Analysts Handbook*, 2d ed., ed. Sumner N. Levine. Homewood, IL: Dow Jones–Irwin, 1988.

Tertzakian, Peter. *A Thousand Barrels a Second: The Coming Oil Break Point and the Challenges Facing an Energy Dependent World*, McGraw Hill, 2006.

The following are proceedings from industry analysis seminars sponsored by the Association for Investment Management and Research (AIMR):

Balog, James, ed. *The Health Care Industry.* Charlottesville, VA: AIMR, 1993.

Bhatia, Sanjiv, ed. *The Consumer Staples Industry.* Charlottesville, VA: AIMR, 1995.

Bhatia, Sanjiv, ed. *The Media Industry.* Charlottesville, VA: AIMR, 1996.

Petrie, Thomas, A. ed. *The Oil and Gas Industries.* Charlottesville, VA: AIMR, 1993.

Shasta, Theodore, ed. *The Automotive Industry.* Charlottesville, VA: AIMR, 1994.

 For Chapter CFA Questions and Problems, please see Appendix A at the end of this text.

Questions

1. Discuss the difference between the top-down and bottom-up approaches. What is the major assumption that causes the difference in these two approaches?
2. What is the benefit of analyzing the market and alternative industries before individual securities?
3. Discuss why you would not expect all industries to have a similar relationship to the economy. Give an example of two industries that have different relationships to the economy.
4. Why would you expect a relationship between economic activity and stock price movements?
5. At a lunch with some business associates, you discuss the reason for the relationship between the economy and the stock market. One of your associates contends that she has heard that stock prices typically turn before the economy does. How would you explain this phenomenon?
6. Explain the following statements: (a) There is a strong, consistent relationship between money supply changes and stock prices. (b) Money supply changes cannot be used to predict stock price movements.
7. You are informed of the following estimates: Nominal money supply is expected to grow at a rate of 7%, and GDP is estimated to grow at 4%. Explain what you think will happen to stock prices during this period and the reason for your expectation.

8. The current rate of inflation is 3%, and long-term Treasury bonds are yielding 7%. You estimate that the rate of inflation will increase to 6%. What do you expect to happen to long-term bond yields? Compute the effect of this change in inflation on the price of a 15-year, 10% coupon bond with a current yield to maturity of 8%.
9. Some observers contend that it is harder to estimate the effect of a change in interest rates on common stocks than on bonds. Discuss this contention.
10. An investor is convinced that the stock market will experience a substantial increase next year because corporate earnings are expected to rise by at least 12%. Do you agree or disagree? Why or why not?
11. Assume the industry you are analyzing is in the fourth stage of the industrial life cycle. How would you react if your industry-economic analysis predicted that sales per share for this industry would increase by 20%? Discuss your reasoning.
12. Discuss at what stage in the industrial life cycle you would like to discover an industry. Justify your decision.
13. Give an example of an industry in Stage 2 of the industrial life cycle. Discuss your reasoning for putting the industry in Stage 2 and any evidence that caused you to select this stage for the industry.

Problems

1. Prepare a table showing the percentage change for each of the last 10 years in (a) the Consumer Price Index (all items), (b) nominal GDP, (c) real GDP (in constant dollars), and (d) the GDP deflator. Discuss how much of nominal growth was due to *real* growth and how much was due to inflation.
2. Evaluate your industry in terms of the five factors that determine an industry's intensity of competition. Based on this analysis, what are your expectations about the industry's profitability in the short run (1 or 2 years) and the long run (5–10 years)?
3. You know the following about your industry (I) and the market (M):

ROE_I:	12%	ROE_M:	16%
RR_I:	0.60	RR_M:	0.55
$Beta_I$:	1.05	$Beta_M$:	1.00

Discuss what difference you would expect in the *P/E*s, and explain why you expect this difference.

4. Based on the Energy Evolution Cycle (Exhibit 8.13), which stage in the cycle do you think the global energy industry is at currently? Are we getting closer or moving further from a break point?
5. Could the Energy Evolution Cycle (Exhibit 8.13) be applied to any other industry? For instance, would you be able to modify the chart such that it might be applicable to another resource-based industry beyond energy?
6. If you were convinced that an energy break point (Exhibit 8.13) is coming within three years, how would you advise your client to act to take advantage of this. Make a list of companies that you might advise your client to buy and a list to sell.
7. Apply the competitive forces analysis (Exhibit 8.14) to a Canadian resource-based industry, a manufacturing industry, and a service industry of your choice.
8. Further to the previous question, do you think the framework is general enough to be applied to any industry, or do you have any suggestions to improve it?

9

Company Analysis and Stock Valuation*

After you read this chapter, you should be able to answer the following questions:

1. Why is it important to differentiate between company analysis and stock valuation?

2. What is the difference between a true growth company and a growth stock?

3. What techniques are useful when estimating the inputs to the various valuation models?

4. What techniques are useful when estimating sales, profit margins, and earnings per share for a company?

5. What factors are considered when estimating the earnings multiplier for a firm?

6. In addition to the earnings multiplier, what are some other relative valuation ratios?

7. How do we compute economic value added (EVA), market value added (MVA), and the franchise value for a firm, and what is the relationship between these value-added measures and changes in the market value of firms?

At this point, you have made two decisions about your equity-market investment. First, after analyzing the economy and stock markets for several countries, you have decided what percent of your portfolio should be invested in common stocks. Second, after analyzing various industries, you have identified those that appear to offer above-average risk-adjusted performance over your investment horizon. The final questions in the fundamental analysis procedure: Which stocks within these desirable industries are the stocks expected to yield returns greater than or equal to its required return?

The chapter begins with a discussion of the difference between company analysis and stock valuation. Company analysis should occur in the context of the prevailing economic and industry conditions. We discuss some competitive strategies that can help firms maximize returns in an industry's competitive environment and review some models used to determine a stock's intrinsic value. This is followed by a review of factors that will help you determine when to sell a stock that you own and discuss the pressures and influences that affect professional stock analysts.

9.1 Company Analysis versus Stock Valuation

The common stocks of good companies are not necessarily good investments. The stock of a firm with superior management and strong performance measured by sales and earnings growth can be priced so high that the stock's intrinsic value is below its current market price and should not be bought. In contrast, a company with lower sales and earnings growth may have a stock market price below its intrinsic value. In this case, although the company is not as good, its stock could be the better investment.

The classic confusion concerns growth companies versus growth stocks. The stock of a growth company is not necessarily a growth stock. Recognition of this difference is absolutely essential for successful investing.

---

* The authors acknowledge comments and suggestions on this chapter by Professor Edgar Norton of Illinois State University.

9.1.1 Growth Companies and Growth Stocks

Historically, growth companies have been defined as those that consistently experience above-average increases in sales and earnings. This definition has some limitations because many firms could qualify due to certain accounting procedures, mergers, or other external events.

In contrast, financial theorists such as Salomon (1963) and Miller and Modigliani (1961) define a **growth company** as a firm with the management ability and the opportunities to make investments that provide returns greater than the firm's required return or its weighted average cost of capital (WACC). For example, a growth company might obtain capital at an average cost of 10%, and management has the ability and the opportunity to invest those funds to return of 15% to 20%. As a result, the firm's sales and earnings grow faster than those of similar risk firms and the overall economy. In addition, these firms with above-average investment opportunities should, and typically do, retain a large portion of its earnings to fund these superior investment projects (i.e., they have low dividend-payout ratios).

Growth stocks are *not* necessarily shares in growth companies. A **growth stock** has a higher expected return than other stocks in the market with similar risk characteristics. The stock achieves this expected superior risk-adjusted return because the market has undervalued it compared to other stocks. Although the stock market prices adjust relatively quickly and accurately to reflect new information, available information is not always perfect or complete. Therefore, imperfect or incomplete information may cause a given stock to be undervalued or overvalued at a point in time.[1]

The price of undervalued stock should eventually increase to reflect its true fundamental value when the correct information becomes available. During this period of price adjustment, the stock's realized return will be more than it should be for a stock with its risk, thus during this period, it will be a growth stock.

If investors recognize a growth company and discount its future earnings stream properly, the current market price of the growth company's stock will reflect its future earnings stream. However, in many instances, overeager investors tend to overestimate the expected growth of earnings and cash flows for the growth company and, therefore, inflate the growth company's stock price. Investors paying the inflated price will earn less than the risk-adjusted return, despite the fact that the company experiences above-average growth of sales and earnings. Studies by Solt and Statman (1989), Shefrin and Statman (1995), and Clayman (1987) have examined the stock price performance for samples of growth companies and found that their stocks have generally not been growth stocks.

9.1.2 Defensive Companies and Stocks

Defensive companies are those whose future earnings are likely to withstand an economic downturn. One would expect them to have relatively low business risk and not excessive financial risk. Typical examples are firms that supply basic consumer necessities, such as public utilities or grocery chains.

There are two closely related concepts of a **defensive stock.** First, a defensive stock's return is not expected to decline during an overall market decline, or it will decline less than the overall market. Second, our CAPM discussion in Chapter 7 indicated that an asset's relevant risk is its covariance with the market portfolio of risky assets—that is, an asset's systematic risk. A stock with low or negative systematic risk (a small positive or negative beta) may be considered a defensive stock according to this theory because its returns are unlikely to be harmed significantly in a bear market.

---

1 An analyst is more likely to find such stocks outside the top tier of companies that are scrutinized by numerous analysts; in other words, look for neglected stocks.

9.1.3   CYCLICAL COMPANIES AND STOCKS

A **cyclical company's** sales and earnings will be heavily influenced by aggregate business activity. Examples would be firms in the steel, automotive, or heavy machinery industries. Such companies will do well during economic expansions and poorly during economic contractions. This volatile earnings pattern is typically a function of the firm's business risk (both sales volatility and operating leverage) and can be compounded by financial risk.

The stock of a cyclical company, however, is not necessarily a cyclical stock. A **cyclical stock return** will experience changes greater than changes in overall market returns. In terms of the CAPM, these would be stocks that have high betas that have high correlation with the aggregate market and greater volatility.

9.1.4   SPECULATIVE COMPANIES AND STOCKS

A **speculative company** is one whose assets involve great risk but that also has a possibility of great gain. A good example of a speculative firm is one involved in oil exploration.

A **speculative stock** possesses a high probability of low or negative returns and a low probability of normal or high returns. Specifically, a speculative stock is one that is overpriced, leading to a high likelihood that it will experience either low or possibly negative returns when the market adjusts the stock price to its true value. Such an expectation might be the case for an excellent growth company whose stock is selling at an extremely high price/earnings ratio (it is substantially overvalued).

9.1.5   VALUE VERSUS GROWTH INVESTING

Some analysts also divide stocks into growth stocks and value stocks. As discussed, growth stocks are companies that have positive earnings surprises and above-average risk-adjusted returns because the stocks are undervalued. If the analyst does a good job in identifying such companies, investors in these stocks will reap the benefits of seeing their stock prices rise after other investors identify their earnings growth potential. **Value stocks** are those that appear to be undervalued for reasons other than earnings growth potential. Value stocks are usually identified by analysts as having low price-earning (P/E) or price-book-value ratios. Notably, in these comparisons between growth and value stocks, the specification of a growth stock is *not* consistent with our preceding discussion. In these discussions, a growth stock is generally specified as a stock of a company that is experiencing rapid growth of sales and earnings (e.g., Research in Motion). As a result of this company performance, the stock typically has a high P/E and price-book-value ratio. Unfortunately, the specification does not consider the critical comparison we advocate between intrinsic value and market price. Therefore, these specifications will not be used in subsequent discussions of valuation.

9.2   Economic, Industry, and Structural Links to Company Analysis

Analysis of companies and their stocks is the final step in the top-down approach to investing. Rather than selecting stocks only on the basis of company-specific factors (as with bottom-up analysis), top-down analysts review the current status and future outlook for domestic and international sectors of the economy. Based on this macroeconomic analysis, they identify industries that offer attractive returns and then value firms in the selected industries. We have summarized this discussion from Web Chapter 20 at www.reilly.nelson.com.

9.2.1   ECONOMIC AND INDUSTRY INFLUENCES

If economic trends are favourable for an industry, the company analysis should focus on firms well-positioned to benefit from these economic trends. Research analysts should become familiar with the cash flow and risk attributes of the firms they are studying because firms within an industry will have varying sensitivities to economic variables, such as economic growth, interest rates, input costs, and exchange rates. Given a period of economic-industry growth, the most attractive firms within the industry may be those with high levels of operating and financial leverage wherein a modest percentage increase in revenue results in a much larger percentage rise in earnings and cash flow.

9.2.2 STRUCTURAL INFLUENCES

Social trends, technology, and political and regulatory influences can also have a major effect on some firms within an industry. Some firms can try to take advantage of demographic changes or shifts in consumer tastes and lifestyles, or they can invest in technology to lower costs and better serve their customers. Such firms grow and succeed despite unfavourable industry or economic conditions. For example, Wal-Mart became a leading retailer because of several smart management decisions. The geographic location of many of its stores allowed it to benefit from regional population growth and lower labour costs. Its competitive strategy of emphasizing everyday low prices appealed to consumers concerned about price and value. Finally, its technologically advanced inventory and ordering systems and its outstanding distribution system gave the company a clear competitive (cost) advantage.

During the initial stage of an industry's life cycle, the original firms in the industry can refine their technologies and move down the learning curve. Subsequent followers may benefit from initial actions, learn from the leaders' mistakes, and take the market lead away from them. Investors need to be aware of such strategies and value them accordingly.

Political and regulatory events can create opportunities in an industry even during weak economic periods. News about the taxation of income trusts resulted in sharp price declines. Some stocks in an industry may deserve lower prices following some political or regulatory event; but if the market also punishes the stock prices of good companies with smaller exposures to the bad news, then an alert analyst will identify buying opportunities of underpriced stocks within an industry.

Remember that although the economy plays a major role in determining overall market trends and industry groups display sensitivity to economic variables, other structural changes may counterbalance the economic effects, or company management may be able to minimize the impact of economic or industry events. Analysts familiar with industry trends and company strategies can issue well-reasoned buy-and-sell recommendations irrespective of the economic forecast.

9.3 Company Analysis

This section outlines various analysis components that should help provide an understanding of a firm's overall *strategic* approach. Given this background, we are in a position to apply several fundamental valuation models.

9.3.1 FIRM COMPETITIVE STRATEGIES

A company's competitive strategy can either be *defensive* or *offensive*. A **defensive competitive strategy** involves positioning the firm to deflect the effect of the competitive forces in the industry. Examples may include investing in capital assets and technology to lower production costs, or creating a strong brand image with increased advertising expenditures.

An **offensive competitive strategy** is one in which the firm attempts to use its strengths to affect the competitive forces in the industry. For example, Wal-Mart used its buying power to obtain price concessions from its suppliers. This cost advantage, coupled with a superior delivery system to its stores, allowed Wal-Mart to grow against larger competitors and eventually become a leading retailer.

As an investor, you must understand what strategies exist, determine each firm's strategy, judge whether the firm's strategy is reasonable for its industry, and, finally, evaluate how successful the firm is in implementing its strategy. For analysts, they must decide whether the firm's management is correctly positioning the firm to take advantage of industry and economic conditions. The analyst's opinion about management's decisions should ultimately be reflected in the analyst's growth estimates for cash flow and earnings.

9.3.2 FOCUSING A STRATEGY

Whichever strategy it selects, a firm must select segments in the industry and tailor its strategy to serve these specific groups. For example, a low-cost strategy would typically exploit cost advantages by being the low-cost producer for the expensive segment of the market. Similarly, a differentiation focus would target the special needs of buyers in specific segments. For example, companies in the athletic-shoe market have attempted to develop shoes for unique sport segments, such as tennis, basketball, aerobics, or walkers and hikers, rather than offering only shoes for runners. Firms thought that participants would be willing to pay a premium for these special shoes. Exhibit 9.1 details some of Porter's ideas for the skills, resources, and company organizational requirements needed to successfully develop a cost leadership or a differentiation strategy.

Next, you must determine whether the strategy can be sustained. As well, you should review the firm's competitive strategy over time; different strategies work during different phases of an industry's life cycle. For example, differentiation strategies may work for firms in an industry during the early growth stages. Subsequently, when the industry is in the mature stage, firms may try the low-cost strategy.

EXHIBIT 9.1	Skills, Resources, and Organizational Requirements Needed to Successfully Apply Cost Leadership and Differentiation Strategies	
Generic Strategy	**Commonly Required Skills and Resources**	**Common Organizational Requirements**
Overall cost leadership	Sustained capital investment and access to capital	Tight cost control
	Process engineering skills	Frequent, detailed control reports
	Intense supervision of labour	Structured organization and responsibilities
	Products designed for ease in manufacture	Incentives based on meeting strict quantitative targets
	Low-cost distribution system	
Differentiation	Strong marketing abilities	Strong coordination among functions in R&D, product development, and marketing
	Product engineering	
	Creative flair	Subjective measurement and incentives instead of quantitative measures
	Strong capability in basic research	
	Corporate reputation for quality or technological leadership	Amenities to attract highly skilled labour, scientists, or creative people
	Long tradition in the industry or unique combination of skills drawn from other businesses	
	Strong cooperation from channels	

Source: Adapted from *Competitive Strategy: Techniques for Analyzing Industries and Competitors* by Michael E. Porter.

Through the analysis process, the analyst begins developing a company's "story." This evaluation is the key to understanding how a company makes money and assists the analyst in deriving a reasonable estimate of the firm's long-run cash flows and its risks.

9.3.3 SWOT ANALYSIS

Another framework for examining and understanding a firm's competitive position and its strategy is a company **SWOT analysis**. Examination of a firm's *s*trengths, *w*eaknesses, *o*pportunities, and *t*hreats should help you evaluate a firm's strategies to exploit its competitive advantages or defend against its weaknesses. Strengths and weaknesses involve identifying the firm's *internal* abilities or lack thereof. Opportunities and threats include *external* situations, such as competitive forces, discovery and development of new technologies, government regulations, and domestic and international economic trends.

The *strengths* of a company give the firm a comparative advantage in the marketplace. Perceived strengths can include good customer service, high-quality products, strong brand image, customer loyalty, innovative R&D, market leadership, or strong financial resources. To remain strengths, they must continue to be developed, maintained, and defended through prudent capital investment policies.

Weaknesses result when competitors have potentially exploitable advantages over the firm. Once identified, the firm can select strategies to mitigate or correct the weaknesses. For example, a domestic producer in a global market can make investments that will allow it to export or produce its product overseas. Another example would be a firm with poor financial resources forming joint ventures with financially stronger firms.

Opportunities, or environmental factors that favour the firm, can include a growing market for the firm's products (domestic and international), shrinking competition, favourable exchange rate shifts, or identification of a new market or product segment.

Threats are environmental factors that can hinder the firm in achieving its goals. Examples would include a slowing domestic economy (or sluggish overseas economies for exporters), additional government regulation, an increase in industry competition, threats of entry, buyers or suppliers seeking to increase their bargaining power, or new technology that can obsolete the industry's product. By recognizing and understanding opportunities and threats, an investor can make informed decisions about how the firm can exploit opportunities and mitigate threats.

Some Lessons from Lynch

Peter Lynch (1989, 1993), the former portfolio manager of Fidelity Investments' highly successful Magellan Fund, looks for the following favourable attributes when he analyzes firms, attributes that may result in favourable stock-market performance:

1. The firm's product is not faddish; it is one that consumers will continue to purchase over time.
2. The company has a sustainable comparative competitive advantage over its rivals.
3. The firm's industry or product has market stability. Therefore, it has little need to innovate or create product improvements or fear that it may lose a technological advantage. Market stability means less potential for entry.
4. The firm can benefit from cost reductions (e.g. a computer manufacturer that uses technology provided by suppliers to deliver a faster and less-expensive product).
5. The firm buys back its shares or management purchases shares, which indicates that its insiders are putting their money into the firm.

Tenets of Warren Buffett

The following tenets are from Robert Hagstrom (2001). The parenthetical comments are based on discussions in the book and Berkshire Hathaway annual report letters.

Business Tenets
- Is the business simple and understandable? This makes it easier to estimate future cash flows with a high degree of confidence. (Does the business have a franchise product or service that is needed or desired, has no close substitute, and is not regulated? This implies that the firm has pricing flexibility.)
- Does the business have a consistent operating history?
- Does the business have favourable long-term prospects?

Management Tenets
- Is management rational?
- Is management candid with its shareholders?
- Does management resist the institutional imperative?
- Is capital allocated to projects that provide returns above the cost of capital? If not, does management pay capital to shareholders through dividends or share repurchase?
- Does management resist imitating the behaviour of other managers?

Financial Tenets
- Focus on return on equity, not earnings per share.
- Calculate owner earnings.
- Look for a company with relatively high sustainable profit margins for its industry.
- Make sure the company has created at least one dollar of market value for every dollar retained.

Market Tenets
- What is the intrinsic value of the business?
- Can the business be purchased at a significant discount to its fundamental intrinsic value?

9.4   Estimating Intrinsic Value

Once the economic, structural forces, industry, company, and competitor analysis is completed, the next step is to estimate the intrinsic value of the firm's common stock.

As we note in Web Chapter 20, we will consider two general approaches to valuation and the following techniques.

Present Value of Cash Flows (PVCF)

1. Present value of dividends (DDM)
2. Present value of free cash flow to equity (FCFE)
3. Present value of free operating cash flow to the firm (FCFF)

Relative Valuation Techniques

1. Price/earnings ratio (*P/E*)
2. Price/cash flow ratio (*P/CF*)
3. Price/book-value-ratio (*P/BV*)
4. Price/sales ratio (*P/S*)

Although we limit our demonstration to Shoppers Drug Mart (ticker symbol: SC), a complete company analysis would cover all the firms in the retail drug store (RDS) industry. Exhibit 9.2 contains historical data for Shoppers Drug Mart that we will require for the present-value of cash flow (PVCF) models.

9.4.1 PRESENT VALUE OF DIVIDENDS

As we note in Web Chapter 20, determining the present value of future dividends is not an easy task. Therefore, analysts make simplifying assumptions such as a constant growth rate on the stock's dividends. Although unrealistic for fast-growing or cyclical firms, this assumption may be appropriate for many mature firms. More complex DDMs exist for more complicated growth forecasts including two-stage and three-stage growth models.[2]

Recall that the constant growth DDM implies that when dividends grow at a constant rate, a stock's price should equal next year's dividend, D_1 divided by investors' required return on the stock (k) minus the dividend growth rate (g):

9.1	**Intrinsic Value** $= D_1/(k - g)$

Next year's dividend (D_1) should equal the current dividend, D_0, increased by the constant dividend growth rate: $D_1 = D_0 (1 + g)$. As we know the current dividend, we need only estimate the dividend growth rate and investors' required return in order to estimate the stock's intrinsic value.

Growth Rate Estimates If the stock has had fairly constant dividend growth over the past 5 to 10 years, one estimate of the constant growth rate is to use the actual growth of dividends over this period or

9.2	**Average Dividend Growth Rate** $= \sqrt[n]{\dfrac{D_n}{D_0}} - 1$

In the case of Shoppers Drug Mart, which began paying dividends in 2005, the 2005 dividend (D_0) was \$0.40 per share and the 2008 dividend (D_2) was \$0.86 per share. The average dividend growth rate was

$$\sqrt[3]{\frac{\$0.86}{0.40}} - 1 = \sqrt[3]{2.15} - 1 = 0.2906$$

or 29.06%. Clearly, blindly plugging historical growth rates into our formulas ignores our analysis of economic, structural, industry, and company influences. Our analysis may have indicated that growth is expected to increase or decrease due to various factors and therefore the historical growth rate may need to be adjusted to reflect our findings.

---

2 These are discussed in Web Chapter 20.

EXHIBIT 9.2   Shoppers Drug Mart Input Data for Various Present Value of Cash Flow Models (dollars in millions, except per-share data)

Year	Dividend per Share	Net Income	Amortization Expense	Capital Spending	Change in Working Capital	Principal Repayment	New Long-term Debt Issued	FCFE	EBIT	Tax Rate	FCFF	100%-Tax Rate	Time
2002	0	209	98	−129	38	−812	652	56	423	30.3	302	69.7	
2003	0	258	96	−178	140	−841	650	125	486	37.2	363	62.8	1
2004	0	169	110	−253	−328	−75	0	−377	537	35.4	−124	64.6	2
2005	0.40	186	129	−275	22	−250	0	−188	599	33.8	273	66.2	3
2006	0.48	422	150	−381	−71	−27	0	93	684	33.3	154	66.7	4
2007	0.64	490	181	−535	230	0	0	370	786	33	403	67	5
2008	0.86	565	220	−766	−548	−300	850	21	883	31	−485	69	6

Source: Information calculated using publicly available data of Shoppers Drug Mart.

Recall from your corporate finance course that future growth can be estimated by calculating the sustainable growth rate.

9.3	$$g = RR \times ROE$$

This of course assumes the firm will maintain a constant debt-equity ratio as it finances asset growth. The sustainable growth calculation from Web Chapter 19 shows Shoppers maintaining a growth rate of around 11.3%.

The dividend growth rate will be influenced by the age of the industry life cycle, structural changes, industry competition, and economic trends. Economic-industry-firm analysis provides valuable information regarding future trends in dividend growth. Averaging the historical growth rate of dividends (29.06%) and the implied sustainable growth estimate of 11.3% indicates a value of 20.18%. We feel that a firm's *ROE* is the critical growth factor and to give this estimate more weight, we will use a conservative 13% for Shoppers' estimated *g* (Shoppers' *ROE* in 2008 was over 16%).

Required Return Estimate We know an investor requires the nominal risk-free interest rate and a risk premium, and if the market is efficient, the return earned should compensate investors for the risk of the investment.

Therefore, we must estimate *future* risk premiums to determine the stock's current intrinsic value. The nominal risk-free estimates would be available from the top-down analysis of the economy. The risk premium must rely on other information, including evaluation of the firm's financial statements and capital market relationships.

We begin by comparing the ratios we examine in Web Chapter 19 that measure business, financial, liquidity, exchange rate, and country risk to the firm's major competitors, its industry, and the overall market. This fundamental comparison should indicate if the firm deserves a higher or lower risk premium. A further analysis requires an estimate of the future, including any information uncovered during the top-down process that would lead to higher or lower risk estimates. Readers are encouraged to review Web Chapter 19 now if they are unfamiliar with ratio analysis.

A market-based risk estimate can be derived using the stock's beta along with estimates of the economy's risk-free rate and the future long-run market return:

9.4	$$E(R_{stock}) = E(RFR) + \beta_{stock}[E(R_{market}) - E(RFR)]$$

Keep in mind that beta is affected by changes in a firm's business and financial risks, as well as other influences, so an investor should increase or lower the historical beta estimate based on his or her analysis of the firm's *future* risk characteristics.

For Shoppers Drug Mart, we make several assumptions regarding the security market line (SML) components. First, the prevailing nominal risk-free rate (*NRFR*) is estimated at about 4%. (Note that this is higher than the rates in mid-2009; we consider this to be anomalous and are using a more conservative long-term estimate.) The expected equity market return (R_M) depends on the expected market risk premium on stocks. As noted earlier, this is a very controversial topic wherein the estimates range substantially; for demonstration purposes we will use a 5% risk premium (0.050). The final estimate is the firm's systematic risk value (beta), based upon the following regression model (the characteristic line):

| 9.5 | $$R_{SC} = \alpha + \beta_{SC}\,R_M$$ |

where:

R_{SC} = monthly return for Shoppers Drug Mart
 α = constant term
β_{SC} = beta coefficient for Shoppers Drug Mart

$$\textbf{equal to }\ \frac{Cov_{SC,M}}{\sigma_M^2}$$

R_M = monthly returns for a market proxy—typically the S&P/TSX Composite Index

When this regression was run using monthly returns (60 observations), the beta coefficient was estimated at 0.50.

Putting together the *RFR* of 0.040 and the market risk premium of 0.050, implies an expected market return (R_M) of 0.090. This, combined with Shoppers' beta of 0.50, indicates the following expected return for Shoppers:

$$\begin{aligned} E(R) &= RFR + \beta_i(R_M - RFR)\\ &= 0.04 + 0.50(0.09 - 0.04)\\ &= 0.04 + 0.025\\ &= 0.065,\ \text{or } 6.5\% \end{aligned}$$

We will round this to 7%, which we consider low given the market risk premium is at the low end of the historical range and that Shoppers' beta is likely somewhat higher than 0.50.

At this point, the analyst would face a problem: the intent was to use the basic DDM, which assumes a constant growth rate for an infinite period and that $k > g$, which is not true in this case. Therefore, the analyst must employ a two- or three-stage growth model. Because of the fairly large difference between the current growth rate of 13% and the long-run constant growth rate of 5% (the conservative, mid-term economic forecast for growth in the retail drug industry), it seems reasonable to use a three-stage growth model, which includes a gradual transition period. We assume that the growth periods are as follows:

g_1 = 3 years (growing at 13% a year)
g_2 = 4 years (during this period it is assumed that the growth rate declines 2% per year for 4 years)
g_3 = constant perpetual growth of 5%

Therefore, beginning with 2009 when dividends were expected to be $0.86, the future dividend payments will be as follows:

Year	HIGH-GROWTH PERIOD			Year	DECLINING-GROWTH PERIOD		
	Gr. Rate	Div.	PV@7%		Gr. Rate	Div.	PV@7%
2010	13%	0.97	0.91	2013	11%	1.38	1.05
2011	13%	1.10	0.96	2014	9%	1.50	1.07
2012	13%	1.24	1.01	2015	7%	1.61	1.07
				2016	5%	1.69	1.05
		Sum	2.88			Sum	4.24

$$\text{Constant Growth Period: } P_{2016} = \frac{1.69\,(1.05)}{0.07 - 0.05} = \frac{1.77}{0.02} = \$88.73$$

Present valued at 7% we get $55.26. The total value of the stock is the sum of the three present-value streams discounted at 7%:

1. Present value of high-growth period dividends	$2.88
2. Present value of declining-growth period dividends	4.24
3. Present value of constant-growth period dividends	55.26
Total present value of dividends	$62.38

The estimated value based on the DDM ($62.38) is higher than the market price in mid-2009 of about $44. This estimated value also implies a *P/E* ratio based on expected earnings in 2009 of about $2.94 per share (i.e., about 21 times earnings) is much higher than the prevailing market *P/E*. In a subsequent section on relative valuation techniques, we compare Shoppers' *P/E* ratio to that of its industry and the market.

9.4.2 PRESENT VALUE OF FREE CASH FLOW TO EQUITY

Similar to the present value of earnings concept (see Web Chapter 20), this technique considers the capital expenditures and the change in working capital required for a growing firm. From our earlier review, recall that free cash flow to equity (FCFE) is as follows:

> **Net Income + Amortization Expense − Capital Expenditures**
> **− Δ in Working Capital − Principal Debt Repayments**
> **+ New Debt Issues**

As these are flows to shareholders, the discount rate used is the firm's cost of equity.

Given the current FCFE values, the alternative forms of the model are similar to those available for the DDM, which in turn depends on the firm's growth prospects. Specifically, if the firm is in its mature, constant-growth phase, it is possible to use a model similar to the reduced form DDM:

9.6

$$\text{Value} = \frac{FCFE_1}{k - g_{FCFE}}$$

where:

FCFE = the expected free cash flow to equity in Period 1

k = the required return on equity for the firm

g_{FCFE} = the expected constant growth rate of free cash flow to equity for the firm

In the case of FCFE, it is necessary to consider the effect of capital expenditures relative to amortization and changes in working capital as well as debt repayments and new debt issues. The historical data in Exhibit 9.2 shows a growth rate in net income that ranged from −34% to 127%. The reason for the dramatic change is the very heavy capital expenditures and the significant working capital requirements during these years. The firm continues to add roughly 1 million square feet of selling space per year (growth of around 11% per year); it is estimated that in 2009 the FCFE will be about $202 million and the FCFF (free cash flow to the firm) will be about $134 million. Such volatility makes it appropriate to use the 13% growth rate going forward. The following example again uses a three-stage growth model with characteristics similar to the dividend growth model.

g_1 = 13% for the three years after 2009

g_2 = a constantly declining growth rate to 5%

k = 7% cost of equity

Beginning with the estimated FCFE value of $202 million in 2009, we estimate the present value of FCFE as follows:

	HIGH-GROWTH PERIOD				DECLINING-GROWTH PERIOD		
Year	Growth Rate	FCFE	PV@7%	Year	Growth Rate	FCFE	PV@7%
2010	13%	202	189	2013	11%	287	219
2011	13%	229	200	2014	9%	312	223
2012	13%	258	211	2015	7%	334	223
				2016	5%	351	219
		Sum	600			Sum	883

$$\text{Constant Growth Period Value} = \frac{351(1.05)}{0.07 - 0.05} = \frac{369}{0.02} = 18,428$$

$$\text{PV@7\%} = \$11,476$$

The total value of FCFE is the sum of the three present-value streams discounted at 7%:

	$Million
1. Present value of high-growth FCFEs	600
2. Present value of declining-growth FCFEs	883
3. Present value of constant-growth FCFEs	11,476
Total present value of FCFE	12,959

With roughly 217 million shares outstanding in 2008, the per-share value, based on the present value of FCFE is $59.72 ($12,959/217). This estimated value implies a P/E ratio of about 20 times estimated 2009 earnings of $2.94 per share.

9.4.3 PRESENT VALUE OF OPERATING FREE CASH FLOW

Also referred to as *free cash flow to the firm (FCFF)* by Damodaran (2006) and the *entity DCF model* by Koller et al. (2005), this model attempts to value the total firm, and then subtracts the value of the firm's debt obligations to arrive at a value for the firm's equity. The operating free cash flow to the firm (FCFF) is discounted at the firm's weighted average cost of capital (WACC) rather than its cost of equity.

Operating free cash flow or free cash flow to the firm is equal to

$$\text{EBIT}(1 - \text{Tax Rate}) + \text{Amortization Expense} \\ - \text{Capital Expenditures} - \Delta \text{ in Working Capital} \\ - \Delta \text{ in other assets}$$

This is the cash flow generated by a company's operations (OFCF) and available to both equity and debt holders. Because it is the cash flow available to *all capital suppliers*, it is discounted at the firm's WACC.

By now you can see that, like the DDM, the OFCF model depends upon the firm's growth prospects. Assuming constant growth, the reduced form model can be used:

9.7
$$\text{Firm Value} = \frac{\text{FCFF}_1}{\text{WACC} - g_{\text{FCFF}}} \quad \text{or} \quad \frac{\text{OFCF}_1}{\text{WACC} - g_{\text{OFCF}}}$$

where:

FCFF_1 = the free cash flow for the firm in Period 1
OFCF_1 = the firm's operating free cash flow in Period 1
WACC = the firm's weighted average cost of capital
g_{FCFF} = the constant infinite growth rate of free cash flow for the firm
g_{OFCF} = the constant infinite growth rate of operating free cash flow

Using information in Exhibit 9.2, the compound annual growth rate for operating free cash flow (free cash flow to the firm) during the seven-year period is not meaningful because it was negative, therefore a more appropriate estimate would be to use the retention rate and tax-adjusted ROIC:

9.8
$$g = RR \times ROIC$$

where:

RR = the average retention rate
$ROIC$ = EBIT(1 − Tax Rate)/Average Total Invested Capital

For Shoppers, the average retention rate is about 73% and

$$ROIC = \frac{\text{EBIT}(1 - \text{Tax Rate})}{\text{Average Total Invested Capital}}$$
$$= \frac{883(0.69)}{(5,188 + 4,389)/2} = \frac{609}{4,789} = 12.72\%$$

Therefore,

$$g = 0.73 \times 0.1272$$
$$= 0.0929, \text{ or } 9.29\%$$

We will round this down to a beginning growth estimate for OFCF/FCFF of 9%.

Calculation of WACC We calculate the discount rate (i.e., the firm's WACC) using the following formula:

9.9 $$\text{WACC} = W_E k + W_D i$$

where:
W_E = the proportion of equity in total capital
k = the after-tax cost of equity (from the SML)
W_D = the proportion of debt in total capital[3]
i = the after-tax cost of debt[4]

You might recall from your corporate finance courses that there are differences of opinion regarding whether the debt and equity weights should be estimated using relative book values or relative market values. Without opening that debate, you should recognize that using market value weights will almost always result in a higher WACC.

WACC Using Book Value Weights

k_e = 0.070 (from prior SML calculation)
k_d = 0.0345 (current interest rate of 5% and recent tax rate of 31% for SC)
    $0.05 \times (1 - 0.31) = 0.0345$
W_d = 0.53 (including leases)
W_e = 0.47
    WACC = $(W_d \times k_d) + (W_e \times k_e)$
        = $(0.53 \times 0.0345) + (0.47 \times 0.070)$
        = 5.12%

WACC Using Market Value Weights

k_e = 0.070 W_e = 0.71
k_d = 0.0345 W_d = 0.29
    WACC = $(W_d \times k_d) + (W_e \times k_e)$
        = $(0.29 \times 0.0345) + (0.71 \times 0.070)$
        = 0.0597, or 5.97%

With the range of 5.12% to 5.97%, we will use the market value WACC and round it up to 6%.

---

3 The proportions of debt and equity capital used in the WACC estimate will be computed using both book value weights that consider the value of capitalized lease payments as debt, and market value weights. The market cap for Shoppers at the calculation date was $9.55 billion.

4 For this estimate, we use the prevailing interest rate on corporate A-rated bonds (5%), and Shoppers recent tax rate of 31%.

With the operating free cash flow growth rate (9%) being greater than the firm's WACC, we cannot use the reduced form model. Therefore, we again employ the three–stage growth model with the following growth assumptions.

Given the firm's WACC, we will use the following growth estimates:

g_1 = 9% in the first year
g_2 = a constantly declining rate to 5%[5]

The specific estimates for future OFCF (or FCFF) are as follows, beginning from the 2009 value of $134 million.

HIGH GROWTH PERIOD

Year	Growth Rate	FCFF	PV@6%
2009		134	126
2010	9%	146	130
2011	7%	156	131
2012	5%	164	130
		Sum	518

$$\text{Constant Growth Period Value} = \frac{164\,(1.05)}{0.06 - 0.05} = 17,220$$

$$PV@6\% = \$13,640$$

Thus, the total value of the firm is:

	$ Million
1. Present value of high growth, declining cash flows	518
2. Present value of constant-growth cash flows	13,640
Total present value of operating FCF (FCFF)	**$14,158**

Recall that the value of equity is the total value of the firm (PV of OFCF) minus the current market value of debt. The values are as follows:

Total present value of operating FCF	$14,158
Minus: Value of debt[6]	4,082
Value of equity	$10,076
Number of common shares	217 million
Value of equity per share	$46.43

The $46.43 value implies a P/E of about 16 times estimated 2009 earnings of $2.94 per share.

To summarize, the valuations derived from the present value of cash flow techniques are as follows:

Present value of dividends	$62.38
Present value of FCFE	$59.72
Present value of OFCF (or the PV of FCFF)	$46.43

---

5 This 5% long-run growth rate assumption implies that we do not believe that FCFF can grow as long at 13% and as fast in the long run as FCFE. Given a beginning growth rate of 9% for one year and a long-run rate of 5% means that the growth rate will decline by 2% per year as shown in the following example.

6 This debt value includes the present value of minimum lease payments.

All of these prices must be compared to the prevailing market price of $44 to determine the investment decision.

9.4.4 RELATIVE VALUATION RATIO TECHNIQUES

In this section, we present the data required to compute the several relative valuation ratios and demonstrate the use of these relative valuation ratio techniques for Shoppers compared to the RDS industry and the S&P/TSX Consumer Staples Index.

Exhibit 9.3 has the basic data required to compute the relative valuation ratios, and Exhibit 9.4 presents the results of relative valuation ratios for Shoppers, its industry, and the aggregate market. Such a comparison helps the analyst determine changes in the relative valuation ratios over time and consider if the current valuation ratio for the company

EXHIBIT 9.3	Growth of the Drug and Pharmaceutical Market						
	CGR	2008	2007	2006	2005	2004	2003
Growth in personal expenditures on drugs and pharmaceuticals*	7.6%	4.3	8.9	9.4	8.2	7.1	7.6
Retail pharmaceutical growth**	7.8%	4.4	7.8	8.7	4.4	8.9	12.9
*Shoppers Drug Mart*** *							
Number of stores		1,149	1,057	987	950	915	870
Growth in number of stores	5.3%	8.7	7.1	3.9	3.8	5.2	3.1
Growth in selling space (millions ft.²)	10.5%	11.8	11.7	10.1	10.2	10.9	8.6
System sales growth	9.6%	11.1	8.9	8.9	8.9	8.4	11.4
Same-store sales growth	5.9%	4.8	5.2	6.5	5.8	6.3	6.9

CGR = compound annual growth rate

Sources: *Statistics Canada
          **IMS Health Canada; Statistics Canada; authors' calculations
          ***Shoppers Drug Mart annual reports; authors' calculations

EXHIBIT 9.4	Profit Margins and Component Expenses for Shoppers and the Retail Drug Store Industry: 2003–2008			
	Shoppers		Food and Staples Retailing	
	Operating Margin (%)	Net Profit Margin (%)	Operating Margin (%)	Net Profit Margin (%)
2008	11.54	6.00	7.69	3.80
2007	11.35	5.82	7.81	3.50
2006	10.63	5.43	7.70	2.62
2005	10.13	5.1	7.83	3.71
2004	13.52	6.69	9.13	4.26
2003	13.22	5.84	9.05	4.22

Source: FPInfomart, industry reports, and FP investors' reports.

(Shoppers) is reasonably based. To aid in the analysis, the time series of the relative valuation ratios for the company, its industry, and the market can be graphed.

9.5 Estimating Company Earnings per Share

Estimating future earnings per share is a function of the sales forecast and the estimated profit margin for a company. It should include an analysis of the relationship of company sales to various relevant economic and industry series in order to assess how the company is performing relative to the economy and to its closest competition.

9.5.1 COMPANY SALES FORECAST

We begin the forecast by obtaining data on Shoppers, the retail drug industry, and personal consumption expenditures for the period 2003 to 2008. These are presented in Exhibit 9.3.

To examine the relationship of Shoppers' sales to the economy, we considered several sources of information. According to Statistics Canada, the compound annual growth rate of personal expenditures on drugs and pharmaceuticals (PCE) was 7.6%, close to the figure reported by IMS Health Canada (an information provider to the pharmaceutical industry) for the growth of the retail pharmacy market.

Looking at the sales growth rate, we can see that Shoppers' sales are growing faster than the PCE, and combined with the rapidly aging population, these increases should continue to fuel Shoppers' growth.

As shown in Exhibit 9.3, the internal sales growth for Shoppers from 2003 resulted from an increase in the number of drug stores (from 870 in 2003 to 1,149 in 2008). The net increase in stores and square footage includes numerous new, large stores and the closing of many smaller stores. As a result, the average size of stores has increased. This is a critical statistic in the retailing industry, and the fact that Shoppers has been able to experience consistent growth in this metric is significant evidence of strong management. Although the firm has continued to see strong growth, we would want to carefully examine Shoppers' strategy for increasing this growth to be more in line with the PCE and retail pharmacy growth.

Sample Estimate of Shoppers' Sales Given the figures for Shoppers' sales growth, and growth in PCE and the retail pharmaceutical market, we could simply make an estimate that is an average of the three. If the figures were not as convincing, we would need to forecast increases in PCE and relate that to the historical relationship between PCE and Shoppers' sales.

Because Shoppers provides data on square footage and the number of stores, we could also make an alternative sales estimate using the company data to support the prior estimate. For example, if we assume store area is increased by 10% in 2009, the firm's total sales area would be roughly 13 million square feet. Assuming a conservative $880 of sales per thousand square feet implies a sales forecast of about $11.4 billion for 2009.

If necessary, another internal estimate is made possible by using the number of stores and sales per store. Shoppers expects to open between 120 and 130 stores during 2009. Assuming that 40 are relocations and 15 are expansions, this results in approximately 1,224 stores at the end of 2009. Assuming sales per store likewise continue to increase from $8 million to $8.40 million implies an estimate of $10.3 billion (1,224 × $8.40 million), an increase of 9% over 2009.

Given these last estimates are higher than the industry and economic forecasts discussed earlier, we will take the more conservative 7.6% estimate. This implies a final sales forecast for 2009 of $10.1 billion.

9.5.2 Estimating the Company Profit Margin

The next step in projecting earnings per share is to estimate the firm's net profit margin, which should consider: (1) identification and evaluation of the firm's specific competitive strategy—that is, either low-cost or differentiation; (2) the firm's internal performance, including general trends and evaluation of any problems that might affect future performance; and (3) the firm's relationship with its industry, which should indicate whether the company's past performance is attributable to its industry or if it is unique to the firm. Evaluation of these should help us understand the firm's past performance and also provide the background to make a meaningful forecasts. In this analysis, we do not consider the company-economy relationship because the significant economy-wide profit factors are reflected in the industry results.

9.6 Shoppers' Competitive Strategies

Over the years, has Shoppers pursued a low-cost strategy, or has the firm attempted to differentiate itself from its competitors in some unique way? Based on its annual reports, Shoppers has pursued both strategies with different segments of its business. The firm's size and buying power allow it to be a cost leader for some of its non-prescription products, such as cosmetics, fragrances, and convenience items. At the same time, Shoppers has attempted to build a very strong franchise in the medical prescription business based on differentiation in service. Computer technology in the prescription area makes it possible for the firm to distinguish itself by providing outstanding service to customers. Service leadership in the growing medical field is a major goal.

9.6.1 The Internal Performance

To predict future values, you need to determine the reason for the overall decline in the industry profit margin and, more importantly, what factors have contributed to Shoppers' strong positive performance.

Industry Factors Industry profit margins have declined due to price discounting by drug chains and an increased presence of Wal-Mart and other larger retailers. The discussion in Chapter 8 suggested this as one of the competitive structure conditions that affect long-run profitability. Industry analysts have observed, however, that price cutting has subsided, and they foresee relative price stability following a period of consolidation. In addition, drugstores have tended toward a more profitable product mix featuring high-profit-margin items, such as cosmetics, which has had a positive influence on profit margins.

Company Performance Shoppers' profit margin has shown consistent improvement, and a major reason has been the change in corporate structure and sales mix. The outlook for profit margins is good because the firm has developed a strong position in the pharmacy business and has invested in service and inventory-control technology that will help the firm experience strong margins on this business. The firm also has emphasized high-profit-margin items, such as greeting cards, photofinishing, and cosmetics.

Specific estimates for Shoppers' future margins typically would begin with an analysis of the firm's relationship with drugstore industry margins using time-series plots, such as those

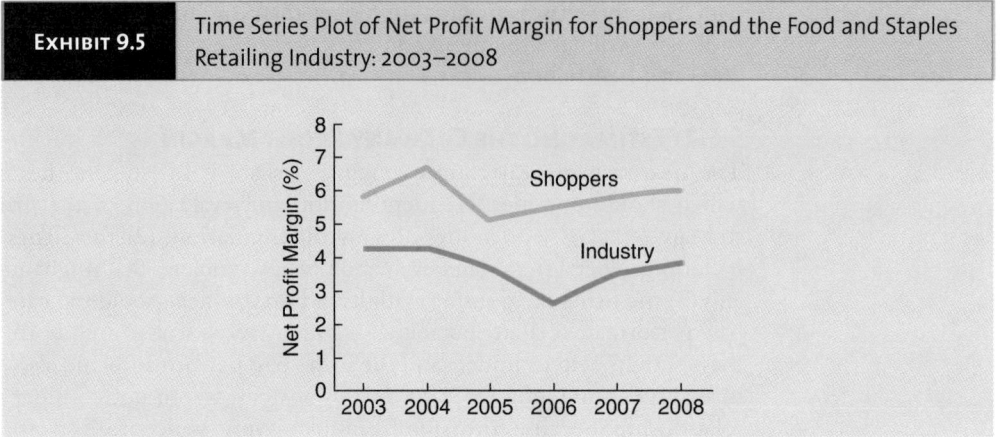

EXHIBIT 9.5   Time Series Plot of Net Profit Margin for Shoppers and the Food and Staples Retailing Industry: 2003–2008

in Exhibit 9.5.[7,8] This time-series plot for the period 2003 to 2008 showed good results for Shoppers versus its industry. You should consider any unique factors that would influence this long-run relationship, such as price wars or an abnormal number of store openings or closings by the firm.

After analysis of the company-industry profit-margin relationship, the firm's common-size income statement should be examined. Looking at Exhibit 19.5 from Web Chapter 19, we can see that the main item of interest—cost of goods sold and other operating expenses—was encouraging. The cost-of-sales percentage remained constant and declined slightly (less than 1%) and as a result, the operating profit margin improved slightly. Finally, the tax rate remained stable at around 31%.

Net Profit Margin Estimate The overall industry outlook is encouraging because of stable prices, an increase in mechanization within the industry, and the inclusion of more high-profit-margin items. Because of Shoppers' strong performance relative to its industry profit margin and a small increase in its margin as shown in Exhibit 9.4, it is estimated that the firm will show a slight increase in 2009. To be conservative though, we will leave our forecast at 6%.

Computing Earnings per Share This margin estimate, combined with the prior sales estimate of $10.1 billion, indicates net income of $606 million. Assuming about 217 million common shares outstanding, earnings should be about $2.79 per share for 2009, which is an increase of 7.3% over 2008. Our next step is to estimate its earnings multiplier.

9.6.2 IMPORTANCE OF QUARTERLY ESTIMATES

Once an estimate of next year's sales and net earnings has been made, it is essential that we also derive an estimate of each of the quarterly results for two reasons. First, this is a way to confirm our annual estimate—do the quarterly estimates required to arrive at the annual estimate seem reasonable? If not, we need to re-evaluate the annual forecast. Second, quarterly

---

7 The FSR industry comparator is comprised of three Canadian companies, two of which are drug retailers. The other company has a different margin structure, and services different aspects of the staples market, therefore a trend comparison to this industry figure is of most use.

8 Both the operating margin and the net-before-tax margin were analyzed; the results indicated that the net profit margins yielded the best relationships, at least over the short term since over the total period the industry margin was declining while Shoppers experienced fairly steady increases as shown in Exhibit 9.5.

forecasts that confirm our annual forecast allow us to evaluate whether the subsequent *actual* results are a positive surprise, negative surprise, or no surprise. If the actual results are a surprise relative to our estimate, we will want to understand the reason for the surprise—for example, did we under- or overestimate sales growth and/or was it due to differences in the profit margin from our estimates? This understanding is needed for an estimated *earnings revision* that reflects the new information from the company—we would probably revise each of our future quarterly estimates to arrive at a new annual estimate.

9.7 Estimating Company Earnings Multipliers

As in our analysis of industry multipliers in Chapter 8, we use two approaches to estimate a company multiplier. First, we estimate the P/E ratio from the relationships between Shoppers, its industry, and the market. This is the macroanalysis. Second, we estimate a multiplier based on its three components: the dividend-payout ratio, the required rate of return, and the rate of growth. We then resolve the estimates derived from each approach and settle on one estimate.

9.7.1 MACROANALYSIS OF THE EARNINGS MULTIPLIER

Exhibit 9.6 shows the mean earnings multiple for the company, the FSR industry, and the aggregate consumer staples market for the period 2003 to 2008. The Shoppers' multiplier has generally followed the industry multiplier with a company-industry ratio between 1.18 and 1.39. The Shoppers' earnings multiplier has been consistently higher than the market multiplier.

This pattern raises the question: Is the higher value for the Shoppers' P/E relative to its industry justified? The microanalyses should provide some insights regarding this question.

9.7.2 MICROANALYSIS OF THE EARNINGS MULTIPLIER

This historical data for the relevant series are contained in Exhibit 9.7. As before, we are looking for estimates of D/E, k, and g to find an earnings multiplier. We will use the historical data in Exhibit 9.7 to determine patterns for the data and to develop future projections.

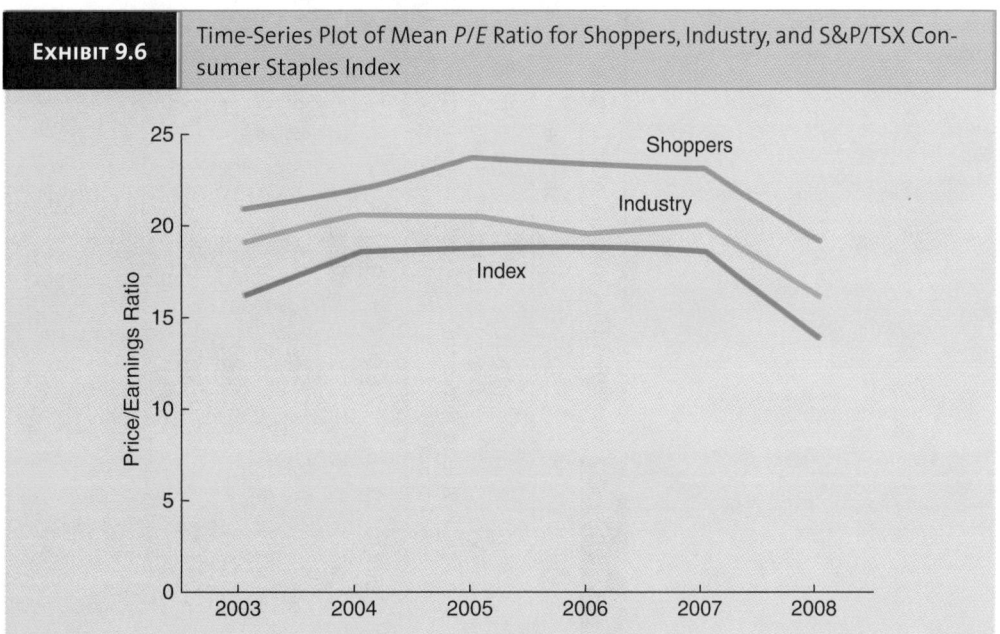

| **EXHIBIT 9.6** | Time-Series Plot of Mean P/E Ratio for Shoppers, Industry, and S&P/TSX Consumer Staples Index |

EXHIBIT 9.7 Variables That Influence the Earnings Multiplier for Shoppers and the Food and Staples Retailers Industry: 2003–2008

Shoppers

	Dividend Payout	(1) Net Profit Margin (%)	(2) Total Asset Turnover	(3) = (1)*(2) Return on Assets (%)	(4) Equity Multiplier	(5) = (3)*(4) Return on Equity (%)
2008	0.31	6.00	1.47	8.82	1.86	16.41
2007	0.27	5.78	1.51	8.73	1.83	15.97
2006	0.23	5.42	1.58	8.56	1.81	15.49
2005	0.18	5.09	1.63	8.30	1.83	15.19
2004	–	4.68	1.59	7.44	1.97	14.66
2003	–	5.82	1.34	7.80	1.96	15.29

Food and Staples Retailing

	Dividend Payout	(1) Net Profit Margin (%)	(2) Total Asset Turnover	(3) = (1)*(2) Return on Assets (%)	(4) Equity Multiplier	(5) = (3)*(4) Return on Equity (%)
2008	0.28	3.8	1.84	6.99	2.61	18.25
2007	0.30	3.5	1.93	6.76	2.93	19.79
2006	0.51	2.62	1.98	5.19	2.91	15.10
2005	0.31	3.71	1.68	6.23	2.94	18.32
2004	0.31	4.26	2.29	9.76	2.68	26.14
2003	0.33	4.22	2.24	9.45	2.72	25.71

Source: FPInfomart, industry reports, and FP investors' reports; authors' calculations.

Comparing Dividend-Payout Ratios The dividend-payout ratio for Shoppers typically has been lower than its industry in the four years Shoppers has paid dividends. This by itself would imply a lower *P/E* ratio for Shoppers than for its industry and the market.

Estimating the Required Rate of Return To find Shoppers' required return (*k*), we need to analyze the firm's fundamental risk characteristics (BR, FR, LR, ERR, and CR) and also derive an estimate based on the SML and a measure of Shoppers' systematic risk (i.e., its beta). Since much of this work was done earlier in this chapter and Web Chapter 19, we will summarize our findings.

Due to its stable sales growth as compared to its industry, Shoppers should have relatively low business risk. Among the several financial risk variables we examined earlier, without considering the financial leases, the financial risk ratios indicate that Shoppers' financial risk as compared to its industry is lower. As we will review in more detail in Web Chapter 19, indicators of market liquidity are: (1) the number of shareholders, (2) the number and market value of shares outstanding, (3) the number of shares traded, and (4) institutional interest in the stock. The firm's liquidity risk is quite low given Shoppers' large number of shareholders, large market capitalization, active trading of its stock, and strong institutional interest. Lastly, Shoppers has very little exchange-rate risk or country risk because the firm has virtually no sales outside Canada. Any exchange-rate risk on goods purchased for resale can be passed on to the consumer.

In summary, Shoppers has below-average business risk and financial risk, low liquidity risk, and virtually no exchange-rate and country risk. This implies that—based on fundamental factors—the overall risk for Shoppers should be lower than the market.

Analysts should also consider market-determined risk (beta) based on the CAPM. Based on our discussion on page 241, the stock's beta derived from five years of monthly data relative to the S&P/TSX Composite for the period ending 2008 was 0.50.

These results are consistent with those derived from an analysis of the fundamental factors—both indicate that Shoppers' risk is below the aggregate market. This means that the required return (*k*) for Shoppers' stock estimated earlier using the CAPM is reasonable—that is, 6.50%. By itself, this lower *k* would suggest an earnings multiplier above the market multiplier.

Estimating the Expected Growth Rate Recall that the expected growth rate (*g*) is determined by the firm's retention rate and its expected return on equity (*ROE*). We have already noted Shoppers' slightly lower dividend payout compared to the industry, which implies a higher retention rate.

Recall that a firm's *ROE* can be estimated using the DuPont model; that is, a firm's *ROE* can be estimated in terms of three ratios: (1) net profit margin (NPM), (2) total asset turnover (TAT), and (3) the financial leverage multiplier. We also know that NPM × TAT = Return on Assets (*ROA*). It is important to examine the relative impact of these two ratios and to compare the *ROA* of alternative firms as a measure of operating performance—that is, profitability and asset efficiency. Shoppers has experienced a slight deterioration in TAT, but this has been offset by an increase in NPM, causing the firm's *ROA* to be relatively stable and above its industry.

Finally, the firm's *ROE* equals the *ROA* times the financial leverage multiplier (total assets/equity). Prior to 2008, both Shoppers and the industry leverage multiplier remained fairly constant after increases in 2005. However, Shoppers remains conservative as compared to the industry.

As a result, the *ROE*s are lower but the financial risk is different—that is, Shoppers has a lower *ROE* but less financial risk.

An analyst would need to *estimate* future components and derive an expected *ROE* that reflects the firm's expected *future* performance; therefore, by combining the average annual *ROEs* and the average of recent retention rates we can derive expected growth rates:

	Retention Rate (3-year average)	ROE (3-year average)	Expected Growth Rate
Shoppers	0.73	15.96%	11.65%
FRS industry	0.64	17.71%	11.33%

Taken alone, this higher expected growth rates for Shoppers would indicate that it should definitely have a higher multiple than its industry.

Computing the Earnings Multiplier Comparing our estimates of D/E, k, and g to comparable values for the industry, we find that Shoppers' earnings multiplier based on the microanalysis should be greater than the multiplier for its industry. Specifically, the exceptional profit margin points toward a higher multiplier for Shoppers, whereas both the lower risk analysis and the higher expected growth rate would indicate a multiplier for Shoppers above that of its industry.

The macroanalysis indicated that the Shoppers' multiplier typically has been above its industry, and the microanalysis supported this relationship. Assuming an industry multiplier of about 16 times, the multiplier for Shoppers should be between 18 and 20, with a tendency toward the upper end of the range.

Estimate of the Future Value for Shoppers Earlier, we estimated 2009 earnings per share for Shoppers of about $2.79 (see page 230) per share. Assuming multipliers of 16-17-18 implies the following estimated future values:

$$16 \times \$2.79 = \$44.64$$
$$17 \times \$2.79 = \$47.43$$
$$18 \times \$2.79 = \$50.22$$

9.7.3   MAKING THE INVESTMENT DECISION

In our prior discussions of valuation, we set forth the following investment-decision rule: calculate the intrinsic value estimate for an investment using the required return as the discount rate. If this intrinsic value is greater than or equal to the investment's current market price, buy it. If intrinsic value is less than the market price, do not buy, and if you own it, sell it.

Therefore, the required comparisons are the estimated values derived using the cash flow and earnings multiple models to the current $44 market price of Shoppers. The following is a summary of these estimated values. Recall that we could not calculate constant-growth models because Shoppers has consistently experienced growth rates above its required return (it is a true growth company).

Present Value of Cash Flow Models

Three-stage DDM	$62.38
Three-stage FCFE	$59.72
Three-stage FCFF (OFCF)	$46.43

Earnings Multiple Models

17 times estimated earnings	$44.64
18 times estimated earnings	$47.43
19 times estimated earnings	$50.22

All of the models are close to or greater than the current market price of $44, but the cash flow models generally indicate a much higher intrinsic value. Therefore, in this case, we have two sets of valuations that indicate different buy recommendations. We do know that Shoppers is an outstanding firm and a true growth company, but based on the valuations can the firm's stock reach the levels predicted by the cash flow models? A sensitivity analysis on the growth factors used might confirm the recommendation.

9.8   Additional Measures of Relative Value

Beyond the well-known price/earnings ratio, analysts also calculate three additional measures of relative value—the price/book value (*P/BV*) ratio, the price/cash flow (*P/CF*) ratio, and the price/sales ratio, which we discuss in Web Chapter 20.

Exhibit 9.8	Relative Value Measures					
	P/BV per Share		**P/CF** per Share		**P/S** per Share	
	Shoppers	Industry	Shoppers	Industry	Shoppers	Industry
2008	3.10	2.00	22.60	12.21	1.10	0.55
2007	3.69	2.72	20.15	12.39	1.34	0.67
2006	3.62	2.75	16.94	11.15	1.26	0.64
2005	3.65	2.89	19.21	11.86	1.21	0.67
2004	3.25	2.95	18.43	10.98	1.47	0.74
2003	2.97	2.84	14.85	11.34	1.23	0.66

Source: FPInfomart, industry reports, and FP investors' reports.

9.8.1   PRICE/BOOK VALUE (*P/BV*) RATIO

The price-to-book-value ratio (*P/BV*) has gained prominence because of the studies by Fama and French (1992); Rosenberg, Reid, and Lanstein (1985); and Fairfield (1994). Book value is a reasonable measure of value for firms that have consistent accounting practice (for example, firms in the same industry), and it can apply to firms with negative earnings or cash flows. You should not attempt to use this ratio to compare firms with different levels of hard assets—for example, a heavy industrial firm and a service firm.

The annual *P/BV* ratios for Shoppers Drug Mart and its industry are in Panel A of Exhibit 9.9. In this instance, the major variable that should cause a difference in the *P/BV* ratio is the firm's return on investment (*ROI*) relative to its cost of capital (its WACC). Assuming that most firms in an industry have comparable WACCs, the major differential should be the firm's *ROI* because the larger the *ROI*-WACC difference, the greater the justified *P/BV* ratio. We will consider this in the subsequent section on EVA.

As shown in Exhibit 9.9, except for in 2008, the *P/BV* ratios for both have remained relatively constant.

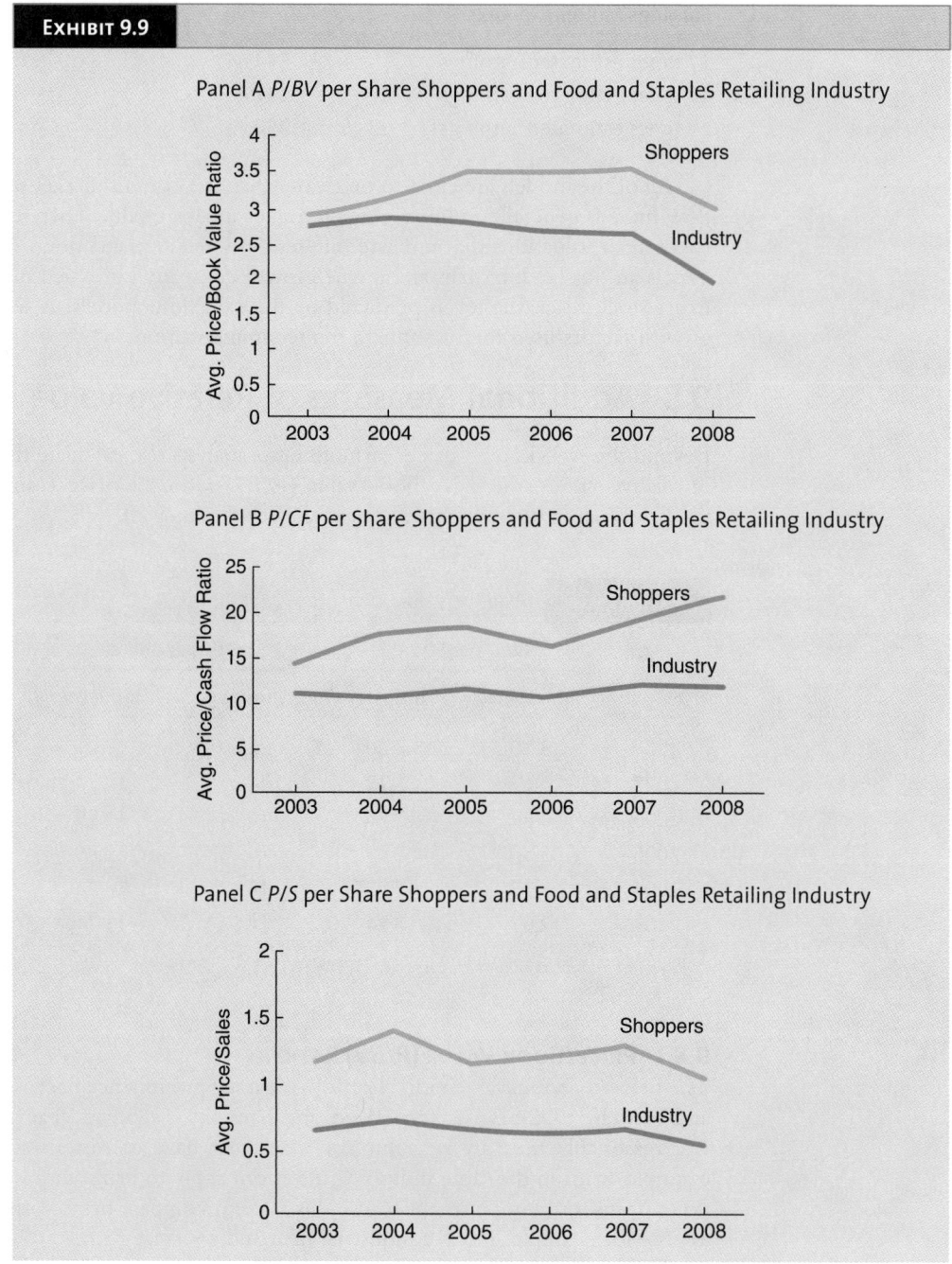

EXHIBIT 9.9

Panel A *P/BV* per Share Shoppers and Food and Staples Retailing Industry

Panel B *P/CF* per Share Shoppers and Food and Staples Retailing Industry

Panel C *P/S* per Share Shoppers and Food and Staples Retailing Industry

9.8.2 PRICE/CASH FLOW (*P/CF*) RATIO

As we note in Web Chapter 20, the price/cash flow ratio has grown in prominence and use because of the contention that a firm's cash flow is less subject to manipulation than its earnings per share and because cash flows are widely used in the present value of cash flow models discussed earlier. An important question is: Which of the several cash flow specifications should an analyst employ? In this analysis, we use the EBITDA cash flow measure equal to net income plus interest, amortization, and taxes because this cash flow measure can be derived for the industry. Although it is certainly legitimate to have a preference for one of the other cash flow measures discussed, a demonstration using this measure should provide a valid comparison for learning purposes.

The time-series graph of the P/CF ratios in Exhibit 9.9, Panel B, shows a general increase for Shoppers and its industry. The industry has remained relatively flat while Shoppers has improved steadily, with the exception of 2006. With the plot of Shoppers' P/CF ratios relative to industry, we see a rapid increase followed by a decrease and recovery. The question becomes, what has happened to the firm's growth rate of cash flow and the risk of these cash flows that would justify this overall volatility in the P/CF ratio relative to the industry?

9.8.3 PRICE/SALES (P/S) RATIO

We note in Web Chapter 20 that the price-to-sales ratio (P/S) has had a long but generally neglected existence followed by a recent reawakening. Those concerned with accounting manipulation point out that sales is one of the purest numbers available. Notably, this ratio equals the P/E ratio times the net profit margin (earnings/sales), which implies that it is heavily influenced by the profit margin of the entity being analyzed in addition to sales growth and sales volatility (risk).

As shown in Panel C of Exhibit 9.9, the P/S ratio for Shoppers Drug Mart has, except for 2008, shown a gradual improvement since 2005 and is higher than the industry figures. However, when the company-to-industry ratio is computed, we once again see some volatility. As before, the analyst must ask whether the growth of sales, the risk related to the sales growth, and the profit margin of Shoppers can justify a much higher P/S ratio than its industry. The positive news is that Shoppers' sales have experienced strong consistent growth relative to its industry and Shoppers has also experienced an increase in its profit margin.

9.8.4 SUMMARY OF RELATIVE VALUATION RATIOS

Notably, the four individual relative valuation variables increased across the board. The widespread increases suggest changes in some aggregate economic variables, such as economic growth and risk factors.

In addition to these overall increases, Shoppers experienced a larger increase than its industry in terms of its P/E ratio, and its P/CF ratio, while lagging in terms of its P/S ratio. An investor who wants to use these ratios to determine relative value or to make an investment decision needs to explain the differences by analyzing the basic valuation factors that affect the ratios.

The following section considers some techniques used to analyze and derive values for growth companies.

9.9 Analysis of Growth Companies

Investment literature contains numerous accounts of the rapid growth of such companies as Research in Motion, Wal-Mart, Apple, Pfizer, and Google, along with stories about investors who became wealthy because of the timely acquisition of these stocks. At the same time, for every successful Wal-Mart or Google, numerous firms did not survive. In addition, there are many instances where the stock price of a true growth company overcompensated for the firm's expected growth, and subsequent returns on the company's stock were below expectations. As noted in Solt and Statman (1989), the common stock of a growth company is *not* always a growth stock.

We have discussed how the DDM *are extremely questionable for a true growth company.* So, the question remains: How do I analyze a growth firm?

9.9.1 GROWTH COMPANY DEFINED

Recall that a growth company has the opportunities and ability to invest in projects that generate returns greater than the firm's cost of capital. Such a condition is considered to be *temporary* because, in a competitive economy, if the returns for a given industry or company exceed the returns expected based on the risk involved, other firms will enter the industry, increase the supply, and eventually drive prices down until the returns earned on capital invested are consistent with the risk involved.

9.9.2 ACTUAL RETURNS ABOVE REQUIRED RETURNS

The notion of a firm consistently earning returns above its required returns needs elaboration. In a state of equilibrium, the returns earned on risky investments by the firm should equal the returns required by investors. Returns above those required for the risk involved are referred to as *pure profits* or *excess profits.*

Excess profits are possible only in a non-competitive environment. Assume that a medical equipment firm is able to earn 20% on its capital, while investors require only 15% from the firm because of its risk. The extra 5% is defined as pure profit, and numerous companies would enter the medical equipment field to enjoy these excess profits. The increased supply of equipment would reduce the price that producers could charge until the marginal returns equalled the required return due to risk.

Those firms deriving excess profits for a number of years have likely done so because of some non-competitive factors, such as patents or copyrights that provide monopoly rights to a process or a manuscript for a specified period. Also, a firm could possess strategies, discussed by Porter, that provide added profits (e.g., a unique marketing technique or other organizational characteristics). Finally, there may be significant barriers to entry, such as capital requirements.

In a purely competitive economy, true growth companies would not exist because competition would not allow continuing excess return investments. The fact is, our economy is not perfectly competitive (although this typically is the best model to use) because there are a number of frictions that restrict competition. Therefore, it is possible for *temporary* true growth companies to exist in our economy. The significant question is: How long can these growth companies earn these excess profits?

9.9.3 ALTERNATIVE GROWTH MODELS[9]

In this section, we consider the full range of growth models, from no growth and negative growth to dynamic true growth. Knowledge of the full range will help you understand the life cycle of true growth companies. To simplify the calculations, we assume the company is all-equity financed. You will note these models are similar to those covered in Web Chapter 20.

No-Growth Firm This mythical company is established with a specified asset base that generates a constant stream of earnings (E) equal to r (equal to the return on assets) times the value of assets. Earnings are calculated after allowing for amortization expense used to maintain the assets at their original value. Therefore,

9.10	$$E = r \times \text{Assets}$$

---

[9] The discussion in this section draws heavily from Salomon (1963), and Miller and Modigliani (1961).

It also is assumed that all earnings of the firm are paid out in dividends; if b is the rate of retention, $b = 0$. Hence,

9.11

$$E = r \times \text{Assets} = \text{Dividends}$$

Under these assumptions, the value of the firm is the discounted value of the perpetual stream of earnings (E). The discount rate (the required return) is specified as k. The firm's return on assets equals its required return $(r = k)$. Therefore, the value of the firm is

9.12

$$V = \frac{E}{k} = \frac{(1 - b)E}{k}$$

In the no-growth case, the earnings stream never changes because the asset base never changes, and the return (r) on the assets never changes. Therefore, the value of the firm never changes, and investors continue to receive k on their investment.

9.13

$$k = E/V$$

Long-Run Growth Models Long-run models differ from the no-growth models because they *assume some of the earnings are reinvested*. In all cases, it is postulated that the market value (V) of an all-equity firm is the capitalized value of three component forms of returns discounted at the rate k.

- $E =$ the level of (constant) net earnings expected from existing assets, without further net investments.
- $G =$ the growth component that equals the present value of capital gains expected from reinvested funds. The return on reinvested funds is equal to r, which equals mk (m is the relative return operator). If m is equal to 1, then $r = k$. If m is greater than 1, the projects that generate these returns are considered true growth investments $(r > k)$. If m is less than 1, the investments are generating returns (r) below the cost of capital $(r < k)$.
- $R =$ the reinvestment of net earnings (E) and is equal to bE, where b is a percent of retention which is between zero (no reinvestment) and unity (total reinvestment; no dividends).

Simple Growth Model This model assumes the firm has growth investment opportunities that provide returns equal to r, where r is greater than k (m is above 1). Further, it is assumed that the firm can invest R dollars per year at these rates and that $R = bE$; R is a *constant dollar amount* because E is the constant earnings at the beginning of the period.

The value of G, the capital gain component, is computed as follows: The first investment of bE dollars yields a stream of earnings equal to bEr dollars, and this is repeated every year. Each of these earnings streams has a present value, as of the year it begins, of bEr/k, which is the present value of a constant perpetual stream discounted at a rate consistent with the risk involved. Assuming the firm does this every year, it has a series of investments, each of which has a present value of bEr/k. The present value of all these series is $(bEr/k)/k$, which equals bEr/k^2. But because $r = mk$, this becomes

9.14 $$\frac{bEmk}{k^2} = \frac{bEm}{k}$$ **(Gross Present Value of Growth Investments)**

To derive these flows, the firm must invest bE dollars each year. The present value of these annual investments is equal to bE/k. Therefore, the *net* present value of growth investments is equal to

9.15 $$\frac{bEm}{k} - \frac{bE}{k}$$ **(Net Present Value of Growth Investments)**

The important variable is the value of m, which indicates the relationship of r to k. Combining this growth component with the capitalized value of the constant earnings stream indicates that the value of the firm is

9.16 $$V = \frac{E}{k} + \left[\frac{bEm}{k} - \frac{bE}{k}\right]$$

This equation indicates that the value of the firm is equal to the capitalized value of the constant earnings stream plus a growth component equal to the *net* present value of reinvestment in growth projects. By combining the first and third terms in Equation 9.16, it becomes

9.17 $$V = \frac{E(1 - b)}{k} + \frac{bEm}{k}$$

Because $E(1 - b)$ is the dividend (D), this model becomes

9.18 $$V = \frac{D}{k} + \frac{bEm}{k}$$ **(Present Value of Constant Dividend plus the Gross Present Value of Growth Investments)**

It can be stated as earnings only by rearranging equation 9.16:

9.19 $$V = \frac{E}{k} + \frac{bE(m - 1)}{k}$$ **(Present Value of Constant Earning plus the Present Value of Excess from Growth Investments)**

Expansion Model The expansion model assumes a firm retains earnings to reinvest but receives a return on its investments that is equal to its cost of capital ($m = 1$, so $r = k$). The effect of such a change can be seen in Equation 9.15, where the net present value of growth investments would be zero. Therefore, Equation 9.16 would become

9.20
$$V = \frac{E}{k}$$

Equation 9.17 would become

9.21
$$V = \frac{E(1 - b)}{k} + \frac{bE}{k} = \frac{E}{k}$$

Equation 9.18 is still valid, but the present value of the growth investment component would be smaller because m would be equal to 1. Finally, the last term in Equation 9.19 would disappear.

This discussion indicates that simply because a firm retains earnings and reinvests them, it is not necessarily beneficial to the stockholder *unless the reinvestment rate is above the required rate ($r > k$)*. Otherwise, the investor in a tax-free world would be as well off with all earnings paid out in dividends. Either way, your return is k.

Negative Growth Model The negative growth model applies to a firm that retains earnings ($b > 0$) and reinvests these funds in projects that generate returns *below* the firm's cost of capital ($r < k$ or $m < 1$). The impact of this on the value of the firm can be seen from Equation 9.15, which indicates that with $m < 1$, the net present value of the growth investments would be *negative*. Therefore, the value of the firm in Equation 9.16 would be *less* than the value of a no-growth firm or an expansion firm. This also can be seen by examining the effect of $m < 1$ in Equation 9.19. The firm is withholding funds from the investor and investing them in projects that generate returns less than those available from comparable risk investments.

Such poor performance may be difficult to uncover because the firm's asset base will grow because it is retaining earnings and acquiring assets. Notably, the earnings of the firm will increase if it earns *any* positive returns on the new assets. However, *the earnings will not grow by as much as they should*. The value of the firm will decline over time when investors discount the below required cash flows from this reinvestment stream at the firm's cost of capital.

What Determines the Capital Gain Component? These equations highlight the factors influencing the capital gain component. Beginning with Equation 9.14, all the equations suggest that the gross present value of growth investments is equal to

$$bEm/k$$

Therefore, three factors influence the size of this capital gain term. The first is b, the percentage of earnings retained for reinvestment. The greater the proportion of earnings retained, the larger the capital gain component. The second factor is m, which is the most critical variable because it indicates the relationship between the firm's return on investments and the firm's required return (i.e., its cost of capital). A value of 1 indicates the firm is earning only its required return. A firm with an *m* greater than 1 is a true growth company. The important question is: How much greater than *k* is the return? The final factor is the time period for the superior investments. How long can the firm make these superior return investments? This critical time factor often is overlooked because we have assumed an infinite horizon to simplify the computations. However, *when analyzing growth companies, this time estimate is clearly a major consideration.* In summary, the three factors that influence the capital gain component are

1. The amount of capital invested in growth investments (*b*)
2. The relative return earned on the funds retained (*m*)
3. The time period for these growth investments

Dynamic True Growth Model A dynamic true growth model applies to a firm that invests a constant *percentage of current earnings* in projects that generate returns above the firm's required rate ($r > k$, $m > 1$). In contrast to the simple growth model where the firm invests a *constant* dollar amount each year, in this model the amount invested is *growing* each year as earnings increase. As a result, the firm's earnings and dividends will grow at a *constant rate* that is equal to *br* (the percentage of earnings retained times the return on investments). In the current model, this would equal *bmk*, where *m* is greater than 1. Given these assumptions, the dynamic growth model for an infinite time period is the dividend discount model:

9.22

$$V = \frac{D_1}{k - g}$$

Applying this model to a true growth company means that earnings and dividends are growing at a constant rate and *the firm is investing larger and larger dollar amounts in projects that generate returns greater than* k. Moreover, the DDM model implicitly assumes that the firm can continue to do this for *an infinite time period*. If the growth rate (*g*) is greater than k, the model blows up and indicates that the firm should have an infinite value. Durand (1957) considered this possibility and concluded that, although many firms had current growth rates above the normal required returns, very few of their stocks were selling for infinite values. He explained this by contending that investors expected the reinvestment rate to decline or they felt that the growing set of investment opportunities would not be available for an infinite time period. Exhibit 9.10 contains a summary of the alternative company characteristics.

9.9.4 The Real World

Because these models are simplified to allow us to develop a range of alternatives, several of them are extremely unrealistic. In the real world, companies generally would combine these models. Unfortunately, most firms have made some investments where $r < k$, and many firms invest in projects that generate returns about equal to their cost of capital. Finally, most firms invest in *some* projects that provide returns above the firm's cost of capital ($r > k$). The crucial questions are (1) how much is invested in these true growth projects? and (2) how long do these true growth opportunities last?

Given this understanding of growth companies and what creates their value, the rest of the chapter considers various models that help you understand how to identify a true growth company and estimate specific values for these growth companies.

EXHIBIT 9.10	Summary of Company Descriptions		
		Retention	Return on Investments
No-growth company		$b = 0$	$r = k$
Long-run growth (assumes reinvestment)			
Negative growth		$b > 0$	$r < k$
Expansion		$b > 0$	$r = k$
Simple long-run growth		$b > 0$	
		(constant $)	$r > k$
Dynamic long-run growth		$b > 0$	
		(constant %)	$r > k$

9.10   Measures of Value Added[10]

In addition to the DDM, which feeds into the *P/E* ratio valuation technique and the supplementary *P/BV* and *P/CF*, ratios, there is also interest in a set of performance measures referred to as "value added" measures. Specifically, they consider *economic profit*, which is analogous to the net present value (NPV) technique used in corporate capital budgeting. These measures examine management performance based on the ability of managers to add value. They are also being considered by security analysts as possible indicators of future equity returns, based on the logic that superior management performance should be reflected in a company's stock returns.

9.10.1 Economic Value Added (EVA)[11]

As noted, EVA is closely related to the net present value (NPV) technique wherein the expected performance of an investment is evaluated by discounting its future cash flows at the firm's weighted average cost of capital (WACC) and comparing this sum to the cost of the project. If the discounted cash flows are greater than its cost, the project is expected to generate a positive NPV, which implies that it will add to the value of the firm and, therefore, it should be undertaken. In the case of EVA, you evaluate the annual performance of management by comparing the firm's net operating profit less adjusted taxes (NOPLAT) to the firm's total cost of capital in dollar terms, including the cost of equity. In this analysis, if the firm's NOPLAT during a specific year exceeds its dollar cost of capital, it has a positive EVA for the year and has added value for its stockholders. In contrast, if the EVA is negative, the firm has not earned enough during the year to cover its total cost of capital and the value of the firm has declined. Specifically, NOPLAT indicates what the firm has earned for all capital suppliers and the dollar cost of capital is what all the capital suppliers required—including the firm's equity holders. The following summarizes the major calculations:[12]

EVA =

(A) Adjusted Operating Profits before Taxes
Minus (B) Cash Operating Taxes
Equals (C) Net Operating Profits Less Adjusted Taxes (NOPLAT)
Minus (D) The Dollar Cost of Capital
Equals (E) Economic Value Added (EVA)

---

10 This section benefited from Peterson and Peterson (1996).

11 EVA is a registered trademark of Stern, Stewart, & Co.

12 For a detailed discussion, see Stewart (1991), or Peterson and Peterson (1996). For summary discussion, see Jones (1995).

In turn, these items are calculated as follows:

Operating Profit (After Depreciation and Amortization)

Add:	Implied Interest on Operating Leases
Add:	Goodwill Amortization
Equals:	*(A) Adjusted Operating Profits before Taxes*

Income Tax Expense

Add:	Decrease in Future Taxes
Add:	Tax Benefit from Interest Expenses
Add:	Tax Benefit from Interest on Leases
Less:	Taxes on Non-operating Income
Equals:	*(B) Cash Operating Taxes*

(A) minus (B) equals: (C) Net Operating Profits Less Adjusted Taxes (NOPLAT)

Capital =

	Net Working Capital (current assets less non-interest-bearing liabilities)
Add:	Net Plant, Property, and Equipment
Add:	Other Assets
Add:	Goodwill
Add:	Accumulated Goodwill Amortized
Add:	Present Value of Operating Leases
Equals:	*Capital*

Weighted Average Cost of Capital (WACC) =

	(Book Value of Debt/Total Book Value) $\times$ (the Market Cost of Debt) (1 − Tax Rate)
	(Book Value of Equity/Total Book Value) $\times$ (Cost of Equity)
	(Cost of equity is based on the CAPM using the prevailing 10-year government bond as the *RFR*, a calculated beta, and a market risk premium between 3% and 6%.)
(D)	Dollar Cost of Capital = Capital $\times$ WACC[13]
(E)	Economic Value Added (EVA) =
(C)	Net Operating Profits Less Adjusted Taxes (NOPLAT)
	Minus (D) Dollar Cost of Capital

EVA Return on Capital The EVA calculation provides a positive or negative dollar value, which indicates whether the firm earned an excess above its cost of capital during the year analyzed. There are two problems with this annual dollar value. First, how does one judge over time if the firm is prospering relative to its past performance? Although you would want the absolute EVA to grow over time, the question is whether the EVA growth rate is adequate for the additional capital provided. Second, how does one compare alternative

---

13 Recall the discussion earlier in this chapter when we calculated the WACC for Shoppers where we made the point that using book-value weights typically resulted in a lower WACC than using market-value weights. A lower WACC means a higher EVA.

firms of different sizes? Both of these concerns can be met by calculating an *EVA return on capital* equal to

EVA Return on Capital = EVA/Capital

You would want this EVA return on capital for a firm to remain constant over time or, ideally, to grow. Using this ratio you can compare firms of different sizes and determine which firm has the largest *economic profit per dollar of capital*.

An Alternative Measure of EVA An alternative but equal way to measure and think about EVA is to compare directly the firm's return on capital employed to the firm's average cost of capital (i.e., its WACC). As noted previously, it is this difference in the actual return earned compared to the firm's required return that identifies a company as a true growth company. Another way to measure EVA is to multiply this EVA spread (return on capital minus WACC) by the amount of capital employed. The appeal of this EVA spread approach is that it concentrates on the factors that create a growth company. Also, it helps the management and analysts recognize that true growth can be created by either (1) increasing the firm's return on capital, or (2) reducing its cost of capital.

9.10.2 MARKET VALUE ADDED (MVA)

In contrast to EVA, which generally is an evaluation of internal performance, MVA is a measure of external performance—how the market has evaluated the firm's performance in terms of the market value of debt and market value of equity compared to the capital invested in the firm.

Market Value Added (MVA) = Market Value of Firm − Invested Capital

Again, to properly analyze this performance, it is necessary to look for positive changes over time—that is, the percent change each year. Subsequently, you need to compare these annual changes in MVA with those for the aggregate stock and bond markets, because these market values can be impacted by interest rate changes and general economic conditions.

9.10.3 RELATIONSHIPS BETWEEN EVA AND MVA

Although EVA is used primarily internally for evaluating management performance, it also is being used by external analysts to evaluate management with the belief that superior internal performance should be reflected in a company's stock performance. Several studies have attempted to determine the relationship between the two variables (EVA and MVA), and the results have not been encouraging. Although the stock of firms with positive EVAs has tended to outperform the stock of negative EVA firms, the differences are typically insignificant and the relationship does not occur every year. This poor relationship may be due to the timing of the analysis (how fast EVA is reflected in stocks) or because the market values (MVAs) are affected by factors other than EVA—for example, MVA can be impacted by market interest rates and by changes in *future* expectations for a firm not considered by EVA. The point is that EVA does an outstanding job of evaluating management's *past* performance in terms of adding value. While one would certainly hope that superior past performance will continue, there is nothing certain about this relationship.

9.10.4 THE FRANCHISE FACTOR

The franchise factor concept is similar to EVA because it recognizes that to add value to a firm, it is necessary to invest in projects that generate returns above its WACC. This technique is directly related to the valuation approach we have been using because the franchise value approach breaks a firm's observed *P/E* ratio down into two components: (1) the *P/E* that is based on the company's ongoing business (its base *P/E*), plus (2) a franchise *P/E* that the market assigns to *the expected value of new and profitable business opportunities*. This can be visualized as:

9.23	**Franchise *P/E* = Observed *P/E* – Base *P/E***

The base *P/E* is the reciprocal of the market discount rate *k* (it is $1/k$). For example, if the stock's market discount rate is 8%, the base *P/E* would be about 12.5 times.

What determines the franchise *P/E*? Not surprisingly, it is a function of the relative return on new business opportunities compared to the firm's cost of equity (the franchise factor) and the size of the superior return opportunities (the growth factor).

9.24	**Incremental Franchise P/E = Franchise Factor × Growth Factor** $$= \frac{R - k}{rk} \times G$$

where:

R = the expected return on the new opportunities
k = the current cost of equity
r = the current *ROE* on investment
G = the present value of the new growth projects relative to the current value of the firm

The critical factors determining the franchise *P/E* are the difference between *R* and *k* and the size of these growth opportunities relative to the firm's current size (i.e., *G*).[14]

9.11 Site Visits and the Art of the Interview

Brokerage house analysts and portfolio managers have access to persons that the typical small investor does not. Analysts frequently have contact with corporate personnel by telephone (conference calls), at formal presentations, or during plant site visits. Though insider trading laws restrict the analyst's ability to obtain material non-public information, these visits facilitate dialogue between the corporation and the investor community. The analyst can gather information about the firm's plans and strategies, which helps the analyst understand the firm's prospects as an investment.

---

14 For further detail and examples of the application, see Leibowitz and Kogelman (1994).

Interviewing is an art. The analyst wants information about the firm, and top management wants to put the firm in the best light possible. Thus, the analyst must be prepared to focus the interview on management's plans, strategies, and concerns. Analysts try to gauge the sensitivity of the firm's revenues, costs, and earnings to different scenarios by asking "what if" questions.

Analysts have frequent contact with the firm's investor relations (IR) department regarding company pronouncements. The chief financial officer and chief executive officer of the firm also meet with security analysts and discuss the firm's planning process and major issues confronting the industry.

The analyst should talk with people other than top managers. Talking with middle managers or factory workers during a plant tour, visiting stores, and talking with customers provide insights beyond those of management. The firm's major customers can provide information regarding product quality and customer satisfaction. The firm's suppliers can furnish information about rising or falling supply orders and the timeliness of payments. Finally, an outstanding source of information is the firm's competitors who will be happy to point out the firm's weaknesses or possible problems. They may even be willing to admit which firm is its toughest competitor.

The idea was always that analysts were able to create a mosaic regarding future expectations for the firm from numerous sources (including the company) and transmit this information to the market by sending research reports to brokerage clients and portfolio managers of pensions and mutual funds. This traditional way of doing research was changed in the United States in 2000 when the SEC issued the Fair Disclosure (FD) guidelines that required all disclosure of "material information" to be made public to all interested parties at the same time. The intent was to level the playing field by ensuring that professional analysts did not have a competitive advantage over non-professional investors. The result of this law is that many firms will not agree to interviews with analysts and will only provide information during large public presentations over the Internet. Canada also introduced a fair disclosure policy (NP51-201) in 2001 although Canadian securities regulation already prohibited selective disclosure ("tipping").

The long-run impact of this FD requirement is not clear in terms of how firms will relate to the professional analyst community. One benefit is that analysts will spend more time with information sources beyond the firm such as trade shows, customers, suppliers, and competitors to build the mosaic.

9.12 When to Sell

Our analysis has focused on determining if a stock should be purchased. In fact, when we make a purchase, a subsequent question gains prominence: When should the stock be sold? Many times holding on to a stock too long leads to a return below expectations or less than what was available earlier. When a stock's price declines immediately following an analyst's valuation and recommendation, is this a further buying opportunity, or does the decline indicate information that is new or was overlooked has significantly decreased the valuation?

The answer to the question of when to sell a stock is contained in the research that convinced the analyst to purchase the stock in the first place. The analyst should have identified the key assumptions and variables driving the expectations for the stock. Analysis of the stock doesn't end when intrinsic value is computed and the research report is written. Once the key value drivers are identified, the analyst must *continually monitor and update* his or her knowledge base about the firm. Notably, if the key value drivers appear to have weakened or there is a major change in management, it is time to re-evaluate, and possibly sell, the stock.

The stock should also be closely evaluated when the current price approaches its intrinsic value estimate. When the stock becomes fairly priced (the undervaluation has been corrected), it may be time to sell it and reinvest the funds in other underpriced stocks. In short, if the "story" for buying the stock still appears to be true, continue to hold it if it has not become fully priced (i.e., market price equal to intrinsic value). If the "story" changes, it may be time to sell the stock. If you know why you bought the stock, and constantly update your valuation to reflect new information, you'll be able to recognize when to sell it.

9.13 Influences on Analysts

Stock analysts and portfolio managers are, for the most part, highly trained individuals who possess expertise in financial analysis and background in their industry. A computer hardware analyst knows as much about industry trends and new product offerings as any industry insider. A pharmaceutical analyst is able to independently determine the market potential of drugs undergoing testing and the Health Canada approval process. So why don't more brokerage house customers and portfolio managers who receive the analysts' expert advice achieve investment success? The following subsections discuss several factors that make it difficult to "beat the market."

9.13.1 EFFICIENT MARKETS

As noted in Chapter 5, the efficient market is difficult to outsmart, especially if you are considering actively traded and frequently analyzed companies. Information about the economy, a firm's industry, and the firm itself is reviewed by numerous analysts, investors, and portfolio managers. Investors look for situations where stocks may not be fairly valued. Notably, because there are numerous, hard-working analysts, it is difficult to successfully, frequently, and consistently find undervalued shares. Put another way, in most instances, the value estimated for a stock will be very close to its market price, which indicates that it is properly valued. The analyst's best place to seek attractive stocks is not among well-known companies and actively traded stocks, because they are analyzed by dozens of Bay Street and Wall Street analysts. Stocks with smaller market capitalizations, those not covered by many analysts, or those whose shares are mainly held by individual investors may be the best places to search for inefficiencies. Smaller capitalization stocks sometimes are too small for time-constrained analysts or too small for purchase by institutional investors.[15] The price of stocks not researched by many analysts ("neglected stocks") may not reflect all relevant information.[16]

9.13.2 PARALYSIS OF ANALYSIS

Just like this chapter, analysts spend a good portion of their time in a relentless search for one more contact or one more piece of information that will ensure the correct stock recommendation. Analysts need to develop a systematic approach for gathering, monitoring, and reviewing relevant information about economic trends, industry competitive forces, and company strategy. The information must be evaluated as a whole to discern patterns that indicate the intrinsic value of the stock rather than searching for one more piece of information.

Because markets are generally efficient, the consensus view about the firm is already reflected in its stock price. As noted previously, to earn above-average returns, there are two requirements: (1) The analyst must have expectations that differ from the consensus, *and*

---

15 According to regulations, mutual funds cannot own more than 10% of a firm's shares. For some large funds, this constraint will make the resulting investment too small to have any significant impact on fund returns, so analysts do not bother to consider such stocks for purchase.

16 Information on the number of analysts covering a stock is available from research firms, such as IBES, Thomson ONE, Zacks, and even Yahoo Finance.

(2) the analyst must be correct. Thus, the analyst should concentrate on identifying what is wrong with the market consensus (i.e., why do you differ from the consensus?), or what surprises may upset the market consensus—that is, work at *estimating earning surprises.*

9.13.3 ANALYST CONFLICTS OF INTEREST

A potential conflict can arise if communication occurs between a firm's investment banking and equity research division. If the investment bankers assist a firm in a stock or bond offering, it will be difficult for an analyst to issue a negative evaluation of the company. Advisory fees have been lost because of a negative stock recommendation. Despite attempts to ensure the independence of stock analysts, firm politics may get in the way.

The analyst is in frequent contact with the top officers of the company he or she analyzes. Although there are guidelines about receiving gifts and favours, it is sometimes difficult to separate personal friendship and impersonal corporate relationships. Corporate officials may try to convince the analyst that his or her pessimistic report is in error or suggest that it glosses over recent positive developments. To mitigate these problems, an analyst should call the company's investor relations department immediately *after* changing a recommendation to explain his or her perspective. The analyst needs to maintain independence and be objective in his or her analysis.

9.14 Global Company and Stock Analysis

As indicated on numerous occasions, a major goal of this text is to demonstrate investment techniques that can be applied globally to markets, industries, and companies around the world. This chapter has been heavily concerned with presenting and demonstrating these techniques to Canadian firms. While space constraints do not allow a full demonstration to international firms, it is important to point out some of the major factors and constraints that analysts and portfolio managers need to acknowledge and adjust for when investing globally. Keep in mind the availability and reliability of data, different accounting conventions and the various risks encountered with currencies, political environments, and the like.

In summary, the good news when investing globally is that the valuation process is the same around the world, and the investment decision in terms of the ultimate comparison of intrinsic value and price is similar. The negative news is that the practice of valuation requires attention to several additional factors that must be considered when valuing an international stock. Therefore, everything you have learned about analysis and valuation is relevant, but it must be applied differently (i.e., the inputs differ), depending on the country.

Summary

1. Fundamental analysis requires a separate analysis of a company followed by the valuation of its stock. A strategic analysis of the firm's goals, objectives, and strategy should put you in a position to properly estimate the intrinsic value of the stock.

2. Typically, growth companies are those that consistently experience above-average increases in sales and earnings or a firm with the management ability and the opportunities to make investments that provide returns greater than the firm's WACC. Growth stocks have a higher expected return than other stocks in the market with similar risk characteristics and are not necessarily stocks

of growth companies. The stock achieves this expected superior risk-adjusted return because the market has undervalued it compared to other stocks.

3. Inputs to the various models require that estimates be made regarding the growth rate (both rate and duration of) and the discount rate appropriate for valuing the stock. Growth rates may be estimated by examining actual growth, estimating sustainable growth, or both. Required returns can be estimated using SML or WACC, depending on what cash flows are being valued.

4. Estimating future earnings per share is a function of the sales forecast and the estimated profit margin for a

company. Several sources of information regarding the company, industry, and economic outlook should be consulted when forecasting sales and profit margins. In estimating profit margins, there needs to be identification and evaluation of the firm's specific competitive strategy, its internal performance, and its relationship with its industry.

5. The P/E ratio can be estimated from the relationships between the firm, its industry, and the market and then computed based on its three components: the dividend-payout ratio, the required rate of return, and the rate of growth.

6. Analysts also calculate three additional relative value measures: price/book value (P/BV), price/cash flow (P/CF), and price/sales (P/S). Price/cash flow has become more popular given concerns that some firms may manipulate earnings per share. Cash flow values are generally less prone to manipulation. An inverse relationship between P/BV ratios and excess rates of return for a cross-section of stocks has been shown but use of the ratio is complicated in that the future book value is not generally available. The price/sales ratio has advantages in that the growth process begins with sales and sales information may be subject to less manipulation than any other data items on the income statement. This particular ratio varies dramatically by industry as do the profit margins in many industries, therefore any analysis using the P/S ratio should be between firms in the same or similar industries.

7. EVA is closely related to NPV but EVA evaluates management's annual performance by comparing the firm's net operating profit less adjusted taxes (NOPLAT) to the firm's total cost of capital in dollar terms, including the cost of equity. If the firm's NOPLAT during a specific year exceeds its dollar cost of capital, it has a positive EVA for the year and has added value for its stockholders. $EVA =$ Adjusted Operating Profits before Taxes − Cash Operating Taxes − Minus the Dollar Cost of Capital. In contrast to EVA, which generally evaluates internal performance, MVA is a measure of external performance or how the market has evaluated the firm's performance. Market Value Added (MVA) = Market Value of Firm − Invested Capital.

To analyze this performance, it is necessary to look for changes over time (as a percent), and they must also be compared to changes in the aggregate stock and bond markets, because these market values can be impacted by interest rate changes and general economic conditions. Similarly, the franchise factor concept recognizes that, to add value to a firm, it is necessary to invest in projects that generate returns above its WACC. The franchise value approach breaks a firm's observed P/E ratio down into a base P/E (reflecting the company's ongoing business), plus a franchise P/E that the market assigns to the expected value of new and profitable business opportunities. Although the stock of firms with positive EVAs has tended to outperform the stocks of negative EVA firms, the differences are typically insignificant and the relationship is not consistent over time. So while EVA is effective in evaluating management's past performance, there is no guarantee of future performance.

Key Terms

cyclical company, p. 233	defensive stock, p. 232	speculative company, p. 233
cyclical stock return, p. 233	growth company, p. 232	speculative stock, p. 233
defensive company, p. 232	growth stock, p. 232	SWOT analysis, p. 236
defensive competitive strategy, p. 234	offensive competitive strategy, p. 234	value stock, p. 233

Suggested Readings

Damodaran, Aswath. *Damodaran on Valuation*, 2nd ed. New York: Wiley, 2006.

Hackel, Kenneth S., and Joshua Livnat. *Cash Flow and Security Analysis*, 2nd ed. Burr Ridge, IL: Irwin Professional Publishing, 1996.

Koller, Tim, Marc Goedhart, and David Wessels. *Valuation: Measuring and Managing the Value of Companies*, 4th ed. New York: Wiley, 2005.

Palepu, Krishna, Victor Bernard, and Paul Healy. *Business Analysis and Valuation*, 3rd ed. Cincinnati, OH: South-Western Publishing, 2008.

Squires, Jan R., ed. *Practical Issues in Equity Analysis*. Charlottesville, VA: AIMR, 2000.

Stowe, John D., Thomas Robinson, Jerald Pinto, and Dennis McLeavey. *Analysis of Equity Investments: Valuation*. Charlottesville, VA: AIMR, 2002.

Sullivan, Rodney N., ed. *Equity Analysis Issues, Lessons and Techniques*. Charlottesville, VA: AIMR, 2003.

For Chapter CFA Questions and Problems, please see Appendix A at the end of this text.

Questions

1. Give an example of a growth company and discuss why you identify it as such. Based on its P/E, do you think it is a growth stock? Explain.
2. Give an example of a cyclical stock and discuss why you have designated it as such. Is it issued by a cyclical company?
3. A biotechnology firm is growing at a compound rate of more than 21% a year. (Its ROE is over 30%, and it retains about 70% of its earnings.) The stock of this company is priced at about 65 times next year's earnings. Discuss whether you consider this a growth company and/or a growth stock.
4. Select a company outside the retail drugstore industry and indicate what economic series you would use for a sales projection. Discuss why this is a relevant series.
5. Select a company outside the retail drugstore industry and indicate what industry series you would use in an industry analysis. (Use one of the industry groups designated by Standard & Poor's.) Discuss why this industry series is appropriate. Were there other possible alternatives?
6. Select a company outside the retail drugstore industry and, based on reading its annual report and other public information, discuss what you perceive to be its competitive strategy (i.e., low-cost producer or differentiation).
7. Discuss a company that is known to be a low-cost producer in its industry and consider why it is a cost leader. Do the same for a firm known for differentiating.
8. Under what conditions would you use a two- or three-stage cash flow model rather than the constant-growth model?
9. What is the rationale for using the price/book value ratio as a measure of relative value?
10. What would you look for to justify a price/book value ratio of 3.0? What would you expect to be the characteristics of a firm with a P/BV ratio of 0.6?
11. Why has the price/cash flow ratio become a popular measure of relative value during the recent past? What factors would help explain a difference in this ratio for two firms?
12. Assume that you uncover two stocks with substantially different price/sales ratios (e.g., 0.5 versus 2.5). Discuss the factors that might explain the difference.
13. Specify the major components for the calculation of economic value added. Describe what a positive EVA signifies.
14. Discuss why you would want to use EVA return on capital rather than absolute EVA to compare two companies or to evaluate a firm's performance over time.
15. Differentiate between EVA and MVA and discuss the relatively weak relationship between these two measures of performance. Is this relationship surprising to you? Explain.
16. Discuss the two factors that determine the franchise value of a firm. Assuming a firm has a base cost of equity of 11% and does not have a franchise value, what will be its P/E?
17. You are told that a company retains 80% of its earnings, and its earnings are growing at a rate of about 8% a year versus an average growth rate of 6% for all firms. Discuss whether you would consider this a growth company.
18. Discuss the reasoning behind the contention that in a completely competitive economy, there would never be a true growth company.
19. Why is it not feasible to use the dividend discount model in the valuation of true growth companies?
20. You are told that a growth company has a P/E ratio of 13 times and a growth rate of 15% compared to the aggregate market, which has a growth rate of 8% and a P/E ratio of 16 times. What does this comparison imply regarding the growth company? What else do you need to know to properly compare the growth company to the aggregate market?
21. Given the alternative companies described in the chapter (negative growth, simple growth, dynamic growth), indicate what your label would be for Shoppers Drug Mart. Justify your label.
22. Indicate and justify a growth label for Magna International.

Problems

1. Select two stocks in an industry of your choice, and perform a common-size income statement analysis over a two-year period.
   a. Discuss which firm is more cost-effective.
   b. Discuss the relative year-to-year changes in gross profit margin, operating profit margin, and net profit margin for each company.
2. Select a company outside the retail drugstore industry, and examine its operating profit margin relative to the operating margin for its industry during the most recent 10-year period. Discuss the annual results in terms of levels and percentage changes.
3. Given Magoo's beta of 1.75 and a risk-free rate of 7%, what is the expected return for Magoo assuming

a. a 15% market return?

b. a 10% market return?

4. Select three companies from any industry except retail drugstores.

a. Compute their *P/E* ratios using last year's average price [(high plus low)/2] and earnings.

b. Compute their growth rate of earnings over the last five years.

c. Look up the most recent beta reported in *Value Line.*

d. Discuss the relationships between *P/E*, growth, and risk.

5. Your client has asked for your advice on the following two investments. Purchase 2,000 shares of common stock or receive real-estate income as follows (year end):

End of Year	Real Estate Cash Flow
1	$38,155
2	$48,020
3	$92,100

The common stock pays no dividends for three years, it is anticipated that the firm will begin paying a $3 dividend in the fourth year and the dividend will grow at 6.6%. Investors demand a 10% return from this stock. The real estate investment yields 14%. What is the value of each of the investments and which investment is better?

6. A company's common stock paid $2 per share in dividend today and is presently selling for $27.86. The cost of equity for this company is 12% per annum. If the dividend is expected to grow at a constant rate per year, what is the anticipated dividend growth rate for this company?

7. Biotronics plans to retain and reinvest all of their earnings for the next 10 years. Investors believe that beginning 11 years from now the firm will begin to pay a dividend of $4.00 per share based on a 30% retention rate. Given a required return of 20%, the stock should sell for what price today?

8. An analyst has estimated the following growth potential for Giant Industries

Now to end of year 3	25% per year
Years 4 and 5	20% per year
Year 6 and beyond	10% per year

The current EPS is $1.60 and shareholders demand a 12% return. Assuming that ROE will remain constant at 30% per year, calculate the value of this stock.

9. You have been asked to examine the following company information

a. Calculate ROE for both years using the three components of the DuPont formula.

b. Using the ROE calculated in Part a, calculate the sustainable-growth rate for 20X2

c. Discuss what impact each of the following would have on the firm's sustainable growth rate:

i. increasing leverage to improve production

ii. issuing long-term debt to reduce accounts payable

iii. increasing the dividend

d. Calculate the FCFF for 20X2.

e. Based on your answer for d, assume the FCFF grows by 20% for the next three years and then 14%. Calculate the current value of the firm's shares. The firm's WACC is 16%.

CLIPPER, INC.: FINANCIAL STATEMENTS FOR YEAR ENDING DECEMBER 31 ($ MILLIONS, EXCEPT PER-SHARE DATA)

	20X1	20X2
Income Statement		
Revenue	5,750	6,140
Cost of goods sold	3,450	3,684
Selling and administrative	1,400	1,484
Amortization expense	120	134
Operating income	780	838
Interest expense	102	131
Income before taxes	678	707
Income taxes	231	240
Net income	447	467
Earnings per share	1.75	1.91
Average shares outstanding (millions)	255	245

	20X1	20X1
Balance Sheet	20X1	20X2
Accounts receivable	900	1,090
Inventories	600	682
Net capital assets	800	920
Total assets	2,300	2,692
Current liabilities	620	667
Long-term debt	320	300
Total liabilities	940	967
Shareholders' equity	1,360	1,725
Total liabilities and shareholder's equity	2,300	2,692
Book value per share	$5.33	$7.04

10

Technical Analysis*

After you read this chapter, you should be able to answer the following questions:

1. How does technical analysis differ from fundamental analysis?

2. What are the underlying assumptions of technical analysis?

3. What main assumption causes a difference between technical analysis and the efficient market hypothesis?

4. What are the advantages and challenges of technical analysis?

5. What is the logic behind contrary-opinion, "follow the smart money," momentum indicators, and stock price and volume techniques?

6. What are the three types of price movements postulated in the Dow Theory, and how are they used?

7. How would a technician use trading volume, support and resistance levels, moving-average lines, and relative-strength ratio?

8. What are some uses of technical analysis in bond and foreign security markets?

The market reacted yesterday to the report of a large increase in the short interest on the TSX.

Although the market declined today, it was not considered bearish because of the light volume.

The market declined today after three days of increases due to profit taking by investors.

These and similar statements appear daily in the business news. All of them have as their rationale one of numerous technical trading rules. *Technical analysts,* or *technicians,* develop technical trading rules from observations of past price movements of the stock market and individual stocks. The philosophy behind technical analysis is in sharp contrast to the efficient market hypothesis that we studied. It also differs from what we learned about fundamental analysis; making investment decisions based on an examination of variables that lead to intrinsic value estimates, which are then compared to prevailing market price. In contrast to both, **technical analysis** involves examining past market data such as prices and trading volume, which leads to an estimate of future price trends and, therefore, an investment decision. Whereas fundamental analysts use economic data that are usually separate from the stock or bond market, technical analysts use data *from the market itself* because they contend that the market is its own best predictor. Therefore, technical analysis is an alternative method of making the investment decision and answering the questions: What securities should an investor buy or sell? When should these investments be made?

Technical analysts see no need to study the multitude of economic, industry, and company variables because they believe that past price movements will signal future price movements. They also believe that a change in the price trend may predict a forthcoming change in the fundamental variables such as earnings and risk before it is perceived by most fundamental analysts. Are technicians correct? Many investors using these techniques claim to have experienced superior returns on many investments. As well, many investment newsletters base their recommendations on technical analysis, and investment firms employ both fundamental and technical analysts.

---

* Walter G. Murphy and Richard T. McCabe, from Merrill Lynch Capital Markets, provided helpful comments and material for this chapter.

Therefore, whether a fan of fundamental analysis or an advocate of the efficient market hypothesis, investors should still have an understanding of the basic philosophy and reasoning behind technical approaches.

10.1   Underlying Assumptions of Technical Analysis

Technical analysts base trading decisions on examinations of prior price and volume data to determine past market trends from which they predict future behaviour for the market as a whole and for individual securities. Several assumptions summarized in Levy (1966) lead to this view of price movements. Certain aspects of these assumptions are controversial, leading fundamental analysts and efficient markets advocates to question their validity. We have italicized those aspects in our list.

1. The market value of any good or service is determined solely by the interaction of supply and demand.
2. Supply and demand are governed by numerous rational and irrational factors. Included in these factors are those economic variables relied on by the fundamental analyst as well as opinions, moods, and guesses. The market weighs all these factors continually and automatically.
3. Disregarding minor fluctuations, *the prices for individual securities and the overall value of the market tend to move in trends, which persist for appreciable lengths of time.*
4. Prevailing trends change in reaction to shifts in supply and demand relationships. These shifts, no matter why they occur, *can be detected sooner or later in the action of the market itself.*

The first two assumptions are almost universally accepted by technicians and non-technicians alike. Almost anyone who has had an introductory economics course would agree that at any point in time, the price of a security (or any good or service) is determined by the interaction of supply and demand. In addition, most observers would acknowledge that supply and demand are governed by many variables. The only difference in opinion might concern the influence of the irrational factors. Certainly, everyone would agree that the market continually weighs all these factors.

In contrast, there is a significant difference of opinion regarding how quickly stock prices adjust to changes in supply and demand. Technical analysts expect stock prices to move in trends that persist for long periods because they believe that new information does *not* come to the market at one point in time but rather enters the market *over a period of time.* This pattern of information access occurs because of different sources of information or because certain investors receive the information or perceive fundamental changes earlier than others. As various groups—ranging from insiders to well-informed professionals to the average investor—receive the information and buy or sell a security accordingly, its price moves gradually toward the new equilibrium. Therefore, technicians do not expect the price adjustment to be as abrupt as fundamental analysts and efficient market supporters do; rather, they expect a *gradual price adjustment* to reflect the gradual dissemination of information.

Exhibit 10.1 shows this process wherein new information causes a decrease in the equilibrium price for a security but the price adjustment is not rapid. It occurs as a trend that persists until the stock reaches its new equilibrium. Technical analysts look for the start of a change so that they can get on the bandwagon early and benefit from the move to the new equilibrium price by buying if the trend is up or selling if the trend is down. Obviously, if there is a rapid adjustment of prices to the new information (as expected by those who espouse an efficient market), the ride on the bandwagon would be so short that investors could not benefit. They do not attempt to predict the new equilibrium value.

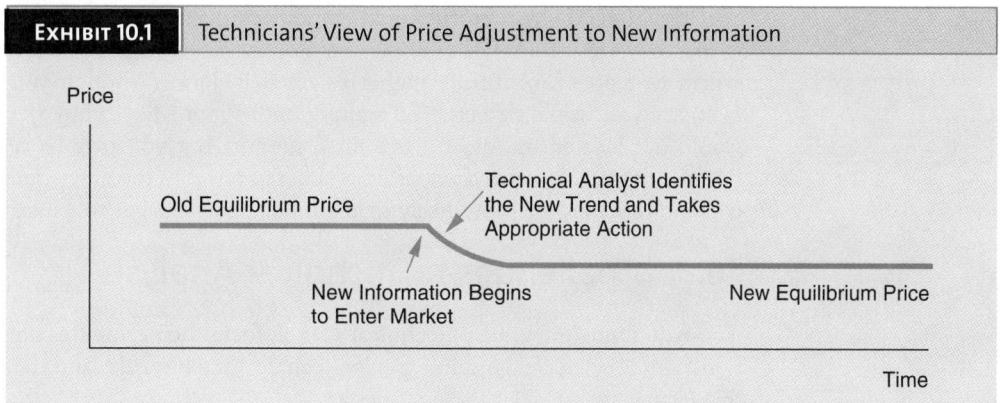

Exhibit 10.1 Technicians' View of Price Adjustment to New Information

10.2 Advantages of Technical Analysis

Although technicians understand the logic of fundamental analysis, they see several benefits in their approach. Most technical analysts admit that a fundamental analyst with good information, good analytical ability, and a keen sense of information's impact on the market should achieve above-average returns. However, this statement requires qualification. According to technical analysts, it is important to recognize that the fundamental analysts can experience superior returns *only* if they obtain new information before other investors and process it *correctly* and *quickly*. Technical analysts do not believe the majority of investors can consistently get new information before other investors and consistently process it correctly and quickly.

In addition, technical analysts claim that a major advantage of their method is that *it is not heavily dependent on financial accounting statements*—the major source of information about the past performance of a firm or industry. As we know from our earlier discussions, the fundamental analyst evaluates such statements to help project future return and risk characteristics for industries and individual securities. The technician contends that there are several major problems with accounting statements:

1. They lack a great deal of information needed by security analysts, such as information related to sales, earnings, and capital utilized by product line and customers.
2. As GAAP allows corporations to choose among several procedures for reporting expenses, assets, or liabilities, vastly different values for expenses, income, return on assets, and return on equity can occur, depending on whether the firm is conservative or aggressive. As a result, it can be difficult to compare statements of two firms within the same industry, much less firms across industries.
3. Many psychological factors and other non-quantifiable variables do not appear in financial statements. Examples include employee training and loyalty, customer goodwill, and general investor attitude toward an industry. Investor attitudes could be important when investors become concerned about the risk from restrictions or taxes on products such as tobacco or alcohol or when firms do business in countries that have significant political risk.

Therefore, because technicians are suspicious of financial statements, they consider it advantageous not to depend on them.

Finally, assume a fundamental analyst determines that a given security is under- or overvalued a long time before other investors. He or she still must determine when to make the purchase or sale. Ideally, the highest return would come from making the transaction just before the change in market value occurs. For example, assume that based on your analysis in February, you expect a firm to report substantially higher earnings in June. Although you could buy the stock in February, you would be better off waiting until about May to buy the stock so that your funds would not be tied up for an extra three months, but you may be reticent to wait that long. Because most technicians do not invest until the move to the new equilibrium is under way, they contend that they are more likely than a fundamental analyst to experience ideal timing.

10.3   Challenges to Technical Analysis

Those doubting the value of technical analysis focus their criticisms on some of its basic assumptions, and they challenge some specific technical trading rules and their long-run usefulness. In this section we consider these challenges.

10.3.1   CHALLENGES TO TECHNICAL ANALYSIS ASSUMPTIONS

The major challenge to technical analysis is based on the results of empirical tests of the efficient market hypothesis (EMH). As discussed in Chapter 5, for technical trading rules to generate superior risk-adjusted returns after taking account of transaction costs, the market would have to be slow to adjust prices to the arrival of new information; that is, it would have to be inefficient (weak-form efficient). Almost all the studies testing the weak-form EMH using statistical analysis have found that prices do not move in trends based on statistical tests of autocorrelation and runs. These results support the EMH.[1]

Regarding the analysis of specific trading rules, as discussed in Chapter 5, numerous technical trading rules exist that have not been or cannot be tested. Still, the vast majority of the results for the trading rules that have been tested support the EMH.

10.3.2   CHALLENGES TO TECHNICAL TRADING RULES

An obvious challenge to technical analysis is that the past price patterns or relationships between specific market variables and stock prices may not be repeated. As a result, a technique that previously worked might miss subsequent market turns. This possibility leads most technicians to follow several trading rules and to seek a consensus of all of them to predict the future market pattern.

Other critics suggest that many price patterns become self-fulfilling prophecies. For example, assume a number of analysts expect a stock currently selling at $40 to go to $50 or more if it should rise above its current pattern and break through its channel at $45. As soon as it reaches $45, enough technicians will buy, thus causing the price to rise to $50, exactly as predicted. In fact, some technicians may place a limit order to buy the stock at such a breakout point. Under such conditions, the increase will probably be only temporary and the price will return to its true equilibrium.

Another problem with technical analysis is that the success of a particular trading rule will encourage many investors to adopt it. It is contended that this popularity and the resulting competition will eventually neutralize the technique. If numerous investors focus on a specific technical trading rule, some of them will attempt to anticipate the price pattern and either ruin the expected historical price pattern or eliminate profits for most traders by

---

1 The two sets of tests of the weak-form EMH are: (1) the statistical analysis of prices to determine if prices moved in trends or were a random walk, and (2) the analysis of specific trading rules to determine if their use could beat a buy-and-hold policy after considering transactions costs and risk.

causing the price to change faster than expected. For example, suppose it becomes known that technicians who employ short-selling data have been enjoying high returns. Based on this knowledge, other technicians will likely start using these data and thus accelerate the stock price pattern following changes in short selling. As a result, this profitable trading rule may no longer be profitable after the first few investors react.

Further, as we will see when we examine specific trading rules, *they all require a great deal of subjective judgment*. Two technical analysts looking at the same price pattern may arrive at widely different interpretations of what has happened and, therefore, will come to different investment decisions. This implies that the use of various techniques is neither completely mechanical nor obvious. Finally, as we will discuss in connection with several trading rules, *the standard values that signal investment decisions can change over time*. Therefore, in some instances technical analysts adjust the specified values that trigger investment decisions to conform to the new environment. In other cases, trading rules have been abandoned because they no longer work.

10.4 Technical Trading Rules and Indicators

Exhibit 10.2 shows a typical stock price cycle that could be an example for the overall stock market or for an individual stock. The graph shows a peak and trough, along with a rising trend channel, a flat trend channel, a declining trend channel, and indications of when a technical analyst would ideally want to trade.

The graph begins with the end of a declining (bear) market that finishes in a **trough**, followed by an upward trend that breaks through the **declining trend channel**. Confirmation that the declining trend has reversed would be a buy signal. The technical analyst would buy stocks that showed this pattern.

The analyst would then expect the development of a **rising trend channel**. As long as the stock price stayed in this rising channel, the technician would hold the stock(s). Ideally, they want to sell at the **peak** of the cycle, but they cannot identify a peak until after the trend changes.

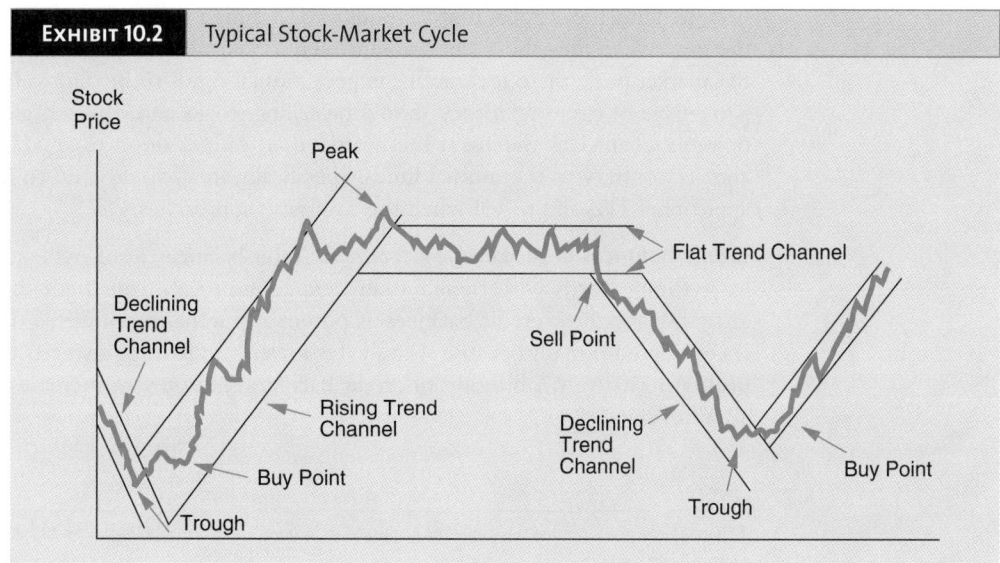

EXHIBIT 10.2 | Typical Stock-Market Cycle

If the stock (or the market) begins trading in a flat pattern, it will necessarily break out of its rising trend channel. At this point, some analysts would sell, but most would hold to see if the stock experiences a period of consolidation and then breaks out of the **flat trend channel** on the upside and begins rising again. Alternatively, if the stock were to break out of the channel on the downside, the technician would take this as a sell signal and would expect a declining trend channel. The next buy signal would come after the trough when the price breaks out of the declining channel and establishes a rising trend. The next question is how to detect these changes in trend and the importance of volume.

There are numerous technical trading rules and a range of interpretations for each of them. Almost all technical analysts watch many alternative rules and decide on a buy or sell decision based on a *consensus* of the signals because complete agreement of all the rules is rare. In the following discussion of several well-known techniques, we have divided the rules into four groups based on the attitudes of technical analysts. The first group includes trading rules used by analysts who like to trade against the crowd using contrary-opinion signals. The second group attempts to emulate astute investors, that is, the smart money. The third group includes popular technical indicators that are not easily classified. Finally, the fourth group contains pure price and volume techniques, including the famous Dow Theory.

10.4.1   CONTRARY-OPINION RULES

Many technical analysts rely on technical trading rules that assume that the majority of investors are wrong as the market approaches peaks and troughs. Therefore, these technicians try to determine when the majority of investors is either strongly bullish or bearish and then trade in the opposite direction.

Mutual Fund Cash Positions Mutual funds hold some part of their portfolio in cash for one of several reasons. One is that they need cash to liquidate shares submitted by fundholders. Another is that new investments in the mutual fund may not have been invested. Third, the portfolio manager might be bearish on the market and want to increase the fund's defensive cash position.

Mutual funds' ratios of cash as a percentage of the total assets in their portfolios (the *cash ratio* or *liquid asset ratio*) are reported in the press, including monthly figures in *Barron's*.[2]

Contrary-opinion technicians believe that mutual funds usually are wrong at peaks and troughs. Thus, they expect mutual funds to have a high percentage of cash near a market trough—the time when they should be fully invested to take advantage of the impending market rise. At the market peak, these technicians expect mutual funds to be almost fully invested with a low percentage of cash when they should be selling stocks and realizing gains. Therefore, contrary-opinion technicians watch for the mutual fund cash position to approach one of the extremes and act contrary to the mutual funds. Specifically, they would tend to buy when the cash ratio approaches 11% and to sell when the cash ratio approaches 4%.

Credit Balances in Brokerage Accounts Credit balances result when investors sell stocks and leave the proceeds with their brokers, expecting to reinvest them shortly. Because technical analysts view these credit balances as potential purchasing power, a decline in these balances is considered bearish because it indicates lower purchasing power as the market approaches a peak. Alternatively, a buildup of credit balances indicates an increase in buying power and is a bullish signal.

---

2 *Barron's* is a prime source for numerous technical indicators. For a readable discussion of relevant data and their use, see Martin E. Zweig (1987).

Investment Advisory Opinions Many technicians believe that if a large proportion of investment advisory services are bearish, this signals the approach of a market trough and the onset of a bull market. Because most advisory services tend to be trend followers, the number of bears usually is greatest when market bottoms are approaching. This trading rule is specified in terms of the percent of advisory services that are bearish/bullish given the number of services expressing an opinion.[3] Exhibit 10.3 shows a time-series plot of the S&P 500 index and the bull/bears difference. Near the end of 2002 there were more bears than bulls, indicating that it might be a good time to buy. In mid- to late 2008, the bulls were at their highest level since 2004, which would recommend selling.

OTC versus NYSE Volume This ratio of trading volume is considered a measure of speculative activity. Speculative trading typically peaks at market peaks. Notably, the interpretation of the ratio has changed—that is, the decision rules have changed. Specifically, during the mid-1990s, the decision rule was in terms of specific percentages—112% was considered heavy speculative trading and an overbought market while 87% was considered low speculative trading and an oversold market. The problem was that the percentages kept increasing because of faster growth in NASDAQ trading volume and dominance of the NASDAQ market by a few large-cap stocks. It was subsequently decided to detect excess speculative activity by using the *direction* of the volume ratio as a guide. For example, if this ratio is increasing, it indicates a bearish speculative environment.

EXHIBIT 10.3	Time-Series Plot of the S&P and the Bullish/Bearish Advisors

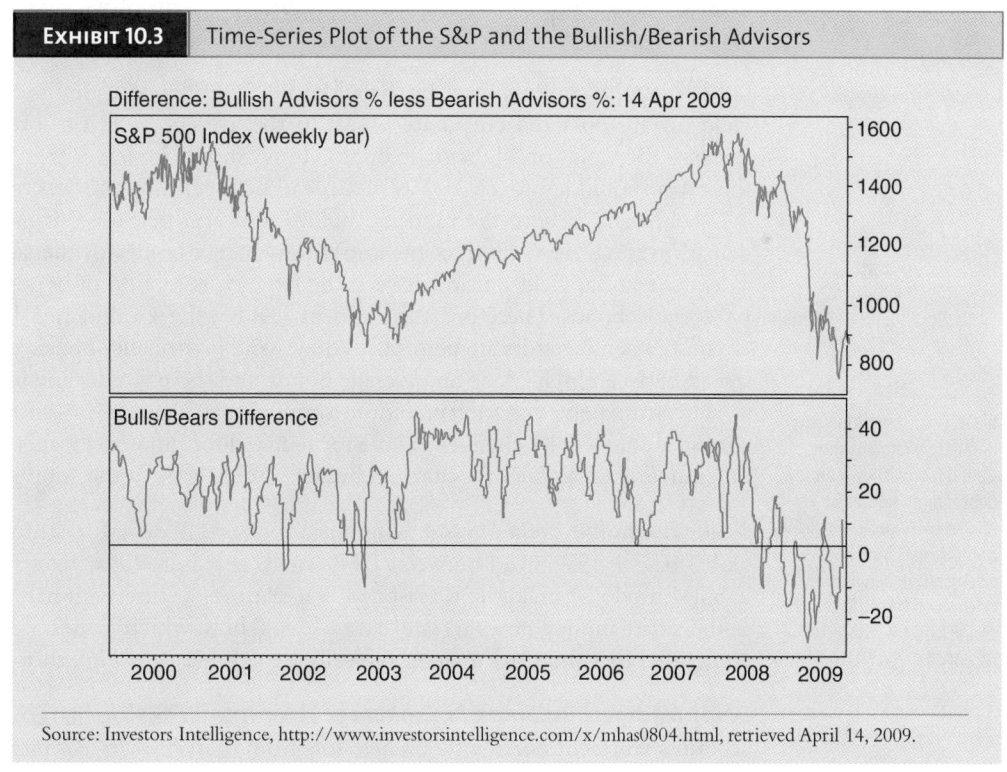

Source: Investors Intelligence, http://www.investorsintelligence.com/x/mhas0804.html, retrieved April 14, 2009.

3 This ratio is compiled by Investors Intelligence, www.investorintelligence.com.

Put–Call Ratio Contrary-opinion technicians use put options, which give the holder the right to sell stock at a specified price for a given time period, as signals of a bearish attitude. A higher put-call ratio indicates a pervasive bearish attitude for investors, which technicians consider a bullish indicator.

This ratio historically fluctuated between 0.60 and 0.40 and was typically substantially less than 1 because investors tend to be bullish and avoid selling short or buying puts. Beginning in 2006, the series experienced a rising trend and has been in the range of 0.80 to 1.20. As of March 2008 the ratio was about 1.14, implying that investors are quite bearish, which would be a strong bullish sign for contrary-opinion technicians.

Futures Traders Bullish on Stock-Index Futures Another relatively popular contrary-opinion measure is the percentage of speculators in stock-index futures who are bullish regarding stocks based on a survey of individual futures traders. These technicians would consider it a bearish sign when more than 70% of the speculators are bullish, and a bullish sign when this ratio declines to 30% or lower.

As we have shown, contrary-opinion technicians have several measures of how the majority of investors are investing that prompt them to take the opposite action. They generally employ several of these series to provide a consensus regarding investors' attitude.

See the current Market Vane bullish indicator at http://online.barrons.com/public/page/9_0210-investorsentimentreadings.html.

10.4.2 FOLLOW THE SMART MONEY

Some technical analysts have created a set of indicators and corresponding rules that they believe indicate the behaviour of smart, sophisticated investors. We discuss three such indicators in this section.

Confidence Index Published by *Barron's*, the Confidence Index is the ratio of the average yield on 10 top-rated corporate bonds to the average yield on intermediate-grade bonds. Because the yields on high-grade bonds always should be lower than on intermediate bonds, this ratio should approach 100 as the spread between the two sets of bonds gets smaller.

Technicians believe the ratio is a bullish indicator because during periods of high confidence, investors are willing to invest in lower-quality bonds for the added yield, which causes a decrease in the yield spread between the large cross-section of bonds relative to the yield on high-grade bonds. Therefore, this ratio of yields—the Confidence Index—will increase. In contrast, when investors are pessimistic, they avoid low-quality bonds, which increases the yield spread between high-grade and average bonds, and there is a decline in the Confidence Index.

Unfortunately, this interpretation assumes that changes in the yield spread are caused almost exclusively by changes in investor demand for different quality bonds. In fact, the yield differences have frequently changed because of changes in the supply of bonds.

IIROC (Investment Industry Regulatory Organization of Canada) publishes monthly debt margin figures at http://www.iiroc.ca/English/ComplianceSurveillance/FinancialCompliance/Documents/MonthlyClientDebtMarginAccounts_en.pdf

T-Bill–Eurodollar Yield Spread A popular measure of investor attitude or confidence on a global basis is the spread between T-bill yields and Eurodollar rates measured as the ratio of T-bill–Eurodollar yields. It is reasoned that at times of international crisis, this spread widens as the smart money flows to safe-haven U.S. T-bills, which causes a decline in this ratio. It is contended that the stock market typically experiences a trough shortly thereafter.

Debit (Margin) Balances in Brokerage Accounts Debit or margin balances in brokerage accounts represent borrowing by investors from their brokers. An increase in margin balances implies buying by these investors and is considered a bullish sign, while a decline in margin balances would indicate selling and would be a bearish indicator.

Monthly data on margin debt is reported in *Barron's*, however, this index does not include borrowing by investors from other sources such as banks. Also, because it is an absolute value, technicians can only look for changes in the trend of borrowing—that is, increases are bullish, declines are bearish.

10.4.3 MOMENTUM INDICATORS

In addition to contrary-opinion and smart-money signals, several indicators of overall market momentum are used to make aggregate market decisions.

Breadth of Market Breadth of market measures the number of issues that have increased each day and the number of issues that have declined. It helps explain the cause of a change of direction in a composite market index such as the S&P/TSX Composite index. As we discussed in Chapter 4, most stock-market indexes are heavily influenced by the stocks of large firms because they are value weighted. Therefore, a stock-market index can experience an overall increase even if the majority of the individual issues do not. Such a divergence can be detected by examining the advance–decline figures for all stocks on the exchange, along with the overall market index.

The advance–decline index is typically a cumulative index of net advances or net declines. Specifically, each day major newspapers and numerous investment websites publish figures on the number of issues on the various exchanges that advanced, declined, or were unchanged. The figures for a five-day sample, as would be reported in *Barron's,* are shown in Exhibit 10.4. These figures, along with changes in the DJIA at the bottom of the table, indicate a strong market decline because the DJIA was dropping and the net decline figure was strong, indicating that the market decrease was broadly based. Even the results on August 28, when the market rallied, were encouraging but short-lived.

Stocks above Their 200-Day Moving Average Technicians often compute moving averages of an index to determine its general trend. To examine individual stocks, the 200-day **moving average** of prices has been fairly popular. From these moving-average indexes for numerous stocks, Media General Financial Services calculates how many stocks currently are trading above their 200-day moving-average index, and this is used as an indicator of general investor sentiment. The market is considered to be *overbought* and subject to a negative correction when more than 70% of the stocks are trading above their 200-day moving average. In contrast, if less than 30% of the stocks are selling above their 200-day moving average, the market is considered to be oversold, which means investors should expect a positive correction. As shown in the top section of Exhibit 10.5, in early 2008, the percent of stocks selling above their 200-day moving average was close to 30%, which indicates an oversold, bullish signal.

Daily information on advances and declines can be found on the TSX website. Under Market Activity click on the "Advancers/Decliners" tab and then scroll down to "Market Summary." You'll see the number of issues advancing and declining, and if you click on the "Issue's Volumes" tab, you'll get the volumes advancing and declining. http://www.tsx.com.

EXHIBIT 10.4	Daily Advance/Decline Volumes on the NASDAQ				
Day	August 25	August 26	August 27	August 28	August 29
Issues traded	2,984	2,999	2,969	2,990	2,993
Advances	625	1,541	1,823	2,090	1,044
Declines	2,221	1,295	980	762	1,808
Unchanged	138	163	166	138	141
Net advances (advances minus declines)	−1,596	246	843	1,328	−764
Cumulative net advances	−1,596	−1,350	−507	821	57
Changes in DJIA	−241.81	+26.62	+89.64	+212.67	−171.63

Source: *Barron's,* "Trading Diary," September 1, 2008, page M63.

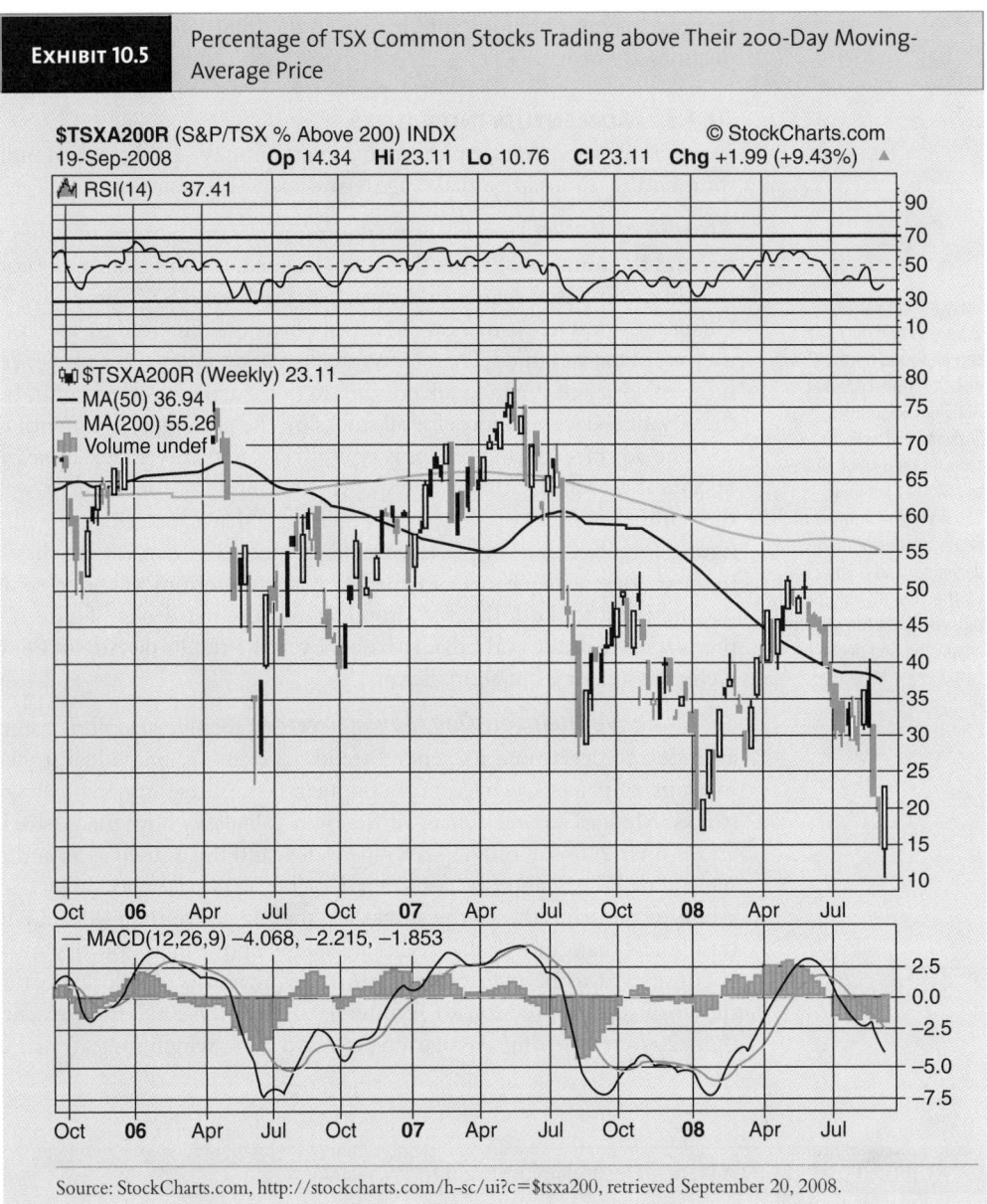

Exhibit 10.5	Percentage of TSX Common Stocks Trading above Their 200-Day Moving-Average Price

Source: StockCharts.com, http://stockcharts.com/h-sc/ui?c=$tsxa200, retrieved September 20, 2008.

10.4.4 STOCK PRICE AND VOLUME TECHNIQUES

Early in this chapter, we examined a hypothetical stock price chart demonstrating market peaks and troughs along with rising and declining trend channels and breakouts from channels that signal new price trends or reversals of the price trends. While price patterns alone are important, most technical trading rules consider both stock price and corresponding volume movements.

Dow Theory Any discussion of technical analysis using price and volume data should begin with the Dow Theory because it was among the earliest work on this topic and remains the basis for many technical indicators.[4] Dow described stock prices as moving in trends analogous to the movement of water. He postulated three types of price movements over time: (1) major trends that are like tides in the ocean, (2) intermediate trends that resemble waves, and (3) short-run movements that are like ripples. Dow Theory theorists attempt to detect the direction of the major price trend (tide), recognizing that intermediate movements (waves) may occasionally move in the opposite direction. They recognize that a major market advance does not go straight up, but rather includes small price declines as some investors decide to take profits.

Exhibit 10.6 shows the typical bullish pattern. The technician would look for every recovery to reach a new peak above the prior peak, and this price rise should be accompanied by heavy trading volume. Alternatively, each profit-taking reversal that follows an increase to a new peak should have a trough above the prior trough, with relatively light trading volume during the profit-taking reversals. When this pattern of price and volume movements changes, the major trend may be entering a period of consolidation (a flat trend) or a major reversal.

Importance of Volume A price movement in one direction means that the net effect on price is in that direction, but the price change alone does not indicate the breadth of the excess demand or supply. Therefore, the technician looks for a price increase on heavy volume relative to the stock's normal trading volume as an indication of bullish activity. Conversely, a price decline with heavy volume is considered bearish. A generally bullish pattern would be when price increases are accompanied by heavy volume and small price reversals occur with light trading volume.

Technicians also use a ratio of upside–downside volume as an indicator of short-term momentum for the aggregate stock market. Each day the stock exchanges announce the volume of trading in stocks that experienced an increase divided by the volume of trading in stocks that declined. These data are reported daily in newspapers and the various stock exchanges. This ratio is used as an indicator of market momentum. Specifically, technicians believe that an upside–downside volume value of 1.75 or more indicates an overbought position that is bearish. Alternatively, a value of 0.75 and lower supposedly reflects an oversold position and is considered bullish. The value as of March 2008 was below 1.00 and thus was providing a bullish signal.

A thorough discussion of the Dow Theory and Charles Dow can be found at StockCharts ChartSchool at http://stockcharts.com/school/doku.php?id=chart_school.

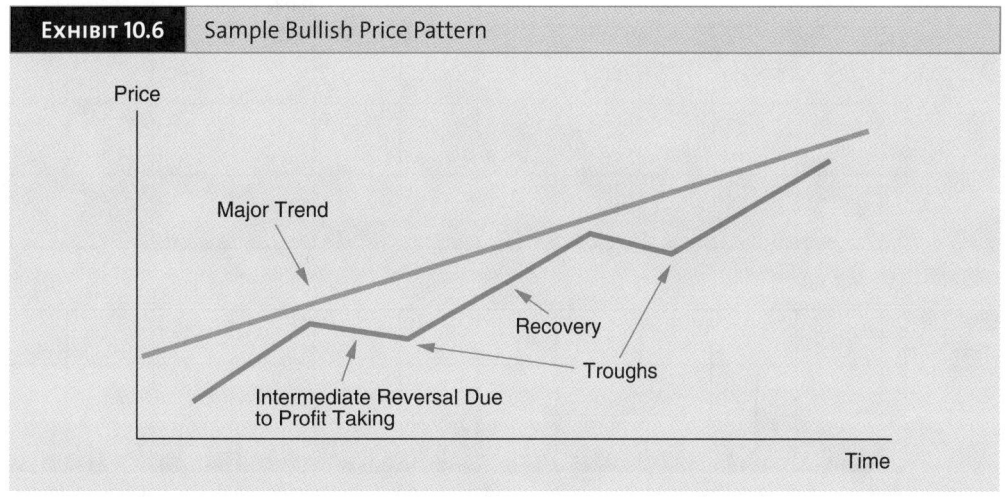

EXHIBIT 10.6	Sample Bullish Price Pattern

---

4 A study that discusses and provides support for the Dow Theory is Glickstein and Wubbels (1983).

Support and Resistance Levels A **support level** is the price range at which the technician would expect a substantial increase in the demand for a stock. Generally, a support level will develop after a stock has enjoyed a meaningful price increase and the stock experiences profit taking. Technicians reason that at some price below the recent peak other investors who did not buy during the first price increase (waiting for a small reversal) will get into the stock. When the price reaches this support price, demand surges and price and volume begin to increase again.

A **resistance level** is the price range at which the technician would expect an increase in the supply of stock and a price reversal. A resistance level develops after a significant decline from a higher price level. After the decline, the stock begins to recover, but the prior decline in price leads some investors who acquired the stock at a higher price to look for an opportunity to sell it near their break-even points. Therefore, the supply of stock owned by these nervous investors is *overhanging* the market. When the price rebounds to the target price set by these investors, this overhanging supply of stock comes to the market and there is a price decline on heavy volume. It is also possible to envision a rising trend of support and resistance levels for a stock. For example, the rising support prices would be a set of higher prices where investors over time would see the price increase and would take the opportunity to buy when there is a "pull back" due to profit taking. In this latter case, there would be a succession of higher support and resistance levels over time.

Exhibit 10.7 contains the daily stock prices for Canadian Tire, with support and resistance lines. The graph shows a gradual decline since March 2008 after reporting flat earnings. In September 2008, the resistance level was at about $60 and dropping, while the support level

EXHIBIT 10.7	Daily Stock Prices and Volume for Canadian Tire Corporation with Indications of Support and Resistance Levels

Source: TMX Money, http://cxa.marketwatch.com/TSX/en/Market/intchart.aspx?symb=CTC&sid=46239, retrieved September 20, 2008.

was about $55 and also dropping. The bearish technician would look for future prices to drop in line with this channel. If prices fell significantly below the rising support line on strong volume, it would signal a possible trend reversal and would be considered a bearish signal. In contrast, an increase above the $60 resistance price line would be bullish.

Moving-Average Lines Earlier, we discussed how technicians use a 200-day moving average as an indicator of the long-run trend and how they examine current prices relative to this trend for signals of a change. In this discussion, we add a 50-day moving-average price line (short-term trend) and consider large volume.

Exhibit 10.8 is a daily stock price chart from Yahoo! Inc. for Shoppers Drug Mart for the year ending September 19, 2008. It also contains 50-day and 200-day moving-average (MA) lines. The MA lines are meant to reflect the overall trend for the price series with the shorter MA line (the 50-day versus 200-day) reflecting shorter trends. Two comparisons involving the MA lines are considered important. The first comparison is the specific prices to the shorter-run 50-day MA line. If the overall price trend of a stock or the market has been down, the moving-average price line generally would lie above current prices. If prices reverse and break through the moving-average line *from below* accompanied by heavy trading volume, most technicians would consider this a *positive* change and speculate that this breakthrough could be a preliminary signal of a reversal of the declining trend. In contrast, if the price of a stock had been rising, the moving-average line would also be rising, but it would be below current prices. If

EXHIBIT 10.8 Daily Stock Prices for Shoppers Drug Mart with 50-Day and 200-Day Moving-Average Lines

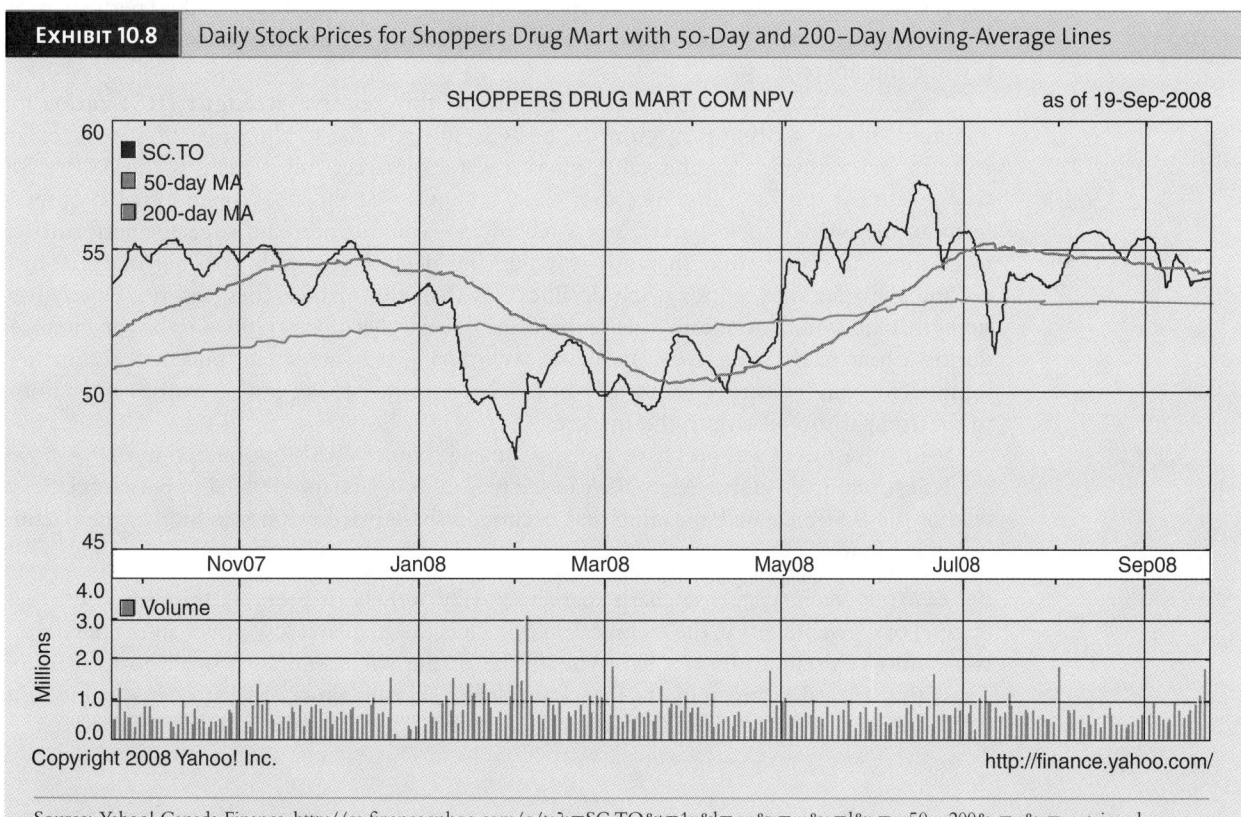

Source: Yahoo! Canada Finance, http://ca.finance.yahoo.com/q/ta?s=SC.TO&t=1y&l=on&z=m&q=l&p=m50,m200&a=v&c=, retrieved September 20, 2008.

current prices declined and broke through the moving-average line *from above* accompanied by heavy trading volume, this would be considered a preliminary bearish pattern that would possibly signal a reversal of the long-run rising trend.

The second comparison is between the 50- and 200-day MA lines. If the 50-day MA line crosses the 200-day MA line from below on good volume, this would be a bullish indicator (buy signal) because it confirms a reversal in trend from negative to positive. In contrast, when the 50-day line crosses the 200-day line from above, it confirms a change to a negative trend and would be a sell signal. In the case of Shoppers, there was a bearish crossing in February 2008, but it was reversed in June 2008 when there was a bullish crossing. Following the bullish crossing, the 50-day line has been above the 200-day line as prices reached a peak of about $57 and were about $54 at the end of the period. There is a cautionary signal to this chart, since the price line has broken through the 50-day line from above several times and is slightly below this MA line at the end of the graph.

Overall, for a *bullish* trend the 50-day MA line should be above the 200-day MA line. Notably, if this positive gap between the 50-day and 200-day lines gets too large (which happens with a fast run-up in price), a technician might consider this an indication that the stock is temporarily overbought, which is bearish in the short run. A *bearish* trend is when the 50-day MA line is always below the 200-day MA line. Still, if the gap gets very large on the downside, it might be considered a signal of an oversold stock, which is bullish for the short run.

Relative Strength Technicians believe that once a trend begins, it will continue until some major event causes a change in direction. They believe this is also true of *relative* performance. If an individual stock or an industry group is outperforming the market, technicians believe it will continue to do so.

Therefore, technicians compute weekly or monthly **relative-strength (RS) ratios** for individual stocks and industry groups. The RS ratio is equal to the price of a stock or an industry index divided by the value for some stock-market index such as the S&P/TSX Composite.[5] If this ratio increases over time, it shows that the stock or industry is outperforming the overall stock market, and a technician would expect this superior performance to continue. Relative-strength ratios work during declining as well as rising markets. In a declining market, if a stock's price declines less than the market does, the stock's relative-strength ratio will continue to rise. Technicians believe that if this ratio is stable or increases during a bear market, the stock should do well during the subsequent bull market. Further, some technicians construct graphs of stocks relative to the stock's industry index in addition to the comparison relative to the market.

Many investment websites have a relative-strength index (RSI) option. Exhibit 10.9 shows the RSI for Shoppers Drug Mart. We can see that in mid-January 2008, Shoppers' stock price fell but the RSI increased, meaning that decline in share price was not as high as the decline in the market.

Bar Charting Technicians use charts that show daily, weekly, or monthly time series of stock prices. For a given interval, the technical analyst plots the high and low prices and connects the two points vertically to form a bar. Typically, he or she will also draw a small horizontal line across this vertical bar to indicate the closing price. Finally, almost all bar charts include the

---

5 In contrast to these relative to market or industry ratios, there are ratios that are relative to the stock itself, which is fundamentally a momentum indicator. These are not the same.

Exhibit 10.9	Relative Strength Index for Shoppers Drug Mart

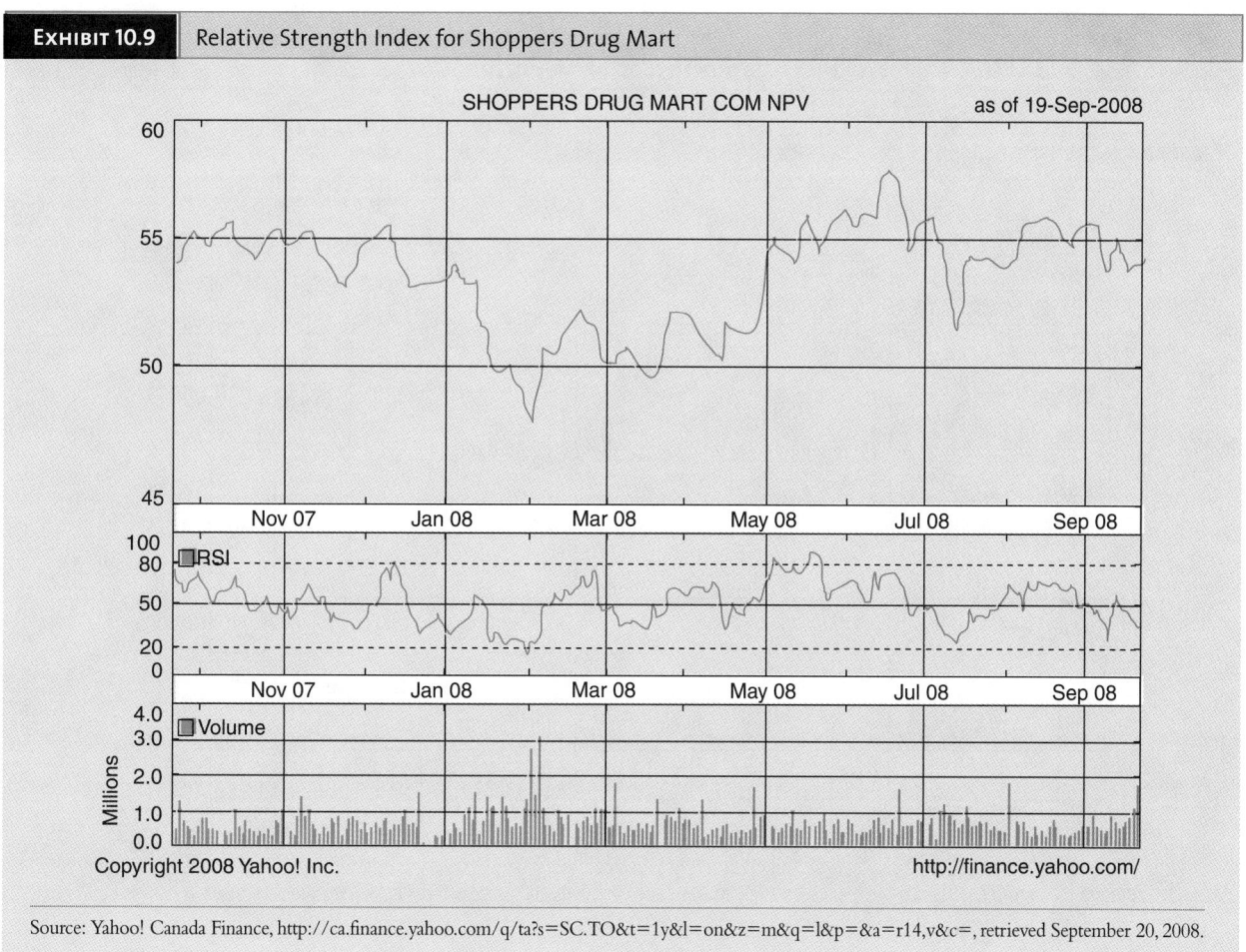

Source: Yahoo! Canada Finance, http://ca.finance.yahoo.com/q/ta?s=SC.TO&t=1y&l=on&z=m&q=l&p=&a=r14,v&c=, retrieved September 20, 2008.

The TSX website has good interactive charts for researching stocks, including an easy-to-use ToolSchool. Go to http://www.tsx.com/, enter a ticker symbol into the "Get Quote" text box, and then select the "Charting" tab on the company's initial page.

volume of trading at the bottom of the chart so that the technical analyst can relate the price and volume movements. Exhibits 10.5 and 10.7 to 10.9 all use the typical bar chart format.

Candlestick Charts A candlestick chart is basically an extension of the bar chart discussed above. In addition to high, low, and closing price for each trading day or period, candlestick charts also include the opening price and indicate the change from open to close by shading whether the market or individual stock went down (dark shading) or up (white bar) for the day or period. The result for Shoppers Drug Mart shown in Exhibit 10.10 is additional information and insight regarding the stock's movements over time.

Multiple-Indicator Charts Thus far we have presented charts that deal with only one trading technique at a time such as moving-average lines or relative-strength rules. In the real world, it is fairly typical for technical charts to contain several indicators that can be used together, like the two MA lines (50- and 200-day) and the RS line, because they can provide added support to the analysis. Technicians include as many price and volume indicators as are reasonable on one chart and then, based on the performance of *several* technical indicators, try to arrive at a consensus about the future movement for the stock. Luckily, many of the charting tools on investment websites allow you to add a number of rules.

Exhibit 10.10	A Typical Candlestick Chart Lists the Daily High, Low, Open, and Close for Shoppers Drug Mart and the S&P/TSX Volume for the Three Months Ending May 9, 2009

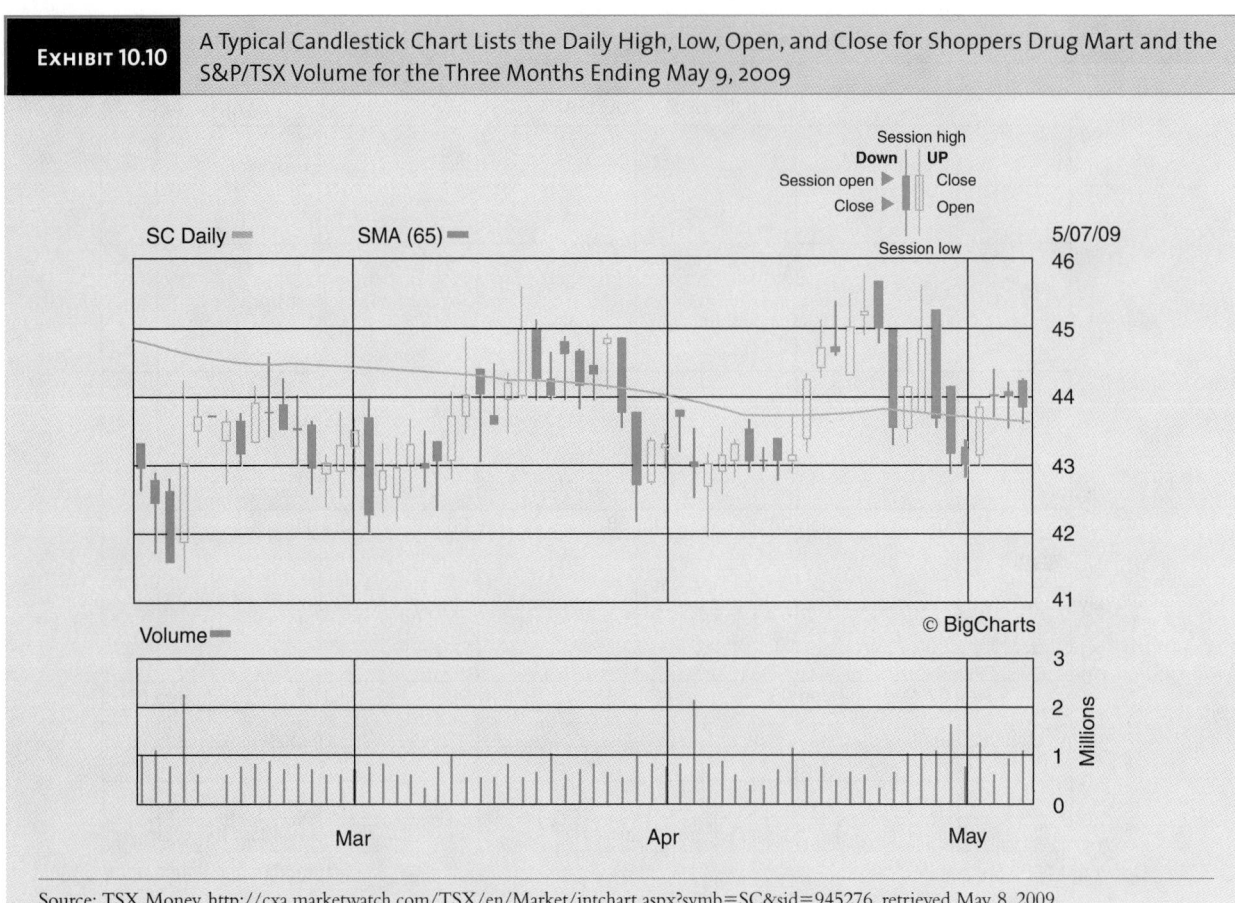

Source: TSX Money, http://cxa.marketwatch.com/TSX/en/Market/intchart.aspx?symb=SC&sid=945276, retrieved May 8, 2009.

Point-and-Figure Charts Another popular graph is the point-and-figure chart. Unlike the bar chart, which typically includes all ending prices and volumes to show a trend, the point-and-figure chart includes only significant price changes, regardless of their timing. The technician determines what price interval to record as significant (one point, two points, and so on) and when to note price reversals.

Suppose a technical analyst wants to chart a volatile stock that is currently selling for $40. Because of its volatility, analysts believe that anything less than a two-point price change is not significant. Also, they consider anything less than a four-point reversal, meaning a movement in the opposite direction, quite minor. Therefore, an analyst may set up a chart similar to Exhibit 10.11, but the new chart would start at 40; it would also progress in two-point increments. If the stock moved to $42, an *X* would be placed in the box above 40, nothing else would be done until the stock rose to $44 or dropped to $38 (a four-point reversal from its high of $42). If it dropped to $38, the analyst would move a column to the right, indicating a reversal in direction, and begin again at 38 (fill in boxes at 42 and 40). If the stock price dropped to $34, the analyst would enter an *X* at 36 and another at 34. If the stock then rose to $38 (another four-point reversal), the analyst would move to the next column and begin at 38, going up (fill in 34 and 36). If the stock then went to $46, the analyst would fill in more *X*s as shown and wait for further increases or a reversal.

EXHIBIT 10.11	Sample Point-and-Figure Chart

50											
48											
46			X								
44			X								
42	X	X	X								
40	X	X	X								
38		X	X								
36		X	X								
34		X	X								
32											
30											

StockCharts.com has a number of free charts to use. Here is a link to a point-and-figure chart for the Bank of Nova Scotia: http://stockcharts.com/def/ servlet/SC.pnf?c=BNS.TO,P.

Depending on how fast the prices rise and fall, this process might take anywhere from two to six months. Given these figures, the technician would attempt to determine trends and look for breakouts to either higher or lower price levels, just as with the bar charts. A long horizontal movement with many reversals but no major trends up or down would be considered a *period of consolidation* wherein the stock is moving from buyers to sellers and back again with no strong consensus about its direction. Once the stock breaks out and moves up or down after a period of consolidation, technical analysts anticipate a major move because previous trading set the stage for it.

Point-and-figure charts provide a compact record of movements because they only consider significant price changes for the stock being analyzed. Therefore, some technicians contend they are easier to work with and give more vivid pictures of price movements.

10.5   Technical Analysis of Foreign Markets

Our discussion thus far has concentrated on Canadian markets, but analysts have discovered that these techniques apply to foreign markets as well. Many investment houses, for instance, prepare separate technical-analysis publications for individual countries such as Japan, Germany, the United States, and the United Kingdom, as well as a summary of all world markets. The examples that follow show that when analyzing other markets, many techniques are limited to price and volume data rather than the more detailed Canadian (and U.S.) market information. The reason is that the detailed information available on the Canadian (and U.S.) market is not always available for other countries.

10.5.1   TECHNICAL ANALYSIS OF FOREIGN EXCHANGE RATES

On numerous occasions, we have discussed the importance of changes in foreign exchange rates on the returns on foreign securities. Because of the importance of these relationships, bond and stock traders in world markets examine the time-series data of various currencies such as the U.S. dollar, the British pound, and the Euro. They also analyze the spread between currencies and typically they examine the time series for the Canadian dollar trade-weighted exchange rate.

10.6 Technical Analysis of Bond Markets

Thus far, we have emphasized the use of technical analysis in stock markets. These techniques can also be applied to the bond market. The theory and rationale for technical analysis of bonds is the same as for stocks, and many of the same trading rules are used. A major difference is that it was generally not possible to consider the volume of trading of bonds because most bonds are traded OTC, where volume was not reported until 2004.

Exhibit 10.12 demonstrates the use of technical-analysis techniques applied to bond-yield series. Specifically, the graph contains a time-series plot of the U.S. 10-year note with a medium-term momentum series. As shown, yields have declined steadily through to March 2008 where the analyst feels the series is bottoming and could experience a rally up to about 4%. Such a technical graph provides important insights to a bond-portfolio manager interested in adjusting his or her bond portfolio.

EXHIBIT 10.12	Time-Series Plot of Yields for the U.S. 10-Year Note with the Medium-Term Momentum Series for the Yields

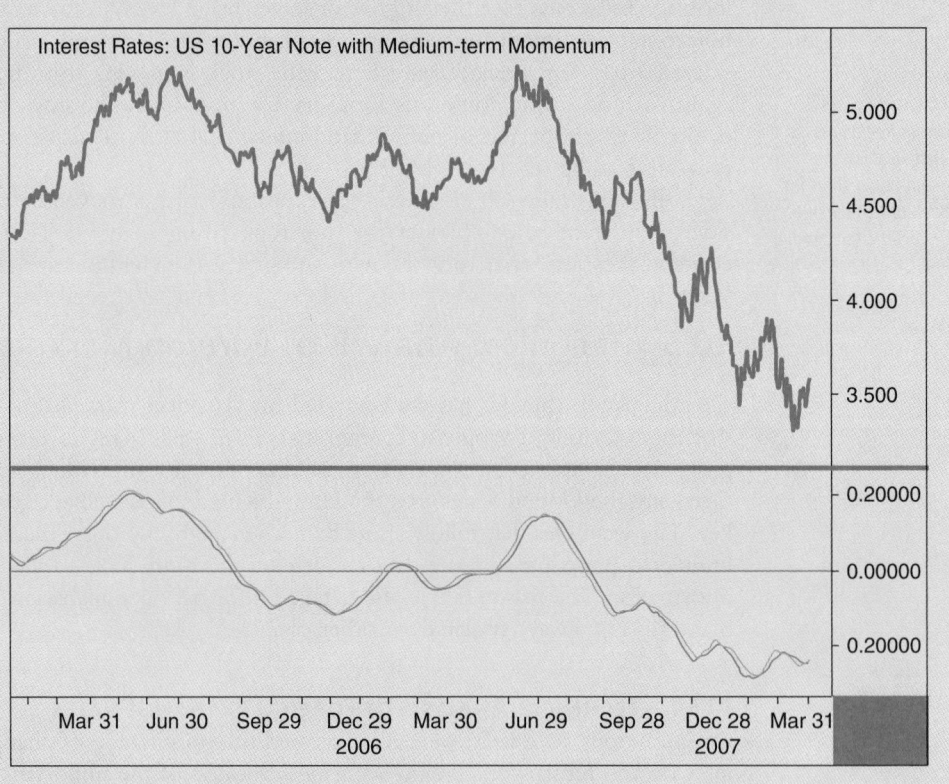

Source: Bloomberg as contained in Walter G. Murphy, Jr., Mary Ann Bartels, and Elias Lanik, "The Global Technician" Merrill Lynch, April 3, 2008, p. 15.

Summary

Numerous investors believe in and use the principles of technical analysis. The fact is, the large investment houses provide extensive support for technical analysis, and a large proportion of the discussion related to securities markets in the media is based on a technical view of the market. Most technicians employ several indicators and attempt to derive a consensus to guide their decision to buy, sell, or do nothing.[6]

1. Fundamental analysts use economic data that are usually separate from the stock or bond market, the technical analyst uses data from the market itself.

2. Like fundamental analysts, technical analysts assume the market value of any good or service is determined by the interaction of supply and demand. Technical analysts also assume that supply and demand are not only governed by economic variables but also by opinions, moods, and guesses. Technical analysts feel security prices and the overall value of the market tend to move in trends that persist for appreciable lengths of time. These trends change in reaction to shifts in supply and demand relationships and, no matter why the shift occurs, can be detected sooner or later in the action of the market itself.

3. Technical analysts and efficient market advocates differ in answering how quickly information is disseminated and how quickly investors adjust security prices to reflect new information. Technical analysts believe that news takes time to travel from the insider and expert to the individual investor. They also believe that price adjustments are not instantaneous. As a result, they contend that security prices move in trends that persist and, therefore, they can use past price trends and volume information along with other market indicators to determine future price trends.

4. A major advantage of technical analysis is that it is not heavily dependent on accounting information and that a transaction (buy or sell) won't occur until a shift has begun. The main challenges of technical analysis include past price patterns not repeating in the future, trading rules that require subjective judgment, and intense competition using a particular rule that will result in the rule becoming ineffective.

5. Contrary-opinion rules assume that the majority of investors are wrong as the market approaches troughs and peaks. Some technicians "follow the smart money," meaning they have developed indicators and rules that they believe indicate the behaviour of the sophisticated investor. Momentum indicators are used to assess the overall mood of the market while price and volume techniques are used to assess price patterns for an individual security.

6. The three types of price movements in the Dow Theory are major trends for long periods (tides), intermediate trends or waves, and short-run movements for very short periods or ripples. The major trend is most important to investors. An intermediate reversal occurs when some investors decide to take profits.

7. Technicians look for price changes on heavy volume as an indication of bullish or bearish activity. A support level is a price at which a technician would expect a substantial increase in price and volume for a stock to reverse a declining trend due to profit taking. A resistance level is a price at which a technician would expect a substantial increase in the supply of a stock to reverse a rising trend. Moving-average lines are used to assess preliminary signals of a price reversal. Relative-strength ratio is used to assess a stock's performance relative to an industry or market index, if it remains stable or increases superior performance is expected to continue.

8. These techniques and trading rules can be applied to both domestic and foreign markets. They can also be used to analyze currency exchange rates and determine the prevailing sentiment in the bond market.

Key Terms

declining trend channel, p. 277
flat trend channel, p. 278
moving average, p. 281
peak, p. 277

relative-strength (RS) ratio, p. 286
resistance levels, p. 284
rising trend channel, p. 277
support level, p. 284

technical analysis, p. 273
trough, p. 277

---

6 An analysis using numerous indicators is the study by Baesel, Shows, and Thorp (1982).

Suggested Readings

Benning, Carl J. "Prediction Skills of Real-World Market Timers." *Journal of Portfolio Management* 23, no. 2 (Winter 1997).

Brown, David P., and Robert H. Jennings. "On Technical Analysis." *Review of Financial Studies* 2, no. 4 (October 1989).

Colby, Robert W., and Thomas A. Mayers. *The Encyclopedia of Technical Market Indicators.* Homewood, IL: Dow Jones–Irwin, 1988.

Deaves, Richer, and Peter Miu. "Investor Overconfidence Meets Momentum, Reversal and Market State." *Canadian Investment Review,* Winter 2007.

DeMark, Thomas R. *The New Science of Technical Analysis.* New York: Wiley, 1994.

Edwards, R. D., and John Magee, Jr. *Technical Analysis of Stock Trends,* 6th ed. Boston: New York Institute of Finance, 1992.

Gerove, Mate. "Can Trading Strategies Effectively Predict the Future?" *Canadian Investment Review,* Winter, 2006.

Jagadeesh, Narasimhan. "Evidence of Predictable Behaviour of Security Returns." *Journal of Finance* 45, no. 3 (July 1990).

Lo, Andrew W., and A. Craig MacKinley. *A Non-Random Walk Down Wall Street.* Princeton, NJ: Princeton University Press, 1999.

Meyers, Thomas A. *The Technical Analysis Course.* Chicago: Probus, 1989.

Pring, Martin J. *Technical Analysis Explained,* 3rd ed. New York: McGraw-Hill, 1991.

Shaw, Alan R. "Market Timing and Technical Analysis." In *The Financial Analysts Handbook,* 2nd ed., ed. Sumner N. Levine. Homewood, IL: Dow Jones–Irwin, 1988.

Zweig, Martin E. *Winning on Wall Street.* New York: Warner Books, 1986.

 For Chapter CFA Questions and Problems, please see Appendix A at the end of this text.

Questions

1. Technical analysts believe that one can use past price changes to predict future price changes. How do they justify this belief?
2. Technicians contend that stock prices move in trends that persist for long periods of time. What do technicians believe happens in the real world to cause these trends?
3. Briefly discuss the problems related to fundamental analysis that are considered advantages for technical analysis.
4. Discuss some disadvantages of technical analysis.
5. If the mutual fund cash position were to increase close to 10%, would a technician consider this cash position bullish or bearish? Give two reasons why the technical analyst would think this way.
6. Assume a significant decline in credit balances at brokerage firms. Discuss why a technician would consider this bearish.
7. If the bearish sentiment index of advisory service opinions were to increase to 61%, discuss why a technician would consider this bullish or bearish.
8. Discuss why an increase in debit balances is considered bullish or bearish.
9. Describe the Dow Theory and its three components. Which component is most important? What is the reason for an intermediate reversal?

10. Describe a bearish price and volume pattern, and discuss why it is considered bearish.
11. Discuss the logic behind the breadth of market index. How is it used to identify a peak in stock prices?
12. During a 10-day trading period, the cumulative net advance index goes from 1,572 to 1,053. During this same period of time, the S&P/TSX Composite index goes from 11,200 to 12,100. As a technician, discuss what this set of events would mean to you.
13. Explain the reasoning behind a support level and a resistance level.
14. What is the purpose of computing a moving-average line for a stock? Describe a bullish pattern using a 50-day moving-average line and the stock volume of trading. Discuss why this pattern is considered bullish.
15. Assuming a stock price and volume chart that also contains a 50-day and a 200-day MA line, describe a bearish pattern with the two MA lines and discuss why it is bearish.
16. Explain how you would construct a relative-strength ratio for an individual stock or an industry group. What would it mean to say a stock experienced good relative strength during a bear market?
17. Discuss why most technicians follow several technical rules and attempt to derive a consensus.

Problems

1. Select a stock on the TSX and construct a daily high, low, and close bar chart for it that includes its volume of trading for 10 trading days.
2. Compute the relative-strength ratio for the stock in Problem 1 relative to the S&P/TSX Composite index. Prepare a table that includes all the data and indicates the computations as follows:

Closing Price			Relative-Strength Ratio
Day	Stock	S&P 500	Stock Price/S&P/TSX Composite

3. Plot the relative-strength ratio computed in Problem 2 on your bar chart. Discuss whether the stock's relative strength is bullish or bearish.
4. Currently, Charlottetown Art Importers is selling at $23 per share. Although you are somewhat dubious about technical analysis, you want to know how technicians who use point-and-figure charts would view this stock. You decide to note one-point movements and three-point reversals. Use $1.00 as a point unit. You gather the following historical price information:

Date	Price	Date	Price	Date	Price
4/1	23.50	4/18	33	5/3	27
4/4	28.50	4/19	35.40	5/4	26.50
4/5	28	4/20	37	5/5	28
4/6	28	4/21	38.50	5/6	28.25
4/7	29.75	4/22	36	5/9	28.15
4/8	30.50	4/25	35	5/10	28.15
4/11	30.50	4/26	35.25	5/11	29.15
4/12	32.15	4/27	33.15	5/12	30.25
4/13	32	4/28	32.85	5/13	29.85

Plot the point-and-figure chart, using Xs for uptrends and Os for downtrends. How would a technician evaluate these movements? Discuss why you would expect a technician to buy, sell, or hold the stock based on this chart.

5. Assume the following daily closings for the S&P/TSX Composite index:

Day	S&P/TSX	Day	S&P/TSX
1	14,010	7	14,220
2	14,100	8	14,130
3	14,165	9	14,250
4	14,080	10	14,315
5	14,070	11	14,240
6	14,150	12	14,310

a. Calculate a four-day moving average for Days 4 through 12.
b. Assume that the index on Day 13 closes at 14,300. Would this signal a buy or sell decision?

6. The cumulative advance-decline line reported in *Barron's* at the end of the month is 21,240. During the first week of the following month, the daily report for the *Exchange* is as follows:

Day	1	2	3	4	5
Issues traded	3,544	3,533	3,540	3,531	3,521
Advances	1,737	1,579	1,759	1,217	1,326
Declines	1,289	1,484	1,240	1,716	1,519
Unchanged	518	470	541	598	596

a. Compute the daily net advance–decline line for each of the five days.
b. Compute the cumulative advance–decline line for each day and the final value at the end of the week.

Analysis and Management of Bonds

CHAPTER 11

Bond Fundamentals

CHAPTER 12

The Analysis and Valuation of Bonds

For most investors, bonds receive limited attention and very little respect. This is surprising when one considers that the total market value of the bond market in other countries is substantially larger than the market value of the stock market. For example, on a global basis, the values are about $69 trillion for bonds versus $54 trillion for stocks. Beyond the size factor, bonds have a reputation for low, unexciting returns. Although this may have been true 40 or 50 years ago, it certainly has not been true during the past 25 years. Specifically, the average annual compound return on government/corporate bonds between 1980 and 2007 was slightly over 10% versus about 14% for common stocks. These returns along with corresponding standard deviations (6% for bonds versus 15% for stocks) and the relatively low correlation between stocks and bonds (about 0.25) indicate that there are substantial opportunities in bonds for individual and institutional investors to enhance their risk-return performance.

The chapters in this part are intended to provide (1) a basic understanding of bonds and the bond markets around the world, (2) background on analyzing returns and risks in the bond market, and (3) insights regarding the valuation of bonds, including numerous new fixed-income securities with very unusual cash flow characteristics.

Chapter 11 describes the global bond market in terms of country participation and the makeup of the bond market in major countries. Also, we examine various characteristics of bonds including many new corporate bond instruments, such as asset-backed securities, zero coupon bonds, high-yield bonds, and inflation protection securities. While the use of these securities globally has generally been limited to the large developed markets, it is certain that they will eventually be used around the world. Finally, we consider sources of price information needed by bond investors.

Chapter 12 is concerned with the analysis and valuation of bonds. This includes a detailed discussion of how one values a bond using a single discount rate or using spot rates. We also evaluate alternative return measures for bonds. Subsequently, we consider what factors affect yields on bonds and what characteristics influence the volatility of bond returns, including the very important concept of bond duration, which is a measure of bond price volatility that is important in active and passive bond portfolio management. We also consider bond convexity and the impact it has on bond price volatility. Notably, these concepts are examined for option-free securities. We also consider how they apply to a growing set of securities with embedded options.

During the past 20 years, there have been more developments related to the valuation and portfolio management of bonds than of stocks. This growth of the fixed-income sector does not detract from the importance of equities but certainly enhances the significance of fixed-income securities. Readers should keep in mind that this growth in size, sophistication, and specialization of the bond market implies numerous and varied career opportunities in the bond area, including trading these securities, valuation, credit analysis, and domestic and global portfolio management.

11

Bond Fundamentals

After you read this chapter, you should be able to answer the following questions:

1. What are some of the basic features of bonds that affect their risk, return, and value?

2. What is the current country structure of the world bond market and how has the makeup of the global bond market changed in recent years?

3. What are the major components of the world bond market and the international bond market?

4. What are bond ratings and what is their purpose? What is the difference between investment-grade bonds and high-yield (junk) bonds?

5. What are the characteristics of bonds in categories such as governments, agencies, and corporate?

6. What are the important characteristics of corporate bond issues developed over the past number of years, such as mortgage-backed securities, other asset-backed securities, zero coupon, and deep discount bonds?

7. How do you read the quotes available for the various bond categories (e.g., governments, municipalities, corporate)?

The global bond market is large and diverse and represents an important investment opportunity. This chapter is concerned with publicly issued, long-term, non-convertible debt obligations of public and private issuers in Canada and major global markets. In later chapters, we consider preferred stock and convertible bonds. An understanding of bonds is helpful in an efficient market because the existence of Canada and foreign bonds increases the universe of investments available for the creation of a diversified portfolio.

In this chapter, we review some basic bond features and examine the structure of the world bond market. Note that the Web Appendix for Chapter 3 reviews some bond terminology.

11.1   Basic Features of a Bond

Public bonds are long-term, fixed-obligation debt securities packaged in convenient, affordable denominations for sale to individuals and institutions. They differ from other debt, such as individual mortgages and privately placed debt obligations, because they are sold to the public rather than channeled directly to a single lender. Bond issues are considered fixed-income securities because they impose fixed financial obligations on the issuers. Specifically, the issuer agrees to

1. Pay a fixed amount of *interest periodically* to the holder of record.
2. Repay a fixed amount of *principal* at the date of maturity.

Normally, interest on bonds is paid semi-annually, although some bond issues pay in intervals as short as a month or as long as a year. The principal is due at maturity; this *par value* of the issue is rarely less than $1,000. A bond has a specified term to maturity, which defines the life of the issue. The public debt market typically is divided into three time segments based on an issue's original maturity:

1. Short-term issues with maturities of one year or less. The market for these instruments is commonly known as the **money market**.
2. Intermediate-term issues with maturities in excess of 1 year but less than 10 years. These instruments are known as **notes**.
3. Long-term obligations with maturities in excess of 10 years, called *bonds*.

The lives of debt obligations change constantly as the issues progress toward maturity. Thus, issues that have been outstanding in the secondary market for any period of time eventually move from long-term to intermediate to short-term. This change in maturity is important because a major determinant of the price volatility of bonds is the remaining life (maturity) of the issue.

11.1.1   BOND CHARACTERISTICS

A bond can be characterized based on (1) its intrinsic features, (2) its type, (3) its indenture provisions, or (4) the features that affect its cash flows and/or its maturity.

Intrinsic Features The coupon, maturity, principal value, and the type of ownership are important intrinsic features of a bond. The **coupon** indicates the income that the bond investor will receive over the life (or holding period) of the issue. This is also termed *interest income*, *coupon income*, or *nominal yield*.

The **term to maturity** specifies the date or the number of years before a bond matures. There are two different types of maturity. The most common is a **term bond**, which has a single maturity date. Alternatively, a **serial bond** issue has a series of maturity dates, perhaps 20 or 25. Each maturity, although a subset of the total issue, is really a small bond issue with generally a different coupon. Municipalities issue most serial bonds.

The **principal**, or **par value**, represents the original value of the obligation. This is generally stated in $1,000 increments from $1,000 to $25,000 or more. The principal value is *not* the same as the bond's market value. The market prices of many issues rise above or fall below their principal values because of differences between their coupons and the prevailing market rate of interest. If the market interest rate is higher than the coupon rate, the bond will sell at a discount to par. If the market rate is below the bond's coupon, it will sell at a premium above par. If the coupon is comparable to the prevailing market interest rate, the market value of the bond will be close to its original principal value.

Finally, bonds differ in terms of ownership. With a **bearer bond**, the holder, or bearer, is the owner, so the issuer keeps no record of ownership. Interest from a bearer bond is obtained by clipping coupons attached to the bonds and sending them to the issuer for payment. In contrast, the issuers of **registered bonds** maintain records of owners and pay the interest directly to them.

Types of Issues In contrast to common stock, companies can have many different bond issues outstanding at the same time. Bonds can have different types of collateral and be either senior, unsecured, or subordinated (junior) securities. Recall that secured (senior) bonds are backed by a legal claim on some specified property of the issuer in the case of default. For example, mortgage bonds are secured by real estate assets; equipment trust certificates, used by railroads and airlines, provide a senior claim on the firm's equipment.

Unsecured bonds (debentures) are backed only by the promise of the issuer to pay interest and principal on a timely basis. As such, they are secured by the general credit of the issuer. **Subordinate (junior) debentures** possess a claim on income and assets that is subordinated to other debentures. Income issues are the most junior type because interest on them is paid only if it is earned. Although income bonds are unusual in the corporate sector, they are very popular municipal issues, where they are referred to as **revenue bonds**. Finally, **refunding issues** provide funds to prematurely retire another issue.

The type of issue has only a minimal impact on comparative yield; it is the credit-worthiness of the issuer that determines bond quality. A study of corporate bond price behaviour by Hickman (1958) found that whether the issuer pledged collateral became important when the bond issue approached default. The collateral and security characteristics of a bond influence yield differentials only when these factors affect the bond's quality ratings.

Indenture Provisions The *indenture* is the contract between the issuer and the bondholder specifying the issuer's legal requirements. A trustee (usually a trust company) acting on behalf of the bondholders ensures that all the indenture provisions are met, including the timely payment of interest and principal. All the details regarding a bond's features, its type, and its maturity are set forth in the indenture.

Features Affecting a Bond's Maturity Investors should be aware of the three alternative call option features that can affect the life (maturity) of a bond. One extreme is a *freely callable* provision that allows the issuer to retire the bond at any time with a typical notification period of 30 to 60 days. The other extreme is a *non-callable* provision wherein the issuer cannot retire the bond prior to its maturity.[1] Intermediate between these is a *deferred call* provision, which means the issue cannot be called for a certain period of time after the date of issue (e.g., 5 to 10 years). At the end of the deferred call period, the issue becomes freely callable. Callable bonds have a **call premium**, which is the amount above maturity value that the issuer must pay to the bondholder for prematurely retiring the bond.

A *non-refunding provision* prohibits a call and premature retirement of an issue from the proceeds of a lower-coupon refunding bond. This is meant to protect the bondholder from a typical refunding, but it is not foolproof. An issue with a non-refunding provision can be called and retired prior to maturity using other sources of funds, such as excess cash from operations, the sale of assets, or proceeds from a sale of common stock. This occurred on several occasions during the 1980s and 1990s when many issuers retired non-refundable high-coupon issues early because they could get the cash from one of these other sources and felt that this was a good financing decision.

Another important indenture provision that can affect a bond's maturity is the **sinking fund**, which specifies that a bond must be paid off systematically over its life rather than only at maturity. There are numerous sinking-fund arrangements, and the bondholder should recognize this as a feature that can change the stated maturity of a bond. The size of the sinking fund can be a percentage of a given issue or a percentage of the total debt outstanding, or it can be a fixed or variable sum stated on a dollar or percentage basis. Similar to a call feature, sinking-fund payments may commence at the end of the first year or may be deferred for 5 or 10 years from date of the issue. The amount of the issue that must be repaid before maturity from a sinking fund can range from a nominal sum to 100%. Further, the sinking-fund feature typically carries a nominal premium but is generally smaller than the straight call premium (e.g., 1%). For example, a bond issue with a 20-year maturity might have a sinking fund that requires that 5% of the issue be retired every year beginning in year 10. By year 20, half of the issue has been retired and the rest is paid off at maturity. At the time of issue, sinking-fund provisions have a small impact on comparative yields but have little effect on subsequent price behaviour.

A sinking-fund provision is an obligation and must be carried out regardless of market conditions. Although a sinking fund allows the issuer to call bonds on a random basis, most bonds are retired for sinking-fund purposes through direct negotiations with institutional holders. Essentially, the trustee negotiates with an institution to buy back the necessary amount of bonds at a price slightly above the current market price.

---

1 The main issuer of non-callable bonds is the Government of Canada. Corporate long-term bonds typically have contained some form of call provision, except during periods of relatively low interest rates (e.g., 1994–2001) when the probability of exercising the option was very low. We discuss this notion in more detail in Chapter 12 in connection with the analysis of embedded options.

11.1.2 RATES OF RETURN ON BONDS

The return on a bond is calculated in the same way as the return on stock or any asset. It is determined by the beginning and ending price and the cash flows during the holding period. Therefore, the holding period return (HPR) for a bond will be

11.1
$$\text{HPR}_{i,t} = \frac{P_{i,t+1} + Int_{i,t}}{P_{i,t}}$$

where:

$\text{HPR}_{i,t}$ = the holding period return for bond i during Period t
$P_{i,t+1}$ = the market price of bond i at the end of Period t
$P_{i,t}$ = the market price of bond i at the beginning of Period t
$Int_{i,t}$ = the interest paid or accrued on bond i during Period t. Because the interest payment is contractual, it accrues over time and if a bond owner sells the bond between interest payments, the sale price includes accrued interest.[2]

The holding period yield (HPY) is:

11.2
$$\text{HPY} = \text{HPR} - 1$$

Note that the only contractual factor is the amount of interest payments. The beginning and ending bond prices are determined by market forces (for a review, see Web Chapter 20). Notably, the ending price is determined by market forces unless the bond is held to maturity, in which case the investor will receive the par value. These price variations mean that bond investors can experience capital gains or losses. The substantial increase in interest rate volatility since the 1960s has caused large price fluctuations in bonds,[3] and as a result, capital gains or losses have become a substantial component of a bond's return.

11.2   The Global Bond Market Structure[4]

The fixed-income securities market is substantially larger than the listed equity exchanges (NYSE, TSX, LSE). Statistics Canada figures indicate that during 2007, 30% of all new security issues in Canada were equity (common and preferred), leaving roughly 70% of financing by way of debt instruments.

Recall from our discussion in Chapter 3 (see Exhibit 3.1) that the global fixed-income securities market has grown substantially, and inclusion of various foreign fixed-income securities is important in reducing risk within a portfolio.

A quick glance at Exhibit 11.1 further emphasizes the size and distribution among select countries of the global bond market.

---

2 The concept of accrued interest will be discussed further in Chapter 12 when we consider the valuation of bonds.
3 The analysis of bond price volatility is discussed in detail in Chapter 12.
4 For a further discussion of global bond markets, see Steward (2005), "International Bond Markets and Instruments"; Steward, Lynch, and Fabozzi (2005), "International Bond Investing and Portfolio Management"; and Malvey (2005), "Global Credit Bond Portfolio Management," all in *The Handbook of Fixed-Income Securities*, 7th ed., ed. Frank J. Fabozzi (New York: McGraw-Hill, 2005).

EXHIBIT 11.1	Selected Indicators on the Size of the Capital Markets, 2006		
	Debt Securities		
	Public	**Private**	**Total**
World	25,780.70	43,420.20	69,200.90
European Union	7,693.40	15,498.90	23,192.30
Euro area	6,580.60	12,180.40	18.761.10
North America	6,941.30	21,449.60	28,390.80
United States	6,234.40	20,815.70	27,050.10
Japan	6,750.60	1,973.10	8,723.70

Source: *Global Financial Stability Report*, April 2008, International Monetary Fund. Extracted from Table 3 Selected Indicators on the Size of the Capital Markets, 2006, page 143; http://www.imf.org/External/Pubs/FT/GFSR/2008/01/pdf/text.pdf

11.2.1   BOND RATINGS

Agency ratings are an integral part of the bond market because most corporate and municipal bonds are rated by one or more of the rating agencies. The exceptions are very small issues and bonds from certain industries, such as bank issues. These are known as *non-rated bonds*. In Canada, there are two bond rating agencies: the Dominion Bond Rating Service (DBRS) and Standard and Poor's Ratings Direct Canada. The three major rating agencies in the United States are Fitch Investors Service, Moody's, and Standard and Poor's.

Bond ratings provide the fundamental analysis for thousands of issues. The rating agencies analyze the issuing organization and the specific issue to determine the probability of default and inform the market of their analyses through their ratings.[5]

The primary question in bond credit analysis is whether the firm can service its debt in a timely manner over the life of a given issue. Consequently, the rating agencies consider expectations over the life of the issue, along with the historical and current financial position of the company. We consider default estimation further when we discuss high-yield (junk) bonds later in this chapter.

Studies by authors such as Belkaoui (1980) and Gentry, Whitford, and Newbold (1988) have examined the relationship between bond ratings and issue quality as indicated by financial variables. The results clearly demonstrated that bond ratings were positively related to profitability, size, and cash flow coverage, and they were inversely related to financial leverage and earnings instability.

The original ratings assigned to bonds have an impact on their marketability and effective interest rate. Generally, the agencies' ratings agree. When they do not, the issue is said to have a *split rating*.[6] Seasoned issues are regularly reviewed to ensure that the assigned rating is still valid. If not, revisions are made either upward or downward. Revisions are usually done in increments of one rating grade. The ratings are based on both the company and the issue. After an evaluation of the creditworthiness of the total company is completed, a company rating is assigned to the firm's most senior unsecured issue. All junior bonds receive lower ratings based on indenture specifications. Also, an issue could receive a higher rating than justified because of credit-enhancement devices, such as the attachment of bank letters of credit, surety, or indemnification bonds from insurance companies.

---

5 For a detailed listing of rating classes and a listing of factors considered in assigning ratings, see "Bond Ratings" in Levine (1988). For a study that examines the value of two bond ratings, see Hsueh and Kidwell (1988). An analysis of the bond-rating industry is contained in Cantor and Packer (1995).

6 Split ratings are discussed in Billingsley, Lamy, Marr, and Thompson (1985); Ederington (1985); and Liu and Moore (1987).

The agencies assign letter ratings depicting what they view as the risk of default of an obligation. The letter ratings range from AAA to D. Exhibit 11.2 describes the various ratings assigned by the major services. Except for slight variations in designations, the

EXHIBIT 11.2	Description of Bond Ratings			
	DBRS	Standard & Poor's	Fitch	Definition
High grade	AAA	AAA	AAA	The highest rating assigned to a debt instrument, indicating an extremely strong capacity to pay principal and interest. Bonds in this category are often referred to as *gilt edge securities*.
	AA	AA	AA	High-quality bonds by all standards with a strong capacity to pay principal and interest. These bonds are rated lower primarily because the margins of protection are less strong than those for AAA bonds.
Medium grade	A	A	A	These bonds possess many favourable investment attributes, but elements may suggest a susceptibility to impairment given adverse economic changes.
	BBB	BBB	BBB	Bonds that are regarded as having adequate capacity to pay principal and interest, but certain protective elements may be lacking in the event of adverse economic conditions that could lead to a weakened capacity for payment.
Speculative	BB	BB	BB	These bonds are considered to have only moderate protection of principal and interest payments during both good and bad times.
	B	B	B	Bonds that generally lack characteristics of other desirable investments. Assurance of interest and principal payments over any long period of time may be small.
Default	CCC	CCC	CCC	Poor-quality issues that may be in default or in danger of default.
	CC	CC	CC	Highly speculative issues that are often in default or possess other marked shortcomings.
			C	The lowest-rated class of bonds. These issues can be regarded as extremely poor in investment quality.
	C	C		Rating given to income bonds on which no interest is being paid.
	D	D	DDD, DD, D	Issues in default with principal or interest payments in arrears. Such bonds are extremely speculative and should be valued only on the basis of their value in liquidation or reorganization.

Sources: *Bond Guide* (New York: Standard & Poor's, monthly); *Bond Record* (New York: Moody's Investors Services, Inc., monthly); *Rating Register* (New York: Fitch Investors Service, Inc, monthly); http://www.dbrs.com/intnlweb/jsp/common/infopagesfaces

meaning and interpretation are basically the same. The U.S. agencies modify the ratings with + and − signs for Fitch and S&P or with numbers (1-2-3) for Moody's. As an example, an A+ (A1) bond is at the top of the A-rated group, while A− (A3) is at the bottom of the A category.

The top four ratings—AAA, AA, A, and BBB—are generally considered to be *investment-grade securities*. The next level of securities is known as *speculative bonds* and includes the BB- and B-rated obligations. The C categories are generally either income obligations or revenue bonds, many of which are trading flat. (Flat bonds are in arrears on their interest payments.) In the case of D-rated obligations, the issues are in outright default, and the ratings indicate the bonds' relative salvage values.[7]

11.3 Types of Bond Issues

In this section, we provide a detailed discussion of the bonds available from the major issuers like sovereigns, agencies, and corporations along with some features of securitized and collateralized debt.

11.3.1 DOMESTIC GOVERNMENT BONDS

Canada A significant percentage of the Canadian dollar fixed-income market is Government of Canada obligations. As described in Chapter 3, the Canadian government issues Treasury bills (T-bills), which mature in less than one year, and two forms of long-term obligations: medium-term bonds, with maturities of 10 years or less, and long-term bonds, with maturities of 10 to 30 years. These bonds are popular because of their high credit quality, substantial liquidity, and non-callable feature.

Short-term T-bills differ from bonds because they are sold at a discount from par to provide the desired yield. The return is the difference between the purchase price and the par at maturity. In contrast, government bonds carry semi-annual coupons that specify the nominal yield of the obligations.

The Bank of Canada provides a comprehensive description of RRBs at http://www.bankofcanada.ca/en/pdf/real_return_eng.pdf.

Real Return Bonds (RRBs) The Government of Canada began issuing these inflation-indexed bonds to appeal to investors who wanted or needed a *real* default-free return. To ensure the investors will receive the promised yield in real terms, the bond principal and interest payments are indexed to the *Consumer Price Index (CPI)*. Because inflation is generally not known until several months after the fact, the index value used has a three-month lag built in—for example, for a bond issued on June 30, 2009, the beginning base index value used would be the CPI value as of March 30, 2009. Following the issuance of an RRB bond, its principal value is adjusted every six months to reflect the inflation since the base period. In turn, the interest payment is computed based on this adjusted principal—that is, the interest payments equal the original coupon times the adjusted principal. The example in Exhibit 11.3 demonstrates how the principal and interest payments are computed. As shown in this example, both the interest payments and the principal payments are adjusted over time to reflect the prevailing inflation, thereby ensuring that the investor receives a real return on these bonds of 3.50%. In the United States, similar bonds are issued by the U.S. Treasury. These bonds, Treasury Inflation Protected Securities, are referred to as TIPS.

---

7 Bonds rated below investment grade are also referred to as "high-yield bonds" or "junk" bonds. These high-yield bonds are discussed in the subsequent section on corporate bonds.

EXHIBIT 11.3	Principal and Interest Payment for a Real Return Bond (RRB)

Par Value—$1,000
Issued on July 15, 2007
Maturity on July 15, 2012
Coupon—3.50%
Original CPI Value—185.00

Date	Index Value[a]	Rate of Inflation	Accrued Principal	Interest Payment[b]
7/15/07	185.00	—	$1,000.00	—
1/15/08	187.78	0.015	1,015.00	$17.76
7/15/08	190.59	0.015	1,030.22	18.03
1/15/09	193.83	0.017	1,047.74	18.34
7/15/09	197.51	0.019	1,067.65	18.68
1/15/10	201.46	0.020	1,089.00	19.06
7/15/10	205.49	0.020	1,110.78	19.44
1/15/11	209.19	0.018	1,130.77	19.79
7/15/11	212.96	0.018	1,151.13	20.14
1/15/12	217.22	0.020	1,174.15	20.55
7/15/12	222.65	0.025	1,203.50	21.06

[a]The CPI index value is for the period three months prior to the date.
[b]Semi-annual interest payment equals 0.0175 (accrued principal).

Notably, these bonds can also be used to derive the prevailing market estimate of the expected rate of inflation during the remaining maturity of the RRB bond. For example, if we assume that when the bond is issued on July 15, 2007, it sells at par for a yield to maturity (YTM) of 3.50%, while a nominal five-year note of equal maturity is sold at a YTM of 5.75%. This differential in promised YTM implies that investors expect an average annual rate of inflation of 2.25% during this five-year period. If a year later the spread increased to 2.45%, it would indicate that investors expect a higher inflation rate during the next four years.

Canada Savings Bonds (CSBs) Like Government of Canada bonds, CSBs are fully guaranteed by the federal government. However, these bonds are not transferrable and may be redeemed at any point in time at their full par value plus accrued interest. There are restrictions on the type of investor that can purchase CSBs (individuals, estates, and certain types of trusts) and the amount that can be purchased. Usually there is a guaranteed minimum interest rate on these bonds. To prevent investors from cashing in the bonds if interest rates should increase, the interest rate on CSBs may be increased. This is not uncommon if the next series of CSBs yield a higher rate. The bonds can also be purchased with two different interest payment options: compound interest and regular interest. The regular-interest bonds simply pay the investor the interest on an annual basis whereas the interest on compound bond is reinvested. Although an investor with a compound-interest bond does not physically receive an annual interest cheque for this amount, it is considered taxable income for that year (imputed interest).

Japan[8] The second-largest country government bond market in the world is Japan's (the United States is the largest). It is controlled by the Japanese government and the Bank of Japan (Japanese Central Bank). Japanese government bonds (JGBs) are an attractive investment vehicle for those favouring the Japanese yen because they are guaranteed by the government of Japan and they are very liquid. There are three maturity segments: medium-term (2, 3, or 4 years), long-term (10 years), and super-long (private placements for 15 and 20 years). Bonds are issued in both registered and bearer form, although registered bonds can be converted to bearer bonds.

At least 50% of the trading in Japanese government bonds will be in the so-called *benchmark* issue of the time. The benchmark issue is selected from 10-year coupon bonds. (As of mid-2008, the benchmark issue was a 1.30% coupon bond maturing in 2018.) The designation of a benchmark issue is intended to assist smaller financial institutions in their trading of government bonds by ensuring these institutions that there is a liquid market in this particular security.

The yield on this benchmark bond is typically about 30 basis points below other comparable Japanese government bonds, reflecting its superior marketability. The benchmark issue changes when a designated issue matures or because of a decision by the Bank of Japan.

United Kingdom[9] The U.K. pound sterling government bond market is made up of jobbers and brokers who act as principals or agents with negotiated commission structures. In addition, there are 27 primary dealers.

Maturities in this market range from short gilts (maturities of less than 5 years) to medium gilts (5 to 15 years) to long gilts (15 years and longer). Government bonds either have a fixed redemption date or a range of dates with redemption at the option of the government after giving appropriate notice. Government bonds are normally registered, although bearer delivery is available.

Gilts are issued through the Bank of England (the British central bank) using the tender method, whereby prospective purchasers tender offering prices at which they hope to be allotted bonds. The price cannot be less than the minimum tender price stated in the prospectus. If the issue is oversubscribed, allotments are made first to those submitting the highest tenders and continue until a price is reached where only a partial allotment is required to fully subscribe the issue. All successful allottees pay the lowest allotment prices.

These issues are extremely liquid and are highly rated because they are guaranteed by the British government. All gilts are quoted and traded on the London Stock Exchange and pay interest semi-annually.

Eurozone[10] The combined value of the Euro sovereign bond market is actually larger in U.S. dollar terms than the Japanese market because it includes several relatively significant markets including Germany, which was the third largest by itself, as well as France and Italy among others. Because the Eurozone includes numerous countries that were previously economically independent, the issuing process for alternative countries differs dramatically except that all of the bonds are denominated in Euros. It is likely that over time the issuing process will become more uniform, but there will always be differences.

11.3.2   GOVERNMENT AGENCY ISSUES

Recall from Chapter 3 that in addition to pure government bonds, the federal government in each country can establish agencies that have the authority to issue their own bonds. The size and importance of these agencies differ among countries. They are a large sector of the U.S.

---

8 For additional discussion, see Viner (1988), Elton and Gruber (1990), and Fabozzi (1990).

9 For further discussion, see European Bond Commission (1989).

10 For additional information on the Eurobond market, see Molinas and Bales (2004).

bond market; a much smaller component of the bond markets in Canada, Japan, and Germany; and nearly non-existent in the United Kingdom. We limit our discussion here to two markets.

United States Agency securities are obligations issued by the U.S. government through either a government agency or a government-sponsored enterprise (GSE). Some of the issues are subject to state and local income tax, whereas others are exempt.[11]

One agency issue is the GNMA ("Ginnie Mae") pass-through certificates, which are obligations of the Government National Mortgage Association. These bonds represent an undivided interest in a pool of federally insured mortgages. The bondholders receive monthly payments from Ginnie Mae that include both principal and interest because the agency "passes through" mortgage payments made by the original borrower (the mortgagee) to Ginnie Mae. The portion of the cash flow that represents the principal repayment is tax-free, but the interest income is subject to tax. Issued with maturities of 25 to 30 years, these typically have an average life of 12 years because, as mortgages in the pool are paid off, payments and prepayments are passed through to the investor. Therefore, unlike most bond issues, the monthly payment is not fixed because of the prepayment schedule that can vary dramatically over time when interest rates change.

Japan The agencies in Japan, referred to as *government associate organizations*, account for about 7% of the total Japanese yen bond market. This agency market includes public debt, but almost twice as much is privately placed with major financial institutions. Public agency debt is issued like government debt.

11.3.3 MUNICIPAL BONDS

Although municipal bonds are not uncommon in Canada and other countries, the characteristics and taxation of these bonds typically are similar to those seen with government bonds and some corporate bonds. However, in the United States the size and popularity of this market deserves some discussion.

U.S. municipalities issue two distinct types of bonds: general obligation bonds and revenue issues. **General obligation bonds (GOs)** are essentially backed by the credit of the issuer and its taxing power. Revenue bonds, in turn, are serviced by the income generated from specific revenue-producing projects of the municipality, such as bridges, toll roads, hospitals, municipal coliseums, and waterworks. Revenue bonds generally provide higher returns than GOs because of their higher default risk. Should a municipality fail to generate sufficient income from a project designated to service a revenue bond, it has no legal debt service obligation until the income becomes sufficient.

GO bonds tend to be issued on a serial basis so that the issuer's cash flow requirements will be steady over the life of the obligation. Therefore, the principal portion of the total debt service requirement generally begins at a fairly low level and builds up over the life of the obligation. In contrast, most municipal revenue bonds are term issues, so the principal value is not due until the final maturity date.[12]

The most important feature of municipal obligations is that the interest payments are exempt from federal income tax and from taxes in the locality and state in which the obligation was issued. This means that their attractiveness varies with the investor's tax bracket.

---

11 Federal National Mortgage Association (Fannie Mae) debentures, for example, are subject to state and local income tax, whereas the interest income from Federal Home Loan Bank bonds is exempt. In fact, a few issues are exempt from federal income tax as well (e.g., public housing bonds).

12 For a more detailed discussion of the municipal bond market, see Feldstein, Fabozzi, Grant, and Kennedy (2005). For discussion of the credit analysis of these bonds, see Feldstein and Grant (2005).

You can convert the tax-free yield of a municipal to an equivalent taxable yield (ETY) using the following equation:

11.3
$$ETY = \frac{i}{1 - t}$$

where:
  ETY = equivalent taxable yield
  i = coupon rate of the municipal obligations
  t = marginal tax rate of the investor

An investor in the 35% marginal tax bracket would find that a 5% yield on a municipal bond selling close to its par value is equivalent to a 7.69% fully taxable yield according to the following calculation:

$$ETY = \frac{0.05}{(1 - 0.35)} = 0.0769$$

Because the tax-free yield is the major benefit of municipal bonds, an investor's marginal tax rate is a primary concern in evaluating them. Although the interest payment on municipals is tax-free, any capital gains are not (that means the ETY formula is correct only for a bond selling close to its par value).

Municipal Bond Insurance A significant feature of the U.S. municipal bond market is *municipal bond insurance*, which provides that an insurance company will guarantee to make principal and interest payments in the event that the issuer of the bonds defaults. The insurance is placed on the bond at date of issue and is *irrevocable* over the life of the issue. The issuer purchases the insurance for the benefit of the investor, and the municipality benefits from lower interest costs due to lower default risk, which causes an increase in the rating on the bond and increased marketability. Those who would benefit from the insurance are small government units that are not widely known and bonds with a complex capital structure.

11.3.4   CORPORATE BONDS
Again, the importance of corporate bonds varies across countries. This market is very diverse and includes debentures, first-mortgage issues, convertible obligations, bonds with warrants, subordinated debentures, income bonds, collateral trust bonds backed by financial assets, equipment trust certificates, and asset-backed securities (ABS) including mortgage-backed bonds.

If we ignore convertible bonds and bonds with warrants, the preceding list of obligations varies by the type of collateral behind the bond. Most bonds have semi-annual interest payments, sinking funds, and a single maturity date. Maturities range from 25 to 40 years, with public utilities generally on the longer end and industrials preferring the 25- to 30-year range. Most corporate bonds provide for deferred calls after 5 to 10 years. The deferment period varies directly with the level of the interest rates. Specifically, during periods of higher interest rates, bond issues typically will carry a 7- to 10-year deferment, while during periods of lower interest rates, the deferment periods decline.

On the other hand, corporate notes—with maturities of five to seven years—are generally non-callable. When interest rates are high, notes become more popular because issuing firms want to avoid long-term obligations during such periods. In contrast, during periods of low interest rates, such as 1997 and 2001–2004, most corporate issues did not include a call provision because corporations did not believe that they would be able to exercise the call option and did not want to pay the required higher yield.

Mortgage Bonds A mortgage bond issuer grants, to the bondholder, a first mortgage lien on some piece of property or possibly all the firm's property. Such a lien provides greater security to the bondholder and a lower interest rate for the issuing firm.

Equipment Trust Certificates Equipment trust certificates are issued by railroads, airlines, and other transportation firms with the proceeds used to purchase equipment (freight cars, railroad engines, and airplanes), which serves as the collateral for the debt. Maturities range from 1 to about 15 years. The fairly short maturities reflect the nature of the collateral, which is subject to substantial wear and tear and tends to deteriorate rapidly.

Equipment trust certificates are appealing to investors because of their attractive yields, low default record, and fairly liquid secondary market.

Collateral Trust Bonds Rather than pledging capital assets or property, a borrower can pledge financial assets, such as stocks, bonds, or notes, as collateral. These pledged assets are held by a trustee for the benefit of the bondholder.

Collateralized Mortgage Obligations (CMOs)[13] These were developed in the early 1980s to offset some of the problems with the traditional mortgage pass-throughs. The main innovation of the CMO instrument is the segmentation of irregular mortgage cash flows to create short-, medium-, and long-term securities. Specifically, CMO investors own bonds that are serviced with the cash flows from mortgages; but rather than the straight pass-through arrangement, the CMO substitutes a *sequential distribution process* that creates a series of bonds with varying maturities to appeal to a wider range of investors.

The prioritized distribution process is as follows:

- Several classes of bonds (referred to as *tranches*) are issued against a pool of mortgages, which are the collateral. For example, assume a CMO issue with four classes (tranches) of bonds. In such a case, the first three (e.g., Classes A, B, C) would pay interest at their stated rates beginning at their issue date and the fourth class would be an accrual bond (referred to as a *Z bond*).
- The cash flows received from the underlying mortgages are applied first to pay the interest on the bonds and then to retire these bonds.
- The classes of bonds are retired sequentially. All principal payments are directed first to the shortest maturity class A bonds until they are completely retired. Then all principal payments are directed to the next shortest maturity bonds (i.e., the class B bonds). The process continues until all the classes have been paid off.
- During the early periods, the accrual bonds (the class Z bonds) pay no interest, but the interest accrues as additional principal, and the cash flow from the mortgages that collateralize these bonds is used to pay interest on and retire the bonds in the other classes. Subsequently, all remaining cash flows are used to pay off the accrued interest, pay any current interest, and then to retire the Z bonds.

---

13 For a detailed discussion, see Crawford (2005).

This prioritized sequential pattern means that the A-class bonds are fairly short term and each subsequent class is a little longer term until the Z-class bond, which is a long-term bond. It also functions like a zero coupon bond for the initial years.

Besides creating bonds that pay interest in a more normal pattern (quarterly or semi-annually) and that have more predictable maturities, these bonds are considered very high-quality securities (AAA) because of the structure and quality of the collateral. To obtain an AAA rating, CMOs are structured to ensure that the underlying mortgages will always generate enough cash to support the bonds issued, even under the most conservative prepayment and reinvestment rates. However, as we witnessed from the general weakness in the U.S. residential markets between 2007 and 2008, many CMOs, even those with mortgages guaranteed by a federal agency, were not without substantial risk. A decline in residential real estate increases the bankruptcy and foreclosure rates, which has a direct impact on the ability of the CMO to meet its required cash flows.

Collateralized debt obligations (CDOs) are similar to CMOs but typically have, as underlying collateral, a portfolio of risky credit instruments such as bonds and loans. Different layers of CDO securities or tranches receive cash flows from the collateral portfolio according to a prioritized payment structure.

The proliferation of CDOs, plain vanilla and exotic, have been blamed, at least in part, for the current financial crisis. See http://www.reuters.com /article/bondsNews/idUSL0 262828420070702?sp= true or http://www. bloomberg.com/apps/ news?pid=20601087& sid=aTzTYtlNHSG8.

Asset-Backed Securities (ABSs) A rapidly expanding segment of the securities market is that of *asset-backed securities*, which involve *securitizing debt*. This is an important concept because it substantially increases the liquidity of these individual debt instruments, whether they be individual mortgages, car loans, or credit card debt. Beyond the mortgage securities, this market is dominated by securities backed by automobile loans and credit card receivables.

Certificates for Automobile Receivables (CARs) These are securities collateralized by loans made to individuals to finance the purchase of cars. These self-amortizing loans typically have monthly payments and relatively short maturities (i.e., two to five years), and they can either be direct loans from a lending institution or indirect loans that are originated by an auto dealer and sold to the ultimate lender. Typically, CARs have fixed monthly or quarterly interest and principal payments, and expected weighted-average lives of one to three years with specified maturities of three to five years. The expected actual life is usually shorter than the specified maturity because of early payoffs that occur when cars are sold or traded in. CAR cash flows are comparable to short-term corporate debt and provide a significant yield premium over General Motors Acceptance Corporation (GMAC) commercial paper, which is the most liquid short-term corporate alternative.

Credit Card Receivables Credit card receivables are considered to be a revolving credit ABS, in contrast to the installment-contract automobile loan or mortgage receivables. Specifically, whereas the mortgage-backed and auto-loan securities amortize principal, the principal payments from credit card receivables are not paid to the investor but are retained by the trustee to reinvest in additional receivables. This allows the issuer to specify a maturity for the security that is consistent with the needs of the issuer and the demands of the investors. When buying a credit card ABS, the indenture specifies (1) the intended maturity for the security; (2) the "lockout period" during which no principal will be paid; and (3) the structure for repaying the principal, which can be accomplished through a single-bullet payment, such as a bond, or distributed monthly with the interest payment over a specified amortization period. For example, a 5-year credit card ABS could have a lockout period of 4 years followed by a 12-month amortization of the principal.

Beyond this standard arrangement, revolving credit securities are protected by early amortization events that can force early repayment if specific payout events occur that are detrimental to the investor (e.g., if there is an increase in the loss rate or if the issuer goes into bankruptcy or receivership). Although this early amortization feature protects the investor from credit problems, it causes an early payment that may not be desirable for the investor.

Variable-Rate Notes Variable-rate notes became popular during periods of high interest rates. As discussed by Fabozzi and Mann (2005), the typical variable-rate note possesses two unique features:

1. After the first 6 to 18 months of the issue's life, during which a minimum rate is often guaranteed, the coupon rate floats, so that every six months it changes to follow some standard. Usually it is pegged 1% above a stipulated short-term rate. For example, the rate might be the preceding three weeks' average 90-day T-bill rate.
2. After the first year or two, the notes are redeemable at par, at the *holder's* option, usually at six-month intervals.

Such notes represent a long-term commitment on the part of the borrower yet provide the lender with all the characteristics of a short-term obligation. However, although the six-month redemption feature provides liquidity, the variable rates can cause these issues to experience wide swings in semi-annual coupons.

Zero Coupon and Deep Discount Bonds The typical corporate bond has a coupon and maturity. In turn, the value of the bond is the present value of the stream of cash flows (interest and principal) discounted at the required YTM. Alternatively, some bonds do not have any coupons or have coupons that are below the market rate at the time of issue. Such securities are referred to as *zero coupon* or *minicoupon bonds* or *original-issue discount (OID) bonds*. A zero coupon discount bond promises to pay a stipulated principal amount at a future maturity date, but it does not promise to make any interim interest payments. Therefore, the price of the bond is the present value of the principal payment at the maturity date using the required discount rate for this bond. The return on the bond is the difference between what the investor pays for the bond at the time of purchase and the principal payment at maturity.

Consider a zero coupon, $10,000 par value bond with a 20-year maturity. If the required rate of return on bonds of equal maturity and quality is 8% and we assume semi-annual discounting, the initial selling price for this bond would be $2,082.89. From the time of purchase to the point of maturity, the investor would not receive any cash flow from the firm. Notably, the investor must pay taxes, however, on the imputed interest on the bond, although no cash is received. Because an investor subject to taxes would experience severe negative cash flows during the life of these bonds, they are primarily of interest to investment accounts not subject to taxes, such as pensions and RRSPs.[14]

A modified form of zero coupon bond is the OID bond where the coupon is set substantially below the prevailing market rate, for example, a 5% coupon on a bond when market rates are 12%. As a result, the bond is issued at a deep discount from par value. Again, taxes must be paid on the implied 12% return rather than the nominal 5%, so the cash flow disadvantage of zero coupon bonds, though lessened, remains.

The Thomson Reuters website has a wealth of information on global debt markets. Check out the league tables at http://www.thomsonreuters.com/business_units/financial/league_tables.

High-Yield Bonds A segment of the corporate bond market that has grown in size, importance, and controversy is **high-yield bonds**, also referred to as *speculative-grade* and *junk bonds*. These are corporate bonds that have been assigned a bond rating as non-investment grade, that is, they have a rating below BBB. The title of speculative-grade bonds is probably the most objective because bonds that are not rated investment grade are speculative grade. The designation of *high-yield bonds* was by Drexel Burnham Lambert (DBL) as an indication

---

14 These bonds will be discussed further in Chapter 12 in the sections on volatility, duration, and immunization.

of the returns available for these bonds relative to government and investment-grade corporate bonds. The *junk bond* designation is obviously somewhat derogatory and refers to the low credit quality of the issues.

Brief History of the High-Yield Bond Market Based on a specification that bonds rated below BBB make up the high-yield market, this segment has existed as long as there have been rating agencies. Prior to 1980, most of the high-yield bonds were referred to as *fallen angels*, meaning they were originally issued as investment-grade securities, but because of changes in the firm over time, the bonds were downgraded into the high-yield sector (BB and below).

The market changed in the early 1980s when DBL began aggressively underwriting high-yield bonds for two groups of clients: (1) small firms that did not have the financial strength to receive an investment-grade rating by the rating agencies, and (2) large and small firms that issued high-yield bonds in connection with leveraged buyouts (LBOs). As a result, the high-yield bond market went from a residual market that included fallen angels to a new-issue market where bonds were underwritten and issued with below-investment-grade ratings. The high-yield bond market exploded in size and activity beginning in 1983 and has had its share of ups and downs. By 2007, the volume of new high-yield bond issues had dropped substantially in light of liquidity and default concerns (to US$165 billion from US$185 billion in 2006). The average size of a new issue in 2007 was over US$550 million.

Distribution of High-Yield Bond Ratings Exhibit 11.4 contains the distribution of ratings for all the bonds contained in the Lehman Brothers High-Yield Bond Index as of December 31 during the period 1994 to 2007. As shown, the heavy concentration by market value is typically in the B class, which contains almost half of all value. There was a strong increase in the BB category that grew from 17% in 1987 to over 48% in 1995, and a subsequent range of 35% to 46%.

EXHIBIT 11.4	High Yield Index Composition by Credit Quality: 1994–2007 (percentage of market value)		
Year	BB	B	CCC/Unrated
1994	42.61	48.00	9.38
1995	48.32	44.60	7.08
1996	45.67	47.36	6.97
1997	38.19	51.07	10.74
1998	35.28	52.04	12.68
1999	33.83	55.82	10.34
2000	36.63	53.94	9.43
2001	46.04	42.35	11.61
2002	41.20	39.70	19.20
2003	35.20	46.40	18.40
2004	39.30	45.10	15.60
2005	41.97	42.77	15.26
2006	35.50	47.76	16.74
2007	36.10	43.06	20.84

Source: Lehman Brothers, *Global Family of Indices* (New York: Lehman Brothers, Annual).

Ownership of High-Yield Bonds The major owners of high-yield bonds have been mutual funds, insurance companies, and pension funds. As of the end of 2007, over 100 mutual funds were either exclusively directed to invest in high-yield bonds or included such bonds in their portfolio. Notably, there has been a shift of ownership away from insurance companies and banks toward mutual funds.

The purpose of this discussion has been to introduce you to high-yield bonds because of the growth in size and importance of this segment of the market for individual and institutional investors. We revisit this topic in Chapter 16 on bond portfolio management, where we review the historical rates of return and alternative risk factors, including the default experience for these bonds.

Japanese Corporate Bond Market The Japanese corporate bond market is made up of two components: (1) bonds issued by industrial firms or utilities and (2) bonds issued by banks to finance loans to corporations.

Japanese corporate bonds are regulated by the *Kisaikai*, a council composed of 22 bond-related banks and seven major securities companies. It operates under the authority of the Ministry of Finance (MOF) and the Bank of Japan (BOJ) to determine bond-issuing procedures, including specifying the coupons on corporate bonds in relation to coupons on long-term government bonds in order to prevent any competition with the government bond market.

As a result of numerous bankruptcies during the 1930s depression, the government mandated that all corporate debt be secured, however, this requirement was abolished in 1988. With the issuance of unsecured debt, there was a need for bond-rating agencies. Currently, there are five major bond-rating agencies operating in Japan.

The Ministry of Finance specifies minimum issuing requirements and controls the issuance system that specifies who can issue bonds and when they can be issued. In addition, lead underwriting managers are predetermined in accordance with a lead manager rotating system that ensures balance among the major securities firms in Japan.

Bank Bonds The substantial issuance of bank bonds is because of the banking system in Japan, which is segmented into the following components:

- Commercial banks (13 big-city banks and 64 regional banks)
- Long-term credit banks (3)
- Mutual loan and savings banks (6)
- Specialized financial institutions

During the post–World War II reconstruction, several banks were permitted to obtain funding by issuing medium- and long-term debentures at rates above yields on government bonds. These funds were used to make mortgage loans to firms in the industrial sector to rebuild plants and equipment. Currently, these financial institutions sell five-year coupon debentures and one-year discount debentures directly to individual and institutional investors. The long-term credit banks are not allowed to take deposits and thus depend on the debentures to obtain funds. These bonds are traded in the OTC market.

Pound Sterling Corporate Bond Market Corporate bonds in the United Kingdom are available in three forms: debentures, unsecured loans, and convertible bonds. The value of securities in each class are about equal. The maturity structure of the corporate bond market is fairly wide and the coupon structure of corporate bonds also is broad with high-coupon bonds in the 10% to 14% range. In contrast, convertible bonds have the low coupons. Almost all U.K. corporate bonds are callable term bonds.

U.K. corporate bonds are issued through both public offerings and private placements. Subsequently, primary dealers have begun trading corporate bonds directly with each other. All corporate bonds are issued in registered form.

Eurozone Corporate Bond Market Corporate bonds in the Eurozone are divided between pure corporate bonds, which include industrial and utility firms (about 15%), and securitized/collaterlized bonds, which include indirect corporate borrowing (about 12%).

11.3.5 INTERNATIONAL BONDS

In Chapter 3 we briefly introduced the two components of each country's international bond market. Recall that *foreign bonds* are issues denominated in the currency of the country in which they are sold but by a borrower of a different nationality. An example would be Canadian dollar–denominated bonds sold in Canada by a Japanese firm (*Maple bonds*). The second component are *Eurobonds*, which are underwritten by international bond syndicates and sold in several national markets. An example would be Eurodollar bonds, which are securities denominated in U.S. dollars, underwritten by an international syndicate, and sold to investors outside the United States. The Euro and U.S. dollar are the most frequently used currencies. The relative size of these two markets (foreign bonds versus Eurobonds) varies by country.

United States The Eurodollar bond market has been much larger than the Yankee bond market. However, because the Eurodollar bond market is heavily affected by changes in the value of the U.S. dollar, it has experienced slower growth during periods when the dollar is weak.

Yankee bonds are issued by foreign firms that register with the SEC and borrow U.S. dollars, using issues underwritten by a U.S. syndicate for delivery in the United States. These bonds are traded in the United States and pay interest semi-annually. Over 60% of Yankee bonds are issued by Canadian corporations and typically have shorter maturities and longer call protection than U.S. domestic issues. These features increase their appeal.

The Eurodollar bond market is dominated by foreign investors, and the centre of trading is in London. Eurodollar bonds pay interest annually. The Eurodollar bond market currently comprises almost 40% of the total Eurobond market.

Japan Historically, the Japanese yen international bond market was dominated by foreign bonds. These *Samurai* bonds are yen-denominated bonds sold by non-Japanese issuers and mainly sold in Japan. The market is fairly small and has limited liquidity. The market has experienced very little growth in terms of yen but substantial growth in U.S. dollar terms because of changes in the exchange rate.

Euroyen bonds are yen-denominated bonds sold in markets outside Japan by international syndicates. This market has grown substantially because of the liberal issue requirements. Its appeal over time is determined by the strength or weakness of the yen relative to other currencies.

United Kingdom Pound sterling foreign bonds are referred to as *bulldog bonds*. Eurosterling bonds are sold in markets outside London by international syndicates.

Similar to other countries, the U.K. international bond market has become dominated by the Eurosterling bonds. The procedure for issuing and trading Eurosterling bonds is similar to that of other Eurobonds.

Eurozone The growth of Eurobonds issued by non-residents has been impressive in recent years. This growth confirmed the popularity of the Euro markets among foreign issuers including issuers domiciled in the United States that accounted for over 7% of the market.

11.4   Obtaining Information on Bond Prices

Historically, the price information available to bond investors has been substantially different from price information available to stock investors. Specifically, stock investors can receive current (within 15 to 20 minutes) transaction prices on major exchanges. In contrast, most bond trading has been done on the over-the-counter (OTC) market, and there was limited reporting of transactions, with the exception of the very liquid government bond market. Fortunately, this environment in the bond market changed dramatically beginning in 2004. In the United States, the National Association of Securities Dealers (NASD), through its Trade Reporting and Compliance Engine (TRACE), began releasing more timely pricing data for a broad group of corporate bonds. Specifically, as of October 2004, NASD expanded the number of corporate bonds for which it reported pricing information, from 4,500 bonds within 45 minutes of the transaction to 17,000 bonds within 30 minutes of the transaction.[15] In 2005 the NASD began reporting transactions on all 23,000 corporate bond issues with the goal to reduce the reporting interval to within 15 minutes of the transaction. Clearly, the price transparency in the corporate bond market has changed significantly, and the transaction cost savings for bond investors has been dramatic. In Canada, the volume is much smaller and transparency issues continue, even with the growth of alternative trading system (ATS) providers (see Chapter 4 for more about ATSs).

In addition to better pricing data, as discussed by Rappaport (2004a), the overall bond market (and especially the corporate bond market) has benefited from the introduction of electronic bond trading through Thomson TradeWeb and MarketAxess, the two leading trading platforms. In early 2004, there was electronic trading in government agency and mortgage-backed securities, but it was not until late 2004 that the volume of trading and the size of corporate bond trading brought transparency to this market. Observers contend that the next frontiers will be electronic trading in high-yield bonds, emerging market debt, and interest rate derivatives.

Given this background, the following discussion considers how investors read and interpret bond price information in newspapers and quote sheets.

11.4.1   INTERPRETING BOND QUOTES

Essentially, all bonds are quoted on the basis of either yield or price. Price quotes are always interpreted as a *percentage of par*. For example, a quote of 98½ is not $98.50 but 98½% of par. The dollar price is derived from the quote, given the par value. If the par value is $5,000, then the price of an issue quoted at 98½ would be $4,925.

Bond Quotes Exhibit 11.5 is a selection of bond quotes for fixed-coupon bonds that appeared on globeinvestor.com. The data pertain to trading activity on October 3, 2008.

The first issue listed is 407 International Inc. This is a 6.05% coupon, with a semiannual coupon frequency. This means that the annual coupon payment for this $1,000 par value bond is $60.50, or $30.25 every six months. The bond matures on July 27, 2009, which is a little less than one year from the beginning of October 2008. The last transaction price for a bond trade on October 3, 2008, was 101.76 of par or $1,017.60, which implies a YTM for this bond (to be explained in detail in Chapter 12) of 3.82%.

The second issue is a bond issued by the Province of Alberta. These bonds, which are due to mature in about two months, are priced quite close to par simply due to the short time remaining before maturity.

---

15 The existence of more bond issues than stock issues is possible because companies can have more than one bond issue, but typically only one stock issue.

EXHIBIT 11.5		**Sample Bond Quotations**							
Issuer	**Bond Type**	**Series**	**Coupon Rate**	**Coupon Freq.**	**Maturity**	**Price**	**Yield**	**Yield Type**	**Duration**
407 INTERNATIONAL INC	CORP	99A1	6.05	S	2009/07/27	101.76	3.82	M	0.78
ALBERTA	PROV		5.00	S	2008/12/16	100.40	2.80	M	0.19
ALTA MUNIC FIN	PROV		4.44	S	2011/12/15	104.25	3.02	M	2.93
BCE INC	CORP	C	7.35	S	2009/10/30	101.61	5.76	M	0.98
CAN REAL RETURN CPN	FEDGOV	RRB	0.00	S	2010/06/01	96.52	2.16	M	2.28
CANADA	FEDGOV		5.00	S	2037/06/01	114.22	4.15	M	15.80
CANADA	FEDGOV		4.25	S	2009/09/01	101.49	2.58	M	0.88
CANADA	FEDGOV		3.75	S	2012/06/01	102.70	2.96	M	3.36
CANADA	FEDGOV		4.00	S	2017/06/01	102.99	3.60	M	7.19

Source: *Report on Business*, http://www.globeinvestor.com/servlet/Page/document/v5/data/bonds?order=a&sort=ISSUER&page=1, retrieved October 3, 2008.

All fixed-income obligations, with the exception of preferred stock, are traded on an *accrued interest basis*. The prices pertain to the value of all *future* cash flows from the bond and exclude interest that has accrued to the holder since the last interest payment date. The actual price of the bond will exceed the quote listed because accrued interest must be added. For example, assume that two months have elapsed since interest was paid on a 7% coupon bond. The current bondholder is entitled to two-sixths (one-third) of the bond's semi-annual interest payment ($35.00) that will be paid in four months time. Therefore, whatever the current price of the bond, an accrued interest value of $11.67 will be added. If a bond is trading "flat," interest is not being paid and accrued interest would not be added.

Summary

1. Each bond has unique intrinsic characteristics and can be differentiated by type of issue and indenture provisions. Major benefits to bond investors include high returns for nominal risk, the potential for capital gains, certain tax advantages, and possibly additional returns from active trading of bonds. Aggressive bond investors must consider market liquidity, investment risks, and interest rate behaviour. We considered high-yield (junk) bonds because of the growth in size and status of this segment of the bond market.

2. The global bond market includes numerous countries. The four major bond markets (the United States, Japan, Europe, and the United Kingdom) have a different makeup in terms of the proportion of governments, agencies, municipals, corporate, and international issues.

The world bond market is large and is continuing to grow due to government deficits around the world and the need for capital by corporations.

3. The various market sectors within the four major bond markets have unique characteristics in terms of liquidity, yield spreads, tax implications, and operating features.

4. To gauge default risk, most bond investors rely on agency ratings. Rating agencies analyze the issuing organization and the specific issue to determine the probability of default and assign a rating. The higher the rating, the less likely there will be default. Speculative-grade and junk bond have bond ratings below BBB. The original ratings assigned impact a bond's marketability and effective interest rate.

5. Governments, agencies, and corporations all issue bonds, each having unique characteristics. The Government of Canada issues short-term obligations (T-bills) through to 30-year bonds, Canada Savings Bonds, and real return bonds. Various agencies of government also issue bonds, though these may or may not be guaranteed by their governments. Corporations issue a wide variety of bonds, typically with more features to provide investors with better returns, less risk, or both.

6. Collateralized mortgage obligations (CMOs) segment the irregular mortgage cash flows to create short-, medium-, and long-term securities. Specifically, CMO investors own bonds that are serviced with the cash flows from mortgages. Asset-backed securities (ABSs) involve securitizing debt, which substantially increases the liquidity of these individual debt instruments whether they be individual mortgages, car loans, or credit card debt. Zero coupon and deep discount bonds do not have any coupons or have coupons that are below the market rate at the time of issue. Both bonds are issued at a deep discount from par value with taxes owing on the implied interest.

7. Bond quotation information varies from vendor to vendor but there is some common information quoted by all. Prices are usually quoted as a percentage of par, the coupon is quoted annually but typically paid semiannually, and the yields are quoted as annual.

Key Terms

bearer bond, p. 298
call premium, p. 299
coupon, p. 298
general obligation (GO) bond, p. 306
high-yield bond, p. 310
money market, p. 297

notes, p. 297
principal (par value), p. 298
public bond, p. 297
refunding issue, p. 298
registered bond, p. 298
revenue bond, p. 298

serial bond, p. 298
sinking fund, p. 299
subordinate (junior) bonds, p. 298
term bond, p. 298
term to maturity, p. 298
unsecured bonds, p. 298

Suggested Readings

Barnhill, Theodore M., William F. Maxwell, and Mark R. Shenkman, eds. *High-Yield Bonds.* New York: McGraw-Hill, 1999.

Fabozzi, Frank J., ed. *Advances and Innovations in the Bond and Mortgage Markets.* Chicago: Probus Publishing, 1989.

Fabozzi, Frank J., ed. *The Handbook of Fixed-Income Securities*, 7th ed. New York: McGraw-Hill, 2005.

Norton, Joseph, and Paul Spellman, eds. *Asset Securitization.* Cambridge, MA: Basil Blackwell, Inc., 1991.

Puffer, Marlene. "Back to Basics: An Overview of Fixed Income Products and New Trends." *Canadian Investment Review*, Fall 2006.

Sundaresan, Suresh. *Fixed-Income Markets and Their Derivatives*, 2nd ed. Cincinnati: South-Western, 2002.

Van Horne, James C. *Financial Market Rates and Flows*, 6th ed. Englewood Cliffs, NJ: Prentice Hall, 2001.

White, Alan. "Risk Swapping: Understanding and Using CDSs and CDDs." *Canadian Investment Review*, Fall 2006.

For Chapter CFA Questions and Problems, please see Appendix A at the end of this text.

Questions

1. Explain the difference between calling a bond and a bond refunding.

2. Identify the three most important determinants of the price of a bond. Describe the effect of each.

3. Given a change in the level of interest rates, discuss how two major factors will influence the relative change in price for individual bonds.

4. Briefly describe two indenture provisions that can affect the maturity of a bond.

5. Explain the differences in taxation of income from Treasury bills, zero coupon bonds, and regular coupon bonds.

6. For several institutional participants in the bond market, explain what type of bond each is likely to purchase and why.

7. Why should investors be aware of the trading volume for bonds in their portfolio?
8. What is the purpose of bond ratings?
9. Based on the data in Exhibit 11.1, discuss the makeup of the Japanese debt market and how and why it differs from the U.S. market.

10. Discuss the positives and negatives of investing in a government agency issue rather than a straight Treasury bond.
11. Discuss the difference between a foreign bond (e.g., a Samurai) and a Eurobond (e.g., a Euroyen issue).

Problems

1. An investor in the 28% tax bracket is trying to decide which of two bonds to purchase. One is a corporate bond carrying an 8% coupon and selling at par. The other is a zero coupon bond yielding 5.5%; this zero coupon bond will be placed in an RSP. Assuming all other relevant factors are equal, which bond should the investor select?
2. What would be the initial offering price for the following (assume semi-annual compounding):
   a. A 15-year zero coupon bond with a yield to maturity (YTM) of 12%.
   b. A 20-year zero coupon bond with a YTM of 10%.
3. The Shamrock Corporation has just issued a $1,000 par value zero coupon bond with an 8% YTM, due to mature 15 years from today (assume semi-annual compounding).

   a. What is the market price of the bond?
   b. If interest rates remain constant, what will be the price of the bond in three years?
   c. If interest rates rise to 10%, what will be the price of the bond in three years?
4. Complete the information requested for each of the following $1,000 face value, zero coupon bonds, assuming semi-annual compounding.

Bond	Maturity (Years)	Yield (Percent)	Price ($)
A	20	12	?
B	?	8	601
C	9	?	350

12

The Analysis and Valuation of Bonds

After you read this chapter, you should be able to answer the following questions:

1. What are the alternative bond yields that are important to investors and how do we compute them?

2. What are the alternative theories that attempt to explain the shape of the term structure of interest rates?

3. What factors affect the volatility of bond price?

4. What is meant by the duration of a bond, how do we compute it, and what factors affect it?

5. What is the convexity for a bond and how do we compute it?

6. Under what conditions is it necessary to consider both duration and convexity when estimating a bond's price volatility?

This chapter is concerned with how one goes about finding the value of bonds and calculating several measures of yields for bonds. It is important to understand why these bond values and yields change over time. A review of bond valuation using the present value model can be found in Web Chapter 20. This background on valuation allows us to understand and compute the expected returns on bonds. After mastering bond yield calculations we consider the different shapes of the yield curve and the alternative theories that explain changes in its shape. We return to bond valuation and acknowledge that when yields change, all bond prices do not change in the same way. Important concepts such as duration and convexity are introduced.

12.1   Bond Valuation and Bond Yields

The value of bonds can be described in terms of dollar values or the rates of return they promise under some set of assumptions. In this section, we describe both the present value model, which computes a specific value for the bond using a single discount value, and the yield model, which computes the promised return based on the bond's current price and a set of assumptions.

12.1.1   THE PRESENT VALUE MODEL

Based on valuation principles, the value of a bond (or any asset) equals the present value of its expected cash flows. The cash flows from a bond are the periodic interest payments to the bondholder and the repayment of principal at maturity. Therefore, the value of a bond is the present value of the semi-annual interest payments plus the present value of the principal payment. Notably, the standard technique is to use a single interest rate discount factor, which is the required return on the bond. We can express this in the following present value formula that assumes semi-annual compounding.[1]

---

1 Most bonds pay interest semi-annually, so it is appropriate to use semi-annual compounding wherein the annual coupon rate is halved and the number of periods is doubled. To be consistent, we should also use semi-annual compounding when discounting the principal payment of a coupon bond or even a zero coupon bond. All our present value calculations assume semi-annual compounding.

$$\boxed{\textbf{12.1}} \qquad P_m = \sum_{t=1}^{2n} \frac{C_i/2}{(1 + i/2)^t} + \frac{P_p}{(1 + i/2)^{2n}}$$

where:

P_m = the current market price of the bond

n = the number of years to maturity

C_i = the annual coupon payment for Bond i

i = the prevailing yield to maturity for this bond issue

P_p = the par value of the bond

BondsOnline is a leading source of bond market information: http://www.bonds-online. com.

The Price-Yield Curve When we know the basic characteristics of a bond in terms of its coupon, maturity, and par value, the only factor that determines its value (price) is the market discount rate, i.e., its required return. As shown, as we increase the required rate, the price declines.

A graph of this relationship is shown in Exhibit 12.1. Besides demonstrating that price moves inverse to yield, the graph shows three other important points:

1. When the yield is less than the coupon rate, the bond will be priced at a *premium* to its par value.
2. When the yield is more than the coupon rate, the bond will be priced at a *discount* to its par value.
3. The price-yield relationship is not a straight line; rather, it is *convex*. As yields decline, the price increases at an increasing rate; as the yield increases, the price declines at a declining rate. This concept of a convex price-yield curve is referred to as *convexity* and will be discussed further in a later section.

12.1.2 THE YIELD MODEL

Instead of determining the value of a bond in dollar terms, investors often price bonds in terms of *yields*, or the promised return under certain assumptions. To compute an expected yield, we use the current market price (P_m) and the expected cash flows to *compute the expected*

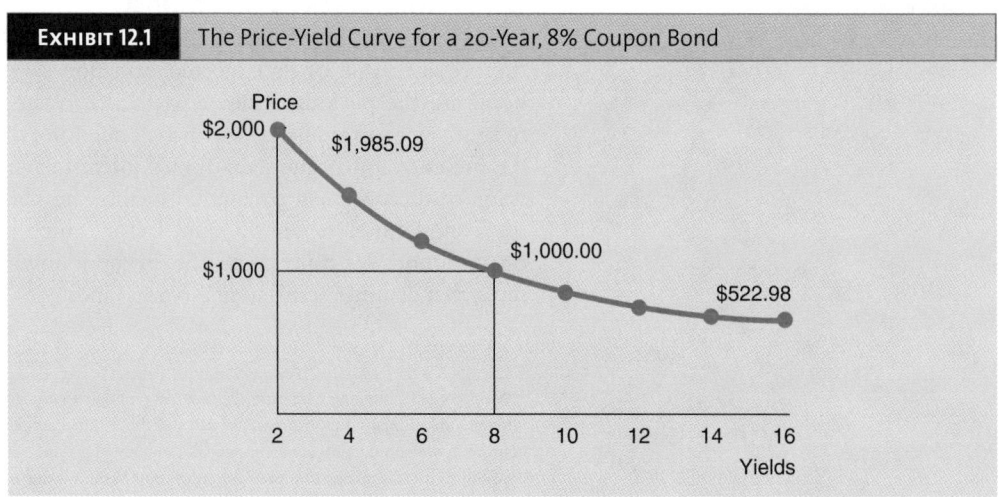

| **EXHIBIT 12.1** | The Price-Yield Curve for a 20-Year, 8% Coupon Bond |

yield on the bond. We can express this approach using the same present value model. The difference is that in Equation 12.1, it was assumed that we knew the appropriate discount rate (the required return), and we computed the estimated value (price) of the bond. In this case, we still use Equation 12.1, but because we know the price of the bond (P_m), we compute the discount rate (yield) that will give us that value (P_m).

$$P_m = \sum_{t=1}^{2n} \frac{C_i/2}{(1 + i/2)^t} + \frac{P_p}{(1 + i/2)^{2n}}$$

where the variables are the same as previously, except

  i = the discount rate that will discount the expected cash flows to equal the current market price of the bond

This i value gives the expected ("promised") yield of the bond under various assumptions to be noted, assuming you pay the price P_m. In the next section, we will discuss several types of bond yields that arise from the assumptions of the valuation model.

   Approaching the investment decision stating the bond's value as a yield figure rather than a dollar amount, we consider the relationship of the computed yield to our required return. If the computed yield is greater than or equal to our required return, we should buy the bond; if the computed yield is less than our required return, we should not buy the bond.

   These approaches to pricing bonds and making investment decisions are similar to the two alternative approaches by which firms make investment decisions: the **net present value (NPV)** method and the **internal rate of return (IRR)** approach, as is reviewed in Chapter 17.

12.2   Computing Bond Yields

Bond investors traditionally have used five yield measures for the following purposes:

Yield Measure	Purpose
Nominal yield	Measures the coupon rate.
Current yield	Measures the current income rate.
Promised yield to maturity	Measures the estimated rate of return for bond held to maturity.
Promised yield to call	Measures the estimated rate of return for bond held to first call date.
Realized (horizon) yield	Measures the estimated rate of return for a bond likely to be sold prior to maturity. It considers specific reinvestment assumptions and an estimated sales price. It also can measure the actual rate of return on a bond during some past period of time.

   Nominal and current yields are mainly descriptive and contribute little to investment decision making. The last three yields are derived from the present value model described previously.

   Nominal yield is the coupon rate of a particular issue. A bond with an 8% coupon has an 8% nominal yield. This provides a convenient way of describing the coupon characteristics of an issue.

Current yield is to bonds what dividend yield is to stocks. It is computed as

| 12.2 | $$CY = C_i / P_m$$ |

where:
    CY = the current yield on a bond
    C_i = the annual coupon payment of Bond i
    P_m = the current market price of the bond

Because this yield measures the current income from the bond as a percentage of its price, it is important to income-oriented investors (e.g., retirees) who want current cash flow from their investment portfolios. Current yield has little use for investors who are interested in total return because it ignores the important capital gain or loss component.

Promised yield to maturity is the most widely used bond yield figure because it indicates the fully compounded return promised to an investor who buys the bond at prevailing prices, *if two assumptions hold true.* The first assumption is that the investor holds the bond to maturity (hence the shortened name, *yield to maturity,* or *YTM*). The second assumption is implicit in the present value calculation. Recall that Equation 12.1 related the current market price of the bond to the present value of all cash flows as follows:

$$P_m = \sum_{t=1}^{2n} \frac{C_i/2}{(1 + i/2)^t} + \frac{P_p}{(1 + i/2)^{2n}}$$

To compute the YTM for a bond, we solve for the rate i that will equate the current price (P_m) to all cash flows from the bond to maturity. Because it is a present value–based calculation, the equation assumes that *all interim cash flows (interest payments) are reinvested at the computed YTM.* This is referred to as a promised YTM because the bond will provide this computed YTM *only* if we meet its conditions:

1. We hold the bond to maturity.
2. We reinvest all the interim cash flows at the computed YTM rate.

If a bond promises an 8% YTM, the coupon income must be reinvested at 8% to realize that promised return. If the coupon payments are spent or if they cannot be reinvested at 8%, then the actual realized yield we earn will be less than the promised yield to maturity. As we will see, if the coupons are reinvested at rates above the YTM, our realized (horizon) return will be greater than the promised YTM. The income earned on this reinvestment of the interim interest payments is referred to as **interest-on-interest**, and is discussed in detail in Homer and Leibowitz (1972, Chapter 1).

The impact of the reinvestment assumption (i.e., the interest-on-interest earnings) on the actual return from a bond varies directly with the bond's coupon and maturity. A higher coupon and/or a longer term to maturity makes the reinvestment assumption more important, that is, such bonds have greater reinvestment risk.

Exhibit 12.2 illustrates the impact of interest-on-interest for an 8%, 25-year bond bought at par to yield 8%. If we invested $1,000 today at 8% for 25 years and reinvested all the coupon payments at 8%, we would have approximately $7,100 at the end of 25 years. We will

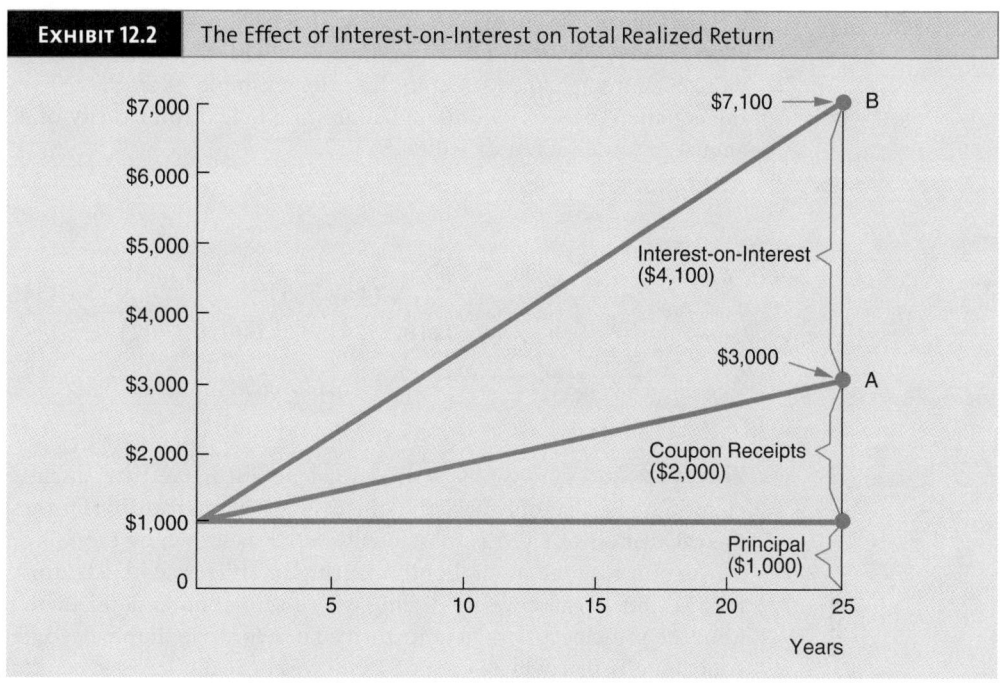

EXHIBIT 12.2 The Effect of Interest-on-Interest on Total Realized Return

call this money at the end of our investment horizon as the **ending-wealth value**. To prove that we would have an ending-wealth value of $7,100, look up the compound interest factor for 4% for 50 payments (assumes semi-annual compounding, the factor is 7.1073). Recall that most bonds pay interest every six months, so semi-annual compounding is used.

Exhibit 12.2 shows that this $7,100 is made up of $1,000 principal return, $2,000 of coupon payments over the 25 years ($80 per year for 25 years), and $4,100 in interest earned on the semi-annual coupon payments reinvested at 4% semi-annually. If we never reinvested any of the coupon payments, we would have an ending-wealth value of only $3,000. This ending-wealth value of $3,000 derived from the beginning investment of $1,000 gives an actual (realized) yield to maturity of only 4.5%. That is, the rate that will discount $3,000 back to $1,000 in 25 years is 4.5%. Reinvesting the coupon payments at some rate between 0 and 8% would cause our ending-wealth position to be above $3,000 and below $7,100; therefore, our actual realized return would be somewhere between 4.5% and 8%. Alternatively, if we managed to reinvest the coupon payments at rates consistently above 8%, our ending-wealth position would be above $7,100, and our realized (horizon) return would be above 8%.

Interestingly, during periods of very high interest rates, we often hear investors talk about "locking in" high yields. These people are subject to *yield illusion* because they do not realize that to achieve the high *promised* yield they must reinvest all the coupon payments at the very high *promised* yields. For example, if we buy a 20-year bond with a promised yield to maturity of 15%, we will realize a 15% yield only if we are able to reinvest all the coupon payments at 15% over the next 20 years.

Computing the Promised Yield to Maturity The promised yield to maturity can be calculated by using the present value model (Equation 12.1) with semi-annual compounding. This technique, used by investment professionals, gives the investor an accurate result.

This model is somewhat complex because the solution requires iteration. However, iteration is rarely performed by hand these days with the advancement of handheld financial calculators and spreadsheets. Using the prior example of an 8%, 20-year bond, priced at $900, the equation gives us a semi-annual promised yield to maturity of 4.545%, which implies an annual promised YTM of 9.09%.[2]

$$900 = 40 \sum_{t=1}^{40} \left(\frac{1}{(1.04545)^t} \right) + 1,000 \left(\frac{1}{(1.04545)^{40}} \right)$$

$$= 40\,(18.2574) + 1,000\,(0.1702)$$

$$= 900$$

YTM for a Zero Coupon Bond In several instances, we have discussed the existence of zero coupon bonds that only have the one cash inflow at maturity. This single cash flow means that the calculation of YTM is substantially easier as shown by the following example.

Assume a zero coupon bond maturing in 10 years with a maturity value of $1,000 selling for $311.80. Because we are dealing with a zero coupon bond, there is only the one cash flow from the principal payment at maturity. Therefore, we simply need to determine what the discount rate is that will discount $1,000 to equal the current market price of $311.80 in 20 semi-annual periods (or 10 years). The equation is as follows:

$$\$311.80 = \frac{\$1,000}{(1 + i/2)^{20}}$$

We will see that $i/2 = 6\%$, which is in semi-annual terms. To get a quote on an annual basis, simply double the semi-annual rate to get the bond equivalent yield (BEY) of 12%. BEY does not consider compounding. To be accurate, we need to consider compounding in order to get the effective yield to maturity or $(1.06 \times 1.06) - 1 = 0.1236$, or 12.36%.

Promised Yield to Call Although investors use promised YTM to value most bonds, they must estimate the return on certain callable bonds with a different measure—the **promised yield to call (YTC)**. Whenever a bond with a call feature is selling at a premium greater than or equal to its call price, the investor should consider valuing the bond in terms of YTC rather than YTM. This is because the marketplace uses the lowest, most conservative yield measure in pricing a bond. As discussed in Homer and Leibowitz (1972, Chapter 4), when bonds are trading at or above a specified **crossover price**, which is approximately the bond's call price plus a small premium that increases with time to call, the yield to call will provide the lowest yield measure.

The crossover price is important because at this price the YTM and the YTC are equal—this is the *crossover yield*. When the bond rises to this price above par, the computed YTM becomes low enough that it would be profitable for the issuer to call the bond and finance the call by

---

2 You will recall from your corporate finance course that you start with one rate (e.g., 4.5% semi-annual) and compute the value of the stream. In this example, the value would exceed $900, so you would select a higher rate until you had a present value for the stream of cash flows of less than $900. Given the discount rates above and below the true rate, you would interpolate between the two rates to arrive at the correct discount rate that would give you a value of $900.

selling a new bond at this prevailing market interest rate.[3] Therefore, the YTC measures the promised return the investor will receive from holding this bond until it is retired at the first available call date, that is, at the end of the deferred call period. Note that if an issue has multiple call dates at different prices (the call price will decline for later call dates), it will be necessary to determine which of these scenarios provides the lowest yield—this is referred to as computing yield to worst. Investors must consider calculating the YTC for their bonds after a period when a number of high-yielding, high-coupon bonds have been issued. Following such a period, interest rates will decline, bond prices will rise, and the high-coupon bonds will subsequently have a high probability of being called—that is, their yields will fall below the crossover yield.

Computing Promised Yield to Call   To compute the YTC by the present value method, we adjust the semi-annual present value equation to give

12.3
$$P_m = \sum_{t=1}^{2nc} \frac{C_i/2}{(1 + i/2)^t} + \frac{P_c}{(1 + i/2)^{2nc}}$$

where:
P_m = the current market price of the bond
C_i = the annual coupon payment for Bond i
nc = the number of years to first call date
P_c = the call price of the bond

Following the present value method, solve for i. Without the aid of a financial calculator or spreadsheet, several interpolations are necessary to get the exact yield. As before, this is a promised yield that requires the two assumptions noted earlier except that instead of holding to maturity, we hold until the first call date.

Realized (Horizon) Yield   The final measure of bond yield, **realized yield** or **horizon yield** (i.e., the actual return over a horizon period) measures the expected return of a bond that we anticipate selling prior to its maturity. In terms of the equation, the investor has a holding period (hp) or investment horizon that is less than n. Realized (horizon) yield can be used to estimate returns attainable from various trading strategies. Although a very useful measure, it requires several estimates not used in the other yield measures. The investor must estimate the (1) expected future selling price of the bond at the end of the holding period and (2) reinvestment rate for the coupon flows prior to selling the bond. This technique is also used by investors to determine their actual yields after selling bonds.

Computing Realized (Horizon) Yield   The realized yields over a horizon holding period are variations on the promised yield equations. The substitution of P_f (future selling price) and hp into the present value model (Equation 12.1) provides the following realized yield model:

12.4
$$P_m = \sum_{t=1}^{2hp} \frac{C_i/2}{(1 + i/2)^t} + \frac{P_f}{(1 + i/2)^{2hp}}$$

Again, we solve for the i that equates the expected cash flows to the current market price.

---

3 An extensive literature on the refunding of bond issues includes studies by Boyce and Kalotay (1979), Harris (1980), Kalotay (1982a), and Finnerty (1983).

We will note from the present value realized yield formula in Equation 12.4 that the coupon flows are implicitly discounted at the computed realized (horizon) yield. In many cases, this is an inappropriate assumption because available market rates might be very different from the computed realized (horizon) yield. Therefore, to derive a realistic estimate of the estimated realized yield, we also need to *estimate our expected reinvestment rate during the investment horizon.*

12.3 Calculating Future Bond Prices

Dollar bond prices need to be calculated in two instances: (1) when computing realized (horizon) yield, we must determine the future selling price (P_f) of a bond if it is to be sold before maturity or first call, and (2) when issues are quoted on a promised yield basis, as with municipals. We can easily convert a yield-based quote to a dollar price by using Equation 12.1, which does not require iteration. (We need only solve for P_m.) The coupon (C_i) is given, as is par value (P_p) and the promised YTM, which is used as the discount rate.

Consider a 10%, 25-year bond with a promised YTM of 12%. We would compute the price of this issue as

$$P_m = \frac{100}{2} \sum_{t=1}^{50} \frac{1}{\left(1 + \dfrac{0.120}{2}\right)^t} + 1{,}000 \, \frac{1}{\left(1 + \dfrac{0.120}{2}\right)^{50}}$$

$$= 50\,(15.7619) + 1{,}000\,(0.0543)$$

$$= \$842.40$$

In this instance, we are determining the prevailing market price of the bond based on the current market YTM. These market yields indicate the consensus of all investors regarding the value of this bond. An investor with a required return on this bond that differs from the market YTM would estimate a different value for the bond.

In contrast to the current market price, we will need to compute a future price (P_f) when estimating the expected realized (horizon) yield performance of alternative bonds. Investors or portfolio managers who consistently trade bonds for capital gains need to compute expected realized (horizon) yield rather than promised yield. They would compute P_f through the following variation of the realized yield equation:

12.5
$$P_f = \sum_{t=1}^{2n-2hp} \frac{C_i/2}{(1 + i/2)^t} + \frac{P_p}{(1 + i/2)^{2n-2hp}}$$

where:
P_f = the future selling price of the bond
P_p = the par value of the bond
n = the number of years to maturity
hp = the holding period of the bond (in years)
C_i = the annual coupon payment of Bond i
i = the expected market YTM at the end of the holding period

This equation is a version of the present value model that is used to calculate the expected price of the bond at the end of the holding period (hp). The term $2n - 2hp$ equals the bond's remaining term to maturity at the end of the investor's holding period, that is, the number of six-month periods remaining after the bond is sold. Therefore, the value of P_f is based on four variables—two that are known and two that must be estimated by the investor.

Specifically, the coupon (C_i) and the par value (P_p) are given. The investor must forecast the length of the holding period and, therefore, the number of years remaining to maturity at the time the bond is sold ($n - hp$). The investor also must forecast the expected market YTM at the time of sale (i). With this information, you can calculate the future price of the bond. The real difficulty (and the potential source of error) in estimating P_f lies in predicting hp and i.

Assume we bought the 10%, 25-year bond just discussed at $842, giving it a promised YTM of 12%. Based on an analysis of the economy and the capital market, we expect this bond's market YTM to decline to 8% in 5 years. Therefore, we want to calculate its future price (P_f) at the end of year 5 to estimate our expected return, assuming we are correct in our assessment of the decline in overall market interest rates. As noted, we estimate the holding period (5 years), which implies a remaining life of 20 years, and the estimated future market YTM of 8%. Using Equation 12.5 gives a future price:

$$P_f = 50 \sum_{t=1}^{40} \frac{1}{(1.04)^t} + 1,000 \frac{1}{(1.04)^{40}}$$

$$= 50(19.7928) + 1,000(0.2083)$$

$$= 989.64 + 208.30$$

$$= \$1,197.94$$

12.3.1 REALIZED (HORIZON) YIELD WITH DIFFERENTIAL REINVESTMENT RATES

The realized yield equation—Equation 12.4—is the standard present value formula with the changes in holding period and ending price. As such, it includes the implicit reinvestment rate assumption that all cash flows are reinvested at the computed i rate. There may be instances where such an implicit assumption is not appropriate, given our expectations for future interest rates. Assume that current market interest rates are very high and we invest in a long-term bond (e.g., a 20-year, 14% coupon) to take advantage of an expected decline in rates from 14% to 10% over a 2-year period. Computing the future price of a 19% 18-year bond yielding 10% (equal to $1,330.95) and using the realized yield equation to estimate the realized (horizon) yield, we will get the following fairly high realized return:

$$P_m = \$1,000$$

$$hp = 2 \text{ Years}$$

$$Pf = \sum_{t=1}^{36} 70/(1 + 0.05)^t + \$1,000/(1.05)^{36}$$

$$= \$1,158.30 + \$172.65$$

$$= \$1,330.95$$

$$\$1{,}000 = \sum_{t=1}^{4} \frac{70}{(1 + i/2)^t} + \frac{1{,}330.95}{(1 + i/2)^4}$$

$$i = 27.5\%$$

As noted, this calculation assumes that all cash flows are reinvested at the computed i (27.5%). However, it is unlikely that during a period when market rates are going from 14% to 10%, we could reinvest the coupon at 27.5%. It is more appropriate and realistic to *explicitly estimate the reinvestment rates and calculate the realized yields based on our ending-wealth position.* This procedure is more precise and realistic, and it is easier because it does not require iteration.

The basic technique calculates the value of all cash flows at the end of the holding period, which is the investor's ending-wealth value. We compare this ending-wealth value to our *beginning-wealth value to determine the compound return that equalizes these two values.* Adding to our prior example, assume we have the following cash flows:

P_m = $1,000
$\quad i$ = interest payments of $70 in 6, 12, 18, and 24 months
$\quad P_f$ = $1,330.95 (the ending market value of the bond)

The ending value of the four interest payments is determined by our assumptions regarding specific reinvestment rates. Assume each payment is reinvested at a different declining rate that holds for its time period (i.e., the first three interest payments are reinvested at progressively lower rates and the fourth interest payment is received at the end of the holding period).

i_1 at 13% for 18 months = $70 × (1 + 0.065)^3 = \$ 84.55$
i_2 at 12% for 12 months = $70 × (1 + 0.06)^2\ \ = \$ 78.65$
$\quad i_3$ at 11% for 6 months = $70 × (1 + 0.055)\ \ = \$ 73.85$
$\quad\quad i_4$ not reinvested = $70 × (1.0)\quad\quad = \underline{\$ 70.00}$

Future value of interest payments = $307.05

Therefore, our total ending-wealth value is

$1,330.95 + $307.05 = $1,638.00

The compound realized (horizon) return is calculated by comparing our ending-wealth value ($1,638) to our beginning-wealth value ($1,000) and determining what interest rate would equalize these two values over a two-year holding period. Using a financial calculator, enter 1,000 as the *PV*, 1,638 as the *FV*, 4 for *N*, then compute $i = 13.13\%$ or an annual rate of 26.26%. This compares to an estimate of 27.5% when we assume an implicit reinvestment rate of 27.5%.

This realized (horizon) yield calculation specifically states the expected reinvestment rates as contrasted to assuming the reinvestment rate is equal to the computed realized yield. The actual assumption regarding the reinvestment rate can be very important.

The steps to calculate an expected realized (horizon) yield can be summarized as follows:

1. Calculate the future value at the horizon date of all coupon payments reinvested at estimated rates.
2. Calculate the expected sales price of the bond at our expected horizon date based on our estimate of the required yield to maturity at the horizon date.

3. Sum the values in Steps 1 and 2 to arrive at the total ending-wealth value.
4. Enter the ending-wealth value as an *FV*, the beginning value (the purchase price of the bond) as a *PV*, the time horizon as *N*, and compute *i* to get the compound rate of interest.

$$\left[\frac{\textbf{Ending-wealth value}}{\textbf{Beginning value}} \right]^{\frac{1}{2n}} - 1$$

5. If all calculations assume semi-annual compounding, double the interest rate derived from Step 4.

12.3.2   PRICE AND YIELD DETERMINATION ON NON-INTEREST DATES

So far, we have assumed that the investor buys (or sells) a bond precisely on the date that interest is due, so the measures are accurate only when the issues are traded on coupon payment dates. However, when the semi-annual model is used, and when more accuracy is necessary, another version of the price and yield model must be used for transactions on non-interest payment dates. Fortunately, the basic models need be extended only one more step because the value of an issue that trades X years, Y months, and so many days from maturity is found by extrapolating the bond value (price or yield) for the month before and the month after the day of transaction. Thus, the valuation process involves full months to maturity rather than years or semi-annual periods.[4]

Accrued Interest Having computed a value for the bond at a non-interest payment date, it is also necessary to consider the notion of *accrued interest*. Because the interest payment on a bond, which is paid every six months, is a contractual promise by the issuer, the bond investor has the right to receive a portion of the semi-annual interest payment if he/she held the bond for some part of the six-month period. For example, assume an 8%, $1,000 par value bond that pays $40 every six months. If you sold the bond two months after the prior interest payment, you have held it for one-third of the six-month period and would have the right to one-third of the $40 ($13.33). This is referred to as the accrued interest on the bond. Therefore, when you sell the bond, there is a calculation of the bond's remaining value until maturity, that is, its price. What you receive is this price *plus* the accrued interest ($13.33).

12.4   What Determines Interest Rates?

The Bank of Canada has a wealth of information about Canadian interest rates and monetary policy. See http://www.bankofcanada.ca.

Now that we have learned to calculate various yields on bonds and to determine the value of bonds using yields and spot rates, the question arises as to what causes differences and changes in yields over time. Market interest rates cause these effects because the interest rates reported in the media are simply the prevailing YTMs for the bonds being discussed. For example, when we hear that the interest rate on long-term government bonds declined from 5.80% to 5.70%, this means that the price of this particular bond increased such that the computed YTM at the former price was 5.80%, but the computed YTM at the new, higher price is 5.70%. Yields and interest rates are the same. They are different terms for the same concept.

We have discussed the inverse relationship between bond prices and interest rates. As demonstrated in Exhibit 12.1, when we change the interest rate (yield) on a bond, we

---

4 For a detailed discussion of these calculations see "Bond Pricing and Return Measures" (Fabozzi, 2005, Chapter 4).

simultaneously change its price in the opposite direction. It is natural to ask which of these is the driving force—bond prices or bond interest rates? It is a simultaneous change, and we can envision either factor causing it. Most practitioners probably envision the changes in interest rates as the causes because they constantly use interest rates to describe changes. They use interest rates because they are comparable across bonds, whereas the price of a bond depends not only on the interest rate but also on the bond's specific characteristics, including its coupon and maturity.

Understanding interest rates and what makes them change is necessary for an investor who hopes to maximize returns from investing in bonds. Therefore, in this section we review our prior discussion of the following topics: what causes overall market interest rates to rise and fall, why alternative bonds have different interest rates, and why the yield spread between alternative bonds changes over time. To accomplish this, we begin with a general discussion of what influences interest rates and then consider the term structure of interest rates (shown by yield curves), which relates the interest rates on a set of comparable bonds to their terms to maturity. The term structure is important because it reflects what investors expect to happen to interest rates in the future and it dictates their current risk attitude.

12.4.1   FORECASTING INTEREST RATES

For now we keep in mind that interest rates are the price for loanable funds and, like any price, they are determined by the supply and demand for these funds. On one side, investors are willing to provide funds (the supply) at prices based on their required rates of return. On the other side, borrowers need funds (the demand).

Although lenders and borrowers have some fundamental factors that determine supply and demand curves, the prices (interest rates) for these funds are affected for short periods by events that shift the curves. Examples include large government bond issues that affect demand for funds, or significant changes in monetary policy that affect the money supply.

Our treatment of interest rate forecasting recognizes that we must be aware of the basic determinants of interest rates and monitor these factors. We also recognize that detailed forecasting of interest rates is a complicated task best left to professional economists. Therefore, our goal as bond investors and bond portfolio managers is to continuously assess the major factors that affect interest rates but rely on the professional economists for detailed insights on such topics as the real RFR and the expected inflation rate.[5]

12.4.2   FUNDAMENTAL DETERMINANTS OF INTEREST RATES

As shown in Exhibit 12.3, average interest rates (yields) for long-term (10-year) U.S. government bonds during the period from 2004 to 2007 went from about 4.71% to 4.95%. These results were similar to those of the United Kingdom and the Euro area, while the rate on Japanese government bonds increased overall from about 1.31% to 1.57%. As a bond investor, we should understand why these differences exist and why interest rates within each country changed.

As we would expect, bond prices increased dramatically during periods when market interest rates dropped, and some bond investors experienced very attractive returns. In contrast, some investors experienced substantial losses during periods when interest rates

---

5 Sources of information on the bond market and interest rate forecasts would include Merrill Lynch's Fixed Income Weekly and World Bond Market Monitor; Goldman Sach's Financial Market Perspectives and The Pocket Chartroom; and the Federal Reserve Bank of St. Louis, Monetary Trends.

EXHIBIT 12.3	Yields of International Long-Term Government Bonds: Quarterly 2004–2007

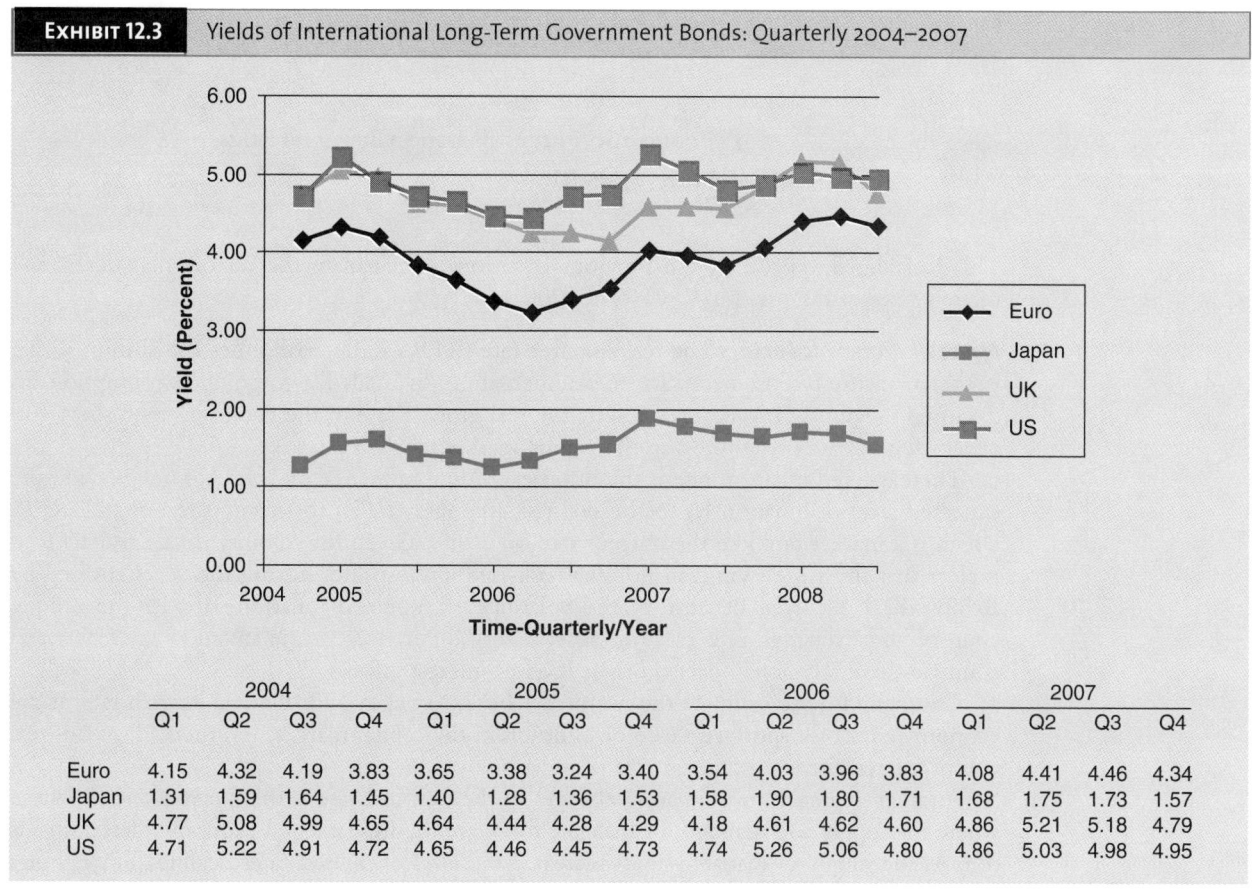

	2004				2005				2006				2007			
	Q1	Q2	Q3	Q4	Q1	Q2	Q3	Q4	Q1	Q2	Q3	Q4	Q1	Q2	Q3	Q4
Euro	4.15	4.32	4.19	3.83	3.65	3.38	3.24	3.40	3.54	4.03	3.96	3.83	4.08	4.41	4.46	4.34
Japan	1.31	1.59	1.64	1.45	1.40	1.28	1.36	1.53	1.58	1.90	1.80	1.71	1.68	1.75	1.73	1.57
UK	4.77	5.08	4.99	4.65	4.64	4.44	4.28	4.29	4.18	4.61	4.62	4.60	4.86	5.21	5.18	4.79
US	4.71	5.22	4.91	4.72	4.65	4.46	4.45	4.73	4.74	5.26	5.06	4.80	4.86	5.03	4.98	4.95

increased. A casual analysis of this chart, which covers about four years, indicates the need for monitoring interest rates. Essentially, the factors causing interest rates (*i*) to rise or fall are described by the following model:

12.6	$$i = RFR + I + RP$$

where:

RFR = the real risk-free rate of interest

I = the expected rate of inflation

RP = the risk premium

The relationship shown in this equation is a simple but complete statement of interest rate behaviour. The more difficult task is estimating the *future* behaviour of such variables as real growth, expected inflation, and economic uncertainty. In this regard, interest rates, like stock prices, are extremely difficult to forecast with any degree of accuracy, as discussed by Fabozzi in "The Structure of Interest Rates" (2005, Chapter 6). Alternatively, we can visualize the source of changes in interest rates in terms of the economic conditions and issue characteristics as follows:

> **12.7**
>
> $$i = f(\text{Economic Forces} + \text{Issue Characteristics})$$
> $$= (RFR + I) + RP$$

This rearranged version of the previous equation helps isolate the factors that determine interest rates, as discussed in Van Horne (2001).

Effect of Economic Factors The real risk-free rate (RFR) is the economic cost of money, that is, the opportunity cost necessary to compensate individuals for forgoing consumption. As discussed previously, it is determined by the real growth rate of the economy with short-run effects due to ease or tightness in the capital market.

The expected inflation rate is the other economic influence on interest rates. We add the expected level of inflation (I) to the real risk-free rate (RFR) to specify the nominal RFR, which is a market rate like the current rate on T-bills. Given the stability of the real RFR, it is clear that the wide swings in nominal risk-free interest rates during the years covered by Exhibit 12.3 occurred because of the volatility of expected inflation. Besides the unique country and exchange rate risk (discussed later), differences in the inflation rates between countries have a major impact on their level of interest rates.

Thus, one way to estimate the nominal RFR is to begin with the real growth rate of the economy, adjust for short-run ease or tightness in the capital market, and then adjust this real rate of interest for the expected rate of inflation.

Another approach to estimating changes in the nominal rate is the macroeconomic view, where the supply and demand for loanable funds are the fundamental economic determinants of i. As the supply of loanable funds increases, the level of interest rates declines, other things being equal. Several factors influence the supply of funds. Government monetary policies imposed by the Bank of Canada have a significant impact on the supply of money. The savings patterns of Canadian and foreign investors also affect the supply of funds. In the case of the U.S., foreign investors have become a stronger influence on the U.S. supply of loanable funds during recent years, as shown by the significant foreign purchases of U.S. securities. We know that this foreign supply of funds to the U.S. bond market has helped reduce the U.S. interest rates and the cost of capital.

Interest rates increase when the demand for loanable funds increases. The demand for loanable funds is affected by the capital and operating needs of the Canadian government, federal agencies, provincial and local governments, corporations, institutions, and individuals. Federal budget deficits increase the demand for loanable funds. Likewise, the level of consumer demand for funds to buy houses, cars, and appliances affects rates, as does corporate demand for funds to pursue investment opportunities. The total of all groups determines the aggregate demand and supply of loanable funds and the level of the nominal RFR.

The Impact of Bond Characteristics A specific bond issue's interest rate is influenced by factors that affect the nominal RFR but also by the unique characteristics of the bond that influences the bond's risk premium (RP). The economic forces that determine the nominal RFR affect all securities, whereas issue characteristics are unique to individual securities, market sectors, or countries. Thus, the differences in the yields of corporate and government bonds are not caused by economic factors but, rather, by different issue characteristics that affect the risk premiums.

Bond investors separate the risk premium into four components:

1. The quality of the issue as determined by its risk of default relative to other bonds
2. The term to maturity of the issue, which can affect price volatility
3. Indenture provisions, including collateral, call features, and sinking-fund provisions
4. Foreign bond risk, including exchange rate risk and country risk

Of the four factors, quality and maturity have the greatest impact on the risk premium for domestic bonds, while exchange rate risk and country risk are important components of risk for foreign bonds.

The credit quality of a bond reflects the ability of the issuer to service its outstanding debt, which is largely captured in the ratings issued by the bond rating firms. As a result, bonds with different ratings have different yields. For example, AAA-rated obligations possess lower risk of default than BBB obligations, so they have a lower required yield.

Notably, the risk premium differences between bonds of different quality levels change dramatically over time, depending on prevailing economic conditions. When the economy experiences a recession or a period of economic uncertainty, the desire for quality increases, and investors sell lower quality debt and bid up prices of higher rated bonds, which increases the difference in yield. This difference in yield is referred to as the quality or credit spread. Dialynas and Edington (1992) contend that this yield spread is also influenced by the volatility of interest rates. This variability in the credit risk premium over time was demonstrated and discussed in Chapter 1 and Web Chapter 20.

Term to maturity also influences the risk premium because it affects the price volatility of the bond. In the section on the term structure of interest rates, we will discuss the typical positive relationship between the term to maturity of a bond issue and its interest rate.

As discussed in Chapter 11, indenture provisions indicate the collateral pledged for a bond, its callability, and its sinking-fund provisions. Collateral gives protection to the investor if the issuer defaults on the bond because the investor has a specific claim on some assets in case of liquidation.

Call features indicate when an issuer can buy back the bond prior to its maturity. An issuer will call the bond when interest rates have declined, so it is not to the advantage of the investor who must reinvest the proceeds at a lower interest rate. Obviously, an investor will charge the issuer for having the call option, and the cost of the option (in the form of a higher yield) will increase with the level of interest rates. Therefore, more protection against having the bond called reduces the risk premium. The significance (value) of call protection increases during periods of high interest rates. As noted by Marshall and Yawitz (1980) and Stanhouse and Stock (1999), when we buy a bond with a high coupon, we want protection from having it called away when rates decline.

As discussed by Kalotay (1981, 1982b), a sinking fund reduces the investor's risk and causes a lower yield for several reasons. First, a sinking fund reduces default risk because it requires the issuer to reduce the outstanding issue systematically. Second, purchases of the bond by the issuer to satisfy sinking-fund requirements provide price support for the bond. These purchases also contribute to a more liquid secondary market for the bond because of the increased trading. Finally, sinking-fund provisions require that the issuer retire a bond before its stated maturity, which reduces the issue's average maturity. The decline in average maturity tends to reduce the risk premium of the bond.

We know that currency exchange rates change over time and that this increases the risk of global investing. The variability of exchange rates vary among countries because the trade balances and rates of inflation differ. Volatile trade balances and inflation rates make exchange rates more volatile, which adds to the uncertainty of future exchange rates and increases the exchange rate risk premium.

In addition to changes in exchange rates, investors also are concerned with the political and economic stability of a country. If investors are unsure about the political or economic environment in a country, they will increase the required risk premium to reflect this country risk.

12.5   The Term Structure of Interest Rates

The Living Yield Curve: To see how the yield curve changes over time, go to http://www.smartmoney. com/onebond/index.cfm? story=yieldcurve.

The term structure of interest rates (or the yield curve, as it is more popularly known) is a static function that relates the term to maturity to the yield to maturity for a sample of bonds at a *given point in time*.[6] Thus, it represents a cross-section of yields for a category of bonds that are comparable in all respects except maturity. Specifically, the quality of the issues should be constant, and ideally we should have issues with similar coupons and call features within a single industry category. We can construct different yield curves for governments, government agencies, AAA utilities, and so on. The accuracy of the yield curve will depend on the comparability of the bonds in the sample.

For example, Exhibit 12.4 shows yield curves in Canada in June of 1997, 2000, 2003, 2005, and May of 2009, the latest available data at the time of this writing. All yield curves, of course, do not have the same shape. Although individual yield curves are static, their behaviour over time is quite fluid. As shown, the 1997 yield curve is apparently upward sloping. The curve flattens in 2000 with short-term yields rising slightly and long-term yields dropping. The curves of 2005 and 2009 closely resemble each other.

The shape of the yield curve can undergo dramatic alterations, following one of the four patterns shown in Exhibit 12.5. The rising yield curve is the most common and tends to prevail when interest rates are at low or modest levels. The declining yield curve tends to occur when rates are relatively high. The flat yield curve rarely exists for any period of time. The humped yield curve prevails when extremely high rates are expected to decline to more normal levels. Note that the slope of the yield curve tends to level off after 15 years.

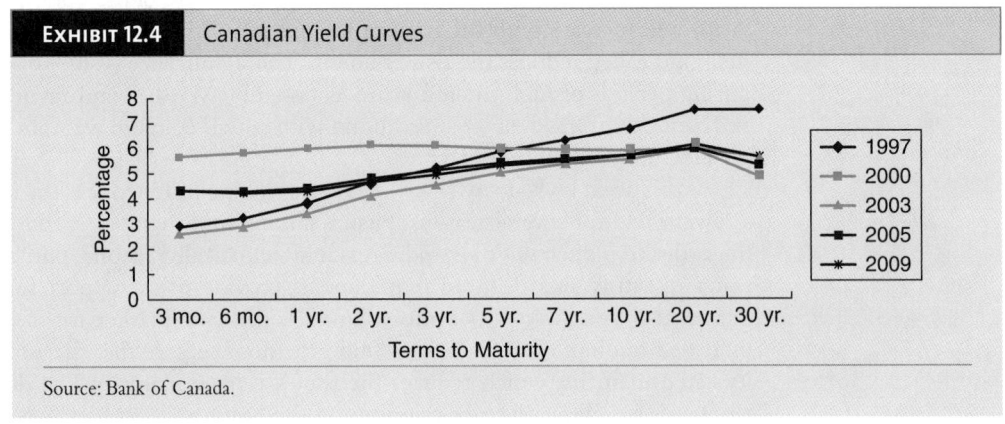

EXHIBIT 12.4   Canadian Yield Curves

Source: Bank of Canada.

---

6 For a discussion of the theory and empirical evidence, see Sundaresan (2002).

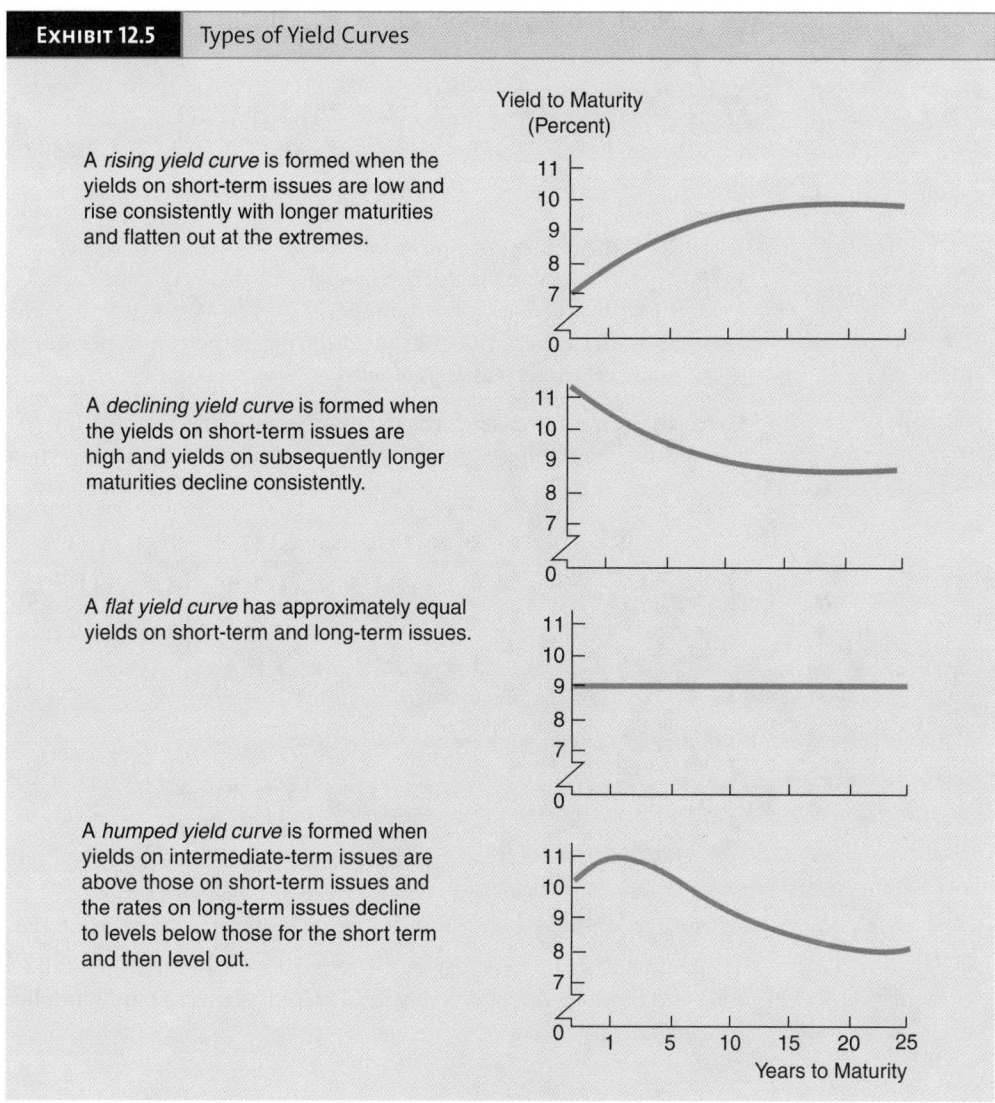

EXHIBIT 12.5   Types of Yield Curves

A *rising yield curve* is formed when the yields on short-term issues are low and rise consistently with longer maturities and flatten out at the extremes.

A *declining yield curve* is formed when the yields on short-term issues are high and yields on subsequently longer maturities decline consistently.

A *flat yield curve* has approximately equal yields on short-term and long-term issues.

A *humped yield curve* is formed when yields on intermediate-term issues are above those on short-term issues and the rates on long-term issues decline to levels below those for the short term and then level out.

Why does the term structure assume different shapes? Three major theories attempt to explain this: the expectations hypothesis, the liquidity preference hypothesis, and the segmented market hypothesis.

12.5.1   EXPECTATIONS HYPOTHESIS

According to the expectations hypothesis, the shape of the yield curve results from the interest rate expectations of market participants. More specifically, it holds that any long-term interest rate simply represents the geometric mean of current and future one-year interest rates expected to prevail over the maturity of the issue. In essence, the term structure involves a series of intermediate- and long-term interest rates, each of which is a reflection of the geometric average of current and expected one-year interest rates. Under such conditions, the equilibrium long-term rate is the rate the long-term bond investor would expect to earn through successive investments in short-term bonds over the term to maturity of the long-term bond.

Generally, this relationship can be formalized as follows:

12.8

$$(1 + {}_tR_n) = [(1 + {}_tR_1)(1 + {}_{t+1}r_1) \cdots (1 + {}_{t+n-1}r_1)]^{1/N}$$

where:

R_n = the actual long-term rate
N = the term to maturity (in years) of the long issue
${}_tR_1$ = the current 1-year rate
${}_{t+i}r1$ = the expected 1-year yield during some future period, $t + i$ (these future 1-year rates are referred to as *forward rates*)

Given the relationship set forth in this equation, the formula for computing the one-period forward rate beginning at time $t + n$ and implied in the term structure at time t is

$$1 + {}_{t+n}r_{1t} = \frac{(1 + {}_tR_{1t})(1 + {}_{t+1}r_{1t})(1 + {}_{t+2}r_{1t}) \cdots (1 + {}_{t+n}r_{1t})(1 + {}_{t+n}r_{1t})}{(1 + {}_tR_{1t})(1 + {}_{t+1}r_{1t}) \cdots (1 + {}_{t+n-1}r_{1t})}$$

$$= \frac{(1 + {}_tR_{n+1})^{n+1}}{(1 + {}_tR_n)^n}$$

12.9

$$_{t+n}r_{1t} = \frac{(1 + {}_tR_{n+1})^{n+1}}{(1 + {}_tR_n)^n} - 1$$

where $_{t+n}r_{1t}$ is the one-year forward rate prevailing at $t + n$, using the term structure at time t.

Assume that the five-year spot rate is 10% (${}_tR_5 = 0.10$) and the four-year spot rate is 9% (${}_tR_4 = 0.09$). The forward one-year rate four years from now implied by these spot rates can be calculated as follows:

$$_{t+n}r_{1t} = \frac{(1 + {}_tR_5)^5}{(1 + {}_tR_4)^4} - 1$$

$$= \frac{(1 + 0.10)^5}{(1 + 0.09)^4} - 1$$

$$= \frac{1.6105}{1.4116} - 1$$

$$= 1.1409 - 1 = 0.1409 = 14.09\%$$

The term structure at time t implies that the one-year spot rate four years from now (during year 5) will be 14.09%. This concept and formula can be used to derive future rates for multiple years. Thus, the two-year spot rate that will prevail three years from now (which is a forward rate) could be calculated using the three-year spot rate and the five-year spot rate. The general formula for computing the j-period forward rate beginning at time $t + n$ as of time t is

12.10
$$_{t+n}r_{jt} = \sqrt[j]{\frac{(1 + {}_tR_{n+j})^{n+j}}{(1 + {}_tR_n)}} - 1$$

As a practical approximation of Equation 12.5, it is possible to use the *arithmetic* average of one-year rates to generate long-term yields.

The expectations theory can explain any shape of yield curve. Expectations for rising short-term rates in the future cause a rising yield curve; expectations for falling short-term rates in the future will cause long-term rates to lie below current short-term rates, and the yield curve will decline. Similar explanations account for flat and humped yield curves.

Consider the following explanation by the expectations hypothesis of the shape of the term structure of interest rates using arithmetic averages:

$_tR_1 = 5\frac{1}{2}\%$ the 1-year rate of interest prevailing now (Period t)

$_{t+1}r_1 = 6\%$ the 1-year rate of interest expected to prevail next year (Period $t + 1$)

$_{t+2}r_1 = 7\frac{1}{2}\%$ the 1-year rate of interest expected to prevail 2 years from now (Period $t + 2$)

$_{t+3}r_1 = 8\frac{1}{2}\%$ the 1-year rate of interest expected to prevail 3 years from now (Period $t + 3$)

Using these values and the known rate on a one-year bond, we compute rates on two-, three-, or four-year bonds (designated R_2, R_3, and R_4) as follows:

$_tR_1 = 5\frac{1}{2}\%$
$_tR_2 = (0.055 + 0.06)/2 = 5.75\%$
$_tR_3 = (0.055 + 0.06 + 0.075)/3 = 6.33\%$
$_tR_4 = (0.055 + 0.06 + 0.075 + 0.085)/4 = 6.88\%$

In this illustration (using the arithmetic average as an approximation of the geometric mean), the yield curve is upward sloping because, at present, investors expect future short-term rates to be above current short-term rates. This is not the formal method for constructing the yield curve. Rather, the yield curve is constructed on the basis of the prevailing promised yields for bonds with different maturities.

The expectations hypothesis attempts to explain why the yield curve is upward sloping, downward sloping, humped, or flat by explaining the expectations implicit in yield curves with different shapes. The evidence is fairly substantial and convincing that the expectations hypothesis is a workable explanation of the term structure. Because of the supporting evidence, its relative simplicity, and the intuitive appeal of the theory, the expectations hypothesis of the term structure of interest rates is rather widely accepted.

Consistent Investor Actions Besides the theory and empirical support, it is also possible to present a scenario wherein investor actions will cause the yield curve postulated by the theory. The expectations hypothesis predicts a declining yield curve when interest rates are expected to fall in the future rather than rise. In a case of expected falling rates, long-term bonds would be considered attractive investments because investors would want to buy them to lock in prevailing higher yields (which are not expected to be as high in the future) or they would buy them to capture the increase in bond prices (as capital gains) that will accompany a decline in rates. By the same reasoning, investors will sell short-term bonds and reinvest the funds in long-term bonds that will experience larger price increases if rates decline. The point is, investor transactions will reinforce the declining shape of the yield curve as they bid up the prices of long-maturity bonds (forcing yields to decline) while short-term bond issues are sold (so prices decline and yields rise). At the same time, there is confirming action by suppliers of bonds. Specifically, government or corporate issuers will avoid selling long bonds at the current high rates, waiting until the rates decline. In the meantime, they will issue short-term bonds, if needed, while waiting for lower rates. Therefore, in the long-term market, we will have an increase in demand and a decline in the supply and vice versa in the short-term market. These shifts between long- and short-term maturities will continue until equilibrium occurs or expectations change.

12.5.2   LIQUIDITY PREFERENCE (TERM PREMIUM) HYPOTHESIS

The theory of liquidity preference holds that long-term securities should provide higher returns than short-term obligations because investors are willing to accept lower yields for short-maturity obligations to avoid the higher price volatility of long-maturity bonds. Another way to interpret the liquidity preference hypothesis is to say that lenders prefer short-term loans, and to induce them to invest in volatile long-term bonds, it is necessary to offer higher yields.

The liquidity preference (also called term premium) theory contends that uncertainty and volatility cause investors to favour short-term issues over bonds with longer maturities because short-term bonds are less volatile and can easily be converted into predictable amounts of cash should unforeseen events occur. This theory argues that the yield curve should generally slope upward and that any other shape should be viewed as a temporary aberration.

This theory can be considered an extension of the expectations hypothesis because the formal liquidity preference position contends that the liquidity premium inherent in the yields for longer maturity bonds should be added to the expected future rate in arriving at long-term yields. Specifically, the liquidity (or term) premium (L) compensates the investor in long-term bonds for the added volatility inherent in long-term bonds compared to short-maturity securities.

Because the liquidity premium (L) is provided to compensate the long-term investor, it is simply a variation of Equation 12.8 as follows:

$$(1 + {}_tR_N) = [(1 + {}_tR_1)(1 + {}_{t+1}r_1 + L_2) \ldots (1 + {}_{t+N-1}r_1 + L_N)]^{1/N}$$

In this specification, the Ls are not the same but would be expected to increase with maturity because the price volatility increases with maturity. The liquidity preference theory has been found to possess some strong empirical support by Kessel (1965), Cagan (1969), and McCulloch (1975).

To see how the liquidity preference theory predicts future yields and how it compares with the pure expectations hypothesis, let us predict future long-term rates from a single set of one-year rates: 6%, 7.5%, and 8.5%. The liquidity preference theory suggests that investors add increasing liquidity premiums to successive rates to derive actual market rates. As an example, they might arrive at rates of 6.3%, 7.9%, and 9.0%.

As a matter of historical fact, the yield curve shows an upward bias, which implies that some combination of the expectations theory and the liquidity preference theory will more accurately explain the shape of the yield curve than either of them alone. Specifically, actual long-term rates consistently tend to be above what is envisioned from the price expectations hypothesis. This tendency implies the existence of a liquidity (term) premium.

12.5.3 SEGMENTED MARKET HYPOTHESIS

A third theory for the shape of the yield curve is the segmented market hypothesis, which enjoys wide acceptance among market practitioners. Also known as the *preferred habitat*, the *institutional theory*, or the *hedging pressure theory*, it asserts that different institutional investors have different maturity needs that lead them to confine their security selections to specific maturity segments. That is, investors supposedly focus on short-, intermediate-, or long-term securities. This theory contends that the shape of the yield curve ultimately is a function of these investment policies of major financial institutions.

In its strongest form, the segmented market theory holds that the maturity preferences of investors and borrowers are so strong that investors never purchase securities outside their preferred maturity range to take advantage of yield differentials. As a result, the short- and long-maturity portions of the bond market are effectively segmented, and yields for a segment depend on the supply and demand *within* that maturity segment.

12.5.4 TRADING IMPLICATIONS OF THE TERM STRUCTURE AND YIELD SPREADS

Information on maturity yields can help us formulate yield expectations by simply observing the shape of the yield curve. If the yield curve is declining sharply, historical evidence suggests that interest rates will probably decline. Expectations theorists would suggest that we need to examine only the prevailing yield curve to predict the direction of interest rates in the future.

Based on these theories, bond investors use the prevailing yield curve to predict the shapes of future yield curves. Using this prediction and knowledge of current interest rates, investors can determine expected yield volatility by maturity sector. As suggested by Hourdouvelis (1988), the maturity segments that are expected to experience the greatest yield changes give the investor the largest potential price-change opportunities.

Another technique that helps bond investors make profitable trades is the analysis of *yield spreads*—the differences in promised yields between bond issues or segments of the market at any point in time. Such differences are specific to the particular issues or segments of the bond market. Thus yield spreads further shape the rates determined by the basic economic forces (*RFR* + *I*).

There are four major yield spreads:

1. Different *segments* of the bond market may have different yields. For example, pure government bonds will have lower yields than government agency bonds, and government bonds have much lower yields than corporate bonds.
2. Bonds in different *sectors* of the same market segment may have different yields. For example, high-grade municipal bonds will have lower yields than good-grade municipal bonds; we will find spreads between AA utilities and BBB utilities, or between AAA industrial bonds and AAA public utility bonds.
3. Different *coupons* or *seasoning* within a given market segment or sector may cause yield spreads. Examples include current coupon government bonds versus deep-discount governments or recently issued AA industrials versus seasoned AA industrials.
4. Different *maturities* within a given market segment or sector also cause differences in yields.

The differences among these bonds cause yield spreads that may be either positive or negative. More importantly, *the magnitude or the direction of a spread can change over time*. These changes in size or direction of yield spreads offer profit opportunities. We say that the spread narrows whenever the differences in yield become smaller; it widens as the differences increase.

12.6   What Determines the Price Volatility for Bonds?

Investing in Bonds is an education site on bonds created by the Securities Industry and Financial Markets Association. See http://www. investinginbonds.com.

In this chapter, we have learned about alternative bond yields, how to calculate them, what determines bond yields (interest rates), and what causes them to change. Now that we understand why yields change, we can logically ask: What is the effect of these yield changes on the prices and rates of return for different bonds? We have discussed the inverse relationship between changes in yields and the price of bonds, so we can now discuss the specific factors that affect the amount of price change for a yield change in different bonds.

A given change in interest rates can cause vastly different percentage price changes for alternative bonds, which implies different interest rate sensitivity. To maximize our return from an expected decline in interest rates, for example, we need to know which bonds will benefit the most from the yield change. This section helps us understand how to make this bond selection decision.

Throughout this section, we talk about bond price changes or bond price volatility interchangeably. **Bond price volatility** is measured as the percentage change in the price of the bond, computed as follows:

$$\frac{\text{EPB}}{\text{BPB}} - 1$$

where:
  EPB = the ending price of the bond
  BPB = the beginning price of the bond

A bond with high price volatility or high interest rate sensitivity is one that experiences a relatively large percentage price change for a given change in yields.

Bond price volatility is influenced by more than yield behaviour alone. Malkiel (1962) used the bond valuation model to demonstrate that the market price of a bond is a function of four factors: (1) its par value, (2) its coupon, (3) the number of years to its maturity, and (4) the prevailing market interest rate. Malkiel's mathematical proofs showed the following relationships between yield (interest rate) changes and bond price behaviour:

1. Bond prices move inversely to bond yields (interest rates).
2. For a given change in yields (interest rates), longer maturity bonds experience larger price changes; thus, bond price volatility is directly related to term to maturity.
3. Bond price volatility increases at a diminishing rate as term to maturity increases.
4. Bond price movements resulting from equal absolute increases or decreases in yield are not symmetrical. A decrease in yield raises bond prices by more than an increase in yield of the same amount lowers prices.
5. Higher coupon issues show smaller percentage price fluctuation for a given change in yield; thus, bond price volatility is inversely related to coupon.

12.6.1   TRADING STRATEGIES

Knowing that coupon and maturity are the major variables influencing a bond's interest rate sensitivity, we can develop some strategies for maximizing returns when interest rates change. Specifically, if we anticipate a drop in interest rates, we know that bond prices will increase, so we want a portfolio of bonds with the *maximum interest rate sensitivity* so that we will enjoy maximum price changes (capital gains) from the change in interest rates. Thus, in this situation, we would attempt to build a portfolio of low-coupon, long-maturity bonds (ideally a long-term zero coupon bond). A portfolio of such bonds should experience the maximum price appreciation for a given decline in market interest rates.

In contrast, if we expect market interest rates to rise, we want a portfolio with *minimum interest rate sensitivity* to minimize the capital losses caused by the increase in rates. Therefore, we would want to change our portfolio to short-maturity bonds with high coupons. This combination should provide minimal price volatility for a change in market interest rates.

12.6.2 DURATION MEASURES

Canadian Bond Rating: DBRS is a leading Canadian bond rating agency. Check it out at http://www.dbrs.com.

Because the price volatility (interest rate sensitivity) of a bond varies inversely with its coupon and directly with its term to maturity, it is necessary to determine the best combination of these two variables to achieve our objective. This effort would benefit from a composite measure that considered both coupon and maturity. A composite measure of the interest rate sensitivity of a bond is referred to as duration. **Macaulay duration**, developed about 70 years ago by Frederick Macaulay (1938), is a measure of the time flow of cash from a bond.

Macaulay Duration Macaulay showed that the duration of a bond was a more appropriate measure of time characteristics than the term to maturity of the bond because duration considers both the repayment of capital at maturity and the size and timing of coupon payments prior to final maturity. Using annual compounding, duration (D) is

12.11

$$D = \frac{\sum_{t=1}^{n} \dfrac{C_t(t)}{(1 + i)^t}}{\sum_{t=1}^{n} \dfrac{C_t}{(1 + i)^t}}$$

where:

t = the time period in which the coupon or principal payment occurs
C_t = the interest or principal payment that occurs in period t
i = the yield to maturity on the bond

The denominator in this equation is the price of a bond as determined by the present value model. The numerator is the present value of all cash flows *weighted according to the time to cash receipt*. The following example, which demonstrates the specific computations for two bonds, shows the procedure and highlights some of the properties of Macaulay duration. Consider the following two sample bonds:

	Bond A	Bond B
Face value	$1,000	$1,000
Maturity	10 years	10 years
Coupon	4%	8%

Assuming annual interest payments and an 8% yield to maturity on the bonds, duration is computed as shown in Exhibit 12.6.[7] If duration is calculated by discounting flows using the YTM of the bond, it is called *Macaulay duration*.

---

7 We assume annual interest payments to reduce the space requirements and computations. In practice we would assume semi-annual payments that would cause a slightly shorter duration since we receive half the payments earlier.

EXHIBIT 12.6	Computation of Macaulay Duration (Assuming 8% Market Yield)

BOND A

(1) Year	(2) Cash Flow	(3) PV at 8%	(4) PV of Flow	(5) PV as % of Price	(6) (1) × (5)
1	$ 40	0.9259	$ 37.04	0.0506	0.0506
2	40	0.8573	34.29	0.0469	0.0938
3	40	0.7938	31.75	0.0434	0.1302
4	40	0.7350	29.40	0.0402	0.1608
5	40	0.6806	27.22	0.0372	0.1860
6	40	0.6302	25.21	0.0345	0.2070
7	40	0.5835	23.34	0.0319	0.2233
8	40	0.5403	21.61	0.0295	0.2360
9	40	0.5002	20.01	0.0274	0.2466
10	1,040	0.4632	481.73	0.6585	6.5850
Sum			$731.58	1.0000	8.1193

Duration = 8.12 Years

BOND B

(1) Year	(2) Cash Flow	(3) PV at 8%	(4) PV of Flow	(5) PV as % of Price	(6) (1) × (5)
1	$ 80	0.9259	$ 74.07	0.0741	0.0741
2	80	0.8573	68.59	0.0686	0.1372
3	80	0.7938	63.50	0.0635	0.1906
4	80	0.7350	58.80	0.0588	0.1906
5	80	0.6806	54.44	0.0544	0.2720
6	80	0.6302	50.42	0.0504	0.3024
7	80	0.5835	46.68	0.0467	0.3269
8	80	0.5403	43.22	0.0432	0.3456
9	80	0.5002	40.02	0.0400	0.3600
10	1,080	0.4632	500.26	0.5003	5.0030
Sum			$1,000.00	1.0000	7.2470

Duration = 7.25 Years

Characteristics of Macaulay Duration This example illustrates several characteristics of Macaulay duration. First, the Macaulay duration of a bond with coupon payments always will be less than its term to maturity because duration gives weight to these interim interest payments.

Second, there is *an inverse relationship between coupon and duration.* A bond with a larger coupon will have a shorter duration because more of the total cash flows come earlier in the form of interest payments. As shown in Exhibit 12.6, the 8% coupon bond has a shorter duration than the 4% coupon bond.

A zero coupon bond or a pure discount bond, such as a T-bill, will have *duration equal to its term to maturity.* In Exhibit 12.6, if we assume a single payment at maturity, duration will equal term to maturity because the only cash flow comes in the final (maturity) year—that is, we receive 100% of cash flows in year n.

Third, there is *generally a positive relationship between term to maturity and Macaulay duration*, but duration increases at a decreasing rate with maturity. Therefore, a bond with longer term to maturity almost always will have a higher duration. The relationship is not direct because as maturity increases the present value of the principal declines in value.

As shown in Exhibit 12.7, the shape of the duration-maturity curve depends on the coupon and the yield to maturity. The curve for a zero coupon bond is a straight line, indicating that duration equals term to maturity. In contrast, the curve for a low-coupon bond selling at a deep discount (due to a high YTM) will turn down at long maturities, which means that under these conditions, the longer maturity bond will have lower duration because the discounted value of the principal payment becomes insignificant, which shifts the weight to the early interest payments, causing a decline in Macaulay duration.

Fourth, all else the same, there is an *inverse relationship between YTM and duration*. A higher yield to maturity of a bond reduces its duration. For example, in Exhibit 12.6, if the YTM had been 12% rather than 8%, the duration for the 4% bond would have gone from 8.12 to 7.75 and the duration of the 8% bond would have gone from 7.25 to 6.80.[8] The combined effect of the inverse relationships between duration and both coupon and yield can be seen with the curve for the bond with a 15% coupon and yield where the duration tops out at about six years. The real-world example of such a bond would be a high-yield bond.

Finally, sinking funds and call provisions can have a dramatic effect on a bond's duration. They can change the total cash flows for a bond and, therefore, significantly change its duration. Between these two factors, the factor that causes the greatest uncertainty is the call feature; it is difficult to estimate when the call option will be exercised because it is a function of changes in interest rates. We consider this further when we discuss the effect of embedded options on the duration and convexity of a bond.

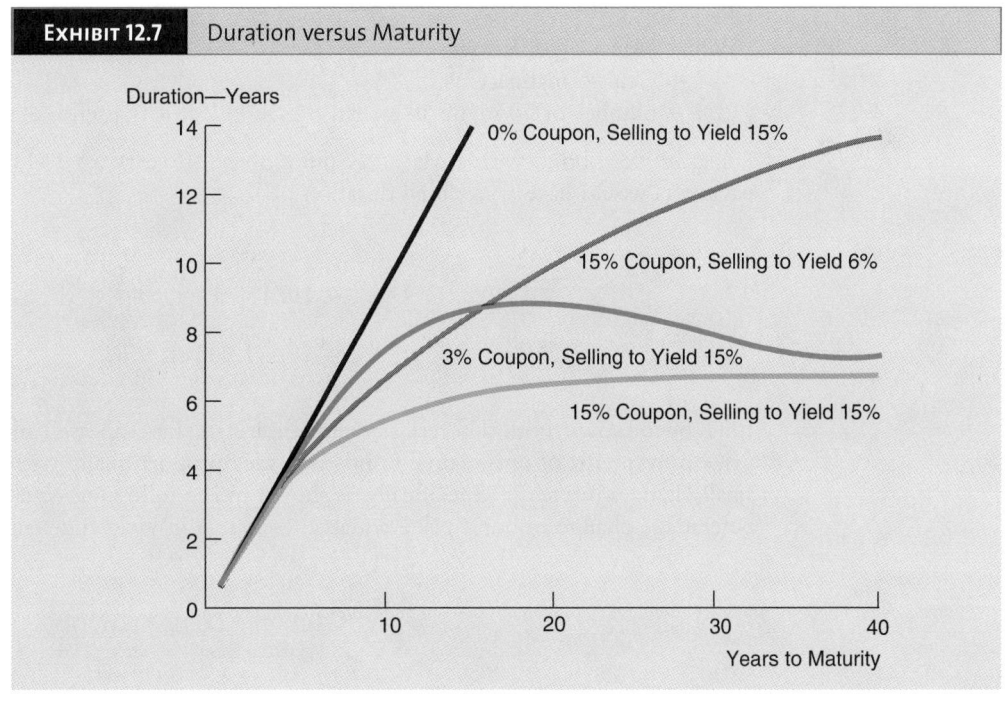

EXHIBIT 12.7 Duration versus Maturity

---

8 These properties are discussed and demonstrated in Reilly and Sidhu (1980) and Fabozzi, Buetow, and Johnson (2005).

A summary of Macaulay duration characteristics is as follows:

- The duration of a zero coupon bond will equal its term to maturity.
- The duration of a coupon bond always will be less than its term to maturity.
- There is an *inverse* relationship between coupon and duration.
- There is generally a *positive* relationship between term to maturity and duration. Note that the duration of a coupon bond increases at a decreasing rate with maturity and the shape of the duration/maturity curve will depend on the coupon and YTM of the bond. Also, the duration of a deep-discount bond will decline at very long maturities (over 20 years).
- There is an *inverse* relationship between yield to maturity and duration.
- Sinking funds and call provisions can cause a dramatic change in the duration of a bond. The effect of embedded options is discussed in a subsequent section.

12.6.3   MODIFIED DURATION AND BOND PRICE VOLATILITY

An adjusted measure of duration called *modified duration* can be used to approximate the interest rate sensitivity of an option-free (straight) bond. Modified duration, D_{mod}, equals Macaulay duration (computed in Exhibit 12.5) divided by 1 plus the current yield to maturity divided by the number of payments in a year.

$$D_{mod} = \frac{D}{1 + \dfrac{i}{m}}$$

where:

D = Macaulay duration
i = yield to maturity
m = number of payments in a year, e.g., $m = 2$ if it is a semi-annual bond

For example, a bond with a Macaulay duration of 10 years, a YTM of 8%, and semi-annual payments would have a modified duration of

$$D_{mod} = 10/\left(1 + \frac{0.08}{2}\right)$$
$$= 10/(1.04) = 9.62$$

It has been shown, both theoretically and empirically by Hopewell and Kaufman (1973), that price movements of option-free bonds will vary proportionally with modified duration for small changes in yields.[9] Specifically, as shown in the following equation, an estimate of the percentage change in bond price equals the change in yield times modified duration:

12.12
$$\frac{\Delta P}{P} \times 100 = -D_{mod} \times \Delta i$$

---

9 The importance of the specification "for small changes in yields" will become clear when we discuss convexity in the next section. Because modified duration is an approximate measure of interest rate sensitivity, the "years" label is not appropriate.

where:
$$\Delta P = \text{the change in price for the bond}$$
$$P = \text{the beginning price for the bond}$$
$$-D_{mod} = \text{the modified duration of the bond}$$
$$\Delta i = \text{the yield change in basis points divided by 100. For example, if interest rates}$$
go from 8.00% to 8.50%, $\Delta i = 50/100 = 0.50$.

Consider a bond with Macaulay $D = 8$ years and $i = 0.10$. Assume that we expect the bond's YTM to decline by 75 basis points (e.g., from 10% to 9.25%). The first step is to compute the bond's modified duration as follows:

$$D_{mod} = 8/\left(1 + \frac{0.10}{2}\right)$$
$$= 8/(1.05) = 7.62$$

The estimated percentage change in the price of the bond using Equation 12.12 is:

$$\%\Delta P = -(7.62) \times \frac{-75}{100}$$
$$= (-7.62) \times (-0.75)$$
$$= 5.72$$

This indicates that the bond price should increase by approximately 5.72% in response to the 75 basis point decline in YTM. If the price of the bond before the decline in interest rates was $900, the price after the decline in interest rates should be approximately $900 × 1.0572 = $951.48.

The modified duration is always a negative value for a non-callable bond because of the inverse relationship between yield changes and bond price changes. Also, remember that this formulation provides an *estimate* or *approximation* of the percent change in the price of the bond. The following section on convexity shows that this formula that uses only modified duration provides an exact estimate of the percentage price change only for very small changes in yields of option-free securities.

Trading Strategies Using Modified Duration We know that the longest duration security provides the maximum price variation. Exhibit 12.8 demonstrates that numerous ways exist to achieve a given level of duration. The following discussion indicates that an active bond investor who wants to adjust his/her portfolio for anticipated interest rate changes can use this measure of interest rate sensitivity to structure a portfolio to take advantage of changes in market yields.

If we expect a *decline* in interest rates, we should *increase* the average modified duration of our bond portfolio to experience maximum price volatility. If we expect an *increase* in interest rates, we should *reduce* the average modified duration of our portfolio to minimize our price decline. Note that the modified duration of our portfolio is the market-value-weighted average of the modified durations of the individual bonds in the portfolio.

EXHIBIT 12.8	Bond Duration in Years for Bond Yielding 6% under Different Terms			
	Coupon Rates			
Years to Maturity	**0.02**	**0.04**	**0.06**	**0.08**
1	0.995	0.990	0.985	0.981
2	4.756	4.558	4.393	4.254
10	8.891	8.169	7.662	7.286
20	14.981	12.980	11.904	11.232
50	19.452	17.129	16.273	15.829
100	17.567	17.232	17.120	17.064
∞	17.167	17.167	17.167	17.167

Source: L. Fisher and R. L. Weil, "Coping with the Risk of Interest Rate Fluctuations: Returns to Bondholders from Naive and Final Strategies," *Journal of Business* 44, no. 4 (October 1971): University of Chicago Press. Reprinted by permission of the University of Chicago Press.

12.6.4   BOND CONVEXITY

Modified duration allows us to estimate bond price changes for a change in interest rates. However, the equation we used to make this calculation (Equation 12.12) is accurate only for *very small changes* in market yields. We will see that the accuracy of the estimate of the price change deteriorates with larger changes in yields because the modified duration calculation is a *linear* approximation of a bond price change that follows a *curvilinear* (convex) function. To understand the effect of this *convexity*, we must consider the price-yield relationship for alternative bonds.[10]

The Price-Yield Relationship for Bonds Because the price of a bond is the present value of its cash flows at a particular discount rate, we can calculate its price at a point in time. The price-yield curve provides a set of prices for a specific maturity/coupon bond at a point in time using a range of yields to maturity. Exhibit 12.9 lists the computed prices for a 12%, 20-year bond assuming yields from 1% to 12%. Discounting the flows from this bond at a yield of 1%, we would get a price of $2,989.47; discounting these same flows at 10% gives a price of $1,171.59. The graph of these prices relative to the yields that produced them (Exhibit 12.10) shows that the price-yield relationship for this bond is not a straight line but is curvilinear or convex.

Three points are important about the price-yield relationship:

1. This relationship can be applied to a single bond, a portfolio of bonds, or any stream of future cash flows.
2. The convex price-yield relationship will differ among bonds or other cash flow streams, depending on the nature of the cash flow stream, that is, its coupon and maturity. For example, the price-yield relationship for a high-coupon, short-term security will be almost a straight line because the price does not change as much for a change in yields (e.g., the 12%, three-year bond in Exhibit 12.9). In contrast, the price-yield relationship for a low-coupon, long-term bond will curve radically (i.e., be very convex), as shown by the zero coupon, 30-year bond in Exhibit 12.9. These differences in convexity are shown graphically in Exhibit 12.11. The curved nature of the price-yield relationship is referred to as the bond's convexity.

---

10   For a further discussion of this topic, see Dunetz and Mahoney (1988) and Fabozzi, Buetow, and Johnson (2005).

Exhibit 12.9	Price Yield Relationships for Alternative Bonds				
A. 12%, 20 Year		**B. 12%, 3 Year**		**C. Zero Coupon, 30 Year**	
Yield	Price	Yield	Price	Yield	Price
1.0%	$2,989.47	1.0%	$1,324.30	1.0%	$741.37
2.0	2,641.73	2.0	1,289.77	2.0	550.45
3.0	2,346.21	3.0	1,256.37	3.0	409.30
4.0	2,094.22	4.0	1,224.06	4.0	304.78
5.0	1,878.60	5.0	1,192.78	5.0	227.28
6.0	1,693.44	6.0	1,162.52	6.0	169.73
7.0	1,533.88	7.0	1,133.21	7.0	126.93
8.0	1,395.86	8.0	1,104.84	8.0	95.06
9.0	1,276.02	9.0	1,077.37	9.0	71.29
10.0	1,171.59	10.0	1,050.76	10.0	53.54
11.0	1,080.23	11.0	1,024.98	11.0	40.26
12.0	1,000.00	12.0	1,000.00	12.0	30.31

Exhibit 12.10	Price-Yield Relationship and Modified Duration at 4% Yield

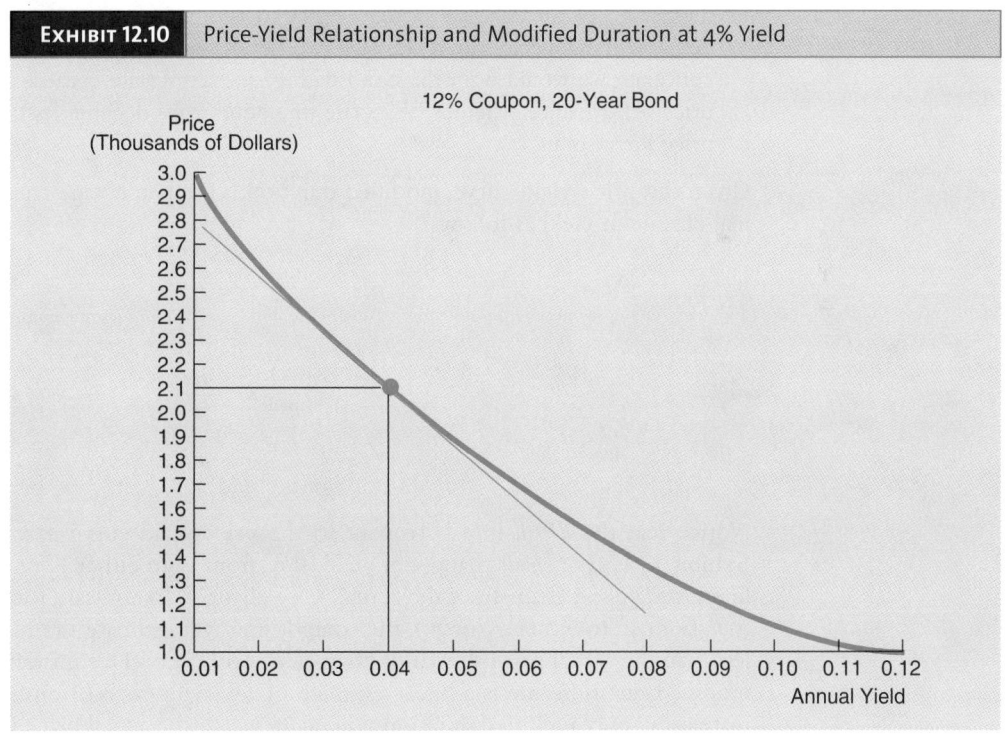

3. As shown by the graph in Exhibit 12.11, because of the convexity of the price-yield relationship (especially the long-term, zero coupon bond) as yield increases, the rate at which the price of the bond declines becomes slower. Similarly, when yields decline, the rate at which the price of the bond increases becomes faster. Therefore, convexity is considered a

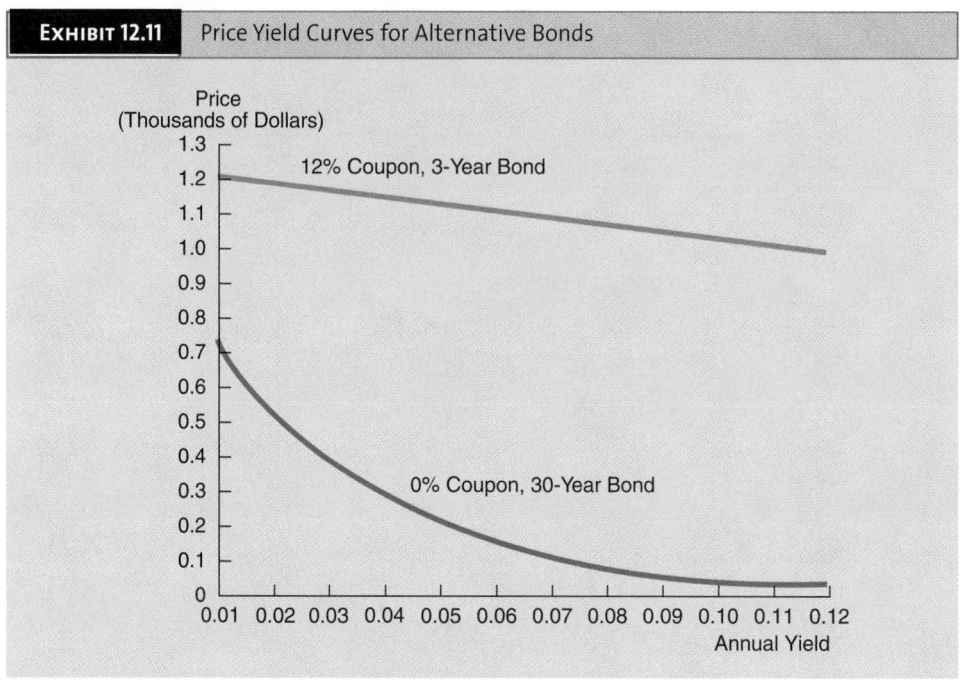

EXHIBIT 12.11 Price Yield Curves for Alternative Bonds

desirable trait. Specifically, if we have two bonds with equal duration but one has greater convexity, we would want the bond with greater convexity because it would have better price performance whether yields rise (the bond price declines less) or yields fall (the bond price increases more).

Given this price-yield curve, modified duration is the percentage change in price for a nominal change in yield as follows:[11]

12.13

$$D_{mod} = \frac{\dfrac{dP}{di}}{P}$$

Notice that the dP/di line is tangent to the price-yield curve *at a given yield* as shown in Exhibit 12.12. For *small* changes in yields (i.e., from $\gamma^\star$ to either γ_1 or γ_2), this tangent straight line gives a good estimate of the actual price changes. In contrast, for larger changes in yields (i.e., from $\gamma^\star$ to either γ_3 or γ_4), the straight line will estimate the new price of the bond at less than the actual price shown by the price-yield curve. This misestimate arises because the modified-duration line is a linear estimate of a curvilinear relationship. Specifically, the estimate using only modified duration will *underestimate* the actual price *increase* caused by a yield decline and *overestimate* the actual price *decline* caused by an increase in yields. This graph, which demonstrates the convexity effect, also shows that price changes are *not* symmetric

---

11 In mathematical terms, modified duration is the first differential of this price-yield relationship with respect to yield.

EXHIBIT 12.12	Price Approximation Using Modified Duration

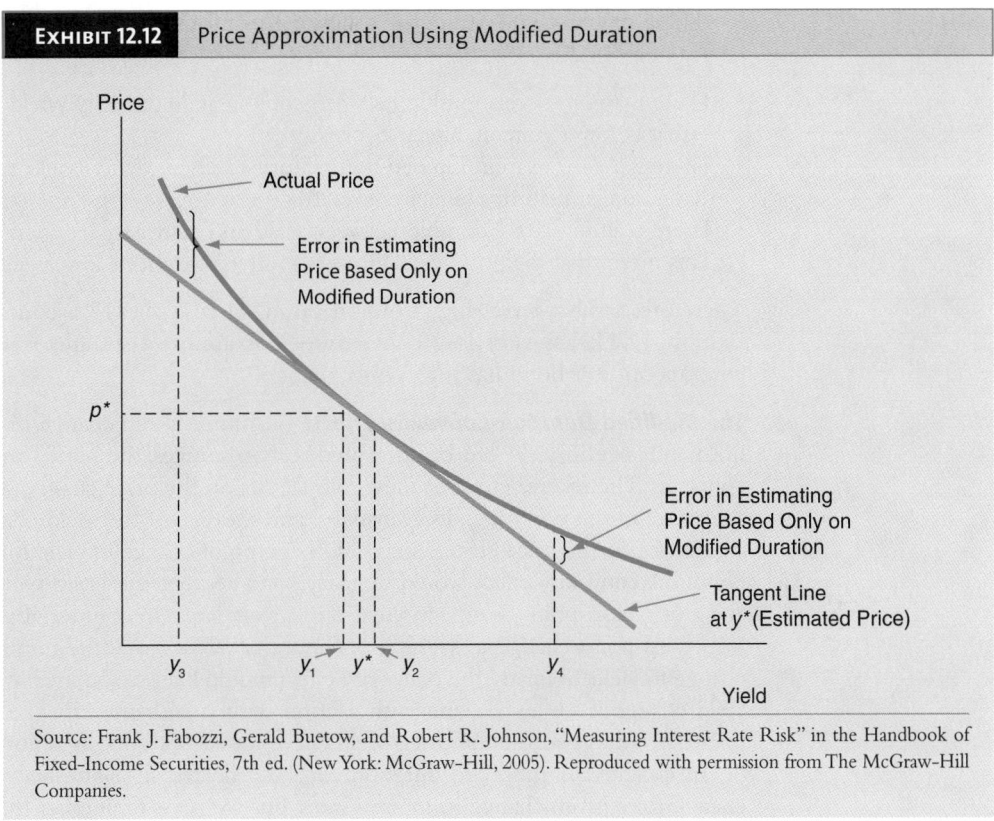

Source: Frank J. Fabozzi, Gerald Buetow, and Robert R. Johnson, "Measuring Interest Rate Risk" in the Handbook of Fixed-Income Securities, 7th ed. (New York: McGraw-Hill, 2005). Reproduced with permission from The McGraw-Hill Companies.

when yields increase or decrease. As shown, when rates decline, there is a larger price error than when rates increase because, due to convexity, when yields decline prices rise at an *increasing* rate, while prices decline at a *decreasing* rate when yields rise.

Determinants of Convexity Convexity is a measure of the curvature of the price–yield relationship. In turn, because modified duration is the slope of the curve at a given yield, convexity indicates changes in duration. Mathematically, convexity is the second derivative of price with respect to yield (d^2P/di^2) divided by price. Specifically, convexity is the percentage change in dP/di for a given change in yield:

12.14

$$\text{Convexity} = \frac{\dfrac{d^2P}{di^2}}{P}$$

Convexity is a measure of how much a bond's price–yield curve deviates from the linear approximation of that curve. As indicated by Exhibit 12.10 and Exhibit 12.12 for *non-callable* bonds, convexity always is a positive number, implying that the price–yield curve lies above the modified-duration (tangent) line. Exhibit 12.11 illustrates the price–yield relationship for two bonds with very different coupons and maturities (yields and prices are shown in Exhibit 12.9).

These graphs demonstrate the following relationship between these factors and the convexity of a bond:

- There is an *inverse* relationship between coupon and convexity (yield and maturity constant)—that is, lower coupon, higher convexity.
- There is a *direct* relationship between maturity and convexity (yield and coupon constant)—that is, longer maturity, higher convexity.
- There is an *inverse* relationship between yield and convexity (coupon and maturity constant). This means that the price-yield curve is more convex at its lower yield (upper left) segment.

Therefore, a short-term, high-coupon bond, such as the 12% coupon, three-year bond in Exhibit 12.11, has very low convexity—it is almost a straight line. In contrast, the zero coupon, 30-year bond has high convexity.

The Modified-Duration-Convexity Effects In summary, the change in a bond's price resulting from a change in yield can be attributed to two sources: the bond's modified duration and its convexity. The relative effect of these two factors on the price change will depend on the characteristics of the bond (i.e., its convexity) and the size of the yield change. For example, if we are estimating the price change for a 300-basis-point change in yield for a zero coupon, 30-year bond, the convexity effect would be fairly large because this bond would have high convexity, and a 300-basis-point change in yield is relatively large. In contrast, if we are dealing with only a 10-basis-point change in yields, the convexity effect would be minimal because it is a small change in yield. Similarly, the convexity effect would likewise be small even if we assume a larger yield change if we are dealing with a bond with small convexity (i.e., a high-coupon, short-maturity bond) because the price-yield curve for such a bond is almost a straight line.

In conclusion, modified duration can help derive an *approximate* percentage bond price change for a given change in interest rates, but we must remember that it is only a good estimate when considering small yield changes. We must also consider the convexity effect on price change when we are dealing with large yield changes and/or when the securities or cash flows have high convexity.

Calculation of Convexity The formula for calculating the convexity of a stream of cash flows looks fairly complex, but it can be broken down into manageable steps. Recall from our convexity equation (12.14) that

$$\text{Convexity} = \frac{d^2P/di^2}{P}$$

In turn,

12.15
$$\frac{d^2P/di^2}{P} = \frac{1}{(1+i)^2}\left[\sum_{t=1}^{n}\frac{CF_t}{(1+i)}(t_2+t)\right]$$

Exhibit 12.13 contains the computations related to this calculation for a 3-year bond with a 12% coupon and 9% YTM assuming annual flows.

The convexity for this bond is very low because it has a short maturity, high coupon, and high yield. Note that the *convexity of a security will vary along the price-yield curve*. We will

EXHIBIT 12.13	Calculation of Convexity

$$\text{Convexity} = \frac{d^2P/di^2}{PV \text{ of Cash Flows}} = \frac{d^2P/di^2}{\text{Price}}$$

$$\frac{d^2P}{di^2} = \frac{1}{(1+i)^2}\left[\sum_{t=1}^{n}(t^2+t)\frac{CF_t}{(1+i)^t}\right]$$

$$\text{Convexity} = \frac{d^2P/di^2}{\text{Price}}$$

Example: 3-Year Bond, 12% Coupon, 9% YTM

(1) Year	(2) CFt	(3) PV @ 9%	(4) PV CF	(5) $t^2 + t$	(4)×(5)
1	120	0.9174	$ 110.09	2	$ 220.18
2	120	0.8417	101.00	6	606.00
3	120	0.7722	92.66	12	1,111.92
4	1,000	0.7722	772.20	12	9,266.40
			Price = $1,075.95		$11,204.50

$$\frac{1}{(1+i)^2} = \frac{1}{(1.09)^2} = \frac{1}{1.19} = 0.84$$

$$\$11,204.50 \times 0.84 = \$9,411.78$$

$$\text{Convexity} = \frac{9,411.78}{1,075.95} = 8.75$$

get a different convexity at a 3% yield than at a 12% yield. In terms of the calculation, the maturity and coupon will be the same, but we will use a different discount rate that reflects where we are on the curve. This is similar to the earlier observation that we will get *a different modified duration at different points on the price-yield curve because the slope* varies along the curve. We also can see this mathematically because, depending on where we are on the curve, we will be using a different market yield, and the Macaulay and modified durations are inverse to the discount rate.[12]

To compute the price change attributable to the convexity effect after we know the bond's convexity, use this equation:

12.16	**Price change due to convexity** $= \frac{1}{2} \times$ **price** $\times$ **convexity** $\times$ $(\Delta$ **in yield**$)^2$

Exhibit 12.14 shows the change in bond price considering the duration effect and the convexity effect for an 18-year bond with a 12% coupon and 9% YTM. For demonstration purposes, we assumed a decline of 100 and 300 basis points in rates.

---

12 Exhibit 12A.1 in the appendix to this chapter is a table that combines the computation of Macaulay and modified duration and convexity using semi-annual cash flows.

Exhibit 12.14	Analysis of Bond Price Change Considering Duration and Convexity

Example: 18–Year Bond, 12% Coupon, 9% YTM
Price: 126.50
Modified Duration: 8.38 (D^*)
Convexity: 107.70
Estimate of Price Change Using Duration:
  Percent Δ Price $= D^* (\Delta$ in YLD/100)
Estimate of Price Change from Convexity:
  Price Change $= \frac{1}{2} \times$ Price $\times$ Convexity $\times (\Delta$ in YLD$)^2$

A. Change in Yield: -100 BP

  Duration Change: $-8.38 \times \left(\dfrac{-100}{100} \right) = +8.38\%$

            $+8.38\% \times 126.50 = +10.60$

  Convexity Change: $\dfrac{1}{2} \times (126.50) \times 107.70 \times (0.01)^2$

            $= 63.25 \times 107.70 \times 0.0001$

            $= 6{,}812.03 \times 0.0001 = 0.68$

  Combined Effect: 126.50

            $\dfrac{+10.60}{137.10}$ (Duration)

            $\dfrac{0.68}{137.78}$ (Convexity)

B. Change in Yield: -300 BP

  Duration Change: $-8.38 \times \left(\dfrac{-300}{100} \right) = +25.14\%$

            $126.50 \times 1.2514 = 158.30 (+31.80)$

  Convexity Effect: $\dfrac{1}{2} \times (126.50) \times 107.70 \times (0.03)^2$

            $6{,}812.03 \times 0.0009 = 6.11$

  Combined Effect: 126.50

            $\dfrac{+131.80}{158.30}$ (Duration)

            $\dfrac{+6.11}{164.41}$ (Convexity)

With the 300-basis-point change, if we considered only the modified-duration effect, we would have estimated that the bond went from 126.50 to 158.30 (a 25.14% increase), when, in fact, the actual price is closer to 164.41, which is about a *30% increase*.

Bonds with Embedded Options The discussions in this chapter have focused on bonds without embedded options. A callable bond is an example of a bond with an option for the issuer to call the bond when certain conditions met. The embedded option will significantly change the duration and convexity of the bond.[13]

---

[13] For a discussion of embedded options, see Chapter 18 of Reilly, Frank, and Keith Brown (2009), *Investment Analysis and Portfolio Management,* 9th ed., South-Western. For a further discussion of the effect of these embedded options, see Fabozzi, Buetow, and Johnson (2005) and Fabozzi, Kalotay, and Williams (2005). Also see Winkelmann (1989).

Summary

1. There are five bond yield measures: nominal yield, current yield, promised yield to maturity, promised yield to call, and realized (horizon) yield.
2. The yield curve (or the term structure of interest rates) shows the relationship between the yields on a set of comparable bonds and the term to maturity. Yield curves exhibit four basic patterns. Three theories attempt to explain the shape of the yield curve: the expectations hypothesis, the liquidity preference (term premium) hypothesis, and the segmented market (preferred habitat) hypothesis.
3. It is important to understand what causes changes in interest rates and how these changes in rates affect the prices of bonds. Differences in bond price volatility are mainly a function of differences in yield, coupon, and term to maturity.
4. Duration is a tool to capture the relationship between yield and bond price. The Macaulay duration measure incorporates coupon, maturity, and yield in one measure. Modified duration (which is directly related to Macaulay duration) provides an estimate of the response of bond prices to changes in interest rates under certain assumptions.
5. The concept of a convex price-yield curve is referred to as convexity. If we have two bonds with equal duration but one has greater convexity, we would want the bond with greater convexity because it would have better price performance whether yields rise (the bond price declines less) or yields fall (the bond price increases more).
6. Because duration provides a straight-line estimate of the curvilinear price-yield function, we must consider duration together with the convexity of a bond for large changes in yields and/or when dealing with securities that have high convexity.

Key Terms

bond price volatility, p. 340
crossover price, p. 324
current yield, p. 322
ending-wealth value, p. 323

interest-on-interest, p. 322
internal rate of return (IRR), p. 321
Macaulay duration, p. 341
net present value (NPV), p. 321

nominal yield, p. 321
promised yield to call (YTC), p. 324
promised yield to maturity (YTM), p. 322
realized yield (or horizon yield), p. 325

Suggested Readings

Deaves, Richard. "Forecasting Canadian Short-Term Interest Rates." *Canadian Journal of Economics* 29, no. 3 (1996): 615–634.

Eavis, Peter. "Time for Fannie, Freddie?" *The Wall Street Journal,* July 8, 2008, C14.

Fabozzi, Frank J. *Bond Markets, Analysis and Strategies,* 5th ed. Upper Saddle River, NJ: 2004.

Fabozzi, Frank J. *Fixed-Income Analysis,* 2nd ed. Hoboken, NJ: John Wiley & Sons, 2007.

Fabozzi, Frank J. *Fixed-Income Mathematics.* Chicago: Probus, 1988.

Fama, Eugene F. "Forward Rates as Predictors of Future Spot Rates." *Journal of Financial Economics* 3, no. 4 (October 1976).

Hagerty, James R., and Serena Ng, "Mortgage Giants Take Beating on Fears over Loan Defaults," *The Wall Street Journal,* July 8, 2008, A1, A14.

Homer, Sidney, and Martin L. Leibowitz. *Inside the Yield Book.* New York: Bloomberg Publishing, 2004.

Miller, Victoria. "Inflation Uncertainty and Optimal Debt Maturity: An Empirical Look at Canadian and U.S. Government Bonds." *Canadian Journal of Administrative* Sciences 14, no. 3 (1997): 246–258.

Sundaresan, Suresh. *Fixed Income Markets and Their Derivates,* 2nd ed. Cincinnati, OH: South-Western, 2002.

Tuckman, Bruce, *Fixed-Income Securities,* 2nd ed. New York: John Wiley & Sons, 2002.

CFA **For Chapter CFA Questions and Problems, please see Appendix A at the end of this text.**

Questions

1. Why does the present value equation appear to be more useful for the bond investor than for the common stock investor?
2. What are the important assumptions made when we calculate the promised yield to maturity? What are the assumptions when calculating promised YTC?
3. a. Define the variables included in the following model:
   $i = (RFR, I, RP)$
   b. Assume that the firm whose bonds you are considering is not expected to break even this year.
   c. Discuss which factor will be affected by this information.
4. We discussed three alternative hypotheses to explain the term structure of interest rates. Briefly discuss the three hypotheses and indicate which one you think best explains the alternative shapes of a yield curve.
5. You expect interest rates to decline over the next six months.
   a. Given our interest rate outlook, state what kinds of bonds you want in our portfolio in terms of duration and explain our reasoning for this choice.
   b. You must make a choice between the following three sets of non-callable bonds. For each set, select the bond that would be best for our portfolio given our interest rate outlook and the consequent strategy set forth in Part a. In each case briefly discuss why you selected the bond.

		Maturity	Coupon	Yield to Maturity
Set 1:	Bond A	15 years	10%	10%
	Bond B	15 years	6%	8%
Set 2:	Bond C	15 years	6%	10%
	Bond D	10 years	8%	10%
Set 3:	Bond E	12 years	12%	12%
	Bond F	15 years	12%	8%

6. At the present time, you expect a decline in interest rates and must choose between two portfolios of bonds with the following characteristics:

	Portfolio A	Portfolio B
Average maturity	10.5 years	10.0 years
Average YTM	7%	10%
Modified duration	5.7 years	4.9 years
Modified convexity	125.18	40.30
Call features	Non-callable	Deferred call features that range from 1 to 3 years

Select one of the portfolios and discuss three factors that would justify your selection.

7. The Francesca Finance Corporation has issued a bond with the following characteristics:
   Maturity—25 years
   Coupon—9%
   Yield to maturity—9%
   Callable—after 3 years @ 109
   Duration to maturity—8.2 years
   Duration to first call—2.1 years
   a. Discuss the concept of call-adjusted duration and indicate the approximate value (range) for it at the present time.
   b. Assuming interest rates increase substantially (i.e., they increase to 13%), discuss what will happen to the call-adjusted duration and the reason for the change.
   c. Assuming interest rates decline substantially (i.e., they decline to 4%), discuss what will happen to the bond's call-adjusted duration and the reason for the change.
   d. Discuss the concept of negative convexity as it relates to this bond.

Problems

1. Four years ago, your firm issued $1,000 par, 25-year bonds, with a 7% coupon rate and a 10% call premium.
   a. If these bonds are now called, what is the *approximate* yield to call for the investors who originally purchased them?
   b. If these bonds are now called, what is the *actual* yield to call for the investors who originally purchased them at par?
   c. If the current interest rate is 5% and the bonds were not callable, at what price would each bond sell?
2. Assume that you purchased an 8%, 20-year, $1,000 par, semi-annual payment bond priced at $1,012.50 when it has 12 years remaining until maturity. Compute:
   a. Its promised yield to maturity.
   b. Its yield to call if the bond is callable in three years with an 8% premium.

3. Calculate the duration of an 8%, $1,000 par bond that matures in three years if the bond's YTM is 10% and interest is paid semi-annually.
   a. Calculate this bond's modified duration.
   b. Assuming the bond's YTM goes from 10% to 9.5%, calculate an estimate of the price change.
4. Two years ago, you acquired a 10-year zero coupon, $1,000 par value bond at a 12% YTM. Recently you sold this bond at an 8% YTM. Using semi-annual compounding, compute the annualized horizon return for this investment.
5. A bond for the Chelle Corporation has the following characteristics:

   Maturity—12 years
   Coupon—10%

   Yield to maturity—9.50%
   Macaulay duration—5.7 years
   Convexity—48
   Non-callable

   a. Calculate the approximate price change for this bond using only its duration assuming its yield to maturity increased by 150 basis points. Discuss the impact of the calculation, including the convexity effect.
   b. Calculate the approximate price change for this bond (using only its duration) if its yield to maturity declined by 300 basis points. Discuss (without calculations) what would happen to your estimate of the price change if this was a callable bond.

EXHIBIT 12A.1	Calculation of Duration and Convexity for an 8% Five-Year Bond Selling to Yield 6%				
Period	Cash Flow	Discount Factor	PV	$PV \times t$	$PV \times t \times (t + 1)$
1	40.00	0.9709	38.83	38.83	77.67
2	40.00	0.9426	37.70	75.41	226.22
3	40.00	0.9151	36.61	109.82	439.27
4	40.00	0.8885	35.54	142.16	710.79
5	40.00	0.8626	34.50	172.52	1,035.13
6	40.00	0.8375	33.50	201.00	1,406.97
7	40.00	0.8131	32.52	227.67	1,821.32
8	40.00	0.7894	31.58	252.61	2,273.50
9	40.00	0.7664	30.66	275.91	2,759.10
10	1,040.00	0.7441	773.86	7,738.58	85,124.34
		Total	1,085.30	9,234.50	95,874.32

$$\text{Macaulay Duration} = \frac{9,234.50}{2 \times 1,085.30} = 4.25$$

$$\text{Macaulay Duration} = \frac{4.25}{1.03} = 4.13$$

$$\text{Convexity} = \frac{95,874.32}{(1.03)^2 \times 2^2 \times 1,085.30} = 20.82$$

Derivative Security Analysis

In recent years, it has been difficult to read the newspaper without encountering at least a passing reference to a scandal attributed to trading in derivative securities. Procter & Gamble's ill-fated swap transactions and the equity index futures trades that brought down Barings Bank give the casual reader the impression that derivatives are highly volatile instruments used only by those investors interested in placing speculative "bets." Of course, nothing could be further from the truth. Although it is true that the companies in these examples either miscalculated or misunderstood the nature of their investment positions, the vast majority of derivative transactions are used by individuals and institutions seeking to reduce the risk exposures generated by their other business ventures.

Derivatives, in their many forms, have become a vital part of modern security markets, trailing only stocks and bonds in terms of importance. Unlike stocks and bonds, however, their widespread use is a relatively recent phenomenon; and misconceptions still exist about how derivatives work and the proper way for investors to trade them. The chapters in this part address this concern by providing the investor with a framework for understanding how derivatives are valued and used in practice. Chapter 13 begins this process by detailing the mechanics of the two basic forms of derivative contract—*forwards* and *options*. After providing an initial description of these instruments and the markets in which they trade, we present the fundamental principles that determine their prices. The chapter concludes with several specific examples of how investors use derivatives to adjust the risk-return characteristics of their stock and bond portfolios.

Chapter 14 further analyzes forward and futures contracts with particular emphasis on the creation of (and subsequent adjustments to) margin accounts and the concept of basis risk. In addition, the calculation of the optimal hedge ratio and the arbitrage-free approach to determining the contract delivery price are discussed along with an examination of some of the features that are designed to offset financial (as opposed to commodity) risk exposures, including interest rate, equity, and currency price movements. The chapter also includes a formal treatment of how option contracts are valued starting with the simple two-state option pricing model and ending with Black-Scholes model. In this development, special attention is paid to the role that price volatility plays in the valuation process.

Lastly, we consider applications involving interest rates, equity prices, and credit risk, along with a discussion of the fundamentals of warrants, convertible securities, and structured notes. The emphasis of this discussion is on the optionlike features of these instruments and how they alter the risk-return dynamics of traditional debt and equity products. We conclude the chapter with a brief discussion of how understanding *real options* can help investors value certain types of complex investments that have embedded derivative-like features, such as oil fields or gold mines.

13

An Introduction to Derivative Markets and Securities

After you read this chapter, you should be able to answer the following questions:

1. What distinguishes a derivative security from more fundamental securities, such as stocks and bonds?

2. What are the important characteristics of forward, futures, and option contracts, and in what sense can they be interpreted as insurance policies?

3. What terminology is used to describe derivative market transactions?

4. What are the similarities and differences between forward and futures contracts?

5. How can derivatives be used in conjunction with stock and Treasury bills to replicate the payoffs to other securities and create arbitrage opportunities for an investor?

6. How do investors use options with the underlying security or in combination with one another to create tailored payoff structures?

7. What differentiates a spread from a straddle, a strangle, or a forward range?

So far, we have seen several ways in which individuals and institutions can design their investments to take advantage of future market conditions. We have also seen how investors can control the volatility associated with their stock and bond positions—at least in part—by forming well-diversified portfolios of securities, thereby reducing or eliminating the unsystematic component of a security's risk.

In this chapter, we begin our investigation of the role played by **derivative securities** in modern investment portfolios. A derivative instrument is one for which the ultimate payoff to the investor depends directly on the value of another security or commodity. Earlier in the text, we briefly described two basic types of derivatives: (1) forward and futures contracts and (2) option contracts.

The growth of the markets in which derivative securities are created and exchanged has been nothing short of phenomenal. The last few decades have seen the emergence of contracts to trade such fundamental products as agricultural commodities, energy, precious metals, currencies, common stock, and bonds. There are even derivatives to trade hypothetical underlying assets (e.g., stock indexes) as well as combination derivatives, such as option contracts that allow the investor to decide at a later date to enter into a futures contract involving another security or commodity. Interest rate swaps, which will be shown in Chapter 14 to be forward contracts on a short-term borrowing or lending rate, are a good example of the prodigious growth of these markets. Starting with the first swap in 1981, the volume of swap market activity had grown in size to almost $200 trillion by 2006.

As we will see, derivative securities can be used by investors in the same way as the underlying assets; an investor believing that a certain common stock will increase in value can benefit from either a purchase of the stock directly or with an option to purchase that stock at a predetermined price. The exact returns will not be equal for these two alternatives, but both will gain from an upward movement in the stock's price. Ultimately, however, the real key to understanding how and why derivatives are used lies in their ability to modify the risk and expected return characteristics of existing investment portfolios. That is, options and futures allow investors to **hedge** (or even increase) the risk of a portfolio in ways that go far beyond the diversification results discussed in the preceding chapters. We will see that derivative securities also allow for the duplication of cash flow patterns that already exist in other forms, thereby creating the possibility of **arbitrage** if two otherwise identical series of cash flows do not carry the same current price.

The balance of this chapter describes the fundamental nature and uses of forward, futures, and option contracts on common stock and bonds.

13.1 Overview of Derivative Markets

As with any financial product, derivatives have a specific terminology that must be understood in order to use these instruments effectively. Unlike many other securities, however, the language used to describe derivatives is often a confusing blend of jargon drawn from the equity, debt, and insurance markets with some unique expressions thrown in for good measure.

Before we examine the relevant details of each contract, we need to understand the basic types of positions available; these are highlighted in Exhibit 13.1. At the broadest level, there are two kinds of derivatives available: (1) forward and futures contracts, and (2) option contracts. While only one forward contract is needed for any particular maturity date and underlying asset, there must be two types of options—calls and puts—in order to offer investors a full range of choices. Finally, an investor can have a long position (i.e., the buyer) or a short position (i.e., the seller).

Recognize that every derivative arrangement that investors might hold in their portfolios can be viewed in terms of one of these six positions, or as a combination of these positions.

13.1.1 THE LANGUAGE AND STRUCTURE OF FORWARD AND FUTURES MARKETS

The most basic derivative product is the **forward contract**. Generally, a forward contract gives its holder both *the right and the full obligation* to conduct a transaction involving another security or commodity—the underlying asset—at a predetermined future date and at a predetermined price. The future date on which the transaction is to be consummated is called the contract's *maturity* (or *expiration*) *date*, while the predetermined price at which the trade takes place is the forward **contract price**. There must always be two parties (sometimes called **counterparties**) to a forward transaction: the eventual buyer (or **long position**), who pays the contract price and receives the underlying security, and the eventual seller (or **short position**), who delivers the security for the fixed price.

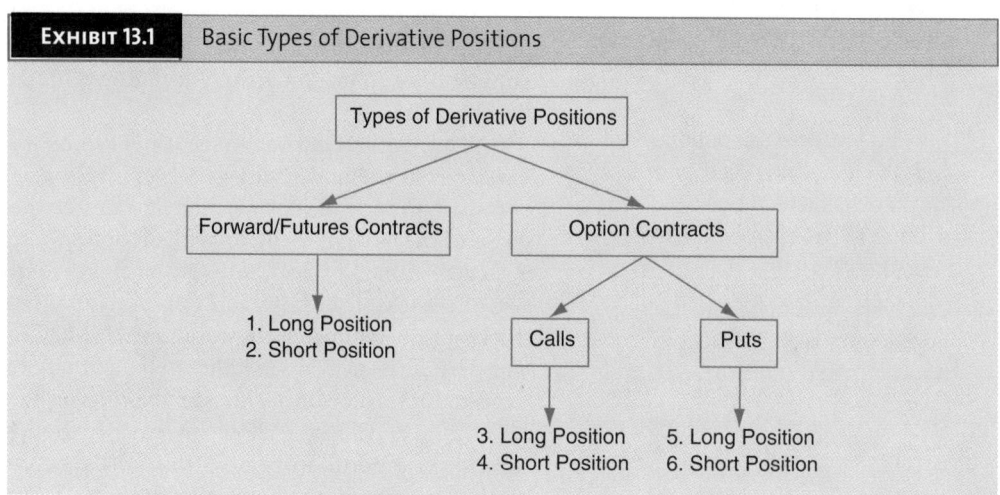

EXHIBIT 13.1 Basic Types of Derivative Positions

Forward and Spot Markets Forward contracts are not securities in the traditional sense; they are more appropriately viewed as *trade agreements* negotiated directly between two parties for a transaction that is scheduled to take place in the future. For example, two investors agree at Date 0 (the present) to transfer a bond from one party to the other at the future Date T. The two agree on which bond and how much of it is to be exchanged, the date and location at which this exchange will take place, and the price at which the bond will be bought and sold. So, the terms that must be considered in forming a forward contract are the same as those necessary for a bond transaction that settled immediately (i.e., a *spot market* transaction), with two exceptions. First, the settlement date agreed to is purposefully set to be in the future. Second, the contract price—which we will call $F_{0,T}$ (forward price set at Date 0 for a contract that matures at Date T)—is usually different from the prevailing spot price (S_0) because of the different time frames involved.

One important way in which spot and forward market transactions are similar is the conditions under which the long and short positions will profit. For example, suppose that at Date T the long position in a bond forward contract must pay \$1,000 ($= F_{0,T}$) for a bond worth $S_T =$ \$1,050 (i.e., the spot price at Date T). Because $F_{0,T} < S_T$, the long position in the contract will profit as he will be able to acquire the bond for \$50 less than its current market value. On the other hand, the short position must deliver the bond at Date T and will lose \$50 on her forward position; she would have profited if S_T had been below the contract price of \$1,000. Thus, just as if the bond had been purchased at Date 0, the long position benefits when bond prices rise, at least relative to the contract price $F_{0,T}$. Conversely, the short position will gain from falling bond prices, just as if she had short sold the bond at Date 0. Even though the timing of the trade's settlement has shifted the "buy low, sell high" philosophy remains.

Forward and Futures Markets Forward contracts are negotiated in the over-the-counter market usually between two private parties—one of which is often a derivatives intermediary, such as a bank—rather than traded through a formal security or commodity exchange. An advantage of this private arrangement is that the terms of the contract are completely flexible; they can be whatever any two mutually consenting counterparties agree to. Another desirable feature to many counterparties is that these arrangements might not require collateral; instead, the parties trust each other to honour their respective commitments at Date T. This lack of collateral means that forward contracts involve *credit* (or *default*) *risk*, which is one reason why banks are often market makers in these instruments.

Forward contracts are often difficult or costly for a counterparty to exit before maturity. Illiquidity is really a by-product of the contract's flexibility because the more specifically tailored an agreement is to an individual's needs, the less marketable it will be to someone else. **Futures contracts** try to solve this problem by standardizing the terms of the agreement (e.g., expiry date, identity and amount of the underlying asset). In contrast to the forward market, both parties in a futures contract trade through a centralized market, called a *futures exchange*. Standardized contracts create contract *homogeneity,* whereby the counterparties can always *unwind* a previous commitment prior to expiration by simply trading their existing position back to the exchange at the prevailing market price.

The *futures price* is analogous to the forward contract price and, at any time during the life of a contract, is set at a level such that a brand-new long or short position would not have to pay an initial premium. However, the futures exchange requires both counterparties to post collateral, or *margin*, to protect itself against the possibility of default. A futures exchange is not a credit-granting institution, so these margin accounts are held by the exchange's *clearinghouse* and are *marked to market* (i.e., adjusted for contract price movements) on a daily basis to ensure that both end users always maintain sufficient collateral to

EXHIBIT 13.2	Popular Futures Contracts and Exchanges

Underlying Asset	Exchange
A. Physical Commodities	
Canola, Western barley	ICE Futures Canada (Winnipeg Commodity Exchange)
Cattle, Hogs, Pork bellies, Lumber, Dairy, Grain and Oilseeds	CME Group (Chicago Mercantile Exchange)
Cocoa, coffee, sugar, Orange Juice, Cotton	Intercontinental Exchange (New York Board of Trade)
Copper, gold, silver, platinum, Crude oil, heating oil, gasoline, natural gas	New York Mercantile Exchange (NYMEX)
B. Financial Securities	
Yen, Euro, Canadian dollar, Swiss franc, British pound, Mexican peso, Australian dollar, Treasury bills, Eurodollar (LIBOR), S&P 500 index, Nikkei 225 index, Russell 2000 index	CME Group (International Monetary Market)
Interest rate derivatives, Index derivatives	Montreal Exchange
Euro LIBOR, British gilt, Japanese government bond, FT-SE 100 index	Euronext.liffe
Euro stock index, Euro stock volatility, credit default derivatives, Inflation derivatives	Eurex

You can find contract specifications for a futures contract on canola at the Winnipeg Commodity Exchange on the ICE (Intercontinental Exchange) website at https://www.theice.com/productguide/ProductDetails.shtml?specId=251.

guarantee their eventual participation. A list of some popular futures contracts, along with the markets where they trade, is shown in Exhibit 13.2. Although generally quite diverse, all of these underlying assets have two things in common: *volatile price movements* and *strong interest* from both buyers and sellers.

13.1.2 INTERPRETING FUTURES PRICE QUOTATIONS: AN EXAMPLE

To illustrate how futures prices are typically quoted in financial markets, consider Exhibit 13.3, a partial list of futures prices for contracts on gold as of October 9, 2008. These futures contract prices are for six different expiration dates.

EXHIBIT 13.3	Gold Futures Contract Price Quotation

Contract	Month	Last	Chg	Open	High	Low	Volume	OpenInt	Exchange
GOLD	Oct '08	**891.0**	−12.1	902.7	902.7	883.0	39	313	COMX
GOLD	Nov '08	**889.8**	−14.0	904.6	910.4	881.1	91	290	COMX
GOLD	Dec '08	**890.5**	−16.0	885.0	914.4	882.9	64,730	208,601	COMX
GOLD	Feb '09	**892.6**	−17.9	912.6	912.9	889.7	4,746	17,678	COMX
GOLD	Apr '09	**901.1**	−12.6	900.2	902.5	895.2	241	18,422	COMX
GOLD	Jun '09	**898.4**	−18.3	917.3	917.3	896.8	20	19,304	COMX

Source: Globeinvestor.com, retrieved October 9, 2008, http://www.globeinvestor.com/v5/content/commodities/groups/Metals.html?action=quote&iFSQsymbols=GC&iFSQtitle=GOLD.

Consider the futures contract that expires in December 2008. The closing (or last) contract price is listed as 890.5 (i.e., $F_{0,T}$). This means that an investor taking a long position in this contract would be committing to buy 100 troy ounces of gold (one contract is for 100 troy ounces) at a price of $890.50 per ounce on the expiration date in December. Conversely, the short position would be committing to sell 100 troy ounces of gold under the same conditions. Recall, that, except for the margin posted with the futures exchange (i.e., the New York Mercantile Exchange or NYMEX for this contract), no money changes hands between the long and short positions at the origination of the contract in October.

Exhibit 13.4 summarizes the net profit for this contract from the long position's point of view, assuming a hypothetical set of gold prices on the December expiration date (i.e., S_T). The most important thing to note is that the payoff to the long position is positive when gold prices increase (relative to the contract price of 890.50), while a loss is incurred when the gold price falls. For instance, if the expiration date price for gold is $900.00, the long position will receive a profit of $9.50 per ounce (= $900 - 890.50$). In that case, the profit is a result of a contract allowing the investor to buy gold that is worth $900 per ounce for the predetermined price of only $890.50. On the other hand, if the December price turns out to be $850.00, the futures contract still obligates the investor to purchase gold for the contract price, thus resulting in a loss of $40.50. This reinforces the fact that the long position benefits when the commodity prices rise and suffers when prices fall, just as would be the case for an investor purchasing a commodity directly in the spot market. Of course, the short position would have payoffs exactly the opposite of those shown in Exhibit 13.4.

The Montreal Exchange has a number of interesting publications and reference manuals. In each section of the Mx productions there are links to useful documents. See www.m-x.ca/english.

EXHIBIT 13.4	Net Profit at Expiry from a Long Gold Futures Contract	
December Gold Price	**Futures Payoff at Expiry**
$875.00	$(875.00 - 890.50) = -15.5$
$880.00	$(880.00 - 890.50) = -10.5$
$890.00	$(890.00 - 890.50) = -0.5$
$890.50	$(890.50 - 890.50) = 0$
$900.00	$(900.00 - 890.50) = 9.5$
$905.00	$(905.00 - 890.50) = 14.5$
$910.00	$(910.00 - 890.50) = 19.5$

The data displayed in Exhibit 13.3 contains other information useful to investors as well. First, recognize that the futures contract prices listed were all lower than they had been the day before (previous close); this can be seen from the negative entries in the "Change" column in comparison with the "Last." This suggests that, although they depend on other factors as well, the futures contract prices are strongly linked to the prevailing price of spot gold ($883.10). Second, notice that the contract prices generally increase the farther into the future the expiration date occurs. Although all prices listed were set on the same day and correspond to the same commodity, the cost of that commodity gets increasingly more expensive, the further forward in time the delivery date is set. We will see later that this relationship is common for some securities and commodities but not for others. Finally, the display also lists the *open interest* and *trading volume* for each contract. Open interest is the number of outstanding contracts while trading volume is the number of those contracts that changed hands that day.

Thus, it appears in this case that the December 2008 contracts are the most abundant and that about 31% (= 64,730 ÷ 208,601) of the number of gold contracts we listed in the exhibit have thus far traded on October 9, 2008.

13.1.3   THE LANGUAGE AND STRUCTURE OF OPTION MARKETS

An **option contract** gives its holder the right—but not the obligation—to either buy or sell an underlying security or commodity at a future date and at a predetermined price. Unlike the forward contract, the option gives the long position the right to decide whether the trade will eventually take place. The option seller (or *writer*) must perform on his side of the agreement if the buyer chooses to exercise the option. Thus, the obligation is inherently one-sided; buyers can do as they please, but sellers are obligated to the buyers under the terms of the agreement. As a result, two types of options are needed: a **call option**—the right to buy the underlying security—and a **put option**—the right to sell that same asset.

Option Contract Terms Two prices are important in evaluating an option position. The **exercise price** (or striking price) is the price the underlying security will be bought or sold for if the option is exercised. The exercise price (X) is to an option what the contract price (i.e., $F_{0,T}$) is to a forward agreement. The second price of interest is the amount the option buyer pays to the seller at Date 0 to buy the contract. This second price is typically called the **option premium**. Note that an option requires an upfront premium payment from buyer to seller while the forward ordinarily does not. This is because the forward contract allows both the long and short positions to "win" at Date T (depending on where S_T settled, relative to $F_{0,T}$), but the option agreement will only be exercised in the buyer's favour; hence the seller must be compensated at Date 0, or she would never agree to the deal. Notice also that although both puts and calls require premium payments, it is quite likely that these two prices will differ. In the analysis that follows, we will define the Date 0 premium to acquire an option expiring at Date T as $C_{0,T}$ for a call and $P_{0,T}$ for a put.

Options can be designed to provide a choice of when the contract can be exercised. **European options** can only be exercised at maturity (Date T), while **American options** can be executed any time up to expiry. For a European-style call option, the buyer will only exercise when on the expiry date, the market value of the underlying asset is greater than the exercise price. On the other hand, a European put will only be exercised when the Date T price of the asset is lower than X. (The decision to exercise an American contract is more complex and will be considered in the next chapter.)

Option Valuation Basics The Date 0 premium for an option can be divided into two components: **intrinsic value** and **time premium**. Intrinsic value represents the value that the buyer would receive from the option if she exercised it immediately. For a call, this is the greater of either zero or the difference between the price of the underlying asset and the exercise price (i.e., max[0, $S_0 - X$]). For a put, intrinsic value would be max[0, $X - S_0$] as X would now represent the proceeds generated from the asset's sale. Options with positive intrinsic value are **in the money**, while ones with zero intrinsic value are **out of the money**. For the special case where $S_0 = X$, the option is **at the money**. The time-premium component is the difference between the whole option premium and the intrinsic component: ($C_{0,T} -$ max[0, $S_0 - X$]) for a call and ($P_{0,T} -$ max[0, $X - S_0$]) for a put. The buyer is willing to pay this extra amount over the option's immediate exercise value because of her ability to complete the transaction at a price of X that will remain in force until Date T. Thus, the time premium is connected to the likelihood that the underlying asset's price will move in the anticipated direction by the contract's maturity.

Although a more complete discussion of valuing option premiums will be deferred until the next chapter, several basic relationships can be seen now. First, because a call buyer is never obligated to exercise, the contract should always at least be worth its intrinsic value. (The situation for put option prices or when the underlying asset pays a dividend can be more complicated and will be discussed later.) In any event, neither a call nor a put option can be worth less than zero. Second, for call options having the same maturity and the same underlying asset, the lower the exercise price, the higher will be the contract's intrinsic value and, hence, the greater its overall premium. Conversely, puts with higher exercise prices are more valuable than those with lower striking prices for the same reason. Third, increasing the amount of time until any option expires will increase the contract's time premium because there is more opportunity for the price of the underlying security to move in the direction anticipated by the investor (i.e., up for a call, down for a put). Finally, because they provide investors with more choices about exercising the agreement, American options are at least as valuable as otherwise comparable European contracts.

Option Trading Markets Like forwards and futures, options trade both in over-the-counter markets and on exchanges. When exchange-traded, the contract seller is required to post a margin account because he is the only one obligated to perform on the contract at a later date. Also, options can be based on a wide variety of underlying securities, including futures contracts or other options. Exhibit 13.5 lists the underlying assets and exchanges where a number of popular option contracts trade.

Exhibit 13.5	Popular Option Contracts and Exchanges
Underlying Asset	**Exchange**

Individual Equities
    S&P 100 index, Dow Jones Industrial Average
    S&P 500 volatility index
	Chicago Board Options Exchange

Individual Equities iShares, iUnits	Montreal Exchange

Yen, Euro, Canadian dollar, Swiss franc,
    British pound, Australian dollar
    Russell 2000 index, Equity Sector index
	Philadelphia Stock Exchange

EuroStoxx ETF, DAX index, SMI index	Eurex

13.1.4 Interpreting Option Price Quotations: An Example

Exhibit 13.6 shows data for a selection of call and put options on Shoppers Drug Mart for October 9, 2008. Unlike the futures contracts, for which there was a single contract price for a given expiration month, Exhibit 13.6 shows several options in any given month with different exercise prices. In fact, the display lists bid and ask premium quotes for both puts and calls, with striking prices ranging from $42 to $50.[1] Notice that as the exercise price falls the calls become more valuable (e.g., higher ask premiums), with the opposite holding true for puts.

---

1 Recall that an investor buys a security from a dealer—in this case, the options exchange—at the ask price, and sells securities to the dealer at the bid price. The difference in these prices, which is the *bid-ask spread*, represents part of the compensation to the exchange for making a market in these contracts.

EXHIBIT 13.6 Shoppers Drug Mart Option Contract Price Quotations

Last Update: Oct. 9, 2008 12:01 Montreal Time (data 15 minutes delayed)

▶ Last Price: 48.010   Net Change: −0.480   Bid Price: 47.990   Ask Price: 48.010   30–Day Historical Volatility: 27%

Calls

Month / Strike	Bid Price	Ask Price	Last Price	Vol.	Impl. Vol.
+ 08 OC 42.000	6.000	6.400	7.450	0	64.27
+ 08 OC 44.000	4.150	4.550	5.550	0	60.16
		...			
+ 08 NO 44.000	5.200	5.600	0.000	0	45.91
+ 08 NO 46.000	3.800	4.150	4.850	0	43.33
+ 08 NO 48.000	2.700	3.000	3.550	0	42.03
+ 08 NO 50.000	1.800	2.050	2.500	0	41.14
		...			
+ 09 JA 44.000	6.000	6.350	0.000	0	38.65
+ 09 JA 46.000	4.700	5.050	5.650	0	37.19
+ 09 JA 48.000	3.600	3.900	4.450	0	36.21
		...			
+ 09 AL 44.000	6.900	7.350	0.000	0	34.40
+ 09 AL 46.000	5.800	6.150	6.650	0	34.04
+ 09 AL 48.000	4.700	5.050	5.550	0	33.44
		...			
Total				0	

Puts

Month / Strike	Bid Price	Ask Price	Last Price	Vol.	Impl. Vol.
+ 08 OC 42.000	0.070	0.250	0.350	0	64.94
+ 08 OC 44.000	0.300	0.450	0.600	0	61.54
		...			
+ 08 NO 44.000	1.200	1.400	0.000	0	46.38
+ 08 NO 46.000	1.800	2.000	1.850	0	44.29
+ 08 NO 48.000	2.600	2.850	2.750	0	43.06
+ 08 NO 50.000	3.700	3.950	3.650	0	41.94
		...			
+ 09 JA 44.000	1.900	2.150	0.000	0	40.02
+ 09 JA 46.000	2.600	2.850	2.600	0	38.92
+ 09 JA 48.000	3.450	3.700	3.400	0	37.80
		...			
+ 09 AL 44.000	2.750	3.000	0.000	0	36.98
+ 09 AL 46.000	3.500	3.700	3.650	0	35.96
+ 09 AL 48.000	4.400	4.600	4.500	0	35.39
		...			
Total				0	

Source: Montreal Exchange, retrieved October 9, 2008, http://www.m-x.ca/nego_cotes_en.php?symbol=SC*#cote.

Consider the fortunes of two different investors, one of whom purchases a Shoppers (SC) November 50 call (i.e., $X = 50$) and the other who buys a November 50 put. When the transaction takes place in October, these investors will pay their sellers the ask prices of $2.05 (i.e., $C_{0,T}$) and $3.95 (i.e., $P_{0,T}$), respectively. In return, the call buyer has the right, but not the obligation, to buy one SC share for $50 by the expiration date in November. As the current SC price is $48.01, this call is out of the money. Thus, the total call premium of $2.05 is a time premium. Similarly, the put buyer has the right to force the sale of one SC share for $50 prior to expiry in November. The put is in the money as this exercise price is higher than the current share price. Therefore, the total put premium of $3.95 can be divided into an intrinsic value component of $1.99 (= 50 − 48.01) and a time premium of $1.96 (= 3.95 − 1.99).

The expiration date net payoffs to these long option positions are listed in Exhibit 13.7 for a variety of possible terminal prices. Looking first at the call option payoffs in Panel A, notice that the investor will only exercise the contract to buy SC shares when the shares trade for more than the exercise price; at price levels at or below the exercise price, the option expires worthless and the investor will simply lose his initial investment. Recognize, though, that while the call is in the money when the share price is above the exercise price, the investor will not realize a profit until the share price rises above $52.05, an amount equal to the exercise price plus the call premium (i.e., $X + C_{0,T}$). For the put payoffs shown in Panel B, the holder will exercise the contract if the share price drops below the exercise price. However, the display also documents that the put investor will not realize a positive net profit until the share price falls below $46.05 (i.e., $X − P_{0,T}$). If the share price remains above $50, the put expires out of the money.

EXHIBIT 13.7	**Net Profit at Expiry from a Long Position in Shoppers Drug Mart Call and Put Option Contracts**

A. Long Call with Exercise Price of 50

November Share Price	Call Payoff at Expiry	Initial Call Premium	Net Profit
48.00	0.00	−2.05	−2.05
49.00	0.00	−2.05	−2.05
50.00	0.00	−2.05	−2.05
52.00	0.00	−2.05	−2.05
52.05	(52.05 − 50) = 2.05	−2.05	0.00
53.00	(53.00 − 50) = 3.00	−2.05	0.95
54.00	(54.00 − 50) = 4.00	−2.05	1.95

B. Long Put with Exercise Price of 50

November Share Price	Put Payoff at Expiry	Initial Put Premium	Net Profit
45.00	(50 − 45.00) = 5.00	−3.95	1.05
46.00	(50 − 46.00) = 4.00	−3.95	0.05
46.05	(50 − 46.05) = 3.95	−3.95	0.00
47.00	(50 − 47.00) = 3.00	−3.95	−0.95
49.00	(50 − 49.00) = 1.00	−3.95	−2.95
50.00	0.00	−3.95	−3.95
51.00	0.00	−3.95	−3.95

13.2 Investing with Derivative Securities

Although we have highlighted many differences between forward and option agreements, the two are quite similar in terms of the benefits to an investor. The ultimate difference between forwards and options lies in the way the investor must pay to receive those benefits.

13.2.1 THE BASIC NATURE OF DERIVATIVE INVESTING

Consider an investor who has decided to purchase a share in SAS Corporation six months from now, to coincide with an anticipated bonus. We assume that both SAS stock forward contracts and call options are available with the market prices of $F_{0,T}$ and $C_{0,T}$ (where $T = 0.5$ year) and that the exercise price of the call, X, equals $F_{0,T}$. If the investor wants to lock in the price now at which the stock purchase will eventually take place, he has two alternatives: a long position in the forward or purchase a call. Exhibit 13.8 compares the Date 0 and Date T cash flow for both possibilities.

Clearly the main difference between these strategies at Date 0 is that the forward position requires no payment or receipt by either party to the transaction whereas investing in the call requires payment of a premium. By paying the premium, the investor does not have to purchase SAS stock at Date T if the terms of the contract turn out to be unfavourable (i.e., $S_T < X$). If the expiration date price of SAS stock is greater than the exercise price, the investor will exercise the call. However, this leads to exactly the same

EXHIBIT 13.8	Exchanges for Long Forward and Long Call Transactions

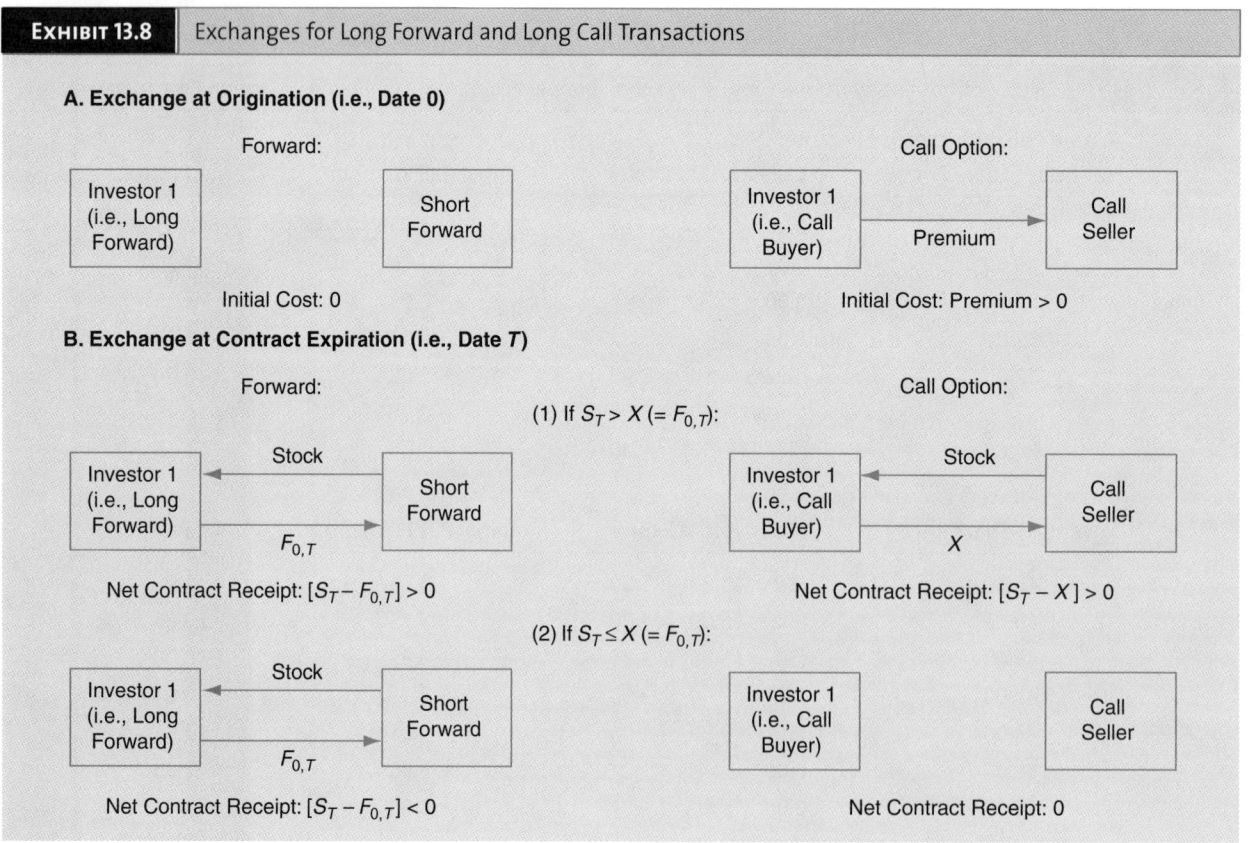

A. Exchange at Origination (i.e., Date 0)

Forward:

Investor 1 (i.e., Long Forward) → Short Forward

Initial Cost: 0

Call Option:

Investor 1 (i.e., Call Buyer) —Premium→ Call Seller

Initial Cost: Premium > 0

B. Exchange at Contract Expiration (i.e., Date T)

Forward:

(1) If $S_T > X (= F_{0,T})$:

Investor 1 (i.e., Long Forward) ←Stock— Short Forward; —$F_{0,T}$→

Net Contract Receipt: $[S_T - F_{0,T}] > 0$

Call Option:

Investor 1 (i.e., Call Buyer) ←Stock— Call Seller; —X→

Net Contract Receipt: $[S_T - X] > 0$

(2) If $S_T \leq X (= F_{0,T})$:

Investor 1 (i.e., Long Forward) ←Stock— Short Forward; —$F_{0,T}$→

Net Contract Receipt: $[S_T - F_{0,T}] < 0$

Call Option:

Investor 1 (i.e., Call Buyer)   Call Seller

Net Contract Receipt: 0

exchange as the long forward contract. It is only when the stock price falls below X (and $F_{0,T}$) on Date T that there is a difference between the two positions; under this condition, the right provided by the option *not* to purchase SAS stock is valuable because the investor in the forward contract will be required to execute that position at a loss. Thus, the call option can be viewed as the "good half" of the long forward position because it allows for the future purchase of SAS stock at a fixed price but doesn't require the transaction to take place.

This is the critical distinction between forward and option contracts. Both positions have been structured to provide the investor with exactly the same amount of "insurance" against a price increase in SAS stock over the next six months. That is, both contracts provide a payoff of $[S_T - X] = [S_T - F_{0,T}]$ whenever S_T exceeds X, which makes the effective purchase price for the stock X. However, with a forward contract, the investor will have to complete the purchase at the expiry date, even if the stock price falls below $F_{0,T}$. For the call, the investor will have to pay the premium at origination but may never exercise. Thus, for the same Date T benefit, the investor's decision between these two "insurance policies" comes down to choosing the certainty of a present premium payment (i.e., long call) versus the possibility of a future payment (i.e., long forward) that could potentially be much larger.

Let's add some numbers to help see this distinction more clearly. Suppose the investor's choices are: (1) pay nothing now and take the long position in a six-month SAS stock forward contract with a contract price of $F_{0,T} = \$45$, or (2) pay a premium of $C_{0,T} = \$3.24$ for a six-month, European call with an exercise price of $X = \$45$. At the time of his decision, we'll assume the SAS stock price (S_0) is $40, which means the call is out of the money and the entire $3.24 is time premium.

Assume now that at expiry, $S_T = \$51$. Both the long forward position and the call will be worth $6 (i.e., $51 - 45$) to the investor, reducing his net purchase price for SAS shares to $45 $(= 51 - 6)$. If, however, $S_T = \$40.75$, the forward contract would require that the investor pay $4.25 $(= 40.75 - 45)$ to his counterparty, which would raise the net cost of his shares to $45. With the call, he could have let the contract expire without exercising it and purchased his SAS shares in the market for only $40.75. Thus, in exchange for the option's front-end expense of $3.24, the investor retains the possibility of paying less than $45 for his eventual stock purchase.

The connection between forward contracts and puts can be made in a similar fashion. Suppose a different investor has decided to liquidate SAS stock from her portfolio in six months' time. Rather than risk a falling stock price over that period, she could arrange now to sell the share at that future date for a predetermined fixed price in one of two ways: a short forward position or the purchase of a put. Exhibit 13.9 illustrates the exchanges for these alternatives. Once again, for the same insurance against SAS stock price declines, the choice comes down to the certainty of paying the put premium versus the possibility of making a potentially larger payment with the forward contract by having to sell her stock for X $(=F_{0,T})$ when that value is considerably less than the stock's Date T market price. Notice once again that the put allows the investor to walk away from her obligation under the short forward position to sell her stock on the expiration date under disadvantageous conditions. Thus, in exchange for a front-end premium payment, the put enables the investor to acquire the "good half" of the short position in a forward contract.

13.2.2 BASIC PAYOFF AND PROFIT DIAGRAMS FOR FORWARD CONTRACTS

Exhibits 13.8 and 13.9 show that the respective expiry date payoffs for long and short positions in a forward contract are $[S_T - F_{0,T}]$ and $[F_{0,T} - S_T]$ and that these values could be either

EXHIBIT 13.9 Exchanges for Short Forward and Long Put Transactions

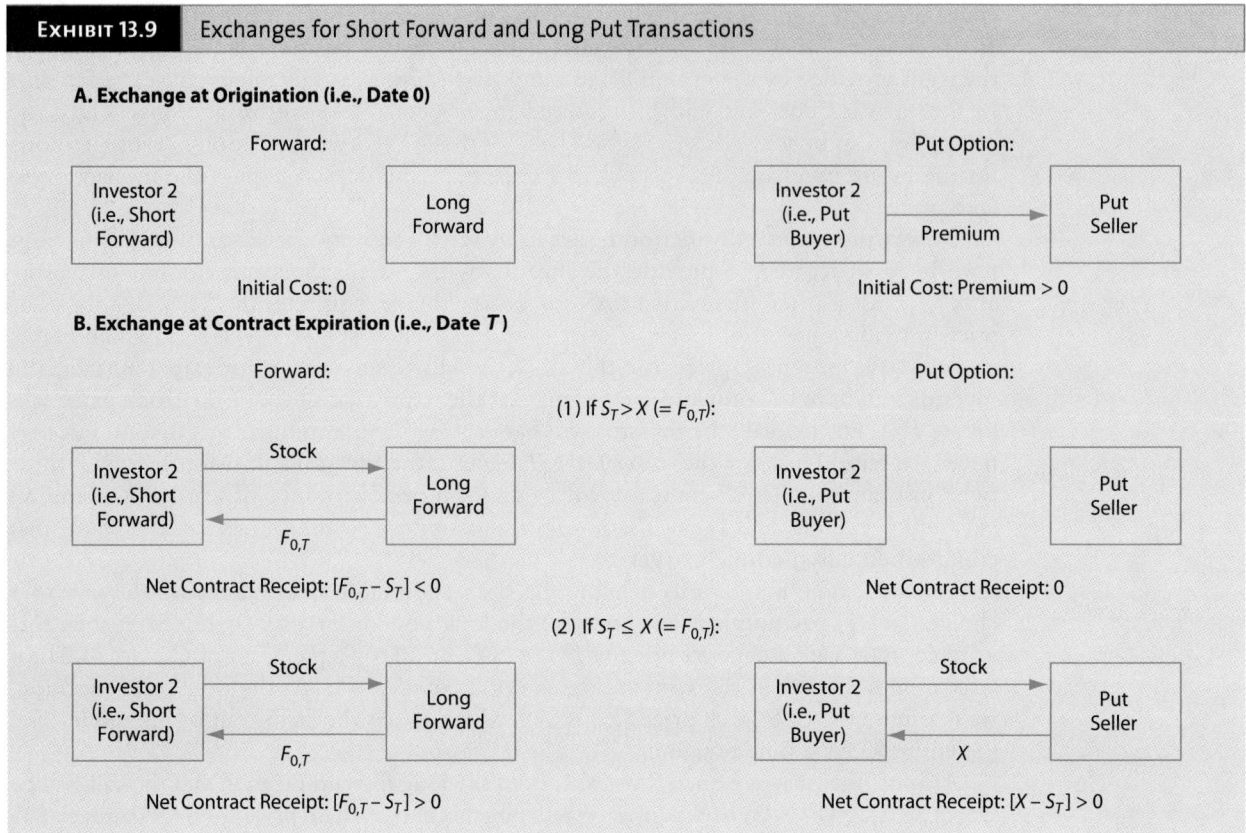

A. Exchange at Origination (i.e., Date 0)

Forward:

Initial Cost: 0

Put Option:

Initial Cost: Premium > 0

B. Exchange at Contract Expiration (i.e., Date T)

Forward:

Put Option:

(1) If $S_T > X (= F_{0,T})$:

Net Contract Receipt: $[F_{0,T} - S_T] < 0$

Net Contract Receipt: 0

(2) If $S_T \leq X (= F_{0,T})$:

Net Contract Receipt: $[F_{0,T} - S_T] > 0$

Net Contract Receipt: $[X - S_T] > 0$

positive or negative depending on the spot price at Date T. These terminal payoffs are plotted against the possible expiration date values of the underlying security price in Exhibit 13.10. There are two interesting items in this display.

First, the payoffs to both long and short positions in the forward contract are *symmetric*, or two-sided, around the contract price. This is a direct result of a contract that fully obligates each party to complete the agreed-upon transaction—even at a financial loss. For instance, in our example, the investor holding a long position in a SAS stock forward contract with a contract price of $45 lost $4.25 when the Date T price of SAS stock was $40.75 but gained $6 when $S_T = \$51$.

Second, the Date T payoffs to the short and long positions are mirror images of each other; forward contracts are *zero-sum games* because the long position gains must be paid by the short position and vice versa. Forward markets reinforce the fundamental financial tenet that long positions benefit from rising prices while short positions benefit from falling prices. Finally, notice that these gains and losses can be quite large. In fact, the short forward position has the potential for unlimited loss while the long forward position has the potential for unlimited gain because there is no theoretical limit on how high the price for the underlying security can rise. Conversely, the loss potential for the long position (and the gain potential for the short position) is limited because the price of the underlying security cannot fall below zero.

13.2.3 BASIC PAYOFF AND PROFIT DIAGRAMS FOR CALL AND PUT OPTIONS

Exhibits 13.8 and 13.9 also show the option premium paid represents a sunk cost to the investor, thus reducing the upside return relative to the comparable forward position. In

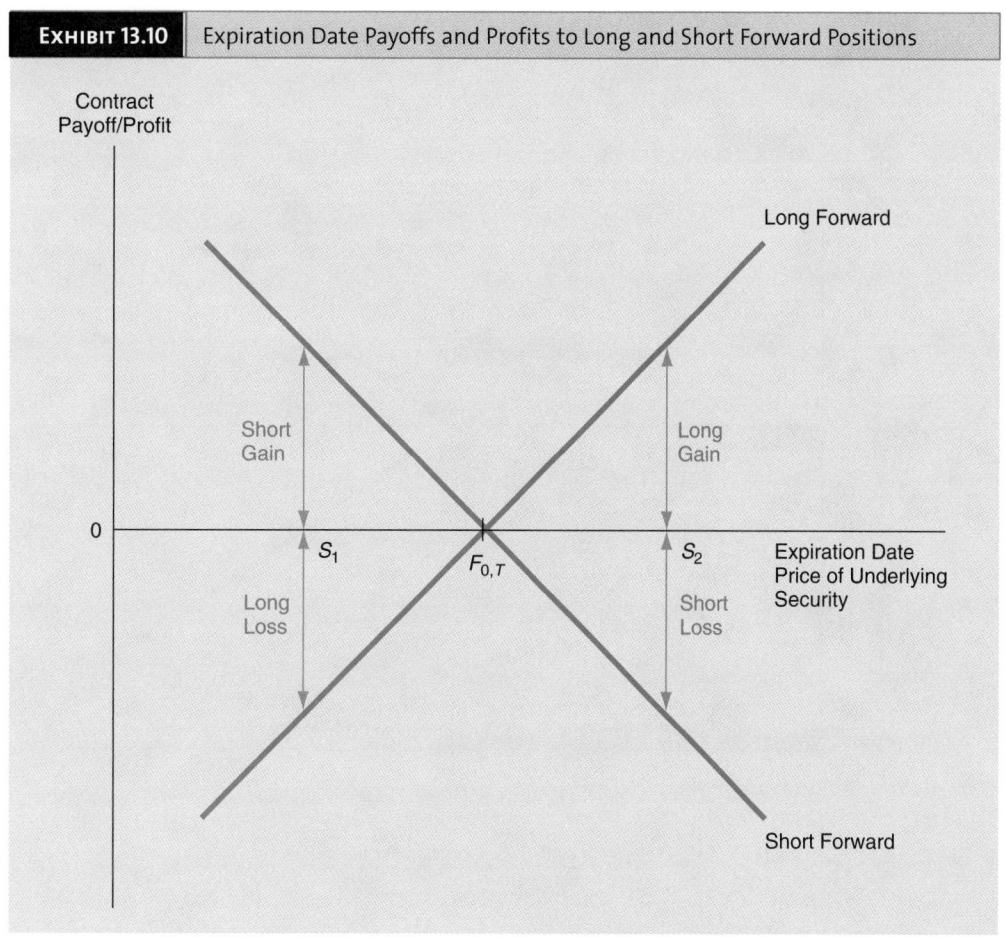

EXHIBIT 13.10   Expiration Date Payoffs and Profits to Long and Short Forward Positions

exchange for this initial fee, the investor receives expiration date payoffs that are decidedly *asymmetric*, or one-sided. Exhibit 13.11 shows the net effect these differences have on the terminal payoffs and net profits to both long and short positions in calls, while Exhibit 13.12 provides a similar illustration for puts. This analysis assumes that both options are European and so they will not be exercised prematurely.

Notice again that the call buyer still benefits whenever the terminal security price (i.e., S_T) exceeds the exercise price of X. However, given that the holder had to pay an initial premium of $C_{0,T}$, the position doesn't generate a positive profit until $S_T > (X + C_{0,T})$.[2] (Recall that this result was shown for the option example in Exhibit 13.7.) When $X < S_T < (X + C_{0,T})$, the option is exercised at a loss, but this loss will be less than the full cost of the option, which is what the long position would incur if the call were not exercised. In fact, when $S_T < X$, the option is out of the money and the buyer who makes the rational decision to let the contract expire will lose $C_{0,T}$.

---

2 The expiration date profits shown in Exhibits 13.11 and 13.12 are somewhat inaccurate as they ignore the timing differential of the two payments (Date 0 and Date T).

EXHIBIT 13.11 Expiration Date Payoffs and Profits to Long and Short Call Positions

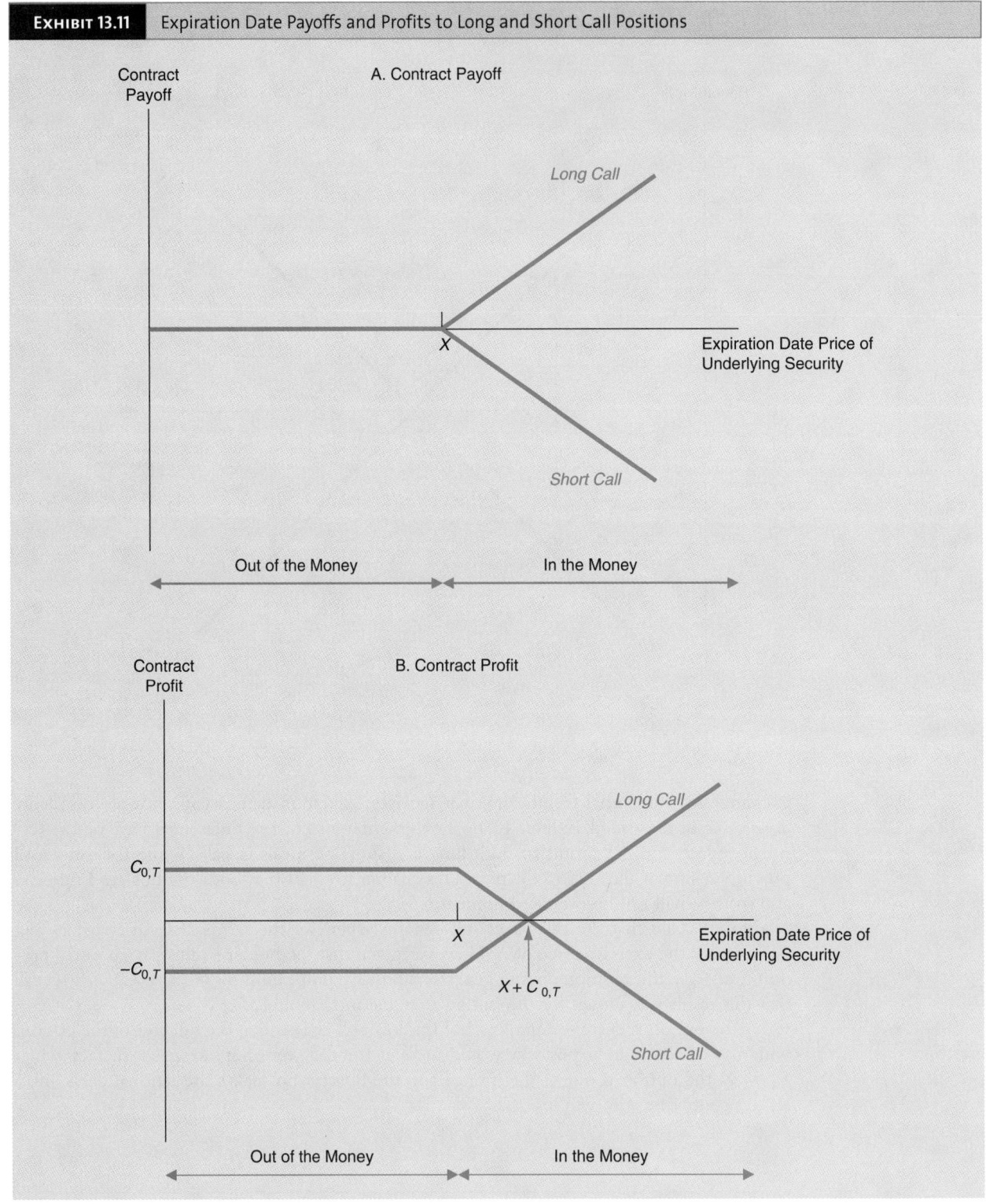

Exhibit 13.12	Expiration Date Payoffs to Long and Short Put Positions

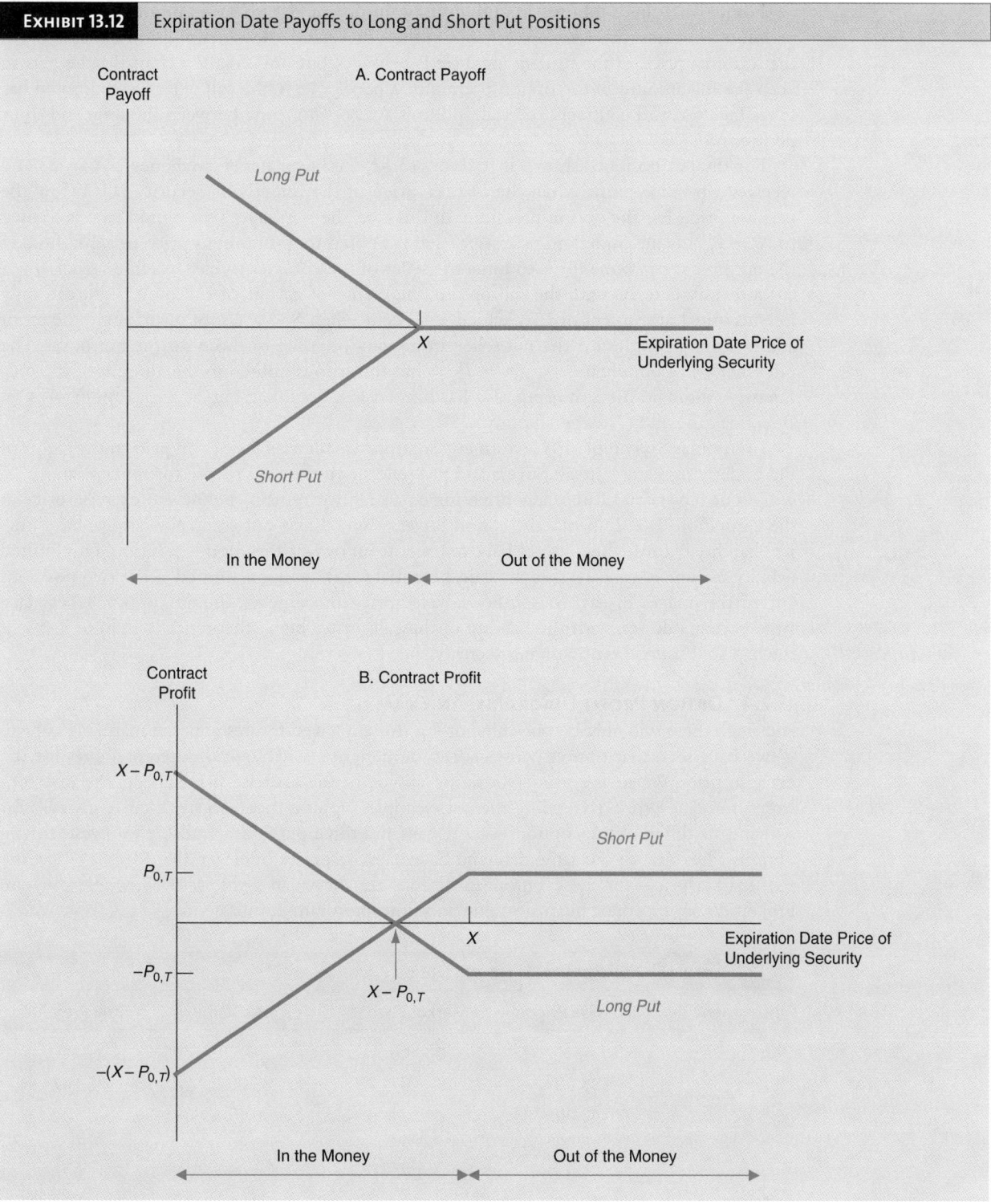

Notice, that the call buyer has unlimited gain potential with losses limited to the option premium no matter how far prices fall. On the other hand, the short position benefits when the terminal price of the underlying asset is below X but only to the extent that he gets to keep the full amount of the option premium. When $S_T > X$, the call seller has unlimited liability. Like forward contracts, the call option is a zero-sum game between the long and short positions.

For the put positions shown in Exhibit 13.12, the buyer benefits whenever $X > S_T$ and receives a positive profit when the Date T price of the underlying security falls below the exercise price, less the option premium. In this case, the put buyer's maximum gain is limited to $X - P_{0,T}$ as the underlying security itself is limited to a minimum price of zero; the best the put holder can hope for is to force the seller of the contract to buy worthless stock for X at the expiry date. As with the call option, the owner of an out-of-the-money put can only lose his initial investment of $P_{0,T}$, which will occur when $S_T > X$. Not surprisingly, the profit and loss opportunities for the put seller are exactly opposite of those for the put buyer. The put seller will gain when $S_T > (X - P_{0,T})$, but this gain is limited to the amount of the premium. A short position in a put also has limited loss potential; but, at a maximum of $X - P_{0,T}$, this can still be a large amount.

In summary, when held as investments, options are *directional views* on price movements of the underlying security. Call buyers and put sellers count on S_T to rise (or remain) above X, while put buyers and call sellers hope for S_T to fall (or remain) below the exercise price at the expiration date. Importantly, option buyers—whether a put or a call—always have limited liability because they do not have to exercise an out-of-the-money position. This limited liability feature also means that the gain potential for the seller is limited as the two positions are mirror images of each other. For adverse price movements, though, option sellers face large potential losses, with the liability of the call writer being theoretically infinite just as if she had sold short the underlying security.

13.2.4 OPTION PROFIT DIAGRAMS: AN EXAMPLE

Although there will only be one value of $F_{0,T}$ for any given futures contract maturing at Date T, we have seen that option contracts can be designed with several different values for the exercise price. We now consider how the choice of the exercise price affects the investor's expiration date profit. Extending the last example, suppose that SAS stock currently sells for $40 and six different SAS options—three calls and three puts—are available to investors. The options all expire on the same date and have exercise prices of either $35, $40, or $45. Current market prices for these European options are shown in Exhibit 13.13, where they are broken down into their intrinsic-value and time-premium components.

EXHIBIT 13.13	Hypothetical Stock and Option Prices			
Instrument	Exercise Price	Market Price	Intrinsic Value	Time Premium
SAS Stock	—	$40.00	—	—
Call: 1	$35.00	8.07	$5.00	$3.07
2	40.00	5.24	0.00	5.24
3	45.00	3.24	0.00	3.24
Put: 1	35.00	1.70	0.00	1.70
2	40.00	3.67	0.00	3.67
3	45.00	6.47	5.00	1.47

Given that $S_0 = \$40$, Call 1 (with $X = 35$) and Put 3 (with $X = 45$) are both \$5 in the money, which leaves \$3.07 and \$1.47, respectively, of time premium. Call 3 and Put 1 are both currently \$5 out of the money and so their market prices are purely time premium; someone buying either of these contracts anticipates that stock prices will move in the desired direction by at least the option price *plus* \$5. Notice that neither of the two at-the-money options, Call 2 and Put 2, have any intrinsic value, but they still sell in the market for different prices. Specifically, the call with $X = \$40$ is more valuable than the comparable put. As we will see shortly, this occurs because of **put–call parity**, which is the formal relationship that must exist between put and call options in efficient capital markets.[3] Finally, the last column of Exhibit 13.13 shows that the time premium is largest for the at-the-money options because, at this point, the greatest amount of uncertainty exists as to whether the option will be in or out of the money (and hence valuable, or not) at expiry.

Exhibit 13.14 compares the expiration date profit diagrams for options with varying exercise prices but similar in every other respect. The payoffs portrayed in Panel A show that, although it is the most expensive, the deepest in-the-money contract (Call 1) becomes profitable the quickest, requiring that S_T rise to \$43.07 ($= 35 + 8.07$). Call 3 is the least expensive to purchase but requires the greatest price movement of the underlying stock—to \$48.24 in this example—before it provides a positive profit to the investor. The Panel B puts tell the same story; Put 1 (the out-of-the-money contract) costs the least but needs the largest price decline to be profitable. In general, by varying the exercise price on a series of options with otherwise identical contract terms, an investor can create just as many different risk-reward trade-offs for herself. This is one of several ways in which derivatives can be used to modify investment risk and to customize a desired payoff structure.

EXHIBIT 13.14 Terminal Profits to Options with Different Exercise Prices

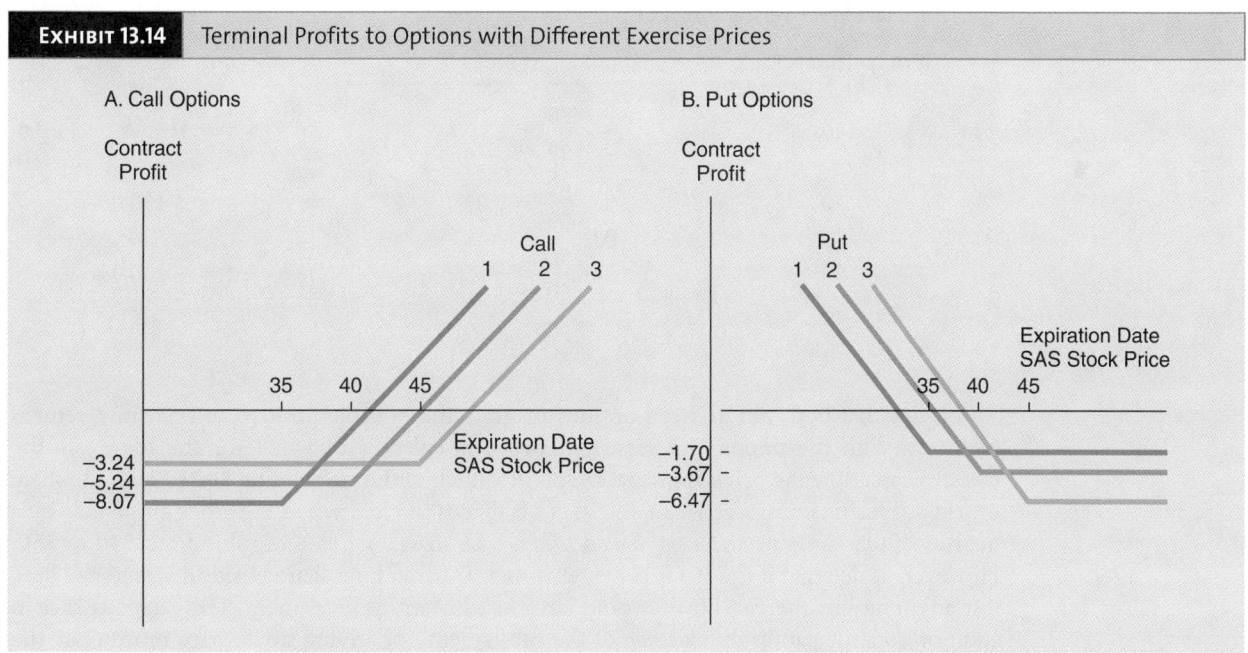

---

3 Put-call parity should always hold for options on non-dividend-paying stock. An at-the-money put can be more valuable than an at-the-money call if the underlying asset has a cash flow (dividend, interest payment).

Options and Leverage As a final extension of this example, we compare the returns to a put or a call option investment with a direct investment (or short sale) in the underlying SAS stock. We will limit the analysis to Call 2 and Put 2, the two at-the-money contracts. Exhibit 13.15 summarizes the holding period returns for various positions assuming three different expiration date stock prices: $30, $40, and $50. Two different comparisons are made: (1) long stock versus long call and (2) short stock versus long put. In calculating the stock position returns, we have measured the change in value of the SAS share as a percentage of the initial price of $40. For the option positions, the terminal payoffs of $\max[0, S_T - 40]$ for the call and $\max[0, 40 - S_T]$ for the put are listed relative to the contract's purchase price.

EXHIBIT 13.15	**Stock and Option Investment Returns**

A. Long Stock versus Long Call

Terminal Stock Price	Long Stock	Long Call
30	$\frac{30}{40} - 1 = -25.0\%$	$\frac{0}{5.24} - 1 = -100.0\%$
40	$\frac{40}{40} - 1 = 0.0\%$	$\frac{0}{5.24} - 1 = -100.0\%$
50	$\frac{50}{40} - 1 = 25.0\%$	$\frac{10}{5.24} - 1 = 90.8\%$

B. Short Stock versus Long Put

Terminal Stock Price	Short Stock	Long Put
30	$1 - \frac{30}{40} = 25.0\%$	$\frac{10}{3.67} - 1 = 172.5\%$
40	$1 - \frac{40}{40} = 0.0\%$	$\frac{0}{3.67} - 1 = -100.0\%$
50	$1 - \frac{50}{40} = -25.0\%$	$\frac{0}{3.67} - 1 = -100.0\%$

Notice that both put and call options magnify the possible positive and negative returns of investing in the underlying security. For an initial cost of $5.24 for the long call, the investor can enjoy the price appreciation of SAS stock without spending $40 to own the share outright. This financial *leverage* manifests itself in a 100% loss when the stock price falls by a quarter of that amount and a 91% gain when SAS shares increase in value from $40 to $50. However, notice that if the stock price remains at $40, the long share position would not have lost anything but the call buyer would have lost his entire investment. This suggests that in addition to anticipating the *direction* of the subsequent underlying stock price movement, the option investor also is taking a view on the *timing* of that movement. If the SAS stock price had stayed at $40 through Date T and then risen to $50 the next day, the shareholder would have experienced a 25% gain, while the buyer of the call would have seen the instrument expire worthless.

13.3 The Relationship between Forward and Option Contracts

The preceding discussion highlighted the fact that positions in forward and option contracts can lead to similar investment payoffs if the price of the underlying security moves in the anticipated direction. This similarity in payoff structures suggests that there is a tractable set of relationships between these instruments. In fact, we will see that the values of five different securities can be linked: a risk-free bond, an underlying asset, a forward contract for the future purchase or sale of that asset, a call, and a put. These relationships, known as put-call parity, specify how the put and call premiums should be set relative to one another. Further, these conditions can be expressed in terms of the connection between these two option types and either the spot or forward market price for the underlying asset. They depend on the assumption that financial markets are free from arbitrage opportunities, meaning that securities (or portfolios of securities) offering identical payoffs with identical risks must sell for the same current price. As such, put-call parity represents a crucial first step in understanding how derivatives are valued in an efficient capital market.[4]

13.3.1 PUT-CALL-SPOT PARITY

Suppose that at Date 0 an investor constructs the following portfolio involving three securities related to Company WYZ:

- Long one WYZ common stock at a price of S_0,
- Long a put to deliver one WYZ stock at an exercise price of X on expiry Date T. Purchase price for the put of $P_{0,T}$,
- Short a call allowing the purchase of one WYZ stock at an exercise price of X on the expiry Date T. Selling price for the call $C_{0,T}$.

We'll assume that both options are European and have the same expiry date and exercise price. However, the specific values of the expiry date and exercise price do not affect the conclusion of our analysis. Further, we will assume initially that WYZ stock does not pay a dividend during the life of the options.

Panel A of Exhibit 13.16 lists the Date 0 investment necessary to construct this portfolio as $(S_0 + P_{0,T} - C_{0,T})$, which is the cost of the long positions in the stock and the put less the proceeds from the sale of the call.[5] Consider also the value that this portfolio will have at the expiry of the two options. Given that the stock's value at Date T (i.e., S_T) is unknown when the investment is made at Date 0, two general outcomes are possible: (1) $S_T \leq X$ and (2) $S_T > X$. Panel B shows the value of each position as well as the net value of the whole portfolio at Date T.

Whenever the Date T value of WYZ stock is below the common exercise price, it is best for the investor to exercise the long put and sell the WYZ share for X instead of its lower market value. In that case, it will not be rational for the call holder to pay X for a share that

---

4 The development of the relationships linking put and call option prices is commonly attributed to Stoll (1969). Others have embellished Stoll's findings in many interesting ways; those subsequent studies include Merton (1973a), Klemkosky and Resnick (1979), and Bharadwaj and Wiggins (2001).

5 In the "arithmetic" of engineering financial portfolios, a plus (+) sign can be interpreted as a long position, and a minus (−) sign represents a short position. Thus, the portfolio investment represented by $(S_0 + P_{0,T} - C_{0,T})$ can also be expressed as (long stock) + (long put) + (short call).

EXHIBIT 13.16	Put-Call-Spot Parity

A. Net Portfolio Investment at Initiation (Date 0)

Portfolio

Long 1 WYZ stock	S_0
Long 1 put option	$P_{0,T}$
Short 1 call option	$-C_{0,T}$
Net investment:	$S_0 + P_{0,T} - C_{0,T}$

B. Portfolio Value at Option Expiration (Date T)

Portfolio	(1) If $S_T \leq X$:	(2) If $S_T > X$:
Long 1 WYZ stock	S_T	S_T
Long 1 put option	$(X - S_T)$	0
Short 1 call option	0	$-(S_T - X)$
Net position:	X	X

is worth less, so the call will expire out of the money. On the other hand, when S_T exceeds X, the holder of the call will exercise the option to buy WYZ stock for X while the put would be out of the money. In either scenario, the net expiration date value of the portfolio is X because the combination of options guarantees that the investor will sell the share of WYZ stock at Date T for the fixed price X. That is, at stock prices lower than X, the investor will choose to sell the share at a profit, although he will be forced to sell at a loss when WYZ trades at a market price higher than X.

The consequence of this is that when the investor commits $(S_0 + P_{0,T} - C_{0,T})$ to construct the portfolio at Date 0, he knows that it will be worth X at Date T. Thus, this particular portfolio has a comparable payoff structure to a Treasury bill, another risk-free, zero coupon security that can be designed to have a face value of X and a maturity date T. In an arbitrage-free capital market, this means that the Date 0 value of the portfolio must be equal to that of the T-bill, which is just the face value X discounted to the present using the risk-free rate. This "no arbitrage" condition can be formalized as follows:

13.1
$$S_0 + P_{0,T} - C_{0,T} = \frac{X}{(1 + RFR)^T}$$

where:

RFR = the annualized risk-free rate

T = the time to maturity (expressed in years)

Defining $[X(1 + RFR)^{-T}]$ as the present value of a T-bill, this equation can be expressed on Date 0 in financial arithmetic terms as:

(Long Stock) + (Long Put) + (Short Call) = (Long T-Bill)

In either form, this condition—known as the *put-call-spot* parity condition—indicates the efficient market linkages between prices for stock, T-bills, puts, and calls.

13.3.2 Put-Call Parity: An Example

Suppose that the current stock price for WYZ stock is $53 and that six-month European call and puts on WYZ stock with an exercise price of $50 sell for $6.74 and $2.51, respectively. Equation 13.1 suggests that we can create a synthetic T-bill by purchasing the stock, buying the put, and selling the call for a net price of $48.77 (= 53.00 + 2.51 − 6.74). At the options' expiration date, this portfolio would have a terminal value of $50. Thus, the risk-free rate implied by this investment can be established by solving the following equation for *RFR:*

$$48.77 = 50 \ (1 + RFR)^{-0.5}$$

or

$$RFR = [(50 \div 48.77)^2 - 1] = 5.11\%$$

If the return on an actual six-month T-bill with a $50 face value is not 5.11%, an investor could exploit the difference. For instance, if the actual T-bill rate is 6.25% and there are no restrictions against using the proceeds from the short sale of any security, an investor wanting a risk-free investment would clearly choose the actual T-bill to lock in the higher return, while someone seeking a loan might attempt to secure a 5.11% borrowing rate by short-selling the synthetic T-bill. Rearranging Equation 13.1, such an artificial short position can be obtained as follows:

$$\textbf{(Short Stock)} + \textbf{(Short Put)} + \textbf{(Long Call)} = \textbf{(Short T-Bill)}$$

With no transaction costs, a financial arbitrage could be constructed by combining a long position in the actual T-bill with a short sale of the synthetic portfolio. Given that the current value of the actual T-bill is $48.51[= $50(1.0625)^{-0.5}]$, this set of transactions would generate the cash flows shown in Exhibit 13.17 and produce a $0.26 profit per each T-bill pair created. As the arbitrage trade did not require the investor to bear any risk (i.e., both the Date 0 and Date *T* values of the net position were known at inception) nor commit any capital, there is nothing in this example to prevent the investor from expanding the size of the trade to increasingly larger levels. However, as additional transactions take place, the price discrepancy will disappear. In this case, the purchase of the actual T-bill and sale of the synthetic (short stock, short put, and long call) will continue until rates are equalized. This is how the markets remain efficient through arbitrage trading.

Another way of seeing this trade is

$$C_{0,T} - P_{0,T} = S_0 - X(1 + RFR)^{-T}$$

Exhibit 13.17	A Put-Call Parity Arbitrage Example

A. Net Initial Investment (Date 0)

Transaction

1. Long actual T-bill at 6.25%	−48.51
2. Short synthetic T-bill at 5.11%:	
Short WYZ stock	53.00
Short put option	2.51
Long call option	−6.74
Net receipt:	0.26

B. Position Value at Option Expiration (Date T)

Transaction	**(1) If $S_T \leq 50$:**	**(2) If $S_T > 50$:**
1. Long actual T-bill at 6.25%	50	50
2. Short synthetic T-bill at 5.11%:		
Short WYZ stock	$-S_T$	$-S_T$
Short put option	$-(50 - S_T)$	0
Long call option	0	$(S_T - 50)$
Net position:	0	0

The "no arbitrage" difference between the call and put prices should equal the difference between the stock price and the present value of the joint exercise price. The market-determined risk-free rate of 6.25% implies that the correct difference between the two derivatives should be $4.49 (= 53 − 48.51), which is $0.26 greater than the $4.23 (= 6.74 − 2.51) actual difference. This discrepancy suggests that, assuming the T-bill is correctly priced, the call price is undervalued relative to the put. Not surprisingly, then, the arbitrage transaction requires the purchase of the call while shorting the put.

13.3.3 Creating Synthetic Securities Using Put-Call Parity

The preceding example shows how a risk-free portfolio could be created by combining three risky securities: stock, a put, and a call. The parity condition developed in the example can be expressed in other useful ways as well. In particular, one of the four assets represented in Equation 13.1 is always *redundant* because it can be defined in terms of the others.

Because the equation can be easily manipulated, this means that if there are not markets in either put or call options, investors can create the desired, but unavailable, pattern of cash flows through the appropriate "packaging" of the other three interrelated assets. Suppose, for example, that a put on WYZ stock does not exist but a call does. Exhibit 13.18 shows the Date 0 and Date T cash flows associated with the portfolio replicating the terminal payoff. Combining both panels of the display, an initial investment of $[X(1 + RFR)^{-T} - S_0 + C_{0,T}]$ leads to a final cash flow that is no less than zero and as large as $X - S_T$ whenever $X > S_T$. Expressed in a more traditional manner, the expiration date payoff to the synthetic put is $\max[0, X - S_T]$.

In practice, the alternative expressions for the put–call parity model are used to identify arbitrage opportunities. Even when a particular derivative instrument trades actively in the market, if its cash flows and risks can be duplicated, this leads to the possibility that the price of the actual instrument and the net cost of the replicating portfolio will differ. From the previous example,

| **Exhibit 13.18** | Replicating a Put Option |

A. Net Portfolio Investment at Initiation (Date 0)

Portfolio	
Long 1 T-bill	$X(1 + RFR)^{-T}$
Short 1 WYZ stock	$-S_0$
Long 1 call option	$C_{0,T}$
Net investment:	$X(1 + RFR)^{-T} - S_0 + C_{0,T}$

B. Portfolio Value at Option Expiration (Date *T*)

Portfolio	(1) If $S_T \le X$:	(2) If $S_T > X$:
Long 1 T-bill	X	X
Short 1 WYZ stock	$-S_T$	$-S_T$
Long 1 call option	0	$(S_T - X)$
Net position:	$X - S_T$	0

the Date T distribution of $\max[0, 50 - S_T]$ could be acquired through the synthetic strategy at a cost of $2.25 (= 48.51 − 53 + 6.74) or through the purchase of the actual put for $2.51.

This is the same $0.26 price differential we saw earlier when designing an arbitrage transaction involving the actual and synthetic T-bill. The put arbitrage would be to short the actual put while buying the replicating portfolio (i.e., long T-bill, short stock, and long call), which is the same set of transactions we used in the T-bill arbitrage. This underscores the important point that the put-call parity model only allows us to make *relative*—rather than absolute— statements about security values. Although we can change our perspective about the misvalued instrument (e.g., T-bill versus put option), the real source of the market inefficiency came from examining the *difference* between the put and call prices in relation to the stock and T-bill prices. Consequently, all four securities need to be included in the arbitrage trade.

13.3.4 ADJUSTING PUT-CALL-SPOT PARITY FOR DIVIDENDS

Another extension of the put-call-spot parity model involves the payment of dividends to the shareholders of WYZ stock. Suppose that in the basic portfolio listed in Exhibit 13.16, WYZ stock pays a dividend of D_T immediately prior to the options expiry at Date T. Assume further that the dividend amount is known when the investment is initiated, a condition that is almost certainly met for values of $T \le 0.25$ per year because Canadian companies typically pay quarterly dividends. The result is that the terminal value of the long stock position will be $(S_T + D_T)$ while the terminal payoffs to the put and call options remain $\max[0, X - S_T]$ and $\max[0, S_T - X]$, respectively, as the holders of the two derivative contracts will not participate directly in the payment of dividends to the shareholder.[6] Thus, the net Date T value of the portfolio acquired originally for $(S_0 + P_{0,T} - C_{0,T})$ is $(X + D_T)$.

---

6 The fact that the expiration date payoff to a call option on both a dividend- and non-dividend-paying stock can be expressed as $\max[0, S_T - X]$ does not mean that the two will generate the same dollar amount of cash flow. This is because the stock's value will be reduced by the payment of the dividend in the former case but not in the latter. Thus, with the lower terminal payout, the call on the dividend-paying stock will be less valuable than an otherwise comparable contract on a non-dividend-paying equity. We will explore this topic more fully in Chapter 14.

With the critical assumption that the dividend payment is known at Date 0, the portfolio long in WYZ stock, long the put, and short the call once again can be viewed as equivalent to a T-bill, now having a face value of $(X + D_T)$. This allows Equation 13.1 to be adapted as follows:

$$S_0 + P_{0,T} - C_{0,T} = \frac{X + D_T}{(1 + RFR)^T} = \frac{X}{(1 + RFR)^T} + \frac{D_T}{(1 + RFR)^T}$$

which can be interpreted as:

(Long Stock) + (Long Put) + (Short Call) = (Long T-Bill) + (Long Present Value of Dividends)

Alternatively, it is often more useful to rearrange this equation as follows:

$$\left\{ S_0 - \frac{D_T}{(1 + RFR)^T} \right\} + P_{0,T} - C_{0,T} = \frac{X}{(1 + RFR)^T}$$

This form of the equation can be compared directly with the no-dividend put-call-spot parity result and shows that the current stock price must be *adjusted downward* by the present value of the dividend. With an initial stock price of $53 and an annualized risk-free rate on a six-month T-bill of 6.25%, a $1 dividend paid just before the expiration of a call and a put option with an exercise price of $50 would result in a theoretical price differential of:

$$C_{0.05} - P_{0.05} = \left\{ 53 - \frac{1}{(1 + 0.0625)^{0.5}} \right\} - \frac{50}{(1 + 0.0625)^{0.5}} = \$3.52$$

This value differs from the parity differential for options on the non-dividend-paying stock, which was shown earlier to be $4.49. Thus, the payment of the dividend has reduced the price of the call relative to the put by $0.97, which is the discounted amount of the $1 cash distribution.

13.3.5 PUT-CALL-FORWARD PARITY

Suppose that instead of buying the stock in the spot market at Date 0, we took a long position in a forward contract allowing us to purchase one WYZ stock at Date T. The future price, $F_{0,T}$, would be established at Date 0. As before, we assume that this transaction is supplemented by the purchase of a put and the sale of a call, each having the same exercise price and expiration date. Exhibit 13.19 summarizes both the initial and terminal cash flows to this position.

Exhibit 13.19	Put-Call-Forward Parity

A. Net Portfolio Investment at Initiation (Date 0)

Portfolio	
Long 1 forward contract	0
Long 1 put option	$P_{0,T}$
Short 1 call option	$-C_{0,T}$
Net investment:	$P_{0,T} - C_{0,T}$

B. Portfolio Value at Option Expiration (Date T)

Portfolio	(1) If $S_T \leq X$:	(2) If $S_T > X$:
Long 1 forward contract	$(S_T - F_{0,T})$	$(S_T - F_{0,T})$
Long 1 put option	$(X - S_T)$	0
Short 1 call option	0	$-(S_T - X)$
Net position:	$(X - F_{0,T})$	$(X - F_{0,T})$

Panel B reveals that this is once again a risk-free portfolio. There are, however, two important differences in its cash flow patterns. First, the net initial investment of $(P_{0,T} - C_{0,T})$ is substantially smaller than when the stock was purchased in the spot market. Second, the riskless terminal payoff of $(X - F_{0,T})$ also is smaller than before as the stock now must be purchased at Date T rather than at Date 0. This intuition leads directly to the *put-call-forward* parity condition:

$$
13.2 \qquad P_{0,T} - C_{0,T} = \frac{X - F_{0,T}}{(1 + RFR)^T} = \frac{X}{(1 + RFR)^T} - \frac{F_{0,T}}{(1 + RFR)^T}
$$

which says that for markets to be free from arbitrage, the difference between put and call prices must equal the discounted difference between the option exercise price and the forward contract price. Just as $F_{0,T}$ did not appear in the spot market version of the parity condition, the current stock price does not appear in Equation 13.2.

This result implies that the only time that put and call prices should be equal to one another in an efficient market is when $X = F_{0,T}$. That is, although the put-call parity result holds for any common exercise price, there is only one value of X for which there would be no net cost to the option combination and that is the prevailing forward price. Recall, for example, that when WYZ stock did not pay a dividend, the theoretical difference between $C_{0,0.5}$ and $P_{0,0.5}$ was \$4.49 (= 53 − 48.51). This meant an investor long the call and short the put with a joint \$50 exercise price would have what amounted to a forward contract to buy WYZ stock in six months at a price of \$50.[7] However, she would have to pay \$4.49 for

---

7 This interpretation follows by noting that the long call position will be exercised when $S_T > 50$ and the short put will be exercised against the investor when $S_T \leq 50$. Therefore, the investor's net option position produces an identical result to holding a long position in a forward contract with a contract price of \$50. Generalizing this result, any time we have a call and a put option on the same underlying stock with a common exercise price and expiration date, the following is true: (long call at X) + (short put at X) = (long forward at X). Similarly, shorting the call and buying the put produces a synthetic short forward position.

this arrangement, suggesting that $50 is a below-market forward price. How much below the prevailing forward contract price is $50? By the future value of $4.49, invested at the prevailing risk-free rate of 6.25%. Thus, the no-arbitrage forward price under these circumstances should be $54.63 [= 50 + 4.49(1 + 0.0625)$^{0.5}$].

Another way to see this result comes from combining the put-call-forward parity condition with the put-call-spot condition. Specifically, inserting the expression for $(P_{0,T} - C_{0,T})$ from the put-call-forward parity condition into the put-call-spot condition leaves

$$S_0 + \left\{ \frac{X}{(1 + RFR)^T} - \frac{F_{0,T}}{(1 + RFR)^T} \right\} = \frac{X}{(1 + RFR)^T}$$

which simplifies to

$$S_0 = \frac{F_{0,T}}{(1 + RFR)^T}$$

In the absence of dividend payments, notice that the share spot price should simply be the discounted value of purchasing the same security in the forward market. Equivalently, this equation can be rewritten so that $F_{0,T} = S_0(1 + RFR)^T$. In the preceding example, the market-clearing (i.e., no net initial cost) contract price for a WYZ stock forward agreement should be $F_{0,0.5} = (53)(1 + 0.0625)^{0.5} = \$54.63$. Finally, when dividends are paid, the equation for the put-call-forward parity condition can be inserted into the dividend-adjusted spot parity condition to produce

$$\left\{ S_0 - \frac{D_T}{(1 + RFR)^T} \right\} = \frac{F_{0,T}}{(1 + RFR)^T}$$

Thus, if a $1 dividend were paid on WYZ stock just prior to the maturity of the contract in six months, the forward price would be adjusted down to $F_{0,0.5} = (53)(1 + 0.0625)^{0.5} - 1 = \$53.63$ to account for the payment to the actual shareholders but not the derivative holder.

13.4　An Introduction to the Use of Derivatives in Portfolio Management

Beyond the unique risk-reward profiles they offer as standalone investments, derivatives also are used widely to modify an existing portfolio's risk. In this section, we review three prominent derivative applications in the management of equity positions: shorting forward contracts, purchasing **protective puts**, and purchasing **equity collars**.

13.4.1 RESTRUCTURING ASSET PORTFOLIOS WITH FORWARD CONTRACTS

Suppose a portfolio manager currently has all of her investable funds committed to a well-diversified portfolio of equity securities designed to reflect the movements of the S&P/TSX

Composite index. Implicit in this investment approach is the manager's belief that she cannot add value by trying to select superior individual securities. She does, however, feel that it is possible to take advantage of perceived trends at a macroeconomic level by switching her funds on a tactical basis between her current equity holding and any of several other portfolios mimicking different asset classes (e.g., fixed-income, cash equivalents).

The stock market has increased steadily over the past several months, and the portfolio has a present market value of $100 million. The manager has now become concerned about the possibility that inflationary pressures will dampen corporate earnings and drive stock prices down. She also feels confident that the uncertainty will be resolved in the coming quarter. Accordingly, she would like to shift her allocation from 100% equity to 100% T-bills for the next three months. There are two ways she can do this. The most direct method would be to sell her stock portfolio and buy $100 million (less the transaction costs) of 90-day T-bills. When the T-bills mature in three months, she could then repurchase her original equity holdings.

The second approach would be to maintain her current stock holdings but convert them into a synthetic risk-free position with a three-month forward contract specifying $100 million of the stock index as the underlying asset. This is a classic example of a *hedge position,* wherein the price risk of the underlying asset is offset (rather than eliminated) by a supplementary derivative transaction. The following table captures the dynamics of this hedge at a basic level.

Economic Event	Actual Stock Exposure	Desired Forward Exposure
Stock prices fall	Loss	Gain
Stock prices rise	Gain	Loss

To neutralize the risk of falling stock prices, the manager requires a hedge position with payoffs that are *negatively correlated* with those of the existing exposure. This requires committing to the short side of the contract.[8]

The primary benefit of converting the portfolio's asset allocation using this approach is that it is far quicker and more cost effective than the physical transformations demanded by the first solution. A 1998 Association for Investment Management and Research seminar found that when all the transaction costs are considered (e.g., trading commissions, market impact, taxes), the average expense of rebalancing an equity portfolio was about 42 basis points of the position's value, while the same trade with an equity forward contract would have cost just 6 basis points. Although a U.S. example, the trading expenses in other countries reflect the same general trend.

This synthetic restructuring is best understood through the effect that it would have on the systematic risk—or beta—of the portfolio. Assume that the original portfolio had a beta of one, matching the volatility for the market portfolio. Combining the long $100 million portfolio and the short a forward covering $100 million of a stock index converts the systematic portion of the portfolio into a synthetic T-bill, which by definition has a beta of zero. Once the contract matures in three months, however, the position reverts to its original risk profile. This is illustrated in Exhibit 13.20. More generally, the short forward position can be designed to allow for intermediate combinations of stock and T-bills as well. To see this, let

---

8 This hedging argument is identical to the point we made in the portfolio formation analysis of Chapter 6 that it is always possible to combine two perfectly negatively correlated assets to create a risk-free position.

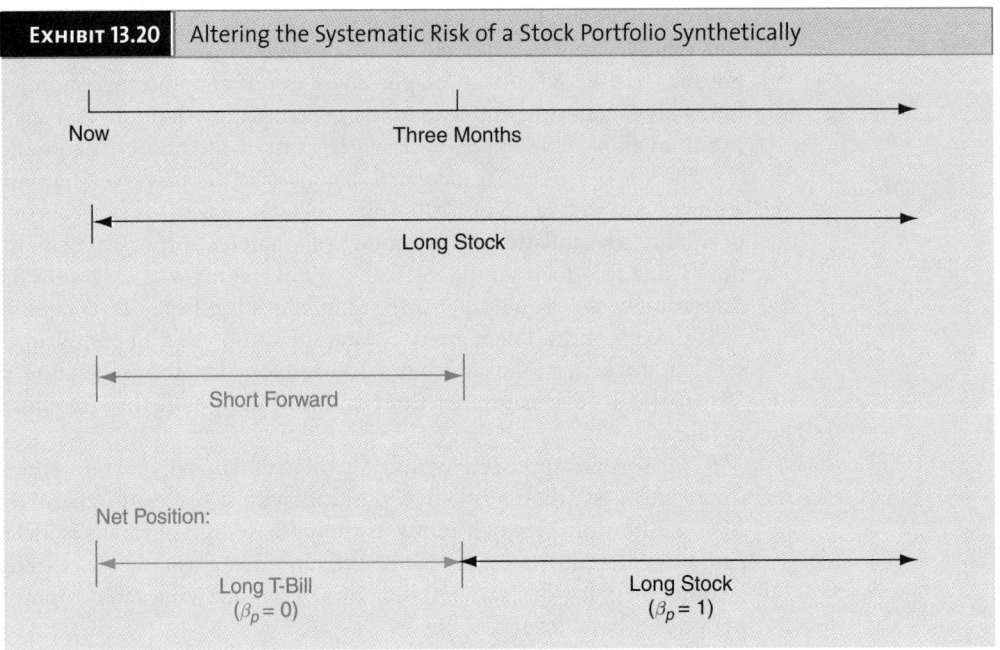

EXHIBIT 13.20 | Altering the Systematic Risk of a Stock Portfolio Synthetically

w_S be the stock allocation so that $(1 - w_S)$ is the allocation to the risk-free asset created synthetically. The net beta for the converted portfolio is simply a weighted average of the systematic risks of its equity and T-bill portions or

13.3

$$\beta_P = (w_S)\beta_S + (1 - w_S)\beta_{RFR}$$

Thus, if the manager had decided to change the original allocation from 100% stock to a "60−40" mix of stock and T-bills, she would have shorted only $40 million of the index forward to leave her with an unhedged equity position totalling $60 million (i.e., $w_S = 0.60$ and $[1 - w_S] = 0.40$). This in turn would leave her with an adjusted portfolio beta of $[(0.6)\,(1) + (0.4)\,(0)] = 0.6$.

13.4.2 PROTECTING PORTFOLIO VALUE WITH PUT OPTIONS

Although the manager's concern in the previous example was to protect her stock portfolio against possible share price declines over the next three months, by shorting the stock index forward contract, she has effectively committed to "selling" her equity position—even if stock prices rise. That is, the manager has surrendered the upside potential of her original holding. Suppose instead that she designed a hedge position correlated to her stock portfolio as follows:

Economic Event	Actual Stock Exposure	Desired Forward Exposure
Stock prices fall	Loss	Gain
Stock prices rise	Gain	*No loss*

In seeking an asymmetric hedge, this manager wants a derivative contract that allows her to sell stock when prices fall but keep her shares when prices rise. As we have seen, she must purchase a put to obtain this exposure.

The purchase of a put to hedge the downside risk of an underlying security holding is called a *protective put* position and is the most straightforward example of a more general set of derivative-based strategies known as *portfolio insurance*.[9] Instead of the short forward position, suppose the manager purchased a three-month, at-the-money put on her $100 million stock portfolio for an up-front premium of $1.324 million. The value of the protective put position (net of the initial cost of the hedge) is calculated in Exhibit 13.21 for several different expiration date prices for the underlying stock portfolio. In particular, notice that with the exercise price set equal to the current portfolio value of $100 million, the put contract exactly offsets any expiration date share price decline while allowing the position to increase in value as stock prices increase. Thus, the put provides the manager with insurance against falling prices with no *deductible*.[10]

Exhibit 13.21	Expiration Date Value of a Protective Put Position		
Potential Portfolio Value	Value of Put Option	Cost of Put Option	Net Protective Put Position
80	(100 − 80) = 20	−1.324	(80 + 20) − 1.324 = 98.676
90	(100 − 90) = 10	−1.324	(90 + 10) − 1.324 = 98.676
100	0	−1.324	(100 + 0) − 1.324 = 98.676
110	0	−1.324	(110 + 0) − 1.324 = 108.676
130	0	−1.324	(130 + 0) − 1.324 = 128.676

Notice that the terminal value of the combined stock and put option portfolio shown in the last column of Exhibit 13.21 resembles the payoff diagram of the long call position illustrated earlier in Exhibit 13.11. This is shown in Exhibit 13.22, which indicates that being long in the stock and long in the put generates the same net payoff as an at-the-money long call holding "elevated" by $100 million. Given the put-call-spot parity results of the previous section, this should come as no surprise. Indeed, the no-arbitrage equation (Equation 13.1) can be rewritten:

$$S_0 + P_{0,T} = C_{0,T} + \frac{X}{(1 + RFR)^T}$$

That is, the protective put method of providing portfolio insurance generates the same expiration date payoff as a long position in a call with equivalent characteristics as the put and a long position in a T-bill with a face value equal to the options' exercise price. It is this final

---

9 The concept and use of portfolio insurance has received a great deal of scrutiny in the research literature. See, for example, the studies by Rubinstein (1985), Kritzman (1986), and Basak (2002).

10 In general, the deductible portion of the portfolio insurance contract can be defined as $[S_0 - X]$. For instance, with an exercise price of 95, the manager would not receive compensation from the hedge until the portfolio value fell below $95 million; she would effectively be self-insuring the first $5 million of losses. Naturally, the larger this deductible amount, the lower the cost of the put option.

EXHIBIT 13.22 Terminal Payoff to an Insured Stock Position

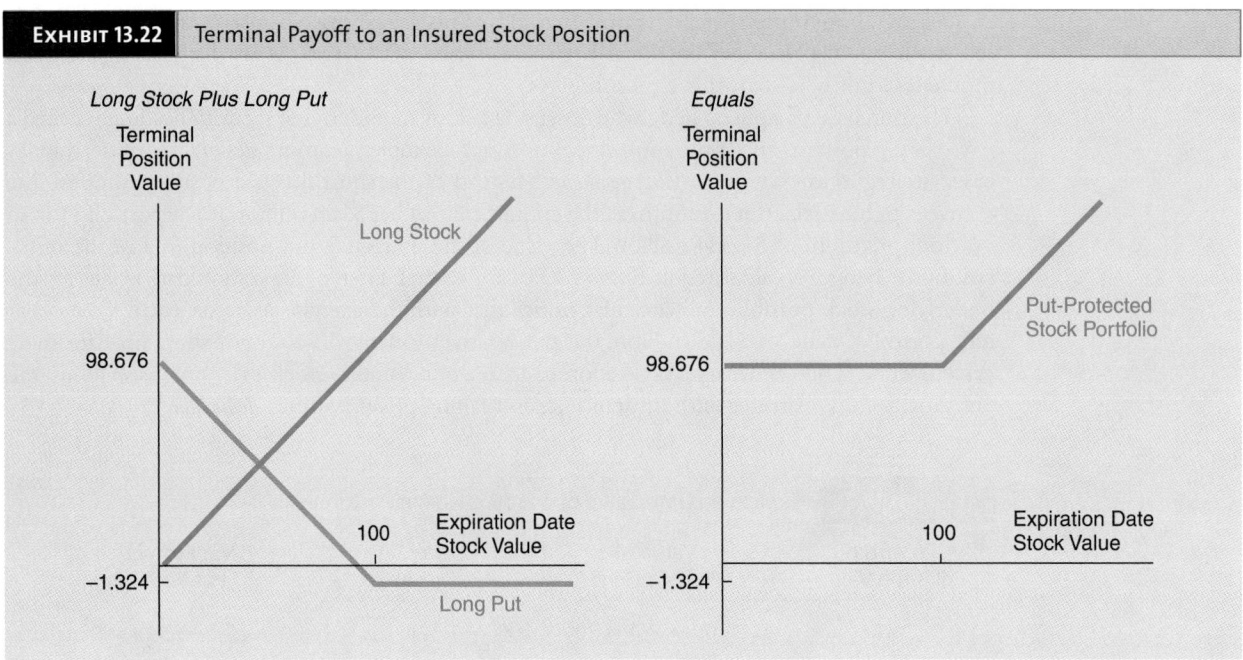

term that provides the elevation to the call payoff diagram in Exhibit 13.22. Thus, the manager has two ways of providing price insurance for her current stock holding: (1) continue to hold her shares and purchase a put, or (2) sell her shares and buy both a T-bill and a call. Her choice between them will undoubtedly come down to considerations such as relative option prices and transaction costs.[11]

13.4.3 AN ALTERNATIVE WAY TO PAY FOR A PROTECTIVE PUT

There is a third alternative for protecting against potential stock price declines, which fits between paying nothing for a hedge but surrendering future stock gains for the next three months (i.e., the short forward position) and keeping those potential gains in exchange for a considerable initial payment (i.e., the protective put position).

Specifically, suppose the manager makes two simultaneous decisions. First, she decides to buy a three-month, out-of-the-money protective put with an exercise price of $97 million and a commensurately lower initial cost of $0.560 million. (Notice that in purchasing an out-of-the-money contract, the manager is creating a $3 million deductible compared to her current portfolio value.) Second, instead of paying cash for the put, our manager sells back to the option dealer a call with a three-month expiration and an exercise price of $108 million that also carries an initial premium of $0.560 million. The simultaneous purchase of an out-of-the-money put and sale of an out-of-the-money call on the same underlying asset and with the same expiration date and market price is a strategy known as a **collar agreement**.

Exhibit 13.23 shows the expiration date outcomes of the manager's equity collar-protected portfolio for several different terminal stock portfolio values. Notice that, like the forward contract hedge, there is no initial out-of-pocket expense associated with this derivative

---

11 Many authors have studied the effect that adding options to an underlying security position has on the risk of the combined portfolio. In particular, see Merton, Scholes, and Gladstein (1978); Bookstaber and Clarke (1981); and Nederlof (1993).

Exhibit 13.23	Expiration Date Value of an Equity Collar-Protected Portfolio			
Potential Portfolio Value	Net Option Expense	Value of Put Option	Value of Call Option	Net Collar-Protected Position
70	(0.56 − 0.56) = 0	(97 − 70) = 27	0	70 + 27 = 97
80	(0.56 − 0.56) = 0	(97 − 80) = 17	0	80 + 17 = 97
90	(0.56 − 0.56) = 0	(97 − 90) = 7	0	90 + 7 = 97
97	(0.56 − 0.56) = 0	0	0	97 + 0 = 97
100	(0.56 − 0.56) = 0	0	0	100 + 0 = 100
108	(0.56 − 0.56) = 0	0	0	108 − 0 = 108
110	(0.56 − 0.56) = 0	0	(108 − 110) = −2	110 − 2 = 108
120	(0.56 − 0.56) = 0	0	(108 − 120) = −12	120 − 12 = 108

combination. Instead, the manager effectively pays for her desired portfolio insurance by surrendering an equivalent amount of the portfolio's future upside potential. Secondly, like the protective put in the last example (and unlike the short forward position), she does retain some of the benefit of a rising stock market. However, this upside gain potential stops at the exercise price of the call. As shown in Exhibit 13.24, the manager has placed a collar around her portfolio for the next three months—its net value will not fall below $97 million and will not rise above $108 million. At any terminal value for the stock portfolio between these extreme

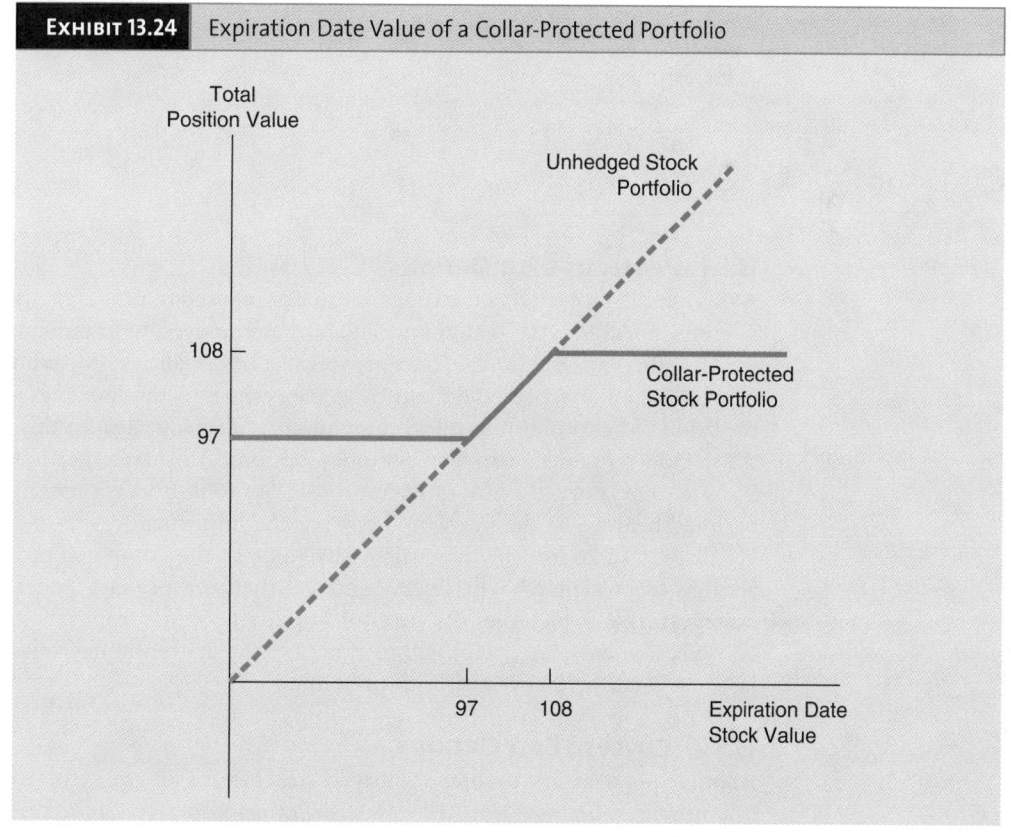

Exhibit 13.24   Expiration Date Value of a Collar-Protected Portfolio

levels, both of the options expire out of the money and no contract settlement payment will be required of either the manager or the dealer.

13.5   Option Trading Strategies

Now that we've had the opportunity to explore the use of derivatives in portfolio management, we will turn our attention to the use of derivatives in *combination* with one another to create customized payoff distributions that do not exist in more fundamental securities, like stocks or bonds. In designing such combinations, the investor usually attempts to exploit a very specific view about future economic conditions. For example, he may feel that a particular company's stock returns will be extraordinarily volatile but have no clear impression about the price movement direction. Or he may feel that another company's shares will trade within a very narrow range around their current price during the next few months. In developing all these strategies, we will return to the hypothetical example of SAS Corporation, which has exchange-traded common stock, as well as call and puts. Current prices for SAS stock and six different derivatives, all of which expire at the same time, are reproduced in Exhibit 13.25.

EXHIBIT 13.25	Hypothetical SAS Corporation Stock and Option Prices				
Instrument		Exercise Price ($)	Market Price ($)	Intrinsic Value ($)	Time Premium ($)
Stock:		—	40.00	—	—
Call:	#1	35.00	8.07	5.00	3.07
	#2	40.00	5.24	0.00	5.24
	#3	45.00	3.24	0.00	3.24
Put:	#1	35.00	1.70	0.00	1.70
	#2	40.00	3.67	0.00	3.67
	#3	45.00	6.47	5.00	1.47

13.5.1   PROTECTIVE PUT OPTIONS

Although the protective put strategy is most often used to provide insurance for price declines in entire portfolios, the technique can also be employed with individual equity positions. To see how this "insured stock" concept works, consider an investor who owns SAS but is concerned that an unexpected downturn in the company's product sales may lead to a decline in the value of her position in the coming months. To hedge against this firm-specific exposure, she decides to purchase an at-the-money put on SAS shares, meaning that she would spend $3.67 to buy Put #2 with an exercise price of $40. If at expiration the price of SAS had declined below $40, the put would pay her the difference.

Exhibit 13.26 lists the expiration date value of the combined protective put position for a range of possible SAS prices. As noted earlier, the primary benefit of the insured stock strategy is that it preserves the investor's upside potential from rising share prices but limits her losses when share prices fall. In this case, the at-the-money put insures her against any losses beyond the $3.67 initial put premium.

13.5.2   COVERED CALL OPTIONS

Another popular way to alter the payoff structure of an equity position involves the sale of call options. When investors sell calls based on an underlying position they own, they are said

Exhibit 13.26	Expiration Date Value of a Protective Put Position		
Potential SAS Stock Value	**Value of Put Option**	**Cost of Put Option**	**Net Protective Put Position**
25	(40 − 25) = 15	−3.67	(25 + 15) − 3.67 = 36.33
30	(40 − 30) = 10	−3.67	(30 + 10) − 3.67 = 36.33
35	(40 − 35) = 5	−3.67	(35 + 5) − 3.67 = 36.33
40	0	−3.67	(40 + 0) − 3.67 = 36.33
45	0	−3.67	(45 + 0) − 3.67 = 41.33
50	0	−3.67	(50 + 0) − 3.67 = 46.33

to be *writing* covered calls. Usually, the purpose of this strategy is to generate additional income for a stock holding that is not expected to change in value much over the near term. By selling a call, an investor receives the premium from the option contract to bolster an otherwise small (or negative) return. The danger is that the stock price rises above the exercise price by the end of the contract's life, causing the shares to be called away.

Suppose now that our investor believes that over the next few months the value of her SAS stock will neither rise nor fall by an appreciable amount. She decides not to insure her position against losses but, instead, to increase the cash flow of the investment by selling an at-the-money call (Call #2) for $5.24. The expiration date values for the covered call position are listed in Exhibit 13.27. The construction of the terminal profit diagram—once again net of the current SAS share price—is depicted in Exhibit 13.28.

Exhibit 13.27	Expiration Date Value of a Covered Call Position		
Potential SAS Stock Value	**Value of Call Option**	**Proceeds from Call Option**	**Net Covered Call Position**
30	0	5.24	(30 − 0) + 5.24 = 35.24
35	0	5.24	(35 − 0) + 5.24 = 40.24
40	0	5.24	(40 − 0) + 5.24 = 45.24
45	−(45 − 40) = −5	5.24	(45 − 5) + 5.24 = 45.24
50	−(50 − 40) = −10	5.24	(50 − 10) + 5.24 = 45.24

Both of these displays show that the expiration date payoff to the covered call position is comparable in form to that of a short a put. This can be seen directly by adjusting the put-call parity condition as follows:

(Long Stock) + (Short Call) = (Long T-bill) + (Short Put)

Notice in Exhibit 13.28 that there are two dimensions to the price risk inherent in this strategy. First, if by the option expiry date, SAS stock has risen above $40, the investor will be

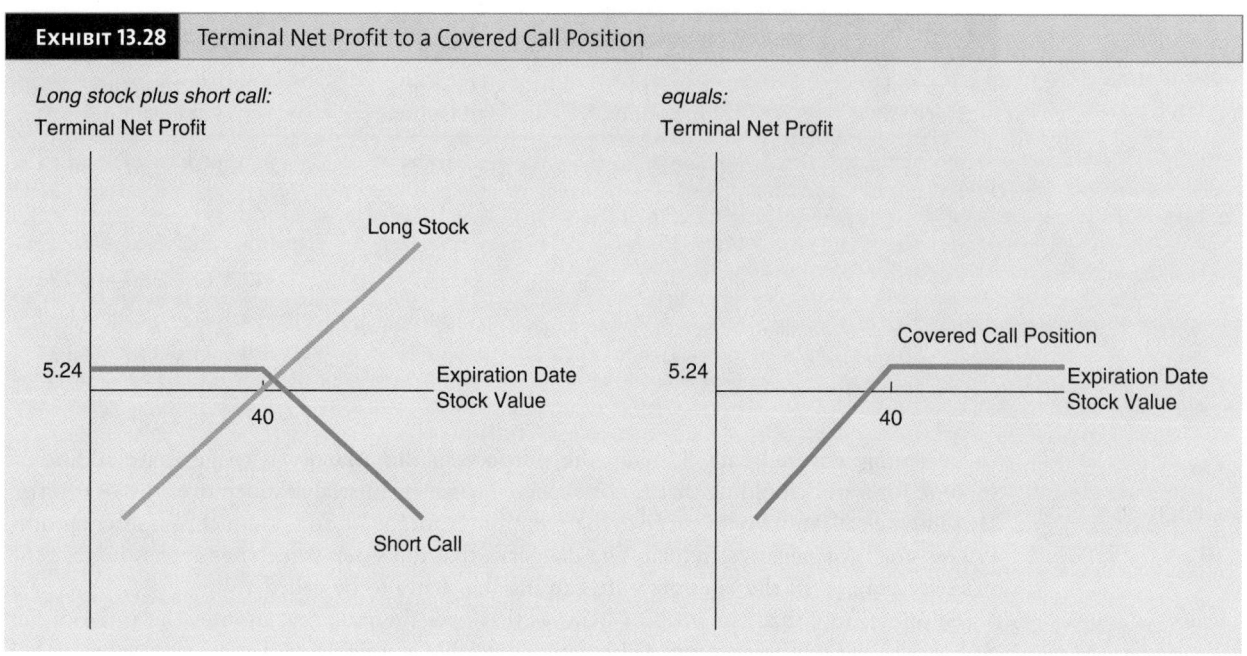

Exhibit 13.28   Terminal Net Profit to a Covered Call Position

forced to sell her shares for less than they are actually worth. However, this will represent a lost opportunity only at prices above $45.24, or the exercise price plus the initial call premium. Second, if SAS stock price declines, her potential loss is not hedged beyond the $5.24 in premium income that she received for selling the call; after prices fall beyond $31.09 (= 40 − 5.24 − 3.67), she would have been better off purchasing the at-the-money protective put. Thus, to be profitable, the covered call strategy requires that the investor guess correctly that share values remain in a reasonably narrow band around their present levels.

13.5.3 Straddles, Strips, and Straps

A *straddle* is the simultaneous purchase (or sale) of a call and a put with the same underlying asset, exercise price, and expiration date. A long straddle requires the purchase of the put and the call, while a short straddle sells both contracts. The long straddle gives the investor a combination that will appreciate in value whether stock prices rise or fall in the future. However, buying two options increases the initial cost; therefore to profit, stock price movements must be more pronounced than if the investor had predicted changes in a single direction. In this sense, a straddle is a *volatility* play; the buyer expects stock prices to move strongly one way or the other, while the seller hopes for lower-than-normal volatility.

Assume that an investor who does not hold SAS stock purchases a put and a call, each with an exercise price of $40. The cost of this purchase will be the combined prices of Call #2 and Put #2, or $8.91 (= 5.24 + 3.67). Recalling that the terminal values of the options are $\max[0, S_T − 40]$ and $\max[0, 40 − S_T]$, respectively, the potential expiration date profits to the straddle position (net of the initial cost, unadjusted for the time value differential) are shown in Exhibit 13.29. These are illustrated in Exhibit 13.30, which also depicts the profit to the seller of the straddle. The breakeven points on this graph occur at $31.09 (= 40 − 8.91) and $48.91 (= 40 + 8.91).

The expiration date values to the long and short positions are mirror images of each other; if the individual options themselves are zero-sum games, so too must be any combination of contracts. The buyer of the straddle is hoping for a dramatic event that will either increase or

Exhibit 13.29	Expiration Date Profits to a Long Straddle Position			
SAS Stock Price at Expiration	Value of Calls	Value of Puts	Cost of Options	Net Profit
20.00	0.00	20.00	−8.91	11.09
25.00	0.00	15.00	−8.91	6.09
30.00	0.00	10.00	−8.91	1.09
35.00	0.00	5.00	−8.91	−3.91
40.00	0.00	0.00	−8.91	−8.91
45.00	5.00	0.00	−8.91	−3.91
50.00	10.00	0.00	−8.91	1.09
55.00	15.00	0.00	−8.91	6.09
60.00	20.00	0.00	−8.91	11.09

Exhibit 13.30	The Straddle Illustrated

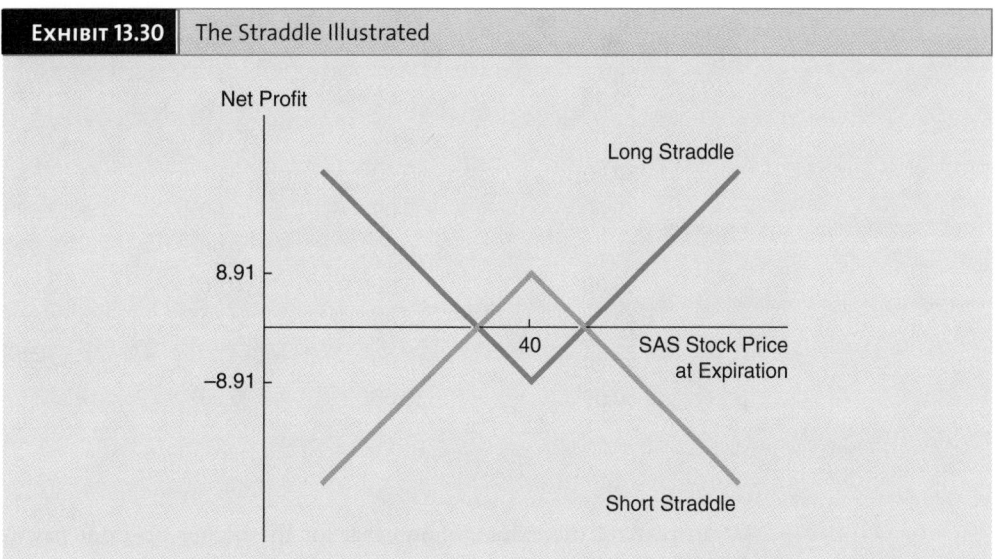

decrease the stock price from its present $40 by at least $8.91. Conversely, the best result for the straddle seller is for SAS stock to continue to trade at its current price through the expiration date (i.e., no volatility at all) so that both options expire worthless. The seller's position demonstrates that it is possible to make money in the stock market even when prices do not change.

The long straddle position assumes implicitly that the investor has no intuition about the likely direction of future stock price movements. A slight modification is overweighting either the put or call position to emphasize a directional belief while maintaining a contract that would profit from a price movement the other way. A long *strap* position is the purchase of two calls and one put with the same exercise price, suggesting an investor who thinks stock prices are more likely to increase. An investor with a more bearish view could create a long *strip* position by purchasing two puts and only one call. The terminal profits to both of these combinations are listed in Exhibit 13.31, which again assumes the use of the two at-the-money SAS contracts.

EXHIBIT 13.31	Expiration Date Profits to Long Strap and Long Strip Positions

A. Strap Position (Two Calls and One Put)

SAS Stock Price at Expiration	Value of Calls	Value of Puts	Cost of Options	Net Profit
20.00	0.00	20.00	−14.15	5.85
25.00	0.00	15.00	−14.15	0.85
30.00	0.00	10.00	−14.15	−4.15
35.00	0.00	5.00	−14.15	−9.15
40.00	0.00	0.00	−14.15	−14.15
45.00	10.00	0.00	−14.15	−4.15
50.00	20.00	0.00	−14.15	5.85
55.00	30.00	0.00	−14.15	15.85
60.00	40.00	0.00	−14.15	25.85

B. Strip Position (Two Puts and One Call)

SAS Stock Price at Expiration	Value of Calls	Value of Puts	Cost of Options	Net Profit
20.00	0.00	40.00	−12.58	27.42
25.00	0.00	30.00	−12.58	17.42
30.00	0.00	20.00	−12.58	7.42
35.00	0.00	10.00	−12.58	−2.58
40.00	0.00	0.00	−12.58	−12.58
45.00	5.00	0.00	−12.58	−7.58
50.00	10.00	0.00	−12.58	−2.58
55.00	15.00	0.00	−12.58	2.42
60.00	20.00	0.00	−12.58	7.42

Panel A of the exhibit shows that for the higher up-front payment of $14.15 [= (2 × 5.24) + 3.67], the strap will accelerate the profit in a rising market relative to the straddle. The settlement payment when SAS stock finishes above $40 on the expiration date is twice as great because the strap has doubled the investor's number of calls. The gross payoff when the price falls below $40 remains the same, however, the net amount received is considerably lower because the extra contract the investor purchased would then be out of the money. The net terminal value of the strip position tells a similar story, only with the acceleration of the profit generated by falling stock prices. The strap is more expensive than the strip under these conditions because SAS is a non-dividend-paying common stock that is expected to increase in price to provide the investor with a positive expected return.

13.5.4 STRANGLES

One final variation on the straddle is an option combination known as a *strangle,* which also involves the simultaneous purchase or sale of a call and a put on the same underlying security with the same expiration date. Unlike the straddle, however, the options used in the strangle do not have the same exercise price; instead, they are selected so that both are out of the money. By buying two out-of-the-money contracts, the investor reduces the original straddle position's initial cost. Offsetting this reduced cost, though, is that stock prices will have to change by a greater amount before the strangle becomes profitable. Thus, the strangle offers a more modest risk-reward structure than the straddle.

Suppose the investor purchased Call #3 and Put #1 for a combined price of $4.94 (= 3.24 + 1.70). If the SAS stock price remained between the put exercise price of $35 and the call exercise price of $45, both contracts would expire worthless and the investor would lose his entire initial investment. Prices would have to decline to $30.06 (= 35 − 4.94) or increase to $49.94 (= 45 + 4.94) before the investor would break even on the position. Exhibit 13.32 shows that these break-even points for the strangle are outside those for the straddle described earlier. Thus, among the set of "volatility bets," the strangle costs less to implement than the straddle but requires greater movement in the underlying security's price before it generates a positive return. Finally, by varying the exercise prices on the two options, the investor can create a strangle position that offers the exact trade-off between initial cost and future expected profit that he desires.

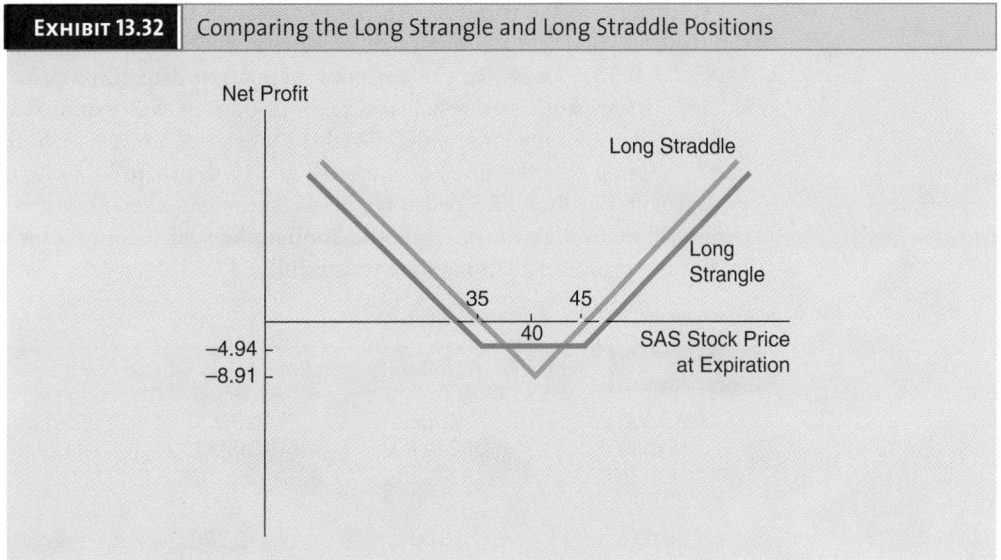

EXHIBIT 13.32 | Comparing the Long Strangle and Long Straddle Positions

13.5.5   CHOOSER OPTIONS

The straddle is a special case of a wider class of option contracts sometimes called *chooser* options. With a chooser option, the investor selects an exercise price and expiration date but doesn't have to decide if the option should be a put or a call until after the contract is purchased. That is, the straddle is just a chooser option for which the decision can be deferred until the expiration date.

At one extreme, if the decision has to be made immediately, the buyer will select the option most likely to be in the money at expiration. For example, the buyer could choose the call with $X = 40$. Thus, a chooser option in this case is worth $5.24. At the other extreme, a chooser option that allows the holder to defer the decision until expiration is, as already noted, equivalent to holding both a put and a call for the entire time to expiration. Consequently, the straddle price of $8.91 is the upper bound of the chooser option value struck at $40. The usual design for the chooser contract requires the holder to make a choice after the initial purchase but before expiration, which would create a position worth somewhere between $5.24 and $8.91.

13.5.6 SPREADS

As described by Black (1975), option spreads are the purchase of one contract and the sale of another, where the options are alike in all respects except for one distinguishing characteristic. In a *money* spread, the investor would sell an out-of-the-money call and purchase an in-the-money call on the same stock and expiration date. Alternatively, a *calendar* (or time) spread requires the purchase and sale of two calls—or two puts—with the same exercise price but different expiration dates. Option spreads are often used when one contract is perceived to be misvalued relative to the other. For instance, if an investor determines that a call with an exercise price of X_1 and an expiration date T is selling at too high a price in the market, he can short it, thereby speculating on an eventual correction. However, if a broad-based increase in the stock market occurs before this contract-specific correction, he stands to lose a great deal because the short call position has unlimited liability. Thus, when he sells the first option, he can hedge some or all of the risk by buying a call with an exercise price of X_2 expiring at T.

Returning to the data for SAS options, assume the investor purchases the in-the-money call (Call #1) and sells the out-of-the-money call (Call #3). This requires a net cash outlay of $4.83 (= 8.07 − 3.24). At the common expiration date, three price ranges should be considered. If SAS stock settles below $35, both options will expire worthless and the investor will lose all of his initial investment. With an SAS price above $45, both contracts will be exercised, meaning that the investor must sell at $45 the share he bought for $35, leaving a $10 gross payoff. Finally, if SAS prices fall between the two exercise prices, the option the investor owns will be in the money while the contract he sold will not. This situation is summarized by the net profit calculations shown in Exhibit 13.33.

EXHIBIT 13.33	Expiration Date Profits to a Bull Money Spread Position			
SAS Stock Price at Expiry	Value of Call #1	Value of Call #3	Cost of Options	Net Profit
20.00	0.00	0.00	−4.83	−4.83
30.00	0.00	0.00	−4.83	−4.83
35.00	0.00	0.00	−4.83	−4.83
40.00	5.00	0.00	−4.83	0.17
45.00	10.00	0.00	−4.83	5.17
50.00	15.00	−5.00	−4.83	5.17
60.00	25.00	−15.00	−4.83	5.17

This combination is sometimes called a *bull* money spread because it will be profitable when stock prices rise. With the initial cost of $4.83, the investor's break-even point occurs when the stock price rises to $39.83 (= 35 + 4.83). His benefit stops increasing if SAS shares reach $45, because this is where the short position in Call #3 becomes a liability. Exhibit 13.34 contrasts this situation with the outright purchase of the in-the-money call. This contract costs $8.07 initially, leading to the higher break-even price of $43.07. It would not have a constraint on the upside profit potential, however, so once a share price of $48.24 is reached [= 45 + (8.07 − 4.83)],

| **EXHIBIT 13.34** | Comparing the Bull Money Spread and Long Call Positions |

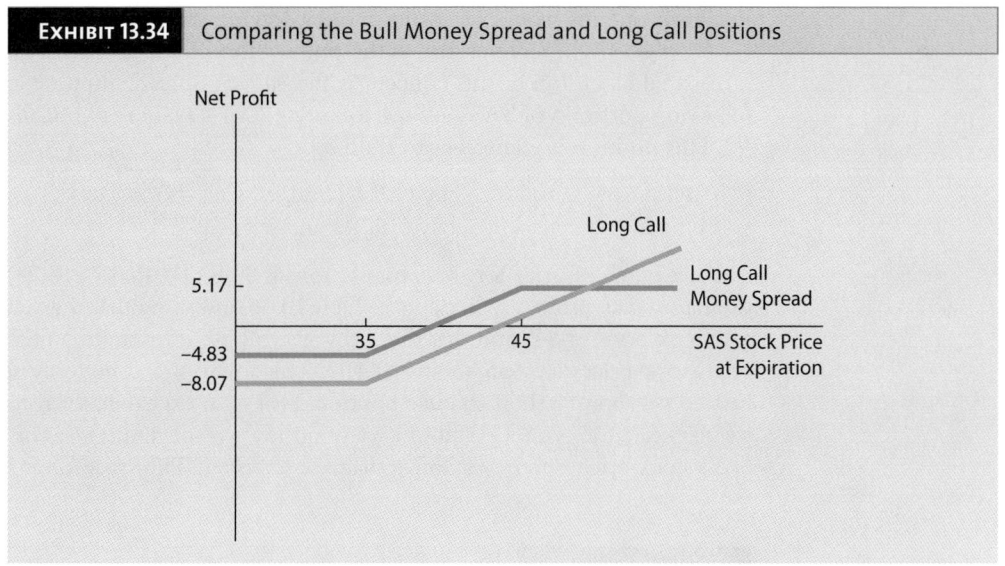

it would become the preferable alternative. Thus, in exchange for a lower initial purchase price, the bull spread investor is giving up the benefits of rising SAS prices after some point—a strategy that makes sense only if he expects the share price to settle within a fairly narrow range.

The profit for a *bear* money spread (the purchase of Call #3 and the sale of Call #1) is the opposite of that for the bull money spread. That is, buying a bear spread is equivalent to selling a bull spread. Consequently, a long bear spread position could be used by an investor who believed stock prices might decline but did not want to be short in the stock. A spread transaction also can be created using puts. For instance, suppose a new investor undertakes the simultaneous purchase of Put #3 and sale of Put #1. Her net cost to acquire the position would be $4.77 (= 6.47 − 1.70), which would then generate the terminal profits displayed in Exhibit 13.35. If SAS stock settled at $45 or higher, both puts would be worthless and the investor would lose all of her initial investment. If the expiration date share price was $35 or

| **EXHIBIT 13.35** | A Bear Money Spread with Put Options |

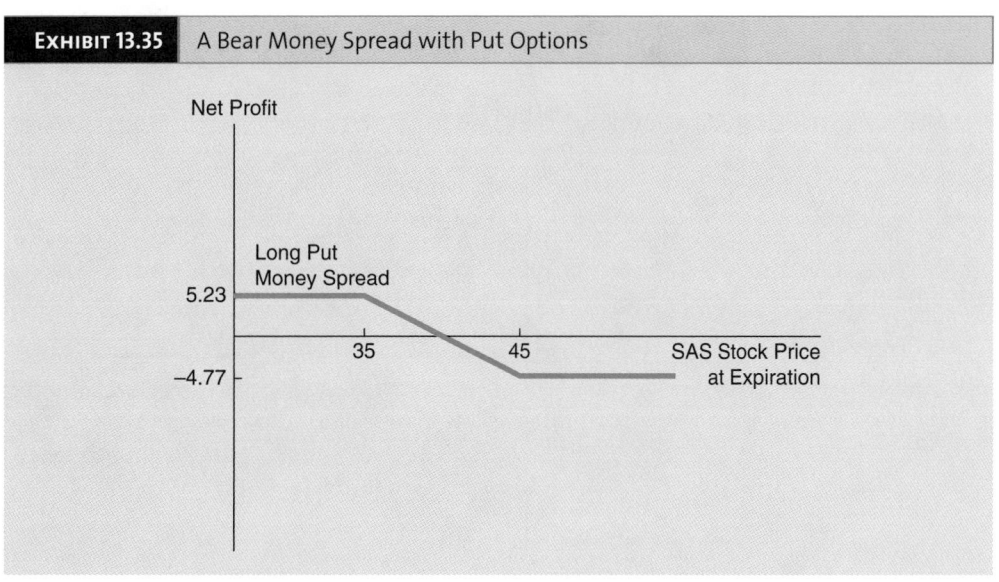

less, both options would be in the money, leaving the investor with a net position of $5.23 (= 45 − 35 − 4.77). Thus, this is the put version of a bear money spread.

A final extension of this concept is the *butterfly* spread. Suppose an investor designed the following portfolio of SAS options: long one Call #1, short two Calls #2, and long one Call #3. This position is equivalent to holding

- a bull money spread (i.e., buy Call #1 and sell Call #2), *and*
- a bear money spread (i.e., buy Call #3 and sell Call #2).

The net purchase price for these transactions is $0.83 [= (8.07 − 5.24) + (3.24 − 5.24)]. The expiration date profits are listed in Exhibit 13.36 and show that the value of the position peaks at a stock price of $40 and that the investor can lose, at most, her initial investment. The break-even stock prices are $35.83 and $44.17. This form of the butterfly spread is equivalent to a hedged version of a short straddle position. That is, in exchange for receiving a smaller potential payoff (i.e., $4.17 vs. $8.91) from a view on low volatility, the investor has limited her losses if SAS's stock price is more explosive than she expected. This trade-off is shown in Exhibit 13.37.

EXHIBIT 13.36	Expiration Date Profits to a Butterfly Spread			
SAS Stock Price at Expiration	Value Bull Spread	Value Bear Spread	Cost of Options	Net Profit
20.00	0.00	0.00	−0.83	−0.83
30.00	0.00	0.00	−0.83	−0.83
35.00	0.00	0.00	−0.83	−0.83
40.00	5.00	0.00	−0.83	4.17
45.00	5.00	−5.00	−0.83	−0.83
50.00	5.00	−5.00	−0.83	−0.83
60.00	5.00	−5.00	−0.83	−0.83

EXHIBIT 13.37	Comparing the Butterfly Spread and Short Straddle Positions

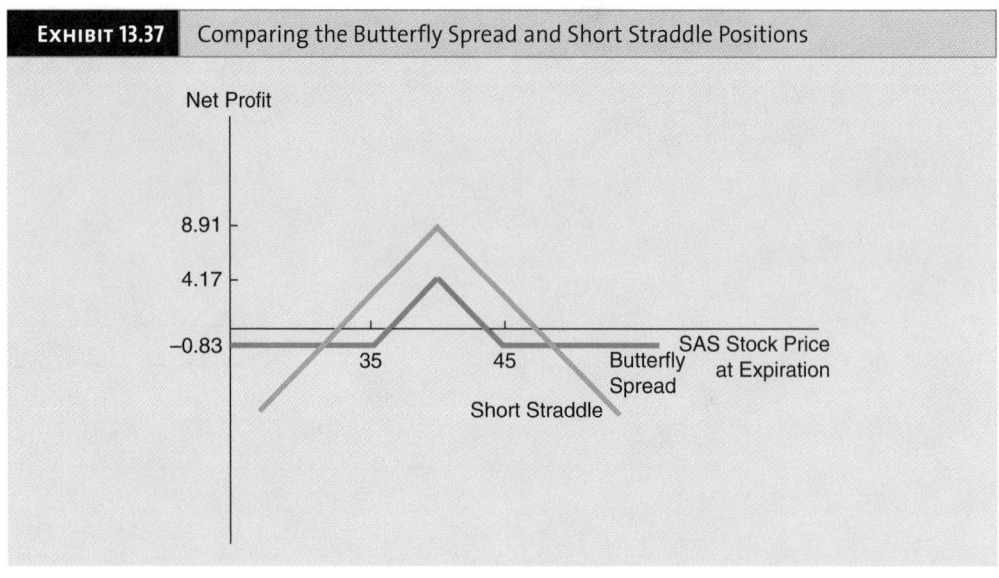

13.5.7 Range Forwards

Earlier we discussed an *equity collar* as a way that a manager could protect her portfolio from adverse movements while allowing for some upside gain potential. We saw that although the equity collar had some of the same attributes as a forward contract (e.g., no upfront premium expense), it was actually a combination of two options—the purchase of an out-of-the money put and sale of an out-of-the-money call. Equity collars are an example of a wider class of option combinations known as range (or flexible) forwards, and they are used to manage the risk of underlying assets other than equity as well.

To see how **range forward** positions might be used in a different context, assume that the treasurer of a multinational corporation knows today that he will have a bill for imported goods that must be paid in three months. This bill, denominated in Australian dollars and requiring payment of AUD$1,000,000, presents a challenge for a Canadian dollar–based company, which must buy the Australian dollars it needs because it does not generate them in the natural flow of business.

After contacting dealers in the OTC market, the treasurer establishes prices and terms for several AUD forward and option contracts. These are listed in Exhibit 13.38, which states prices on a direct (i.e., CAD/AUD) basis. The treasurer could lock in a three-month forward rate of CAD 0.80/AUD without cost in two ways. First, he could commit to a long position in the AUD forward with a contract amount of AUD$1,000,000. Second, he could buy the AUD call struck at CAD 0.80/AUD and pay for it by selling the AUD put at the same exercise rate. Recall that the put-call parity model indicates that buying a call and selling a put with the same exercise rate is equivalent to a long forward position. Further, this second strategy would generate a zero-cost forward (i.e., $C_0 = P_0$) only when the common exercise rate is set equal to the prevailing forward rate.

Exhibit 13.38	Hypothetical AUD Derivative Prices and Terms			
Derivative	Contract/Exercise Price (CAD/AUD)	Expiration	AUD Amount	Price (CAD/AUD)
Forward:	0.80	3 months	1,000,000	—
Calls:	0.77	3 months	1,000,000	0.034
	0.80	3 months	1,000,000	0.015
	0.83	3 months	1,000,000	0.004
Puts:	0.77	3 months	1,000,000	0.004
	0.80	3 months	1,000,000	0.015
	0.83	3 months	1,000,000	0.034

As a third alternative, what if the treasurer (1) bought the 0.83 call for CAD $0.004 per AUD and (2) sold the 0.77 put for the same price? Once again, this would be a costless combination of options; however, as the two options do not have a common exercise price, this combination is not equivalent to the actual forward—it is a range forward. At the expiration date, one of three things will happen: (1) if the spot FX rate is greater than CAD 0.83/AUD, the treasurer will exercise his call and buy AUD at that level; (2) if the spot FX rate is less than CAD 0.77/AUD, the dealer to whom the treasurer sold the put will force him to buy Australian dollars for CAD 0.77 per AUD, and (3) if the spot FX rate is between these extremes, both options will finish out of the money and the treasurer will buy the required currency at the regular market price. This payoff scheme is contrasted with the regular forward contract in Exhibit 13.39.

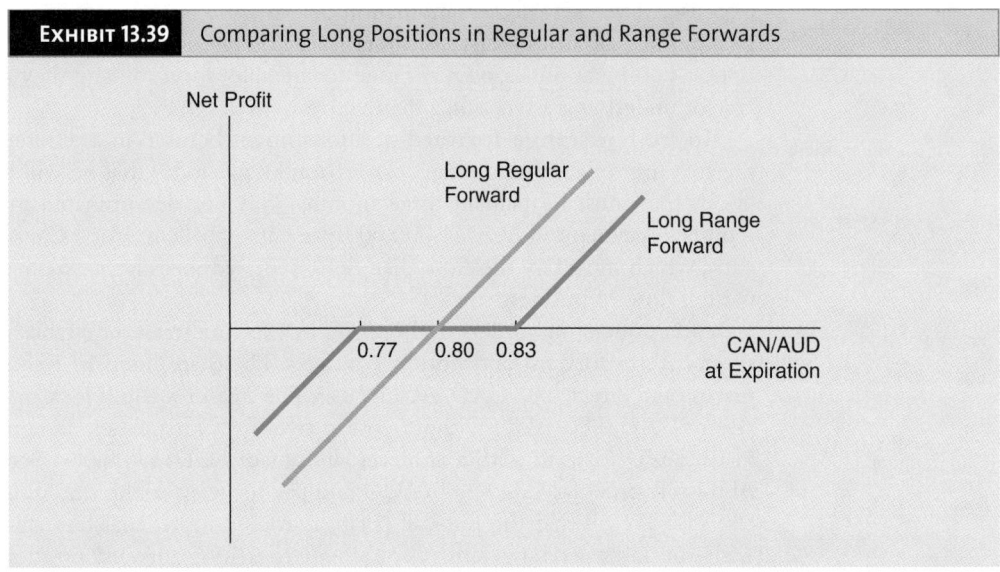

EXHIBIT 13.39   Comparing Long Positions in Regular and Range Forwards

If the treasurer takes a long position in the regular forward contract, he will buy his Australian dollars at CAD 0.80/AUD, whether or not the prevailing exchange rate in three months is above or below this level. Thus, although he is protected against a weakening dollar, he cannot benefit if the domestic currency strengthens. With a long position in the range forward, though, in exchange for worse FX insurance—namely, a maximum purchase CAD 0.83/AUD—he could pay as little as CAD 0.77/AUD if the dollar gets stronger. Finally, many zero-cost range forwards could be created; for any desired out-of-the-money call, there will be an out-of-the-money put at some exercise price that has the same premium. In fact, the actual forward contract can be viewed as a zero-cost range forward for which the put and the calls are both struck at CAD 0.80/AUD.

Summary

1. A derivative security is one for which the ultimate payoff to the investor depends directly on the value of another security or commodity.

2. Forward and option contracts can be viewed as insurance policies that an investor can hold against adverse price movements in his underlying position. The basic difference between these contracts lies in how the investor must pay for the desired insurance. Forwards typically do not require any initial payment but do obligate the investor to the possibility of an unfavourable transaction at a future date. Conversely, options provide asymmetrical terminal payoffs, but the investor must pay an up-front premium.

3. Derivatives have a specific terminology that is a blend of jargon. Forward and futures contracts, and option contracts offer investors a full range of choices. The buyer has a long position while the seller has a short position, the buyer and seller are sometimes called counterparties (forwards). The future date on which the transaction is to be consummated is called the maturity or expiration date, the predetermined price at which the trade takes place is the contract price if a forward, and an exercise price if an option.

4. A forward contract gives its holder both the right and the full obligation to conduct a transaction involving the underlying asset at a predetermined future date and at a

predetermined price. An advantage of forwards is that the contract terms can be whatever any two mutually consenting counterparties agree to. In contrast to forwards, both parties in a futures contract trade through a centralized market using standardized contracts. The futures exchange requires both counterparties to post collateral, or *margin,* to protect itself against the possibility of default.

5. There are well-defined relationships that must exist in an efficient capital market between the prices of forward and option contracts. The put-call parity conditions delineate the linkages between five different securities: the underlying asset (e.g., stock), T-bills, forward contracts, call options, and put options. An important consequence of these relationships is that one of these securities is always redundant because its cash flow patterns can be replicated by the remaining instruments. This leads to another important use for derivatives: arbitrage investing. Through their ability to help create synthetic replicas of existing securities, derivatives provide investors with the possibility of riskless excess returns when the synthetic and actual instruments sell for different prices.

6. Although forward, futures, and option contracts play important roles as stand-alone investments, the real advantage of derivatives is their ability to modify the risk-return characteristics of a collection of existing securities in a cost-effective manner. This use of forwards and options to restructure a portfolio synthetically has two dimensions: (1) It is possible to combine derivatives with the underlying position to replicate the cash flows of another traded instrument, and (2) derivatives can be used with the original portfolio to create a payoff structure that is otherwise unavailable.

7. A straddle is the simultaneous purchase or sale of a call and a put with the same underlying asset, exercise price, and expiration date. A strangle is also the simultaneous purchase or sale of a call and a put on the same underlying security with the same expiration date but the options used do not have the same exercise price. The options selected for strangles typically are out of the money, which reduces the original straddle position's initial cost but that means stock prices will have to change by a greater amount before the strangle becomes profitable. Option spreads are the purchase of one contract and the sale of another, where the options are alike in all respects except for one distinguishing characteristic. Option spreads are often used when one contract is perceived to be misvalued relative to the other. Range forwards are used to manage the risk of underlying assets and often are a trading strategy based on a variation of the put-call parity model where, for the same underlying asset but different exercise prices, a call option is purchased and a put option is sold (or vice versa).

Key Terms

American option, p. 364
arbitrage, p. 360
at the money, p. 364
call option, p. 364
collar agreement, p. 388
contract price, p. 360
counterparty, p. 360
derivative security, p. 359
equity collar, p. 384

European option, p. 364
exercise (or striking) price, p. 364
forward contract, p. 360
futures contract, p. 361
hedge, p. 359
in the money, p. 364
intrinsic value, p. 364
long position, p. 360
option contract, p. 364

option premium, p. 364
out of the money, p. 364
protective put, p. 384
put option, p. 364
put-call parity, p. 375
range forward, p. 399
short position, p. 360
time premium, p. 364

Suggested Readings

Bookstaber, Richard M., and Roger G. Clarke. "Options Can Alter Portfolio Return Distributions," *Journal of Portfolio Management* 7, no. 3 (Spring 1981): 63–70.

Brown, Keith C., ed. *Derivative Strategies for Managing Portfolio Risk.* Charlottesville, VA: AIMR, 1993.

Burns, Terrence E., ed. *Derivatives in Portfolio Management.* Charlottesville, VA: AIMR, 1998b.

Chance, Don M., and Robert Brooks. *An Introduction to Derivatives and Risk Management,* 7th ed. Mason, OH: Southwestern Publishing, 2007.

Moriarty, Eugene, Susan Phillips, and Paula Tosini. "A Comparison of Options and Futures in the Management of Portfolio Risk," *Financial Analysts Journal* 37, no. 1 (January–February 1981).

For Chapter CFA Questions and Problems, please see Appendix A at the end of this text.

Questions

1. Explain why the difference between put and call prices depends on whether or not the underlying security pays a dividend during the life of the contracts.

2. When comparing futures and forward contracts, it has been said that futures are more liquid but forwards are more flexible. Explain what this statement means and comment on how differences in contract liquidity and design flexibility might influence an investor's preference in choosing one instrument over the other.

3. Compare and contrast the gain and loss potential for investors holding the following positions: long forward, short forward, long call, short call, long put, and short put. Indicate what the terms *symmetric* and *asymmetric* mean in this context.

4. Explain how call and put options can represent a leveraged way of investing in the stock market and also enable investors to hedge their risk completely. Specifically, under what circumstances will the addition of an option increase the risk of an existing portfolio and under what circumstances will it decrease portfolio risk?

5. It has been said that, from an investor's perspective, a long position in a call option represents the "good half" of a long position in a forward contract. Explain what is meant by this statement. Also, describe what the "bad half" of the long forward position would have to be for this statement to be true.

6. Discuss the difficulties that having options in a security portfolio create for the measurement of portfolio risk. Specifically, explain why standard deviation is a deficient statistic for capturing the essence of risk in a put-protected portfolio. How could the standard deviation statistic be modified to account for this concern?

7. If the current price of a non-dividend-paying stock is $32 and a one-year futures contract on that stock has a contract price of $35, explain how an investor could create an "off-market" long position in a forward contract at an exercise price of $25. Would this synthetic contract require a cash payment from either the long or short position? If so, explain which party would have to make the payment and how that payment should be calculated.

8. Straddles have been described as "volatility plays." Explain what this means for both long and short straddle positions. Given the fact that volatility is a primary factor in how options are priced, under what conditions might an investor who believes that markets are efficient ever want to create a straddle?

9. Put-call-forward parity and range forward positions both involve the purchase of a call option and the sale of a put option (or vice versa) on the same underlying asset. Describe the relationship between these two trading strategies. Is one a special case of the other?

Problems

1. The common stock of Osprey Enterprises serves as the underlying asset for the following derivative securities: (1) forward contracts, (2) European call options, and (3) European put options.

   a. Assuming that all Osprey derivatives expire at the same date in the future, complete a table similar to the following for each of the following contract positions:

      (1) A long position in a forward with a contract price of $50

      (2) A long position in a call option with an exercise price of $50 and a front-end premium expense of $5.20

Expiration Date Osprey Stock Price	Expiration Date Derivative Payoff	Initial Derivative Premium	Net Profit
25	_____	_____	_____
30	_____	_____	_____
35	_____	_____	_____
40	_____	_____	_____
45	_____	_____	_____
50	_____	_____	_____
55	_____	_____	_____

60	____	____	____
65	____	____	____
70	____	____	____
75	____	____	____

   (3) A short position in a call option with an exercise price of $50 and a front-end premium receipt of $5.20

In calculating net profit, ignore the time differential between the initial derivative expense or receipt and the terminal payoff.

  b. Graph the net profit for each of the three derivative positions, using net profit on the vertical axis and Osprey's expiration date stock price on the horizontal axis. Label the break-even (i.e., zero profit) point(s) on each graph.

  c. Briefly describe the belief about the expiration date price of Osprey stock that an investor using each of these three positions implicitly holds.

2. Refer once again to the derivative securities using Osprey common stock as an underlying asset discussed in Problem 1.

  a. Assuming that all Osprey derivatives expire at the same date in the future, complete a table similar to the following for each of the following contract positions:

    (1) A short position in a forward with a contract price of $50

    (2) A long position in a put option with an exercise price of $50 and a front-end premium expense of $3.23

    (3) A short position in a put option with an exercise price of $50 and a front-end premium receipt of $3.23

Expiration Date Osprey Stock Price	Expiration Date Derivative Payoff	Initial Derivative Premium	Net Profit
25	____	____	____
30	____	____	____
35	____	____	____
40	____	____	____
45	____	____	____
50	____	____	____
55	____	____	____
60	____	____	____
65	____	____	____
70	____	____	____
75	____	____	____

In calculating net profit, ignore the time differential between the initial derivative expense or receipt and the terminal payoff.

  b. Graph the net profit for each of the three derivative positions, using net profit on the vertical axis and Osprey's expiration date stock price on the horizontal axis. Label the break-even (i.e., zero profit) point(s) on each graph.

  c. Briefly describe the belief about the expiration date price of Osprey stock that an investor using each of these three positions implicitly holds.

3. Suppose that an investor holds a share of Osprey common stock, currently valued at $50. She is concerned that over the next few months the value of her holding might decline and she would like to hedge that risk by supplementing her holding with one of three different derivative positions, all of which expire at the same point in the future:

    (1) A short position in a forward with a contract price of $50

    (2) A long position in a put option with an exercise price of $50 and a front-end premium expense of $3.23

    (3) A short position in a call option with an exercise price of $50 and a front-end premium receipt of $5.20

  a. Using a table similar to the following, calculate the expiration date value of the investor's combined (i.e., stock and derivative) position. In calculating net portfolio value, ignore the time differential between the initial derivative expense or receipt and the terminal payoff.

  b. For each of the three hedge portfolios, graph the expiration date value of her combined position on the vertical axis, with potential expiration date share prices of Osprey stock on the horizontal axis.

  c. Assuming that the options are priced fairly, use the concept of put-call parity to calculate the zero-value contract price (i.e., $F_{0,T}$) for a forward agreement on Osprey stock. Explain why this value differs from the $50 contract price used in Part a and Part b.

Expiration Date Osprey Stock Price	Expiration Date Derivative Payoff	Initial Derivative Premium	Combined Terminal Position Value
25	____	____	____
30	____	____	____
35	____	____	____
40	____	____	____

45	_____	_____	_____
50	_____	_____	_____
55	_____	_____	_____
60	_____	_____	_____
65	_____	_____	_____
70	_____	_____	_____
75	_____	_____	_____

4. You strongly believe that the price of Breener Inc. stock will rise substantially from its current level of $137, and you are considering buying shares in the company. You currently have $13,700 to invest. As an alternative to purchasing the stock itself, you are also considering buying call options on Breener stock that expire in three months and have an exercise price of $140. These call options cost $10 each.
   a. Compare and contrast the size of the potential payoff and the risk involved in each of these alternatives.
   b. Calculate the three-month rate of return on both strategies assuming that at the option expiration date Breener's stock price has (1) increased to $155 or (2) decreased to $135.
   c. At what stock price level will the person who sells you the Breener call option break even? Can you determine the maximum loss that the call option seller may suffer, assuming that he does not already own Breener stock?

5. The common stock of Company XYZ is currently trading at a price of $42. Both a put and a call option are available for XYZ stock, each having an exercise price of $40 and an expiration date in exactly six months. The current market prices for the put and call are $1.45 and $3.90, respectively. The risk-free holding period return for the next six months is 4%, which corresponds to an 8% annual rate.
   a. For each possible stock price in the following sequence, calculate the expiration date payoffs (net of the initial purchase price) for the following positions: (1) buy one XYZ call option, and (2) short one XYZ call option:

   $$20, 25, 30, 35, 40, 45, 50, 55, 60$$

   Draw a graph of these payoff relationships, using net profit on the vertical axis and potential expiration date stock price on the horizontal axis. Be sure to specify the prices at which these respective positions will break even (i.e., produce a net profit of zero).
   b. Using the same potential stock prices as in Part a, calculate the expiration date payoffs and profits (net of the initial purchase price) for the following positions: (1) buy one XYZ put option, and (2) short one XYZ put option. Draw a graph of these relationships, labelling the prices at which these investments will break even.

c. Determine whether the $2.45 difference in the market prices between the call and put options is consistent with the put-call parity relationship for European contracts.

6. Consider Commodity Z, which has both exchange-traded futures and option contracts associated with it. As you look in today's paper, you find the following put and call prices for options that expire exactly six months from now:

Exercise Price	Put Price	Call Price
40	$0.59	$8.73
45	1.93	—
50	—	2.47

   a. Assuming that the futures price of a six-month contract on Commodity Z is $48, what must be the price of a put with an exercise price of $50 in order to avoid arbitrage across markets? Similarly, calculate the "no arbitrage" price of a call with an exercise price of $45. In both calculations, assume that the yield curve is flat and the annual risk-free rate is 6%.
   b. What is the "no arbitrage" price differential that should exist between the put and call options having an exercise price of $40? Is this differential satisfied by current market prices? If not, demonstrate an arbitrage trade to take advantage of the mispricing.

7. As an options trader, you are constantly looking for opportunities to make an arbitrage transaction (i.e., a trade in which you do not need to commit your own capital or take any risk but can still make a profit). Suppose you observe the following prices for options on DRKC Co. stock: $3.18 for a call with an exercise price of $60, and $3.38 for a put with an exercise price of $60. Both options expire in exactly six months, and the price of a six-month T-bill is $97.00 (for face value of $100).
   a. Using the put-call-spot parity condition, demonstrate graphically how you could synthetically re-create the payoff structure of a share of DRKC stock in six months using a combination of puts, calls, and T-bills transacted today.
   b. Given the current market prices for the two options and the T-bill, calculate the no-arbitrage price of a share of DRKC stock.
   c. If the actual market price of DRKC stock is $60, demonstrate the arbitrage transaction you could create to take advantage of the discrepancy. Be specific as to the positions you would need to take in each security and the dollar amount of your profit.

8. You are currently managing a stock portfolio worth $55 million and you are concerned that, over the next four months, equity values will be flat and may even fall. Consequently, you are considering two different strategies

for hedging against possible stock declines: (1) buying a protective put, and (2) selling a *covered call* (i.e., selling a call option based on the same underlying stock position you hold). An over-the-counter derivatives dealer has expressed interest in your business and has quoted the following bid and offer prices (in millions) for at-the-money call and put options that expire in four months and match the characteristics of your portfolio:

	Bid	Ask
Call	$2.553	$2,573
Put	1.297	1.317

a. For each of the following expiration date values for the unhedged equity position, calculate the terminal values (net of initial expense) for a protective put strategy.

35, 40, 45, 50, 55, 60, 65, 70, 75

b. Draw a graph of the protective put net profit structure in Part a and demonstrate how this position could have been constructed by using call options and T-bills, assuming a risk-free rate of 7%.

c. For each of these same expiration date stock values, calculate the terminal net profit values for a covered call strategy.

d. Draw a graph of the covered call net profit structure in Part c and demonstrate how this position could have been constructed by using put options and T-bills, again assuming a risk-free rate of 7%.

9. In mid-May, there are two outstanding call option contracts available on the stock of ARB Co.:

Call #	Exercise Price	Expiration Date	Market Price
1	$50	August 19	$8.40
2	60	August 19	3.34

a. Assuming that you form a portfolio consisting of *one* Call #1 held long and *two* Calls #2 held short, complete the following table showing your intermediate steps. In calculating net profit, be sure to include the net initial cost of the options.

Price of ARB Stock at Expiration ($)	Profit on Call #1 Position	Profit on Call #2 Position	Net Profit on Total Position
40	—	—	—
45	—	—	—
50	—	—	—
55	—	—	—
60	—	—	—
65	—	—	—
70	—	—	—
75	—	—	—

b. Graph the net profit relationship in Part a, using stock price on the horizontal axis. What is (are) the break-even stock price(s)? What is the point of maximum profit?

c. Under what market conditions will this strategy (which is known as a *call ratio spread*) generally make sense? Does the holder of this position have limited or unlimited liability?

10. In developing the butterfly spread position, we showed that it could be broken down into two call option money spreads. Using the price data for SAS stock options from Exhibit 13.25 (page 390), demonstrate how a butterfly payoff structure similar to that shown in Exhibit 13.37 (page 398) could be created using put options. Be specific as to the contract positions involved in the trade and show the expiration date net payoffs for the combined transaction.

Derivatives: Analysis and Valuation

Having laid the foundation for the existence of futures and options contracts and introduced options strategies in Chapter 13, in this chapter we continue our discussion on the valuation of futures and options. We start with an overview of futures trading and hedging with futures. We then move on to analyze valuation of futures and discuss applications of interest rate futures and stock-index futures. Further, we present three approaches to option pricing: the binomial option pricing, the extended binomial option pricing, and the Black-Scholes option valuation models. Finally, we extend our coverage to other derivatives including swaps and option-like securities such as warrants, convertible bonds, and callable bonds.

Derivatives have indeed become an important investment and risk management tool globally that no one can ignore. According to the Futures Industry Association, in 2007, over 15 billion futures and options contracts took place on 54 exchanges worldwide and the top three categories are derivatives based on equity index, individual equity, and interest rate (see Exhibit 14.1)

14.1 An Overview of Forward and Futures Trading

Recall from our discussion in Chapter 13 that forward contracts are agreements negotiated directly between two parties in the OTC (i.e., non-exchange-traded) markets. A typical participant in a forward contract is a commercial or investment bank that, serving the role of the market maker, is contacted directly by the customer. Forward contracts are individually designed agreements, tailored to the specific needs of the ultimate end user. Futures contracting, on the other hand, is somewhat more complicated. An investor wishing either to buy or to sell in the futures market gives his order to a broker (a *futures commission merchant*), who then passes it to a trader on the floor of an exchange (the *trading pit*) or through an electronic trading network. After a trade has been agreed on, details of the deal are passed to the **exchange clearinghouse**, which catalogues the transaction. The ultimate end users in a futures contract never deal with each other directly, but transact

EXHIBIT 14.1	Global Exchange-Traded Derivatives Volume by Category		
Category	2007	2006	% Change
Equity Index	5,616,816,347	4,454,222,902	26.10%
Individual Equity	4,091,923,113	2,876,486,897	42.25%
Interest Rate	3,740,876,650	3,193,410,504	17.14%
Agriculture	645,643,564	489,031,853	32.02%
Energy	496,408,289	385,965,150	28.61%
Foreign Currency	334,707,898	240,053,180	39.43%
Precious Metals	105,092,237	102,298,908	2.73%
Industrial Metals	150,976,113	116,383,437	29.72%
Others	4,226,619	4,360,194	−3.06%
Total	**15,186,670,830**	**11,862,213,025**	**28.03%**

Note: Based on the number of futures and options traded and/or cleared by 54 exchanges worldwide.

Source: Futures Industry Association, http://www.futuresindustry.org/downloads/fimag/2007/marapr/mar-apr_volume.pdf

Futures Industry Association: Industry trends and statistics worldwide can be found at http://www.futuresindustry.org.

ICE Futures Canada is Canada's commodity exchange. Check out https://www.theice.com/futures_canada.jhtml.

The Commodity Futures Trading Commission regulates commodity futures and option markets in the United States. See http://www.cftc.gov.

with the clearinghouse, which is also responsible for overseeing the delivery process, settling daily gains and losses, and guaranteeing the overall transaction. Exhibit 14.2 highlights the differences in how these contracts are created.[1]

As an example, consider the traditional agricultural commodity futures that have been traded for more than 150 years beginning with the creation of the Chicago Board of Trade (CBT), the world's oldest and largest derivatives exchange. Futures contracts based on a wide array of commodities and securities have been created and now trade on almost 100 exchanges worldwide. Exhibit 14.4 lists the leading futures exchanges in the United States and the world, ranked by trading volume. Notice that two of the top four and three of the top nine exchanges in the world are located in the United States.[2] While the leading exchange outside of the United States is the Korean Exchange; the volume at the Canadian derivatives market, the Montreal Exchange, is negligible.[3]

Canada's commodities futures market is ICE Futures Canada, formerly the Winnipeg Commodity Exchange. Its products are canola and Western barley. Exhibit 14.3 shows the volume of futures and options in recent years.

The main trade-off between forward and futures contracts is *design flexibility* versus *credit and liquidity risks*, as highlighted by the following comparison.

---

1 For a more detailed discussion of the futures trading process, see Clarke (1992); some of this discussion is based on his book.

2 The Chicago Mercantile Exchange (CME) and Chicago Board of Trade (CBOT) merged in 2007 under the CME Group. In 2008, CME Group acquired the New York Mercantile Exchange (NYMEX).

3 According to the Futures Industry Association (http://www.futuresindustry.org/default.asp), the volume of derivatives, including futures and options, at the Montreal Exchange in 2007 is 42,742,210 and is about 1.5% of the CME Group. Montreal's futures and options trading was ranked 32nd in the world. Thus in our discussions in this chapter, we will use more United States examples than Canadian ones.

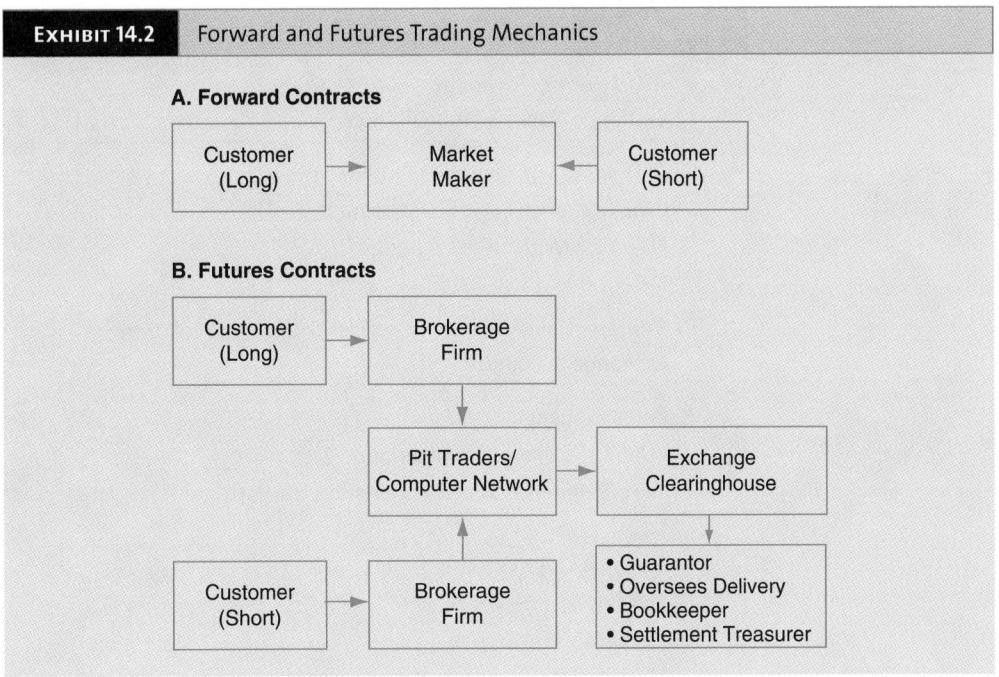

| **Exhibit 14.2** | Forward and Futures Trading Mechanics |

A. Forward Contracts

Customer (Long) → Market Maker ← Customer (Short)

B. Futures Contracts

Customer (Long) → Brokerage Firm → Pit Traders/Computer Network → Exchange Clearinghouse
Customer (Short) → Brokerage Firm → Pit Traders/Computer Network

Exchange Clearinghouse:
- Guarantor
- Oversees Delivery
- Bookkeeper
- Settlement Treasurer

	Futures	Forwards
Design flexibility:	Standardized	Can be customized
Credit risk:	Clearinghouse risk	Counterparty risk
Liquidity risk:	Depends on trading	Negotiated exit

These differences represent extremes; some forward contracts, particularly in foreign exchanges, are quite standard and liquid while some futures contracts now allow for greater flexibility in terms of the agreement. Also, forwards require less managerial oversight and intervention—especially on a daily basis—because of the lump-sum settlement at delivery (i.e., no margin accounts or marked-to-market settlement), a feature that is often important to unsophisticated or infrequent users of these products.

Exhibit 14.3	ICE Futures Canada Volumes			
	Futures		**Options**	
	Canola	Western Barley	Canola	Western Barley
2008	3,132,188	167,381	21,206	5
2007	3,169,182	214,672	17,067	4,774
2006	2,607,354	195,024	26,523	1,080

Source: ICE Futures Canada, https://www.theice.com/futures_canada.jhtml.

EXHIBIT 14.4	Leading Futures Exchanges Ranked by Relative Trading Volume

A. U.S. Futures Exchanges (2007 Data)

Exchange Name & Abbreviation	Trading Volume
CME Group: Chicago Mercantile (CME)	1,775.4
CME Group: Chicago Board of Trade (CBT)	1,029.6
New York Mercantile Exchange (NYM)	353.4
ICE Futures U.S. (ICE)	53.8

B. International Futures Exchanges & Groups (2007 Data)

Exchange & Country	Trading Volume
Korea Exchange, Korea	2,709.1
EUREX, Germany & Switzerland	1,899.9
LIFFE, Belgium, France, Netherlands, UK, Portugal	949.0
BM&F, Brazil	426.4
National Stock Exchange, India	379.9
Bolsa de Valores, Brazil	367.7
JSE, South Africa	329.6
Mexican Derivatives Exchange, Mexico	229.0
Dalian Commodity Exchange, China	185.6
OMX Nordic Exchange, Denmark, Finland, Norway	142.5
ICE Futures Europe	138.5

Source: Futures Industry Association. Reprinted with permission.

14.2 Hedging with Forwards and Futures

14.2.1 HEDGING AND THE BASIS

The New York Mercantile Exchange is the world's largest commodity futures exchange and the leading exchange for energy and precious metals. See http://www.nymex.com.

The goal of a *hedge* transaction is to create a position that, once added to an investor's portfolio, will offset the price risk of another, more fundamental holding. The word "offset" is used here rather than "eliminate" because the hedge transaction attempts to neutralize an exposure that remains on the balance sheet. We express this concept with the following chart, which assumes that the underlying exposure results from a long commodity position:

Economic Event	Actual Commodity Exposure	Desired Hedge Exposure
Commodity prices fall	Loss	Gain
Commodity prices rise	Gain	Loss

In this case, a short position in a forward contract based on the same commodity would provide the desired negative price correlation. By virtue of holding a short forward position against the long position in the commodity, the investor has entered into a **short hedge**. A **long hedge** is created by supplementing a short commodity holding with a long forward position.

The basic premise behind any hedge is that as the price of the underlying commodity changes, so too will the price of a forward contract based on that commodity. The hope of the hedger is that the spot and forward prices change in a predictable way relative to one another. For instance, the short hedger in the preceding example is hoping that if commodity prices fall and reduce the value of her underlying asset, the forward contract price also will fall by the same amount to create an offsetting gain on the derivative. Thus, a critical feature that affects the quality of a hedge transaction is how spot and forward prices change over time.

Defining the Basis To understand better the relationship between spot and forward price movements, it is useful to develop the concept of the **basis**. At any Date t, the basis is the spot price minus the forward price for a contract maturing at Date T:

14.1
$$B_{t,T} = S_t - F_{t,T}$$

where:
S_t = the Date t spot price
$F_{t,T}$ = the Date t forward price for a contract maturing at Date T

Potentially, a different level of the basis may exist on each trading Date t. Two facts always are true, however. First, the *initial basis* at Date 0 $(B_{0,T})$ always will be known since both the current spot and forward contract prices can be observed. Second, the *maturity basis* at Date T $(B_{T,T})$ always is zero whenever the commodity underlying the forward contract matches the asset held exactly. For this to occur, the forward price must *converge* to the spot price as the contract expires $(F_{T,T} = S_T)$.

Consider again the investor who hedged her long position in a commodity by agreeing to sell it at Date T through a short position in a forward contract. The value of the combined position is $(F_{0,T} - S_0)$. If the investor decides to liquidate her entire position (including the hedge) prior to maturity, she will have to (1) sell her commodity position on the open market for S_t, and (2) buy back her short forward position for the new contract price of $F_{t,T}$. The profit from the short hedge liquidated at Date t is

14.2
$$B_{t,T} - B_{0,T} = (S_t - F_{t,T}) - (S_0 - F_{0,T})$$

The term $B_{t,T}$ often is called the *cover basis* because that is when the forward contract is closed out, or covered.

14.2.2   Understanding Basis Risk

Equation 14.2 highlights an important fact about hedging. Once the hedge position is formed, the investor no longer is exposed to the absolute price movement of the underlying asset alone. Instead, she is exposed to **basis risk** because the terminal value of her combined position is defined as the cover basis minus the initial basis. Notice that only the cover basis is unknown at Date 0, and so her real exposure is to the **correlation** between subsequent changes in the spot and forward contract prices. If these movements are highly correlated, the basis risk will be quite small. In fact, it is usually possible to design a forward contract that reduces basis risk to zero, as $F_{T,T} = S_T$. However, basis risk is a possibility when contract terms are standardized, and is most likely to occur in the futures market where standardization is the norm.

To illustrate the concept of basis risk, suppose the investor wishes in October to hedge a long position of 75,000 pounds of coffee she is planning to sell in February. Coffee futures contracts do exist as follows but with delivery months in either December or March.

Coffee Futures Quotations

Dec '07	135.85	137.40	134.10	135.20	−.65	106,550
March '08	139.00	140.90	137.80	138.80	−.70	34,298

Source: From the *Wall Street Journal,* October 5, 2007. Copyright 2007 by DOW JONES & CO INC. Reproduced with permission of DOW JONES & CO INC in the format Other Book via Copyright Clearance Center.

With each contract requiring the delivery of 37,500 pounds of coffee, she decides to short two of the March contracts, specifically intending to liquidate her position a month early. Suppose that on the date she initiates her short hedge, the spot coffee price was $1.3162 per pound and the March futures contract price was $1.3880 per pound. This means that her initial basis was −7.18 cents, which she hopes will move toward zero in a smooth and predictable manner. Suppose, in fact, that when she closes out her combined position in February, coffee prices have declined so that $S_t = \$1.2978$ and $F_{t,T} = \$1.3092$, leaving a cover basis of −1.14 cents. This means the basis has increased in value, or *strengthened,* which is to the short hedger's advantage. The net February selling price for her coffee is $1.3766 per pound, which is equal to the spot price of $1.2978 plus the net futures profit of $0.0788 = (1.3880 − 1.3092)$. Notice that this is lower than the original futures price but considerably higher than the February spot price. Thus, the short hedger has benefited by exchanging pure price risk for basis risk.

Although it is difficult to generalize, substantial indirect evidence exists that minimizing basis risk is the primary goal of most hedgers. For example, Brown and Smith (1995) noted that the phenomenal growth of OTC products to manage interest rate risk—despite the existence of exchange-traded contracts—is a response to the desire to create customized solutions. Further, a survey by Jesswein, Kwok, and Folks (1995) showed that corporate risk managers preferred to hedge their firms' foreign exchange exposure with forward contracts rather than with futures by a ratio of about five to one. However, Bali, Hume, and Martell (2007) showed that hedging with futures does not necessarily reduce a firm's return.

14.3 Valuation of Forward and Futures

We will consider how forward and futures contracts are priced in an efficient capital market. Given that these instruments are not really securities in the same sense that stocks and bonds are, the notion of traditional security valuation is not quite appropriate. Instead, valuation involves specifying the proper relationship between the forward contract price and the spot price for the underlying position. We develop the "no arbitrage" result that the forward contract price should be equal to the spot price plus the cumulative costs of transporting the underlying security or commodity from the present to the future delivery date.

14.3.1 THE COST TO CARRY MODEL

We can understand the intuition for the relationship between spot and forward prices with an example: You have agreed at Date 0 to deliver 5,000 bushels of corn to your counterparty at Date T. What is a fair price $(F_{0,T})$ to charge? One way to look at this question is to consider how much it will cost you to fulfill your obligation. If you wait until Date T to purchase the corn on the spot market, you have a *speculative* position, because your purchase price (S_T) will be unknown when you commit to a selling price.

Alternatively, suppose you buy the corn now for the current cash price of S_0 per bushel and store it until you have to deliver it at Date T. Under this scheme, the forward contract price you would be willing to commit to would have to be high enough to cover (1) the present cost of the corn and (2) the cost of storing the corn until contract maturity. In general, these storage costs, denoted here as $SC_{0,T}$, can involve several things, including commissions paid for the physical warehousing of the commodity ($PC_{0,T}$) and the cost of financing the initial purchase of the underlying asset ($i_{0,T}$) but less any cash flows received ($D_{0,T}$) by owning the asset between Dates 0 and T. Thus, in the absence of arbitrage opportunities, the forward contract price should be equal to the current spot price plus the **cost of carry** necessary to transport the asset to the future delivery date:

14.3	$$F_{0,T} = S_0 + SC_{0,T} = S_0 + (PC_{0,T} + i_{0,T} - D_{0,T})$$

Notice that even if the funds needed to purchase the commodity at Date 0 are not borrowed, $i_{0,T}$ accounts for the opportunity cost of committing one's own financial capital to the transaction.

14.3.2 CONTANGO AND BACKWARDATED

This cost of carry model is useful in practice because it applies in a wide variety of cases. For some commodities, such as corn or cattle, physical storage is possible but the costs are enormous. Also, neither of these assets pays periodic cash flows. In such situations, it is quite likely that $F_{0,T} > S_0$ and the market is said to be in **contango**. On the other hand, common stock is costless to store but often pays a dividend. This cash flow sometimes makes it possible for the basis to be positive (i.e., $F_{0,T} < S_0$), meaning that $SC_{0,T}$ can be negative. There is another reason why $SC_{0,T}$ might be less than zero. For certain storable commodities that do not pay a dividend, $F_{0,T} < S_0$ can occur when there is a premium placed on currently owning the commodity. This premium, called a **convenience yield**, results from a small supply of the commodity at Date 0 relative to what is expected at Date T after, say, a crop harvest. Although it is extremely difficult to quantify, the convenience yield can be viewed as a potential negative storage cost component that works in a manner similar to $D_{0,T}$. A futures market in which $F_{0,T} < S_0$ is said to be **backwardated**.

Equation 14.3 implies that there should be a direct relationship between contemporaneous forward and spot prices; indeed, this positive correlation is the objective of any well-designed hedging strategy. A related question involves the relationship between $F_{0,T}$ and the spot price expected to prevail at the time the contract matures (i.e., $E(S_T)$). There are three possibilities. First, the *pure expectations* hypothesis holds that, on average, $F_{0,T} = E(S_T)$, so futures prices serve as unbiased forecasts of future spot prices. When this is true, futures prices serve an important *price discovery* function for participants in the applicable market. Conversely, $F_{0,T}$ could be less than $E(S_T)$, a situation that Keynes (1930) and Hicks (1939) argued would arise whenever short hedgers outnumber long hedgers. In that case, a risk premium in the form of a lower contract price would be necessary to attract a sufficient number of long speculators. For reasons that are not entirely clear, this situation is termed *normal backwardation*. Finally, a *normal contango* market occurs when the opposite is true, specifically, when $F_{0,T} > E(S_T)$.

The existence of a risk premium in the futures market is widely debated. Kamara (1984) surveyed the early literature on the subject and found the evidence from the commodity markets to be mixed. He concluded that although the normal backwardation hypothesis was supported, futures markets are mainly driven by risk-averse hedgers who have been able to acquire "cheap" insurance. Krehbiel and Collier (1996) examined the price behaviour in the

Eurodollar and Treasury bill futures markets and found evidence consistent with the existence of risk premia that were necessary to balance net hedging and net speculative positions. Finally, Brooks (1997) documented that the risk premia priced into Eurodollar futures contracts have a substantial impact on the pricing of interest rate swaps, which can be viewed as portfolios of Eurodollar contracts.

14.4 Financial Futures

To find out more about the Chicago Mercantile Exchange, a leading financial and commodity derivative exchange, go to http://www.cmegroup.com.

Originally, forward and futures markets were organized largely around trading agricultural commodities, such as corn and wheat. Although markets for these products remain strong, the most significant recent developments involve the use of financial securities as the asset underlying the contract. Exhibit 14.1 shows that the top three most heavily traded derivative contracts globally are all financial, namely, equity index, individual equity, and interest rate. In this section, we introduce financial futures through two applications. The T-bond/T-note futures spread are an example of interest rate futures, and the **stock-index arbitrage** is an application of stock index futures.

14.4.1 Interest Rate Futures

Interest rate forwards and futures were among the first derivatives to specify a financial security as the underlying asset. The earliest versions of these contracts were designed to lock in the forward price of a particular fixed-coupon bond, which in turn locks in its yield.

A T-Bond/T-Note (NOB) Futures Spread Frequently, speculators in the bond market have a clear view on a change in the overall shape of the yield curve but can be less certain as to the actual direction in future rate movements. Suppose we think the yield curve—which is currently upward sloping across all maturities—will flatten, but we are not sure how this might occur:

- Short-term rates rise and long-term rates fall.
- Short- and long-term rates both rise, but short-term rates rise by more.
- Short- and long-term rates both fall, but short-term rates fall by less.

Clearly, taking a long or short position in a single futures contract linked to a single point on the yield curve is too risky, given our view; we could be right about the shape shift but guess wrong about direction. One way to mitigate this unwanted risk is to go both long and short in contracts representing different points on the yield curve. This is known as the Treasury "Notes over Bond" **spread** (or "NOB" spread) strategy.

Suppose in mid-February we observe the following price quotes (along with their implied yields to maturity) for T-bond and T-note futures contracts maturing in June:

Contract	Settle Price	Implied Yield
20-yr., 6% T-bond	103–02	5.74%
10-yr., 6% T-note	104–02	5.47%

Notice that our expectation of a flattening yield curve is identical to the view that the 27 basis point yield gap (= 0.0574 − 0.0547) between the longer- and shorter-term contracts will shrink. If we also feel this will occur by mid-June, the appropriate strategy would be:

- Go long in one Treasury bond futures.
- Go short in one Treasury note futures.

The net profit from this joint position when we close out the two contracts is calculated as the sum of the profits on the short T-note position and the long T-bond contract, or

$$\left[\frac{104.0625 - \text{June T} - \text{Note Price}}{100} + \frac{\text{June T} - \text{Bond Price} - 103.0625}{100} \right](\$100,000)$$

To see how this combined position would pay off if our view is correct, assume rates increase to 6.00% by June. In this case, both futures contracts will sell at par and so our net profit will be

$$\text{Net Profit} = [0.040625 - 0.030625](\$100,000) = \$1,000$$

Notice that this same calculation can be done on a "price tick" basis:

$$\text{Net Profit} = \{[(104-02) - (103-02)] - [(100-00) - (100-00)]\}(\$31.25)$$
$$= (32 \text{ Ticks})(\$31.25) = \$1,000$$

which is equivalent to the change in the number of ticks in the NOB spread multiplied by the dollar value of a tick (i.e., \$31.25).

In Canada, interest rate futures are available at the Montreal Exchange. Products include BAX (Three-Month Canadian Bankers' Acceptance Futures) and OBX (Options on Three-Month Canadian Bankers' Acceptance Futures), and CGB (Ten-Year Government of Canada Bond Futures).

The Montreal Exchange is Canada's derivatives market. Find it at http://www.m-x.ca.

14.4.2 Stock Index Futures

Another important form of financial futures contracting specifies an equity index as the underlying asset. In this section, we consider the basics of stock index futures trading and discuss two applications for these instruments, including a popular form of computer-assisted trading known as stock index arbitrage.

Canadian stock index futures traded at the Montreal Exchange include S&P/TSX market index SXF (S&P Canada 60 Futures) and sartorial indices such as gold (SXA), financial (SXB), and energy (SXY). Exhibit 14.5 shows the volume and open interest of SXF in recent years.

Stock Index Futures Contract Fundamentals Like interest rate futures, stock index futures were originally intended to provide a hedge against movements in an underlying financial asset. As detailed in Chapter 4 and the introductory example in Chapter 13, the underlying financial asset for a stock index futures contract is a hypothetical creation that does not exist in practice and therefore cannot be delivered to settle a contract. Thus, stock index futures can only be settled in cash, similar to the Eurodollar (i.e., LIBOR) contract.

Stock index futures are intended to provide general hedges against stock market movements and can be applied to either whole (i.e., diversified) portfolios or individual stocks. Hedging an individual stock with an index futures contract is done in an attempt to isolate the unsystematic portion of that security's risk. Additionally, stock index futures often are used to convert entire stock portfolios into synthetic riskless positions to exploit an apparent mispricing between stock in the cash and futures markets. This strategy, commonly called stock index arbitrage, is the most prominent example of a wider class of computer-assisted trading schemes known as *program trading.*

EXHIBIT 14.5	SXF: S&P Canada 60 Futures

Source: Montreal Exchange, http://www.m-x.ca

Exhibit 14.6 lists quotes for futures contracts on several U.S. stock indices, including the Dow Jones Industrial Average, S&P 500, NASDAQ 100, and Russell 1000. Contracts for indices representing global markets (e.g., Nikkei 225 [Japan], DAX 30 [Germany], Euro Stoxx 50) are traded actively but not shown in the display. For example, an investor planning in October to buy stock the following June can hedge against the risk of his eventual purchase price increasing by entering into the long position in the June 2008 S&P 500 contract. Given the settlement price of 1,573.90, he has obligated himself to the theoretical purchase of 250 shares of the S&P 500 on the day before the third Friday of June for $393,475 (= 1,573.90 × 250). The minimum contract price movement is 0.10 index points, which equals $25. Thus, if the actual level of the index on the contract settlement date turned out to be 1,576.10, the long position would gain $550, or $25 times 22 ticks [i.e., (1,576.10 − 1,573.90) ÷ 0.10], thereby reducing the net purchase price for his desired equity position. Finally, notice that a "mini" version of the S&P 500 futures contract requiring the hypothetical purchase or sale of only 50 shares is also available.

Stock Index Futures Valuation and Index Arbitrage Earlier, we established that the key to understanding the pricing of futures contracts is the concept of arbitrage. To see how this works for index contracts, suppose that at Date 0 an investor (1) purchases a portfolio of stock representing the underlying stock index for S_0, and (2) goes short a stock index future (with an expiration date of T) for $F_{0,T}$. Assume further that the funds for the long position are borrowed at the risk-free rate of RFR. On unwinding this position at Date t, the net profit (Π) is given by

$$\Pi = (F_{0,T} - F_{t,T}) + (S_t - S_0 - S_0 RFR_t + S_0 d_t) = (F_{0,T} - F_{t,T}) + [S_t - S_0 (1 + RFR_t - d_t)]$$

where:

   d_t = the dividend yield accruing to the stocks comprising the index between Dates 0 and t

In other words, the profit we make on this short hedge in stock index futures will consist of two components: the net difference in the futures position and the net difference in the underlying index position (after adding borrowing costs and subtracting dividends received from the initial purchase).

EXHIBIT 14.6	Stock Index Futures Quotations					
Open	High	Contact hi lo	Low	Settle	Chg	Open Interest
DJ Industrial Average (CBT)-$10 x index						
Dec	14059	14090	14025	**14041**	−11	27,586
Mini DJ Industrial Average (CBT)-$5 x index						
Dec	14057	14090	14026	**14041**	−11	90,300
March'08	14150	14153	14125	**14139**	−11	34
S&P 500 Index (CME)-$250 x index						
Dec	1550.80	1554.70	1548.10	**1552.20**	1.50	573,448
June'08	1574.50	1575.30	1571.30	**1573.90**	1.60	874
Mini S&P 500 (CME)-$50 x index						
Dec	1550.75	1554.75	1548.00	**1552.25**	1.50	1,864,257
March'08	1562.75	1565.75	1559.50	**1563.50**	1.75	2,706
Nasdaq 100 (CME)-$100 x index						
Dec	2121.00	2129.00	2109.00	**2123.0**	2.25	45,983
Mini Nasdaq 100 (CME)-$20 x index						
Dec	2121.3	2128.8	2108.5	**2123.0**	2.3	380,611
March'08	2140.0	2151.3	2132.5	**2146.0**	2.8	64
Russell 1000 (ICE-US)-$500 x index						
Dec	844.00	845.00	844.00	**845.20**	1.00	7,668
U.S. Dollar Index (ICE-US)-$1,000 x index						
Dec	78.56	78.65	78.22	**78.38**	−0.8	37,188
March'08	78.50	78.36	78.36	**78.31**	−0.8	2,824

Source: From the *Wall Street Journal*, October 5, 2007. Copyright 2007 by DOW JONES & CO INC. Reproduced with permission of DOW JONES & CO INC in the format Other Book via Copyright Clearance Center.

Now assume the long position in the stock portfolio is held until the expiration of the futures contract (i.e., Date $t = T$) so that the futures price and index level will converge. That is, at Date T, we will have $F_{T,T} = S_T$, which means that the short hedge profit (Π) equation can be written

$$\Pi = [F_{0,T} - S_0 - S_0(RFR_t - d_T)]$$

As before, $RFR_t - d_T$ is called the net cost of carry and represents the difference between the borrowing cost paid and the dividend received.

If the dividend yield is known at Date 0, this position is riskless and requires no initial investment. Thus, buying and selling among arbitrageurs trading in both markets should ensure that $\Pi = 0$. The futures price set at Date 0 will be

14.4
$$F_{0,T} = S_0 + S_0(RFR_t - d_T)$$

EXHIBIT 14.7	Stock Index Futures Valuation Example				
	S&P at Expiration is:				
	1,220	1,240	1,260	1,280	1,300
Net futures profit	42.50	22.50	2.50	(17.50)	(37.50)
Net index profit	(30.00)	(10.00)	10.00	30.00	50.00
Dividend	18.75	18.75	18.75	18.75	18.75

As discussed earlier, the futures price could be set below the spot level of the index (i.e., a backwardated market) if $(RFR_t - d_T) < 0$. That is, the index futures contract will be priced lower than the current level of the stock index whenever the dividends received by holding stock exceed the borrowing cost.

To see how this parity relationship helps establish the appropriate futures price, assume that one share of the S&P 500 index can be purchased for \$1,250.00 and that the dividend yield and risk-free rate over the holding period are 1.5% and 2.5%, respectively. Under these conditions, the contract price on a six-month S&P 500 futures should be

$$F_{0,0.5} = 1,250 + 1,250(0.025 - 0.015) = 1,262.50$$

Now suppose that we construct a short hedge position by (1) purchasing the index at 1,250.00 and (2) shorting the futures at 1,262.50. If the position is held to expiry, our profit at various expiration date levels of the S&P will be as shown in Exhibit 14.7. Notice that our net profit remains constant no matter the level of the index at the expiration date. This net profit can be expressed as

$$(31.25) \div (1,250) = 2.5\%$$

which is the assumed cost of borrowing.

14.5   An Overview of Option Markets and Contracts

The Chicago Board of Trade is a leading futures and futures-options exchange. Go to http://www.cmegroup.com.

We have discussed the primary difference between forward and futures contracts. Futures are standardized and trade on exchanges, while forward contracts have negotiable terms and therefore must be arranged in the OTC market. Option contracts offer investors similar trading alternatives. The most important features of how these contracts are traded and quoted in the financial press are highlighted in the following sections.

14.5.1   OPTION MARKET CONVENTIONS

Option contracts have been traded for centuries in the form of separate agreements or embedded in other securities. Malkiel (2007), for example, tells the story of how call options were used to speculate on flower prices during the tulip bulb frenzy in 17th-century Holland. Then, and for most of the time until now, options were arranged and executed in private transactions.

Collectively, these private transactions represent the OTC market for options and agreements can be structured around any terms or underlying asset to which two parties can agree. This has been a particularly useful mechanism when the underlying asset is too illiquid to support a widely traded contract. Also, recall that credit risk is a paramount concern in this market because OTC agreements typically are not collateralized. This credit risk is one-sided with an option agreement because the buyer worries about the seller's ability to honour his obligations, but the seller has received everything he will get up front and is not concerned about the buyer's creditworthiness.

As in all security markets, OTC options ultimately are created in response to the needs and desires of the corporations and individual investors who use them. Financial institutions, such as money-centre banks and investment banks, serve as market makers by facilitating the arrangement and execution of these deals. Over the years, various trade associations of broker dealers in OTC options have emerged (and, in some cases, faded), including the Put and Call Brokers and Dealers Association, which helped arrange private stock option transactions, and the International Swap and Derivatives Association, which monitors the activities of market makers for interest rate and foreign exchange derivatives. These trade groups create a common set of standards and language to govern industry transactions.

In April 1973, the Chicago Board of Trade opened the Chicago Board Options Exchange (CBOE). Specializing in stock and stock index options, the CBOE has introduced two important aspects of market uniformity. Foremost, contracts offered by the CBOE are standardized in terms of the underlying common stock, the number of shares covered, the delivery dates, and the range of available exercise prices. This standardization was meant to help develop a secondary market for the contracts. The rapid increase in trading volume on the CBOE and other options exchanges suggests that this feature is desirable compared to OTC contracts that must often be held to maturity due to a lack of liquidity.

The centralization of the trading function also necessitated the creation of the **Options Clearing Corporation (OCC)**, which acts as the guarantor of each CBOE-traded contract. Therefore, end users in option transactions ultimately bear the credit risk of the OCC. For this reason, even though the OCC is independent of the exchange, it demands that the option seller post margin to guarantee future performance. The option buyer will not have a margin account because a future obligation to the seller is non-existent. Finally, this central market structure makes monitoring, regulation, and price reporting much easier than in the decentralized OTC markets.

14.5.2 PRICE QUOTATIONS FOR EXCHANGE-TRADED OPTIONS

Equity Options Options on the common stock of individual companies have traded on the CBOE since 1973. Several other markets, including the American (AMEX) and Philadelphia (PHLX) Exchanges, began trading their own contracts shortly afterward. The CBOE remains the largest exchange in terms of option market volume with a market share of 33%, with the AMEX second at around 10%. Options on each of these exchanges are traded similarly, with a typical contract for 100 shares of stock. Because exchange-traded contracts are not issued by the company whose common stock is the underlying asset, they require secondary transactions in the equity if exercised.[4]

Panel A of Exhibit 14.8 displays price and volume statistics for a sample of the most actively traded equity options on October 16, 2007. Options for both individual equities and

---

4 Call options issued directly by the firm whose common stock is the underlying assets are called *warrants*. We will discuss these later in Section 14.9.1.

Exhibit 14.8 | Stock Option Quotations

A. Most Active Individual Stock and ETF Options

<HELP> for explanation.   Msg: A. LOPEZ
Enter #<Equity><go> or #<Corp><go> for selection.

Most Actives by Volume

PAGES   Page   1/3
1—Most Active   U.S. Exchange: US Opt Comp   1 1—Today , 2—Previous   * Ex-Date
2—Most Up   1 1—Name. 2—Ticker   1 1—Net, 2—Percent   * Split
3—Most Down   1 1—Equity, 2—Index   * Ex & Split

Options (Only U.S. Index options avail)

	Name			Last	Chng	Vol			Name			Last	Chng	Vol
1)	PG	Oct07	C65	PG+JM	5.93 −.17	181852	15)	MO	Jan08	C70	MO+AN	3.21 +.16	25499
2)	INTC	Oct07	C27½	INQ+JY	.13 −.01	42098	16)	YHOO	Jan09	P25	VYH+ME	2.57 +.35	25150
3)	IWM	Nov07	P82	IOW+WD	2.18 +0.21	41669	17)	YHOO	Oct07	C27½	YHQ+JY	.95 −.44	24164
4)	INTC	Oct07	P25	INQ+VE	.14 +.07	37354	18)	IWM	Oct07	P83	IOW+VE	1.21 +.22	22994
5)	AAPL	Oct07	C170	APU+JN	2.67 +.57	36250	19)	MSFT	Jan08	C30	MSQ+AK	1.72 +.19	22893
6)	YHOO	Oct07	P25	YHQ+VE	.37 +.05	35795	20)	XLF	Jan08	C39	XLF+AM	.25 −.14	22600
7)	IWM	Oct07	P81	IOW+VC	.38 +.03	35712	21)	INTC	Nov07	C27½	INQ+KY	.39 +.01	22182
8)	YHOO	Oct07	C30	YHQ+JF	.27 −.22	32374	22)	IMB	Nov07	P15	IMB+WC	.95 +.25	21809
9)	INTC	Oct07	C25	INQ+JE	1.02 −.13	32251	23)	SMH	Nov07	P35	SMH+WG	.67 −.08	21119
10)	PG	Oct07	C60	PG+JL	10.95 −.05	31005	24)	IWM	Nov07	P76	IOW+WX	.74 +.04	20602
11)	SPY	Oct07	P153	SYH+VW	.70 +.15	28796	25)	SPY	Oct07	C156	SYH+JZ	.36 −.38	20543
12)	NOK	Oct07	C35	NAY+JG	1.40 −.35	28483	26)	F	Nov07	P8	F+WK	.20 +.07	20520
13)	IWM	Oct07	P82	IOW+VD	.65 +.05	28249	27)	IWM	Oct07	P75	IOW+VW	.02 −.02	20036
14)	YHOO	Oct07	P25	YHO+PE	1.84 +.23	25661	28)	IWM	Oct07	P80	IOW+VB	.21 +.01	19183

Australia 61 2 9777 8600   Brazil 5511 3048 4500   Europe 44 20 7330 7500   Germany 49 69 920410
Hong Kong 852 2977 6000   Japan 81 3 3201 8900   Singapore 65 6212 1000   U.S. 1 212 318 2000   Copyright 2007 Bloomberg L.P.
H426–565–0 16–Oct–2007 13:22: 41

B. Stock Options for Microsoft (MSFT)

<HELP> for explanation, <MENU> for similar functions. 120×228 sMsg:A. LOPEZ
Enter #<Equity><GO> for selection. Note: All values in USD

Pages: MOST ACTIVE OPTIONS ON   Page 1 of 3
1—Most Active   MICROSOFT CORP   Total   Call   Put
2—Most Up   T T—today or P—previous   Volume   105,181   89,375   15,806
3—Most Down   V V—volume   O—open inter.   Open Int.   3686944   2178493   1508451

Underlying:	Last	Volume	1–Day	Chg	Open	High	Low	Yest.	2–Day	Ch
MSFT	U.S. 30.35	35607907	+.31	30.24	30.58	30.23	30.04	+.18		

	Option			Symbol	Last	Chng	Vol		Option			Symbol	Last	Chng	Vol
1)	Jan08	30	Calls	AK	1.72	+ .19	22893	17)	Apr08	32.5	Calls	DZ	1.20	+ .09	990
2)	Oct07	30	Calls	JK	.52	+ .16	17363	18)	Jan08	35	Calls	AL	.19	+ .04	693
3)	Jan08	25	Calls	AJ	5.80	+ .40	14982	19)	Jan09	25	Calls	AE	7.20	+ .20	540
4)	Jan08	27.5	Calls	AY	3.55	+ .30	10192	20)	Jan09	27.5	Calls	AY	5.50	+ .25	534
5)	Oct07	30	Puts	VK	.14	− .11	4132	21)	Jan08	32.5	Puts	MZ	2.50	− .24	521
6)	Nov07	30	Puts	WK	.72	− .14	3982	22)	Jan08	40	Calls	AH	.03	− .01	491
7)	Nov07	30	Calls	KK	1.14	+ .17	3867	23)	Oct07	27.5	Puts	VY	.01	unch	402
8)	Jan08	32.5	Calls	AZ	.60	+ .07	3334	24)	Nov07	27.5	Calls	KY	3.15	+ .35	329
9)	Jan09	32.5	Calls	AZ	2.75	+ .17	3195	25)	Oct07	32.5	Calls	JZ	.01	− .01	286
10)	Jan10	35	Calls	AL	3.15	+ .16	3001	26)	Apr08	32.5	Puts	PZ	2.86	− .24	259
11)	Nov07	32.5	Puts	WZ	2.35	− .28	2397	27)	Oct07	27.5	Calls	JY	2.90	+ .33	189
12)	Apr08	35	Calls	DL	.55	+ .08	2058	28)	Nov07	35	Calls	KL	.05	− .01	156
13)	Nov07	32.5	Calls	KZ	.25	+ .03	1904	29)	Jan10	30	Puts	MK	3.25	− .20	139
14)	Apr08	30	Puts	PK	1.51	− .20	1770	30)	Nov07	27.5	Puts	WY	.15	− .02	114
15)	Jan08	30	Puts	MK	1.11	− .15	1594	31)	Apr08	22.5	Calls	DX	8.50	+ .40	110
16)	Apr08	30	Calls	DK	2.44	+ .23	1529	32)	Apr08	37.5	Calls	DU	.23	+ .02	108

Australia 61 2 9777 8600   Brazil 5511 3048 4500   Europe 44 20 7330 7500   Germany 49 69 920410
Hong Kong 852 2977 6000   Japan 81 3 3201 8900   Singapore 65 6212 1000   U.S. 1 212 318 2000   Copyright 2007 Bloomberg L.P.
H426-565–0 16–Oct–2007 13: 24: 42

Source: © 2007 Bloomberg L.P. All rights reserved. Reprinted with permission.

exchange traded funds are included in this list. Several of the names represented—Procter & Gamble (PG), Intel (INTC), Microsoft (MSFT), Russell 2000 iShares (IWM)—also rank among the most actively traded stocks and ETFs. To interpret this exhibit, suppose that an investor wanted to buy an option on Microsoft common stock. The highlighted entry indicates that on this day the MSFT call with an exercise price of 30 and an expiration date in January 2008 traded at a price of $1.72 per share of the underlying stock. By convention, stock options expire on the Saturday following the third Friday of the designated month. Panel B of Exhibit 14.8 provides more details for this contract, along with many other MSFT options available on this date.

To consider the dynamics of a specific option transaction in more detail, assume that on October 16, 2007, an investor bought the MSFT January 2008 30 call. Based on the last reported price, her contract would cost a total of $172.00, calculated as the stated per-share price of 1.72 multiplied by 100 shares. In exchange for that payment, the holder of this American-style call would then be able to exercise the option in mid-January—or any time before then—by paying $3,000 (= 30 × 100) and would receive 100 Microsoft shares from the option seller, who is obligated to make that exchange at the buyer's request. That is rational only if the mid-January price of MSFT is greater than $30. If the MSFT price closes below $30, the investor will simply let the call expire.

Finally, notice that with the prevailing Microsoft share price being $30.35 (which is shown in Panel B), the investor could immediately recover $0.35 of the $1.72 she paid for the contract. Her time premium of $1.37 (= 1.72 − 0.35) preserves her right to buy MSFT stock at a price of $30 for the next three months, even if the market value of those shares moves higher.[5] Consider another investor who sells the January 30 Microsoft put, the details of which are also highlighted in Panel B of Exhibit 14.8. In return for an upfront receipt of $111 (= 1.11 × 100), he must stand ready to buy 100 shares of stock in mid-January for $3,000 if the option holder chooses to exercise his option to sell. The stock price will, of course, have to fall from its current level before this can occur. The investor in this case has sold an out-of-the-money contract and hopes that it will stay out of the money through expiration, letting the passing of time decay the time premium to zero. As we saw earlier, the front-end premium is all that sellers of put or call options ever receive, and they hope to retain as much of it possible. Like the long position in the call, the short put position benefits from an increase in MSFT share prices.

Finally, notice that most of the options listed in both panels of Exhibit 14.8 expire within a few months of the quotation date. In fact, the expiration dates available for these exchange-traded contracts are the two nearest term months (October and November for Microsoft) and up to three additional months from a quarterly cycle beginning in either January, February, or March.

In the case of Microsoft options, January 2008 and April 2008 (which is part of the quarterly cycle beginning in January) are the additional months most frequently listed. Exhibit 14.9 gives quotations for Long-Term Equity Anticipation Securities (LEAPS), which are simply regular call and put options with longer expiration dates. Like the contracts just described, LEAPS are also traded on the CBOE and have comparable terms.

---

5 Recall from Chapter 13 that a call option's value can be divided into two components: the *intrinsic value,* which is the greater of either zero or the stock price minus the striking price, and the *time premium*. In this example, the Microsoft call is said to be *in the money* because it has positive intrinsic value, whereas an option with no intrinsic value is *out of the money.*

Exhibit 14.9 Long-Term Equity Anticipation Securities (LEAPS) Quotations for MSFT

Calls	Last Sale	Net	Bid	Ask	Vol	Open Int	Puts	Last Sale	Net	Bid	Ask	Vol	Open Int
09 Jan 20.00 (VMF AD-E)	11.30	0.0	11.25	11.45	0	16996	09 Jan 20.00 (VMF MD-E)	0.35	0.0	0.37	0.39	0	40936
09 Jan 22.50 (VMF AX-E)	9.00	0.0	9.15	9.30	0	7656	09 Jan 22.50 (VMF MX-E)	0.75	0.0	0.64	0.68	0	51145
09 Jan 25.00 (VMF AE-E)	7.20	−0.15	7.20	7.30	420	49868	09 Jan 25.00 (VMF ME-E)	1.06	0.0	1.04	1.08	0	85265
09 Jan 27.00 (VMF AY-E)	5.46	0.0	5.45	5.60	0	37927	09 Jan 27.50 (VMF MY-E)	1.85	0.0	1.64	1.69	0	60892
09 Jan 30.00 (VMF AF-E)	3.90	0.0	3.90	4.00	0	160002	09 Jan 30.00 (VMF MF-E)	2.53	0.0	2.52	2.56	0	104238
09 Jan 32.00 (VMF AZ-E)	2.73	+0.08	2.68	2.74	108	33312	09 Jan 32.50 (VMF MZ-E)	3.95	0.0	3.70	3.80	0	19663
09 Jan 35.00 (VMF AG-E)	1.76	+0.11	1.73	1.80	10	57738	09 Jan 35.00 (VMF MG-E)	6.50	0.0	5.30	5.40	0	10574
09 Jan 40.00 (VMF AH-E)	0.65	+0.08	0.63	0.68	60	71701	09 Jan 40.00 (VMF MH-E)	10.60	0.0	9.45	9.75	0	25
10 Jan 20.00 (VMF AD-E)	12.00	0.0	11.90	12.20	0	1242	10 Jan 20.00 (VMF MD-E)	0.66	0.0	0.67	0.75	0	1465
10 Jan 25.00 (VMF AJ-E)	7.75	0.0	8.30	8.55	0	1543	10 Jan 25.00 (VMF MJ-E)	1.72	0.0	1.59	1.79	0	7359
10 Jan 30.00 (VMF AK-E)	5.20	0.0	5.25	5.55	0	23695	10 Jan 30.00 (VMF MK-E)	3.50	0.0	3.15	3.30	0	21327
10 Jan 35.00 (VMF AL-E)	3.00	0.0	3.00	3.20	0	3245	10 Jan 35.00 (VMF ML-E)	5.35	0.0	5.70	6.00	0	143
10 Jan 40.00 (VMF AH-E)	1.64	0.0	1.62	1.70	0	2468	10 Jan 40.00 (VMF MH-E)	10.74	0.0	9.50	9.90	0	120

Source: Chicago Board Options Exchange (www.cboe.com); October 16, 2007. Provided as a courtesy by Chicago Board Options Exchange, Incorporated.

The LEAPS quotes allow us to see the effect that time to expiration has on the value of an option. The highlighted entries in the display show prices for four different calls and puts for MSFT. Each contract has an exercise price of 30, but the expiration dates are either 1.25 years (January 2009) or 2.25 years (January 2010) in the future. For both calls and puts, the value of the contract increases as the expiration date is pushed farther out (e.g., $3.90 for the January 2009 call versus $5.20 for the January 2010). Of course, because these contracts have the same exercise price ($30) and underlying stock price ($30.35), the intrinsic value is the same as discussed earlier. Thus, the difference in the contract prices is purely because of additional time premium.

Stock Index Options As we saw in Chapter 13, options on stock indices, such as S&P 100 or 500, are patterned closely after equity options. However, they differ in one important way: Index options can only be settled in cash. This is because of the underlying index, which is a hypothetical portfolio that would be quite costly to duplicate in practice. First traded on the CBOE in 1983, index options are popular with investors for the same reason as stock index futures: They provide a relatively inexpensive and convenient way to take an investment or hedging position in a broad-based indicator of market performance. Index puts are particularly useful in portfolio insurance applications, such as the protective put strategy described earlier and again at the end of this chapter.

Prices for two widely traded contracts—the S&P 500 and Russell 2000 index options—are listed in Exhibit 14.10. They are interpreted the same way as individual equity option prices, with each contract specifying the transfer of 100 "shares" of the underlying index. For example, the November 2007 SPX index call option with an exercise price of 1,540 is out of the money, given that the index level on October 16, 2007, was 1,538.53. This contract could be purchased at the ask price for $3,460 (= 34.60 × 100) and would only be exercised to acquire $154,000 worth of the index if the S&P rises above 1,540 by the expiration date. In contrast, a November 2007 RUT index put option with an exercise price of 830 is in the money given the current index level of 823.35. In exchange for an upfront payment of $2,570 (= 25.70 × 100), the owner of this put contract would be able to sell $83,000 worth of the index, assuming the Russell 2000 index remained below 830 at the expiration date.

Options on Futures Contracts Although they have existed for decades in the OTC markets, options on futures contracts have only been exchange-traded since 1982. Also known as futures options, they give the holder the right, but not the obligation, to enter into a futures contract on an underlying security or commodity at a later date and at a predetermined price. Purchasing a call on a futures contract allows for the acquisition of a long position in the futures market, while exercising a put would create a short futures position. On the other hand, the call seller would be obligated to enter into the short side of the futures contract if the option holder decided to exercise the contract, while the put seller might be forced into a long futures position. Futures options exist for a wide variety of underlying assets, including agricultural, metal, and energy commodities; Treasury bonds and notes; foreign currencies; and stock indices.

The Montreal Exchange is Canada's options market where options on equity and exchange traded funds (ETFs) are available. Exhibit 14.11 shows the volume, including the specific volume of options on various ETFs. The most popular is the option on XIU, the EFT of the S&P/TSX 60 large-cap index. Exhibit 14.12 is a chart of trading volume by sector. Materials, energy, and financials are the three dominating sectors.

EXHIBIT 14.10   Stock Index Option Quotations for SPX and RVT

Panel A. Standard & Poor's 500 Index (SPX)

Calls	Last sale	Net	Bid	Ask	Vol	Open Int	Puts	Last sale	Net	Bid	Ask	Vol	Open Int
07 Oct 1530.00 (SXM JF-E)	16.00	−4.00	15.20	17.20	148	21354	07 Oct 1530.00 (SXM VF-E)	7.50	+3.20	5.70	7.70	8120	19974
07 Oct 1535.00 (SXM JG-E)	12.20	−5.30	11.50	13.50	12596	22052	07 Oct 1535.00 (SXM VG-E)	8.80	+1.80	7.80	8.80	8166	11786
07 Oct 1540.00 (SXM JH-E)	9.50	−7.50	8.70	10.70	1194	11174	07 Oct 1540.00 (SXM VH-E)	10.20	+2.20	10.20	11.00	7006	21385
07 Oct 1545.00 (SXM JI-E)	7.00	−6.00	6.30	8.30	1183	10047	07 Oct 1545.00 (SXM VI-E)	13.50	+4.70	12.50	14.00	3044	6731
07 Nov 1530.00 (SXM KF-E)	41.80	−6.20	39.30	41.30	1560	990	07 Nov 1530.00 (SXM WF-E)	28.00	+4.30	26.40	28.40	6174	4583
07 Nov 1535.00 (SXM KG-E)	41.60	−9.00	36.20	38.20	2	32	07 Nov 1535.00 (SXM WG-E)	28.20	+2.80	28.30	30.20	620	16656
07 Nov 1540.00 (SXM KH-E)	33.80	−7.60	32.60	34.60	98	791	07 Nov 1540.00 (SXM WH-E)	31.00	+0.50	30.20	32.20	481	14958
07 Nov 1545.00 (SXM KI-E)	30.30	−5.90	30.10	32.10	4463	2172	07 Nov 1545.00 (SXM WI-E)	33.40	+1.40	32.70	34.70	5892	1340

Panel B. Russell 2000 Index (RUT)

Calls	Last sale	Net	Bid	Ask	Vol	Open Int	Puts	Last sale	Net	Bid	Ask	Vol	Open Int
07 Oct 810.00 (RUZ JB-E)	17.60	−1.85	16.40	17.00	76	3436	07 Oct 810.00 (RUZ VB-E)	3.20	+0.90	3.10	3.40	348	9736
07 Oct 820.00 (RUZ JD-E)	10.45	−1.60	9.60	10.10	291	8973	07 Oct 820.00 (RUZ VD-E)	5.90	+1.70	6.00	6.40	564	13292
07 Oct 830.00 (RUZ JF-E)	5.00	−2.05	4.80	5.20	2664	8384	07 Oct 830.00 (RUZ VF-E)	11.20	+3.70	11.20	11.70	2280	6912
07 Oct 840.00 (RUZ JH-E)	2.20	−2.50	2.10	2.45	3757	8907	07 Oct 840.00 (RUZ VH-E)	17.30	+3.30	18.40	19.00	186	9572
07 Nov 810.00 (RUZ KB-E)	33.95	−0.80	32.60	33.20	18	3034	07 Nov 810.00 (RUZ WB-E)	17.80	+1.80	17.40	18.00	83	3562
07 Nov 820.00 (RUZ KD-E)	27.00	−1.80	26.20	26.80	141	1456	07 Nov 820.00 (RUZ WD-E)	19.25	−0.35	20.90	21.50	50	13731
07 Nov 830.00 (RUZ KF-E)	21.65	−0.70	20.40	21.00	43	2820	07 Nov 830.00 (RUZ WF-E)	25.30	+0.30	25.10	25.70	346	5897
07 Nov 840.00 (RUZ KH-E)	15.60	−3.90	15.40	15.90	55	7152	07 Nov 840.00 (RUZ WH-E)	30.40	+0.80	30.00	30.50	284	9923

Source: Chicago Board Options Exchange (www.cboe.com); October 16, 2007. Provided as a courtesy by Chicago Board Options Exchange, Incorporated.

Exhibit 14.11   Volume of the Canadian Equity Options Market

ETF Options	Volume YTD 2008	Volume YTD 2007	% Variation
XIU (LT included)	661,286	364,924	81.20%
COW	64	N/A	N/A
HXD	3,882	N/A	N/A
HXU	7,665	N/A	N/A
XGD/XGL (LT included)	58,438	89,435	−34.7%
XFN	195,820	101,499	92.9%
XIT	3,248	14,989	−78.3%
XMA	5,811	59,371	−90.2%
XEG/XEX (LT included)	80,838	158,178	−48.9%
Subtotal	1,017,052	788,396	29.0%
Equity Derivatives			
Equity Options	14,003,555	11,903,402	17.6%
Long-Term Options	630,044	730,658	−13.8%
Subtotal	14,633,599	12,634,060	15.8%
Subtotal Equity Opt. + ETF	**15,650,651**	**13,422,456**	**16.6%**

XIU: iShares CDN LargeCap 60 Index
COW: Claymore Global Agriculture
HXD: Horizons BetaPro S&P/TSX 60 Bear Plus Fund
HXU: Horizons BetaPro S&P/TSX 60 Bull Plus Fund
XGD: iUnits S&P/TSX Capped Gold Index Fund
XFN: iUnits S&P/TSX Capped Financials Index Fund
XIT: iUnits S&P/TSX Capped Information Technology Index Fund
XMA: iUnits S&P/TSX Capped Materials Index Fund
XEG: iUnits S&P/TSX Capped Energy Index Fund

Source: Montreal Exchange, December 2008, http://www.m-x.ca/f_stat_en/0812_stats_en.pdf.

Exhibit 14.12   Canadian Options Volume by Sector

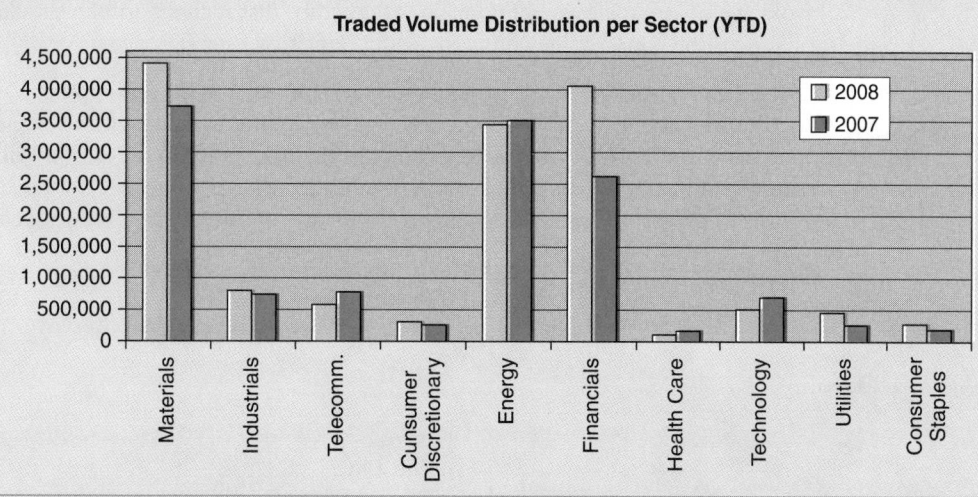

Source: Montreal Exchange, December 2008, http://www.m-x.ca/f_stat_en/0812_stats_en.pdf.

14.6 The Fundamentals of Option Valuation

The key to understanding how options are valued is to recognize that they are risk reduction tools. The theoretical value of an option depends on combining it with its underlying security to create *synthetic risk-free portfolio*. That is, it always is theoretically possible to use the option as a perfect *hedge* against fluctuations in the value of the asset on which it is based. Recall that this was essentially the same approach we used in Chapter 13 to establish the put–call parity relationships.

14.6.1 THE BASIC BINOMIAL APPROACH

While the mathematics associated with option valuation can be complex, the fundamental intuition behind the process is straightforward. Suppose we have just purchased one WYZ Corp. stock for $50. The stock is not expected to pay a dividend during the time we plan to hold it, and we have forecast that in one year the stock price will either rise to $65 or fall to $40. This can be summarized as follows:

Today	One Year

$$50 \begin{array}{c} \diagup \ 65 \\ \diagdown \ 40 \end{array}$$

Suppose further that we can either buy or sell a call option on WYZ stock with an exercise price of $52.50. Assuming this is a European-style contract that expires in exactly one year, it will have the following possible expiration date values:

Today	One Year

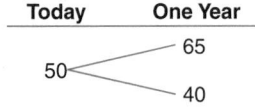

$$C_0 \begin{array}{c} \diagup \ \max[0, 65 - 52.5] = 12.50 \\ \diagdown \ \max[0, 40 - 52.5] = 0 \end{array}$$

The dilemma is determining what the contract should sell for today (i.e., C_0). This question can be answered in three intuitive steps:

1. Creating a riskless hedge portfolio combining options with the underlying security.
2. Invoking a no-arbitrage assumption about the return that such a portfolio should earn.
3. Solving for the option value consistent with the first two steps.

Both the binomial and Black-Scholes models are consistent with this approach.

Based on the above, we first design a hedge portfolio consisting of one WYZ stock held long and some number of call options (i.e., h) so that the combined position will be riskless. The number of call options needed can be established by ensuring that the portfolio has the same value at expiration no matter which of the two forecasted stock values occurs, or

$$65 + (h)(12.50) = 40 + (h)(0)$$

leaving

$$h = \frac{(65 - 40)}{(0 - 12.5)} = -2.00$$

There are both *direction* and *magnitude* dimensions to this number. The negative sign indicates that in order to create negative correlation between two assets that are naturally positively correlated, call options must be *sold* to hedge a long stock position. Further, given that the range of possible expiration date option outcomes (i.e., 12.5 − 0) is only half as large as the range for WYZ stock (i.e., 65 − 40), twice as many options must be sold as there is stock in the hedge portfolio. The value *h* is known as the *hedge ratio*.[6] Thus, the risk-free hedge portfolio can be created by purchasing one share and selling two call options.

The second step in the option valuation process assumes capital markets that are free from arbitrage so that all riskless investments are priced to earn the risk-free rate over the time until expiration. The hedge portfolio costing $[50 − (2)(C_0)]$ today would grow to the certain value of \$40 by the following formula:

$$[50 - (2.00)(C_0)](1 + RFR)^T = 40$$

where:

RFR = the annualized risk-free rate

T = the time to expiration (i.e., one year)

Our third step is to estimate RFR and solve for C_0. If the one-year T-bill yield is 8%, the C_0 can be solved as follows:

$$C_0 = \frac{50 - 40/1.08}{2.00} = \$6.48$$

This bit of algebraic manipulation is the third and final step in determining the call's fair market value. That is, \$6.48 represents the fundamental value of a one-year call option on WYZ stock, given both the prevailing market prices for two other securities (i.e., stock and T-bills) and the investor's forecast of future share values. Because the security prices are observable, the investor's forecast of future share values becomes the critical element in determining if this present value is a reasonable estimate. Finally, because the call option is currently out of the money, this amount is purely a time premium.

14.6.2 THE BINOMIAL APPROACH EXPANDED

A crucial element of this approach is that future changes in the underlying asset's price always can be simplified to one of two possibilities: an up movement or a down movement. Rendleman and Bartter (1979) and Cox, Ross, and Rubinstein (1979) show this analytical development is part of a more general valuation methodology known as the *two-state option pricing model*. One difficulty with the preceding examples though is that they required the investor to specify cash amounts for each of the future potential stock prices

---

6 In some valuation models (e.g., Black-Scholes), the hedge ratio is expressed as the option's potential volatility divided by that of the stock. In this example, that would be $(0 - 12.5) \div (65 - 40) = -0.5$, meaning that the option is half as volatile in dollar terms as the share of stock. Of course, this alternative calculation is just the reciprocal of the value of $h = -2.00$.

in all the sub-periods demanded by the forecast. This can be a daunting task as the number of terminal outcomes is allowed to expand with the time to expiration of the contract.

Forecasting Price Changes To simplify this process, suppose an investor focuses her estimates on how stock prices change between sub-periods, rather than on the dollar levels. That is, beginning with today's known stock price, for the next sub-period she forecasts: (1) one plus the percentage change for an up *(u)* movement, and (2) one plus the percentage change for a down *(d)* movement. Further, to limit the number of required forecasts, suppose she also assumes that the same values for *u* and *d* apply to every up and down price change in all subsequent sub-periods. With these assumptions, the investor need only forecast three things: *u, d,* and *N*—the total number of sub-periods.

Exhibit 14.13 shows the effect that these modifications—which represent the essence of the **binomial option pricing model**—have on the forecasted stock price and option value trees. Consistent with the four-outcome version of the preceding example, this illustration allows for three sub-periods (i.e., *N* = 3). The upper panel of the display shows that after an up and a down movement during the first two sub-periods, the initial stock price of *S* will have changed to *(ud)S*. Of course, the values *(ud)S* and *(du)S* are equal, meaning that the forecast does not depend on whether the stock price begins its journey by rising or falling. As before, once *u, d,* and *N* are determined, the expiration date payoffs to the option (i.e., C_{uuu}, C_{uud}, C_{udd}, and C_{ddd}) are established.

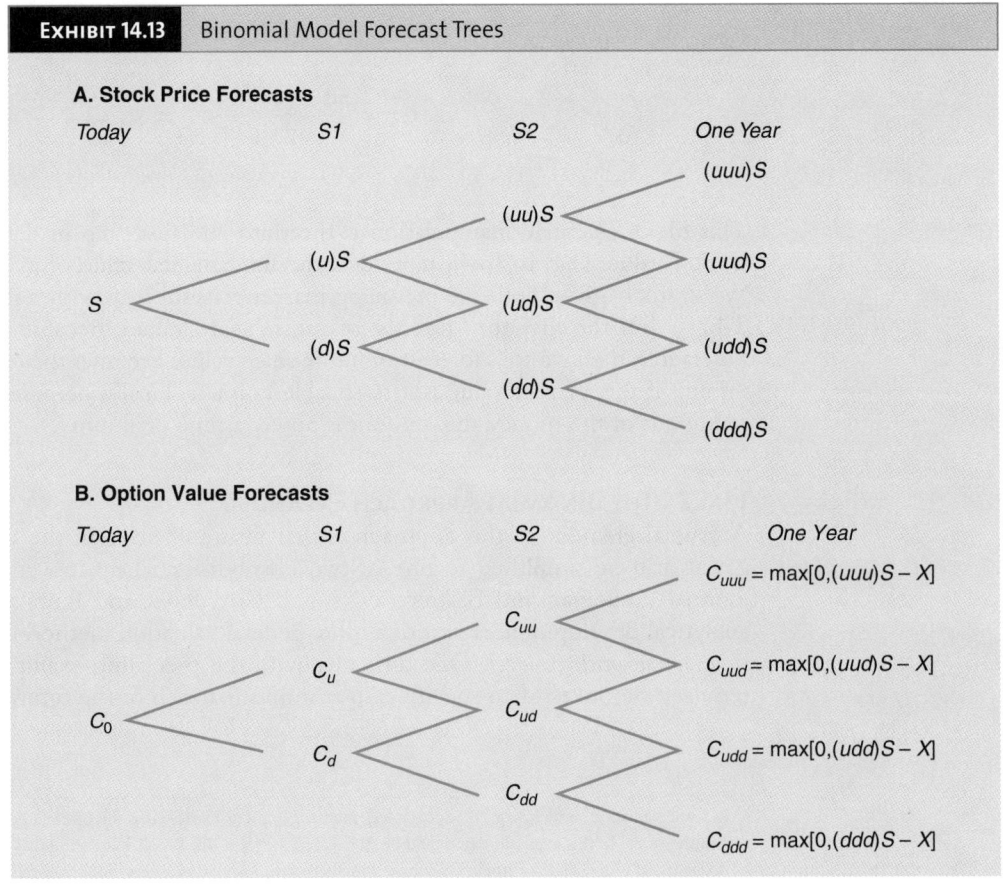

EXHIBIT 14.13 Binomial Model Forecast Trees

A. Stock Price Forecasts

B. Option Value Forecasts

As before, the initial value for the call, C_0, can be solved by working backward through the tree and solving for each of the remaining intermediate option values. However, another distinct advantage of the binomial model is that these intermediate values are much easier to compute. In fact, in the *j*th state in any sub-period, the value of the option can be calculated by

14.5
$$C_j = \frac{(p)C_{ju} + (1 - p)C_{jd}}{r}$$

Where

$$p = \frac{r - d}{u - d}$$

and

r = one plus the risk-free rate over the sub-period.

Generalizing the Model Equation 14.5 can be extended by recognizing that the value generated for *Cj* is one of the inputs for valuing the option in the preceding sub-period. Thus, the formula for an option in Sub-period *t* can be inserted into the right-hand side of the formula for Sub-period *t* − 1. Carrying this logic all the way back to Date 0, the binomial option valuation model becomes

14.6
$$C_0 = \left\{ \sum_{j=0}^{N} \frac{N!}{(N - j)!j!} p^j (1 - P)^{N-j} \max[0, (u^j d^{N-j})S - X] \right\} \div r^N$$

where

$$N! = [(N)(N - 1)(N - 2) \ldots (2)(1)]$$

To interpret Equation 14.6, the ratio $[N! \div (N - j)!j!]$ is the "combinatorial" way of stating how many distinct paths lead to a particular terminal outcome, $pj(1 - p)^N - j$ is the probability of getting to that outcome, and $\max[0, (u^j d^{N - j})S - X]$ is the payoff associated with that outcome. Letting *m* be the smallest integer number of up moves guaranteeing that the option will be in the money at expiration (i.e., $u^m d^{N-m})S > X$), this formula can be reduced further to

14.7
$$C_0 = \left\{ \sum_{j=m}^{N} \frac{N!}{(N - j)!j!} p^j (1 - p)^{N-j} [(u^j d^{N-j})S - X] \right\} \div r^N$$

For example, assume the investor has gathered contract terms and price data and has made her forecasts as follows: $S = 50.00, X = 52.50, T = $ *one year, RFR = 8 percent (through expiration), u = 1.09139, d = 0.92832, and N = 3.* By these forecasts, the investor has divided the one-year life of the option into three sub-periods and estimated up and down moves during any sub-period as slightly greater than 9% and 7%, respectively. Also, the values for r and p implied by these forecasts are 1.026 [= $(1.08)^{0.33}$] and 0.599 [= $(1.026 - 0.92832) \div (1.09139 - 0.92832)$]. Using Equation 14.7, which ignores the two terminal option outcomes that are equal to zero, the value of a one-year European-style call option with an exercise price of $52.50 is

$$C_0 = \frac{(3)(0.599)^2(0.401)(2.79) + (1)(0.599)^3(12.50)}{(1.026)^3} = \$3.60$$

This is the same value the three-step approach used in the previous example. Finally, the hedge ratio for any state j becomes

$$h_j = \frac{(u - d)S_j}{C_{jd} - C_{ju}}$$

Thus, a stock held long could be hedged initially by shorting 1.78 call options [= (1.09139 − 0.92832)(50) ÷ (0.95 − 5.53)], a position that would be rebalanced to 1.32 calls after one sub-period if the first price change was positive.

14.7 The Black-Scholes Valuation Model

The binomial model is a *discrete* method for valuing options because it allows security price changes to occur in distinct upward or downward movements. Prices can also change *continuously* throughout time. This was the approach taken by Black and Scholes (1973) in developing their celebrated equation for valuing European-style options.[7] This assumption is not completely realistic because it presumes that security prices change when markets are closed (e.g., at night, on weekends). However, the advantage of the Black-Scholes approach—identical in spirit to the basic three-step, riskless hedge method outlined earlier—is that it leads to a relatively simple, closed-form equation capable of valuing options accurately under a wide array of circumstances.

Assuming the continuously compounded risk-free rate and the stock's variance (i.e., σ^2) remain constant until the expiration date T, Black and Scholes used the riskless hedge intuition to derive the following formula for valuing a call option on a non-dividend-paying stock:

14.8	$$C_0 = SN(d_1) - X(e^{-\{RFR\}T})N(d_2)$$

where $e^{-(RFR)T}$ is the discount function for continuously compounded variables,

$$d_1 = [(\ln(S/X) + (RFR + 0.5\sigma^2)[T])] \div (\sigma[T]^{1/2})$$

---

7 For a detailed analysis of the mathematics underlying the Black-Scholes model, see Hull (2009).

and

$$d_2 = d_1 - \sigma[T]^{1/2}$$

with $\ln(\cdot)$ being the natural logarithm function. The variable $N(d)$ is the cumulative probability of observing a value drawn from the standard normal distribution (i.e., one with a mean of zero and a standard deviation of one) equal to or less than d. As the standard normal distribution is symmetric around zero, a value of $d = 0$ would lead to $N(d) = 0.5000$; positive values of d would then have cumulative probabilities greater than 50%, with negative values of d leading to cumulative probabilities of less than one-half.

Values for $N(d)$ can be determined in two ways. First, an investor can use a table of calculated values for the standard normal distribution, such as the one shown in the Appendix E at the end of this book. For example, if the value for d_1 is 0.65, $N(d_1)$ could be determined by finding the entry corresponding to the 0.6 row and the 0.05 column, or 0.7422. This means 74.22% of the observations in the standard normal distribution have a value of 0.65 or less. If d_1 had been -0.65, the value of $N(-d_1) = 1 - N(d_1) = 1 - 0.7422 = 0.2578$, which must be the case as the distribution is symmetric.

A second approach to calculating cumulative normal probabilities is approximating them with the following formula following Carr (1988).

$$N(d) \approx \begin{cases} 0.5e^{-(d^2)/2 - 281/(83-351/d)} & \text{if } d < 0 \\ 1 - 0.5e^{-(d^2)/2 - 281/(83-351/d)} & \text{if } d \geq 0 \end{cases}$$

For example, with $d = 0.65$, we have an approximate probability of

$$N(0.65) \approx 1 - 0.5e^{-(0.65^2)/2 - 281/(83+351/0.65)} = 0.7422$$

14.7.1 PROPERTIES OF THE MODEL

The **Black–Scholes valuation model** reveals that the option's value is a function of five variables:

1. Current security price
2. Exercise price
3. Time to expiration
4. Risk-free rate
5. Security price volatility.

Functionally, the Black–Scholes model holds that $C = f(S, X, T, RFR, \sigma)$. The first and fourth factors are observable market prices, and the second and third variables are defined by the contract itself. Thus, the only variable an investor must provide is the volatility factor. As noted earlier, the estimate of σ embeds the investor's forecast of future stock prices.

The value of the call option will increase with increases in each of the five factors *except* the exercise price. Exhibit 14.14 summarizes these relationships. The intuition behind the first three relationships in the middle column of the exhibit is straightforward: An increase in the

EXHIBIT 14.14	Factors Affecting Black-Scholes Option Values	
	Will Cause An Increase/Decrease In:	
An Increase In:	**Call Value**	**Put Value**
Security price (S)	Increase	Decrease
Exercise price (X)	Decrease	Increase
Time to expiration (T)	Increase	Increase or decrease
Risk-free rate (RFR)	Increase	Decrease
Security volatility (a)	Increase	Increase

underlying asset's price (i.e., S) will increase the call's intrinsic value; a larger exercise price (i.e., X) will reduce the intrinsic value. Also, the longer the option has until expiry, the more valuable the time premium component. This is because a greater opportunity exists for the contract to finish in the money. On the other hand, the relationships between C, RFR, and σ are less obvious. An increase in RFR will increase the call's value because this reduces the present value of X, an expense that the call holder must pay at expiry to exercise the contract. Similarly, when the volatility of the underlying asset's price increases, the call becomes more valuable because this increases the probability that the option will be deeper in the money at expiry.[8]

Another useful facet of the Black-Scholes model is that the hedge ratio at any moment is simply $N(d_1)$, the partial derivative of the call's value with respect to the stock price (i.e., $\delta C/\delta S$). Under this interpretation, $N(d_1)$ is the change in the option's value given a one dollar change in the underlying security's price. For this reason, $N(d_1)$ often is called the option's **delta**, and it indicates the number of stock that can be hedged by a single call—the exact reciprocal of the previous interpretation of the hedge ratio, h. Finally, although the Black-Scholes model was developed several years before the binomial framework, the former is actually an extension of the latter. As the number of sub-periods (i.e., N) approaches infinity, the up or down price movements begin to occur on a continuous basis. If the values of u and d are then set equal to $e^{\sigma[\Delta T]1/2}$ and $e^{-\sigma[\Delta T]1/2}$, respectively, the binomial model collapses to become the Black-Scholes formula.

An Example Consider the following values for the five input variables: $S = 40$, $X = 40$, $T =$ one year, $RFR = 9\%$, and $\sigma = 0.30$. To calculate the Black-Scholes value of a European-style call option under these conditions, first calculate:

$$d_1 = (\ln(40/40) + (0.09 + 0.5(0.3)^2)[1]) \div (0.3[1]^{1/2}) = 0.45$$

and

$$d_2 = 0.45 - 0.3[1]^{1/2} = 0.15$$

---

8 In more technical terms, these relationships can be summarized as $\delta C/\delta S > 0$, $\delta C/\delta RFR > 0$, $\delta C/\delta T > 0$, $\delta C/\delta \sigma > 0$, and $\delta C/\delta X < 0$.

so that

$$N(d_1) = 1 - 0.5e^{-(0.45^2)/2 - 281/(83+351/0.45)} = 0.6736$$

and

$$N(d_2) = 1 - 0.5e^{-(0.15^2)/2 - 281/(83+351/0.15)} = 0.5596$$

Thus,

$$C_0 = (40)(0.6736) - 40(e^{-.09})(0.5596) = \$6.49$$

$N(d_1)$ says that the call option will change in value by about \$0.67 for every dollar of a change in the underlying asset, suggesting a hedge ratio of 1.5 calls short for every stock held long. Exhibit 14.15 shows how both the option's value and $N(d_1)$ change as the security's value changes—with the other factors held constant. Notably, the hedge ratios range in value from 0 to 1, and increase as stock prices increase. Therefore, the deeper in the money the option is, the closer its price movements will come to duplicating those of the stock itself. The relationship between stock prices and call option prices for this example is shown in Exhibit 14.16. The delta, or hedge ratio, associated with a given stock price is simply the slope of a line tangent to the call option price curve.

14.7.2 Estimating Volatility

Just as the dividend growth rate (i.e., g) was a crucial element in establishing the fundamental value of common stock, option valuation depends critically on an accurate forecast of the underlying asset's future price level. In the Black-Scholes framework, this means selecting the proper σ, the standard deviation of returns to the underlying asset. This value can be estimated in two ways. First, it can be calculated in the traditional manner using historical returns. Specifically, calculate the Day t *price relative* as $Rt = \ln(Pt \div Pt-1)$. If a series of price relatives are

Exhibit 14.15	Example of Black-Scholes Valuation		
	Stock Price (\$)	Call Value (\$)	Hedge Ratio
	25	0.44	0.1321
	30	1.51	0.3054
	35	3.60	0.5020
	40	6.49	0.6736
	45	10.19	0.8003
	50	14.42	0.8837
	55	18.98	0.9347

Note: Assumes $X = 40$, $T = 1$ year, $RFR = 9\%$, and $\sigma = 0.30$.

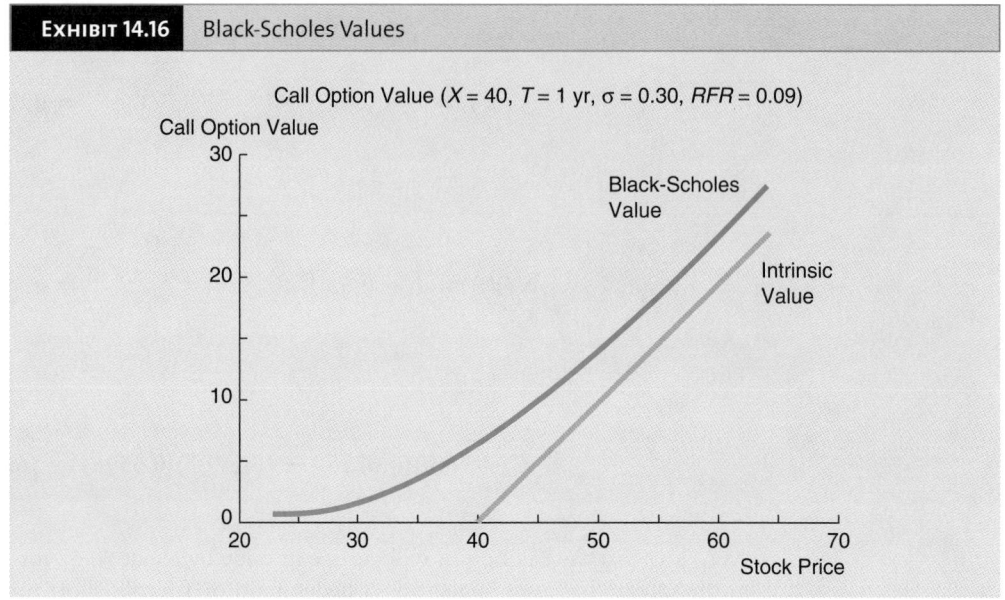

EXHIBIT 14.16   Black-Scholes Values

Call Option Value ($X = 40$, $T = 1$ yr, $\sigma = 0.30$, $RFR = 0.09$)

calculated for a sequence of N days in the recent past, the mean and standard deviation of this series can be calculated as

$$\bar{R} = \left(\frac{1}{N} \right) \sum_{t=1}^{N} R_t \text{ and } \sigma^2 \left(\frac{1}{N-1} \right) \sum_{t=1}^{N} (R_t - \bar{R})^2$$

The factor σ is expressed in terms of daily price movements. To annualize this value, σ can be multiplied by the square root of the number of trading days in the year (usually assumed to be 250), which then becomes the estimate of volatility employed in the Black–Scholes formula. The advantage of historical volatility is that it is easy to compute and requires no prior assumption about stock market efficiency; the main disadvantage is the presumption that future stock price behaviour will continue as it has in the past, a sometimes questionable assumption. Exhibit 14.17 lists 30-day historical volatilities for a representative sample of optionable stocks during November 2004 and May 2007.

Rather than relying on historical price movements we can use a second volatility estimation approach, which involves the Black–Scholes equation. Recall that if all five input factors—S, X, T, RFR, and σ—are known, we can solve for the value of the call option. However, if we know the current price of the option (call it C^*) and the four other variables, we can calculate the level of σ that forces the Black–Scholes value to equal C^*. That is, the volatility implied by current market prices is determined by finding σ^* such that $C^* = f(S, X, T, RFR, \sigma^*)$. Accordingly, the value σ^* is known as the **implied volatility**. No simple closed-form solution exists for performing this calculation; it must be done by trial and error.

Implied volatility is advantageous because it calculates the same volatility forecast investors use to set option prices. The disadvantage of implied volatility is its presumption that markets are efficient in that the option price set in the market corresponds directly to that generated by the Black–Scholes equation. Beckers (1981) has shown that implied volatilities do a better job than historical volatilities of predicting future stock price movements; however, Figlewski (1989b) and

EXHIBIT 14.17	Historical Volatility Estimates		
		30–day Volatility Estimate (%)	
Company	Ticker	November 2004	May 2007
Altria	MO	36.96	11.30
Amazon.com	AMZN	32.66	36.57
Applied Materials	AMAT	27.98	30.76
Bank of America	BAC	12.44	8.58
Continental Airlines	CAL	18.95	33.01
Cisco Systems	CSCO	32.82	31.71
Citigroup	C	14.87	16.63
Coca-Cola	KO	9.16	12.65
Dell Computer	DELL	31.97	41.13
Duke Energy	DUK	20.97	15.93
eBay	EBAY	25.81	21.15
General Electric	GE	14.27	10.07
Halliburton	HAL	28.23	23.74
Intel	INTC	26.23	21.41
Merck	MRK	34.18	14.46
Oracle	ORCL	20.91	18.52
Pfizer	PFE	22.00	9.65
Tivo	TIVO	69.25	41.20
Wal-Mart	WMT	23.22	9.61
Xerox	XRX	26.10	20.34

Source: Chicago Board Options Exchange, October 16, 2007. Provided as a courtesy by Chicago Board Options Exchange, Incorporated.

Szakmary, Ors, Kim, and Davidson (2003) caution that σ^* can be "noisy" because it picks up not only the true level of volatility but also any misestimate inherent in the valuation process.

Brown, Harlow, and Tinic (1989) estimated the volatilities implied by the S&P 500 index call option contract for the 121-day period surrounding the stock market crash in October 1987. These calculations are reproduced in Exhibit 14.18. The time variable is denominated relative to "Black Monday" (i.e., Day 0). To see how much market risk changed with the crash, the *average* implied volatility measure for the period Day -60 to Day -5 (i.e., the period beginning approximately two-and-a-half months before the crash) was 18.9%. The comparable statistic for the period from Day $+5$ to Day $+60$ was 43.3%. Moreover, on Black Monday itself, the implied volatility rose to 145%, more than seven-and-a-half times its precrash level!

The concept of implied volatility is also the foundation of a popular measure of stock market sentiment. Introduced by Whaley (1993), the **Volatility Index (VIX)** is calculated as a weighted average of the implied volatility estimates from options on the S&P 500 index using a wide range of exercise prices. VIX purports to measure investor expectations of near-term (i.e., 30-day) volatility in the stock market, with higher levels of the index indicating greater investor wariness about future economic conditions. In a typical year, the VIX can range

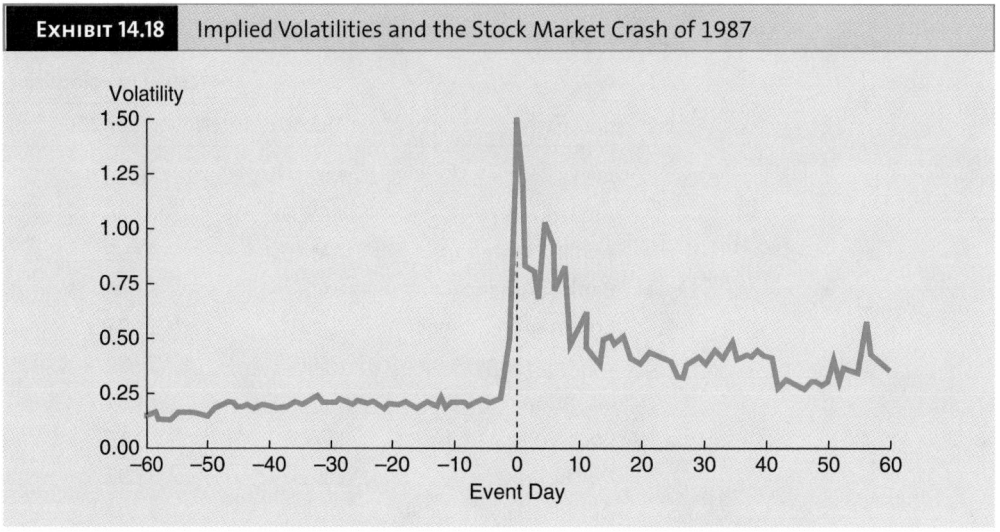

EXHIBIT 14.18 Implied Volatilities and the Stock Market Crash of 1987

between 10.00% and 45.00%. Futures and options contracts using the VIX as the underlying asset have traded on the CBOE since 2004 and 2006, respectively. Exhibit 14.19 shows the VIX around the time of the outbreak of the global financial crisis. The index started to rise from early September 2008, and reached its heights in mid-fall, before leveling off in December.

14.7.3 VALUING EUROPEAN-STYLE PUT OPTIONS

Converting the discounting process for the T-bill to be a continuous function, the put-call-spot parity model of Chapter 13 can be expressed in terms of the value of a put option.

$$P_0 = C_0 + X(e^{-(RFT)T}) - S$$

EXHIBIT 14.19 SPX Market Volatility Index

CBOE SPX MARKET VOLATILITY INDE
as of 28-Jan-2009

Copyright 2009 Yahoo! Inc.   http ://finance.yahoo.com/

This formula implies that if we know the prices of the security, the call option, and the T-bill, we can solve for the value of the put option. If the Black-Scholes value for C is inserted into this expression, we have

$$P_0 = [SN(d_1) - X(e^{-(RFR)T})N(d_2)] + X(e^{-(RFR)T}) - S$$

which can be manipulated to equal

14.9
$$P_0 = X(e^{-(RFR)T})N(-d_2) - SN(-d_1)$$

where all the notation is the same as before. Equation 14.9 is the Black-Scholes put option valuation model.

The comparative statics of put option valuation were shown in the final column of Exhibit 14.14. The value of the put will increase with higher levels of X but decline with an increase in S because of the effect these movements have on the contract's intrinsic value. Like the call option, the put's value benefits from an increase in σ because this increases the likelihood that the contract will finish deep in the money. Also, an increase in the risk-free rate reduces the present value of X, which hurts the holder of the put who receives the exercise price if the contract is executed. Finally, the sign of $\delta P/\delta T$ could be either positive or negative depending on the trade-off between the longer time over which the security price could move in the desired direction and the reduced present value of the exercise price received by the seller at expiration.

14.7.4 PROBLEMS WITH BLACK-SCHOLES VALUATION

The Black-Scholes option valuation model is popular with investors for at least two reasons: It is computationally convenient and it produces reasonable values under a wide variety of conditions. There are, however, circumstances in which the model is less than desirable. In one of the earliest empirical tests of the Black-Scholes equation, MacBeth and Merville (1979) showed that implied volatilities tended to be overly large when the associated call options were in the money and too small for out-of-the-money contracts. Assuming that at-the-money options are priced fairly by the market, this suggested that in-the-money options were priced higher by investors than their Black-Scholes values, with the opposite being true for the out-of-the-money contracts.

Thus, for the authors' sample of stocks, the Black-Scholes model overvalued out-of-the-money call options and undervalued in-the-money contracts. Interestingly, in two different studies, Rubinstein (1985b, 1994) found evidence that both supported and contradicted these results.

In general, any violation of the assumptions upon which the Black-Scholes model is based could lead to a misvaluation of the option contract. For instance, because stock prices do not change continuously, less actively traded stocks might have options that are priced differently in the market than those stocks that trade frequently. Figlewski (1989a) has noted how such market imperfections as brokerage fees, bid-ask spreads, and inflexible position sizes can create arbitrageable differences between option values and prices. He cautioned that Black-Scholes values should be viewed as approximations, best suited for comparing prices of different contracts.

Further, Black (1989) has observed that other conditions of the model are almost certain to be violated in practice, such as the assumption that the risk-free rate and volatility level remain constant until the expiration date.

14.8 Swaps

14.8.1 INTEREST RATE SWAPS

Forward Rate Agreement An extremely active OTC market exists for products designed to manage an investor's or an issuer's interest rate risk. The **forward rate agreement (FRA)** is the most basic of the OTC interest rate contracts.[9] In an FRA, two parties agree today to a future exchange of cash flows based on two different interest rates. One of the cash flows is tied to a yield that is fixed at the deal's origination (the fixed rate); the other is determined at some later date (the floating rate). On the contract's settlement date, the difference between the two interest rates is multiplied by the FRA's **notional principal** and prorated to the length of the holding period. The London Interbank Offer Rate (LIBOR) is frequently used as the floating rate index, making FRAs the OTC equivalent of the Eurodollar futures contracts with two important exceptions: (1) FRAs typically require no collateral account, and (2) they are not marked to market on a daily basis.

Go to http://www.isda.org, the website of the International Swaps and Derivatives Association.

Interest Rate Swaps FRAs represent a one-time-only solution to an interest rate risk management problem as they have a single settlement date. In fact, both investors and borrowers are routinely exposed to interest rate movements at regular intervals over an extended period of time. For example, assume that Counterparty A is an institutional investor who currently holds a three-year bond paying a semi-annual coupon of 4.80%. He feels that interest rates are likely to rise in the near term, and although he does not want to sell this position, he is concerned about a reduction in the bond's value. Instead, the investor decides to convert his investment into a synthetic floating-rate note whose coupons will rise with future LIBOR increases. He accomplishes this by agreeing to pay the fixed rate on a three-year **interest rate swap** contract with Counterparty B (i.e., the swap dealer). The terms of this agreement can be summarized as follows:

- Origination date: October 23, 2007
- Maturity date: October 23, 2010
- Notional principal: $30 million
- Fixed-rate payer: Counterparty A (i.e., the investor)
- Swap fixed rate: 4.546% (semi-annual, 30/360 bond basis)
- Fixed-rate receiver: Counterparty B (i.e., the swap dealer)
- Floating rate: Six-month LIBOR (money market basis)
- Settlement dates: October 23 and April 23
- LIBOR determination: Set in advance, paid in arrears.

This "fixed-for-floating" transaction—the most basic form of a swap—is often called a *plain vanilla* agreement. Exhibit 14.20 illustrates the approximate effect (ignoring slight day count differentials) of combining the swap with the underlying bond position, while Exhibit 14.21 lists the precise settlement cash flows from the investor's perspective for a hypothetical time series of six-month LIBOR. In this agreement, the fixed-rate payer makes the net settlement payment when the day count-adjusted level of LIBOR is less than 4.546%; the fixed-rate receiver makes the settlement payment when LIBOR exceeds 4.546%.

Plain vanilla swaps are generally used for the same reason as FRAs—namely, to restructure the cash flows of an interest-sensitive asset or liability. In this example, the investor has reduced the price sensitivity (i.e., duration) of his asset by converting the fixed-rate coupon into one that adjusts to shifting market conditions without having to actually sell what might be a highly

---

9 Some of the discussion in this section is based on work by Brown and Smith (1995).

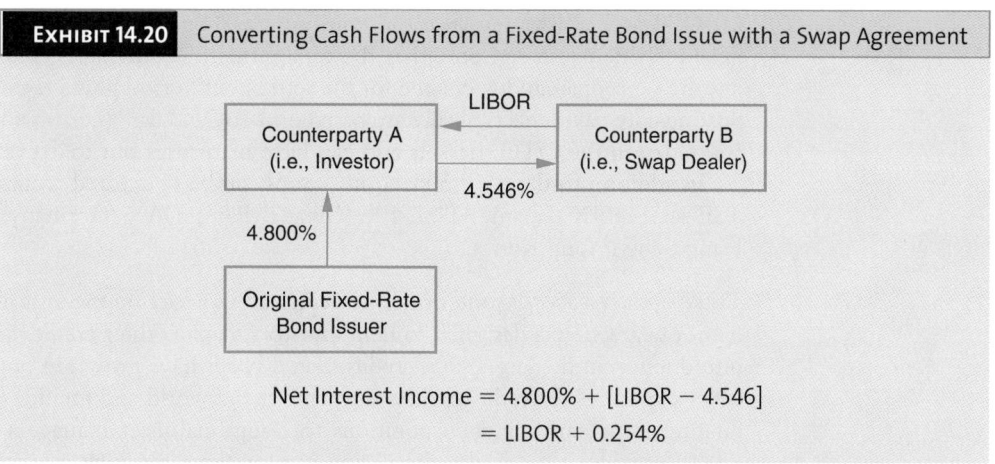

EXHIBIT 14.20 Converting Cash Flows from a Fixed-Rate Bond Issue with a Swap Agreement

Net Interest Income = 4.800% + [LIBOR − 4.546]
= LIBOR + 0.254%

EXHIBIT 14.21 Settlement Cash Flows for a Three-Year Plain Vanilla Interest Rate Swap (Fixed-Payer's Perspective)

Settlement Date	Number of Actual Days	Number of 30/360 Days	Current LIBOR	Fixed-Rate Payment	Floating-Rate Receipt	Net Payment (Receipt)
10/23/2007	—	—	4.25%	—	—	—
4/23/2008	183	180	4.40%	681,900	648,125	33,775
10/23/2008	183	180	4.90%	681,900	671,000	10,900
4/23/2009	182	180	5.05%	681,900	743,167	(61,267)
10/23/2009	183	180	4.60%	681,900	770,125	(88,225)
4/23/2010	182	180	4.35%	681,900	697,667	(15,767)
10/23/2010	183	180	4.20%	681,900	663,375	18,525

illiquid bond. Given A's original coupon rate of 4.8%, the net annualized cash flow he will receive after accounting for the swap position will be (again ignoring day count differentials):

Fixed-Rate Bond Coupon Receipt = 4.800%
Swap: (1) LIBOR Receipt = LIBOR
         (2) Fixed Payment = (4.546%)
Net Interest Income: = LIBOR + 0.254%

Thus, the net impact of combining the swap with the fixed-rate bond is to convert that security into a variable-rate asset paying a coupon of LIBOR plus 25.4 basis points.

14.8.2 EXTENSIONS OF SWAPS

Although interest rate swaps are by far the most prevalent OTC rate contracts, other extensions of this concept that are important for portfolio managers have been developed as well. All these variations preserve the essential feature of a swap contract by exchanging cash flows based on two different rates or prices.

Equity Index–Linked Swaps Similar in form to interest rate swaps, equity index–linked swaps or **equity swaps** are equivalent to portfolios of forward contracts calling for the exchange of cash flows based on two different investment rates: (1) a variable-debt rate (e.g., three-month

LIBOR) and (2) the return to an equity index (e.g., Standard and Poor's 500). The index-linked payment is based on either the total return (i.e., dividends plus capital gain or loss) or just the percentage index change for the settlement period plus a fixed spread adjustment. The floating-rate payments typically are based on LIBOR "flat" (i.e., no adjustment). Equity swaps are traded in the OTC markets and can have maturities out to 10 years or beyond.

In addition to the S&P 500, equity swaps can be structured around other indexes, such as TSE 35, TOPIX (Japan), FT-SE 100 (Great Britain), DAX (Germany), CAC 40 (France), and Hang Seng (Hong Kong).

Credit-Related Swaps One of the newest swap contracting extensions has been the development of agreements designed to help investors manage their credit risk exposures. From their introduction in the late 1990s, credit-related swaps have grown in popularity. These contracts cover exposures to credit markets throughout the world and include as end-users institutions ranging from banks and corporations to traditional asset managers and hedge funds. Hull (2009) provides a detailed examination of how these products are structured and valued.

One of the first attempts to provide credit risk protection in the derivatives market was the **total return swap**. As with equity swaps, total return swaps provide for the periodic exchange of cash flows based on (1) a variable-debt rate (e.g., LIBOR) and (2) the total return (i.e., periodic interest and any capital gain or loss) to a *reference entity* specified by the agreement. The reference entity can be either a specific bond obligation or a portfolio (index) of bonds. When an individual security is designated as the reference entity, it is possible to design the total return swap to allow for physical delivery of the bond at maturity in exchange for a payment of the bond's initial value. However, neither party in the swap transaction is required to own the reference entity, nor does the maturity or notional principal in the agreement need to match those of the underlying security.

Credit Default Swap and Collateralized Debt Obligation One drawback of using total return swaps to manage credit risk is that they require cash flow exchanges for events—such as general interest rate movements—that have nothing to do with the default potential of the reference entity. A **credit default swap (CDS)** addresses this shortcoming by making the payment of any compensation for loss *contingent on the actual occurrence of a credit-related event*. This contingent payment makes the credit default contract closer in form to an insurance policy than a traditional swap agreement. The *protection buyer* pays an annual premium in exchange for the *protection seller's* obligation to make a settlement payment if a credit-related event occurs to the reference entity during the life of the swap. The range of credit-related events covered by a CDS agreement can be wide, but typically includes bankruptcy, failure to pay in a timely fashion, and a default-rating downgrade resulting from a corporate restructuring. Now the explosive growth of this unregulated derivative has been widely blamed as one of the reasons of the 2008 global financial crisis. The Bank of International Settlement estimated that by December 2007, total notional value of outstanding CDS reached a record of $57.9 trillion. One would not fully appreciate the grandeur of this astronomical figure until it is pointed out it was greater than the world GDP in 2007: $54.3 trillion.[10] Thus it is not surprising that troubles of CDS would easily be of a global size. Due to the global financial crisis, the notional value of CDS contracted to $41.9 trillion in December 2008, though.

But how were CDS connected to the financial crisis? The answer is **collateralized debt obligations (CDOs)**. CDS sold by financial institutions such as AIG had been used as a tool

---

10   Nicholas Varchaver and Katie Benner, "The $55 Trillion Question," *Fortune*, September 30, 2008.

to manage the risk of CDOs. So it is time now to revisit CDOs. As discussed in Chapter 11, CDOs are considered part of the asset-backed security (ABS) market because they are backed by cash-flow generating assets similar to mortgages, car loans, or credit card accounts. They deserve special attention for four reasons: (1) their rapid growth since 2000, (2) the substantial diversity of assets that are used to back the securities, (3) the diversity of credit quality within a CDO issue in terms of credit rating, and (4) the significant problems generated by these securities caused by credit problems for the tranches with low credit ratings, and liquidity problems for the tranches with high credit ratings.

As noted, in contrast to most ABSs that are backed by one specific type of asset (mortgages, car loans, etc.), the CDO is generally backed by a diversified pool of several assets including investment-grade or high-yield bonds, domestic bank loans, emerging market bonds, residential and commercial mortgages, and even other CDOs. The reason for creating many CDOs is to allow an institution to reduce its capital requirements by removing some high-risk loans from its balance sheet. Beyond a diverse set of assets, the CDO is typically structured into tranches similar to the collaterialized mortgage obligations, but in this case the tranches differ by credit quality—that is, the issuers use credit enhancement techniques to create tranches that are rated from AAA to BBB or lower. Similar to other ABSs, the issuer, in consultation with the rating agencies, determines what credit enhancements are required to attain a given rating for a tranche. Therefore, investors can benefit from higher returns but can also select their desired credit risk based on the ratings assigned.

The U.S. Treasury has been working on the regulatory reform of derivatives such as credit default swaps. See http://www.ustreas.gov.

The problems in these securities began in 2006 when during the real estate "boom," mortgage loans were made to numerous individuals with very low credit scores resulting in subprime mortgage loans that were subsequently put into CDOs. In 2007 and 2008, there were a high proportion of defaults on these sub-prime loans that reduced the value of these tranches. Even the highly rated tranches that were protected by the credit-enhancement techniques could not be traded—they were very illiquid because of a general flight to Treasury securities and away from complicated securities with credit ratings that were being questioned. As a result, there were significant price declines because of either credit or liquidity problems. At the outbreak of the crisis, how CDOs and CDSs had caused the decline and fall of financial institutions such as AIG was widely reported.[11]

14.9 Option-Like Securities

A popular investment strategy in recent years has involved the creation of security "packages" in which derivatives are combined with, or embedded into, more basic instruments, such as stocks or bonds. In this section, we take a detailed look at three important variations on this theme: (1) warrants, (2) convertible bonds, and (3) callable bonds.

14.9.1 WARRANTS

A **warrant** is an equity call option issued directly by the company whose stock serves as the underlying asset. The key feature that distinguishes it from an ordinary call option is that, if exercised, the company will create new shares of stock to give to the warrant holder. Thus, the exercise of a warrant will increase the total number of outstanding shares, which reduces the value of each individual share. Because of this dilutive effect, the warrant is not as valuable as an otherwise comparable option contract. Indeed, the valuation of warrants is complicated by many factors, such as how and when the number of outstanding warrants will be

---

11 See, for example, Bill Saporiot, "How AIG Became Too Big to Fail," *Time* magazine, March 19, 2009.

exercised, what the company's current capital structure looks like, and what the company plans to do with the new funds if and when the warrant is exercised.

Galai and Schneller (1978) proposed a simple warrant valuation model in which a firm is presently financed with all equity and the warrants it issues are European-style. On its expiration date T, the warrant will be worth

$$W_T = \max \left[\frac{V_T + N_w X}{N + N_w} - X, 0 \right]$$

where:

N = the current number of outstanding shares
N_W = the number of new shares created if the warrants are exercised
V_T = the value of the firm before the warrants are exercised
X = the exercise price.

They show that this terminal value can be rewritten as

14.10
$$W_T = \left[\frac{1}{1 + (N_w/N)} C_T \right]$$

where:

C_T = the expiration date value of a regular call option with otherwise identical terms as the warrant

Consequently, at any point prior to expiration, the value of the warrant should be equal to the value of the call deflated (i.e., diluted) by the factor $[1 + (N_w/N)]^{-1}$.

Although warrants can be issued as stand-alone instruments, more frequently a company will attach them to a bond issue to lower its initial funding cost. Warrants created in this manner usually can be detached from the debt instrument by the buyer and traded separately. Suppose a firm with 1,000,000 common stock outstanding at a current share price of $100 attempts to raise an additional $10 million by issuing a 10-year, annual coupon bond. Assume further that the yield it would have to pay for a straight debt issue is 8.50%. The firm could lower this borrowing cost by attaching European-style equity warrants to the bond. If the warrants mature in exactly one year and have an exercise price of $115 per share, and the firm eventually hopes to raise an additional $5.75 million with these warrants, it will have to create new derivative contracts to cover 50,000 shares ($5.75 million ÷ $115).

Assuming that the one-year risk-free rate is 7% and the volatility of the firm's stock is 25%, the Black-Scholes value for a one-year call option to buy one share at $X = \$115$ can be calculated as $7.09, meaning the warrants are worth $6.75 (= 7.09 ÷ [1 + (50,000/1,000,000)]) per share. If each warrant allows for the purchase of one share and the face value of a single bond is $1,000, the firm will issue 10,000 bonds with five warrants attached to each. With an 8.50% coupon, the total proceeds generated from the sale of each bond with the warrants attached would be $1,033.75, or $1,000 for the bond and

$33.75 (= 5 \times \$6.75)$ for the warrants. Thus, the firm can reduce its funding cost to 8.00%—the solution to the yield to maturity in the following bond calculation:

$$1033.75 = \sum_{t=1}^{10} \frac{85}{(1+i)^t} + \frac{1000}{(1+i)^{10}}$$

Packaging warrants with bonds to reduce debt expenses for the issuer and enhance return potential for the investor can be done in a variety of ways. A recent trend in financial markets is for a firm to attach to its bonds an option that is based on an underlying asset other than the company's own stock such as foreign exchange and stock index transactions. For instance, Rogalski and Seward (1991) detail the development of the market for *foreign currency exchange warrants,* which give the holder the right, but not the obligation, to purchase a fixed number of U.S. dollars for a price denominated in a foreign currency. Although called warrants, these contracts are closer in form to traditional call options on the USD (or, equivalently, put options on the foreign currency) because they do not result in any direct change to the issuing firm's capital structure. That is, no dilutive valuation effect exists for these derivatives because there are no new stock issued. Beyond that, these instruments generally can be settled only in cash but can be detached and traded separately from the original bond.[12]

14.9.2   CONVERTIBLE BONDS

A convertible security gives its owner the right, but not the obligation, to convert the existing investment into another form. Typically, the original security is either a bond or a preferred stock, which can be exchanged into common stock according to a predetermined formula. A convertible security is a hybrid issue consisting of a regular bond or preferred stock holding and a call option that allows for the conversion. Similar to warrants, they have been popular with issuers because they generally lead to a lower initial borrowing cost and represent a future supply of equity capital. In fact, McGuire (1991) and Schmidt (2003) have noted that these securities often are used in connection with mergers and venture capital deals, because they help align managerial incentives and generate capital without immediately diluting the equity base of the acquiring firm. On the other hand, investors in convertibles gain the upside potential of common stock while actually holding a less-risky asset.

A convertible bond can be viewed as a pre-packaged portfolio containing two distinct securities: a regular bond and an option to exchange the bond for a pre-specified number of the issuing firm's common stock. Thus, a convertible bond represents a hybrid investment involving elements of both the debt and equity markets.

From the investor's standpoint, there are both advantages and disadvantages to this packaging. Although the buyer receives equity-like returns with a "guaranteed" terminal payoff equal to the bond's face value, she must also pay the option premium, which is embedded in the price of the security. Lummer and Riepe (1993) argue that the risk-return dynamics that convertible bonds offer are sufficiently unique as to merit their own asset class. On the other side, the issuer of a convertible bond increases the company's leverage while providing a potential source of equity financing in the future. **Conversion ratio** is the number of shares of common stock for which a convertible security may be exchanged, and **conversion parity price** is the price at which common stock can be obtained by surrendering the convertible instrument at par value.

---

12 For additional information about how warrants are used in capital markets, see Francis, Toy, and Whittaker (2000) and Howe and Su (2001).

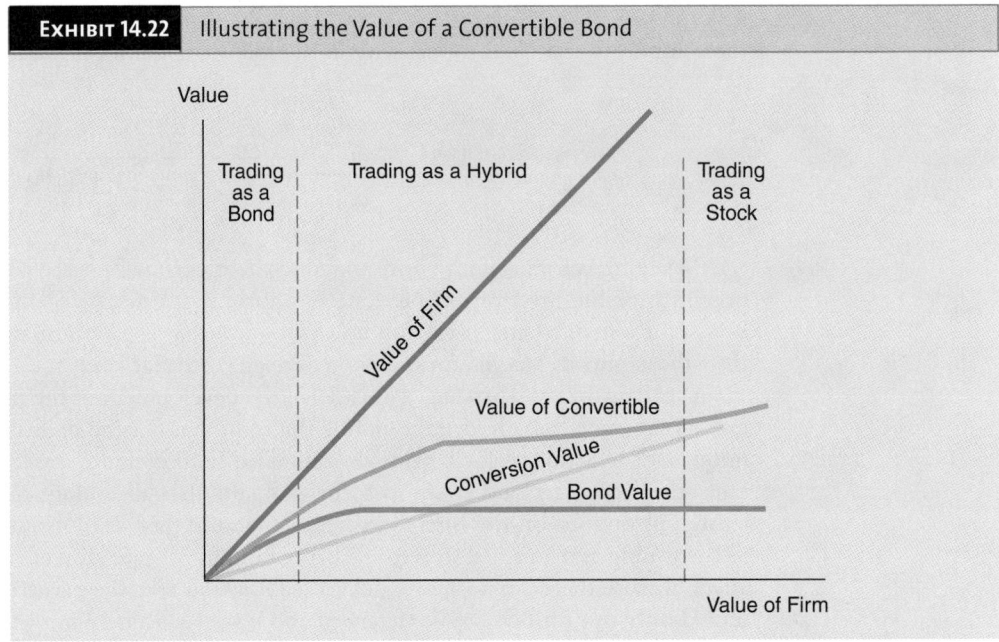

EXHIBIT 14.22 Illustrating the Value of a Convertible Bond

Exhibit 14.22 illustrates the value of a convertible bond in a more general way. Because it cannot sell for more than the company's assets, the value of the firm is an upper bound for the value of a convertible. The "straight" bond value component is relatively flat for a wide range of firm values because, at some point, higher firm values do not benefit bondholders who receive only their promised payments. However, at fairly low firm values, the value of the bond drops off as bankruptcy becomes more likely. Conversion value rises directly with the value of the firm. The value of the convertible shows that when firm value is low, the convertible will act more like a bond, trading for only a slight premium over the bond value. Alternatively, when firm values are high, the convertible will act more like a stock, selling for only a slight premium over the conversion value. In the middle range, the convertible will trade as a hybrid security that acts somewhat like a bond and somewhat like a stock.

14.9.3 CALLABLE BONDS

The discussion and presentation thus far regarding Macaulay and modified durations and convexity in Chapter 12 have been concerned with option-free bonds. A callable bond is different because it provides the issuer with an option to call the bond under certain conditions and pay it off with funds from a new issue sold at a lower yield. Observers refer to this as a bond with an *embedded option*. As discussed in Chapter 12, the duration of a bond can be seriously affected by an embedded call option if interest rates decline substantially below a bond's coupon rate. In such a case, the issuer will likely call the bond, which will dramatically change the maturity and the duration of the bond. For example, assume a firm issues a 30-year bond with a 9% coupon with a deferred call provision whereby the bond can be called in six years at 109% of par. If the bond is issued at par, its original *duration to maturity* will be about 11 years. A year later, if rates decline to about 7%, its duration to maturity will still be over *10 years* because duration is inversely related to yield and yields have declined. Notably, at a yield of 7%, this bond will probably trade at *yield to call* because at a 7% yield the firm will likely exercise its option and call the bond in five years. Notably, the bond's *duration to first call* would be about *four years.* Clearly, there is a significant difference between duration to maturity (over 10 years) and duration to first call (about 4 years).

To understand the impact of the call feature on the duration and convexity of a bond, it is important to consider what determines the price of a callable bond. A callable bond is a combination of a non-callable bond plus a *call option* that was *sold to the issuer,* which allows the issuer to call the bond under the conditions discussed earlier. Because the call option is owned by the issuer, it has negative value for the investor in the bond. Thus the bondholder's position is

> **14.11** **Long a callable bond = Long a non-callable bond**
> **+ A short position in a call option**

Therefore, the value (price) of a callable bond is equal to

> **14.12** **Callable bond price = Non-callable bond price − call option price**

Given this valuation, anything that increases the value of the call option will reduce the value of the callable bond.[13] The point is, when interest rates decline, the right-hand side of this equation experiences a conflict between the value of the non-callable bond that increases in value, and the value of the call option that also increases, but this has a negative effect on the bond price. Notably, if the value of the call option increases faster than the value of the non-callable bond, the overall value of the callable bond will *decline* when interest rates decline and this is referred to as *negative duration*—that is, in contrast to the usual inverse relationship between yield changes and bond price changes, in this case yield changes and price changes both decline.

Summary

1. Forward and futures contracts have become an important feature of the modern investment landscape. They are the most fundamental type of derivative instruments available. Forwards and futures differ primarily in the areas of design flexibility and collateralization. Forward agreements generally are more flexible but carry more credit risk, while the process of marking margin accounts to market on a daily basis makes futures contracts more secure (to the exchange, at least) even as the standardization of contract terms makes them less adaptable to the end user.

2. Hedging is key to understanding forward-based contracting and that the basis is the most important concept in understanding hedging. In particular, the basis, which is defined as the difference between spot and forward prices at any point in time, contains the essence of a short hedge position so that the hedger effectively trades the price risk of the underlying asset for the basis risk inherent in the spot-forward combination.

3. The cost of carry model suggests that in order to avoid arbitrage, the forward price should be equal to the spot price plus the cost of transporting the underlying asset to the future delivery date. These carrying costs can include commissions for physical storage, an opportunity cost for the net amount of invested capital, and a premium for the convenience of consuming the asset now.

4. Interest rate futures and stock index futures are financial futures. Interest rate futures hedges against interest rate

---

13 For a further discussion of the effect of these embedded options, see Fabozzi, Buetow, and Johnson (2005) and Fabozzi, Kalotay, and Williams (2005). Also see Winkelmann (1989).

risks. Stock index futures are intended to provide general hedges against stock market movements and can be applied to either diversified portfolios, sectorial portoflios, or individual stocks.

5. We discuss the binomial, the expanded binomial, and the Black-Scholes models, and they are all based on the same three-step evolution. The first step is combining options with the underlying asset in order to create a riskless position. This usually requires the sale (purchase) of multiple calls (puts) to offset to the full cash exposure of a single share of stock held long. This hedge ratio changes with movements in the underlying asset's price and the passage of time; therefore, the riskless hedge portfolio needs to be rebalanced frequently. Once it is formed, however, the option's value can be established by assuming that the hedge portfolio should earn the risk-free rate (i.e., the no-arbitrage condition) and solving for the option value that makes this assumption true.

6. The Black-Scholes model is extremely flexible. Although originally created for European-style call options on non-dividend-bearing stock, this model extends easily to valuing put options and options on dividend-paying stocks. We also discuss how volatility, the only user-provided variable in the valuation model, is either estimated directly from a historical series of asset prices or implied from option prices themselves.

7. We discuss swaps with an examination of the market for OTC interest rate agreements. Although forward rate agreements are the most basic product in this category, interest rate swaps are the most popular. We also explained equity index-linked swaps and credit-related swaps.

8. Lastly we analyze several ways in which derivatives can be embedded into other securities to create customized payoff distributions. Warrants are call options on common stock issued directly by the company itself. Convertible bonds can be set up to allow for conversion into common stock at the investor's option. Callable bonds provides the issuer with an option to call the bond.

Key Terms

backwardated, p. 413
basis, p.411
basis risk, p. 411
binomial option pricing model, p. 428
Black-Scholes valuation model, p. 431
collateralized debt obligations (CDOs), p. 440
contango, p. 413
convenience yield, p. 413
conversion parity price, p. 443

correlation p. 411
conversion ratio, p. 443
cost of carry, p. 413
credit default swap (CDS), p. 440
delta, p. 432
equity swap, p. 439
exchange clearinghouse, p. 407
forward rate agreement (FRA), p. 438
implied volatility, p. 434
interest rate swap, p. 438

long hedge, p. 410
notional principal, p. 438
Options Clearing Corporation (OCC), p. 419
short hedge, p. 410
spread, p. 414
stock index arbitrage, p. 415
total return swap, p. 440
Volatility Index (VIX), p. 435
warrant, p. 441

Suggested Readings

Futures

Gagnon, Louis, and Greg Lypny. "Hedging Short-Term Interest Risk under Time-Varying Distributions: Introduction." *The Journal of Futures Markets* 15, no. 7 (1995): 767.

McDonald, Robert L. *Derivatives Markets*. Boston, MA: Pearson Education, 2003.

Park, Tae H, and Lorne N. Switzer. "Bivariate Garch Estimation of the Optimal Hedge Ratios for Stock Index Futures: A Note." *The Journal of Futures Markets* 15, no. 1 (1995): 61.

Park, Tae H, and Lorne N. Switzer. "Index Participation Units and the Performance of Index Futures Markets: Evidence from the Toronto 35 Index Participation Units Market." *The Journal of Futures Markets* 15, no. 2 (1995): 187.

Siegel, Daniel, and Diane F. Siegel. *Futures Markets*. Hinsdale, IL: Dryden Press, 1990.

Smithson, Charles W., and Clifford W. Smith, Jr. *Managing Financial Risk*, 3rd ed. New York: McGraw-Hill, 1998.

Stulz, Reve M. *Risk Management and Derivatives*. Mason, OH: South-Western Publishing, 2003.

Telser, Lester G. "Futures Trading and the Storage of Cotton and Wheat." *Journal of Political Economy* 66 (June 1958).

Working, Holbrook. "Economic Functions of Futures Markets." In *Selected Writings of Holbrook Working*. Chicago: Chicago Board of Trade, 1977.

Options

Briys, Eric, Huu Minh Mai, Mondher Bellalah, and François De Varenne. *Options, Futures, and Exotic Derivatives*. New York: Wiley, 1998.

Chance, Don M. *Analysis of Derivatives for the CFA Program.* Charlottesville, VA: AIMR, 2003.

Cox, John C., and Mark Rubinstein. *Option Markets.* Englewood Cliffs, NJ: Prentice Hall, 1985.

Doidge, Craig, and Jason Z. Wei. "Volatility Forecasting and the Efficiency of the Toronto 35 Index Options Market." *Revue Canadienne des Sciences de l'administration* 15, no. 1 (1998): 28–38.

Dubofsky, David A., and Thomas W. Miller. *Derivatives: Valuation and Risk Management.* New York: Oxford University Press, 2003.

Gagnon, Louis. "Exchange Traded Financial Derivatives in Canada: Finally off the Launching Pad," *Canadian Investment Review,* Fall 1990.

Gagnon, Louis, and Greg Lypny. "The Benefits of Dynamically Hedging the Toronto 35 Stock Index." *Revue Canadienne des Sciences de l'Administration* 14, no. 1 (1997): 69–78.

Jarrow, Robert, and Stuart Turnbull. *Derivative Securities,* 2nd ed. Cincinnati, OH: Thomson Learning, 2000.

Khoury, Nabil, and Klaus P. Fischer. "The Effect of Multiple Listings on the Bid-Ask Spread in Option Markets: The Case of Montreal Exchange." *The Journal of Futures Markets* 22, no. 10 (2002): 939–957.

Swaps

Buetow, Gerald W., Jr., and Frank J. Fabozzi. *Valuation of Interest Rate Swaps and Swaptions.* New York: John Wiley, 2000.

Chance, Don M., and Pamela P. Peterson. *Real Options and Investment Valuation.* Charlottesville, VA: Research Foundation of AIMR, 2002.

Eckl, S., J. N. Robinson, and D. C. Thomas. *Financial Engineering: A Handbook of Derivative Products.* Cambridge, MA: Basil Blackwell, 1991.

Finnerty, John D. "An Overview of Corporate Securities Innovation." *Journal of Applied Corporate Finance* 4, no. 4 (Winter 1992).

Kat, Harry M. Structured Equity Derivatives; The Definitive Guide to Exotic Options and Structured Notes. London: Wiley, 2001.

CFA For Chapter CFA Questions and Problems, please see Appendix A at the end of this text.

Questions

1. We have futures contracts on Treasury bonds, but we do not have futures contracts on individual corporate bonds. We have cattle and hog futures but no chicken futures. Explain why the market has developed in this manner. What do you think are the most important characteristics for the success of a new futures contract concept?

2. "Hedgers trade price risk for basis risk." What is meant by this statement? In particular, explain the concept of the basis in a hedge transaction and how forward and futures contracts can be selected to minimize risk.

3. Suppose you are a derivatives trader specializing in creating customized commodity forward contracts for clients and then hedging your position with exchange-traded futures contracts. Your latest position is an agreement to deliver 100,000 U.S. gallons (approximately 378,541 litres) of unleaded gasoline to a client in three months.

    a. Explain how you can hedge your position using gasoline futures contracts.

    b. In calculating your hedge ratio, how must you account for the different valuation procedures used for forward and futures contracts? That is, what difference does it make that forward contracts are valued on a discounted basis while futures contracts are marked to market without discounting?

    c. If the only available gasoline futures contracts call for the delivery of 42,000 U.S. gallons (approximately 159,000 litres) and mature in either two or four months, describe the nature of the basis risk involved in your hedge.

4. A multinational corporation is about to embark on a major financial restructuring program. One critical stage will be the issuance of seven-year Eurobonds sometime within the next month. The CFO is concerned with recent instability in capital markets and with the particular event that market yields rise prior to issuance, forcing the corporation to pay a higher coupon rate on the bonds. It is decided to hedge that risk by selling 10-year Treasury note futures contracts. Notice that this is a classic cross hedge wherein 10-year Treasury notes are used to manage the risk of 7-year Eurobonds.

    Describe the nature of the basis risk in the hedge. In particular what specific events with respect to the shape of the Treasury yield curve and the Eurobond spread over Treasuries could render the hedge ineffective? In other words, under what circumstances would the hedge fail and make the corporation worse off?

5. You own an equally weighted portfolio of 50 different stocks worth about $5,000,000. The stocks are from several different industries, and the portfolio is reasonably well diversified. Which do you think would provide you with the best overall hedge: a single position

in an index future or 50 different positions in futures contracts on the individual stocks? What are the most important factors to consider in making this decision?

6. It is often stated that a stock index arbitrage trade is easier to implement when the stock index futures contract price is above its theoretical level than when it is below that value. What institutional realities might make this statement true? Describe the steps involved in forming the arbitrage transaction in both circumstances. To the extent that the statement is valid, what does it suggest about the ability of the stock index futures market to remain efficient?

7. "Although options are risky investments, they are valued by virtue of their ability to convert the underlying asset into a synthetic risk-free security." Explain what this statement means, being sure to describe the basic three-step process for valuing option contracts.

8. Explain why a change in the time to expiration (i.e., T) can have either a positive or negative impact on the value of a European-style put option. In this explanation, it will be useful to contrast the put's reaction with that of a European-style call, for which an increase in T has an unambiguously positive effect.

9. On October 19, 1987, the stock market (as measured by the Dow Jones Industrial Average) lost almost one-quarter of its value in a single day. Nevertheless, some

traders made a profit buying call options on the stock index and then liquidating their positions before the market closed. Explain how this is possible, assuming that it was not a case of the traders taking advantage of spurious upward ticks in stock prices.

10. "When the yield curve is upward-sloping, the fixed rate on a multiyear swap must be higher than the current level of LIBOR. With a downward-sloping yield curve, the opposite will occur." Explain what is meant by this statement and why it must be true.

11. Total return swaps and credit default swaps were both developed as tools to help investors manage for credit risk. In practice, however, credit default swaps are used far more widely. Compare the relevant features of both derivative agreements and explain the reason for this difference in popularity.

12. We have seen that equity warrants are not as valuable as an otherwise identical call option on the stock of the same company. Explain why this must be the case. Also, what is the incentive for a firm to issue a warrant rather than issuing stock directly?

13. Bonds and preferred stock that are convertible into common stock are said to provide investors with both upside potential and downside protection. Explain how one security can possess both attributes. What implications do these features have for the way a convertible security is priced?

Problems

1. It is March 9, and you have just entered into a short position in a soybean meal futures contract. The contract expires on July 9 and calls for the delivery of 100 tonnes of soybean meal. Further, because this is a futures position, it requires the posting of a $3,000 initial margin and a $1,500 maintenance margin; for simplicity, however, assume that the account is marked to market on a monthly basis. Assume the following represent the contract delivery prices (in dollars per tonne) that prevail on each settlement date:

March 9 (initiation)	$173.00
April 9	179.75
May 9	189.00
June 9	182.50
July 9 (delivery)	174.25

a. Calculate the equity value of your margin account on each settlement date, including any additional equity required to meet a margin call. Also compute the amount of cash that will be returned to you on July 9,

and the gain or loss on your position, expressed as a percentage of your initial margin commitment.

b. Assuming that the underlying soybean meal investment pays no dividend and requires a storage cost of 1.5% (of current value), calculate the current (i.e., March 9) spot price for a tonne of soybean meal and the implied May 9 price for the same tonne. In your calculations, assume that an annual risk-free rate of 8% prevails over the entire contract life.

c. Now suppose that on March 9 you also entered into a long forward contract for the purchase of 100 tonnes of soybean meal on July 9. Assume further that the July forward and futures contract prices always are identical to one another at any point in time. Calculate the cash amount of your gain or loss if you unwind both positions in their respective markets on May 9 and June 9, taking into account the prevailing settlement conditions in the two markets.

2. You are a coffee dealer anticipating the purchase of 82,000 pounds of coffee in three months. You are concerned that the price of coffee will rise, so you take a long position in coffee futures. Each contract covers

37,500 pounds, and so, rounding to the nearest contract, you decide to go long in two contracts. The futures price at the time you initiate your hedge is 55.95 cents per pound. Three months later, the actual spot price of coffee turns out to be 58.56 cents per pound and the futures price is 59.20 cents per pound.

a. Determine the effective price at which you purchased your coffee. How do you account for the difference in amounts for the spot and hedge positions?

b. Describe the nature of the basis risk in this long hedge.

3. A bond speculator currently has positions in two separate corporate bond portfolios: a long holding in Portfolio 1 and a short holding in Portfolio 2. All the bonds have the same credit quality. Other relevant information on these positions includes:

Portfolio	Bond	Market Value (Mil.)	Coupon Rate	Compounding Frequency	Maturity	Yield to Maturity
1	A	$6.0	0%	Annual	3 yrs	7.31%
	B	$4.0	0%	Annual	14 yrs	7.31%
2	C	$11.5	4.6%	Annual	9 yrs	7.31%

Treasury bond futures (based on $100,000 face value of 20-year T-bonds having an 8% semi-annual coupon) with a maturity exactly six months from now are currently priced at 109–24 with a corresponding yield to maturity of 7.081%. The "yield betas" between the futures contract and Bonds A, B, and C are 1.13, 1.03, and 1.01, respectively. Finally, the modified duration for the T-bond underlying the futures contract is 10.355 years.

a. Calculate the modified duration (expressed in years) for each of the two bond portfolios. What will be the *approximate* percentage change in the value of each if all yields increase by 60 basis points on an annual basis?

b. Without performing the calculations, explain which of the portfolios will *actually* have its value impacted to the greatest extent (in absolute terms) by the shift in yields. (Hint: This explanation requires knowledge of the concept of *bond convexity*.)

c. Assuming the bond speculator wants to hedge her *net* bond position, what is the optimal number of futures contracts that must be bought or sold? Start by calculating the optimal hedge ratio between the futures contract and the two bond portfolios separately and then combine them.

4. An investment bank engages in stock index arbitrage for its own and customer accounts. On a particular day, the S&P index at the New York Stock Exchange is 602.25 when the futures contract for delivery in 90 days is 614.75. If the annualized 90-day interest rate is 8.00% and the (annualized) dividend yield is 3%, would program trading involving stock index arbitrage possibly take place? If so, describe the transactions that should be undertaken and calculate the profit that would be made per each "share" of the S&P 500 index used in the trade.

5. Assuming that a one-year call option with an exercise price of $38 is available for the stock of the DEW Corp., consider the following price tree for DEW stock over the next year:

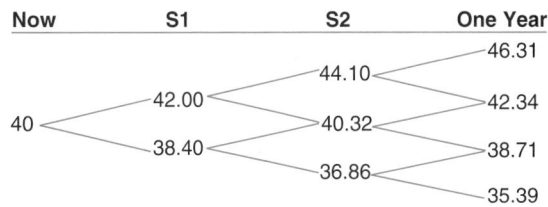

Now	S1	S2	One Year
40	42.00	44.10	46.31
	38.40	40.32	42.34
		36.86	38.71
			35.39

a. If the sequence of stock prices that DEW stock follows over the year is $40.00, $42.00, $40.32, and $38.71, describe the composition of the initial riskless portfolio of stock and options you would form and all the subsequent adjustments you would have to make to keep this portfolio riskless. Assume the one-year risk-free rate is 6%.

b. Given the initial DEW price of $40, what are the probabilities of observing each of the four terminal stock prices in one year? (Hint: In arriving at your answer, it will be useful to consider (1) the number of different ways that a particular terminal price could be achieved and (2) the probability of an up or down movement.)

c. Use the binomial option model to calculate the present value of this call option.

d. Calculate the value of a one-year put option on DEW stock having an exercise price of $38; be sure your answer is consistent with the correct response to Part c.

6. Following is a two-period price tree for a share of stock in SAB Corp.:

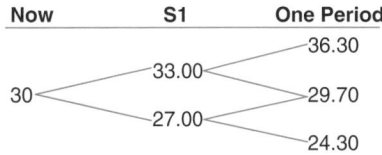

Now	S1	One Period
30	33.00	36.30
	27.00	29.70
		24.30

Using the binomial model, calculate the current fair value of a regular call option on SAB stock with the following characteristics: $X = 28$, $RFR = 5\%$ (per period). You should also indicate the composition of the implied riskless hedge portfolio at the valuation date.

7. Consider the following questions on the pricing of options on the stock of ARB Inc.:

a. A share of ARB stock sells for $75 and has a standard deviation of returns equal to 20% per year. The current risk-free rate is 9% and the stock pays two dividends: (1) a $2 dividend just prior to the option's expiration day, which is 91 days from now (i.e., exactly one-quarter of a year); and (2) a $2 dividend 182 days from now (i.e., exactly one-half year). Calculate the Black-Scholes value for a European-style call option with an exercise price of $70.

b. What would be the price of a 91-day European-style put option on ARB stock having the same exercise price?

c. Calculate the change in the call option's value that would occur if ARB's management suddenly decided to suspend dividend payments and this action had no effect on the price of the company's stock.

d. Briefly describe (without calculations) how your answer in Part a would differ under the following separate circumstances: (1) the volatility of ARB stock increases to 30%, and (2) the risk-free rate decreases to 8%.

8. Consider the following data relevant to valuing a European-style call option on a non-dividend-paying stock: $X = 40$, RFR = 9%, T = six months (i.e., 0.5), and $\sigma = 0.25$.

a. Compute the Black-Scholes option and hedge ratio values for the series of hypothetical current stock price levels shown in Exhibit 14.15.

b. Explain why the values in Part a differ from those shown in Exhibit 14.15.

c. For $S = 40$, calculate the Black-Scholes value for a European-style put option. How much of this value represents time premium?

9. Consider the following price data for TanCo. stock in two different sub-periods:

Sub-period A: 168.375; 162.875; 162.5; 161.625; 160.75; 157.75; 157.25; 157.75; 161.125; 162.5; 157.5; 156.625; 157.875; 155.375; 150.5; 155.75; 154.25; 155.875; 156; 152.75; 150.5; 150.75

Sub-period B: 122.5; 124.5; 121.875; 120.625; 119.5; 118.125; 117.75; 119.25; 122.25; 121.625; 120; 117.75; 118.375; 115.625; 117.75; 117.5; 118.5; 117.625; 114.625; 110.75

a. For each sub-period, calculate the annualized historical measure of stock volatility that could be used in pricing an option for TanCo. In your calculations, you may assume that there are 250 trading days in a year.

b. Suppose now that you decide to gather additional data for each sub-period. Specifically, you obtain information for a call option with a current price of $12.25 and the following characteristics: $X = 115$; $S = 120.625$; time to expiration = 62 days; RFR = 7.42%; and dividend yield = 3.65%. Here the risk-free rate and dividend yields are stated on an annual basis. Use the volatility measure from Sub-period B and the Black-Scholes model to obtain the "fair value" for this call option. Based on your calculations, is the option currently priced as it should be? Explain.

Portfolio Management

In Part 6, we apply these same valuation principles and practices as in Part 5 to the analysis and management of common stocks. The objective is to be in position to make the critical risk-return decision at the market-industry-company stock level. Chapter 15 offers a discussion of how the equity portfolio management decision fits into the investor's overall asset allocation strategy. We first distinguish between passive and active investment strategies and the various approaches under each. Passive strategies are based on the market index and can be done with full replication, sampling, or programming techniques. Active strategies can be classified under fundamental approaches, technical approaches, or others. After discussing the integrated approach to asset allocation, we examine strategic, tactical, and insured allocation strategies.

In Chapter 16, we consider five major categories of bond portfolio management strategies in detail: passive management strategies, active management strategies, core-plus management strategies, matched-funding strategies, and contingent and structured strategies. During the past 20 years, there have been more developments related to the valuation and portfolio management of bonds than of stocks. This growth of the fixed-income sector does not detract from the importance of equities but certainly enhances the significance of fixed-income securities. Finally, readers should keep in mind that this growth in size, sophistication, and specialization of the bond market implies numerous and varied career opportunities in the bond area, including trading these securities, valuation, credit analysis, and domestic and global portfolio management.

Chapters 17 deals with professional asset management, and Chapter 18 is concerned with the evaluation of portfolio performance. The discussions of both of these topics are designed to address the needs of individual and institutional investors alike; both individual and institutional investors periodically need the services of a professional money manager and both types of investors also need to be aware of how one evaluates the performance of a portfolio.

Because many investors employ professional asset managers to manage their assets, Chapter 17 is an important wrap-up to their asset allocation and portfolio construction process. After a broad overview of the different ways that professional asset management firms can be organized, the chapter describes how the asset management industry has changed over time and how professional managers are compensated for their expertise. Particular emphasis is paid to the role of *investment companies* (also more commonly called mutual funds), which manage the majority of assets held by individual investors. The discussion includes a description of the major forms of investment companies and the general types of funds available, such as money market, growth, aggressive growth, income, balanced, and bond funds. It is argued that almost any investment objective can be met by investing in one or several investment companies. The chapter also provides a detailed examination of how *alternative asset* investments—hedge funds and private equity—are structured and managed. These investments are among the fastest-growing segments of the money management industry.

We conclude Chapter 17 with a discussion of ethical and regulatory issues that arise when hiring a professional asset manager. We argue that most of these issues arise from the *classical principal-agent problem* that defines many economic relationships. After first examining the myriad regulations that govern the behaviour of professional portfolio managers, we then describe the set of standards that the industry has adopted voluntarily in an effort to foster an atmosphere of trust and responsibility. The chapter ends with several examples of ethical conflicts that can arise when investors employ professional money managers. Two issues that are of special concern are designing compensation contracts to provide managers with the proper incentives to act in the investor's best interest and the proper use of trading commission fees.

We conclude the part with Chapter 18, which deals with the evaluation of portfolio performance. Perhaps the most important concept to understand from this discussion is that any meaningful evaluation of an investment manager's performance must consider both the return and the riskiness of the portfolio. Thus we review in detail the major *risk-adjusted*

portfolio performance models, i.e., the Sharpe measure, the Jensen measure, and the information ratio. We then discuss evaluation techniques beyond risk-adjusted measures, including attribution analysis, market timing analysis, and style analysis.

In evaluation of portfolio performance, selecting an appropriate benchmark is important. We consider potential problems with the traditional performance measures including a review of Roll's benchmark problem and its effect

on these performance models. It is demonstrated that this benchmark problem has become more significant with the growth of global investing. Also, because the factors that determine success in bonds differ from what is important in equities, we review alternative models used to evaluate the performance of bond portfolio managers. The chapter finishes with a consideration of how investment performance results should be presented so as to be consistent with industry practice.

Equity Portfolio Management Strategies

After you read this chapter, you should be able to answer the following questions:

1. What are the two generic equity portfolio management styles?

2. What is a portfolio's tracking error and how is it useful in the construction of a passive equity investment?

3. What are the strategies for constructing passive and active equity portfolios, respectively?

4. What stock characteristics differentiate value-oriented and growth-oriented investment styles?

5. What is style analysis and what does it indicate about a manager's investment performance?

6. What are the differences between the integrated, strategic, tactical, and insured approaches to asset allocation?

Recent chapters have reviewed how to analyze industries and companies, how to estimate a stock's intrinsic value, and how technical analysis can assist in stock picking. In this chapter, we move on to the management of a portfolio of stocks. There are two generic equity portfolio management styles: active and passive. If an investor believes that the capital markets are fairly efficient and thus trusts in the collective wisdom of the players in the marketplace, she may want to take a passive strategy by following the market through buying or replicating an equity index. If, however, an investor doesn't believe the market is always 100% efficient, and that there is room for him to beat the market, he may choose to take an active strategy by buying and selling stocks according to his best judgment. Bond portfolio management strategies will be explored in the next chapter.

15.1 An Overview

Equity portfolio management strategies can be placed into either a passive or an active category. One way to distinguish between these strategies is to decompose the total actual return that the portfolio manager attempts to produce:

$$
\begin{aligned}
\textbf{Total Actual Return} \\
= [\textbf{Expected Return}] + [\textbf{``Alpha''}] \\
\textbf{15.1} \quad = \underbrace{[\textbf{Risk-Free Rate} + \textbf{Risk Premium}]}_{\textbf{Passive}} + [\textbf{``Alpha''}] \\
\underbrace{\hphantom{= [\textbf{Risk-Free Rate} + \textbf{Risk Premium}] + [\textbf{``Alpha''}]}}_{\textbf{Active}}
\end{aligned}
$$

Passive portfolio managers just try to capture the expected return consistent with the risk level of their portfolios. In contrast, active managers attempt to "beat the market" by forming portfolios capable of producing actual returns that exceed risk-adjusted expected returns. The difference between the actual and expected return is often called the portfolio's alpha and it represents the amount of value that the active manager has added (if positive) or subtracted (if negative) to the investment process.

Passive equity portfolio management typically holds stocks so that the portfolio's returns will track those of a benchmark index over time. Accordingly, this approach is generally referred to as *indexing* and there is no attempt on the manager's part to generate an alpha return component. While indexing is often thought to be a long-term buy-and-hold strategy, occasional portfolio rebalancing is necessary as the composition of the underlying benchmark changes and cash distributions must be reinvested. However, because the purpose of the passive portfolio is to mimic an index, the passive manager is judged by how well he or she tracks the target—that is, minimizes the deviation between stock portfolio and index returns.

Conversely, *active equity portfolio management* is an attempt by the manager to outperform an equity benchmark on a risk-adjusted basis. The active manager can employ any of several specific investment strategies to do this, but broadly speaking there are two main ways to try to add alpha: *tactical adjustments* (e.g., equity style or sector timing) or *security selection* (i.e., stock picking) skills. Notice that so-called hybrid investment strategies that may appear to fall into the middle ground between the passive and active categories (e.g., enhanced indexing) are really just more modest variations of an active approach to equity portfolio management. Further, *hedge funds* are actively managed portfolios that often pursue a "pure alpha" (i.e., absolute return) strategy in which the manager seeks to isolate the alpha component of return; these strategies are discussed in Chapter 17.

When deciding to follow either strategy (or some combination of the two), an investor must assess the trade-off between the low-cost but less-exciting alternative of indexing versus the potentially more lucrative alternative of active investing, which almost certainly will have higher management fees and trading costs. Sharpe (1991) argued that these higher expenses will *always* make active management the inferior alternative. Sorensen, Miller, and Samak (1998) noted that the critical factor in this evaluation is the stock-picking skill of the portfolio manager. Using pension fund performance data, they showed that the optimal allocation to indexing declines as managerial skill increases. However, they also concluded that some indexing is appropriate for most risk objective classes. Alford, Jones, and Winkelmann (2003) support this position by arguing that a disciplined approach to active management—which they term structured portfolio management—is likely to be the most effective method for investors. Finally, Harlow and Brown (2006) showed that the active versus passive management decision for many investors comes down to their ability to identify superior managers in advance.

Exhibit 15.1 reports the amount of money in the U.S. equity and fixed-income markets using active and passive strategies for two recent years. The data are compiled from a survey of almost 1,000 professional managers on behalf of their clients. The main conclusion is that both active and passive funds play a prominent role with investors. Further, while active management strategies control the largest percentage of investor wealth, passively managed investment products are growing in importance at a rapid pace, particularly in the equity market.

Exhibit 15.1	Active and Passive Investment in U.S. Equity and Fixed-Income Markets		
Strategy	**2005 (Billions)**	**2004 (Billions)**	**% Change**
Active Equity	$1,979.5	$1,905.1	3.9
Passive Equity	1,098.5	983.1	11.7
Active Fixed Income	1,780.8	1,628.5	9.4
Passive Fixed Income	225.8	207.4	9.9

Source: *Pensions & Investment Money Manager Directory*, May 29, 2006, and May 30, 2005.

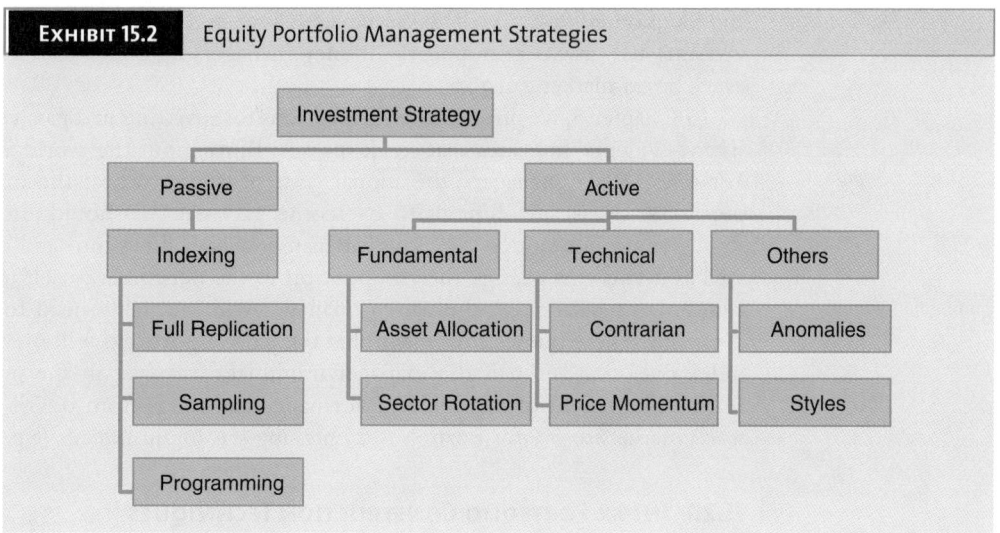

EXHIBIT 15.2 Equity Portfolio Management Strategies

Exhibit 15.2 provides a taxonomy of the strategies. To take a passive strategy, i.e., following a market index, one can fully replicate the index, invest in a sample of the stocks in the index, or invoke programming techniques. Possibilities for the active strategy are more versatile but we can basically classify those under three categories: fundamental, technical, and others such as anomalies and styles. Through economic and industry analysis, one may be able to predict the performance of countries, industry sectors, or asset classes, and take buying or selling actions accordingly. From a technician's point of view, an active strategy is to uncover the momentum of stocks and the market, and depending on whether the trend is predicted to continue or reverse, he can make his trades. Beyond fundamental and technical, there are other strategies. One can take advantage of market anomalies such as January effects or *P/E* effects or adopt a particular investment style focusing on growth stocks or value stocks. Details of each of the above will be examined in the following sections.

15.2 Passive Equity Portfolio Management Strategies

Passive equity portfolio management attempts to design a set of stock holdings that *replicates* the performance of a specific benchmark. As discussed in Chapter 2, the portfolio manager who earns higher returns by violating the client's policy statement should be fired. Similarly, a passive manager who is not really passive should also be dismissed. A passive manager earns a fee by constructing a portfolio that closely tracks the returns to a particular equity index meeting the client's needs and objectives. If the manager tries to outperform the benchmark, he or she clearly violates the passive premise of the portfolio.

Chapter 4 contained a summary of many of the different market indices that a passive manager can attempt to replicate. North American equity indices include S&P/TSX in Canada, and the S&P 500, the Major Market index, the NASDAQ Composite index, and the Wilshire 5000 in the U.S. Benchmarks also exist for various sectors of the stock market, such as those for small capitalization stocks (Russell 2000), for value- or growth-oriented stocks (Russell Growth index and the Russell Value index), for numerous developed world regions (such as the EAFE index), and for collections of smaller countries (emerging markets). Fernholz, Garvy, and Hannon (1998), as well as Khorana, Nelling, and Trester (1998), have noted that as passive investing has grown in popularity, money managers have created an index fund for virtually every broad market category.

In Chapter 5, we presented several reasons for investing in a passive equity portfolio. Consistent evidence indicates that stock markets throughout the world are often fairly efficient. For many active managers, the annual costs of trying to beat the market (1% to 2% of the portfolio's assets) are difficult to overcome. However, it should also be noted that passive strategies are not costless to employ. Because of cash flows into and out of an index fund, as well as events that change the composition of the benchmark itself (e.g., mergers, bankruptcies, index rebalancing), the passive manager will inevitably need to buy and sell securities over time. These transactions mean that the passive portfolio will inevitably underperform its index over time, even if the manager minimizes turnover in the portfolio for every other reason. The extent of this underperformance can range from 0.05% to 0.25% in developed stock markets to 3% for portfolios mimicking less liquid indices (e.g., emerging markets).

15.2.1 INDEX PORTFOLIO CONSTRUCTION TECHNIQUES

There are three basic techniques for constructing a passive index portfolio: full replication, sampling, and quadratic optimization or programming. The **full replication** technique, wherein all the securities in the index are purchased in proportion to their weights in the index, helps ensure close tracking. However, it may be suboptimal as the transaction costs arising from the need to buy many securities and the frequent reinvestment of dividends will detract from performance.

The second technique, **sampling**, addresses the problem of numerous stock issues. Statistical theory teaches us that we don't need to ask everyone in Canada his or her opinion to determine who might win an election. Thus, opinion pollsters query only a small sample of the population to gauge public sentiment. Similarly, with sampling, a portfolio manager would only need to buy a representative sample of stocks that comprise the benchmark index. Stocks with larger index weights are purchased according to their weight in the index; smaller issues are purchased so that their aggregate characteristics (e.g., beta, industry distribution, dividend yield) approximate the underlying benchmark. With fewer stocks to purchase, larger positions can be taken in the issues acquired, which should lead to proportionately lower commissions. Further, the reinvestment of dividend cash flows will be less problematic because fewer securities need to be purchased to rebalance the portfolio. The disadvantage of sampling is that portfolio returns will almost certainly not track the returns for the benchmark index as closely as with full replication.

Rather than obtaining a sample based on industry or security characteristics, **quadratic optimization** or programming techniques can be used to construct a passive portfolio. With quadratic programming, historical information on price changes and correlations between securities are input to a computer program that determines the composition of a portfolio that will minimize return deviations from the benchmark. A problem with this technique is that it relies on *historical* price changes and correlations, and if these factors change over time, the portfolio may experience very large differences from the benchmark.

Sometimes customized passive portfolios, called **completeness funds**, are constructed to complement active portfolios that do not cover the entire market. For example, a large pension fund may allocate some of its holdings to active managers expected to outperform the market. Many times, these active portfolios are overweighted in certain market sectors or stock types. In this case, the pension fund sponsor may want the remaining funds to be invested passively to "fill the holes" left vacant by the active managers. The performance of the completeness fund will be compared to a customized benchmark that incorporates the characteristics of the stocks not covered by the active managers.

For example, suppose a pension fund hires three active managers to invest part of the fund's money. One manager emphasizes small-capitalization Canadian stocks, the second invests only in Pacific Rim countries, and the third invests in Canadian stocks with low *P/E* ratios. To ensure adequate diversification, the pension fund may want to passively invest the remaining assets in a completeness fund that will have a customized benchmark that includes large- and mid-capitalization Canadian stocks, Canadian stocks with normal to high *P/E* ratios, and international stocks outside the Pacific Rim.

Still other passive portfolios and benchmarks exist for investors with certain unique needs and preferences. Some investors may want their funds to be invested only in stocks that pay dividends or in a company that produces a product or service that the investor deems socially responsible. Mossavar-Rahmani (1988) and Dialynas (2001) show that benchmarks can be produced that reflect these desired attributes, and passive portfolios can be constructed to track the performance of the customized benchmark over time so that investors' special needs can be satisfied.

15.2.2 TRACKING ERROR AND INDEX PORTFOLIO CONSTRUCTION

If the goal of forming a passive portfolio is to replicate a particular equity index, the success of such a fund lies not in the absolute returns it produces but in how closely its returns match those of the benchmark. That is, the goal of the passive manager should be to minimize the portfolio's return volatility or **tracking error** relative to the index.

Tracking error can be defined as the extent to which return fluctuations in the managed portfolio are *not correlated* with return fluctuations in the benchmark. A flexible and straight-forward way of measuring tracking error can be developed as follows. Using the Chapter 6 notation:

w_i = investment weight of Asset i in the managed portfolio
R_{it} = return to Asset i in Period t
R_{bt} = return to the benchmark portfolio in Period t

We can define the Period t return to managed portfolio as

$$R_{pt} = \sum_{i=1}^{N} w_i R_{it}$$

where:

N = number of assets in the managed portfolio

With these definitions, the Period t *return differential* between the managed portfolio and the benchmark is

15.2
$$\Delta_t = \sum_{i=1}^{N} w_i R_{it} - R_{bt} = R_{pt} - R_{bt}$$

Given the returns to the N assets in the managed portfolio and the benchmark, Δ is a function of the investment weights that the manager selects. Also, not all of the assets in the benchmark need be included in the managed portfolio (i.e., $w = 0$ for some assets).

For a sample of T return observations, the variance of Δ can be calculated as follows:

15.3	$$\sigma_\Delta^2 = \frac{\sum_{t=1}^{T}(\Delta_t - \bar{\Delta})^2}{(T-1)}$$

Finally, the standard deviation of the return differential is

$$\sigma_\Delta = \sqrt{\sigma_\Delta^2} = \textbf{periodic tracking error}$$

so that *annualized tracking error (TE)* can be calculated as

15.4	$$TE = \sigma_\Delta \sqrt{P}$$

where P is the number of return periods in a year (e.g., $P = 12$ for monthly returns, $P = 252$ for daily returns).

Suppose an investor has formed a portfolio designed to track a particular benchmark. Over the last eight quarters, the returns to this portfolio, as well as the index returns and the return difference between the two, were:

Period	Manager	Index	Difference (Δ)
1	2.3%	2.7%	−0.4%
2	−3.6	−4.6	1.0
3	11.2	10.1	1.1
4	1.2	2.2	−1.0
5	1.5	0.4	1.1
6	3.2	2.8	0.4
7	8.9	8.1	0.8
8	−0.8	0.6	−1.4

The periodic average and standard deviation of the manager's return differential (i.e., "delta") relative to the benchmark are

Average

$$\Delta = [-0.4 + 1.0 + \cdots + 0.8 - 1.4] \div 8 = 0.2\%$$

$$\sigma = \sqrt{(-0.4 - 0.2)^2 + (1.0 - 0.2)^2 + \cdots + (-1.4 - 0.2)^2}$$
$$\div \sqrt{(8-1)} = 1.0\%$$

Thus, the manager's annualized tracking error for this two-year period is 2.0% (= $1.0\% \times \sqrt{4}$).

Generally speaking, there is an inverse relationship between a passive portfolio's tracking error relative to its index and the time and expense necessary to create and maintain the portfolio. For example, full replication of the S&P 500 would have virtually no tracking error but would involve positions in 500 different stocks and require frequent rebalancing. As smaller samples are used to replicate the S&P index's return performance, the expense of forming the managed portfolio would decline but the potential tracking error is likely to increase. Thus, the art of being a manager of a passive equity portfolio lies in balancing the costs (larger tracking error) and the benefits (easier management, lower trading commissions) of using smaller samples. Exhibit 15.3 estimates the tracking error that occurs from such sampling.

Alford, Jones, and Winkelmann (2003) have also shown that tracking error can be a useful way to categorize a fund's investment style. They argue that money managers can be classified using the following chart with regard to the tracking errors of their portfolios compared to the relevant benchmark:

Investment Style	Tracking Error Range
Passive	Less than 1.0% (0.5% or lower is normal)
Structured	Between 1.0% and 3.0%
Active	Over 3.0% (5.0% to 15.0% is normal)

They also document that structured portfolio managers, who can be viewed as active managers with the tightest controls on the permissible level of their tracking errors, tend to produce superior risk-adjusted returns to those active managers whose investment mandates allow them to stray farther from their indices.

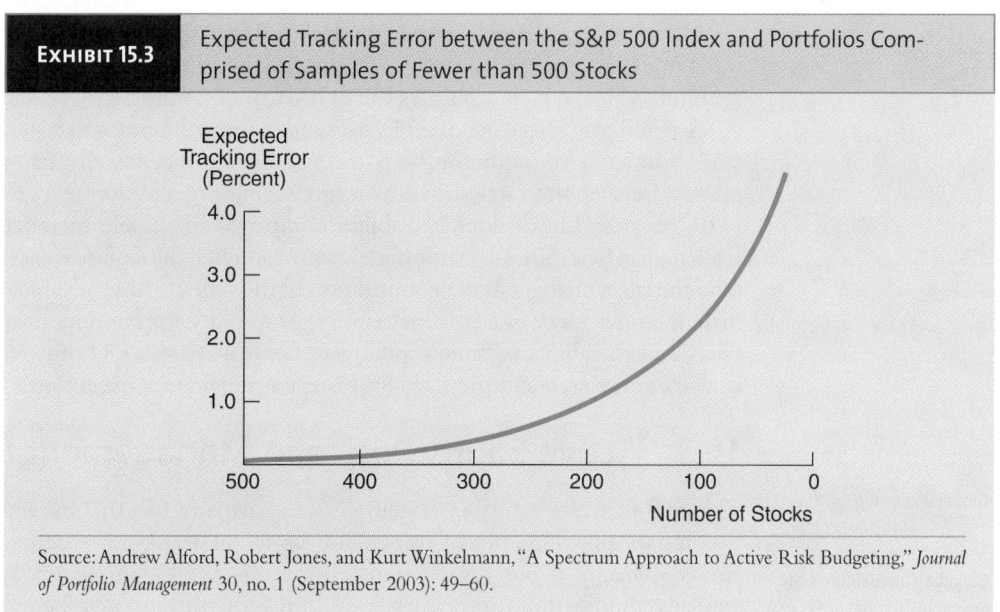

EXHIBIT 15.3 Expected Tracking Error between the S&P 500 Index and Portfolios Comprised of Samples of Fewer than 500 Stocks

Source: Andrew Alford, Robert Jones, and Kurt Winkelmann, "A Spectrum Approach to Active Risk Budgeting," *Journal of Portfolio Management* 30, no. 1 (September 2003): 49–60.

15.2.3 METHODS OF INDEX PORTFOLIO INVESTING

Although investors can construct their own passive investment portfolios that mimic a particular equity index, there are at least two prepackaged ways to accomplish this goal that are typically more convenient and less expensive for the small investor. These are (1) buying shares in an *index mutual fund* or (2) buying shares in an *exchange-traded fund* (*ETF*).

Index Funds As we discuss in Chapter 17, mutual funds represent established security portfolios managed by professional investment companies (e.g., Fidelity, Vanguard, Putnam, AIM) in which investors can participate. The investment company is responsible for deciding how the fund is managed. For an indexed portfolio, the fund manager will typically attempt to replicate the composition of the particular index exactly (full replication). Since changes to most equity indices occur infrequently, index funds tend to generate low trading and management expense ratios. An example is Vanguard's 500 Index Fund (VFINX), which is designed to mimic the S&P 500 index.

The advantage of index mutual funds is that they provide an inexpensive way for investors to acquire a diversified portfolio that emphasizes the desired market or industry within the context of a traditional money management product. As with any mutual fund, the disadvantages are that investors can only liquidate their positions at the end of the trading day (i.e., no intraday trading), usually cannot short sell, and may have unwanted tax repercussions if the fund has an unforeseen need to sell a portion of its holdings, thereby realizing capital gains.

Exchange-Traded Funds As discussed in Chapter 3, ETFs are a more recent development in the world of indexed investment products. There are several notable example of ETFs, including (1) market-index ETFs such as Standard & Poor's 500 Depository Receipts (SPDRs or "spider" as they are sometimes called), which are based on a basket of all the securities held in that index; (2) regional or country ETFs, which re-create indexed positions in several global developed and emerging equity markets such as Brazil, Mexico, Japan, India, and China; and (3) sector ETFs, which invest in baskets of stocks from specific industry sectors. In Canada, ETFs are also gaining popularity. As of May 2009, Barclay Global Investors reported on its website that it offered 28 iShares on the TSX, including 6 Canadian equity and 6 Canadian bonds ETFs. With a total net asset value of over CDN$8.9 billion, the iShares CDN LargeCap 60 Index Fund (symbol: XIU) is the largest. Its management expense ratio is 0.17%. It also offered sector ETFs such as the iShares CDN Financial Sector Index Fund (symbol: XFN), which replicates the performance of the S&P/TSX Capped Financial Index.

A significant advantage of ETFs over index mutual funds is that they can be bought and sold (and short sold) like common stock through an organized exchange or in an over-the-counter market. Further, they are backed by a sponsoring organization (e.g., for SPDRs, the sponsor is PDR Services LLC, a limited liability company whose sole member is the American Stock Exchange where SPDR shares trade) who can alter the composition of the underlying portfolio to reflect changes in the composition of the index. Other advantages relative to index funds include no payment of a management fee, the ability for continuous trading while markets are open, and the ability to time capital gain tax realizations. ETF disadvantages include the brokerage commission and the inability to reinvest dividends except on a quarterly basis.

15.3 Active Equity Portfolio Management Strategies

The goal of active equity management is to earn a return that exceeds the return of a passive benchmark portfolio, net of transaction costs, on a risk-adjusted basis. The job of an active equity manager is not easy. If transaction costs and fees total 1.5% of the portfolio's assets annually, the portfolio must earn 1.5% more than the passive benchmark just to keep pace

Yahoo Exchange Traded Funds Centre provides comprehensive information on ETFs at http://ca.finance.yahoo.com/etf.

GlobeFund of the *Globe and Mail* provides comprehensive information on Canadian mutual funds at http://www.globefund.com.

EXHIBIT 15.4	Performance of Active Mutual Funds vs. S&P 500: January 1980–June 2004

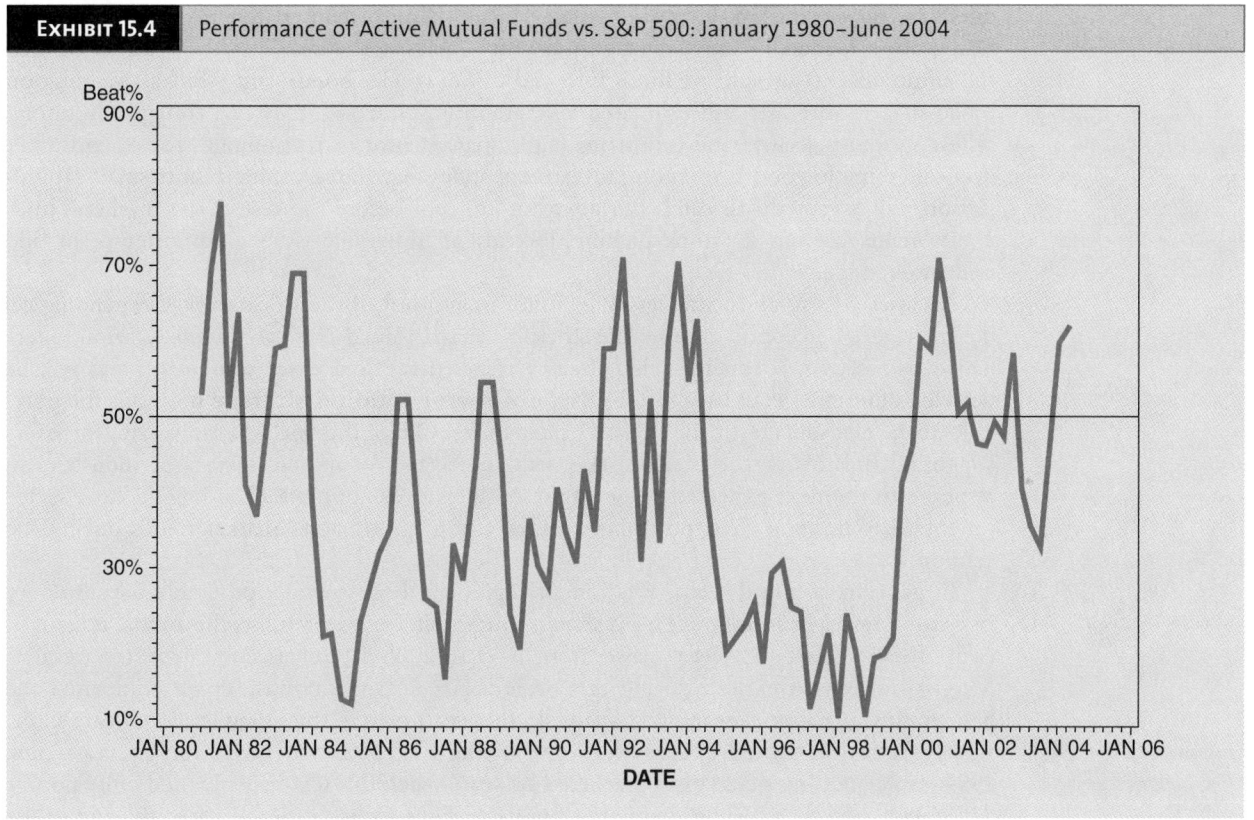

with it. Further, if the manager's strategy involves overweighting specific market sectors in anticipation of price increases, the active portfolio's risk may exceed that of the passive benchmark, so the active portfolio's return will have to exceed the benchmark by an even wider margin to compensate for its higher risk.

Exhibit 15.4 shows the percentage of U.S.-domiciled mutual funds that were able to produce annual returns in excess of the S&P 500 index over nearly a 25-year period. Notice that the average fund manager was not able to outperform the broad index for the majority of this period; the percentage of active funds whose return exceeded that of the index was less than 50% in 64 of the 98 quarters represented in the sample. However, we can also see that the percentage of active managers beating the market was never zero and occasionally rose as high as 70%, which is impressive given that there were more than 5,600 domestic equity funds by the end of 2003. Indeed, evidence provided by Brown and Goetzmann (1995) and Chen, Jegadeesh, and Wermers (2000) show that fund managers possess significant stock-picking skills that can translate into superior and persistent investment returns.

15.3.1 FUNDAMENTAL STRATEGIES

As we saw in Chapter 8, the top-down investment process begins with an analysis of broad country and asset class allocations and progresses down through sector allocation decisions to the bottom level where individual securities are selected. Alternatively, a bottom-up process simply emphasizes the selection of securities without any initial market or sector analysis. Active equity management based on fundamental analysis can start from either direction, depending on what the manager thinks is mispriced relative to his or her valuation models. Generally, active managers use three generic themes. First, they can try to time the equity market by shifting funds into and out of stocks, bonds, and T-bills depending on broad market forecasts and estimated risk premiums. Second, they can shift funds among different equity sectors and industries (e.g., financial stocks, technology stocks, consumer cyclicals, durable goods) or among investment styles (e.g., large capitalization, small capitalization, value, growth) to catch the next hot concept before the rest of the market. Third, equity managers can do stock picking, looking at individual issues in an attempt to find undervalued stocks.

An asset class rotation strategy shifts funds in and out of the stock market depending on the manager's perception of how the stock market is valued compared to the various alternative asset classes. Formally, such a strategy is called **tactical asset allocation** and will be described in more detail later in the chapter. A **sector rotation strategy** positions the portfolio to take advantage of the market's next move. Often, this means emphasizing or overweighting (relative to the benchmark portfolio) certain economic sectors or industries in response to the next expected phase of the business cycle. Exhibit 15.5 suggests how sector rotators may position their portfolios to take advantage of stock market trends during the economic cycle.

In general, asset and sector rotation strategies can be extremely profitable but also very risky for a manager to follow. This is shown in Exhibit 15.6, which lists the annual returns in each of several asset and sector classes from 1991 to 2006. The chart documents the tremendous volatility that existed during this period. For instance, bonds, which comprised the best-performing asset class in 2002, made up the worst class in the following four years. Conversely, large-cap growth stocks were one of the best places to invest for six years (i.e., 1994–1999), but this period was bracketed by years when this sector performed quite poorly. The message is clear: While there are impressive gains to be made by correctly timing the hottest (or the coldest) market sectors, a manager must be right substantially more than he or she is wrong. Because this is an extremely difficult thing to do consistently, many investors choose to interpret Exhibit 15.6 as ultimately extolling the virtue of asset and sector class diversification.

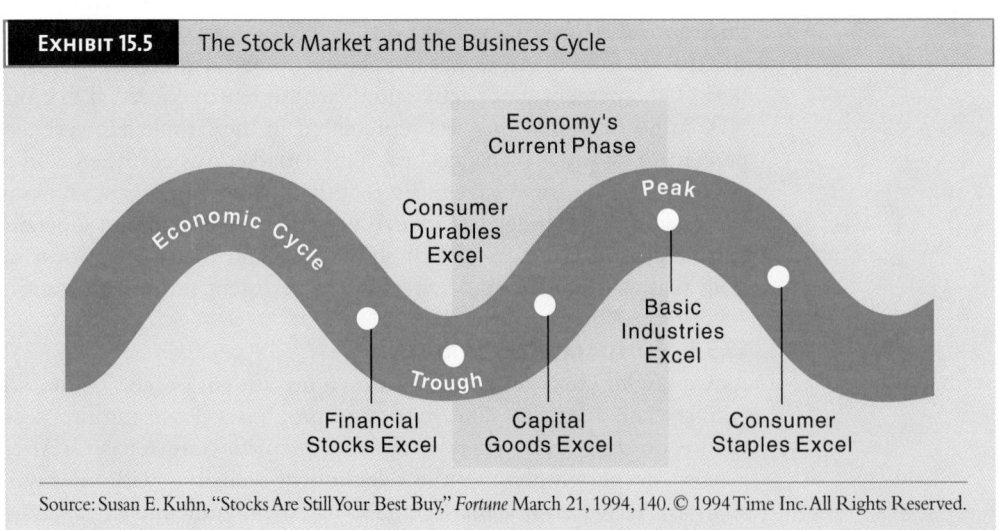

EXHIBIT 15.5   The Stock Market and the Business Cycle

Source: Susan E. Kuhn, "Stocks Are Still Your Best Buy," *Fortune* March 21, 1994, 140. © 1994 Time Inc. All Rights Reserved.

Exhibit 15.6 Asset and Sector Class Return Performance: 1991–2006

1991	1992	1993	1994	1995	1996	1997	1998	1999	2000	2001	2002	2003	2004	2005	2006
SG 48.2%	SV 26.52%	F 32.57%	F 7.78%	LV 33.04%	LG 21.72%	LV 31.35%	LG 35.84%	SG 39.03%	SV 21.54%	SV 14.54%	B 10.25%	SG 41.54%	SV 21.04%	F 14.02%	F 26.86%
S 39.94%	S 18.02%	SV 21.84%	LG 3.12%	L 32.60%	L 20.95%	L 29.85%	L 26.53%	LG 30.33%	B 11.63%	B 8.44%	SV −9.81%	S 40.49%	F 20.25%	LV 7.13%	SV 21.90%
SV 36.59%	LV 13.28%	S 17.86%	L 0.85%	LG 32.18%	LV 20.19%	SV 28.50%	F 20.00%	F 26.96%	LV 8.32%	S 5.15%	LV −14.84%	SV 39.54%	S 17.93%	L 6.42%	LV 20.50%
LG 36.44%	SG 9.04%	LV 16.97%	SV −1.11%	SG 28.01%	SV 19.95%	LG 28.37%	LV 16.80%	S 21.01%	S 0.52%	SG −4.14%	F −15.56%	F 39.17%	LV 15.60%	LG 5.56%	S 17.87%
L 29.99%	L 8.94%	SG 13.34%	S −1.31%	S 25.73%	S 16.41%	S 21.51%	SG 6.79%	L 19.92%	L −6.66%	LV −4.95%	S −20.21%	LV 27.30%	SG 14.74%	SV 5.51%	L 14.96%
LV 23.06%	B 7.40%	L 9.91%	LV −1.53%	SV 23.43%	SG 12.78%	SG 14.44%	B 8.70%	LV 7.92%	F −13.96%	L −11.32%	L −22.26%	L 27.00%	LG 11.12%	S 5.49%	SG 13.77%
B 16.00%	LG 5.19%	B 9.75%	SG −1.72%	B 18.46%	F 6.05%	B 9.64%	S 1.14%	SV −0.54%	SG −17.29%	LG −18.09%	LG −30.16%	LG 26.76%	LG 8.96%	SG 5.31%	LG 9.00%
F 12.14%	F −12.18%	LG 3.17%	B −2.92%	F 11.21%	B 3.64%	F 1.78%	SV −4.35%	B −0.82%	LG −22.07%	F −21.21%	SG −32.39%	B 4.10%	B 4.34%	B 2.43%	B 4.33%

Legend:
L = Large Stocks (Russell 1000 Index)
LG = Large Growth Stocks (Russell 1000 Growth Index)
LV = Large Value Stocks (Russell 1000 Value Index)
S = Small Stocks (Russell 2000 Index)
SG = Small Growth Stocks (Russell 2000 Growth Index)
SV = Small Value Stocks (Russell 2000 Value Index)
F = Foreign Stocks (MSCI EAFE Index)
B = Bonds (Lehman Brothers Aggregate Bond Index)

Source: Frank Russell Company.

A fundamental stock picker operating on a pure bottom-up basis will form a portfolio of equities that can be purchased at a substantial discount to what his or her valuation model indicates they are worth. As discussed in Chapter 9, these models might be based on absolute judgments about the company's future (i.e., discounted cash flow) or relative assessments of how attractive the stock is compared with shares in otherwise similar firms (i.e., relative price multiples). In either case, it is usually true that the active manager will find stock picking to be a more reliable, although less profitable, way to invest than market timing.

Finally, a recent trend in fundamental equity management is the development of the so-called **130/30 strategy**. Fowler (2007) explains that funds based on this approach are allowed to take long positions up to 130% of the portfolio's original capital and have short positions up to 30%. Relative to "long only" portfolios, these *enhanced active* funds let managers exploit their expertise in two ways. First, as Jacobs and Levy (2007) note, the use of the short positions creates the leverage needed to extend the long holdings beyond the original capital limit, potentially increasing both risk and expected returns compared to the fund's benchmark. Second, and more importantly, 130/30 strategies enable managers to make full use of their fundamental research to buy stocks they identify as undervalued as well as short those that are overvalued. Thus, these strategies expand the ways in which investors can capture available alpha opportunities.

15.3.2 TECHNICAL STRATEGIES

Earlier, we discussed the role that technical analysis plays in the stock evaluation process. As we saw, assessing past stock price trends to surmise what information they imply about future price movements was one of the primary tools of this analytical approach. Active managers can form equity portfolios on the basis of past stock price trends by assuming that one of two things will happen: (1) past stock price trends will continue in the same direction, or (2) they will reverse themselves.

A **contrarian** investment strategy is based on the belief that the best time to buy (sell) a stock is when the majority of other investors are the most bearish (bullish) about it. The contrarian investor will attempt to always purchase the stock when it is near its lowest price and sell it (or even short sell it) when it nears its peak. Implicit in this approach is the belief that stock returns are *mean reverting*, indicating that, over time, stocks will be priced so as to produce returns consistent with their risk-adjusted expected (i.e., mean) returns. DeBondt and Thaler (1985) demonstrated the potential benefits of forming active portfolios based on this notion. They showed that investing on an *overreaction hypothesis* could provide consistently superior returns.

At the other extreme, active portfolios can also be formed on the assumptions that recent trends in past prices will continue. A **price momentum** strategy, as it is more commonly called, assumes that stocks that have been hot will stay hot, while cold stocks will also remain so.

Although there may well be sound economic reasons for these trends to continue (e.g., company revenues and earnings that continue to grow faster than expected), it may also be the case that investors periodically *underreact* to the arrival of new information. Thus, a pure price momentum strategy focuses on the trend of past prices alone and makes purchase and sale decisions accordingly. Chan, Jegadeesh, and Lakonishok (1999) investigated the profitability of this approach. They divided all of the stocks traded in U.S. markets over a five-year period into ten different portfolios based on their past six-month price movements and calculated returns over the following year. Panel A of Exhibit 15.7 shows these returns for each of the portfolios, from the one with the most positive past price trend (#10) to the worst price trend (#1). The data appear to justify the price momentum strategy in that the portfolios with the highest (lowest) level of price momentum generated the highest (lowest) subsequent returns. Also, the last column shows that a momentum-based hedge fund long in the best-trend portfolio and short in the worst-trend one would also have been quite profitable.

EXHIBIT 15.7 Profitability of Momentum Strategies: 1994–1998

	1 (Low)	2	3	4	5	6	7	8	9	10 (High)	10-1 (PPS)
A. Classification Based on Prior Six-Month Return											
1994	−12.00	−6.10	0.40	2.10	0.50	−0.90	−1.80	3.10	−4.50	−6.40	5.40
1995	35.70	27.40	32.30	35.00	32.30	32.20	30.30	36.70	35.30	42.10	6.40
1996	11.90	15.60	17.90	20.20	27.90	22.50	22.00	21.90	20.40	15.30	3.40
1997	7.20	5.70	14.80	20.80	26.60	32.80	35.60	37.30	37.50	23.80	16.60
1998	−2.30	−4.40	−7.00	−3.30	−0.40	0.00	4.50	0.10	−0.80	4.40	6.70
1994–1998 average	8.10	7.64	11.68	14.96	17.38	17.32	18.12	19.82	17.58	15.84	7.74
B. Classification Based on Standardized Unexpected Earnings											
1994	−2.30	−2.40	−6.80	−1.00	−4.60	−1.20	−0.10	−3.30	0.90	−2.00	0.30
1995	36.70	25.40	27.80	31.00	33.40	27.50	36.10	36.90	38.60	40.60	3.90
1996	16.30	17.90	19.20	16.30	21.90	19.60	23.10	22.70	24.70	18.40	2.10
1997	25.50	21.70	23.50	22.80	24.10	24.50	25.20	28.40	29.60	28.10	2.60
1998	−3.20	−5.20	−1.30	4.40	−0.60	5.00	−0.10	−0.60	0.00	−6.20	−3.00
1994–1998 average	14.60	11.48	12.48	14.70	14.84	15.08	16.84	16.82	18.76	15.78	1.18

Source: Copyright © 1999, Association for Investment Management and Research. Reproduced and republished from "The Profitability of Momentum Strategies," from the November/December 1999 issue of the *Financial Analyst's Journal*, with permission from the CFA Institute. All Rights Reserved.

Copyright 1999, CFA Institute. Reproduced and republished from the Financial Analysts Journal with permission from CFA Institute. All rights reserved.

15.3.3　Anomalies and Attributes

The price momentum strategies just discussed could either be based on pure price trend analysis or supported by the underlying economic fundamentals of the company. An **earnings momentum** strategy is a somewhat more formal active portfolio approach that purchases and holds stocks that have accelerating earnings and sells (or short sells) stocks with disappointing earnings. The notion behind this strategy is that, ultimately, a company's share price will follow the direction of its earnings, which is one measure of the firm's economic success. In practice, investors judge the degree of momentum in a firm's earnings by comparing the company's actual *earnings per share* (*EPS*) to some level of what was expected. Two types of expected earnings are used most frequently: (1) those generated by a statistical model and (2) the consensus forecast of professional stock analysts. Panel B of Exhibit 15.7 shows that earnings momentum strategies were generally successful, although not to the same degree as price momentum strategies.

In our examination of market efficiency (Chapter 5), we saw several anomalies that suggested a role for active equity management. Two of these—the weekend effect and the January effect—involved investing during particular times of the year. While conceptually viable, the limitations inherent in these anomalies do not produce particularly effective portfolio strategies. That is, managers investing in stocks only in January are not likely to be able to justify their annual fees, while the number of transactions implied by the weekend effect (i.e., buy every Monday, sell every Friday) generally makes for a cost-ineffective portfolio. Remember, however, that whether or not these calendar-related anomalies produce successful active portfolios, they still are useful rules for trades that an investor plans to make anyway.

A more promising approach to active anomaly investing involves forming portfolios based on various characteristics of the companies themselves. Two characteristics we have seen to matter in the stock market are the total capitalization of the firm's outstanding equity (i.e., firm size) and the financial position of the firm, as indicated by its various financial ratios (e.g., *P/E*, *P/BV*). Two general conclusions can be made about these firm characteristics. First, over time, firms with smaller market capitalizations produce bigger risk-adjusted returns than those with large market capitalizations. Second, over time, firms with lower *P/E* and *P/BV* ratios produce bigger risk-adjusted returns than those with higher levels of those ratios. In fact, we saw in Chapter 7 that low and high levels of these ratios are used in practice to define value and growth stocks, respectively.

Another reason why these firm-specific attributes may be important to active investors is that the term *sector* considered earlier in the context of rotation strategies also can be defined by different stock attributes. Because the market seems to favour some attributes more than others, sector rotation may involve overweighting stocks with certain characteristics, such as small- or large-capitalization stocks, high or low *P/E* stocks, or stocks classified more generally as value or growth stocks. For example, Panel A of Exhibit 15.8 shows the difference in returns to portfolios invested in small- and large-cap stocks on a monthly basis from 1991 to 2007. The graph shows the large-cap portfolio return minus the small-cap return, so any net return above the horizontal axis indicates a period when the former outperformed the latter. Notice the consistent firm size rotation and spread in returns that occurred in this period; in given months, both large- and small-cap stocks outperformed the other by over 30%. Keep in mind, however, that small-cap stocks are almost always riskier than large-cap stocks. This is shown in Panel B of Exhibit 15.8 as the difference in the standard deviations of the large- and small-cap portfolios.

Similar analysis reveals the potential benefits of forming active global portfolios around financial ratios. Over a 20-year period, Fama and French (1998) divided the stocks in 13 world markets using several different ratios, including *P/E* and *P/BV.* They formed portfolios of stocks based on the highest and lowest 30% of each ratio and measured returns and standard

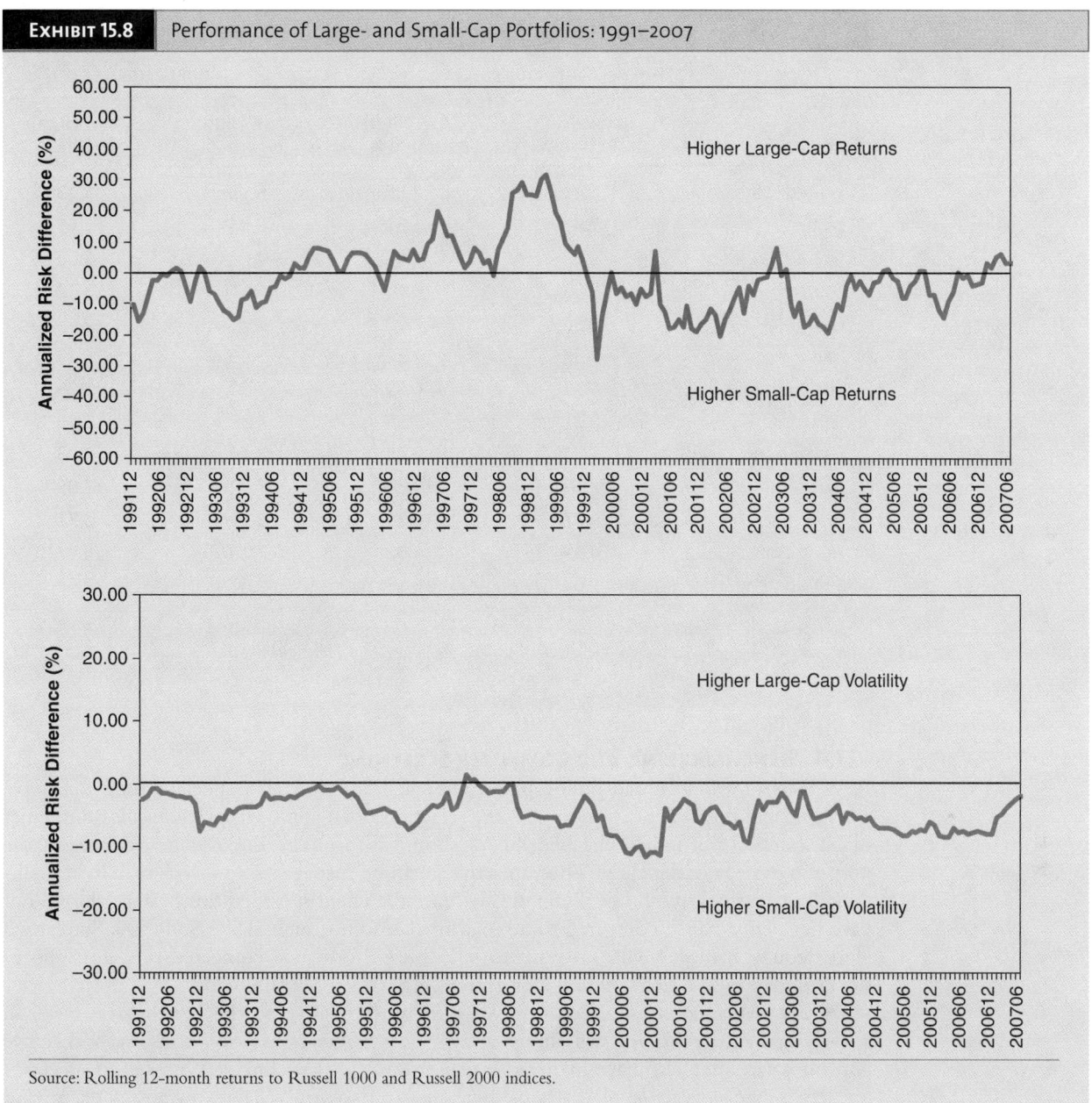

| EXHIBIT 15.8 | Performance of Large- and Small-Cap Portfolios: 1991–2007 |

Source: Rolling 12-month returns to Russell 1000 and Russell 2000 indices.

deviations. Exhibit 15.9 summarizes their findings. For each country and each ratio, the display reports the average annual return differential between the lowest ratio portfolio and the highest ratio portfolio, as well as difference in standard deviation for those two portfolios. Two facts are clear from these results. First, over time, portfolios with the lowest P/E and P/BV ratios produced the highest returns everywhere in the world except Italy. Second, those low-ratio portfolios also tended to be more volatile, although this finding was far less uniform across countries. As we will see shortly, these results are important for understanding the differences between the value and growth investment styles.

EXHIBIT 15.9	Performance of Ratio-Based Stock Portfolios: 1975–1995			
	P/E Ratio		*P/BV* Ratio	
Country	(Low–High) Return %	(Low–High) Std Dev %	(Low–High) Return %	(Low–High) Std Dev %
United States	6.71	2.87	6.79	1.13
Japan	7.47	−1.52	9.85	−2.75
United Kingdom	2.65	5.32	4.62	2.09
France	6.98	4.70	7.64	5.72
Germany	0.55	−10.20	2.75	−2.40
Italy	−5.37	−12.32	−5.99	−15.12
The Netherlands	5.11	0.59	2.30	12.06
Belgium	2.22	2.59	4.39	0.99
Switzerland	1.54	2.63	3.49	1.43
Sweden	8.19	17.67	8.02	12.05
Australia	9.67	−0.70	12.32	3.71
Hong Kong	4.99	4.02	7.16	8.47
Singapore	2.09	−5.13	9.67	9.18

Source: Eugene F. Fama and Kenneth R. French, "Value versus Growth: The International Evidence," *Journal of Finance* 53, no. 6 (December 1998): 1975–1999. Reprinted with permission of Blackwell Publishing.

15.3.4 BENCHMARKING AND COMPUTER SCREENING

Regardless of which broad philosophical approach adopted, an important issue for active managers and their clients to resolve is the selection of an appropriate *benchmark* (sometimes called a *normal* portfolio). The benchmark should incorporate the average qualities of the portfolio strategy of the client. Thus, an active portfolio manager who invests mainly in small-capitalization stocks with low *P/E* ratios because the client specified this strategy should not have her performance compared to a broad market index, such as the S&P 500. Similarly, a global equity manager will not want to have his performance compared to a portfolio of stocks drawn from a single country, or even a single region in the world.

Active managers must overcome two difficulties relative to the benchmark. First, an actively managed portfolio will almost always have higher transaction costs. Second, active portfolios can often also have higher risk than the passive benchmark. One key to success is for active managers to *be consistent* in their area of expertise. Market gyrations occur, and investment styles go in and out of favour. Successful long-term investing requires that we maintain our investment philosophy and composure while others are deviating from theirs. Another key to success is to *minimize the trading activity* of the portfolio. Attempts to time price movements over short horizons will result in lower profits because of growing commissions.

Finally, notice that most active equity strategies are inherently quantitative in nature. This suggests that computer-assisted portfolio formation procedures can be quite useful. In fact, the existence of computer databases has encouraged the use of computer screening and other quantitatively based methods of evaluating stocks. These screening methods search for portfolios of stocks with certain characteristics rather than examining individual stocks to determine whether they are underpriced. The simplest computer screens identify groups of stocks based on a set of attributes. Screens also are used to narrow the list of thousands of stocks to a manageable few that can then be evaluated using more traditional analytical means. Indeed, some managers let the computers do all the work.

15.4 Investment Styles

15.4.1 VALUE VERSUS GROWTH INVESTING

Morningstar Canada is a leading mutual fund research firm and this is its Canadian mutual funds site: http://www.morningstar.ca.

An important development in active equity management during the last several years has been the creation of portfolio strategies based on value- and growth-oriented investment styles. Indeed, it is now common for money management firms to define themselves as "value stock managers" or "growth stock managers" when selling their services. Exhibit 15.10 indicates how pervasive these styles have become. Using the Morningstar Inc. classifications, the number of growth- and value-oriented funds grew dramatically, particularly toward the end of the reporting period. The chart shows that the available number of growth fund products expanded by more than 18% per year over this period, with large-cap portfolios being the most prevalent. Value fund availability did not increase quite as much but still expanded by almost 16% annually.

The distinction between value and growth investing can be best appreciated by considering the thought process of a representative manager for each style.[1] In Web Chapter 19, we show that the price-earnings ratio for any company can be expressed as:

15.5
$$P/E \text{ Ratio} = \frac{(\text{Current Price per Share})}{(\text{Earning per Share})}$$

EXHIBIT 15.10	Number of Growth and Value Mutual Funds: 1991–2007				
	2007	**2003**	**2000**	**1995**	**1991**
Growth–Oriented Funds					
Large-cap	1,751	1,245	651	174	117
Mid-cap	985	784	415	106	79
Small-cap	843	672	383	77	42
Total	3,579	2,701	1,449	357	238
Annual % Increase (1991–2007)	18.5%				
Value-Oriented Funds					
Large-cap	1,405	946	615	211	133
Mid-cap	407	301	212	69	60
Small-cap	427	270	193	47	25
Total	2,239	1,517	1,020	327	218
Annual % Increase (1991–2007)	15.7%				

Source: Fidelity Management and Research. Adapted from Table 1 in Keith C. Brown, W.V. Harlow, and Hanjiang Zhang, "Staying the Course: Performance Persistence and the Role of Investment Style Consistency in Professional Asset Management," Working Paper, June 23, 2008.

---

1 This motivation is based on an excellent overview of value, and growth-oriented investment styles that can be found in Christopherson and Williams (1995).

where the earnings per share (EPS) measure can be based on either current or forecasted firm performance. In broad terms, value and growth managers will focus on different aspects of this equation when deciding whether a stock should be added to an existing portfolio. Specifically, a growth-oriented investor will

- focus on the EPS component (i.e., the denominator) of the P/E ratio and its economic determinants;
- look for companies that he or she expects to exhibit rapid EPS growth in the future; and
- often implicitly assume that the P/E ratio will remain constant over the near term, meaning that the stock price will rise as forecasted earnings growth is realized.

On the other hand, a value-oriented investor will

- focus on the price component (i.e., the numerator) of the P/E ratio; he or she must be convinced that the price of the stock is "cheap" by some means of comparison;
- not care a great deal about current earnings or the fundamental drivers of earnings growth; and
- look for undervalued stocks and often implicitly assume that the P/E ratio is below its natural level and that the market will soon "correct" this situation by increasing the stock price with little or no change in earnings.

The conceptual difference between value and growth investing may be reasonably straightforward, but classifying individual stocks into the appropriate style is not always simple in practice. Because detailed company valuations are time-consuming to produce, most analysts rely on more easily obtained financial indicators—such as P/E and P/BV ratios, dividend yields, and EPS growth rates—to define both an individual equity holding as well as the style benchmark portfolio. Exhibit 15.11 shows one approach along these lines for classifying firms according to style and market capitalization. Notice that value stocks are defined as those that are relatively cheap (e.g., low P/BV, high yield) and with modest growth opportunities (e.g., regulated firms) while growth stocks tend to be more expensive, reflecting their superior earnings potential (e.g., technology firms).

| Exhibit 15.11 | Characteristics of Growth and Value Stocks |

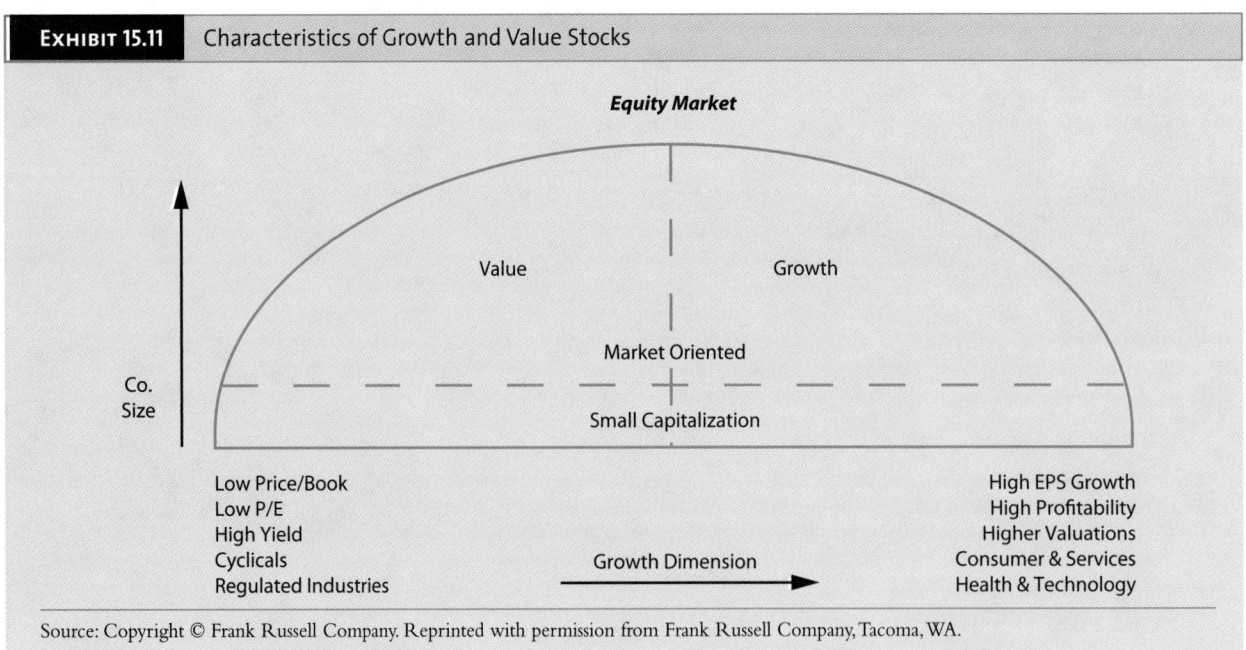

Source: Copyright © Frank Russell Company. Reprinted with permission from Frank Russell Company, Tacoma, WA.

EXHIBIT 15.12	Large-cap Value Fund versus Small-cap Growth Fund

Top Stock Holdings of Growth and Value Mutual Funds (As of Septemeber 30, 2008)
Value Fund: TD Dividend Income-I

Company	Ticker	Market Cap ($ Bil)	P/E	P/BV	Est. Growth EPS (%)	Div. Yield (%)	Beta
Bank of Nova Scotia	BNS	45.1	12.3	2.5	4.05	3.12	0.74
Canadian Oil Sands Trust	COS.UN	18.3	11.0	4.4	1.6	9.3	1.62
Royal Bank of Canada	RY	60.6	12.8	2.6	4.42	4.2	0.80
Currency (Canada)							
Manulife Financial Coporation	MFC	54.4	13.3	2.2	2.68	2.7	0.64
Canadian Imperial Bank of Commerce	CM	19.1	9.0	1.7	9.91	6.1	0.78
Bank of Montreal	BMO	20.9	10.8	1.3	4.22	6.7	0.69
Toronto–Dominion Bank	TD	43.2	14.3	1.5	5.82	3.9	0.75
EnCana Corporation	ECA	97.9	27.6	4.8	4.86	2.2	1.22
Brookfield Asset Management, Inc. A	BAM.A	15.7	20.8	2.5	1.23	1.9	0.87
	Average:	*41.69*	*14.66*	*2.61*	*4.31*	*4.46*	*0.90*

Growth Fund: Manulife ML Elite Canadian Small Cap

Company	Ticker	Market Cap ($ Bil)	P/E	P/BV	Est. Growth EPS (%)	Div. Yield (%)	Beta
Major Drilling Group International Inc.	MDI	0.68	12.1	3.12	3.14	n.a.	1.29
Jaguar Mining Inc.	JAG	0.35	−11.9	3.25	−0.49	n.a.	1.12
Highpine Oil & Gas	HPX	0.58	−1.4	0.71	−7.14	n.a.	1.38
Transat A.T. Inc. B	TRZ.B	0.45	6.5	1.85	2.6	2.2	0.50
Canada Bread Company, Limited	CBY	1.44	14.6	1.93	3.91	0.5	0.11
BMTC Grp	GBT.A	0.56	9.4	2.79	2.04	1.97	0.28
WFI Industries	WFI	0.32	36.7	16.28	0.82	n.a.	0.47
Glacier Ventures	GVC	0.29	2.9	0.33	1.19	n.a.	0.14
North West Company Fund Trust Unit	NWF.UN	0.77	15.4	3.27	1.11	5.28	0.40
TriStar Oil & Gas Ltd.	TOG	1.61	−123.0	3.01	−0.14	n.a.	1.40
	Average:	*0.71*	*−3.87*	*3.65*	*0.70*	*2.49*	*0.71*

Sources: Financials are from Morningstar.ca (large cap) and Mint Global database (small cap); betas are from FT.Com; and Fund Valuation & Holdings are from Morningstar.com.

To get a better feel for the types of stock portfolios these two investment styles might produce, Exhibit 15.12 shows the contrast between a large-cap income fund, the TD Dividend Income Fund, and a small-cap growth fund, the Manulife ML Elite Canadian Small Cap Fund. We show the top 10 holdings of each fund and relevant financials. The two funds have very different holdings. The large-cap value fund is of big-name companies and the small-cap growth fund holds less-known, smaller firms. The average market capitalization of the top 10 holdings of the large-cap value fund is almost $42 billion and the average dividend yield 4.46%, while those of the small-cap growth fund are $710 million and 2.49%.

Although investors appear to pay somewhat more attention to growth-oriented strategies, research has shown that a value approach to portfolio management tends to provide superior returns. Siegel (2005) uses data of S&P 500 companies from 1957—the beginning year of the index—to 2002, to demonstrate that value investing is superior to growth investing. He cautioned investors of the investment trap of companies in the "the bold and the new" as stocks of companies in new technologies and growing sectors can be overpriced. Capaul, Rowley, and Sharpe (1993) studied the performance of value and growth portfolios (defined by relative P/BV ratios) in six countries: the United States, the United Kingdom, Japan, France, Germany, and Switzerland. Over a 10-year period ending in June 1992, they demonstrated that global value stocks outperformed global growth stocks by an average of 3.3% per year. Further, value stocks outperformed growth stocks in each of the six countries considered separately. More recent evidence provided by Chan and Lakonishok (2004) supports this conclusion.

It is tempting to conclude that value is unambiguously superior to growth as an investment style. However, the higher average returns of value investing do not occur with much consistency from one investment period to another. Panel A of Exhibit 15.13 shows that there are significant differences in the value-growth return spread (based on the rolling annual performance of the Russell 1000 Value and Growth indices) over time. The spread ranged from over 50% in favour of value investing to more than 30% to the advantage of the growth style. Conversely, Panel B shows that the spread between value and growth return standard deviations, while itself volatile, is consistently negative, meaning that the growth strategy is consistently riskier than the value approach.

15.4.2 Style Analysis

As we have seen, there are many approaches to managing an equity portfolio. But do we simply take the words of the fund managers or financial firms when they declare they are following a particular style? How do we know, for instance, if a mutual fund that claims a strategy of investing in large-cap growth firms actually implemented such a strategy? Returns-based **style analysis** is a technique to answer such a question. Effectively, style analysis determines the combination of long positions in a collection of passive indices that best mimics the past performance of a security portfolio.

The process of returns-based style analysis involves using the past returns to a manager's portfolio along with those to a series of indices representing different investment styles in an effort to determine the relationship between the fund and those specific styles. Generally speaking, the more highly correlated a fund's returns are with a given style index, the greater the weighting that style is given in the statistical assessment. The goals of the analysis are to better understand the underlying influences responsible for the portfolio's performance and to properly classify the manager's strategy when comparing his or her investment prowess with that of other managers. Thus, regardless of whatever investment objective a manager might profess to follow, style analysis allows the portfolio to speak for itself.

Exhibit 15.14 shows a simple *style grid* that could be used to classify a manager's performance along two dimensions: firm size (large, mid, and small cap) and relative value (value, blend, growth) characteristics. An investor whose portfolio produced returns best mimicked by the returns to indices representing a small-cap value style (such as Manager a) would be plotted in the lower left quadrant of the grid. These grids are also useful in establishing the implicit investment style for any of the popular stock market indicators. For example, Exhibit 15.15 shows the style plot points for the S&P 500, S&P Midcap, Wilshire 5000, NASDAQ Composite, Russell 3000 (R3), Russell 2000 (R2), and Russell 1000 (R1), among others.[2] Note that the S&P 500

---

2 Exhibit 15.15 also plots the investment style for various subsets of the Russell indices. For example, R1V and R1G are, respectively, the value and growth halves of the Russell 1000. They are created by ranking the 1,000 companies in the index by their price-to-book ratios and assigning those with the lowest (highest) ratios to the value (growth) subindex.

EXHIBIT 15.13	Performance of Value and Growth Portfolios: 1991–2007

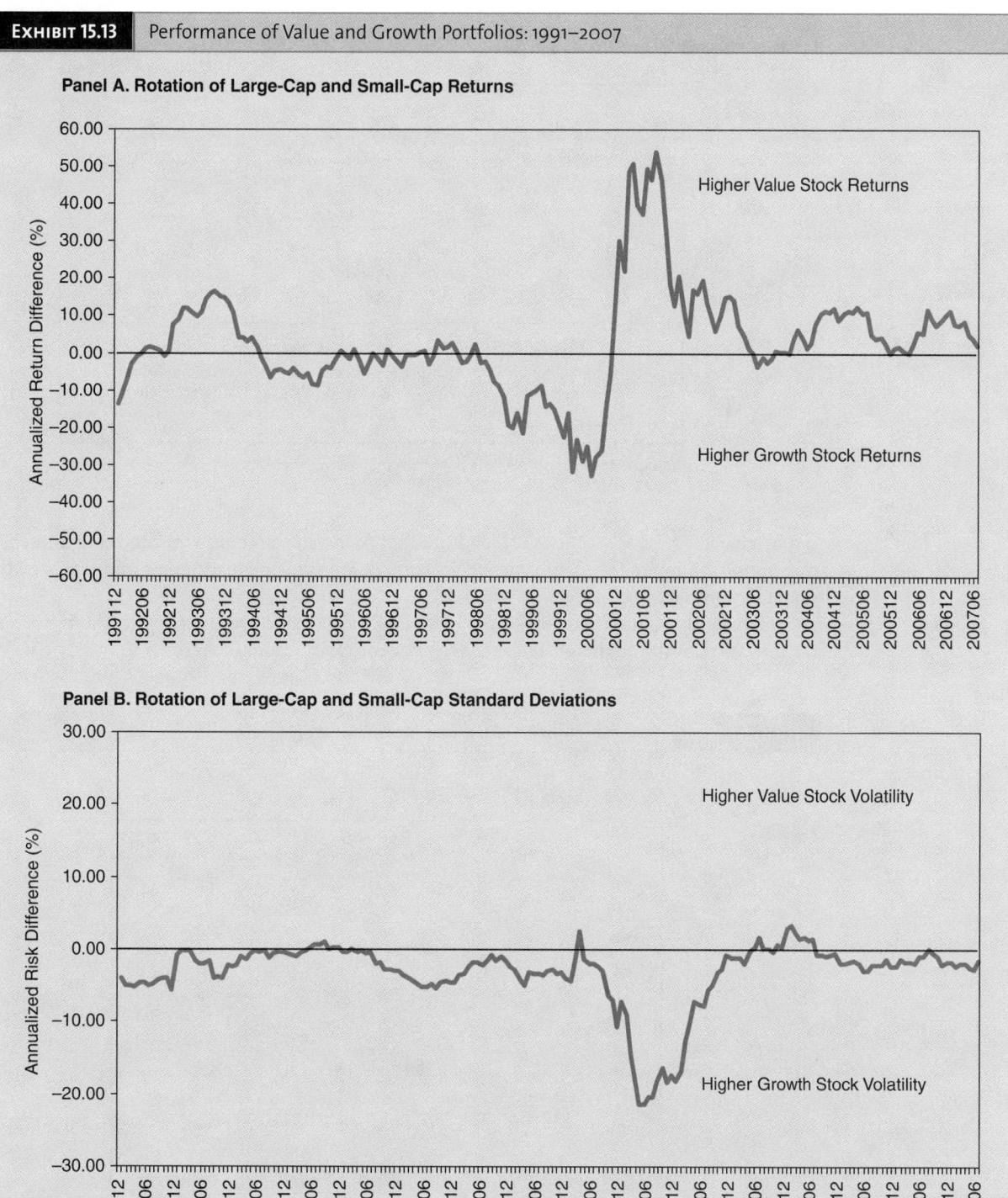

Panel A. Rotation of Large-Cap and Small-Cap Returns

Panel B. Rotation of Large-Cap and Small-Cap Standard Deviations

Source: Rolling 12-month returns to Russell 1000 Value and Growth indices.

EXHIBIT 15.14   A Style Analysis Grid

	Value ←		→ Growth
Large	Large-Cap Value	Large-Cap Blend	Large-Cap Growth
	Mid-Cap Value	Mid-Cap Blend	Mid-Cap Growth
Small	•*Manager A* Small-Cap Value	Small-Cap Blend	Small-Cap Growth

---

can be characterized as a large–cap, blend (i.e., between value and growth) fund, and as such, it may not be the appropriate performance benchmark for someone managing a mid-cap, growth-oriented portfolio.

Formally, style analysis relies on the *constrained least squares* procedure, with the returns to the manager's portfolio designated as the dependent variable and the returns to the style index

---

EXHIBIT 15.15   Investment Style of Popular Stock Market Indicators

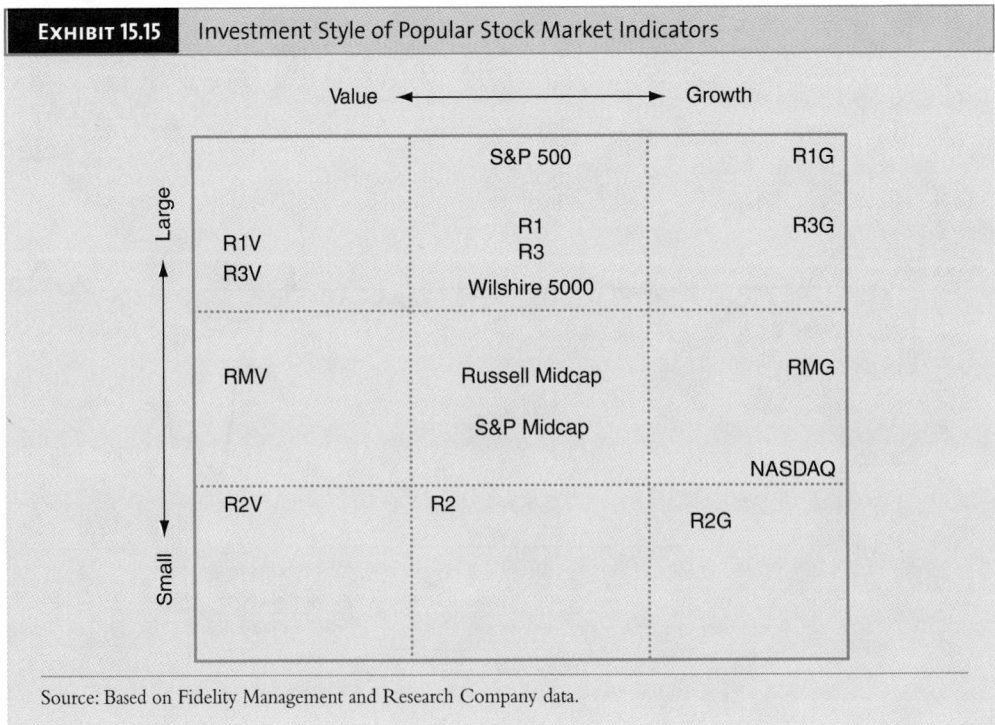

Source: Based on Fidelity Management and Research Company data.

portfolios as the independent variables. In practice, there are often three constraints employed: (1) no intercept term is specified, (2) the coefficients must sum to one, and (3) all the coefficients must be non-negative. As developed by Sharpe (1992), returns-based style analysis is simply an application of an asset class factor model:

$$15.6 \qquad R_{pt} = [b_{p1}F_{1t} + b_{p2}F_{2t} + \ldots + b_{pn}F_{nt}] + e_{pt}$$

where:

R_{pt} = the tth period return to the portfolio of Manager p
F_{jt} = the tth period return to the jth style factor
b_{pj} = the sensitivity of Portfolio p to Style Factor j
e_{pt} = the portion of the return variability in Portfolio p not explained by variability in the set of factors

As with any regression equation, the coefficient of determination can be defined as

$$15.7 \qquad R^2 = 1 - [\sigma^2(e_p)/\sigma^2(R_p)]$$

Because of the way the factor model is designed, R^2 can be interpreted as the percentage of Manager p's return variability due to the portfolio's *style*, with $(1 - R^2)$ due to his or her *selection* skills.

The benchmark portfolios that are selected as style analysis factors should be consistent with the manager's pronounced style. This suggests that a different set of indices might be specified for a domestic equity fund than for an international bond fund. Also, an effective benchmark portfolio should be easy to measure, available as a realistic investment alternative to an actively managed portfolio, and as uncorrelated as possible with the other style indices.

To illustrate how this process can be implemented, Sharpe measured the investment styles of two large institutional equity portfolios—Vanguard Trustee's U.S. Fund and Fidelity Magellan Fund—over a five-year interval. Both portfolios performed well during the period, generating respective average annual returns of 15.5% and 20.6%. However, Exhibit 15.16 shows that the portfolio managers followed very different styles. The bar charts indicate the extent to which each portfolio's returns were correlated with the underlying style factors. Accordingly, the Trustees' Fund is best thought of as being a small-cap value fund over this period while the Magellan Fund was a small- to mid-cap growth portfolio with some global exposure. Also, security selection accounted for a relatively small amount of Magellan's return variability (2.7%) but was more of a consideration (7.8%) in the Trustees' portfolio.

Finally, style analysis can also be used to determine whether a manager is able to maintain a consistent investment style over time. This can be accomplished by re-estimating the optimal combination of mimicking style indices as additional performance data become available and then overlaying the plot points on the same grid. Exhibit 15.17 shows the connected sequence of plot points—or "snail trails" as they are sometimes called—for four different mutual funds managed by a leading investment company. Two of these funds (I and II) have

EXHIBIT 15.16	Style Analysis for Two Mutual Funds

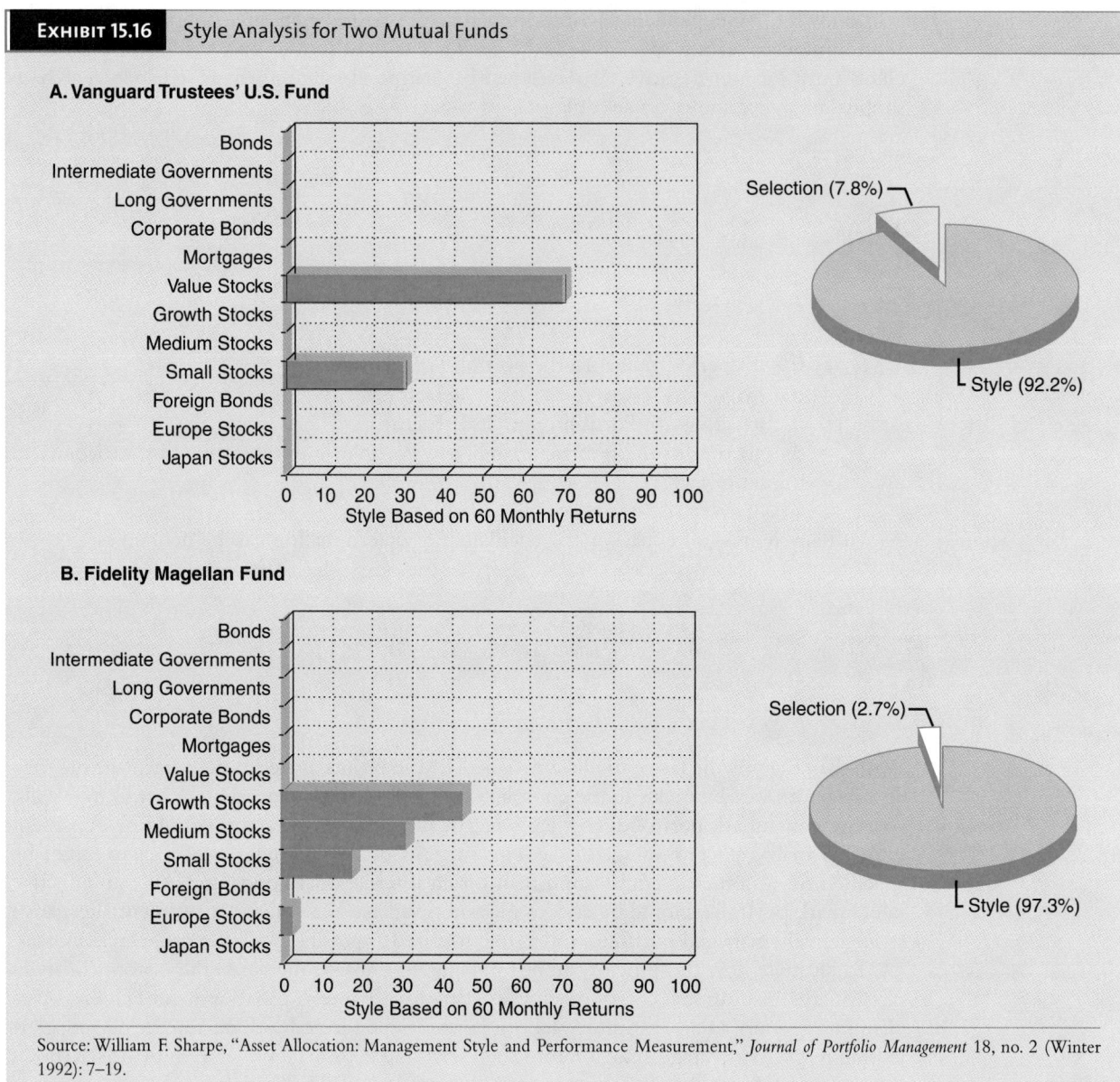

Source: William F. Sharpe, "Asset Allocation: Management Style and Performance Measurement," *Journal of Portfolio Management* 18, no. 2 (Winter 1992): 7–19.

well-defined style mandates and have been able to achieve relatively stable investment policies. The other two—III and IV—have exhibited considerable *style drift*, which in both cases is consistent with their flexible investment missions. Of course, an investor needs to be cautious about a manager whose portfolio exhibits unintentional style drift.

15.5   Asset Allocation Strategies

Investment Industry Regulatory Organization of Canada:http://www.iiroc.ca.

An equity portfolio does not stand in isolation; many times the equity portfolio is part of a balanced portfolio that contains holdings in various long- and short-term debt securities (such as bonds and T-bills) in addition to equities.

Exhibit 15.17	Mutual Fund Styles over Time

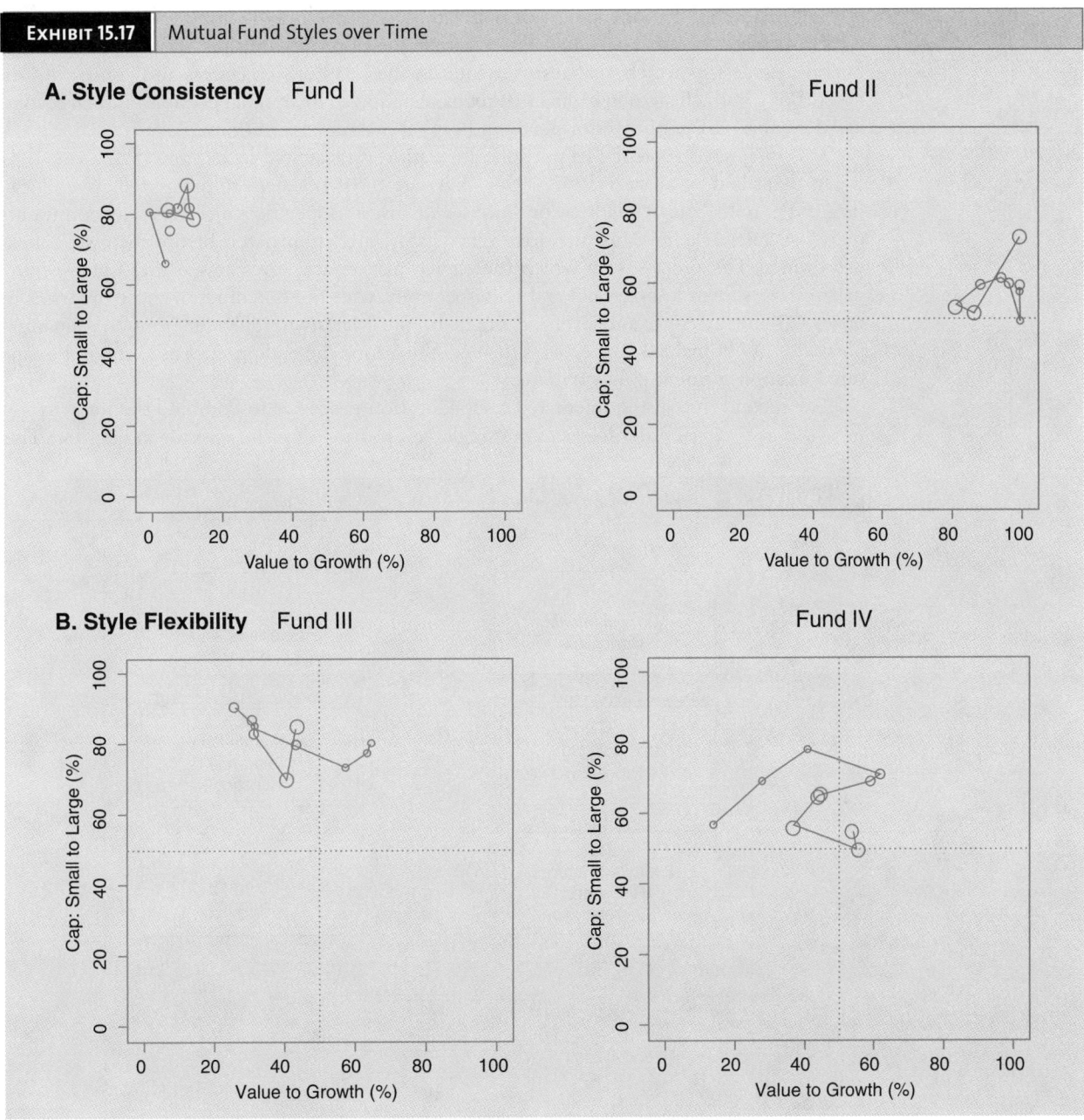

In such situations, the portfolio manager must consider more than just the composition of the equity or the bond component of the portfolio. The manager also must determine the appropriate mix of asset categories in the entire portfolio. There are four general strategies for determining the asset mix of a portfolio: the integrated, strategic, tactical, and insured asset allocation methods.

15.5.1 Integrated Asset Allocation

The integrated asset allocation strategy separately examines (1) capital market conditions and (2) the investor's objectives and constraints. These factors are then combined to establish the portfolio asset mix that offers the best opportunity for meeting the investor's needs given the capital market forecast. The actual returns from the portfolio are then used as inputs to an iterative process in which changes over time in the investor's objectives and constraints are noted along with changes in capital market expectations. The optimal portfolio is then revised based on this update of investor needs and capital market expectations.

This integrated approach to portfolio formation is illustrated in Exhibit 15.18.

As described by Sharpe (1987, 1990), there are three key steps to integrated asset allocation. First, both capital market conditions and investor-specific objectives and constraints (e.g., risk tolerance, investment horizon, tax status) are summarized before the asset mix is determined. The processes by which the capital market and investor-specific data are summarized are shown in boxes C2 and I2, respectively, with the outcomes of those processes in boxes C3 and I3. An example of C3 might be the Markowitz efficient frontier containing portfolios of optimal risk–expected return combinations; the end product of I3 might be captured in an investment policy statement.

The second step in the integrated asset allocation process is to combine the information from the first step in order to select the single best portfolio for the investor in question. This

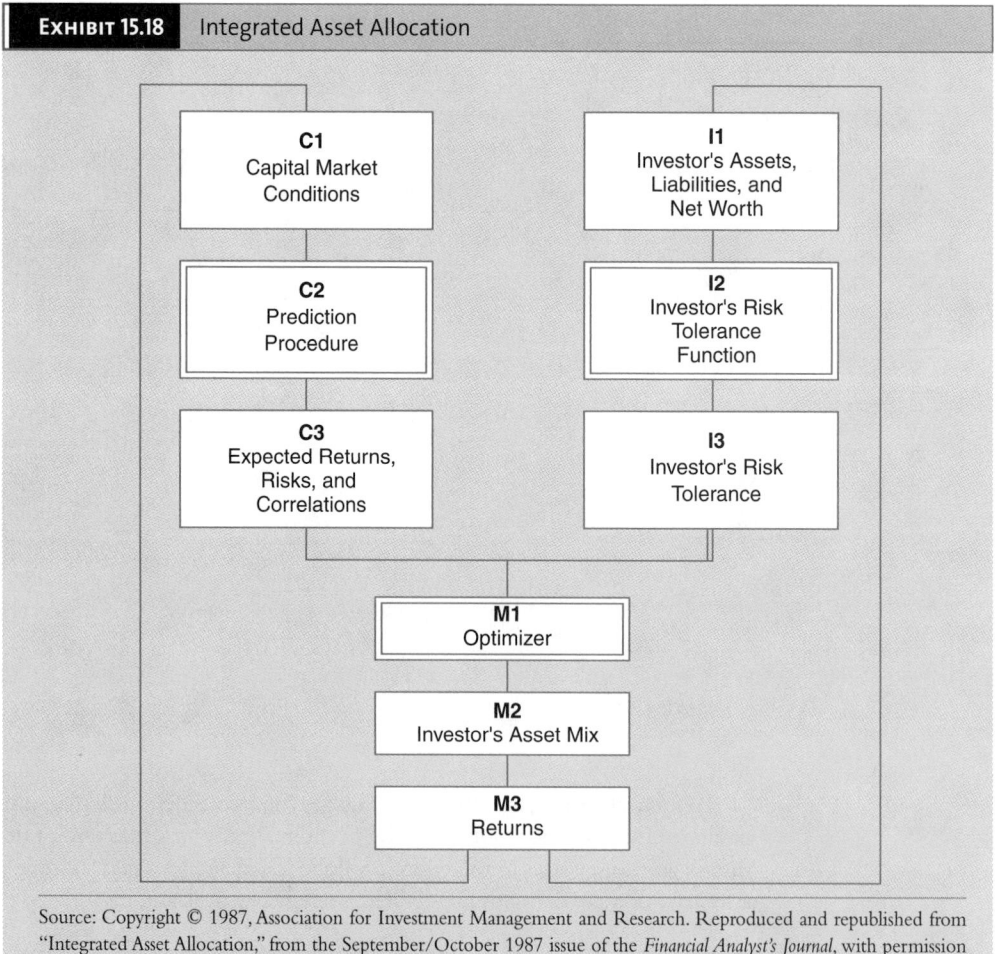

EXHIBIT 15.18   Integrated Asset Allocation

C1 Capital Market Conditions

I1 Investor's Assets, Liabilities, and Net Worth

C2 Prediction Procedure

I2 Investor's Risk Tolerance Function

C3 Expected Returns, Risks, and Correlations

I3 Investor's Risk Tolerance

M1 Optimizer

M2 Investor's Asset Mix

M3 Returns

Source: Copyright © 1987, Association for Investment Management and Research. Reproduced and republished from "Integrated Asset Allocation," from the September/October 1987 issue of the *Financial Analyst's Journal*, with permission from the CFA Institute. All Right Reserved.

Copyright 1987, CFA Institute. Reproduced and republished from the Financial Analysts Journal with permission from CFA Institute. All rights reserved.

is captured by the optimizer box in M1, with the resulting asset mix being shown in M2. One simple way of seeing how M1 might work would be to calculate the *expected utility (EU)* of each prospective asset mix using the following formula:

15.8

$$EU_{pk} = ER_p - \left(\frac{\sigma_p^2}{RT_k}\right) = ER_p - \text{(Risk Penalty)}$$

where ER_p and σ_p^2 are the expected return and variance for Portfolio p (which come from C3) and RT_k is the risk-tolerance factor for Investor k (which comes from I3). The risk-tolerance factor is an estimate intended to capture the essence of an investor's attitude toward risk bearing. Notice that the higher this number, the more risk tolerant the investor is and, hence, the less Portfolio p has its expected return "penalized" by its risk level. The optimal asset mix for any particular investor is then the one that generates the highest level of expected utility.

As an example of the first two stages of the integrated asset allocation process, Panel A of Exhibit 15.19 shows the expected returns and variances for three different potential asset mixes (C3), while Panel B lists risk-tolerance factors for two investors (I3). Panel C shows the result of the expected utility calculations that combine this information (M2). For instance, the expected utility generated by Portfolio A for Investor 1 is 5.6 (= 7 − 7/5), which is the largest value of the three potential allocations and therefore his optimal asset mix. Conversely, Investor 2 is more tolerant of risk and finds that Portfolio C, which generates an expected utility level of 8.5 (= 9 − 20/40), is her optimal allocation. Notice that the risk-tolerance factor effectively deflates the risk penalty, allowing more risk-tolerant investors to pursue more volatile portfolios with higher expected returns.

Exhibit 15.19	Optimal Portfolio Selection: An Example

A. Prospective Efficient Portfolios (C3)

Portfolio	Asset Mix Stock	Bond	ER	σ^2
A	20%	80%	7%	7%
B	50	50	8	13
C	80	20	9	20

B. Risk-Tolerance Factors (I3)

Investor	RT	
1	5	(i.e., *less* tolerant)
2	40	(i.e., *more* tolerant)

C. Expected Utility Results (M2)

	A	B	C
Investor #1 *EU*	5.6	5.4	5.0
Investor #2 *EU*	6.8	7.7	8.5

The third stage of the integrated portfolio process occurs after enough time has passed that the optimal portfolio's actual performance can be compared with the manager's original expectations. This evaluation process is represented by Box M3 in Exhibit 15.18. Following this assessment, the manager can then make adjustments to the portfolio by including any new information into the optimization process. Adjustments to the initial asset mix can result from either a fundamental change in capital market conditions (e.g., increased inflation) or a change in the investor's circumstances (e.g., increased risk tolerance). It is this feedback loop that makes portfolio management a *dynamic* process.

15.5.2 STRATEGIC ASSET ALLOCATION

Strategic asset allocation is used to determine the long-term policy asset weights in a portfolio. Typically, long-term average asset returns, risk, and covariances are used as estimates of future capital market results. Efficient frontiers are generated using this historical return information, and the investor decides which asset mix is appropriate for his or her needs during the planning horizon. This results in a *constant-mix* asset allocation with periodic rebalancing to adjust the portfolio to the specified asset weights.

The strategic allocation process is similar to the integrated asset allocation process shown in Exhibit 15.18 but without the feedback loops. That is, as just described, the manager will determine the long-term asset allocation that is best suited for a particular investor. However, once this asset mix is established, the manager does not constantly attempt to adjust the allocation according to temporary changes in market and investor circumstances. Thus, as Ezra (1998) points out, the strategic allocation should define the basic nature of the trade-off between opportunity and safety that confronts the investor.

As an example, Brown, Garlappi, and Tiu (2008) examined the asset allocation patterns of college and university endowment funds in the United States and Canada. Exhibit 15.20 shows both the average actual and strategic (i.e., target) investment proportions for their fund sample in 2002 and 2005. There are several interesting things to note. First, endowment fund managers made some dramatic adjustments in the targeted investment proportions over these years; for instance, the strategic allocations to both U.S. equity (49.6% to 44.7%) and U.S. fixed-income (25.1% to 21.5%) *declined* significantly. Second, at the same time, managers apparently made an explicit decision to shift these assets to investments in the foreign equity and hedge fund categories. Finally, planned investments in the rest of the asset classes listed remained relatively stable, which is consistent with the idea of a strategic allocation as a long-term view.

15.5.3 TACTICAL ASSET ALLOCATION

Unlike an investor's strategic allocation, which is set with a long-term focus and modified infrequently, a tactical approach to asset allocation constantly adjusts the asset class mix in the portfolio in an attempt to take advantage of changing market conditions. With tactical asset allocation, these adjustments are driven solely by perceived changes in the relative values of the various asset classes; the investor's risk tolerance and investment constraints are assumed to be constant over time. In Exhibit 15.18, it is equivalent to an integrated approach but removes the feedback loop involving investor-specific information (i.e., I2).

Tactical asset allocation is often based on the premise of *mean reversion*, which as we have seen, holds that whatever a security's return has been in the recent past, it will eventually revert to its long-term average (mean) value. This assessment is usually done on a comparative basis. For instance, suppose that the ratio of stock and bond returns is normally 1.2, reflecting the greater degree of risk in the equity market. Then, if in the most recent investment period, stock returns were double those of bond returns, the tactical investor might determine that bonds

EXHIBIT 15.20	Strategic and Tactical Asset Allocations for University Endowment Funds

A. 2005 Year-End Data (709 Funds)

Asset Class	Actual Allocation	Strategic Allocation	Tactical Adjustment
U.S. Equity	45.7%	44.7%	+1.0%
Non–U.S. Equity	12.7	12.8	−0.1
U.S. Fixed Income	20.5	21.5	−1.0
Non-U.S. Fixed Income	0.9	1.0	−0.1
Real Estate—Public	1.2	1.3	−0.1
Real Estate—Private	2.0	2.2	−0.2
Hedge Funds	8.9	9.0	−0.1
Private Equity—Venture Capital	0.8	1.5	−0.7
Private Equity—Buyout	1.6	2.5	−0.9
Natural Resources	1.0	1.2	−0.2
Cash	3.4	1.6	+1.8
Other	1.4	0.8	+0.6

B. 2002 Year-End Data (535 Funds)

Asset Class	Actual Allocation	Strategic Allocation	Tactical Adjustment
U.S. Equity	46.4%	49.6%	−3.2%
Non–U.S. Equity	10.2	10.6	−0.4
U.S. Fixed Income	25.9	25.1	+0.8
Non-U.S. Fixed Income	1.1	0.7	+0.4
Real Estate—Public	1.2	1.0	+0.2
Real Estate—Private	1.4	1.2	+0.2
Hedge Funds	5.6	4.9	+0.7
Private Equity—Venture Capital	1.0	1.9	−0.9
Private Equity—Buyout	1.2	1.9	−0.7
Natural Resources	0.4	0.3	+0.1
Cash	4.0	1.6	+2.4
Other	1.6	1.2	+0.4

Source: Adapted from Keith C. Brown, Lorenzo Garlappi, and Cristian Tiu, "Does Asset Allocation Determine Portfolio Performance? Evidence From University Endowment Funds," Working Paper, June 11, 2008.

were now undervalued relative to stock and most likely to be the best-performing asset class in the coming period. Accordingly, he should then overweight the fixed-income component of his portfolio, shifting, say, from a 60%–40% initial mix of stocks and bonds to a 50%–50% split.

For the preceding description, notice that tactical asset allocation is an inherently *contrarian* method of investing. That is, the investor adopting this approach will always be buying the asset class that is currently out of favour—on a relative basis, at least—and selling the asset class with the highest market value. In the preceding example, this was the case when the investor underweighted his stock allocation after stock prices rose substantially compared to bond prices. DuBois (1992) notes that how frequently the investor chooses to adjust the asset class mix in the portfolio will depend on several factors, such as the general level of volatility in the capital markets, the relative size of the equity and fixed-income risk premiums, and changes in the fundamental macroeconomic environment.

15.5.4 INSURED ASSET ALLOCATION

Insured asset allocation likewise results in continual adjustments in the portfolio allocation. Insured asset allocation assumes that expected market returns and risks are constant over time, while the investor's objectives and constraints change as his or her wealth position changes. For example, rising portfolio values increase the investor's wealth and consequently his or her ability to handle risk, which means the investor can increase his or her exposure to risky assets. Declines in the portfolio's value lower the investor's wealth, consequently decreasing his or her ability to handle risk, which means the portfolio's exposure to risky assets must decline. Often, insured asset allocation involves only two assets, such as common stocks and T-bills. As stock prices rise, the asset allocation increases the stock component. As stock prices fall, the stock component of the mix falls while the T-bill component increases. This is opposite of what would happen under tactical asset allocation. Insured asset allocation is like the integrated approach without the feedback loop on the capital market side (i.e., C2 in Exhibit 15.18). It is sometimes called a *constant proportion* strategy because of the shifts that occur as wealth changes.

15.5.5 SELECTING AN ACTIVE ALLOCATION METHOD

Which asset allocation strategy is used depends on the perceptions of the variability in the client's objectives and constraints and the perceived relationship between past and future capital market conditions. If we believe that capital market conditions are relatively constant over time, we might use insured asset allocation. If we believe that the client's goals, risk preferences, and constraints are constant, we likewise might use tactical asset allocation. Integrated asset allocation assumes that both the investor's needs and capital market conditions are variable and therefore must be constantly monitored. Under these conditions, the portfolio mix must be updated constantly to reflect current changes in these parameters.

Summary

1. Passive equity portfolios attempt to track the returns of an established benchmark, such as the S&P/TSX, or some other benchmark that meets the investor's needs. Active portfolios attempt to add value relative to their benchmark by market timing and/or by seeking to buy undervalued stocks. Index mutual funds and exchange-traded funds are popular ways for small investors to make passive investments.

2. Tracking error, which is defined as the standard deviation of the difference between the returns to a managed fund and a benchmark, is a convenient way to categorize various management styles. Portfolios with tracking errors of less than 1% are generally considered to be passive, while active equity strategies often have tracking errors in excess of 5%.

3. There are several methods for constructing and managing a passive portfolio, including full replication of a benchmark or sampling. Also, several active management strategies exist, including sector rotation, the use of factor models, quantitative screens, and linear programming methods.

4. A growth-oriented investor focuses on the earnings per share (EPS) component of the *P/E* ratio and its economic determinants. They look for companies that he or she expects to exhibit rapid EPS growth in the future; and often implicitly assume that the *P/E* ratio will remain constant over the near term, meaning that the stock price will rise as forecasted earnings growth is realized. A value-oriented investor focuses on the price component (i.e., the numerator) of the *P/E* ratio. He or she must be convinced

that the price of the stock is "cheap" by some means of comparison, not caring a great deal about current earnings or the fundamental drivers of earnings growth. Such an investor often implicitly assumes that the *P/E* ratio of a "cheap" stock is below its natural level and that the market will soon "correct" this situation by increasing the stock price with little or no change in earnings.

5. Regardless of whatever investment objective a manager might profess to follow, style analysis allows the portfolio to speak for itself. The process of returns-based style analysis involves using the past returns to a manager's portfolio along with those to a series of indices representing different investment styles in an effort to determine the relationship between the fund and those specific styles. The more highly correlated a fund's returns are with a given style index, the greater the weighting that style is given in the statistical assessment.

6. Because equity portfolios typically are used with other assets in an investor's overall portfolio, we reviewed several common asset allocation strategies, including integrated asset allocation, strategic asset allocation, tactical asset allocation, and insured asset allocation. The basic difference between these strategies is whether they rely on current market expectations or long-run projections, and whether the investor's objectives and constraints remain constant over the planning horizon or change with market conditions.

Key Terms

130/30 strategy, p. 466
completeness fund, p. 458
contrarian, p. 466
earnings momentum, p. 468

full replication, p. 458
price momentum, p. 466
quadratic optimization, p. 458
sampling, p. 458

sector rotation strategy, p. 464
style analysis, p. 474
tactical asset allocation, p. 464
tracking error, p. 459

Suggested Readings

Ammann, Manuel, and Heinz Zimmermann. "Tracking Error and Tactical Asset Allocation." *Financial Analysts Journal* 57, no. 2 (March/April 2001): 32–43.

Bernstein, Richard. *Style Investing: Unique Insight into Equity Management.* New York: Wiley, 1995.

Burns, Terrence E. *Asset Allocation in a Changing World.* Charlottesville, VA: AIMR, 1998a.

Dreman, David M. *Contrarian Investment Strategies: The Next Generation.* New York: Simon & Schuster, 1998.

Hopkins, Peter J. B., and C. Hayes Miller. *Country, Sector, and Company Factors in Global Equity Portfolios.* Charlottesville, VA: Research Foundation of AIMR, 2001.

Li, Bin, and Lawrence Krzanowski. "What Determines the Holding Period of an Investor?" *Canadian Investment Review* 13, no. 3 (October 2000): 18+.

Potvin, Paul. "Passive Management, the TSE 300 and the Toronto 35 Stock Indexes." *Canadian Investment Review* 5, no. 1: (April 1992): 61–65.

Sharpe, William F. "Expected Utility Asset Allocation," *Financial Analysts Journal* 63, no. 5 (September/October 2007): 18–30.

Siegel, Jeremy. *The Future for Investors: Why the Tried and the True Triumph Over the Bold and the New.* Crown Business, New York., 2005.

Singer, Jonathan. "Does Size Matter?" *Canadian Investment Review* 18, no. 1 (April 2005): 31–32.

CFA   **For Chapter CFA Questions and Problems, please see Appendix A at the end of this text.**

Questions

1. Why have passive portfolio management strategies increased in use over time?

2. What is meant by an indexing portfolio strategy and what is the justification for this strategy? How might it differ from another passive portfolio?

3. Briefly describe four techniques considered active equity portfolio management strategies.

4. Describe several techniques for constructing a passive portfolio.

5. Discuss three strategies active managers can use to add value to their portfolios.
6. How do trading costs and market efficiencies affect the active manager? How may an active manager try to overcome these obstacles to success?
7. Discuss how the four asset allocation strategies differ from one another.
8. Describe the difference between a price momentum strategy and an earnings momentum strategy. Under what conditions would you expect the two approaches to produce similar portfolios?
9. What are the trade-offs involved when constructing a portfolio using a full replication versus a sampling method?
10. Because of inflationary expectations, you expect natural resource stocks, such as mining companies and oil firms, to perform well over the next three to six months. As an active portfolio manager, describe the various methods available to take advantage of this forecast.

Problems

1. Given the monthly returns that follow, how well did the passive portfolio track the S&P 500 benchmark? Find the R^2, alpha, and beta of the portfolio. Compute the average return differential with and without sign.

Month	Portfolio Return	S&P 500 Return
January	5.0%	5.2%
February	−2.3	−3.0
March	−1.8	−1.6
April	2.2	1.9
May	0.4	0.1
June	−0.8	−0.5
July	0.0	0.2
August	1.5	1.6
September	−0.3	−0.1
October	−3.7	−4.0
November	2.4	2.0
December	0.3	0.2

2. Consider the following trading and performance data for four different equity mutual funds:

	Fund W	Fund X	Fund Y	Fund Z
Assets under Management, avg. for past 12 months (mil)	$289.4	$653.7	$1,298.4	$5,567.3
Security Sales, past 12 months (mil)	$37.2	$569.3	$1,453.8	$437.1
Expense Ratio	0.33%	0.71%	1.13%	0.21%
Pretax Return, 3-yr. avg.	9.98%	10.65%	10.12%	9.83%
Tax-adjusted Return, 3-yr. avg.	9.43%	8.87%	9.34%	9.54%

a. Calculate the portfolio turnover ratio for each fund.
b. Which two funds are most likely to be actively managed and which two are most likely passive funds? Explain.
c. Calculate the tax cost ratio for each fund.
d. Which funds were the most and least tax efficient in the operations? Why?

3. As the chief investment officer for a money management firm specializing in taxable individual investors, you are trying to establish a strategic asset allocation for two different clients. You have established that Ms. A has a risk-tolerance factor of 8 while Mr. B's risk-tolerance factor is 27. The characteristics for four model portfolios follow:

	Asset Mix			
Portfolio	Stock	Bond	ER	Σ^2
1	5%	95%	8%	5%
2	25	75	9	10
3	70	30	10	16
4	90	10	11	25

a. Calculate the expected utility of each prospective portfolio for each of the two clients.
b. Which portfolio represents the optimal strategic allocation for Ms. A? Which portfolio is optimal for Mr. B? Explain why there is a difference in these two outcomes.
c. For Ms. A, what level of risk tolerance would leave her indifferent between having Portfolio 1 or Portfolio 2 as her strategic allocation? Demonstrate.

4. Consider the annual returns produced by two different active equity portfolio managers (A and B) as well as those to the stock index with which they are both compared:

Period	Manager A	Manager B	Index
1	12.8%	13.9%	11.8%
2	−2.1	−4.2	−2.2
3	15.6	13.5	18.9
4	0.8	2.9	−0.5
5	−7.9	−5.9	−3.9
6	23.2	26.3	21.7
7	−10.4	−11.2	−13.2
8	5.6	5.5	5.3
9	2.3	4.2	2.4
10	19.0	18.8	19.7

a. Did either manager outperform the index, based on the average annual return differential that he or she produced relative to the benchmark? Demonstrate.

b. Calculate the tracking error for each manager relative to the index. Which manager did a better job of limiting his or her client's unsystematic risk exposure? Explain.

CANADIAN MUTUAL FUND PROJECT

The objective of this project is to give the students a general understanding of the practice of portfolio management by studying selected Canadian mutual funds. Through the project, the students also become familiar with various categories of mutual funds and the information available about Canadian mutual funds. The project can be done on an individual or a group basis.

Most of the information needed to complete the project is available online, in particular, at GlobeFund.com of the *Globe and Mail* and Morningstar.ca of Morningstar Canada. It may be useful to obtain the annual report of the fund at www.sedar.com, although it is not essential for this project. SEDAR is the filing system of the Canadian Securities Administrators (CSA) to which mutual fund companies submit their reports.

Preparation

Choose one mutual fund from each of the following six categories as classified by GlobeFund.com: growth, growth and income, international growth, aggressive growth, income, and capital preservation. Limit your choice to funds covered by both GlobeFund.com and Morningstar.ca, although the latter has a more extensive classification system. Each fund you choose should have been around for at least 10 years. You may want to include funds that you or people you know have bought. It would make the research more relevant. You may also want to include both highly ranked funds and underperforming funds in order to learn from their successes and failures.

Tasks

Below is a list of questions for each of the funds you selected. Most of the questions are fact-finding. Create a summary table to record the facts you've found across the six funds. Open-ended questions for you to comment and discuss are in *italics*.

The Company

- What is the name of the mutual fund company?
- How much are the total net assets managed by the company?
- What is its ranking of total net assets of the company?
- Who are the portfolio managers and what are their qualifications?
- How many different funds does this company hold?

The Fund

- What is the name of the fund?
- What is the fund's category or asset class?
- What is the fund's asset value?

Fund Objectives

- What are the fund's objectives?
- What is the fund's management style? Morningstar.ca reports the style of most of the five-star funds. If you can't find the style of your fund, see if you can tell from the objectives of the fund.
- What is the benchmark for the fund?
- *Based on the objectives and management style, do you think the benchmark is suitable for the fund or not, and why? If not, what is a suitable benchmark?*

Fund Risk and Return

- What are the management expense ratio (MER) of the fund, a competing fund, and the average in the same category?
- What are the one-, three-, and five-year return of the fund and the benchmark?
- What is the volatility measure as stated on GlobeFund.com (low, medium, high)? *Do you agree with this considering the current economic situation?*
- What are the betas of the fund and the benchmark? GlobeFund.com reports three-year beta of the funds.
- *How would you interpret the betas of the fund versus the benchmark?*
- Use a chart to show the price movement of the fund and the benchmark during the past five years.
- *Report and comment on your observations of the above chart.*

Asset Allocation

Most of the following can be answered with a self-explanatory pie chart or table.
- What is the asset allocation of the fund? Report value and percentage in equity, fixed income, and cash. What are the sectoral weightings of the fund? Report value and percentage of the top five sectors.
- What is the geographic composition of the fund? Report value and percentage of the top five regions or countries.
- What are the value and percentage of the top 10 holdings?
- *Given your understanding of the objective of the fund and where the global economy and industry are going, do you think the above four aspects of allocations of the funds are reasonable? Would you recommend any adjustments and why?*

Current Issues

- Do an online search to find any analyst's report and any recent news on the fund and the fund company.
- *Based on the above, discuss three internal or external developments that are important to the investors, e.g., turnover of fund managers, mergers and acquisition of the mutual fund company, changes in regulations.*
- *Was the fund impacted by the global financial crisis in any way? What did the fund manager do to cope with or to take advantage of the crisis? If you were the fund manager, what would you do?*

Evaluation

- What is the fund's five-star ranking by GlobeFund.com and Morningstar.ca, respectively?
- *Compare and contrast the ranking system of the above two sources.*
- *As an individual investor, evaluate GlobeFund.com and Morningstar.ca as providers of mutual fund information. What are the strengths and weaknesses of each?*

Overall

- *Based on the table that you have compiled, compare and contrast your answers for each fact-finding question. List and discuss the three most interesting observations.*
- *In relation to today's economy, are there any specific types of funds that a highly risk averse investor should shy away from during this time?*
- *Which funds are most vulnerable/resilient to a global/national recession?*
- *Based on your personal investment objectives and risk tolerance, what type of fund best suits you? Why?*

16

Bond Portfolio Management Strategies

In this chapter, we shift our attention to an examination of the most widely used bond portfolio management strategies. After a brief discussion of how bonds have performed as an asset class in recent years and how fixed-income investment styles are typically classified, we will see that these strategies can be classified into one of five broad approaches: passive, active, core-plus, matched-funding, and contingent and structured active management. In the following sections, we describe these approaches in more detail and give examples of how each is used in practice.

16.1 Bond Portfolio Performance, Style, and Strategy

The volatile pattern of interest rates in recent decades has provided increasingly attractive returns to bond investors of all types. Active bond portfolio managers in particular have found the frequent opportunities to realize capital gains that resulted from those rates shifts to be especially attractive. However, despite the generally favourable economic climate that has prevailed for most of the last 25 years, fixed-income portfolios generally produced both less return and less volatility than other asset classes (e.g., domestic equity, foreign equity). Reilly and Wright (2004) confirmed this in their examination of the investment performance of 36 classes of long-term securities over the 21-year time horizon that began in 1980. Exhibit 16.1, which summarizes their findings, shows that bond portfolios—as represented by the Lehman Brothers U.S. Government Bond (LBG), U.S. Corporate Bond (LBC), and U.S. Aggregate Bond (LBA) indices—fall at the lower end of the risk-return spectrum measured by the capital market line, making them a conservative choice within an investor's overall asset allocation strategy. On the other hand, the relatively low historical correlation between fixed-income and equity securities—Reilly and Wright (2004) calculated this to be 0.27—have made bond portfolios an excellent tool for diversifying risk as well.

In Chapter 15, we saw that it was useful to classify the investment *style* of equity portfolios along two dimensions: market capitalization and relative valuation (i.e., value vs. growth). Similarly, the investment style of a bond portfolio can be summarized by its two most important characteristics: *credit quality* and *interest rate sensitivity*. Exhibit 16.2 shows how the 3 × 3 style grid can be adjusted to accommodate these

After you read this chapter, you should be able to answer the following questions:

1. How is the investment style box defined for fixed-income portfolios?

2. What are the five major classes of bond portfolio management strategies?

3. What are the two main types of passive bond portfolio management strategies?

4. What are the main active bond portfolio management strategies and what is core-plus bond portfolio management?

5. How does a matched-funding approach to bond portfolio management work and what are the techniques?

6. What is meant by a contingent immunization approach to bond portfolio management?

| **EXHIBIT 16.1** | Risk-Return Comparison Between Bond Portfolios and Other Asset Classes |

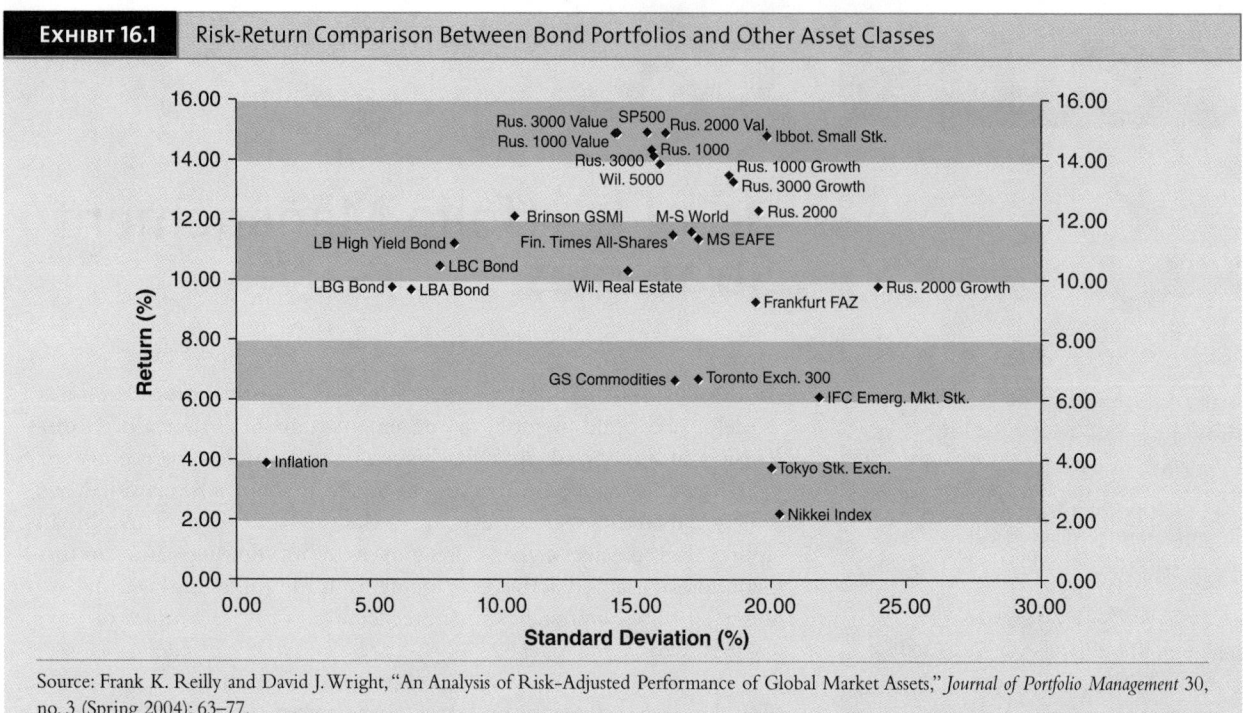

Source: Frank K. Reilly and David J. Wright, "An Analysis of Risk-Adjusted Performance of Global Market Assets," *Journal of Portfolio Management* 30, no. 3 (Spring 2004): 63–77.

| **EXHIBIT 16.2** | Fixed-Income Investment Style Grid |

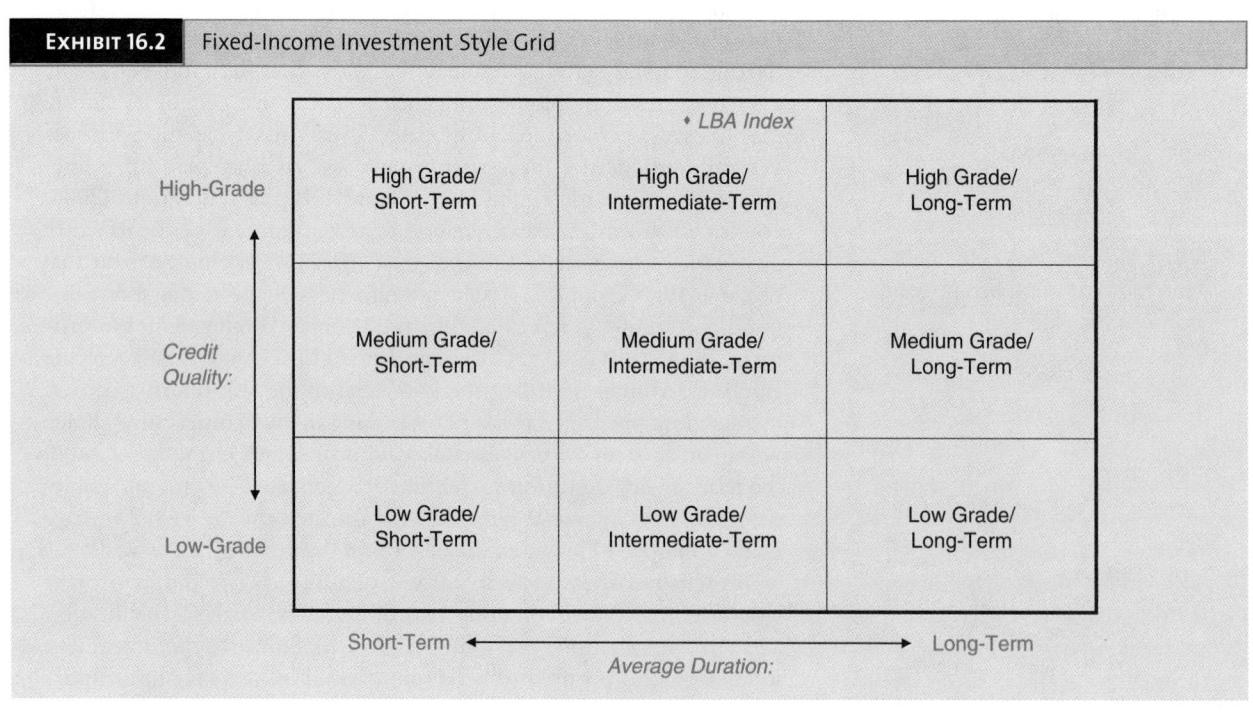

Royal Bank's Fixed Income Education Centre:
https://www6.royalbank.com/educationcentre/english/fixed-income.html.

dimensions. Specifically, the average credit quality of the portfolio can be classified as *high grade* (e.g., government, agency, AAA-rated or AA-rated corporate bonds), *medium grade* (e.g., A-rated or BBB-rated), or *low grade* (e.g., below BBB-rated), based on the profile of the composite holding. On the other hand, we established previously that average duration is an effective way to measure the portfolio's price sensitivity to interest rate changes. Accordingly, the second dimension of the bond portfolio's investment style can be separated as *short-term* (e.g., duration less than 3.0 years), *intermediate-term* (e.g., duration between 3.0 and 6.5 years), or *long-term* (e.g., duration above 6.5 years). For example, the Lehman Brothers U.S. Aggregate Bond index is purposely constructed to mimic the profile of the investment grade fixed-income security market in the United States, which typically consists of 70% to 80% government, agency, or AAA-rated bonds. Also, the LBA index is structured to maintain an average duration of between 4.0 and 5.0 years. Thus, it would plot in the middle cell of the top row of the style grid in Exhibit 16.2 and would be classified as a high-grade/intermediate-term portfolio.

Just as the inherent investment style of one bond portfolio compared to another can vary widely, so too can the underlying strategic approach adopted by the managers who formed those portfolios. As is often the case, the nature of the investor's problem usually dictates the way in which the manager will go about designing the bond portfolio that solves that problem. Consequently, an investor who wants a specific amount of cash in the near future will likely have a very different strategy for assembling a fixed-income portfolio compared to someone whose goal is to maximize capital gains resulting from an anticipated shift in interest rates. Exhibit 16.3, which is based in part on the development in Leibowitz (1986a), indicates that bond portfolio strategies can be divided into the five broad groups mentioned earlier.

EXHIBIT 16.3 Bond Portfolio Investment Strategies

1. Passive Management Strategies
   a. Buy and hold
   b. Indexing
2. Active Management Strategies
   a. Interest rate anticipation
   b. Valuation analysis
   c. Credit analysis
   d. Yield spread analysis
   e. Sector/country analysis
   f. Prepayment/option analysis
   g. Other (e.g., liquidity, currency, anomaly capture)
3. Core-Plus Management Strategies
   a. Enhanced indexing
   b. Active/passive "plus" sectors
4. Matched-Funding Strategies
   a. Dedicated: exact cash match
   b. Dedicated: optimal cash match
   c. Classical immunization
   d. Horizon matching
5. Contingent & Structured Strategies
   a. Contingent immunization
   b. Structured management

Prior to the 1960s, only the first two strategic approaches—passive and active—were widely available and most bond portfolios were managed on a buy-and-hold basis with the intention of producing a steady stream of cash flow for the investor. The early 1970s saw a growing level of curiosity with alternative active bond portfolio management approaches, while the late 1970s and early 1980s were characterized by record-breaking inflation and interest rates as well as extremely volatile yields across all spectrums of the bond market. This, in turn, led to the introduction of many new financial instruments in response to the increase in rate volatility (e.g., adjustable-rate bonds and mortgages). Since the mid-1980s, matched-funding techniques, core-plus strategies, and contingent bond management approaches have been developed to meet the increased needs of institutional investors, such as pension funds and insurance companies. Finally, beginning in the mid-1990s, it has become increasingly common to see bonds combined with positions in derivative securities in the management of sophisticated fixed income portfolios; this topic will be explored in later chapters.

16.2   Passive Management Strategies

PC-Bond Analytics is a leading provider of Canadian fixed income indices. Go to http://www.canadianbondindices.com.

Two specific passive portfolio management strategies exist. First is a **buy-and-hold strategy** in which a manager selects a portfolio of bonds based on the objectives and constraints of the client with the intent of holding these bonds to maturity. In the second passive strategy—**indexing**—the objective is to construct a portfolio of bonds that will be matched as closely as possible to the performance of a specified bond index, such as the Canadian DEX Universe Bond Index, or the Lehman Brothers Corporate/Government Bond Index (U.S.).

16.2.1   BUY-AND-HOLD STRATEGY

The simplest portfolio management strategy is to buy and hold. While obviously not unique to bond investors, this approach involves finding fixed-income securities with the desired levels of credit quality, coupon rate, term to maturity or duration, and other important indenture provisions, such as call and sinking fund features. Buy-and-hold investors do not consider active trading as a viable alternative to achieve abnormal returns but, rather, look for bond issues whose maturity/duration characteristics approximate their stipulated investment horizon in order to reduce price and reinvestment risk. Many successful bond investors and portfolio managers follow a modified buy-and-hold strategy wherein they purchase an issue with the intention of holding it to maturity, but still look for opportunities to trade into a more desirable position should the occasion to do so arise. Of course, if the buy-and-hold approach is modified too much, it becomes an active strategy.

Whether the manager follows a strict or modified buy-and-hold approach, the critical concept is finding investment vehicles that possess the desired attributes. The strategy does not restrict the investor to accept whatever the market has to offer, nor does it imply that selectivity is unimportant. Attractive high-yielding issues with desirable features and quality standards are actively sought. For example, these investors recognize that agency issues or asset-backed securities generally provide attractive incremental returns relative to Government of Canada bonds with little sacrifice in quality, or that various call and put features can materially impact the risk and realized yield of an issue. Thus, successful buy-and-hold investors use their knowledge of market and issue characteristics to seek out attractive realized yields. Aggressive buy-and-hold investors also incorporate timing considerations into their strategy by using their knowledge of market rates, yield spreads, and expectations.

Finally, recognize that there is an important fundamental difference between managing a bond portfolio and a stock portfolio on a buy-and-hold basis. Since bonds eventually mature with the passing of time whereas stock shares do not, the bond manager is faced with the need to periodically reinvest the funds from a matured issue. However, it is possible for the stock manager to employ a "pure" buy-and-hold strategy in which he never adjusts the portfolio's composition once it is formed. Fixed-income portfolio managers often address this concern by forming a **bond ladder** in which they divide their investment funds evenly across the portfolio into instruments that mature at regular intervals. For instance, for a manager with an intermediate-term investment focus, instead of investing all of her funds in a five-year zero-coupon security—which would become a four-year security after one year had passed—she could follow a laddered approach and buy equal amounts of bonds maturing in annual intervals between one and nine years. The idea would then be to hold each bond to maturity, but to reinvest the proceeds from a maturing bond into a new instrument with a maturity at the far end of the ladder (i.e., to reinvest a maturing bond in a brand-new nine-year issue). In this way, the desired maturity/duration target for the portfolio can be maintained over time without having to continually adjust the investment weights for the remaining positions.

16.2.2 INDEXING STRATEGY

In our earlier discussion of efficient capital markets, we cited numerous empirical studies that have demonstrated that the majority of money managers have not been able to match the risk-adjusted return performance of common stock and bond indices. As a result, many clients have opted to index some part of their bond portfolios, which means that the portfolio manager builds a portfolio that will match the performance of a selected bond market index, such as a Canadian index, the DEX Universe bond index, or an American one, such as a Lehman Brothers index, a Merrill Lynch index, or a Salomon Brothers index. In such a case, the bond index manager is judged not on the basis of his ability to produce abnormal returns relative to the index, but by how closely his portfolio produces returns that match those of the index. When describing similar concepts for stock index managers in Chapter 15, we saw that **tracking error** was a useful tool to judge how closely the returns of a managed portfolio match (i.e., "track") those of the targeted index. Recall that tracking error is measured as the standard deviation of the *difference* in returns produced by the managed portfolio and the index over time. An annualized tracking error statistic of 1% or less usually indicates that an index fund manager is doing a good job matching the performance of the index.

As with stock index funds, when designing an actual bond portfolio that attempts to mimic a hypothetical index, managers can follow two different paths: *full replication* or *stratified sampling*. While it is quite common when constructing stock index funds to fully replicate the underlying index, it is more likely that the bond index fund manager will follow a sampling approach, wherein a smaller number of instruments are held in the actual portfolio than appear in the index. One reason for this is that bond indices often contain several thousand specific issues and are adjusted frequently, making them both impractical and expensive to replicate. The goal of the stratified sampling approach is to create a bond portfolio that matches the important characteristics of the underlying index—such as credit quality, industry composition, maturity/duration, or coupon rate—while maintaining a portfolio that is more cost effective to manage. To the extent that the manager is not able to match these characteristics over time, the tracking error of the indexed portfolio will typically increase.

When initiating an indexing strategy, the selection of an appropriate market index is clearly a very important decision, chiefly because it directly determines the client's risk-return results. Consequently, it is important for investors to be acquainted with the main characteristics (e.g., maturity/duration, credit quality) of their selected index. Reilly and Wright (1994, 1997, 2005) have examined many aspects of the major bond indices, such as their risk-return characteristics and the correlation between them over time. Also, Dialynas and Murata (2006) and Volpert (2001) discuss how the characteristics of indices affect their performance in different interest rate environments. For bond indices, it is also important to be aware of how the aggregate bond market and the indices change over time. Reilly, Kao, and Wright (1992) demonstrated that the market experienced significant shifts in composition, maturity, and duration since 1975, which can significantly impact the tracking error performance of an indexed portfolio.[1]

16.2.3 BOND INDEXING IN PRACTICE: AN EXAMPLE

To see how two actual managers have responded to the challenge of forming a bond portfolio designed to track one of the leading indices, we consider the several aspects of the Vanguard Total Bond Index Fund (ticker: VBMFX) and the iShare Lehman U.S. Aggregate (ticker: AGG) exchange-traded fund over a recent investment period. Both of these portfolios were specifically created to mimic the performance of the Lehman Brothers U.S. Aggregate index—whose formal ticker symbol is LBUSTRUU—and represent the two methods widely used in practice to create indexed portfolios for retail investors (i.e., index mutual funds and ETFs).

Exhibit 16.4 summarizes many of the most important structural characteristics for these funds, as well as for the underlying index. Notice that both managers have adopted a stratified sampling approach to replicating the index, which contains over 9,000 separate bond

Exhibit 16.4	Indexed Bond Investing: Index Fund versus ETF, January 2008		
	Lehman U.S. Aggregate Index (LBUSTRUU)	**Vanguard Total Bond Index Fund (VBMFX)**	**iShare Lehman U.S. Aggregate ETF (AGG)**
Style Classification (Credit Grade/Duration)	High Grade/ Intermediate-Term	High Grade/ Intermediate-Term	High Grade/ Intermediate-Term
# of Holdings	9,195	2,300	166
Annual Turnover (%)	—	64	483
Annual Yield (%)	4.6	4.9	4.8
Avg. Duration (yrs.)	4.4	4.4	4.6
Avg. Maturity (yrs.)	7.0	7.0	7.1
Credit Quality (% of Portfolio):			
Govt/Agency/AAA	79.3	79.8	74.4
AA	5.3	5.5	7.7
A	8.4	7.9	9.6
BBB	7.1	6.8	7.7
Other/Not Rated	0.0	0.0	0.7
Tracking Error (%/yr.):			
(1/04 – 12/07)	—	0.19	0.61
Expense Ratio (%)	—	0.20	0.20

Source: Prepared by the authors using data from Morningstar, Inc. and Fidelity Investments.

---

1 For further discussion on how bond market dynamics change over time, see Van Horne (2001) and Zhon (2001). For more on how these changes impact the management of an indexed portfolio, see Mossavar-Rahmani (1991) and Fabozzi (2007, chapter 23).

issues. However, there is a wide disparity in how these managers implemented their sampling methods, which can be seen by the fact that the VBMFX holds 2,300 names while AGG attempts to mimic the index by holding only 166 distinct security positions. Not surprisingly, AGG also has a substantially higher portfolio turnover statistic than VBMFX—483% versus 64%—which is undoubtedly a by-product of trying to keep the ETF's portfolio composition aligned with that of the much larger index.

This difference in sampling approaches also leads to slight differences in the relevant investment characteristics of the portfolios. Generally speaking, the index mutual fund maintains a bond portfolio that is closer to the index in terms of average duration (Index: 4.4, VBMFX: 4.4, AGG: 4.6) and credit quality, as measured by the percentage of the portfolio carrying a rating of AAA or higher (Index: 79.3, VBMFX: 79.8, AGG: 74.4). These discrepancies lead, in turn, to a small difference in the tracking error statistic produced by each manager, with VBMFX and AGG having annualized values of 0.19% and 0.61%, respectively. Thus, although the exchange traded fund's tracking error was roughly three times greater than that for the index mutual fund, both statistics fall well within the range of what is considered normal for a passive approach to investing. Finally, the expense ratios for both indexed vehicles are identical (i.e., 20 basis points) and much smaller than what would be typical for an actively managed bond portfolio.

16.3   Active Management Strategies

Find listings of bonds in Canada from corporate to government at the Globe and Mail investor site at http://www.globeinvestor.com/servlet/Page/document/v5/data/bonds.

As we have seen with active equity portfolio management, the active fixed-income manager will attempt to hold a collection of bonds that produce superior risk-adjusted returns (i.e., alpha) compared to the index against which her investment performance is measured. Of course, to beat a benchmark, the active manager must form a portfolio that differs from the holdings comprising the index in a meaningful way. Thus, active bond management strategies are closely tied to the manager's view of what factors or market conditions will be the source of the incremental alpha returns she seeks.

Layard-Liesching (2001) analyzed the investment attributes of several potential sources of alpha for the active bond portfolio manager, all of which depend on some structural barrier that prevents the bond market from being fully efficient. These characteristics are summarized in Exhibit 16.5. He compares each active strategy on four dimensions: (1) scalability (i.e., how large a position can be taken); (2) sustainability (i.e., how far into the future the strategy can be successfully employed); (3) risk-adjusted performance; and (4) extreme values (i.e., how exposed the strategy is to the chance of a large loss). For instance, in the interest rate anticipation category, he argues that duration-based active bets—in which the manager increases or decreases the average duration level of the active portfolio on the belief that the yield curve will either shift down or up, respectively—are highly scalable because they can be implemented with virtually any securities available in the market. However, they also offer the lowest chance of sustainable performance as well as the worst risk-adjusted returns. By contrast, credit risk bets—where the manager takes a position in a bond that she thinks has a substantially different default potential than has been priced by the market—are a much more sustainable and reliable source of potential alpha. Finally, notice that while valuation analysis offers the active manager reasonable alpha potential, it is a more limited strategy from a scalability standpoint because it relies on identifying pricing errors in specific bond issues.[2]

---

2 Additional discussions of active bond portfolio strategies can be found in Malvey (2005), Fong (2001), Squires (1997a), and Churchill (1994).

| EXHIBIT 16.5 | Characteristics of Active Bond Portfolio Strategies | | | | |

Source	Scalability	Sustainability	Risk-Adjusted Performance*	Extreme Values
Interest Rate Anticipation:				
Duration	High	Very Weak	1	Yes
Yield Curve Shape	Low	Very Weak	3	No
Valuation Analysis:				
Security Selection	Low	Medium	5	No
Anomaly Capture	Low	Weak	7	Yes
Credit Risk:	High	Strong	8	Yes
Yield Spread Analysis:				
Optionality	Medium	Medium	7	Yes
Prepayment	Medium	Medium	6	Yes
Liquidity	Low	Strong	3	Yes
Global & Tactical:				
Sector Allocation	High	Strong	6	No
Country Allocation	High	Strong	5	No
Currency	High	Medium	2	Yes

*1 = Low, 10 = High (Note: This list is subjective; investors should make their own assessment of these criteria.)

Source: Adapted from Ronald Layard-Liesching, "Exploiting Opportunities in Global Bond Markets," in *Core-Plus Bond Management* (Charlottesville, VA: AIMR), 2001.

In the remainder of this section, we will explore four categories of active bond strategies—interest rate anticipation, valuation analysis, credit risk, and yield spread analysis—in more detail, as well as describe bond swaps as a means to implement a specific active strategic view.

16.3.1 INTEREST RATE ANTICIPATION

Interest rate anticipation is perhaps the riskiest active management strategy because it involves relying on uncertain forecasts of future interest rates. The idea is to preserve capital when an increase in interest rates is anticipated and achieve attractive capital gains when interest rates are expected to decline. Such objectives usually are attained by altering the portfolio's duration structure (i.e., reducing portfolio duration when interest rates are expected to increase and increasing the portfolio duration when a decline in yields is anticipated). Thus, the risk in such portfolio restructuring is largely a function of these duration alterations. When durations are shortened, substantial income could be sacrificed and capital gain opportunities could be lost if interest rates decline rather than rise. Similarly, the portfolio shifts prompted by anticipation of a decline in rates are very risky. Assuming that we are at a peak in interest rates, it is likely that the yield curve is downward sloping, which means that bond coupons will decline with maturity. Therefore, the investor is sacrificing current income by shifting from high-coupon short bonds to longer duration bonds. At the same time, the portfolio is purposely exposed to greater price volatility that could work against the portfolio if an unexpected increase in yields occurs. Note that the portfolio adjustments prompted by anticipation of an increase in rates involve less risk of an absolute capital loss. When we reduce the maturity, the worst that can happen is that interest income is reduced and/or capital gains are forgone (opportunity cost).

Once future (expected) interest rates have been determined, the procedure relies largely on technical matters. Assume that we expect interest rates to increase and want to preserve our capital by reducing the duration of our portfolio. A popular choice would be high-yielding, short-term obligations, such as T-bills. Although our primary concern is to preserve capital, we would nevertheless look for the best return possible given the maturity constraint. Liquidity also is important because, after interest rates increase, yields may experience a period of stability before they decline, and we would want to shift positions quickly to benefit from the higher income and/or capital gains.

To illustrate this process, suppose that the yield curve for Government of Canada bonds is currently flat across all maturities at 4.75%. We have observed the following "paired" transaction by an active bond portfolio manager:

Bond	Transaction	Type	Maturity (yrs.)	Coupon Rate (%)	Modified Duration
1	Buy	Canadian Govt.	7	8	5.438
2	Sell	Canadian Govt.	13	0	12.698

What does this trade suggest about the manager's view as to how the yield curve is likely to change in the future? First, and foremost, by switching out of a long-maturity, zero-coupon bond into an intermediate-maturity, high-coupon bond, the manager has significantly shortened the modified duration of the position and, presumably, of the entire portfolio. Thus, this trade is consistent with a view that the yield curve will shift up. Further, the manager will also benefit if the shape of the yield curve either stays flat or becomes upward sloping because he has replaced a bond whose future cash flow is paid out at one point in the future (i.e., 13 years) with a shorter-term instrument that makes payments every six months for the next seven years. Finally, notice that by using one Government of Canada bond to replace another, the manager has not introduced any credit risk into the portfolio that might conflict with his interest rate anticipation view.

An alternative way to shorten maturities is to use a *cushion bond*—a high-yielding, long-term bond that carries a coupon substantially above the current market rate and that, due to its current call feature and call price, has a market price lower than what it should be given current market yields. As a result, its yield is higher than normal. An example would be a 10-year bond with a 12% coupon, currently callable at 110. If current market rates are 8%, a non-callable bond would have a price of about 127; however, because of its call price, it will stay close to 110, and its yield will be about 10% rather than 8%. Bond portfolio managers look for cushion bonds when they expect a modest increase in rates because such issues provide attractive current income *and* protection against capital loss. Because these bonds are trading at an abnormally high yield, market rates would have to rise to that abnormal level before their price would react.

The portfolio manager who anticipates higher interest rates, therefore, has two simple strategies available: shorten the portfolio's duration or look for an attractive cushion bond as described by Homer and Leibowitz (2004, chapter 5). In either case, we would want to invest in very liquid issues.

Investors anticipating a decline in interest rates take a totally different stance. The significant risk involved in restructuring a portfolio to take advantage of a decline in interest rates is balanced by the potential for substantial capital gains and holding period returns. When lower interest rates are expected, we should increase the portfolio's duration because the longer the duration, the greater the positive price volatility. Also, liquidity is important because we want to be able to close out the position quickly when the rate drop ends.

Notably, because interest rate sensitivity is critical, it is important to recall that the higher the quality of an obligation, the more sensitive it is to interest rate changes. Therefore, high-grade securities should be used, such as Federal Government, agencies, or corporates rated AAA through BBB. Finally, we want to concentrate on non-callable issues or those with strong call protection because of the substantial call risk discussed in Chapter 11 in connection with the analysis of duration and convexity.

16.3.2 VALUATION ANALYSIS

With **valuation analysis**, the manager attempts to select bonds based on their intrinsic value, which is determined based on their characteristics and the average value of these characteristics in the marketplace. For example, a bond's rating will dictate a certain spread relative to comparable Government of Canada bonds: long maturity might add 60 basis points relative to short maturity (i.e., the maturity spread); a given deferred call feature might require a higher or lower yield; a specified sinking fund would likewise mean higher or lower required yields. Given all the bond characteristics and their cost in terms of yield, we would determine the bond's required yield and, therefore, its implied intrinsic value. We would compare these derived bond values to the prevailing market prices to determine which bonds are under-valued or overvalued. Based on our confidence in the characteristic costs, we would buy the undervalued issues and ignore or sell the overvalued issues.

Success in valuation analysis is based on understanding the characteristics that are important in valuation and being able to accurately *estimate* the yield cost of these characteristics with the understanding that these yield costs change over time.

16.3.3 CREDIT ANALYSIS

A **credit analysis** strategy involves projecting changes in the credit ratings assigned to bonds by the various rating agencies discussed in Chapter 11.[3] These rating changes are affected by internal changes in the entity (e.g., changes in important financial ratios) and by changes in the external environment (i.e., changes in the firm's industry and the economy). During periods of strong economic expansion, even financially weak firms may survive and prosper. In contrast, during severe economic contractions, normally strong firms may find it very difficult to meet financial obligations. Therefore, historically there has been a strong cyclical pattern to rating changes: typically, downgrades increase during economic contractions and decline during economic expansions.

To use credit analysis as a portfolio management strategy, it is necessary to project rating changes prior to the announcement by the rating agencies. This can be quite challenging because the market adjusts rather quickly to bond rating changes, especially to downgrades. Therefore, we want to purchase bond issues expected to be upgraded and sell or avoid those bond issues expected to be downgraded.

Credit Analysis of High-Yield (Junk) Bonds One of the most obvious opportunities for credit analysis is the analysis of high-yield (junk) bonds. Several studies have shown the yield differential between junk bonds (rated below BBB) and Treasury securities ranges from about 200 basis points to almost 1,000 basis points.

Although the spreads have changed, a study by Mody and Taylor (2003) indicated that the average credit quality of high-yield bonds also varied over time as revealed by interest coverage changes over the business cycle. Also, the credit quality of bonds *within* rating categories changed over the business cycle as demonstrated by Reilly and Gentry (2004).

---

3 For a discussion of changes in the aggregate financial risk of U.S. corporations and the opportunities this has created, see Reilly and Gentry (2004). For a presentation on credit analysis that emphasizes changes in credit ratings, see Fabozzi (2005a, chapter 32). For a set of readings on global credit analysis, see Squires (1998b).

Changes in credit quality make credit analysis of high-yield bonds more important, but also more difficult. This means bond analysts and portfolio managers need to engage in detailed credit analysis to select bonds that will survive. Given the spread in promised yields, if a portfolio manager can—through rigorous credit analysis—avoid bonds with a high probability of default or downgrade, high-yield bonds will provide the investor substantial rates of return; see Vine (2001) and Fabozzi (2005a).

Exhibit 16.6 lists the cumulative default rates for bonds with different ratings and for various time periods after issue. Over 10 years—the holding period that is widely used in practice for comparative purposes—the default rate for BBB investment-grade bonds is only 4.44%, but the default rate increases to almost 15% for BB-rated bonds, to over 30% for B-rated bonds, and to almost 50% for CCC-rated bonds. These default rates do not mean investors should avoid high-yield bonds, but they do indicate that extensive credit analysis is a critical component for success within this risky sector of the fixed-income market.

Investing in Defaulted Debt Beyond high-yield bonds with high credit risk and high default rates, a new set of investment opportunities has evolved—investing in defaulted debt. While this sector requires an understanding of legal procedures surrounding bankruptcy as well as economic analysis, Altman (1993) has noted that the returns have generally been consistent with the risk.

Credit Analysis Models The credit analysis of high-yield bonds can use a statistical model or basic fundamental analysis that recognizes some of the unique characteristics of these bonds. Altman and Nammacher (1987) suggest that a modified *Z-score model* (normally used to predict the probability of bankruptcy within two years) can also be used to predict default for these high-yield bonds or as a gauge of changes in credit quality. The Z-score model combines traditional financial measures with a multivariate technique known as *multiple discriminant analysis* to derive a set of weights for the specified variables. The result is an overall credit score (zeta score) for each firm. The model is of the form

$$\textbf{Zeta} = a_0 + a_1 X_1 + a_2 X_2 + a_3 X_3 + \ldots + a_n X_n$$

where:

$$\text{Zeta} = \text{the overall credit score}$$
$$X_1 \ldots X_n = \text{the explanatory variables (ratios and market measures)}$$
$$a_0 \ldots a_n = \text{the weightings or coefficients}$$

The final model used in this analysis included the following seven financial measures:

X_1 = profitability: earnings before interest and taxes (EBIT)/total assets (TA)
X_2 = stability of profitability measure: the standard error of estimate of EBIT/TA (normalized for 10 years)
X_3 = debt service capabilities (interest coverage): EBIT/interest charges
X_4 = cumulative profitability: retained earnings/total assets
X_5 = liquidity: current assets/current liabilities
X_6 = capitalization levels: market value of equity/total capital (five-year average)
X_7 = size: total tangible assets (normalized)

Exhibit 16.7 illustrates the Z-score calculations for two companies whose bonds were rated below investment grade as of December 2007: Amazon.com (BB rating) and General Motors (B rating). Z-scores typically range from −5.0 to +20.0, with higher scores (i.e., above +3.0) indicating that bankruptcy over the next two years is unlikely while

EXHIBIT 16.6 Cumulative Average Default Rates by Bond Rating: 1981–2007 (%)

Rating	1	2	3	4	5	6	7	8	9	10	11	12	13	14	15
AAA	0.00	0.00	0.09	0.18	0.28	0.41	0.48	0.59	0.63	0.67	0.67	0.67	0.67	0.73	0.79
AA+	0.00	0.06	0.06	0.13	0.20	0.28	0.35	0.35	0.35	0.35	0.35	0.35	0.35	0.35	0.35
AA	0.00	0.00	0.00	0.09	0.18	0.25	0.35	0.48	0.60	0.72	0.81	0.88	1.03	1.10	1.14
AA–	0.02	0.09	0.20	0.32	0.45	0.61	0.76	0.86	0.96	1.08	1.21	1.35	1.41	1.53	1.60
A+	0.05	0.10	0.25	0.45	0.61	0.77	0.95	1.10	1.29	1.46	1.66	1.88	2.08	2.31	2.51
A	0.07	0.18	0.30	0.42	0.60	0.80	1.00	1.21	1.42	1.73	1.98	2.12	2.26	2.35	2.61
A–	0.06	0.20	0.32	0.49	0.73	1.02	1.44	1.71	1.95	2.12	2.19	2.32	2.42	2.53	2.65
BBB+	0.15	0.46	0.91	1.30	1.74	2.22	2.58	2.91	3.36	3.71	4.07	4.27	4.62	5.14	5.72
BBB	0.23	0.54	0.85	1.39	1.95	2.47	2.95	3.48	3.93	4.44	5.00	5.44	5.93	6.12	6.50
BBB–	0.31	1.02	1.78	2.78	3.74	4.60	5.25	5.87	6.33	6.91	7.42	7.94	8.54	9.37	10.03
BB+	0.52	1.41	2.85	4.20	5.41	6.71	7.88	8.41	9.36	10.21	10.82	11.41	11.85	12.35	13.07
BB	0.81	2.50	4.62	6.53	8.38	10.13	11.52	12.79	13.82	14.62	15.71	16.63	17.10	17.19	17.28
BB–	1.44	4.16	7.04	9.90	12.32	14.66	16.52	18.35	19.87	21.03	21.93	22.62	23.51	24.22	24.87
B+	2.53	6.97	11.22	14.92	17.65	19.74	21.64	23.29	24.70	26.11	27.32	28.29	29.29	30.31	31.19
B	6.27	12.74	17.75	21.27	23.84	26.03	27.44	28.52	29.43	30.43	31.40	32.36	33.42	34.20	35.04
B–	9.06	16.94	22.75	26.66	29.44	31.56	33.38	34.53	35.25	35.73	36.26	36.64	36.84	37.07	37.32
CCC/C	25.59	34.06	39.04	41.86	44.50	45.62	46.67	47.25	48.86	49.76	50.50	51.26	51.87	52.50	52.50
Investment grade	0.10	0.30	0.52	0.81	1.11	1.42	1.69	1.95	2.19	2.44	2.66	2.85	3.05	3.24	3.47
Speculative grade	2.81	6.54	10.00	12.92	15.23	17.23	18.87	20.25	21.46	22.54	23.52	24.34	25.12	25.79	26.43
All rated	0.98	2.30	3.53	4.62	5.52	6.32	6.98	7.56	8.06	8.53	8.96	9.31	9.66	9.98	10.32

—Time horizon (years)—

Source: *2007 Annual Global Corporate Default Study and Rating Transitions* (New York: Standard & Poor's, February 2008): p. 11 (Table 8). Reprinted with permission.

EXHIBIT 16.7	Altman's Z-Score Analysis

A. Amazon.com Inc.

<HELP> for explanation, <MENU> for similar functions.   Corp AZS

ALTMAN'S Z – SCORE MODEL

AMZN US	Amazon.Com Inc
Total Assets	6485.00
Working Capital	1450.00
Retained Earnings	−1870.00
Earn Before Int & Taxes	655.00
Market Value of Equity	39927.84
Total Liabilities	5288.00
Sales to Total Assets	2.29
Total Shareholders' Equity	1197.00

Financial Health Assessment and Outlook

Reference Date	12/2007	Calculate: A	
Credit Rating	BB	Altman's Zscore	7.02
		Health Grade	C+

Australia 61 2 9777 8600   Brazil 5511 3048 4500   Europe 44 20 7330 7500   Germany 49 69 9204 1210   Hong Kong 852 2977 6000
Japan 81 3 3201 8900   Singapore 65 6212 1000   U.S. 1 212 318 2000   Copyright 2008 Bloomberg Finance L.P.
H464–414–0 02–Mar–2008 13:03:27

B. General Motors Corp.

<HELP> for explanation, <MENU> for similar functions.   Corp AZS

ALTMAN'S Z – SCORE MODEL

GM US	General Motors Corp
Total Assets	148883.00
Working Capital	−9720.00
Retained Earnings	−53356.00
Earn Before Int & Taxes	−4390.00
Market Value of Equity	14089.22
Total Liabilities	184363.00
Sales to Total Assets	1.22
Total Shareholders' Equity	−35480.00

Financial Health Assessment and Outlook

Reference Date	12/2007	Calculate: A	
Credit Rating	B	Altman's Zscore	0.59
		Health Grade	F

Australia 61 2 9777 8600   Brazil 5511 3048 4500   Europe 44 20 7330 7500   Germany 49 69 9204 1210   Hong Kong 852 2977 6000
Japan 81 3 3201 8900   Singapore 65 6212 1000   U.S. 1 212 318 2000   Copyright 2008 Bloomberg Finance L.P.
H464–414–0 02–Mar–2008 13:02:52

Source: © 2008 Bloomberg L.P. All rights reserved. Reprinted with permission.

lower scores (i.e., below $+1.8$) suggest an increased potential for business failure. In this case, Amazon.com's Z-score shows that it is in a relatively strong financial position given its credit rating, while General Motors' Z-score indicates the opposite. The fact that Amazon.com survived the recent global financial crisis and the subsequent recession while General Motors went bankrupt in 2009 and was taken over by the government seems to be consistent with the prediction of the Z-score. It is important to note, however, that these scores are best interpreted as they change over time, rather than as a single observation. Thus, the active bond manager following a credit analysis strategy might use this as a tool to help predict rating upgrades and downgrades before they occur.[4] Altman and Levallee (1980) constructed a Canadian discriminant analysis model with five ratios: sales/total assets ratio, total debt/total assets ratio, current assets/current liabilities ratio, net profit after tax/total debt ratio, and rate of growth of equity versus rate of asset growth.

In contrast to using a composite credit score model, many analysts simply adapt their basic corporate bond analysis techniques *to the unique needs of high-yield bonds,* which have characteristics of common stock as shown by Reilly and Wright (1994, 2001). Fabozzi (2005a, chapter 32) claims that the analysis of high-yield bonds is the same as with any bond except that the following areas of analysis should be expanded:

1. What is the firm's *competitive position* in terms of cost and pricing? This can be critical to a small firm.
2. What is the firm's *cash flow* relative to cash requirements for interest, research, growth, and periods of economic decline? Also, what is the firm's *borrowing capacity* that can serve as a safety net and provide flexibility?
3. What is the *liquidity value of the firm's assets*? Are these assets available for liquidation (are there any claims against them)? In many cases, asset sales are a critical part of the strategy for a leveraged buyout.
4. How good is the *total management team*? Is the management team committed to and capable of operating in the high-risk environment of this firm?
5. What is the firm's *financial leverage* on an absolute basis and on a market-adjusted basis (using market value of equity and debt)?

16.3.4 YIELD SPREAD ANALYSIS

As discussed in Chapter 12, spread analysis assumes normal relationships exist between the yields for bonds in alternative sectors (e.g., the spread between high-grade versus low-grade industrial or between industrial versus utility bonds). A bond portfolio manager would monitor these relationships and, when an abnormal relationship occured, execute various sector swaps. The crucial factor is developing the background to know the normal yield relationship and to evaluate the liquidity necessary to buy or sell the required issues quickly enough to take advantage of the temporary yield abnormality.

Dialynas and Edington (1992) consider several specific factors that affect the aggregate spread. The generally accepted explanation of changes in the yield spread is that it is related to the economic environment. Specifically, the spread widens during periods of economic uncertainty and recession because investors demand larger risk premiums. In contrast, the spread will decline during periods of economic confidence and expansion. Although not denying the existence of such a relationship, the authors contend that a more encompassing

---

4 For more on the analysis of default rates for high-yield bonds, see Jonsson and Fridson (1996), Helwege and Kleinman (1997), and Fridson, Garman, and Wu (1997).

factor is the impact of interest rate (yield) volatility. They contend that yield volatility will affect the spread via three effects: (1) yield volatility and the behaviour of embedded options, (2) yield volatility and transactional liquidity, and (3) the effect of yield volatility on the business cycle.

Recall that a callable bond's value equals the value of the non-callable bond minus the value of the call option. Therefore, if the option value goes up, the value of the callable bond will decline and its yield will increase. When yield volatility increases, the call option value increases resulting in a decline in the price of the callable bond and an increase in the bond's yield and its yield spread relative to government bonds. Similarly, an increase in yield volatility raises the uncertainty facing bond dealers thus causing them to increase their bid-ask spreads that reflect the transactional liquidity for these bonds. This liquidity will have a bigger effect on non-government bonds, so their yield spread relative to government bonds will increase. Finally, interest rate volatility causes uncertainty for business executives and consumers regarding their cost of funds. This typically will precede an economic decline that will, in turn, lead to an increase in the yield spread.

It is possible to have a change in yield spread for reasons other than economic uncertainty. If greater yield volatility occurs when in a period of economic stability, the yield spread will increase due to the embedded option effect and the transactional liquidity effect. This analysis implies that when examining yield spreads, we should pay particular attention to interest rate (yield) volatility.

16.3.5   IMPLEMENTING AN ACTIVE BOND TRANSACTION

Once a bond manager has decided on the specifics of an active strategy, the next step is to create a portfolio (or alter an existing one). A popular approach involves the use of **bond swaps**, which entail liquidating a current position and simultaneously buying a different issue in its place with similar attributes and a better chance for improved return. These trades can be executed to increase current yield, to increase yield to maturity, to take advantage of shifts in interest rates or the realignment of yield spreads, to improve the quality of a portfolio, or for tax purposes. Some swaps are highly sophisticated and require advanced modelling, however, most are fairly simple transactions with obvious goals and risk. They go by such names as *profit takeouts, substitution swaps, intermarket spread swaps,* or *tax swaps.* Although many of these transactions involve low risk (e.g., the pure yield pickup swap), others entail substantial risk (e.g., the rate anticipation swap). Regardless of the risk involved, all trades have one basic purpose: portfolio improvement. In fact, Boyd and Mercer (2005) demonstrate that these swaps lead to a substantial improvement in risk-adjusted performance relative to standard bond benchmarks.

Most bond swaps involve several different types of risk. One obvious risk is that the market will move against us while the transaction is in progress. Interest rates may move up over the holding period and cause us to incur a loss. Alternatively, yield spreads may fail to respond as anticipated. Possibly the new bond may not be a true substitute and so, even if our expectations and interest rate forecasts are correct, the swap may be unsatisfactory because the wrong issue was selected. Finally, if the work-out time is longer than anticipated, the realized yield might be less than expected. As noted by Homer and Leibowitz (2004) and Fabozzi, Mann, and Choudhry (2005, chapter 55), we must be willing to accept such risks to improve our portfolio. The following subsections consider two of the more popular bond swaps.

Pure Yield Pickup Swap   This swap involves trading out of a low-coupon bond into a comparable higher coupon bond to realize an automatic and instantaneous increase in current yield and yield to maturity. An example of such a trade would be an investor who currently holds a 30-year, AA-rated 10% issue that is trading at an 11.5% yield. Assume that a comparable 30-year, AA-rated obligation bearing a 12% coupon priced to yield 12% becomes available. The investor would realize some book loss if the original issue was bought at par but is able to improve current yield and yield to maturity simultaneously if the new obligation is held to maturity.

The investor need not predict rate changes, and the swap is not based on any imbalance in yield spread. The object simply is to seek higher yields. Quality and maturity stay the same as do all other factors *except coupon*. The major risk is that future reinvestment rates may not be as high as expected, and, therefore, the total terminal value of the investment (capital recovery, coupon receipts, and interest-on-interest) may fall short of expectations. This reinvestment risk can be evaluated by analyzing the results with a number of reinvestment rates to determine the minimum reinvestment rate that would make the swap viable.

Substitution Swap This swap is generally short term and relies heavily on interest rate expectations. Consequently, it is subject to considerably more risk than pure yield pickup swaps. Substitution swaps assume a short-term imbalance in yield spreads between issues that are perfect substitutes and that the imbalance will be corrected in the near future. For example, an investor might hold a 30-year, 12% issue yielding 12% and be offered a comparable 30-year, 12% bond that is yielding 12.20%. Because the issue offered will trade at a price less than $1,000 for every issue sold, the investor can buy more than one of the offered obligations.

We would expect the yield spread imbalance to be corrected by having the yield on the offering bond decline to the level of our current issue. Thus, we would realize capital gains by switching out of our current position into the higher yielding obligation.

Although a modest increase in current income occurs as the yield imbalance is corrected, attractive capital gains are possible, causing a differential in *realized yield*. The work-out time will have an important effect on the differential realized return. Even if the yield is not corrected until maturity, 30 years later, we will still experience a small increase in realized yield (about 10 basis points). In contrast, if the correction takes place in one year, the differential realized return is much greater. After the correction has occurred, we would have additional capital for a subsequent swap or other investment. Several risks are involved in this swap. In addition to the pressure of the work-out time, market interest rates could move against us, the yield spread may not be temporary, and the issue may not be a viable swap candidate (i.e., the spread may be due to the issue's lower quality).

16.3.6 ACTIVE GLOBAL BOND INVESTING

Global capital markets at *Financial Times*: http://www.ft.com/markets/capitalmarkets.

An active approach to global fixed-income management must consider three interrelated factors: (1) the local economy in each country that includes the effect of domestic and international demand, (2) the impact of this total demand and domestic monetary policy on inflation and interest rates, and (3) the effect of the economy, inflation, and interest rates on the exchange rates among countries.[5] Based on the evaluation of these factors,

---

5 For a detailed discussion of the benefits of international bond investing as well as what is involved in the analysis, see Steward (2005), Munves (2005), Malvey (2005), and Steward, Lynch, and Fabozzi (2005). Also see Churchill (1994), Squires (1996; 1997a, b; 2000a), and Jost (2002).

a portfolio manager must decide on the relative weight for each country. In addition, one might consider an allocation within each country among government, and corporate bonds.

16.4   Core-Plus Management Strategies

Beyond a pure passive strategy designed to mimic an index or any of the several active management strategies we have just seen, there has been increased interest among professional bond investors in an approach that combines the two styles. Specifically, **core-plus bond portfolio management** places a significant part (i.e., 70% to 80%) of the funds in a passively managed portfolio of high-grade securities reflecting a broad representation of the overall bond market; this is the "core" of the strategy. The remainder of the funds would then be managed actively in the "plus" portion of the portfolio, where it is felt that the manager's selection skills offer a higher probability of achieving positive abnormal rates of return.

Typically, the core portion of the portfolio is effectively managed as an index fund based on the belief that the designated core sectors of the bond market are efficient to the point where it is not worth the time and cost to attempt to derive substantial excess returns from them. Examples of market sectors that are often included in this definition include the U.S. broad market sector or the U.S. government/corporate sector, both of which are dominated by issues that carry a credit rating of AAA or higher. (The difference between these two core sectors is that the former includes the rapidly growing markets for mortgage-backed and asset-backed bonds.) Not surprisingly, then, the plus sectors consist of those segments of the global bond market that are regarded as being less efficient and therefore more likely to be sources of alpha in the managed portfolio. This would include high-yield bonds, foreign bonds from developed countries, and emerging market debt.

From the preceding description, it should be clear that a core-plus approach can also be considered a form of **enhanced indexing**, depending on how much of the portfolio is placed in the core portion and how actively the plus sectors are managed. As Davidson (2001) points out, the core-plus bond manager attempts to combine a substantial *beta* investment—that is, the funds invested to mimic the systematic risk exposure of the benchmark index—with the *alpha* potential associated with selecting bonds from the actively managed sectors.

Thus, an important feature of the plus sectors is that they have the possibility of delivering high risk-adjusted returns over time that are not driven by systematic movements in the general bond market. This means that plus sector investments often have *high total risk*, as measured by their standard deviation of returns, but also *low correlations* with the other fixed-income sectors representing the core of the portfolio. As we have seen, high-yield bonds are a good example of a plus sector because they tend to have very high standard deviations that make them equivalent to equity investments in many respects, but have very low correlations (e.g., 0.30 or lower) with the investment-grade bond sector.

Relative to a passive index strategy, a core-plus approach offers three potential advantages: (1) higher returns that occur from exploiting market inefficiencies outside the traditional core sectors, (2) increased opportunities for exploiting the manager's security selection skills, and (3) the ability to alter the composition of the fixed-income asset class in a manner consistent with the insights and views of the manager. Of course, these additional sources of alpha come at the expense of additional sources of risk. The incremental risk that the core-plus approach introduces into the passive portfolio can be particularly significant in no-growth or declining-growth economic scenarios given that much of the plus investing is likely to be done in lower credit grade instruments whose market values will be affected the most under those circumstances. Further, there may be a number of other risks associated with investments in the plus sectors—such as prepayment and liquidity risks—that are not as prevalent in the core portion of the portfolio. Finally, Dopfel (2003) cautions asset managers against the risks associated with changing correlations between stock and bond markets.

16.5 Matched-Funding Management Strategies

Securities Industry and Financial Markets Association's bond site: http://www. investinginbonds.com.

The goal for many bond market participants is simply to increase the wealth of their overall portfolios while providing risk diversification benefits across asset classes. For these investors, the passive, active, and core-plus strategies are all potentially appropriate management styles, depending on their underlying beliefs about how efficient the bond market is. Other investors, however, face a more precise investment problem in which a specific set of liabilities needs to be met. For instance, life insurance companies have a series of future payments they are obligated to make, which they can predict with a reasonable degree of accuracy given their actuarial forecasts. Further, defined-benefit pension funds can also predict fairly precisely the future retirement benefits they must pay—in both amount and timing—to their constituents. For these investors, the bond portfolios they construct should take into account the nature of the liabilities that those assets are intended to fund.

Matched-funding strategies are a form of **asset–liability management** whereby the characteristics of the bonds held in the portfolio are coordinated with those of the liabilities the investor is obligated to pay. As we will see, these matching techniques can range from an attempt to exactly match the levels and timing of the required cash payments to more general approaches that focus on other investment characteristics, such as setting the average duration or investment horizon of the bond portfolio equal to that of the underlying liabilities. An important assumption underlying all of the matched-funding techniques we will examine is that the investor's *liabilities are predictable* with some degree of precision.

16.5.1 DEDICATED PORTFOLIOS

Dedication refers to bond portfolio management techniques that are used to service a prescribed set of liabilities. Such a "dedicated" portfolio can be created in several ways. We will discuss two alternatives. A **pure cash-matched dedicated portfolio** is the most conservative strategy. Specifically, its objective is to develop a bond portfolio that will provide a stream of payments from coupons, sinking funds, and maturing principal that exactly matches the specified liability schedules. An example of typical liability stream for a retired-lives component of a person system is shown in Exhibit 16.8. The goal is to build a portfolio that will generate sufficient funds in advance of each scheduled payment to ensure that the payment will be met. One alternative is to find a number of zero-coupon Government bonds that will exactly cash match each liability. Such an exact cash match portfolio is referred to as a *total passive* portfolio because it is designed so that any prior receipts would not be reinvested (i.e., it assumes a zero reinvestment rate).

Dedication with reinvestment is similar to the pure cash-matched technique except it is assumed that the bonds and other cash flows do not have to exactly match the liability stream. Any inflows that precede liability claims can be reinvested at some reasonably

EXHIBIT 16.8	A Prescribed Schedule of Liabilities

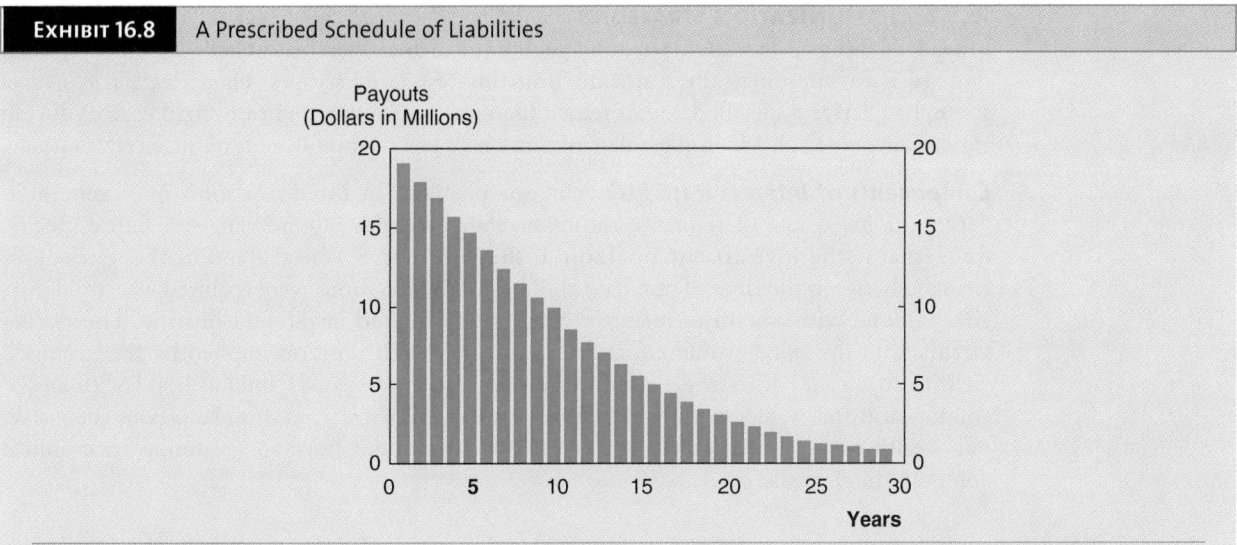

Source: Copyright 1986, Association for Investment Management and Research. Reproduced and republished from "The Dedicated Bond Portfolio in Pension Funds—Part I: Motivations and Basics," in the *Financial Analysts Journal,* January/February 1986, with permission from the CFA Institute. All Rights Reserved.

Copyright 1986, CFA Institute. Reproduced and republished from the Financial Analysts Journal with permission from CFA Institute. All rights reserved.

conservative rate. This allows the portfolio manager to consider a much wider set of bonds that may have higher return characteristics. In addition, the ability to reinvest within each period and between periods also will generate a higher return for the asset portfolio. As a result, the net cost of the portfolio will be lower, with almost equal safety, assuming the reinvestment rate assumption is conservative. An example would be to assume a reinvestment rate of 4% in an environment where market interest rates are currently ranging from 5% to 8%.

Potential problems exist with both of these approaches. When selecting bonds for these portfolios, it is critical to be aware of call/prepayment possibilities (refundings, calls, sinking funds) with specific bonds or mortgage-backed securities. The possibility of prepayment becomes very important following periods of historically high rates. A prime example was the period 1982 to 1986, when interest rates went from over 18% to under 8%. Because of this substantial rate change, many dedicated portfolios constructed without adequate concern for complete call protection were negatively affected when numerous bonds were called that were not expected to be called under normal conditions. For example, deep discount bonds (which typically provide implicit call protection), when rates were 16% to 18%, went to par and above when rates fell below 10% and were subsequently called. Obviously, the reinvestment of these proceeds at the lower rates caused many dedicated portfolios to be underfunded. Therefore, it is necessary to find bonds with complete call protection or to consider deep discount bonds under conservative interest rate conditions.

Although quality also is a legitimate concern, it is probably not necessary to invest only in government bonds if the portfolio manager diversifies across industries and sectors. A diversified portfolio of AA or A industrial bonds can provide a current and total annual return of 40 to 60 basis points above government bonds. This differential over a 30-year period can have a significant impact on the net cost of funding a liability stream.

16.5.2 IMMUNIZATION STRATEGIES

Instead of using a dedicated portfolio technique, a manager may decide that the optimal strategy is to immunize the portfolio from interest rate changes. *Immunization techniques* attempt to derive a specified rate of return (generally close to the current market rate) during a given investment horizon regardless of what happens to the future level of interest rates.

Components of Interest Rate Risk A major problem in bond portfolio management is deriving a given rate of return to satisfy an ending-wealth requirement at a future specific date—that is, the **investment horizon**. If the yield curve were flat and market rates never changed between the time of purchase and the date when funds were required, we could purchase a bond with a term to maturity equal to the desired investment horizon. The ending wealth from the bond would equal the promised wealth position implied by the promised yield to maturity. For example, assume we purchase a 10-year, $1 million bond with an 8% coupon at its par value. If the yield curve was flat and there were no changes in the curve, our wealth position at the end of our 10-year investment horizon (assuming semi-annual compounding) would be

$$\$1,000,000 \times (1.04)^{20} = \$2,191,123$$

We can get the same answer by taking the $40,000 semi-annual coupon and compounding it to the end of the period at 4% and adding the $1,000,000 principal at maturity. Unfortunately, in the real world, the yield curve is not typically flat and interest rates are constantly changing. Consequently, the bond portfolio manager faces **interest rate risk** between the time of investment and the future target date. Interest rate risk is the uncertainty regarding the ending-wealth value of the portfolio due to changes in market interest rates between the time of purchase and the investor's horizon date. Notably, interest rate risk involves two component risks: **price risk** and **coupon reinvestment risk**.

Price risk occurs if interest rates change before the horizon date and the bond is sold prior to maturity. In such cases, the realized market price for the bond will differ from the *expected* price. If rates increased after purchase, the realized price for the bond in the secondary market would be below expectations, whereas if rates declined, the bond's realized price would be above expectations. Because we do not know whether interest rates will increase or decrease, we are uncertain about the bond's future price.

The coupon reinvestment risk arises because the yield to maturity calculation implicitly assumes that all coupons will be reinvested at the promised yield to maturity. If, after buying the bond, interest rates decline, the coupons will be reinvested at rates below the initial promised yield, and the ending wealth will be below expectations. In contrast, if interest rates increase, the coupons will be reinvested at rates above expectations, and the ending wealth will be above expectations. Again, because we are uncertain about future rates, we are uncertain about these reinvestment rates.

Classical Immunization and Interest Rate Risk Fisher and Weil (1971), as well as Bierwag and Kaufman (1977) and Bierwag (1977), showed that price risk and reinvestment risk are affected inversely by a change in market rates and that duration is the time period when these two risks are of equal magnitude, but in opposite directions. An increase in interest rates will cause an ending price below expectations, but the reinvestment rate for interim cash flows will be above expectations. A decline in market interest rates will cause the reverse situation. Clearly, a bond portfolio manager with a specific investment horizon will attempt to eliminate these two components of interest rate risk. The process intended to eliminate interest rate risk is referred to as **immunization** and was discussed by Redington (1952). It has been specified in detail by Fisher and Weil (1971) as follows:

> A portfolio of investments in bonds is *immunized* for a holding period if its value at the end of the holding period, regardless of the course of interest rates during the holding period, must be at least as large as it would have been had the interest-rate function been constant throughout the holding period. If the realized return on an investment in bonds is sure to be at least as large as the appropriately computed yield to the horizon, then that investment is immunized [p. 411].

Fisher and Weil found a significant difference between the *promised* yields and the *realized* returns on bonds for the period 1925 to 1968, indicating the importance of immunizing a bond portfolio. They showed that it is possible to immunize a bond portfolio if we can assume that any change in interest rates will be the same for all maturities—that is, if forward interest rates change, all rates will change by the same amount (there is a parallel shift of the yield curve). Given this assumption, Fisher and Weil proved that *a portfolio of bonds is immunized from interest rate risk if the duration of the portfolio is always equal to the desired investment horizon*.

The authors simulated the effects of applying the immunization concept (a duration-matched strategy) compared to a naïve portfolio strategy where the portfolio's maturity was equal to the investment horizon. They compared the ending-wealth ratio for the duration matched and for the naïve strategy portfolios to a wealth ratio that assumed no change in the interest rate structure. In a perfectly immunized portfolio, the actual ending wealth should equal the expected ending wealth implied by the promised yield, so these comparisons should indicate which portfolio strategy does a superior job of immunization. The duration-matched strategy results were consistently closer to the promised yield results; however, the results were not perfect. The duration portfolio was not perfectly immunized because the basic assumption did not always hold; when interest rates changed, all interest rates did not change by the same amount.

The Mechanics of Bond Immunization: A Simple Illustration[6] Suppose that an investor has a liability that she needs to pay off in exactly three years. Thus, her desired investment horizon is three years, which can also be considered as the duration of the liability she faces. Suppose further that the yield curve is currently flat at 10% but that it declines to 8% as soon as her initial investment is made. She considers four alternative bond investments to fund this liability:

(A)   Purchase a 10-year bond paying a 9% annual coupon and sell it in three years
(B)   Purchase three consecutive one-year "pure discount" (i.e., zero-coupon) bonds
(C)   Purchase a three-year, pure discount bond
(D)   Purchase a four-year bond paying a 34.85% annual coupon and sell it in three years

Under these assumptions, the promised yield for each of these prospective investments is 10% at the time she makes her initial decision. So the relevant question to consider is: What will be the realized yields (RY) for all four positions at the end of her three-year investment horizon?

---

6 The authors gratefully acknowledge Professor Robert Radcliffe's contribution to this example.

For *Bond A,* the initial investment (per $1,000 of face value) is:

$$P_0 = \sum_{t=1}^{10} \frac{90}{(1 + 0.10)^t} + \frac{1,000}{(1 + 0.10)^{10}} = \$938.55$$

Because this position will not have matured by Year 3, it will have to be sold at the prevailing market rate (assumed to then be 8%). Also, she will be able to reinvest the coupons she receives prior to her planning horizon. Thus, the ending wealth in this position is the combination of:

(i) Sale of Bond:

$$P_3 = \sum_{t=1}^{7} \frac{90}{(1 + 0.08)^t} + \frac{1,000}{(1 + 0.08)^7} = \$1,052.06, \text{ and}$$

(ii) Reinvested Coupon Payments:

$$90(1 + 0.08)^2 + 90(1 + 0.08) + 90 = \$292.18$$

or $1,344.24. This means the investor's realized yield in *Bond A* would be:

$$RY_A = \sqrt[3]{\frac{1,344.24}{938.55}} - 1 = 12.72\%$$

For *Bond B,* assume for simplicity that the bondholder invests $1,000 initially at 10% and then reinvests the total annual proceeds for two more years at 8%:

Year 1: (1,000.00)(1 + 0.10) = $1,100.00
Year 2: (1,100.00)(1 + 0.08) = $1,188.00
Year 3: (1,188.00)(1 + 0.08) = $1,283.04

Thus, her realized yield from this "rollover" strategy would be:

$$RY_B = \sqrt[3]{\frac{1,283.04}{1,000.00}} - 1 = 8.66\%$$

The initial purchase price of *Bond C* (per $1,000 face value) is:

$$P_0 = (1,000) \div (1 + 0.10)^3 = \$751.31$$

so the realized yield would be:

$$RY_C = \sqrt[3]{\frac{1000.00}{751.31}} - 1 = 10.00 \text{ percent}$$

Finally, *Bond D* is similar to Bond A in that it must be sold prior to maturity and its coupons must be reinvested. The initial price for this security is:

$$P_0 = \sum_{t=1}^{4} \frac{348.50}{(1 + 0.10)^t} + \frac{1,000}{(1 + 0.10)^4} = \$1,787.71$$

The ending-wealth level in Year 3 combines:

(i) Sale of Bond:

$$P_3 = (1,000 + 348.50) \div (1 + 0.08) = \$1,248.61, \text{ and}$$

(ii) Coupon Payments:

$$348.50(1 + 0.08)^2 + 348.50(1 + 0.08) + 348.50 = \$1,131.37$$

or \$2,379.98 and, thus, the realized yield would be:

$$RY_D = \sqrt[3]{\frac{2,379.98}{1,787.71}} - 1 = 10.00\%$$

Notice that only for Bonds C and D does the yield to maturity prevailing at the time of the original investment decision (i.e., the *promised* or *expected* return) equal the *actual* rate of return over the three-year investment horizon. To see why this is the case, it is easy to confirm that the duration statistics for each of these bonds are:

> Bond A: 6.89 years
> Bond B: 1.00 year (per bond)
> Bond C: 3.00 years
> Bond D: 3.00 years

Because the investor's planning horizon was three years, the only bonds that actually produced the expected yield of 10% were the two having durations of three years. That is, by investing in a bond that pays out the "average" cash flow at precisely the time it is desired, it is possible to completely offset the effects of a subsequent change in interest rates. If interest rates fall (rise) after purchase, the bond price will rise (fall) by exactly enough to offset the decline (increase) in income from reinvested coupons; the portfolio was *immunized*.

On the other hand, when the investor tried to fund a three-year liability with a longer duration bond (i.e., Bond A), she had to sell the bond to get the majority of her cash out of the position. This resulted in a situation where the price risk component dominated the reinvestment risk component (i.e., *net price risk*). This produced a higher actual return than she was promised (12.72 versus 10%) because rates in the market fell, which benefited the bond's price more than it hurt coupon reinvestment potential. Conversely, when she tried to fund the three-year liability with a series of shorter duration positions (i.e., Bond B), she received her cash back sooner than she needed it and therefore faced a *net reinvestment risk* problem, which in this case led to a lower realized yield as rates fell. However, the important point here is that with either Bond A or Bond B, the investor faces uncertainty over the outcome of her investment, as can be seen from the fact that her realized yield differed from her promised yield.

In summary, given that bond risk caused by changing interest rates can be split into price risk and reinvestment risk, the following general statements can be made:

If *Duration* > *Investment Horizon,* the investor faces *Net Price Risk* (Bond A)
If *Duration* < *Investment Horizon,* the investor faces *Net Reinvestment Risk* (Bond B)
If *Duration* = *Investment Horizon,* the investor is *immunized* (Bonds C and D)

Finally, it should be noted that setting the duration of an asset equal to the duration of the liability will just immunize an investment against the *next* interest rate movement. However, the position will remain immunized to subsequent yield changes *as long as it is rebalanced promptly*; this is demonstrated in the Appendix to this chapter.

Application of Classical Immunization Stonewall Insurance Ltd. (a pseudonym for a real company) is a property and casualty insurance firm that operates as an offshore subsidiary of a construction firm based in the U.S. Stonewall's primary function is to provide worker's compensation insurance benefits to the employees of the parent firm. Although the construction firm has an excellent safety record, there are occasional worksite accidents that require compensation benefits to be paid. These payments can range from a few months to several years; the parent firm conservatively plans for payments to continue an average of 3.50 to 4.50 years. Thus, they consider this to be the duration range of the potential liabilities (i.e., planning horizon) they face.

The uncertainty of both the size and length of the benefit claims that Stonewall is liable for makes the implementation of a cash-matched portfolio solution impractical. (It is typically the case that property and casualty insurance firms have less predictable liabilities than life insurance companies.) Instead, the firm's solution to this asset-liability management problem is to assemble a bond portfolio that has a duration statistic (expressed in modified form, in this case) of around 4 years. Details of the specific securities they held as of January 2008 are shown in Exhibit 16.9. Notice in particular that the portfolio holds 27 separate positions—mostly corporate bonds—with an aggregate market value of $23 million and an average credit grade of between A1 (Moody's) and AA-(Standard & Poor's). More importantly, however, the portfolio has been assembled to have a modified duration of 3.91 years, which closely matches the target horizon period implied by their projected liabilities. Thus, the position is effectively immunized; an unexpected increase or decrease in interest rates at this point in time would have approximately equal and offsetting effects on the value of both Stonewall's assets and liabilities, leaving the firm's net worth unaffected by the rate movement.

EXHIBIT 16.9 Immunized Bond Portfolio of Stonewall Insurance Ltd., January 2008

Category	Sector	Issuer	Ticker Symbol	CUSIP	Maturity	Coupon	Call Date (Price)	Par Value (000s)	Bid Yield	Bid Price	Total Bond Value	Accrued Interest	Total Pos. Value	% of Ttl Position	Mod. Dur.	Convex	Moody Rating	S&P Rating
Agency 4.40%	—	Federal Home Loan Bank	FHLB	3133XD7E5	9/21/2012	5.250%	3/21/08 (100.000)	1000	5.237%	100.0454	$1,000,453.89	1.458	$1,015,037.22	4.395%	4.078	19.988	Aaa	AAA
Corporate 95.60%	Aerospace:	McDonnell Douglas	BA	580169AM2	4/1/2012	9.750%	Not Callable	1000	5.097%	117.5649	$1,175,648.71	2.438	$1,200,023.71	5.196%	3.480	15.230	A2	A+
	Conglomerates:	Emerson Electric	EMR	EC9551796	5/1/2013	4.500%	MW (+10)	584	5.142%	97.0320	$566,666.79	0.750	$571,046.79	2.473%	4.636	25.403	A2	A
		General Dynamics	GD	369550AK4	5/15/2013	4.250%	MW (+25)	1000	4.870%	97.0952	$970,952.10	0.543	$976,382.66	4.228%	4.710	26.058	A2	A
	Consumer-Products:	Procter & Gamble	PG	742718DA4	8/15/2014	4.950%	MW (+10)	500	4.480%	102.6626	$513,312.85	1.870	$522,662.85	2.263%	5.516	36.530	Aa3	AA-
		Anheuser Busch	BUD	035229CY7	1/15/2015	5.000%	MW (+20)	500	4.979%	100.1212	$500,606.01	2.306	$512,133.79	2.218%	5.742	39.969	A2	A
	Consumer-Restaurants:	McDonald's	MCD	58013MDU5	6/1/2013	4.125%	MW (+15)	1000	4.538%	98.0330	$980,330.29	0.344	$983,767.79	4.260%	4.778	26.708	A3	A
	Consumer-Retail:	Target	TGT	87612EAH9	3/1/2012	5.875%	MW (+20)	500	4.857%	103.7907	$518,953.59	1.958	$528,745.25	2.290%	3.609	15.869	A2	A+
		Target	TGT	87612EAM8	6/15/2013	4.000%	MW (+15)	500	5.305%	93.8903	$469,451.51	2.178	$480,340.40	2.080%	4.698	26.340	A2	A+
		Wal-Mart Stores	WMT	931142BT9	5/1/2013	4.550%	Not Callable	1000	4.480%	100.3232	$1,003,232.41	0.758	$1,010,815.74	4.377%	4.658	25.607	Aa2	AA
	Energy:	Seariver Maritime	XOM	812293AB4	9/1/2012	0.000%	1/11/08 (88.708)	1000	4.520%	81.1732	$811,731.95	0.000	$811,731.95	3.515%	4.564	23.057	Aaa	AAA
		MidAmerican Energy	BRK	595620AD7	10/1/2014	4.650%	MW (+15)	1000	4.968%	98.1880	$981,879.94	1.163	$993,504.94	4.302%	5.653	38.053	A2	A-
	Financial-Diversified:	General Electric Capital	GE	36962GVS0	11/15/2010	6.875%	Not Callable	1000	4.135%	107.3425	$1,073,425.27	0.878	$1,082,209.99	4.686%	2.590	8.334	Aaa	AAA
	Financial-Global:	Merrill Lynch	MER	590118ES3	4/27/2008	7.000%	Not Callable	1000	5.533%	100.4513	$1,004,512.75	1.244	$1,016,957.20	4.404%	0.314	0.251	A1	A+
		Goldman Sachs	GS	38141GDQ4	10/15/2013	5.250%	Not Callable	500	5.120%	100.6361	$503,180.67	1.108	$508,722.34	2.203%	4.891	28.618	Aa3	AA-
		Morgan Stanley	MS	61748AAE6	4/1/2014	4.750%	Not Callable	500	5.855%	94.2768	$471,383.79	1.188	$477,321.29	2.067%	5.233	32.721	A1	A+
	Financial-Regional:	BankBoston	BAC	06606HD87	4/15/2008	6.375%	Not Callable	1000	5.072%	100.3593	$1,003,593.21	1.346	$1,017,051.55	4.404%	0.282	0.217	Aa1	AA
		Bank of America	BAC	060505BM5	6/15/2014	5.375%	Not Callable	1000	5.138%	101.2915	$1,012,915.24	2.926	$1,042,179.13	4.513%	5.255	33.778	Aa1	AA
	Healthcare:	AstraZeneca	AZN	046353AA6	6/1/2014	5.400%	MW (+15)	1000	4.925%	102.5818	$1,025,817.60	0.450	$1,030,317.60	4.462%	5.366	34.345	A1	AA-
		Bristol-Myers Squibb	BMY	110122AL2	8/15/2013	5.250%	MW (+15)	1000	4.622%	103.0727	$1,030,727.10	1.983	$1,050,560.43	4.549%	4.751	27.189	A1	A+
		Merck	MRK	589331AK3	3/1/2015	4.750%	MW (+15)	1000	4.865%	99.3048	$993,047.96	1.583	$1,008,881.29	4.369%	5.914	41.945	Aa3	AA-
	Industrial Equipment:	Caterpillar	CAT	149123BG5	9/15/2009	7.250%	MW (+10)	1000	4.146%	105.0517	$1,050,517.44	2.135	$1,071,864.67	4.642%	1.574	3.350	A2	A
	Office Equipment:	Pitney Bowes	PBI	72447WAU3	8/15/2014	4.875%	MW (+15)	1000	5.125%	98.6053	$986,053.02	1.842	$1,004,469.69	4.350%	5.487	36.212	A1	A+
	Mortgage:	Federal Natl. Mort. Assn.	FNMA	31360QP2	4/25/2019	10.450%	Serial Calls	23	4.571%	117.7500	$26,564.44	1.074	$26,806.74	0.116%	2.940	5.041	Aaa	AAA
	Technology:	Intl. Business Machines	IBM	459200BZ6	1/26/2009	5.400%	Not Callable	1000	4.651%	100.7690	$1,007,689.68	2.325	$1,030,939.68	4.464%	1.007	1.536	A1	A+
	Telecommunications:	Verizon NJ	VZ	92344UAA3	1/17/2012	5.875%	MW (-30)	1000	4.716%	104.2198	$1,042,197.95	2.676	$1,068,961.84	4.629%	3.494	14.992	A3	A
		BellSouth Corp.	BLS	079860AB8	10/15/2011	6.000%	MW (+20)	1000	4.918%	103.6902	$1,036,901.92	1.267	$1,049,568.59	4.545%	3.331	13.494	A2	A

Portfolio Summary

Number of Bond Issues	27
Total Portfolio Market Value	$23,093,005.12
Total Portfolio Par Value	$22,606,560.04
Wght. Avg. Bond Yield to Maturity	4.863%
Wght. Avg. Bond Coupon	5.445%
Portfolio Modified Duration	3.905
Portfolio Convexity	21.687
Wght. Avg. Moody's Rating	A1
Wght. Avg. S&P Rating	AA-

515

This example also helps highlight some practical challenges an investor must face when designing an immunization strategy. First of all, except for the special case of a zero-coupon bond, an immunized portfolio will require frequent rebalancing. As shown in the Appendix to this chapter, such rebalancing will be necessary with every significant shift in the yield curve, but it will also be required by the passing time. For instance, even if market rates do not change, after a year has passed (i.e., January 2009) the modified duration of the bond portfolio will be substantially lower than 3.91 years. (Because duration declines more slowly than maturity as time passes, the January 2009 modified duration level for the firm will be somewhat higher than 2.91 years.) Of course, because the target investment horizon would still be 4.00 years, this decay in the portfolio's duration would leave the firm in a position of net reinvestment risk and therefore adversely exposed to a subsequent downward movement in the yield curve. Thus, to remain immunized over time, the bond manager for Stonewall will periodically need to rebalance the portfolio to maintain the original duration target.

Second, in Chapter 12 we discussed the fact that duration changes inversely with changes in interest rates. In fact, it is this property that makes the relationship between a bond's price and its yield a convex function rather than a straight line. Consequently, the manager of an immunized bond portfolio should also pay attention to the convexity statistic of the position. Specifically, in addition to duration matching the company's assets and liabilities, the manager should attempt to construct a bond portfolio that has *greater convexity* than the firm's liabilities. When the convexity of the assets exceeds that of the liabilities at a time when the durations are matched, it will be the case that the *actual* decline in value for an upward rate movement will be less severe for the assets than for the liabilities. While it is difficult to know if the convexity level of 21.69 for Stonewall's portfolio accomplishes that goal without knowing more about the precise characteristics of its projected obligations, Kritzman (1992) demonstrates that for two portfolios with the same duration, the one with cash flows that are more spread out (i.e., less concentrated around the duration date) will have greater convexity. Thus, the bond ladder approach adopted by Stonewall's managers (e.g., maturity dates ranging from 2009 to 2015) is likely to produce a more successful outcome that a portfolio that concentrated its cash flow payments around January 2012 (i.e., the current date plus 4.00 years).

Finally, because certain segments of the fixed-income market can be illiquid, there sometimes is a problem purchasing the bonds we have identified as optimal for our portfolio. For example, can we purchase the long-duration bonds we have targeted at a price we consider to be acceptable? Further, bonds possessing the particular characteristics we need to match the target horizon exactly may not be available. Thus, Stonewall's modified duration statistic of 3.91 is likely as close as the manager could get to the target horizon of 4.00 given the nature of the bond market at the time of the example. In summary, it is important to recognize that classical immunization is generally *not* a passive strategy because it is subject to all of these practical issues that demand the attention of the manager.

16.5.3   Horizon Matching

Horizon matching is a combination of two of the techniques just discussed: cash-matching dedication and immunization. As shown in Exhibit 16.10, the liability stream is divided into two segments. In the first segment, the portfolio is constructed to provide a cash match for the liabilities during this horizon period (e.g., the first five years). The second segment is the remaining liability stream following the end of the horizon period—in the example, it is the 25 years following 2015. During this second time period, the liabilities are covered by a duration-matched strategy based on immunization principles. As a result, Leibowitz (1986b)

| **EXHIBIT 16.10** | The Concept of Horizon Matching |

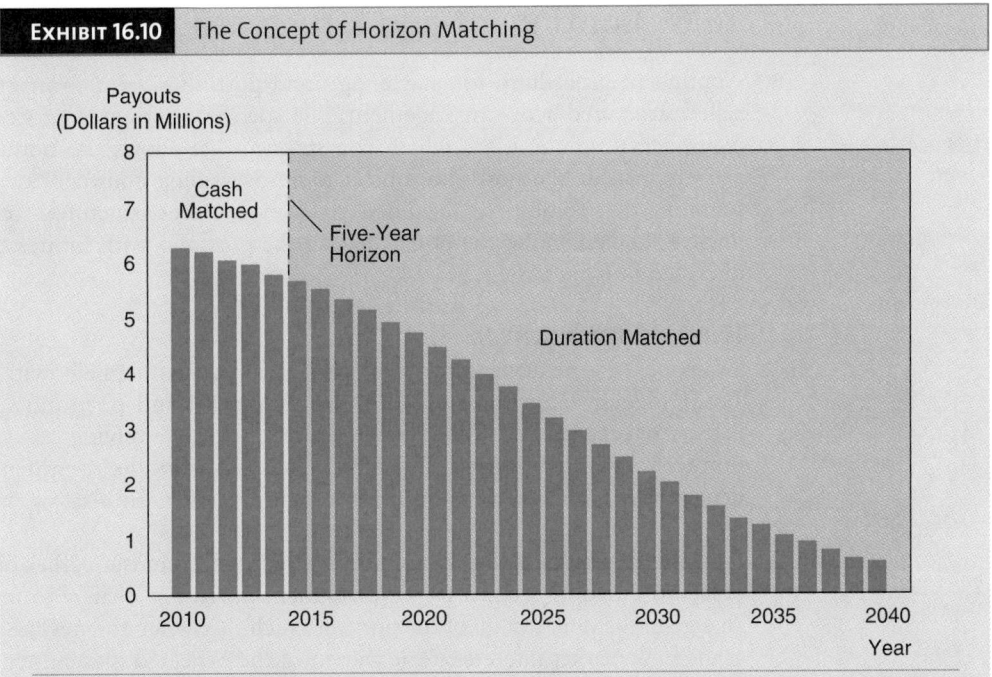

Source: "Horizon Matching: A New Generalized Approach for Developing Minimum Cost Dedicated Portfolios." Copyright 1983 Salomon Brothers Inc. This chart was prepared for Salomon Brothers Inc. by Martin Leibowitz, a former Managing Director; Thomas E. Klaffky, Managing Director; Steven Mandel, a former Managing Director; and Alfred Weinberger, a former Director. Although the information in this chart has been obtained from sources that Salomon Brothers Inc. believed to be reliable, SSB does not guarantee their accuracy, and such information may be incomplete or condensed. All figures included in this chart constitute SSB's judgment as of the original publication date. Reprinted with permission from SalomonSmithBarney.

contends that the client receives the certainty of cash matching during the early years and the cost saving and flexibility of duration-matched flows thereafter.

Horizon matching also helps alleviate one of the problems with classical immunization: the potential for non-parallel shifts in the yield curve. Most of the problems related to non-parallel shifts are concentrated in the short end of the yield curve because this is where the most severe curve reshaping typically occurs. Because the near-term horizon is cash-matched, however, these irregular rate changes are not of concern. Further, we know that the long end of the yield curve tends toward parallel shifts.

An important decision when using horizon matching is the length of the horizon period. The trade-off when making this decision is between the safety and certainty of cash matching and the lower cost and flexibility of duration-based immunization. The portfolio manager should provide the client with a set of horizon alternatives and the costs and benefits of each of them and allow the client to make the decision.

As part of their discussion on horizon matching, Leibowitz, Klaffky, Mandel, and Weinberger (1983) point out that it also is possible to consider *rolling out* the cash-matched segment over time. Specifically, after the first year the portfolio manager would restructure the portfolio to provide a cash match during the original Year 6, which means that we would still have a five-year horizon. The ability and cost of rolling out depends on movements in interest rates; ideally we would still want to see parallel shifts in the yield curve.

16.6   Contingent and Structured Management Strategies

Contingent procedures for managing bond portfolios are a form of what has come to be called structured active management. The specific contingent procedure we discuss here is contingent immunization, which is a strategy that allows the bond manager flexibility to actively manage the portfolio subject to an overriding constraint that the portfolio remains immunized at some predetermined yield level. Other structured strategies, which typically involve supplementing the bonds held in the portfolio with futures or option contracts, was discussed in Chapters 13 and 14.

16.6.1   CONTINGENT IMMUNIZATION

Subsequent to the developments of classical immunization, Leibowitz and Weinberger (1982, 1983) suggest a portfolio strategy that allows a bond portfolio manager to pursue the highest returns available through active strategies while relying on classical bond immunization techniques to ensure a given minimal return over the investment horizon. That is, their new procedure allows active portfolio management with a safety net provided by classical immunization.

To understand contingent immunization, recall from our earlier discussion that when the portfolio duration is equal to the investment horizon, a change in interest rates will cause a change in the dollar value of the portfolio such that when the new asset value is compounded at the new market interest rate, it will equal the expected (desired) ending-wealth value. This required change in value occurs *only* when the modified duration of the portfolio is equal to the remaining time horizon, which is why the modified duration of the portfolio must be maintained at the horizon value.

Consider the following example of this process. Assume that our desired ending-wealth value is $206.3 million. Given this specific ending value and the number of years to our horizon value, it is possible to determine how much we must invest today to attain that ending value if we assume a rate of return on the portfolio. Obviously, this is just the reverse of the price compounding exercise—that is, we compute the present value of the ending value at the expected yield for the horizon period.[7] In this case, we assume a five-year horizon and a 15% return, meaning that we compute the present value of $206.3 million at 15% for five years or 7.5% for 10 periods assuming semi-annual compounding. The present value equals $100 million—this is the required initial investment under these assumptions to attain the desired ending value.

Assuming the five-year horizon, we can do it for other interest rates as follows:

Percent	Present Value Factor[a]	Required Investment ($ Mil.)	Percent	Present Value Factor[a]	Required Investment ($ Mil.)
10	0.6139	$126.65	16	0.4632	$95.56
12	0.5584	115.20	18	0.4224	87.14
14	0.5083	104.86	20	0.3855	79.53
15	0.4852	100.00			

[a]Present value for 10 periods (5 years) at one-half the annual percentage rate.

---

7 The article on this topic was written when interest rates were at historically high levels of about 14% to 16%, which explains the high example rates. The concepts would be the same with lower rates.

| EXHIBIT 16.11 | Classical Immunization |

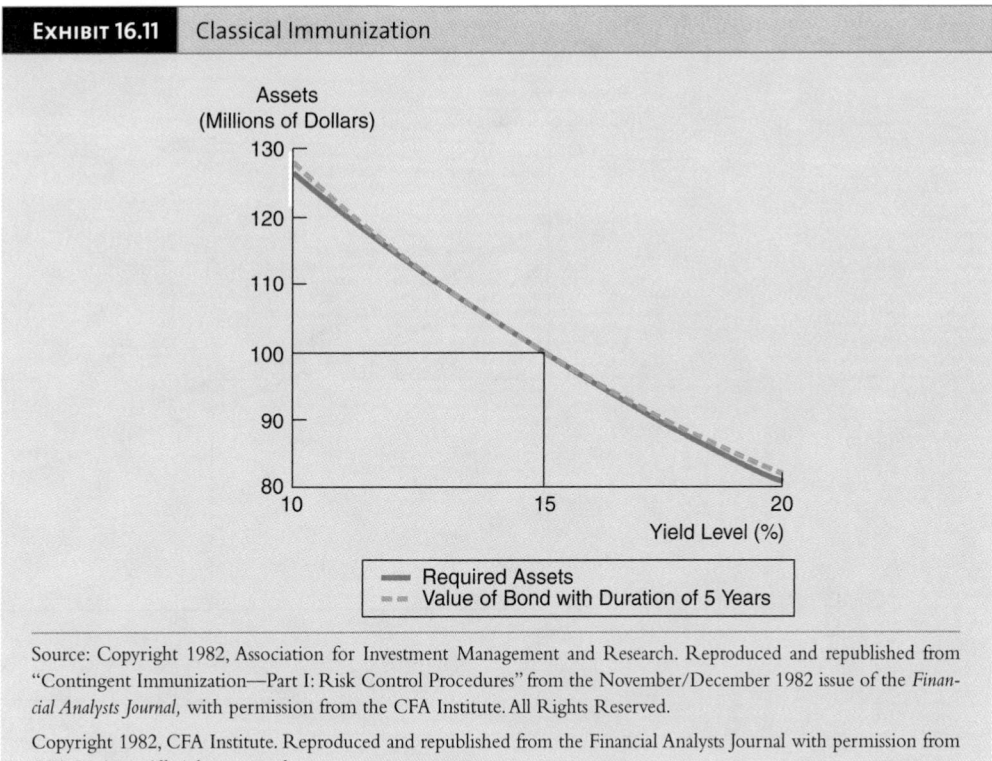

Source: Copyright 1982, Association for Investment Management and Research. Reproduced and republished from "Contingent Immunization—Part I: Risk Control Procedures" from the November/December 1982 issue of the *Financial Analysts Journal,* with permission from the CFA Institute. All Rights Reserved.

Copyright 1982, CFA Institute. Reproduced and republished from the Financial Analysts Journal with permission from CFA Institute. All rights reserved.

Exhibit 16.11 reflects these calculations—that is, the dark line indicates the required initial amount that must be invested at every yield level to attain $206.3 million in five years. Clearly, at lower yields we need a larger initial investment (e.g., $126 million at 10%), and it declines with higher yields (e.g., it is less than $80 million at 20%). The dotted line in Exhibit 16.11 indicates that the price sensitivity of a portfolio with a modified duration of five years will have almost exactly the price sensitivity required.

Contingent immunization requires that the client be willing to accept a potential return below the current market return. This is referred to as a *cushion spread,* or the difference between the current market return and some floor rate. This cushion spread in required yield provides flexibility for the portfolio manager to engage in active portfolio strategies. For example, if current market rates are 15%, the client might be willing to accept a floor rate of 14%. Assuming the client initiated the fund with $100 million, accepting this lower rate will mean that the portfolio manager does not have the same ending-asset requirements. Specifically, at 14% the required ending-wealth value would be $196.72 million (7% for 10 periods) compared to the $206.3 million at 15%. Because of this lower floor rate (and lower ending-wealth value), it is possible to experience some declines in the value of the portfolio while attempting to do better than the market through active management strategies.

Exhibit 16.12 shows the value of assets required at the beginning assuming a 14% required return and the implied ending-wealth value of $196.72 million. Notably, assuming current market rates of 15%, the required value of assets at the beginning would be $95.45 million (present value of $196.72 million at 15% for five years). The difference between the client's initial fund of $100 million and the required assets of $95.56 million is the dollar cushion available to the portfolio manager. As noted, this dollar cushion arises

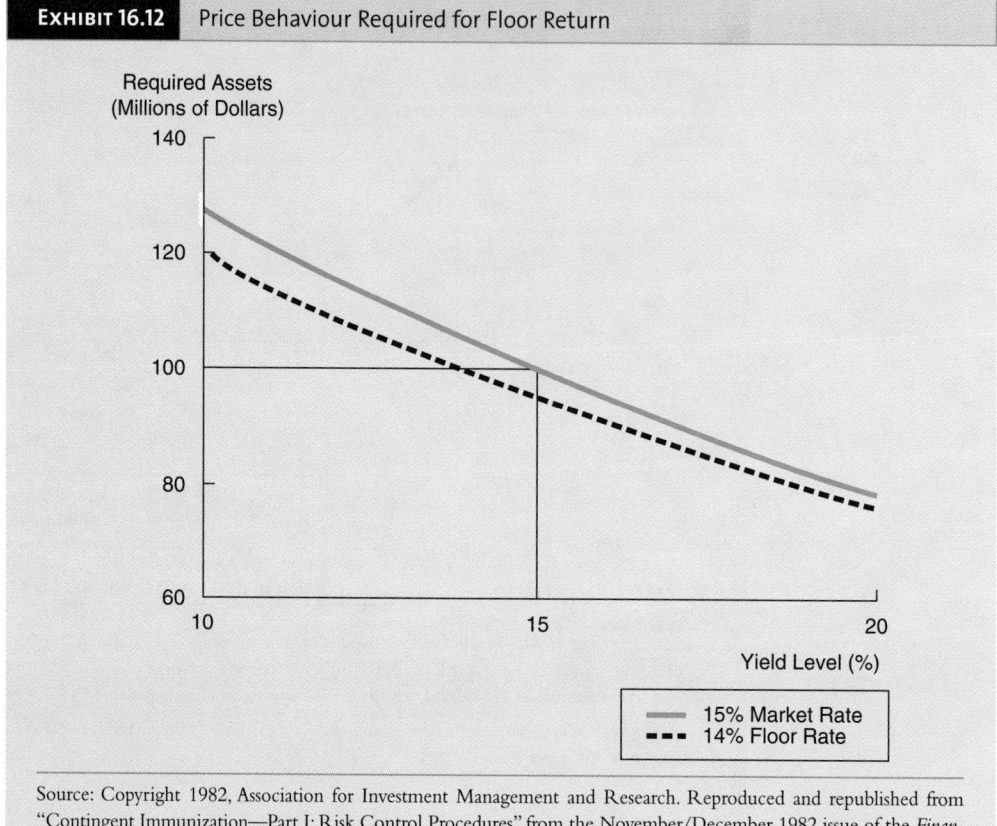

EXHIBIT 16.12   Price Behaviour Required for Floor Return

Source: Copyright 1982, Association for Investment Management and Research. Reproduced and republished from "Contingent Immunization—Part I: Risk Control Procedures" from the November/December 1982 issue of the *Financial Analysts Journal,* with permission from the CFA Institute. All Rights Reserved.

Copyright 1982, CFA Institute. Reproduced and republished from the Financial Analysts Journal with permission from CFA Institute. All rights reserved.

because the client has agreed to a lower investment rate and, therefore, a lower ending-wealth value. Therefore, the manager effectively now has a $4.55 million (= 100 − 95.45) "side fund" with which to pursue active management strategies in an attempt to add alpha to the overall portfolio.

At this point, the manager can engage in various active portfolio management strategies to increase the ending-wealth value of the portfolio above that required at 14%. For example, assume that the portfolio manager believes that market rates will decline. Under such conditions, they might consider buying a 30-year bond with a modified duration greater than the investment horizon of five years and, therefore, has greater price sensitivity to changes in market rates. Hence, if rates decline as expected, the value of the long-duration portfolio will experience a rapid increase above the initial value. In contrast, if rates increase, the portfolio value will decline rapidly. In this case, depending on how high rates go, the portfolio value could fall to a value below that needed to reach the desired ending-wealth value of $196.72 million.

Exhibit 16.13 shows what happens to the portfolio value if we assume an instantaneous change in interest rates when the fund is established. Specifically, if rates decline from 15%, the portfolio of long-duration, 30-year bonds would experience a large increase in value and develop a *safety margin*—a portfolio value above the required value. In contrast, if rates increase, the portfolio value will decline until it reaches the asset value required at 14%. When the value of the portfolio reaches this point of minimum return (referred to as a *trigger point*), it is nec-

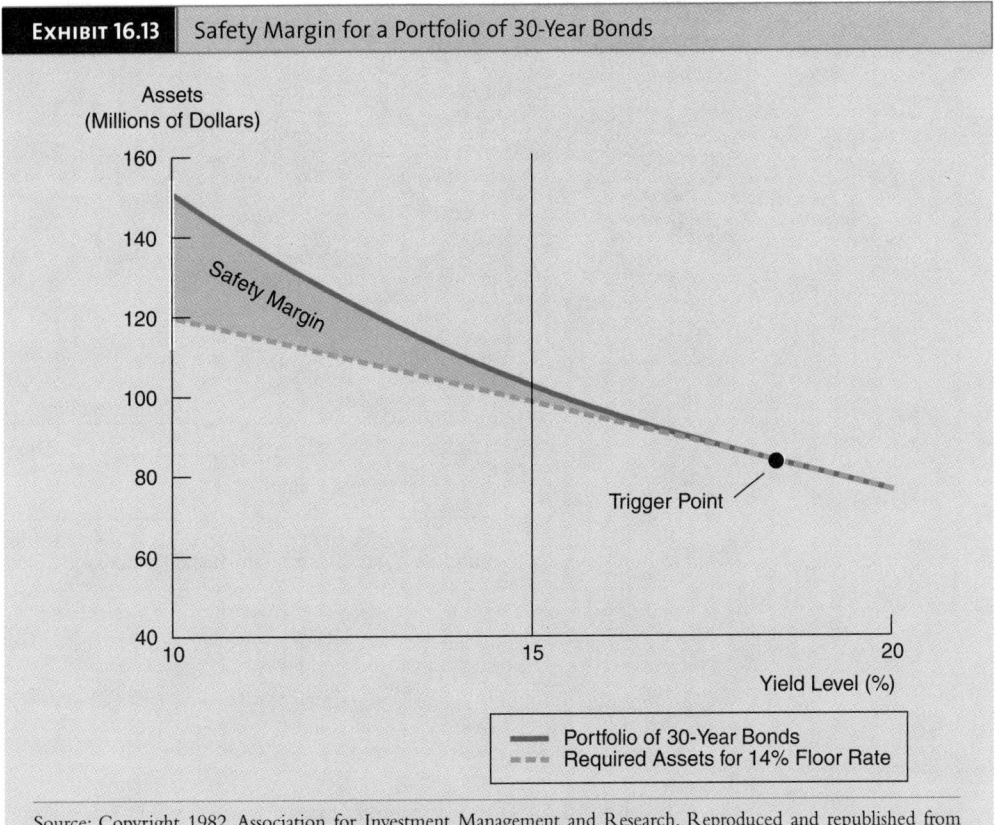

EXHIBIT 16.13 Safety Margin for a Portfolio of 30-Year Bonds

Source: Copyright 1982, Association for Investment Management and Research. Reproduced and republished from "Contingent Immunization—Part I: Risk Control Procedures" from the November/December 1982 issue of the *Financial Analysts Journal,* with permission from the CFA Institute. All Rights Reserved.

Copyright 1982, CFA Institute. Reproduced and republished from the Financial Analysts Journal with permission from CFA Institute. All rights reserved.

essary to stop active portfolio management and use classical immunization with the remaining assets to ensure that we attain the desired ending-wealth value (i.e., $196.72 million).

Potential Return The concept of potential return is helpful in understanding the objective of contingent immunization. This is the return the portfolio would achieve over the entire investment horizon if, at any point, the assets on hand were immunized at the prevailing market rate. Exhibit 16.14 shows the various rates of return based on dollar asset values shown in Exhibit 16.13. If the portfolio were immediately immunized when market rates were 15%, its potential return would naturally be 15%. Alternatively, if yields declined instantaneously to 10%, the portfolio's asset value would increase to $147 million (see Exhibit 16.13). If this $147 million portfolio were immunized at the market rate of 10% over the remaining five-year period, the portfolio would grow to a total value of $239.45 million (using 5% compound growth factor for 10 periods). This ending value of $239.45 million represents an 18.25% realized (horizon) rate of return on the original $100 million portfolio.

In contrast, if interest rates increase, the portfolio value will decline substantially and the potential return will decline. For example, if market rates rise to 17% (i.e., a yield change of 2%), the asset value of the 30-year bond portfolio will decline to $88 million (see Exhibit 16.13). If this portfolio of $88 million were immunized for the remaining five years at the prevailing market rate of 17%, the ending value would be $199 million. This ending value implies a potential return of 14.32% for the total period.

EXHIBIT 16.14 The Potential Return Concept

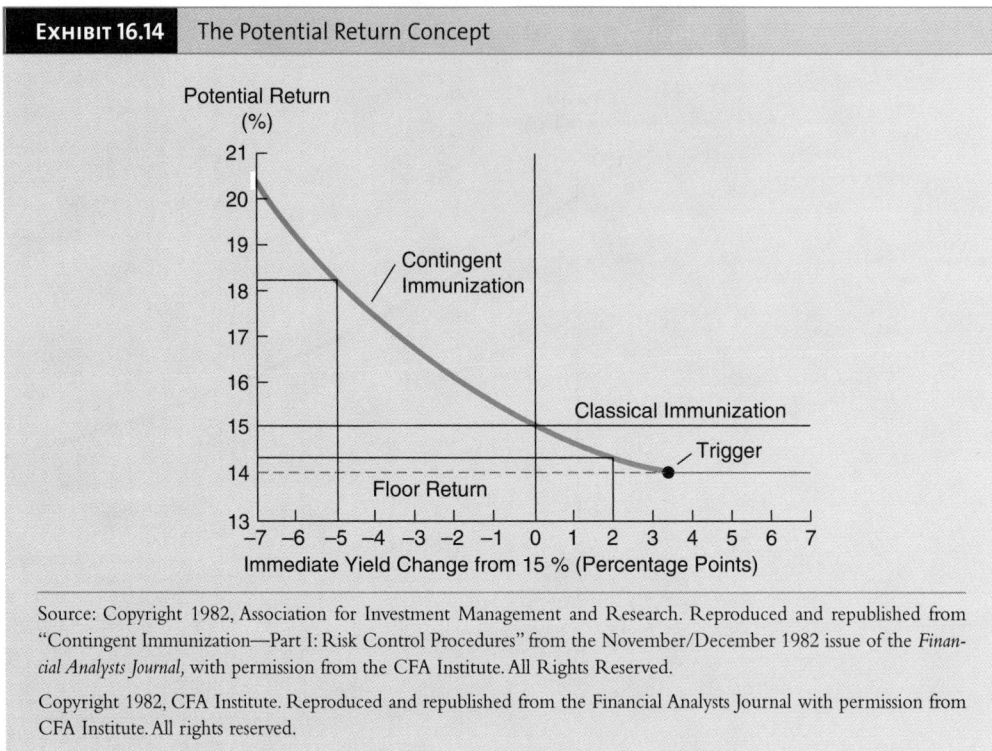

Source: Copyright 1982, Association for Investment Management and Research. Reproduced and republished from "Contingent Immunization—Part I: Risk Control Procedures" from the November/December 1982 issue of the *Financial Analysts Journal,* with permission from the CFA Institute. All Rights Reserved.

Copyright 1982, CFA Institute. Reproduced and republished from the Financial Analysts Journal with permission from CFA Institute. All rights reserved.

As Exhibit 16.13 shows, if interest rates rose to 18.50%, the 30-year bonds would decline to a value of $81.16 million (the trigger point) and the portfolio would have to be immunized. At this point, if the remaining assets of $81.16 million were immunized at this current market rate of 18.50%, the value of the portfolio would grow to $196.59 million (using 9.25% compound growth for 10 periods). This ending value implies that the potential return for the portfolio would be exactly 14% as shown in Exhibit 16.14. Regardless of what happens to subsequent market rates, the portfolio has been immunized at the floor rate of 14%. That is a major characteristic of the contingent immunized portfolio; if there is proper monitoring we will always know the trigger point where we must immunize to be assured of receiving a return no less than the minimum rate of return specified.

Monitoring the Immunized Portfolio Clearly, monitoring the contingent immunized portfolio is crucial to ensure that, if the asset value falls to the trigger point, the appropriate action is taken to ensure that the portfolio is immunized at the floor-level rate. This can be done using a chart as in Exhibit 16.15. The top line is the current market value of the portfolio over time. The bottom line is the required value of the immunized floor portfolio. Specifically, the bottom line is *the required value of the portfolio* if we were to immunize at *today's rates* to attain the necessary ending-wealth value. This required minimum portfolio value is *the present value of the promised ending-wealth value at the prevailing market rate.*

To demonstrate how this floor portfolio would be constructed, consider again our example where we derived a promised ending-wealth value in five years of $196.72 million based on an initial investment of $100 million and an acceptable floor rate of 14%. If one year after the initiation of the portfolio, market rates were 10%, we would need a minimum portfolio value of roughly $133.14 million to get to $196.72 million in four years (present value of $196.72 million promised ending-wealth value at 5% for eight periods, assuming

Exhibit 16.15	Contingent Immunization Floor Portfolio over Time

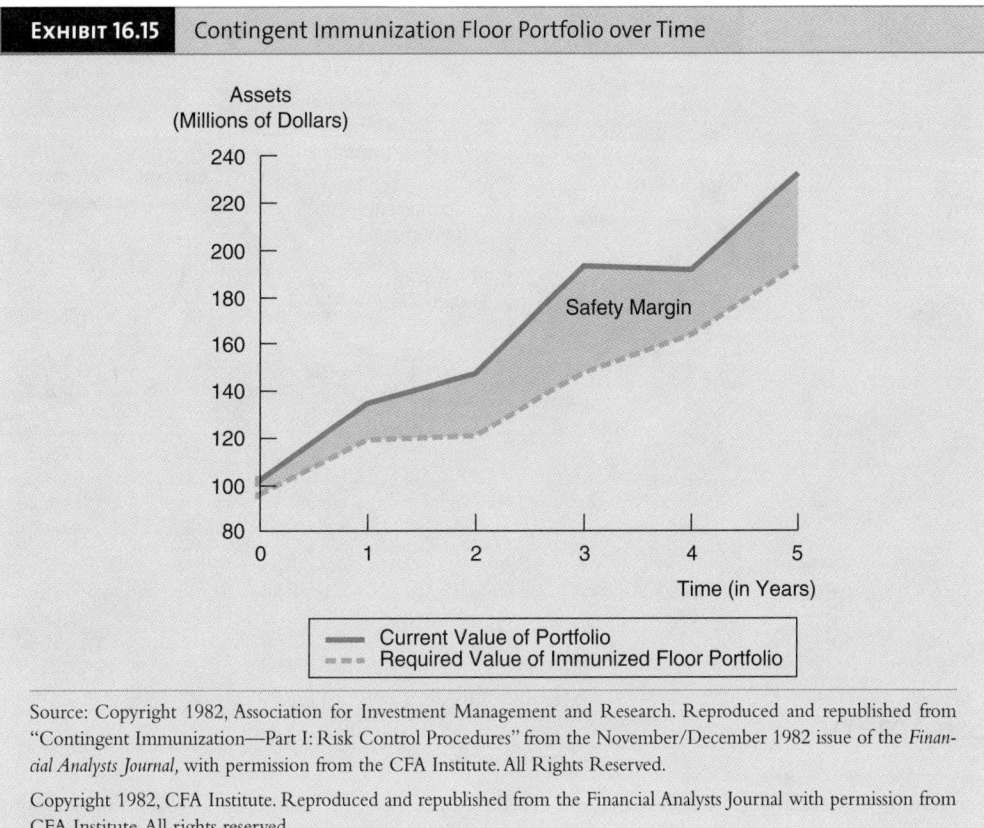

Source: Copyright 1982, Association for Investment Management and Research. Reproduced and republished from "Contingent Immunization—Part I: Risk Control Procedures" from the November/December 1982 issue of the *Financial Analysts Journal,* with permission from the CFA Institute. All Rights Reserved.

Copyright 1982, CFA Institute. Reproduced and republished from the Financial Analysts Journal with permission from CFA Institute. All rights reserved.

semi-annual compounding). The logic is that $133.14 million invested at 10% for four years will equal $196.72 million.

If the active manager had originally predicted correctly that market rates would decline and had structured a long-duration portfolio under these conditions, the *actual* value of the portfolio would be much higher than this *minimum required* value, and there would be a safety margin. A year later (after Year 2), we would determine the assets needed at the rate prevailing at that point in time. Assuming interest rates had by then increased to 12%, we could determine that we would need a floor portfolio of about $138.69 million. Specifically, this is the present value of the $196.72 million for three years at 12%, assuming semi-annual compounding. Again, we would expect the actual portfolio value to be greater than this required floor portfolio, so we still have a safety margin. If we ever reached the point where the actual portfolio value was equal to the required floor value, we would stop the active management and immunize what was left *at the current market rate* to ensure that the ending value of the portfolio would be $196.72 million.

In summary, the contingent immunization strategy encompasses the opportunity for a bond portfolio manager to engage in various active portfolio strategies if the client is willing to accept a floor return (and ending-wealth value) that is below what is currently available. The graph in Exhibit 16.16 describes the trade-offs involved in contingent immunization. Specifically, by allowing for a slightly lower minimum target rate, the client is making it possible to experience a much higher potential return from active management by the portfolio manager.

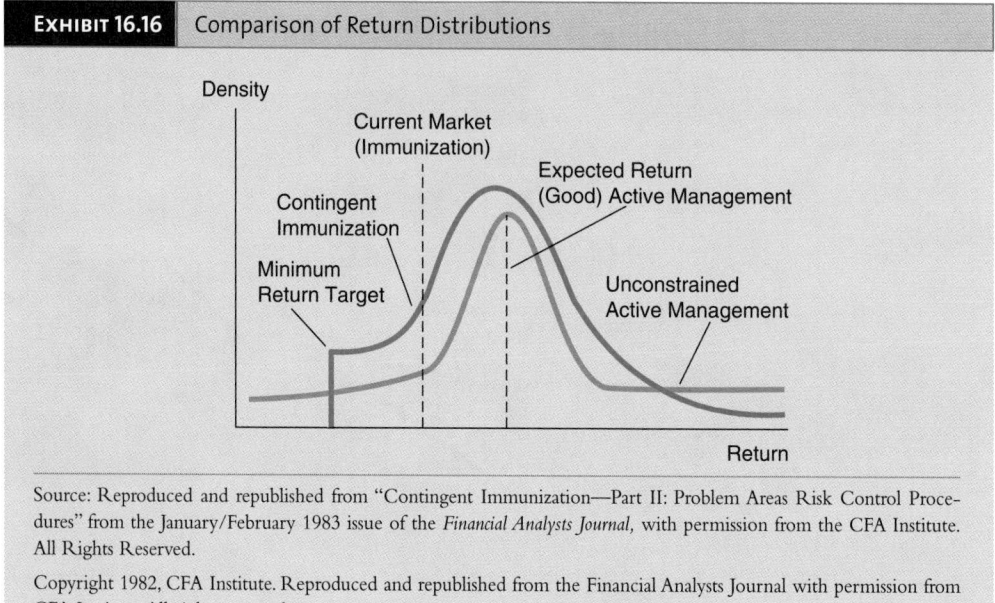

EXHIBIT 16.16 Comparison of Return Distributions

Source: Reproduced and republished from "Contingent Immunization—Part II: Problem Areas Risk Control Procedures" from the January/February 1983 issue of the *Financial Analysts Journal*, with permission from the CFA Institute. All Rights Reserved.

Copyright 1982, CFA Institute. Reproduced and republished from the Financial Analysts Journal with permission from CFA Institute. All rights reserved.

Summary

1. The investment style of a bond portfolio can be summarized by its two most important characteristics: credit quality and interest rate sensitivity. A 3 × 3 style grid can be used to accommodate these dimensions. The average credit quality of the portfolio can be classified as high, medium, or low grade. The second dimension of the bond portfolio's investment style can be separated as short-, intermediate-, or long-term.

2. During the past few decades, there has been a significant increase in the number and variety of bond portfolio strategies available to individual investors and professional managers. These strategies, which can range from being quite simple to quite complex to implement and maintain, can be classified into five separate categories: passive management techniques, active management techniques, core-plus management techniques, matched-funding techniques, and contingent and structured techniques.

3. Passive approaches to managing a bond portfolio can take two forms. Buy-and-hold investors simply choose a selection of bonds with the desired set of characteristics (e.g., duration, coupon rate, credit quality) and replace them when they mature. By contrast, an investor following an indexed approach constructs a portfolio that mimics the contents of a particular bond index. The construction of an indexed portfolio can either fully replicate the underlying benchmark or follow a stratified sampling approach that attempts to reproduce the index characteristics with a smaller number of instruments.

4. Active bond management strategies attempt to exceed the risk-return performance produced by a bond index over time. The active manager does this by assembling a collection of bonds that differs from those in the benchmark in a manner consistent with his view of future bond market conditions. The number of active strategies available is numerous and includes interest rate anticipation, valuation analysis, credit analysis, yield spread analysis, and global and tactical techniques. Core-plus bond management can be viewed as type of enhanced indexing that combines passive and active techniques.

5. Many institutional investors (e.g., pension funds, insurance companies) employ matched-funding strategies when the investment problem they confront involves forming a portfolio of assets designed to pay off a specific set of liabilities. Immunization techniques based on matching the durations of the organization's assets and liabilities are particularly useful in providing protection against adverse interest rate movements. Other techniques include dedicated portfolios and horizontal matching.

6. Finally, contingent immunization is a form of structured active management that combines a classical immunization approach with some active management techniques.

Key Terms

asset–liability management, p. 508
bond ladder, p. 495
bond swap, p. 505
buy-and-hold strategy, p. 494
core-plus bond portfolio
    management, p. 507
coupon reinvestment risk, p. 510

credit analysis, p. 500
dedication, p. 508
dedication with reinvestment, p. 508
enhanced indexing, p. 507
immunization, p. 511
indexing, p. 494
interest rate anticipation, p. 498

interest rate risk, p. 510
investment horizon, p. 510
price risk, p. 510
pure cash-matched dedicated
    portfolio, p. 508
tracking error, p. 495
valuation analysis, p. 500

Suggested Readings

Altman, Edward I., and Mario Y. Levallee. "Business Failure Classification in Canada." *Journal of Business Administration* 12, no. 1 (1980): 147–164.

Booth, Laurence. "The Case against Foreign Bonds." *Canadian Investment Review* 11, no. 2 (July 1998): 23.

Dattatreya, Ravi E., and Frank J. Fabozzi. *Active Total Return Management of Fixed-Income Portfolios,* rev. ed. Burr Ridge, IL: Irwin Professional, 1995.

Edwards, Greg. "A Simple Model for Bond Portfolio Performance Attribution." *Canadian Investment Review* 10, no. 1 (April 1997): 14–17.

Fabozzi, Frank J., ed. *Fixed-Income Readings for the Chartered Financial Analysts Program,* 2nd ed. New Hope, PA: Frank J. Fabozzi Associates, 2004.

Fabozzi, Frank J., Lionel Martellini, and Philippe Priaulet, eds. *Advanced Bond Portfolio Management.* Hoboken, NJ: John Wiley, 2006.

Fridson, Martin. *High-Yield Bonds: Assessing Risk and Identifying Value in Speculative Grade Securities.* Chicago: Probus, 1989.

Leibowitz, Martin L., William S. Krasker, and Ardavan Nozari. "Spread Duration: A New Tool for Bond Portfolio Management," *Journal of Portfolio Management* 16, no. 3 (Spring 1990).

Marmer, Harry, Martin Den Hayer, and Barry McInerney. "The Uses of Real Return Bonds." *Canadian Investment Review* 10, no. 4 (January 1997): 40.

Prisman, Eliezer Z., and Yisong Tian. "Immunization in Markets with Tax-Clientele Effects: Evidence from the Canadian Market." *Journal of Financial and Quantitative Analysis* 29, no. 2 (1994): 301.

Sherrerd, Katrina F., ed. *Fixed-Income Management for the 21st Century.* Charlottesville, VA: Association for Investment Management and Research,

For Chapter CFA Questions and Problems, please see Appendix A at the end of this text.

Questions

1. How would you explain to a casual observer why high-yield bond returns are more correlated to common stock returns than to investment-grade bond returns?

2. You begin with an investment horizon of four years and a portfolio with a duration of four years with a market interest rate of 10%. A year later, what is your investment horizon? Assuming no change in interest rates, what is the duration of your portfolio relative to your investment horizon? What does this imply about your ability to immunize your portfolio?

3. During a conference with a client, the subject of classical immunization is introduced. The client questions the fee charged for developing and managing an immunized portfolio. The client believes it is basically a passive investment strategy, so the management fee should be substantially lower. What would you tell the client to show that it is not a passive policy?

Problems

1. The par yield curve for Canadian government bonds is currently flat across all maturities at 5.50%. You have observed the following "paired" transaction by your bond portfolio manager:

Bond	Transaction	Type	Credit Spread (bp)	Maturity (yrs.)	Coupon Rate (%)	Modified Duration
G	Buy	Canadian Govt.	—	15	0	14.599
H	Sell	Corporate	100	7	8	5.386

Briefly discuss what this paired trade suggests to you about the manager's implied view as to: (i) the general direction of future interest rate movement, (ii) the future shape of the par yield curve, and (iii) the future level of corporate bond credit spreads.

2. Answer the following questions assuming that at the initiation of an investment account, the market value of your portfolio is $200 million, and you immunize the portfolio at 12% for six years. During the first year, interest rates are constant at 12%.
   a. What is the market value of the portfolio at the end of Year 1?
   b. Immediately after the end of the year, interest rates decline to 10%. Estimate the new value of the portfolio, assuming you did the required rebalancing (use only modified duration).

3. Compute the Macaulay duration (refer to Chapter 12) under the following conditions:
   a. A bond with a five-year term to maturity, a 12% coupon (annual payments), and a market yield of 10%.
   b. A bond with a four-year term to maturity, a 12% coupon (annual payments), and a market yield of 10%.
   c. Compare your answers to Parts a and b, and discuss the implications of this for classical immunization.

4. Compute the Macaulay duration (refer to Chapter 12) under the following conditions:
   a. A bond with a four-year term to maturity, a 10% coupon (annual payments), and a market yield of 8%.
   b. A bond with a four-year term to maturity, a 10% coupon (annual payments), and a market yield of 12%.
   c. Compare your answers to Parts a and b. Assuming it was an immediate shift in yields, discuss the implications of this for classical immunization.

5. Evaluate the following pure-yield pickup swap: You currently hold a 20-year, Aa-rated, 9.0% coupon bond priced to yield 11.0%. As a swap candidate, you are considering a 20-year, Aa-rated, 11% coupon bond priced to yield 11.5%. (Assume reinvestment at 11.5%.)

	Current Bond	Candidate Bond
Dollar investment		
Coupon		
i on one coupon		
Principal value at year end		
Total accrued		
Realized compound yield		

Value of swap: _____ basis points in one year

6. Evaluate the following substitution swap: You currently hold a 25-year, 9.0% coupon bond priced to yield 10.5%. As a swap candidate, you are considering a 25-year, Aa-rated, 9.0% coupon bond priced to yield 10.75%. (Assume a one-year work-out period and reinvestment at 10.5%.)

	Current Bond	Candidate Bond
Dollar investment		
Coupon		
i on one coupon		
Principal value at year end		
Total accrued		
Realized compound yield		

Value of swap: _____ basis points in one year

7. A university endowment fund has sought your advice on its fixed-income portfolio strategy. The characteristics of the portfolio's current holdings are listed below:

Bond	Credit Rating	Maturity (yrs.)	Coupon Rate (%)	Modified Duration	Convexity	Market Value of Position
A	U.S. Govt	3	0	2.727	9.9	$30,000
B	A1	10	8	6.404	56.1	30,000
C	Aa2	5	12	3.704	18.7	30,000
D	Agency	7	10	4.868	32.1	30,000
E	Aa3	12	0	10.909	128.9	30,000
						$150,000

   a. Calculate the modified duration for this portfolio (i.e., Mod D_p).
   b. Suppose you learn that the implied sensitivity (i.e., modified duration) of the endowment's liabilities is about 6.50 years. Identify whether the bond portfolio is: (i) immunized against interest rate risk, (ii) exposed

to net price risk, or (iii) exposed to net reinvestment risk. Briefly explain what will happen to the net position of the endowment fund if in the future there is a significant parallel upward shift in the yield curve.

c. Briefly describe how you could increase the convexity of the portfolio while keeping the modified duration at the same level.

d. Your current active view for the fixed-income market over the coming months is that Treasury yields will decline and corporate credit spreads will also decrease. Briefly discuss how you could restructure the existing portfolio to take advantage of this view.

BOND IMMUNIZATION AND PORTFOLIO REBALANCING

Suppose that you have decided to fund a three-year liability with a *portfolio* of bonds and that the only individual securities that you have to choose from are a two-year zero-coupon bond and a four-year zero-coupon bond. The current interest rate is 10%. Therefore:

$$\text{Price of two-year bond (i.e., Bond 2)} = (1,000) \div (1.1)^2 = \$826.35$$
$$\text{Price of four-year bond (i.e., Bond 4)} = (1,000) \div (1.1)^4 = \$683.01$$

In order to form a portfolio with duration of three years, you must purchase identical amounts of Bond 2 and Bond 4 as each of these zero-coupon instruments will have duration equal to its maturity. Consequently, you will need to buy 1.0 units of Bond 2 and $(826.45 \div 683.01) = 1.21$ units of Bond 4 for a total initial investment of \$1,652.89 [$826.45 + (1.21)(683.01)$]. The duration of your bond portfolio can then be calculated:

$$D = (826.45 \div 1,652.89)(D_2) + (826.45 \div 1,652.89)(D_4)$$
$$= (0.5)(2.00) + (0.5)(4.00) = 3.00$$

Assume now that immediately after you make your initial purchases, interest rates fall to 8%. If you do not rebalance your portfolio, what is your realized yield after three years? To establish this, compute: Terminal Value of Portfolio:

(i) Allow two-year bond to mature and reinvest for one year: $(1,000)(1.08) = \$1,080.00$
(ii) Sell 1.21 four-year bonds: $(1.21)(1,000 \div 1.08) = \$1,120.37$

so that your total terminal value is \$2,200.37, and the realized yield is:

$$\sqrt[3]{\frac{2,200.37}{1,652.89}} - 1 = 10.00\%$$

Therefore, your actual return is equal to the original promised return (i.e., the yield to maturity) of 10%. By investing so that the duration of the portfolio was equal to your horizon date, you have immunized yourself against the *first* interest rate change and locked in the initial promised yield of 10%.

Now, continuing with the assumption that interest rates decline immediately after your initial purchases, suppose that you decide to *rebalance* your portfolio. To understand how you can do this, you need to first establish the new bond prices:

$$\text{Price of Bond 2} = (1,000) \div (1.08)^2 = \$857.34$$
$$\text{Price of Bond 4} = (1,000) \div (1.08)^4 = \$735.03$$

To see why you need to rebalance, calculate the new duration of your portfolio:

Value of Investment in Bond 2 = 857.34

Value of Investment in Bond 4 = (1.21)(735.03) = 889.39

Value of Total Investment = \$1,746.73

so:

$$D = (857.34 \div 1{,}746.73)(D_2) + (889.39 \div 1{,}746.73)(D_4)$$
$$= (0.4908)(2.00) + (0.5092)(4.00) = 3.02$$

Notice that even though the change in interest rates didn't change the duration of the individual bonds it did increase the duration of the portfolio slightly since it altered the relative market values of Bond 2 and Bond 4. To correct the problem (i.e., to rebalance the portfolio), you need to *shorten* the overall duration by selling some of Bond 4 and purchasing some more of Bond 2. To accomplish this, you must once again invest equal dollar amounts in each security, or \$873.365 [(.5)(1,746.73)]. This in turn means that you must own the following number of each instrument:

Number of Bond 2 to be held = (873.365 ÷ 857.39) = 1.0186

Number of Bond 4 to be held = (873.365 ÷ 735.03) = 1.1882

After completing this step, you have rebalanced your portfolio to immunize against future changes in interest rate movements. By once again holding equal amounts of each bond, you have reset the duration of the portfolio to your original investment horizon of three years. An important assumption here is that this rebalancing can be done costlessly. If you must pay brokerage fees, the total dollar value of your portfolio, and hence your actual return, will be reduced accordingly.

By rebalancing your portfolio you have tampered with the composition of your initial investment. However, by doing so, have you also changed the realized yield that you will receive? Put another way, when you rebalance your portfolio at the new yield to maturity of 8%, will you still end up with the original yield of 10%? To answer this, calculate the terminal value of the rebalanced portfolio: (i) Allow 1.0182 two-year bonds to mature and reinvest for one year: (1.0182)(1,000)(1.08) = \$1,099.66; and (ii) sell 1.1882 four-year bonds: (1.1882)(1,000 ÷ 1.08) = \$1,100.19. Thus, your total terminal value of the rebalanced investment is \$2,200.31, and the realized yield is:

$$\sqrt[3]{\frac{2{,}199.85}{1{,}652.89}} - 1 = 10.00\%$$

Therefore, rebalancing your portfolio when interest rates change has *two effects*: (i) you immunize yourself against the next interest rate change, and (ii) your actual return is still equal to the yield to maturity that prevailed at the time of your original investment. Finally, it should be noted that although we assumed that the interest rate changed immediately after the initial purchase, the fundamentals of rebalancing also apply to yield curve shifts that occur at any point in the duration of the investment.

Professional Money Management, Alternative Assets, and Industry Ethics

So far, we have discussed how investors can analyze the aggregate market, various industry sectors, and individual companies, as well as their stocks and bonds to include in their investment portfolios. We have also examined alternative investment vehicles, such as options, warrants, convertibles, and futures that expand an investor's risk–return possibilities. This chapter introduces another possibility to the investor: entrusting one's money to a professional portfolio manager. Using a professional manager can range from having an account with an investment advisor, purchasing shares (or units) in an established security portfolio managed by an investment company, or becoming a limited partner in an organization managed by a general partner. In any form, professionally managed investments often represent a substantial portion of an individual's total holdings.

Both individual and institutional (e.g., pension plans, university endowments) investors alike seek the services of professional money managers for several reasons. First and foremost, it is often presumed that these managers may possess superior investment skills that will lead to higher returns than investors could obtain on their own. Beyond that, there are a number of additional benefits that professional managers supply, such as offering access to asset classes and investment strategies that might otherwise be unavailable or providing a cost-effective way to choose among a wide variety of diversified portfolios spanning the risk–return spectrum. However, these relationships also create potential conflicts of interest between the goals of the investor and those of the manager that need to be considered.

We begin by explaining how asset management firms are typically organized and charge for their services. We then explore three different types of professional money management firms: traditional private management firms, investment (i.e., fund) companies, and "alternative asset" companies (i.e., hedge funds, private equity firms) created through limited partnership vehicles. We pay particular attention to the contrast between investment companies, which are the most prevalent ways in which investors employ professional counsel, and alternative asset vehicles, which represent the most rapidly growing segment of the industry.

17.1 The Asset Management Industry: Structure and Evolution

There are two basic ways that traditional professional asset management firms are organized. In the most straightforward structure, individuals as well as institutional investors make contracts directly with a **management and advisory firm** for its services. These services can range from providing standard banking transactions (e.g., savings accounts, personal loans) to advising clients on structuring their own portfolios to actually managing the investment funds themselves. Although banking and financial advice were once the main services these firms offered, there has recently been a dramatic shift toward the *assets under management* (AUM) approach. In that arrangement, the management firm becomes the custodian of the investor's capital, usually with full discretion as to how those funds are invested. Each client of the management firm has a *separate account* so that the assets of each client will be accounted for separately regardless of whether the firm employs a single "model" portfolio (see Panel A of Exhibit 17.1).

A second approach to asset management involves the *commingling* investment capital from several clients. An **investment company** invests a pool of funds belonging to many individuals in a single portfolio of securities. In exchange for this capital, the investment company issues to each investor new shares or units representing his or her proportional ownership of the mutually held securities portfolio or *fund*. For example, assume an investment company sells 10 million units at $10 per unit, thereby raising $100 million. If the fund's purpose is to emphasize large-cap common stocks, the manager would invest the proceeds of the fund share sale ($100 million less any brokerage fees) in the stock of such companies. Each investor who bought units would then own the appropriate percentage of the overall fund, rather than any portion of the shares in the portfolio themselves (see Panel B of Exhibit 17.1).

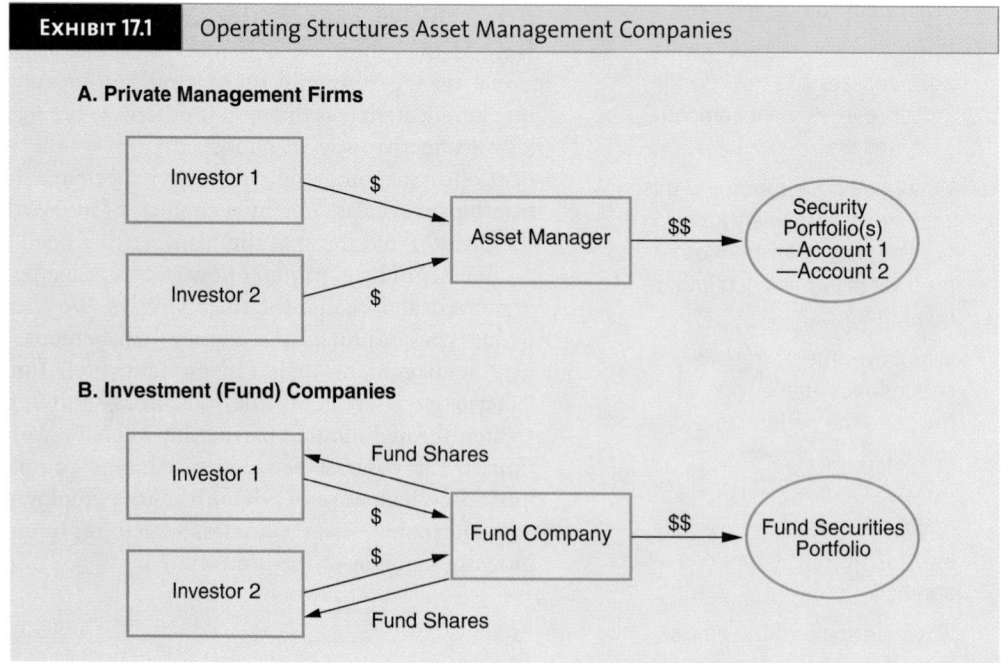

| **EXHIBIT 17.1** | Operating Structures Asset Management Companies |

A. Private Management Firms

B. Investment (Fund) Companies

Up-to-date information on the Canadian mutual fund industry can be found on the Investment Funds Institute of Canada web site at http://www.ific.ca.

There are important differences between these two organizational forms. Private management and advisory firms typically develop a personal relationship with their clients, getting to know the specific investment objectives and constraints of each. The assets held in the various separate accounts can then be tailored to these special needs, even if a general blueprint portfolio is used for all clients. This special attention comes at a cost, and for this reason private management firms are primarily used by investors such as pension fund sponsors and individuals with high net worth. Conversely, a mutual fund offered by an investment company is formed as a general solution to an investment problem and then marketed to investors who might fit that profile. The primary clients who seek professional asset management through investment companies are individual investors with relatively small pools of capital.

It is not unusual for professional asset management firms to combine these two structures by offering private advisory services as well as publicly traded funds. For instance, consider Dundee Wealth, a Canadian multi-asset, independent advisory firm. Founded over 30 years ago, Dundee Wealth has seen its business grow to the point where it managed almost $66 billion by mid-2008. The majority of this capital is invested in the firm's various public mutual fund portfolios, but Dundee Wealth also has $2.9 billion AUM from private clients (this includes retirement funds, public funds and unions, foundations and endowments, and individual investors).[1]

The AUM growth that Dundee Wealth has experienced during the past few years has been typical for the entire industry. According to the Investment Funds Institute of Canada (http://statistics.ific.ca/English/Reports/MonthlyStatistics.asp) there has been an increase in the number of large asset management firms, defined as those organizations with AUM of more than $100 billion. In 2001, there were no such Canadian firms; by 2008, there were two. Much of this asset growth can be explained by the strong performance of global equity markets during this period, but another important contributing factor was the consolidation trend that marked the industry. This consolidation trend is likely to continue, because the competition among existing asset management firms for the flow of new investment capital is expected to increase significantly.[2]

17.2   Private Management and Advisory Firms

While larger management companies offer a broader range of services and products, the majority of private management and advisory firms are still much smaller and more narrowly focused on a particular niche of the market. To examine one typical organization in greater detail, consider Prudent Capital Management (PCM),[3] a growth-oriented equity and fixed-income manager located in Southern California. PCM utilizes a "bottom-up" security selection process, with its portfolio managers looking for companies that have exceptional profitability, market share, return on equity, and earnings growth. PCM's clients include both institutional investors and individuals with high net worth (between $2 million and $5 million in assets) in both separate and commingled accounts. The firm offers management of both taxed and non-taxed products. Exhibit 17.2 shows the myriad investment products that PCM offers, along with the minimum investment accepted in each.

---

1 This, and much more, information is available from Dundee Wealth's public home page at http://www.dundeewealth.eu/en.

2 Good economic analysis of the professional asset management business can be found in Hurley et al. (1995) and Brinson (2005).

3 Prudent Capital Management is a pseudonym for a real firm whose name has been changed by request. However, all of the subsequent information reported is real.

EXHIBIT 17.2	Representative Private Management Firm Investment Products		
	Large-Cap	**Mid-Cap**	**Small-Cap**
Equity:	$5 million	$5 million	
	$2 million	$5 million	$10 million
	Commingled fund (Delaware Business Trust)	Commingled fund (Delaware Business Trust)	Commingled fund (closed)
	$2 million for sponsored program affiliates	$2 million for sponsored program affiliates	
Balanced:	$5 million		
	$2 million for sponsored program affiliates		
Concentrated:	$5 million		
	$2 million for sponsored program affiliates		
Tax-Sensitive Management:	$5 million		
	Equity, balanced, fixed		
	$2 million for sponsored program affiliates		
Concentrated:	$5 million		
Tax-Sensitive Management:	$2 million for sponsored program affiliates		
Active Fixed Income:	$5 million		
	Separately managed		
	$2 million for sponsored program affiliates		

Like the industry as a whole, PCM saw the assets under its management increase steadily over the past several years. Panel A of Exhibit 17.3 shows that over a recent five-year period, the firm's AUM grew by almost 80%, from $11.8 billion to $21.2 billion. During the same period, the median separate account size jumped from $24.8 million to over $39 million. This suggests that PCM's clients tend to be institutional investors, and the client profile summarized in Panel B of Exhibit 17.3 confirms this. The company offers services to more than 350 clients, but the majority of these are—and the vast majority of the assets come from—institutional investors. Perhaps because of the minimum investment restrictions, relatively few of the clients are individual investors and the assets they represent are slightly less than 3% (535 ÷ 21,165) of PCM's business.

Panel C of Exhibit 17.3 shows fee schedules representative of both the equity and fixed-income management services that PCM offers. Typical of the entire industry, these fees are not flat amounts but are expressed as percentages of invested capital on an annual basis. They are also graduated on a declining scale so that the more capital an investor commits to the firm,

Exhibit 17.3	Representative Private Management Firm: AUM, Clients, and Fees

A. AUM

Date	Assets Managed ($ Mil.)	No. of Institutional Clients	ACCOUNT SIZE	
			Average ($ Mil.)	Median ($ Mil.)
Year 5	21,165.0	207	97.5	39.3
Year 4	18,441.0	206	85.1	34.9
Year 3	17,608.0	226	74.2	30.6
Year 2	17,808.0	233	72.3	30.4
Year 1	14,578.0	237	61.5	27.8
Year 0	11,833.0	230	51.4	24.8

B. Clients

	No. of Clients	Assets ($ Mil.)
Corporate retirement funds	126	7,937.0
Public funds	35	3,881.0
Unions (Taft-Hartley)	18	1,442.0
Foundations, endowments, associations	66	1,656.0
Commingled funds	4	1,682.0
General insurance accounts	N/A	N/A
Limited partnership	N/A	N/A
Mutual funds	18	3,411.0
Individuals: IRAs and other	75	535.0
Other	5	186.0
Taxable corporate	17	435.0

C. Fee Schedule

Large-Cap Growth Equity Accounts	**Fixed-Income Accounts**
• 1.00% on the first $10,000,000	• 0.375% on the first $25,000,000
• 0.75% on the next $10,000,000	• 0.30% over $25,000,000
• 0.50% above $20,000,000	

Source: Data adapted from Nelson's Directory of Investment Managers.

the lower his or her average cost would be. An individual with $15 million would pay annual fees of $137,500 (10,000,000 × 0.01 + 5,000,000 × 0.0075), or 0.92% of total invested capital. On the other hand, the fee paid by a pension fund with $115 million under management would be $650,000 (10,000,000 × 0.01 + 10,000,000 × 0.0075 + 95,000,000 × 0.005), or 0.57%. One advantage to the investor of having the fee schedule tied directly to AUM is that as the management firm performs better for the client, its fees will increase. This reward system helps to align the incentives of the investor and the manager.

17.2.1 INVESTMENT STRATEGY AT A PRIVATE MONEY MANAGEMENT FIRM

Recall from our earlier description that the private money management firm would hold each client's assets in a separate account and those portfolios would likely be heavily influenced by the firm's overall investment philosophy. It is this investment philosophy—along with the returns it produces—that attracts clients to a particular money manager in the first place. We show the investment strategy and major holdings for two of PCM's model portfolios, one in equities and one in fixed-income securities, in Exhibit 17.4.

The investment approach outlined in Panel A of Exhibit 17.4 makes it clear that clients choosing to invest in PCM's large-cap growth stock product will have their money invested primarily in technology companies. While the specific stock allocations might vary from one client to another, the same fundamental orientation toward stock selection will be applied to

---

| **EXHIBIT 17.4** | Investment Strategy at a Representative Private Management Firm |

A. Large-Cap Growth Equity Portfolio

Investment Approach:

Our focused, fundamental research process is primarily based on the ideas from our in-house analysts. Our analysts operate as specialists. They direct their expertise on specific industries and sectors covering seven key growth sectors: technology/components, technology/systems, telecom, health care, retail, consumer, and finance.

Our investment process seeks out companies that have at least one or more catalysts for growth. The catalysts may be identified as new products, exploitation of demographic trends, proprietary products, gaining market share, and/or changing cost structure, in order to attain or maintain very strong earnings per share growth.

We search for companies that have significant management ownership, well-thought-out management goals and growth plans supported by stringent controls, and a commitment to enhancing shareholder value. We also seek out companies with a proven track record (at least three to five years) of superior revenue and earnings growth, strong pre-tax margins, low levels of debt, exceptional profitability, market share, high return on equity, high reinvestment rates, and attractive valuations relative to their industry and the market in general.

Largest Holdings: 1. Microsoft   6. Motorola
2. Nokia   7. Sun Microsystems
3. Cisco Systems   8. EMC
4. Qualcomm   9. Amgen
5. Genentech   10. Flextronics

Benchmark Used: Russell 1000 Growth index

B. Active Fixed Income

Investment Approach:

We believe that superior risk-adjusted returns can be achieved by capturing changes in relative value through active yield curve management, sector rotation, and prudent security selection. We follow a disciplined process designed to add incremental value over long periods of time by taking advantage of relative value opportunities without accepting excessive interest rate risk. Our process is not dependent on forecasts of future interest rates or economic events. Rather our decisions are based on current conditions, analyzed in the context of historical relationships. Our performance record has been built employing this process. We expect that in the future, market conditions will offer similar opportunities. While markets will change, our process will not.

Largest Holdings: 1. A–Baa rated corporates (56.9%)
2. Treasury/agencies (33.6%)
3. Aaa–Aa rated corporates (9.5%)

Benchmark Used: Lehman Government/Corporate index

Source: Data adapted from *Nelson's Directory of Investment Managers.*

all accounts. Similarly, a client choosing to invest in PCM's core fixed-income product will end up holding a portfolio of bonds split between government and investment-grade corporates. The stated investment process at PCM requires extensive interaction between the firm's portfolio managers and security analysts. At the time in question, PCM employed 11 equity portfolio managers, 10 equity analysts, 3 equity traders, and 6 additional manager/analysts.

17.3   Organization and Management of Investment Companies

An investment company typically is a corporation that has as its major assets the portfolio of marketable securities referred to as a fund. The management of the securities portfolio and most of the other administrative duties are handled by a separate **investment management company** hired by the board of directors of the investment company. This legal description oversimplifies the typical arrangement. The actual management usually begins with an investment advisory firm that starts an investment company and selects a board of directors for the fund. Subsequently, this board of directors hires the investment advisory firm as the fund's portfolio manager.

The contract between the investment company (the portfolio of securities) and the investment management company details the duties and compensation of the management company. The major duties of the investment management company include investment research, the management of the portfolio, and administrative duties, such as issuing securities and handling redemptions and dividends. The management fee is generally stated as a percentage of the total value of the fund and typically ranges from 1/4 to 1/2 of 1%, with a sliding scale as the size of the fund increases.

To achieve economies of scale, many management companies launch numerous funds with different characteristics in order to appeal to many investors with different risk-return preferences. In addition, it allows investors to switch among funds as economic or personal conditions change. This "family of funds" promotes flexibility and increases the total capital managed by the investment firm.

17.3.1   VALUING INVESTMENT COMPANY SHARES

When clients have their invested capital held in separate accounts, the value of any given account can be calculated by simply totalling the market value of the securities held in the portfolio, less fees. When the securities are held jointly, as they are in an investment company, the value of the clients' investment is simply the number of shares or units held in the fund multiplied by the per-share unit value (**net asset value** or **NAV**). NAV is the total market value of all the fund's assets divided by the total number of fund units outstanding, or

$$\text{Fund NAV} = \frac{\text{Total Market Value of Fund Portfolio} - \text{Fund Expenses}}{\text{Total Fund Shares Outstanding}}$$

The NAV is analogous to the share price of a corporation's common stock; like common stock, the NAV of the fund units will increase as the value of the underlying assets (the fund security portfolio) increases.

Using the earlier example, a fund with a $100 million large-cap stock portfolio and 10 million units outstanding would have an NAV of $10. If during the holding period, the value of the stock portfolio increased to $112.5 million and the fund incurred $0.1 million in trading expenses and management fees, what would be the NAV? Assuming no new units were sold during the period, the net value of the total investment fund is $112.4 million, which leaves a net asset value per unit of $11.24 ([112,500,000 − 100,000] ÷ 10,000,000). Thus, the NAV provides an immediate reflection of the investment company's market value net of operating expenses. Had the fund made any capital gain or dividend distributions to its investors, these too would be reflected in the NAV calculation because they would reduce the value of the fund portfolio. For publicly traded funds, NAVs are calculated and reported on a daily basis.

17.3.2 CLOSED-END VERSUS OPEN-END INVESTMENT COMPANIES

An **open-end investment company** (often referred to as a **mutual fund**) differs from a closed-end investment company (typically referred to as a *closed-end fund*) in the way each operates *after* the initial public offering.

Like any other public firm, a **closed-end investment company** will see its units trade in the secondary market, and the price of its units will be determined by supply and demand. Thus to buy or sell closed-end fund units, you must execute the trade in the market where the units are listed (e.g., TSX, NYSE). The typical closed-end investment company offers no further shares and does not repurchase the shares on demand, therefore, new investment dollars are only available for the investment company if it makes another public sale of securities. Unit repurchases by the investment company are rare.

A listing of Canadian closed-end funds can be found at http://globefunddb. theglobeandmail.com/ gishome/plsql/gis.show_ closed_end_rep.

The closed-end fund's NAV is computed twice daily based on prevailing market prices for the portfolio securities. The *market price* of the units is determined by the relative supply and demand for the units in the secondary market. As with stocks, when buying or selling closed-end fund units, you pay or receive this market price plus or minus a regular trading commission. You should recognize that *the NAV and the market price of a closed-end fund are almost never the same!* Over the long run, closed-end funds typically sell at a discount to NAV (historically they sell between 5% and 20% below the NAV).

This typical discount prompts questions from investors: Why do these funds sell at a discount? Why do the discounts differ between funds? What are the returns available to investors from funds that sell at large discounts? This final question arises because an investor purchasing a portfolio at a price below market value (i.e., below NAV) expects an above-average dividend yield. Still, the total return on the fund depends on what happens to the discount during the holding period. If the discount relative to the NAV declines, the investment should generate positive excess returns. If the discount increases, the investor will likely experience negative excess returns. The analysis of these discounts remains a major question of modern finance.[4]

The interest in closed-end funds has led Thomas J. Herzfeld Advisors, a firm that specializes in closed-end funds, to create an index that tracks the market price performance of a sample of U.S. closed-end funds that invest principally in U.S. equities. The price-weighted series is based on fund market values rather than on NAVs. In addition to its market price index, Herzfeld also computes the average discount from NAV. The lower right-hand graph in Exhibit 17.5 indicates that the average discount from NAV changes over time and has a major impact on the market performance of the index. For example, during the period 2006 to 2007, this value changed from a discount of 4% to a premium of about 5%. Despite this, the performance of the Herzfeld closed-end average at the end of this period was ahead of the DJIA.

---

4 Studies over the years include research by Lee, Shleifer, and Thaler (1991); Barclay, Holderness, and Pontiff (1993); Malkiel (1995); Klibanoff, Lamont, and Wizman (1998); and Berk and Stanton (2007).

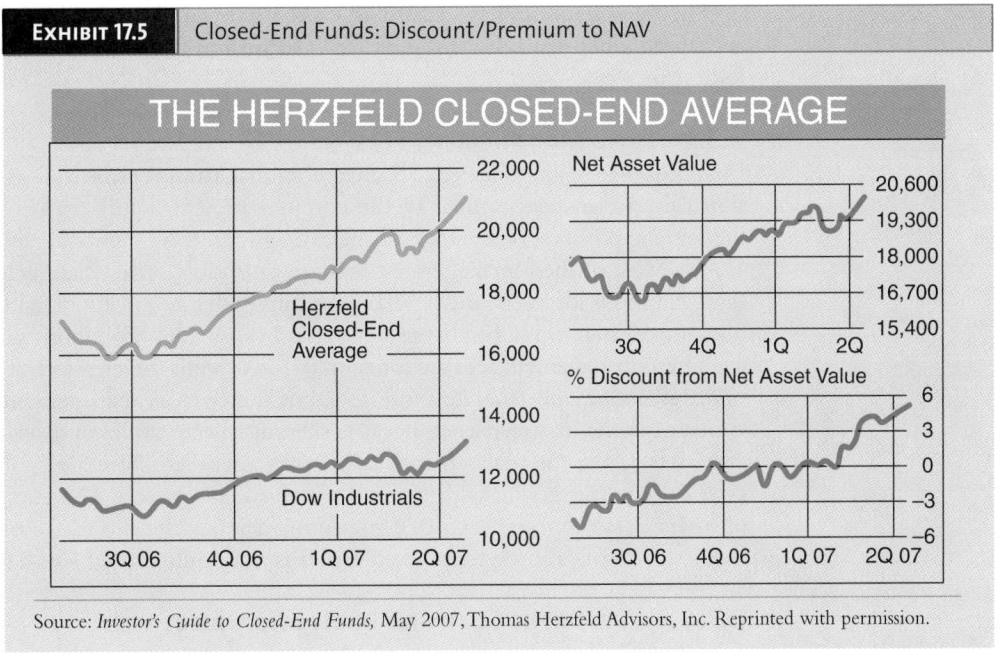

| **EXHIBIT 17.5** | Closed-End Funds: Discount/Premium to NAV |

Source: *Investor's Guide to Closed-End Funds,* May 2007, Thomas Herzfeld Advisors, Inc. Reprinted with permission.

Open-end investment companies, or mutual funds, continue to sell and repurchase units after their initial public offerings. They stand ready to sell additional units of the fund at the NAV, with or without sales charge, or to buy back (redeem) shares of the fund at the NAV, with or without redemption fees.

Load versus No-Load Open-End Funds One distinction of open-end funds is that some charge a sales fee for unit sales. The offering price for a unit of a *load fund* equals the NAV of the unit plus a sales charge, which can be as large as 7.5% to 8.0% of the NAV. A fund with an 8% sales charge (load) would give an individual who invested $1,000 in the fund units worth only $920. Generally these two funds do not charge a redemption fee, which means the units can be redeemed at their NAV. These funds typically are quoted with a NAV and an offering price. The NAV price is the redemption (bid) price, and the offering (ask) price equals the NAV divided by 1.0 minus the percent load. For example, if the NAV of a fund with an 8% load is $8.50 a share, the offering price would be $9.24 ($8.50/0.92). The 74-cent differential is really 8.7% of the NAV. The load percentage typically declines with the size of the order.

A **no-load fund** imposes no initial sales charge, so it sells shares at their NAV. Some of these funds charge a small redemption fee of about one-half of 1%. The number of no-load funds has increased substantially in recent years, with many of these funds being sponsored through banks.

Between the full-load fund and the pure no-load fund, several variations exist. The first is the **low-load fund**, which imposes a front-end sales charge when the fund is bought, but it is typically in the 3% range rather than 7% to 8%. Generally, low-load funds are used for bond funds or equity funds offered by management companies that also offer no-load funds. Alternatively, some funds—previously charging full loads—have reduced their loads.[5]

---

5 A U.S. innovation is the **12b-1 plan**, named after a 1980 SEC ruling. This plan permits funds to deduct as much as 0.75% of average net assets *per year* to cover distribution costs, such as advertising, brokers' commissions, and general marketing expenses. Many no-load funds are adopting these plans, as are a few low-load funds. An investor must read the prospectus or use an investment service that reports charges in substantial detail to determine if the fund has a 12b-1 plan.

Finally, some funds have instituted **contingent, deferred sales loads** in which a sales fee is charged when the fund is sold if it is held for less than some time period, perhaps three or four years.

17.3.3 FUND MANAGEMENT FEES

In addition to selling charges, all charge annual **management fees** to compensate professional fund managers. Similar to the compensation structure for private management firms, the fee is typically a percentage of the average funds net assets varying from about 0.25% to 1.00%. Most of these management fees are on sliding scales that decline with the size of the fund. A fund with assets under $1 billion might charge 1%, funds with assets between $1 billion and $5 billion might charge 0.50%, and those over $5 billion would charge 0.25%.

These management fees are a major factor driving the creation of new funds. More assets under management generate more fees, but the costs of management do not increase at the same rate as the managed assets because substantial economies of scale exist in managing financial assets. Once the research staff and management structure are established, the incremental costs do not rise in line with the assets under management. The cost of managing $1 billion of assets is *not* twice the cost of managing $500 million. Finally, one consequence of the industry consolidation we discussed earlier is that mutual fund fees have been declining.

17.3.4 INVESTMENT COMPANY PORTFOLIO OBJECTIVES

A mutual fund can be created around any portfolio of assets. As a practical matter, however, mutual funds tend to exist for only the more liquid asset classes, such as stocks and bonds. There are four broad fund objective categories: equity funds, bond funds, hybrid funds, and money market funds. Each of these strategies is described briefly here, a more detailed listing of many of the popular subcategories within these objective classes can be found on the Canadian Investment Funds Standards Committee website (http://www.cifsc.org/en/historicaldefinitions.php).

As the category title suggests, equity funds invest almost exclusively in common stocks. Within that broad mission, however, substantial differences can be found, including funds that focus on specific industries, collection of industries, security characteristics, or even geographic areas. With several thousand to choose from, any investor can almost certainly find an equity fund that matches his or her desired investment strategy.

Bond funds concentrate on various types of bonds to generate high current income with minimal risk. They are similar to common stock funds; however, their investment policies differ. Some funds concentrate on government or high-grade corporate bonds, others hold a mixture of investment-grade bonds, and some concentrate on high-yield (junk) bonds. Management strategies also can differ, ranging from buy and hold to extensive trading of the portfolio bonds.

Balanced funds diversify outside a single market by combining common stock with fixed-income securities, including government bonds, corporate bonds, convertible bonds, or preferred stock. The ratio of stocks to fixed-income securities will vary by fund, as stated in each fund's prospectus. **Flexible portfolio** (or *asset allocation*) **funds** seek high total returns by investing in a mix of stocks, bonds, and money-market securities.

Money market funds were created in 1973 when short-term interest rates were at record levels. These funds attempt to provide current income, safety of principal, and liquidity by investing in diversified portfolios of short-term securities, such as T-bills, banker acceptances, and commercial paper. They typically are no-load funds that impose no penalty for early withdrawal, and some allow holders to write cheques against their account. Changes in their growth rate are usually associated with investor attitudes toward the stock market. When investors are bullish toward stocks, they withdraw funds from their money market accounts to invest; when they are uncertain, they shift from stocks to the money funds.

17.3.5 Breakdown by Fund Characteristics

The two major means of mutual fund distribution are (1) by a sales force and (2) by direct purchase from the fund or direct marketing. Sales forces include brokers, commission-based financial planners, or dedicated sales forces. Almost all mutual funds purchased from these sources charge sales fees (loads) from which salespeople are compensated.

Investors typically purchase directly marketed fund units through the mail, telephone, bank wire, or Internet. These direct sales funds usually impose a low sales charge or none at all. In the past, they had to be sold directly because a broker had no incentive to sell a no-load fund. This has changed recently because some brokerage firms have developed agreements with specific no-load funds whereby they will sell these funds to their clients and collect a fee from the fund. Given the investor preference for no-load funds and the increasing availability, this trend toward direct marketed funds should continue.

17.3.6 Global Investment Companies

We cannot express enough that serious thought should be given to global diversification of investment portfolios. Funds that invest in foreign securities are generally called *international* or *global funds.* International funds often hold only foreign stocks from such countries as the United States, Germany, Japan, Singapore, and Korea, while global funds contain both Canadian and foreign securities. Both international and global funds fall into familiar categories: money funds, government and corporate bond funds, and equity funds. In turn, an international equity fund might limit its focus to a segment of the global market, such as the European Fund, Pacific Basin Fund, or Emerging Market Fund, or to a single country.

Although most global or international funds are open-end (either load or no load), a significant number are closed-end funds, including most of the single country and the emerging-market funds. These funds have opted to be closed-end so that they are not subject to the potential for major investor liquidations that require the sale of stocks in the portfolio on a potentially illiquid foreign stock exchange.

A final alternative that all investors should appreciate is the large number of foreign investment companies that offer both domestic and global products in their local markets. In fact, the Investment Company Institute reported that of $21.76 trillion invested worldwide in open-end investment companies at the end of 2006, over 52% of these assets were controlled by firms located outside the United States.

17.3.7 Mutual Fund Organization and Strategy: An Example

The Dreyfus Corporation, established in 1951 and headquartered in New York City, is one of the leading mutual fund companies in the United States, managing more than $200 billion as of December 2007.[6] The Dreyfus Appreciation Fund (DGAGX) is a one of several equity-oriented portfolios that the company offers to its institutional and retail investors. The Appreciation Fund, which follows a large-cap blend investment style, is different than many of the other funds in the Dreyfus family in that it is not managed in-house by portfolio managers that it employs directly. Rather, DGAGX is managed by Fayez Sarofim, a Houston, Texas, money manager who has run his own private management firm since 1958 and serves Dreyfus as a subinvestment advisor. A portion of Bloomberg's description of DGAGX is shown in Exhibit 17.6. Notice that DGAGX has about $4.6 billion (Panel A) of assets under management and is a no-load fund that also does not charge a 12b-1 fee

---

6 Much of the information contained in this example is available from Dreyfus Corporation's Web site at http://www.dreyfus.com.

EXHIBIT 17.6	Description of Dreyfus Appreciation Fund (DGAGX)

Panel A. Overview

Screen Printed
DGAGX US
DREYFUS APPRECIATION FD INC

DESCRIPTION
Objective - Blue Chip

EquityDES
Page 1/4

Dreyfus Appreciation Fund, Inc. is an open-end fund incorporated in the USA. The Fund's objective is long-term capital growth consistent with the preservation of capital. Its secondary goal is current income. The Fund invests at least 80% of its net assets in the common stock of United States and foreign

Bloomberg Classification Data	
Asset Class	Equity
Style	Blue Chip
Market Cap Focus	Multi-cap
Geographic Focus	Global

Performance/Percentile Ranking		
as of 12/3/07	Return	Rank
3) TRA 1 Month	.06	94
YTD	6.70	40
1 Year	9.40	41
2006	16.26	84
5 Year	9.82	30

Current / Operational Data		
1)GP NAV	$	46.70
Assets(mil) 10/31/07	S	4556.00
Inception Date	1/18/84	

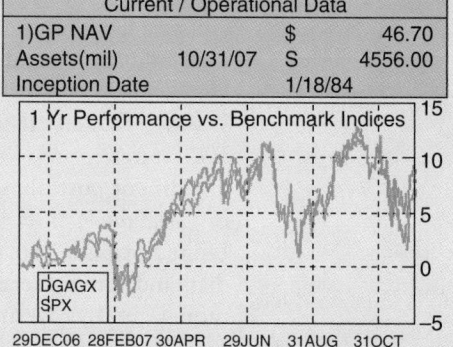

1 Yr Performance vs. Benchmark Indices

DGAGX
SPX

29DEC06 28FEB07 30APR 29JUN 31AUG 31OCT

{ FPC<GO> } FOR FUND PERFORMANCE CHARTS AND { FSRC<GO> } FOR FUND SEARCH
Subadvisor: Fayez Sarofim & Co.

Australia 61 2 9777 8600   Brazil 5511 3048 4500   Europe 44 20 7330 7500   Germany 49 69 920410   Hong Kong 852 2977 6000
Japan 81 3 3201 8900   Singapore 65 6212 1000   U.S. 1 212 318 2000   Copyright 2007 Bloomberg Finance L.P.
H445–82–1 04–Dec–2007 10:40:31

Panel B. Management & Fee Structure

Page

DGAGX US
DREYFUS APPRECIATION FD INC

DESCRIPTION
Fund Type - Open-End Fund

EquityDES
Page 2/4

Contact Details
Fund Manager
11)FAYEZ SHALABY SAROFIM
Management Company
Dreyfus Corp/The
Address
Dreyfus Funds
200 Park Avenue
New York, NY 10166
USA
Telephone   1-800-645-6561 Domestic
1-516-794-5452 Intl
Web Site
7)www.dreyfus.com
Transfer Agent
Dreyfus Transfer Inc

Isin	US2619701079	Valor	N.A.
Cusip	261970107	Sicovam	N.A.
Sedol	2291244 US	WPK	N.A.

Fees & Expenses		
Front Load	.000	%
Back Load	.000	%
Early Withdraw	.000	%
Current Mgmt Fee	.550	%
Performance Fee		%
Expense Ratio	.920	%
12b1 fee	.000	%
Min Investment	$	2500
Min Subsequent	$	100
Min IRA	$	750

Distributions – Irreg			
6)DVD		Income	Capital Gain
YTD	$	.02	.00
2006	$	.62	1.79
2005	$	.54	.00
2004	$	.52	.00
2003	$	.41	.00
2002	$	.30	.02

Pricing Source
  NASDAQ

Australia 61 2 9777 8600   Brazil 5511 3048 4500   Europe 44 20 7330 7500   Germany 49 69 920410   Hong Kong 852 2977 6000
Japan 81 3 3201 8900   Singapore 65 6212 1000   U.S. 1 212 318 2000   Copyright 2007 Bloomberg Finance L.P.
H445–82–1 04–Dec–2007 10:42:46

Source: © 2007 Bloomberg L.P. All rights reserved. Reprinted with permission.

(Panel B). However, investors do pay an annual management fee of 0.55% of the portfolio's assets, and the expense ratio, which accounts for the total cost of running the fund, is 0.92% of AUM.

One of the reasons why Dreyfus chose to enter into this arrangement was to allow investors who would not otherwise have sufficient capital to gain access to a private manager with an outstanding long-term performance record. Fayez Sarofim's investment philosophy is somewhat unique among mutual fund managers, in that he preaches a patient approach to portfolio formation that seeks to keep turnover below 15% per annum. The firm describes its investment approach as follows:

> Our investment philosophy leads us to construct a portfolio comprised predominantly of large capitalization, US-based, multinational companies. These companies are global leaders in structurally attractive industries. They benefit from increasing global market share, ongoing product introduction or innovation, and productivity enhancements—three key drivers of long-term earnings growth. In addition, their financial strength allows them to make profitable investments at any point in the economic cycle. We believe these businesses are most capable of generating superior growth in earnings, dividends, and cash flow over time, leading to greater capital appreciation. Investing in high quality companies at reasonable prices also produces two additional advantages for our clients—low portfolio turnover and a higher likelihood of preservation of capital.[7]

One interesting concept implied in this statement of philosophy is that Fayez Sarofim can be considered a global portfolio manager, even though the majority of the stocks he selects are from companies domiciled in the United States. The equity holdings of DGAGX are designed to mimic the portfolios that Sarofim assembles for his own private clients, and thus follows the same philosophy. Panel A of Exhibit 17.7 shows the top 10 holdings of the fund as of March 2009. Not surprisingly, all of these stocks (e.g., Exxon Mobil, Procter & Gamble, Phillip Morris) fit the profile of being large companies with dominant global franchises. Although not shown on either exhibit, the DGAGX portfolio has a lower level of systematic risk than the market, with a beta coefficient of 0.86. Finally, while Panel B of the exhibit shows that DGAGX underperformed the S&P 500 index (which is a relevant comparison for a large-cap blend fund manager) until December 2007, it is important to note that this particular period in the market was led by low-quality, small-cap, and value stocks, which were aided by a recovering economy and unusually low interest rates and easy credit. The strategy did result in better performance than the S&P 500 Index thereafter.

The investment structures just described—private management firms and investment companies—are extremely efficient ways for investors to gain access to a number of different asset classes and strategies. This is particularly true when the desired asset class investments are in liquid markets, such as with stocks, bonds, or money market securities. Recently, however, individual and institutional investors alike have become interested in committing their financial capital in non-traditional asset classes. These **alternative asset** classes can include a wide variety of investment opportunities, but the most notable ones are hedge funds, private equity, real estate, or natural resources and commodities. In this section, we will take a detailed look at hedge funds and private equity investments.

Alternative asset investing can take place either through the creation of separate accounts for each investor or through the commingling of investor capital into a single pool of assets

---

7 The complete statement of the Fayez Sarofim investment philosophy can be found on the firm's Web site (http://www.sarofim.com).

Exhibit 17.7 DGAGX Portfolio Holdings and Performance

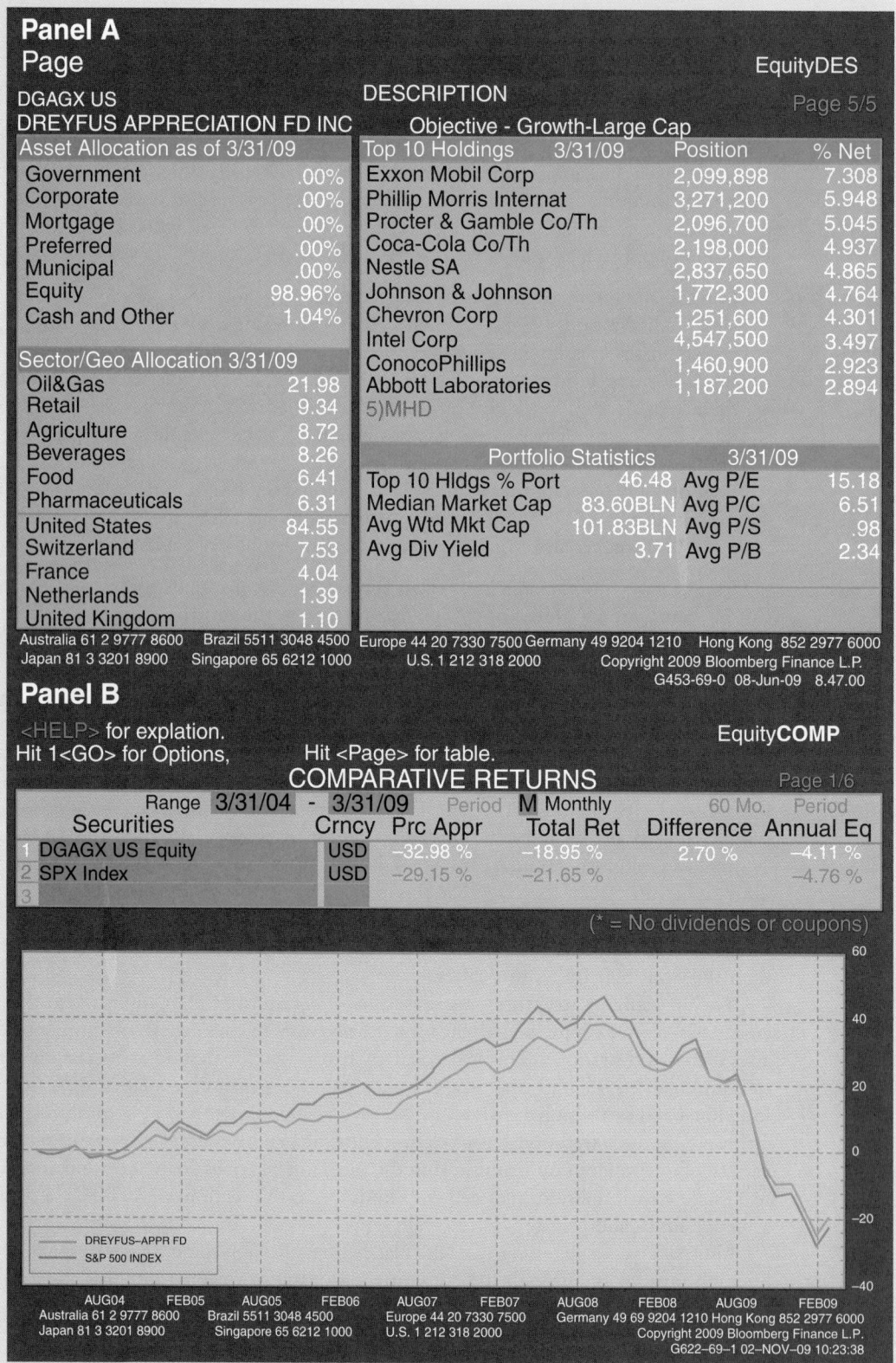

Panel A

Page

DGAGX US
DREYFUS APPRECIATION FD INC

EquityDES

Page 5/5

DESCRIPTION
Objective - Growth-Large Cap

Asset Allocation as of 3/31/09

Government	.00%
Corporate	.00%
Mortgage	.00%
Preferred	.00%
Municipal	.00%
Equity	98.96%
Cash and Other	1.04%

Sector/Geo Allocation 3/31/09

Oil&Gas	21.98
Retail	9.34
Agriculture	8.72
Beverages	8.26
Food	6.41
Pharmaceuticals	6.31
United States	84.55
Switzerland	7.53
France	4.04
Netherlands	1.39
United Kingdom	1.10

Top 10 Holdings 3/31/09	Position	% Net
Exxon Mobil Corp	2,099,898	7.308
Phillip Morris Internat	3,271,200	5.948
Procter & Gamble Co/Th	2,096,700	5.045
Coca-Cola Co/Th	2,198,000	4.937
Nestle SA	2,837,650	4.865
Johnson & Johnson	1,772,300	4.764
Chevron Corp	1,251,600	4.301
Intel Corp	4,547,500	3.497
ConocoPhillips	1,460,900	2.923
Abbott Laboratories	1,187,200	2.894
5)MHD		

Portfolio Statistics		3/31/09	
Top 10 Hldgs % Port	46.48	Avg P/E	15.18
Median Market Cap	83.60BLN	Avg P/C	6.51
Avg Wtd Mkt Cap	101.83BLN	Avg P/S	.98
Avg Div Yield	3.71	Avg P/B	2.34

Australia 61 2 9777 8600   Brazil 5511 3048 4500   Europe 44 20 7330 7500 Germany 49 9204 1210   Hong Kong 852 2977 6000
Japan 81 3 3201 8900   Singapore 65 6212 1000   U.S. 1 212 318 2000   Copyright 2009 Bloomberg Finance L.P.
G453-69-0 08-Jun-09 8.47.00

Panel B

<HELP> for explation.
Hit 1<GO> for Options,   Hit <Page> for table.

EquityCOMP

COMPARATIVE RETURNS

Page 1/6

Securities		Crncy	Prc Appr	Total Ret	Difference	Annual Eq
Range 3/31/04 - 3/31/09	Period	M Monthly	60 Mo.	Period		
1 DGAGX US Equity		USD	−32.98 %	−18.95 %	2.70 %	−4.11 %
2 SPX Index		USD	−29.15 %	−21.65 %		−4.76 %
3						

(* = No dividends or coupons)

Australia 61 2 9777 8600   Brazil 5511 3048 4500   Europe 44 20 7330 7500   Germany 49 69 9204 1210 Hong Kong 852 2977 6000
Japan 81 3 3201 8900   Singapore 65 6212 1000   U.S. 1 212 318 2000   Copyright 2009 Bloomberg Finance L.P.
G622−69−1 02−NOV−09 10:23:38

Source: © 2009 Bloomberg Finance L.P. All rights reserved. Used with permission.

(recall Exhibit 17.1). Most often, though, an alternative asset investment is structured as a commingled collection of assets (i.e., Panel B), with the important difference that it is usually formed as a **limited partnership** rather than as a mutual fund. In a limited partnership, one or more *general partners* are responsible for running the organization and assuming its legal obligations, while the remaining *limited partners* are only liable to the extent of their investments. For example, in a hedge fund or private equity partnership, the general partner develops, implements, and maintains the investment portfolio around an initial strategy, while the limited partners (e.g., high-net-worth individuals, pension funds, endowment funds) provide the majority of the capital but have no direct involvement in the actual investment process.

Of course, one of the reasons that investors consider hiring professional asset managers is the belief that they will be able to deliver superior investment performance relative to simple indexed investments. In the parlance of the asset management industry, investors feel that professional managers can consistently add *alpha*, which is defined as the difference between a fund's actual and expected (e.g., CAPM, benchmark) return. In fact, one of the reasons for the impressive recent development of the alternative assets market is the growing belief that they are better able to produce superior returns than traditional investment structures, such as mutual funds. This argument is summarized in Exhibit 17.8, which illustrates an "excess returns" form of the Security Market Line (SML) for several different asset classes. Notice that standard "long only" positions in U.S. stocks and bonds plot virtually on the SML—indicating very little possibility for adding alpha—while the alternative asset classes (i.e., hedge funds, private equity) have substantially more potential in that area.

EXHIBIT 17.8	Security Market Line for Traditional and Alternative Asset Classes

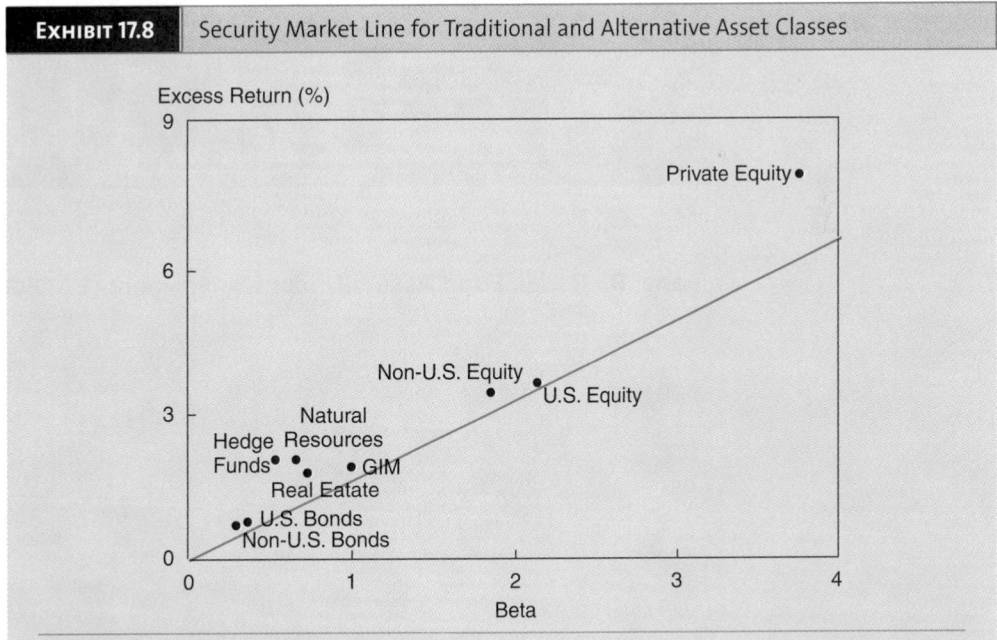

Note: GIM = Global Investment Market.

Source: Brian D. Singer, Renato Staub, and Kevin Terhaar, "Determining the Appropriate Allocation to Alternative Investments," *Hedge Fund Management* (Charlottesville, VA: CFA Institute, 2002), 10. Copyright © 2002 CFA Institute: Reproduced and republished from *Financial Management Journal* with permission from the CFA Institute. All Rights Reserved.

Copyright 2002, CFA Institute. Reproduced and republished from the CFA Institute Conference Proceedings with permission from CFA Institute. All rights reserved.

17.4 Hedge Funds and Private Equity

One of the most significant developments in the professional asset management industry over the past 20 years has been the emergence of the global market for hedge fund investing. Exhibit 17.9 shows that the increase in both the number of hedge funds in existence, as well as the assets under management those funds control, has been nothing short of phenomenal. There were about 600 funds at the start of the 1990s controlling less than $40 billion in assets; by 2006 there were over 9,000 active funds controlling an estimated $1.34 trillion in assets. This represents AUM expansion of about 23% per annum over the past several years.

Despite this recent surge in growth, hedge fund investing is not new. In fact, Lhabitant (2002) notes that use of the term "hedge fund" originated in 1949, when Alfred Winslow

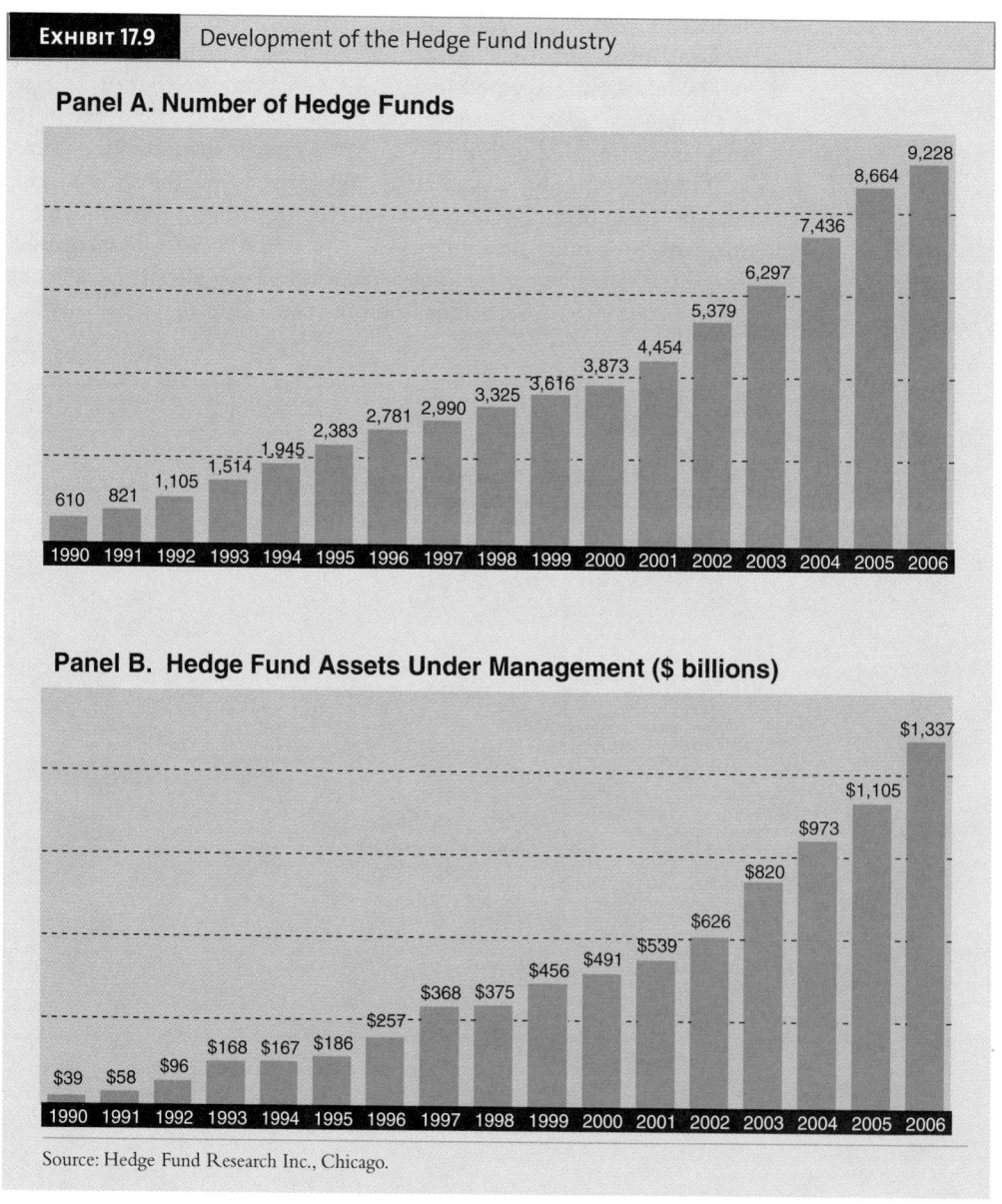

EXHIBIT 17.9 Development of the Hedge Fund Industry

Panel A. Number of Hedge Funds

Panel B. Hedge Fund Assets Under Management ($ billions)

Source: Hedge Fund Research Inc., Chicago.

Jones tested his security selection skills by forming a portfolio that combined both long and short position in the equity market with the use of financial leverage to enhance returns. Jones did this using a partnership structure that avoided SEC restrictions and also included an incentive fee for superior performance. Despite the fact that the performance of this original hedge fund was indeed spectacular—it outperformed the best mutual fund of the era by almost 90% over a 10-year period—Jones's strategy was not widely imitated for several decades. However, that situation has certainly changed.

17.4.1   CHARACTERISTICS OF A HEDGE FUND

Regardless of how a hedge fund is structured (limited partnership, limited liability company, or unit trusts), it should be noted that typical hedge fund investments are far less liquid than mutual fund (or even closed-end fund) shares; there are severe limitations on when and how often investment capital can be contributed to or removed. The appeal, though, of a limited partnership is that these hedge funds are generally less restricted in how and where they can make investments, which is perhaps the biggest reason why investors believe that these vehicles have the ability to deliver abnormally large returns on a consistent basis. They also tend to be less correlated with traditional asset class investments, providing investors with additional diversification benefits.

Exhibit 17.10 highlights several important features related to the way hedge funds are structured. Notice that the average hedge fund only permits investors to enter or exit a few times a year (i.e., monthly and quarterly, respectively) compared to the daily ownership adjustments allowed by mutual funds and that most hedge funds allow managers to use leverage (71%), short sell (82%), and derivatives (69%). By contrast, Almazan et al. (2004) document that the vast majority of mutual fund managers cannot employ these investment tools.

Lastly, notice that the hedge fund manager typically receives compensation in two components: a regular management fee (e.g., 1% of AUM) and a performance allocation fee, which normally amounts to 20% of the fund's profits beyond a certain pre-specified return level (i.e., hurdle rate). In calculating this performance fee, it is typical for investors to require that any past losses be recouped before managers receive the additional payout; this arrangement is known as a *high water mark*. Finally, as a tangible signal to investors of belief in their abilities, most hedge fund managers put a substantial amount of their own capital into the fund.

Although some information is dated, the Alternative Investment Management Association (AIMA) has a few hedge fund publications worth reviewing at http://www.aima-canada.org/aima_can_publications.html.

17.4.2   HEDGE FUND STRATEGIES

Saying you are invested in a hedge fund is a little like saying you play a sport—it is a statement that conveys some information but could mean many different things. In fact, several investment strategies are often included under the hedge fund designation, and these vary greatly in the risk and expected return profiles they imply. Within a given strategic category, there can be as many interpretations of how the portfolio should be designed as there are fund managers. Nevertheless, we describe below some common features that define the more popular hedge fund strategies.[8]

 I. *Equity-Based Strategies*
  • *Long–short equity:* The original and perhaps most basic form of hedge fund investing. Managers attempt to identify misvalued stocks and take long positions in the undervalued ones and short positions in the overvalued ones. Because investors participate in both the long and the short side of the market, one major advantage of the long–short strategy is the ability to generate "double alpha" (i.e., profit from price corrections for both undervalued and overvalued securities), unlike the long-only possibilities in the mutual fund industry.

---

8 The following list of hedge fund strategies, which draws from the discussion in Nicholas (1999), is intended to be representative rather than exhaustive. Alternative lists of strategies can be found at the following websites: http://www.greenwichai.com and http://www.thehfa.org.

Exhibit 17.10	Characteristics of Hedge Fund Investments		
	Mean	**Median**	**Mode**
Fund Size	$83 million	$26.5 million	$20 million
Fund Age	6.8 years	6.2 years	8.0 years
Minimum Investment Required	$649,000	$250,000	$1,000,000
Number of Entry Dates per Year	22	12	12
Number of Exit Dates per Year	17	4	4
Management Fee	1.4%	1.0%	1.0%
Performance Allocation ("Fee")	17.2%	20.0%	20.0%

	YES
Fund has hurdle rate (of those with a performance allocation)	14%
Fund has high water mark	93%
Fund has audited financial statements or audited performance	95%
Manager has $500,000 of own money in fund	78%
Fund can handle "hot issues"	56%
Fund is diversified	44%
Fund can short sell	82%
Fund can use leverage	71%
Fund uses derivatives for hedging only, or none	69%

Level of turnover	Low (0–25%) = 17%	Medium (26–75%) = 26%	High (>75%) = 58%	
Capitalization of underlying investments	Small ($1–$500m) = 12%	Medium ($500–$1,000m) = 4%	Large (>$1,000m) = 10%	Mixed = 73%

Source: © 2004 Greenwich Alternative Investments, LLC.

- *Equity market neutral:* Like the long–short strategy, returns are generated by exploiting perceived pricing inefficiencies between securities. However, equity market neutral strategies also attempt to limit the overall volatility exposure of the fund by taking offsetting risk positions on the long and short side, an effort that might also involve adopting derivative positions. Absent leverage, these portfolios are expected to produce returns of 2% to 4% above the risk-free rate, which has led some investors to refer to them as *absolute return* strategies.

II. *Arbitrage-Based Strategies*

- *Fixed-income arbitrage:* Returns are generated by taking advantage of bond pricing disparities caused by changing market events, investor preferences, or fluctuations in the fixed-income market. Because the valuation disparities between related instruments (e.g., coupon-bearing bonds and zero-coupon government strips) are typically small, managers usually employ leverage to enhance their overall returns. The ability to generate alpha is driven largely by the manager's skill at building quantitative models, as well as structuring and managing fixed-income portfolios.
- *Convertible arbitrage:* Seeks to profit from disparities in the relationship between prices for convertible bonds and the underlying common stock. A typical position involves purchasing

the convertible bond and short selling the underlying stock, thereby isolating the conversion option embedded in the bond. Returns are generated in several ways, including interest income on the convertible bonds, interest on the proceeds of related equity short sales, and the price appreciation of the convertible bonds as they gradually assume the value of the equity into which they are exchangeable. Like fixed-income arbitrage, convertible arbitrage positions often utilize leverage to enhance returns.

- *Merger (risk) arbitrage:* Returns depend on the magnitude of the spread on merger transactions, which are directly related to the likelihood that the deal will not be completed due to regulatory, financial, or company-specific reasons. As the probability of the merger improves, the spread narrows, generating profits for the position. Merger arbitrage investors essentially bet that their subjective assessment of whether the proposed deal is ultimately completed is superior to that of the other investors in the market.

III. *Opportunistic Strategies*

- *High yield and distressed:* When companies are distressed, their securities can be purchased at deep discounts. If and when a turnaround materializes, security prices will approach their intrinsic value, generating profits for the distressed manager. *Emerging market* investing can be viewed as a global application of this strategy using sovereign securities instead of corporate instruments.

- *Global macro:* This broad class of strategies seeks to profit from changes in global economies, typically brought about by shifts in government policy that impact interest rates, in turn affecting currency, stock, and bond markets. Fund managers typically use a "top-down" global approach to identifying opportunities and often participate in all major markets—equities, bonds, currencies, and commodities—though not always at the same time. The strategy uses leverage and derivatives to enhance returns, but also might hedge exposures on a situational basis.

- *Managed futures:* This strategy uses long and short positions in a variety of futures contracts, both to take "directional" positions on certain economic or company-specific events (e.g., changing conditions in stock or bond markets) and to exploit pricing discrepancies between various contracts. The assets underlying these futures positions may involve commodities, equities, interest rates, or foreign currencies. These strategies frequently employ a substantial degree of financial leverage.

- *Special situations:* Special situation returns occur due to the outcomes of significant events that occur during the normal life cycle of a corporation. These strategies may involve investing in companies around the time of bankruptcies, financial restructurings or recapitalizations, spin-offs, or carve-outs. Given the underlying reason for the investment, positions are usually directional and not fully hedged. Depending on the manager's specific strategy, *event-driven* returns are realized when the catalyst necessary to generate the position's intrinsic value (e.g., the spin-off of an operating division) takes place.

IV. *Multiple Strategies*

- *Fund of funds:* Although not formally a separate strategic category, this investment vehicle acts like a mutual fund of hedge funds, giving investors access to managers that might otherwise be unavailable to them. The primary benefit to the investor of a fund of funds position is that it is a convenient method for achieving a well-diversified allocation to the hedge fund investment space. A fund of funds can offer either a concentration in a particular strategy (e.g., long–short equity) and then diversify across different hedge fund managers—this is a *multiple manager* approach—or it can diversify across strategies, which is the *multiple strategy* approach. The primary disadvantage to the fund of funds investor is that there will be an extra layer of fees necessary to compensate the fund of funds manager; this additional fee can be as high as 3% of the AUM.

17.4.3   RISK ARBITRAGE INVESTING: A CLOSER LOOK

A popular hedge fund strategy involves taking equity positions in companies that are the target of a merger or takeover attempt. These risk arbitrage investments require managers to compare their own subjective judgment about the ultimate success of the proposed takeover with the success probability implied by the market price of the target firm's stock following the announcement of the prospective deal. If the manager thinks the takeover is more likely to occur than the market does, she will buy shares in the target firm. Conversely, the manager might short sell the target firm shares if she thinks the proposed deal is less likely to be completed.

To understand how a manager can establish the market's consensus forecast for the success of an announced takeover, consider the following hypothetical example. Suppose the shareholders of Company XYZ receive an unsolicited cash tender offer for $30 per share. At the time of the offer—which we assume was a complete surprise—XYZ's shares traded for $20. Suppose further that shortly after the takeover announcement—which still must be approved by regulatory authorities—the price of XYZ's shares rises to $28. Brown and Raymond (1986) showed that a simple estimate of the market's *implied probability* that the takeover bid will ultimately be successful is (28 − 20) ÷ (30 − 20), or 80%. In this situation, the risk arbitrage hedge fund manager must think the deal has better than a four-in-five chance of being completed in order to justify purchasing XYZ stock for $28 in the hope of selling at the tender offer price of $30; if the deal falls apart, the manager can assume that XYZ's shares will return to $20. Exhibit 17.11 compares the implied probabilities for a sample of proposed takeovers that were ultimately completed (both competing and non-competing) to a sample of deals that failed. Investors in the market are very good at discriminating between "good" and "bad" deals as far as three months prior to the final resolution.

Panel A of Exhibit 17.12 summarizes the relevant aspects of JP Morgan Chase (JPM) Bank's takeover of Hambrecht & Quist (HQ), a San Francisco–based investment bank specializing in

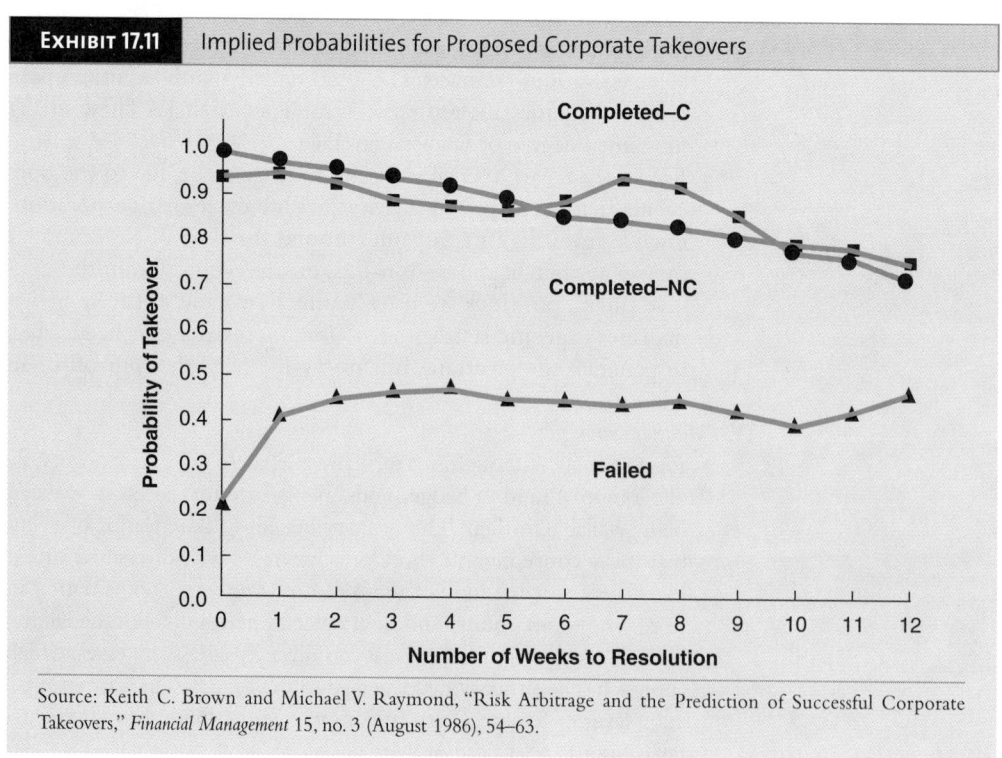

EXHIBIT 17.11   Implied Probabilities for Proposed Corporate Takeovers

Source: Keith C. Brown and Michael V. Raymond, "Risk Arbitrage and the Prediction of Successful Corporate Takeovers," *Financial Management* 15, no. 3 (August 1986), 54–63.

EXHIBIT 17.12	JP Morgan Chase's Takeover of Hambrecht & Quist

A. Tender Offer Details

<HELP> for explanation.
<MENU> to return

N090 **Equity CACS**

More Deal Info ▾	Target Info ▾	Acquirer Info ▾	Acquisition Detail
Target: JP Morgan H&Q Industry: Finance–Invest Bnkr/Brkr Country: United States	HQ US		Price: SIC Code: SEC BROKER/DLR
Acquirer: JPMorgan Chase & Co Industry: Money Center Banks Country: United States	JPM US		Price: 39.28 USD SIC Code: NATL COML BANK

Announced Date: 9/28/99
Completion Date: 12/10/99
            Status: Completed

% owned:
% acquired: 100.00

Currency: USD
Annd tot. value: 1222.2290 Mln
Final tot. val: 1222.2290 Mln
Paym't Type: Cash
  Cash Terms: 50.0000 /Sh.
Stock Terms:
    Net Debt:
Nature of Bid: Friendly

Announced premium: 22.35%

Arbitrage profit:
Cash Value:
Acct'g meth:

Action ID: 4845653

TENDER OFFER EFF: 12/08/99 (94.5%). ACQ'R N/C FROM HAMBRECHT & QUIST GROUP UPON COMPLETION.

Australia 61 2 9777 8600   Brazil 5511 3048 4500   Europe 44 20 7330 7500   Germany 49 69 920410
Hong Kong 852 2977 6000   Japan 81 3 3201 8900   Singapore 65 6212 1000   U.S. 1 212 318 2000   Copyright 2004 Bloomberg Finance L.P.
G469–10–0 08–Nov–04 16:36:43

B. HQ Share Price Movements

HQ US $ **Acquired**
Screen Printed

Equity GP

T r a d e   L i n e   HQ US Equity   1/4

| Range | 8/ 1/99 – 12/ 9/99 | Period | D Daily | Base Currency: | USD |
Upper Chart: 3 Trade Line   Moving Averages
Lower Chart: V Volume Histogram   Moving Average 15   1) News

Close/Trade/USD
Last   50.00
High 12/09/99 50.00
Average   46.1481
Low 08/10/99 34.6876

Volume   12200
SMAVG on Volume(15) 60966.6680

Australia 61 2 9777 8600   Brazil 5511 3048 4500   Europe 44 20 7330 7500   Germany 49 69 920410
Hong Kong 852 2977 6000   Japan 81 3 3201 8900   Singapore 65 6212 1000   U.S. 1 212 318 2000   Copyright 2004 Bloomberg Finance L.P.
G469–10–0 08–Nov–04 16:38:11

Source: © 2007 Bloomberg L.P. All rights reserved. Reprinted with permission.

transactions involving technology firms. In an effort to bolster its equity business, JPM made a tender offer of $50 per share for all of the outstanding shares of HQ, which at the time of the announcement were trading for $39.28. This represents a tender premium of $10.72, and capturing as much of this premium as possible is the goal of the risk arbitrage investor. However, Panel B indicates that within a day of the announcement, HQ shares were already trading for $48.69. This means that the market had already assessed the probability of this friendly takeover attempt to be 88% [= (48.69 − 39.28) ÷ (50 − 39.28)]. Thus, a hedge fund manager who did not already own HQ stock would have to be extremely confident that this deal would ultimately be completed to purchase shares at that point.

17.4.4　HEDGE FUND PERFORMANCE

Nicholas (2005) studied the performance of several of the strategies that defined the early hedge fund market. His findings are summarized in Exhibit 17.13, which plots a Capital Market Line (CML) comparing total risk and return characteristics over the period from 1990 to 2004. During this time, all of the indicated strategies plotted above the CML, demonstrating the ability of hedge fund managers to add a positive alpha to their investors over and above the returns that investments in traditional products such as Treasury bills or the S&P 500 equity index produced. There is also tremendous variation in the level of risk inherent in the myriad strategies; arbitrage-based strategies and those that take both long and short positions (e.g., equity market neutral) tend to exhibit far less volatility than those that adopt directional positions (e.g., macro and event-driven strategies). Clearly, not all hedge funds are the same when it comes to their risk and return profiles, a fact that participants in this market need to understand.

EXHIBIT 17.13	HFRI Index Risk–Return Comparison

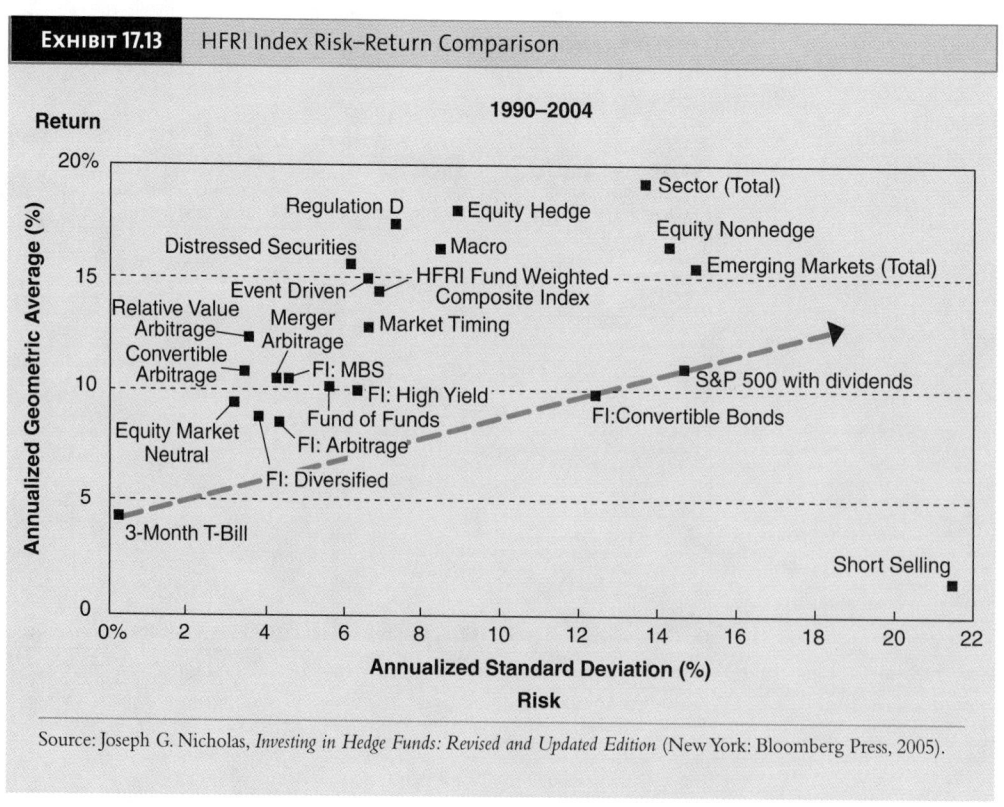

Source: Joseph G. Nicholas, *Investing in Hedge Funds: Revised and Updated Edition* (New York: Bloomberg Press, 2005).

While these CML results are encouraging for potential hedge fund investors, keep in mind that they represent comparisons based on long-term averages over one specific time period. Investors should also be aware that the returns to these strategies show a high degree of variability on a year-to-year basis, in both an absolute and a relative sense. Exhibit 17.14, which lists the annual returns and rankings for 10 different broad hedge fund categories, documents this *strategy rotation* effect. Some of the swings represented in the display can be dramatic. For example, emerging markets (EM) was the worst performing strategy in 1995, posting a loss of 16.9%. However, it was the best performing strategy during the following year, returning 34.5%. Similar patterns exist throughout the exhibit; for instance, the long/short equity (LS) strategy performed well in 2003 and 2004, but lost money in 2002. Finally, notice that there are only 2 (of 14) years in which every strategy class earned positive returns.

17.4.5   PRIVATE EQUITY

Like hedge funds, **private equity** can also include a wide variety of different investment vehicles and strategies. A private equity investment refers to any ownership interest in an asset (or collection of assets) that is not tradable in a public market. This non-tradeability feature has two immediate consequences. First, private equity transactions typically fund either new companies that do not have sufficient operating histories to issue common stock on an exchange or established firms that are seeking to change their organizational structure or are experiencing financial distress. Second, private equity investments are generally far less liquid than public stock holdings and are therefore considered to be long-term positions within an investor's overall portfolio.

The security market dynamics illustrated in Exhibit 17.8 showed that, on average, private equity are among the highest risk and highest reward investments available. This risk-return trade-off is one thing that distinguishes private equity as a separate asset class as is the fact such investments are not perfectly correlated with the other traditional asset classes (as shown in Exhibit 17.15, which lists expected return, standard deviation, and correlation statistics for several different asset classes based on data from the 10-year period ending in 2005). While the private and public equity markets in the United States are highly correlated (i.e., a correlation coefficient of 0.50), the same is not as true for private equity with bonds (0.05) or real estate (0.15). Thus, in addition to their potential to deliver high returns, private equity investments also serve as an important source of diversification.

The combination of higher risk, less liquidity, high minimum initial investments (usually millions of dollars), and capital "lock ups" (minimum time commitments) often precludes small investors from participating in the private equity market. Further, cash distributions from a fund may occur on a sporadic basis and only after an extended period of time. Thus, even when the investment risks are diversified across a well-designed collection of holdings, private equity deals are designed for those investors who can afford to have the funds committed for a lengthy period of time and be able to absorb the possibility that they may lose all of their initial capital. This best describes institutional investors, such as public and corporate pension funds or endowments, and high-net-worth individual investors.

Organization of the Private Equity Market   The main tenant of the early forms of private equity organizations was that combining a pool of investment capital with skilled management could simultaneously benefit start-up companies and produce superior returns for investors. From these early experiments came the model most often used today: the limited partnership format, which allows for a separation between the main sources of the investment capital and the source of the investment expertise (e.g., the company serving as general partner that organizes the fund).

EXHIBIT 17.14 Hedge Fund Strategy Return Performance: 1994–2008

1994	1995	1996	1997	1998	1999	2000	2001	2002	2003	2004	2005	2006	2007	2008
DS 14.9%	GM 30.7%	EM 34.5%	GM 37.1%	MF 20.6%	LS 47.2%	CA 25.6%	ED 20.0%	MF 18.3%	EM 28.8%	ED 15.6%	EM 17.4%	EM 20.5%	EM 20.3%	MF 18.3%
EM 12.5%	ED 26.1%	GM 25.6%	EM 26.6%	LS 17.2%	EM 44.8%	DS 15.8%	GM 18.4%	DS 18.1%	ED 25.1%	EM 12.5%	DS 17.0%	ED 15.6%	GM 17.4%	DS 14.9%
MF 12.0%	LS 23.0%	ED 25.6%	LS 21.5%	MN 13.3%	ED 22.2%	MN 15.0%	CA 14.6%	GM 14.7%	GM 18.0%	LS 11.6%	ED 11.7%	LS 14.4%	LS 13.7%	RA -3.3%
RA 5.3%	CA 16.6%	CA 17.9%	ED 20.7%	RA 5.6%	CA 16.0%	RA 14.7%	MN 9.3%	MN 7.4%	LS 17.3%	GM 8.5%	LS 9.7%	CA 14.3%	RA 8.8%	GM -4.6%
ED 0.7%	FI 12.5%	LS 17.1%	MN 14.8%	ED -1.7%	MN 15.3%	GM 11.7%	FI 8.0%	EM 7.4%	MF 14.1%	FI 6.9%	GM 9.3%	GM 13.5%	MN 9.3%	LS -19.8%
FI 0.3%	RA 11.9%	MN 16.6%	CA 14.5%	GM -3.6%	RA 13.2%	FI 6.3%	EM 5.8%	FI 5.8%	CA 12.9%	MN 6.5%	MN 6.1%	MN 11.2%	ED 8.4%	ED -20.5%
MN -2.0%	MN 11.0%	FI 15.9%	RA 9.8%	CA -4.4%	FI 12.1%	MF 4.2%	RA 5.7%	CA 4.1%	RA 9.0%	MF 6.0%	RA 3.1%	FI 8.7%	DS 6.1%	FI -28.8%
GM -5.7%	MF -7.1%	RA 13.8%	FI 9.3%	DS -6.0%	GM 5.8%	LS 2.1%	MF 1.9%	ED -0.7%	FI 8.0%	RA 5.5%	FI 0.6%	RA 8.2%	MF 6.0%	EM -30.4%
CA -8.1%	DS -7.4%	MF 12.0%	MF 3.1%	FI -8.2%	MF -4.7%	ED 2.0%	DS -3.6%	LS -1.6%	MN 7.1%	CA 2.0%	MF -0.1%	MF 8.1%	CA 5.2%	CA -31.6%
LS -8.1%	EM -16.9%	DS -5.5%	DS 0.4%	EM -37.7%	DS -14.2%	EM -5.5%	LS -3.7%	RA -3.5%	DS -32.6%	DS -7.7%	CA -2.6%	DS -6.6%	FI 3.8%	MN -40.3%

Legend:
CA	=	Convertible Arbitrage
DS	=	Dedicated Short Bias
ED	=	Event Driven—Distressed
EM	=	Emerging Markets
FI	=	Fixed-Income Arbitrage
GM	=	Global Macroeconomic
LS	=	Long/Short Equity
MF	=	Managed Futures
MN	=	Equity Market Neutral
RA	=	Risk Arbitrage
		Event Driven—Risk Arbitrage

Source: © Credit Suisse Tremont Index LLC. All rights reserved.

EXHIBIT 17.15	Asset Class Return, Risk, and Correlations Statistics							

Asset Class	Expected Return	Standard Deviation	Correlations:					
			U.S. Equity	Non-U.S. Equity	U.S. Bonds	Hedge Funds	Real Estate	Private Equity
U.S. Stock	8.9%	16.4%	1.00					
Non-U.S. Stock	8.9	17.5	0.67	1.00				
U.S. Bonds	5.2	5.3	0.05	−0.13	1.00			
Hedge Funds	6.9	6.5	0.51	0.48	0.06	1.00		
Real Estate	7.9	13.6	0.53	0.47	−0.12	0.37	1.00	
Private Equity	*13.1*	*30.1*	*0.50*	*0.45*	*0.05*	*0.40*	*0.15*	*1.00*

Source: University of Texas Investment Management Company, *Asset Allocation Review 2005.*

While private equity investments can be defined to include *any* non–public ownership interest, these transactions are typically classified into three different subcategories:[9]

I. *Venture Capital:* Focuses on investments in start-up firms, early stage businesses, and new products and services created by established businesses. For the past two decades, venture investments have often been concentrated in the technology (e.g., Internet, telecommunications, software) and health care industries. Venture capital funds tend to specialize by stage of investing, as determined by the time frame in a company's development:
- *Seed:* An entrepreneur has a new idea or product, but no established organization or operating structure. Investors at this stage (who are sometimes called "angels") tend to provide limited financial capital and other physical resources to help the entrepreneur develop a coherent business plan.
- *Early Stage:* The business organization has moved beyond the planning stage and has now been formed. It has employees and products that are in the developmental stage. Early-stage investors commit capital once companies complete the business plan and have at least part of the management team in place.
- *Later Stage:* The firm now has an established infrastructure in place, as well as a viable product that is either ready for the market or already producing revenues. Later-stage investors usually provide financing for the expansion of a company that is already producing and shipping a product and increasing its sales volume.

II. *Buyouts:* Involves the acquisition of a product line, set of assets, or business from an established company. The company being acquired can be either a public or a private firm of virtually any size and payment for the transaction can involve both debt and equity.[10] A change in the ownership control of the company being acquired is almost always a feature of a buyout transaction, which can also include recapitalizations, spin-offs, carve-outs, consolidations, and roll-ups. Firms seek buyout financing for several reasons, including a desire to expand their options, to divest themselves of a business unit that no longer fits the strategic plan, or to affect a change in management or ownership. When a public firm is bought out and taken private, there also may be less scrutiny of its operations by outside parties (e.g., regulators, financial analysts).

---

9 These descriptions of the various types of private equity investments are adapted from Ennis Knupp (2004), which also provides an excellent overview of the industry.
10 A transaction that involves the uses of debt to fund the acquisition of a company is called a *leveraged buyout,* or LBO.

III. *Special Situations:* Includes investments in distressed companies or firms with unique opportunities that may be available on a one-time basis (e.g., an investment subsidy resulting from a change in a governmental regulation). Two important classes in this category are:

- *Distressed Debt:* Investors acquire multiple classes of the debt or equity of a publicly traded firm that is in or near bankruptcy. The goal of distressed investors is to create new value in the firm through an infusion of capital and a reorganization of its operations. In a reorganization, distressed investors often forgive the debt obligations of the company in exchange for enough equity to compensate them; this is why distressed debt funds are considered equity investors. However, these funds can also profit by liquidating a firm, which is why they are sometimes called "vulture capitalists."
- *Mezzanine Financing:* Investors provide a middle-level of funding that is subordinated to senior debt but ranks above the existing equity. A typical mezzanine investment includes a subordinated loan to the company—at an interest rate higher than the yield on the senior debt—along with the receipt of some form of equity participation (e.g., warrants, common stock, preferred stock). Thus, like distressed debt investors, mezzanine financiers are providing both private debt and private equity funding.

From the preceding descriptions, it should be clear that not all of these categories will produce investments with the same risk-return trade-offs. Venture capital commitments are generally considered to be the riskiest private equity transactions because they are often made before the organization in question has created a viable source of revenue. Buyouts can also involve a considerable amount of risk—especially when a large amount of leverage is used in the transaction—but they have the advantage of involving companies with established product markets, which typically makes them somewhat more predictable than venture-related deals. Finally, special situation investments such as mezzanine transactions fall on the safer end of the private equity spectrum because they involve a commitment of capital with a senior claim on the firm's resources.

There has been a significant increase in private equity investments over the past 10 to 15 years, particularly in the amount of buyout activity. Venture capital investing appears to have peaked during the technology-related boom in the equity market that occurred in the late 1990s. As Acharya et al. (2007) point out, this trend reflects the simultaneous impact of several factors in place during this period: (i) the influx of a substantial amount of new investment capital as institutional investors shifted their strategic asset allocation policies toward alternative assets, (ii) the availability of relatively inexpensive credit, which made debt financing a cheap source of funds, and (iii) relatively high valuations in the equity market. McKinsey & Company found that the market pool for private equity grew to $76 billion in 2007.

Information on venture capital and private equity in Canada can be found at http://www.cvca.ca.

The Private Equity Investment Process To better understand the dynamics of private equity investing, consider the hypothetical company illustrated in Exhibit 17.16. Suppose initially that two young entrepreneurs have developed a better and more cost-effective way to search for websites. After exhausting their personal savings and bank loans to develop the business—which is sometimes called *zero-stage capital*—they turn to a venture capital firm to provide the additional seed and early-stage funding they need to advance their idea to the next level. Following an evaluation of their business plan, Venture Partners Fund agrees to provide financial capital and operating expertise to help launch the Internet Search Engine Company or ISE (i.e., Step 1a). In exchange for these resources, Venture Partners receives an equity stake in the new company.

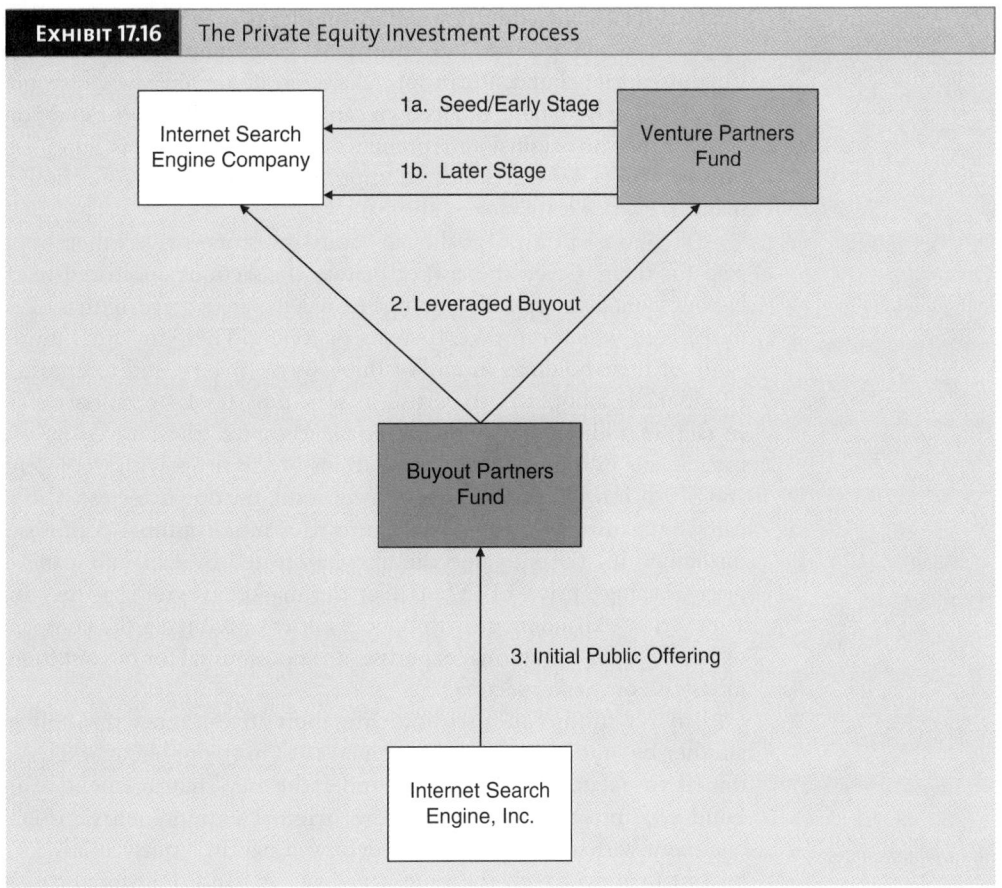

EXHIBIT 17.16   The Private Equity Investment Process

As venture capital investing is extremely risky because the enterprise is unlikely to have an established stream of revenues or profits, the Venture Partners Fund must evaluate the firm on the basis of their *potential* for future success. Typically, only two or three out of ten first-stage ventures become profitable and only one in ten becomes a huge success (e.g., Apple Computer, Genentech, Federal Express). Thus, venture capital firms attempt to mitigate their risk by diversifying their investments across a portfolio of start-up companies. Another method to reduce risk is for the venture funds to limit their exposure to a given start-up by providing funding in stages as the company demonstrates its capacity for success. Thus, Venture Partners Fund decides it will provide only later-stage equity capital to help ISE expand its operations once the firm has established a viable product (i.e., Step 1b).

While venture capital funds help companies develop and grow, they will ultimately want to liquidate their equity holdings in order to create a return on their investment and provide capital to fund new ventures. A typical holding period for their successful investments is between three and seven years. Generally, there are two ways that a venture fund can "exit" one of the companies in their investment portfolio: (i) through a buyout arranged with another private equity investor, or (ii) through an initial public offering (IPO) of common stock to the public equity market. Assuming that ISE has developed a solid support base for its product among users and advertisers, now suppose that it has attracted the interest of Buyout Partners Fund, a firm specializing in doing leveraged buyouts of privately held companies. Using both debt and its own capital, Buyout Partners Fund purchases all of the existing equity from the original entrepreneurs and Venture Partners Fund (i.e., Step 2). Like the venture capitalists, buyout funds attempt to diversify their collection of investments across as many as two or three dozen companies.

Of course, a primary goal of all equity investors is to sell their holdings for more than they paid for them. Given the risk of private transactions compared to the public stock market, buyout capitalists typically attempt to receive an average return of two-to-three times their initial cost, which can take 10 years or longer. These investors must be able to increase the value of their holdings in any of three ways. (i) First and foremost, buyout funds provide a considerable amount of expertise in how a particular business can be run more effectively. In fact, in addition to supplying financial capital, these investors often become very active participants in the day-to-day operations of the firms with the intention of increasing operating cash flows (i.e., EBITDA). (ii) Second, buyout firms can also unlock value in a company by adjusting its capital structure to a more optimal combination of debt and equity financing. (iii) Finally, value can also be created by expanding the cash flow multiple (i.e., price-earnings, price-EBITDA) that the market is willing to pay for a firm, which can be achieved by expanding growth opportunities or reducing the company's level of risk. Because of this need for operational expertise, it is not unusual for buyout funds to specialize in certain industries or market sectors.

Buyout funds can also liquidate their investments through either a private sale to another buyout investor or through an IPO in the public market. Assume that ISE has continued to expand its operations under the new management team that Buyout Partners Fund put into place to replace the original entrepreneurs. After continuing to run the company with a combination of debt and private equity funds for a number of years, the buyout firm now feels the time is right to expand the capital base further by selling additional shares of stock to the general public (i.e., Step 3). As a result of the IPO event, the company now becomes ISE, Inc., a publicly traded corporation. An immediate advantage to Buyout Partners Fund is that the IPO creates a broader and more liquid market for their ownership shares. However, it is frequently the case in an initial stock offering that the existing owners (i.e., Buyout Partners) are restricted from selling their positions for six months or more.

Returns to Private Equity Funds Although average annual returns for these investments tend to be quite high over time, the initial years of a new private equity commitment usually produce negative returns. This is because the organizational expenses incurred by the fund's general partner are drawn from invested capital, as well as the fact that the less-successful investments in the portfolio tend to be recognized quickly and written down. However, as the better-performing investments increase in value over time and are sold at a profit, the returns to the private equity fund tend to increase dramatically.

This return pattern is known as the **J-curve effect** and is illustrated in Exhibit 17.17. The performance measure in this exhibit is the internal rate of return (IRR), which is the most widely used statistic for private market investments. In the early years of a fund's operations, these IRR calculations are usually based on valuation estimates, since the portfolio companies are themselves illiquid assets that trade infrequently. As these assets are sold over time, the IRR statistics become based on the actual cash distributions to the investors.

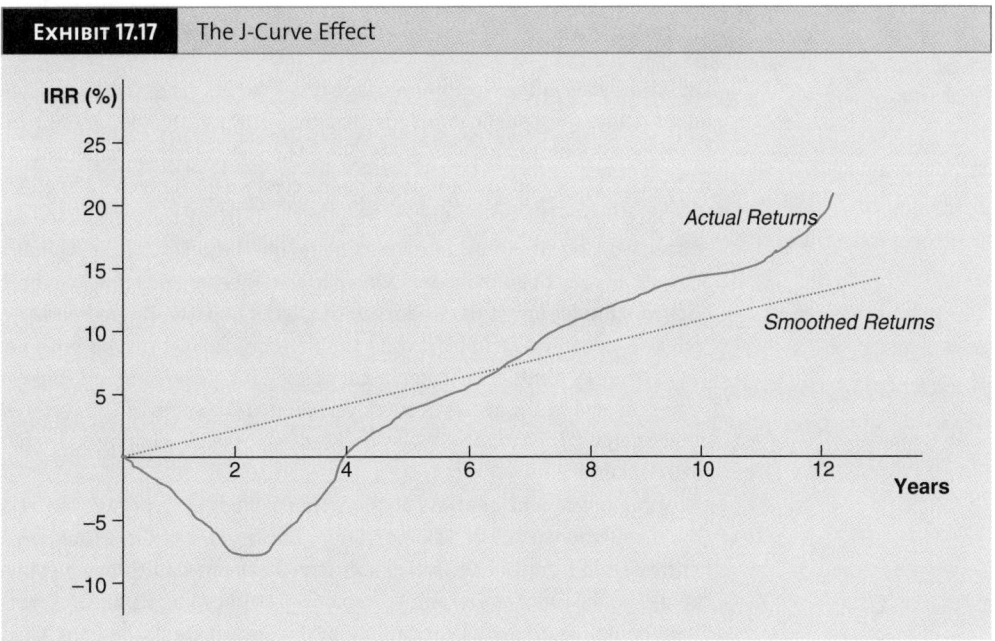

EXHIBIT 17.17   The J-Curve Effect

17.5   Ethics and Regulation in the Professional Asset Management Industry

The issue of ethical behaviour arises any time an individual is hired to perform a service for or look after the interests of another. Economists often refer to this potential conflict as the *principal-agent problem,* which can be summarized as follows: A principal (owner of the assets) hires an agent (manager) to manage her assets. She rightfully expects that the manager will make decisions that are in her best interest. Although the agent is being paid to protect the owner's assets, the manager also has the incentive to take actions that may be in his best interest rather than the client's. For instance, the manager might misuse the owner's assets in both subtle ways (e.g., generating unnecessary expenses for first-class travel or office furnishings) and more blatant ways (e.g., expropriation of resources).

This sort of **agency conflict** occurs frequently in financial relationships. The shareholders of a corporation (i.e., principals) are the owners of the firm's assets, but they usually hire professional managers (i.e., agents) to run the company. Thus, the shareholders face the constant challenge of how they can keep the managers' incentives aligned with theirs. This topic is particularly important for the investment management business because the entire industry is based on handling someone else's money, meaning that agency issues are always present. In this section, we consider how the industry addresses these conflicts, both from a legal (i.e., regulatory) and ethical standpoint.

17.5.1   REGULATION IN THE ASSET MANAGEMENT INDUSTRY

With professional portfolio managers entrusted with the management of trillions of dollars, it is not surprising that the investment industry is highly regulated to ensure a minimum level

Ethical Conflicts in the Profession of Security Analyst

Recent decades in the North American stock markets seem to end in scandals and crashes. Naturally, the investing public demands that those responsible be brought to justice. The end of the 1980s saw Dennis Levine, Ivan Boesky, and Michael Milken go to jail and Drexel Burnham Lambert go bankrupt. The end of the 1990s saw the collapse of the tech bubble.

Once again the guilty had to be punished. The Attorney General for New York State, Eliot Spitzer, working from tips, uncovered many unethical kinds of behaviour on the part of security analysts and portfolio managers. One particularly egregious practice on the part of security analysts working for investment banks with a large underwriting/corporate finance business (called "sell-side" organizations as opposed to "buy-side" for institutions with no underwriting business such as mutual funds and insurance companies) was to recommend highly to clients stocks of companies covered by the analyst's employer when at the same time privately disparaging the stock to other analysts. The stock price was boosted by these glowing recommendations and would eventually collapse.

Some prominent analysts such as Henry Blodget (who worked at Merrill Lynch) and Jack Grubman (who worked at Salomon Smith Barney-part of Citi Group) were censured and permanently barred from the securities industry. Grubman had to pay a total of $15 million to settle charges against him. In December 2002, Spitzer forced a $1.4 billion settlement on ten large Wall Street banks (Bear Stearns, Credit Suisse First Boston, Deutsche Bank, Goldman Sachs, J.P. Morgan Chase, Lehman Brothers, Merrill Lynch, Morgan Stanley, Salomon Smith Barney and UBS Warburg) for participating in and encouraging this kind of unethical behaviour. To prevent this behaviour from recurring, new rules were enacted and agreed to by the banks. Security analysts working for sell-side institutions were to be insulated from pressures by the investment bankers. In addition, money from the $1.4 billion fine was to be used to pay independent analysts to cover firms listed on the exchanges.

The distinction between sell-side and buy-side analysts continues in the present. Sell-side research suffers from a presumption of bias whereas buy-side research does not. The Spitzer settlement may have cured one problem but created another. The major unresolved issue in security analysis is who pays for it? Before 2002, the investment banks paid security analysts very large compensation to act as sales people for the underwriting side of the bank. Since the Spitzer settlement this had to stop and many listed companies are no longer covered by analysts. Thus, one can argue that as a result, the market is less well-informed and less efficient.

Prepared by Francis Tapon, University of Guelph

A brief description of the role of the securities commissions, the Canadian Securities Regulators, and the Investment Industry Regulatory Organization of Canada can be found on the IFIC website at https://www.ific.ca/Content/Content.aspx?id=91.

of acceptable practice. These regulations, which often involve a complex interaction between provincial and federal laws, have the primary purpose of ensuring that portfolio managers act in the best interests of their investors. At their most basic level, these regulations are written to promote adequate disclosure of information related to the investment process and to provide various antifraud protections.

One of the appreciable advantages that the hedge fund industry enjoys is that it is relatively free from regulatory prohibitions that might otherwise impede the investment process. These funds tend to adopt a limited liability format (e.g., limited partnership, limited liability company) purposely to avoid having to register with securities commissions. This freedom allows hedge fund managers to employ certain strategic tools (e.g., leverage, short selling) that are not available to traditional fund managers.

17.5.2   STANDARDS FOR ETHICAL BEHAVIOUR

Many developed economies are founded on the notion of financial market discipline. In such a system, government intervention is necessary to remedy situations when market forces fail to adequately protect investor interests. Unfortunately, we know that such failures do occur. Investors are well aware of the securities scandals of the 1980s that made Ivan Boesky and Michael Milken household names. Market-timing trading scandals tainted the mutual fund industry in 2003, and rogue traders have been exposed in many different portfolio management positions.

Transgressions of this nature confirm that although regulations can punish those found in violation of the law, they cannot prevent all such abuses from occurring in the first place. Absolute prevention requires self-regulation on the part of the asset manager in the form of a strict set of personal ethical standards. Prentice (2007) and Jennings (2000) have stressed that the desire of individuals and firms in the investment management business to maintain their reputation with clients is a major motivating factor in the practice of self-regulation.[11]

The margin note reads:

> The CFA Institute Code and Standards are available at: http://www.cfainstitute.org/centre/codes/ethics.

The CFA (i.e., Chartered Financial Analysts) Institute—formerly known as the Association for Investment Management and Research (AIMR)—has developed for its worldwide membership of security analysts and money managers a rigorous *Code of Ethics* and *Standards of Professional Conduct* based on these principals. The *Code of Ethics* stipulates that members of the CFA Institute must:

- Act with integrity, competence, diligence, respect, and in an ethical manner with the public, clients, prospective clients, employers, employees, colleagues in the investment profession, and other participants in the global capital markets.
- Place the integrity of the investment profession and the interests of clients above their own personal interests.
- Use reasonable care and exercise independent professional judgment when conducting investment analysis, making investment recommendations, taking investment actions, and engaging in other professional activities.
- Practise and encourage others to practise in a professional and ethical manner that will reflect credit on ourselves and the profession.
- Promote the integrity of, and uphold the rules governing, capital markets.
- Maintain and improve their professional competence and strive to maintain and improve the competence of other investment professionals.

The specific standards of practice suggested by these ethical mandates provide asset managers with precisely defined conduct and actions that are acceptable (or, more to the point, unacceptable) in daily practice. For example, the general principle that managers should use proper care becomes a specific requirement that they must be able to justify the suitability of any investment decision made on behalf of a particular client. The CFA Institute expects all of its members, which includes everyone holding the CFA designation, to uphold these standards on a voluntary basis. Violations deemed severe enough can result in the loss of a manager's charter.

To further promote ethical behaviour in the asset management industry, the CFA Institute recently launched the Centre for Financial Market Integrity. The stated purpose in creating the centre was "to develop timely, practical solutions to global capital market issues, while advancing investors' interests by promoting the highest standards of ethics and professionalism within the investment community worldwide."[12] The centre's guiding principles—which stress the fact that

---

11 For interesting discussions of the investing public's perception of ethics in the asset management industry, see Lummer (1994) and Ware (2000).

12 A more complete description of the centre's goals and activities can be found at http://www.cfainstitute.org/centre.

investors should come first in all of the manager's activities, from investment decisions to financial reporting—are listed in Exhibit 17.18. In recognition of the unique place of trust that portfolio managers enjoy, one recent initiative that the centre has undertaken on behalf of the worldwide constituency of the CFA Institute has been the creation of a comprehensive *Asset Manager Code of Professional Conduct*. Established in 2005, the *Asset Manager Code* sets forth minimum standards for providing asset management services to clients. It seeks to extend the voluntary standards of practice governing individual conduct to a set of rules that pertains to entire investment management firms. Although many firms already have such standards in place, others (including both traditional managers and hedge funds) do not, and this is the niche the new *Code* is designed to fill.

17.5.3   EXAMPLES OF ETHICAL CONFLICTS

Many ethical breaches, such as plagiarizing research reports or falsifying performance statements, are unambiguously wrong. Other lapses are not as clear-cut. We will conclude this section with a discussion of three examples of how possible conflicts between the manager and the investor can arise from accepted business practices.

Incentive Compensation Schemes   The first example is related to the way in which managers are compensated for their services. We saw earlier in the chapter that traditional asset management companies—both public and private—typically receive fees based on AUM, while hedge fund managers also receive a performance allocation fee tied directly to the portfolio's performance. The fund managers are often compensated with a base salary and bonus that depends on the performance of their portfolios relative to those of their peers. Brown, Harlow, and Starks (1996) argued that this arrangement is analogous to a golf or tennis tournament where the players with the best relative performance at the end of the competition receive the largest payoffs. They documented that mutual fund managers with the worst relative performance midway through a compensation period were more likely to increase the risk of the portfolio in an effort to increase their final standing. Of course, altering fund risk to enhance their own compensation suggests that some managers may not always act in their clients' best interests.

> IFIC and other interested associations are keeping close watch on the soft dollar debate. For the latest comments, perform an Internet search for "IFIC soft dollars."

EXHIBIT 17.18	Guiding Principles for Ethical Behaviour in the Asset Management Industry

- Investors come first. The interests of the investing client must always take precedence over the interests of investment professionals and their employers.
- Investment professionals must act ethically and in accordance with the highest professional standards. They must:
  - Act with integrity in all their dealings
  - Maintain independence and objectivity
  - Continuously strive to maintain and improve their professional knowledge and competence.
- Investors need complete, accurate, timely, and transparent information from securities issuers.
- Financial statements should be reported from the perspective of the shareholder who bears the ultimate risk, and with the shareholder's best interests held paramount.
  - Financial statements should be fully transparent and report the fair values of all assets, liabilities, exchanges, and transactions that could potentially impact the investor.
  - All assets and liabilities should be included in the balance sheet, with no hidden assets, hidden debt, or hidden obligations.
- Markets should move toward one set of global, high-quality standards for reporting financial information.
- Self-regulation is generally the preferred method for promoting fair and efficient markets. However, we recognize that some circumstances require additional regulation in order to ensure adequate investor protection.

Source: *CFA* Centre for Financial Market Integrity.

Copyright CFA Institute. Reproduced and republished from What We Stand For, The CFA Centre for Financial Market Integrity with permission from CFA Institute. All rights reserved.

Soft Dollar Arrangements A second potential ethical dilemma for professional asset managers involves the use of **soft dollars**. Soft dollars are generated when a manager commits the investor to paying a brokerage commission that is higher than the simple cost of executing a security trade in exchange for the manager receiving additional bundled services from the broker. A typical example of this practice would be for a manager to route her equity trades through a full service broker in order to receive security research reports that the brokerage firm produces. It may not be hard for the manager to justify how this additional research benefits the investor—who, of course, is ultimately paying for the service—but the story is quite different if, instead of research, the manager receives from the broker "perks," such as office equipment, secretarial services, or even payment for personal travel. In 1998, the CFA Institute adopted a comprehensive set of voluntary standards designed to give its members guidance on the permissible uses of soft dollar arrangements.

Marketing Investment Management Services A final example of an ethical dilemma that confronts professional asset management organizations is how and when to advertise their services. Conventional wisdom holds that it would be in the investors' best interests for any particular investment management company to build a steady awareness over time of its relative merits. However, in their consumer (i.e., investor) survey in the mutual fund market, Capon, Fitzsimons, and Prince (1996) documented that the main factor in the decision of which fund's shares to buy was the immediate past total return performance of the portfolio. Zweig (2000) observed that a consequence of this tendency has been the development of a situation in which mutual funds time their advertisements around relative peaks in their performance. Further, firms that run a family of funds can choose which portfolio or manager they want to promote on a situational basis, while still maintaining continuous brand awareness for the entire complex. Despite the usual disclaimers to the effect that "past returns are not an indication of future performance," the decision to always promote the "hot hand" is likely to be effective, but it is also likely to result in a misallocation of investor capital.

In summary, it is important for investors to recognize that potential ethical conflicts will exist any time they hire professional investment managers. Investors are protected by the series of regulations that oversee the security industry as well as the strict standards imposed by trade associations such as the CFA Institute. Of course, perhaps the best protection that investors have is the vast majority of the thousands of investment advisors and managers throughout the world who are unwilling to do anything that would jeopardize their personal and professional reputations.

17.6   What Do You Want from a Professional Asset Manager?

What functions do you want your portfolio manager to perform for you? The list probably includes some or all of the following:

1. Help determine your investment objectives and constraints (e.g., return goals, risk tolerance) and develop a portfolio that is consistent with them.
2. Diversify your portfolio to eliminate unsystematic risk.
3. Maintain your portfolio diversification within your desired risk class while allowing flexibility so that you can shift between alternative investment instruments as desired.
4. Attempt to achieve a risk-adjusted performance level that is superior to that of your relevant benchmark; some investors may be willing to sacrifice diversification for superior returns in limited segments of their portfolios.

5. Administer the account, keep records of costs and transactions, provide timely information for tax purposes, and reinvest dividends if desired.
6. Maintain ethical standards of behaviour at all times.

Not all of the types of asset management organizations we have discussed in this chapter address each of these goals; mutual funds do not determine your risk preference for you and alternative asset investments are seldom well diversified. However, once you determine your risk-return preferences, you can choose a mutual fund from a large and growing variety of alternatives designed to meet almost any investment goal. In general, these types of managers are consistent in meeting their stated goals for investment strategies, risk, and returns. Private asset management companies are oriented toward providing similar services (including investment policy development) for clients who have larger amounts of investable capital.

Diversifying your portfolio to eliminate unsystematic risk is one of the major benefits of both private management companies and mutual funds. Many mutual funds provide *instant diversification,* which is especially beneficial to small investors who do not have the resources to form their own large-scale portfolios. Although diversification varies among funds, typically a large percentage of existing portfolios have a correlation with the market above 0.80. Therefore, most mutual funds provide excellent diversification, especially if they state this goal as an explicit objective.

The third function your portfolio manager might perform for you is to maintain the diversification of your portfolio within your desired risk class. It should not be too surprising that both types of traditional asset manager (i.e., private management companies and mutual funds) generally maintain the stability of their correlation with the market over time because few managers change the makeup of reasonably well-diversified portfolios very much. Strong evidence exists regarding the consistency of the risk class mandates for portfolios regardless of whether the overall performance is better or worse than average. On the other hand, hedge fund portfolios often vary significantly within the broad context of their designated strategy as managers attempt to add the maximum amount of alpha (i.e., the difference between actual and expected return).

Mutual funds have met the desire for flexibility to change investment instruments by creating numerous funds within a given management company. Typically, investment groups will allow you to shift between portfolios in their family of funds without a charge simply by calling the company. Therefore, you can shift between an aggressive stock fund, a money market fund, and a bond fund for much less than it would cost you in time and money to buy and sell numerous individual issues. By their nature, both private management companies and hedge funds tend to restrict an investor's ability to make these sorts of changes; accordingly, both of these management types are considered to be less liquid than mutual funds.

The fourth function of your portfolio manager is to provide risk-adjusted performance that is superior to your benchmark, which implies that it is superior to a naive buy-and-hold investment policy. The rapid development of the alternative asset industry over the past several years suggests two things in this regard. First, investors increasingly view these managers as being better suited to produce positive and consistent alphas than traditional managers. Second, it is becoming more and more difficult for many traditional asset managers to generate superior risk-adjusted returns because of the many constraints imposed on their investment process (e.g., short sale prohibitions, leverage restrictions).

The fifth function of a portfolio manager is account administration. All managers provide this service to some degree. However, private management companies are the most likely to see all (or substantially all) of a client's assets and so these firms are in the best position to administer the account most effectively. Conversely, most mutual funds also provide many valuable administrative services. For instance, they allow automatic reinvestment of dividends with no charge and supply annual statements of dividend income and capital gain distribution that can be used to prepare tax returns. Given their partnership format, hedge funds and private equity funds also provide investors with necessary tax information as well as periodic accounting of investment activity.

The final function that you should expect from your portfolio manager is ethical behaviour that strictly follows the prevailing regulations and standards of conduct in the industry. For all investors, this is—and should be—a non-negotiable requirement of any manager, regardless of the organizational form of the company. As we have seen, professional asset management is a fiduciary business, and those managers whose conduct violates the trust of those whose wealth they protect and grow will not last long. In extreme cases, they may even suffer legal consequences.

In summary, as an investor, you probably want your portfolio manager to perform a broad array of functions. Typically, however, no single manager is equipped to provide all of the services that you may require. Therefore, it is quite common for investors to form a "portfolio" of managers with different talents and capabilities (e.g., a hedge fund manager to provide superior risk-adjusted returns, an index mutual fund manager to provide diversification for the majority of your assets). Given what we know about the value of diversifying our financial capital across different asset classes and securities, it should come as no surprise that the same principle holds for portfolio management skills as well.

Summary

1. There are two primary types of asset management companies. Management and advisory firms hold the assets of individual and institutional investors in separate accounts while investment companies pool and manage the assets collectively. In recent years, the industry has undergone considerable structural change with a trend toward consolidating AUM in large, multiproduct companies. This has had a beneficial effect for investors of reducing management fees.

2. Traditional asset management companies typically receive fees based on AUM, while hedge fund managers also receive a performance allocation fee tied directly to the portfolio's performance. The fund managers are often compensated with a base salary and bonus that depends on the performance of their portfolios relative to those of their peers.

3. Net asset value (NAV) per share is calculated by determining the market value of a fund's holdings (securities, cash, and any accrued earnings) less any liabilities, divided by the number of shares outstanding.

4. Investors in investment companies receive units representing their proportional ownership in the underlying portfolio of stocks, bonds, or other securities. These fund units can either be traded in the secondary market (closed-end) or sold directly back to the investment company (mutual fund) at the prevailing net asset value.

5. Some mutual funds charge a sales or load fee from which salespeople are compensated. A fee to purchase the fund (front-end load) is usually a percentage of the NAV. Other funds may charge a small redemption fee. No-load funds have become popular in recent years, many sponsored

through banks. In addition to selling charges, all levy annual management fees (usually a percent of average net assets and may be on a sliding scale) to compensate the fund managers. These management fees are a major factor driving the creation of new funds. More AUM generate more fees, although the costs of management do not increase at the same rate because substantial economies of scale in managing financial assets.

6. In recent years there has been rapid development of alternative investments, such as hedge funds and private equity. These are generally less restricted in what strategies they can follow and investment techniques they can employ. As a consequence of this additional level of flexibility, many investors have come to regard hedge funds as being in a unique position to produce superior risk-adjusted returns. Private equity typically funds either new companies or established firms seeking funds. Although often illiquid, private equity are among the highest risk and reward investments available.

7. Hedge funds employ a number of different investment strategies that vary in the risk and return profiles. Managers using a long–short equity strategy attempts to identify misvalued stocks and take long or short positions accordingly in order to generate "double alpha." An equity market neutral strategy attempts to limit the volatility exposure by taking offsetting risk positions on the long and short side, perhaps by using derivatives. These portfolios are expected to produce returns of 2% to 4% above the risk-free rate (an absolute return strategy) if no leverage is employed. Arbitrage-based hedge funds look for disparities in bond pricing (fixed-income), between prices for convertible

bonds and the underlying common stock (convertible) or the magnitude of the spread on merger transactions (merger or risk). Given the typically small price disparities on fixed income and convertibles, managers usually use leverage to enhance overall returns. Merger arbitrage manager returns depend on whether the proposed deal is ultimately completed and whether their analysis is superior to that of the other investors in the market. A number of opportunistic strategies such as high yield/distressed, global macro, and managed futures exist. Should a turnaround occur with distressed firms, security prices will approach their intrinsic value, generating profits for the distressed fund managers. Global macro managers seek to profit from changes in global economies and typically use leverage and derivatives to enhance returns. A managed futures strategy uses long and short positions in a variety of futures contracts to take "directional" positions on certain events and to exploit pricing discrepancies. These strategies frequently employ a substantial degree of financial leverage.

8. Venture capital focuses on investments in start-up firms, early-stage businesses, and new products and services created by established businesses. Buyouts involve the acquisition of a product line, set of assets, or business from an established company. Venture capital commitments are generally considered to be the riskiest transactions because they are often made before the organization in question has created a viable source of revenue. Buyouts can also involve a considerable amount of risk but they have the advantage of involving companies with established product markets, which typically makes them somewhat more predictable than venture-related deals.

9. Issues of ethical behaviour arise any time one person is hired to perform a service for another. The professional asset management industry protects investors through a series of government regulations and voluntary standards of practice imposed by trade associations on their members. The primary purpose of these regulations and standards is to ensure that managers deal with all investors fairly and equitably and that information about investment performance is accurately reported. Two areas of particular concern in the investment community involve manager compensation arrangements and the use of soft dollars.

Key Terms

12b-1 plan, p. 539
agency conflict, p. 559
alternative asset, p. 543
balanced fund, p. 540
closed-end investment company, p. 538
contingent, deferred sales load, p. 540
flexible portfolio fund, p. 540

investment company, p. 532
investment management company, p. 537
J-curve effect, p. 558
limited partnership, p. 545
low-load fund, p. 539
management and advisory firm, p. 532
management fee, p. 540

money market fund, p. 540
mutual fund, p. 538
net asset value (NAV) per share, p. 537
no-load fund, p. 539
open-end investment company, p. 538
private equity, p. 553
soft dollars, p. 563

Suggested Readings

CFA Institute. *Standards of Practice Handbook,* 9th ed. Charlottesville, VA, 2006.

CFA Institute. *Points of Inflection: New Directions for Portfolio Management.* Charlottesville, VA, 2004.

Keswani, Aneeland, and David Stolin, "Which Money Is Smart? Mutual Fund Buys and Sells of Individual and Institutional Investors." *The Journal of Finance,* 63, no. 1 (February 2008).

Khorana, Aja, Henri Servaes, and Peter Tufano, "Mutual Fund Fees around the World," HBS Finance Working Paper No. 901023, July 2007.

Lakonishok, Josef, Andrei Shleifer, and Robert W. Vishny. "The Structure and Performance of the Money Management Industry." In *Brookings Papers on Economic Activity.* Washington, DC: Brookings Institute, 1992.

Oberlechner, Thomas. *The Psychology of Ethics in the Finance and Investment Industry.* Charlottesville, VA: Research Foundation of CFA Institute, 2007.

Pozen, Robert C. *The Mutual Fund Business,* 2nd ed. Boston, MA: Houghton Mifflin, 2002.

For Chapter CFA Questions and Problems, please see Appendix A at the end of this text.

Questions

1. What are the differences between a management and advisory firm and an investment company? Describe the approach toward portfolio management adopted by each organization.
2. It has been suggested that the professional asset management community is rapidly becoming dominated by a fairly small number of huge, multiproduct firms. Discuss whether the data presented on the IFIC website (http://statistics.ific.ca/English/Reports/Monthly Statistics.asp) supports that view.
3. Closed-end funds generally invest in securities and financial instruments that are relatively illiquid whereas most mutual funds invest in widely traded stocks and bonds. Explain the difference between closed-end and open-end funds and why this liquidity distinction matters.
4. What is the difference between a load fund and a no-load fund?

5. Should you care about how well a mutual fund is diversified? Why or why not?
6. As an investigator evaluating how well mutual fund managers select undervalued stocks or project market returns, discuss whether net or gross returns are more relevant.
7. You are told that Fund X experienced *above-average* performance over the past two years. Do you think it will continue over the next two years? Why or why not?
8. Most money managers have a portion of their compensation tied to the performance of the portfolios they manage. Explain how this arrangement can create an ethical dilemma for the manager.
9. What are soft dollar arrangements? Describe one potential way they can be used to transfer wealth from the investor to the manager.

Problems

1. Suppose ABC Mutual Fund had no liabilities and owned only four stocks as follows:

Stock	Shares	Price	Market Value
W	1,000	$12	$12,000
X	1,200	15	18,000
Y	1,500	22	33,000
Z	800	16	12,800
			$75,800

The fund began by selling 50,000 units at $8.00 per unit. What is its NAV?

2. Suppose you are considering investing $1,000 in a load fund that charges a fee of 8%, and you expect your investment to earn 15% over the next year. Alternatively, you could invest in a no-load fund with similar risk that charges a 1% redemption fee. You estimate that this no-load fund will earn 12%. Given your expectations, which is the better investment and by how much?

3. Consider the recent performance of the Closed Fund, a closed-end fund devoted to finding undervalued, thinly traded stocks:

Period	NAV	Premium/Discount
0	$10.00	0.0%
1	11.25	−5.0
2	9.85	+2.3
3	10.50	−3.2
4	12.30	−7.0

Here price premiums and discounts are indicated by pluses and minuses, respectively, and Period 0 represents Closed Fund's initiation date.

a. Calculate the average return per period for an investor who bought 100 units of the Closed Fund at the initiation and then sold her position at the end of Period 4.
b. What was the average periodic growth rate in NAV over that same period?
c. Calculate the periodic return for another investor who bought 100 units of Closed Fund at the end of Period 1 and sold his position at the end of Period 2.
d. What was the periodic growth rate in NAV between Periods 1 and 2?

4. CMD Asset Management has the following fee structure for clients in its equity fund:
   1.00% of first $5 million invested
   0.75% of next $5 million invested

0.60% of next $10 million invested

0.40% above $20 million

a. Calculate the annual dollar fees paid by Client 1, which has $27 million under management, and Client 2, which has $97 million under management.

b. Calculate the fees paid by both clients as a percentage of their assets under management.

c. What is the economic rationale for a fee schedule that declines (in percentage terms) with increases in assets under management?

5. Suppose that at the start of the year, a no-load mutual fund has a net asset value of $27.15 per unit. During the year, it pays its unitholders a dividend distribution of $1.12 per unit and finishes the year with an NAV of $30.34.

a. What is the return to an investor who holds 257.876 units of this fund in his RRSP?

b. What is the after-tax return for the same investor if these units were held in an ordinary account? For simplicity, assume that the investor has a combined federal and provincial tax rate of 41% and the effective tax rate on dividend income is 24%.

c. If the investment company allowed the investor to automatically reinvest his cash distribution in additional fund units, how many additional units could the investor acquire? Assume that the distribution occurred at year end and that the proceeds from the distribution can be reinvested at the year-end NAV.

6. The Focus Fund is a mutual fund that holds long-term positions in a small number of non-dividend-paying stocks. Their holdings at the end of two recent years are as follows:

| Stock | YEAR 1 | | YEAR 2 | |
	Shares	Price	Shares	Price
A	100,000	$45.25	100,000	$48.75
B	225,000	25.38	225,000	24.75
C	375,000	14.50	375,000	12.38
D	115,000	87.13	115,000	98.50
E	154,000	56.50	154,000	62.50
F	175,000	63.00	175,000	77.00
G	212,000	32.00	212,000	38.63
H	275,000	15.25	275,000	8.75
I	450,000	9.63	450,000	27.45
J	90,000	71.25	90,000	75.38
K	87,000	42.13	87,000	49.63
L	137,000	19.88	0	27.88
M	0	17.75	150,000	19.75
Cash		$3,542,000		$2,873,000
Expenses		$ 730,000		$ 830,000

At the end of both years, Focus Fund had 5,430,000 units outstanding.

a. Calculate the net asset value for a unit of the Focus Fund at the end of Year 1, being sure to include the cash position in the net total portfolio value.

b. Immediately after calculating its Year 1 NAV, Focus Fund sold its position in Stock L and purchased its position in Stock M (both transactions were done at Year 1 prices). Calculate the Year 2 NAV for Focus Fund and compute the growth rate in the unit value on a percentage basis.

c. At the end of Year 2, how many units of the Focus Fund could the manager redeem without having to liquidate her stock positions (i.e., using only the cash account)?

d. If immediately after calculating the Year 2 NAV, the manager received investor redemption requests for 500,000 units, how many shares of each stock would she have to sell in order to maintain the same proportional ownership position in each stock? Assume that she liquidates the entire cash position before she sells any stock holdings.

7. Mutual funds can effectively charge sales fees in one of three ways: front-end load fees, annual fees, or deferred (i.e., back-end) load fees. Assume that the SAS Fund offers its investors the choice of the following sales fee arrangements: (1) a 3% front-end load, (2) a 0.50% annual deduction taken at the end of the year, or (3) a 2% back-end load, paid at the liquidation of the investor's position. Also, assume that SAS Fund averages NAV growth of 12% per year.

a. If you start with $100,000 in investment capital, calculate what an investment in SAS would be worth in three years under each of the proposed sales fee schemes. Which scheme would you choose?

b. If your investment horizon were 10 years, would your answer in Part a change? Demonstrate.

c. Explain the relationship between the timing of the sales charge and your investment horizon. In general, if you intend to hold your position for a long time, which fee arrangement would you prefer?

18

Evaluation of Portfolio Performance

After you read this chapter, you should be able to answer the following questions:

1. What is the peer group comparison method of evaluating an investor's performance?

2. What are the risk-adjusted performance measures, i.e., the Treynor measure, the Sharpe measure, the Jensen measure, and the information ratio? How do they relate to one another?

3. What are other tools for evaluating portfolio performance beyond risk-adjusted measurements?

4. What are the challenges to benchmarking, and what are the important characteristics that any useful benchmark should possess?

5. How do bond portfolio performance measures differ from equity portfolio performance measures?

6. What are time-weighted and dollar-weighted returns, and which should be reported under the CFA Institute's presentation standards?

This chapter outlines the theory and practice of evaluating the performance of an investment portfolio. We begin this discussion by examining a most simple assessment technique, *peer group comparison*, which is still widely used today, but it does not adjust for the risk exposure of the portfolio, which is a severe shortcoming. We then present four risk-adjusted portfolio performance evaluation techniques (referred to as composite performance measures) that comprise the basic "toolkit" for measuring risk-adjusted performance. Following this discussion of the most prevalent tools, we discuss evaluation techniques beyond risk-adjusted measures, including attribution analysis, a technique designed to establish the source of a portfolio manager's skill, and a measure for market timing skills.

In evaluation of portfolio performance, selecting an appropriate benchmark is important. We will discuss the challenges of benchmarking and present the characteristics of useful benchmarks. We will also consider how measuring the performance of a bond portfolio differs from that of a portfolio of stocks. Finally, we examine industry standards for calculating returns and reporting portfolio performance to investors.

18.1 Peer Group Comparisons

At one time, investors evaluated portfolio performance almost entirely on the basis of the rate of return. They were aware of the concept of risk but did not know how to measure it, so they could not consider it explicitly. Developments in portfolio theory in the early 1960s showed investors how to quantify risk in terms of the variability of returns. Still, because no single measure combined both return and risk, the two factors had to be considered separately, as Friend, Blume, and Crockett (1970) did by grouping portfolios into similar risk classes based on return variance and then compared the returns for alternative portfolios directly within these risk classes.

A **peer group comparison**, which Kritzman (1990) describes as the most common manner of evaluating portfolio managers, collects the returns produced by a representative universe of investors over a specific period of time and displays them in a simple boxplot format. The universe is typically divided into percentiles, showing the relative ranking of a given investor.

For instance, a portfolio manager who produced a one-year return of 12.4% would be in the 10th percentile if only 9 other portfolios in a universe of 100 produced a higher return. Although these comparisons can get quite detailed, it is common for the boxplot graphic to include the maximum and minimum returns, as well as the returns falling at the 25th, 50th (i.e., the median), and 75th percentiles.

Exhibit 18.1 shows the returns from periods of varying length for a representative investor—labelled here as "U.S. Equity with Cash"—relative to its peer universe of other U.S. domestic equity managers.[1] Also included in the comparison are the periodic returns to three indexes of the overall market: Standard and Poor's 500, Russell 1000, and Russell 3000. The display shows return quartiles for investment periods ranging from 5 to 10 years. The investor in question (indicated by the large dot) performed admirably, finishing above the median in each of the comparison periods. The manager of this portfolio produced the largest nine-year return (16.5%), well above the median return of 13.0%. Notice, however, that although the investor's 10-year average return exceeds the 9-year level (16.6%), it falls below the 5th percentile, which is no longer the best.

There are several potential problems with the peer group comparison method of evaluating an investor's performance. First, the boxplots shown in Exhibit 18.1 do not make any explicit adjustment for the risk level of the portfolios in the universe. Investment risk is only *implicitly* considered to the extent that all the portfolios in the universe have essentially the same level of volatility. This is not likely to be the case for any sizable peer group, particularly if the universe mixes portfolios with different investment styles. Second, it is almost impossible to form a truly comparable peer group that is large enough to make the percentile rankings valid and meaningful. Finally, by focusing on nothing more than relative returns, such a comparison loses sight of whether the investor in question has accomplished his individual objectives and satisfied his investment constraints.

18.2   Risk-Adjusted Composite Performance Measures

Morningstar and the *Globe and Mail* each has a five-star evaluation system for mutual funds. Go to http://www.morningstar.ca or http://www.globefund.com.

This section describes in detail the four major composite equity portfolio performance measures that combine risk and return performance into a single value. We describe each measure and then demonstrate how to compute it and interpret the results. We also compare the measures and discuss how they differ and why they rank portfolios differently.

18.2.1   TREYNOR PORTFOLIO PERFORMANCE MEASURE

Treynor (1965) developed a measure of performance that would apply to all investors, regardless of their risk preferences. Building on developments in capital market theory, the **Treynor measure** introduced a risk-free asset that could be combined with different portfolios to form a portfolio possibility line. He showed that rational, risk-averse investors would always prefer the portfolio line with the largest slope because this would place them on the highest indifference curve. The slope of this portfolio possibility line (designated T) is equal to[2]

18.1

$$T_i = \frac{\overline{R_i} - \overline{RFR}}{\beta_i}$$

where:

$\overline{R_i}$ = the average rate of return for Portfolio i during a specified time period

$\overline{RFR}$ = the average rate of return on a risk-free investment during the same time period

β_i = the slope of the fund's characteristic line during that time period

1 This example comes from Singer (1996) and was based on data from the Frank Russell Company.

2 The terms used in the formula differ from those used by Treynor but are consistent with our earlier discussion. Also, our discussion is concerned with general portfolio performance rather than being limited to mutual funds.

EXHIBIT 18.1 An Illustrative Peer Group Comparison

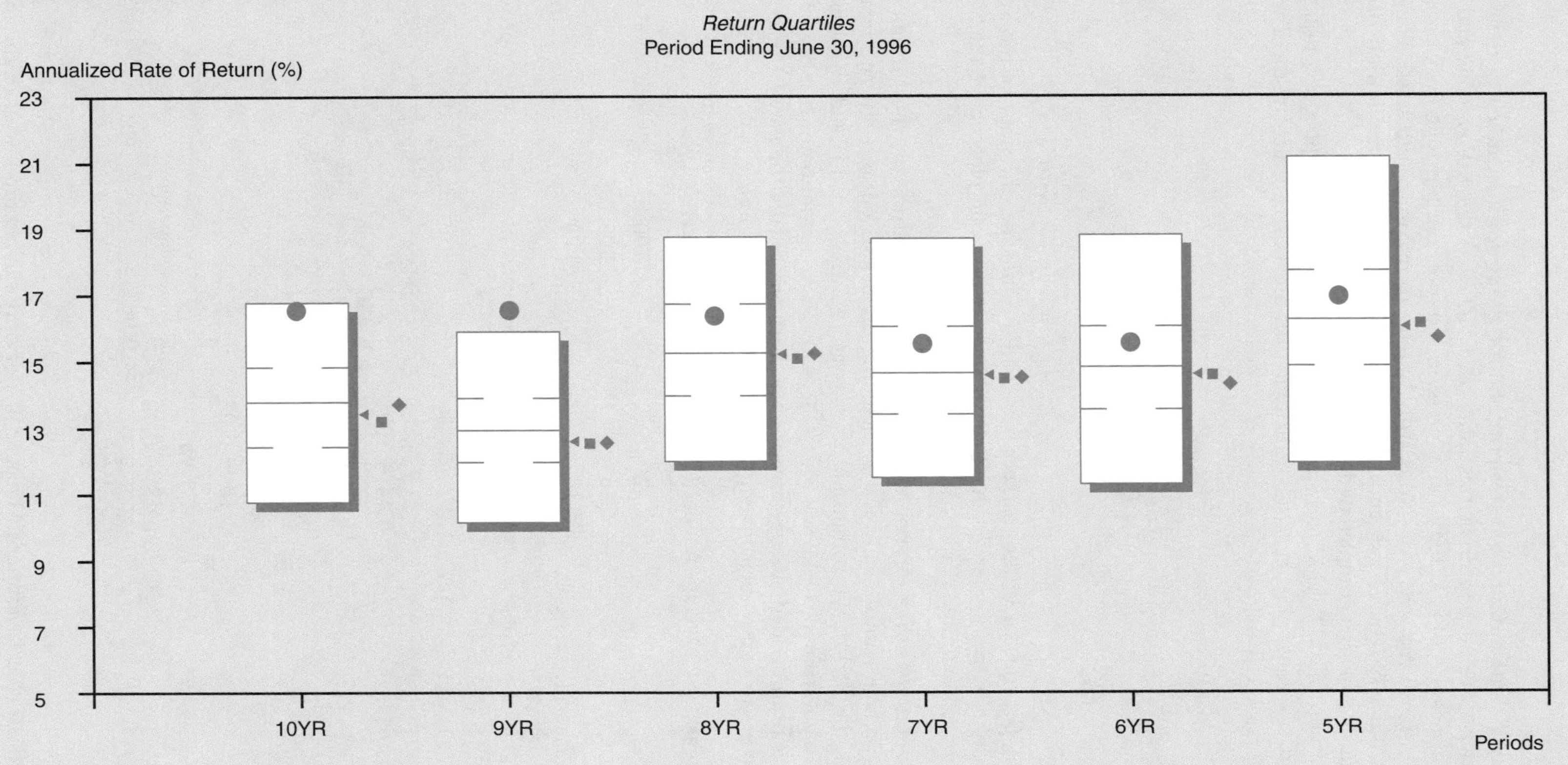
Return Quartiles
Period Ending June 30, 1996
Annualized Rate of Return (%)
23
21
19
17
15
13
11
9
7
5
10YR
9YR
8YR
7YR
6YR
5YR
Periods

	10YR	9YR	8YR	7YR	6YR	5YR
5th percentile	16.8	15.9	18.8	18.7	18.8	21.2
25th percentile	14.8	13.9	16.7	16.0	16.0	17.7
Median	13.8	13.0	15.2	14.6	14.8	16.2
75th percentile	12.5	12.0	14.0	13.4	13.5	14.8
95th percentile	10.8	10.1	12.0	11.5	11.3	11.9
◂ Russell 1000	13.5	12.7	15.3	14.6	14.6	16.1
■ Russell 3000	13.2	12.5	15.1	14.5	14.6	16.2
◆ S&P 500 index	13.8	12.6	15.3	14.6	14.3	15.7
● U.S. equity with cash portfolio	16.6	16.5	16.4	15.6	15.6	17.0

Source: Brian Singer, "Valuation of Portfolio Performance: Aggregate Return and Risk Analysis," *The Journal of Performance Measurement* 1, no. 1 (Fall 1996): 6–16.

As noted, a larger T value indicates a better portfolio for all investors, regardless of their risk preferences. Because the numerator of this ratio ($\overline{R_i} - \overline{RFR}$) is the *risk premium* and the denominator is a measure of risk, the total expression indicates the portfolio's *risk premium return per unit of risk*. All risk-averse investors would prefer to maximize this value. The risk variable beta measures systematic risk and tells us nothing about the diversification of the portfolio. It *implicitly assumes* a completely diversified portfolio.

Comparing a portfolio's T value to a similar measure for the market portfolio indicates whether the portfolio would plot above the security market line (SML). Calculate the T value for the aggregate market as follows:

$$T_M = \frac{\overline{R_M} - \overline{RFR}}{\beta_M}$$

In this expression, β_M equals 1.0 (the market's beta) and T_M indicates the slope of the SML. Therefore, a portfolio with a higher T value than the market portfolio plots above the SML, indicating superior risk-adjusted performance.

Demonstration of Comparative Treynor Measures Suppose that during the most recent 10-year period, the average annual total return (including dividends) on an aggregate market portfolio, such as the S&P/TSX composite index, was 14% ($\overline{R_M} = 0.14$) and the average nominal return on government T-bills was 8% ($\overline{RFR} = 0.08$). As administrator of a large pension fund that has been divided among three money managers during the past 10 years, we must decide whether to renew their investment management contracts.

Investment Manager	Average Annual Rate of Return	Beta
W	0.12	0.90
X	0.16	1.05
Y	0.18	1.20

You compute T values for the market portfolio and for each of the individual portfolio managers as follows:

$$T_M = \frac{0.14 - 0.08}{1.00} = 0.060$$

$$T_W = \frac{0.12 - 0.08}{0.90} = 0.044$$

$$T_X = \frac{0.16 - 0.08}{1.05} = 0.076$$

$$T_Y = \frac{0.18 - 0.08}{1.20} = 0.083$$

These results indicate that Investment Manager W not only ranked the lowest of the three managers but did not perform as well as the aggregate market on a risk-adjusted basis. In

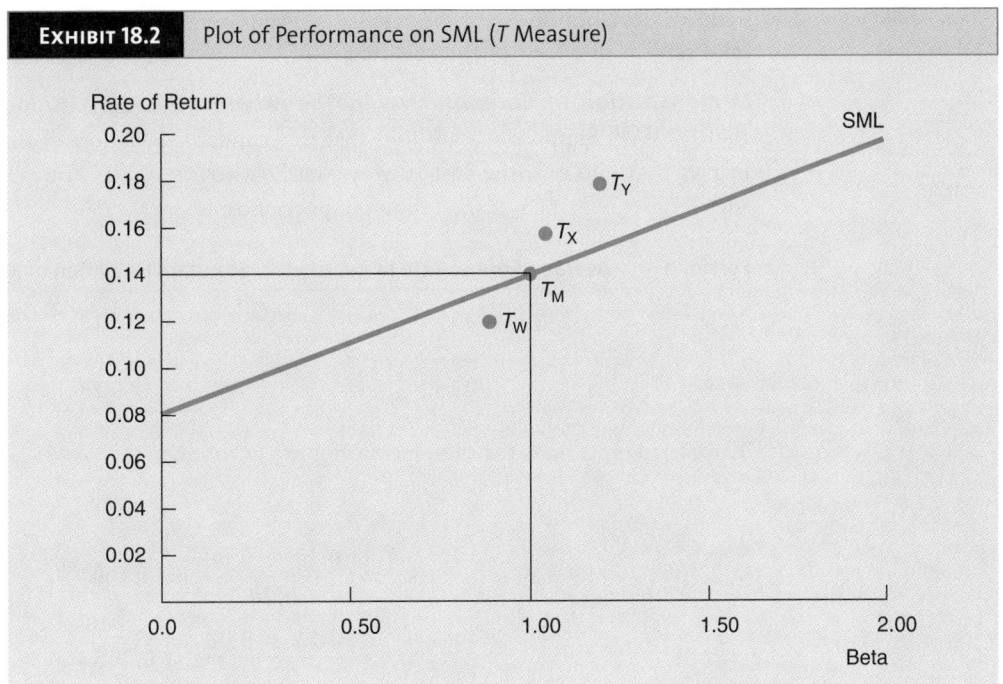

EXHIBIT 18.2   Plot of Performance on SML (*T* Measure)

contrast, both X and Y beat the market portfolio, and Manager Y performed somewhat better than Manager X. Both of their portfolios plotted above the SML, as shown in Exhibit 18.2.

18.2.2   SHARPE PORTFOLIO PERFORMANCE MEASURE

Sharpe (1966) likewise conceived of a composite measure to evaluate the performance of mutual funds. The measure followed closely his earlier work on the capital asset pricing model (CAPM), dealing specifically with the capital market line (CML).

The **Sharpe measure** of portfolio performance (designated *S*) is stated as follows:

18.2
$$S_i = \frac{\overline{R}_i - \overline{RFR}}{\sigma_i}$$

where in addition to the earlier notation:

σ_i = the standard deviation of the rate of return for Portfolio i during the time period.

This performance measure clearly is similar to the Treynor measure; however, it seeks to measure the *total risk* of the portfolio by using the standard deviation of returns rather than considering only the systematic risk summarized by beta. Because the numerator is the portfolio's risk premium, this measure indicates the *risk premium return earned per unit of total risk*. As such, this portfolio performance measure uses the CML to compare portfolios, whereas the Treynor measure examines portfolio performance in relation to the SML. Finally, the standard deviation in S_i can be calculated using either (1) total portfolio returns or (2) portfolio returns in excess of the risk-free rate.[3]

Demonstration of Comparative Sharpe Measures Again, assume that $\overline{R}_M = 0.14$ and $\overline{RFR} = 0.08$. Suppose we are told that the standard deviation of the annual return for the market portfolio over the past 10 years was 20% ($\sigma_M = 0.20$). You want to examine the risk-adjusted performance of the following portfolios:

Portfolio	Average Annual Rate of Return	Standard Deviation of Return
D	0.13	0.18
E	0.17	0.22
F	0.16	0.23

The Sharpe measures for these portfolios are as follows:

$$S_M = \frac{0.14 - 0.08}{0.20} = 0.300$$

$$S_D = \frac{0.13 - 0.08}{0.18} = 0.278$$

$$S_E = \frac{0.17 - 0.08}{0.22} = 0.409$$

$$S_F = \frac{0.16 - 0.08}{0.23} = 0.348$$

The D portfolio had the lowest risk premium return per unit of total risk, failing to perform as well as the market portfolio. In contrast, Portfolios E and F performed better than the aggregate market, and Portfolio E did better than Portfolio F.

Given the market portfolio results during this period, it is possible to draw the CML. If we plot the results for Portfolios D, E, and F on this graph, as shown in Exhibit 18.3, we see that Portfolio D plots below the line, whereas the E and F portfolios are above the line, indicating superior risk-adjusted performance.

18.2.3 JENSEN PORTFOLIO PERFORMANCE MEASURE

Like the T and S measures just discussed, the **Jensen measure** (Jensen, 1968) was originally based on the capital asset pricing model (CAPM), which calculates the expected one-period return on any security or portfolio by the following expression:

| 18.3 |

$$E(R_j) = RFR + \beta_j[E(R_M) - RFR]$$

---

3 The Sharpe measure was formulated using the total risk (i.e., σ) of a portfolio, but recently Sharpe (1994, 2007) and Lo (2002) have suggested using the standard deviation of the excess portfolio return (i.e., σ_{ER}) instead. With this adjustment, the measure becomes $S_i = [\overline{R}_i - \overline{RFR}] \div \sigma_{ER}$. The advantage of this approach will be clear shortly when we discuss the *information ratio* performance measure.

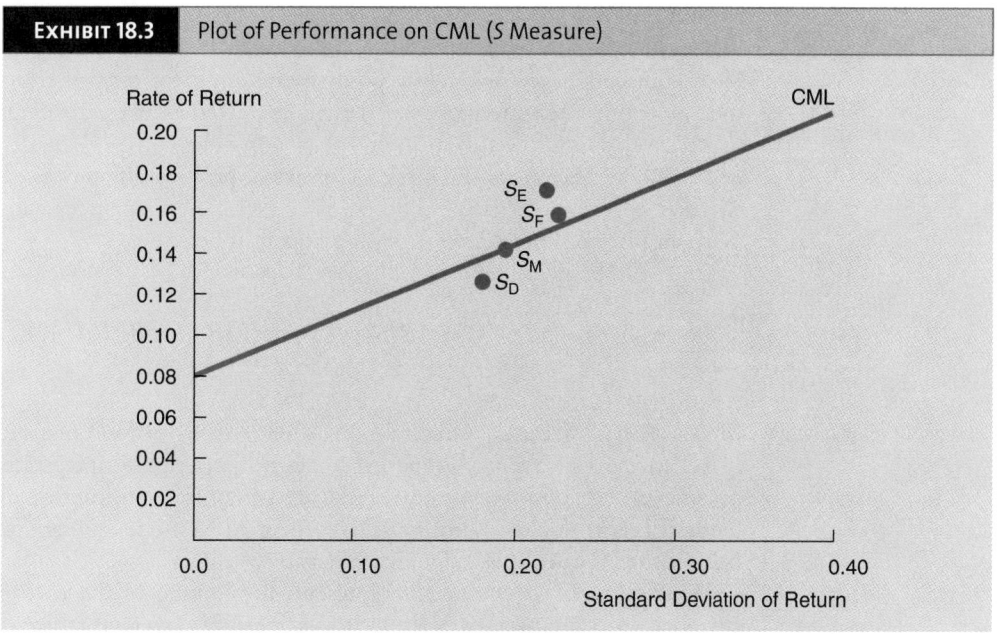

EXHIBIT 18.3   Plot of Performance on CML (*S* Measure)

where:

$E(R)$ = the expected return on security or Portfolio j

RFR = the one-period risk-free interest rate

β_j = the systematic risk (beta) for security or Portfolio j

$E(R_M)$ = the expected return on the market portfolio of risky assets

The expected return and the risk-free return vary for different periods. Consequently, we are concerned with the time series of expected rates of return for Security or Portfolio j. Moreover, assuming the asset pricing model is empirically valid, you can express Equation 18.3 in terms of *realized* rates of return as follows:

$$R_{jt} = RFR_t + \beta_j[R_{mt} - RFR_t] + e_{jt}$$

This equation states that the realized rate of return on a security or portfolio during a given time period should be a linear function of the risk-free rate of return during the period, plus a risk premium that depends on the systematic risk of the security or portfolio during the period plus a random error term (e_{jt}).

Subtracting the risk-free return from both sides, we have

$$R_{jt} - RFR = \beta_j[R_{mt} - RFR_t] + e_{jt}$$

so that the risk premium earned on the jth portfolio is equal to β_j times a market risk premium plus a random error term. An intercept for the regression is not expected if all assets and portfolios were in equilibrium.

Alternatively, superior portfolio managers who forecast market turns or consistently select undervalued securities earn higher risk premiums over time than those implied by this model. Such managers have consistently positive random error terms because the actual returns for their portfolios consistently exceed their expected returns. To detect this superior performance, we must allow for an intercept (a non-zero constant) that measures any positive or negative difference from the model. Consistent positive differences cause a positive intercept, whereas consistent negative differences (inferior performance) cause a negative intercept. With an intercept included, the earlier equation becomes

18.4
$$R_{jt} - RFR_t = \alpha_j + \beta_j[R_{mt} - RFR_t] + e_{jt}$$

In Equation 18.4, the α_j value indicates whether the portfolio manager is superior or inferior in her investment ability. A superior manager has a significant positive α_j (or "alpha") value because of the consistent positive residuals. In contrast, an inferior manager's returns consistently fall short of expectations based on the CAPM model giving consistently negative residuals. In such a case, α_j is a significant negative value.

Therefore, the α coefficient represents how much of the managed portfolio's return is attributable to the manager's ability to derive above-average returns adjusted for risk. Superior risk-adjusted returns indicate that the manager is good at either predicting market turns or selecting undervalued issues for the portfolio, or both.

Applying the Jensen Measure To estimate alpha, one can use Equation 18.4 as a linear regression model. Collect the time series of excess return of the portfolio and that of excess return of the market. The estimated intercept would be an estimated alpha. Please see the time series data set in Exhibit 18.5 and the discussions in Section 18.2.6 for an example.

There is also an alternative way to estimate Jensen by relying on average returns similar to Treynor and Sharpe. If we move alpha to the left of Equation 18.4, express all variables in terms of averages, and recognize that the average of the random error term e_{jt} is zero, then we have

$$\alpha_j = \overline{R}_j - [\overline{RFR} + \beta_j(\overline{R}_m - \overline{RFR})]$$

where the bars above the variables indicate average.

Now we can see that alpha is simply the difference between the average realized return and the average return required by the CAPM. This expression provides us with a simplified approach to estimate Jensen's alpha. For instance, the annual average return of a portfolio over a number of years is 6.5%, the average risk-free is rate 3%, the average market return is 5%, and the beta of the portfolio is 1.1. Applying the above equation will generate an estimate of alpha of 1.3% because

$$6.5 - [3 + 1.1(5 - 3)] = 1.3$$

Like the Treynor measure, the Jensen measure does not directly consider the portfolio manager's ability to diversify because it calculates risk premiums in terms of systematic risk. As noted earlier, to evaluate the performance of a group of well-diversified portfolios such as mutual funds, this is likely to be a reasonable assumption, because such portfolios can be correlated with the market at rates above 0.90.

Finally, the Jensen performance measure is flexible enough to allow for alternative models of risk and expected return than the CAPM. Specifically, risk-adjusted performance (i.e., α) can be computed relative to any of the multifactor models discussed in Chapter 7 as follows:

18.5
$$R_{jt} - RFR_t = \alpha_j + [b_{jt}F_{1t} + b_{j2}F_{2t} + \ldots + b_{jk}F_{kt}] + e_{jt}$$

where F_{kt} represents the Period t return to the kth common risk factor.

18.2.4   THE INFORMATION RATIO PERFORMANCE MEASURE

Closely related to the statistics just presented is a fourth widely used performance measure: the **information ratio**. This statistic measures a portfolio's average return in excess of that of a comparison or **benchmark portfolio** divided by the standard deviation of this excess return. Formally, the information ratio (*IR*) for portfolio j is calculated as:

18.6
$$IR_j = \frac{\overline{R}_j - \overline{R}_b}{\sigma_R} = \frac{\overline{ER}_j}{\sigma_{ER}}$$

where:
$\overline{R}_b$ = the average return for the benchmark portfolio during the period
σ_{ER} = the standard deviation of the excess return during the period

To interpret *IR*, the mean excess return in the numerator represents the investor's ability to use her talent and information to generate a portfolio return that differs from that of the benchmark against which her performance is being measured (e.g., the S&P/TSX Composite index). Conversely, the denominator measures the amount of residual (unsystematic) risk that the investor incurred in pursuit of those excess returns. The coefficient σ_{ER} is sometimes called the *tracking error* of the investor's portfolio, and it is a "cost" of active management in that fluctuations in the periodic *ERj* values represent random noise, beyond an investor's control, that could hurt performance. Thus, the *IR* can be viewed as a benefit-to-cost ratio that assesses the quality of the investor's information deflated by unsystematic risk generated by the investment process.

Goodwin (1998) noted that the Sharpe ratio is a special case of the *IR* where the risk-free asset is the benchmark portfolio, although this interpretation violates the spirit of a statistic that should have a value of zero for any passively managed portfolio. He also showed that if excess portfolio returns are estimated with historical data using the same single-factor regression equation used to compute Jensen's alpha, the *IR* simplifies to

$$IR_j = \frac{\alpha_j}{\sigma_e}$$

where:

σ_e = the standard error of the regression[4]

Finally, he showed that an information ratio based on periodic returns measured T times per year could be annualized as follows:

$$\text{Annualized } IR = \frac{(T)\alpha_j}{\sqrt{T}\sigma_e} = \sqrt{T}(IR)$$

For instance, an investor that generated a quarterly ratio of 0.25 would have an annualized IR of $0.50 = (\sqrt{4} \times 0.25)$.

18.2.5 COMPARING THE COMPOSITE PERFORMANCE MEASURES

Find top ranking mutual funds in the US and other countries at the "Mutual Fund" link under "Market Data" of Bloomberg.
www.bloomberg.com

Each of the portfolio performance statistics just described is widely used in practice and has its own strengths and weaknesses. The primary advantages and disadvantages of the S, α, and IR measures are listed in Exhibit 18.4. The important thing to recognize is that no one of these measures dominates the others and they all provide at least slightly different information useful to investors in the assessment of a portfolio's risk-adjusted performance. Consequently, it is generally advisable to compute all of them in order to provide a complete performance picture.

The Sharpe ratio is the simplest measure to compute, requiring just a few straightforward calculations based on the portfolio returns themselves. In its original form, S uses the standard deviation of total returns, whereas the Treynor ratio uses the portfolio's systematic risk (i.e., beta) coefficient. As we demonstrated in Chapter 7, beta can also be calculated directly from the returns to the portfolio and the market index, but that is a somewhat more involved process. For a completely diversified portfolio, T and S give identical performance rankings because total risk and systematic risk are the same. However, a poorly diversified portfolio could have a high ranking based on the Treynor ratio, which ignores unsystematic risk, but a much lower ranking based on the Sharpe measure, which does not. Any difference in rankings produced by T and S comes directly from a difference in portfolio diversification levels.

A disadvantage of the Treynor and Sharpe measures is that they only produce *relative*, not absolute, performance rankings. For example, the Sharpe values for Portfolios E and F in Exhibit 18.3 show that both managers generated risk-adjusted returns above the market. Further, E's risk-adjusted performance measure (0.409) is larger than F's (0.348). What we cannot say with certainty, however, is whether any of these differences are statistically significant. The same dilemma exists when comparing the performance of Portfolios X and Y using the Treynor measures illustrated in Exhibit 18.2.

The Jensen's alpha measure is typically the most difficult to compute because it requires a formal regression analysis. Offsetting that drawback are three substantial advantages relative to the T and S measures. First, it is easier to understand: An alpha value of 0.02 indicates that the manager generated a return of 2% per period more than what was expected given the

---

4 The development of this form of the information ratio is credited to Treynor and Black (1973).

EXHIBIT 18.4   Comparing the Portfolio Performance Measures

Performance Measure	Risk-Adjustment Measure	Advantages	Disadvantages
Treynor Ratio (T)	Portfolio beta relative to market index proxy	• Simple and intuitive "benefit-cost" comparison of the risk-return trade-off • Linked conceptually to the SML and capital market theory • Relatively simple to calculate and widely used in practice	• Permits only relative assessments of performance for different portfolios • Difficult to interpret and assess statistical significance • Ignores unsystematic risk in a portfolio
Sharpe Ratio (S)	(i) Standard deviation of total portfolio return; or (ii) Standard deviation of portfolio return in excess of risk-free rate	• Simple and intuitive "benefit-cost" comparison of the risk-return trade-off • Linked conceptually to the CML and capital market theory • Simplest to calculate and widely used in practice	• Permits only relative assessments of performance for different portfolios • Difficult to interpret and assess statistical significance • Ignores diversification potential of portfolio
Jensen's Alpha (α)	(i) Portfolio beta relative to market index proxy; or (ii) Portfolio betas relative to multiple risk factors	• Most rigorous risk-adjustment process separating systematic and unsystematic risk components • Can be adapted to either CAPM or multifactor models of the risk-return trade-off • Intuitive interpretation of measure that permits statistical significance assessment	• More difficult computation requiring formal regression analysis • Diversification of portfolio assessed in separate measure from performance • Alpha level and significance can vary greatly depending on specification of return-generating model
Information Ratio (IR)	Standard deviation of portfolio return in excess of return to style-class benchmark index (i.e., tracking error)	• Direct comparison of portfolio performance compared to benchmark in investment style class • Simple and intuitive measure of the "benefit-cost" trade-off involved with active management • Flexible design permitting multiple benchmark comparisons	• Permits only relative assessments of performance for different portfolios in a style class • Difficult to interpret and assess statistical significance • Implicitly assumes that portfolio and benchmark have similar levels of systematic risk

portfolio's risk level. On the other hand, a Sharpe ratio of 0.409 means that the portfolio manager generated *0.409 units of excess return per unit of total risk,* which is more challenging language to interpret. Second, because α is estimated from a formal statistical process, it is possible to make statements about the statistical significance of the manager's skill level, or the difference in skill between two different managers. Third, Jensen's alpha can be computed relative to any of several different risk–return models, in contrast to S, which focuses on total risk and ignores the return-generating process altogether, and T, which is locked into beta as the specific estimate of systematic risk.

Finally, because the information ratio is similar in form to T and S, it shares many of the same strengths and weakness of those two ratios. The primary advantage that differentiates IR from the other composite measures is that it provides a direct comparison between the return performance of the portfolio manager and that of the specific benchmark index against which she is competing. Because investors can often own this benchmark portfolio directly—either through index mutual funds or exchange-traded funds—the IR measure calculates the risk-adjusted value added by the active portfolio manager relative to a passive investment alternative.

18.2.6 APPLICATION OF PORTFOLIO PERFORMANCE MEASURES

To apply these measures, we selected 30 open-end mutual funds from the nine investment style classes described in Chapter 15 and used monthly data for the five-year period from April 2002 to March 2007. The monthly rates of return for one of these funds (Neuberger Berman Partners) and the S&P 500 are contained in Exhibit 18.5. The total return for each month is computed as follows:

$$R_{it} = \frac{EP_{it} + Div_{it} + Cap.Dist._{it} - BP_{it}}{BP_{it}}$$

where

R_{it} = the total rate of return on Fund i during month t
EP_{it} = the ending price for Fund i during month t
Div_{it} = the dividend payments made by Fund i during month t
$Cap.Dist._{it}$ = the capital gain distributions made by Fund i during month t
BP_{it} = the beginning price for Fund i during month t

These return computations do not take into account any sales charges by the funds.

The arithmetic average annual rate of return for Neuberger Berman Fund (ticker: NPRTX) was 10.72% versus 6.88% for the market, and the fund's beta was greater than 1.00 (1.157). Using the average annual rate of T-bills of 2.46% as the $\overline{RFR}$, the Treynor measure for the NPRTX (T_i) was substantially bigger than the comparable measure for the market T_M (7.132 vs. 4.420), primarily because the S&P index performed modestly over this five-year period. Likewise, the standard deviation of returns of the Neuberger Berman fund was greater than the market's (15.72 vs. 12.26), but the Sharpe measure for the fund (S) was still bigger than the measure for the market (S_M) (0.525 vs. 0.360).

Finally, a one-factor regression of the fund's annual risk premium ($R_{it} - RFR_t$) and the market's annual risk premium ($R_m - RFR_t$) indicated a positive intercept (constant) value of 0.261 but was not statistically significant. If this intercept value had been significant, NPRTX's risk-adjusted annual rate of return would have averaged about a quarter percent above the market on a reliable basis.

EXHIBIT 18.5	Example of Computing Portfolio Evaluation Measures Using Neuberger Berman Partners (NPRTX) Fund				
	R_{it}	R_{mt}	RFR_t	$R_{it} - RFR_t$	$R_{mt} - RFR_t$
April 2002	−3.47	−6.10	0.15	−3.62	−6.25
May 2002	−1.16	−0.78	0.14	−1.30	−0.92
June 2002	−8.35	−7.13	0.13	−8.48	−7.26
July 2002	−11.19	−7.40	0.15	−11.34	−7.55
August 2002	0.54	0.70	0.14	0.40	0.56
September 2002	−11.88	−10.90	0.14	−12.02	−11.04
October 2002	5.51	8.86	0.14	5.37	8.72
November 2002	8.90	5.90	0.12	8.78	5.78
December 2002	−7.41	−5.88	0.11	−7.52	−5.99
January 2003	−1.28	−2.66	0.10	−1.38	−2.76
February 2003	−1.04	−1.52	0.09	−1.13	−1.61
March 2003	0.52	1.03	0.10	0.42	0.93
⋮	⋮	⋮	⋮	⋮	⋮
⋮	⋮	⋮	⋮	⋮	⋮
⋮	⋮	⋮	⋮	⋮	⋮
April 2006	2.31	1.21	0.36	1.95	0.85
May 2006	−4.48	−2.83	0.43	−4.91	−3.26
June 2006	−1.43	0.16	0.40	−1.83	−0.24
July 2006	−1.30	0.56	0.40	−1.70	0.16
August 2006	2.57	2.42	0.42	2.15	2.00
September 2006	−0.70	2.65	0.41	−1.11	2.24
October 2006	4.88	3.25	0.41	4.47	2.84
November 2006	5.92	1.84	0.42	5.50	1.42
December 2006	0.25	1.38	0.40	−0.15	0.98
January 2007	1.48	1.41	0.44	1.04	0.97
February 2007	−1.05	−2.19	0.38	−1.43	−2.57
March 2007	0.87	1.00	0.43	0.44	0.57
Average (annual)	10.72	6.88	2.46	8.25	4.42
Standard deviation	15.72	12.26	0.45		
Beta	1.157				
S_i	0.525				
S_m	0.360				
T_i	7.132				
T_m	4.420				
Jensen alpha (1 factor)	0.261				
R^2_{im}	0.813				

Total Sample Results The overall results in Exhibit 18.6 indicate that active fund managers performed much better than has been documented in earlier performance studies. A primary factor for this outcome was the abnormally poor performance of the index during the first part of the sample period. Also, our sample was rather casually selected because we intended

EXHIBIT 18.6 Performance Measures for 30 Selected Mutual Funds

Fund	Ticker	Style Class	Average Annual Rate of Return	Standard Deviation	Beta	R^2	Treynor		Sharpe		Jensen (1 Factor)	
AllianceBerstein Growth	AGRYX	Large Growth	6.15	14.63	1.016	0.722	3.630	(27)	0.252	(27)	−0.067	(27)
American Century Sm Val	ASVIX	Small Value	12.25	13.46	0.898	0.666	10.898	(13)	0.727	(14)	0.485	(12)
Buffalo Small Cap	BUFSX	Small Growth	12.21	19.34	1.301	0.677	7.497	(19)	0.504	(19)	0.334	(15)
Aim Constellation	CSTGX	Large Growth	4.66	13.36	1.011	0.861	2.174	(30)	0.165	(30)	−0.189	(30)
Dreyfus Appreciation	DGAGX	Large Blend	4.69	10.63	0.813	0.883	2.734	(28)	0.209	(28)	−0.114	(28)
DFA Tax-Managed Value	DTMMX	Mid Value	10.94	14.33	1.090	0.869	7.782	(18)	0.592	(17)	0.305	(16)
Fidelity Magellan	FMAGX	Large Growth	4.64	12.67	1.001	0.938	2.176	(29)	0.172	(29)	−0.187	(29)
Goldman Sachs Mid Value	GCMAX	Mid Value	13.76	10.55	0.700	0.658	16.138	(2)	1.070	(2)	0.683[a]	(5)
Heartland Value	HRTVX	Small Blend	15.96	17.45	1.049	0.541	12.869	(6)	0.774	(12)	0.739	(2)
Hotchkis&WileyLrgVal	HWLIX	Large Value	13.23	13.21	0.971	0.806	11.080	(12)	0.815	(9)	0.539[a]	(10)
Janus Twenty	JAVLX	Large Growth	9.91	12.39	0.862	0.728	8.640	(15)	0.601	(16)	0.303	(17)
DWS Dreman High Rtn	KDHBX	Large Value	7.27	13.48	0.976	0.787	4.928	(25)	0.357	(25)	0.041	(25)
Columbia Acorn	LACAX	Mid Growth	14.21	13.47	0.933	0.717	12.591	(7)	0.872	(5)	0.635[a]	(6)
Lazard Mid Cap	LZMIX	Mid Value	11.46	11.82	0.880	0.831	10.228	(14)	0.761	(13)	0.426[a]	(14)
Morgan Stanley Small Value	MCVAX	Small Value	13.96	14.16	0.961	0.693	11.954	(8)	0.811	(10)	0.604[a]	(8)
Munder Mid Cap Select	MGOYX	Mid Growth	13.43	12.73	0.802	0.594	13.662	(5)	0.861	(6)	0.618[a]	(7)
Numeric Investors Mid Cap	NIGVX	Mid Blend	12.23	11.94	0.839	0.740	11.635	(9)	0.818	(8)	0.505[a]	(11)
Neuberger Berman Partners	NPRTX	Large Blend	10.72	15.72	1.157	0.813	7.132	(21)	0.525	(18)	0.261	(20)
Wells Fargo Small Cap Op	NVSOX	Small Growth	13.29	13.97	0.949	0.692	11.415	(11)	0.775	(11)	0.553	(9)
Allianz OCC Value	PDLIX	Large Value	9.42	17.89	1.374	0.885	5.067	(24)	0.389	(24)	0.074	(24)
JPMorgan Small Growth	PGSGX	Small Growth	10.17	15.75	0.984	0.585	7.835	(16)	0.489	(21)	0.280	(19)
T. Rowe Price Small Value	PRSVX	Small Value	14.78	13.31	0.796	0.534	15.476	(3)	0.925	(3)	0.733[a]	(3)
RS Partners	RSPFX	Small Blend	20.41	12.84	0.673	0.407	26.674	(1)	1.398	(1)	1.248[a]	(1)
Royce Premier	RYPRX	Mid Growth	14.82	13.45	0.856	0.606	14.425	(4)	0.919	(4)	0.714[a]	(4)
Wells Fargo Large Growth	SLGIX	Large Growth	7.62	11.98	0.866	0.783	5.955	(22)	0.431	(23)	0.111	(23)
TCW Diversified Value	TGDVX	Large Value	10.61	13.54	1.042	0.887	7.819	(17)	0.602	(15)	0.295	(18)
Tweedy, Browne American	TWEBX	Large Value	5.59	9.65	0.697	0.784	4.479	(26)	0.324	(26)	0.003	(26)
Van Kampen Mid Growth	VGRAX	Mid Growth	9.42	14.02	0.954	0.695	7.293	(20)	0.496	(20)	0.228	(21)
Vanguard Primecap	VPMCX	Large Growth	8.90	14.43	1.119	0.902	5.754	(23)	0.446	(22)	0.124	(22)
JPMorgan Mid Cap Equity	VSNGX	Mid Blend	11.77	11.22	0.814	0.789	11.430	(10)	0.830	(7)	0.476[a]	(13)
Average Fund			10.95	13.58	0.946	0.736	9.379		0.630		0.359	
S&P 500			6.88	12.26	1.000	1.000	4.420		0.360		0.000	
90–day T-bill rate			2.46	0.45								

[a]Significant at the 0.05 level.

it for demonstration purposes only. The mean annual return for all the funds was above the market return (10.95 vs. 6.88). Considering only the return, 25 of the 30 funds outperformed the market.

The R^2 statistic comparing a portfolio with the market can serve as a measure of diversification. The closer the R^2 is to 1.00, the more completely diversified the portfolio. The average R^2 for our sample was fairly high at 0.736, although the range was quite large, from 0.407 to 0.938. This suggests that many of the funds were reasonably well diversified, with 24 of the 30 portfolios having R^2 values greater than 0.65. (Recall that a typical individual stock would have an R^2 value of around 20% to 30%.)

The two risk measures (standard deviation and beta) also show a wide degree of dispersion but generally are consistent with expectations. Specifically, 23 of the 30 funds had larger standard deviations than the market, and the mean standard deviation was larger (13.58 vs. 12.26). Only 10 of the funds had a beta of 1.00 or greater; the average beta was 0.946.

The various performance measures ranked the performance of individual funds consistently, if somewhat differently. (These rankings are listed in parentheses beside each measure.) Only four out of 30 funds had a lower Treynor ratio than that of the market; only six funds had a lower Sharpe as well. Also, 26 of the 30 Jensen's alpha values using the Single-Index Market Model were positive, with 11 of these being statistically significant. The mean Jensen alpha value of 0.359 indicates that the average manager in the sample was able to produce a return of about 36 basis points per month more than what would have been expected given the risk level of the fund. The mean values for the Sharpe and Treynor measures were considerably higher than the aggregate market figure. These results confirm that, overall, this sample of funds produced much better risk-adjusted performance than the market during this time period.

One might expect the best performance by funds with low diversification because they apparently are attempting to beat the market by being unique in their security selection or market timing. This seems to be true for some of the top-performing funds, such as RS Partners Fund, whereas portfolios that produced returns more closely aligned with overall market, such as the Fidelity Magellan Fund, were among the worst performing funds. It appears that during this period it was often better to not look like the market portfolio, although this is not always the case.

Exhibit 18.7 reports information ratios for these 30 funds. To interpret the display, consider that the TCW Diversified Value Fund had a monthly *IR* value of 0.223, which was calculated by dividing its alpha (0.295) by its regression standard error (1.32). This statistic is then annualized to 0.772 by multiplying the monthly *IR* by the square root of 12. Notice that 26 of the 30 funds had positive *IR* levels, which follows directly from the number of funds that had a positive Jensen's alpha. The mean annualized *IR* for the sample was 0.563, which exceeded the Grinold-Kahn standard for "good" performance of 0.500. Thus, on average, even after accounting for tracking error costs, this collection of funds added substantial value to its investors.

Potential Bias of One-Parameter Measures Friend and Blume (1970) pointed out that the composite measures of performance should be independent of alternative measures of risk because they are *risk-adjusted* measures. However, their analysis of the relationship between the composite measures and two definitions of risk (standard deviation and beta) for 200 random stock portfolios indicated that the risk-adjusted performance of low-risk portfolios was better than the comparable performance for high-risk portfolios. Subsequently, Klemkosky (1973) examined the relationship between composite performance measures and risk measures using actual mutual fund data. The results showed a *positive*

EXHIBIT 18.7	Information Ratios for 30 Funds				
Fund	Alpha	Standard Error	IR	Annualized IR	Rank
AllianceBerstein Growth	−0.067	2.25	−0.030	−0.103	(27)
American Century Sm Val	0.485	2.27	0.214	0.741	(15)
Buffalo Small Cap	0.334	3.21	0.104	0.360	(19)
Aim Constellation	−0.189	1.45	−0.131	−0.452	(29)
Dreyfus Appreciation	−0.114	1.06	−0.108	−0.375	(28)
DFA Tax-Managed Value	0.305	1.51	0.202	0.701	(16)
Fidelity Magellan	−0.187	0.91	−0.205	−0.709	(30)
Goldman Sachs Mid Value	0.683	1.80	0.380	1.316	(2)
Heartland Value	0.739	3.44	0.214	0.743	(14)
Hotchkis&WileyLrgVal	0.539	1.70	0.318	1.100	(3)
Janus Twenty	0.303	1.88	0.161	0.559	(17)
DWS Dreman High Rtn	0.041	1.81	0.023	0.079	(25)
Columbia Acorn	0.635	2.09	0.304	1.053	(5)
Lazard Mid Cap	0.426	1.42	0.301	1.042	(6)
Morgan Stanley Small Value	0.604	2.28	0.264	0.916	(10)
Munder Mid Cap Select	0.618	2.37	0.261	0.905	(11)
Numeric Investors Mid Cap	0.505	1.78	0.284	0.985	(8)
Neuberger Berman Partners	0.261	1.98	0.132	0.457	(18)
Wells Fargo Small Cap Op	0.553	2.25	0.245	0.850	(12)
AllianzOCC Value	0.074	1.76	0.042	0.145	(24)
JPMorgan Small Growth	0.280	2.96	0.095	0.328	(21)
T. Rowe Price Small Value	0.733	2.65	0.277	0.958	(9)
RS Partners	1.248	2.90	0.430	1.491	(1)
Royce Premier	0.714	2.46	0.290	1.005	(7)
Wells Fargo Large Growth	0.111	1.62	0.068	0.236	(23)
TCW Diversified Value	0.295	1.32	0.223	0.772	(13)
Tweedy, Browne American	0.003	1.31	0.003	0.009	(26)
Van Kampen Mid Growth	0.228	2.25	0.101	0.351	(20)
Vanguard Primecap	0.124	1.32	0.095	0.328	(22)
JPMorgan Mid Cap Equity	0.476	1.50	0.317	1.098	(4)
Mean	0.359	1.98	0.163	0.563	
Median	0.319	1.84	0.208	0.721	

relationship between the composite performance measures and the risk involved. This was especially true for the Treynor and Jensen measures. He concluded that although a bias might exist, one could not be certain of its direction. More recently, Leland (1999) has shown that alpha can be biased downward for those portfolios designed to limit downside risk.

Measuring Performance with Multiple Risk Factors Equation 18.5 showed in general terms how the Jensen's alpha measure could be estimated relative to multifactor models of risk and expected return. Exhibit 18.8 shows the Jensen measures calculated for the 30 mutual funds using two different versions of the Fama-French model discussed in Chapter 7:

$$R_{jt} - RFR_t = \alpha_j + \{[b_{j1}(R_{mt} - RFR_t) + b_{j2}SMB_t + b_{j3}HML_t] + b_{j4}MOM_t\} + e_{jt}$$

Specifically, alphas are computed relative to: (1) a three-factor model including the market $(R_{mt} - RFR)$, firm size (SMB), and relative valuation (HML) variables; and (2) a four-factor model that also includes the return momentum (MOM) variable.

The performance results in Exhibits 18.8 and 18.9 showed that the vast majority of the active mutual fund managers in the sample were able to outperform the market on a risk-adjusted basis over the April 2002 to March 2007 period. However, it is possible that some of this superior performance was an illusion because the S&P 500 index was not the appropriate benchmark for many of the portfolios. In fact, the style classifications for the 30 funds in Exhibit 18.6 show that only two portfolios followed the large-cap blend style, the category for which the S&P 500 index applies. Thus, the advantage of measuring a fund's alpha using a multifactor approach is that it is designed to control for both market (i.e., R_{mt}), style (i.e., SMB and HML), and momentum (i.e., MOM) risk influences.

Although not listed in Exhibit 18.8, the average annual returns (i.e., risk premia) for the SMB, HML, and MOM factors were 0.40%, 0.60%, and 0.18%, respectively.

This indicates that in the stock market as a whole over this investment period, small stocks outperformed large stocks (i.e., a positive mean SMB return), value stocks outperformed growth stocks (i.e., a positive mean HML return), and high-momentum stocks outperformed low-momentum stocks (i.e., a positive mean MOM return). For this particular collection of 30 funds, the mean factor betas—0.954 for the market factor, 0.302 for the SMB factor, 0.109 for the HML factor, and 0.026 for the MOM factor—indicate that the average fund has less systematic market risk than average and is oriented toward holding smaller, more value-oriented stocks that exhibit positive return momentum.

The Jensen alpha results for both the three-factor and four-factor models show some important differences with the comparable findings from the one-factor model reported in Exhibit 18.6. In particular, the mean value for alpha is now slightly negative in each case (0.012 and 0.014, respectively). Also, 15 (rather than 26) of the funds had positive alpha values, but only one (rather than 11) of the funds with positive alphas had statistically significant outperformance with the three-factor model. Further, two of the funds (CSTGX and TWEBX) exhibited statistically significant underperformance when measured against the four-factor model. For instance, HRTVX, a small-cap blend fund, had a large positive alpha of 0.739 when in Exhibit 18.6 its performance was measured relative to a large-cap blend index (i.e., S&P 500), but relative to models that take investment style and momentum into account, its alpha was reduced to −0.126 (three-factor) and −0.119 (four factor). This highlights the fact that the one-factor and multifactor Jensen measures produce similar but distinct performance rankings and should therefore be considered as different from one another as the Sharpe and Treynor measures.

EXHIBIT 18.8	Performance Measures for 30 Funds Using Multifactor Models

Fund	Style Class	Factor Betas				Jensen Alpha (3-Factor)	Rank	Jensen Alpha (4-Factor)	Rank
		$R_{mt} - RFR$	SMB	HML	MOM				
AGRYX	Large Growth	1.132	0.197	−0.461	0.283	−0.154	(21)	−0.170	(23)
ASVIX	Small Value	0.841	0.588	0.396	−0.075	−0.129	(19)	−0.125	(19)
BUFSX	Small Growth	1.064	0.898	0.068	−0.209	−0.179	(23)	−0.167	(21)
CSTGX	Large Growth	1.088	0.108	−0.343	0.195	−0.274	(28)	−0.285[a]	(28)
DGAGX	Large Blend	0.889	−0.412	0.060	0.026	−0.150	(20)	−0.152	(20)
DTMMX	Mid Value	1.117	0.160	0.343	−0.025	−0.170	(22)	−0.168	(22)
FMAGX	Large Growth	1.025	−0.135	−0.215	0.049	−0.191	(25)	−0.193	(24)
GCMAX	Mid Value	0.824	0.217	0.350	0.120	0.175	(5)	0.168	(5)
HRTVX	Small Blend	0.920	1.020	0.528	−0.138	−0.126	(18)	−0.119	(18)
HWLIX	Large Value	0.907	0.214	0.326	−0.134	0.133	(9)	0.141	(8)
JAVLX	Large Growth	0.964	−0.100	−0.201	0.159	0.244	(3)	0.235	(3)
KDHBX	Large Value	1.058	−0.312	0.508	−0.065	−0.326	(30)	−0.322	(30)
LACAX	Mid Growth	0.952	0.531	0.115	0.081	0.148	(7)	0.143	(7)
LZMIX	Mid Value	0.857	0.258	0.102	−0.021	0.113	(10)	0.114	(10)
MCVAX	Small Value	0.908	0.560	0.305	−0.061	0.042	(15)	0.046	(15)
MGOYX	Mid Growth	0.920	0.488	−0.007	0.234	0.173	(6)	0.159	(6)
NIGVX	Mid Blend	0.886	0.330	0.166	0.067	0.079	(12)	0.076	(12)
NPRTX	Large Blend	1.185	0.244	0.249	0.000	−0.210	(26)	−0.210	(26)
NVSOX	Small Growth	0.920	0.562	0.131	0.008	0.075	(14)	0.074	(13)
PDLIX	Large Value	1.194	0.004	0.365	−0.335	−0.243	(27)	−0.224	(27)
PGSGX	Small Growth	1.015	0.754	−0.136	0.187	−0.186	(24)	−0.196	(25)
PRSVX	Small Value	0.808	0.735	0.292	0.073	0.077	(13)	0.073	(14)
RSPFX	Small Blend	0.731	0.604	0.583	0.030	0.479[a]	(1)	0.477	(1)
RYPRX	Mid Growth	0.849	0.589	0.041	0.057	0.276	(2)	0.272	(2)
SLGIX	Large Growth	0.917	0.075	−0.440	0.171	0.141	(8)	0.131	(9)
TGDVX	Large Value	0.989	0.131	0.244	−0.106	−0.046	(16)	−0.040	(16)
TWEBX	Large Value	0.708	0.042	0.309	−0.047	−0.320[a]	(29)	−0.317[a]	(29)
VGRAX	Mid Growth	1.048	0.344	−0.151	0.204	−0.076	(17)	−0.088	(17)
VPMCX	Large Growth	1.058	0.087	−0.254	−0.027	0.080	(11)	0.082	(11)
VSNGX	Mid Blend	0.853	0.271	0.000	0.085	0.183	(4)	0.178	(4)
	Mean	0.954	0.302	0.109	0.026	−0.012		−0.014	

[a]Significant at the 0.05 level.

Relationship among Performance Measures Exhibit 18.9 contains the matrix of rank correlation coefficients among the Treynor, Sharpe, Jensen (one-factor, three-factor, and four-factor), and Information Ratio measures. The striking feature is that all of these statistics are positively correlated with one another, but not perfectly so. (The two multifactor Jensen measures produced virtually identical rankings for this fund sample.) This suggests that although the measures provide a generally consistent assessment of portfolio performance when taken as a whole, they remain distinct at an individual level. The exhibit reinforces our earlier point that it is best to consider these composites collectively and that the user must understand what each means.

Exhibit 18.9	Correlations between Alternative Portfolio Performance Measures					
	Treynor	Sharpe	Jensen (1-Factor)	Jensen (3-Factor)	Jensen (4-Factor)	Information Ratio
Treynor	—					
Sharpe	0.978	—				
Jensen (1-factor)	0.976	0.979	—			
Jensen (3-factor)	0.773	0.795	0.734	—		
Jensen (4-factor)	0.780	0.803	0.743	0.997	—	
Information Ratio	0.879	0.953	0.919	0.744	0.754	—

18.3   Other Performance Measures

Go to "Data and Directories" of the Pension and Investment site http://www.pionline. com/ to find mutual fund and fund manager performance ranking.

Beyond the above risk-adjusted composite measurements, there are three other performance measures to help us evaluate the skills of portfolio managers. *Performance attribution analysis* reveals the sources of the performance, and *market timing analysis* measures market timing skills of the managers. A third measure is *style analysis*, which is a technique to examine if a portfolio manager has adhered to a particular investment style she professed to follow. Style analysis has already been discussed in Chapter 15 and will not be repeated here.

18.3.1   PERFORMANCE ATTRIBUTION ANALYSIS

As we have seen, portfolio managers can add value for their investors in either of two ways: selecting superior securities or demonstrating superior timing skills by allocating funds to different asset or sector classes. **Attribution analysis** attempts to distinguish which of these factors is the source of the portfolio's overall performance. This method compares the manager's total return to the return for a predetermined benchmark policy portfolio and decomposes the difference into an *allocation effect* and a *selection effect*. The most straightforward way to measure these two effects is as follows:

18.7

$$\text{Allocation Effect} = \sum_i [(w_{ai} - w_p i) \times (R_{pi} - R_p)]$$
$$\text{Selection Effect} = \sum_i [(w_{ai}) \times (R_{ai} - R_{pi})]$$

where:

w_{ai}, w_{pi} = the investment proportions of the ith *market segment* (e.g., asset class, industry group) in the manager's portfolio and the policy portfolio, respectively

R_{ai}, R_{pi} = the investment return to the ith market segment in the manager's portfolio and the policy portfolio, respectively

R_p = the total return to the policy portfolio

The allocation effect measures the manager's decision to over- or underweight a particular market segment (i.e., $[w_{ai} - w_{pi}]$) in terms of that segment's return performance relative to the overall return to the benchmark (i.e., $[R_{pi} - R_p]$). Good timing skill is therefore a matter of investing more money in those market segments that end up producing greater than average returns. The selection effect measures the manager's ability to form specific market segment portfolios that generate superior returns relative to how the comparable market segment is defined in the benchmark portfolio (i.e., $[R_{ai} - R_{pi}]$) weighted by the manager's actual market segment investment proportions. The manager's total value-added performance is the sum of the allocation and selection effects.[5]

An Example Consider an investor whose top–down portfolio strategy consists of two dimensions. First, he decides on a broad allocation across three asset classes: Canadian stocks, Canadian long-term bonds, and cash equivalents, such as T-bills or commercial paper. Once this judgment is made, the investor's second general decision is choosing which specific stocks, bonds, and cash instruments to buy. As a policy benchmark, he selects a hypothetical portfolio with a 60% allocation to the S&P/TSX Composite index, a 30% investment in the DEX Long Bond index, and a 10% allocation to 90-day T-bills.

Suppose that at the start of the investment period, the investor believes equity values are somewhat inflated relative to the fixed-income market. Compared to the benchmark, he therefore decides to underweight stocks and overweight bonds and cash. The investment proportions he chooses are 50% in equity, 38% in bonds, and 12% in cash. Further, he decides to concentrate on equities in the interest rate–sensitive sectors, such as utilities and financial companies, while deemphasizing the technology and consumer durables sectors. Finally, he resolves to buy shorter duration bonds of a higher credit quality than are contained in the benchmark bond index and to buy commercial paper rather than T-bills.

The manager has made active investment decisions involving both the allocation of assets and the selection of individual securities. To determine if either (or both) of these decisions proved to be wise ones, at the end of the investment period he can calculate his overall and segment-specific performance. Exhibit 18.10 summarizes these returns for the investor's actual and benchmark asset class portfolios, as well as the investment weightings for each. The overall returns can be computed as:

> **Overall Manager Return** = $(0.50 \times 0.097) + (0.38 \times 0.091) + (0.12 \times 0.056)$
> = **8.98%**

---

5 Bailey, Richards, and Tierney (2007) argue that a better way to measure the selection effect is to multiply the market segment return differential by the benchmark for that segment, or $\Sigma_i[(w_{pi}) \times (R_{ai} - R_{pi})]$. A drawback of this approach is that the allocation and selection effects no longer sum to the total value-added return. To balance the equation, he calculates an *interaction effect* as $\Sigma_i[(w_{ai} - w_{pi}) \times (R_{ai} - R_{pi})]$ to measure residual performance.

EXHIBIT 18.10	Asset Class Performance Attribution Analysis					
	Investment Weights			Returns		
Asset Class	Actual	Benchmark	Excess	Actual	Benchmark	Excess
Stock	0.50	0.60	−0.10	9.70%	8.60%	1.10%
Bonds	0.38	0.30	0.08	9.10	9.20	−0.10
Cash	0.12	0.10	0.02	5.60	5.40	0.20

and

$$
\begin{aligned}
\textbf{Overall Benchmark Return} \ &= \ (0.60 \times 0.086) + (0.30 \times 0.092) \\
&\quad + (0.10 \times 0.054) \\
&= \ 8.46\%
\end{aligned}
$$

Thus, the manager beat the policy benchmark by 52 basis points ($= 0.0898 - 0.0846$) over this particular investment horizon.

The goal of attribution analysis is to isolate the reason for this value-added performance. The manager's allocation effect can be computed by multiplying the excess asset class weight by that class's relative investment performance:

$$
\begin{aligned}
[-0.10 \times (0.086 - 0.0846)] + [0.08 \times (0.092 - 0.0846)] \\
+ [0.02 \times (0.054 - 0.0846)] = -0.02\%
\end{aligned}
$$

This shows that if the investor had made just his market timing decisions and not picked different securities than those in the benchmark, his performance would have lagged behind the policy return by two basis points. This total allocation effect can be broken down further into an equity allocation return of −2 basis points [$=-0.10 \times (0.086 - 0.0846)$], a bond allocation return of 6 basis points [$= 0.08 \times (0.092 - 0.0846)$], and a cash allocation return of −6 basis points [$= 0.02 \times (0.054 - 0.0846)$]. Therefore, the decision to underweight stock and overweight cash (asset classes that generated returns above and below the benchmark, respectively) resulted in diminished performance that more than offset the benefit of overweighting bonds.

Because the investor knows that he outperformed the benchmark overall, a negative allocation effect must mean that he exhibited positive security selection skills. His selection effect can be computed as:

$$
\begin{aligned}
[0.50 \times (0.097 - 0.086)] - [0.38 \times (0.091 - 0.092)] \\
+ [0.12 \times (0.056 - 0.054)] \\
= 0.54\%
\end{aligned}
$$

In this example, the investor formed superior stock and cash portfolios, although his bond selections did not perform quite as well as the DEX index. One important caveat is that because the returns are not risk-adjusted, it is possible that the asset class portfolios formed by the investor are riskier than their benchmark counterparts. This is almost certainly true for a cash portfolio that holds short-term corporate debt obligations instead of T-bills, so the investor should expect a somewhat higher return that has nothing to do with his skill. Finally, the investor's total incremental return of 52 basis points can be decomposed as:

$$\text{Total Value Added} = \text{Allocation Effect} + \text{Selection Effect}$$
$$= -0.02\% + 0.54\% = 0.52\%$$

Using a procedure similar to the one just described, Brinson, Hood, and Beebower (1986) examined the performance of a group of 91 large U.S. pension plans from 1974 to 1983. The mean annual return for this sample was 9.01%, compared to 10.11% for their benchmark. Thus, active management cost the average plan 110 basis points of return per year. This "value subtracted" return increment consisted of a -77-basis-point allocation effect and a -33-basis-point selection effect. They concluded that a plan's initial strategic asset allocation choice, rather than any of its active management decisions, was the primary determinant of portfolio performance. In a follow-up study, Brinson, Singer, and Beebower (1991) reached a similar conclusion for a different group of 82 pension plans over the 1977 to 1987 period. For this new sample, the total active return shortfall dropped to -7 basis points, which was divided into an 18-basis-point selection effect and a -25-basis-point allocation effect.

18.3.2   MEASURING MARKET TIMING SKILLS

As we saw in Chapter 15, *tactical asset allocation* (*TAA*) attempts to produce active value-added returns solely through allocation decisions. Instead of trying to pick superior individual securities, TAA managers adjust their asset class exposures based on perceived changes in the relative valuations of those classes. This means that the relevant performance measurement criterion for a TAA manager is how well she is able to time broad market movements. There are two reasons why attribution analysis is ill-suited for this task. First, by design, a TAA manager indexes her actual asset class investments and so the selection effect is not relevant. Second, TAA might entail dozens of changes to asset class weightings during an investment period, which could render meaningless an attribution effect computed on the average holdings. Because of these problems, many analysts consider a regression-based method for measuring timing skills to be a superior approach.

Weigel (1991) tested the market-timing skills of a group of 17 U.S.-based TAA managers. His methodology was motivated by the pioneering work of Merton (1981) and Hendriksson and Merton (1981) and assumed that perfect market-timing ability was equivalent to owning a lookback call option that pays at expiration the return to the best-performing asset class among stocks, bonds, and cash. That is, in Period t, a manager with perfect market-timing skills would have a return (R_{at}) equal to

$$R_{at} = RFR_t + \max\ [R_{st} - RFR_t,\ R_{bt} - RFR_t, 0]$$

where R_{st} and R_{bt} are the Period t returns to the stock and bond benchmark portfolios, respectively. Controlling for stock and bond price movements in a manner comparable to Jensen's method, the following regression equation can be calculated:

$$(R_{at}RFR_t) = \alpha + \beta_b(R_{bt} - RFR_t) + \beta_s(R_{st} - RFR_t)$$
$$+ \gamma\{\max[R_{st} - RFR_t, R_{bt} - RFR_t, 0]\} + e_t$$

The average value for γ, which measures the proportion of the perfect timing option that the TAA managers were able to capture, was 0.30. This value was statistically significant, meaning that these managers had reliable, although not perfect, market-timing skills. Also, the average alpha was -0.5% per quarter, indicating that these same managers had negative non-market-timing skills (e.g., hedging strategies).

Many other studies have examined the market-timing ability of portfolio managers who are not exclusively TAA practitioners. Kon (1983) and Chang and Lewellen (1984) concluded that mutual fund managers generally possess negative market-timing skills, a position supported by Bauer and Dahlquist (2001). Coggin, Fabozzi, and Rahman (1993) carried this analysis further by looking at both the timing and selectivity skills of a group of U.S. equity pension fund managers. They demonstrated that their sample of managers possessed positive, but small, selection skills and negative timing skills. From these studies, it is reasonable to conclude that only those managers explicitly trying to time market movements have a chance of doing so.

18.4   The Challenges of Benchmarking

All the performance measures just described are only as good as their data inputs. Of course, an analyst should use judgment and be patient in the evaluation process. It is not possible to evaluate a portfolio manager on the basis of a quarter or even a year. An evaluation should extend over several years and cover at least a full market cycle, which allows one to determine whether the manager's performance differs during rising and declining markets as Ferson and Schadt (1996) demonstrate.

Many of the equity portfolio performance measures we have discussed are derived from the CAPM and assume the existence of a market portfolio at the point of tangency on the Markowitz efficient frontier. Theoretically, the market portfolio is an efficient, completely diversified portfolio. As we discussed in Chapter 7, this market portfolio must contain all risky assets in the economy and all components must be market-value weighted. The problem arises in finding a realistic proxy for this theoretical market portfolio. Analysts typically use the S&P 500 index as the proxy for the market portfolio because it contains a fairly diversified portfolio of stocks, and the sample is market-value weighted. Unfortunately, it does not represent the true composition of the market portfolio. Specifically, it includes only common stocks and most of them are listed on the NYSE. Notably, it excludes many other risky assets that theoretically should be considered, such as numerous domestic stocks, foreign stocks, foreign and domestic bonds, real estate, alternative assets, and collectibles.

This lack of completeness was highlighted in several articles by Roll (1977a, 1978, 1980, 1981), who detailed the problem with the market proxy and pointed out its implications for measuring portfolio performance. Although a detailed discussion of Roll's critique will not be repeated here, we need to consider his major problem with the measurement of the market portfolio, which he refers to as a **benchmark error**. He showed that if the proxy for the market portfolio is not a truly efficient portfolio, then the SML using this proxy may not be the true SML—the true SML could have a higher slope. In such a case, a portfolio plotted above the SML and derived using a poor benchmark could actually plot below the SML that uses the true market portfolio.

Another problem is that the beta could differ from that computed using the true market portfolio. For example, if the true beta were larger than the beta computed using the proxy, the true position of the portfolio would shift to the right. In an empirical test, Brown and Brown (1987) documented a considerable amount of ranking reversal when the definition of the market portfolio was changed in a Jensen's alpha analysis of a sample of well-established mutual funds. Terhaar (2001) also showed how the benchmark error problem can affect attribution analysis.

18.4.1 THE GLOBAL BENCHMARK PROBLEM

Emerging Markets at *Financial Times*: http://www.ft.com/ markets/emerging.

To illustrate the impact of the benchmark problem in global capital markets, consider what happens to the individual measures of risk when the world equity market is employed to estimate the beta coefficient from the SML. Exhibit 18.11 contains beta estimates for the 30 stocks in the Dow Jones Industrial Average (DJIA) using the S&P 500, which is the typical proxy for stocks of companies domiciled in the United States, and the Morgan Stanley Capital International (MSCI) World Stock index, which is a market-value-weighted index that contains stocks from around the world. These findings were calculated using weekly returns from two different three-year periods: 2002 to 2004 and 2005 to 2007. The percentage difference between the U.S. beta and the world beta is also shown, using the higher of the two risk estimates as the base.

There are two major differences in the various beta statistics. First, for many stocks, the beta estimates change a great deal over time. For example, General Electric's U.S. and world betas during the period 2002 to 2004 were 1.14 and 1.17, respectively. However, during the period 2005 to 2007, both of these values substantially decreased (to 0.67 and 0.52, respectively). Second, although the mean and median values for the U.S. and world beta estimates appear to be somewhat similar during both time periods, the "% Difference" columns show that there are some substantial differences in betas estimated for the same stock over the same time period when two different definitions of the benchmark portfolio are employed. For instance, the U.S. and world beta estimates for Johnson & Johnson differed by almost 12% in the period 2002 to 2004 and then by almost 15% in the period 2005 to 2007. Overall, the median size of this discrepancy increased over time—from 5.2% to 13.0%—which is a sizable difference. It indicates that the specification of the proper benchmark remains a critical issue in the performance evaluation process.

Managed Funds at *Financial Times*: http://funds.ft.com/funds.

Reilly and Akhtar (1995) examined the effect of the choice of a benchmark on global performance measurement by plotting SMLs for six different indexes over three time horizons: 1983 to 1988, 1989 to 1994, and 1983 to 1994. Four country-specific benchmarks—the S&P 500 (U.S.), the Nikkei (Japan), the FTAll Shares (England), and the FAZ (Germany)—and two aggregate benchmarks—M-S World and Brinson GSMI—were used in the analysis. The results indicate that using alternative market proxies for different countries generates SMLs that differ substantially during a given time period and that these SMLs tend to be very unstable over time. For instance, the Nikkei SML had the largest risk premium during the period 1983 to 1988 but a negative risk premium during the period 1989 to 1994, which clearly is contrary to capital market theory. Finally, the S&P 500 provided investors with the biggest performance hurdle over the whole sample period, which was mostly due to the high risk premiums in the United States during the period 1989 to 1994.

| EXHIBIT 18.11 | Beta Estimates for Dow Jones Industrials Stock Using Domestic and World Stock Market Indices: 2002–2004 & 2005–2007 |

Stock	Ticker	2002–2004			2005–2007		
		Beta-US	Beta-World	% Diff	Beta-US	Beta-World	% Diff
3M Company	MMM	0.73	0.71	2.7	0.83	0.73	12.0
Alcoa	AA	1.35	1.53	11.8	1.63	1.72	5.2
Altria Group	MO	0.53	0.51	3.8	0.73	0.60	17.8
American Express	AXP	1.39	1.50	7.3	1.30	1.05	19.2
American Intl Group	AIG	1.34	1.38	2.9	1.01	0.77	23.8
AT&T	T	1.08	1.13	4.4	0.79	0.68	13.9
Boeing	BA	0.86	0.92	6.5	0.87	0.78	10.3
Caterpillar	CAT	1.20	1.26	4.8	1.70	1.67	1.8
Citigroup	C	1.29	1.45	11.0	1.10	0.84	23.6
Coca-Cola	KO	0.55	0.56	1.8	0.61	0.49	19.7
Du Pont	DD	0.96	0.93	3.1	1.24	1.09	12.1
ExxonMobil	XOM	0.74	0.72	2.7	1.27	1.23	3.1
General Electric	GE	1.14	1.17	2.6	0.67	0.52	22.4
General Motors	GM	1.02	1.12	8.9	1.68	1.58	6.0
Hewlett-Packard	HPQ	1.57	1.68	6.5	1.02	0.84	17.6
Home Depot	HD	1.06	1.06	0.0	1.29	1.10	14.7
Honeywell	HON	1.32	1.37	3.6	1.34	1.24	7.5
Intel	INTC	1.51	1.65	8.5	1.31	1.16	11.5
Intl Business Machines	IBM	1.23	1.36	9.6	0.90	0.74	17.8
Johnson & Johnson	JNJ	0.68	0.60	11.8	0.47	0.40	14.9
JPMorgan	JPM	1.67	1.89	11.6	1.23	0.99	19.5
McDonald's	MCD	0.84	0.94	10.6	0.92	0.81	12.0
Merck	MRK	0.90	0.86	4.4	0.71	0.67	5.6
Microsoft	MSFT	1.17	1.24	5.6	0.86	0.79	8.1
Pfizer	PFE	0.90	0.85	5.6	1.04	1.00	3.8
Procter & Gamble	PG	0.39	0.28	28.2	0.43	0.33	23.3
United Technologies	UTX	0.83	0.83	0.0	0.99	0.96	3.0
Verizon	VZ	0.80	0.83	3.6	0.93	0.78	16.1
Wal-Mart Stores	WMT	0.87	0.74	14.9	0.85	0.71	16.5
Walt Disney	DIS	1.19	1.25	4.8	0.81	0.76	6.2
	Mean:	1.04	1.08	6.8	1.02	0.90	13.0
	Median:	1.04	1.09	5.2	0.96	0.80	13.0

18.4.2   IMPLICATIONS OF THE BENCHMARK PROBLEMS

Several points are significant regarding this benchmark criticism. First, the problems noted by Roll, which are increased with global investing, do not negate the value of the CAPM as a *normative* model of equilibrium pricing; the theory is still viable. The problem is one of *measurement* when using the theory to evaluate portfolio performance. We need to find a better proxy for the market portfolio or to adjust measured performance for benchmark errors. Roll (1981) and Grinold (1992) have made several suggestions to help overcome this problem. Finally, the multiple markets index (MMI), developed by Brinson, Diermeier, and Schlarbaum (1986), is a major step toward a truly comprehensive world market portfolio.

Alternatively, the analyst might consider giving greater weight to the Sharpe portfolio performance measure because it does not depend on the market portfolio. Although the evaluation process based on these statistics generally uses a benchmark portfolio as an example of an unmanaged portfolio for comparison purposes, the risk measure for the portfolio being evaluated does not directly depend on a market portfolio.

18.4.3   REQUIRED CHARACTERISTICS OF BENCHMARKS

Concurrent with the search for a global market portfolio, there has also been a search for appropriate **normal portfolios**, which are customized benchmarks that reflect the specific styles of alternative managers. Bailey, Richards, and Tierney (2007) consider this a critical need of pension plans and endowments who hire multiple managers with widely divergent styles. They point out that if a broad market index is used rather than a specific benchmark portfolio, it is implicitly assumed that the portfolio manager does not have an investment style, which is quite unrealistic. Also, it does not allow the plan sponsors to determine if the money manager is consistent with his or her stated investment style. The authors contend that any useful benchmark should have the following characteristics:

- *Unambiguous:* The names and weights of securities comprising the benchmark are clearly delineated.
- *Investable:* The option is available to forgo active management and simply hold the benchmark.
- *Measurable:* It is possible to calculate the return on the benchmark on a reasonably frequent basis.
- *Appropriate:* The benchmark is consistent with the manager's investment style or biases.
- *Reflective of current investment opinions:* The manager has current investment knowledge (be it positive, negative, or neutral) of the securities that make up the benchmark.
- *Specified in advance:* The benchmark is constructed prior to the start of an evaluation period.
- *Owned:* The manager should accept accountability for benchmark performance.

If a benchmark does not possess all of these properties, it is considered flawed as an effective management tool. One example of a flawed benchmark is the use of the median manager from a broad universe of managers or even a limited universe of managers. This criticism is spelled out in detail by Bailey (1992), who argues that the manager universe is inadequate on almost every characteristic. Finally, Dialynas (2001) considers the special problems of creating benchmarks for fixed-income portfolios.

18.5   Evaluation of Bond Portfolio Performance

As it was for stocks, bond performance measurement can also be divided into attempts to assess how portfolio managers performed relative to investor expectations and why the managers produced the performance they did. We now consider techniques that address both of these questions.[6]

---

6 A good overview of this area and a discussion of the historical development of the various performance measures are contained in Fong (2001).

18.5.1   RETURNS-BASED BOND PERFORMANCE MEASUREMENT

Early attempts to analyze fixed-income performance often involved peer group comparisons of the returns generated by bond portfolio managers with comparable investment styles. Kritzman (1983) examined the ranking for 32 bond managers over two five-year periods. He determined each manager's percentile ranking in each period, and correlated the rankings. The results revealed no relationship between levels of performance in the two periods and no relationship between past and future performance, even when comparing the best and worst performers. He concluded that it is necessary to look at something besides past performance to determine superior bond portfolio managers.

Of course, peer group comparisons are potentially flawed because they do not account for investment risk directly. In principle, the Jensen's alpha approach described in previous sections can be employed to measure the performance of *any* asset portfolio. In practice, however, when the assets in the portfolio change from stocks to bonds, it is likely that a straightforward application of the conventional risk models will not produce the most meaningful results. Fama and French (1993) addressed this issue by expanding their three-factor equation to include two additional factors specifically related to how returns are generated for fixed-income securities:

18.8
$$R_{jt} - RFR_t = \alpha_j + [b_{j1}(R_{mt} - RFR_t) + b_{j2}SMB_t + b_{j3}HML_t]$$
$$+ [b_{j4}TERM_t + b_{j4}DEF_t] + e_{jt}$$

The two additional risk factors are defined as follows: (1) TERM is the term premium built into the slope of the Treasury yield curve and is calculated as the difference between the long-term and short-term government bond yields, and (2) DEF is the default premium and is calculated by the credit spread between the long-term corporate and government bond yields. As in Chapter 7, *SMB*, i.e. small minus big, is the return to a portfolio of small capitalization stocks less the return to a portfolio of large capitalization stocks, and *HML*, i.e., high minus low, is the return to a portfolio of stocks with high ratios of book-to-market values less the return to a portfolio of low book-to-market value stocks.

Fama and French (1993) tested this model using seven different bond portfolios over the 342-month period from July 1963 to December 1991. The seven bond portfolios were formed with the following securities: 1- to 5-year Treasuries (1–5G) 6- to 10-year Treasuries (6–10G), Aaa-rated corporates, Aa-rated corporates, A-rated corporates, Baa-rated corporates, and low-grade corporates rated below Baa (LG). Their findings are summarized in Exhibit 18.12.

Although both stock and bond risk factors were included, the two bond factors provide the dominant explanation for how these bond portfolio returns varied over time. While all of the portfolios groups had significant positive exposures to TERM and DEF, only a few of the categories also had significant loadings on the stock market variables. Further, the reported alpha coefficients in the last row are quite small and were insignificant for all of the corporate bond portfolios. Because these portfolios represent the performance of indexed fixed-income investments, these results are what we would expect. However, the same process can be used to assess the value added by active bond managers as well.

EXHIBIT 18.12	Risk Factor and Jensen's Alpha Estimates for Seven Bond Portfolios: 1963–1991							
	Bond Portfolios							
	Government		Corporate					
Risk Factor:	1–5FG	6–10G	Aaa	Aa	A	Baa	LG
$(R_m - RFR)$	−0.02[a]	−0.04[a]	−0.02[a]	0.00	0.00	0.02	0.18[a]
SMB	0.00	−0.02	−0.02[a]	−0.01[a]	0.00	0.05[a]	0.08[a]
HML	0.00	−0.02	−0.02[a]	−0.00	0.00	0.04[a]	0.12[a]
TERM	0.47[a]	0.75[a]	1.03[a]	0.99[a]	1.00[a]	0.99[a]	0.64[a]
DEF	0.27[a]	0.32[a]	0.97[a]	0.97[a]	1.02[a]	1.05[a]	0.80[a]
Portfolio Alpha:	0.09[a]	0.11[a]	−0.00	−0.00	−0.00	0.02	−0.07

[a]Significant at the 0.05 level.

Source: Eugene F. Fama and Kenneth R. French, "Common Risk Factors in the Returns on Stocks and Bonds," *Journal of Financial Economics* 33, no. 1 (January 1993): 3–56.

18.6 Reporting Investment Performance

Performance presentation standards can be found at CFA Institute:

http://www.cfainstitute.org.

The performance measures described in this chapter represent the essential elements of how any investor's performance should be evaluated. However, before the various composite statistics can be calculated, a more fundamental question must be addressed: How should the returns used in the evaluation process be reported to the investor? We conclude our discussion by exploring two dimensions of this problem. First, we consider the issue of how returns should be computed for a portfolio that experiences infusions and withdrawals of cash during the investment period. Second, we will briefly summarize the **performance presentation standards (PPS)** created by the CFA Institute, an international organization of over 90,000 investment practitioners and educators in more than 100 countries.

18.6.1 TIME-WEIGHTED RETURNS

As we saw in Chapter 1, the holding period yield (HPY) for any investment position was determined by that position's market value at the end of the period divided by its initial value: Ending Value of Investment

$$ HPY = \frac{\text{Ending Value of Investment}}{\text{Beginning Value of Investment}} - 1 $$

For any security or portfolio, we also saw that there are two basic reasons why the ending and beginning values could differ: the receipt of cash payments (e.g., dividends) or a change in price (e.g., capital gains) during the period. Thus, for most investment positions, calculating returns during any given time frame is a reasonably straightforward matter.

For professional money managers and management companies, however, there is another reason why the beginning and ending value of a portfolio can differ, and it has nothing to do with the manager's investment prowess. If the investor either withdraws or adds to her initial investment capital during the period, the ending value of the position will reflect these changes.

Of course, it would be unfair to credit the manager with having produced high returns that were due to additional capital commitments. Similarly, it would be equally unfair to penalize him for reductions in the ending value of the investment that were caused by the investor removing funds from her account. Consequently, an evaluation of the manager's true performance must take these contributions and withdrawals into account.

Consider two portfolio managers (A and B) who have exactly identical investment styles and stock-picking abilities. Indeed, we will assume that over a two-period investment horizon, they produce exactly the same capital gains with the investment capital entrusted to them: 25% in Period 1, and 5% in Period 2. Further, suppose that each manager receives from his respective investor $500,000 to invest. The difference is that Manager A receives all of these funds immediately whereas Manager B's investor commits only $250,000 initially and the remaining $250,000 at the end of the first period.

The immediate effect of this investment timing difference can be seen by calculating the terminal (Period 2) value of each portfolio:

$$\textbf{Portfolio A: } 500,000[(1 + 0.25)(1 + (0.05)] = \$656,250$$

and

$$\textbf{Portfolio B: } 250,000[(1 + 0.25)(1 + 0.05)] + 250,000(1 + 0.05) = \$590,625$$

Obviously, Manager B's portfolio is worth less than Manager A's, but this is a result of the way the investment funds were committed rather than of any differences in the performance of the two managers. Accordingly, the managers' performance evaluation should not be affected by the investors' decisions concerning the timing of their capital commitments. In other words, Manager B should not be held accountable for the fact that investor B did not have all of her funds invested during the high-return environment of the first period.

18.6.2 DOLLAR-WEIGHTED RETURNS

One common method of computing average returns that we have seen is to use a discounted cash flow approach to calculate an investment's internal return. For the two managers in this example, these calculations generate the following returns:

$$\textbf{Manager A: } 500,000 = \frac{656,250}{(1 + r_{dA})^2} \text{ , or } r_{dA} = 14.56\%$$

and

$$\textbf{Manager B: } 250,000 = \frac{-250,000}{(1 + r_{dB})^1} + \frac{590,625}{(1 + r_{dB})^2} \text{ , or } r_{dB} = 11.63\%$$

These returns (r_{dA} and r_{dB}) are **dollar-weighted returns** and are sometimes called **money-weighted returns** because they are the discount rates that set the present value of future cash flows (including future investment contributions and withdrawals) equal to the level of the initial investment. Unfortunately, in this case, dollar-weighted returns give an inaccurate impression of Manager B's ability; he did not actually perform 2.93% (= 0.1456 − 0.1163) worse than Manager A. Thus, while this internal rate of return method gives an accurate assessment of *Investor* B's return, it is a misleading measure of *Manager* B's talent.

A better way of evaluating a manager's performance would be to consider how well he did regardless of the size or timing of the investment funds involved. For both managers in this example, the **time-weighted return** is simply the geometric average of (one plus) the periodic returns:

$$r_{tA} = r_{tB} = \sqrt[2]{(1 + 0.25)(1 + 0.05)} - 1 = 14.56\%$$

Dollar-weighted and time-weighted returns are only the same when there are no interim investment contributions within the evaluation period. This was the case for Manager A. For Manager B, the dollar-weighted return understates the true (time-weighted) performance because of the way the investor deployed her funds.

18.6.3 PERFORMANCE PRESENTATION STANDARDS

The preceding example underscores the fact that there may not always be a straightforward answer to a seemingly simple question. Although Portfolio B had a dollar-weighted return of 11.63%, its manager generated an average return of 14.56%. Which should be reported to the investor? The U.S. Securities and Exchange Commission (SEC) has established regulations[7] to guard against the publication of outright fraudulent claims, but Lawton and Remington (2007) point out that the following reporting practices have been historically permissible:

- Present returns only for the best-performing portfolios as though those returns were fully representative of the manager's expertise in a given strategy or style.
- Base portfolio market values on unsubstantiated estimates of asset prices or present simulated returns as though they had actually been earned.
- Inflate returns by annualizing partial-period returns.
- Select the most favourable measurement period, calculating returns from a low point to a high point.
- Choose as a benchmark the particular index the selected portfolios have outperformed by the greatest margin during the measurement period.
- Portray growth in assets under management (AUM) in a way that masks the difference between investment returns and client contributions.

---

7 The Ontario Securities Commission (OSC) and the Investment Dealers Association of Canada (IDA), also have regulations (e.g., http://www.osc.gov.on.ca/FastAnswers/Inquiries/Scams/fa_scams.jsp; see also the Mutual Fund Dealers Association of Canada's (MFDA) http://www.bcsc.bc.ca/uploadedFiles/Amendments_to_MFDA_Rule_5.3_Rule_2.8.pdf about performance reporting), but to date, there no studies examining what could be dubious but permissible in practice in Canada.

Largely as a result of such abuses, the investment community has recently begun to demand the adoption of a more rigorous set of reporting guidelines.

In an effort to fulfill the call for uniform, accurate, and consistent performance reporting, the CFA Institute (formerly known as the Association for Investment Management and Research, or AIMR) has developed a comprehensive set of performance presentation standards (PPS).

Introduced in 1987, formally adopted in 1993, and modified in 1999, the AIMR-PPS quickly became the accepted practice within the investment management community. However, early versions of these standards tended to have country-specific elements that made them difficult to translate to a fully global platform. Consequently, in 1999 the CFA Institute also adopted a companion set of global investment performance standards (GIPS), which were intended to serve the following purpose:

> A global investment performance standard leads to readily accepted presentations of investment performance that (1) present performance results that are readily comparable among investment management firms without regard to geographical location and (2) facilitate a dialogue between investment managers and their prospective clients about the critical issues of how the investment management firm achieved performance results and determines future investment strategies.[8]

By 2005, the GIPS had been adopted by 25 countries throughout North America, Europe, Africa, and the Asia Pacific region. They have replaced the original AIMR-PPS and are now considered the definitive set of standards for reporting investment performance.

Although a detailed analysis of these standards (which are revised frequently) is beyond our current scope, it is worth noting several of the fundamental principles on which they are based:

- Total return, including realized and unrealized gains plus income, must be used when calculating investment performance.
- Time-weighted rates of return must be used.
- Portfolios must be valued at least monthly, and periodic returns must be geometrically linked.
- If composite return performance is presented, this composite must contain all actual fee-paying accounts, including all terminated accounts for periods up through the last full reporting period the account was under management. Composite results may not link simulated or model portfolios with actual performance.
- Performance must be calculated after the deduction of trading expenses (e.g., broker commissions and SEC fees), if any.
- For taxable clients, taxes on income and realized capital gains must be recognized in the same period they were incurred and must be subtracted from results regardless of whether taxes are paid from assets outside the account.
- Annual returns for all years must be presented. Performance of less than one year must not be annualized. A 10-year performance record (or a record for the period since firm inception if less than 10 years) must be presented.

---

8 See *Global Investment Performance Standards* (Charlottesville, VA: CFA Institute, February 2005).

- Performance presentation must disclose whether performance results are calculated gross or net of investment management fees and what the firm's fee schedule is. Presentation should also disclose any use of leverage (including derivatives) and any material change in personnel responsible for investment management.

In addition to the preceding requirements, CFA Institute also encourages managers to disclose the volatility of the aggregate composite return and to identify benchmarks that parallel the risk or investment style the composite is expected to track. Exhibit 18.13 shows a sample performance presentation that is in compliance with the standards.

EXHIBIT 18.13	A Sample Performance Presentation

Sample 1 Investment Firm
Balanced Composite
1 January 1995 through 31 December 2004

Year	Gross-of-Fees Return (%)	Net-of-Fees Return (%)	Benchmark Return (%)	Number of Portfolios	Internal Dispersion (%)	Total Composite Assets (CAD Million)	Total Firm Assets (CAD Million)
1995	16.0	15.0	14.1	26	4.5	165	236
1996	2.2	1.3	1.8	32	2.0	235	346
1997	22.4	21.5	24.1	38	5.7	344	529
1998	7.1	6.2	6.0	45	2.8	445	695
1999	8.5	7.5	8.0	48	3.1	520	839
2000	−8.0	−8.9	−8.4	49	2.8	505	1,014
2001	−5.9	−6.8	−6.2	52	2.9	499	995
2002	2.4	1.6	2.2	58	3.1	525	1,125
2003	6.7	5.9	6.8	55	3.5	549	1,225
2004	9.4	8.6	9.1	59	2.5	575	1,290

Sample 1 Investment Firm has prepared and presented this report in compliance with the Global Investment Performance Standards (GIPS★).

Notes:

1. Sample 1 Investment Firm is a balanced portfolio investment manager that invests solely in Canadian securities. Sample 1 Investment Firm is defined as an independent investment management firm that is not affiliated with any parent organization. For the periods from 2000 through 2004, Sample 1 Investment Firm has been verified by Verification Services Inc. A copy of the verification report is available upon request. Additional information regarding the firm's policies and procedures for calculating and reporting performance results is available upon request.

2. The composite includes all nontaxable balanced portfolios with an asset allocation of 30% S&P/TSX and 70% Scotia Canadian Bond Index Fund, which allow up to a 10% deviation in asset allocation.

3. The benchmark: 30% S&P/TSX; 70% Scotia Canadian Bond Index Fund rebalanced monthly.

4. Valuations are computed and performance reported in Canadian dollars.

5. Gross-of-fees performance returns are presented before management and custodial fees but after all trading expenses. Returns are presented net of nonreclaimable withholding taxes. Net-of-fees performance returns are calculated by deducting the highest fee of 0.25% from the quarterly gross composite return. The management fee schedule is as follows: 1.00% on first CAD25M; 0.60% thereafter.

6. This composite was created in February 1995. A complete list and description of firm composites is available upon request.

7. For the periods 1995 and 1996, Sample 1 Investment Firm was not in compliance with the GIPS standards because portfolios were valued annually.

8. Internal dispersion is calculated using the equal-weighted standard deviation of all portfolios that were included in the composite for the entire year.

Source: Copyright 2005, CFA Institute. Reproduced and republished from Global Investment Performance Standards (GIPS), 2005, with permission from the CFA Institute. All rights reserved.

Copyright 1991, CFA Institute. Reproduced and republished from Global Investment Performance Standards with permission from CFA Institute. All rights reserved.

Summary

1. Peer group comparison is the most common manner of evaluating portfolio managers. It collects the returns produced by a representative universe of investors over a specific period of time and displays them in a simple boxplot format. The universe is typically divided into percentiles, showing the relative ranking of a given investor. Its main drawback is that it does not take risk into consideration.

2. Several techniques have been derived to evaluate equity portfolios in terms of both risk and return (composite measures). The Treynor measure considers the excess returns earned per unit of systematic risk. The Sharpe measure indicates the excess return per unit of total risk. The Jensen and Information Ratio measures likewise evaluate performance in terms of the systematic risk involved and show how to determine whether the difference in risk-adjusted performance (good or bad) is statistically significant.

3. Beyond risk-adjusted measurements, performance attribution analysis reveals the sources of the performance, and market-timing analysis measures market-timing skills of the managers. A third measure is style analysis (discussed in Chapter 15), which is a technique to examine whether a portfolio manager has adhered to a particular investment style she professed to follow.

4. Richard Roll challenged the validity of all techniques that assume a market portfolio that theoretically includes all risky assets, but which then use a proxy such as the S&P 500 that is limited to U.S. common stocks. This criticism does not invalidate the normative asset pricing model, only its application because of measurement problems related to the proxy for the market portfolio. The measurement problem is increased in an environment where global investing is the norm. Any useful benchmark should be unambiguous, investable, measureable, appropriate, reflective of current investment opinions, specified in advance, and owned.

5. Although the techniques for evaluating equity portfolio performance have been in existence for almost 50 years, comparable techniques for examining bond portfolio performance were initiated more recently. While it is possible to adapt equity risk models for the evaluation of bond managers, it is often necessary to consider separately the several important decision variables related to bonds: the overall market factor, the impact of maturity-duration decisions, the influence of sector and quality factors, and the impact of individual bond selection.

6. There are two ways to compute returns for a portfolio that experiences infusions and withdrawals of cash during the investment period. Time-weighted return calculates the geometric average of (one plus) the holding period yields to an investment portfolio. Dollar-weighted return calculates the discount rate that sets the present value of a future set of cash flows equal to the investment's current value. Time-weighted returns should be reported under the CFA Institute's performance presentation standards.

Key Terms

attribution analysis, p. 587
benchmark error, p. 591
benchmark portfolio, p. 577
dollar-weighted return, p. 598
information ratio, p. 577

Jensen measure, p. 574
normal portfolio, p. 594
peer group comparison, p. 569
performance presentation
    standards (PPS), p. 596

Sharpe measure, p. 573
time-weighted return, p. 598
Treynor measure, p. 570

Suggested Readings

Amenc, Noel, and Veronique LeSourd. *Portfolio Theory and Performance Analysis.* West Sussex, England: Wiley, 2003.

Appelt, Timothy. "Active Management: What Is the Right Performance Benchmark." *Canadian Investment Review* 5, no. 1 (April 1992): 67–72.

Athanassakos, George, Peter Carayannopoulos, and Marie Racine. "How Effective Is Aggressive Portfolio Management" Mutual Fund Performance in Canada, 1985–1996. *Canadian Investment Review* 15, no. 3 (October 2002): 39, 41+.

Bacon, Carl. *Practical Portfolio Performance Measurement and Attribution.* West Sussex, England: Wiley, 2004.

Curwood, Bruce. "Measuring Performance: A New Direction. Fiduciaries Often Use Flawed Methodologies to Evaluate Manager Performance. There Is a Better Way." *Canadian Investment Review* 13, no. 1 (April 2000): 28+.

DeFusco, Richard A., Dennis Mc Leavey, Jerald A. Pinto, and David E. Runkle. *Quantitative Methods for Investment Analysis*, 2nd ed. Charlottesville, VA: CFA Institute, 2004.

Feibel, Bruce J. *Investment Performance Measurement*. Hoboken, NJ: Wiley, 2003.

Khoury, Nabil, Marc Veilleux, and Robert Viau. "A Performance Attribution Model for Fixed-Income Portfolios." *Canadian Investment Review* 16, no. 3 (October 2003): 11–18.

Sharpe, William F. "The Sharpe Ratio." *Journal of Portfolio Management* 21, no. 1 (October 1994): 49.

Sherrerd, Kartrina F., ed. *Benchmarks and Attribution Analysis*. Charlottesville, VA: Association for Investment Management and Research, 2001.

Vos, Wilfred. "Measuring Mutual Fund Performance." *Canadian Investment Review* 10, no. 4 (January 1997): 33.

CFA **For Chapter CFA Questions and Problems, please see Appendix A at the end of this text.**

Questions

1. Describe two major factors that a portfolio manager should consider before designing an investment strategy. What types of decisions can a manager make to achieve these goals?

2. Compare and contrast four prominent approaches to measuring investment performance on a risk-adjusted basis. In developing your answer, comment on the conditions under which each measure will be most useful.

3. The Sharpe and Treynor performance measures both calculate a portfolio's average excess return per unit of risk. Under what circumstances would it make sense to use both measures to compare the performance of a given set of portfolios? What additional information is provided by a comparison of the rankings achieved using the two measures?

4. Describe how the Jensen measure of performance is calculated. Under what conditions should it give a similar set of portfolio rankings as the Sharpe and Treynor measures? Is it possible to adjust the Jensen measure so that a portfolio's alpha value is measured relative to an empirical

form of the arbitrage pricing theory rather than the capital asset pricing model? Explain.

5. The information ratio (*IR*) has been described as a benefit-cost ratio. Explain how the *IR* measures portfolio performance and whether this analogy is appropriate.

6. Performance attribution analysis is an attempt to divide a manager's "active" residual return into an allocation effect and a selection effect. Explain how these two effects are measured and why their sum must equal the total value-added return for the manager. Is this analysis valid if the actual portfolio in question is riskier than the benchmark portfolio to which it is being compared?

7. It has been contended that the derivation of an appropriate model for evaluating the performance of a bond manager is more difficult than an equity portfolio evaluation model because more decisions are required. Discuss some of the specific decisions that need to be considered when evaluating the performance of a bond portfolio manager.

Problems

1. The following portfolios are being considered for investment. During the period under consideration, *RFR* = 0.07.

Portfolio	Return	Beta	Σ_i
P	0.15	1.0	0.05
Q	0.20	1.5	0.10
R	0.10	0.6	0.03
S	0.17	1.1	0.06
Market	0.13	1.0	0.04

a. Compute the Sharpe measure for each portfolio and the market portfolio.

b. Compute the Treynor measure for each portfolio and the market portfolio.

c. Rank the portfolios using each measure, explaining the cause for any differences you find in the rankings.

2. You have been assigned the task of comparing the investment performance of five different pension fund managers. After gathering 60 months of excess returns (i.e., returns in excess of the monthly risk-free rate) on each fund as well as the monthly excess returns on

the entire stock market, you perform the regressions of the form:

$$(R_{fund} - RFR)_t = \alpha + \beta(R_{mkt} - RFR)_t + e_t$$

You have prepared the following summary of the data, with the standard errors for each of the coefficients listed in parentheses.

Portfolio	α	β	R^2	Mean	σ
	Regression Data			$(R_{Fund} - RFR)$	
ABC	0.192	1.048	94.1%	1.022%	1.193%
	(0.11)	(0.10)			
DEF	−0.053	0.662	91.6	0.473	0.764
	(0.19)	(0.09)			
GHI	0.463	0.594	68.6	0.935	0.793
	(0.19)	(0.07)			
JKL	0.355	0.757	64.1	0.955	1.044
	(0.22)	(0.08)			
MNO	0.296	0.785	94.8	0.890	0.890
	(0.14)	(0.12)			

a. Which fund had the highest degree of diversification over the sample period? How is diversification measured in this statistical framework?
b. Rank these funds' performance according to the Sharpe, Treynor, and Jensen measures.
c. Because you know that according to the CAPM the intercept of these regressions (i.e., alpha) should be zero, this coefficient can be used as a measure of the value added provided by the investment manager. Which funds have statistically outperformed and underperformed the market using a two-sided 95% confidence interval? (Note: The relevant t-statistic using 60 observations is 2.00.)

3. You have just gathered the following performance data for three different money managers, based on a regression of their excess returns relative to those for the S&P 500 index. Each manager's performance was measured over the same three-year period, but the return period for each was different.

Manager	Alpha	Beta	Std. Error of Regression	Return Period
A	0.058%	0.95	0.533%	Weekly
B	0.115	1.12	5.884	Biweekly
C	0.250	0.78	2.165	Monthly

a. Calculate the information ratio for each manager, ignoring the difference in return reporting periods.
b. Calculate the annualized information ratio for each manager.
c. Rank the managers' performance according to your answers in Parts a and b. Which manager performed the best? Explain.

4. Consider the following historical performance data for two different portfolios: the S&P 500 and the 90-day T-bill.

Investment Vehicle	Average Rate of Return	Standard Deviation	Beta	R^2
Fund 1	26.40%	20.67%	1.351	0.751
Fund 2	13.22	14.20	0.905	0.713
S&P 500	15.71	13.25		
90-day T-bill	6.20	0.50		

a. Calculate the Fama overall performance measure for both funds.
b. What is the return to risk for both funds?
c. For both funds, compute the measures of (1) selectivity, (2) diversification, and (3) net selectivity.
d. Explain the meaning of the net selectivity measure and how it helps you evaluate investor performance. Which fund had the best performance?

5. You are evaluating the performance of two portfolio managers and you have gathered annual return data for the past decade:

Year	Manager X Return (%)	Manager Y Return (%)
1	−1.5	−6.5
2	−1.5	−3.5
3	−1.5	−1.5
4	−1.0	3.5
5	0.0	4.5
6	4.5	6.5
7	6.5	7.5
8	8.5	8.5
9	13.5	12.5
10	17.5	13.5

a. For each manager, calculate: (i) the average annual return, (ii) the standard deviation of returns, and (iii) the semi-deviation of returns.
b. Assuming that the average annual risk-free rate during the 10-year sample period was 1.5%, calculate the Sharpe ratio for each portfolio. Based on these computations, which manager appears to have performed the best?

6. Consider the following performance data for two portfolio managers (A and B) and a common benchmark portfolio:

	Benchmark		Manager A		Manager B	
	Weight	Return	Weight	Return	Weight	Return
Stock	0.6	−5.0%	0.5	−4.0%	0.3	−5.0%
Bonds	0.3	−3.5	0.2	−2.5	0.4	−3.5
Cash	0.1	0.3	0.3	0.3	0.3	0.3

a. Calculate: (1) the overall return to the benchmark portfolio; (2) the overall return to Manager A's actual portfolio; and (3) the overall return to Manager B's actual portfolio. Briefly comment on whether these managers have under- or outperformed the benchmark fund.

b. Using attribution analysis, calculate (1) the *selection effect* for Manager A, and (2) the *allocation effect* for Manager B. Using these numbers in conjunction with your results from Part a, comment on whether these managers have added value through their selection skills, their allocation skills, or both, and justify your conclusion.

7. For each of the last six quarters, Managers L and M have provided you with the total dollar value of the funds they manage, along with the quarterly contributions or withdrawals made by their clients. (Note: Contributions are indicated by positive numbers, withdrawals by negative numbers.)

	Manager L		Manager M	
Quarter	Total Funds Under Management	Contributions/ Withdrawals	Total Funds Under Management	Contributions/ Withdrawals
Initial	$500,000	—	$700,000	—
1	527,000	12,000	692,000	−35,000
2	530,000	7,500	663,000	−35,000
3	555,000	13,500	621,000	−35,000
4	580,000	6,500	612,000	−35,000
5	625,000	10,000	625,000	−35,000

For each manager, calculate:
a. her dollar-weighted or money-weighted return;
b. her time-weighted return.

Valuation Principles
and Practices

APPENDIX  A

CFA Questions and Problems

CHAPTER 1

Examination Level I

1. The table below gives current information on the interest rates for two two-year and two eight-year maturity investments. The table also gives the maturity, liquidity, and default risk characteristics of a new investment possibility (Investment 3). All investments promise only a single payment (a payment at maturity). Assume that premiums relating to inflation, liquidity, and default risk are constant across all time horizons.

Investment	Maturity (in Years)	Liquidity	Default Risk	Interest Rate (%)
1	2	High	Low	2.0
2	2	Low	Low	2.5
3	7	Low	Low	r_3
4	8	High	Low	4.0
5	8	Low	High	6.5

Based on the information in the above table, address the following:

A. Explain the difference between the interest rates on Investment 1 and Investment 2.

B. Estimate the default risk premium.

C. Calculate upper and lower limits for the interest rate on Investment 3, r_3

The table below gives the annual total returns on the MSCI Germany Index from 1993 to 2002. The returns are in the local currency. Use the information in this table to answer Problem 2.

MSCI GERMANY INDEX TOTAL RETURNS, 1993–2002

Year	Return (%)
1993	46.21
1994	−6.18
1995	8.04
1996	22.87
1997	45.90
1998	20.32
1999	41.20
2000	−9.53
2001	−17.75
2002	−43.06

Source: Ibbotson EnCorr Analyzer™.

2. To describe the compound rate of growth of the MSCI Germany Index, calculate the geometric mean return.

3. A. Explain the relationship among arithmetic mean return, geometric mean return, and variability of returns.
   B. Contrast the use of the arithmetic mean return to the geometric mean return of an investment from the perspective of an investor concerned with the investment's terminal value.
   C. Contrast the use of the arithmetic mean return to the geometric mean return of an investment from the perspective of an investor concerned with the investment's average one-year return.

4. An analyst expects a risk-free return of 4.5%, a market return of 14.5%, and the returns for Stocks A and B that are shown in the following table:

STOCK INFORMATION

Stock	Beta	Analyst's Estimated Return (%)
A	1.2	16
B	0.8	14

   A. Show on a graph:
      i. Where Stocks A and B would plot on the security market line (SML) if they were fairly valued using the capital asset pricing model (CAPM).
      ii. Where Stocks A and B actually plot on the same graph according to the returns estimated by the analyst and shown in the table.
   B. State whether Stocks A and B are undervalued or overvalued if the analyst uses the SML for strategic investment decisions.

Examination Level III

5. An investor is considering adding three new securities to his internationally focused fixed-income portfolio. The securities under consideration are as follows:
   • 1-year U.S. Treasury note (non-callable)
   • 10-year BBB/Baa rated corporate bond (callable)
   • 10-year mortgage-backed security (MBS; government-backed collateral)
   The investor will invest equally in all three securities being analyzed or will invest in none of them at this time. He will only make the added investment provided that the expected spread/premium of the equally weighted investment is at least 0.5% (50 bps) over the 10-year Treasury bond. The investor has gathered the following information:

Real risk-free interest rate	1.2%
Current inflation rate	2.2%
Spread of 10-year over 1-year Treasury note	1.0%
Long-term inflation expectation	2.6%
10-year MBS prepayment risk spread (over 10-year Treasuries)[a]	95 bps
10-year call risk spread	80 bps
10-year BBB credit risk spread (over 10-year Treasuries)	90 bps

[a]This spread implicitly includes a maturity premium in relation to the 1-year T-note as well as compensation for prepayment risk.

   Using only the information given, address the following problems using the risk premium approach:
   A. Calculate the expected return that an equal-weighted investment in the three securities could provide.
   B. Calculate the expected total risk premium of the three securities, and determine the investor's probable course of action.

6. Swennson, who manages a domestic equities portfolio of Swedish shares, has had fairly volatile returns for the last five years. Nevertheless, Swennson claims that his returns over the long run are good. Another Swedish equity manager, Mattsson, has had less volatile returns. Their records are as follows:

Year	Swennson (%)	Mattsson (%)
1	27.5	5.7
2	−18.9	4.9
3	14.6	7.8
4	−32.4	−6.7
5	12.3	5.3

Assume no interim cash flows.
A. Calculate the annualized rates of return for Swennson and Mattsson.
B. State which manager achieved a higher return over the five-year period.

CHAPTER 1 Appendix

Examination Level I

The following provides the annual total returns on the MSCI Germany Index and also gives the annual total returns on the JP Morgan Germany five- to seven-year government bond index (JPM 5–7 Year GBI, for short). During the period given in the table, the International Monetary Fund Germany Money Market Index (IMF Germany MMI for short) had a mean annual total return of 4.33%. Use that information and the information in the table to answer Problems A1 and A2.

Year	MSCI Germany Index (%)	JPM Germany 5–7 Year GBI (%)
1993	46.21	15.74
1994	−6.18	−3.40
1995	8.04	18.30
1996	22.87	8.35
1997	45.90	6.65
1998	20.32	12.45
1999	41.20	−2.19
2000	−9.53	7.44
2001	−17.75	5.55
2002	−43.06	10.27

Source: Ibbotson EnCorr Analyzer™.

A1. Calculate the annual returns and the mean annual return on a portfolio 60% invested in the MSCI Germany Index and 40% invested in the JPM Germany GBI.

A2. A. Calculate the coefficient of variation for
  i. the 60/40 equity/bond portfolio described in Problem A1.
  ii. the MSCI Germany Index.
  iii. the JPM Germany 5–7 Year GBI.
 B. Contrast the risk of the 60/40 equity/bond portfolio, the MSCI Germany Index, and the JPM Germany 5–7 Year GBI, as measured by the coefficient of variation.

A3. Calculate the covariance of the returns on Bedolf Corporation (R_B) with the returns on Zedock Corporation (R_Z), using the following data:

PROBABILITY FUNCTION OF BEDOLF AND ZEDOCK RETURNS

	$R_z = 15\%$	$R_z = 10\%$	$R_z = 5\%$
$R_B = 30\%$	0.25	0	0
$R_B = 15\%$	0	0.50	0
$R_B = 10\%$	0	0	0.25

Note: Entries are joint probabilities.

Examination Level II

A4. The estimated betas for AOL Time Warner (NYSE: AOL), J.P. Morgan Chase & Company (NYSE: JPM), and The Boeing Company (NYSE: BA) are 2.50, 1.50, and 0.80, respectively. The risk-free rate of return is 4.35% and the equity risk premium is 8.04%. Calculate the required rates of return for these three stocks using the CAPM.

Examination Level III

A5. Assume that the domestic volatility (standard deviation) of the German bond market (in euros) is 5.5%. The volatility of the euro against the U.S. dollar is 11.7%.
   A. What would the dollar volatility of the German market be for a U.S. investor if the correlation between the bond market returns and exchange rate movements were zero?
   B. Suppose the dollar volatility of the German bond market is 13.6%. What can you conclude about the correlation between German bond market movements and exchange rate movements? What might explain this correlation?

A6. Indicate whether the following statement is correct, and explain your reasoning: "The best diversification vehicle is an asset with high volatility and low correlation with the portfolio."

CHAPTER 2

Examination Level II

The following information relates to Questions 1–6.

James Stephenson, age 55 and single, is a surgeon who has accumulated a substantial investment portfolio without a clear long-term strategy in mind. Two of his patients who work in financial markets comment as follows:

- James Hrdina: "My investment firm, based on its experience with investors, has standard investment policy statements in five categories. You would be better served to adopt one of these standard policy statements instead of spending time developing a policy based on your individual circumstances."
- Charles Gionta: "Developing a long-term policy can be unwise given the fluctuations of the market. You want your investment advisor to react continuously to changing conditions and not be limited by a set policy."

Stephenson hires a financial advisor, Caroline Coppa. At their initial meeting, Coppa compiles the following notes:

> Stephenson currently has a $2.0 million portfolio that has a large concentration in small-capitalization U.S. equities. Over the past five years, the portfolio has averaged 20% annual total return on investment. Stephenson hopes that, over the long term, his portfolio will continue to earn

20% annually. When asked about his risk tolerance, he described it as "average." He was surprised when informed that U.S. small-cap portfolios have experienced extremely high volatility.

He does not expect to retire before age 70. His current income is more than sufficient to meet his expenses. Upon retirement, he plans to sell his surgical practice and use the proceeds to purchase an annuity to cover his post-retirement cash flow needs.

Both his income and realized capital gains are taxed at a 30% rate. No pertinent legal or regulatory issues apply. He has no pension or retirement plan but does have sufficient health insurance for post-retirement needs.

1. The comments about investment policy statements made by Stephenson's patients are *best* characterized as:

	Hrdina	Gionta
A.	Correct	Correct
B.	Incorrect	Correct
C.	Incorrect	Incorrect

2. In formulating the return objective for Stephenson's investment policy statement, the *most* appropriate determining factor for Coppa to focus on iscc
   A. Return desires.
   B. Ability to take risk.
   C. Return requirement.

3. Stephenson's willingness and ability to accept risk can be *best* characterized as:

	Willingness to Accept Risk	Ability to Accept Risk
A.	Below average	Above average
B.	Above average	Below average
C.	Above average	Above average

4. Stephenson's tax and liquidity constraints can be *best* characterized as:

	Tax Constraint	Liquidity Constraint
A.	Significant	Significant
B.	Significant	Insignificant
C.	Insignificant	Insignificant

5. Stephenson's time horizon is *best* characterized as:
   A. Short-term and single-stage.
   B. Long-term and single-stage.
   C. Long-term and multistage.

6. Stephenson's return objective and risk tolerance are *most* appropriately described as:

	Return Objective	Risk Tolerance
A.	Below average	Above average
B.	Above average	Below average
C.	Above average	Above average

Examination Level III

7. Louise and Christopher Maclin live in London, United Kingdom, and currently rent an apartment in the metropolitan area. Christopher Maclin, aged 40, is a supervisor at Barnett Co. and earns an annual

salary of £80,000 before taxes. Louise Maclin, aged 38, stays home to care for their newborn twins. She recently inherited £900,000 (after wealth-transfer taxes) in cash from her father's estate. In addition, the Maclins have accumulated the following assets (current market value):

- £5,000 in cash
- £160,000 in stocks and bonds
- £220,000 in Barnett common stock

The value of their holdings in Barnett stock has appreciated substantially as a result of the company's growth in sales and profits during the past ten years. Christopher Maclin is confident that the company and its stock will continue to perform well.

The Maclins need £30,000 for a down payment on the purchase of a house and plan to make a £20,000 non–tax deductible donation to a local charity in memory of Louise Maclin's father. The Maclins' annual living expenses are £74,000. After-tax salary increases will offset any future increases in their living expenses.

During discussions with their financial advisor, Grant Webb, the Maclins express concern about achieving their educational goals for their children and their own retirement goals. The Maclins tell Webb:

- They want to have sufficient funds to retire in 18 years when their children begin their four years of university education.
- They have been unhappy with the portfolio volatility they have experienced in recent years. They state that they do not want to experience a loss in portfolio value greater than 12% in any one year.
- They do not want to invest in alcohol and tobacco stocks.
- They will not have any additional children.

After their discussions, Webb calculates that in 18 years the Maclins will need £2 million to meet their educational and retirement goals. Webb suggests that their portfolio be structured to limit shortfall risk (defined as expected total return minus two standard deviations) to no lower than a negative 12% return in any one year. Maclin's salary and all capital gains and investment income are taxed at 40% and no tax-sheltering strategies are available. Webb's next step is to formulate an investment policy statement for the Maclins.

A. i. Formulate the risk objective of an investment policy statement for the Maclins.
   ii. Formulate the return objective of an investment policy statement for the Maclins. Calculate the pretax rate of return that is required to achieve this objective. Show your calculations.
B. Formulate the constraints portion of an investment policy statement for the Maclins, addressing *each* of the following:
   i. Time horizon.
   ii. Liquidity requirements.
   iii. Tax concerns.
   iv. Unique circumstances.
   Note: Your response to Part B should not address legal and regulatory factors.

8. Sam Nakusi is managing a balanced portfolio of fixed income and equity securities worth £1,000,000. The portfolio's pretax expected return is 6.0%. The percentage of return composed of interest, dividends, and realized capital gain as well as the associated tax rates are listed below. Assume the portfolio's cost basis equals market value.

HYPOTHETICAL TAX PROFILE AND EXAMPLE

Tax Profile	Annual Distribution Rate (p) (%)	Tax Rate (T) (%)
Interest (i)	20	35
Dividends (d)	30	15
Capital gain (cg)	40	25

What is the expected future accumulation in 15 years assuming these parameters hold for that time period?
A. £1,930,929
B. £1,962,776
C. £1,994,447

9. *Worden Technology, Inc.*: Based in London, Worden Technology, Inc. is an established company with operations in North America, Japan, and several European countries. The firm has £16 billion in total assets and offers its employees a defined-benefit pension plan. Worden's pension plan currently has assets of £8.88 billion and liabilities of £9.85 billion. The plan's goals include achieving a minimum expected return of 8.4% with expected standard deviation of return no greater than 16.0%. Next month, Worden will reduce the retirement age requirement for full benefits from 60 years to 55 years. The median age of Worden Technology's workforce is 49 years.

Angus Williamson, CFA, manages the pension plan's investment policy and strategic asset allocation decisions. He has heard an ongoing debate within Worden Technology about the pension plan's investment policy statement. Exhibit A.1 compares two IPSs under consideration.

EXHIBIT A.1	Investment Policy Statements	
	IPS X	**IPS Y**
Return requirement	Plan's objective is to outperform the relevant benchmark return by a substantial margin.	Plan's objective is to match relevant benchmark return.
Risk tolerance	Plan has a high risk tolerance because of the long-term nature of the plan and its liabilities.	Plan has a low risk tolerance because of its limited ability to assume substantial risk.
Time horizon	Plan has a very long time horizon because of its infinite life.	Plan has a shorter time horizon than in the past because of plan demographics.
Liquidity requirement[a]	Plan has moderate liquidity needs to fund monthly benefit payments.	Plan has minimal liquidity needs.

[a]Assume Worden will not contribute to its pension plan over the next several years.

Identify which investment policy statement, X or Y, contains the appropriate language for each of the following components of Worden Technology's pension plan:
A. Return requirement
B. Risk tolerance
C. Time horizon
D. Liquidity
Justify your choice in each instance.

10. For the following types of investors, appraise the importance of using the specified asset class for strategic asset allocation.
A. Long-term bonds for a life insurer and for a young investor.
B. Common stock for a bank and for a young investor.
C. Domestic tax-exempt bonds for an endowment and for a mid-career professional.
D. Private equity for a major foundation and for a young investor.

11. Evaluate the most likely effects of the following events on the investor's investment objectives, constraints, and financial plan.
A. A childless working married couple in their late 20s adopts an infant for whom they hope to provide a university education.

B. An individual decides to buy a house in one year. He estimates that he will need $102,000 at that time for the down payment and closing costs on the house. The portfolio from which those costs will be paid has a current value of $100,000 and no additions to it are anticipated.

C. A foundation with a €150,000,000 portfolio invested 60% in equities, 25% in long-term bonds, and 15% in absolute return strategies has approved a grant totalling €15,000,000 for the construction of a radio telescope observatory. The foundation anticipates a new contribution from a director in the amount of €1,000,000 toward the funding of the grant.

12. Duane Rogers, as chief investment officer for the Summit PLC defined benefit pension scheme, has developed an economic forecast for presentation to the plan's board of trustees. Rogers projects that U.K. inflation will be substantially higher over the next three years than the board's current forecast.

Rogers recommends that the board immediately take the following actions based on his forecast:

A. Revise the pension scheme's investment policy statement to account for a change in the U.K. inflation forecast.

B. Reallocate pension assets from domestic (U.K.) to international equities because he also expects inflation in the United Kingdom to be higher than in other countries.

C. Initiate a program to protect the pension scheme's financial strength from the effects of U.K. inflation by indexing benefits paid by the scheme.

State whether *each* recommended action is correct or incorrect. Justify *each* of your responses with *one* reason.

13. Briefly discuss the properties that a valid benchmark should have.

14. Kim Lee Ltd., an investment management firm in Singapore managing portfolios of Pacific Rim equities, tells you that its benchmark for performance is to be in the top quartile of its peer group (Singapore managers running portfolios of Pacific Rim equities) over the previous calendar year. Is this a valid benchmark? Why or why not?

CHAPTER 3

Examination Level II

1. You are provided with annual rates of return for a portfolio and relevant benchmark index for the years 2008 to 2012. Calculate the tracking error for the portfolio.

Year	Portfolio Return (%)	Benchmark Return (%)
2008	12	14
2009	14	10
2010	20	12
2011	14	16
2012	16	13

2. Consider a German firm that wishes to invest Euro funds for a period of one year. The firm has a choice of investing in a euro bond with one year to maturity, paying an interest rate of 3.35%, and a U.S. dollar bond with one year to maturity, paying an interest rate of 2.25%. The current exchange rate is €1.12 per U.S. dollar, and the one-year forward exchange rate is €1.25 per U.S. dollar. Should the German firm invest in Euro bonds or in U.S. dollar bonds?

Examination Level III

3. Is currency risk a barrier to international investment?

4. Consider a U.S. pension fund with the following performance:

	Percentage Total Portfolio (%)	Total Dollar Return (%)	Standard Deviation of Return (%)	Correlation with U.S. Stock Index
U.S. equity	90	10	15	0.99
Foreign equity	10	11	20	−0.10

Is the risk-return performance of the foreign portfolio attractive?

CHAPTER 4

Examination Level I

1. Compared to a producer, the consumer is *most likely* to pay the largest part of a tax increase if the elasticity of demand and elasticity of supply, respectively, are more:

	Elasticity of Demand	Elasticity of Supply
A.	Elastic	Elastic
B.	Elastic	Inelastic
C.	Inelastic	Elastic

2. An analyst gathered the following year-end price level data for an economy:

Year End	Price Level
2000	174.0
2004	190.3
2005	196.8

The economy's annual inflation rate for 2005 and the compounded annual inflation rate for the 2000–2005 period are *closest* to:

	2005 Inflation (%)	2000–2005 Inflation (%)
A.	3.42	2.49
B.	3.42	2.62
C.	6.50	2.49

3. You decide to sell short 100 shares of Charlotte Horse Farms when it is selling at its yearly high of 56. Your broker tells you that your margin requirement is 45% and that the commission on the purchase is $155. While you are short the stock, Charlotte pays a $2.50 per share dividend. At the end of one year, you buy 100 shares of Charlotte at 45 to close out your position and are charged a commission of $145. What is your rate return on the investment?

4. An investor acquires 100 shares of BP Amoco (BP) at a price of $70 per share using 50% margin. If the price of the shares increases 15%, the total market value of the position is:
A. $4,550 and the investor's equity is $3,500.
B. $8,050 and the investor's equity is $3,500.
C. $8,050 and the investor's equity is $4,550.

5. You are given the following information regarding prices for a sample of stocks.

Stock	Number of Shares	Price	
		T	T + 1
A	1,000,000	60	80
B	10,000,000	20	35
C	30,000,000	18	25

A. Construct a *price-weighted* index for these three stocks, and compute the percentage change in the index for the period from T to T + 1.

B. Construct a *value-weighted* index for these three stocks, and compute the percentage change in the index for the period from T to T + 1.

C. Briefly discuss the difference in the results for the two indexes.

6. A. Given the data in Problem 5, construct an equal-weighted index by assuming $1,000 is invested in each stock. What is the percentage change in wealth for this portfolio?

B. Compute the percentage of price change for each of the stocks in Problem 5. Compute the arithmetic mean of these percentage changes. Discuss how this answer compares to the answer in Part A.

C. Compute the geometric mean of the percentage changes in Part B. Discuss how this result compares to the answer in Part B.

Examination Level III

7. An analyst is estimating various measures of spread for Airnet Systems, Inc. (NYSE: ANS). The following is a sample of quotes in ANS on the New York Stock Exchange on 10 March 2004 between 10:49:00 and 10:57:00.

Time	Bid Price ($)	Ask Price ($)
10:49:44	4.69	4.74
10:50:06	4.69	4.75
10:50:11	4.69	4.76
10:50:14	4.70	4.76
10:54:57	4.70	4.75
10:56:32	4.70	4.75

Source: Trade and Quote (TAQ) database, NYSE.

A buyer-initiated trade in ANS was entered at 10:50:06 and was executed at 10:50:07 at a price of $4.74. For this trade, answer the following:

A. What is the quoted spread?

B. What is the effective spread?

C. When would the effective and quoted spreads be equal?

8. An investment manager placed a limit order to buy 500,000 shares of Alpha Corporation at $21.35 limit at the opening of trading on 8 February. The closing market price of Alpha Corporation on 7 February was also $21.35. The limit order filled 40,000 shares, and the remaining 460,000 shares were never filled. Some good news came out about Alpha Corporation on 8 February, and its price increased to $23.60 by the end of that day. However, by the close of trading on 14 February, the price had declined to $21.74. The investment manager is analyzing the missed trade opportunity cost using the closing price on 7 February as the benchmark price.

A. What is the estimate of the missed trade opportunity cost if it is measured at a one-day interval after the decision to trade?

B. What is the estimate of the missed trade opportunity cost if it is measured at a one-week interval after the decision to trade?

C. What are some of the problems in estimating the missed trade opportunity cost?

9. Famed Investments has a C$25 million portfolio. It follows an active approach to investment management and, on average, turns the portfolio over twice a year. That is, it expects to trade 200% of the value of the portfolio over the next year. Every time Famed Investments buys or sells securities, it incurs execution costs of 75 basis points, on average. It expects an annual return before execution costs of 8%. What is the expected return net of execution costs?

CHAPTER 5

Examination Level III (Case)

Rimfire Investment Management (RIM) is a large mutual fund organization with a tradition of providing individual investors with low-cost mutual fund alternatives. In recent years, RIM funds have experienced relatively poor performance and the result has been a decline in both assets under management and the number of investor accounts.

Donald Tolar, CFA, and Maria Bonetti have been charged with the task of recommending changes to the investment research and management functions at RIM. Tolar, Bonetti, and others in RIM management are concerned with deficiencies in three areas: research process and recommendations, asset management, and client education. These concerns have surfaced from conversations with, and surveys of, current, past, and prospective shareholders of RIM mutual funds. Some managers wonder if decision-making topics found in behavioral finance readings might be useful for addressing these deficiencies.

Bonetti believes behavioral finance can provide insight. She begins with RIM's chief economist. Two years ago he forecast GDP growth to be strong because the Federal Reserve would keep interest rates low, but instead GDP was marginally positive as the Fed increased rates in order to keep inflation in check. The chief economist blamed his inaccurate forecast on the Fed's decision to raise interest rates.

Tolar mentions that some of RIM's portfolio managers attempt to earn abnormal returns by trading arbitrage situations, but they recognize they are exposed to adverse risk faced by all arbitrageurs. In discussions with Tolar, one portfolio manager states that the specific risks to arbitrage can be managed and provide opportunity for profitable trading. To give an example, the manager first comments that "trading friction is beneficial to arbitrageurs because it provides higher returns," and in a second comment states that "fundamental risk is partially made better by shorting a substitute stock."

At the client level, one recommkendation is to improve RIM's services by providing financial planning advice to clients. This service will be accomplished either "in house" with RIM employees acting as financial advisors, or else "out-sourced" to financial planning groups that include the RIM mutual fund family as a component in their asset allocation advice to their clients.

Bonetti believes providing financial planning advice will lead to additional clients investing in RIM funds. In addition, the alternative will provide clients with a "psychological call option." If the investment choice turns out well, the client can take credit for the good decision. If it turns out badly, then the client can reduce the level of regret by blaming the financial advisor.

Bonetti notes that an examination of client portfolios shows that many clients with access to defined contribution plans, such as 401(k) and 403(b) plans, have made poor choices. Many portfolios exhibit poor diversification with an excess amount in the employee's own company stock. In addition, some plan participants with long time horizons have excess amounts in stable value funds rather than equity funds that will likely grow in value and provide an inflation hedge.

To increase the amount of funds that clients commit to equities, Tolar will meet with plan sponsors to educate them about the benefits to plan participants of proper diversification. He also will suggest that plan sponsors make available more equity fund choices because such an expansion of choices might result in participants having a higher allocation to equities.

Bonetti remarks "Well, now that we have considered client issues, let's get on with solving the problem of some funds generating poor risk/return performance. One approach to solve the problem is to offer an

Alpha fund whose mission is to 'exploit chronic market inefficiencies,' including arbitrage opportunities and other behavioral biases. In order to accomplish that goal the firm has set two guidelines: First, in order to provide a wide selection of opportunities, arbitrage positions will be limited to a one-year time horizon. And second, as a price target is approached, the position will be reduced, and any upward price target revision requires justification."

1. The chief economist's response to his forecast error describes an ego defence mechanism *best* identified as the:
   A. "If only" defence.
   B. "Ceteris paribus" defence.
   C. "I was almost right" defence.

2. Are the portfolio manager's two comments regarding arbitrage risk correct?
   A. Yes.
   B. No. Only the first comment is correct.
   C. No. Only the second comment is correct.

3. The "psychological call option" Bonetti describes is an example of:
   A. Regret framing.
   B. Cognitive heuristics.
   C. Self-attribution bias.

4. The tendency of some individual investors to have a significant portion of funds allocated to stable value funds is indicative of:
   A. Anchoring.
   B. Money illusion.
   C. Myopic loss aversion.

5. The solution Bonetti proposed to the problem of poor asset allocation choices seeks to exploit:
   A. Status quo bias.
   B. Myopic loss aversion.
   C. The endorsement effect.

6. Are Alpha fund's guidelines consistent with its mission?
   A. Yes.
   B. No. Only the first guideline is consistent.
   C. No. Only the second guideline is consistent.

7. The information in the table below pertains to a New Zealand pension plan sponsor.

NEW ZEALAND PENSION PLAN SPONSOR ACCOUNT VALUATIONS AND RETURNS
YEAR OF 2002 (ALL VALUES SHOWN IN NZ$ NET-OF-FEES)

Asset Category	Beginning Value	Ending Value	Actual Return	Benchmark Return
Domestic equities	143,295,254	149,799,531	4.54%	4.04%
Equity Mgr A	93,045,008	97,473,950	4.76	4.61
Equity Mgr B	50,250,246	52,325,581	4.13	4.31
International equities	35,762,987	38,049,834	6.39	5.96
Int'l Equity Mgr A	20,453,512	21,791,172	6.54	5.82
Int'l Equity Mgr B	15,309,475	16,258,662	6.20	6.02
Domestic fixed income	43,124,151	43,961,750	2.16	2.56
Fixed-Income Mgr A	24,900,250	25,298,654	1.60	1.99
Fixed-Income Mgr B	18,223,900	18,663,096	2.41	2.55
Total fund	222,182,392	231,811,115	4.33	4.22

Based on the information given in the table, address the following:
A. Which asset classes and managers have done relatively well and which have done relatively poorly as judged by returns alone?
B. Characterize the overall performance of the pension plan sponsor.
C. Assuming that relative outperformance or underperformance as indicated in the table is representative of performance over a substantial time period, would you recommend any changes? If so, what changes would you consider?

8. Investment markets are highly competitive and professional investors now dominate the marketplace. What should the average performance of all investors be, compared with market indexes? If international investment managers, as a group, beat some national market index, what does it tell us about the performance of local investment managers? Would you reach the opposite conclusion if international managers underperform, as a group, relative to some local market index?

CHAPTER 6

Examination Level I

1. An investor has an equal amount invested in each of the following four securities:

Security	Expected Annual Rate of Return
W	0.10
X	0.12
Y	0.16
Z	0.22

The investor plans to sell Security Y and use the proceeds to purchase a new security that has the same expected return as the current portfolio. The expected return for the investor's new portfolio, compared to the current portfolio, will be:
A. Lower regardless of changes in the correlation of returns among the securities.
B. The same regardless of changes in the correlation of returns among the securities.
C. lower only if the correlation of the new security with Securities W, X, and Z is lower than the correlation of Security Y with the other securities.

2. An investor currently holds a portfolio that is expected to return 12%. The investor is planning to sell one of the securities included in the current portfolio that has an expected return of 14% and use the proceeds to purchase a security that has an expected return of 13%. Compared to the investor's current portfolio, the expected return for the investor's revised portfolio will be:
A. Above 12% whether or not any change occurs in the standard deviation of the portfolio.
B. Below 12% whether or not any change occurs in the standard deviation of the portfolio.
C. Below 12% only if the standard deviation of the new security is higher than the standard deviation of the security that was sold.

Examination Level II

Mean–Variance Analysis

3. Given the large-cap stock index and the government bond index data in the following table, calculate the expected mean return and standard deviation of return for a portfolio 75% invested in the stock index and 25% invested in the bond index.

ASSUMED RETURNS, VARIANCES, AND CORRELATIONS

	Large-Cap Stock Index	Government Bond Index
Expected return	15%	5%
Variance	225	100
Standard deviation	15%	10%
Correlation	0.5	

For Problems 4 and 5, assume the following:
- Each stock has the same variance of return, denoted σ^2.
- The correlation between all pairs of stocks is the same, p.
- Stocks are equally weighted.

4. Suppose 0.3 is the common correlation of returns between any two stocks in a portfolio containing 100 stocks. Also, suppose the average variance of stocks in the portfolio is 625 (corresponding to a standard deviation of return of 25%). Calculate the portfolio standard deviation of return.

5. Suppose the average variance of return of all stocks in a portfolio is 625 and the correlation between the returns of any two stocks is 0.3. Calculate the variance of return of an equally weighted portfolio of 24 stocks. Then state that variance as a percent of the portfolio variance achievable given an unlimited number of stocks, holding stock variance and correlation constant.

CHAPTER 7

Examination Level I

1. An analyst gathered the following information about McGettrick Enterprises and the market:

Beta for McGettrick common stock	1.1
Estimated annual rate of return for McGettrick common stock	12.8%
Market risk premium	8.0%
Risk-free rate of return	4.0%

The common stock of Jimma Industries has the same estimated annual rate of return as McGettrick stock but has a higher covariance of returns with the market portfolio. Based on the security market line, are the stocks of McGettrick and Jimma, respectively, *most likely* valued appropriately? McGettrick stock is:
A. Undervalued and Jimma stock is overvalued.
B. Properly valued and Jimma stock is overvalued.
C. Properly valued and Jimma stock is undervalued.

2. An analyst gathered the following information:

Estimated rate of return for a stock	13%
Expected rate of return for the market portfolio	12%
Risk-free rate of return	3%

If the covariance of the returns on the stock with the returns on the market portfolio is equal to the variance of the returns on the market portfolio, the analyst's *most* appropriate conclusion is that the stock is:
A. Undervalued.
B. Properly valued.
C. Overvalued.

3. You expect an *RFR* of 10% and the market return (R_M) of 14%. Compute the expected (required) return for the following stocks, and plot them on an SML graph.

Stock	Beta $E(R)$
U	0.85
N	1.25
D	−0.20

4. An investor whose portfolio is located on the capital market line to the left of the market portfolio *most likely* has
   A. Lower unsystematic risk than the market portfolio.
   B. Higher unsystematic risk than the market portfolio.
   C. Less than 100% of his wealth invested in the market portfolio.

Examination Level II

Multifactor Models

5. Suppose that the expected return on the stock in the following table is 11%. Using a two-factor model, calculate the stock's return if the company-specific surprise for the year is 3%.

Variable	Actual Value (%)	Expected Value (%)	Stock's Factor Sensitivity
Change in interest rate	2.0	0.0	−1.5
Growth in GDP	1.0	4.0	2.0

CHAPTER 8

Examination Level II

1. In the past 20 years, the best-performing stock markets have been found in countries with the highest economic growth rates. Should the current growth rate guide you in choosing stock markets if the world capital market is efficient?

2. Here is some return information on firms of various sizes and their price-to-book (value) ratios. Based on this information, what can you tell about the *size* and *value* style factors?

Stock	Size	P/BV	Return (%)
A	Huge	High	4
B	Huge	Low	6
C	Medium	High	9
D	Medium	Low	12
E	Small	High	13
F	Small	Low	15

3. During the period 1960–2007, earnings of the S&P 500 Index companies have increased at an average rate of 8.18% per year and the dividends paid have increased at an average rate of 5.9% per year. Assume that:
   • Dividends will continue to grow at the 1960–2007 rate.
   • The required return on the index is 8%.
   • Companies in the S&P 500 Index collectively paid $27.73 billion in dividends in 2007.

Estimate the aggregate value of the S&P 500 Index component companies at the beginning of 2008 using the Gordon growth model.

CHAPTER 9

Examination Level I

1. You are analyzing the last five years of earnings per share data for a company. The figures are $4.00, $4.50, $5.00, $6.00, and $7.00. At what compound annual rate did EPS grow during these years?

2. An analyst expects that ka company's net sales will double and the company's net income will triple over the next five-year period starting now. Based on the analyst's expectations, which of the following *best* describes the expected compound annual growth?
   A. Net sales will grow 15% annually and net income will grow 25% annually.
   B. Net sales will grow 20% annually and net income will grow 40% annually.
   C. Net sales will grow 25% annually and net income will grow 50% annually.

3. Which of the following is an appropriate method of computing free cash flow to the firm?
   A. Add operating cash flows plus capital expenditures and deduct after-tax interest payments.
   B. Add operating cash flows plus after-tax interest payments and deduct capital expenditures.
   C. Deduct both after-tax interest payments and capital expenditures from operating cash flows.

4. An analyst gathered the following information about a company:

Current dividend (D_0) per share on common stock	€3.00
Expected annual growth rate for years 1 and 2	20%
Expected annual growth rate for year 3 and thereafter	9%
Expected risk-free rate of return	6%
Expected return on the market portfolio	11%
Beta for common stock	1.2

The value of a share of the company's common stock is *closest* to:
   A. €110.
   B. €120.
   C. €132.

5. An analyst gathered the following annual data for a company:

Net profit margin	3%
Total asset turnover	2.0
Total assets to equity	3.0
Net income for 2005	$20,000,000
Dividends paid on common stock during 2005 (D_0)	$5,000,000
Shares of common stock outstanding	2,000,000
Required rate of return on company's common stock	17.5%

If the growth rate in dividends is constant, the value of a share of the company's common stock at the end of 2005 is *closest* to:
A. $22.
B. $63.
C. $71.

Examination Level II

6. Do Pham is evaluating Phaneuf Accelerateur by using the FCFF and FCFE valuation approaches. Pham has collected the following information (currency in euros):
   - Phaneuf has net income of €250 million, depreciation of €90 million, capital expenditures of €170 million, and an increase in working capital of €40 million.
   - Phaneuf will finance 40% of the increase in net fixed assets (capital expenditures less depreciation) and 40% of the increase in working capital with debt financing.
   - Interest expenses are €150 million. The current market value of Phaneuf's outstanding debt is €1,800 million.
   - FCFF is expected to grow at 6.0% indefinitely, and FCFE is expected to grow at 7.0%.
   - The tax rate is 30%.
   - Phaneuf is financed with 40% debt and 60% equity. The before-tax cost of debt is 9%, and the before-tax cost of equity is 13%.
   - Phaneuf has 10 million outstanding shares.
   A. Using the FCFF valuation approach, estimate the total value of the firm, the total market value of equity, and the per-share value of equity.
   B. Using the FCFE valuation approach, estimate the total market value of equity and the per-share value of equity.

7. Watson Dunn is planning to value BCC Corporation, a provider of a variety of industrial metals and minerals. Dunn uses a single-stage FCFF approach. The financial information Dunn has assembled for his valuation is as follows:
   - The company has 1,852 million shares outstanding.
   - The market value of its debt is $3.192 billion.
   - The FCFF is currently $1.1559 billion.
   - The equity beta is 0.90; the equity risk premium is 5.5%; the risk-free rate is 5.5%.
   - The before-tax cost of debt is 7.0%.
   - The tax rate is 40%.
   - To calculate WACC, he will assume the company is financed 25% with debt.
   - The FCFF growth rate is 4%.
   Using Dunn's information, calculate the following:
   A. WACC.
   B. Value of the firm.
   C. Total market value of equity.
   D. Value per share.

8. Suppose an analyst uses an equity index as a comparison asset in valuing a stock. In making a decision to recommend purchase of an individual stock, which price multiple(s) would cause concern about the impact of potential overvaluation of the equity index?

Examination Level III

9. David Burke is considering investing in a mutual fund that is classified generically under the term "growth and income." In preparation for his CFA exams, Burke studied style investing. Using publicly available data sources, he gathered the following information about the mutual fund in question. How should he characterize the fund based on what he has learned in his CFA exam preparation?

	Fund	Market Benchmark
Number of stocks	80	600
Weighted-average market cap	$37 billion	$40 billion
Dividend yield	2.5%	2.1%
P/E	16	19
P/B	1.6	1.9
EPS growth (5-year projected)	11%	12%
Sector		
Consumer Discretionary	16%	10%
Consumer Staples	9	12
Energy	9	9
Finance	15	20
Health Care	9	7
Industrials	12	9
Information Technology	8	7
Materials	5	8
Telecommunications	7	10
Utilities	10	7

CHAPTER 11

Examination Level I

1. An assistant portfolio manager reviewed the prospectus of a bond that will be issued next week on January 1 of 2000. The call schedule for this $200 million, 7.75% coupon 20-year issue specifies the following:

> The Bonds will be redeemable at the option of the Company at any time in whole or in part, upon not fewer than 30 nor more than 60 days' notice, at the following redemption prices (which are expressed in percentages of principal amount) in each case together with accrued interest to the date fixed for redemption:
>
> If redeemed during the 12 months beginning January 1,
>
> | | |
> |---|---|
> | 2000 through 2005 | 104.00% |
> | 2006 through 2010 | 103.00% |
> | 2011 through 2012 | 101.00% |
> | from 2013 on | 100.00% |
>
> provided, however, that prior to January 1, 2006 the Company may not redeem any of the Bonds pursuant to such option, directly or indirectly, from or in anticipation of the proceeds of the issuance of any indebtedness for money borrowed having an interest cost of less than 7.75% per annum.

The prospectus further specifies that:

> The Company will provide for the retirement by redemption of $10 million of the principal amount of the Bonds each of the years 2010 to and including 2019 at the principal amount thereof, together with accrued interest to the date of redemption. The Company may also provide for the redemption of up to an additional $10 million principal amount . . . annually . . . such optional right being non-cumulative.

The assistant portfolio manager made the following statements to a client after reviewing this bond issue. Comment on each statement. (*When answering this question, remember that the assistant portfolio manager is responding to statements just before the bond is issued in 2000.*)

A. "My major concern is that if rates decline significantly in the next few years, this issue will be called by the Company in order to replace it with a bond issue with a coupon rate less than 7.75%."

B. "One major advantage of this issue is that if the Company redeems it *for any reason* in the first five years, investors are guaranteed receiving a price of 104, a premium over the initial offering price of 100."

C. "A beneficial feature of this issue is that it has a sinking fund provision that reduces the risk that the Company won't have enough funds to pay off the issue at the maturity date."

D. "A further attractive feature of this issue is that the Company can accelerate the payoff of the issue via the sinking fund provision, reducing the risk that funds will not be available at the maturity date."

E. In response to a client question about what will be the interest and principal that the client can depend on if $5 million par value of the issue is purchased, the assistant portfolio manager responded: "I can construct a schedule that shows every six months for the next 20 years the dollar amount of the interest and the principal repayment. It is quite simple to compute— basically it is just multiplying two numbers."

2. There are some securities that are backed by a pool of loans. These loans have a schedule of interest and principal payments every month and give each borrower whose loan is in the pool the right to pay off their respective loan at any time at par. Suppose that a portfolio manager purchased one of these securities. Can the portfolio manager rely on the schedule of interest and principal payments in determining the cash flow that will be generated by such securities (assuming no borrowers default)? Why or why not?

3. Suppose a portfolio manager purchases $1 million of par value of a Treasury inflation protection security. The real rate (determined at the auction) is 3.2%.

A. Assume that at the end of the first six months the CPI-U is 3.6% (annual rate). Compute the (i) inflation adjustment to principal at the end of the first six months, (ii) the inflation-adjusted principal at the end of the first six months, and (iii) the coupon payment made to the investor at the end of the first six months.

B. Assume that at the end of the second six months the CPI-U is 4.0% (annual rate). Compute the (i) inflation adjustment to principal at the end of the second six months, (ii) the inflation-adjusted principal at the end of the second six months, and (iii) the coupon payment made to the investor at the end of the second six months.

Examination Level II

4. In 1998 there were several developments in Europe leading to the liberalization of the European telecommunication industry. In October 1998, Moody's Investors Service published a report ("Rating Methodology: European Telecoms") addressing the issues in the rating of European telecommunication companies. Below are quotes from the report followed by questions that should be answered.

A. "We look carefully at a company's general funding strategy—the debt and equity markets the company accesses, and the sources of bank financing it arranges. . . . This becomes more important the lower down the rating scale, particularly in the case of high yield issuers. . . . " Why is the funding strategy of high-yield issuers of particular concern to Moody's analysts?

B. "As a very general rule of thumb, the larger the company's cushion of cash and assets above fixed payments due, the more able it will be to meet maturing debt obligations in potentially adverse conditions, and the higher the rating. In many cases, the size of this cushion may be less important than its predictability or sustainability. Moody's views the telecom industry as having generally very predictable revenue streams, which accounts for the relatively high level of ratings of the telecom industry compared to other industries." Explain why "predictability and sustainability" may be more important than size of a coverage ratio.

C. In discussing the financial measures it uses, the report explains the importance of "cash flow to debt figures." The report stated, "We also look at adjusted retained cash flow which includes any items which we view as non-discretionary to gauge the financial flexibility of a company, . . ." What is meant by "financial flexibility of a company"?

D. The quote in the previous part ends with "as well as adjusted debt figures which include unfunded pension liabilities and guarantees." Why would Moody's adjust debt figures for these items?

E. In the report, Moody's looks at various measures considered in ratings such as coverage ratios and capitalization ratios, and shows these ratios for a sample of European telecom companies. In each case when discussing ratios, Moody's notes the "loose correlation" between ratings and ratios; that is, it is not necessarily the case that companies with the best ratios will always receive a better rating. Moody's noted that "inconsistencies underscore the limitations of ratio analysis." Explain why one might expect a loose correlation between ratios and ratings.

5. Krane Products Inc. is a manufacturer of ski equipment. The company has been in operation since 1997. Ms. Andrews is a credit analyst for an investment management company. She has been asked to analyze Krane Products as a possible purchase for the bond portfolio of one of her firm's accounts. At the time of the analysis, Krane Products Inc. was rated BB by S&P. The bonds of the company trade in the market with the same spread as other comparable BB bonds. Ms. Andrews collected financial data for Krane Products Inc. for the years 2000 and 1999 and computed several financial ratios. Information for selected ratios is given below:

Ratios	2000	1999
EBIT interest coverage	3.8	2.7
EBITDA interest coverage	5.9	4.1
Funds from operations/Total debt	28.3%	24.5%
Free operating cash flow/Total debt	19.2%	1.2%
Pretax return on capital	24.4%	17.1%
Operating income/Sales	25.5%	19.5%
Long-term debt/Capitalization	55.0%	57.4%
Total debt/Capitalization	57.1%	59.5%

Based on the first three quarters of fiscal year 2001, Ms. Andrews projected the following ratios for 2001:

Ratios	2001
EBIT interest coverage	4.5
EBITDA interest coverage	6.9
Funds from operations/Total debt	41.5%
Free operating cash flow/Total debt	22.5%
Pretax return on capital	24.2%
Operating income/Sales	25.12%
Long-term debt/Capitalization	40.5%
Total debt/Capitalization	45.2%

Ms. Andrews obtained from S&P information about median ratios by credit rating. These ratios are reproduced below:

	AAA	AA	A	BBB	BB	B
EBIT interest coverage	12.9	9.2	7.2	4.1	2.5	1.2
EBITDA interest coverage	18.7	14.0	10.0	6.3	3.9	2.3
Funds from operations/Total debt	89.7	67.0	49.5	32.3	20.1	10.5
Free operating cash flow/Total debt	40.5	21.6	17.4	6.3	1.0	(4.0)
Pretax return on capital	30.6	25.1	19.6	15.4	12.6	9.2
Operating income/Sales	30.9	25.2	17.9	15.8	14.4	11.2
Long-term debt/Capitalization	21.4	29.3	33.3	40.8	55.3	68.8
Total debt/Capitalization	31.8	37.0	39.2	46.4	58.5	71.4

What do you think Ms. Andrews' recommendation will be with respect to the purchase of the bonds of Krane Products Inc.? Explain why.

Examination Level III

6. Other than changes in the rate of inflation, specify two factors that impact the yields available on inflation-indexed bonds.

7. Consider a collateralized debt obligation (CDO) that has a $250 million structure. The collateral consists of bonds that mature in seven years, and the coupon rate for these bonds is the seven-year Treasury rate plus 500 bps. The senior tranche comprises 70% of the structure and has a floating coupon of LIBOR plus 50 bps. There is only one junior tranche that comprises 20% of the structure and has a fixed coupon of 7-year Treasury rate plus 300 bps. Compute the rate of return earned by the equity tranche in this CDO if the seven-year Treasury rate is 6% and the LIBOR is 7.5%. There are no defaults in the underlying collateral pool. Ignore the collateral manager's fees and any other expenses.

CHAPTER 12

Examination Level I

1. Determine whether the yield to maturity of a 6.5% 20-year bond that pays interest semiannually and is selling for $90.68 is 7.2%, 7.4%, or 7.8%.

2. The following yields and prices were reported in the financial press. Are any of them incorrect assuming that the reported price and coupon rate are correct? If so, explain why. (No calculations are needed to answer this question.)

Bond	Price	Coupon Rate (%)	Current Yield (%)	Yield to Maturity (%)
A	100	6.0	5.0	6.0
B	110	7.0	6.4	6.1
C	114	7.5	7.1	7.7
D	95	4.7	5.2	5.9
E	75	5.6	5.1	4.1

3. A. Which of the following three bonds has the greatest dependence on reinvestment income to generate the computed yield? Assume that each bond is offering the same yield to maturity. (No calculations are needed to answer this question.)

Bond	Maturity	Coupon Rate (%)
X	25 years	0
Y	20 years	7
Z	20 years	8

B. Which of the three bonds in Part. A has the least dependence on reinvestment income to generate the computed yield? Assume that each bond is offering the same yield to maturity. (No calculations are needed to answer this question.)

4. James Smith and Donald Robertson are assistant portfolio managers for Micro Management Partners. In a review of the interest rate risk of a portfolio, Smith and Robertson discussed the riskiness of two Treasury securities. Following is the information about these two Treasuries:

Bond	Price	Modified Duration
A	90	4
B	50	6

Smith noted that Treasury bond B has more price volatility because of its higher modified duration. Robertson disagreed noting that Treasury bond A has more price volatility despite its lower modified duration. Which manager is correct?

5. An investor holds two bonds in her portfolio as follows:

Bond	Market Value ($)	Duration
3-year, 6% coupon	300,521	2.67
10-year, 5% coupon	567,000	6.11

The portfolio's duration is *closest* to:
A. 4.51.
B. 5.11.
C. 5.45.

6. A bond with a par value of $1,000 has a duration of 6.2. If the yield on the bond is expected to change from 8.80% to 8.95%, the estimated new price for the bond following the expected change in yield is *best* described as being:
A. 0.93% lower than the bond's current price.
B. 1.70% lower than the bond's current price.
C. 10.57% lower than the bond's current price.

Examination Level II

7. You are the financial consultant to a pension fund. After your presentation to the trustees of the fund, you asked the trustees if they have any questions. You receive the two questions below. Answer each one.

A. "The yield curve is upward-sloping today. Doesn't this suggest that the market consensus is that interest rates are expected to increase in the future and therefore you should reduce the interest rate risk exposure for the portfolio that you are managing for us?"

B. "I am looking over one of the pages in your presentation that shows spot rates and I am having difficulty in understanding it. The spot rates at the short end (up to three years) are increasing with maturity. For maturities greater than three years but less than eight years, the spot rates are declining with maturity. Finally, for maturities greater than eight years the spot rates are virtually the same for each maturity. There is simply no expectations theory that would explain that type of shape for the term structure of interest rates. Is this market simply unstable?"

CHAPTER 13

Examination Level I

1. You are provided with the following information on put and call options on a stock:
   Call price, c_0 = $6.64
   Put price, p_0 = $2.75
   Exercise price, X = $30
   Days to option expiration = 219
   Current stock price, S_0 = $33.19

   Put–call parity shows the equivalence of a call/bond portfolio (fiduciary call) and a put/underlying portfolio (protective put). Illustrate put–call parity assuming stock prices at expiration (S_T) of $20 and of $40. Assume that the risk-free rate, r, is 4%.

2. You simultaneously purchase an underlying priced at $77 and write a call option on it with an exercise price of $80 and selling at $6.
   A. What is the term commonly used for the position that you have taken?
   B. Determine the value at expiration and the profit for your strategy under the following outcomes:
      i. The price of the underlying at expiration is $70.
      ii. The price of the underlying at expiration is $75.
      iii. The price of the underlying at expiration is $80.
      iv. The price of the underlying at expiration is $85.
   C. Determine the following:
      i. The maximum profit.
      ii. The maximum loss.
      iii. The expiration price of the underlying at which you would realize the maximum profit.
      iv. The expiration price of the underlying at which you would incur the maximum loss.
   D. Determine the break-even price at expiration.

3. Suppose you simultaneously purchase an underlying priced at $77 and a put option on it, with an exercise price of $75 and selling at $3.
   A. What is the term commonly used for the position that you have taken?
   B. Determine the value at expiration and the profit for your strategy under the following outcomes:
      i. The price of the underlying at expiration is $70.
      ii. The price of the underlying at expiration is $75.
      iii. The price of the underlying at expiration is $80.
      iv. The price of the underlying at expiration is $85.
      v. The price of the underlying at expiration is $90.
   C. Determine the following:
      i. The maximum profit.
      ii. The maximum loss.
      iii. The expiration price of the underlying at which you would incur the maximum loss.
   D. Determine the breakeven price at expiration.

4. The recent price per share of Dragon Vacations Inc. is $50 per share. Calls with exactly six months left to expiration are available on Dragon with strikes of $45, $50, and $55. The prices of the calls are $8.75, $6.00, and $4.00, respectively. Assume that each call contract is for 100 shares of stock and that at initiation of the strategy the investor purchases 100 shares of Dragon at the current market price. Further assume that the investor will close out the strategy in six months when the options expire, including the sale of any stock not delivered against exercise of a call, whether the stock price goes up or goes down. If the closing price of Dragon stock in six months is exactly $60, the profit to a covered call using the $50 strike call is *closest* to:
   A. $400.
   B. $600.
   C. $1,600.

Examination Level II

5. A security is currently worth $225. An investor plans to purchase this asset in one year and is concerned that the price may have risen by then. To hedge this risk, the investor enters into a forward contract to buy the asset in one year. Assume that the risk-free rate is 4.75%.
   A. Calculate the appropriate price at which this investor can contract to buy the asset in one year.
   B. Four months into the contract, the price of the asset is $250. Calculate the gain or loss that has accrued to the forward contract.
   C. Assume that eight months into the contract, the price of the asset is $200. Calculate the gain or loss on the forward contract.
   D. Suppose that at expiration, the price of the asset is $190. Calculate the value of the forward contract at expiration. Also indicate the overall gain or loss to the investor on the whole transaction.
   E. Now calculate the value of the forward contract at expiration assuming that at expiration, the price of the asset is $240. Indicate the overall gain or loss to the investor on the whole transaction. Is this amount more or less than the overall gain or loss from Part D?

Examination Level III

6. The trustees of a pension fund would like to examine the issue of protecting the bonds in the fund's portfolio against an increase in interest rates using options and futures. Before discussing this with their external bond fund manager, they decide to ask four consultants about their recommendations as to what should be done at this time. It turns out that each of them has a different recommendation. Consultant A suggests selling covered calls, Consultant B suggests doing nothing at all, Consultant C suggests selling interest rate futures, and Consultant D suggests buying puts. The reason for their different recommendations is that although all consultants understand the pension fund's objective of minimizing risk, they differ with one another in regards to their outlook on future interest rates. One of the consultants believes interest rates are headed downward, one has no opinion, one believes that the interest rates would not change much in either direction, and one believes that the interest rates are headed upward. Based on the consultants' recommendations, could you identify the outlook of each consultant?

7. You are bullish about an underlying that is currently trading at a price of $80. You choose to go long one call option on the underlying with an exercise price of $75 and selling at $10, and go short one call option on the underlying with an exercise price of $85 and selling at $2. Both the calls expire in three months.
   A. What is the term commonly used for the position that you have taken?
   B. Determine the value at expiration and the profit for your strategy under the following outcomes:

      i. The price of the underlying at expiration is $89.

      ii. The price of the underlying at expiration is $78.

      iii. The price of the underlying at expiration is $70.

   C. Determine the following:

      i. The maximum profit.

      ii. The maximum loss.

   D. Determine the breakeven underlying price at expiration of the call options.

   E. Verify that your answer to Part D above is correct.

8. A stock is currently trading at a price of $114. You construct a butterfly spread using calls of three different strike prices on this stock, with the calls expiring at the same time. You go long one call with an exercise price of $110 and selling at $8, go short two calls with an exercise price of $115 and selling at $5, and go long one call with an exercise price of $120 and selling at $3.

   A. Determine the value at expiration and the profit for your strategy under the following outcomes:

      i. The price of the stock at the expiration of the calls is $106.

      ii. The price of the stock at the expiration of the calls is $110.

      iii. The price of the stock at the expiration of the calls is $115.

      iv. The price of the stock at the expiration of the calls is $120.

      v. The price of the stock at the expiration of the calls is $123.

   B. Determine the following:

      i. The maximum profit.

      ii. The maximum loss.

      iii. The stock price at which you would realize the maximum profit.

      iv. The stock price at which you would incur the maximum loss.

   C. Determine the breakeven underlying price at expiration of the call options.

CHAPTER 14

Examination Level II

1. A. In what sense does a convertible bond typically have multiple embedded options?

   B. Why is it complicated to value a convertible bond?

2. In the October 26, 1992, prospectus summary of the Staples 5% convertible subordinated debentures due 1999, the offering stated: "Convertible into Common Stock at a conversion price of $45 per share . . ." Since the par value is $1,000, what is the conversion ratio?

3. Mary Craft is expecting large-capitalization stocks to rally close to the end of the year. She is pessimistic, however, about the performance of small-capitalization stocks. She decides to go long one December futures contract on the Dow Jones Industrial Average at a price of 9,020 and short one December futures contract on the S&P Midcap 400 Index at a price of 369.40. The multiplier for a futures contract on the Dow is $10, and the multiplier for a futures contract on the S&P Midcap 400 is $500. When Craft closes her position toward the end of the year, the Dow and S&P Midcap 400 futures prices are 9,086 and 370.20, respectively. How much is the net gain or loss to Craft?

4. A. The current price of gold is $300 per ounce. Consider the net cost of carry for gold to be zero. The risk-free interest rate is 6%. What should be the price of a gold futures contract that expires in 90 days?

   B. Using Part A above, illustrate how an arbitrage transaction could be executed if the futures contract is priced at $306 per ounce.

   C. Using Part A above, illustrate how an arbitrage transaction could be executed if the futures contract is priced at $303 per ounce.

5. Consider the following information on put and call options on a stock:

    Call price, c_0 = \$4.50
    Put price, p_0 = \$6.80
    Exercise price, X = \$70
    Days to option expiration = 139
    Current stock price, S_0 = \$67.32
    Risk-free rate, r = 5%

A. Use put-call parity to calculate prices of the following:
   i. Synthetic call option.
   ii. Synthetic put option.
   iii. Synthetic bond.
   iv. Synthetic underlying stock.
B. For each of the synthetic instruments in Part A, identify any mispricing by comparing the actual price with the synthetic price.
C. Based on the mispricing in Part B, illustrate an arbitrage transaction using a synthetic call.
D. Based on the mispricing in Part B, illustrate an arbitrage transaction using a synthetic put.

6. A stock currently trades at a price of \$100. The stock price can go up 10% or down 15%. The risk-free rate is 6.5%.
A. Use a one-period binomial model to calculate the price of a call option with an exercise price of \$90.
B. Suppose the call price is currently \$17.50. Show how to execute an arbitrage transaction that will earn more than the risk-free rate. Use 100 call options.
C. Suppose the call price is currently \$14. Show how to execute an arbitrage transaction that replicates a loan that will earn less than the risk-free rate. Use 100 call options.

Examination Level III

7. A company has issued floating-rate notes with a maturity of one year, an interest rate of LIBOR plus 125 basis points, and total face value of \$50 million. The company now believes that interest rates will rise and wishes to protect itself by entering into an interest rate swap. A dealer provides a quote on a swap in which the company will pay a fixed rate 6.5% and receive LIBOR. Interest is paid quarterly, and the current LIBOR is 5%. Indicate how the company can use a swap to convert the debt to a fixed rate. Calculate the overall net payment (including the loan) by the company. Assume that all payments will be made on the basis of 90/360.

CHAPTER 15

Examination Level III

1. Contrast the elements in the strategic asset allocation process that are relatively stable to those that frequently change.

2. Wendy Willet is chief investment officer of the Allright University Endowment (AUE) based in the United States. The strategic asset allocation of AUE is as follows, where percentages refer to proportions of the total portfolio:

Global equities		60%
U.S. equities	30%	
Ex-U.S. equities	30%	
Global fixed income		40%
U.S. bonds	30%	
Ex-U.S. bonds	10%	

Exhibit A.2 gives Willet's expectations.

Exhibit A.2	Expected Return for Asset Classes		
Asset Class		**Long-Term**	**Short-Term**
Global equities		A	B
U.S. equities		8%	14%
Ex-U.S. equities		10	10
Global fixed income		C	D
U.S. bonds		6%	8%
Ex-U.S. bonds		5	4

AUE runs a top-down global tactical asset allocation program that looks first at the overall allocation between global equities and global fixed income, then at the asset allocation within global
equities and global fixed income. Assume that the asset classes' risk characteristics are constant.
A. Calculate the long-term and short-term expectations for global equities (*A* and *B*, respectively)
   and global fixed income (*C* and *D*, respectively).
B. Determine and justify the changes in portfolio weights (in relation to the policy portfolio
   target weights) that would result from a global tactical asset allocation program.

3. Juan Varga is concerned about the performance and investment positions of an investment firm he
   hired five years ago. The firm, Galicia Investment Management, has been tasked with managing an
   active portfolio with a developed market mandate (MSCI World countries). Galicia is a well-
   known value manager. Varga performs some returns-based style analysis and finds the following
   results for the last two years (each quarterly snapshot is the result of a regression using the prior
   36 months return data).

	MSCI World Value (%)	**MSCI World Growth (%)**	**Other (%)**
1Q 2002	83	16	1
2Q 2002	77	20	3
3Q 2002	79	19	2
4Q 2002	68	29	3
1Q 2003	55	40	5
2Q 2003	48	45	7
3Q 2003	52	45	3
4Q 2003	55	43	2

What reasonable conclusions can Varga reach regarding the Galicia investment process?

4. Shawn Miller plans to use returns-based style analysis to analyze his global portfolio. He will use
   style indices as a proxy for style in the analysis and is debating whether to use indices like Dow
   Jones (which categorizes stocks as value, growth, or neutral) or like MSCI (which categorizes
   stocks only as value or growth).
   A. What are the benefits and drawbacks of each method?
   B. Does it matter which type Miller chooses for a returns-based style analysis?

CHAPTER 16

Examination Level III

1. The table below shows the active return for six periods for a bond portfolio. Calculate the portfolio's tracking risk for the six-period time frame.

Period	Portfolio Return	Benchmark Return	Active Return
1	14.10%	13.70%	0.400%
2	8.20	8.00	0.200
3	7.80	8.00	−0.200
4	3.20	3.50	−0.300
5	2.60	2.40	0.200
6	3.30	3.00	0.300

2. You are the manager of a portfolio consisting of three bonds in equal par amounts of $1,000,000 each. The first table below shows the market value of the bonds and their durations. (The price includes accrued interest.) The second table contains the market value of the bonds and their durations one year later.

INITIAL VALUES

Security	Price	Market Value	Duration	Dollar Duration
Bond #1	$106.110	$1,060,531	5.909	?
Bond #2	98.200	981,686	3.691	?
Bond #3	109.140	1,090,797	5.843	?
Portfolio dollar duration =				?

AFTER 1 YEAR

Security	Price	Market Value	Duration	Dollar Duration
Bond #1	$104.240	$1,042,043	5.177	?
Bond #2	98.084	980,461	2.817	?
Bond #3	106.931	1,068,319	5.125	?
Portfolio dollar duration =				?

As manager, you would like to maintain the portfolio's dollar duration at the initial level by rebalancing the portfolio. You choose to rebalance using the existing security proportions of one-third each. Calculate:
A. The dollar durations of each of the bonds.
B. The rebalancing ratio necessary for the rebalancing.
C. The cash required for the rebalancing.

Use the Following Information to Answer Questions 3–8

The State Retirement Board (SRB) provides a defined benefit pension plan to state employees. The governors of the SRB are concerned that their current fixed-income investments may not be appropriate because the average age of the state employee workforce has been increasing. In addition, a surge in retirements is projected to occur over the next 10 years.

Chow Wei Mei, the head of the SRB's investment committee, has suggested that some of the future pension payments can be covered by buying annuities from an insurance company. She proposes that the

SRB invest a fixed sum to purchase annuities in seven years time, when the number of retirements is expected to peak. Chow argues that the SRB should fund the future purchase of the annuities by creating a dedicated fixed-income portfolio consisting of corporate bonds, mortgage-backed securities, and risk-free government bonds.

Chow states:

> Statement #1: "To use a portfolio of bonds to immunize a single liability, and remove all risks, it is necessary only that 1) the market value of the assets be equal to the present value of the liability and 2) the duration of the portfolio be equal to the duration of the liability."

Chow lists three alternative portfolios that she believes will immunize a single, seven-year liability. All bonds in Exhibit A.3 are option-free government bonds.

EXHIBIT A.3	Alternative Portfolios for Funding an Annuity Purchase in 7 Years	
Portfolio	**Description**	**Portfolio Yield to Maturity (%)**
A	Zero-coupon bond with a maturity of 7 years	4.20
B	Bond with a maturity of 6 years	4.10
	Bond with a maturity of 8 years	
C	Bond with a maturity of 5 years	4.15
	Bond with a maturity of 9 years	

Chow then states:

> Statement #2: "Because each of these alternative portfolios immunizes this single, seven-year liability, each has the same level of reinvestment risk."

The SRB governors would like to examine different investment horizons and alternative strategies to immunize the single liability. The governors ask Chow to evaluate a contingent immunization strategy using the following assumptions:

- The SRB will commit a $100 million investment to this strategy.
- The horizon of the investment is 10 years.
- The SRB will accept a 4.50% return (semiannual compounding).
- An immunized rate of return of 5.25% (semiannual compounding) is possible.

Marshall Haley, an external consultant for the SRB, has been asked by the governors to advise them on the appropriateness of its investment strategies. Haley notes that, although state employee retirements are expected to surge over the next 10 years, the SRB will experience a continual stream of retirements over the next several decades. Hence, the SRB faces a schedule of liabilities, not a single liability. In explaining how the SRB can manage the risks of multiple liabilities, Haley makes the following statements:

> Statement #1: "When managing the risks of a schedule of liabilities, multiple liability immunization and cash flow matching approaches do not have the same risks and costs. Whereas cash flow matching generally has less risk of not satisfying future liabilities, multiple liability immunization generally costs less."

Statement #2: "Assuming that there is a parallel shift in the yield curve, to immunize multiple liabilities, there are three necessary conditions: i) the present value of the assets be equal to the present value of the liabilities; ii) the composite portfolio duration be equal to the composite liabilities duration; and iii) I cannot remember the third condition."

Statement #3: "Horizon matching can be used to immunize a schedule of liabilities."

3. Is Chow's Statement #1 correct?
   A. Yes.
   B. No, because credit risk must also be considered.
   C. No, because the risk of parallel shifts in the yield curve must also be considered.

4. Is Chow's Statement #2 correct?
   A. No, Portfolio B is exposed to less reinvestment risk than Portfolio A.
   B. No, Portfolio B is exposed to more reinvestment risk than Portfolio C.
   C. No, Portfolio C is exposed to more reinvestment risk than Portfolio B.

5. Which of the following is *closest* to the required terminal value for the contingent immunization strategy?
   A. $100 million.
   B. $156 million.
   C. $168 million.

6. Is Haley's Statement #1 correct?
   A. Yes.
   B. No, because multiple liability immunization is generally less risky than cash flow matching.
   C. No, because cash flow matching is generally less costly than multiple liability immunization.

7. The condition that Haley cannot remember in his Statement #2 is that the:
   A. Cash flows in the portfolio must be dispersed around the horizon date.
   B. Cash flows in the portfolio must be concentrated around the horizon date.
   C. Distribution of durations of individual assets in the portfolio must have a wider range than the distribution of the liabilities.

8. The *most* appropriate description of the strategy that Haley suggests in his Statement #3 is to create a portfolio that:
   A. Has cash flows concentrated around the horizon date.
   B. Is duration matched but uses cash flow matching in the later years of the liability schedule.
   C. Is duration matched but uses cash flow matching in the initial years of the liability schedule.

CHAPTER 17

Examination Level I

1. A. Briefly explain the concept of the *efficient market hypothesis* (EMH) and each of its three forms—*weak, semistrong*, and *strong*—and briefly discuss the degree to which existing empirical evidence supports each of the three forms of the EMH.
   B. Briefly discuss the implications of the efficient market hypothesis for investment policy as it applies to:
      i. Technical analysis in the form of charting, and
      ii. Fundamental analysis.
   C. Briefly explain *two* major roles or responsibilities of portfolio managers in an efficient market environment.
   D. Briefly discuss whether active asset allocation among countries could consistently outperform a world market index. Include a discussion of the implications of *integration versus segmentation* of international financial markets as it pertains to portfolio diversification, but ignore the issue of stock selection.

Use the Following Information to Answer Question 2

Global Leveraged Equity Fund (GLEF) has three classes of shares, each holding the same portfolio of securities but having a different expense structure. The following table summarizes the expenses of these classes of shares.

EXPENSE COMPARISON FOR THREE CLASSES OF GLEF

	Class A	Class B*	Class C
Sales charge (load) on purchases	5%	None	None
Deferred sales charge (load) on redemptions	None	4% in the first year, declining by 1% each year thereafter	1% for the initial 2 years only
Annual expenses:			
Distribution fee	0.25%	0.50%	0.50%
Management fee	0.50%	0.50%	0.50%
Other expenses	0.50%	0.50%	0.50%
	1.25%	1.50%	1.50%

*Class B shares automatically convert to Class A shares 72 months (6 years) after purchase.

Assume that expense percentages given will be constant at the given values. Assume that the deferred sales charges are computed on the basis of NAV.

An investor is considering the purchase of GLEF shares. The investor expects equity investments with risk characteristics similar to GLEF to earn 9% per year. He decides to make his selection of fund share class based on an assumed 9% return in each year, gross of any of the expenses given in the preceding table.

2. Decide which class of shares of GLEF is best for the investor if he plans to liquidate his investment toward the end of
   A. Year 1.
   B. Year 3.
   C. Year 5.
   D. Year 15.

Examination Level II

3. Which of the following statements clearly *conflicts* with the recommended procedures for compliance presented in the CFA Institute *Standards of Practice Handbook?*
   A. Firms should disclose to clients the personal investing policies and procedures established for their employees.
   B. Prior approval must be obtained for the personal investment transactions of all employees.
   C. For confidentiality reasons, personal transactions and holdings should not be reported to employers unless mandated by regulatory organizations.
   D. Personal transactions should be defined as including transactions in securities owned by the employee and members of his or her immediate family and transactions involving securities in which the employee has a beneficial interest.

Examination Level III

4. The Medical Research Foundation (MRF) has just learned that it will receive a $45 million cash gift in three months. The gift will greatly increase the size of the foundation's endowment from its

current $10 million. The foundation's grant-making (spending) policy has been to pay out virtually all of its annual net investment income. Because MRF's investment approach has been conservative, the endowment portfolio now consists almost entirely of fixed-income assets. The finance committee understands that these actions are causing the real value of foundation assets and the real value of future grants to decline because of inflation effects. Until now, the finance committee has believed it had no alternative to these actions, given the large immediate cash needs of the research programs being funded and the size of the foundation's capital base. The foundation's annual grants must at least equal 5% of its assets' market value to maintain its U.S. tax-exempt status, a requirement that is expected to continue indefinitely. No additional gifts or fundraising activity are expected for the foreseeable future.

Given the change in circumstances that the cash gift will make, the finance committee wishes to develop new grant-making and investment policies. Annual spending must at least meet the 5% of market value requirement, but the committee is unsure how much higher spending can or should be. The committee wants to pay out as much as possible because of the critical nature of the research being funded; however, it understands that preserving the real value of the foundation's assets is equally important in order to preserve its future grantmaking capabilities. You have been asked to assist the committee in developing appropriate policies. Exhibit A.4 summarizes the capital markets data.

Recommend and justify a long-term asset allocation.

EXHIBIT A.4	Capital Markets Annualized Return Data	
Asset	1926–1992 Average	1993–2000 Consensus Forecast
U.S. Treasury bills	3.7%	4.2%
Intermediate-term U.S. T-bonds	5.2	5.8
Long-term U.S. T-bonds	4.8	7.7
U.S. corporate bonds (AAA)	5.5	8.7
Non-U.S. bonds (AAA)	N/A	8.4
U.S. common stocks (large cap)	10.3	9.0
U.S. common stocks (small cap)	12.2	12.0
Non-U.S. common stocks (all)	N/A	10.1
Venture capital	N/A	15.5
Real estate	N/A	8.5
U.S. inflation	3.1%	3.5%

5. Katrina Lowry works for the pension department of National Software. Her supervisor has asked her to evaluate the different style alternatives for a large-cap mandate and to highlight their differences.
   A. State the three main large-cap styles.
   B. Describe the basic premise and risks of each style identified in Part A.

6. Ian Parkinson, as chief pension officer of a large defined-benefit plan, is considering presenting a recommendation that the pension plan make its first investments in three different types of hedge funds: (1) market neutral, (2) convertible arbitrage, and (3) global macro.

   An analyst who works for Parkinson comes by with the table given below and makes the following comment: "The returns for global macro are very impressive. In fact, there are other strategies that have significantly outperformed the S&P 500, equity market-neutral, and convertible arbitrage over the past 15 years. I think that, based on their returns, we should focus specifically on the other strategies."

PERFORMANCE OF HEDGE FUND STRATEGIES AND TRADITIONAL ASSETS 1990–2004

Fund or Asset	Annual Return (%)	Annual Standard Deviation (%)	Sharpe Ratio	Minimum Monthly Return (%)	Correlation with S&P 500	Correlation with Lehman Gov./Corp. Bond
HFCI	13.46	5.71	1.61	6.92	0.59	0.17
Event driven	13.46	5.59	1.64	−9.37	0.59	0.07
Equity hedge	15.90	9.34	1.24	−9.70	0.64	0.10
Equity market neutral	9.24	2.50	1.98	−1.07	0.09	0.24
Merger/risk arbitrage	9.07	4.86	0.99	−8.78	0.48	0.10
Distressed	15.28	6.07	1.81	−9.71	0.42	0.04
Fixed-income arbitrage	7.62	3.61	0.92	−6.61	0.06	−0.06
Convertible arbitrage	10.23	3.96	1.50	−3.42	0.19	0.13
Global macro	16.98	8.38	1.51	−5.41	0.26	0.34
Short selling	−0.61	19.39	−0.25	−14.62	−0.76	−0.01
S&P 500	10.94	14.65	0.45	−14.46	1.00	0.13
Lehman Gov./Corp. Bond	7.77	4.46	0.78	−4.19	0.13	1.00
MSCI World	7.08	14.62	0.19	−13.32	0.86	0.09
Lehman Global Bond	8.09	5.23	0.73	−3.66	0.11	0.74

Note: HFCI is the Hedge Fund Composite Index and was constructed by equally weighting the EACM 100, the HFR Fund Weighted Composite Index, and Credit Suisse/Tremont Hedge Fund Index.

Source: CISDM (2005c).

A. Describe the three alternative strategies that Parkinson is considering, and evaluate each with respect to their level of market risk and credit risk. Interpret their correlations with the S&P 500 and the Lehman Government/Corporate Bond indices as presented in the table above.

B. Critique the analyst's statement.

CHAPTER 18

Examination Level III

1. A plan sponsor is considering two U.K. investment managers, Manchester Asset Management and Oakleaf Equities, for the same mandate. Manchester will produce on average an annual value-added return of 1.5% over the benchmark, with variability of the excess returns of 2.24%. Oakleaf is expected to produce a higher annual value-added return of 4%, but with variability of excess returns around 10%. Using the information in the following table, determine which manager has a larger chance of underperforming the benchmark over periods of 1, 5, and 10 years. Explain the factor(s) causing the manager you identify to have a larger chance of underperforming for a given time period.

PROBABILITY OF A MANAGER OUTPERFORMING A BENCHMARK GIVEN
VARIOUS LEVELS OF INVESTMENT SKILL

Years	Information Ratio					
	0.20	0.30	0.40	0.67	0.80	1.00
1.0	57.93	61.79	65.54	74.75	78.81	84.03
5.0	67.26	74.88	81.45	93.20	96.32	98.73
10.0	73.65	82.86	89.70	98.25	99.43	99.92
20.0	81.70	91.01	96.32	99.86	99.98	99.99

2. You are a plan sponsor trying to decide between two equity portfolio managers. As you review the information you have gathered during your search, you notice that the two managers have similar investment styles and similar returns for the equity portion of their portfolios. However, the first manager, Acorn Asset Management, keeps its cash level very low, typically around 1% of assets. But the second manager, Zebra Investments, has much more cash in the portfolio and usually keeps approximately 10% in cash for clients' accounts.

Contrast Zebra and Acorn in terms of cash level in the accounts relative to overall portfolio performance. Are there time periods when higher or lower cash levels could be beneficial to an equity portfolio?

3. The Dennett Electronics Pension Plan had the following quarterly returns during the last two years:

1Q Year 1	+4.76%
2Q Year 1	+12.08%
3Q Year 1	−4.88%
4Q Year 1	+7.14%
1Q Year 2	−13.57%
2Q Year 2	+17.65%
3Q Year 2	+1.08%
4Q Year 2	+0.97%

Calculate the following:
A. Annual performance for Year 1.
B. Annual performance for Year 2.
C. Cumulative performance for the two-year period.
D. Annualized compound performance for the two-year period.

4. Renner, Williams, & Woods specializes in management of equity and balanced individual, personal accounts with an emphasis on income generation. Because most of its clients are elderly and care little about performance as long as they receive a steady, monthly income stream, Renner, Williams, & Woods decides that there is no reason to show a benchmark when presenting composite investment performance. Is this decision permissible under the GIPS standards?

Web CHAPTER 19

Examination Level I

1. Defining total asset turnover as revenue divided by average total assets, all else equal, impairment write-downs of long-lived assets owned by a company will most likely result in an increase for that company in
A. The debt-to-equity ratio but not the total asset turnover.
B. The total asset turnover but not the debt-to-equity ratio.
C. Both the debt-to-equity ratio and the total asset turnover.

2. Income tax expense reported on a company's income statement equals taxes payable, plus the net increase in
   A. Deferred tax assets and deferred tax liabilities.
   B. Deferred tax assets, less the net increase in deferred tax liabilities.
   C. Deferred tax liabilities, less the net increase in deferred tax assets.

3. When both the timing and amount of tax payments is uncertain, analysts should treat deferred tax liabilities as
   A. Equity.
   B. Liabilities.
   C. Neither liabilities nor equity.

4. Compared to an identical company that uses an operating lease, a company that uses a finance lease will *most likely* produce a reported return on equity (*ROE*) that
   A. Starts lower but rises during the life of the lease.
   B. Starts higher but declines during the life of the lease.
   C. Starts lower and remains so during the life of the lease.

5. An analyst gathered the following data for a company:

	2003	2004	2005
ROE	19.8%	20.0%	22.0%
Return on total assets	8.1%	8.0%	7.9%
Total asset turnover	2.0	2.0	2.1

   Based only on the information above, the *most* appropriate conclusion is that, over the period 2003 to 2005, the company's
   A. Net profit margin and financial leverage have decreased.
   B. Net profit margin and financial leverage have increased.
   C. Net profit margin has decreased but its financial leverage has increased.

6. A decomposition of ROE for Integra SA is as follows:

	2005	2004
ROE	18.90%	18.90%
Tax burden	0.70	0.75
Interest burden	0.90	0.90
EBIT margin	10.00%	10.00%
Asset turnover	1.50	1.40
Leverage	2.00	2.00

   Which of the following choices *best* describes reasonable conclusions an analyst might make based on this ROE decomposition?
   A. Profitability and the liquidity position both improved in 2005.
   B. The higher average tax rate in 2005 offset the improvement in profitability, leaving ROE unchanged.
   C. The higher average tax rate in 2005 offset the improvement in efficiency, leaving ROE unchanged.

Examination Level II

The Following Information Relates to Questions 7–13

Quentin Abay, CFA, is an analyst for a private equity firm interested in purchasing Bickchip Enterprises, a conglomerate. His first task is to determine the trends in ROE and the main drivers of the trends using DuPont analysis. To do so he gathers the data in Exhibit A.5.

EXHIBIT A.5	Selected Financial Data for Bickchip Enterprises (€ Thousands, except ratios)		
	2009	2008	2007
Revenue	72,448	66,487	55,781
Earnings before interest and tax	6,270	4,710	3,609
Earnings before tax	5,101	4,114	3,168
Net income	4,038	3,345	2,576
Asset turnover	0.79	0.76	0.68
Assets/Equity	3.09	3.38	3.43

After conducting the DuPont analysis, Abay believes that his firm could increase the ROE without operational changes. Further, Abay thinks that ROE could improve if the company divested segments that were generating the lowest returns on capital employed (total assets less non-interest-bearing liabilities). Segment EBIT margins in 2009 were 11% for Automation Equipment, 5% for Power and Industrial, and 8% for Medical Equipment. Other relevant segment information is presented in Exhibit A.6.

EXHIBIT A.6	Segment Data for Bickchip Enterprises (€ Thousands)					
	Capital Employed			Capital Expenditures (Excluding Acquisitions)		
Operating Segments	2009	2008	2007	2009	2008	2007
Automation Equipment	10,705	6,384	5,647	700	743	616
Power and Industrial	15,805	13,195	12,100	900	849	634
Medical Equipment	22,870	22,985	22,587	908	824	749
	49,380	42,564	40,334	2,508	2,416	1,999

Abay is also concerned with earnings quality, so he intends to calculate Bickchip's cash-flow-based accruals ratio and the ratio of operating cash flow before interest and taxes to operating income. To do so, he prepares the information in Exhibit A.7.

EXHIBIT A.7	Earnings Quality Data for Bickchip Enterprises (€ Thousands)		
	2009	2008	2007
Net income	4,038	3,345	2,576
Net cash flow provided by (used in) operating activity[a]	9,822	5,003	3,198
Net cash flow provided by (used in) investing activity	(10,068)	(4,315)	(5,052)
Net cash flow provided by (used in) financing activity[b]	(5,792)	1,540	(2,241)
Average net operating assets	43,192	45,373	40,421
[a]includes cash paid for taxes of:	(1,930)	(1,191)	(1,093)
[b]includes cash paid for interest of:	(1,169)	(596)	(441)

7. Over the three-year period presented in Exhibit A.5, Bickchip's return on equity is *best* described as:
   A. Stable.
   B. Trending lower.
   C. Trending higher.

8. Based on the DuPont analysis, Abay's belief regarding ROE is *most likely* based on:
   A. Leverage.
   B. Profit margins.
   C. Asset turnover.

9. Based on Abay's criteria, the business segment *best* suited for divestiture is:
   A. Medical equipment.
   B. Power and industrial.
   C. Automation equipment.

10. Bickchip's cash-flow-based accruals ratio in 2009 is *closest* to:
    A. 9.9%.
    B. 13.4%.
    C. 23.3%.

11. The cash-flow-based accruals ratios from 2007 to 2009 indicate:
    A. Improving earnings quality.
    B. Deteriorating earnings quality.
    C. No change in earnings quality.

12. The ratio of operating cash flow before interest and taxes to operating income for Bickchip for 2009 is *closest* to:
    A. 1.6.
    B. 1.9.
    C. 2.1.

13. Based on the ratios for operating cash flow before interest and taxes to operating income, Abay should conclude that:
    A. Bickchip's earnings are backed by cash flow.
    B. Bickchip's earnings are not backed by cash flow.
    C. Abay can draw no conclusion due to the changes in the ratios over time.

Web CHAPTER 20

Examination Level I

1. Credit analysts are likely to consider which of the following in making a rating recommendation?
   A. Business risk, but not financial risk.
   B. Financial risk, but not business risk.
   C. Both business risk and financial risk.

The Following Data Relate to Questions 2–4

Abitibi-Consolidated Inc. (TSX: A) is a Montreal, Canada–headquartered manufacturer of newsprint, groundwood papers, and lumber. In 2001, Abitibi reported the following results:

From the Income Statement (and Footnotes)

- Net sales was CAD$6.032 million.
- Net income was CAD$289 million.
- Net interest expense was CAD$470 million.
- The effective income tax rate was 29%.
- 440 million common shares were outstanding.

From the Balance Sheet (and Footnotes)

- Total assets were CAD$11,707 million (including CAD1,420 million of goodwill and approximately CAD$379 million of deferred charges).
- Total liabilities (claims senior to common equity) were CAD$8,442 million.

From the Statement of Cash Flows

- Depreciation and amortization was CAD$707 million.
- Other noncash expenses netted to CAD$91 million.
- Net investment in working capital (excluding cash and short-term debt) was CAD$50 million.
- Net investment in fixed capital approximated CAD$425 million.
- Net borrowing was −CAD$20 million (debt repayments exceeded new issuance).

Other

- The closing share price on 15 April 2002 was CAD$13.89.

2. A. Calculate P/E and P/S.
   B. Identify and explain one possible advantage and drawback of P/S compared to P/E.
   C. Identify and calculate one financial ratio that is relevant for evaluating the cost structure of Abitibi. Explain how that ratio relates to P/S.

3. A. Calculate P/B.
   B. Identify and explain one possible advantage and drawback of P/B compared to P/E.
   C. Calculate tangible book value per share and the price to tangible book value ratio.

4. A. Calculate P/CF using the CF approximation with EPS, depreciation, and amortization.
   B. Identify and explain one possible advantage and drawback of P/CF compared to P/E.

Examination Level II

5. Consider a company that pays out all its earnings. The required return for the firm is 13%.
   A. Compute the intrinsic P/E value of the company if its ROE is 15%.
   B. Compute the intrinsic P/E value of the company if its ROE is 20%.
   C. Discuss why your answers to Parts A and B differ or do not differ from one another.
   D. Suppose that the company's ROE is 13%. Compute its intrinsic P/E value.
   E. Would the answer to Part D change if the company retained half of its earnings instead of paying all of them out? Discuss why or why not.

6. Mohan Gupta is the portfolio manager of an India-based equity fund. He is analyzing the value of Tata Chemicals Ltd. (Bombay Stock Exchange: TATACHEM). Tata Chemicals is India's leading manufacturer of inorganic chemicals, and also manufactures fertilizers and food additives. Gupta has concluded that the DDM is appropriate to value Tata Chemicals.

   During the last five years (fiscal year ending 31 March 2004 to fiscal year ending 31 March 2008), the company has paid dividends per share of Rs. 5.50, 6.50, 7.00, 8.00, and 9.00, respectively. These dividends suggest an average annual growth rate in DPS of just above 13%. Gupta has decided to use a three-stage DDM with a linearly declining growth rate in Stage 2. He considers Tata Chemicals to be an average growth company, and estimates Stage 1 (the growth stage) to be 6 years and Stage 2 (the transition stage) to be 10 years. He estimates the growth rate to be 14% in Stage 1 and 10% in Stage 3. Gupta has estimated the required return on equity for Tata Chemicals to be 16%. Estimate the current value of the stock.

7. Casey Hyunh is trying to value the stock of Resources Limited. To easily see how a change in one or more of her assumptions affects the estimated value of the stock, she is using a spreadsheet model. The model has projections for the next four years based on the following assumptions.
   - Sales will be $300 million in Year 1.
   - Sales will grow at 15% in Years 2 and 3 and 10% in Year 4.
   - Operating profits (EBIT) will be 17% of sales in each year.

- Interest expense will be $10 million per year.
- Income tax rate is 30%.
- Earnings retention ratio would stay at 0.60.
- The per-share dividend growth rate will be constant from Year 4 forward and this final growth rate will be 2% less than the growth rate from Year 3 to Year 4.

The company has 10 million shares outstanding. Hyunh has estimated the required return on Resources' stock to be 13%.

A. Estimate the value of the stock at the end of Year 4 based on the above assumptions.
B. Estimate the current value of the stock using the above assumptions.
C. Hyunh is wondering how a change in the projected sales growth rate would affect the estimated value. Estimate the current value of the stock if the sales growth rate in Year 3 is 10% instead of 15%.

CREDITS FOR APPENDIX A

Chapter 1 questions 1, 2, 3, 4 p. 601; Chapter 1 Appendix questions A1, A2, A3 p. 602; Chapter 4 questions 1, 2, 4 p. 606; Chapter 6 questions 1, 2 p. 609; Chapter 7 questions 1, 2, 4 p. 610; Chapter 9 questions 1, 2, 3, 4, 5 p. 611; Chapter 11 question 1 p. 612, Questions 2, 3 p. 213; Chapter 12 questions 1, 2, p. 612, Questions 3, 4, 5, 6 p. 615; Chapter 13 questions 1, 2 p. 615, Questions 3, 4 p. 616; Chapter 17 question 1 p. 620; Chapter 19 questions 1, 2, 3, 4, 5, 6 p. 623; Chapter 20 questions 1, 2, 3, 4 p. 625: Copyright 2009, CFA Institute. Reproduced and republished from *2009 Level I CFA Program Curriculum* with permission from CFA Institute. All rights reserved.

Chapter 1 Appendix question A4 p. 603; Chapter 2 questions 1, 2, 3 p. 603, questions 4, 5, 6 p. 604; Chapter 6 questions 3, 4, 5 p. 609; Chapter 7 question 5 p. 610; Chapter 8 question 3 p. 610; Chapter 9 questions 6, 7 p. 611, question 8 p. 612; Chapter 11 questions 4, 5 p. 613; Chapter 12 question 7 p. 615; Chapter 13 question 5 p. 616; Chapter 14 questions 1, 2, 3, 4, 5, 6 p. 617; Chapter 17 question 3 p. 621; Chapter 19 question 7 p. 623, questions 8, 9, 10, 11 p. 624, questions 12, 13 p. 625; Chapter 20 questions 6, 7 p. 625: Copyright 2010, CFA Institute. Reproduced and republished from *2010 Level II CFA Program Curriculum* with permission from CFA Institute. All rights reserved.

Chapter 1 questions 5, 6 p. 602; Chapter 2 questions 7, 8 p. 604, questions 9, 10, 11, 12 p. 605, questions 13, 14 p. 606; Chapter 4 questions 7, 8, 9 p. 607; Chapter 5 questions 1, 2, 3, 4, 5, 6, 7 p. 608; Chapter 9 question 9 p. 612; Chapter 11 questions 6, 7 p. 614; Chapter 13 questions 6, 7, 8 p. 616; Chapter 14 question 7 p. 617; Chapter 15 questions 1, 2, 3, 4 p. 618; Chapter 16 questions 1, 2 p. 618, questions 3, 4, 5, 6, 7, 8 p. 620; Chapter 17 questions 4, 5, 6 p. 621; Chapter 18 questions 1, 2, 3 p. 622, question 4 p. 623: Copyright 2010, CFA Institute. Reproduced and republished from *2010 Level III CFA Program Curriculum* with permission from CFA Institute. All rights reserved.

Chapter 1 Appendix questions A5, A6 p. 603; Chapter 3 questions 1, 2, 3 p. 606; Chapter 5 question 8 p. 609; Chapter 8 questions 1, 2 p. 610; Chapter 17 question 2 p. 620; Chapter 20 question 5 p. 625: Solnik, GLOBAL INVESTMENTS, © 2009 Pearson Education, Inc. Reproduced by permission of Pearson Education, Inc.

Chapter 4 question 3 p. 606, questions 5, 6 p. 607; Chapter 7 question 3 p. 610: *From Investment Analysis and Portfolio Management*, Eighth Edition, by Frank K. Reilly, CFA and Keith C. Brown.

HOW TO BECOME A CFA® CHARTERHOLDER

As mentioned in the section on career opportunities, the professional designation of Chartered Financial Analyst (CFA) is becoming a significant requirement for a career in investment analysis and/or portfolio management. For that reason, this section presents the history and objectives of CFA Institute and general guidelines for acquiring the CFA designation. If you are interested in the program, you can write or e-mail CFA Institute for more information.

The CFA examinations were first offered in 1963 by the Institute of Chartered Financial Analysts (ICFA), which was formed in 1959 to enhance the professionalism of those involved in various aspects of the investment decision-making process and to recognize those who achieve a high level of professionalism. The ICFA combined with the Financial Analysts Federation in 1990 to form the Association for Investment Management and Research, which became CFA Institute in early 2004.

The mission of CFA Institute is to lead the investment profession globally by setting the highest standards of ethics, education, and professional excellence. As applied to the CFA program, the focus of CFA Institute is:

- To develop and keep current a "body of knowledge" applicable to the investment decision-making process. The principal components of this knowledge are financial accounting, economics, both debt and equity securities analysis, portfolio management, ethical and professional standards, and quantitative techniques.
- To administer a study and examination program for eligible candidates, the primary objectives of which are to assist the candidate in mastering and applying the body of knowledge and to test the candidate's competency in the knowledge gained.
- To award the professional CFA designation to those candidates who have passed three examination levels (encompassing a total of 18 hours of testing over a minimum of 2 years), who meet stipulated standards of professional conduct, and who otherwise are eligible for membership in CFA Institute.
- CFA Institute also provides a useful and informative program of continuing education through seminars, publications, and other formats that enable members, candidates, and others in the investment constituency to be more aware of and to better utilize the changing and expanding body of knowledge.

- Importantly, CFA Institute also sponsors and enforces a *Code of Ethics and Standards of Professional Conduct* that apply to enrolled candidates and to all members.

To enter the CFA program an applicant must have a bachelor's degree (or the equivalent work experience). Students who confirm they are in their final year of a degree program may register and enroll for Level I of the CFA program. Student candidates can take the CFA Level I exam and receive results but will not be allowed to enroll for the Level II exam until confirmation of a degree has been provided. A candidate may sit for all three examinations without having had investment experience per se or having joined a member society or chapter of CFA Institute. However, after passing the three examination levels, the CFA Charter will not be awarded unless or until the candidate:

- Has at least four years of acceptable work experience, and
- Has been accepted for regular membership in CFA Institute and has applied for regular membership in an affiliated society.

The curriculum of the CFA study program covers:

1. Ethical and Professional Standards
2. Quantitative Methods
3. Economics
4. Financial Statement Analysis
5. Corporate Finance
6. Analysis of Debt Investments
7. Analysis of Equity Investments
8. Analysis of Derivatives
9. Analysis of Alternative Investments
10. Portfolio Management and Wealth Planning

Members and candidates are typically employed in the investment field. From 1963 to July 2008, over 100,000 charters have been awarded. There were more than 175,000 candidate registrations for the 2008 CFA Program. If you are interested in learning more about the CFA Program, CFA Institute has a booklet that describes the program and includes an application form. The address is: CFA Institute, Attn: Information Central, P.O. Box 3668, Charlottesville, Virginia, 22903, USA. You may also find more information at CFA Institute website (http://www.cfainstitute.org), or by requesting a booklet by e-mail to info@cfainstitute.org.

Copyright CFA Institute. Reproduced and republished from the CFA Institute with permission from CFA Institute. All rights reserved.

CODE OF ETHICS AND STANDARDS OF PROFESSIONAL CONDUCT

Preamble

The CFA Institute Code of Ethics and Standards of Professional Conduct (Code and Standards) are fundamental to the values of CFA Institute and essential to achieving its mission to lead the investment profession globally by setting high standards of education, integrity, and professional excellence. High ethical standards are critical to maintaining the public's trust in financial markets and in the investment profession. Since their creation in the 1960s, the Code and Standards have promoted the integrity of CFA Institute members and served as a model for measuring the ethics of investment professionals globally, regardless of job function, cultural differences, or local laws and regulations. All CFA Institute members (including holders of the Chartered Financial Analyst® [CFA®] designation) and CFA candidates must abide by the Code and Standards and are encouraged to notify their employer of this responsibility. Violations may result in disciplinary sanctions by CFA Institute. Sanctions can include revocation of membership, candidacy in the CFA Program, and the right to use the CFA designation.

The Code of Ethics

Members of CFA Institute (including Chartered Financial Analyst® [CFA®] charterholders and candidates for the CFA designation ["Members and Candidates"]) must:

- Act with integrity, competence, diligence, respect, and in an ethical manner with the public, clients, prospective clients, employers, employees, colleagues in the investment profession, and other participants in the global capital markets.
- Place the integrity of the investment profession and the interests of clients above their own personal interests.
- Use reasonable care and exercise independent professional judgment when conducting investment analysis, making investment recommendations, taking investment actions, and engaging in other professional activities.
- Practice and encourage others to practice in a professional and ethical manner that will reflect credit on themselves and the profession.
- Promote the integrity of, and uphold the rules governing, capital markets.
- Maintain and improve their professional competence and strive to maintain and improve the competence of other investment professionals.

Standards of Professional Conduct

I. Professionalism

A. Knowledge of the Law. Members and Candidates must understand and comply with all applicable laws, rules, and regulations (including the CFA Institute Code of Ethics and Standards of Professional Conduct) of any government, regulatory organization, licensing agency, or professional association governing their professional activities. In the event of conflict, Members and Candidates must comply with the more strict law, rule, or regulation. Members and Candidates must not knowingly participate or assist in and must dissociate from any violation of such laws, rules, or regulations.

B. Independence and Objectivity. Members and Candidates must use reasonable care and judgment to achieve and maintain independence and objectivity in their professional activities. Members and Candidates must not offer, solicit, or accept any gift, benefit, compensation, or consideration that reasonably could be expected to compromise their own or another's independence and objectivity.

C. Misrepresentation. Members and Candidates must not knowingly make any misrepresentations relating to investment analysis, recommendations, actions, or other professional activities.

D. Misconduct. Members and Candidates must not engage in any professional conduct involving dishonesty, fraud, or deceit or commit any act that reflects adversely on their professional reputation, integrity, or competence.

II. Integrity of Capital Markets

A. Material Nonpublic Information. Members and Candidates who possess material nonpublic information that could affect the value of an investment must not act or cause others to act on the information.

B. Market Manipulation. Members and Candidates must not engage in practices that distort prices or artificially inflate trading volume with the intent to mislead market participants.

III. Duties to Clients

A. Loyalty, Prudence, and Care. Members and Candidates have a duty of loyalty to their clients and must act with reasonable care and exercise prudent judgment. Members and Candidates must act for the benefit of their clients and place their clients' interests before their employer's or their own interests.

Copyright CFA Institute. Reproduced and republished from the CFA Institute Code of Ethics and Standards of Professional Conduct with permission from CFA Institute. All rights reserved.

In relationships with clients, Members and Candidates must determine applicable fiduciary duty and must comply with such duty to persons and interests to whom it is owed.

B. Fair Dealing. Members and Candidates must deal fairly and objectively with all clients when providing investment analysis, making investment recommendations, taking investment action, or engaging in other professional activities.

C. Suitability.

1. When Members and Candidates are in an advisory relationship with a client, they must:
   a. Make a reasonable inquiry into a client's or prospective clients' investment experience, risk and return objectives, and financial constraints prior to making any investment recommendation or taking investment action and must reassess and update this information regularly.
   b. Determine that an investment is suitable to the client's financial situation and consistent with the client's written objectives, mandates, and constraints before making an investment recommendation or taking investment action.
   c. Judge the suitability of investments in the context of the client's total portfolio.
2. When Members and Candidates are responsible for managing a portfolio to a specific mandate, strategy, or style, they must only make investment recommendations or take investment actions that are consistent with the stated objectives and constraints of the port folio.

D. Performance Presentation. When communicating investment performance information, Members or Candidates must make reasonable efforts to ensure that it is fair, accurate, and complete.

E. Preservation of Confidentiality. Members and Candidates must keep information about current, former, and prospective clients confidential unless:

1. The information concerns illegal activities on the part of the client or prospective client.
2. Disclosure is required by law.
3. The client or prospective client permits disclosure of the information.

IV. Duties to Employers

A. Loyalty. In matters related to their employment, Members and Candidates must act for the benefit of their employer and not deprive their employer of the advantage of their skills and abilities, divulge confidential information, or otherwise cause harm to their employer.

B. Additional Compensation Arrangements. Members and Candidates must not accept gifts, benefits, compensation, or consideration that competes with, or might reasonably be expected to create a conflict of interest with, their employer's interest unless they obtain written consent from all parties involved.

C. Responsibilities of Supervisors. Members and Candidates must make reasonable efforts to detect and prevent violations of applicable laws, rules, regulations, and the Code and Standards by anyone subject to their supervision or authority.

V. Investment Analysis, Recommendations, and Action

A. Diligence and Reasonable Basis. Members and Candidates must:

1. Exercise diligence, independence, and thoroughness in analyzing investments, making investment recommendations, and taking investment actions.
2. Have a reasonable and adequate basis, supported by appropriate research and investigation, for any investment analysis, recommendation, or action.

B. Communication with Clients and Prospective Clients. Members and Candidates must:

1. Disclose to clients and prospective clients the basic format and general principles of the investment processes used to analyze investments, select securities, and construct portfolios and must promptly disclose any changes that might materially affect those processes.
2. Use reasonable judgment in identifying which factors are important to their investment analyses, recommendations, or actions and include those factors in communications with clients and prospective clients.
3. Distinguish between fact and opinion in the presentation of investment analysis and recommendations.

C. Record Retention. Members and Candidates must develop and maintain appropriate records to support their investment analysis, recommendations, actions, and other investment-related communications with clients and prospective clients.

VI. Conflicts of Interest

A. Disclosure of Conflicts. Members and Candidates must make full and fair disclosure of all matters that could reasonably be expected to impair their independence and objectivity or interfere with respective duties to their clients, prospective clients, and employer. Members and Candidates must ensure that such disclosures are prominent, are delivered in plain language, and communicate the relevant information effectively.

B. Priority of Transactions. Investment transactions for clients and employers must have priority over investment transactions in which a Member or Candidate is the beneficial owner.

C. Referral Fees. Members and Candidates must disclose to their employer, clients, and prospective clients, as appropriate, any compensation, consideration, or benefit received from, or paid to, others for the recommendation of products or services.

VII. Responsibilities as a CFA Institute Member or CFA Candidate

A. Conduct as Members and Candidates in the CFA Program. Members and Candidates must not engage in any conduct that compromises the reputation or integrity of CFA Institute or the CFA designation or the integrity, validity, or security of the CFA examinations.

B. Reference to CFA Institute, the CFA designation, and the CFA Program. When referring to CFA Institute, CFA Institute membership, the CFA designation, or candidacy in the CFA Program, Members and Candidates must not misrepresent or exaggerate the meaning or implications of membership in CFA Institute, holding the CFA designation, or candidacy in the CFA Program.

INTEREST TABLES

TABLE D.1 Present Value of $1: PVIF $= 1/(1 + k)^t$

Period	1%	2%	3%	4%	5%	6%	7%	8%	9%	10%	12%	14%	15%	16%	18%	20%	24%	28%	32%	36%
1	.9901	.9804	.9709	.9615	.9524	.9434	.9346	.9259	.9174	.9091	.8929	.8772	.8696	.8621	.8475	.8333	.8065	.7813	.7576	.7353
2	.9803	.9612	.9426	.9246	.9070	.8900	.8734	.8573	.8417	.8264	.7972	.7695	.7561	.7432	.7182	.6944	.6504	.6104	.5739	.5407
3	.9706	.9423	.9151	.8890	.8638	.8396	.8163	.7938	.7722	.7513	.7118	.6750	.6575	.6407	.6086	.5787	.5245	.4768	.4348	.3975
4	.9610	.9238	.8885	.8548	.8227	.7921	.7629	.7350	.7084	.6830	.6355	.5921	.5718	.5523	.5158	.4823	.4230	.3725	.3294	.2923
5	.9515	.9057	.8626	.8219	.7835	.7473	.7130	.6806	.6499	.6209	.5674	.5194	.4972	.4761	.4371	.4019	.3411	.2910	.2495	.2149
6	.9420	.8880	.8375	.7903	.7462	.7050	.6663	.6302	.5963	.5645	.5066	.4556	.4323	.4104	.3704	.3349	.2751	.2274	.1890	.1580
7	.9327	.8706	.8131	.7599	.7107	.6651	.6227	.5835	.5470	.5132	.4523	.3996	.3759	.3538	.3139	.2791	.2218	.1776	.1432	.1162
8	.9235	.8535	.7894	.7307	.6768	.6274	.5820	.5403	.5019	.4665	.4039	.3506	.3269	.3050	.2660	.2326	.1789	.1388	.1085	.0854
9	.9143	.8368	.7664	.7026	.6446	.5919	.5439	.5002	.4604	.4241	.3606	.3075	.2843	.2630	.2255	.1938	.1443	.1084	.0822	.0628
10	.9053	.8203	.7441	.6756	.6139	.5584	.5083	.4632	.4224	.3855	.3220	.2697	.2472	.2267	.1911	.1615	.1164	.0847	.0623	.0462
11	.8963	.8043	.7224	.6496	.5847	.5268	.4751	.4289	.3875	.3505	.2875	.2366	.2149	.1954	.1619	.1346	.0938	.0662	.0472	.0340
12	.8874	.7885	.7014	.6246	.5568	.4970	.4440	.3971	.3555	.3186	.2567	.2076	.1869	.1685	.1372	.1122	.0757	.0517	.0357	.0250
13	.8787	.7730	.6810	.6006	.5303	.4688	.4150	.3677	.3262	.2897	.2292	.1821	.1625	.1452	.1163	.0935	.0610	.0404	.0271	.0184
14	.8700	.7579	.6611	.5775	.5051	.4423	.3878	.3405	.2992	.2633	.2046	.1597	.1413	.1252	.0985	.0779	.0492	.0316	.0205	.0135
15	.8613	.7430	.6419	.5553	.4810	.4173	.3624	.3152	.2745	.2394	.1827	.1401	.1229	.1079	.0835	.0649	.0397	.0247	.0155	.0099
16	.8528	.7284	.6232	.5339	.4581	.3936	.3387	.2919	.2519	.2176	.1631	.1229	.1069	.0930	.0708	.0541	.0320	.0193	.0118	.0073
17	.8444	.7142	.6050	.5134	.4363	.3714	.3166	.2703	.2311	.1978	.1456	.1078	.0929	.0802	.0600	.0451	.0258	.0150	.0089	.0054
18	.8360	.7002	.5874	.4936	.4155	.3503	.2959	.2502	.2120	.1799	.1300	.0946	.0808	.0691	.0508	.0376	.0208	.0118	.0068	.0039
19	.8277	.6864	.5703	.4746	.3957	.3305	.2765	.2317	.1945	.1635	.1161	.0829	.0703	.0596	.0431	.0313	.0168	.0092	.0051	.0029
20	.8195	.6730	.5537	.4564	.3769	.3118	.2584	.2145	.1784	.1486	.1037	.0728	.0611	.0514	.0365	.0261	.0135	.0072	.0039	.0021
25	.7798	.6095	.4776	.3751	.2953	.2330	.1842	.1460	.1160	.0923	.0588	.0378	.0304	.0245	.0160	.0105	.0046	.0021	.0010	.0005
30	.7419	.5521	.4120	.3083	.2314	.1741	.1314	.0994	.0754	.0573	.0334	.0196	.0151	.0116	.0070	.0042	.0016	.0006	.0002	.0001
40	.6717	.4529	.3066	.2083	.1420	.0972	.0668	.0460	.0318	.0221	.0107	.0053	.0037	.0026	.0013	.0007	.0002	.0001	*	*
50	.6080	.3715	.2281	.1407	.0872	.0543	.0339	.0213	.0134	.0085	.0035	.0014	.0009	.0006	.0003	.0001	*	*	*	*
60	.5504	.3048	.1697	.0951	.0535	.0303	.0173	.0099	.0057	.0033	.0011	.0004	.0002	.0001	*	*	*	*	*	*

*The factor is zero to four decimal places.

TABLE D.2 Present Value of an Annuity of $1 per Period for n Periods: $\text{PVIF A} = \sum_{t=1}^{n} \dfrac{1}{(1+k)^t} = \dfrac{1 - \dfrac{1}{(1+k)^n}}{k}$

Number of Payments	1%	2%	3%	4%	5%	6%	7%	8%	9%	10%	12%	14%	15%	16%	18%	20%	24%	28%	32%
1	0.9901	0.9804	0.9709	0.9615	0.9524	0.9434	0.9346	0.9259	0.9174	0.9091	0.8929	0.8772	0.8696	0.8621	0.8475	0.8333	0.8065	0.7813	0.7576
2	1.9704	1.9416	1.9135	1.8861	1.8594	1.8334	1.8080	1.7833	1.7591	1.7355	1.6901	1.6467	1.6257	1.6052	1.5656	1.5278	1.4568	1.3916	1.3315
3	2.9410	2.8839	2.8286	2.7751	2.7232	2.6730	2.6243	2.5771	2.5313	2.4869	2.4018	2.3216	2.2832	2.2459	2.1743	2.1065	1.9813	1.8684	1.7663
4	3.9020	3.8077	3.7171	3.6299	3.5460	3.4651	3.3872	3.3121	3.2397	3.1699	3.0373	2.9137	2.8550	2.7982	2.6901	2.5887	2.4043	2.2410	2.0957
5	4.8534	4.7135	4.5797	4.4518	4.3295	4.2124	4.1002	3.9927	3.8897	3.7908	3.6048	3.4331	3.3522	3.2743	3.1272	2.9906	2.7454	2.5320	2.3452
6	5.7955	5.6014	5.4172	5.2421	5.0757	4.9173	4.7665	4.6229	4.4859	4.3553	4.1114	3.8887	3.7845	3.6847	3.4976	3.3255	3.0205	2.7594	2.5342
7	6.7282	6.4720	6.2303	6.0021	5.7864	5.5824	5.3893	5.2064	5.0330	4.8684	4.5638	4.2883	4.1604	4.0386	3.8115	3.6046	3.2423	2.9370	2.6775
8	7.6517	7.3255	7.0197	6.7327	6.4632	6.2098	5.9713	5.7466	5.5348	5.3349	4.9676	4.6389	4.4873	4.3436	4.0776	3.8372	3.4212	3.0758	2.7860
9	8.5660	8.1622	7.7861	7.4353	7.1078	6.8017	6.5152	6.2469	5.9952	5.7590	5.3282	4.9464	4.7716	4.6065	4.3030	4.0310	3.5655	3.1842	2.8681
10	9.4713	8.9826	8.5302	8.1109	7.7217	7.3601	7.0236	6.7101	6.4177	6.1446	5.6502	5.2161	5.0188	4.8332	4.4941	4.1925	3.6819	3.2689	2.9304
11	10.3676	9.7868	9.2526	8.7605	8.3064	7.8869	7.4987	7.1390	6.8052	6.4951	5.9377	5.4527	5.2337	5.0286	4.6560	4.3271	3.7757	3.3351	2.9776
12	11.2551	10.5753	9.9540	9.3851	8.8633	8.3838	7.9427	7.5361	7.1607	6.8137	6.1944	5.6603	5.4206	5.1971	4.7932	4.4392	3.8514	3.3868	3.0133
13	12.1337	11.3484	10.6350	9.9856	9.3936	8.8527	8.3577	7.9038	7.4869	7.1034	6.4235	5.8424	5.5831	5.3423	4.9095	4.5327	3.9124	3.4272	3.0404
14	13.0037	12.1062	11.2961	10.5631	9.8986	9.2950	8.7455	8.2442	7.7862	7.3667	6.6282	6.0021	5.7245	5.4675	5.0081	4.6106	3.9616	3.4587	3.0609
15	13.8651	12.8493	11.9379	11.1184	10.3797	9.7122	9.1079	8.5595	8.0607	7.6061	6.8109	6.1422	5.8474	5.5755	5.0916	4.6755	4.0013	3.4834	3.0764
16	14.7179	13.5777	12.5611	11.6523	10.8378	10.1059	9.4466	8.8514	8.3126	7.8237	6.9740	6.2651	5.9542	5.6685	5.1624	4.7296	4.0333	3.5026	3.0882
17	15.5623	14.2919	13.1661	12.1657	11.2741	10.4773	9.7632	9.1216	8.5436	8.0216	7.1196	6.3729	6.0472	5.7487	5.2223	4.7746	4.0591	3.5177	3.0971
18	16.3983	14.9920	13.7535	12.6593	11.6896	10.8276	10.0591	9.3719	8.7556	8.2014	7.2497	6.4674	6.1280	5.8178	5.2732	4.8122	4.0799	3.5294	3.1039
19	17.2260	15.6785	14.3238	13.1339	12.0853	11.1581	10.3356	9.6036	8.9501	8.3649	7.3658	6.5504	6.1982	5.8775	5.3162	4.8435	4.0967	3.5386	3.1090
20	18.0456	16.3514	14.8775	13.5903	12.4622	11.4699	10.5940	9.8181	9.1285	8.5136	7.4694	6.6231	6.2593	5.9288	5.3527	4.8696	4.1103	3.5458	3.1129
25	22.0232	19.5235	17.4131	15.6221	14.0939	12.7834	11.6536	10.6748	9.8226	9.0770	7.8431	6.8729	6.4641	6.0971	5.4669	4.9476	4.1474	3.5640	3.1220
30	25.8077	22.3965	19.6004	17.2920	15.3725	13.7648	12.4090	11.2578	10.2737	9.4269	8.0552	7.0027	6.5660	6.1772	5.5168	4.9789	4.1601	3.5693	3.1242
40	32.8347	27.3555	23.1148	19.7928	17.1591	15.0463	13.3317	11.9246	10.7574	9.7791	8.2438	7.1050	6.6418	6.2335	5.5482	4.9966	4.1659	3.5712	3.1250
50	39.1961	31.4236	25.7298	21.4822	18.2559	15.7619	13.8007	12.2335	10.9617	9.9148	8.3045	7.1327	6.6605	6.2463	5.5541	4.9995	4.1666	3.5714	3.1250
60	44.9550	34.7609	27.6756	22.6235	18.9293	16.1614	14.0392	12.3766	11.0480	9.9672	8.3240	7.1401	6.6651	6.2402	5.5553	4.9999	4.1667	3.5714	3.1250

TABLE D.3 Future Value of $1 at the End of n Periods: $FVIF_{k,n} = (1 + k)^n$

Period	1%	2%	3%	4%	5%	6%	7%	8%	9%	10%	12%	14%	15%	16%	18%	20%	24%	28%	32%	36%
1	1.0100	1.0200	1.0300	1.0400	1.0500	1.0600	1.0700	1.0800	1.0900	1.1000	1.1200	1.1400	1.1500	1.1600	1.1800	1.2000	1.2400	1.2800	1.3200	1.3600
2	1.0201	1.0404	1.0609	1.0816	1.1025	1.1236	1.1449	1.1664	1.1881	1.2100	1.2544	1.2996	1.3225	1.3456	1.3924	1.4400	1.5376	1.6384	1.7424	1.8496
3	1.0303	1.0612	1.0927	1.1249	1.1576	1.1910	1.2250	1.2597	1.2950	1.3310	1.4049	1.4815	1.5209	1.5609	1.6430	1.7280	1.9066	2.0972	2.3000	2.5155
4	1.0406	1.0824	1.1255	1.1699	1.2155	1.2625	1.3108	1.3605	1.4116	1.4641	1.5735	1.6890	1.7490	1.8106	1.9388	2.0736	2.3642	2.6844	3.0360	3.4210
5	1.0510	1.1041	1.1593	1.2167	1.2763	1.3382	1.4026	1.4693	1.5386	1.6105	1.7623	1.9254	2.0114	2.1003	2.2878	2.4883	2.9316	3.4360	4.0075	4.6526
6	1.0615	1.1262	1.1941	1.2653	1.3401	1.4185	1.5007	1.5869	1.6771	1.7716	1.9738	2.1950	2.3131	2.4364	2.6996	2.9860	3.6352	4.3980	5.2899	6.3275
7	1.0721	1.1487	1.2299	1.3159	1.4071	1.5036	1.6058	1.7138	1.8280	1.9487	2.2107	2.5023	2.6600	2.8262	3.1855	3.5832	4.5077	5.6295	6.9826	8.6054
8	1.0829	1.1717	1.2668	1.3686	1.4775	1.5938	1.7182	1.8509	1.9926	2.1436	2.4760	2.8526	3.0590	3.2784	3.7589	4.2998	5.5895	7.2058	9.2170	11.703
9	1.0937	1.1951	1.3048	1.4233	1.5513	1.6895	1.8385	1.9990	2.1719	2.3579	2.7731	3.2519	3.5179	3.8030	4.4355	5.1598	6.9310	9.2234	12.166	15.916
10	1.1046	1.2190	1.3439	1.4802	1.6289	1.7908	1.9672	2.1589	2.3674	2.5937	3.1058	3.7072	4.0456	4.4114	5.2338	6.1917	8.5944	11.805	16.059	21.646
11	1.1157	1.2434	1.3842	1.5395	1.7103	1.8983	2.1049	2.3316	2.5804	2.8531	3.4785	4.2262	4.6524	5.1173	6.1759	7.4301	10.657	15.111	21.198	29.439
12	1.1268	1.2682	1.4258	1.6010	1.7959	2.0122	2.2522	2.5182	2.8127	3.1384	3.8960	4.8179	5.3502	5.9360	7.2876	8.9161	13.214	19.342	27.982	40.037
13	1.1381	1.2936	1.4685	1.6651	1.8856	2.1329	2.4098	2.7196	3.0658	3.4523	4.3635	5.4924	6.1528	6.8858	8.5994	10.699	16.386	24.758	36.937	54.451
14	1.1495	1.3195	1.5126	1.7317	1.9799	2.2609	2.5785	2.9372	3.3417	3.7975	4.8871	6.2613	7.0757	7.9875	10.147	12.839	20.319	31.691	48.756	74.053
15	1.1610	1.3459	1.5580	1.8009	2.0789	2.3966	2.7590	3.1722	3.6425	4.1772	5.4736	7.1379	8.1371	9.2655	11.973	15.407	25.195	40.564	64.358	100.71
16	1.1726	1.3728	1.6047	1.8730	2.1829	2.5404	2.9522	3.4259	3.9703	4.5950	6.1304	8.1372	9.3576	10.748	14.129	18.488	31.242	51.923	84.953	136.96
17	1.1843	1.4002	1.6528	1.9479	2.2920	2.6928	3.1588	3.7000	4.3276	5.0545	6.8660	9.2765	10.761	12.467	16.672	22.186	38.740	66.461	112.13	186.27
18	1.1961	1.4282	1.7024	2.0258	2.4066	2.8543	3.3799	3.9960	4.7171	5.5599	7.6900	10.575	12.375	14.462	19.673	26.623	48.038	85.070	148.02	253.33
19	1.2081	1.4568	1.7535	2.1068	2.5270	3.0256	3.6165	4.3157	5.1417	6.1159	8.6128	12.055	14.231	16.776	23.214	31.948	59.567	108.89	195.39	344.53
20	1.2202	1.4859	1.8061	2.1911	2.6533	3.2071	3.8697	4.6610	5.6044	6.7275	9.6463	13.743	16.366	19.460	27.393	38.337	73.864	139.37	257.91	468.57
21	1.2324	1.5157	1.8603	2.2788	2.7860	3.3996	4.1406	5.0338	6.1088	7.4002	10.803	15.667	18.821	22.574	32.323	46.005	91.591	178.40	340.44	637.26
22	1.2447	1.5460	1.9161	2.3699	2.9253	3.6035	4.4304	5.4365	6.6586	8.1403	12.100	17.861	21.644	26.186	38.142	55.206	113.57	228.35	449.39	866.67
23	1.2572	1.5769	1.9736	2.4647	3.0715	3.8197	4.7405	5.8715	7.2579	8.9543	13.552	20.361	24.891	30.376	45.007	66.247	140.83	292.30	593.19	1178.6
24	1.2697	1.6084	2.0328	2.5633	3.2251	4.0489	5.0724	6.3412	7.9111	9.8497	15.178	23.212	28.625	35.236	53.108	79.496	174.63	374.14	783.02	1602.9
25	1.2824	1.6406	2.0938	2.6658	3.3864	4.2919	5.4274	6.8485	8.6231	10.834	17.000	26.461	32.918	40.874	62.668	95.396	216.54	478.90	1033.5	2180.0
26	1.2953	1.6734	2.1566	2.7725	3.5557	4.5494	5.8074	7.3964	9.3992	11.918	19.040	30.166	37.856	47.414	73.948	114.47	268.51	612.99	1364.3	2964.9
27	1.3082	1.7069	2.2213	2.8834	3.7335	4.8223	6.2139	7.9881	10.245	13.110	21.324	34.389	43.535	55.000	87.259	137.37	332.95	784.63	1800.9	4032.2
28	1.3213	1.7410	2.2879	2.9987	3.9201	5.1117	6.6488	8.6271	11.167	14.421	23.883	39.204	50.065	63.800	102.96	164.84	412.86	1004.3	2377.2	5483.8
29	1.3345	1.7758	2.3566	3.1187	4.1161	5.4184	7.1143	9.3173	12.172	15.863	26.749	44.693	57.575	74.008	121.50	197.81	511.95	1285.5	3137.9	7458.0
30	1.3478	1.8114	2.4273	3.2434	4.3219	5.7435	7.6123	10.062	13.267	17.449	29.959	50.950	66.211	85.849	143.37	237.37	634.81	1645.5	4142.0	10143
40	1.4889	2.2080	3.2620	4.8010	7.0400	10.285	14.974	21.724	31.409	45.259	93.050	188.88	267.86	378.72	750.37	1469.7	5455.9	19426	66520	*
50	1.6446	2.6916	4.3839	7.1067	11.467	18.420	29.457	46.901	74.357	117.39	289.00	700.23	1083.6	1670.7	3927.3	9100.4	46890	*	*	*
60	1.8167	3.2810	5.8916	10.519	18.679	32.987	57.946	101.25	176.03	304.48	897.59	2595.9	4383.9	7370.1	20555	56347	*	*	*	*

*FVTFA > 99,999

Table D.4 Sum of an Annuity of $1 per Period for n Periods: $FVIFA = \sum_{t=1}^{n}(1+k)^{t-1} = \dfrac{(1+k)^{n-1}}{k}$

Number of Period	1%	2%	3%	4%	5%	6%	7%	8%	9%	10%	12%	14%	15%	16%	18%	20%	24%	28%	32%	36%
1	1.0000	1.0000	1.0000	1.0000	1.0000	1.0000	1.0000	1.0000	1.0000	1.0000	1.0000	1.0000	1.0000	1.0000	1.0000	1.0000	1.0000	1.0000	1.0000	1.0000
2	2.0100	2.0200	2.0300	2.0400	2.0500	2.0600	2.0700	2.0800	2.0900	2.1000	2.1200	2.1400	2.1500	2.1600	2.1800	2.2000	2.2400	2.2800	2.3200	2.3600
3	3.0301	3.0604	3.0909	3.1216	3.1525	3.1836	3.2149	3.2464	3.2781	3.3100	3.3744	3.4396	3.4725	3.5056	3.5724	3.6400	3.7776	3.9184	4.0624	4.2096
4	4.0604	4.1216	4.1836	4.2465	4.3101	4.3746	4.4399	4.5061	4.5731	4.6410	4.7793	4.9211	4.9934	5.0665	5.2154	5.3680	5.6842	6.0156	6.3624	6.7251
5	5.1010	5.2040	5.3091	5.4163	5.5256	5.6371	5.7507	5.8666	5.9847	6.1051	6.3528	6.6101	6.7424	6.8771	7.1542	7.4416	8.0484	8.6999	9.3983	10.146
6	6.1520	6.3081	6.4684	6.6330	6.8019	6.9753	7.1533	7.3359	7.5233	7.7156	8.1152	8.5355	8.7537	8.9775	9.4420	9.9299	10.980	12.135	13.405	14.798
7	7.2135	7.4343	7.6625	7.8983	8.1420	8.3938	8.6540	8.9228	9.2004	9.4872	10.089	10.730	11.066	11.413	12.141	12.915	14.615	16.533	18.695	21.126
8	8.2857	8.5830	8.8923	9.2142	9.5491	9.8975	10.259	10.636	11.028	11.435	12.299	13.232	13.726	14.240	15.327	16.499	19.122	22.163	25.678	29.731
9	9.3685	9.7546	10.159	10.582	11.026	11.491	11.978	12.487	13.021	13.579	14.775	16.085	16.785	17.518	19.085	20.798	24.712	29.369	34.895	41.435
10	10.462	10.949	11.463	12.006	12.577	13.180	13.816	14.486	15.192	15.937	17.548	19.337	20.303	21.321	23.521	25.958	31.643	38.592	47.061	57.351
11	11.566	12.168	12.807	13.486	14.206	14.971	15.783	16.645	17.560	18.531	20.654	23.044	24.349	25.732	28.755	32.150	40.237	50.398	63.121	78.998
12	12.682	13.412	14.192	15.025	15.917	16.869	17.888	18.977	20.140	21.384	24.133	27.270	29.001	30.850	34.931	39.580	50.894	65.510	84.320	108.43
13	13.809	14.680	15.617	16.626	17.713	18.882	20.140	21.495	22.953	24.522	28.029	32.088	34.351	36.786	42.218	48.496	64.109	84.852	112.30	148.47
14	14.947	15.973	17.086	18.291	19.598	21.015	22.550	24.214	26.019	27.975	32.392	37.581	40.504	43.672	50.818	59.195	80.496	109.61	149.23	202.92
15	16.096	17.293	18.598	20.023	21.578	23.276	25.129	27.152	29.360	31.772	37.279	43.842	47.580	51.659	60.965	72.035	100.81	141.30	197.99	276.97
16	17.257	18.639	20.156	21.824	23.657	25.672	27.888	30.324	33.003	35.949	42.753	50.980	55.717	60.925	72.939	87.442	126.01	181.86	262.35	377.69
17	18.430	20.012	21.761	23.697	25.840	28.212	30.840	33.750	36.973	40.544	48.883	59.117	65.075	71.673	87.068	105.93	157.25	233.79	347.30	514.66
18	19.614	21.412	23.414	25.645	28.132	30.905	33.999	37.450	41.301	45.599	55.749	68.394	75.836	84.140	103.74	128.11	195.99	300.25	459.44	700.93
19	20.810	22.840	25.116	27.671	30.539	33.760	37.379	41.446	46.018	51.159	63.439	78.969	88.211	98.603	123.41	154.74	244.03	385.32	607.47	954.27
20	22.019	24.297	26.870	29.778	33.066	36.785	40.995	45.762	51.160	57.275	72.052	91.024	102.44	115.37	146.62	186.68	303.60	494.21	802.86	1298.8
21	23.239	25.783	28.676	31.969	35.719	39.992	44.865	50.422	56.764	64.002	81.698	104.76	118.81	134.84	174.02	225.02	377.46	633.59	1060.7	1767.3
22	24.471	27.299	30.536	34.248	38.505	43.392	49.005	55.456	62.873	71.402	92.502	120.43	137.63	157.41	206.34	271.03	469.05	811.99	1401.2	2404.6
23	25.716	28.845	32.452	36.617	41.430	46.995	53.436	60.893	69.531	79.543	104.60	138.29	159.27	183.60	244.48	326.23	582.62	1040.3	1850.6	3271.3
24	26.973	30.421	34.426	39.082	44.502	50.815	58.176	66.764	76.789	88.497	118.15	158.65	184.16	213.97	289.49	392.48	723.46	1332.6	2443.8	4449.9
25	28.243	32.030	36.459	41.645	47.727	54.864	63.249	73.105	84.700	98.347	133.33	181.87	212.79	249.21	342.60	471.98	898.09	1706.8	3226.8	6052.9
26	29.525	33.670	38.553	44.311	51.113	59.156	68.676	79.954	93.323	109.18	150.33	208.33	245.71	290.08	405.27	567.37	1114.6	2185.7	4260.4	8233.0
27	30.820	35.344	40.709	47.084	54.669	63.705	74.483	87.350	102.72	121.09	169.37	238.49	283.56	337.50	479.22	681.85	1383.1	2798.7	5624.7	11197.9
28	32.129	37.051	42.930	49.967	58.402	68.528	80.697	95.338	112.96	134.20	190.69	272.88	327.10	392.50	566.48	819.22	1716.0	3583.3	7425.6	15230.2
29	33.450	38.792	45.218	52.966	62.322	73.639	87.346	103.96	124.13	148.63	214.58	312.09	377.16	456.30	669.44	984.06	2128.9	4587.6	9802.9	20714.1
30	34.784	40.568	47.575	56.084	66.438	79.058	94.460	113.28	136.30	164.49	241.33	356.78	434.74	530.31	790.94	1181.8	2640.9	5873.2	12940	28172.2
40	48.886	60.402	75.401	95.025	120.79	154.76	199.63	259.05	337.88	442.59	767.09	1342.0	1779.0	2360.7	4163.2	7343.8	22728	69377	*	*
50	64.463	84.579	112.79	152.66	209.34	290.33	406.52	573.76	815.08	1163.9	2400.0	4994.5	7217.7	10435	21813	45497	*	*	*	*
60	81.669	114.05	163.05	237.99	353.58	533.12	813.52	1253.2	1944.7	3034.8	7471.6	18535	29219	46057	*	*	*	*	*	*

*FVIF > 99,999

E

STANDARD NORMAL PROBABILITIES

z	0.00	0.01	0.02	0.03	0.04	0.05	0.06	0.07	0.08	0.09
0.0	.5000	.5040	.5080	.5120	.5160	.5199	.5239	.5279	.5219	.5359
0.1	.5398	.5438	.5478	.5517	.5557	.5596	.5636	.5675	.5714	.5753
0.2	.5793	.5832	.5871	.5910	.5948	.5987	.6026	.6064	.6103	.6141
0.3	.6179	.6217	.6255	.6293	.6331	.6368	.6406	.6443	.6480	.6517
0.4	.6554	.6591	.6628	.6664	.6700	.6736	.6772	.6808	.6844	.6879
0.5	.6915	.6950	.6985	.7019	.7054	.7088	.7123	.7157	.7190	.7224
0.6	.7257	.7291	.7324	.7357	.7389	.7422	.7454	.7486	.7517	.7549
0.7	.7580	.7611	.7642	.7673	.7704	.7734	.7764	.7794	.7823	.7852
0.8	.7881	.7910	.7939	.7967	.7995	.8023	.8051	.8078	.8106	.8133
0.9	.8159	.8186	.8212	.8238	.8264	.8289	.8315	.8340	.8365	.8389
1.0	.8413	.8438	.8461	.8485	.8508	.8531	.8554	.8577	.8599	.8621
1.1	.8643	.8665	.8686	.8708	.8729	.8749	.8770	.8790	.8810	.8830
1.2	.8849	.8860	.8888	.8907	.8925	.8943	.8962	.8980	.8997	.9015
1.3	.9032	.9049	.9066	.9082	.9099	.9115	.9131	.9147	.9162	.9177
1.4	.9192	.9207	.9222	.9236	.9251	.9265	.9279	.9292	.9306	.9319
1.5	.9332	.9345	.9357	.9370	.9382	.9394	.9406	.9418	.9429	.9441
1.6	.9452	.9463	.9474	.9484	.9495	.9505	.9515	.9525	.9535	.9545
1.7	.9554	.9564	.9573	.9582	.9591	.9599	.9608	.9616	.9625	.9633
1.8	.9641	.9649	.9656	.9664	.9671	.9678	.9686	.9693	.9699	.9706
1.9	.9713	.9719	.9726	.9732	.9738	.9744	.9750	.9756	.9761	.9767
2.0	.9772	.9778	.9783	.9788	.9793	.9798	.9803	.9808	.9812	.9817
2.1	.9821	.9826	.9830	.9834	.9838	.9842	.9846	.9850	.9854	.9857
2.2	.9861	.9864	.9868	.9871	.9875	.9878	.9881	.9884	.9887	.9890
2.3	.9893	.9896	.9898	.9901	.9904	.9906	.9909	.9911	.9913	.9916
2.4	.9918	.9920	.9922	.9925	.9927	.9929	.9931	.9932	.9934	.9936
2.5	.9938	.9940	.9941	.9943	.9945	.9946	.9948	.9949	.9951	.9952
2.6	.9953	.9955	.9956	.9957	.9959	.9960	.9961	.9962	.9963	.9964
2.7	.9965	.9966	.9967	.9968	.9969	.9970	.9971	.9972	.9973	.9974
2.8	.9974	.9975	.9976	.9977	.9977	.9978	.9979	.9979	.9980	.9981
2.9	.9981	.9982	.9982	.9983	.9984	.9984	.9985	.9985	.9986	.9986
3.0	.9987	.9987	.9987	.9988	.9988	.9989	.9989	.9989	.9990	.9990

Acharya, Viral A., Julian Franks, and Henri Servaes. 2007. "Private Equity: Boom or Bust?" *Journal of Applied Corporate Finance* 19, no. 4 (Fall): 44–53.

Alford, A., R. Jones, and K. Winkelmann. 2003. "A Spectrum Approach to Active Risk Budgeting." *Journal of Portfolio Management* 30: 49–60.

Almazan, Andres, Keith C. Brown, Murray Carlson, and David A. Chapman. 2004. "Why Constrain Your Mutual Fund Manager?" *Journal of Financial Economics* 73, no. 2 (August): 289–321.

Altman, Edward I. 1968. "Financial Ratios, Discriminant Analysis and the Prediction of Corporate Bankruptcy." *Journal of Finance* 23, no. 4 (September): 589–609.

Altman, Edward I. 1993. "Defaulted Bonds: Demand, Supply, and Performance, 1987–1992." *Financial Analysts Journal* 49, no. 3 (May–June): 55–60.

Altman, Edward I., and Edith Hotchkiss. 2006. *Corporate Financial Distress and Bankruptcy,* 3rd ed. New York: Wiley.

Altman, Edward I., and Mario Y. Levallee. 1980. Business Failure Classification in Canada. *Journal of Business Administration* 12, no. 1: 147–164.

Altman, Edward I., and Scott A. Nammacher. 1987. *Investing in Junk Bonds.* New York: Wiley.

Altman, Edward I., and Herbert Rijken. 2006. "A Point-in-Time Perspective on Through-the-Cycle Ratings. *Financial Analysts Journal* 62, no. 1 (January–February).

Amenc, Noel, and Veronique LeSourd. 2003. *Portfolio Theory and Performance Analysis.* West Sussex, England: Wiley.

Ammann, Manuel, and Heinz Zimmermann. 2001. "Tracking Error and Tactical Asset Allocation." *Financial Analysts Journal* 57, no. 2 (March–April): 32–43.

Ang, Andrew, Robert J. Hodrick, Yuhang Xing, and Xiaoyan Zhang. 2006. "The Cross-Section of Volatility and Expected Returns." *Journal of Finance* 61, no. 1 (February): 259–299.

Appelt, Timothy. 1992. "Active Management: What Is the Right Performance Benchmark?" *Canadian Investment Review* 5, no. 1 (April): 67–72.

Arbel, Avner, and Paul Strebel. 1983. "Pay Attention to Neglected Firms!" *Journal of Portfolio Management* 9, no. 2 (Winter): 37–42.

Ariely, Dan. 2008. *Predictably Irrational: The Hidden Forces that Shape Our Decisions,* New York: Harper Collins.

Arnott, Robert D., Jason C. Hsu, and John M. West. 2008. *The Fundamental Index,* New York: Wiley.

Athanassakos, George, Peter Carayannopoulos, and Marie Racine. 2002. "How Effective Is Aggressive Portfolio Management? Mutual Fund Performance in Canada, 1985–1996." *Canadian Investment Review* 15, no. 3 (October): 39, 41+.

Auger, Robert, and Denis Parisien, 1991. "Understanding Asset Allocation," *Canadian Investment Review* 4, no. 1 (Spring).

Bacon, Carl. 2004. *Practical Portfolio Performance Measurement and Attribution.* West Sussex, England: Wiley.

Baesel, Jerome, George Shows, and Edward Thorp. 1982. "Can Joe Granville Time the Market?" *Journal of Portfolio Management* 8, no. 3 (Spring): 5–9.

Bailey, Jeffrey V. 1992. "Are Manager Universes Acceptable Performance Benchmarks?" *Journal of Portfolio Management* 18, no. 3 (Spring): 9–13.

Bailey, Jeffery V., Thomas M. Richards, and David E. Tierney. 2007. "Evaluating Portfolio Performance." In *Managing Investment Portfolio: A Dynamic Process,* 3rd ed., ed. John L. Maginn, Donald L. Tuttle, Jerald E. Pinto, and Dennis W. McLeavey. Hoboken, NJ: Wiley.

Bali, Turan G., Susan R. Hume, and Terrence F. Martell. 2007. "A New Look at Hedging With Derivatives: Will Firms Reduce Market Risk Exposure?" *Journal of Futures Markets* 27, no. 11 (November): 1053–1083.

Ball, Ray. 1995. "The Theory of Stock Market Efficiency: Accomplishments and Limitations." *Journal of Applied Corporate Finance* 8, no. 1 (Spring): 4–18.

Balog, James, ed. 1993. *The Health Care Industry.* Charlottesville, VA: AIMR.

Banz, R. W. 1981. "The Relationship between Return and Market Value of Common Stocks." *Journal of Financial Economics* 9, no. 1 (March): 3–18.

Barber, Brad, and Terrance Odean. 1999. "The Courage of Misguided Convictions: The Trading Behavior of Individual Investors." *Financial Analysts Journal* 55, no. 6 (November–December): 41–55.

Barber, Brad, and Terrance Odean. 2000. "Trading Is Hazardous to Your Wealth: The Common Stock Investment Performance of Individual Investors." *Journal of Finance* 55, no. 2 (April): 773–806.

Barber, Brad, and Terrance Odean. 2001. "Boys Will Be Boys: Gender, Overconfidence, and Common Stock Investment." *Quarterly Journal of Economics* 116, no. 1 (February): 261–292.

Barberis, Nicholas, and Richard Thaler. 2003. "A Survey of Behavioral Finance." *Handbook of the Economics of Finance,* ed. G.M. Constantianides, M. Harris, and Rene Stulz. New York: Elsevier Science.

Barclay, Michael, Clifford Holderness, and Jeffrey Pontiff. 1993. "Private Benefits from Block Ownership and Discounts on Closed-End Funds." *Journal of Financial Economics* 33, no. 3 (June): 263–292.

Barclay, Michael, Terrence Hendershott, and D. Timothy McCormick. 2003. "Competition among Trading Venues: Information and Trading on Electronic Communications Networks." *Journal of Finance* 58, no. 6 (December).

Barnhill, Theodore M., William F. Maxwell, and Mark R. Shenkman, eds. 1999. *High-Yield Bonds*. New York: McGraw-Hill.

Baruch, Lev. 1989. "On the Usefulness of Earnings and Earnings Research: Lessons and Directions from Two Decades of Empirical Research." *Journal of Accounting Research* 27 (Supplement).

Basak, Suleyman. 2002. "A Comparative Study of Portfolio Insurance." *Journal of Economic Dynamics and Control* 26, no. 7–8 (July): 1217–1241.

Basu, Senjoy. 1977. "Investment Performance of Common Stocks in Relation to Their Price-Earnings Ratios: A Test of the Efficient Market Hypothesis." *Journal of Finance* 32, no. 3 (June): 663–682.

Battalio, Robert H. 1997. "Third Market Broker-Dealers: Cost Competitors or Cream Skimmers?" *Journal of Finance* 52, no. 1 (March): 341–352.

Battalio, Robert, Jason Greene, and Robert Jennings. 1997. "How Do Competing Specialists and Preferencing Dealers Affect Market Quality?" *Review of Financial Studies* 10: 969–993.

Bauer, Richard J., and Julie R. Dahlquist. 2001. "Market Timing and Roulette Wheels." *Financial Analysts Journal* 57, no. 1 (January–February): 28–40.

Beard, Allison. 2001. "Short Selling Goes from Strength to Strength." *Financial Times,* March 16, p. 29.

Beard, Craig, and Richard Sias. 1997. "Is There a Neglected-Firm Effect?" *Financial Analysts Journal* 53, no. 5 (September–October): 19–23.

Beckers, Stan. 1981. "Standard Deviations Implied in Option Prices as Predictors of Future Stock Price Variability." *Journal of Banking and Finance* 5, no. 3 (September): 363–381.

Belkaoui, Ahmed. 1980. "Industrial Bond Ratings: A New Look." *Financial Management* 9, no. 3 (Fall): 44–52.

Benesh, Gary A., and Pamela P. Peterson. 1986. "On the Relation between Earning Changes, Analysts' Forecasts and Stock Price Fluctuations." *Financial Analysts Journal* 42, no. 6 (November–December): 29–39.

Benning, Carl J. 1997. "Prediction Skills of Real-World Market Timers." *The Journal of Portfolio Management* 23, no. 2 (Winter): 55–65.

Benveniste, L. M., A. J. Marcus, and W. J. Wilhelm. 1992. "What's Special about the Specialist?" *Journal of Financial Economics* 32, no. 1 (August): 61–86.

Berk, Jonathan B., and Richard Stanton. 2007. "Managerial Ability, Compensation, and the Closed-End Fund Discount." *Journal of Finance* 62, no. 2 (April): 529–556.

Berkowitz, Stephen A., Louis D. Finney, and Dennis Logue. 1988. *The Investment Performance of Corporate Pension Plans*. New York: Quorum Books.

Bernard, Victor L., and Jacob K. Thomas. 1989. "Post-Earnings–Announcements Drift: Delayed Price Response or Risk Premium?" *Journal of Accounting Research* 27 (Supplement).

Bernstein, Richard. 1995. *Style Investing: Unique Insight into Equity Management*. New York: Wiley.

Bharadwaj, Anu, and James B. Wiggins. 2001. "Box Spread and Put-Call Parity Tests for the S&P 500 Index LEAPS Market." *Journal of Derivatives* 8, no. 4 (Summer): 62–71.

Bhatia, Sanjiv, ed. 1995. The Consumer Staples Industry. Proceedings of the AIMR Seminar "Industry Analysis: Consumer Staples," March 28–29, 1995, St. Louis, Missouri. Charlottesville, VA: AIMR.

Bhatia, Sanjiv, ed. 1996. The Media Industry. Proceedings of the AIMR Seminar "The Media Industry," January 31–February 1, 1996, New York, New York. Charlottesville, VA: AIMR.

Bierwag, G. O. 1977. "Immunization, Duration, and the Term Structure of Interest Rates." *Journal of Financial and Quantitative Analysis* 12, no. 5 (December): 725–742.

Bierwag, G. O., and George G. Kaufman. 1977. "Coping with the Risk of Interest Rate Fluctuations: A Note." *Journal of Business* 50, no. 3 (July): 364–370.

Billingsley, Randall S., R. Lamy, M. Marr, and T. Thompson. 1985. "Split Ratings and Bond Reoffering Yields." *Financial Management* 14, no. 2 (Summer): 59–65.

Black, Fischer. 1972. "Capital Market Equilibrium with Restricted Borrowing." *Journal of Business* 45, no. 3 (July): 444–455.

Black, Fischer. 1975. "Fact and Fantasy in the Use of Options." *Financial Analysts Journal* 31, no. 4 (July–August): 36–41, 61–72.

Black, Fischer. 1989. "How to Use the Holes in Black-Scholes." *Journal of Applied Corporate Finance* 1, no. 4 (Winter): 67–73.

Black, Fischer, and Myron Scholes. 1973. "The Pricing of Options and Corporate Liabilities." *Journal of Political Economy* 81, no. 2 (May–June): 637–654.

Black, Fischer, and Myron Scholes. 1979. "The Effects of Dividend Yield and Dividend Policy on Common Stock Prices and Returns." *Journal of Financial Economics* 1, no. 1 (March): 1–22.

Blythe, Scott. 2003. "Can Bonds Go Electronic?" *Canadian Investment Review* 16, no. 2 (Summer): 49–50.

Bookstaber, Richard M., and Roger G. Clarke. 1981. "Options Can Alter Portfolio Return Distributions." *Journal of Portfolio Management* 7, no. 3 (Spring): 63–70.

Booth, Laurence. 1998. "The Case against Foreign Bonds." *Canadian Investment Review* 11, no. 2 (July): 23.

Boyce, W. M., and A. J. Kalotay. 1979. "Optimum Bond Calling and Refunding." *Interfaces* (November): 36–49.

Boyd, Naomi E., and Jeffrey M. Mercer. 2005. "Gains from Bond Swap Strategies." Working Paper, George Washington University.

Branch, Ben. 1977. "A Tax Loss Trading Rule." *Journal of Business* 50, no. 2 (April): 198–207.

Branch, Ben, and Kyun Chun Chang. 1985. "Tax-Loss Trading—Is the Game Over or Have the Rules Changed?" *Financial Review* 20, no. 1 (February): 55–69.

Brealey, Richard A., and Stewart C. Myers. 2004a. *Principles of Corporate Finance,* 8th ed. New York: McGraw-Hill.

Brealey, Richard A., and Stewart C. Myers. 2004b. *Fundamentals of Corporate Finance,* 4th ed. New York: McGraw Hill.

Brennan, Michael. 1969. "Capital Market Equilibrium with Divergent Borrowing and Lending Rules." *Journal of Financial and Quantitative Analysis* 4, no. 1 (March): 4–14.

Brennan, Michael J., and A. Subramanyam. 1996. "Market Microstructure and Asset Pricing on the Compensation for Illiquidity in Stock Returns." *Journal of Financial Economics* 41, no. 3 (July): 341–344.

Brigham, Eugene. 2007. *Fundamentals of Financial Management,* 10th ed. Mason, OH: South-Western.

Brinson, Gary P. 2005. "The Future of Investment Management." *Financial Analysts Journal* 61, no. 4 (July–August) 24–28.

Brinson, Gary P., Jeffrey J. Diermeier, and G. G. Schlarbaum. 1986. "A Composite Portfolio Benchmark for Pension Plans." *Financial Analysts Journal* 42, no. 2 (March–April): 15–24.

Brinson, Gary P., L. Randolph Hood, and Gilbert L. Beebower. 1986. "Determinants of Portfolio Performance." *Financial Analysts Journal* 42, no. 4 (July–August): 39–44.

Brinson, Gary P., Brian D. Singer, and Gilbert L. Beebower. 1991. "Determinants of Portfolio Performance II: An Update." *Financial Analysts Journal* 47, no. 3 (May–June): 40–48.

Briys, Eric, Huu Minh Mai, Mondher Bellalah, and François De Varenne. 1998. *Options, Futures, and Exotic Derivatives.* New York: Wiley.

Brooks, Robert. 1997. *Interest Rate Modeling and the Risk Premiums in Interest Rate Swaps.* Charlottesville, VA: Research Foundation of the Institute of Chartered Financial Analysts.

Brockman, Paul, Charles Mossman, and Dennis Olson. 1997. "What's the Value of Fundamental Analysis?" *Canadian Investment Review* 10, no. 3 (Fall): 10.

Brown, David P., and Robert H. Jennings. 1989. "On Technical Analysis." *Review of Financial Studies* 2, no. 4 (October).

Brown, Keith C., ed. 1993. *Derivative Strategies for Managing Portfolio Risk.* Charlottesville, VA: AIMR.

Brown, Keith C., and Gregory D. Brown. 1987. "Does the Composition of the Market Portfolio Really Matter?" *Journal of Portfolio Management* 13, no. 2 (Winter): 26–32.

Brown, Keith C., and W. V. Harlow. 2005. "Staying the Course: Performance Persistence and the Role of Investment Style Consistency in Professional Asset Management," Working Paper.

Brown, Keith C., W. V. Harlow, and Laura T. Starks. 1996. "Of Tournaments and Temptations: An Analysis of Managerial Incentives in the Mutual Fund Industry." *Journal of Finance* 51, no. 1 (March): 85–110.

Brown, Keith C., W. V. Harlow, and Seha M. Tinic. 1989. "How Rational Investors Deal with Uncertainty (or, Reports of the Death of Efficient Market Theory Are Greatly Exaggerated)." *Journal of Applied Corporate Finance* 2, no. 3 (Fall): 45–58.

Brown, Keith C., and Michael V. Raymond. 1986. "Risk Arbitrage and the Prediction of Successful Corporate Takeovers." *Financial Management* 15, no. 3 (August): 54–63.

Brown, Keith C., and Donald J. Smith. 1995. *Interest Rate and Currency Swaps: A Tutorial.* Charlottesville, VA: Research Foundation of Institute of Chartered Financial Analysts.

Brown, Keith C., Lorenzo Garlappi, and Cristian Tiu. 2008. "The Troves of Academe: Asset Allocation, Risk Budgeting and the Investment Performance of University Endowment Funds," Working Paper, August 8.

Brown, Ken. 2000. "Fund Diversification Dies a Not Very Slow Death." *Wall Street Journal,* February 7, pp. R1, R5.

Brown, Stephen J., and William Goetzmann. 1995. "Performance Persistence." *Journal of Finance* 50, no. 3 (June): 679–698.

Buetow, Gerald W., Jr., and Frank J. Fabozzi. 2000. *Valuation of Interest Rate Swaps and Swaptions.* New York: Wiley.

Burmeister, Edwin, Richard Roll, and Stephen A. Ross. 1994. "A Practitioner's Guide to Arbitrage Pricing Theory." In *A Practitioner's Guide to Factor Models,* ed. John Peavy. Charlottesville, VA: Research Foundation of the Institute of Chartered Financial Analysts.

Burns, Terrence E. 1998a. *Asset Allocation in a Changing World.* Charlottesville, VA: AIMR.

Burns, Terence E., ed. 1998b. *Derivatives in Portfolio Management.* Charlottesville, VA: AIMR.

Byrnes, Nanette, and David Henry. 2001. "Confused about Earnings?" *BusinessWeek,* November 26, pp. 77–84.

Byrnes, Nanette, Mike McNamee, Diane Brady, Louis Lavelle, and Christopher Palmeri. 2002. "Accounting in Crisis." *BusinessWeek,* January 28, pp. 44–48.

Cagan, Phillip. 1969. *Essays on Interest Rates.* New York: Columbia University Press for the National Bureau of Economic Research.

Campbell, John Y., and John Ammer. 1993. "What Moves the Stock and Bond Markets? A Variance Decomposition for Long-Term Asset Returns." *Journal of Finance* 48, no. 1 (March): 3–38.

Campbell, John Y., Martin Lettau, Burton G. Malkiel, and Yexiao Xu. 2001. "Have Individual Stocks Become More Volatile?: An Empirical Exploration of Idiosyncratic Risk." *Journal of Finance* 56, no. 1 (February): 1-43.

Campbell, John Y., Christopher Polk, and Tuomo Vuolteenaho. 2007. "Growth or Glamour? Fundamentals and Systematic Risk in Stock Return," Working Paper (February). Retrieved at http://personal.lse.ac.uk/polk/research/gorg20070219.pdf.

Cantor, Richard, and Frank Packer. 1995. "The Credit Rating Industry." *Journal of Fixed Income* 5, no. 3 (December): 10–34.

Capaul, Carlo, Ian Rowley, and William F. Sharpe. 1993. "International Value and Growth Stock Returns." *Financial Analysts Journal* 49, no.1 (January–February): 27–36.

Capon, N., G. Fitzsimons, and R. Prince. 1996. "An Individual Level Analysis of the Mutual Fund Investment Decision." *Journal of Financial Services Research* 10: 59–82.

Carhart, Mark M. 1997. "On Persistence in Mutual Fund Performance." *Journal of Finance* 52, no. 1 (March): 57–82.

Carr, Peter. 1988. "A Calculator Program for Option Values and Implied Standard Deviations." *Journal of Financial Education* 17, no. 1 (Fall): 89–93.

CFA Institute. 2004. *Points of Inflection: New Directions for Portfolio Management.* Charlottesville, VA: CFA Institute.

CFA Institute. 2006. *Standards of Practice Handbook,* 9th ed. Charlottesville, VA.

Chan, Louis, Narasimhan Jegadeesh, and Josef Lakonishok. 1999. "The Profitability of Momentum Strategies." *Financial Analysts Journal* 55, no. 6 (November–December): 80–90.

Chan, Louis, and Josef Lakonishok. 2004. "Value and Growth Investing: Review and Update." *Financial Analysts Journal* 60, no. 1 (January–February): 71–86.

Chan, Wesley. 2003. "Stock Price Reaction to News and No-News: Drift and Reversal after Headlines." *Journal of Financial Economics* 70, no. 2 (November): 223–260.

Chance, Don M. 2003. *Analysis of Derivatives for the CFA Program.* Charlottesville, VA: AIMR.

Chance, Don M., and Rober Brooks. 2007. *An Introduction to Derivatives and Risk Management,* 7th ed. Mason, OH: Southwestern Publishing.

Chance, Don M., and Pamela P. Peterson. 2002. *Real Options and Investment Valuation.* Charlottesville, VA: Research Foundation of AIMR.

Chang, Eric C., and Wilbur G. Lewellen. 1984. "Market Timing and Mutual Fund Investment Performance." *Journal of Business* 57, no. 1 (January): 57–72.

Chemmanur, Thomas, and An Yan. 2004. "A Theory of Corporate Spin-offs." *Journal of Financial Economics* 72, no. 2 (May): 259–290.

Chen, H. L., N. Jegadeesh, and R. Wermers. 2000. "An Examination of the Stockholdings and Trades of Mutual Fund Managers." *Journal of Financial and Quantitative Analysis* 35 (September): 343–368.

Chen, Nai-fu, Richard Roll, and Stephen A. Ross. 1986. "Economic Forces and the Stock Market." *Journal of Business* 59, no. 3 (April): 383–404.

Chowdhury, M., J. S. Howe, and J. C. Lin. 1993. "The Relation between Aggregate Insider Transactions and Stock Market Returns." *Journal of Financial and Quantitative Analysis* 28, no. 3 (September): 431–437.

Christie, William. 1990. "Dividend Yield and Expected Returns." *Journal of Financial Economics* 28, no. 1 (November–December): 95–125.

Christopherson, Jon A., and C. Nola Williams. 1995. "Equity Style: What It Is and Why It Matters." In *The Handbook of Equity Style Management,* ed. T. Daniel Coggin and Frank J. Fabozzi. New Hope, PA: Frank J. Fabozzi Associates.

Churchhill, Dwight D., ed. 1994. *Fixed-Income Management: Techniques and Practices.* Charlottesville, VA: AIMR.

Clarke, Roger G. 1992. *Options and Futures: A Tutorial.* Charlottesville, VA: Research Foundation of the Institute of Chartered Financial Analysts.

Clayman, Michelle. 1987. "In Search of Excellence: The Investor's Viewpoint." *Financial Analysts Journal* 43, no. 3 (May/June): 54–63.

Coggin, Daniel T., Frank J. Fabozzi, and Shafiqur Rahman. 1993. "The Investment Performance of U.S. Equity Pension Fund Managers: An Empirical Investigation." *Journal of Finance* 48, no. 3 (July): 1039–1055.

Cohen, Abby J. 1996. "Economic Forecasts and the Asset Allocation Decision." In *Economic Analysis for Investment Professionals.* Charlottesville, VA: AIMR, November.

Colby, Robert W., and Thomas A. Mayers. 1988. *The Encyclopedia of Technical Market Indicators.* Homewood, IL: Dow Jones–Irwin.

Cox, John C., Stephen A. Ross, and Mark Rubinstein. 1979. "Option Pricing: A Simplified Approach." *Journal of Financial Economics* 7, no. 3 (September): 229–264.

Cox, John C., and Mark Rubinstein. 1985. *Option Markets.* Englewood Cliffs, NJ: Prentice Hall.

Crawford, Alexander. 2005. "Collateralized Mortgage Obligations." In *The Handbook of Fixed-Income Securities,* 7th ed., ed. Frank J. Fabozzi. New York: McGraw-Hill.

Curwood, Bruce. 2000. "Measuring Performance: A New Direction. Fiduciaries Often Use Flawed Methodologies to Evaluate Manager Performance. There Is a Better Way." *Canadian Investment Review* 13, no. 1 (April): 28+.

Damodaran, Aswath. 2002. *Investment Valuation,* 2nd ed. New York: Wiley.

Damodaran, Aswath. 2006. *Damodaran on Valuation,* 2nd ed. New York: Wiley.

Danielson, M. G. 1998. "A Simple Valuation Model and Growth Expectations." *Financial Analysts Journal* 54, no. 3 (May–June): 50–57.

Dattatreya, Ravi E., and Frank J. Fabozzi. 1995. *Active Total Return Management of Fixed-Income Portfolios,* rev. ed. Burr Ridge, IL: Irwin Professional.

Davidson, Steve. 2001 "Core Plus Bond Strategies: The Investor Search for Higher Returns." *Community Banker* 2, no. 7 (July).

Deaves, Richard. 1996. "Forecasting Canadian Short-Term Interest Rates." *Canadian Journal of Economics* 29, no. 3: 615–634.

Deaves, Richard, and Peter Miu. 2007. "Investor Overconfidence Meets Momentum, Reversal and Market State." *Canadian Investment Review* 20, no. 4 (Winter).

DeBondt, Werner F. M., and Richard Thaler. 1985. "Does the Stock Market Overreact?" *Journal of Finance* 40, no. 3 (July): 793–805.

DeFusco, Richard A., Dennis W. McLeavey, Jerald E. Pinto, and David E. Runkle. 2004. *Quantitative Methods for Investment Analysis,* 2nd ed. Charlottesville, VA: CFA Institute.

Degennaro, Ramon P., and Cesare Robotti. 2007. "Financial Market Frictions." *Economic Review* 92, no. 3 (Third Quarter): 1–16.

DeMark, Thomas R. 1999. *The New Science of Technical Analysis.* New York: Wiley.

Desai, H., and P. Jain. 1999. "Firm Performance and Focus: Long-Run Stock Market Performance Following Spin-offs." *Journal of Financial Economics* 54, no. 1 (February): 75–102.

De Servigney, Arnaud, and Olivier Renault. 2004. *Measuring and Managing Credit Risk.* New York: McGraw-Hill.

Dialynas, Chris P. 2001. "The Active Decisions in the Selection of Passive Management and Performance Bogeys." In *The Handbook of Fixed-Income Securities,* 6th ed., ed. Frank J. Fabozzi. New York: McGraw-Hill.

Dialynas, Chris P., and Alfred Murata. 2006. "The Active Decisions in the Selection of Passive Management and Performance Bogeys." In *Active Bond Portfolio Management,* ed. Frank J. Fabbozi, Lionel Martellini, and Philippe Priaulet. Hoboken, NJ: John Wiley.

Dialynas, Chris P., and David H. Edington. 1992. "Bond Yield Spreads—A Postmodern View." *Journal of Portfolio Management* 19, no. 1 (Fall): 60–75.

Diermeier, Jeffrey J. 1990. "Capital Market Expectations: The Macro Factors." In *Managing Investment Portfolios: A Dynamic Process,* 2nd ed., ed. John L. Maginn and Donald L. Tuttle. Boston: Warren, Gorham, & Lamont.

Dimson, E. 1979. "Risk Management When Shares Are Subject to Infrequent Trading." *Journal of Financial Economics* 7, no. 2 (June): 197–226.

Doidge, Craig, and Jason Z. Wei. 1998. "Volatility Forecasting and the Efficiency of the Toronto 35 Index Options Market." *Revue Canadienne des Sciences de l'administration* 15, no. 1: 28–38.

Dopfel, Frederick E. 2003. "Asset Allocation in a Lower Stock-Bond Correlation Environment." *Journal of Portfolio Management* 30, no. 1 (Fall).

Doupnik, Timothy, and Hector Perera. 2007. *International Accounting,* 1st ed. New York: McGraw-Hill.

Dreman, David M. 1998. *Contrarian Investment Strategies: The Next Generation.* New York: Simon & Schuster.

Dubofsky, David A., and Thomas W. Miller. 2003. *Derivatives: Valuation and Risk Management.* New York: Oxford University Press.

DuBois, Charles H. 1992. "Tactical Asset Allocation: A Review of Current Techniques." In *Active Asset Allocation,* ed. R. Arnott and F. Fabozzi. Chicago: Probus.

Dudley, William C., and Edward F. McKelvey. January 1997. "The Brave New Business Cycle: No Recession in Sight." *U.S. Economics Research,* Goldman Sachs.

Dumbolena, I. G., and J. M. Shulman. 1988. "A Primary Rule of Detecting Bankruptcy: Watch the Cash." *Financial Analysts Journal* 44, no. 5 (September–October): 74–78.

Dunetz, Mark L., and James M. Mahoney. 1988. "Using Duration and Convexity in the Analysis of Callable Bonds." *Financial Analysts Journal* 44, no. 3 (May–June): 53–73.

Durand, David. 1957. "Growth Stocks and the Petersburg Paradox." *Journal of Finance* 12, no. 3 (September): 348–363.

Easley, David, Nicholas Kiefer, and Maureen O'Hara. 1996. "Cream-Skimming or Profit Sharing? The Curious Role of Purchased Order Flow." *Journal of Finance* 51, no. 3 (July): 811–833.

Eavis, Peter. 2008. "Time for Fannie, Freddie?" *Wall Street Journal,* July 8, C14.

Eckl, S., J. N. Robinson, and D. C. Thomas. 1991. *Financial Engineering: A Handbook of Derivative Products.* Cambridge, MA: Basil Blackwell.

Ederington, L. H. 1985. "Why Split Ratings Occur." *Financial Management* 14, no. 1 (Spring): 37–47.

Edwards, R. D., and John Magee, Jr. 1992. *Technical Analysis of Stock Trends,* 6th ed. Boston: New York Institute of Finance.

Edwards, Greg. 1997. "A Simple Model for Bond Portfolio Performance Attribution." *Canadian Investment Review* 10, no. 1 (April): 14–17.

Elton, Edwin J., and Martin J. Gruber, eds. 1990. *Japanese Capital Markets.* New York: Harper & Row.

Elton, Edwin J., Martin J. Gruber, and Christopher R. Blake. 1996. "The Persistence of Risk-Adjusted Mutual Fund Performance." *Journal of Business* 69, no. 2 (April): 133–157.

Elton, Edwin J., Martin J. Gruber, Stephen J. Brown, and William N. Goetzmann. 2010. *Modern Portfolio Theory and Investment Analysis,* 8th ed. New York: Wiley.

Elton, Edwin J., Martin J. Gruber, and Joel Rentzler. 1983. "A Single Examination of the Empirical Relationship between Dividend Yields and Deviations from the CAPM." *Journal of Banking and Finance* 7, no. 1 (March): 135–146.

Ennis Knupp & Associates. 2004. *Private Equity Overview.* (January).

European Bond Commission. 1989. *The European Bond Markets: An Overview and Analysis for Issuers and Investors.* Chicago: Probus.

Evans, John, and Stephen Archer. 1968. "Diversification and the Reduction of Dispersion: An Empirical Analysis." *Journal of Finance* 23, no. 5 (December): 761–767.

Ezra, D. Don. 1998. "Strategic Asset Allocation and Total Portfolio Returns." In *Asset Allocation in a Changing World.* Charlottesville, VA: AIMR.

Fabozzi, Frank J. 1988. *Fixed-Income Mathematics.* Chicago: Probus.

Fabozzi, Frank J., ed. 1989. *Advances and Innovations in the Bond and Mortgage Markets.* Chicago: Probus.

Fabozzi, Frank J., ed. 1990. *The Japanese Bond Markets.* Chicago: Probus.

Fabozzi, Frank J., and Steven V. Mann. 2005. "Floating-Rate Securities." In *The Handbook of Fixed-Income Securities,* 7th ed., ed. Frank J. Fabozzi. New York: McGraw-Hill.

Fabozzi, Frank J., ed. 2005 *The Handbook of Fixed-Income Securities,* 7th ed. New York: McGraw-Hill.

Fabozzi, Frank J., Lionel Martellini, and Philippe Priaulet, eds. 2006. *Advanced Bond Portfolio Management.* Hoboken, NJ: John Wiley.

Fabozzi, Frank J. 2007. *Fixed-Income Analysis,* 2nd ed. Hoboken, NJ: Wiley.

Fabozzi, Frank J., ed. 2004. *Fixed-Income Readings,* 2nd ed. Hoboken, NJ: Wiley.

Fabozzi, Frank J. 2009. *Bond Markets, Analysis and Strategies,* 7th ed. Upper Saddle River, NJ: Pearson Prentice Hall.

Fabozzi, Frank J., Steven V. Mann, and Mourad Choudhry. 2005. "Interest Rate Swaps and Swaptions." In *The Handbook of Fixed-Income Securities,* 7th ed. New York: McGraw-Hill.

Fabozzi, Frank J., Gerald W. Buetow, and Robert R. Johnson. 2005. "Measuring Interest Rate Risk." In *The Handbook of Fixed-Income Securities,* 7th ed., ed. Frank J. Fabozzi. New York: McGraw-Hill.

Fabozzi, Frank J. 2005a. "Dedicated Bond Portfolios." In *The Handbook of Fixed-Income Securities,* 7th ed., ed. Frank J. Fabozzi. New York: McGraw-Hill.

Fabozzi, Frank J. 2005b. "Bond Immunization: An Asset/Liability Optimization Strategy." In *The Handbook of Fixed-Income Securities,* 7th ed., ed. Frank J. Fabozzi. New York: McGraw-Hill.

Fabozzi, Frank J., Andrew J. Kalotay, and George O. Williams. 2005. "Valuation of Bonds with Embedded Options." In *The Handbook of Fixed-Income Securities,* 7th ed., ed. Frank J. Fabozzi. New York: McGraw-Hill.

Fabozzi, Frank J., and Christopher K. Ma. 1988. "The Over-the-Counter Market and New York Stock Exchange Trading Halts." *Financial Review* 23, no. 4 (November): 427–437.

Fairfield, Patricia. 1994. "P/E, P/B, and the Present Value of Future Dividends." *Financial Analysts Journal* 50, no. 4 (July–August): 23–31.

Fama, Eugene F. 1970. "Efficient Capital Markets: A Review of Theory and Empirical Work." *Journal of Finance* 25, no. 2 (May): 383–417.

Fama, Eugene F. 1972. "Components of Investment Performance." *Journal of Finance* 27, no. 3 (June): 551–567.

Fama, Eugene F. 1976. "Forward Rates as Predictors of Future Spot Rates." *Journal of Financial Economics* 3, no. 4 (October): 361–377.

Fama, Eugene F. 1991. "Efficient Capital Markets: II." *Journal of Finance* 46, no. 5 (December): 1575–1617.

Fama, Eugene. 1998. "Market Efficiency, Long-Term Returns, and Behavioral Finance." *Journal of Financial Economics* 49, no. 3 (September): 283–306.

Fama, Eugene F., L. Fisher, M. Jensen, and R. Roll. 1969. "The Adjustment of Stock Prices to New Information." *International Economic Review* 10, no. 1 (February): 1–21.

Fama, Eugene F., and Kenneth French. 1989. "Business Conditions and Expected Returns on Stocks and Bonds." *Journal of Financial Economics* 25, no. 1 (November): 23–49.

Fama, Eugene F., and Kenneth French. 1992. "The Cross Section of Expected Stock Returns." *Journal of Finance* 47, no. 2 (June): 427–465.

Fama, Eugene F., and Kenneth R. French. 1993. "Common Risk Factors in the Returns on Stocks and Bonds." *Journal of Financial Economics* 33, no. 1 (January): 3–56.

Fama, Eugene F., and Kenneth R. French. 1998. "Value versus Growth: The International Evidence." *Journal of Finance* 53, no. 6 (December): 1975–1999.

Fama, Eugene F., and Merton H. Miller. 1972. *The Theory of Finance.* New York: Holt, Rinehart and Winston.

Farrell, James L. 1985. "The Dividend Discount Model: A Primer." *Financial Analysts Journal* 41, no. 6 (November–December): 16–25.

Farrell, James L., Jr. 1997. *Portfolio Management Theory and Application,* 2nd ed. New York: McGraw-Hill.

Feibel, Bruce J. 2003. *Investment Performance Measurement.* Hoboken, NJ: Wiley.

Feldstein, Sylvan G., and Alexander M. Grant, Jr. 2005. "Guidelines in the Credit Analysis of General Obligation and Revenue Municipal Bonds." In *The Handbook of Fixed-Income Securities,* 7th ed., ed. Frank J. Fabozzi. New York: McGraw-Hill.

Feldstein, Sylvan, Frank J. Fabozzi, Alexander M. Grant, Jr., and Patrick M. Kennedy. 2005. "Municipal Bonds." In *The Handbook of Fixed-Income Securities,* 7th ed., ed. Frank J. Fabozzi. New York: McGraw-Hill.

Fernholz, Robert, Robert Garvy, and John Hannon. 1998. "Diversity-Weighted Indexing." *Journal of Portfolio Management* 24, no. 2 (Winter): 74–82.

Ferson, Wayne E., and Rudi W. Schadt. 1996. "Measuring Fund Strategy and Performance in Changing Economic Conditions." *Journal of Finance* 52, no. 2 (June): 425–461.

Figlewski, Stephen. 1989a. "Options Arbitrage in Imperfect Markets." *Journal of Finance* 44, no. 5 (December): 1289–1311.

Figlewski, Stephen. 1989b. "What Does an Option Pricing Model Tell Us about Option Prices?" *Financial Analysts Journal* 45, no. 5 (September–October): 12–15.

Finnerty, John D. 1983. "Evaluating the Economics of Refunding High-Coupon Sinking-Fund Debt." *Financial Management* 12, no. 1 (Spring): 5–10.

Finnerty, John D. 1992. "An Overview of Corporate Securities Innovation." *Journal of Applied Corporate Finance* 4, no. 4 (Winter).

Finnerty, John D., and Dean Leistikow. 1993. "The Behavior of Equity and Debt Risk Premiums." *Journal of Portfolio Management* 19, no. 4 (Summer): 73–84.

Fisher, Irving. 1961. *The Theory of Interest.* New York: Augustus M. Kelley. (Orig. publ. Macmillan, 1930)

Fisher, Kenneth L. 1984. *SuperStocks.* Woodside, CA: Business Classics.

Fisher, Lawrence. 1959. "Determinants of Risk Premiums on Corporate Bonds." *Journal of Political Economy* 67, no. 3 (June): 217–237.

Fisher, Lawrence, and James H. Lorie. 1977. *A Half Century of Returns on Stocks and Bonds.* Chicago: University of Chicago Graduate School of Business.

Fisher, Lawrence, and Roman L. Weil. 1971. "Coping with the Risk of Interest-Rate Fluctuations: Returns to Bondholders from Naive and Optimal Strategies." *Journal of Business* 44, no. 4 (October): 408–431.

Fisher, Phillip A. 1984. *Common Stocks and Uncommon Profits.* Woodside, CA: PSR Publications. (Orig. publ. Harper, 1958)

Fogler, H. Russell. 1993. "A Modern Theory of Security Analysis." *Journal of Portfolio Management* 19, no. 3 (Spring): 6–14.

Fong, H. Gifford. 2001. "Bond Management: Past, Current, and Future." In *The Handbook of Fixed-Income Securities,* 6th ed., ed. Frank J. Fabozzi. New York: McGraw-Hill.

Foster, F. D., and S. Viswanathan. 1993. "The Effects of Public Information and Competition on Trading Volume and Price Volatility." *Review of Financial Studies* 6, no. 1 (Spring): 23–56.

Fowler, Gordon B., Jr. 2007. "Understanding 130/30 Equity Strategies." *CFA Institute Conference Proceedings Quarterly* (September): 11–16.

Francis, Jack Clark, William W. Toy, and J. Gregg Whittaker. 2000. *The Handbook of Equity Derivatives.* New York: John Wiley.

Fridson, Martin. 1989. *High-Yield Bonds: Assessing Risk and Identifying Value in Speculative Grade Securities.* Chicago: Probus.

Fridson, Martin, and Fernando Alvarez. 2002. *Financial Statement Analysis,* 3rd ed. New York: Wiley.

Fridson, Martin, Christopher Garman, and Sheng Wu. 1997. "Real Interest Rates and the Default Rate on High-Yield Bonds." *Journal of Fixed Income* 7, no. 2 (September): 27–34.

Friedman, Milton. 1969. *The Optimum Quantity of Money and Other Essays.* Chicago: Aldine.

Friedman, Milton, and Leonard J. Savage. 1948. "The Utility Analysis of Choices Involving Risk." *Journal of Political Economy* 56, no. 3 (August): 279–304.

Friedman, Milton, and Anna J. Schwartz. 1963. "Money and Business Cycles." *Review of Economics and Statistics* 45, no. 1, part 2, supplement (February): 32–78.

Friend, Irwin, and Marshall Blume. 1970. "Measurement of Portfolio Performance under Uncertainty." *American Economic Review* 60, no. 4 (September): 561–575.

Friend, Irwin, Marshall Blume, and Jean Crockett. 1970. *Mutual Funds and Other Institutional Investors.* New York: McGraw-Hill.

Gagnon, Louis, and Greg Lypny. 1995. "Hedging Short-Term Interest Risk under Time-Varying Distributions: Introduction." *The Journal of Futures Markets* 15, no. 7: 767.

Gagnon, Louis, and Greg Lypny. 1997. "The Benefits of Dynamically Hedging the Toronto 35 Stock Index." *Revue Canadienne des Sciences de l'Administration* 14, no. 1: 69–78.

Gagnon, Louis. 1990. "Exchange Traded Financial Derivatives in Canada: Finally off the Launching Pad." *Canadian Investment Review* 3, no. 2 (Fall): 63–70.

Galai, Dan, and Meir I. Schneller. 1978. "Pricing Warrants and the Value of the Firm." *Journal of Finance* 33, no. 5 (December): 1333–1342.

Gastineau, Gary. 2001. "Exchange-Traded Funds: An Introduction." *Journal of Portfolio Management* 27, no. 3 (Spring): 88–96.

Gentry, James A., Paul Newbold, and David T. Whitford. 1985a. "Classifying Bankrupt Firms with Funds Flow Components." *Journal of Accounting Research* 23, no. 1 (Spring).

Gentry, James A., Paul Newbold, and David T. Whitford. 1985b. "Predicting Bankruptcy: If Cash Flow's Not the Bottom Line, What Is?" *Financial Analysts Journal* 41, no. 5 (September–October): 47–56.

Gentry, James A., David T. Whitford, and Paul Newbold. 1988. "Predicting Industrial Bond Ratings with a Profit Model and Funds Flow Components." *Financial Review* 23, no. 3 (August): 269–286.

Gerov, Matey. 2006. "Quantitative Trading: The Predictive Power and Economic Effectiveness of Trading Trading Strategies." *Canadian Investment Review* 19, no. 4 (Winter): 8–16.

Gibbons, Michael. 1982. "Multivariate Tests of Financial Models: A New Approach." *Journal of Financial Economics* 10, no. 1 (March): 3–28.

Glickstein, David A., and Rolf E. Wubbels. 1983. "Dow Theory Is Alive and Well." *Journal of Portfolio Management* 9, no. 3 (Spring): 28–32.

Global Investment Performance Standards. 2005. Charlottesville, VA: CFA Institute.

Goff, Delbert C., Heather Hulburt, Terrill R. Keasler, and Joe Walsh. 2008. "Isolating the Information Content of Equity Analysts' Recommendation Changes, Post Reg FD." *Financial Review* 43, no. 2 (May): 303–321.

Goldman Sachs. 2007. "Introducing the GS SUSTAIN." Retrieved at http://www.unglobalcompact.org/docs/summit2007/gs_esg_embargoed_until030707pdf.pdf

Goodman, D. A., and John W. Peavy, III. 1983. "Industry Relative Price-Earnings Ratios as Indicators of Investment Returns." *Financial Analysts Journal* 39, no. 2 (March–April): 60–66.

Goodwin, Thomas H. 1998. "The Information Ratio." *Financial Analysts Journal* 54, no. 4 (July–August): 34–43.

Gordon, Myron J. 1962. *The Investment, Financing, and Valuation of the Corporation.* Homewood, IL: Irwin.

Grabbe, J. Orlin. 1986. *International Financial Markets.* New York: Elsevier Science.

Greenberg, Herb. 2000. "Alphabet Dupe: Why EBITDA Falls Short." *Fortune* 10 (July): 240–241.

Grinold, Richard C. 1992. "Are Benchmark Portfolios Efficient?" *Journal of Performance Management* 19, no. 1 (Fall): 34–40.

Grinold, Richard C., and Ronald N. Kahn. 1994. "Multiple-Factor Models for Portfolio Risk." In *A Practitioner's Guide to Factor Models,* ed. John Peavy. Charlottesville, VA: Research Foundation of the Institute of Chartered Financial Analysts.

Grinold, Richard C., and Ronald N. Kahn. 2008. *Active Portfolio Management,* 2nd ed. New York: McGraw-Hill.

Hackel, Kenneth S., and Joshua Livnat. 1996. *Cash Flow and Security Analysis,* 2nd ed. Burr Ridge, IL: Irwin Professional.

Hackel, Kenneth S., and Joshua Livnat. 1996. *Cash Flow and Security Analysis,* 2nd ed. Burr Ridge, IL: Irwin Professional Publishing.

Hagerty, James R., and Serena Ng. 2008. "Mortgage Giants Take Beating on Fears over Loan Defaults," *Wall Street Journal*, July 8, A1, A14.

Hagstrom, Robert G. 2001. *The Essential Buffett.* New York: Wiley.

Hamao, Yasushi. 1989. "Japanese Stocks, Bonds, Inflation, 1973–1987." *Journal of Portfolio Management* 16, no. 2 (Winter): 20–26.

Handa, Puneet, S. P. Kothari, and Charles Wasley. 1989. "The Relation between the Return Interval and Betas: Implications of the Size Effect." *Journal of Financial Economics* 23, no. 1 (June): 79–100.

Handa, Puneet, and Robert A. Schwartz. 1996. "How Best to Supply Liquidity to a Securities Market." *Journal of Portfolio Management* 22, no. 2 (Winter): 44–51.

Hanks, Sara. 1990. "SEC Ruling Creates a New Market." *Wall Street Journal,* May 16, p. A12.

Harlow, W. V., and Keith C. Brown. 2006. "The Right Answer to the Wrong Question: Identifying Superior Active Portfolio Management." *Journal of Investment Management* 4, no. 4 (Fourth Quarter): 15–40.

Harris, Larry. 2003. *Trading and Exchanges.* New York: Oxford University Press.

Harris, R. S. 1980. "The Refunding of Discounted Debt: An Adjusted Present Value Analysis." *Financial Management* 9, no. 4 (Winter): 7–12.

Hartford, Tim. 2008. *The Logic of Life,* New York: Random House.

Hawthorne, Fran. 1986. "The Battle of the Bond Indexes." *Institutional Investor* 20, no. 4 (April).

Helfert, Erich A. 2002. *Techniques of Financial Analysis,* 11th ed. New York: McGraw-Hill/Irwin.

Helwege, Jean, and Paul Kleiman. 1997. "Understanding Aggregate Default Rates of High-Yield Bonds." *Journal of Fixed Income* 7, no. 1 (June): 55–62.

Hendriksson, Roy D., and Robert C. Merton. 1981. "On Market Timing and Investment Performance: Statistical Procedures for Evaluating Forecasting Skills." *Journal of Business* 54, no. 4 (October): 513–534.

Henry, David. 2001. "The Numbers Game." *BusinessWeek,* May 14, pp. 100–110.

Hickman, W. Braddock. 1958. *Corporate Bond Quality and Investor Experience.* Princeton, NJ: Princeton University Press.

Hicks, John. 1939. *Value and Capital.* Oxford, UK: Clarendon Press.

Higgins, Robert C. 2005. *Analysis for Financial Management,* 8th ed. New York: McGraw-Hill/Irwin.

Hirschleifer, David. 2001. "Investor Psychology and Asset Pricing." *Journal of Finance* 56, no. 4 (August): 1533–1597.

Homer, Sidney, and Martin L. Leibowitz. 2004. *Inside the Yield Book: The Book that Changed Bond Analysis.* New York: Bloomberg.

Hopewell, Michael H., and George Kaufman. 1973. "Bond Price Volatility and Term to Maturity: A Generalized Respecification." *American Economic Review* 63, no. 4 (September): 749–753.

Hopewell, Michael H., and Arthur L. Schwartz, Jr. 1978. "Temporary Trading Suspensions in Individual NYSE Securities." *Journal of Finance* 33, no. 5 (December): 1355–1373.

Hopkins, Peter J. B., and C. Hayes Miller. 2001. *Country, Sector, and Company Factors in Global Equity Portfolios.* Charlottesville, VA: Research Foundation of AIMR.

Hourdouvelis, Gikas A. 1988. "The Predictive Power of the Term Structure during Recent Monetary Regimes." *Journal of Finance* 43, no. 2 (June): 339–356.

Howe, John S., and Tie Su. 2001. "Discretionary Reductions in Warrant Exercise Prices." *Journal of Financial Economics* 61, no. 2 (August): 227–252.

Hsueh, L. Paul, and David S. Kidwell. 1988. "Bond Ratings: Are Two Better Than One?" *Financial Management* 17, no. 1 (Spring): 46–53.

Huang, Roger. 2002. "The Quality of ECN and Nasdaq Market-Maker Quotes." *Journal of Finance* 57, no. 3 (June): 1285–1319.

Hughes, Pamela S., and Ehsan Zargar. 2006. "Exchange Demutualization." Blake, Cassels and Graydon LLP (May). Retrievable at http://www.blakes.ca/english/publications/bsra/v143/Paper-Exchange_Demutualization-May2006.pdf.

Hull, John. 2009. *Options, Futures, and Other Derivatives,* 7th ed. Upper Saddle River, NJ: Pearson Education.

Hurley, M., S. Meers, B. Bornstein, and N. Strumingher. 1995. *The Coming Evolution of the Investment Management Industry: Opportunities and Strategies.* New York: Goldman Sachs, October.

Ibbotson Associates. *Stocks, Bonds, Bills, and Inflation.* Chicago: Ibbotson Associates, annual.

Ibbotson, Roger G., and Paul D. Kaplan. 2000. "Does Asset Allocation Policy Explain 40, 90, or 100 Percent of Performance?" *Financial Analysts Journal* 56, no. 1 (January–February): 26–33.

Ibbotson, Roger G., Jody L. Sindelar, and Jay R. Ritter. 1994. "The Market Problems with the Pricing of Initial Public Offerings." *Journal of Applied Corporate Finance* 7, no. 1 (Spring): 66–74.

Ineichen, Alexander M. 2000. "Twentieth Century Volatility." *Journal of Portfolio Management* 27, no. 1 (Fall): 93–101.

Ip, Greg. 1998. "What's Behind the Trailing Performance of the Dow Industrials vs. the S & P 500?" *Wall Street Journal,* August 20, pp. C1, C17.

Ip, Greg. 2001. "If Big Board Specialists Are an Anachronism, They're a Profitable One." *Wall Street Journal,* March 12, pp. A1, A10.

Ivkovic, A., and N. Jegadeesh. 2004. "The Timing and Value of Forecast and Recommendation Revisions." *Journal of Financial Economics* 73, no. 3 (September): 433–463.

Jacobs, Bruce I., and Kenneth N. Levy. 2007. "20 Myths about Enhanced Active 120-20 Strategies." *Financial Analysts Journal* 63, no. 4 (July–August): 19–26.

Jain, Prom C. 1988. "Response of Hourly Stock Prices and Trading Volume to Economic News." *Journal of Business* 61, no. 2 (April).

James, Christopher, and Robert Edmister. 1983. "The Relation between Common Stock Returns, Trading Activity, and Market Value." *Journal of Finance* 38, no. 4 (September): 1075–1086.

Jarrow, Robert, and Stuart Turnbull. 2000. *Derivative Securities,* 2nd ed. Cincinnati, OH: Thomson Learning.

Jegadeesh, Narasimhan. 1990. "Evidence of Predictable Behavior of Security Returns." *Journal of Finance* 45, no. 3 (July): 881–898.

Jegadeesh, Narasimhan, J. Kim, S. Krische, and C. M. Lee. 2004. "Analyzing the Analysts: When Do Recommendations Add Value?" *Journal of Finance* 59, no. 3 (June): 1083–1124.

Jennings, Marianne M. 2000. "Professional Responsibilities, Ethics, and the Law." In *Ethical Issues for Today's Firm.* Charlottesville, VA: AIMR.

Jensen, Gerald R., Robert R. Johnson, and Jeffrey M. Mercer. 1997. "New Evidence on Size and Price-to-Book Effects in Stock Returns." *Financial Analysts Journal* 53, no. 6 (November–December): 34–42.

Jensen, Michael C. 1968. "The Performance of Mutual Funds in the Period 1945–1964." *Journal of Finance* 23, no. 2 (May): 389–416.

Jensen, Michael C., and Clifford W. Smith, Jr., eds. 1986. "Symposium on Investment Banking and the Capital Acquisition Process." *Journal of Financial Economics* 15, no. 1/2 (January–February): 3–29.

Jensen, Michael C., and Jerald B. Warner. 1988. "The Distribution of Power among Corporate Managers, Shareholders, and Directors." *Journal of Financial Economics* 20, no. 1/2 (January–March): 3–24.

Jesswein, Kurt, Chuck C. Y. Kwok, and William R. Folks. 1995. "What New Currency Risk Products Are Companies Using and Why?" *Journal of Applied Corporate Finance* 8, no. 3 (Fall): 103–114.

Jones, Christopher S. 2001. "Extracting factors from Heteroskedastic Asset Returns." *Journal of Financial Economics* 62, no. 2 (November): 293–325.

Jones, C. N., G. Kaul, and M. L. Lipson. 1994. "Information, Trading and Volatility." *Journal of Financial Economics* 36, no. 1 (August): 127–154.

Jones, C. P., R. J. Rendleman, Jr., and H. A. Latané. 1985. "Earnings Announcements: Pre- and Post-Responses." *Journal of Portfolio Management* 11, no. 3 (Spring): 28–32.

Jones, Thomas P. 1995. "The Economic Value-Added Approach to Corporate Investments." In *Corporate Financial Decision Making and Equity Analysis.* Charlottesville, VA: AIMR.

Jonsson, Jon G., and Martin S. Fridson. 1996. "Forecasting Default Rates on High-Yield Bonds." *Journal of Fixed Income* 6, no. 1 (June): 69–77.

Jorion, Philippe. 1991. "The Pricing of Exchange Rate Risk in the Stock Market." *Journal of Financial and Quantitative Analysis* 26, no. 3 (September): 363–376.

Jost, Kathryn Dixon, ed. 2001. *Best Execution and Portfolio Performance.* Charlottesville, VA: AIMR.

Jost, Kathryn Dixon, ed. 2002. *Fixed-Income Management for the 21st Century.* Charlottesville, VA: AIMR.

Kalotay, A. J. 1981. "On the Management of Sinking Funds." *Financial Management* 10, no. 2 (Summer): 34–40.

Kalotay, A. J. 1982a. "On the Structure and Valuation of Debt Refundings." *Financial Management* 11, no. 1 (Spring): 41–42.

Kalotay, A. J. 1982b. "Sinking Funds and the Realized Cost of Debt." *Financial Management* 11, no. 1 (Spring): 43–54.

Kamara, Avraham. 1984. "The Behavior of Futures Prices: A Review of Theory and Evidence." *Financial Analysts Journal* 40, no. 4 (July–August): 68–75.

Kan, J. 1997. *Handbook of Canadian Security Analysis,* Volume One. New York: Wiley.

Kan, J. 2000. *Handbook of Canadian Security Analysis,* Volume Two. New York: Wiley.

Kaplan, S. N., and R. S. Ruback. 1995. "The Valuation of Cash Flow Forecasts: An Empirical Analysis." *Journal of Finance* 50, no. 4 (September): 1059–1093.

Kaplan, Paul D. 1998. "Asset Allocation Models Using the Markowitz Approach." Retrieved at http://corporate.morningstar.com/ib/documents/MethodologyDocuments/IBBAssociates/Markowitz Approach.pdf.

Kat, Harry M. 2001. *Structured Equity Derivatives: The Definitive Guide to Exotic Options and Structured Notes.* London: Wiley.

Kessel, Reuben A. 1965. "The Cyclical Behavior of the Term Structure of Interest Rates." Occasional Paper 91. New York: National Bureau of Economic Research.

Keswani, Aneeland, and David Stolin. 2008. "Which Money Is Smart? Mutual Fund Buys and Sells of Individual and Institutional Investors." *The Journal of Finance* 63, no. 1 (February): 85–118.

Keynes, John Maynard. 1930. *A Treatise on Money.* London: Macmillan.

Khorana, Ajay, Edward Nelling, and Jeffrey Trester. 1998. "The Emergence of Country Index Funds." *Journal of Portfolio Management* 24, no. 4 (Summer): 78–84.

Khorana, Aja, Henri Servaes, and Peter Tufano, 2007. "Mutual Fund Fees around the World," HBS Finance Working Paper No. 901023 (July).

Khoury, Nabil, and Klaus P. Fischer. 2002. "The Effect of Multiple Listings on the Bid-Ask Spread in Option Markets: The Case of Montreal Exchange." *The Journal of Futures Markets* 22, no. 10: 939–957.

Khoury, Nabil, Marc Veilleux, and Robert Viau. 2003. "A Performance Attribution Model for Fixed-Income Portfolios." *Canadian Investment Review* 16, no. 3 (October): 11–18.

King, Michael R., and Maksym Padalko, 2007. "Outing Insiders: A Look at Price and Volume Dynamics Ahead of Canadian Merger Announcements." *Canadian Investment Review* 20, no. 1 (Spring): 16–23.

Klemkosky, Robert C. 1973. "The Bias in Composite Performance Measures." *Journal of Financial and Quantitative Analysis* 8, no. 3 (June): 505–514.

Klemkosky, Robert C., and Bruce G. Resnick. 1979. "Put-Call Parity and Market Efficiency. *Journal of Finance* 34, no. 5 (December): 1141–1155.

Klibanoff, Peter, Owen Lamont, and Thierry A. Wizman. 1998. "Investor Reaction to Salient News in Closed-End Country Funds." *Journal of Finance* 53, no. 2 (April): 673–699.

Koller, Tim, Marc Goedhart, and David Wessels. 2005. *Valuation: Measuring and Managing the Value of Companies,* 4th ed. New York: Wiley.

Kon, Stanley J. 1983. "The Market-Timing Performance of Mutual Fund Managers." *Journal of Business* 56, no. 3 (July): 323–347.

Kooli, M., and M. J. Suret. 2004. "The Aftermarket Performance of Initial Public Offerings in Canada." *Journal of Multinational Financial Management* 14, no.1: 47–66.

Korkie, B., and H. Turtle. 1998. "The Canadian Investment Opportunity Set. 1967–1993." *Canadian Journal of Administrative Sciences* 15, no. 3 (September): 213–229.

Kostovetsky, Leonard. 2003. "Index Mutual Funds and Exchange-Traded Funds." *Journal of Portfolio Management* 29, no. 4 (Summer): 80–92.

Krehbiel, Tim, and Roger Collier. 1996. "Normal Backwardation in Short-Term Interest Rate Markets." *Journal of Futures Markets* 16, no. 8 (December): 899–913.

Kritzman, Mark. 1983. "Can Bond Managers Perform Consistently?" *Journal of Portfolio Management* 9, no. 4 (Summer): 54–56.

Kritzman, Mark. 1986. "What's Wrong with Portfolio Insurance?" *Journal of Portfolio Management* 13, no. 1 (Fall): 13–17.

Kritzman, Mark P. 1990. "Quantitative Methods in Performance Measurement." In *Quantitative Methods for Financial Analysis,* 2nd ed., ed. S. Brown and M. P. Kritzman. Homewood, IL: Dow Jones–Irwin.

Kritzman, Mark. 1992. "What Investors Need to Know about Duration and Convexity." *Financial Analysts Journal* 48, no. 6 (November–December): 17–20.

Kryzanowski, Lawrence, Skander Lasrak, and Ian Rakita. 2005. "The Behaviour of Prices, Trades, and Spreads for Canadian IPOs," *Multinational Finance Journal* 9, no. 3/4: 213–234.

Kryzanowski, Lawrence, Simon Lalancette, and Minh Chau To. 1997. "Performance Attribution Using an APT with Prespecified Macrofactors and Time-Varying Risk Premia and Betas," *Journal of Financial and Quantitative Analysis* 32, no. 2 (June): 205–224 .

Lakonishok, Josef, Andrei Shleifer, and Robert W. Vishny. 1992. "The Structure and Performance of the Money Management Industry." In *Brookings Papers on Economic Activity.* Washington, DC: Brookings Institute.

Lawton, Philip, and W. Bruce Remington. 2007. "Global Investment Performance Standards." In *Managing Investment Portfolio: A Dynamic Process,* 3rd ed., ed. John L. Maginn, Donald L. Tuttle, Jerald E. Pinto, and Dennis W. McLeavey. Hoboken, NJ: Wiley.

Layard-Liesching, Ronald. 2001. "Exploiting Opportunities in Global Bond Markets." In *Core-Plus Bond Management,* Association for Investment Management and Research. Charlottesville, VA: 30–38.

Lee, Charles. 2003. "Fusion Investing." In *Equity Valuation in a Global Context.* Charlottesville, VA: AIMR.

Lee, Charles, Andrei Shleifer, and Richard Thaler. 1991. "Investor Sentiment and the Closed- End Fund Puzzle." *Journal of Finance* 46, no. 1 (March): 76–110.

Lehmann, Bruce N., and David M. Modest. 1988. "The Empirical Foundations of the Arbitrage Pricing Theory." *Journal of Financial Economics* 21, no. 3 (September).

Leibowitz, Martin L. 1986a. "The Dedicated Bond Portfolio in Pension Funds—Part I: Motivations and Basics." *Financial Analysts Journal* 42, no. 1 (January–February): 68–75.

Leibowitz, Martin L. 1986b. "The Dedicated Bond Portfolio in Pension Funds—Part II: Immunization, Horizon Matching, and Contingent Procedures." *Financial Analysts Journal* 42, no. 2 (March–April): 47–57.

Leibowitz, Martin L. 1997. *Sales Driven Franchise Value.* Charlottesville, VA: Research Foundation of the Institute of Chartered Financial Analysts.

Leibowitz, Martin L., Thomas E. Klaffky, Steven Mandel, and Alfred Weinberger. 1983. *Horizon Matching: A New Generalized Approach for Developing Minimum-Cost Dedicated Portfolios.* New York: Salomon Brothers.

Leibowitz, Martin L., and Stanley Kogelman. 1994. *Franchise Value and the Price-Earnings Ratio.* Charlottesville, VA: Research Foundation of the Institute of Chartered Financial Analysts.

Leibowitz, Martin L., William S. Krasker, and Ardavan Nozari. 1990. "Spread Duration: A New Tool for Bond Portfolio Management." *Journal of Portfolio Management* 16, no. 3 (Spring): 46–53.

Leibowitz, Martin L., and Alfred Weinberger. 1982. "Contingent Immunization—Part I: Risk Control Procedures." *Financial Analysts Journal* 38, no. 6 (November–December): 17–32.

Leibowitz, Martin L., and Alfred Weinberger. 1983. "Contingent Immunization—Part II: Problem Areas." *Financial Analysts Journal* 39, no. 1 (January–February): 35–50.

Leland, Hayne E. 1999. "Beyond Mean-Variance: Performance Measurement in a Nonsymmetrical World." *Financial Analysts Journal* 55, no. 1 (January–February): 27–36.

Lessard, Donald R. 1988. "International Diversification." In *The Financial Analyst's Handbook,* 2nd ed., ed. Sumner N. Levine. Homewood, IL: Dow Jones–Irwin.

Levine, Sumner N., ed. 1988. "Bond Ratings." In *The Financial Analyst's Handbook,* 2nd ed. Homewood, IL: Dow Jones–Irwin.

Levy, Robert A. 1966. "Conceptual Foundations of Technical Analysis." *Financial Analysts Journal* 22, no. 4 (July/August): 83.

Lhabitant, Francois-Serge. 2002. *Hedge Funds: Myths and Limits.* Hoboken, NJ: Wiley.

Li, Bin, and Lawrence Krzanowski. 2000. "What Determines the Holding Period of an Investor? *Canadian Investment Review* 13, no. 3 (October): 18+.

Lintner, John. 1965. "Security Prices, Risk and Maximal Gains from Diversification." *Journal of Finance* 20, no. 4 (December): 587–615.

Litzenberger, Robert, and K. Ramaswamy. 1979. "The Effect of Personal Taxes and Dividends on Capital Asset Prices: Theory and Empirical Evidence." *Journal of Financial Economics* 7, no. 2 (June): 163–196.

Liu, P., and W. T. Moore. 1987. "The Impact of Split Bond Ratings on Risk Premia." *The Financial Review* 22, no. 1 (February).

Lo, Andrew W. 2002. "The Statistics of Sharpe Ratios." *Financial Analysts Journal* 58, no. 4 (July–August): 36–52.

Lo, Andrew W., and A. Craig MacKinley. 1999. *A Non-Random Walk down Wall Street.* Princeton, NJ: Princeton University Press.

Loomis, Carol J. 1996. "Short Sellers and the Seamy Side of Wall Street." *Fortune,* July 22, pp. 66–72.

Lorie, James. 1975. "Diversification: Old and New." *Journal of Portfolio Management* 1, no. 2 (Winter): 25–28.

Loughran, T., J. Ritter and K. Rydqvist. 2008. "Initial Public Offerings: International Insights," *Pacific-Basin Finance Journal* 2: 165–199. Updated March 20, 2008; available at http://bear.cba.ufl.edu/ritter/Int2008.pdf.

Lowenstein, Roger. 1995. *Buffett: The Making of an American Capitalist.* New York: Random House.

Ludvigson, Sydney C., and Serena Ng. 2007. "The Empirical Risk-Return Relation: A Factor Analysis Approach." *Journal of Financial Economics* 83, no. 1 (January): 171–222.

Lummer, Scott L. 1994. "Public Perception of the Investment Industry: Trends and Counteractions." In *Good Ethics: The Essential Element of a Firm's Success,* ed. K. Baker. Charlottesville, VA: AIMR.

Lummer, Scott L., and Mark W. Riepe. 1993. "Convertible Bonds as an Asset Class: 1957–1992." *Journal of Fixed Income* 3, no. 2 (September): 47–56.

Lynch, Peter. 1989. *One Up on Wall Street.* New York: Simon & Schuster.

Lynch, Peter. 1993. *Beating the Street.* New York: Simon & Schuster.

Macaulay, Frederick R. 1938. *Some Theoretical Problems Suggested by the Movements of Interest Rates, Bond Yields, and Stock Prices in the United States since 1856.* New York: National Bureau of Economic Research.

MacBeth, James D., and Larry J. Merville. 1979. "An Empirical Examination of the Black-Scholes Call Option Pricing Model." *Journal of Finance* 34, no. 5 (December): 1173–1186.

Madhaven, Ananth, and George Sofianos. 1998. "An Empirical Analysis of NYSE Specialist Trading." *Journal of Financial Economics* 48, no. 2 (May): 189–210.

Malkiel, Burton G. 1962. "Expectations, Bond Prices, and the Term Structure of Interest Rates." *Quarterly Journal of Economics* 76, no. 2 (May): 197–218.

Malkiel, B. G. 1995. "The Structure of Closed-End Fund Discounts Revisited." *The Journal of Portfolio Management* 21, no. 4: 32–38.

Malkiel, Burton G. 2007. *A Random Walk down Wall Street.* 9th ed. New York: Norton.

Malkiel, Burton G., and John G. Cragg. 1970. "Expectations and the Structure of Share Prices." *American Economic Review* 60, no. 4 (September): 601–617.

Malvey, Jack. 2005. "Global Credit Bond Portfolio Management." In *The Handbook of Fixed-Income Securities,* 7th ed., ed. Frank J. Fabozzi. New York: McGraw-Hill.

Mandelker, Gershon M., and S. Ghon Rhee. 1984. "The Impact of Degrees of Operating and Financial Leverage on the Systematic Risk of Common Stock." *Journal of Financial and Quantitative Analysis* 19, no. 1 (March): 45–57.

Marin, Jose M., and Jacques P. Oliver. 2008. "The Dog That Did Not Bark: Insider Trading and Crashes," *The Journal of Finance* 63, no. 5 (October): 2429–2476.

Mankiw, N. G., Kneebone, R. D., McKenzie, K. J., and N. Rowe. 2008. *Principles of Macroeconomics,* 4th Canadian Edition. Toronto: Nelson Publishing.

Markowitz, Harry. 1952. "Portfolio Selection." *Journal of Finance* 7, no. 1 (March): 77–91.

Markowitz, Harry. 1959. *Portfolio Selection—Efficient Diversification of Investments.* New York: Wiley.

Marmer, Harry, Martin Den Hayer, and Barry McInerney. 1997. "The Uses of Real Return Bonds." *Canadian Investment Review* 10, no. 4 (January): 40.

Marshall, William, and Jess B. Yawitz. 1980. "Optimal Terms of the Call Provision on a Corporate Bond." *Journal of Financial Research* 3, no. 3 (Fall): 203–211.

Masinn, John L., Donald L. Tuttle, Jerold E. Pinto, and Dennis W. McLeavy. 2007. *Managing Investment Portfolios: A Dynamic Process,* 3rd ed. Hoboken, NJ: John Wiley & Sons.

McConnell, John J., and Gary Sanger. 1989. "A Trading Strategy for New Listings on the NYSE." *Financial Analysts Journal* 40, no. 1 (January–February): 38–39.

McCulloch, J. Huston. 1975. "An Estimate of the Liquidity Premium." *Journal of Political Economy* 83, no. 1 (January–February): 95–119.

McDonald, Robert L. 2003. *Derivatives Markets.* Boston, MA: Pearson Education.

McGuire, S. R. 1991. *The Handbook of Convertibles.* New York: Simon & Schuster.

Merton, Robert C. 1973a. "The Relationship between Put and Call Option Prices: Comment." *Journal of Finance* 28, no. 1 (March): 183–184.

Merton, Robert C. 1973b. "Theory of Rational Option Pricing." *Bell Journal of Economics and Management* 4, no. 1 (Spring): 141–183.

Merton, Robert C., Myron S. Scholes, and Mathew L. Gladstein. 1978. "The Returns and Risk of Alternative Call Option Portfolio Investment Strategies." *Journal of Business* 51, no. 2: 183–242.

Merton, Robert C. 1981. "On Market Timing and Investment Performance: An Equilibrium Theory of Value for Market Forecasts." *Journal of Business* 54, no. 3 (July): 363–406.

Metcalf, Cherie, Angela Redish, and Ronald Shearer. 1998. "New Estimates of the Canadian Money Stock, 1871–1967." *The Canadian Journal of Economics* 31, no. 1 (February): 104–124.

Meyers, Thomas A. 1989. *The Technical Analysis Course.* Chicago: Probus.

Miller, Janet T., ed. 2001. *Investment Counseling for Private Clients, III.* Charlottesville, VA: AIMR.

Miller, Merton H., and Franco Modigliani. 1961. "Dividend Policy, Growth, and the Valuation of Shares." *Journal of Business* 34, no. 4 (October): 411–433.

Miller, Merton H., and Myron Scholes. 1982. "Dividends and Taxes: Some Empirical Evidence." *Journal of Political Economy* 90, no. 4 (December): 1118–1141.

Miller, Robert E., and Frank K. Reilly. 1987. "Examination of Mispricing, Returns, and Uncertainty for Initial Public Offerings." *Financial Management* 16, no. 2 (January): 33–38.

Miller, Victoria. 1997. "Inflation Uncertainty and Optimal Debt Maturity: An Empirical Look at Canadian and U.S. Government Bonds." *Canadian Journal of Administrative* Sciences 14, no. 3: 246–258.

Milligan, John W. 1990. "Two Cheers for 144A." *Institutional Investor* 24, no. 9 (July): 117–119.

Mishkin, Frederic S., and Apostolos Serletis, 2008. *The Economics of Money, Banking, and Financial Markets*, Third Canadian Edition: Toronto: Addison Wesley.

Mitchell, Roger S., ed. 2000. *Investment Counseling for Private Clients, II.* Charlottesville, VA: AIMR.

Mody, Ashoka, and Mark P. Taylor. 2003. "The High-Yield Spread as a Predictor of Real Economic Activity: Evidence of a Financial Accelerator for the United States." *IMF Staff Papers* 50, no. 3: 373–402.

Molinas, César, and Gioia Bales. 2004. "Size and Structure of the World Bond Market: 2004." Merrill Lynch Global Fixed Income Research Team.

Moore, Geoffrey, and John P. Cullity. 1988. "Security Markets and Business Cycles." In *The Financial Analyst's Handbook,* 2nd ed., ed. Sumner N. Levine. Homewood, IL: Dow Jones–Irwin.

Moriarty, Eugene, Susan Phillips, and Paula Tosini. 1981. "A Comparison of Options and Futures in the Management of Portfolio Risk." *Financial Analysts Journal* 37, no. 1 (January–February): 61–67.

Mossavar-Rahmani, Sharmin. 1988. "Customized Benchmarks in Structured Management." *Journal of Portfolio Management* 13, no. 4 (Summer): 65–68.

Mossavar-Rahmani, Sharmin. 1991. *Bond Index Funds.* Chicago: Probus.

Mossavar-Rahmani, Sharmin. 2005. "Indexing Fixed-Income Assets." In *The Handbook of Fixed-Income Securities,* 7th ed., ed. Frank J. Fabozzi. New York: McGraw-Hill.

Mossin, J. 1966. "Equilibrium in a Capital Asset Market." *Econometrica* 34, no. 4 (October): 768–783.

Munves, David. 2005. "The Eurobond Market." In *The Handbook of Fixed-Income Securities,* 7th ed., ed. Frank J. Fabozzi. New York: McGraw-Hill.

Nederlof, Maarten L. 1993. "The Comparison of Strategies Using Derivatives." In *Derivative Strategies for Managing Portfolio Risk,* ed. K. Brown. Charlottesville, VA: AIMR.

Nicholas, Joseph G. 1999. *Investing in Hedge Funds: Strategies for the New Marketplace.* Princeton, NJ: Bloomberg Press.

Nicholas, Joseph G. 2005. *Investing in Hedge Funds: Revised and Updated Edition.* New York: Bloomberg Press.

Norton, Joseph, and Paul Spellman, eds. 1991. *Asset Securitization.* Cambridge, MA: Basil Blackwell.

Oberlechner, Thomas. 2007. *The Psychology of Ethics in the Finance and Investment Industry.* Charlottesville, VA: Research Foundation of CFA Institute.

Odean, Terrance. 1998. "Are Investors Reluctant to Realize Their Losses?" *Journal of Finance* 53, no. 5 (October): 1775–1798.

Odean, Terrance. 1999. "Do Investors Trade Too Much?" *American Economic Review* 89 (December): 1279–1298.

Olsen, Robert A. 1998. "Behavioral Finance and Its Implications for Stock-Price Volatility." *Financial Analysts Journal* 54, no. 2 (March–April): 10–18.

Otuteye, Eben. 1991. "How Economic Forces Explain Canadian Stock Returns." *Canadian Investment Review,* vol. 4 (Spring 1991).

Palepu, Krishna, Victor Bernard, and Paul Healy. 2007. *Business Analysis and Valuation.* Cincinnati, OH: South-Western.

Park, Tae H., and Lorne N. Switzer. 1995. "Bivariate Garch Estimation of the Optimal Hedge Ratios for Stock Index Futures: A Note." *The Journal of Futures Markets* 15, no. 1: p. 61.

Park, Tae H., and Lorne N. Switzer. 1995. "Index Participation Units and the Performance of Index Futures Markets: Evidence from the Toronto 35 Index Participation Units Market." *The Journal of Futures Markets* 15, no. 2: p. 187.

Parnes, Dror. 2007. "Applying Credit Score Models to Multiple States of Nature," *Journal of Fixed Income* 17, no. 3 (Winter): 57–71.

Peavy, John W., III, and David A. Goodman. 1983. "The Significance of P/Es for Portfolio Returns." *Journal of Portfolio Management* 9, no. 2 (Winter).

Peavy, John, ed. 1994. *A Practitioner's Guide to Factor Models.* Charlottesville, VA: Research Foundation of the CFA Institute.

Penman, S. H. 1996. "The Articulation of Price-Earnings Ratios and Market-to-Book Ratios and the Evaluation of Growth." *Journal of Accounting Research* 34, no. 2 (Spring).

Penman, Stephen. 2007. *Financial Statement Analysis and Security Valuation,* 3rd ed. New York: McGraw-Hill.

Peters, Donald J. 1991. "Valuing a Growth Stock." *Journal of Portfolio Management* 17, no. 3 (Spring): 49–51.

Peterson, Pamela P., and David Peterson. 1996. "Company Performance Measures of Value Added." Charlottesville, VA: Research Foundation of the Institute of Chartered Financial Analysis.

Petrie, Thomas A., ed. 1993. *The Oil and Gas Industries.* Proceedings from the fourth AIMR Industry seminar, November 12–13, 1992, in Houston, Texas. Charlottesville, VA: AIMR.

Pettit, R. R., and P. C. Venkatesh. 1995. "Insider Trading and Long-Run Return Performance." *Financial Management* 24, no. 2 (Summer): 88–103.

Pierce, Douglas, and Vance Roley. 1985. "Stock Prices and Economic News." *Journal of Business* 59, no. 1 (Summer).

Pierce, Phyllis S., ed. *The Business One Irwin Investor's Handbook.* Burr Ridge, IL: Dow Jones Books, published annually.

Pompian, Michael M. 2006. *Behaviorial Finance and Wealth Management: How to Build Optimal Portfolios that Account for Investor Biases.* Hoboken, NJ: John Wiley & Sons.

Porter, Michael E. 1980a. *Competitive Strategy: Techniques for Analyzing Industries and Competitors.* New York: Free Press.

Porter, Michael E. 1980b. "Industry Structure and Competitive Strategy: Keys to Profitability." *Financial Analysts Journal* 36, no. 4 (July–August).

Porter, Michael E. 1985. *Competitive Advantage: Creating and Sustaining Superior Performance.* New York: Free Press.

Porter, Michael E. 1988. "How to Conduct an Industry Analysis." In *The Financial Analysts Handbook,* 2nd ed., ed. Sumner N. Levine. Homewood, IL: Dow Jones–Irwin.

Potvin, Paul. 1992. "Passive Management, the TSE 300 and the Toronto 35 Stock Indexes." *Canadian Investment Review* 5, no. 1 (April): 61–65.

Power, William. 1993. "Short Sellers Set to Catch Tumbling Overhead Stocks." *Wall Street Journal,* December 28, pp. C1, C2.

Pozen, Robert C. 2001. *The Mutual Fund Business,* 2nd ed. Boston, MA: Houghton Mifflin.

Prentice, Robert A. 2007. "Ethical Decision Making: More Needed Than Good Intentions." *Financial Analysts Journal* 63, no. 6 (November–December): 17–30.

Pring, Martin J. 1991. *Technical Analysis Explained,* 3rd ed. New York: McGraw-Hill.

Prisman, Eliezer Z., and Yisong Tian. 1994. "Immunization in Markets with Tax-Clientele Effects: Evidence from the Canadian Market." *Journal of Financial and Quantitative Analysis* 29, no. 2: p. 301.

Puffer, Marlene. 2006. "Back to Basics: An Overview of Fixed Income Products and New Trends." *Canadian Investment Review* 19, no. 3 (Fall): 22–27.

Rappaport, Liz. 2004. "Electronic Platforms See Surge in Trading of Corporate Bonds." *Wall Street Journal,* November 3, p. C5.

Redington, F. M. 1952. "Review of the Principles of Life—Office Valuations." *Journal of the Institute of Actuaries* 78: 286–340.

Reilly, Frank K., and Rashid A. Akhtar. 1995. "The Benchmark Error Problem with Global Capital Markets." *Journal of Portfolio Management* 22, no. 1 (Fall): 33–52.

Reilly, Frank K., and James A. Gentry. 2004. "The Growing Importance of Credit Analysis." Working paper, University of Notre Dame.

Reilly, Frank K., Wenchi Kao, and David J. Wright. 1992. "Alternative Bond Market Indexes." *Financial Analysts Journal* 48, no. 3 (May–June): 44–58.

Reilly, Frank K., and Dominic R. Marshall. 1999. "Using P/E/ Growth Ratios to Select Stocks." Paper presented at Financial Management Association Meeting, Seattle, October.

Reilly, Frank K., and Rupinder Sidhu. 1980. "The Many Uses of Bond Duration." *Financial Analysts Journal* 36, no. 4 (July–August): 58–72.

Reilly, Frank K., and David J. Wright. 1984. "Block Trades and Aggregate Stock Price Volatility." *Financial Analysts Journal* 40, no. 2 (March–April): 54–60.

Reilly, Frank K., and David J. Wright. 1988. "A Comparison of Published Betas." *Journal of Portfolio Management* 14, no. 3 (Spring): 64–69.

Reilly, Frank K., and David J. Wright. 1994. "An Analysis of High-Yield Bond Benchmarks." *Journal of Fixed Income* 3, no. 4 (March): 6–25.

Reilly, Frank K., and David J. Wright. 1995. "Global Bond Markets: An Analysis of Alternative Benchmarks and Risk-Return Performance." Paper presented at Midwest Finance Association Meeting, Chicago, March.

Reilly, Frank K., and David J. Wright. 1997. "Introducing a Comprehensive U.S. Treasury Bond Market Benchmark." In *Yield Curve Dynamics,* ed. Ronald J. Ryan. Chicago: Glen Lake.

Reilly, Frank K., and David J. Wright. 1999. "An Analysis of High-Yield Bond Indices." In *High-Yield Bonds,* ed. Theodore M. Barnhill, Jr., William F. Maxwell, and Mark R. Shenkman. New York: McGraw-Hill.

Reilly, Frank K., and David J. Wright. 2001. "Unique Risk-Return Characteristics of High-Yield Bonds." *Journal of Fixed Income* 11, no. 2 (September): 65–82.

Reilly, Frank K., and David J. Wright. 2002. "Alternative Small-Cap Stock Benchmarks." *The Journal of Portfolio Management* 28, no. 3 (Spring): 82–95.

Reilly, Frank K., and David J. Wright. 2004. "Analysis of Risk-Adjusted Performance for Global Market Assets." *Journal of Portfolio Management* 30, no. 3 (Spring): 63–77.

Reilly, Frank K., and David J. Wright. 2005. "Bond Market Indexes." In *The Handbook of Fixed-Income Securities,* 7th ed., ed. Frank J. Fabozzi. New York: McGraw-Hill.

Reilly, Frank K., David J. Wright, and Edward I. Altman. 1998. "Including Defaulted Bonds in the Capital Markets Asset Spectrum." *Journal of Fixed Income* 8, no. 3 (December): 33–48.

Reilly, Frank K., David J. Wright, and Kam C. Chan. 2000. "Bond Market Volatility Compared to Stock Market Volatility." *Journal of Portfolio Management* 27, no. 1 (Fall): 82–92.

Reilly, Frank K., David J. Wright, and Robert R. Johnson. 2005. "An Analysis of the Interest Rate Sensitivity of Common Stocks." Paper presented at Financial Management Association European Meeting June 6, Siena, Italy.

Reilly, Frank K., David J. Wright, and Robert R. Johnson. 2007. "Analysis of the Interest Rate Sensitivity of Common Stocks." *The Journal of Portfolio Management* 33, no. 3: 85–107.

Reilly, Frank K., and Thomas Zeller. 1974. "An Analysis of Relative Industry Price–Earnings Ratios." *Financial Review,* 17–33.

Reinganum, Marc R. 1981. "The Arbitrage Pricing Theory: Some Empirical Results." *Journal of Finance* 36, no. 2 (May): 313–321.

Reinganum, Marc R. 1983. "Portfolio Strategies Based on Market Capitalization." *Journal of Portfolio Management* 9, no. 2 (Winter).

Reinganum, Marc R. 1992. "A Revival of the Small-Firm Effect." *Journal of Portfolio Management* 18, no. 3 (Spring): 55–62.

Rendleman, Richard J., Jr., and Brit J. Bartter. 1979. "Two-State Option Pricing." *Journal of Finance* 34, no. 5 (December): 1093–1110.

Rendleman, Richard J., Jr., Charles P. Jones, and Henry A. Latané. 1982. "Empirical Anomalies Based on Unexpected Earnings and the Importance of Risk Adjustments." *Journal of Financial Economics* 10, no. 3 (November): 269–287.

Rogalski, Richard J., and James K. Seward. 1991. "Corporate Issues of Foreign Currency Warrants." *Journal of Financial Economics* 30, no. 2 (December): 347–366.

Rogowski, Robert J., and Eric H. Sorensen. 1985. "Deregulation in Investment Banking: Shelf Registration, Structure and Performance." *Financial Management* 14, no. 1 (Spring): 5–15.

Roll, Richard. 1977. "A Critique of the Asset Pricing Theory's Tests." *Journal of Financial Economics* 4, no. 4 (March): 129–176.

Roll, Richard. 1978. "Ambiguity When Performance Is Measured by the Securities Market Line." *Journal of Finance* 33, no. 4 (September): 1051–1069.

Roll, Richard. 1980. "Performance Evaluation and Benchmark Error I." *Journal of Portfolio Management* 6, no. 4 (Summer): 5–12.

Roll, Richard. 1981. "Performance Evaluation and Benchmark Error II." *Journal of Portfolio Management* 7, no. 2 (Winter): 17–22.

Rosenberg, Barr, Kenneth Reid, and Ronald Lanstein. 1985. "Persuasive Evidence of Market Inefficiency." *Journal of Portfolio Management* 11, no. 3 (Spring): 9–17.

Rosenberg, Michael R. 2005. "International Fixed-Income Investing: Theory and Practice." In *The Handbook of Fixed-Income Securities,* 7th ed., ed. Frank J. Fabozzi. New York: McGraw-Hill.

Rosenberg, Michael R. 1996. *Currency Forecasting.* Burr Ridge, IL: Irwin Professional Publishing.

Ross, Stephen. 1976. "The Arbitrage Theory of Capital Asset Pricing." *Journal of Economic Theory* 13, no. 2 (December): 341–360.

Ross, Stephen. 1977. "Return, Risk, and Arbitrage." In *Risk and Return in Finance,* ed. I. Friend and J. Bicksler, pp. 189–218. Cambridge, MA: Ballinger.

Rubinstein, Mark. 1985a. "Alternative Paths to Portfolio Insurance." *Financial Analysts Journal* 41, no. 4 (July–August): 42–52.

Rubinstein, Mark. 1985b. "Nonparametric Tests of Alternative Options Pricing Models Using All Reported Trades and Quotes on the 30 Most Active CBOE Options Classes from August 23, 1976, through August 31, 1978." *Journal of Finance* 40, no. 2 (June): 455–480.

Rubinstein, Mark. 1994. "Implied Binomial Trees." *Journal of Finance* 49, no. 3 (July): 771–818.

Rueschhoff, Norlin, and David Strupeck. 2000. "Equity Returns: Local GAAP versus US GAAP for Foreign Issuers from Developing Countries." *Journal of International Accounting* 33, no. 3 (Spring).

Sadka, Ronnie E., and Anna Scherbina. 2007. "Analysts Disagreement, Mispricing, and Liquidity." *The Journal of Finance* 62, no. 5 (October).

Salomon, Ezra. 1963. *The Theory of Financial Management.* New York: Columbia University Press.

Saporiot, Bill. 2009. "How AIG Became Too Big to Fail," *Time* magazine, March 19.

Schmidt, Klaus M. 2003. "Convertible Securities and Venture Capital Finance." *Journal of Finance* 58, no. 3 (June): 1139–1166.

Schulz, Ellen R. 1996. "Workers Put Too Much in Their Employer's Stock." *Wall Street Journal,* September 13, pp. C1, C25.

Schwert, G. William. 1989. "Why Does Stock Market Volatility Change over Time?" *Journal of Finance* 44, no. 5 (December): 1115–1153.

Senchack, A. J., Jr., and John D. Martin. 1987. "The Relative Performance of the PSR and PER Investment Strategies." *Financial Analysts Journal* 43, no. 2 (March–April): 46–56.

Shackalford, Aaron L., ed. 1997. *Economic Analysis for Investment Professionals.* Charlottesville, VA: AIMR.

Shanken, Jay. 1985. "Multivariate Tests of the Zero Beta CAPM." *Journal of Financial Economics* 14, no. 3 (September): 327–348.

Sharpe, William F. 1964. "Capital Asset Prices: A Theory of Market Equilibrium under Conditions of Risk." *Journal of Finance* 19, no. 3 (September): 425–442.

Sharpe, William F. 1966. "Mutual Fund Performance." *Journal of Business* 39, no. 1, part 2 (January): 119–138.

Sharpe, William F. 1984. "Factor Models, CAPMs, and the APT." *Journal of Portfolio Management* 11, no. 1 (Fall): 21–25.

Sharpe, William F. 1987. "Integrated Asset Allocation." *Financial Analysts Journal* 43, no. 5 (September–October): 25–32.

Sharpe, William F. 1990. "Asset Allocation." In *Managing Investment Portfolios: A Dynamic Process,* 2nd ed., ed. John L. Maginn and Donald L. Tuttle. Boston: Warren, Gorham, & Lamont.

Sharpe, William. 1991. "The Arithmetic of Active Management." *Financial Analysts Journal* 47, no. 1 (January–February): 7–9.

Sharpe, William F. 1992. "Asset Allocation: Management Style and Performance Measurement." *Journal of Portfolio Management* 18, no. 2 (Winter): 7–19.

Sharpe, William F. 1994. "The Sharpe Ratio." *Journal of Portfolio Management* 21, no. 1 (Fall): 49–59.

Sharpe, William F. 2007a. "Expected Utility Asset Allocation," *Financial Analysts Journal* 63, no. 5 (September–October): 18–30.

Sharpe, William F. 2007b. *Investors and Markets: Portfolio Choices, Asset Prices, and Investment Advice.* Princeton, NJ: Princeton University Press.

Shasta, Theodore, ed. 1994. *The Automotive Industry: January 25–26, 1994, Chicago, Illinois.* Charlottesville, VA: AIMR.

Shaw, Alan R. 1988. "Market Timing and Technical Analysis." In *The Financial Analyst's Handbook,* 2nd ed., ed. Sumner N. Levine. Homewood, IL: Dow Jones–Irwin.

Shefrin, Hersh. 2001. "Behavioral Corporate Finance." *Journal of Applied Corporate Finance* 14, no. 3 (Fall): 113–124.

Shefrin, Hersh. 2005. *A Behavioral Approach to Asset Pricing Theory.* Amsterdam: Elsevier-North Holland.

Shefrin, Hersh, and Meir Statman. 1995a. "Behavioral Capital Asset Pricing Theory." *Journal of Financial and Quantitative Analysis* 30, no. 3 (September).

Shefrin, Hersh, and Meir Statman. 1995b. "Making Sense of Beta, Size, and Book-to-Market." *Journal of Portfolio Management* 21, no. 2 (Winter): 26–34.

Shermer, Michael. 2008. *The Mind of the Market.* New York: Times Books.

Sherrerd, Katrina F., ed. 2001. *Benchmarks and Attribution Analysis.* Charlottesville, VA: AIMR.

Sherrerd, Katrina F., ed. 2002. *Fixed-Income Management for the 21st Century.* Charlottesville, VA: Association for Investment Management and Research.

Shiller, Robert J. 1984. "Stock Prices and Social Dynamics." *Brookings Papers on Economic Activity,* 2: 457–498. Washington, DC: Brookings Institute.

Siegel, Daniel, and Diane F. Siegel. 1990. *Futures Markets.* Hinsdale, IL: Dryden Press.

Siegel, Jeremy J. 1991. "Does It Pay Stock Investors to Forecast the Business Cycle?" *Journal of Portfolio Management* 18, no. 1 (Fall): 27–34.

Siegel, Jeremy. 2005. *The Future for Investors: Why the Tried and the True Triumph Over the Bold and the New.* New York: Crown Business.

Siegel, Laurence B., and Paul D. Kaplan. 1990. "Stocks, Bonds, Bills, and Inflation around the World." In *Managing Institutional Assets,* ed. Frank J. Fabozzi. New York: Harper & Row.

Singer, Brian. 1996. "Valuation of Portfolio Performance: Aggregate Return and Risk Analysis." *Journal of Performance Measurement* 1, no. 1 (Fall): 6–16.

Singer, Brian D., Renato Staub, and Kevin Terhaar. 2002. "Determining the Appropriate Allocation to Alternative Investments." In *Hedge Fund Management,* Charlottesville, VA: AIMR.

Singer, Jonathan. 2005. "Does Size Matter?" *Canadian Investment Review* 18, no. 1 (April): 31–32.

Smith, Clifford W., Jr. 1986. "Investment Banking and the Capital Acquisition Process." *Journal of Financial Economics* 15, no. 1–2 (January–February): 3–29.

Smithson, Charles W., and Clifford W. Smith, Jr. 1998. *Managing Financial Risk,* 3rd ed. New York: McGraw-Hill.

Solin, Daniel. 2007. *Smartest Investment Book You Ever Read,* Canadian Edition. Toronto: Viking Canada.

Solnik, Bruno. 1993. *Predictable Time-Varying Components of International Asset Returns.* Charlottesville, VA: AIMR.

Solnik, Bruno, and Dennis McLeavey. 2004. *International Investments,* 5th ed. Reading, MA: Addison-Wesley.

Solt, Michael, and Meir Statman. 1989. "Good Companies, Bad Stocks." *Journal of Portfolio Management* 15, no. 4 (Summer): 39–44.

Sorensen, Eric H., Keith L. Miller, and Vele Samak. 1998. "Allocating between Active and Passive Management." *Financial Analysts Journal* 54, no. 4 (September–October): 18–31.

Steward, Christopher. 2005. "International Bond Markets and Instruments." In *The Handbook of Fixed-Income Securities*, 7th ed., ed. Frank J. Fabozzi. New York: McGraw-Hill.

Stowe, John D., Thomas Robinson, Jerald Pinto, and Dennis McLeavey. 2002. *Analysis of Equity Investments: Valuation.* Charlottesville, VA: AIMR.

Strong, Robert. 2006. *Portfolio Construction, Management, and Protection,* 4th ed. Cincinnati: Thomson South-Western.

Strong, Robert. 2008. *Portfolio Construction, Management, and Protection,* 5th ed. Cincinnati: Thomson South-Western.

Squires, Jan R., ed. 1996. *Global Portfolio Management.* Charlottesville, VA: AIMR.

Squires, Jan R., ed. 1997a. *Global Bond Management.* Charlottesville, VA: AIMR.

Squires, Jan R., ed. 1997b. *Managing Currency Risk.* Charlottesville, VA: AIMR.

Squires, Jan R., ed. 1998a. *Asset Allocation in a Changing World.* Charlottesville, VA: AIMR.

Squires, Jan R., ed. 1998b. *Credit Analysis around the World.* Charlottesville, VA: AIMR.

Squires, Jan R., ed. 2000a. *Global Bond Management II: The Search for Alpha.* Charlottesville, VA: AIMR.

Squires, Jan R., ed. 2000b. *Practical Issues in Equity Analysis.* Charlottesville, VA: AIMR.

Stambaugh, Robert. 1982. "On the Exclusion of Assets from Tests of the Two-Parameter Model: A Sensitivity Analysis." *Journal of Financial Economics* 10, no. 4 (November): 237–268.

Standard and Poor's Corporation. 2008. *Corporate Ratings Criteria.* New York: Standard & Poor's.

Stanhouse, Bryan, and Duane Stock. 1999. "How Changes in Bond Call Features Affect Coupon Rates." *Journal of Applied Corporate Finance* 12, no. 1 (Spring): 92–99.

Statman, Meir. 1987. "How Many Stocks Make a Diversified Portfolio?" *Journal of Financial and Quantitative Analysis* 22, no. 3 (September): 353–363.

Steward, Christopher. 2005. "International Bond Markets and Instruments." In *The Handbook of Fixed-Income Securities,* 7th ed., ed. Frank J. Fabozzi. New York: McGraw-Hill.

Steward, Christopher, J. Hank Lynch, and Frank J. Fabozzi. 2005. "International Bond Portfolio Management." In *The Handbook of Fixed-Income Securities,* 7th ed., ed. Frank J. Fabozzi. New York: McGraw-Hill.

Stewart, G. Bennett, III. 1991. *The Quest for Value.* New York: Harper Business.

Stickney, Clyde P., Paul Brown, and James Wahlen. 2004. *Financial Reporting and Statement Analysis,* 5th ed. Mason, OH: South-Western.

Stoll, Hans R. 1969. "The Relationship between Put and Call Option Prices." *Journal of Finance* 24, no. 5 (December): 801–824.

Stoll, Hans R., and Robert E. Whaley. 1983. "Transaction Costs and the Small Firm Effect." *Journal of Financial Economics* 12, no. 1: 57–79.

Stowe, John D., Thomas Robinson, Jerald Pinto, and Dennis McLeavey. 2002. *Analysis of Equity Investments: Valuation.* Charlottesville, VA: AIMR.

Stulz, Rene M. 2003. *Risk Management and Derivatives.* Mason, OH: South-Western.

Sullivan, Rodney N., ed. 2003. *Equity Analysis Issues, Lessons and Techniques.* Charlottesville, VA: AIMR.

Sundaresan, Suresh. 2002. *Fixed-Income Markets and Their Derivatives,* 2nd ed. Cincinnati, OH: South-Western.

Szakmary, Andrew, Evren Ors, Jin Kyoung Kim, and Wallace N. Davidson. 2003. "The Predictive Power of Implied Volatility: Evidence from 35 Futures Markets." *Journal of Banking and Finance* 27, no. 11 (November): 2151–2175.

Telser, Lester G. 1958. "Futures Trading and the Storage of Cotton and Wheat." *Journal of Political Economy* 66 (June).

Terhaar, Kevin. 2001. "Return, Risk, and Performance Attribution." In *Benchmarks and Attribution Analysis,* ed. Katrina Sherrerd. Charlottesville, VA: AIMR.

Tertzakian, Peter. 2006. *A Thousand Barrels a Second: The Coming Oil Break Point and the Challenges Facing an Energy Dependent World.* New York: McGraw Hill.

Tobin, James. 1958. "Liquidity Preference as Behavior Towards Risk." *Review of Economic Studies* 25, no. 2 (February): 65–85.

Tole, Thomas. 1982. "You Can't Diversify without Diversifying." *Journal of Portfolio Management* 8, no. 2 (Winter): 5–11.

Treynor, Jack L. 1965. "How to Rate Management of Investment Funds." *Harvard Business Review* 43, no. 1 (January–February): 63–75.

Treynor, Jack L., and Fischer Black. 1973. "How to Use Security Analysis to Improve Security Selection." *Journal of Business* 46, no. 1 (January): 66–86.

Tuckman, Bruce. 1995. *Fixed-Income Securities.* New York: Wiley.

Tuckman, Bruce. 2002. *Fixed-Income Securities,* 2nd ed. New York: John Wiley & Sons.

Van Horne, James C. 2001. *Financial Market Rates and Flows,* 6th ed. Englewood Cliffs, NJ: Prentice Hall.

Varchaver, Nicholas, and Katie Benner. 2008. "The $55 Trillion Question," *Fortune,* September 30.

Vine, Allen A. 2001. "High-Yield Analysis of Emerging Markets Debt." In *The Handbook of Fixed-Income Securities,* 6th ed., ed. Frank J. Fabozzi. New York: McGraw-Hill.

Viner, Aron. 1988. *Inside Japanese Financial Markets.* Homewood, IL: Dow Jones–Irwin.

Volpert, Kenneth E. 2001. "Managing Indexed and Enhanced Indexed Bond Portfolios." In *The Handbook of Fixed-Income Securities,* 6th ed., ed. Frank J. Fabozzi. New York: McGraw-Hill.

Vos, Wilfred. 1997. "Measuring Mutual Fund Performance." *Canadian Investment Review* 10, no. 4 (January): 33.

Walter, John R. 1989. "Monetary Aggregates: A User's Guide." Federal Reserve Bank of Richmond *Economic Review* (January–February): 53–61.

Ware, James W. 2000. "Drawing the Line in a Gray Area." In *Ethical Issues for Today's Firm.* Charlottesville, VA: AIMR.

Weigel, Eric J. 1991. "The Performance of Tactical Asset Allocation." *Financial Analysts Journal* 47, no. 5 (September–October): 63–70.

Weiss, Gary. 1996. "The Secret World of Short Sellers." *BusinessWeek,* August 5, pp. 62–68.

Whaley, Robert E. 1993. "Derivatives on Market Volatility: Hedging Tools Long Overdue." *Journal of Derivatives* 1 (Fall): 71–84.

White, Alan. 2006. "Risk Swapping: Understanding and Using CDSs and CDDs." *Canadian Investment Review* 19, no. 3 (Fall): 37–46.

Williams, J. B. 1938. *The Theory of Investment Value.* Cambridge, MA: Harvard University Press.

Winkelmann, Kurt. 1989. "Uses and Abuses of Duration and Convexity." *Financial Analysts Journal* 45, no. 5 (September–October): 72–75.

Womack, Kent L. 1996. "Do Brokerage Analysts' Recommendations Have Investment Value?" *Journal of Finance* 51, no. 1 (March): 137–167.

Wood, Arnold S., ed. 1995. *Behavioral Finance and Decision Theory in Investment Management.* Charlottesville, VA: AIMR.

Working, Holbrook. 1977. "Economic Functions of Futures Markets." In *Selected Writings of Holbrook Working.* Chicago: Chicago Board of Trade.

Zhou, Chunsheng. 2001. "Credit Rating and Corporate Defaults." *Journal of Fixed Income* 11, no. 3 (December): 30–40.

Zweig, Martin E. 1986. *Winning on Wall Street.* New York: Warner Books.

Zweig, Martin E. 1987. *Understanding Technical Forecasting.* New York: Dow Jones.

Zweig, Martin E. 2000. "You Get the Clients You Deserve." In *Ethical Issues for Today's Firm.* Charlottesville, VA: AIMR.

130/30 strategy An active equity portfolio management approach that allows short positions up to a certain percentage (e.g., 30) of captial and an equal percentage of leveraged long positions.

12b-1 plan A fee charged by some funds, named after the U.S. Securities and Exchange Commission rule that permits it. Such fees pay for distribution costs, such as advertising, or for brokers' commissions. The fund's prospectus details any 12b-1 charges that apply.

A

Abnormal rate of return The amount by which a security's actual return differs from its expected rate of return which is based on the market's rate of return and the security's relationship with the market.

Accumulation phase Phase in the investment life cycle during which individuals in the early-to-middle years of their working career attempt to accumulate assets to satisfy short-term needs and longer term goals.

Actuarial rate of return The discount rate used to find the present value of a defined benefit pension plan's future obligations and thus determine the size of the firm's annual contribution to the plan.

Agency conflict An ethical problem that can arise any time one person (i.e., agent) is hired to perform a service or act in the interest of another (i.e., principal).

Alpha A term commonly used to describe a manager's abnormal rate of return, which is the difference between the return the portfolio actually produced and the expected return given its risk level.

Alternative asset A non-traditional (i.e., not common stocks or bonds) asset class investment, including hedge funds, private equity, real estate, and commodities.

Alternative trading system (ATS) A non-traditional, computerized trading system that competes with or supplements dealer markets and traditional stock exchanges. While they facilitate trading in shares, they do not provide listing services.

American Depository Receipts (ADRs) Certificates of ownership issued by a U.S. bank that represent indirect ownership of a certain number of shares of a specific foreign firm. Shares are held on deposit in a bank in the firm's home country.

American option An option contract that can be exercised at any time until its expiration date.

Analysis effect The difference in performance of a security portfolio from that of a chosen index due to acquisition of temporarily mispriced issues that then move to their correct prices.

Anomalies Security price relationships that appear to contradict a well-regarded hypothesis; in this case, the efficient market hypothesis.

Arbitrage A trading strategy designed to generate a guaranteed profit from a transaction that requires no capital commitment or risk bearing on the part of the trader. A simple example of an arbitrage trade would be the simultaneous purchase and sale of the same security in different markets at different prices.

Arbitrage pricing theory (APT) A theory that posits that the expected return to a financial asset can be described by its relationship with several common risk factors. The multifactor APT can be contrasted with the single-factor CAPM.

Arithmetic mean (AM) A measure of mean annual rates of return equal to the sum of annual holding period rates of return divided by the number of years.

Asset allocation The process of deciding how to distribute an investor's wealth among different asset classes for investment purposes.

Asset backed securities (ABS) These are securitized debt that can be backed by a range of assets beyond the traditional mortgage assets. The other assets include car loans, credit card debt, student loans, or home equity loans.

Asset class Securities that have similar characteristics, attributes, and risk-return relationships.

Asset-liability management A matched-funding approach to portfolio management where the characteristics (e.g., cash flow amount, duration) of the assets are coordinated with those of the liabilities that the investor faces.

Assets under management (AUM) The total market value of the assets managed by an investment firm.

At the money A special case of an option where the exercise price and the price of the underlying asset are identical.

Attribution analysis An assessment technique designed to establish whether a manager's performance relative to a benchmark resulted from market timing or security selection skills.

Autocorrelation test A test of the efficient market hypothesis that compares security price changes over time to check for predictable correlation patterns.

Average tax rate A person's total tax payment divided by his or her total income.

B

Backwardated A situation in a futures market where the current contract price is less than the current spot price for the underlying asset.

Balance sheet A financial statement that shows what assets the firm controls at a fixed point in time and how it has financed these assets.

Balanced fund A mutual fund with, generally, a three-part investment objective: (1) to conserve the investor's principal, (2) to pay current income, and (3) to increase both principal and income. The fund aims to achieve this by owning a mixture of bonds, preferred stocks, and common stocks.

Basis The difference between the spot price of the underlying asset and the futures contract price at any point in time (e.g., the *initial* basis at the time of contract origination, the *cover* basis at the time of contract termination).

Basis of an asset For tax purposes, the cost of an asset.

Basis risk The residual exposure to the price volatility of an underlying asset that results from a cross hedge transaction.

Bearer bond An unregistered bond for which ownership is determined by possession. The holder receives interest payments by clipping coupons attached to the security and sending them to the issuer for payment.

Behavioural finance Involves the analysis of various psycho-logical traits of individuals and how these traits affect how they act as investors, analysts, and portfolio managers.

Benchmark error Situation where an inappropriate or incorrect benchmark is used to compare and assess portfolio returns and management.

Benchmark portfolio A comparison standard of risk and assets included in the policy statement and similar to the investor's risk preference and investment needs, which can be used to evaluate the investment performance of the portfolio manager.

Beta A standardized measure of systematic risk based upon an asset's covariance with the market portfolio.

Binomial option pricing model A valuation equation that assumes the price of the underlying asset changes through a series of discrete upward or downward movements.

Black-Scholes valuation model A valuation equation that assumes the price of the underlying asset changes continuously through the option's expiration date.

Bond insurance. Insurance policies written by commercial insurance companies wherein the insurance company agrees to pay the bondholder principal and/or coupon interest that is due on a bond that is not paid by the issuer. These policies were originally issued only on municipal bonds, but have subsequently been written for corporate bonds and collateralized issues. Insured bond issues generally receive the bond rating equal to that held by the insurance company.

Bond ladder A strategy for managing a fixed-income portfo-lio where the investment funds are divided evenly among bonds that mature at regular intervals surrounding the desired time horizon.

Bond price volatility The percentage changes in bond prices over time.

Bond swap An active bond portfolio management strategy that exchanges one position for another to take advantage of some difference between them.

Business risk The variability of operating income arising from the characteristics of the firm's industry. Two sources of business risk are sales variability and operating leverage.

Buy-and-hold strategy A passive portfolio management strategy in which securities (bonds or stocks) are bought and held to maturity.

C

Call market A market in which trading for individual stocks only takes place at specified times. All the bids and asks available at the time are combined and the market administrators specify a single price that will possibly clear the market at that time.

Call option Option to buy an asset within a certain period at a specified price called the *exercise price*.

Call premium Amount above par that an issuer must pay to a bondholder for retiring the bond before its stated maturity.

Call provisions Specifies when and how a firm can issue a call for bonds outstanding prior to their maturity.

Capital appreciation A return objective in which the investor seeks to increase the portfolio value, primarily through capital gains, over time to meet a future need rather than dividend yield.

Capital asset pricing model (CAPM) A theory concerned with deriving the expected or required rates of return on risky assets based on the assets' systematic risk relative to a market portfolio.

Capital market instruments Fixed-income or equity investments that trade in the secondary market.

Capital market line (CML) The line from the intercept point that represents the risk-free rate tangent to the original efficient frontier; it becomes the new efficient frontier since investments on this line dominate all the portfolios on the original Markowitz efficient frontier.

Capital preservation A return objective in which the investor seeks to minimize the risk of loss; generally a goal of the risk-averse investor.

Characteristic line Regression line that indicates the systematic risk (beta) of a risky asset.

Closed-end investment company An investment company that issues only a limited number of shares, which it does not redeem (buy back). Instead, shares of a closed-end fund are traded in securities markets at prices determined by supply and demand.

Coefficient of variation (CV) A measure of relative variability that indicates risk per unit of return. It is equal to: standard deviation divided by the mean value. When used in investments, it is equal to: standard deviation of returns divided by the expected rate of return.

Coincident indicators A set of economic variables whose values reach peaks and troughs at about the same time as the aggregate economy.

Collar agreement A hedging arrangement where an underlying asset is protected against decreases in value by the simultaneous purchase of a put option and sale of a call option.

Collateral trust bonds A mortgage bond wherein the assets backing the bond are financial assets like stocks and bonds.

Collateralized debt obligations (CDOs). They are consid-ered part of the asset-backed securities (ABSs) market because they are backed by the cash flows from a portfolio of securities. In contrast to the specific securities such as mortgages, credit card debt, and auto loans, CDOs are unique because they will generally include a variety of debt with a diversity of credit ratings. Finally, there are typically several tranches with different credit ratings from AAA to non-investment grade.

Collateralized mortgage obligation (CMO) A debt security based on a pool of mortgage loans that provides a relatively predictable term by paying of tranches in specified order.

Commission brokers Employees of a member firm who buy or sell securities for the customers of the firm.

Common stock An equity investment that represents ownership of a firm, with full participation in its success or failure. The firm's directors must approve dividend payments.

Common size statements The normalization of balance sheet and income statement items to allow for more meaningful comparison of different-size firms. Balance sheet items are divided by total assets; income statement items are divided by total sales.

Competitive bid An underwriting alternative wherein an issuing entity (governmental body or a corporation) specifies the type of security to be offered (bonds or stocks) and the general characteristics of the issue, and the issuer solicits bids from competing investment banking firms with the understanding that the issuer will accept the highest bid from the bankers.

Competitive environment The level of intensity of competition among firms in an industry, determined by an examination of five competitive forces.

Competitive strategy The search by a firm for a favourable competitive position within an industry within the known competitive environment.

Completely diversified portfolio A portfolio in which all unsystematic risk has been eliminated by diversification.

Completeness fund A specialized index used to form the basis of a passive portfolio whose purpose is to provide diversification to a client's total portfolio by excluding those segments in which the client's active managers invest.

Composite measure An investment performance statistic that considers both the return and risk associated with a portfolio (e.g., Sharpe measure, Treynor measure, Jensen measure).

Consolidation phase Phase in the investment life cycle during which individuals who are typically past the midpoint of their career have earnings that exceed expenses and invest them for future retirement or estate planning needs.

Construct the portfolio Given the strategy and economic outlook, what specific stocks and/or bonds will be put into the portfolio at the present time that are consistent with the client's policy statement.

Contango A situation in a futures market where the current contract price is greater than the current spot price for the underlying asset.

Contingent deferred sales load A mutual fund that imposes a sales charge when the investor sells or redeems shares. Also referred to as *rear-end loads* or *redemption charges*.

Continual monitoring The constant evaluation of the economic environment, the policy statement, and the port-folio to ensure that it is consistent with the policy state-ment. Also involves evaluating performance to determine if changes are required in the portfolio, the strategy, or the policy statement.

Continuous market A market where stocks are priced and traded continuously by an auction process or by dealers when the market is open.

Contract price The transaction price specified in a forward or futures contract.

Contrarian An investment strategy that attempts to buy (sell) securities on which the majority of other investors are bearish (bullish).

Convenience yield An adjustment made to the theoretical forward or futures contract delivery price to account for the preference that consumers have for holding spot positions in the underlying asset.

Conversion parity price The price at which common stock can be obtained by surrendering the convertible instrument at par value.

Conversion premium The excess of the market value of the convertible security over its equity value if immediately converted into common stock. Typically expressed as a percentage of the equity value.

Conversion ratio The number of shares of common stock for which a convertible security may be exchanged.

Conversion value The value of the convertible security if converted into common stock at the stock's current market price.

Convertible bonds A bond with the added feature that the bondholder has the option to turn the bond back to the firm in exchange for a specified number of common shares of the firm.

Convexity A measure of the degree to which a bond's price-yield curve departs from a straight line. This characteristic affects estimates of a bond's price volatility for a given change in yields.

Core-plus bond portfolio management This is a combination approach to bond portfolio management wherein a significant (core) part of the portfolio (e.g., 70–75%) of the portfolio is managed passively in a widely recognized sector of the bond market, such as an aggregate bond index or a government/corporate sector. The rest of the portfolio would be actively managed in one or several "plus" sectors that are less efficient than the core component—for example, high-yield bonds, foreign bonds, or emerging market debt.

Correlation coefficient A standardized measure of the rela-tionship between two variables that ranges from −1.00 to +1.00.

Cost of carry The net amount that would be required to store a commodity or security for future delivery, usually calculated as physical storage costs plus financial capital costs less dividends paid to the underlying asset.

Counterparty A participant to a derivative transaction.

Country risk Uncertainty due to the possibility of major political or economic change in the country where an investment is located. Also called *political risk.*

Coupon Indicates the interest payment on a debt security. It is the coupon rate times the par value that indicates the interest payments on a debt security.

Coupon reinvestment risk The component of interest rate risk due to the uncertainty of the rate at which coupon payments will be reinvested.

Covariance A measure of the degree to which two variables, such as rates of return for investment assets, move together over time relative to their individual mean returns.

Covered call A trading strategy in which a call option is sold as a supplement to a long position in an underlying asset or portfolio of assets.

Covered interest arbitrage A trading strategy involving borrowing money in one country and lending it to another designed to exploit price deviations from the interest rate parity model.

Credit analysis An active bond portfolio management strategy designed to identify bonds that are expected to experience changes in rating. This strategy is critical when investing in high-yield bonds.

Credit default swap (CDS) An agreement in which the protection buyer makes periodic premium payments in exchange for the protection seller's obligation to make a settlement payment that is contingent on the occurrence of a credit-related event to a predetermined reference entity, usually a specific bond or bond index.

Cross hedge A trading strategy in which the price volatility of a commodity or security position is hedged with a forward or futures contract based on a different underlying asset or different settlement terms.

Crossover price The price at which the yield to maturity equals the yield to call. Above this price, yield to call is the appropriate yield measure; below this price, yield to maturity is the appropriate yield measure.

Cross-sectional analysis An examination of a firm's performance in comparison to other firms in the industry with similar characteristics to the firm being studied.

Cross-sectional return studies Studies wherein investigators look for public information that can be used to predict the cross-sectional distribution of risk-adjusted returns—e.g., is there an inverse relationship between market-value size of a firm and future risk-adjusted rates of return for its stock.

Current income A return objective in which the investor seeks to generate income rather than capital gains; generally a goal of an investor who wants to supplement earnings with income to meet living expenses.

Current yield A bond's yield as measured by its current income (coupon) as a percentage of its market price.

Cyclical change An economic trend arising from the ups and downs of the business cycle.

Cyclical company A firm whose earnings rise and fall with general economic activity.

Cyclical stock return A stock with a high beta; its gains typically exceed those of a rising market and its losses typically exceed those of a falling market.

D

Debentures Bonds that promise payments of interest and principal but pledge no specific assets. Holders have first claim on the issuer's income and unpledged assets. Also known as *unsecured bonds.*

Declining trend channel The range defined by security prices as they move progressively lower.

Dedication A portfolio management technique in which the portfolio's cash flows are used to retire a set of liabilities over time.

Dedication with reinvestment A dedication strategy in which portfolio cash flows may precede their corresponding liabilities. Such cash flows can be reinvested to earn a return until the date the liability is due to be paid.

Defensive company Firms whose future earnings are likely to withstand an economic downturn.

Defensive competitive strategy Positioning the firm so that its capabilities provide the best means to deflect the effect of the competitive forces in the industry.

Defensive stock A stock whose return is not expected to decline as much as that of the overall market during a bear market (a beta less than one).

Defined benefit pension plan A pension plan to which the company contributes a certain amount each year and promises to pay employees a specified income after they retire. The benefit size is based on factors such as workers' salary and time of employment.

Defined contribution pension plan A pension plan in which worker benefits are determined by the size of employees' contributions to the plan and the returns earned on the fund's investments.

Delta The change in the price of the option with respect to a one dollar change in the price of the underlying asset; this is the option's *hedge ratio,* or the number of units of the underlying asset that can be hedged by a single option contract.

Derivative security An instrument whose market value ultimately depends upon, or derives from, the value of a more fundamental investment vehicle called the underlying asset or security.

Diffusion index for stocks An indicator of the number of stocks rising during a specified period of time relative to the number of stocks declining and not changing price.

Discount A bond selling at a price below par value due to capital market conditions.

Discounted cash flow valuation techniques A type of approach to value the stock based upon the present value of some measure of cash flow, including dividends, operating cash flow, and free cash flow.

Discriminant analysis A statistical technique that identifies a linear combination of variables that can best separate two groups. This is used in credit analysis to find an linear equation of financial indicators that can best separate healthy companies from and failed ones.

Dividend discount model (DDM) A technique for estimating the value of a stock issue as the present value of all future dividends.

Dollar-weighted return The discount rate that sets the present value of a future set of cash flows equal to the investment's current value; also known as the *internal rate of return.*

Downside risk The volatility in a portfolio based on returns that fall below a minimum acceptable threshold level, which is specified by the investor.

DuPont system A method of examining *ROE* by breaking it down into three component parts: (1) profit margin, (2) total asset turnover, and (3) financial leverage.

Duration A measure of the interest rate sensitivity of a bond's market price taking into consideration its coupon and term to maturity. The percent change in price for 100 basis point change in yield.

Duration strategy A portfolio management strategy employed to reduce the interest rate risk of a bond portfolio by matching the modified duration of the portfolio with its investment horizon. For example, if the investment horizon is 10 years, the portfolio manager would construct a portfolio that has a modified duration of 10 years. This strategy is referred to as *immunization of the portfolio.*

E

Earnings momentum A strategy in which portfolios are constructed of stocks of firms with rising earnings.

Earnings multiplier model A technique for estimating the value of a stock issue as a multiple of its future earnings per share.

Earnings surprise A company announcement of earnings that differ from analysts' prevailing expectations.

EBITDA Earnings before interest, taxes, depreciation, and amortization.

Economic value added (EVA) Internal management performance measure that compares net operating profit to total cost of capital. Indicates how profitable company projects are as a sign of management performance.

Effective duration Direct measure of the interest rate sensitivity of a bond (or any financial instrument) based upon price changes derived from a pricing model.

Efficient capital market A market in which security prices rapidly reflect all information about securities.

Efficient frontier The set of portfolios that has the maximum rate of return for every given level of risk, or the minimum risk for every potential rate of return.

Electronic Communication Network (ECN) A computerized trading system that matches buy and sell orders, usu-ally for retail and small institutional trading. ECNs act for customers as a broker—they do not buy or sell from their own accounts.

Electronic Crossing System (ECS) An electronic trading system that matches large buy and sell orders.

Empirical duration Measures directly the interest rate sensitivity of an asset by examining the percentage price change for an asset in response to a change in yield during a specified period of time.

Ending-wealth value The total amount of money derived from investment in a bond until maturity, including principal, coupon payments, and income from reinvestment of coupon payments.

Enhanced indexing A portfolio management strategy that attempts to outperform a designated benchmark on a risk-adjusted basis by combining passive (i.e, indexed) and active management approaches.

Equipment trust certificates Mortgage bonds that are secured by specific pieces of transportation equipment like boxcars and planes.

Equity collar An option-based hedging strategy that protects a stock position from price declines by purchasing a put option that is paid for by the sale of a call option.

Equity swap A swap transaction in which one cash flow is tied to the return to an equity portfolio position, often an index such as the Standard and Poor's 500, while the other is based on a floating-rate index.

Estimated rate of return The rate of return an investor anticipates earning from a specific investment over a particular future holding period.

Eurobonds Bonds denominated in a currency not native to the country in which they are issued.

European option An option contract that can only be exercised on its expiration date.

Event study Research that examines the reaction of a security's price to a specific company, world event, or news announcement.

Exchange clearinghouse The functional unit attached to a futures exchange that guarantees contract performance, oversees delivery, serves as a bookkeeper, and calculates settlement transactions.

Exchange rate risk Uncertainty due to the denomination of an investment in a currency other than that of the investor's own country.

Exchange-traded fund (ETF) A tradable depository receipt that gives investors a pro rata claim to the returns associated with a portfolio of securities (often designed to mimic an index, such as the S&P/TSX Composite Index) held in trust by a financial institution.

Exercise price The transaction price specified in an option contract; also known as the *striking price*.

Expected return The return that analysts' calculations suggest a security should provide, based on the market's rate of return during the period and the security's relationship to the market.

Expense ratio The percentage of a fund's assets deducted annually for expenses, including management fees, administrative fees, and operating costs, but not including security trading fees.

Expiry The expiration date of a derivative security.

Extended DuPont System A method of examining *ROE* by breaking it down into five component parts.

External efficiency A market in which prices adjust quickly to new information regarding supply or demand. Also referred to as *informational efficiency*.

F

Fiduciary A person who supervises or oversees the investment portfolio of a third party, such as in a trust account, and makes investment decisions in accordance with the owner's wishes.

Filter rule A trading rule that recommends security transactions when price changes exceed a previously determined percentage.

Financial risk The variability of future income arising from the firm's fixed financing costs, for example, interest payments. The effect of fixed financial costs is to magnify the effect of changes in operating profit on net income or earnings per share.

Fixed-income investments Loans with contractually mandated payment schedules from firms or governments to investors.

Flat trend channel The range defined by security prices as they maintain a relatively steady level.

Flexible portfolio fund Mutual fund that allows managers to shift assets between stocks, bonds, and cash acccording to changing market conditions; also known as *asset allocation* fund.

Floating-rate note (FRN) Short- to intermediate-term bonds with regularly scheduled coupon payments linked to a variable interest rate, most often LIBOR.

Floor agreement A contract that on each settlement date pays the holder the greater of the difference between the floor rate and the reference rate or zero; it is equivalent to a series of put options on the reference rate.

Floor brokers Independent members of an exchange who act as brokers for other members.

Forward contract An agreement between two counterparties that requires the exchange of a commodity or security at a fixed time in the future at a predetermined price.

Forward discount A situation where, from the perspective of the domestic country, the spot exchange rate is smaller than the forward exchange rate with a foreign country.

Forward premium A situation where, from the perspective of the domestic country, the spot exchange rate is larger than the forward exchange rate with a foreign country.

Forward rate A short-term yield for a future holding period implied by the spot rates of two securities with different maturities.

Forward rate agreement (FRA) A transaction in which two counterparties agree to a single exchange of cash flows based on a fixed and floating rate, respectively.

Franchise factor A firm's unique competitive advantage that makes it possible for a firm to earn excess returns (rates of return above a firm's cost of capital) on its capital projects. In turn, these excess returns and the franchise factor cause the firm's stock price to have a P/E ratio above its base P/E ratio that is equal to $1/k$.

Free cash flow to equity This cash flow measure equals cash flow from operations minus capital expenditures and debt payments.

Full replication A technique for constructing a passive index portfolio in which all securities in an index are purchased in proportion to their weights in the index.

Futures contract An agreement that provides for the future exchange of a particular asset at a specified delivery date in exchange for a specified payment at the time of delivery.

G

General obligation (GO) bond A municipal issue serviced from and guaranteed by the issuer's full taxing authority.

Generally accepted accounting principles (GAAP) Accounting principles formulated by the Canadian Institute of Chartered Accountants and used to construct financial statements.

Geometric mean (GM) The nth root of the product of the annual holding period returns for n years minus 1.

Gifting phase Phase in the investment life cycle during which individuals use excess assets to financially assist relatives or friends, establish charitable trusts, or construct trusts to minimize estate taxes.

Growth company A company that consistently has the opportunities and ability to invest in projects that provide rates of return that exceed the firm's cost of capital. Because of these investment opportunities, it retains a high proportion of earnings, and its earnings grow faster than those of average firms.

Growth stock A stock issue that generates a higher rate of return than other stocks in the market with similar risk characteristics.

H

Hedge A trading strategy in which derivative securities are used to reduce or completely offset a counterparty's risk exposure to an underlying asset.

Hedge fund An investment vehicle designed to manage a private, unregistered portfolio of assets according to any of several strategies. The investment strategy often employs arbitrage trading and significant financial leverage (e.g., short selling, borrowing, derivatives) while the compensation arrangement for the manager typically specifies considerable profit participation.

Hedge ratio The number of derivative contracts that must be transacted to offset the price volatility of an underlying commodity or security position.

High-yield bond A bond rated below investment grade. Also referred to as *speculative-grade bonds* or *junk bonds*.

Holding period return (HPR) The total return from an investment, including all sources of income, for a given period of time. A value of 1.0 indicates no gain or loss. Equal to ending wealth/beginning wealth.

Holding period yield (HPY) The total return from an investment for a given period of time stated as a percentage. Equal to HPR-1.

I

Immunization A bond portfolio management technique of matching modified duration to the investment horizon of the portfolio to eliminate interest rate risk.

Implied volatility The standard deviation of changes in the price of the underlying asset that can be inferred from an option's market price in relation to a specific valuation model.

In the money An option that has positive intrinsic value.

Incentive compensations A scheme for paying investment managers according to the performance of the portfolio, often based on the level of assets under management.

Income bonds Debentures that stipulate interest payments only if the issuer earns the income to make the payments by specified dates.

Income statement A financial statement that shows the flow of the firm's sales, expenses, and earnings over a period of time.

Indenture The legal agreement that lists the obligations of the issuer of a bond to the bondholder, including payment schedules, call provisions, and sinking funds.

Indexing A passive bond portfolio management strategy that seeks to match the composition, and therefore the performance, of a selected market index.

Index fund A fund whose purpose is to track the performance of the specified market series (index) over time.

Industry life cycle analysis An analysis that focuses on the industry's stage of development.

Information An attribute of a good market that includes providing buyers and sellers with timely, accurate information on the volume and prices of past transactions and on all currently outstanding bids and offers.

Information ratio Statistic used to measure a portfolio's average return in excess of a comparison, benchmark portfolio divided by the standard deviation of this excess return.

Informationally efficient market A more technical term for an efficient capital market that emphasizes the role of information in setting the market price.

Initial public offering (IPO) A new issue by a firm that has no existing public market.

Interest rate anticipation An active bond portfolio management strategy designed to preserve capital or take advantage of capital gains opportunities by predicting interest rates and their effects on bond prices.

Interest rate parity The relationship that must exist in an efficient market between the spot and forward foreign exchange rates between two countries and the interest rates in those countries.

Interest rate risk The uncertainty of returns on an investment due to possible changes in interest rates over time.

Interest rate swap An agreement calling for the periodic exchange of cash flows, one based on an interest rate that remains fixed for the life of the contract and the other that is linked to a variable-rate index.

Interest-on-interest Bond income from reinvestment of coupon payments.

Intermarket trading system (ITS) A computerized system that connects competing exchanges and dealers who trade stocks listed on an exchange. Its purpose is to help customers find the best market for these stocks at a point in time.

Internal liquidity (solvency) ratios Financial ratios that measure the ability of the firm to meet future short-term financial obligations.

Internal rate of return (IRR) The discount rate at which cash outflows of an investment equal cash inflows.

International domestic bonds Bonds issued by a foreign firm, denominated in the firm's native currency, and sold within its own country.

Intrinsic value The portion of a call option's total value equal to the greater of either zero or the difference between the current value of the underlying asset and the exercise price; for a put option, intrinsic value is the greater of either zero or the exercise price less the underlying asset price. For a stock, it is the value derived from fundamental analysis of the stock's expected returns or cash flows.

Investment The current commitment of dollars for a period of time in order to derive future payments that will compensate the investor for the time the funds are committed, the expected rate of inflation, and the uncertainty of future payments.

Investment company A firm that sells shares of the company and uses the proceeds to buy portfolios of stock, bonds, or other financial instruments.

Investment decision process Estimation of intrinsic value for comparison with market price to determine whether or not to invest.

Investment horizon The time period used for planning and forecasting purposes or the future time at which the investor requires the invested funds.

Investment management company A company separate from the investment company that manages the portfolio and performs administrative functions.

Investment strategy A decision by a portfolio manager regarding how he or she will manage the portfolio to meet the goals and objectives of the client. This will include either active or passive management and, if active, what style in terms of top-down or bottom-up or fundamental versus technical.

J

January effect A frequent empirical anomaly where risk-adjusted stock returns in the month of January are signifi-cantly larger than those occurring in any other month of the year.

J-curve effect The tendency for the returns to private equity funds to be negative initially and then positive in later years as the more profitable investments are realized.

Jensen measure An absolute measure of a portfolio's risk-adjusted performance, computed as the intercept in a regression equation where the excess returns to a manager's portfolio and the market index are, respectively, the dependent and independent variables.

L

Lagging indicators A set of economic variables whose values reach peaks and troughs after the aggregate economy.

Leading indicators A set of economic variables whose values reach peaks and troughs in advance of the aggregate economy.

Limit order An order that lasts for a specified time to buy or sell a security when and if it trades at a specified price.

Limited partnership A business organization with one or more general partners, who manage the business and assume legal debts and obligations, and one or more limited partners, who are liable only to the extent of their investments.

Liquid Term used to describe an asset that can be quickly converted to cash at a price close to fair market value.

Liquidity The ability to buy or sell an asset quickly and at a reasonable price based on information.

Liquidity preference hypothesis. One of the alternative explanations for the different shapes of the term structure of interest rates. This hypothesis holds that long-term securities should provide higher promised yields than short-term securities because of the higher price volatility of long-maturity (high duration) bonds.

Liquidity risk Uncertainty due to the ability to buy or sell an investment in the secondary market.

Long hedge A long position in a forward or futures contract used to offset the price volatility of a short position in the underlying asset.

Long position The buyer of a commodity or security or, for a forward contract, the counterparty who will be the eventual buyer of the underlying asset.

Long-term, high-priority goal A long-term financial investment goal of personal importance that typically includes achieving financial independence, such as being able to retire at a certain age.

Lower priority goal A financial investment goal of lesser personal importance, such as taking a luxurious vacation or buying a car every few years.

Low-load fund A mutual fund that imposes a moderate front-end sales charge when the investor buys the fund, typically about 3% to 4%.

M

Macaulay duration A measure of the time flow of cash from a bond where cash flows are weighted by present values discounted by the yield to maturity.

Maintenance margin The required proportion that the investor's equity value must be to the total market value of the stock. If the proportion drops below this percent, the investor will receive a margin call.

Management and advisory firm A firm that provides a range of services from standard banking transactions (savings accounts, personal loans) to advising individual and institutional investors on structuring their portfolios and managing investment funds.

Management effect A combination of the interest rate anticipation effect, the analysis effect, and the trading effect.

Management fee The compensation an investment company pays to the investment management company for its services. The average annual fee is about 0.5% of fund assets.

Maple bonds Canadian dollar–denominated bonds sold in Canada by a foreign corporation or governments.

Margin The percent of cost a buyer pays in cash for a security, borrowing the balance from the broker. This introduces leverage, which increases the risk of the transaction.

Margin account The collateral posted with the futures exchange clearinghouse by an outside counterparty to insure its eventual performance; the *initial* margin is the deposit required at contract origination while the *maintenance* margin is the minimum collateral necessary at all times.

Margin call A request by an investor's broker for additional capital for a security bought on margin if the investor's equity value declines below the required maintenance margin.

Marginal tax rate The part of each additional dollar in income that is paid as tax.

Marked to market The settlement process used to adjust the margin account of a futures contract for daily changes in the price of the underlying asset.

Market The means through which buyers and sellers are brought together to aid in the transfer of goods and/or services.

Market order An order to buy or sell a security immediately at the best price available.

Market portfolio The portfolio that includes all risky assets with relative weights equal to their proportional market values.

Market risk premium The amount of return above the risk-free rate that investors expect from the market in general as compensation for systematic risk.

Market value added (MVA) External management performance measure to compare the market value of the company's debt and equity with the total capital invested in the firm.

Maturity strategy A portfolio management strategy employed to reduce the interest rate risk of a bond portfolio by matching the maturity of the portfolio with its investment horizon. For example, if the investment horizon is 10 years, the portfolio manager would construct a portfolio that will mature in 10 years.

Mean rates of return The average of an investment's returns over an extended period of time.

Modified duration A measure of Macaulay duration divided by one plus the bond's periodic yield used to approximate the bond's price volatility.

Money market The market for short-term debt securities with maturities of less than one year.

Money market fund A fund that invests in short-term securities sold in the money market. (Large companies, banks, and other institutions also invest their surplus cash in the money market for short periods of time.) In the entire investment spectrum, these are generally the safest, most stable securities available. They include Treasury bills, banker acceptances, and commercial paper (short-term IOUs of large corporations).

Mortgage bonds Bonds that pledge specific assets such as buildings and equipment. The proceeds from the sale of these assets are used to pay off bondholders in case of bankruptcy.

Moving average The continually recalculating average of security prices for a period, often 200 days, to serve as an indication of the general trend of prices and also as a benchmark price.

Multifactor model An empirical version of the APT where the investor chooses the exact number and identity of the common risk factors used to describe an asset's risk-return relationship. Risk factors are often designated as *macroeconomic* variables (e.g., inflation, changes in gross domestic product) or *microeconomic* variables (e.g., security-specific characteristics like firm size or book-to-market ratios).

Mutual fund An investment company that pools money from shareholders and invests in a variety of securities, including stocks, bonds, and money market securities. A mutual fund ordinarily stands ready to buy back (redeem) its shares at their current net asset value, which depends on the market value of the fund's portfolio of securities at the time. Mutual funds generally continuously offer new shares to investors.

N

Nasdaq InterMarket A trading system that includes Nasdaq market makers and ECNs that quote and trade stocks listed on the NYSE and the AMEX. It involves dealers from the Nasdaq market and the Intermarket Trading System (ITS). In many ways, this has become what had been labelled the third market.

National Association of Securities Dealers Automated Quotation (Nasdaq) system An electronic system for providing bid-ask quotes on OTC securities.

Near-term, high-priority goal A short-term financial investment goal of personal importance, such as accumulating funds for making a house down payment or buying a car.

Negotiated sales An underwriting arrangement wherein the sale of a security issue by an issuing entity (governmental body or a corporation) is done using an investment banking firm that maintains an ongoing relationship with the issuer. The characteristics of the security issue are determined by the issuer in consultation with the investment banker.

Net asset value (NAV) per share The market value of an investment company's assets (securities, cash, and any accrued earnings) after deducting liabilities, divided by the number of shares outstanding.

Net present value (NPV) A measure of the excess cash flows expected from an investment proposal. It is equal to the present value of the cash *inflows* from an investment proposal, discounted at the required rate of return for the investment, minus the present value of the cash *outflows* required by the investment, also discounted at the investment's required rate of return. If the derived net present value is a positive value (i.e., there is an excess net present value), the investment should be acquired because it will provide a rate of return above its required returns.

New issue Common stocks or bonds offered by companies for public sale.

No-load fund A mutual fund that sells its shares at net asset value without adding sales charges.

Nominal yield A bond's yield as measured by its coupon rate.

Normal portfolio A specialized or customized benchmark constructed to evaluate a specific manager's investment style or philosophy.

Notes Intermediate-term debt securities with maturities longer than 1 year but less than 10 years.

Notional principal The principal value of a swap transac-tion, which is not exchanged but is used as a scale factor to translate interest rate differentials into cash settlement payments.

O

Objectives The investor's goals expressed in terms of risk and return and included in the policy statement.

Offensive competitive strategy A strategy whereby a firm attempts to use its strengths to affect the competitive forces in the industry and, in so doing, improves the firm's relative position in the industry.

Open-end investment company The more formal name for a mutual fund, which derives from the fact that it continuously offers new shares to investors and redeems them (buys them back) on demand.

Operating efficiency ratios Financial ratios intended to indicate how efficiently management is utilizing the firm's assets in terms of dollar sales generated per dollar of assets. Primary examples would be: total asset turnover, fixed asset turnover, or equity turnover.

Operating leverage The use of fixed-production costs in the firm's operating cost structure. The effect of fixed costs is to magnify the effect of a change in sales on operating profits.

Operating profitability ratios Financial ratios intended to indicate how profitable the firm is in terms of the percent of profit generated from sales. Alternative measures would include: operating profit (EBIT)/net sales; pretax profit (EBT)/net sales; and net profit/sales.

Optimal portfolio The portfolio on the efficient frontier that has the highest utility for a given investor. It lies at the point of tangency between the efficient frontier and the curve with the investor's highest possible utility.

Option-adjusted duration An estimate of the duration of a bond that specifically adjusts for the existence of an embedded put and/or call option in the bond. It can be envisioned as the duration of a non-callable bond minus the duration of an embedded call option or plus the duration of an embedded put option.

Options Clearing Corporation (OCC) A company designed to guarantee, monitor margin accounts, and settle exchange-traded option transactions.

Option contract An agreement that grants the owner the right, but not the obligation, to make a future transaction in an underlying commodity or security at a fixed price and within a predetermined time in the future.

Option premium The initial price that the option buyer must pay to the option seller to acquire the contract.

Option-adjusted spread A type of yield spread that considers changes in the term structure and alternative estimates of the volatility of interest rates. It is spread after adjusting for embedded options.

OTC Electronic Bulletin Board (OTCBB) A regulated quotation service that displays real-time quotes, last-sale prices, and volume information for a specified set of over-the-counter (OTC) securities that are not traded on the formal Nasdaq market.

Out of the money An option that has no intrinsic value.

Overfunded plan A defined benefit pension plan in which the present value of the pension liabilities is less than market value of the plan's assets.

Over-the-counter (OTC) In Canada, where most trading in bonds occurs; that is, there is no formal market—just a network of dealers standing ready to buy and sell.

Overweighted A condition in which a portfolio, for whatever reason, includes more of a class of securities than the relative market value alone would justify.

P

Par value *See* Principal.

Payback The time required for the added income from the convertible security relative to the stock to offset the conversion premium.

Peak The culmination of a bull market when prices stop rising and begin declining.

Peer group comparison A method of measuring portfolio performance by collecting the returns produced by a representative universe of investors over a specific period of time.

Performance presentation standards (PPS) A comprehensive set of reporting guidelines created by the CFA Institute (formerly known as the Association for Investment Management and Research, or AIMR), in an effort to fulfill the call for uniform, accurate, and consistent performance reporting.

Perpetuity An investment without any maturity date. It provides returns to its owner indefinitely.

Personal trust An amount of money set aside by a grantor and often managed by a third party, the trustee. Often constructed so one party receives income from the trust's investments and another party receives the residual value of the trust after the income beneficiaries' death.

Policy effect The difference in performance of a bond portfolio from that of a chosen index due to differences in duration, which result from a fund's investment policy.

Policy statement A statement in which the investor specifies investment goals, constraints, and risk preferences.

Portfolio A group of investments. Ideally, the investments should have different patterns of returns over time.

Portfolio turnover The total dollar value of securities sold from a portfolio in a year divided by the average assets under management for the fund during the same period.

Preferred stock An equity investment that stipulates the dividend payment either as a coupon or a stated dollar amount. The firm's directors may withhold dividend payments.

Premium A bond selling at a price above par value due to capital market conditions.

Price continuity A feature of a liquid market in which there are small price changes from one transaction to the next due to the depth of the market.

Price momentum A portfolio strategy in which you acquire stocks that have enjoyed above-market stock price increases.

Price risk The component of interest rate risk due to the uncertainty of the market price of a bond caused by changes in market interest rates.

Price-earnings (P/E) ratio The number by which expected earnings per share is multiplied to estimate a stock's value; also called the *earnings multiplier.*

Price-weighted index An index calculated as an arithmetic mean of the current prices of the sampled securities.

Price-yield curve This is created by plotting the set of computed prices for a specific bond against an alternative set of potential yields. It generally shows the convexity of the curve.

Primary market The market in which newly issued securities are sold by their issuers, who receive the proceeds.

Principal (par value) The original value of the debt underlying a bond that is payable at maturity.

Private equity An ownership interest in a company or collection of assets that is not publicly traded on an exchange or in the over-the-counter market.

Private placement A new issue sold directly to a small group of investors, usually institutions.

Promised yield to call (YTC) A bond's yield if held until the first available call date, with reinvestment of all coupon payments at the yield-to-call rate.

Promised yield to maturity (YTM) The most widely used measure of a bond's yield that states the fully compounded rate of return on a bond bought at market price and held to maturity with reinvestment of all coupon payments at the yield to maturity rate.

Protective put A trading strategy in which a put option is purchased as a supplement to a long position in an underlying asset or portfolio of assets; the most straight-forward form of *portfolio insurance.*

Public bond A long-term, fixed-obligation debt security in a convenient, affordable denomination for sale to individuals and financial institutions.

Pure cash-matched dedicated portfolio A conservative dedicated portfolio management technique aimed at developing a bond portfolio that will provide cash payments that exactly match the specified liability schedules.

Put options Options to sell a security (stock or bond) within a certain period at a specified price.

Put-call parity The relationship that must exist in an efficient market between the prices for put and call options having the same underlying asset, exercise price, and expiration date.

Q

Quadratic optimization A technique that relies on historical correlations in order to construct a portfolio that seeks to minimize tracking error with an index.

Quality financial statements Financial statements that most knowledgeable observers (analysts, portfolio managers) would consider conservatively prepared in terms of sales, expenses, earnings, and asset valuations. The results reported would reflect reasonable estimates and indicate what truly happened during the period and the legitimate value of assets and liabilities on the balance sheet.

R

Range forward A trading strategy based on a variation of the put-call parity model where, for the same underlying asset but different exercise prices, a call option is purchased and a put option is sold (or vice versa).

Rate anticipation effect The difference in return because of changing the duration of the portfolio during a period as compared with the portfolio's long-term policy duration.

Real estate investment trusts (REITs) Investment funds that hold portfolios of real estate investments.

Real options Options embedded in a firm's real assets that give managers valuable decision-making flexibility, such as the right to either undertake or abandon an investment project.

Real risk-free rate (RRFR) The basic interest rate with no accommodation for inflation or uncertainty. The pure time value of money.

Realized capital gains Capital gains that result when an appreciated asset is sold; realized capital gains are taxable.

Realized yield The expected compounded yield on a bond that is sold before it matures assuming the reinvestment of all cash flows at an explicit rate. Also called *horizon yield* for the yield realized during an investment horizon period.

Refunding issue Bonds that provide funds to prematurely retire another bond issue. These bonds can be either a junior or senior issue.

Registered bond A bond for which ownership is registered with the issuer. The holder receives interest payments by check directly from the issuer.

Relative valuation techniques A type of approach to value the stock based upon its current price relative to variables considered to be significant to valuation, such as earnings, cash flow, book value, or sales

Relative-strength (RS) ratio The ratio of a stock price or an industry index value to a market indicator series, indicating the stock's or the industry's performance relative to the overall market.

Required rates of return The return that compensates inves-tors for their time, the expected rate of inflation, and the uncertainty of the return.

Resistance level A price at which a technician would expect a substantial increase in the supply of a stock to reverse a rising trend.

Return prediction studies Studies wherein investigations attempt to predict the time series of future rates of return using public information. An example would be predicting above-average returns for the stock market based on the aggregate dividend yield—e.g., high dividend yield indicates above average future market returns.

Revenue bond A bond that is serviced by the income generated from specific revenue-producing projects of the municipality such as toll roads or athletic stadiums.

Rising trend channel The range defined by security prices as they move progressively higher.

Risk The uncertainty that an investment will earn its expected rate of return.

Risk averse The assumption about investors that they will choose the least risky alternative, all else being equal.

Risk premium (RP) The increase over the nominal risk-free rate that investors demand as compensation for an investment's uncertainty.

Risk-free asset An asset with returns that exhibit zero variance.

Risky asset An asset with uncertain future returns.

Runs test A test of the weak-form efficient market hypothesis that checks for trends that persist longer in terms of positive or negative price changes than one would expect for a random series.

S

Sampling A technique for constructing a passive index portfolio in which the portfolio manager buys a representative sample of stocks that comprise the benchmark index.

Seasoned equity issues New equity shares offered by firms that already have stock outstanding.

Secondary market The market in which outstanding securities are bought and sold by owners other than the issuers. Purpose is to provide liquidity for investors.

Sector rotation strategy An active strategy that involves purchasing stocks in specific industries or stocks with specific characteristics (low *P/E*, growth, value) that are anticipated to rise in value more than the overall market.

Secured (senior) bond A bond backed by a legal claim on specified assets of the issuer.

Security-market index An index created as a statistical mea-sure of the performance of an entire market or segment of a market based on a sample of securities from the market or segment of a market.

Security market indicator series An index created as a statistical measure of the performance of an entire market or segment of a market based on a sample of securities from the market or segment of a market.

Security market line (SML) The line that reflects the combination of risk and return of alternative investments. In CAPM, risk is measured by systematic risk (beta).

Semistrong-form efficient market hypothesis The belief that security prices fully reflect all publicly available information, including information from security transactions and company, economic, and political news.

Separation theorem The proposition that the investment decision, which involves investing in the market portfolio on the capital market line, is separate from the financing decision, which targets a specific point on the CML based on the investor's risk preference.

Serial bond A bond issue that has a series of maturity dates. Typical for municipal bonds.

Settlement price The price determined by the exchange clearinghouse with which futures contract margin accounts are marked to market.

Sharpe measure A relative measure of a portfolio's benefit-to-risk ratio, calculated as its average return in excess of the risk-free rate divided by the standard deviation of portfolio returns.

Short hedge A short position in a forward or futures contract used to offset the price volatility of a long position in the underlying asset.

Short position The seller of a commodity or security or, for a forward contract, the counterparty who will be the eventual seller of the underlying asset.

Short sale The sale of borrowed securities with the intention of repurchasing them later at a lower price and earning the difference.

Sinking fund Bond provision that requires the issuer to redeem some or all of the bond systematically over the term of the bond rather than in full at maturity.

Small-firm effect A frequent empirical anomaly where risk-adjusted stock returns for companies with low market capitalization (i.e., share price multiplied by number of outstanding shares) are significantly larger than those generated by high market capitalization (large cap) firms.

Soft dollars A form of compensation to a money manager generated when the manager commits the investor to paying higher brokerage fees in exchange for the manager receiving additional services (e.g., stock research) from the broker.

Specialist The major market maker on stock exchanges who acts as a broker or dealer to ensure the liquidity and smooth functions of the secondary stock market.

Speculative company A firm with a great degree of business and/or financial risk, with commensurate high earnings potential.

Speculative stock A stock that appears to be highly overpriced compared to its intrinsic valuation.

Spending phase Phase in the investment life cycle during which individuals' earning years end as they retire. They pay for expenses with income from social security and returns from prior investments and invest to protect against inflation.

Spot rate The required yield for a cash flow to be received at some specific date in the future—for example, the spot rate for a flow to be received in one year, for a cash flow in two years, and so on.

Spread A trading strategy where long and short positions in two call (or two put) option contracts having the same underlying asset but different exercise prices or expiration dates are combined to create a customized return distribution.

Standard deviation A measure of variability equal to the square root of the variance.

Statement of cash flows A financial statement that shows the effects on the firm's cash flow of income flows and changes in its balance sheet.

Static yield spread Yield spreads over the total term structure.

Stock index arbitrage A trading strategy involving a long position in a stock portfolio and a short position in a stock index futures contract (or vice versa) designed to exploit a mispricing in the futures contract relative to the underlying index.

Straddle A trading strategy requiring the simultaneous purchase of a call option and a put option having the same exercise price, underlying asset, and expiration date. Variations of this theme include *strips, straps, strangles,* and *chooser options.*

Strong-form efficient market hypothesis The belief that security prices fully reflect all information from both public and private sources.

Structural change Economic trend occurring when the economy is undergoing a major change in organization or in how it functions.

Structured note A bond with an embedded derivative designed to create a payoff distribution that satisfies the needs of a specific investor clientele.

Style analysis An attempt to explain the variability in the observed returns to a security portfolio in terms of the movements in the returns to a series of benchmark portfolios designed to capture the essence of a particular security characteristic such as size, value, and growth.

Style grid A graph used to classify and display the investment style that best defines the nature of a security portfolio.

Subordinate (junior) bonds Debentures that, in case of default, entitle holders to claims on the issuer's assets only after the claims of holders of senior debentures and mortgage bonds are satisfied.

Support level A price at which a technician would expect a substantial increase in price and volume for a stock to reverse a declining trend that was due to profit taking.

Sustainable growth rate A measure of how fast a firm can grow using internal equity and debt financing and a constant capital structure. Equal to retention rate $\times ROE$.

Swap spread A measure of the risk premium for an interest rate swap, calculated as the difference between the agreement's fixed rate and the yield on a Treasury bond with the same maturity.

SWOT analysis An examination of a firm's *Strengths, Weaknesses, Opportunities,* and *Threats.* This analysis helps an analyst evaluate a firm's strategies to exploit its competitive advantages or defend against its weaknesses.

Systematic risk The variability of returns that is due to macroeconomic factors that affect all risky assets. Because it affects all risky assets, it cannot be eliminated by diversification.

T

Tactical asset allocation An investment strategy that adjusts the investor's mix of stocks and bonds by increasing the allocation to the asset class that is relatively undervalued.

Tax cost ratio Based on the ratio of the portfolio's tax-adjusted and pretax returns, the measure indicates the average annual percentage of a taxable investor's assets that have been consumed by taxes over the measurement period.

Tax efficiency The extent to which the investor controls the tax consequences of the security trades in a portfolio by balancing capital gains and capital losses.

Technical analysis Estimation of future security price movements based on past price and volume movements.

Term bond A bond that has a single maturity date.

Term structure of interest rates The relationship between term to maturity and yield to maturity for a sample of comparable bonds at a given time. Popularly known as the *yield curve.*

Term to maturity Specifies the date or the number of years before a bond matures or expires.

Third market Over-the-counter trading of securities listed on an exchange.

Tick The minimum price movement for the asset underlying a forward or futures contract; for Treasury bonds, one tick equals 1/32 of 1 percent of par value.

Time premium The difference between an option's total market value and its intrinsic value.

Timely and accurate information Information needed to enter a market to buy or sell a good or service quickly at a price justified by the prevailing supply and demand, based on the volume and prices of past transactions and all currently outstanding bids and offers.

Time-series analysis An examination of a firm's performance data over a period of time.

Time-weighted return The geometric average of (one plus) the *holding period yields* to an investment portfolio.

Total return A return objective in which the investor wants to increase the portfolio value to meet a future need by both capital gains and current income reinvestment.

Total return swap An agreement providing for the periodic exchange of cash flows based on a floating-rate index and the total return (i.e., interest plus capital gain or loss) to a predetermined reference entity, usually a specific bond or bond index.

Tracking error The standard deviation of the difference in returns between an active investment portfolio and its benchmark portfolio; also called *tracking error volatility.*

Trading effect The difference in performance of a bond portfolio from that of a chosen index due to short-run changes in the composition of the portfolio.

Trading rule A formula for deciding on current transactions based on historical data.

Trading turnover The percentage of outstanding shares traded during a period of time.

Transaction cost The cost of executing a trade. Low costs characterize an operationally efficient market.

Treasury bill A negotiable, government, non-interest-bearing security with original maturities of one year or less. Medium-term bonds have 3- to 10-year maturities; and long-term bonds are typically issued with initial maturities over 10 years.

Treynor measure A relative measure of a portfolio's performance calculated as its average return in excess of the risk-free rate divided by its beta coefficient.

Trough The culmination of a bear market at which prices stop declining and begin rising.

U

Underfunded plan A defined benefit pension plan in which the present value of the fund's liabilities to employees exceeds the value of the fund's assets.

Underweighted A condition in which a portfolio, for whatever reason, includes less of a class of securities than the relative market value alone would justify.

Unrealized capital gains Capital gains that reflect the price appreciation of currently held unsold assets.

Unsecured bonds Bonds that promise payments of interest and principal but pledge no specific assets. Holders have first claim on the issuer's income and unpledged assets. Also known as *debentures*.

Unsystematic risk Risk that is unique to an asset, derived from its particular characteristics. It can be eliminated in a diversified portfolio.

Unweighted index An indicator series affected equally by the performance of each security in the sample regardless of price or market value. Also referred to as an *equal-weighted series*.

Unwind The negotiated termination of a forward or futures position before contract maturity.

V

Valuation analysis An active bond portfolio management strategy designed to capitalize on expected price increases in temporarily undervalued issues.

Valuation process Part of the investment decision process in which you estimate the value of a security.

Value stocks Stocks that appear to be undervalued for reasons besides earnings growth potential. These stocks are usually identified based on high dividend yields, low *P/E* ratios, or low price-to-book ratios.

Value-weighted index An index calculated as the total market value of the securities in the sample. Market value is equal to the number of shares or bonds outstanding times the market price of the security.

Variable-rate note A debt security for which the interest rate changes to follow some specified short-term rate, for example, the T-bill rate; see *Floating rate note*.

Variance A measure of variability equal to the sum of the squares of a return's deviation from the mean, divided by the total number of returns.

Volatility index (VIX) A measure of investor expectations of near-term volatility in the stock market calculated as a weighted average of the implied volatilities estimated from Standard & Poor's 500 option contracts.

W

Warrant An instrument that allows the holder to purchase a specified number of shares of the firm's common stock from the firm at a specified price for a given period of time.

Weak-form efficient market hypothesis The belief that security prices fully reflect all security market information.

Y

Yankee bonds U.S. dollar-denominated bonds sold in the United States by a foreign firm or government.

Yield The promised rate of return on an investment under certain assumptions.

Yield illusion The erroneous expectation that a bond will provide its stated yield to maturity without recognizing the implicit reinvestment assumption related to coupon payments.

Yield spread The difference between the promised yields of alternative bond issues or market segments at a given time relative to yields on Treasury issues of equal maturity.

Yield to worst Given a bond with multiple potential maturity dates and prices due to embedded call options, the practice is to calculate a yield to maturity for each of the call dates and prices and select the lowest yield (the most conservative possible yield) as yield to worst.

Z

Zero coupon bond A bond that pays its par value at maturity but no periodic interest payments. Its yield is determined by the difference between its par value and its discounted purchase price. Also called *original issue discount (OID) bonds*.

*Numbers in italics refer to chapters or appendices on the www.reilly.nelson.com website. Web chapter references are preceded
by a *W* (e.g., *W19*-4–5 refers to pages 4–5 in Web Chapter 19). Appendix references will have either a *1A* or a *3A* (e.g., *1A*-3 refers to page 3
in Web Appendix 1A). A page reference followed by an "n" (e.g., 201n) refer to a footnote on that page.